JAN 0 4 2010

PAGES PACKED WITH ESSENTIAL INFORMATION

"Value-packed, unbeatable, accurate, and comprehensive."

—*The Los Angeles Times*

"The guides are aimed not only at young budget travelers but at the independent traveler; a sort of streetwise cookbook for traveling alone."

—*The New York Times*

"Unbeatable; good sight-seeing advice; up-to-date info on restaurants, hotels, and inns; a commitment to money-saving travel; and a wry style that brightens nearly every page."

—*The Washington Post*

THE BEST TRAVEL BARGAINS IN YOUR BUDGET

"All the dirt, dirt cheap."

—*People*

"Let's Go follows the creed that you don't have to toss your life's savings to the wind to travel—unless you want to."

—*The Salt Lake Tribune*

REAL ADVICE FOR REAL EXPERIENCES

"The writers seem to have experienced every rooster-packed bus and lunar-surfaced mattress about which they write."

—*The New York Times*

"[Let's Go's] devoted updaters really walk the walk (and thumb the ride, and trek the trail). Learn how to fish, haggle, find work—anywhere."

—*Food & Wine*

"A world-wise traveling companion—always ready with friendly advice and helpful hints, all sprinkled with a bit of wit."

—*The Philadelphia Inquirer*

A GUIDE WITH A SPIRIT AND A SOCIAL CONSCIENCE

"Lighthea   [Let's Go] helps the novic

—*...rnal-Constitution*

"The seri   ...tions to respect
the cultu   ...s a volunteer, a
student, c

—*San Francisco Chronicle*

LET'S GO PUBLICATIONS

TRAVEL GUIDES

Australia
Austria & Switzerland
Brazil
Britain
California
Central America
Chile
China
Costa Rica
Costa Rica, Nicaragua & Panama
Eastern Europe
Ecuador
Egypt
Europe
France
Germany
Greece
Guatemala & Belize
Hawaii
India & Nepal
Ireland
Israel
Italy
Japan
Mexico
New Zealand
Peru
Puerto Rico
Southeast Asia
Spain & Portugal with Morocco
Thailand
USA
Vietnam
Western Europe
Yucatan Peninsula

ROADTRIP GUIDE

Roadtripping USA

ADVENTURE GUIDES

Alaska
Pacific Northwest
Southwest USA

CITY GUIDES

Amsterdam
Barcelona
Berlin, Prague & Budapest
Boston
Buenos Aires
Florence
London
London, Oxford, Cambridge & Edinburgh
New York City
Paris
Rome
San Francisco
Washington, DC

POCKET CITY GUIDES

Amsterdam
Berlin
Boston
Chicago
London
New York City
Paris
San Francisco
Venice
Washington, DC

LET'S GO

ITALY

RESEARCHERS

DANIEL K. BILOTTI   BERYL LIPTON
EMILY CHERTOFF   JUSTIN MONTICELLO
MATEO CORBY   PAIGE PAVONE
ASHLEY GRAND   FABIAN POLIAK
MARYKATE JASPER   JULIA ROONEY
KENNETH G. SAATHOFF

LAUREN CARUSO MANAGING EDITOR
RAÚL CARRILLO EDITOR
SARA O'ROURKE ASSOCIATE EDITOR
MARY POTTER ASSOCIATE EDITOR
MATT ROLLER ASSOCIATE EDITOR
GRETCHEN KRUEGER MAP EDITOR
BEATRICE FRANKLIN RESEARCH MANAGER
CLAIRE SHEPRO RESEARCH MANAGER

EDITORS

COURTNEY A. FISKE   RUSSELL FORD RENNIE
SARA PLANA   CHARLIE E. RIGGS
OLGA I. ZHULINA

HOW TO USE THIS BOOK

COVERAGE LAYOUT. Welcome to *Let's Go Italy 2010*. Our book begins in Rome, still the center of Italian pride, hope, and *la dolce vita*. From there, we travel to the rugged, alpine north; the flashy (and occasionally trashy) Mediterranean coast; and the top of the boot, containing beautiful lakes and cutting edge fashion. We visit the northeastern shores of Venice, Verona, and spots immortalized in literature; central Italy for culinary and artistic delights; and Campania, for lovers, ruins, and the occasional mobster. Finally, we move to the sunbaked southern heel, explosive Sicily, and mythic Sardinia. Black tabs on the side of each page and our extensive **Index** (p. 512) will help you navigate Italy's regions.

TRANSPORTATION INFO. Sections on intercity transportation generally list all major destinations, followed by trip duration, frequency, time range of departures, and price. A typical listing: Trains to Rome (1hr., 13 per day 4:30am-7pm, €10). For more general info on travel, consult the **Essentials** (p. 8) section.

COVERING THE BASICS. Discover Italy (p. 1), contains **Let's Go Picks** (our favorite places in Italy) and **Suggested Itineraries** to help you plan your trip. Essentials (p. 8) provides logistical information and useful tips for travelers in Italy. **Life and Times** (p. 37) explains Italy's 3000 years of history, culture, and customs. Along your Italian trek, reference the useful **Italian phrasebook** and **menu reader** in the **Appendix** (p. 505). For information on study abroad, volunteer, and work opportunities in Italy, consult Beyond Tourism (p. 63).

PRICE DIVERSITY. Our researchers list establishments in order of value from best to worst, with absolute favorites denoted by the Let's Go thumbs-up (🖐). Since the cheapest price does not always mean the best value, we have incorporated a system of price ranges for food and accommodations (p. XII).

LANGUAGE AND OTHER QUIRKS. The English translations for cities are listed when applicable, followed by their Italian name. For pronunciation help, consult the phonetic spelling in each city introduction, or the Appendix (p. 505). In text and on maps, the names of streets and **piazze** have been shortened to the standardized abbreviations chart on the inside back cover.

PHONE CODES AND TELEPHONE NUMBERS. Phone codes for each city appear opposite the name of the city and are denoted by the ☎ icon. Phone numbers in text are also preceded by the ☎ icon.

RESEARCHERS

Daniel K. Bilotti
Milan

Fame seemed to follow Danny wherever he went, bumping into both John Malkovich and Furious Pete. We were a little concerned when he said he was most looking forward to embarrassing America abroad—but we're pretty sure he failed in that regard, and succeeded in most others, including charming us with great coverage of Milan.

Emily Chertoff
Rome

When we saw Emily's pre-departure *Roman Holiday*-esque haircut, we knew she would fit right into the Eternal City. She battled British soccer fans and unreliable Lazian buses to bring the most chic, unique establishments to our pages. And, of course, she managed it all while sharing her witty and articulate take on the scenes around her.

Mateo Corby
Sicily, Calabria

The memories of most RWs fade long after they have stepped off their route—not so with Mateo. Blazing through Sicily and Calabria in record time, this supersonic bomber also provided precise copy. He experienced *la dolce vita* in a way most never will—so quickly he was able to meet every backpacker on the lava-seared island at least twice. "Isa nice!"

Ashley Grand
Rome, Sardinia

Ashley braved the summer heat—and the tourist hordes—in Rome to bring readers the inside pulse of the heart of *la città eterna*. The Poli-Sci major also got to see the flipside of Italy while rubbing shoulders with the *sardo* in rural Sardinia. Ashley finished her route just in time to study abroad in yet another cultural capital—Buenos Aires.

Marykate Jasper
Florence

Already familiar with the inner workings of Let's Go, Marykate used her knowledge of format and flair to produce stellar copy. Despite enduring the inconsistencies of the Florence tourist office, the vagaries of Tuscan transportation, and the indignity of the Kimono of Shame, she kept us in stitches with her punny sense of humor.

Beryl Lipton *Florence*

Beryl tackled the art-historic center of Florence, getting into fashion shows and onto restaurant rooftops. Her steady consumption of gelato made us worry about her dietary health; her command of the Florentine nightlife scene, however, led us to think she was probably strengthened by all of that fresh dairy goodness—or maybe just on a sugar high.

Paige Pavone *Liguria, Tuscany, Umbria*

Those pretty boys under the Tuscan sun never knew what hit 'em. Paige intrepidly toured the soul of Italy and sent back excellent, clever copy. Mastering Tuscan slang and rooting through the touristy Riviera to find the hottest of seaside spots, Paige got the inside scoop on the most path-not-taken of places. *Grazie mille!* Your coverage=*ganza!*

Justin Monticello *Rome*

Between finding each hilarious anecdote and legend about Ancient Rome and wrangling a discount for LG readers at nearly every establishment he visited—you're welcome—Justin still found time to do unbelievable nightlife research and satisfy his cravings with the best pizza in the world. We suspect magic. Or a lot of espresso. Magic espresso?

Julia Rooney *Emilia-Romagna, Friuli, Le Marche, Trentino, Veneto*

This former track star's painterly eye led her on a veggie-pizza-fueled whirlwind from rainy beaches up north to Giotto's Scrovegni Chapel in Padua to Italy's party capital, Rimini. Julia truly hit her stride in Venice, returning home energized, practically fluent in Italian, and with plenty of artistic inspiration. Her plaque now resides in the LG Hall of Fame.

Kenneth G. Saathoff *Piedmont, Valle D'Aosta, The Lake Country, Lombardy*

This crafty outdoorsman with dashing good looks took his mountaineering skills and prolific prose on the road. He composed copy to rival the *canti* of Dante, the novels of Stendhal, and the magna opera of all others who had drawn inspiration from the beautiful scene. Braving euro-less days and a language barrier (at first), Kenny G prevailed.

Fabian Poliak *Campania, Puglia, Basilicata, Abruzzo, Molise*

Fabian had a special touch for the Wild South. Not even twin Swedish blondes or equally lascivious nuns could deter this well-traveled *gaucho* from his goal: creating nightlife and outdoors coverage where there once was none. Always down for another adventure, Fabian learned Italian on the fly and developed a motto that researchers will use for years to come: "There is no such thing as the wrong street."

ACKNOWLEDGMENTS

TEAM ITALY THANKS: Our super RWs!!!!!!! ▨Lauren for devotion, patience, and TLC. Prod! Gretchen for map perfection. ▨Jonathan for salvation. Team France for playing second fiddle. Kansas...for nothing. NOS. Sara for being clutch. Middle school R&B ballads. Gelfand for the help at the end. Ditto Gordon. We done!!!

RAÚL THANKS: Mama. Mary Potter for being a saint. The Jungle. Mateo and Fabian for hilarious and sometimes very touching marginalia. Weezy F Baby for that last push. Sammy G for always caring. LG of LG—the tension was awkward. Brain Break. ZEM. RIP Rolldiggity, you understood me best.

MARY THANKS: *Grazie mille* Mommer 'n em & ▨Thomas Aquinas, Rennie & Sharon, Lauren, Ra-Raúl, mat-roller & sara-o. Char, Dee Dee & marycat, Julia, FRITA, the studs at LGHQ, the blocktopus+▨popkins, the Bro-tel, and all members of the little bookgroup that couldn't.

SARA THANKS: Lauren for schmeeks, Hwack, and being (my) superior. MPMP for my fresh pond map, ETC. Raúl. City Pod+Dube for lunch and other failed plans. LGHQ. Lyle&Brit for girls' nights. Family and friends for readership. ▨Nelly for TACK, surrealism, and other Awkward Moments. Siblings for fun, friendship, and bonding over chaos. Dad and Mom, as always.

GRETCHEN THANKS: Team Italia, for hard work, creativity, and patience. My RWs, for editing maps with care. Meg, shoop! Becca and Elissa, for laughing and appreciating little things. Illiana, for advice about life after graduating. Derek, for the music and for teaching me about maps. MNDC, for all the good times. Trish, Justine, and Eliz, for the love. My family.

Editor
Raúl Carrillo
Associate Editors
Sara O'Rourke
Mary Potter
Matt Roller
Managing Editor
Lauren Caruso
Map Editor
Gretchen Krueger
Research Manager
Beatrice Franklin, Claire Shepro
Editors
Courtney A. Fiske, Sara Plana, Russell Ford Rennie, Charlie E. Riggs, Olga I. Zhulina
Typesetter
C. Alexander Tremblay

LET'S GO

Publishing Director
Laura M. Gordon
Editorial Director
Dwight Livingstone Curtis
Publicity and Marketing Director
Vanessa J. Dube
Production and Design Director
Rebecca Lieberman
Cartography Director
Anthony Rotio
Website Director
Lukáš Tóth
Managing Editors
Ashley Laporte, Iya Megre, Mary Potter, Nathaniel Rakich
Technology Project Manager
C. Alexander Tremblay
Director of IT
David Fulton-Howard
Financial Associates
Catherine Humphreville, Jun Li

President
Daniel Lee
General Manager
Jim McKellar

CONTENTS

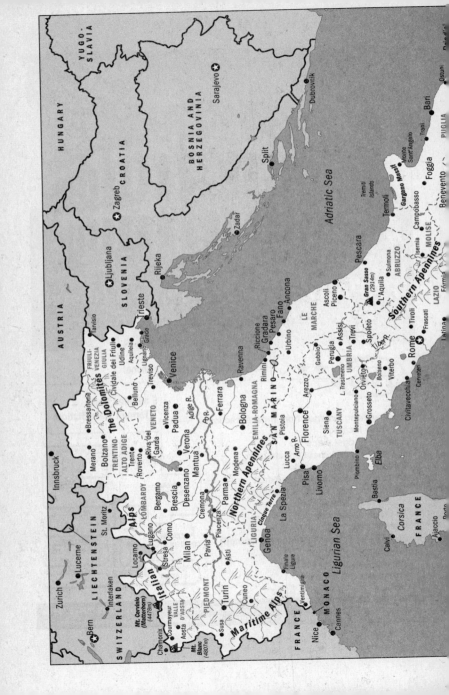

Italy

Our researchers list establishments in order of value from best to worst, honoring our favorites with a *Let's Go* thumbs-up (⊠). Because the best *value* is not always the cheapest *price*, we have incorporated a system of price ranges based on a rough expectation of what you will spend. For **accommodations,** we base our range on the cheapest price for which one traveler can stay for one night. For **restaurants** and other dining establishments, we estimate the average amount one traveler will spend in one sitting. The table below tells you what you'll typically find in Italy at the corresponding price range, but keep in mind that no system can allow for the quirks of individual establishments.

ACCOMMODATIONS	RANGE	WHAT YOU'RE *LIKELY* TO FIND
❶	under €20	Campgrounds, dorm rooms, *suores* (rooms in religious institutions), or dorm-style rooms. Expect bunk beds and a communal bath. You may have to provide or rent towels and sheets.
❷	€20-30	Upper-end hostels or lower-end *pensioni*. You may have a private bathroom, or there may be a sink in your room and a communal shower in the hall.
❸	€31-45	A small room with a private bath, probably in a budget hotel or *pensione*. Should have decent amenities, such as phone and TV. Breakfast may be included in the price of the room.
❹	€46-65	Similar to ❸, but may have more amenities or be in a convenient location.
❺	above €65	Large hotels or upscale chains. If it's a ❺ and it doesn't have the perks you want, you've paid too much.

FOOD	RANGE	WHAT YOU'RE *LIKELY* TO FIND
❶	under €7	Probably a fast-food stand, *gelateria*, bar, cafe, or pizzeria. Rarely ever a sit-down meal.
❷	€7-15	Sit-down pizzerias and most affordable *trattore*. Should include *primi* and *secondi*.
❸	€16-25	Similar to ❷, but nicer setting and a more elaborate menu. May offer a cheaper lunch *menù*, and a pizza could be a less expansive alternative to a *primo* or *secondo* combination.
❹	€26-33	As in ❸, higher prices are likely related to better service, but in these restaurants, the food will tend to be fancier or more elaborate, or the location will be especially convenient or historic. While few restaurants in this price range will have a dress code, T-shirts, jeans, or shorts may be frowned upon.
❺	above €33	Venerable reputation, a 90-page wine list, or the freshest seafood and a harbor view. Elegant attire may be expected.

DISCOVER ITALY

The classic images of Italy—the vespas, the Vatican, the *vino*—are all enjoyable, but don't let them define your experience. Instead, stomp through volcanic ruins, masquerade with budget-friendly Bacchus, and saunter down cobblestone streets—in stilettos, of course. Slap on your Frauda sunglasses, slip into D&G, douse yourself in Gucci perfume, and indulge in some good ol' Italian elegance. Meet those eccentric restaurant owners, learn Italy's local secrets, and explore her untainted nature. In between action-packed adventures, don't forget to step back, as Italians often do, and experience *la dolce far niente* (literally, the sweetness of doing nothing). Don't just come to Italy to confirm the spaghetti-and-meatballs image; come to discover something you can't send home on a postcard. Discover the chaos, energy, and allure. Discover Italy.

FACTS AND FIGURES	
ITALY 2009 POPULATION: 58 million	**REGULAR CHURCHGOERS:** 18½ million
NUMBER OF CELL PHONES: 63 million	**REGULAR SOCCER FANS:** 30 million
MONEY THROWN INTO ROME'S TREVI FOUNTAIN EACH DAY: about €3000	**WORLD'S RICHEST INSTITUTION AND SMALLEST COUNTRY:** Vatican City
ANNUAL WINE CONSUMPTION PER PERSON: 26 gallons	**ANNUAL BREAD CONSUMPTION PER PERSON:** 26 kg

READY, SET... DON'T GO YET!

Tourism enters overdrive in June, July, and August. Hotels are booked solid, rates skyrocket, and rows of lounge chairs take over pristine beaches. Around *Ferragosto*, a national holiday on August 15, Italians head to the coast, leaving a flood of closed businesses in their wake. Some larger cities avoid this summer hibernation and remain enjoyable in August, but late May through July make for a livelier trip. Traveling to Italy in early May or early September assures a calmer, cooler, cheaper vacation, with temperatures averaging a comfortable 25°C (77°F). Depending on the destination, a trip in April offers the advantages of lower prices and smaller crowds. The best weather for hiking in the Alps is from June to September; ski season generally lasts from December through late March, although some locations stay open year-round.

MOSAICS TO MODERNISM

Unsurprisingly, Italy, the birthplace of the Renaissance, is home to impressive art collections. The most important are found in the country's largest cities; however, virtually every small town has its own *museo archeologico* or *pinacoteca* (art gallery) that showcases collections that range from Greek pottery shards and Roman mosaics to Futurist paintings. Don't head to these if you're looking for a high concentration of famous works, but avoiding the crowds and finding that lone Caravaggio or da Messina in a regional museum can be a more rewarding experience than a barrage of masterworks. Also, note that some of Italy's greatest artwork is held within the sacred walls of her many churches.

CITY	PRINCIPAL ART COLLECTIONS
Florence	Uffizi Gallery (p. 309) Museo dell'Opera del Duomo (p. 316)
Milan	Pinacoteca di Brera (p. 190)
Naples	Museo Archeologico Nazionale (p. 397)
Rome	Sistine Chapel (p. 115) Vatican Museums (p. 115) Galleria Borghese (p. 116) Museo Nazionale d'Arte Antica (p. 119)
Reggio di Calabria	Museo Nazionale (p. 433)
Siena	Pinacoteca Nazionale (p. 329) Museo dell'Opera Metropolitana (p. 329)
Trieste	Museo Revoltella (p. 266)
Turin	Museo Egizio (p. 141) Galleria Sabauda (p. 141)
Venice	Collezione Peggy Guggenheim (p. 241) Gallerie dell'Accademia (p. 241)

SO MUCH MORE THAN PIZZA

Pizza, beloved internationally as a quick takeout meal, is much more than fast food on its home turf. Originating in **Naples** (p. 385) in the 1800s after introduction of tomatoes, pizza has evolved beyond the basic *Margherita*. Italy's pizzerias may be good, but don't be afraid to branch out. Even pasta, an integral part of the Italian diet for thousands of years, faces competition for its claim as the Italian carb of choice. Italy's famous creamy rice dish, *risotto*, incorporates local specialties: wine and truffles in Piedmont, seafood in the Veneto, and saffron in Milan. In northern regions such as **Trentino-Alto Adige** (p. 255), polenta and gnocchi (potato and flour dumplings) enjoy popularity. To go beyond the nationwide staples, begin your regional tour of Italian cuisine with **Piedmont's** (p. 133) white truffles. Watch your wallet, though, because these 'white diamonds' go for US$850-1500 per lb. This region also saw the invention of Nutella, which is now consumed internationally in greater amounts than all peanut butter brands combined. **Genoa** (p. 155) flaunts colorful pesto, which gets its name from *pestatura* (a method of grinding using a mortar and pestle); imitations are marketed worldwide, but the best basil leaves—and therefore the best pesto—hail from Liguria. The **Friuli-Venezia Giulia region** (p. 263) has a subtle Slavic flair, apparent in ingredients like yogurt, fennel, cumin, and paprika. **Treviso**, in the Veneto region, is famous for its tiramisu, a heavenly espresso-and-rum-soaked cake layered with mild *mascarpone* cheese. Its name, which literally means "pick me up," is rumored to have originated from its use by tired prostitutes. Check out **Tuscany's** (p. 296) saltless bread, whose popularity comes as a surprise to many; several theories explain the lack of salt, including one that claims a 12th-century salt price-hike protest that changed from boycott to tradition after prices came back down. Centuries ago, **Florence** (p. 296) birthed gelato, a milk-based frozen treat now available throughout the country. In the heart of Emilia-Romagna, **Bologna** (p. 271), birthplace of *tortellini bolognese* sauce, reigns as Italy's culinary capital, while **Parma** (p. 279) boasts tender prosciutto. The region is perhaps most famous for its *parmigiano-reggiano* cheese. Besides Naples' pizza, southern Italy offers seafood, olive oil, and *granita*, **Sicily's** (p. 442) slushy version of gelato, and *cipolle rosse* (red onions) from Tropea. To find the perfect wine to compliment your meal, see **In Vino Veritas** (p. 59).

BICEP CURLS GET THE GIRLS

Sandwiched between the Mediterranean and Adriatic Seas, the Italian coastline stretches over 2000 mi. In the northwest, the famous beaches of **Liguria** (p. 155) form the Italian Riviera, home to the glitterati-packed resorts of **San Remo** (p. 173). Farther down, the hidden gem, **Ponza** (p. 129), provides a relaxing daytrip from sweaty Rome. Swing south along the Amalfi Coast to beach towns like **Positano** (p. 411) and **Capri** (p. 406) that offer sparkling waters, lapping against cliffs and lemon groves. After getting your dose of high culture in Venice's art museums, don't miss the nearby beach towns like **Caorle** (p. 265). On the Salento Peninsula, **Gallipoli's** (p. 429) emerald waters entice visitors. On the east coast, **Rimini** (p. 287) attracts a large student population with its beaches during the day as well as a smoking night club scene. Calabria and Sicily offer visitors variety, from the dark stone coasts of African-influenced Pantelleria to the resort towns of **Cefalù** (p. 453).

TAKE A HIKE!

Italy presents plenty of opportunities for the outdoor adventurer, whether you get your kicks staring into the fiery mouth of a volcano or strolling through the Tuscan countryside. The **Aeolian Islands** are home to both active and inactive volcanoes, while nearby **Mt. Etna** (p. 470) offers far-reaching views. Hike, bike, or ski through **Abruzzo National Park** (p. 380), the southern Apennines, the northeastern **Dolomites** (p. 255), or Calabria's **Sila Massif** (p. 437). Slow things down by taking Grandma on a walk through the **Chianti region** (p. 324) of Tuscany, which offers travelers a less strenuous experience; walk along country roads past vineyards, olive groves, and ancient castles, all while enjoying views of the surrounding hills and valleys.

TAKE A BREAK ON A LAKE

Northern Italy is home to the gorgeous **Lake Country** (p. 200). A trek along **Stresa's** (p. 215) scenic trails will alleviate any stress, leaving you ready to hit the clubs in **Desenzano** (p. 206), reportedly home of the best *discoteche* on Lake Garda. *Mangia* in **Menaggio** to get a taste of some authentic regional cuisine. Be prepared to shell out a few extra euro for this paradise; however, the lakeside view from your balcony will remind you that it's worth it.

HOW TO RUIN A PERFECTLY GOOD TRIP

The Roman Empire may have fallen 1500 years ago, but it continues to bring global commerce into Rome. Some crumbling and wonderfully preserved arches, aqueducts, and amphitheaters give a sense of majesty, mystery, and poetry. Although many Italian cities, including **Spoleto** (p. 357), **Rimini** (p. 287), and **Aosta** (p. 147) boast some sort of Roman relic, the most impressive ruins are scattered through the streets of **Rome** itself (p. 74) where travelers can admire the famous Colosseum, Pantheon, and Roman Forum. Daytrips from Rome lead to the extravagant Villa Adriana in **Tivoli** (p. 131). Farther south, **Naples** (p. 385) boasts a world-renowned archaeological museum and miles of subterranean Roman aqueducts open for exploration. Near Naples, **Pompeii** (p. 402) is a city eternally petrified in AD 79, when an eruption of Mt. Vesuvius covered it in lava. A neighboring excavation site, **Herculaneum** (p. 405), features another surprisingly intact 2000-year-old town. Across the peninsula, **Brindisi** is home to the

DISCOVER

column marking the end of the Appian Way, an ancient road that led to Rome. Italy also has numerous relics of pre-Roman inhabitants. Etruscan artifacts can be found in many Tuscan towns like **Fiesole** (p. 323). Sicily's proximity to Greece led to the establishment of many Greek colonies, which were the first great civilizations in Italy, including **Agrigento** (p. 476), and **Syracuse** (p. 471). Evidence of more ancient civilizations can be found in **Alberobello's** *trulli*, and **Sardinia's** *nuraghi* (p. 499).

LET'S GO PICKS

BEST PLACE TO SHOW UP BACCHUS HIMSELF: In the vineyards of the **Chianti** region (p. 324).

BEST PLACE TO CORPSE-WATCH: Pace through the huge **Cappuchin Catacombs** (p. 450) in Palermo, where 8000 bodies rest in their moth-eaten Sunday best. Or check out the partially decayed body of **Ötzi**, a 5000-year-old Iceman in Bolzano.

BEST PLACE TO SLEEP LIKE A ROCK: The white-washed, conical *trulli* of **Alberobello** (p. 424) are mortarless abodes used as residences and churches.

BEST PLACE TO SAY A HAIL MARY TO ATONE FOR BACCHANALIAN EXCESS: The **Vatican** (p. 105) offers confession in numerous languages.

BEST PLACE TO REVEL IN INSOMNIA: Wild bars and themed clubs dominate the beachside party town of **Rimini** (p. 287).

BEST PLACE TO GET BLOWN AWAY: Scale **Mt. Vesuvius** (p. 402), Europe's only active volcano; investigate—but not too closely—**Mt. Etna's** (p. 470) lava-seared wilderness.

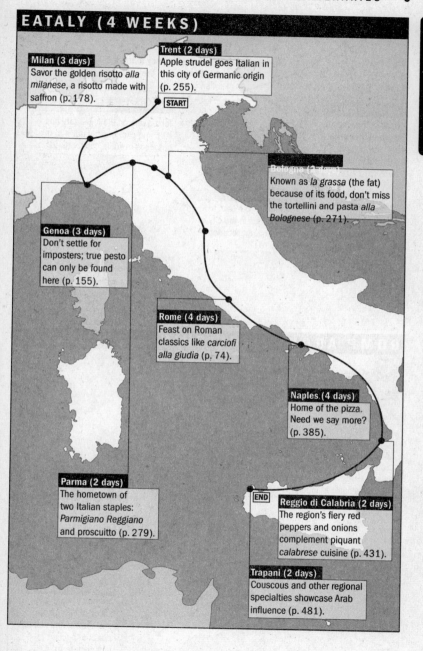

EATALY (4 WEEKS)

Milan (3 days)
Savor the golden risotto *alla milanese*, a risotto made with saffron (p. 178).

Trent (2 days)
Apple strudel goes Italian in this city of Germanic origin (p. 255).

START

Bologna (2 days)
Known as *la grassa* (the fat) because of its food, don't miss the tortellini and pasta *alla Bolognese* (p. 271).

Genoa (3 days)
Don't settle for imposters; true pesto can only be found here (p. 155).

Rome (4 days)
Feast on Roman classics like *carciofi alla giudia* (p. 74).

Naples (4 days)
Home of the pizza. Need we say more? (p. 385).

Parma (2 days)
The hometown of two Italian staples: *Parmigiano Reggiano* and proscuitto (p. 279).

END

Reggio di Calabria (2 days)
The region's fiery red peppers and onions complement piquant *calabrese* cuisine (p. 431).

Trapani (2 days)
Couscous and other regional specialties showcase Arab influence (p. 481).

DEBEACHERY (3 WEEKS)

Milan (3 days)
Bar-hop from trendy to trendier neighborhoods in the capital of Italian fashion (p. 178).

Alassio (2 days)
Bask on beaches by day and dance on them by night at internationally attended clubs (p. 170).

Rimini (3 days)
Take a ride on the legendary bus #11 and club hop 'till dawn in this notorious nightlife capital (p. 287).

Elba (3 days)
Soothe a Rimini hangover lounging on the pristine *spiagge* of this Tuscan island (p. 342).

Rome (5 days)
Pledge your soul to Bacchus in the city of eternal intoxication (p. 74).

Naples (5 days)
Swerve into southern Italy's fast lane and the gorgeous Amalfi Coast (p. 385).

ROMP AROUND THE RUINS (2 WEEKS)

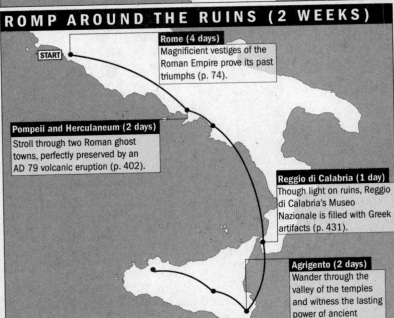

START

Rome (4 days)
Magnificient vestiges of the Roman Empire prove its past triumphs (p. 74).

Pompeii and Herculaneum (2 days)
Stroll through two Roman ghost towns, perfectly preserved by an AD 79 volcanic eruption (p. 402).

Reggio di Calabria (1 day)
Though light on ruins, Reggio di Calabria's Museo Nazionale is filled with Greek artifacts (p. 431).

Agrigento (2 days)
Wander through the valley of the temples and witness the lasting power of ancient architecture (p. 476).

BEST OF ITALY (4 WEEKS)

Turin (3 days)
Enjoy the cultural offerings, hot nightlife, and nearby outdoor adventures in this rising star of the North (p. 133).

Milan (3 days)
Party it up in this fast-paced financial and fashion center that hasn't forgotten its past (p. 178).

Trieste (2 days)
Sample sapphire seas and sauerkraut in this multicultural hidden gem (p. 263).

START

Venice (5 days)
Dreams come true drifting down Venice's romantic canals (p. 222).

Florence (5 days)
This Renaissance city is brimming with world-class art, awe-inspiring churches, and high-class shopping (p. 296).

Rome (5 days)
After more than 2700 years, powerful history and lively nightlife still echo in *la città eterna* (p. 74).

Naples (3 days)
Grab a slice in pizza's hometown and don't miss nearby Herculaeum and Pompeii (p. 385).

Catania (2 days)
Climb Mt. Etna and discover this Sicilian treasure's mixed architecture and lively student population (p. 464).

END

ESSENTIALS

PLANNING YOUR TRIP

ENTRANCE REQUIREMENTS
Passport (see opposite page). Required for citizens of Australia, Canada, Ireland, New Zealand, the UK, and the US.
Visa (p. 10). Required only for citizens of Australia, Canada, Ireland, New Zealand, the UK, and the US for stays over 90 days.
Work Permit (p. 10). Required for all foreigners planning to work in Italy.

EMBASSIES AND CONSULATES

ITALIAN CONSULAR SERVICES ABROAD

Australia: 12 Grey St., Deakin, Canberra ACT 2600 (☎+61 262 733 333; www.ambcanberra.esteri.it/Ambasciata_Canberra). **Consulates:** 509 St. Kilda Rd., Melbourne VIC 3004 (☎+61 039 867 5744; www.consmelbourne.esteri.it); The Gateway, Level 45, 1 Macquarie Pl., Sydney NSW 2000 (☎+61 029 392 7900; www.conssydney.esteri.it).

Canada: 275 Slater St., 21st fl., Ottawa, ON K1P 5H9 (☎+1-613-232-2401; www.ambottawa.esteri.it). **Consulate:** 3489 Drummond St., Montreal, QC H3G 1X6 (☎+1-514-849-8351; www.consmontreal.esteri.it).

Ireland: 63/65 Northumberland Rd., Dublin (☎+353 16 60 17 44; www.ambdublino.esteri.it).

New Zealand: 34-38 Grant Rd., P.O. Box 463, Thorndon, Wellington (☎+64 44 735 339; www.italy-embassy.org.nz). **Consulate:** 102 Kitchener Rd., PO Box 31 121 Auckland (☎+649 489 9632).

UK: 14 Three Kings Yard, London W1K 4EH (☎+44 207 312 2200; www.embitaly.org.uk). **Consulates:** 32 Melville Street, Edinburgh EH3 7HA (☎+44 131 226 3631; www.consedimburgo.esteri.it); Rodwell Tower, 111 Piccadilly, Manchester M1 2HY (☎+44 161 236 9024; www.consmanchester.esteri.it).

US: 3000 Whitehaven St., N.W., Washington, DC 20008 (☎+1-202-612-4400; www.ambwashingtondc.esteri.it). **Consulates:** 600 Atlantic Ave., Boston, MA 02110 (☎+1-617-722-9201; www.consboston.esteri.it); 500 N. Michigan Ave., Ste. #1850, Chicago, IL 60611 (☎+1-312-467-1550; www.conschicago.esteri.it); 690 Park Ave., New York, NY 10021 (☎+1-212-737-9100; www.consnewyork.esteri.it).

CONSULAR SERVICES IN ITALY

Australia: V. Antonio Bosio 5, Rome 00161 (☎06 85 27 21, emergency ☎800 87 77 90; www.italy.embassy.gov.au). Open M-F 9am-5pm.

Canada: V. Zara 30, Rome 00198 (☎06 85 44 41; www.dfait-maeci.gc.ca/canada-europa/italy/menu-en.asp). Open M-Th 8:30-11:30am.

Ireland: P. di Campitelli 3, Rome 00186 (☎06 69 79 121; www.ambasciata-irlanda.it). Open M-F 10am-12:30pm and 3-4:30pm.

New Zealand: V. Zara 28, Rome 00198 (☎06 44 17 171; www.nzembassy.com). Open M-F 8:30am-12:45pm and 1:45-5pm. **Consulate:** V. Guido d'Arezzo 6, Milan 20145 (☎02 48 01 25 44). Open M-F 8:30am-5pm.

UK: V. XX Settembre 80a, Rome 00187 (☎06 42 20 00 01; www.britain.it). Open M-F Sept.-May 9am-5pm; June-Aug. 8am-2pm. Closed UK and Italian holidays.

US: V. Vittorio Veneto 121, Rome 00187 (☎06 46 741; www.usembassy.it). Consular services open M-F 8:30am-12:30pm. Closed US and Italian holidays. **Consulate:** V. Principe Amedeo 2/10, Milan 20121 (☎02 29 03 51). Open M-F 8:30am-noon.

ESSENTIALS

TOURIST OFFICES

Italian Government Tourist Board (ENIT) provides information on Italy's culture, natural resources, history, and leisure activities. Visit their website, www. italiantourism.com, for info. Call ☎+1-212-245-4822 for a free copy of *General Information for Travelers to Italy*. The main office in Rome (☎06 49 71 11; sedecentrale@cert.enit.it) can help locate any local office not listed online.

Australia: 44 Market St., Sydney NSW 2000 (☎+29 26 21 666; enitour@ihug.com.au).

Canada: 175 E. Bloor St., Ste. 907 South Tower, Toronto, ON M4W 3R8 (☎+1-416-925-4882; enit.canada@on.aibn.com).

UK: 1 Princes St., London W1B 2AY (☎+20 7408 1254; www.italiantouristboard.co.uk).

US: 630 5th Ave., Ste. 1565, New York, NY 10111 (☎+1-212-245-5618; www.italiantourism.com).

DOCUMENTS AND FORMALITIES

PASSPORTS

REQUIREMENTS

Citizens of Australia, Canada, Ireland, New Zealand, the UK, and the US need valid passports to enter Italy and to re-enter their home countries. Returning home with an expired passport is illegal and may result in a fine.

NEW PASSPORTS

Citizens of Australia, Canada, Ireland, New Zealand, the UK, and the US can apply for a passport at any passport office or at selected post offices and courts of law. Citizens of these countries may also download passport applications from the official website of their country's government or passport office. Any new passport or renewal applications must be filed well in advance of the departure date; rush services may be available for a very steep fee. Note, however, that even "rushed" passports still take up to two weeks to arrive.

PASSPORT MAINTENANCE

Photocopy the page of your passport with your photo as well as your visas, traveler's check serial numbers, and any other important documents. Carry one set of copies in a safe place, apart from the originals, and leave another set at home. If you lose your passport, immediately notify the local police and your home country's nearest embassy or consulate. To expedite its replacement, you must show ID and proof of citizenship; it also helps to know all information previously recorded in the passport. In an emergency, ask for immediate temporary traveling papers that will permit you to re-enter your home country.

ONE EUROPE. European unity has come a long way since 1958, when the European Economic Community (EEC) was created to promote European solidarity and cooperation. Since then, the EEC has become the European Union (EU), a mighty political, legal, and economic institution. On May 1, 2004, 10 South, Central, and Eastern European countries—Cyprus, the Czech Republic, Estonia, Hungary, Latvia, Lithuania, Malta, Poland, Slovakia, and Slovenia—were admitted into the EU, joining the original 15: Austria, Belgium, Denmark, Finland, France, Germany, Greece, Ireland, Italy, Luxembourg, the Netherlands, Portugal, Spain, Sweden, and the UK. On January 1, 2007, two others, Bulgaria and Romania, came into the fold, bringing the tally of member states to 27.

What does this have to do with the average non-EU tourist? The EU's policy of **freedom of movement** means that most border controls have been abolished and visa policies harmonized. Under this treaty, formally known as the **Schengen Agreement,** you're still required to carry a passport (or government-issued ID card for EU citizens) when crossing an internal border, but, once you've been admitted into one country, you're free to travel to other participating states. Most EU states are already members of Schengen (minus Bulgaria, Cyprus, Ireland, Romania, and the UK), as are Iceland and Norway. In 2009, Cyprus, Liechtenstein, and Switzerland will bring the number of Schengen countries to 27. Britain and Ireland have also formed a **common travel area,** abolishing passport controls between the UK and the Republic of Ireland.

For more important consequences of the EU for travelers, see **The Euro** (p. 12) and **Customs in the EU** (see opposite page).

VISAS, INVITATIONS, AND WORK PERMITS

VISAS

EU citizens do not need a visa. Citizens of Australia, Canada, New Zealand, and the US do not need a visa for stays of up to 90 days, but this three-month period begins upon entry into any of the countries that belong to the EU's **freedom of movement** zone. For more information, see **One Europe** (above). Those staying longer than 90 days may purchase a visa at the Italian consulate or embassy. A visa costs about €60 and allows the holder to spend between 90 and 365 additional days in Italy, depending on the type of visa. Double-check entrance requirements at the nearest Italian embassy or consulate (p. 8) for up-to-date info before departure. US citizens can also consult http://travel.state.gov.

Foreign nationals planning to spend over 90 days in Italy should apply within eight working days of arrival for a *permesso di soggiorno* (permit of stay). Generally, non-EU tourists are required to get a permit at a police station or foreign office *(questura)* if staying longer than 20 days or taking up residence in a location other than a hotel, official campsite, or boarding house.

Entering Italy to study requires a special visa. For more information, see the **Beyond Tourism** chapter (p. 63) or visit www.ambwashingtondc.esteri.it.

WORK PERMITS

Admittance to a country as a traveler does not include the right to work, which is authorized only by a work permit. For more information on the regulations related to obtaining a work permit, see the **Beyond Tourism** chapter (p. 63).

IDENTIFICATION

When you travel, always carry at least two forms of identification on your person, including a photo ID. A passport and a driver's license or birth certificate will usually suffice. Never carry all of your IDs together; split them up in case of theft or loss and keep photocopies in your luggage and at home.

STUDENT, TEACHER, AND YOUTH IDENTIFICATION

The **International Student Identity Card** (ISIC), the most widely accepted form of student ID, provides discounts on some sights, accommodations, food, and transportation; access to a 24hr. emergency help line; and insurance benefits for US cardholders (see **Insurance**, p. 17). Applicants must be full-time secondary or post-secondary school students at least 12 years old. Because of the proliferation of fake ISICs, some services (particularly airlines) require additional proof of student identity.

The **International Teacher Identity Card** (ITIC) offers teachers the same insurance coverage as the ISIC and similar but limited discounts. To qualify for the card, teachers must be currently employed and have worked a minimum of 18hr. per week for at least one school year. For travelers who are under 26 years old but are not students, the **International Youth Travel Card** (IYTC) also offers many of the same benefits as the ISIC.

CUSTOMS

Upon entering Italy, you must declare certain items from abroad and pay a duty on the value of those articles if they exceed the allowance established by Italy's customs service. Goods and gifts purchased at duty-free shops abroad are not exempt from duty or sales tax; "duty-free" means that you won't pay tax in the country of purchase. Duty-free allowances were abolished for travel between EU member states on June 30, 1999, but still exist for those arriving from outside the EU. Upon returning home, you must likewise declare all articles acquired abroad and pay a duty on the value of articles in excess of your home country's allowance. In order to expedite your return, make a list of any valuables brought from home and register them with customs before traveling abroad. It's a good idea to keep receipts for all goods acquired abroad.

> **CUSTOMS IN THE EU.** As well as freedom of movement of people (see opposite page), travelers in the European Union can also take advantage of the freedom of movement of goods. This means that there are no customs controls at internal EU borders (i.e., you can take the blue customs channel at the airport), and travelers are free to transport whatever legal substances they like as long as it is for their own personal (non-commercial) use.

MONEY

CURRENCY AND EXCHANGE

The currency chart below is based on August 2008 exchange rates between local currency and Australian dollars (AUS$), Canadian dollars (CDN$), European Union euro (EUR€), New Zealand dollars (NZ$), British pounds (UK£), and US dollars (US$). Check the currency converter on websites like www.xe.com or www.bloomberg.com for the latest exchange rates.

ESSENTIALS

EURO (€)	
AUS$1 = €0.59	€1 = AUS$1.71
CDN$1 = €0.64	€1 = CDN$1.56
NZ$1 = €0.48	€1 = NZ$2.10
UK£1 = €1.16	€1 = UK£0.86
US$1 = €0.71	€1 = US$1.43

As a general rule, it's cheaper to convert money in Italy than at home. While currency exchange will probably be available in your arrival airport, it's wise to bring enough foreign currency to last for at least 24-72 hours.

When changing money abroad, try to go only to banks or money chargers (*cambio*) that have at most a 5% margin between their buy and sell prices. Since you lose money with every transaction, it makes sense to convert large sums at one time (unless the currency is depreciating rapidly).

TRAVELER'S CHECKS

Traveler's checks are one of the safest and most convenient means of carrying funds. However, they can also be one of the most frustrating means of spending money since fewer and fewer shops outside of tourist areas accept traveler's checks. American Express (in Australia ☎ +61 2 9271 8666, in New Zealand +64 9 367 4567, in the UK +44 1273 696 933, in the US and Canada +1-800-221-7282; elsewhere, call the US collect at +1-336-393-1111) and Visa (in the UK ☎ +44 0800 895 078, in the US +1-800-227-6811; elsewhere, call the UK collect at +44 2079 378 091) are the most-recognized brands. Many banks and agencies sell them for a small commission. Check issuers provide refunds if the checks are lost or stolen, and many provide additional services, such as toll-free refund hotlines abroad, emergency message services and assistance with lost and stolen credit cards or passports. Ask about toll-free refund hotlines and the location of refund centers when purchasing checks, and always carry emergency cash.

THE EURO. As of January 1, 2009, the official currency of 16 members of the European Union—Austria, Belgium, Cyprus, Finland, France, Germany, Greece, Ireland, Italy, Luxembourg, Malta, the Netherlands, Portugal, Slovakia, Slovenia, and Spain—will be the euro.

The currency has some important—and positive—consequences for travelers hitting more than one euro-zone country. For one thing, money-changers across the euro-zone are obliged to exchange money at the official, fixed rate (below) and at no commission (though they may still charge a small service fee). Second, euro-denominated traveler's checks allow you to pay for goods and services across the euro-zone, again at the official rate and commission-free. At the time of printing, €1 = US$1.58 = CDN$1.59 = NZ$2.08. For more info, check a currency converter, visit www.xe.com or www.europa.eu.int.

CREDIT, DEBIT, AND ATM CARDS

Where they are accepted, credit cards often offer superior exchange rates—up to 5% better than the retail rate used by banks and other currency exchange establishments. Credit cards may also offer services such as insurance or emergency help and are sometimes required to reserve hotel rooms or rental cars. **EuroCard** and **Carte Bleue** are the most frequently accepted; **American Express** cards work at some ATMs and at AmEx offices and major airports.

The use of ATM cards is widespread in Italy. Depending on the system that your home bank uses, you can most likely access your personal bank account from abroad. Cirrus and BankMate are two of the most common financial networks. ATMs get the same wholesale exchange rate as credit cards, but there is often a limit on the amount of money you can withdraw per day (around US$500). There is also typically a surcharge of US$1-5 per withdrawal.

The two major international money networks are **MasterCard/Maestro/Cirrus** (for ATM locations ☎+1-800-424-7787 or www.mastercard.com) and **Visa/PLUS** (for ATM locations ☎+1-800-847-2911 or www.visa.com). Most ATMs charge a transaction fee that is paid to the bank that owns the ATM.

PINS AND ATMS. To use a cash or credit card to withdraw money from a cash machine (ATM) in Europe, you must have a four-digit Personal Identification Number (PIN). If your PIN is longer than four digits, ask your bank whether you can just use the first four or whether you'll need a new one. Credit cards don't usually come with PINs, so, if you intend to hit up ATMs in Europe with a credit card to get cash advances, call your credit-card company before leaving to request one.

Travelers with alphabetic, rather than numerical, PINs may also be thrown off by the lack of letters on European cash machines. The following are the corresponding numbers to use: 1 = QZ; 2 = ABC; 3 = DEF; 4 = GHI; 5 = JKL; 6 = MNO; 7 = PRS; 8 = TUV; and 9 = WXY. Note that if you mistakenly punch the wrong code into the machine three times, it will swallow your card for good.

GETTING MONEY FROM HOME

If you run out of money while traveling, the easiest and cheapest solution is to have someone back home make a deposit to your bank account. Otherwise, consider one of the following options.

WIRING MONEY

It is possible to arrange a **bank money transfer,** which means asking a bank back home to wire money to a bank in Italy. This is the cheapest way to transfer cash, but it's also the slowest, usually taking several days or more. Note that some banks may only release your funds in local currency, potentially sticking you with a poor exchange rate; inquire about this in advance. Money transfer services like Western Union are faster and more convenient than bank transfers—but convenience comes at a price. **Western Union** has many locations worldwide. To find one, visit www.westernunion.com, or call in Australia ☎+1 800 173 833, in Canada and the US +1-800-325-6000, in the UK +44 0800 833 833, or in Italy at 800 788 935. To wire money using a credit card (Discover, MasterCard, Visa), call in Canada and the US ☎+1-800-CALL-CASH, in the UK +44 0800 833 833. Money transfer services are also available to **American Express** cardholders and at selected **Thomas Cook** offices.

US STATE DEPARTMENT (US CITIZENS ONLY)

In serious emergencies only, the US State Department will forward money within hours to the nearest consulate, which will then disburse it according to instructions for a US$30 fee. If you wish to use this service, you must contact the Overseas Citizens Services division of the US State Department (☎+1-202-501-4444, from US 888-407-4747).

COSTS

The cost of your trip will vary considerably, depending on where you go, how you travel, and where you stay. The most significant expenses will probably be your round-trip (return) airfare to Italy (see **Getting to Italy: By Plane,** p. 19) and a railpass or bus pass. Before you go, spend some time calculating a reasonable daily budget.

STAYING ON A BUDGET

To give you a general idea, a bare-bones day in Italy (camping or sleeping in hostels/guesthouses, buying food at supermarkets) would cost about US$50 (€32); a slightly more comfortable day (sleeping in hostels and the occasional budget hotel, eating one meal per day at a restaurant, going out at night) would cost US$90 (€57); and, for a luxurious day, the sky's the limit. Don't forget to factor in emergency reserve funds (at least US$200) when planning how much money you'll need.

TIPPING AND BARGAINING

At many Italian restaurants, a service charge *(servizio)* or cover *(coperto)* is included in the bill. Locals sometimes do not give tips, but it is appropriate for foreign visitors to leave an additional 5-10% at restaurants for the waiter. Taxi drivers expect about a 5-10% tip, though Italians rarely tip them. Bargaining is common in Italy, but use discretion. Haggling is appropriate at markets, with vendors, and unmetered taxi fares (settle the price before getting in), but elsewhere, it is usually inappropriate. Hotel negotiation is more successful in uncrowded *pensioni*. To get lower prices, show little interest. Don't offer what you can't pay; you're expected to buy once the merchant accepts your price.

TAXES

The **Value Added Tax** (**VAT;** *imposto sul valore aggiunta,* or IVA) is a sales tax levied in the EU. Foreigners making any purchase over €155 are entitled to an additional 20% VAT refund. Some stores take off 20% on-site. Others require that you fill out forms at the customs desk upon leaving the EU and send receipts from home within six months. Not all storefront "Tax-Free" stickers imply an immediate, on-site refund, so ask before making a purchase.

PACKING

Pack lightly: lay out only what you absolutely need, then take half the clothes and twice the money. The **Travelite FAQ** (www.travelite.org) is a good resource for tips on traveling light. The online **Universal Packing List** (http://upl.codeq.info) will generate a customized list of suggested items based on your trip length, the expected climate, your planned activities, and other factors.

Converters and Adapters: In Italy, electricity is 230 volts AC, enough to fry any 120V North American appliance. 220/240V electrical appliances won't work with a 120V current, either. Americans and Canadians should buy an adapter (which changes the shape of the plug; US$10-20) and a converter (which changes the voltage; US$10-20). Don't make the mistake of using only an adapter (unless appliance instructions explicitly state otherwise). Australians and New Zealanders (who use 230V at home) won't need a converter but will need a set of adapters to use anything electrical. For more on all things adaptable, check out http://kropla.com/electric.htm.

SAFETY AND HEALTH

GENERAL ADVICE

In any type of crisis, the most important thing to do is **stay calm.** Your country's embassy abroad (p. 8) is usually your best resource in an emergency; registering with that embassy upon arrival in the country is a good idea. The government offices listed in the **Travel Advisories** box (see next page) can provide information on the services they offer their citizens in case of emergencies abroad.

LOCAL LAWS AND POLICE

In Italy you will mainly encounter two types of police: the *polizia* (☎ 113) and the *carabinieri* (☎ 112). The *polizia* are a civil force under the command of the Ministry of the Interior, whereas the *carabinieri* fall under the auspices of the Ministry of Defense and are considered a military force. Both, however, generally serve the same purpose—to maintain security and order in the country. In the case of attack or robbery both will respond to inquiries for help.

DRUGS AND ALCOHOL

Needless to say, **illegal drugs** are best avoided altogether. In Italy, drugs including marijuana, cocaine, and heroin are illegal. An increase in cocaine and heroin addiction and trafficking have led Italian authorities to respond harshly to drug-related offenses. If you carry **prescription drugs,** bring copies of the prescriptions and a note from a doctor, and have them accessible at international borders. The drinking age in Italy is 16. Drinking and driving is prohibited and can result in a prison sentence. The legal blood alcohol content (BAC) for driving is under 0.05%, significantly lower than US standards, which limit BAC to 0.08%.

SPECIFIC CONCERNS

NATURAL DISASTERS

Italy is crossed by several fault lines, the chief one running from Sicily to Friuli-Venezia Giulia in the northeast. The country's principal cities do not lie near these faults, though smaller tourist towns like Assisi do and thus may experience **earthquakes** (most recently in 1997).

DEMONSTRATIONS AND POLITICAL GATHERINGS

Americans should be mindful while traveling in Italy, as there is some anti-American sentiment. No matter where you travel in Italy, you will likely encounter some sort of anti-American or, more likely, anti-Bush statements. It is best to err on the side of caution and sidestep these discussions. In general, use discretion and avoid being too vocal about your citizenship.

TERRORISM

Terrorism has not been as serious a problem in Italy as in other European countries, though the general threat of terrorism still exists. Exercise common sense and caution when in crowded, public areas like train or bus stations and open spaces like *piazze* in larger cities. The box on **travel advisories** on the next page lists offices to contact and webpages to visit to get the most updated list of your home country's government's advisories about travel.

PERSONAL SAFETY

EXPLORING AND TRAVELING

To avoid unwanted attention, try to blend in as much as possible. Respecting local customs (in many cases, dressing more conservatively than you would at home) may ward off would-be hecklers. Familiarize yourself with your surroundings before you set out and walk with purpose. Check maps indoors rather than on the street. If you're traveling alone, be sure someone at home knows your itinerary and never tell anyone you meet that you're by yourself. When walking at night, stick to busy, well-lit streets. If you ever feel uncomfortable, leave the area as quickly and directly as you can.

There is no surefire way to avoid all the threatening situations that you might encounter while traveling, but a good **self-defense course** will give you concrete ways to react to unwanted advances. **Impact, Prepare,** and **Model Mugging** can refer you to local self-defense courses in Australia, Canada, Switzerland, and the US. Visit the website at www.modelmugging.org for a list of chapters.

If you are using a **car,** learn local driving signals and always wear a seatbelt. Study route maps before you hit the road and, if you plan on spending a significant amount of time driving, consider bringing spare parts. For long drives in desolate areas, invest in a cellular phone (p. 29) and a roadside assistance program (p. 27). Park your vehicle in a garage or well-traveled area and use a steering-wheel locking device in larger cities. Sleeping in your car is the most dangerous way to get your rest. See p. 28.

TRAVEL ADVISORIES. The following government offices provide travel information and advisories by telephone, by fax, or via the web:

Australian Department of Foreign Affairs and Trade: ☎+61 2 6261 1111; www.dfat.gov.au.

Canadian Department of Foreign Affairs and International Trade (DFAIT): ☎+1-800-267-8376; www.dfait-maeci.gc.ca. Call for their free booklet, *Bon Voyage...But.*

New Zealand Ministry of Foreign Affairs: ☎+64 44 39 80 00; www.mfat.govt.nz.

United Kingdom Foreign and Commonwealth Office: ☎+44 20 7008 1500; www.fco.gov.uk.

US Department of State: ☎+1-888-407-4747; http://travel.state.gov. Visit the website for the booklet, *A Safe Trip Abroad.*

POSSESSIONS AND VALUABLES

Never leave your belongings unattended; crime occurs in even the most safe-looking hostel or hotel. Bring your own padlock for hostel lockers and don't ever store valuables in a locker. Be particularly careful on **buses** and **trains.**

There are a few steps you can take to minimize the financial risk associated with travel. First, **bring as little with you as possible.** Second, buy a few combination **padlocks** to secure your belongings either in your pack or in a hostel or train-station locker. Third, **carry as little cash as possible.** Carry traveler's checks and ATM/credit cards in a **money belt**—not a "fanny pack"—along with your passport and ID cards. Fourth, **keep a small cash reserve separate from your primary stash.** This should be about US$50 (US dollars or euros are best) sewn into or stored deep in your pack, along with your traveler's check numbers, photocopies of your passport, your birth certificate, and other important documents.

In large cities, **con artists** often work in groups and may involve children. Beware of certain classics: sob stories that require money, rolls of bills "found" on the street, mustard spilled (or saliva spit) onto your shoulder to distract you while they snatch your bag. **Never let your passport and your bags out of your sight.**

PRE-DEPARTURE HEALTH

In your passport, write the names of any people you wish to be contacted in case of a **medical emergency** and list any allergies or medical conditions. Matching a prescription to a foreign equivalent is not always easy, safe, or possible, so, if you take **prescription drugs,** consider carrying up-to-date prescriptions or a statement from your doctor stating the medication's trade name, manufacturer, chemical name, and dosage. While traveling, be sure to keep all medication with you in your carry-on luggage.

IMMUNIZATIONS AND PRECAUTIONS

Travelers over two years old should make sure that the following vaccines are up to date: MMR (for measles, mumps, and rubella); DTaP or Td (for diphtheria, tetanus, and pertussis); IPV (for polio); Hib (for *haemophilus influenzae* B); and HepB (for Hepatitis B). Adults traveling to the developing world on trips longer than four weeks should consider the following additional immunizations: Hepatitis A vaccine and/or immune globulin (IG), typhoid and cholera vaccines, particularly if traveling off the beaten path, as well as a rabies vaccine and yearly influenza vaccines. For recommendations on immunizations, consult the Centers for Disease Control and Prevention (CDC; below) in the US or the equivalent in your home country and check with a doctor for guidance.

INSURANCE

Travel insurance covers four basic areas: medical/health problems, property loss, trip cancellation/interruption, and emergency evacuation. Though regular insurance policies may well extend to travel-related accidents, you may consider purchasing separate travel insurance if the cost of potential trip cancellation, interruption, or emergency medical evacuation is greater than you can absorb. Prices for travel insurance purchased separately generally run about US$50 per week for full coverage, while trip cancellation/interruption may be purchased separately at a rate of US$3-5 per day, depending on length of stay.

STAYING HEALTHY

Common sense is the simplest prescription for good health while you travel. Drink lots of fluids to prevent dehydration, and wear sturdy, broken-in shoes.

ONCE IN ITALY

ENVIRONMENTAL HAZARDS

Arid summer weather in the south creates prime conditions for heat exhaustion and dehydration. Be especially careful at Pompeii; there may no longer be a threat of volcanic eruption, but a lack of water fountains and shade create new dangers. Trekking at high altitudes in the Dolomites, the Alps, and on Mt. Vesuvius and Mt. Etna should not be done too hastily; be especially careful in winter to protect yourself against hypothermia and frostbite.

ESSENTIALS

Heat exhaustion and dehydration: Heat exhaustion leads to nausea, excessive thirst, headaches, and dizziness. Avoid it by drinking plenty of fluids, eating salty foods (e.g., crackers), abstaining from dehydrating beverages (e.g., alcohol and caffeinated beverages), and wearing sunscreen. Continuous heat stress can eventually lead to heatstroke, characterized by a rising temperature, severe headache, delirium, and cessation of sweating. Victims should be cooled off with wet towels and taken to a doctor.

INSECT-BORNE DISEASES

Many diseases are transmitted by insects—mainly mosquitoes, fleas, ticks, and lice. Be aware of insects in wet or forested areas, especially while hiking and camping. Wear long pants and long sleeves, tuck your pants into your socks, and use a mosquito net. Use insect repellents such as DEET and soak or spray your gear with permethrin (licensed in the US only for use on clothing). **Mosquitoes**—responsible for malaria, dengue fever, and yellow fever—can be particularly abundant in wet, swampy, or wooded areas like those found in Liguria and Trentino-Alto Adige. **Ticks**—which can carry Lyme and other diseases—can be particularly dangerous in rural and forested regions, especially in Friuli-Venezia Giulia, the Veneto, and Trentino-Alto Adige.

FOOD- AND WATER-BORNE DISEASES

Prevention is the best cure: be sure that your food is properly cooked and the water you drink is clean. Watch out for food from markets or street vendors that may have been cooked in unhygienic conditions. Other culprits are raw shellfish, unpasteurized milk, and sauces containing raw eggs. Buy bottled water or purify your own water by bringing it to a rolling boil or treating it with **iodine tablets;** note, however, that boiling is more reliable. While Italy's water is relatively clean (the ancient Roman aqueduct water still provides Rome with a reliable water source), it is important to be wary in places like some campgrounds and trains where water is not clean. The sign *"acqua non potabile"* means the water is not drinkable; the sign *"acqua potabile"* means the water is sanitary. Even as a developed nation, Italy experienced an outbreak of stomach flu due to contaminated drinking water in Taranto in 2006.

OTHER INFECTIOUS DISEASES

The following diseases exist all over the world. Travelers should know how to recognize them and what to do if they suspect they have been infected.

AIDS and HIV: For detailed info on Acquired Immune Deficiency Syndrome (AIDS) in Italy, call the 24hr. National AIDS Hotline at ☎+1-800-342-2437. Note that Italy screens incoming travelers for AIDS, primarily those planning extended visits for work or study, and denies entrance to those who test HIV-positive. Contact the consulate of Italy for info.

Sexually transmitted infections (STIs): Gonorrhea, chlamydia, genital warts, syphilis, herpes, HPV, and other STIs are easier to catch than HIV and can be just as serious. Though condoms may protect you from some STIs, oral or even tactile contact can lead to transmission. If you think you may have contracted an STI, see a doctor immediately.

OTHER HEALTH CONCERNS

MEDICAL CARE ON THE ROAD

Although quality of care varies by region, Italy overall conforms to standards of modern health care. Medical facilities tend to be better in the north and in private hospitals and clinics. Doctors speak English in most large cities; if they don't, they may be able to arrange for a translator. *Let's Go* lists info on how to access medical help in the **Practical Information** sections of most cities.

Those concerned about obtaining medical assistance abroad may wish to employ special support services. The **MedPass** from **GlobalCare, Inc.,** 6875 Shiloh Rd. East, Alpharetta, GA 30005, USA (☎+1-800-860-1111; www.globalcare. net), provides 24hr. international medical assistance, support, and evacuation resources. The **International Association for Medical Assistance to Travelers** (**IAMAT;** US ☎+1-716-754-4883, Canada +1-519-836-0102; www.iamat.org) lists English-speaking doctors worldwide, and offers detailed info on immunization requirements and sanitation. If your regular insurance policy does not cover travel abroad, you may wish to purchase additional coverage (p. 17).

GETTING TO ITALY

BY PLANE

When it comes to airfare, a little effort can save you a bundle. Courier fares are the cheapest options for travelers whose plans are flexible enough to deal with the restrictions. Tickets sold by consolidators and standby seating are also good deals, but last-minute specials, airfare wars, and charter flights often beat these fares. The key is to hunt around, be flexible, and ask about discounts. Students, seniors, and those under 26 should never pay full price for a ticket.

FLIGHT PLANNING ON THE INTERNET. The Internet may be the budget traveler's dream when it comes to finding and booking bargain fares, but the array of options is overwhelming. Many airline sites offer special last-minute deals. Look for sale fares on www.alitalia.com and www.flyairone.it.
STA (www.statravel.com) and **StudentUniverse** (www.studentuniverse.com) provide quotes on student tickets, while **Orbitz** (www.orbitz.com), **Expedia** (www.expedia.com), and **Travelocity** (www.travelocity.com) offer full travel services. **Priceline** (www.priceline.com) lets you specify a price and obligates you to buy any ticket that meets or beats it; **Hotwire** (www.hotwire. com) offers bargain fares but won't reveal the airline or flight times until you buy. Other sites that compile deals include www.bestfares.com, www. lowestfare.com, www.onetravel.com, and www.travelzoo.com.
SideStep (www.sidestep.com) and **Booking Buddy** (www.bookingbuddy. com) are online tools that can help sift through multiple offers; these two let you enter your trip information once and search multiple sites.
Air Traveler's Handbook (www.faqs.org/faqs/travel/air/handbook) is an indispensable resource on the Internet; it has a comprehensive list of links to everything you need to know before you board a plane.

AIRFARES

Airfares to Italy peak between April and early September; holidays are also expensive. The cheapest times to travel are from late September to mid-December and January to March. Midweek (M-Th morning) round-trip flights tend to be cheaper than weekend flights, but they are generally more crowded and less likely to permit frequent-flier upgrades. Not fixing a return date ("open return") or arriving in and departing from different cities ("open-jaw") can be pricier than round-trip flights. Flights into Rome and Milan tend to be cheaper.

If Italy is only one stop on a more extensive globe-hop, consider a round-the-world (RTW) ticket. Tickets usually include at least five stops and are valid for about a year; prices range US$1200-5000. Try **Northwest Airlines/KLM** (☎+1-800-225-2525; www.nwa.com) or **Star Alliance,** a consortium of 16 airlines including United Airlines (www.staralliance.com).

Fares for round-trip flights to Rome and Milan from the US or Canadian east coast cost US$700-1200, US$500-700 in the low season (mid-Sept. to mid-Dec. and Jan.-Mar.); from the US or Canadian west coast US$800-1600/600-1000; from the UK, UK£175-300/125-200; from Australia AUS$1700-2600/1320-2000; from New Zealand NZ$2000-3000/1800-2400.

BUDGET AND STUDENT TRAVEL AGENCIES

While knowledgeable agents specializing in flights to Italy can make your life easy and help you save, they may not spend the time to find you the lowest possible fare—they get paid on commission. Travelers holding ISICs and IYTCs (p. 11) qualify for big discounts from student travel agencies. Most flights from budget agencies are on major airlines, but in peak season some may sell seats on less reliable chartered aircraft.

STA Travel, 5900 Wilshire Blvd., Ste. 900, Los Angeles, CA 90036, USA (24hr. reservations and info ☎+1-800-781-4040; www.statravel.com). A student and youth travel organization with over 150 offices worldwide (check their website for a listing of all their offices), including US offices in Boston, Chicago, Los Angeles, New York, Seattle, San Francisco, and Washington, D.C. Ticket booking, travel insurance, railpasses, and more. Walk-in offices are located throughout Australia (☎+61 392 075 900), New Zealand (☎+64 93 09 97 23), and the UK (☎+44 8701 630 026).

The Adventure Travel Company, 124 MacDougal St., New York, NY, 10021, USA (☎+1-800-467-4595; www.theadventuretravelcompany.com). Offices across Canada and the US including Champaign, New York, San Diego, Seattle, and San Francisco.

USIT, 19-21 Aston Quay, Dublin 2, Ireland (☎+353 1602 1904; www.usit.ie). Ireland's leading student/budget travel agency has 20 offices throughout Northern Ireland and the Republic of Ireland. Offers programs to work, study, and volunteer worldwide.

Wasteels, Skoubogade 6, 1158 Copenhagen K., Denmark (☎+453 3314 4633; www.wasteels.com). A huge chain with 180 locations across Europe. Sells Wasteels BIJ tickets discounted 30-45% off regular fare, 2nd-class international point-to-point train tickets with unlimited stopovers for those under 26 (sold only in Europe).

COMMERCIAL AIRLINES

The commercial airlines' lowest regular offer is the **APEX (Advance Purchase Excursion)** fare, which provides confirmed reservations and allows "open-jaw" tickets. Generally, reservations must be made seven to 21 days ahead of departure, with seven- to 14-day minimum-stay and up to 90-day maximum-stay restrictions. These fares carry hefty cancellation and change penalties. Book peak-season APEX fares early. Use **Expedia** (www.expedia.com) or **Travelocity** (www.travelocity.com) to get an idea of low published fares, then use the resources outlined here to try to beat those fares. Low-season fares should be appreciably cheaper than the high-season (mid-June to Aug.) ones listed here.

Let's Go treats 🗲**budget airlines** (see opposite page) separately from commercial airlines. For travelers who don't place a premium on convenience, we recommend these no-frills airlines as the best way to jet around Europe. Even if you live outside the continent, you can save money by finding the absolute cheapest flight to Europe and then using budget airlines to reach your final destination.

TRAVELING FROM NORTH AMERICA

The most common ways to cross the pond are those you've probably heard of. Standard commercial carriers will probably offer the most convenient flights, but they may not be the cheapest.

American: ☎+1-800-433-7300; www.aa.com.

United: ☎+1-800-538-2929; www.ual.com.

Northwest: ☎+1-800-447-4747; www.nwa.com.

Lufthansa: ☎+1-800-399-5838; www.lufthansa.com.

British Airways: ☎+1-800-247-9297; www.britishairways.com.

Air France: ☎+1-800-237-2747; www.airfrance.us.

Alitalia: ☎+1-800-223-5730; www.alitaliausa.com.

TRAVELING FROM IRELAND AND THE UK

Cheapflights (www.cheapflights.co.uk) publishes bargains on airfare from the British Isles, but British and Irish globetrotters really looking to save should always fly on budget airlines. The following commercial carriers occasionally offer discounted fares or specials.

Aer Lingus: Ireland ☎+353 818 365 000; www.aerlingus.ie. Flights from Dublin, Cork, Kerry, and Shannon to Bologna, Milan, Naples, Rome, and Venice (EUR€30-200).

KLM: UK ☎+44 8705 074 074; www.klmuk.com. Cheap tickets between UK airports and over 23 Italian destinations (UK£60-200).

TRAVELING FROM AUSTRALIA AND NEW ZEALAND

Qantas Air: Australia ☎+61 13 13 13, New Zealand +64 800 808 767; www.qantas.com.au. Flights from Australia and New Zealand to Rome.

Singapore Air: Australia ☎+61 13 10 11, New Zealand +64 800 808 909; www.singaporeair.com. Flies from Auckland, Christchurch, Melbourne, and Sydney to Rome.

Thai Airways: Australia ☎+61 86 62 22 66, New Zealand +64 93 77 38 86; www.thaiair.com. Flies from Auckland, Melbourne, Perth, and Sidney to Rome.

BUDGET AIRLINES

Low-cost carriers are the latest big thing in Europe. With their help, travelers can often snag tickets for illogically low prices (i.e., less than the price of a meal in the airport food court), but you get what you pay for: namely, minimalist service and no frills. In addition, many budget airlines fly out of smaller regional airports several kilometers out of town. You'll have to buy shuttle tickets to reach the airports of many of these airlines, so plan on adding an hour or so to your travel time. After round-trip shuttle tickets and fees for services that might come standard on other airlines, that €1 sale fare can suddenly jump to €20-100. Prices vary dramatically; shop around, book months ahead, pack light, and stay flexible to nab the best fares. For a more detailed list of these airlines by country, check out www.whichbudget.com.

bmibaby: UK ☎0871 224 0224, elsewhere +44 870 126 6726; www.bmibaby.com. Round-trip London to Naples (UK£35-140) and Venice (UK£40-100).

easyJet: ☎+44 871 244 2366, UK£0.10 per min.; www.easyjet.com. London to Bologna, Milan, Naples, Pisa, Rome, Turin, and Venice (UK£25-200).

Ryanair: Ireland ☎0818 30 30 30, UK 0871 246 0000, elsewhere +353 1249 7791; www.ryanair.com. The cheapest flights (from £10 with taxes) from Dublin, Glasgow, Liverpool, London, and Shannon to over a dozen destinations throughout Italy.

BY TRAIN

Traveling to Italy by train from within Europe can be as expensive as a flight, but allows travelers to watch the country unfold before them, and allows the possibility of spontaneous stopovers before reaching their ultimate destination. For info on traveling within Italy by rail, see **By Train**, p. 24.

MULTINATIONAL RAILPASSES

EURAIL PASSES. Eurail is **valid** in most of Western Europe but **not** the UK. Standard **Eurail Passes,** valid for a consecutive number of days, are best for those planning to spend an extended period of time on trains. **Eurail Global Pass,** valid for any 10 or 15 (not necessarily consecutive) days in a two-month period, is more cost-effective for those traveling long distances less frequently. **Eurail Pass Saver** provides first-class travel for travelers in groups of two or more people. **Eurail Pass Youth** provides parallel second-class perks for 12- to 25-year-olds. Passholders receive a timetable for routes and a map with details on possible bike rental, car rental, hotel, and museum discounts, as well as reduced fares or free passage on many boat, bus, and private railroad lines.

The **Eurail Selectpass** is a slimmed-down version of the Eurail Pass: it allows five to 15 days of unlimited travel in any two-month period within three to five bordering countries.

SHOPPING FOR A EURAIL. Passes are designed by the EU itself and must be sold at uniform prices determined by the EU. Some agents tack on a US$10 handling fee, and others offer certain bonuses, so shop around. Prices usually go up each year, so if you're planning to travel early in the year, save cash by purchasing before January 1 (you'll have 3 months to validate your pass).

Eurail passes should be bought before leaving; only a few places in major European cities sell them, usually at marked-up prices. You can get a replacement for a lost pass if you have purchased insurance under the **Pass Security Plan** (US$12). Eurail Passes are available through travel agents, student travel agencies like STA (p. 19), **Rail Europe** (US ☎+1-888-382-7245, Canada +1-800-361-7245; www.raileurope.com), or **Flight Centre** (US ☎+1-866-967-5351, Canada +1-877-967-5302; www.flightcentre.com). You can also buy directly from Eurail's website, www.eurail.com.

FURTHER READING AND RESOURCES ON TRAIN TRAVEL
Info on rail travel and railpasses: www.raileurope.com.
Point-to-point fares and schedules: www.raileurope.com/us/rail/fares_schedules/index.htm. Allows you to calculate railpass savings.
European Railway Server: www.railfaneurope.net. Links to rail servers located throughout Europe.

BY BUS AND BOAT

Though European trains are popular, in some cases buses prove a better option. Often cheaper than railpasses, international bus passes allow unlimited travel on a hop-on, hop-off basis between major European cities. Amsterdam, Athens, Istanbul, London, Munich, and Oslo are centers for lines that offer long-distance rides across Europe. Bus travel within Italy has its own benefits and disadvantages; in remote parts of the country private companies offer cheap fares and are often the only option, though schedules may be unreliable.

Eurolines, 4 Vicarage Rd., Edgbaston, Birmingham B15 3ES, UK (☎+44 0870 514 3219; www.eurolines.com). The largest operator of Europe-wide coach services. Unlimited 15-day (high season UK£195, under 26 and over 60 UK£165; low season UK£149/129); 30-day (high season UK£290/235; low season UK£209/169); or 60-day (high season UK£333/259; low season UK£265/211) travel passes that offer unlimited transit between 35 major European cities.

Busabout, 258 Vauxhall Bridge Rd., London SW1V 1BS, UK (☎+44 0207 950 1661; www.busabout.com). Offers 5 interconnecting bus circuits covering 60 cities and towns in Europe. Unlimited (consecutive-day) Passes, Flexipasses, and Add On Passes are available. Unlimited standard/student passes are valid for 2 weeks (US$469/419), 4 weeks (US$739/659), 6 weeks (US$919/819), 8 weeks (US$1049/939), 12 weeks (US$1319/1179), or for the season (US$1649/1469).

BORDER CROSSINGS

The surrounding countries of France, Switzerland, and Austria can make great daytrips from Italy's border cities. Multiple-country rail passes are available through RailEurope (www.raileurope.com). For more info on cross-border transportation in Europe, see opposite page.

As a part of the EU, Italy only requires that travelers present a valid passport and ID to travel between EU nations. When traveling to France and Austria, no currency exchange is necessary; yet, Switzerland uses the Swiss franc (CHF).

GETTING AROUND ITALY

Fares are either **one-way** or **round-trip.** "Period returns" require you to return within a specific number of days; "day return" means you must return on the same day. Unless stated otherwise, *Let's Go* always lists single fares. Round-trip fares on trains and buses in Italy are typically double the one-way fare.

BY PLANE

With 25 major airports throughout Italy, there is no excuse for not making that hop, skip, and jump up to Venice to rendezvous with your newfound Italian lover. The main Italian hubs are Rome, Milan, Bergamo, Verona, Bologna, Genoa, Pisa, Florence, Turin, Venice, Naples, Bari, and Palermo, but suitable airports exist in nearly every corner of the country. The recent emergence of no-frills airlines has made hopscotching around Europe by air more affordable and convenient. Though these flights often feature inconvenient hours or serve less-popular regional airports, with one-way flights running as low as US$30, it's never been faster or easier to jet set across the Continent. **Ryanair** and **easyjet** (p. 21) are just two among many cheap airlines that fly throughout Italy and beyond. The **Star Alliance European Airpass** offers economy class fares as low as US$65 for travel within Europe to more than 965 airports in 42 countries. The pass is available to non-European passengers on Star Alliance carriers, including Air Canada, Austrian Airlines, BMI British Midland, Lufthansa,

Scandinavian Airlines System, Thai International, and United Airlines, as well as on certain partner airlines. See www.staralliance.com for more info. In addition, a number of European airlines offer discount coupon packets. Most are available as tack-ons for transatlantic passengers, but some are stand-alone offers. Most must be purchased before departure, so research in advance.

BY TRAIN

Trenitalia (☎89 20 21; www.trenitalia.com) is the main provider of railway transportation throughout Italy. Trenitalia is owned by Ferrovie dello Stato (FS), which is owned by the Italian government. Other (somewhat less reliable) companies include **Ferrovia Nord,** which runs several lines originating in Milan and expanding into the north, and **Ferrovie Sud-Est (FSE),** which runs mainly in Puglia. Local rail in some parts of Italy shuts down on Sunday, leaving buses as the principle weekend transportation option.

Several types of trains ride the Italian rails. The **locale** (sometimes called a **regionale**) stops at every station along a particular line, often taking twice as long. The **diretto** makes fewer stops than the *locale*, while the **espresso** only stops at major stations. The air-conditioned, more expensive, **InterCity (IC),** or **rapido,** train travels only to the largest cities; a few routes may require reservations. Tickets for the fast, comfortable, and pricey **Eurostar** trains (1st- and 2nd-class trains) require reservations. Eurail passes are valid without a supplement on all trains except the Eurostar. All InterRail holders must also purchase supplements (€2-20) for trains like Eurostar and InterCity. Train tickets may be purchased from *biglietterie* and automated ticket machines, which have instructions in English. There are often discounts for those under 26 or those traveling in a group of six or more.

Towns listed in parentheses on European schedules require a train switch at the town listed immediately before the parentheses. Note that unless stated otherwise, *Let's Go* lists one-way fares.

In general, trains in Italy are cheap enough not to warrant buying a national pass. **Eurail** sells a **National Pass** for Italy (Youth and Saver options also available). The **Italy pass** is available for three to 10 days in a two-month period, and costs US$225-424, US$191-361 for the Saver pass, and US$186-346 for the Youth pass. The Euro Domino pass became the InterRail **One Country Pass** in 2007 and is available to anyone who has lived in Europe for at least six months; it is only valid in one country (designated when bought). Passes can be bought for three to eight days within one month. A three-day pass is €109, under 26 €71; an eight-day pass costs €229/149. Reservations must be paid for separately. Supplements are included for many high-speed trains. The pass can be purchased online at www.interrailnet.com. In addition to simple railpasses, many countries (as well as Eurail) offer **rail-and-drive passes,** which combine car rental with rail travel—a good option for travelers who wish to visit cities accessible by rail and to make trips into the surrounding areas.

 NEED VALIDATION? Before boarding, always validate your ticket in the validation machines, colored yellow or orange. Failure to validate may result in steep fines, and train operators do not accept ignorance as an excuse.

BY FERRY

The islands of Sicily and Sardinia, as well as the smaller islands along the coasts, are connected to the mainland and to each other by **ferries** *(traghetti)* and the more expensive **hydrofoils** *(aliscafi);* international trips are generally made by ferry. Italy's largest private ferry service, **Tirrenia** (www.gruppotirrenia. it), runs ferries to Sardinia, Sicily, Tunisia, and Albania. Other major ferry companies (**Siremar, Toremar, Saremar, Caremar, Moby Lines,** and **Corsica Ferries**) and the **SNAV** (www.snav.it) hydrofoil services travel between major ports like Ancona, Bari, Brindisi, Civitavecchia, Genoa, La Spezia, Naples, and Trapani. Ferry services also depart for the Tremiti, Pontine, and Aeolian Islands. Ferry service is also prevalent in the Lake Country.

BY BUS AND METRO

DON'T TRASH IT! Hold on to your (validated!) bus, metro, and train tickets throughout your entire journey. *Controllori* will spontaneously board at any given time to check for freeloaders and dole out hefty fines.

Though notoriously unreliable and uncomfortable, **buses** *(autobus)* are often cheaper than trains. Two bus systems exist within Italy: *pullman* or intercity, which run between towns and regions, and intra-city, which provide local transportation. Tickets can generally be purchased at private bus company offices near the bus station or departure point, or onboard. In many rural areas, where stops are unmarked, it is crucial to find out exactly where to stand to flag down the bus. On rare occasions, the tickets are actually sold by the side of the road out of a salesperson's car near where the bus will stop. Intra-city bus tickets are usually sold at *tabaccherie*, and must be validated using the orange machines immediately upon entering the bus. Failure to do so will result in fines around €30, but occasionally as high as €500 upon inspection. The websites www.bus. it and www.italybus.it are both helpful resources for finding bus companies in specific regions and routes to small towns.

Most large cities, including Rome, Naples, and Milan, have fast and cheap **metro systems** that connect major tourist destinations. Along with buses, the metro is the best form of local transport. The metro usually operates from 6am until midnight, and tickets usually cost approximately €1. Cabins and stations get packed during rush hour, so guard personal belongings carefully, as theft is rampant. Tickets are sold in stations at counters or from automated machines. Remember to validate them, or risk a heavy fine.

FERMATA FRENZY. Taking the bus in Italy is easy, affordable, and a great way to get around, but most bus stops that aren't in major *piazze* are only *"fermata prenotata"* stops, meaning the bus driver won't stop there unless he/she sees somebody waiting or someone onboard requests a stop. Drivers often miss travelers waiting quietly on the side of the road, so make your presence known. Wave your hands, step out on the curb, and make eye contact; you might feel silly but you'll feel worse if the bus drives right by.

ESSENTIALS

BY CAR

With a vast network of narrow, winding roads, loosely enforced speed limits, and aggressive native drivers, touring Italy by **car** is a memorable experience. Despite the initial intimidation that may come from cruising bumper to bumper on a cliffside road along the Amalfi coast, with a little bit of courage and a decent helping of driving competence, car travel opens up corners of Italy that are not easily reached by—or inaccessible altogether to—the average explorer.

RENTING

While the Italian bus and train systems are quite effective in negotiating travel between the major cities, travelers looking to explore smaller cities and rural villages might find renting a car to be a more viable option. A single traveler won't save by renting a car (especially considering the high gas prices), but four usually will. If you can't decide between train and car travel, you may benefit from a combination of the two; RailEurope and other railpass vendors offer **rail-and-drive** packages. **Fly-and-drive** packages are often available from travel agents or airline-rental agency partnerships.

RENTAL AGENCIES

You can generally make reservations before you leave by calling major international offices in your home country. It's a good idea to cross-check this information with local agencies as well. The local desk numbers are included in town listings; for home-country numbers, call your toll-free directory.

To rent a car from most establishments in Italy, you need to be at least 18 years old. Some agencies require renters to be 25, and most charge those 18-24 an additional insurance fee of €12 per day. Small local operations occasionally rent to people under 21, but be sure to ask about the insurance coverage and deductible, and always check the fine print. Rental agencies in Italy include:

Auto Europe (Italy, Canada, and the US ☎+1-888-223-5555; www.autoeurope.com).

Avis (Australia ☎13 63 33, Canada and the US +1-800-352-7900, Italy 19 91 00 133, New Zealand 0800 655 111, UK 0870 010 0287; www.avis.com).

Budget (Canada ☎+1-800-268-8900, UK 8701 565 656, US +1-800-472-3325, www.budget.com).

Europe by Car (US ☎+1-800-223-1516; www.europebycar.com).

Hertz (Canada ☎+1-800-654-3001; +1-US 800-654-3001; www.hertz.com).

COSTS AND INSURANCE

Rental car prices start at around US$39 a day from national companies. Expect to pay more for larger cars and for four-wheel-drive. Cars with **automatic transmission** can cost up to US$100 per day more than cars with manual transmission (stick shift), and, in some places, automatic transmission is hard to find in the first place. It is often difficult to find an automatic four-wheel-drive. Remember that if you are driving a conventional rental vehicle on an unpaved road, you are almost never covered by insurance; ask about this before leaving the rental agency.

DRIVING PERMITS AND CAR INSURANCE

INTERNATIONAL DRIVING PERMIT (IDP)

If you plan to drive a car while in Italy, you must be over 18 and have an **International Driving Permit (IDP)**, though certain regions will allow travelers to drive with a valid American or Canadian license for a limited number of months. It may be a good idea to get one anyway, in case you're in a situation (e.g., an accident or stranded in a small town) where the police do not know English; information on the IDP is printed in 11 languages, including Italian.

Your IDP, valid for one year, must be issued in your own country before you depart. An application for an IDP usually requires one or two photos, a current local license, an additional form of identification, and a fee. To apply, contact your home country's automobile association. Be vigilant when purchasing an IDP online or anywhere other than your home automobile association. Many vendors sell permits of questionable legitimacy for higher prices.

CAR INSURANCE

Most credit cards cover standard insurance. If you rent, lease, or borrow a car, you will need a **green card,** or **International Insurance Certificate,** to certify that you have liability insurance and that it applies abroad. Green cards can be obtained at car rental agencies, car dealers (for those leasing cars), some travel agents, and some border crossings. Rental agencies may require you to purchase theft insurance in countries that they consider to have a high risk of auto theft.

ON THE ROAD

Driving in Italy is similar to driving in the rest of Europe: vehicles drive on the right, pass on the left, and follow international rules and road signs established by the Geneva Convention. Roads range from the *autostrade*—superhighways with 130kph (80 mph) speed limit, increased to 150kph (93 mph) in some areas—to the narrow and sometimes unpaved *strade comunali* (local roads). Mountain roads can have steep cliffs and narrow curves; exercise caution if you must drive in the Dolomites or the Apennines. Highways usually charge expensive tolls, often best paid with a credit card. In cities the speed limit is usually 50kph (31 mph). Headlights must be on when driving on the *autostrada*. For more driving rules and regulations, check *Moto Europa* (www.ideamerge.com/motoeuropa) or *In Italy Online* (www.initaly.com/travel/info/driving.htm).

CAR ASSISTANCE

The **Automobile Club d'Italia** (ACI) is at the service of all drivers in Italy, with offices located throughout the country (www.aci.it). In case of breakdown, call ☎116 for assistance from the nearest ACI. On superhighways use the emergency telephones placed every 2km. For long drives in desolate areas, invest in a roadside assistance program and a cell phone, but be aware that use of phones en route is only permitted with a hands-free device.

BY BOAT, BICYCLE, MOPED, ETC.

Renting a **bike** is easy in Italy; look for *noleggio* signs. If you want to bring your own, some airlines will count a bike as your second piece of luggage; many now charge extra (one-way US$80-160). Bikes must be packed in a cardboard box with the pedals and front wheel detached; many airlines sell bike boxes at the airport (US$15). Most ferries let you take your bike for free or for a nominal fee, and you can always ship your bike on trains. Renting a bike beats bringing your own if you plan to stay in one or two regions, and some hostels rent bicycles for low prices. *Let's Go* lists bike rental stores in the **Transportation** section of towns and cities whenever possible. **Ciclismo Classico,** 30 Marathon St., Arlington, MA 02474, USA (☎+1-800-866-7314; www.ciclismoclassico. com), offers beginner to advanced level trips across Italy, including Sardinia, the Amalfi Coast, Southern Italy, Sicily, Piedmont, and the Veneto.

Scooters or **mopeds** are available for rent in major cities, as well as in smaller or rural locations. Often a *motorino* (scooter) is the most convenient method of transportation to reach sights in places with unreliable bus or train connections. Rental companies are required by law to provide a helmet, which the driver must wear. Gas and insurance may or may not be included in the rental price. Even if riding a scooter is exhilarating, always exercise caution; practice in empty streets before you hit the open road and keep with the flow of traffic instead of just following street signs. Drivers in Italy—especially those enthusiastic southerners—are notorious for ignoring traffic laws.

Some of Italy's grandest scenery can be seen only by **foot.** *Let's Go* features many daytrips, but native inhabitants and fellow travelers are the best source for tips. Professionally run hiking and walking tours are often your best bet for navigating *la bell'Italia.* Hiking tours generally range from six to nine days long and cost from US$2800-4000. Check out Ciclismo Classico (see above) for hiking options along the Amalfi Coast, and through Tuscany or Cinque Terre. The **Backpack Europe** website (www.backpackeurope.com) provides links to great hiking, walking, and kayaking options throughout Italy.

BY THUMB

> **!** **LET'S NOT GO.** Let's Go never recommends hitchhiking as a safe means of transportation. None of this information is intended to do so.

Let's Go strongly urges you to consider the risks before you choose to hitchhike. Hitching means entrusting your life to a stranger and risking assault, sexual harassment, theft, and unsafe driving. For women traveling alone (or even in pairs), hitching is just too dangerous. Note that it is illegal to walk along the highway. Some travelers head to service areas *(le aree di servizio)* to get rides. Italian speakers will have an easier time getting where they want to go; knowing the Italian name of the destination is essential. Most Western European countries, including Italy, offer a ride service which pairs drivers with riders; the fee varies by destination. **Eurostop International** (www.eurostop.be) is one of the largest. Or try **Viaval** (www.viavai.com/autostop).

KEEPING IN TOUCH

BY EMAIL AND INTERNET

While Internet is a relatively common amenity throughout Italy, Wi-Fi is not, and as a general rule, the prevalence of both decreases the further you travel from urban areas. In large towns, it may be possible to find Internet but not Wi-Fi. In smaller towns, even a basic Internet connection may be hard to come by. Rates range from €2-6 per hour. While it's possible in some places to forge a remote link with your home server, in most cases this is a much slower (and more expensive) option than using free **web-based email accounts** (e.g., www.gmail.com and www.hotmail.com). **Internet cafes** and the occasional free Internet terminal at a public library or university are listed in the **Practical Information** sections of major cities. For additional cybercafes in Italy, check out http://cafe.ecs.net.

BY TELEPHONE

CALLING HOME FROM ITALY

Prepaid phone cards are a common and relatively inexpensive means of calling abroad. Each comes with a Personal Identification Number (PIN) and a toll-free access number. You call the access number and then follow the directions to enter your PIN. To buy prepaid phone cards, check online for the best rates; www.callingcards.com is a good place to start. Online providers generally send your access number and PIN via email, with no actual "card" involved. You can also call home with prepaid phone cards purchased in Italy.

PLACING INTERNATIONAL CALLS. To call Italy from home or to call home from Italy, dial:
1. The **international dialing prefix.** To call from **Australia**, dial 0011; **Canada** or the **US**, 011; **Ireland, New Zealand,** or the **UK,** 00; **Italy,** 00.
2. The **country code** of the country you want to call. To call **Australia,** dial 61; **Canada** or the **US,** 1; **Ireland,** 353; **New Zealand,** 64; the **UK,** 44; **Italy,** 39.
3. The **city/area code.** *Let's Go* lists the city/area codes for cities and towns in Italy opposite the city or town name, next to a ☎, as well as in every phone number. If the first digit is a zero (e.g., 020 for London), omit the zero when calling from abroad (e.g., dial 20 from **Canada** to reach **London**).
4. The **local number.**

Another option is to purchase a **calling card,** linked to a major national telecommunications service in your home country. Calls are billed collect or to your account. To call home with a calling card, contact the operator for your service provider in Italy by dialing the appropriate toll-free access number.

CALLING WITHIN ITALY

The simplest way to call within the country is to use a coin-operated phone. Prepaid phone cards (available at newspaper kiosks and tobacco stores, or *tabaccherie*), usually save time and money in the long run.

CELLULAR PHONES

Cellular phones *(telefonini)* are a convenient and inexpensive option for those planning longer visits to Italy. Given the prevalence of cell phones in Italy, pay phones are increasingly hard to come by, making cell phones a good alternative for tourists. You won't necessarily have to deal with cell phone plans and bills; prepaid minutes are widely available and phones can be purchased cheaply or even rented, avoiding the hassle of pay phones and phone cards.

The international standard for cell phones is **Global System for Mobile Communication** (GSM). To make and receive calls in Italy you will need a GSM-compatible phone and a **SIM (Subscriber Identity Module) card,** a country-specific, thumbnail-sized chip that gives you a local phone number and plugs you into the local network. For more info on GSM phones, check out www.telestial.com, www.orange.co.uk, www.roadpost.com, or www.planetomni.com.

TIME DIFFERENCES

Italy is one hour ahead of Greenwich Mean Time (GMT). The country observes Daylight Saving Time, which starts on the last Sunday in March, when clocks

ESSENTIALS

are moved ahead one hour, making Italy two hours ahead of GMT. Clocks are put back one hour on the last Sunday of October.

The following table applies from late October to early April.

4AM	5AM	6AM	7AM	8AM	1PM	10PM*
Vancouver Seattle Los Angeles	Denver	Chicago	Boston New York Toronto	New Brunswick	**Rome**	Sydney Canberra Melbourne

*Australia observes Daylight Saving Time from October to March, the opposite of the Northern Hemisphere. Therefore, it is 8hr. ahead of Rome from March to October and 10hr. ahead from October to March, for an average of 9hr.

BY MAIL

SENDING MAIL HOME FROM ITALY

Airmail is the best way to send mail home from Italy. **Aerogrammes,** printed sheets that fold into envelopes and travel via airmail, are available at post offices. Write "airmail" or *"per posta aerea"* on the front. Most post offices charge exorbitant fees or simply refuse to send aerogrammes with enclosures. Surface mail is by far the cheapest and slowest way to send mail. It takes one to two months to cross the Atlantic and one to three to cross the Pacific—good for heavy items you won't need for a while, such as souvenirs. Delivery times and package shipping costs vary; inquire at the post office (*ufficio postale*).

SENDING MAIL TO ITALY

To ensure timely delivery, mark envelopes "airmail," *"par avion,"* or *"per posta aerea."* In addition to the standard postage system whose rates are listed below, **Federal Express** (Australia ☎+61 13 26 10, Canada and the US +1-800-463-3339, Ireland +353 800 535 800, New Zealand +64 800 733 339, the UK +44 8456 0708 09; www.fedex.com) handles express mail services to Italy.

There are several ways to arrange pick up of letters sent to you while you are abroad. Mail can be sent via **Fermo Posta** (General Delivery) to almost any city or town in Italy with a post office, and it is generally reliable, if occasionally untimely. Address **Poste Restante** letters like so:

Dante ALIGHIERI

c/o Ufficio Postale Centrale

FERMO POSTA

48100 Ravenna

Italy

The mail will go to a special desk in the central post office, unless you specify a post office by street address or postal code. Note that the postal service may ignore this specification. It is usually safer and quicker, though more expensive, to send mail express or registered. Bring your passport (or other photo ID) for pickup; there may be a small fee. If the clerks insist that there is nothing for you, ask them to check under your first name as well. *Let's Go* lists post offices in the **Practical Information** section for each city and most towns.

ACCOMMODATIONS

HOSTELS

Many hostels are laid out dorm-style, often with large single-sex rooms and bunk beds, though private rooms that sleep two to four are becoming more common. They sometimes provide bike or moped rentals, lockers, transportation to airports, breakfast and other meals, laundry facilities, and Internet. However, there can be drawbacks: some hostels close during certain daytime "lockout" hours, have a curfew, don't accept reservations, impose a maximum stay, or, less frequently, require that you do chores. In Italy, a dorm bed in a hostel will average around €15-25 and a private room around €25-30.

A HOSTELER'S BILL OF RIGHTS. There are certain standard features that we do not include in our hostel listings. Unless we state otherwise, you can expect that every hostel has no lockout, no curfew, free sheets, free hot showers, some system of secure luggage storage, and no key deposit.

HOSTELLING INTERNATIONAL

Joining the youth hostel association in your own country (listed below) automatically grants you membership privileges in **Hostelling International (HI)**, a federation of national hosteling associations. Non-HI members may be allowed to stay in some hostels, but will have to pay extra to do so. HI hostels are scattered throughout Italy, and are typically less expensive than private hostels. HI's umbrella organization's website (www.hihostels.com), which lists the web addresses and phone numbers of all national associations, can be a great place to begin researching hosteling in a specific region. Other comprehensive hosteling websites include www.hostels.com and www.hostelplanet.com.

Most HI hostels also honor **guest memberships**—you'll get a blank card with space for six validation stamps. Each night you'll pay a nonmember supplement (one-sixth the membership fee) and earn one guest stamp; six stamps make you a member. A new membership benefit is the **FreeNites program,** which allows hostelers to gain points toward free rooms. Most student travel agencies (p. 19) sell HI cards, as do all of the national hosteling organizations listed below. All prices listed below are valid for a one-year membership.

Australian Youth Hostels Association (AYHA), 422 Kent St., Sydney, NSW 2000 (☎+61 2 9261 1111; www.yha.com.au). AUS$52, under 18 AUS$19.

Hostelling International-Canada (HI-C), 205 Catherine St., Ste. 400, Ottawa, ON K2P 1C3 (☎+1-613-237-7884; www.hihostels.ca). CDN$35, under 18 free.

Hostelling International Northern Ireland (HINI), 22-32 Donegall Rd., Belfast BT12 5JN (☎+44 28 9032 4733; www.hini.org.uk). UK£15, under 25 UK£10.

Youth Hostels Association of New Zealand Inc. (YHANZ), Level 1, 166 Moorhouse Ave., P.O. Box 436, Christchurch (☎+64 3379 9970, in NZ 0800 278 299; www.yha.org.nz). NZ$40, under 18 free.

Youth Hostels Association (England and Wales), Trevelyan House, Dimple Rd., Matlock, Derbyshire DE4 3YH (☎+44 8707 7088 68; www.yha.org.uk). UK£16, under 26 UK£10.

Hostelling International-USA, 8401 Colesville Rd., Ste. 600, Silver Spring, MD 20910 (☎+1-301-495-1240; www.hiayh.org). US$28, under 18 free.

HOTELS, GUESTHOUSES, AND PENSIONS

Hotel singles in Italy cost about US$40-80 (€25-50) per night, doubles US$ 60-140 (€40-90). In many lower budget establishments, you'll typically share a hall bathroom; a private bathroom will cost extra. Some hotels offer "full pension" (all meals) and "half pension" (no lunch). Smaller guesthouses and pensions are often cheaper than hotels. If you make **reservations** in writing, indicate your night of arrival and the number of nights you plan to stay. The hotel will send you a confirmation and may request payment for the first night.

OTHER TYPES OF ACCOMMODATIONS

BED AND BREAKFASTS (B&BS)

For a cozy alternative to impersonal hotel rooms, B&Bs (private homes with rooms available to travelers) range from acceptable to sublime. In Italy, B&Bs, singles generally cost €20-50 and doubles generally cost €70-90. Any number of websites provide listings for B&Bs; check out **Bed & Breakfast Inns Online** (www.bbonline.com), **InnFinder** (www.inncrawler.com), **InnSite** (www.innsite.com), or **BedandBreakfast.com** (www.bedandbreakfast.com).

AGRITURISMO

Frequently omitted by mainstream travel guides and ignored by local tourist offices, *agriturismo* is a pleasurable, leisurely, and inexpensive way to visit the Italian countryside. Local families open their homes to guests and provide reasonably-priced meals. The host family and guests gather around the table each night, sharing bottles of homemade wine, fresh vegetables from the garden, and stories that last far into the night. These houses, however, are usually only accessible by car—a tranquil remoteness that simply adds to their charm, provided that you can reach them. If you're looking to truly experience the laid-back Italian lifestyle, hearty cuisine, local wines, and sweeping countryside vistas, *agriturismo* is the best way to spend your time and money. To find *agriturismo* options in your region, consult local tourist offices or check out the **Associazione Nazionale per l'Agriturismo, l'Ambiente e il Territorio** (www.agriturist.it).

UNIVERSITY DORMS

Many **colleges** and **universities** open their residence halls to travelers when school is not in session; some do so even during term time. Getting a room may take a couple of phone calls and require advanced planning, but rates tend to be low and many offer free local calls and Internet access. For a list of student housing opportunities in Italian cities, write to The Italian Ministry of Education, Vle. Trastevere 76/A, 00153 Rome (☎06 58 491; www.pubblica.istruzione.it), and ask for a "Guide for Foreign Students."

LONG-TERM ACCOMMODATIONS

Travelers planning to stay in Italy for extended time periods may find it most cost-effective to locate an **apartment** for rent (*affittasi*). A good place to check for apartments is **craigslist** (www.craigslist.org), a forum for renters and rentees where you can see others' listings or post your own housing needs. For regional listings, try http://affittistudenti.studenti.it and www.secondamano.it. If it's Rome you're after, look at http://liveinrome.com. For listings in Rome, Florence, and Venice, check www.romepower.com.

CAMPING

Over 1700 campgrounds in Italy are designated between one and four stars; a four-star campground includes amenities such as a market, swimming pool, and a bar. Costs vary, but are generally under €10 per person. Some campgrounds offer bungalows as a cheap alternative for travelers without tents; others even have tents to rent. Camping is legal only at designated sites. A regional guide can be found through **Easy Camping** (☎33 96 09 41 04; easycamping.it). Reservations are recommended at some sites. Campgrounds are listed in the **Accommodations** section when available.

THE GREAT OUTDOORS

The **Great Outdoor Recreation Page** (www.gorp.com) provides excellent general information for travelers planning on camping or enjoying the outdoors.

 LEAVE NO TRACE. *Let's Go* encourages travelers to embrace the "Leave No Trace" ethic, minimizing their impact on natural environments and protecting them for future generations. Trekkers and wilderness enthusiasts should set up camp on durable surfaces, use cookstoves instead of campfires, bury human waste away from water supplies, bag trash and carry it out with them, and respect wildlife and natural objects. For more detailed information, contact the **Leave No Trace Center for Outdoor Ethics**, P.O. Box 997, Boulder, CO 80306, USA (☎+1-800-332-4100 or 303-442-8222; www.lnt.org).

USEFUL RESOURCES

A variety of publishing companies offer guidebooks to meet the educational needs of novice or expert hikers. For info about camping, hiking, and biking, write or call the publishers listed below to receive a free catalog. Campers heading to Europe should consider buying an **International Camping Carnet.** Similar to a hostel membership card, it's required at a few campgrounds and sometimes provides discounts. It is available in North America from the **Family Campers and RVers Association** and in the UK from **The Caravan Club** (both below). For Italian information, consult the **Touring Club Italiano (TCI),** C. Italia 10, Milan (☎02 85 261; www.touringclub.com).

NATIONAL PARKS

Trekking through a national park can be a welcome escape from the touristed mayhem of Italy's big cities. With 22 national parks and more than five times as many regional parks and nature reserves, Italy protects nearly 10% of its land. Whether you seek mountains, lakes, forests, or oceans, Italy's parks have something to offer. Bears and lynxes inhabit the **Parco Nazionale d'Abruzzo** (www.parcoabruzzo.it; see p. 380), accessible by both car and train from Rome. The beautiful coast of the **Parco Nazionale delle Cinque Terre** (www.parconazionale-5terre.it; see p. 168) can be reached by bus, train, and boat. **Federparchi,** V. Cristoforo Colombo 163, 00147 Rome (☎06 51 60 49 40; www.parks.it.) publishes *Parchi,* a magazine devoted to the parks, their preservation, and other environmental concerns in Italy and throughout Europe. Its thorough website lists news, events, and other info for the parks.

WILDERNESS SAFETY

Staying **warm, dry,** and **well hydrated** is key to a happy and safe wilderness experience. For any hike, pack a first-aid kit, a reflector, a whistle, high-energy food, extra water, raingear, a hat, mittens, and extra socks. For warmth, wear wool or insulating synthetic materials designed for the outdoors.

Check weather forecasts often and pay attention to the skies when hiking, as weather patterns can change suddenly. Always let someone—a friend, your hostel, or a park ranger—know when and where you are going. See **Safety and Health**, p. 15, for information on outdoor medical concerns.

ORGANIZED ADVENTURE TRIPS

Organized adventure tours offer another way of exploring the wild. Activities include hiking, biking, skiing, canoeing, kayaking, rafting, climbing, photo safaris, and archaeological digs. Tourism bureaus can often suggest parks, trails, and outfitters. Organizations that specialize in camping and outdoor equipment like REI and EMS (above) also are good sources for info.

La Boscaglia (☎05 16 26 41 69; www.boscaglia.it). Offers walking tours and treks throughout Italy. Must pay a membership fee to participate (about €20

Specialty Travel Index, P.O. Box 458, San Anselmo, CA 94979, USA (US ☎1-888-624-4030, elsewhere 415-455-1643; www.specialtytravel.com).

SPECIFIC CONCERNS

SUSTAINABLE TRAVEL

In Italy, attention is often focused on cultural restoration while natural resources are overlooked and under appreciated. As the number of travelers on the road rises, the detrimental effect they can have on natural environments is an increasing concern. *Let's Go* promotes the philosophy of sustainable travel. Through a sensitivity to issues of ecology and sustainability, today's travelers can be a powerful force in preserving and restoring the places they visit.

Ecotourism, a rising trend in sustainable travel, focuses on the conservation of natural habitats—mainly, on how to use them to build up the economy without exploitation or overdevelopment. Travelers can make a difference by doing advance research, by supporting organizations and establishments that pay attention to their carbon "footprint," and by patronizing establishments that strive to be environmentally friendly. Recently, ecotourism has been getting more creative, interesting and diverse. Opportunities in Italy can be found at **www.ecoturismo-italia.it,** an Italian nonprofit that works in conjunction with other international organizations. For information on environmental conservation, see the resources below or the **Beyond Tourism** (p. 63) section of this book.

WOMEN TRAVELERS

Women exploring on their own inevitably face additional safety concerns. Single women can consider staying in singles that lock from the inside in hostels or in religious organizations with single-sex dorms. It's a good idea to stick to centrally located accommodations and to avoid traveling alone at night. Always carry extra cash for a phone call, bus, or taxi. Look as if you know where you're going and approach older women or couples for directions if you're lost or feeling uncomfortable. Generally, the less you look like a tourist, the better off you'll be. Your best answer to verbal harassment is no answer at all; feigning deafness, sitting motionless, and staring straight ahead at nothing in particular will usually do the trick. The extremely persistent can sometimes be dissuaded by a firm, loud, and very public *"Vai via"* or *"Vattene"* ("Go Away!"). Don't hesitate to seek out a *poliziotto* (police officer) or a passerby if you are being harassed. A self-defense course will both prepare you for a potential attack and raise your level of awareness of your surroundings (see **Personal Safety,** p. 16).

GLBT TRAVELERS

It is difficult to characterize the Italian attitude toward gay, lesbian, bisexual, and transgender (GLBT) travelers. Homophobia is still in issue in some regions. Rome, Florence, Milan, and Bologna all have easily accessible gay scenes. Away from the larger cities, however, gay social life may be difficult to find. **Out and About** (www.planetout.com) offers a comprehensive site addressing gay travel concerns. The online newspaper **365gay.com** also has a travel section (www.365gay.com/travel/travelchannel.htm). **Babilonia** and **Guida Gay Italia** (www.guidagay.com) can be found at newsstands, and **Pride** and **GayClubbing** (both free) can be found at most gay venues. Travelers can also expect the larger cities to have gay *discoteche* and bars.

Arcigay, V. Don Minzoni 18, 40121 Bologna (☎051 64 93 055; www.arcigay.it). National organization provides resources for homosexuals and helps combat homophobia throughout the peninsula. Holds dances and other special events. Website contains addresses and phone numbers of city centers.

Gay.It, S.p.A., V. Ravizza 22/E, 56121 Pisa (www.gay.it). Provides info on gay life in Italy. Associated website in English (www.gayfriendlyitaly.com) gives regional info on nightlife, homophobia, gay events, and more.

TRAVELERS WITH DISABILITIES

Those with disabilities should inform airlines and hotels of their disabilities when making reservations; some time may be needed to prepare special accommodations. Call ahead to restaurants, museums, and other facilities to find out if they are wheelchair-accessible. Guide-dog owners should inquire as to the quarantine policies of each destination country.

Rail is probably the most convenient form of transport for disabled travelers in Europe: many stations have ramps, and some trains have wheelchair lifts, special seating areas, and specially equipped toilets. All Eurostar, some InterCity (IC), and some EuroCity (EC) trains are **wheelchair-accessible,** and CityNightLine trains and Conrail trains feature special compartments. For those who wish to rent cars, some major **car-rental** agencies (e.g., Hertz) offer hand-controlled vehicles. Look for pamphlets on accessibility from local tourist offices; a list of publications and where to find them can be found at **www.**

coinsociale.it/tourism/services/guide.php. A good wheelchair accessible tour of Rome is available at www.slowtrav.com/italy/accessible/rome/index.htm.

USEFUL ORGANIZATIONS

Accessible Italy, V. C. Manetti 34, 47891 Dogana, Repubblica di San Marino (☎378 05 49 94 11 11; www.accessibleitaly.com). Provides tours to Italy for travelers with disabilities. Proceeds go toward improving handicap-access to attractions in Italy. Also organizes handicap-accessible weddings in Italy.

The Guided Tour, Inc., 7900 Old York Rd., Ste. 114B, Elkins Park, PA 19027, USA (☎+1-800-783-5841; www.guidedtour.com). Organizes travel programs in Italy for persons with developmental and physical challenges.

MINORITY TRAVELERS

Like much of Western Europe, Italy has experienced a wave of immigration from Africa, Eastern Europe, and South America in recent years that has spurred some racial tension, especially over competition in the local economy. Particularly in southern Italy, travelers belonging to racial minorities or members of non-Christian religions may feel unwelcome or experience some hostility. Tension has always existed in Italy regarding gypsies from Romania and other parts of Eastern Europe. In terms of safety, there is no easy answer. Men and women should always travel in groups and avoid unsafe parts of town. The best answer to verbal harassment is often not to acknowledge it. A number of advocacy groups for immigrant rights have sprouted up throughout Italy, including **Associazione Almaterra** (☎01 12 46 70 02; www.arpnet.it/alma/) and **NOSOTRAS** (☎05 52 77 63 26; www.nosotras.it).

DIETARY CONCERNS

With all of Italy's delicious carnivorous offerings, vegetarians may feel left out. While there are not many strictly vegetarian restaurants in Italy, it is not difficult to find vegetarian meals. To avoid confusion in restaurants, make sure you tell your waiter *"Non mangio carne"* (I don't eat meat). Before you head to Italy, check out the **Italian Vegetarian Association (AVI),** V. XXV Aprile 41, 20026 Novate Milanese, Milano (www.vegetariani.it), which also offers *Good Vegetarian Food* (Italian Vegetarian Association, 2004; €12), a guide to vegetarian tourism up and down the peninsula.

Lactose intolerance also does not have to be an obstacle to eating well in Italy. In restaurants ask for items without *latte* (milk), *formaggio* (cheese), *burro* (butter), or *crema* (cream); or order the cheeseless *pizza marinara*.

Travelers who keep **kosher** should contact synagogues in larger cities for info on kosher restaurants. Check out www.shamash.org/kosher/ for an extensive database of kosher establishments in Italy. A good resource is the *Jewish Travel Guide*, edited by Michael Zaidner (Vallentine Mitchell; US$18). Travelers looking for **halal** restaurants may find www.zabihah.com a useful resource.

LET'S GO ONLINE. Plan your next trip on our newly redesigned website, **www.letsgo.com.** It features the latest travel info on your favorite destinations, as well as tons of interactive features: make your own itinerary, read blogs from our researcher-writers, browse our photo library, watch exclusive videos, check out our newsletter, find travel deals, and buy new guides.

LIFE AND TIMES

From Michelangelo to Armani, Italy has carved a distinct path through the centuries, consistently setting a world standard for innovation and elegance. Defined by the legacy of the Roman Empire and the prominence of the Catholic Church, its artistic, intellectual, and cultural developments have carried forward from ancient times to form the foundations of a modern civilization. As a result, modern Italy boasts more UNESCO World Heritage Sites than any other country in the world. Despite this distinction, the country's history has been marked as much by its unresolved conflict as by its accomplishments. Haunted by centuries of foreign rule, fragmented governments, and regional disputes, Italy's allegiances are often torn between past and present, local and national. Even in the last century Italy has continued to rely on its past tradition, struggling to overcome the vestiges of fascism, delaying the passage of women's suffrage until 1945, and strictly observing the Catholic custom. Though both Roman rule and the Risorgimento came close to uniting the country's varied regions, distinct regional identities and social tensions between North and South persist. Italy is today in constant negotiation between tradition and progress, unity and independence, as it endeavors to transform its triumphant past into an equally glorious future the Italian way—slowly but surely.

HISTORY AND POLITICS

ITALY BEFORE ROME (UNTIL 753 BC)

Italy before Rome? Impossible! That's what most might think at least. In fact, a somewhat lengthy and quasi-exciting and rich history proceeded the grand Empire.

Archaeological excavations at Isernia date Italy's earliest inhabitants to the Paleolithic Era (100,000-70,000 BC). Perhaps the most important discovery has been **Ötzi**, a 5000-year-old iceman (p. 261) found in 1991 encased deep inside the icy Dolomites, just chillin'. The Bronze Age brought the development of more sophisticated settlements, and by the seventh century BC, the **Etruscans** had established their stronghold in present-day Tuscany, conquering much of Italy in the process. Though initially powerful, their growth was gradually checked by an increasing Greek presence along the Mediterranean coast. And so the Greco-Roman rivalry commenced. Forming what the Romans would later call **Magna Graecia,** the Greeks established colonies along the coast of Puglia, at Cumae in Campania, and throughout Calabria and Sicily. By the third century BC, however, the power of both Greeks and Etruscans declined as a third force swelled on the mainland—the Romans. By conquering *Magna Graecia*, the Romans inherited their predecessors' cultural history. It was only a matter of time before they set up their legacy.

ANCIENT ROME (753 BC-AD 476)

THE MONARCHY (753-509 BC)

Though numerous stories recount the founding of Rome, the tale of the brothers **Romulus** and **Remus** is by far the most famous. According to legend, one of the seven Vestal Virgins, priestesses who protect Rome's Eternal Flame, conceived the twins Romulus and Remus when she lost her virginity to Mars, the god of war. In a fury over the shame his niece brought to the family name, the priestesses's royal uncle ordered the infants killed. The servant commissioned for the task found himself unable to do so, and instead laid the children in a basket by the Tiber River. Various accounts describe their rescue, though one of the most common depictions is of Romulus and Remus suckling at the teats of a she-wolf who adopted them (an excellent example can be found in a sculpture dating to 500 BC, in the Musei Capitolini; p. 117). In 753 BC, the brothers founded Rome together on the Palatine Hill. While Romulus was building the wall around the Palatine, however, Remus challenged the height of the wall by showing he could jump over it. Angered by this insult, Romulus killed his brother and became the first king of Rome, which was named in his honor. Despite the early successes of Romulus and his successors, Etruscan kings eventually forced themselves back into power. By 616 BC, their **Tarquin** dynasty, short-lived though it may have been, was infamous for its tyranny. This era of kings ended in 509 BC, when Prince Sextus Tarquinius raped the noblewoman Lucretia, compelling her relative Lucius Brutus to expel the Tarquins and establish the **Roman Republic.**

THE REPUBLIC (509-27 BC)

The end of the monarchy and the foundation of the Republic raised new debates over equality. The Republic faced social struggles between upper-class patricians, who enjoyed full participation in the Senate, and middle- and lower-class plebeians, who were denied political involvement. In 450 BC, the **Laws of the Twelve Tables,** the first codified Roman laws, made a slight concession to the lower classes, requiring that the law be made public and allowing them some political liberties.

As the Republic made efforts to placate those within its territory, it continued in its efforts to dominate those outside it. The defeat of Tarentum (modern day Taranto) in 272 BC completed the Roman conquest of mainland Italy. Never satisfied, the Romans went on to conquer **Sicily** in 241 BC and to wrest **Sardinia** in 238 BC from the **Carthaginians,** an extremely successful Phoenician colony. With this conquest, the Romans gained control of all of modern-day Italy.

The spoils of war that supposedly enriched Rome actually undermined its stability by creating further class inequality. In 133 BC Tiberius Gracchus, the first of the two **Gracchi brothers,** attempted to push through land reforms, but was assassinated. Ten years later his brother Gaius again attempted reforms with the same results. Demands for land redistribution led to riots against the patrician class and then to the **Social War** in 91 BC. The patrician general **Sulla** saw his chance for glory in the unrest, defeated his rivals in 82 BC, and quickly named himself dictator.

In 73 BC, **Spartacus,** an escaped gladiatorial slave, led an army of 70,000 slaves and impoverished farmers on a two-year rampage around the Italian peninsula. Sulla's close associates, **Marcus Crassus** and **Pompey the Great,** quelled the uprising and took control of Rome for themselves. They joined forces with ambitious **Julius Caesar,** the conqueror of Gaul, but their alliance rapidly fell apart as their absolute power corrupted them absolutely. By 45 BC, Caesar had defeated his "allies" and emerged as the Republic's leader, naming himself Dictator for Life. Angered by Caesar's pandering to the poor, an aristocratic coalition, led by **Brutus,** assassinated the reform-oriented leader on the Ides (15th) of March, 44 BC. Caesar's death created yet another power vacuum as would-be successors struggled for the helm. In 31 BC, Octavian, Caesar's adopted heir, emerged victorious over Marc Antony and his exotic mistress Cleopatra; he was granted the title **Augustus** (meaning "majestic") in 27 BC.

THE EMPIRE (27 BC-AD 476)

As the center of the world's largest and most powerful empire, Rome eventually reached as far as modern Britain in the north and Iran in the east. Political power and economic prosperity brought about great cultural achievement, and Roman civilization and language made a lasting impact on every corner of the Empire, and often beyond.

Augustus was the first of the Empire's **Julio-Claudian** rulers (27 BC-AD 68). Superficially following Republican traditions, he did not call himself *rex* (king), but *princeps* (first citizen). His principate (27 BC-AD 14) is considered the Golden Age of Rome, and this period of relative stability and prosperity, the *Pax Romana* (Roman Peace), continued until AD 180. During this time, Augustus extended Roman law and civic culture, beautified Rome, and reorganized its administration. For all of his excellent reforms, Augustus ran a tight ship. He even exiled his daughter, **Julia,** for reasons of promiscuity.

The Empire continued to expand despite the fact that two of its emperors during this time, **Caligula** (AD 37-41) and **Nero** (AD 54-68), were violent, economically irresponsible, and likely mad: a veritable trifecta of political incompetence. Following a series of civil wars after Nero's death in AD 68, the **Flavian** dynasty (AD 69-96) ushered in a period of prosperity, extended to new heights by **Trajan** (AD 98-117), who conquered the regions at the borders of the Black Sea. By this point, the Empire had reached astounding geographical limits, encompassing Western Europe, the Mediterranean islands, England, North Africa, and part of Asia. Following Trajan, **Hadrian** (AD 117-130) established the **Antonine** dynasty, which lasted until AD 193. The Antonines, especially philosopher-emperor **Marcus Aurelius,** were known for their enlightened leadership. When **Septimius Severus** (AD 146-211) won the principate after yet another civil war, he founded the robust **Severan** dynasty (AD 193-235).

Weak governments and rapid inflation led to near anarchy in the AD third century, until a formerly obscure general, **Diocletian** (AD 284-305), divided the empire into two eastern and two western regions, each with its own ruler. As a result of his persecution of Christians, Diocletian's reign became known as the "Age of Martyrs." While Diocletian's economically successful four-part empire eventually crumbled under his successor, **Constantine** (AD 272-337), Christian fortune took a turn for the better. Before the Battle of the Milvian Bridge in AD 312, he claimed he saw a cross of light in the sky, emblazoned with the words "by this sign you shall conquer." When victory followed, he converted to Christianity and issued the **Edict of Milan** in AD 313 abolishing religious discrimination. In AD 330 he began the process of moving the capital to Byzantium, renaming the city **Constantinople** (present-day Istanbul) in his honor. These changes split the Empire permanently into the stronger, wealthier Byzantine Empire and the down-sized Roman Empire, which struggled to integrate a large barbarian immigrant population. **Alaric,** king of the Visigoths, sacked Rome in AD 410, dealing a crushing blow to Roman morale. Roman leadership proved little help in this situation: Emperor **Honorius** so uninformed of the state of his Empire that he believed news of the imminent fall of Rome referred to the death of his pet rooster, Roma. The final symbolic blow came in AD 476 when the German chief **Odoacer** crowned himself king and put the last western emperor, Romulus Augustulus, under house arrest.

MIDDLE AGES (476-1375 AD)

Though sometimes called the "Dark Ages," the near millennium between the fall of Rome and the emergence of the Renaissance was not, in fact, a cultural wasteland. Instead, this complex period of secular and religious power struggles resulted in the establishment of institutions like the royal court and feudal society. External influences from barbarian tribes, Arabic kingdoms, and the Germanic empire brought a blast of fresh air to counteract the former empire's decay.

While the East continued to thrive as the **Byzantine Empire,** the fall of the Roman Empire in the West left room for the growing strength of the papacy. **Pope Gregory I** (the Great; also known for the Gregorian chant; see p. 54) began to negotiate treaties independent of the Emperor instead of relying on him for protection. With Arabs and Byzantines advancing on Italian territory, the Pope called upon the barbarian chieftain **Charlemagne** to uphold **Roman Catholicism.** Adding Italy to the Holy Roman Empire (not to be confused with the fallen Roman Empire), Charlemagne was crowned emperor of Christian Europe by Pope Leo III on Christmas Day, AD 800. Pope Urban II increased the Church's strength by launching the **First Crusade** to liberate the Holy Land in 1095.

Charlemagne's successors were unable to maintain the new Empire, and in the following centuries, Italy became a playing field for petty wars. The instability of the 12th, 13th, and 14th centuries resulted in a division of power between city-states and rival families, leading to intense regional divisions that still exist today. Both European ruling houses and the Vatican enjoyed setting Italians, most notably the **Guelphs** and **Ghibellines** in the 12th and 13th centuries, against each other. The pro-papal Guelphs managed to expel the imperial-minded Ghibellines from major northern cities by the mid-13th century. The victorious Guelphs then split into two rival factions, the **Blacks** and the **Whites,** and battled for dominion. After the Whites exiled the Blacks from Florence in 1300, the Blacks came back with a vengeance in 1302 and expelled the Whites. Politically minded Florentine poet **Dante Alighieri** was permanently exiled to Ravenna for his loyalty to the Whites, and wrote *La Divina Commedia* (p. 52) as an attempt to vindicate himself in the eyes of his fellow Florentines.

Church separated from state when Holy Roman Emperor **Henry IV** (1084-1105) denounced **Pope Gregory VII** (1073-85) as a "false monk." Gregory in turn threatened the Emperor's nobles with excommunication. The terrified Emperor gave in to the Pope, but then came back with an army that defeated the Church's forces. The destabilization of Church power reached its zenith during the **Babylonian Captivity** (1309-77), when the papacy was moved from Rome to Avignon and was supposedly held "captive" by the French kings. The disorder and confusion sparked the **Great Schism** (1378-1417), when three popes simultaneously claimed the holy title. The conflict was overshadowed by an outbreak of the **Black Death** (also called the bubonic plague) in 1347, which killed one-third of Europe's population, and recurred in Italy each July over the next two centuries.

RENAISSANCE (1375-1540)

After the Middle Ages came the great rebirth, or **Rinascimento** (Renaissance), growing out of a rediscovery of Greek and Latin texts and a new emphasis on high culture. Pinpointing its origins has always been problematic, though historian Hans Baron has argued that the Italian tendency toward friendly competition spurred the rise of **civic humanism** by compelling city officials to bid for the best minds of the era, creating a market for intelligence.

Rising out of medieval obscurity were the exalted **Medici** clan in Florence, the **Visconti** in Milan, and the **House of Este** in Ferrara. When not stabbing each other in cathedrals, these ruling families instituted a series of humanist-minded economic and social reforms. **Cosimo** and **Lorenzo (Il Magnifico)** consolidated power and broadened the scope of the Medici family's activities from banking and warring to patronizing the arts. They engaged in a high-stakes political battle with sword-wielding **Pope Julius II** to bring Michelangelo to Florence and would have prevailed were it not for his Sistine Chapel commission (p. 49).

Just as things were getting interesting, an ascetic Dominican friar set out to spoil the fun. Infamous **Girolamo Savonarola** was ferociously opposed to what he perceived as the excesses of the Church. In 1497, Savonarola's followers did the priest's bidding by collecting and burning thousands of "immoral" books and other objects of vanity, including cosmetics, fine dresses, and musical instruments. The event became known as **The Bonfire of the Vanities**, and participants ranged from enraged Florentine clergy to a reformed Botticelli, who even threw several of his own paintings of mythological figures onto the pyre. Savonarola's power over the Florentine public pushed him into such great criticism of the clergy that **Pope Alexander VI** tried to silence the friar by excommunicating him. Savonarola persevered until the fickle Florentines—tired of his nagging—tortured and hanged him from the top of the **Palazzo Vecchio**, and burned him at the stake.

Power-hungry princes continued the Italian tradition of petty warfare, leaving the door open for foreign invasion. The weakened cities yielded in the 16th century to the invading Spanish armies of **Charles V.** The fighting continued until 1559 when Spain finally gained control over all Italian cities except Venice. Despite the political unrest plaguing Italy at the time, several prominent Italians embarked to make a splash on the world scene. **Christopher Columbus,** a native of Genoa funded by Queen Isabella of Spain, set sail in 1492 to discover a faster route to Asia, inadvertently opening the door to a whole New World of exploration with his discovery of the Caribbean. The Florentine **Amerigo Vespucci** made his own expeditions across the Atlantic, leaving his name on both Americas, and **Galileo Galilei,** despite the Church's opposition, suggested that the Earth spins around the sun. During Galileo's trial for heresy, he recanted, but mumbled *"eppur si muove"* ("but it does move") after the Inquisition ruled him guilty. He died under house arrest in 1642.

FOREIGN RULE (1540-1815)

Once the seat of the mightiest empire of the Western world, by the 18th century the Italian peninsula could no longer support the economic demands of the Holy Roman Empire. **Charles II,** the last Spanish Habsburg ruler, died in 1700, sparking the War of the Spanish Succession. Italy, weak and decentralized, became the booty in battles between the Austrian Habsburgs and the French and Spanish Bourbons.

A century later, **Napoleon** decided to solve the disputes the easy way: he began taking all the spoils for himself. During his march through Europe, the little emperor united much of Italy into the Italian Republic and incidentally fostered national sovereignty. Napoleon declared himself the monarch of the newly united **Kingdom of Italy** in 1804. After Napoleon's fall in 1815 at the **Battle of Waterloo**, the **Congress of Vienna** carved up Italy, unsurprisingly granting considerable control to Austria. Exiled, Napoleon spent his last days amidst the charms of Elba (p. 342), an island off the Tuscan coast. Despite his exile, the consequences of his unification efforts would have a permanent impact on the Italian landscape.

THE ITALIAN NATION (1815-PRESENT)

UNIFICATION

Following the Congress of Vienna, a long-standing grudge against foreign rule sparked the **Risorgimento,** a nationalist movement that culminated in political unification in 1860. **Giuseppe Mazzini, Giuseppe Garibaldi,** and **Camillo Cavour,** the movement's leaders, are honored on countless street signs throughout the country. **Vittorio Emanuele II,** whose name also crowds Italian maps, was crowned as the first ruler of the independent Kingdom of Italy in 1860. He expanded the nation by annexing the north and central regions, with Rome and the Veneto joining in 1870.

Though Italy was united under a single name, tensions arose between the different regions. The north sought to protect its money from the needs of the agrarian south, and cities were wary of surrendering power to a central administration. The defiant **Pope Pius IX** (1846-78), who had lost power to the kingdom, refused to acknowledge Italian acquisition of Rome and began calling himself a prisoner in the Vatican. Despite these tensions, nationalism increased during **World War I,** as Italy fought against Austria, having been promised territory for its alliance with Russia, Britain, and France.

THE FASCIST REGIME

The chaotic aftermath of WWI paved the way for fascism under **Benito Mussolini,** *Il Duce* ("the leader"), who promised strict order and stability. He established the world's first fascist regime in 1919 and expelled all opposing parties. As Mussolini initiated domestic development programs and aggressive foreign policies, sentiments toward the fascist leader ran the gamut from intense loyalty to belligerent discontent. In 1940, Italy entered **World War II** on the side of its **Axis** ally, Nazi Germany. Success for the Axis powers came quickly but was short-lived: the Allies landed in Sicily in 1943, pushing Mussolini from power. Later that year, Mussolini established the **Republic of Salò,** a Nazi puppet state based in Salò (p. 206). As a final indignity, he and his mistress, **Claretta Petacci,** were captured in Milan and executed, their naked bodies hung upside-down in public. In 1945, after nearly three years of occupation, Italy was finally freed from Nazi control, but tension persisted between supporters of a more liberal government and those who favored a return to fascism.

POST-WAR POLITICS

The end of WWII did little but highlight the Italian peninsula's intense factions. In the 63 years since the end of the war, Italy has changed governments more than 60 times, with no evidence to suggest the trend is slowing. The **Constitution,** adopted in 1948, established a democratic Republic, with a president, a prime minister, a bicameral parliament, and an independent judiciary. The **Christian Democratic Party (DC)** soon triumphed over the **Socialists (PSI)** as the primary player in the government. Over 300 parties fought for supremacy in parliament; unsurprisingly, none could claim a majority.

Ultimately, tenuous party compromises were formed, and the coalition system that exists to this day was arranged.

Italian economic recovery began with industrialization in the 1950s—Lamborghini billboards and factory smokestacks quickly appeared alongside old cathedral spires and large glowing crucifixes on northern cities' skylines. Despite the **Southern Development Fund,** which was established to build roads, construct schools, and finance industry, the traditionally agrarian south lagged behind the more industrial north during this period of growth; the resulting economic inequality contributed to much of the regional strife that persists today. Economic success gave way to violence in the late 1960s, especially the *autunno caldo* (hot autumn) of 1969, a season of strikes, demonstrations, and riots by university students and factory workers, which foreshadowed greater violence in the 70s. During the period of *Strategia della Tensione* (Strategy of Tension) in the early 70s, right-wing terrorists detonated bombs as public manifestations of political discontent, typically trying to blame them on political opponents. The most shocking episode was the 1978 kidnapping and murder of ex-Prime Minister **Aldo Moro** by a group of left-wing terrorists, the *Brigate Rosse* (Red Brigades). The demonstrations and violence of the 70s challenged the conservative Social Democrats. In 1983, **Bettino Craxi** became Italy's first Socialist prime minister, but fell from grace in a corruption scandal, avoiding jail time by fleeing to Tunisia, where he died in 2000.

RECENT DEVELOPMENTS

Italians have always been enamored with powerful, charismatic leaders. Living up to expectations, Italian government officials have rarely shied away from questionable maneuvers intended to bring them more power. Recognizing corruption in his own government, **Luigi Scalfaro,** elected in 1992, launched the *Mani Pulite* (Clean Hand) campaign. With the help of anti-corruption judge **Antonio di Pietro,** he uncovered the *Tangentopoli* (Bribesville) scandal, an unprecedented political crisis that found over 1200 public officials guilty of bribery. Fallout from the investigation included the 1993 bombing of the Uffizi Gallery in Florence, suicides of 10 indicted officials, and the murders of anti-Mafia investigators. Out of the ruins of the old system came the origins of the modern, (generally) less corrupt political system.

ENTER BERLUSCONI. The election of media tycoon **Silvio Berlusconi** as prime minister in 1994 raised eyebrows. The self-made billionaire's empire included three private TV channels, political influence over three state-run channels, a major newspaper, and the AC Milan soccer team. The fragile web of coalitions that enabled Berlusconi's election collapsed after just eight months, forcing him to resign.

Shortly after the collapse of Berlusconi's government, the platform of the reactionary Northern League became separatist under the extremist (and some say racist) **Umberto Bossi.** Aiming to push the economy to meet the European Union's economic standards, the Northern League called for a split from the south in order to create the **Republic of Padania,** a nation for northerners only. The 1996 elections brought the center-left coalition, **l'Ulivo** (Olive Tree), to power, with **Romano Prodi,** a Bolognese professor, economist, and non-politician, serving as prime minister. Ultimately, Prodi helped stabilize Italian politics. For the first time in modern history, Italy was run by two equal coalitions: the center-left l'Ulivo and the center-right **Il Polo** (Berlusconi's Freedom Alliance, without the Northern League). Despite Prodi's optimism, his coalition lost a vote of confidence in 1998.

Prodi was succeeded by former communist **Massimo D'Alema.** D'Alema and **Carlo Ciampi** introduced fiscal reforms and pushed a "blood and tears" budget that qualified Italy for entrance into the European Monetary Union in January 1999. Despite D'Alema's successes, he stepped down in May 2000 and was replaced by former Treasury Minister **Giuliano Amato**. Nicknamed "Dr. Subtle," Amato is one of the people credited with the institution of the 1999 budget reforms. Perhaps the nickname also derives from Amato's ability to avoid scandal; he was one of few to emerge unscathed from corruption crack-downs in the early 90s.

BERLUSCONI: TAKE TWO. Somehow or another Italy's richest man, Berlusconi, secured his re-election as prime minister again in May 2001. Downplaying corruption charges, he won 30% of the popular vote to head Italy's 59th government since WWII with his **Forza Italia** party. Berlusconi reaffirmed his commitment to the US, courting President George W. Bush in several meetings and sending 2700 troops to Iraq, in spite of left-wing opposition. In European foreign policy, the Prime Minister focused more on domestic than on European issues, creating some tension between Italy and its neighbors. Most notable was Berlusconi's 2004 comparison of one German European Parliament member to a guard in a Nazi concentration camp, a comment which caused considerable discord between the governments of Italy and Germany, and caused a miffed Chancellor Gerhard Schroeder to cancel his summer holiday in Italy.

BERLUSCONI: TAKE THREE? Berlusconi's unpopularity mounted as a result of troop deployment in Iraq, and an economic recession caused some to call for the reinstitution of lira. Berlusconi resigned again as Prime Minister in April 2005, only to form a new coalition several days later. History repeated itself as Romano Prodi won over Berlusconi in the national elections of April 2006, much like he did 10 years earlier. Prodi did not find ruling the Italians to be any easier. A controversy over funding the Italian troops in Afghanistan in early 2007 followed by a dispute over expanding the US Army Base in Vicenza (p. 250), pushed Prodi to the limit. He offered his resignation to President Giorgio Napolitano in February 2007. Napolitano did not accept the resignation enthusiastically and called for a vote of confidence in the legislature. After a narrow survival of the vote of no confidence, Prodi decided to remain in office. However, a short time later in January 2008, a new crisis caused Prodi to lose a vote of confidence. In an early election that was scheduled for April 2008, Berlusconi regained his post as Prime Minister.

PEOPLE

DEMOGRAPHICS

Despite the stereotype of large families, Italian women today have an average of only 1.3 babies each, contributing to a lag in population growth that has persisted for several decades. In fact, with a death rate that narrowly outstrips its birth rate and increasing immigration, Italy's population is barely growing at all, holding approximately steady at its current 58 million. Immigration from China, Africa, Eastern Europe, and Middle Eastern countries functions to counteract the dwindling number of Italians in the workforce. Although some consider immigration to be necessary for the economy, many Italians associate undocumented migrant labor with sex work or drug trafficking, despite efforts by the government to eliminate illegal immigration. The situation is only made worse by Italy's aging population distribution. Altogether, these problematic statistics present a perfect storm of population crisis, which represents a legitimate threat to the traditional Italian way of life.

LANGUAGE

A descendant of Latin, Italian is part of the family of Romance languages, which includes French, Spanish, Portuguese, and Romanian. Due to the number and variety of dialects that exist in various regions of the country (a vestige of Italy's past division into city-states), many Italians, especially those in the South, will ironically claim that the first foreign language they learn is Italian. The claim is not unfounded: the throaty **Neapolitan** of southern Italy may indeed sound foreign to a northerner, and even be difficult to understand. Ligurians use a mix of Italian, Catalan, and French. Many Tuscan dialects substitute an "h" for every "c;" an American might be called an "Amerihano." **Sardo,** spoken in Sardinia, bears little resemblance to standard Italian, constituting a separate language in itself. In the northern region of Friuli-Venezia Giulia, you may encounter as many as four languages spoken in one small city—Slovene, Italian, German, and Friulian coexist in Canale. Conversely, citizens in some northern regions do not speak any Italian at all: the population of Valle d'Aosta speaks mainly French, and Trentino-Alto Adige has a German-speaking minority. Standard Italian, developed in the 13th and 14th centuries as a literary dialect, today serves as the language used by schools, media, and literature. North of Rome, dialects are dying out in favor of this standard language, but accents persist. Locals do their best to employ standard Italian with foreigners, although some may be hesitant to do so. Many Italians, especially older people or those living in rural areas, do not speak English, but most young people, big-city dwellers, and those in the tourist industry do.

TALK TO THE HAND. Italians don't just talk with their mouths, they also use hand gestures. When dialects (or basic language skills) fall short, these are universal and instantly understood. To express frustration, as in, "*Mamma mia*, are you seriously going to fine me even though the signs says I can park here on Sundays?" put your hands together in a prayer-like position and shake them down and up, imploringly. Indignant? Hold all your fingers together, point them upward, and shake your wrist lightly back and forth. Don't care? Point your palm downwards and drag your fingers outwards from where your chin and neck meet. Ask around for more gems. Don't get confused; the best of friendships could go south if an inexperienced gesturer were to offer up the wrong finger 🖕.

LISTEN WITH YOUR EYES. First published in 1958 and re-released in 2005 by Chronicle Books, Bruno Munari's *Speak Italian: The Fine Art of the Gesture* waves its hands in every conceivable Italian way and provides a "supplement to the Italian dictionary" by demystifying Italian hand gestures. A fun collection of photos accompanied by explanations in Italian and English, this book will give you "words" when you find yourself speechless in the stickiest of situations.

RELIGION

As the home of the pope, Italy has been the center of the Roman Catholic faith for almost 2000 years. The **Lateran Pacts,** a treaty in 1929 between Pope Pius XI and Benito Mussolini, made the Vatican City a sovereign state within the city of Rome. It is the traditional and administrative capital of the Catholic

Church. The treaty also made Catholicism the official religion of Italy, which it remained until 1984. Unsurprisingly, roughly 90% of Italians identify themselves as Catholic, although only 40% consider themselves active members of the church. Additionally, the country is home to a substantial number of Protestants and nearly a million Muslims.

The death of **Pope John Paul II** in April 2005 stirred Catholics around the globe. Tens of thousands flooded the square in front of St. Peter's Basilica (p. 140) as the College of Cardinals gathered in the Sistine Chapel (p. 49) to elect a new Pope. Sworn to secrecy (a full transcript of the voting will not be made public for 100 years), the Cardinals locked inside the chapel cast four votes per day until a two-thirds majority was reached. After each round of voting, smoke from the chimneys of the Sistine Chapel signaled the results—gray smoke for failure to reach a consensus, and white smoke for a successful election. The process could have taken up to three and a half months (as it did in AD 180), but **Cardinal Ratzinger** of Munich (now **Pope Benedict XVI**) was elected on the second day of voting. At 78, Cardinal Ratzinger became the oldest elected pope since Clement XII in 1730. Though his past career indicated he might be overly dogmatic, Benedict has in fact displayed a softer touch. His first encyclical, *Deus Caritas Est* (God is Love), stressed the love of God and neighbor as the core of Christian life. Yet, he has also placed great emphasis on opposing what he calls "the dictatorship of relativism" in the West and advocating the Church's conservative position on social issues like abortion, birth control, and same-sex marriage, putting the Church at odds with many progressive activists.

The Church continues to play a substantial role in the lives of ordinary Italians. Most Italians continue to celebrate the feast day of their town's patron saint in annual celebrations, but church attendance is declining. Currently about one-third of the nation attends weekly services. Nevertheless, Italians are very conscientious about respecting churches, cathedrals, and other religious domains. In general, tourists are not allowed in religious spaces unless dressed modestly: covered shoulders for women and long pants for men. Furthermore, some churches do not allow visitors to take pictures because camera flashes damage fragile paintings and mosaics. When visiting churches, remember that the buildings are places of worship first, and tourist attractions second.

ART AND ARCHITECTURE

In Italy, great works of art and architecture seem to spring from every street corner. In Rome, the Colosseum (p. 96) hovers above a city bus stop; in Florence, couples flirt in front of the *duomo* (p. 310); in Sicily, diners sit beneath Greek columns. Modern Italians may seem immune to this stunning visual history, but to anyone who hasn't grown up amid ancient ruins and medieval fortresses, it's a feast for the senses.

ANCIENT ITALIAN ART

GREEKS. In the eighth century BC, the Greeks established colonies in southern Italy, covering the region with magnificent **temples** and **theaters.** The best-preserved examples of Greek ruins are in Sicily—not Greece!—in the Valle dei Templi at Agrigento (p. 479) and Taormina (p. 460). Italy is also home to Roman copies of Greek **statues** and original Greek **bronzes;** the prized *Bronzi di Riace*, recovered from the Ionian Sea in 1972 after 2500 years underwater, are now in Reggio di Calabria's Museo Nazionale della Magna Grecia (p. 433).

AND ETRUSCANS. The history of native Italian art begins with the Etruscans, a people who lived on the Italian peninsula before the Romans. Loosely influenced by Greek art and inspired by both the everyday and the afterlife, Etruscan artwork is best known for its narrative quality; beneficial, as the Etruscan language is largely undeciphered. The Etruscan works that remain today include decorated **funeral statues, tomb paintings,** and **ceramic ash burial urns,** all of which depict Etruscan scenes and legends. However, because the Romans either destroyed or melted down a large portion of Etruscan sculptures and bronzes, our modern perception of Etruscan art as solely funerary is skewed. Just like their art, the Etruscans mysteriously disappeared in the third century BC. The Museum at the Villa Giulia (p. 118) in Rome houses many Etruscan gems.

AND ROMANS (OH MY!). Roman art (200 BC-AD 500) is known for its vivid portrayal of the political aims and cultural values of Imperial Rome. Sculptures, architecture, and other masterpieces fall into two principle categories: private household art and art in service of the state. Although art historians have traditionally used Greek statues as benchmarks for beauty and artistic skill, the sculpted portraiture developed by the Romans deserves separate recognition. Portraits of the **Republican period** (510-27 BC) were brutally honest, immortalizing wrinkles, scars, and even warts. The later **imperial sculpture** (27 BC-AD 476) tended to blur the distinction between mortal and god in powerful, idealized images like *Augustus of Prima Porta* (Vatican Museums; p. 115). Later in the period, Roman art developed a flattened style of **portraiture,** with huge eyes looking out in an "eternal stare." The government sponsored **statues, monuments,** and **literary narratives** to commemorate leaders, heroes, and victories. Augustus was perhaps the best master of this form of self-promotion, as evidenced by his impressive **mausoleum** and **Ara Pacis** (Altar of Peace), both gracing the Piazza Augusto Imperatore in Rome (p. 120). Roman monuments evolved into decorated concrete forms with numerous arches and columns, like the **Colosseum** (p. 96) and the **Pantheon** (p. 102).

Upper-class Romans had an appetite for sumptuous interior decoration. Scenes depicting gods and goddesses, exotic beasts, and street entertainers decorated villas, courtyards, and shops. Some wealthy patrons had their walls adorned with **frescoes,** which used the Greek technique of painting onto wet plaster walls to create a time-resistant effect. It was also popular to hire craftsmen to fashion wall and floor **mosaics,** works of art created using thousands of finely shaded *tesserae* (geometrically-shaped fragments of colored pottery, tile or glass) cemented with mortar.

EARLY CHRISTIAN AND BYZANTINE ART

Fearing persecution, early Christians in Rome, Naples, and Syracuse hid inside haunting **catacombs** to worship their Christian God. But following Emperor Constantine's **Edict of Milan** (AD 313), the religion quickly became Rome's faith *du jour*. Even the Roman magistrate's basilica was altered to accommodate Christian services. **Transepts** were added to many Roman churches, creating crucifixshaped architecture. Except for a few **sarcophagi** and **ivory reliefs,** Christian art slowly transitioned from sculpture to pictorial forms in order to depict religious narratives for the illiterate. Ravenna (p. 283) is a veritable treasure trove of the first Byzantine Golden Age, which ran from AD 526 to 726. Examples of these "instructional" mosaics can be seen in Ravenna's octagonal **Basilica of San Vitale** (p. 285), a UNESCO World Heritage Site that is one of the first churches to boast a free-standing *campanile* (bell tower).

MIDDLE AGES

ROMANESQUE. Although true classical Roman style was not revived until the Renaissance, rounded Roman arches, heavy columns, and windowless churches came back into style in the period from AD 800 to 1200. The earliest Italian example of Romanesque architecture is Milan's **Basilica di Sant'Ambrogio** (p. 191), notable for its squat nave and groin vaults. In Tuscany, competition among Italian cities (particularly Florence and Pisa) resulted in great architectural feats, most notably **San Miniato al Monte** and the **Duomo** in Pisa with its famously leaning *campanile* (p. 490). In the south, most notably in **Cattedrale di Monreale** (p. 449), sculptural detailings and intricate mosaics reflect Arab, Byzantine, and Norman influences on the Romanesque style.

GOTHIC. Beginning in the late 13th century, the Gothic movement filtered into Italy from France. Artists and architects rejoiced at the fantastic spaces and light created by the new vaulted technology and giant, multi-colored rose windows. The most impressive Gothic cathedrals include the **Basilica di San Francesco** (p. 333) in Assisi, the **Basilica di Santa Maria Gloriosa dei Frari** (p. 240) in Venice, and the **Santa Maria Novella** (p. 312) in Florence. Secular structures like Florence's **Ponte Vecchio** (p. 318) followed this stylistic trend too. The **Palazzo Ducale** (p. 238) in Venice, spanning several canals with ornate bridges, represents the brilliant marriage of airy, lace-like Islamic stonework and Gothic style. In sculpture, **Nicola Pisano** (c. 1220-78) created pulpits at both Pisa and Siena that combined Roman reliefs, Gothic form, and early Byzantine mosaics. By the end of the 13th century, Italians were bored by the emaciated torsos of suffering martyrs. **Cimabue** (c. 1240-1302) and **Duccio** (c. 1255-1318) introduced new dimensions and brighter colors to their works, though bleeding Christians remained their subject of choice. Straddling the late Gothic and early Renaissance, **Giotto** (c. 1267-1337) is credited with noting that humans—not giants—look at pictures. He placed his work at eye level, putting the viewer on equal footing with his realistically rendered holy subjects. His masterpieces are on display at the Basilica di San Francesco and the **Scrovegni Chapel** (p. 248).

RENAISSANCE

EARLY RENAISSANCE. **Donatello's** (1386-1466) *David* (c. 1430; at the **Bargello** in Florence; p. 315, a now-world-famous free-standing nude, marked the "rebirth" of sculpture without boundaries. His wooden *Mary Magdalene* in Florence similarly represents a departure from earlier, restrained traditions, emphasizing the woman's fallen and repentant side, depicting her in rags and with a sorrowful facial expression. Just as Donatello's expressive portraiture became a model for artists to come, **Brunelleschi's** (1377-1446) mathematical studies of ancient Roman architecture became the cornerstone of Renaissance building. His engineering talent allowed him to raise the dome over **Santa Maria del Fiore** (p. 310) and showcase his mastery of proportions in the **Pazzi Chapel**. **Lorenzo Ghiberti** (c. 1381-1455) designed two sets of bronze doors for the baptistry in Florence, defeating Brunelleschi's doors in the contest of 1401. **Leon Battista Alberti** (1404-72), a champion of visual perspective, designed Florence's **Santa Maria Novella** (p. 312) and Rimini's **Tempio Malatestiano** (p. 291), prototypes for future Renaissance palaces and churches. In painting, **Sandro Botticelli** (1444-1510) and his *The Birth of Venus* (p. 310), depicting the goddess floating on her tidal foam, epitomize the Italian Renaissance. **Masaccio** (1401-28) filled chapels with angels and gold-leaf and is credited with the first use of the mathematical laws of perspective. His figures in the **Brancacci Chapel** of Florence served as models for Michelangelo and Leonardo. An unlikely artist, **Fra Angelico** (c. 1400-55) personified the tension between medieval and Renaissance Italy. Though a member of a militant branch of Dominican friars which opposed humanism on principle, Fra Angelico's works, seen at the **Museo della Chiesa di San Marco** in Florence, exhibit the techniques of space and perspective endorsed by humanistic artists.

HIGH RENAISSANCE. From 1450 to 1520, the torch of distinction passed between two of art's greatest figures: Leonardo and Michelangelo. Branching out from the disciplines of sculpture and painting, **Leonardo da Vinci** (1452-1519) excelled in subjects ranging from geology, engineering, and musical composition to human dissection and armaments design. *The Last Supper*, or *Il Cenacolo* (p. 190), in Milan, pays a level of attention to the individuality of its figures previously unrivalled for that particular biblical subject. His experimentations with *chiaroscuro*, or contrasts between light and shadow that highlight contours, and *sfumato*, which is a smoky or hazy effect of brushwork, secured his place as the century's great artistic innovator.

Michelangelo Buonarroti (1475-1564) was an artistic jack of all trades, despite what he told Julius II after painting the Sistine Chapel ceiling: "I am not a painter!" Julius was so fond of the artist's work on the ceiling that he commissioned *The Last Judgment* for the wall above the chapel's altar. Michelangelo painted like a sculptor, boldly emphasizing musculature and depth, and sculpted like a painter, with lean, smooth strokes. The artist also completed architectural designs for the **Laurentian Library** (p. 315) in Florence and the dome on **St. Peter's Basilica** (p. 105) in Rome. Classic examples of his sculptures include the *Pietà* in St. Peter's and the *David* and unfinished *Slaves* in Florence's Accademia (p. 313).

Other prominent Renaissance artists include **Raffaello** (1483-1520), a draftsman who created technically perfect figures. His frescoes in the papal apartments of the Vatican, including the *School of Athens* (p. 116), show his debt to classical standards. In addition to Michelangelo, the Venetian Renaissance school of artistic thought produced **Giorgione**, known as "The Great" (1478-1510); **Giovanni Bellini** (c. 1430-1516), the pre-eminent teacher within the school; and Bellini's protégé, the prolific **Titian** (1488-1576). Titian's works are notable for their realistic facial expressions and rich colors. In the **High Renaissance,** the greatest architect after Michelangelo was **Donato Bramante** (1444-1514), famed for his work on the *Tempietto of St. Peter* in Rome.

MANNERISM

A heightened sense of aestheticism led to Mannerism, the style that dominated the High Renaissance from the 1520s until the birth of the Baroque style around 1590. Starting in Rome and Florence, Mannerist artists experimented with juxtapositions of color and scale. For example, **Parmigianino** (1503-40) created the *Madonna of the Long Neck*, a piece emblematic of the movement's self-conscious distortions. Another painter, **Jacopo Tintoretto** (1518-94), a Venetian Mannerist, was the first to paint multiple light sources within a single composition. The Mannerist period is also known for its architecture, designed by artisans such as **Giulio Romano** (c. 1499-1546) who rejected the Renaissance (see opposite page) deal of harmony. The villas and churches of architect **Andrea Palladio** (1508-80) were also remarkably innovative, particularly the Villa Rotonda outside Vicenza. His other lasting contribution, the *Four Books of Architecture*, promoted his work and influenced countless architects.

BAROQUE AND ROCOCO

A 17th-century stylistic hybrid born of the Counter-Reformation and monarchy, Baroque composition combined Mannerism's intense emotion with the Renaissance's grandeur to achieve a new expressive theatricality. Heavy on drama, emotion, and richness, Baroque art attempted to inspire faith in the Catholic Church and respect for earthly power. Painters of this era favored naturalism, a commitment to portraying nature in its raw state. **Caravaggio** (1573-1610), the epitome of Baroque painters, relied heavily on *chiaroscuro* and naturalism to create dramatically unsettling images. It is even rumored that he used the corpse of a prostitute recovered from Rome's Tiber River as a model for the Virgin Mary's body in *Death of the Virgin* (1606). **Gianlorenzo Bernini** (1598-1680), a prolific **High Baroque** sculptor and architect, designed the overwhelming colonnade of St. Peter's Piazza and the awesome *baldacchino* inside. Drawing inspiration from Hellenistic works, Bernini's sculptures were orgies of movement, portraying violent interactions of light and space. **Francesco Borromini** (1599-1667), Bernini's rival, was even more adept than his rival at shaping the walls of his buildings into lively, serpentine architectural masterpieces, as in his **San Carlo alle Quattro Fontane** (p. 108). Toward the end of the Baroque period, however, this grand style began to give way to the delicacy and elaborate ornamentation of **Rococo**, a light and graceful method originating in 18th-century France. Rococo motifs include seashells, clouds, flowers, and vines carved into woodwork and stone edifices. **Giovanni Battista Tiepolo** (1696-1770), with his brilliant palette and vibrant frescoes, was a prolific Venetian painter of allegories and the premier exemplar of the Italian Rococo style.

NINETEENTH-CENTURY ART

With the decline of Rococo came French-influenced **Neoclassicism,** which abandoned the overly detailed Rococo and dramatic Baroque methods in favor of a purer, more ancient construction. At first, the shift was almost too subtle to notice, primarily because the Neoclassical artists had no new materials on which they could base their Neotraditional works. With the early 17th-century discovery and excavation of Herculaneum and Pompeii, however, Neoclassical artists quickly found their ancient muses in the forms of recovered artifacts. One such Neoclassical artist was the sculptor **Antonio Canova** (1757-1822) who explored the formal Neoclassical style in his giant statues and bas-reliefs. His most famous work is the statue of *Pauline Borghese*, which displays Neoclassical grace and purity of contour. Rebelling against the strict Neoclassical style, **Telemaco Signorini** (1835-1901), **Giovanni Fattori** (1825-1908), and **Silvestro Lega** (1826-1895) spearheaded the **Macchiaioli** group in Florence (c. 1855-65)—a group anticipating French Impressionism that believed a painting's meaning lay in its *macchie* (spots) of color rather than in its narrative. A technique called "blotting," which abruptly juxtaposed patches of color through manipulations with a dry paint brush, was used to depict politicized scenes of battle and outspoken responses to everyday life.

TWENTIETH-CENTURY ART

The Italian **Futurist** painters, sculptors, and architects of the early 20th century brought Italy to the cutting edge of art. Inspired by **Filippo Tommaso Marinetti's** (1876-1944) *Futurist Manifesto* of 1909, these Italian artists loved to glorify danger, war, and the 20th-century machine age. With pieces displayed in the 1912 Futurist exhibition in Paris, painters **Gino Severini** (1883-1966) and **Carlo Carrà** (1881-1966) and sculptor **Umberto Boccioni** (1882-1916) went beyond

Cubism to celebrate the dynamism and energy of modern life by depicting several aspects of moving forms. The work of **Giorgio de Chirico** (1888-1978), some of which is currently on display at the Collezione Peggy Guggenheim in Venice (p. 241), depicts eerie scenes dominated by mannequin figures, empty space, and steep perspective. Although his mysterious and disturbing style, called *Pittura Metafisica*, was never successfully imitated, de Chirico inspired early Surrealist painters. Other 20th-century Italian artists include **Amadeo Modigliani** (1884-1920), a sculptor and painter who was highly influenced by African art and Cubism, and **Marcello Piacentini** (1881-1960) who created fascist architecture that imposed sterility upon classical motifs. In 1938, Piacentini designed the looming **EUR** in Rome (Esposizione Universale Roma) as an impressive reminder of the link between Mussolinian fascism and Roman imperialism.

In the Postwar Era, Italian art lacked unity but still produced noteworthy artists. **Lucio Fontana** (1899-1968) started **Spatialism**, a movement to bring art beyond the canvas towards a synthesis of color, sound, movement, time, and space. His *taglio* (slash) canvases of the mid-1950s created a new dimension for the 2D surface with a simple linear cut. Conceptual artist **Piero Manzoni** (1933-63) created a scandal in 1961 when he put his feces in 90 small cans labeled *Artist's Shit*, setting the price of the excrements at their weight in gold. In May 2007 Sotheby's sold a can for €124,000. In the late 1960s **Arte Povera** bridged the gap between art and life by integrating cheap everyday materials into pieces of art. **Michelangelo Pistoletto** (1933-) caused a clamor with his *Venus in Rags* (1967), a plaster cast of a classical Venus facing a pile of old rags, on display at the **Castello di Rivoli Museo d'Arte Contemporanea** (p. 141) in Turin. While eclipsed by its Renaissance past, contemporary art in Italy thrives in select museums and at the bi-annual **Venice Biennale** (p. 245), showcasing the recent work of artists from Italy and around the world.

LITERATURE

SEX, DRUGS, AND ROMAN MYTHOLOGY

The Romans stole their religion and mythology from anyone and everyone. Though much Roman folklore comes from their own early traditions and Etruscan beliefs, much more of their mythology is a filtered form of Greek mythology. It is important to remember that Greek civilization across the Mediterranean flourished centuries before Rome. When Greek poets were reciting the Odyssey and Iliad, Rome was still an obscure farming village. During the last two centuries of the Roman Republic, roughly the last two centuries BC, interaction between the Greeks and Romans increased because the Romans were conquering the Greeks. When they were not forcing the city-states into submission, they took the time to embrace the Greek mythological system in the form of beautiful poems typically depicting lustful and petty gods. Until this time, the Romans had relied only on boring and ambiguous agricultural gods, as well as the famous story of Romulus and Remus (p. 37).

LATIN LOVERS

ET IN ARCADIA EGO. As they gained dominance over the Hellenized Mediterranean, the Romans discovered the refined joys of literature. **Plautus** (c. 259-184 BC) and **Terrence** (d. 159 BC), for example, adapted Greek comedies into Latin while giving them their own Roman flair. The lyric, though occasionally obscene, poetry of **Catullus** (84-54 BC) demonstrates the complex relationship between Greece and Rome. **Cicero** (106-43 BC), a fiery and complicated Roman politician, orator, and author, whose prose has been central to Latin education since ancient times, is the definitive example of classical Latin. History buffs should check out the writing of **Julius Caesar** (100-44 BC), who gave a first-hand account of the expansion of Rome's empire in his Gallic Wars.

WHEN IN ROME. As a result of Augustus's patronage and the relative peace and prosperity of the time, Augustan Rome produced an array of literary talents. **Livy** (c. 59 BC-AD 17) wrote a mammoth history of Rome from the city's founding to his own time in *Ab Urbe Condita* (From the Founding of the City). Coining the phrase *carpe diem*, **Horace** (65-8 BC) wrote on love, wine, service to the state, hostile critics, and the pleasure of pastoral life in his Odes. **Ovid** (43 BC-AD 17) gave the world the *Metamorphoses*, a beautiful and sometimes racy collection of poetry. For unknown reasons, he angered Augustus so much that he was eventually exiled to modern-day Romania where he eventually died a broken man. **Suetonius's** (c. AD 69-130) *De Vita Caesarum* presents tabloid biographies of the first twelve Emperors, and **Tacitus's** (c. AD 55-116) *Histories* offers a biting synopsis of Roman war, diplomacy, scandal, and rumor during AD 69, the year of notorious Emperor Nero's death. It is widely considered stylistically the greatest work of history in Latin.

DARK AGES TO CULTURAL REBIRTH

DARK TIMES. Between classical antiquity and the Renaissance, authors usually remained anonymous, with the exception of notable religious figures like **St. Thomas Aquinas** (1225-74). By the 13th century, Christianity had become the uniting factor of much of chaotic Europe. While this religious zeal was sometimes oppressive, it also ensured the survival of ancient texts and ideas, since monks of this period typically spent their days and nights copying ancient texts. Despite this tendency to preserve ancient thoughts, writers of the Dark Ages also began using a degraded form of Latin. Adding to this evolution of literature were troubadour songs (usually detailing romance at court) and Carolingian and Arthurian adventure stories which developed at the intersection of northern Italy, southern France, and northern Spain. These served as models for the medieval verses delivered by singers and poets who traveled throughout Europe. The invasion of Norman and Arab rulers into Sicily and southern Italy (1091-1224) also introduced diverse literary traditions.

ABANDON ALL HOPE, YE WHO ENTER HERE! Although the tumult of medieval life discouraged most literary musing in the late 13th century, three Tuscan writers, known as the *Tre Corone* (Three Crowns), resuscitated the written art: **Dante, Petrarch,** and **Boccaccio.** Although scholars do not agree on the precise dates of the literary Renaissance, many argue that the work of Dante Alighieri (1265-1321) marked its inception. Considered the father of modern Italian literature, Dante was one of the first poets in all of Europe to write using the *volgare* (common vernacular; Florentine, in Dante's case) instead of Latin. In his epic poem *La Divina Commedia*, he roams the three realms of the afterlife *(Inferno, Purgatorio, Paradiso)* with Virgil as his guide, meeting famous historical and mythological figures and his true love, Beatrice. In the work, Dante calls for social reform and indicts all those who contributed to Florence's moral downfall, including Popes and political figures—especially those who ordered his own political exile. **Petrarch** (1304-74), the second titan of the 13th century, more clearly belongs to the literary Renaissance. A scholar of classical Latin and a key proponent of humanist thought, he wrote sonnets to a married woman named Laura, collected in *Il Canzoniere*. The third member of this literary triumvirate, **Giovanni Boccaccio** (1313-75), wrote the *Decameron*, a collection of 100 stories that range in tone from suggestive to vulgar. In one, a gardener has his way with an entire convent.

RENAISSANCE MEN. The 14th century saw the rise of **la Commedia dell'Arte**, a form of improvised theater with a standard plot structure and characters. Each character had its own mask and costume and a few fixed personality traits. The most famous character, *Arlecchino* (Harlequin), was easily identified by his diamond-patterned costume. By the 15th and 16th centuries, Italian authors were reviving classical sources in new ways. **Alberti** (1404-72) and **Palladio** (1508-80) wrote treatises on architecture and art theory. In 1528 **Baldassare Castiglione** (1478-1529) wrote *Il Cortegiano*, which instructed the Renaissance man on etiquette and other fine points of behavior. At the pinnacle of the Renaissance, **Ludovico Ariosto's** (1474-1533) *Orlando Furioso* (1516) described a whirlwind of military victories and unrequited love, and **Niccolò Machiavelli** (1469-1527) wrote *Il Principe* (The Prince), a grim assessment of what it takes to gain political power. In the spirit of the Renaissance, specialists in other fields tried writing: **Giorgio Vasari** (1511-74) stopped redecorating Florence's churches to produce the ultimate primer on art history and criticism, *The Lives of the Artists;* **Benvenuto Cellini** (1500-71) wrote about his art in *The Autobiography;* and **Michelangelo** (1475-1564) proved to be a prolific composer of sonnets.

MODERN TIMES

The 19th century brought Italian unification and the need for one language. Nationalistic "Italian" literature, an entirely new concept, grew slowly. *Racconti* (short stories) and poetry became popular in the 1800s. **Giovanni Verga's** (1840-1922) brutally honest depiction of destitute Italians ushered in a new tradition of portraying the common man in art and literature, a movement known as *verismo* (contemporary, all-too-tragic realism). In 1825, **Alessandro Manzoni's** (1785-1873) historical novel, *I Promessi sposi*, established the Modernist novel as a major avenue of Italian literary expression. **Carlo Collodi's** (1826-1890) *Storia di un burattino* (Adventures of a Marionette), also called *Le avventure di Pinocchio*, continues to enchant children, now in its innocuous Disney classic format, with the precocious and sometimes diabolic antics of a puppet.

POSTMODERNISM. Twentieth-century Italian writers sought to undermine the concept of objective truth that was so dear to the *verismo* movement. Nobel Prize winner **Luigi Pirandello** (1867-1936) deconstructed theatrical convention and explored meta-theater in works like *Sei personaggi in cerca d'autore* (*Six Characters in Search of an Author*, 1921). During the terror of Mussolini, antifascist fiction exploded as writers related their horrific personal and political experiences under the dictator. The most prolific of these writers, **Alberto Moravia** (1907-90), wrote the ground-breaking *Gli indifferenti* (*The Time of Indifference*), which was promptly censored for its subtle attacks on the fascist regime. **Primo Levi** (1919-87) wrote *Se questo è un uomo* (1947) about his experience as a prisoner in Auschwitz. Several female writers also gained popularity, including **Grazia Deledda** (1875-1936), **Elsa Morante** (1912-85), and **Natalia Ginzburg** (1916-91). Writers such as **Cesare Pavese** (1908-50) and **Beppe Fenoglio** (1922-63) brought the cinematic trend of *neorealismo* to the novel. **Italo Calvino** (1923-85) exemplified the postmodern era with the magic realism of *Il barone rampante* (*The Baron in the Trees*, 1957) and by questioning the act of reading and writing in *Se una notte d'inverno un viaggiatore* (*If On A Winter's Night A Trav-*

eler, 1979). In 1997, playwright **Dario Fo's** (b. 1926) satires brought him both a denunciation by the Catholic Church and the Nobel Prize for literature.

MUSIC

GREGORY'S FAMOUS CHANTING MONKS

Biblical psalms are some of the earliest known songs of both Italian and Western culture. Roman and Ambrosian rites (Italy's medieval liturgies), which originated in Jewish liturgy, were characterized by monophonic vocal **plainchant,** also known as plainsong. Although the Ambrosian chant can still be heard in Milan, it is the Roman Gregorian chant that prevails. The **Gregorian Chant,** named for **Pope Gregory I** (c. 540-609) is characterized by a repeated reciting note, interrupted only by periodic deviations. Further advancements were made by Italian monk **Guido d'Arezzo** (c. 995-1050), who came up with the modern system of staff-notation and explored the emerging concept of polyphony. Blind organist and composer **Francesco Landini** (c. 1335-97) made significant contributions to the development of the song during the 14th century **Ars Nova** period. This era also brought *madrigales*, musical poems, and *caccia*, musical and poetic narratives describing hunting scenes.

OPERA LIRICA: THE FAT LADY SINGS

Italy's most cherished musical art form was born in Florence in the mid-1590s, nurtured in Venice and Naples, and popularized in Milan's famed Teatro alla Scala (p. 189). Conceived by the **Camerata,** a circle of Florentine writers, noblemen, and musicians including Vincenzo Galilei (famed music theorist and father of Galileo, c. 1525-91), **opera lirica** originated as an attempt to recreate the dramas of ancient Greece by setting lengthy poems to music. The earliest surviving opera is *Euridice* (1600), a collage of compositions by **Jacobo Peri** (1561-1633), **Ottavio Rinuccini** (1562-1621), and **Giulio Caccini** (c. 1550-1618). Opera found a perfect equilibrium between music and poetry for the first time in *L'Orfeo* (1607), a breakthrough piece by **Claudio Monteverdi** (1567-1643), who drew freely from history and juxtaposed high drama, love scenes, and uncouth humor. Still-popular **Alessandro Scarlatti** (1660-1725) was arguably the most talented composer of Italian operas, pioneering advances in the overture during the 17th century. Meanwhile, the simple and toneful aria became the dominant form of opera, and castrated men the singers of choice. These *castrati*, thanks to their masculine strength of voice and feminine tone, became the most celebrated and envied group of singers in all of Europe.

BAROQUE: THE BIRTH OF VIVALDI AND THE VIOLIN

The Baroque period, known for its heavy ornamentation and emphasis on musical contrasts, saw the birth of the string orchestra. The violin's modern form was perfected by **Antonio Stradivari** (1644-1737) and became popular in pieces by fellow Cremonese Monteverdi and his contemporaries. In 1698, Florentine **Bartolomeo Cristofori** (1655-1731) invented the pianoforte. The work of violinist **Antonio Vivaldi** (1675-1741), who composed over 600 concertos, continues to awe contemporary audiences, with innovative works like *The Four Seasons* (1725). Vivaldi established the concerto's present form, in which an orchestra accompanies a soloist through three movements.

VIVA VERDI!

LAYING THE GROUNDWORK. Despite its convoluted plots and powerful, dramatic music, 19th-century Italian opera had not yet adopted the French tradition of visual spectacle. A famous composer of tragedies and comedies and a master of the light, flexible *bel canto* (beautiful song), **Gioacchino Rossini** (1792-1868) composed *Cinderella* in 1817. Rossini's rough contemporary, **Giacomo Puccini** (1858-1924), helped further the reputation of Italian opera with his brilliant orchestral works and world-famous operas, including *La Bohème* (1896), *Tosca* (1900), and *Madama Butterfly* (1904).

AND, OF COURSE, THE MAN HIMSELF. **Giuseppe Verdi** (1813-1901), whose lyrical half-century domination of Italian opera emphasized human themes and the human voice, remains the crowning musical figure of 19th-century Italy and, along with his German contemporary Wagner, of all of opera. *Nabucco* (1842), a pointed and powerful *bel canto*, typifies Verdi's early works. The opera's chorus, *Va pensiero*, became the hymn of Italian freedom and unity during the Risorgimento. Verdi also produced the touching, personal dramas and memorable melodies of *Rigoletto* (1851), *La Traviata* (1853), and *Il Trovatore* (1853) in mid-career. His later work brought the grand and heroic conflicts of *Aïda* (1871), the dramatic thrust of *Otello* (1887), and the mercurial comedy *Falstaff* (1893). Verdi's support of the Risorgimento in the 1850s encouraged patriots to invoke his name—a convenient acronym for "Vittorio Emanuele, *Re d'Italia*" (King of Italy)—as their popular battle cry: *"Viva Verdi!"*

TWENTIETH-CENTURY OPERA. In the 20th century, **Ottorino Respighi** (1879-1936) explored his fascination with orchestral color in the popular *Roman Trilogy* (1924-29). The Italian-American composer, **Gian Carlo Menotti** (1911-2007) wrote Pulitzer Prize-winning operas *The Consul* (1950) and *The Saint of Bleecker Street* (1954). **Luigi Dallapiccola** (1904-75) achieved success with surrealist choral works, including *Canti di prigionia* (*Songs of Prison*, 1941), which protested fascism. His student, avant-garde composer **Luciano Berio** (1925-2003), pioneered the composition of electronic music. Grammy-winning tenor **Luciano Pavarotti** (1935-2007) made his world debut in the 60s and helped bring opera into mainstream popular culture with his televised operas in the 1990s. **Andrea Bocelli** (b. 1958) has continued to bridge the expanse between opera and pop with chart-topping songs such as *"Con Te Partirò"* in 19995. Visitors looking to experience Italian opera firsthand can visit Milan's Teatro alla Scala (p. 189), Rome's Teatro dell'Opera, and Palermo's Teatro Massimo (p. 448), or one of Italy's countless other opulent opera houses.

ARRIVEDERCI, VERDI

More recent Italian music has reversed its centuries-long role as a groundbreaker, drawing inspiration instead from American pop culture. Melodic rockers of the 60s included **Enzo Iannacci**, a dentist-turned-musician; the crooning, politically-minded, Genoese **Fabrizio De Andre**, and **Adriano Celentano**, whose career spanned 40 years. Emerging in the 60s and 70s, **Lucio Battisti** now enjoys a popularity rivalling that of the Beatles in his own country. In the 70s and 80s, **Eduardo Bennato** used rock to spread a progressive political message; his successor **Vasco Rossi**, drew an unprecedented 300,000-member crowd to a free concert he gave in 2004. **Eros Ramazzotti** gained universal appeal by recording every album in Spanish as well as Italian, often teaming up with Cher and Tina Turner. Italians **Laura Pausini, Elisa**, and **L'Aura** followed suit by recording English albums. More recently, **Jovanotti's** rap has entered the global scene, along with socially conscious **Frankie-Hi-NRG** and **99 Posse**. For a more relaxed beat, try **Lucio Dalla**'s internationally popular *Caruso*.

FILM

OLDIES AND GOLDIES

Italy's golden position within the film industry began in 1905, when **Filoteo Alberini** released *La Presa di Roma (The Taking of Rome)*. This film ushered in the Italian "super-spectacle," an extravagant recreation of historical events through film. Throughout the early 20th century, most Italian film followed this melodramatic pattern, and many Italian film stars were consequently thought of as superhuman. Before WWI, celebrated actors like **Francesca Bertini** (1888-1985), **Pina Menichelli** (1890-1984), and **Lyda Borelli** (1884-1959) epitomized the Italian diva.

SEEING IS BELIEVING

No one ever accused Benito Mussolini of missing out on an opportunity. Recognizing film's potential as propaganda in the late 30s, Mussolini revived an industry that had been in decline since the golden age of the silent era by creating the gargantuan **Cinecittà Studios**, Rome's answer to Hollywood. Yet the boost to the industry came at a price: Mussolini also enforced a few "imperial edicts" that dictated the production of films, one of which even forbade laughing at the Marx Brothers's 1933 film, *Duck Soup*. Films created under fascist rule between the years 1936 and 1943 glorified Italian military conquests (linking them to Classical Roman success) and portrayed comfortable middle-class life. This era of Italian film is often referred to as the era of *telefoni bianchi* (white telephones) in reference to the common prop. Rare compared to their black cousins, these phones were a symbol of prosperity, and during the short-lived glory days of Italian Fascism, these films kept the chaos in other parts of Europe out of sight, out of mind. A few renegade leaders in the film industry, however, opposed fascist rule. **Luigi Chiarini,** for instance, was instrumental in the founding of Italy's *Centro Sperimentale della Cinematografia*, the film school that despite funding by Mussolini's government, slowly shifted away from propaganda and became the alma mater of many neorealist directors.

NEOREALISM

The fall of fascism brought the explosion of **neorealismo** in cinema in the 1940s, which rejected contrived sets and professional actors, emphasizing instead on-location shooting and "authentic" drama based in reality. These low-budget productions created a film revolution and brought Italian cinema international prestige. Neorealists first gained attention in Italy with **Luchino Visconti's** (1906-76) French-influenced *Ossessione* (1942). Because fascist censors suppressed this so-called "resistance" film, it wasn't until **Roberto Rossellini's** (1906-77) film *Roma, città aperta* (1945) that neorealist films gained international exposure. The film began his Neorealistic WWII Trilogy, which also included *Paisà* (1946) and *Germania anno zero* (1948). **Vittorio De Sica's** 1948 *Ladri di biciclette* (The Bicycle Thief) was perhaps the most successful neorealist film. The film's simple plot explored the human struggle against fate. A demand for Italian comedy gave birth to **neorealismo rosa**, a more comic version of the intense and often dismally authentic glimpse into daily Italian life. Actor **Totò** (1898-1967), the illegitimate son of a Neapolitan duke, was Italy's Charlie

Chaplin. With his dignified antics and clever lines, Totò charmed audiences and provided subtle commentary on Italian society.

THE GOLDEN AGE

The golden age of Italian cinema, which took place in the 60s, began *la commedia all'italiana*, during which the prestige and economic success of Italian movies was at its height. **Mario Monicelli** (*I Soliti Ignoti*, 1958; *La Grande guerra*, 1959) brought a more cynical tone to the portrayal of daily Italian life, which was in a stage of rapid transformation and social unease. Italian comedy struggled to portray cultural stereotypes with as much wit as its public demanded. Actors **Marcello Mastroianni, Vittorio Gassman,** and **Alberto Sordi** gained fame portraying self-centered characters lovable for their frailties.

By the 1960s, post-neorealist directors like **Federico Fellini** (1920-93) and **Michelangelo Antonioni** (1912-2007) valued careful cinematic construction over mere real-world experience. With the Oscar-winning *La Strada* (1954), Fellini went beyond neorealism, scripting the vagabond life of two street performers, Gelsomina and Zampanò, in the most poetic of terms. Fellini's *8½* (1963) interwove dreams with reality in a semi-autobiographical exploration of the demands of the artist that has earned a place in the international cinematic canon. His *La Dolce Vita* (1959) was condemned by both religious and political authorities for its portrayal of decadently stylish celebrities in 50s Rome on the Via Veneto. The film coined the term *paparazzi* and glamorized dancing in the Trevi Fountain (p. 104), an act that is now legally off-limits. Antonioni's haunting trilogy, *L'Avventura* (1959), *La Notte* (1960), and *L'Eclisse* (1962) presents a stark world of estranged couples and isolated aristocrats. His *Blow-Up* was a 1966 English-language hit about miming, murder, and mod London. Controversial writer-director **Pier Paolo Pasolini** (1922-75) may have spent as much time on trial for his politics as he did making films. An ardent Marxist, he set his films in the underworld of shanty neighborhoods, poverty, and prostitution. His later films include scandalous adaptations of famous literary works including famous works, *Il Decameron* (1971) and *The Arabian Nights* (1974).

INTROSPECTION

Aging directors and a lack of funds led Italian film into an era characterized by nostalgia and self-examination. **Bernardo Bertolucci's** (b. 1940) *Il conformista* (1970) investigates fascist Italy by focusing on one "comrade" struggling to be normal. Other major Italian films of this era include **Vittorio de Sica's** (1901-74) *Il Giardino dei Finzi-Contini* (1971) and **Francesco Rosi's** *Cristo si è fermato a Eboli* (1979), both of which are adaptations of classic post-war, anti-fascist novels. In the 80s, the **Taviani brothers,** Paolo and Vittorio, catapulted to fame with *La notte di San Lorenzo* (1982), which depicted an Italian village during the last days of WWII, and *Kaos* (1984), a film based on stories by **Pirandello.** Inheriting the *commedia all'italiana* tradition of the golden age, actor-directors like **Nanni Moretti** (b. 1953) and **Maurizio Nichetti** (b. 1948) delighted audiences with macabre humor in the 80s and early 90s. Both men usually choose projects that required them to play neurotic, introspective, or ridiculous characters. In his psychological comedy-thriller *Bianca* (1984), Moretti stars as a slightly deranged high school math teacher, and in *Volere Volare* (1991), Nichetti plays a confused cartoon sound designer who turns into an animated figure.

BUONGIORNO, PRINCIPESSA!

Oscar-winners **Gabriele Salvatores** (for *Mediterraneo*, 1991) and **Giuseppe Tornatore** (for *Nuova Cinema Paradiso*, 1988) have earned the attention and affection of audiences worldwide. Oscars have been bestowed upon a handful of other contemporary Italian filmmakers, as well. In 1996 **Massimo Troisi's** (b. 1953) *Il Postino* won Best Original Score and was nominated in four additional categories, including Best Picture, Screenplay, Director, and Actor. Three years later **Roberto Benigni** (b. 1952) won several Oscars for *La vita è bella (Life is Beautiful)*, which juxtaposed the tragedy of the Holocaust with a father's devoted love for his son. Most recently, **Nanni Moretti** snagged the Palm D'Or at Cannes in 2001 for the film, *La Stanza del Figlio (The Son's Room)*, and **Leonardo Pieraccioni** (b. 1965) released *Il Paradiso all'improvviso (Suddenly Paradise)* to international acclaim in 2003.

DESIGN

From the Roman aqueducts to Leonardo's flying machine to Dolce & Gabbana's spacesuit-inspired winter 2008 line, Italians have always had a penchant for design. Compare **Enzo Ferrari's** original 1929 cars to Ford's Model T's, **Bialetti's** 1930 art deco Moka Express coffeemaker to one by Mr. Coffee, or a Gucci leather shoe to the American sneaker, and it's obvious that Italians designers deserve the prestige they enjoy. Aside from cars and appliances that achieve statuesque beauty, Italian design produced the **Vespa**—still adored by Italians and hated by fearful tourists—in 1946, and the 1957 **Fiat**, a tiny 2-door car. Before the days of sleek laptops, **Olivetti's** 1969 Valentine typewriter by designer **Ettore Sottass** combined style and practicality. This combination of streamlined beauty and simple functionality frequently characterizes Italian design.

 FASHION FOR POCKET CHANGE. Save 25-75% at end-of-season sales. These happen in January and July and last until the collection sells out. Many stores also offer previews of the next collection at this time.

Equally stunning and more widely recognized is Italian fashion design. Italian domination began in 1881 when **Cerruti** opened his doors and began his lasting impact on Italian fashion, serving as a mentor and teacher for later designers such as **Giorgio Armani.** Still-famous **Salvatore Ferragamo,** whose love affair with shoes would later produce Dorothy's ruby slippers in *The Wizard of Oz* (1939), opened his first shoe shop in his parents' home in 1912. The illustrious **Fendi** line began as a tiny fur and leather business in Rome at the end of WWI, but was revolutionized by the five Fendi sisters who took control after WWII. Two years later, **Guccio Gucci** opened a leather store in Florence originally intended as a saddle shop that later moved to Rome and became an international fashion powerhouse. In the early 50s, **Gian Battista Giorgini** organized a series of runway shows that re-introduced the phrase "Made in Italy" as a universally accepted indication of quality and established Milan as a fashion capital on par with Paris. Italy soon became host to now-famous designers such as **Max Mara** (1951), **Valentino** (1962), the **Giorgio Armani Company** (1975), **Versace** (1978), and **Dolce & Gabbana** (1985), all of whose designs litter the red carpet, often overshadowing the stars they adorn. To become a star for the day, go shopping in **Milan** (see **Milan: Shopping,** p. 192), and find out what makes this the fashion capital of the world. Take notes on the classic cuts, quality fabrics, and liberal use of black that make Italians so effortlessly stylish. If you have assimilated to Italian culture and decided that football (p. 60) is your passion, take a look at Dolce & Gabbana's AC Milan uniforms or their 2006 men's underwear campaign featuring well-cut *calcio* stars.

FOOD AND WINE: LA DOLCE VITA

MANGIAMO!

In Italy, food preparation is an art form, and culinary traditions constitute a crucial part of the culture. Each region of Italy has a distinct culinary identity to complement its personality that often includes its own unique shape of pasta. The words *"Buon appetito!"* and *"Cin cin!"* chime around the table as friends and families sit down to dine. As much an institution as the meal itself, the after-dinner *passeggiata* (promenade) attracts Italians into the main square late into the evening. Small portions and leisurely paced meals help keep locals looking svelte despite their rich cuisine.

Breakfast is the least elaborate meal in Italy. Often taken at a neighborhood bar, *la colazione* consists—at most—of a quick coffee and a *cornetto* (croissant). For *il pranzo* (lunch), Italians usually grab a *panino* (sandwich) or salad. Lunch is generally the most important meal of the day in rural regions, where daily work comes in two shifts and is separated by a lengthy lunch and *pisolino* (nap). Most common in northern cities, Italians will end a none-too-stressful day at work with an *aperitivo* (aperitif) around 5 or 6pm. Try a *spritz*, a northern specialty made with *prosecco*, *campari*, or *aperol* and a splash of mineral water. *La cena* (dinner) usually begins at 8pm, although in Naples it's not unheard of to go for a midnight pizza. Traditionally, dinner is the lengthiest meal of the day, usually lasting through much of the evening and consisting of an *antipasto* (appetizer), a *primo piatto* (starch-based first course like pasta or *risotto*), a *secondo piatto* (meat or fish), and a *contorno* (vegetable side dish). Finally, *la cena* is capped off with the *dolce* (dessert), then *caffè* (espresso), and often an after-dinner liqueur. Many restaurants offer a fixed-price *menù turistico* including *primo*, *secondo*, bread, water, and wine. While the cuisine may vary regionally, the importance of relaxing over a meal does not. For example, many restaurants in Bologna do not seat more than one party per table per night, and dinners throughout Italy can last for hours. It's easy to see why Italians champion the Slow Food movement to combat Americanized fast food.

IN VINO VERITAS

Despite its reputation for living in the shadow of wine-loving French neighbors, Italy is the world's leading exporter of vintage spirits. Today, over 2000 varieties of grapes are grown in Italy's warm climes and rocky hills before *la vendemmia* (the grape harvest) in September or October. To make red wine, *rosso*, vintners pump the juice and skins into glass, oak, or steel fermentation vats; white wines, *biancos*, are made from skinless grapes. Whether a wine is *dolce* (sweet) or *secco* (dry) is largely determined by the ripeness and sugar content of its grape. After fermentation, the wine is racked and clarified to remove sediment. The wine is then stored in barrels or vats until bottling.

CORK YOUR WALLET! Wine snobs may spend €50 on a bottle of aged *riserva*, but wines in the €6-12 range can often be sublime. The most respected wine stewards in the nation regularly rank inexpensive wines above their costly cousins. Expense can equal quality, but it's wiser to go for the high end of a lower-grade wine than the low end of a higher-grade wine.

IT'S ALL IN THE NAME. Look for one of four classifications on your bottle to determine the wine's quality. Independently tested wine will bear the label

DOCG (*Denominazione di Origine Controllata e Garantita*); wines that follow regional regulations are labeled DOC (*Denominazione di Origine Controllata*); the label IGT (*Indicazione Geografica*) means that a wine has been produced in a specific area; and *Vino da Tavola* is a catch-all term for otherwise unclassifiable table wines.

Wine tasting is made easy by *enoteche* (wine bars), especially government-run bars, which serve as regional exhibition and tasting centers in order to promote local vineyards and sponsor educational events. *Cantine* (wine cellars) do not typically offer tastings unless accompanied by a wine bar. If touring by car, ask the local tourist office about *Strade del Vino* (wine roads). **Tuscany** (see p. 325), birthplace of the *Movimento del Turismo del Vino* (wine tourism), is especially accessible for wine tasting. Reservations are recommended at some vineyards, so be sure to call ahead.

WAKE UP AND SMELL THE CAFFÈ!

THE ART OF ESPRESSO. Italians drink coffee at breakfast, lunch, dinner, and any time in between—and still manage to close shop in the afternoon for a snooze. But espresso in Italy isn't just a beverage; it's an experience, from the harvesting of the beans to the savoring of the beverage. High altitude *Arabica* beans compose 60-90% of most Italian blends, while the remaining 10-40% are made of woody-flavored *robusta* beans. Italians are partial to a high concentration of *robusta* beans because they emit oils that produce a thick, foamy *crema* under the heat and pressure of the espresso machine. Espresso beans are roasted longer than other coffee beans, and give the drink fuller volume. After roasting, the beans are then ground, tapped into a basket, and mixed with hot, pressurized water. In a good cup of espresso, the foamy *crema* should be caramel-colored and thick enough to support a spoonful of sugar for a good couple of seconds. Heavy *crema* prevents the drink's rich aroma from diffusing into the air and is the sign of a quality brew.

COFFEE STAINED. While Italians drink coffee with every meal, they do not drink cappuccino after 10am. If you order a cappuccino after lunch or dinner, you might as well open your map on the table and wave your country's flag; every Italian in the surrounding area will know you're a tourist.

SO A GUY WALKS INTO A BAR... In Italy a *"bar"* doesn't refer to a beer-serving nightspot but to an establishment where you can get a coffee and a bite to eat. For alcohol, head to *un bar americano* or a *discoteca*.

SPORTS AND RECREATION

ANCIENT TIMES. The Romans liked their athletic spectacles fast and violent. Gladiatorial combat originated as part of a funeral custom: gifts to the dead were offered in amphitheaters across the Empire. Examples include a site at **Pompeii (p. 402)** and, of course, the Roman **Colosseum (p. 96)**. Romans also hosted *venationes* (wild beast hunts), and even giant mock naval battles. Greek athletics, like wrestling, running, and javelin throwing, were slower to catch on in the Capital of the Ancient World—perhaps there just wasn't enough killing.

SOCCER. Slightly less violent—and only slightly—today's *calcio* ("soccer" to Americans, "football" to everyone else) surpasses all other sports in popularity and competes with politics, fashion, and religion as national pastime. **La Squadra Azzurra** (The Blue Team) is a source of pride: there are claims that Italy's 1982 World Cup victory inspired more national unity than any of the country's political movements. However, Italian *calcio* fans, or *tifosi*, are also divided by their undying devotion to local teams. Enthusiasm peaks in June for the **Coppa Italia** championship. During games between big-city rivals like Naples, Milan, and Rome, don't be surprised to find hauntingly empty streets and bars stifled with fans either commiserating or celebrating in communal agony or ecstasy. To become one with the mob, catch a game at Rome's **Stadio Olimpico (p. 121)**.

WORLD CUP 2006. Veni, Vidi, Vici: Italy came. Italy saw. Italy conquered. Despite French player Zinedine Zidane's "head-butt felt 'round the world" in the final match, the Italian national team officially became ■**the world's best soccer team in 2006.** The victory served as Italian football's saving grace: around the same time as the Cup, *Calciopoli*, or the **Serie A scandal**, incriminated Juventus and other teams in Italy's professional soccer league for fixing match results.

CYCLING. Home to both cyclists and cycling aficionados, Italy hosts the annual **Giro d'Italia**, a 21-stage cross-country race, in May. Second only to the Tour de France, the race was inaugurated in 1909 and has since been interrupted only twice—by the First and Second World Wars. The Giro's victor receives the **maglia rosa**, whose pink hue represents the color of paper used by *La Gazzetta dello Sport*, Italy's top sports newspaper.

SKIING. From December to April, skiers flock to the Italian Alps and Apennines. Head to resorts near **Turin** (p. 133), host of the 2006 Winter Olympics, or to the **Aosta Valley** (p. 147) for summer skiing, helicopter skiing, and a large assortment of other exciting possibilities. Annual World Cup competitions at Italian ski slopes appeal to less adventurous ski fans.

FESTIVALS AND HOLIDAYS

Though most Italians work 35hr. per week, take 2hr. lunch breaks, close some businesses on Mondays, and take elaborate month-long coastal vacations each August, they still enjoy a seemingly constant stream of festivity. Despite often religious origins, celebrations aren't necessarily pious. Revelry during **Carnevale,** which is particularly enthusiastic in Venice, prepares Italian towns for Lent with 10 days of celebration. At **Scoppio del Carro**, held in **Florence** on Easter Sunday, Florentines set off a cart of explosives in keeping with medieval tradition (except for the addition of the mechanical dove used to light the cart). Countless other quirky local festivals pay homage to medieval customs, often in the form of jousts and period costumes. The following is a list of national festivals. For a complete list, write to the **Italian Government Tourist Board** (p. 9).

DATE	FESTIVAL
Jan. 1	Capodanno (New Year's Day)
Jan. 6	Epifania (Epiphany)
Palm Su to Easter Su (Apr. 5-12, 2009)	Settimana Santa (Holy Week)
Apr. 10, 2009	Venerdi Santo (Good Friday)
Apr. 12, 2009	Pasqua (Easter Sunday)
Apr. 13, 2009	Pasquetta (Easter Monday)
Apr. 25	Festa della Liberazione (Liberation Day)

LIFE AND TIMES

DATE	FESTIVAL
May 1	Festa del Lavoro (Labor Day)
June 2	Festa della Repubblica (Republic Day)
Aug. 15	Ferragosto (Feast of the Assumption)
Nov. 1	Ognissanti (All Saints' Day)
Nov. 2	Giorno dei Morti (All Souls' Day)
Dec. 8	Immacolata (Day of Immaculate Conception)
Dec. 24	Le Farchie di Natale (Christmas Eve)
Dec. 25	Natale (Christmas Day)
Dec. 26	Festa di Santo Stefano (Saint Stephen's Day)
Dec. 31	Festa di San Silvestro (New Year's Eve)

BEYOND TOURISM

A PHILOSOPHY FOR TRAVELERS

HIGHLIGHTS OF BEYOND TOURISM IN ITALY

TRACK endangered dolphins near the volcanic island of Ischia (p. 65).
PLANT grapevines on a vineyard in Naples recently reclaimed from the mob (p. 65).
LEARN LATIN for free from Father Reginald Foster *et carpe diem.*
COOK traditional Tuscan cuisine with locals at culinary classes in Florence (p. 69).

As a tourist, you are always a foreigner. Sure, hostel-hopping and sightseeing can be great fun, but connecting with a foreign country through studying, volunteering, or working can extend your travels beyond tourist traps. We don't like to brag, but this is what's different about a *Let's Go* traveler. Instead of feeling like a stranger in a strange land, you can understand Italy like a local. Instead of being that tourist asking for directions, you can be the one who gives them (and correctly!). All the while, you get the satisfaction of leaving Italy in better shape than you found it (after all, it's being nice enough to let you stay here). It's not wishful thinking—it's Beyond Tourism.

As a **volunteer** in Italy, you can take part in everything from preserving rare Neolithic rock art in an alpine valley to teaching English to school children in Sardinia. This chapter is full of ideas on how to get involved, whether you're looking to pitch in for a day or run away from home for a whole new life in Italian activism.

The powers of **studying** abroad are beyond comprehension: it actually makes you feel sorry for those poor tourists who don't get to do any homework while they're here. Aside from being home to some of the oldest universities in Europe, Italy hosts a slew of unique educational institutions, from art schools in Florence to archaeological camps in Rome. A little research in advance is all you need to discover your ideal study abroad program.

Working abroad immerses you in a new culture and can bring some of the most meaningful relationships and experiences of your life. Yes, we know you're on vacation, but these aren't your normal desk jobs. (Plus, it doesn't hurt that it helps pay for more globetrotting.) Opportunities in Italy include interning at a museum in Venice or teaching English in schools around the country.

 SHARE YOUR EXPERIENCE. Have you had a particularly enjoyable volunteer, study, or work experience that you'd like to share with other travelers? Post it to our website, www.letsgo.com!

VOLUNTEERING

Feel like saving the world this week? Volunteering can be a powerful and fulfilling experience, especially when combined with the thrill of traveling in a new place. Whatever shape your philanthropic cravings may take, opportunities to satisfy them exist throughout Italy. As the former home to the ancient Etruscans, Greeks, and numerous iterations of the Roman Empire, Italy has more than its share of relics and tourists who want to explore them. As the country strives both to share its ancient treasures and protect them, demand is high for volunteers willing to assist in the preservation effort. Even with minimal prior experience, hundreds of opportunities exist for English speakers interested in the art, architecture, and culture of the many groups that have occupied the Italian peninsula throughout history.

Most people who volunteer in Italy do so on a short-term basis at organizations that make use of drop-in or once-a-week volunteers. The best way to find opportunities that match your interests and schedule may be to check with local or national volunteer centers similar to those listed below, which organize work camps devoted to a number of cultural and environmental causes. Opportunities range from programs for community development to camps dedicated to ecological and historical preservation. Demand for volunteers among these programs varies depending on the time of year and the duration of a volunteer's stay, so it's always best to check with an organization before making any definitive plans. As always, read up before heading out.

Those looking for longer, more intensive volunteer opportunities usually choose to go through a parent organization that takes care of logistical details and often provides a group environment and support system—for a fee. There are two main types of organizations—religious and secular—although there are rarely restrictions on participation for either. Websites like **www.volunteerabroad.com**, **www.servenet.org**, and **www.idealist.org** allow you to search for volunteer openings both in your country and abroad.

I HAVE TO PAY TO VOLUNTEER? Many volunteers are surprised to learn that some organizations require large fees or "donations," but don't go calling them scams just yet. While such fees may seem ridiculous at first, they often keep the organization afloat, covering airfare, room, board, and administrative expenses for the volunteers. (Other organizations must rely on private donations and government subsidies.) If you're concerned about how a program spends its fees, request an annual report or finance account. A reputable organization won't refuse to inform you of how volunteer money is spent. Pay-to-volunteer programs might be a good idea for young travelers who are looking for more support and structure (such as pre-arranged transportation and housing) or anyone who would rather not deal with the uncertainty of creating a volunteer experience from scratch.

ECOTOURISM

Italy's expansive coastline and mild mainland environment play host to thousands of visitors annually. Tourists and locals alike are able to play a role in preserving the environment that has made Italy such a popular travel destination. Taking advantage of opportunities to work with wildlife and restore local habitats can be a great way to experience Italian culture at its best.

Canadian Alliance for Development Initiatives and Projects (CADIP), 129-1271 Howe St., Vancouver, British Columbia, V6Z 1R3, Canada (☎+1-604-628-7400; www.cadip.org). Offers over 100 2- to 3-week projects in Italy with an emphasis on environmental and historical preservation. Room and board provided by the program. Most projects 18+. US$285; some projects have extra fees.

Ecovolunteer: Common Dolphin Research, CTS-Centro Turistico Studentesco e Giovanile, Dept. Ambiente, V. Albalonga 3, 00183 Rome (☎06 64 96 03 27; www.ecovolunteer.org). Volunteers in the Gulf of Naples live on a research boat while tracking dolphins and other marine mammals. 1-week programs June-Oct. 18+. Program fee €750-850 per week. Student discounts available.

Greenwood Cooperation Society (Società Cooperativa Greenwood), V. Pozzillo 21, 87045 Dipignano (☎0984 44 55 26; www.scgreenwood.it). Conducts research in National Park of Calabria and encourages ecotourism. Volunteers help with ecological studies, like studying and tracking wolves with GPS devices and topographic maps. Check website for current studies. €350 covers food, camping, and research supplies.

Lega Italiana Protezione Uccelli (LIPU), LIPU Sede Nazionale, V. Trento 49, 43100 Parma (☎05 21 27 30 43; www.lipu.it/tu_voluntario.htm). Volunteers at this bird sanctuary nurse injured animals back to health and help with grounds maintenance.

Parco Nazionale d'Abruzzo, Lazio e Molise, V. Roma s.n.c., 67030 Villetta Barrea, AQ (☎08 64 89 102; www.parcoabruzzo.it). Hosts over 100 summer volunteers for 1-3 weeks. Responsibilities range from park maintenance to visitor assistance. 18+. Program fee 1 week €110, 2 weeks €170, 3 weeks €230.

World-Wide Opportunities on Organic Farms (WWOOF Italia), V. Casavecchia 109, 57022 Castagneto Carducci, Livorno (www.wwoof.it). Provides a list of organic farms that introduce volunteers to tasks like harvesting olives, grapes, and even bamboo. Knowledge of farming not necessary, although volunteers should be physically capable and willing to work hard. Required €25 membership fee.

ART, CULTURE, AND RESTORATION

Italy's rich cultural heritage, which dates back to Ancient Rome, is increasingly in danger of crumbling or being overrun by modern life. Volunteers looking for a labor-intensive way to engage with Italy's historical past should research groups that specialize in landmark preservation.

Archeo Venezia, Cannaregio 1376/a, 30121 Venezia (☎41 71 05 15; www.archeove.com). Offers 1-week programs in archeological field work, including ceramics, metalwork, and painting. €150-330. Fee includes room and board.

Footsteps of Man, Ple. Donatori di Sangue 1, 25040 Cerveno, Brescia, Italy (☎03 64 43 39 83; www.rupestre.net/field/index.html). Accepts volunteers for a minimum stay of 7 days to analyze rock art in the Italian Alps, with over 300,000 samples dating from the Neolithic era to the Middle Ages. Training provided. 16+. €370 per week.

ResponsibleTravel.com, 3rd Floor, Pavilion House, 6 Old Steine, Brighton BN1 1EJ, UK (☎+44-127-360-0030; www.responsibletravel.com). Various volunteer opportunities including cultural and environmental preservation projects of variable length. Program fee €460-975, depending on project.

YOUTH AND THE COMMUNITY

Community-based projects are among the most rewarding volunteer experiences. Programs listed below promote interactive humanitarian work through

English language programs and projects aimed at assisting the disadvantaged. Due to their one-on-one nature, knowledge of Italian is often necessary.

Agape Centro Ecumenico, Segreteria di Agape, Borgata Agape 1, 10060 Prali, Torino (☎01 21 80 75 14; www.agapecentroecumenico.org). Help maintain this international Protestant conference center in the Italian Alps. Clean and cook for the center for as little as 2 days to as long as 5 weeks in return for free room and board during spring and summer. Knowledge of Italian useful. 18+.

Global Volunteers, 375 East Little Canada Rd., St. Paul, MN 55117, USA (☎+1-800-487-1074; www.globalvolunteers.org). Teach English to students in southern Italy. 2-week sessions available throughout the year. Program fee US$2695-2995.

Pueblo Inglés, Rafael Calvo 18, 4A, Madrid 28010, Spain (☎+34 913 913 400; www.puebloingles.com). Week-long program in Umbria hires native English-speaking volunteers to provide English-language immersion for Italians. Room and board provided. Ages 22-80; alternative opportunities for ages 13-18. Free.

Service Civil International, 5505 Walnut Level Rd., Crozet, VA 22932, USA (☎+1-434-823-9003; www.sci-ivs.org). Places volunteers in small, 2- to 4-week work camps that range from festival assistance to social work to environmental or historical restoration. Long-term opportunities are also available. 18+. Program fee €50-150.

United Planet, 11 Arlington St., Boston, MA 02116, USA (☎+1-617-267-7763; www.unitedplanet.org). Places volunteers in 6-month to 1-year programs, including many aimed at helping children and the disabled in Italy. 18+. Maximum age varies by program. Fee of US$5000 for 6 months and $8000 for 1 year includes local transportation costs, training, a monthly stipend, and room and board with a host family.

Volunteers for Peace, 1034 Tiffany R., Belmont, VT 05730, USA (☎+1-802-259-2759; www.vfp.org). Provides info on volunteer programs. Most programs 18+. Program fee US$300.

STUDYING

It's hard to dread the first day of school when Rome is your campus and heaping bowls of *pasta al dente* and creamy *gelato alla fragola* make up your meal plan. A growing number of students report that studying abroad is the highlight of their university, or post-educational experience. If you've never studied abroad, you don't know what you're missing—and if you have studied abroad, your former destination certainly could not hold a candle to Italy's many sunny cities. Either way, opportunities to immerse yourself in *la dolce vita italiana*—while hitting the books every once and awhile—can be found in every corner of the beautiful, bold, and boisterous boot.

Study-abroad programs range from basic language and culture courses to university-level classes, often for college credit. In order to choose a program that best fits your needs, research as much as you can before making your decision—determine costs and duration, as well as what kind of students participate in the program and what sorts of accommodations are provided.

In programs that have large groups of students who speak the same language, there is a trade-off. You may feel more comfortable in the community, but you will not have the same opportunity to practice a foreign language or to befriend other international students. For accommodations, dorm life provides a better opportunity to mingle with fellow students, but there is less of a chance to experience the local scene. If you live with a family, you could potentially build lifelong friendships with natives and experience day-to-day life in more depth, but you might also get stuck sharing a room with their pet iguana. Conditions can vary greatly from family to family.

VISA INFORMATION. Italian bureaucracy often gives international visitors the run-around, but there are ways to minimize paperwork confusion. Just remember that all **non-EU citizens** are required to obtain a visa for any stay longer than three months. For info and applications, contact the Italian embassy or consulate in your country. Before applying for a student visa, however, be sure to obtain the following documentation: valid passport, visa application form (available from most embassy websites), four passport-size photographs, proof of residency, and complete documentation on the course or program in which you are participating. If you are under the age of 18, you will also need an affidavit of financial support from parents, and your parents' most recent bank statement. All **non-EU citizens** are also required to register with the *Ufficio degli Stranieri* (Foreigners' Bureau) at the *questura* (local police headquarters) to receive a *permesso di soggiorno* (permit to stay) within eight days of arrival. The kit required to complete the *permesso di soggiorno* can be obtained and submitted at most major *ufficio postali* (post offices). The same documentation is necessary for the *permesso di soggiorno* as for the visa; additionally, applicants must have the required *permesso di soggiorno* form and a *Marco da Bollo*, which costs €15 and is available at most Italian *tabaccherie*. **EU citizens** must apply for a *permesso di soggiorno* within three months, but they do not need a visa to study in Italy. Once you find a place to live, bring your *permesso di soggiorno* (it must have at least one year's validity) to a records office. This certificate will both confirm your registered address and expedite travel into and out of Italy.

UNIVERSITIES

Most university-level study-abroad programs are conducted in Italian, but many programs offer classes in English as well as lower-level language courses. Savvy linguists may find it cheaper to enroll directly in a university abroad, although getting college credit may be more difficult. You can search **www.studyabroad.com** for various semester-abroad programs that meet your criteria, including your desired location and focus of study. If you're a college student, your friendly neighborhood study-abroad office is often the best place to start.

AMERICAN PROGRAMS

American Institute for Foreign Study (AIFS), College Division, River Plaza, 9 W. Broad St., Stamford, CT 06902, USA (☎+1-800-727-2437; www.aifsabroad.com). Organizes programs for high-school and college study in universities in Italy.

CET Academic Programs: Italian Studies Program in Siena, Florence, and Sicily, 1920 N St. NW, Ste. 200, Washington, D.C. 20036, USA (☎+1-800-225-4262; www.cetacademicprograms.com). Only open to the public for the summer term, this Vanderbilt University program offers art history courses and traveling seminars. Summer program US$7790-8490. Includes medical insurance and housing.

Council on International Educational Exchange (CIEE), 300 Fore St., Portland, ME 04101, USA (☎+1-207-553-4000 or +1-800-40-STUDY/407-8839; www.ciee.org). A comprehensive resource for work, academic, and internship programs in Italy.

International Association for the Exchange of Students for Technical Experience (IAESTE), Politecnico di Milano, Centro per le Relazioni Internazionali, Piazza Leonardo da Vinci 32, 20133 Milan (☎2 23 99 97 64; www.iaeste.org). Offers hands-on technical internships in Italy. You must be a college student studying science, technology, or engineering. Most programs last 8-12 weeks.

School for International Training (SIT) Study Abroad, 1 Kipling Rd., P.O. Box 676, Brattleboro, VT 05302, USA (☎+1-888-272-7881 or +1-802-258-3212; www.sit.edu/studyabroad). Semester-long programs cost about US$6800. Also runs **The Experiment in International Living** (☎+1-800-345-2929; www.usexperiment.org), which offers 3- to 5-week summer programs for high-school students that involve cross-cultural homestays, community service, ecological adventure, and language training. US$6800.

LANGUAGE SCHOOLS

Enrolling at a language school has two major perks: a slightly less rigorous courseload and the ability to teach you exactly what those kids in Milan are calling you under their breath. There can be great variety in language schools—independently run, affiliated with a larger university, local, international—but one thing is constant: they rarely offer college credit. Their programs are also good for younger high-school students who might not feel comfortable with older students in a university program.

Centro Culturale Giacomo Puccini, V. Amerigo Vespucci 173, 55049 Viareggio (☎05 84 43 02 53; www.centropuccini.it). 2- to 24- week language courses at all levels. Pro-

fessional Italian and cultural courses available. 16+. Additional accommodations fee for apartment or homestay. Program costs €260-2520. €70 registration fee.

Centro Fiorenza, V.S. Spirito 14, 50125 Florence (☎05 52 39 82 74; www.centro-fiorenza.com). Students live in Florence and are immersed in Italian. Program also offers courses on the island of Elba, although hotel accommodations there are expensive. 1- to 5-week course (20 lessons per week) from €185. Enrollment fee €55.

Eurocentres, 56 Eccleston Sq., London SW1V 1PH, UK (☎+44 20 7963 8450; www.eurocentres.com). Language programs with homestays in Florence.

Istituto Venezia, Campo S. Margherita 3116/a, Dorsoduro, 30123 Venice (☎04 15 22 43 31; www.istitutovenezia.com). Language and art history classes at all levels, taught in small groups. Courses 1-24 weeks. Language classes also taught in Trieste. Accommodation arrangements upon request; costs and housing types vary, but start at €220.

Italiaidea, V. dei Due Macelli 47, 1st fl., 00187 Rome (☎06 60 94 13 14; www.italiaidea.com). 1-week to 6-month Italian language and culture courses near the Spanish Steps for individuals and groups of 10 or fewer. Courses qualify for credit at many American universities. Students live in private homes, homestay, or apartments; reserve ahead. Program costs €300-1200. €50 registration fee.

Koinè, V. de' Pandolfini 27, I-50122 Florence (☎05 52 13 881; wwww.koinecenter.com). Language lessons (group and individual), cultural lessons, wine tastings, and cooking lessons. Courses offered in Florence, Lucca, Bologna, Cortona, and Elba. 1-4 week courses €190-4780. Accommodations not included. Deposit €150.

Language Immersion Institute, State University of New York at New Paltz, 1 Hawk Dr., New Paltz, NY 12561, USA (☎+1-845-257-3500; www.newpaltz.edu/lii). Short, intensive summer language courses and some overseas courses in Italian. Program fees are around US$1000 for a 2-week course, not including accommodations.

ITALIAN SCHOOLS: SPECIAL INTEREST

FINE ARTS

Aegean Center for the Fine Arts, Paros 84400, Cyclades, Greece (☎+30 22 84 02 32 87; www.aegeancenter.org). Italian branch located in Pistoia. Instruction in arts, literature, creative writing, voice, and art history. Classes taught in English. Fees cover housing in 16th-century villa, meals, and excursions to Rome, Venice, and Greece. University credit on individual arrangement. 14-week program in the fall €8500.

Art School in Florence, Studio Art Centers International, Palazzo dei Cartelloni, Via Sant'Antonio 11, 50123 Florence (☎+1-212-248-7225; www.saci-florence.org). Affiliated with Bowling Green State University. Studio arts, art history, Italian studies. Apartment housing. 6 credits summer US$5550; 15 credits semester US$14,900.

Scuola Arte del Mosaico, V. Francesco Negri 14, 48110 Ravenna (☎34 96 01 45 66; www.sira.it/mosaic/studio.htm). Participants learn the history and techniques behind both ancient and modern mosaics, and get to create their own. 5-day course (40hr.) for beginner and intermediate levels conducted in English. Program fee €660.

COOKING IN LA CUCINA

Apicius, The Culinary Institute of Florence, V. Guelfa 85, Florence 50129 (☎05 52 65 81 35; www.apicius.it). Professional and non-professional food and wine studies in historic Florence. Cooking courses in English; Italian language classes available. Prices for weekly, non-professional programs €1265-5750. Include room and board. Masters in Italian cuisine €10,550. Enrollment fee €115.

Cook Italy, (☎34 90 07 82 98; www.cookitaly.com). Region- or dish-specific cooking classes. Venues include Bologna, Cortona, Florence, Lucca, Rome, and Sicily. Courses 3- to 6- nights from €950. Housing, meals, and recipes included.

The International Kitchen, 330. N. Wabash #2613, Chicago, IL 60611, USA (☎+1-800-945-8606; www.theinternationalkitchen.com). A leading provider of cooking school vacations to Italy. Traditional cooking instruction in beautiful settings for individuals and groups. Program locations include the Amalfi Coast, Liguria, Tuscany, and Venice. Courses 2-10 nights. Programs start at US$400.

ROCKIN' RELICS

Aestiva Romae Latinitatis, Summer Latin in Rome, P. Reginald Foster OCD, Tersianum, P. S. Pancrazio 5A, I-00152 Rome. Free 6-week summer Latin program in Rome with legendary Father Reginald Foster, an American priest who works in the "Latin Letters" section of the Vatican's Secretariat of State. Foster has taught this program for nearly 25 years. Lessons in written and conversational Latin for intermediate and advanced students. Optional lesson "sub arboribus" (under the trees in the monastery garden) given in the evenings. Write for info and application materials.

ArchaeoSpain, PO Box 1331, Farmington, CT 06034 USA (☎+1-866-932-003; www.archaeospain.com). Archeology buffs help out in Rome at Monte Testaccio. Once an ancient pottery dump, the site is now the best record of ancient Roman commerce. English speakers and all ages welcome. University credit on individual arrangement. 2-week program US$2745. Housing and meals included.

WORKING

Nowhere does money grow on trees (though *Let's Go*'s researchers aren't done looking), but there are still some pretty good opportunities to earn a living and travel at the same time. As with volunteering, work opportunities tend to fall into two categories. Some travelers want long-term jobs that allow them to integrate into a community, while others seek out short-term jobs to finance the next leg of their travels. In Italy, short-term work in agriculture, the service sector, and tourism is the easiest to come by. Though job hunters must navigate the inevitable challenge of Italy's soaring unemployment rates and the premium that Italian employers place on both practical experience and advanced degrees, take heart: with a little research in advance, long-term opportunities are not out of the realm of possibility. **Transitions Abroad** (www.transitionsabroad.com) offers updated online listings for work over any time span.

Check out weekly job listings in *Corriere della Sera*'s "Corriere Lavoro" (online at trovolavoro.it) or *Il Sole 24 Ore*'s "Cercolavoro Giovani," which specializes in listings for recent university graduates. **GoAbroad.com** (www.internabroad.com/Italy.cfm) has a user-friendly online database of internship listings in Italy. **Youth Info Centers Informagiovani** (www.informagiovani-italia.com) in each region target both Italians and visitors and offer free information on work regulations, employment trends, volunteer programs, and study opportunities. Note that working abroad often requires a special work visa.

MORE VISA INFORMATION. Working legally in Italy as a foreigner is a bureaucratic challenge regardless of your nationality. **EU passport holders** do not require a special visa to live or work in Italy. They do require a permit to stay *(permesso di soggiorno per lavoro)*, which grants permission to remain in Italy for the duration of employment. To obtain a *permesso di soggiorno*, EU citizens must register at the local police headquarters *(questura)* within eight days of arrival for a permit to search for work *(ricevuta di segnalazione di siggiorno)*. **Non-EU citizens** seeking work in Italy must possess an Italian work permit *(autorizzazione al lavoro in Italia)* before entering the country. Only a prospective employer can begin the process, guaranteeing that the individual has been offered a position. Permits are authorized by the Provincial Employment Office and approved by the police headquarters before being forwarded to the employer and prospective employee. The prospective employee must then present the document, along with a valid passport, in order to obtain a work visa. **Non-EU citizens** must also obtain both the *permesso di soggiorno* and a workers' registration card—*libretto di lavoro*—which will function as an employment record for up to ten years. Visit the **Italian Ministry of Foreign Afffairs** website (www.esteri.it) or the **US Embassy** site (http://italy.usembassy.gov) for more information.

BEYOND TOURISM

LONG-TERM WORK

If you're planning on spending a substantial amount of time (more than 3 months) working in Italy, search for a job well in advance. International placement agencies are often the easiest way to find employment abroad, especially for those interested in teaching. Although they are often only available to college students, **internships** are a good way to ease into working abroad. Many say the interning experience is well worth it, despite low pay (if you're lucky enough to be paid at all). Because Italian students typically spend more years in university than their American, British, and Australian counterparts, *stage* (internships) are not as prevalent. Strong language skills will certainly make you a more desirable candidate. Be wary of advertisements for companies claiming to be able get you a job abroad for a fee—often the same listings are available online or in newspapers.

Center for Cultural Interchange, 746 N. LaSalle Dr., Chicago, IL 60610, USA (☎312-944-2544; www.cci-exchange.com/abroad/intern.shtml). 1-3 month volunteer internships in Florence. Opportunities in business, accounting and finance, tourism, and social service. At least 2 years of college-level Italian required. US$7090-10,590. Tuition includes Italian language course, health insurance, and homestay with half-board.

English Yellow Pages, V. Belisario 4/B, 00187 Rome (☎06 474 0861 and 06 97 61 75 28; www.englishyellowpages.it). Resources for English-speaking expats in Italy run by an American who relocated to Italy in 1982 to teach English. Includes job listings, classifieds, photos, blogs, and more.

Global Experiences, 168 West St., Annapolis, MD 21401, USA (☎877-432-27623; www.globalexperiences.com). Arranges internships with companies in Florence, Rome, Verona, and Milan. 8-week programs start at €4000 and include intensive language training, accommodation, emergency medical travel insurance, and full-time on-site support.

Institute for the International Education of Students, 33 N. LaSalle St., 15th fl., Chicago, IL 60602, USA (☎800-995-2300; www.iesabroad.org). Internships for academic credit in Rome, Milan, and Siena based on availability, background, skills, and language ability. Past assignments in fashion, photography, journalism, business consulting, and psychological research. Semester-long programs from around US$17,000. Includes tuition for up to 19 credits, orientation, housing, and medical insurance.

Peggy Guggenheim Collection, Palazzo Venier dei Leoni, Dorsoduro 701, 30123 Venice (☎041 2405 401; www.guggenheim-venice.it). Interns assist museum operations such as gallery preparation, tour guidance, workshops with children, and administrative matters for 1-3 months. Offers a stipend. Italian skills a plus.

World Endeavors, 3015 E. Franklin Ave., Minneapolis, MN 55406, USA (☎+1-866-802-9678; www.worldendeavors.com/Italy). 3- to 6-month internships in Florence in a wide variety of fields from craft apprenticeships to sports management with professional football teams. 4-month internships start at US$4700 and include intensive Italian training and various English-speaking support services.

TEACHING ENGLISH

While some elite private American schools offer competitive salaries, let's just say that teaching jobs abroad pay more in personal satisfaction and emotional fulfillment than in actual cash. Perhaps this is why volunteering as a teacher instead of getting paid is a popular option. Even then, teachers often receive some sort of a daily stipend to help with living expenses. In almost all cases, you must have at least a bachelor's degree to be a full-fledged teacher, although college undergraduates can often get summer positions teaching or tutoring. Though the demand for English teachers in Italy is high, the competition is stiff. Finding a teaching job as a non-EU citizen can be especially tough.

Many schools require teachers to have a **Teaching English as a Foreign Language (TEFL)** certificate. You may still be able to find a teaching job without one, but certified teachers often find higher-paying jobs. Some schools within Italy that grant TEFLs will even offer both classroom instruction and practical experience or a leg up in job placement when you earn your certificate. The Italian-impaired don't have to give up their dream of teaching, either. Private schools usually hire native English speakers for English-immersion classrooms where no Italian is spoken. (Teachers in public schools will more likely work in both English and Italian.) Placement agencies or university fellowship programs are the best resources for finding teaching jobs. The alternative is to contact schools directly or to try your luck once you arrive in Italy. In the latter case, the best time to look is several weeks before the start of the school year, or as early as February or March for summer positions.

Associazione Culturale Linguista Educational (ACLE), V. Roma 54, 18038 San Remo, Imperio (☎01 84 50 60 70; www.acle.org). Non-profit association working to bring theater, arts, and English language instruction to Italian schools. Employees create theater programs in schools, teach English at summer camps, and help convert a medieval home into a student art center. Knowledge of Italian useful. On-site accommodations and cooking facilities included. Ages 20-30. Camp counselor salary of €220-260.

International Schools Services (ISS), 15 Roszel Rd., P.O. Box 5910, Princeton, NJ 08543, USA (☎+1-609-452-0990; www.iss.edu). Hires teachers for more than 200 overseas schools, including in Italy. Candidates should have teaching experience and a bachelor's degree. 2-year commitment is the norm.

Office of Overseas Schools, US Department of State, 2201 C St. NW, Washington, D.C. 20520, USA (☎+1-202-647-4000; www.state.gov/m/a/os). Provides an extensive list of general info about teaching overseas. See also the **Office of English Language Programs** (http://exchanges.state.gov/education/engteaching).

AU PAIR WORK

Au pairs are typically women (although sometimes men) aged 18-27 who work as live-in nannies, caring for children and doing light housework in foreign countries in exchange for room, board, and a small spending allowance or stipend. One perk of the job is that it allows you to get to know Italy without the high expenses of traveling. Drawbacks, however, can include mediocre pay and long hours. Unfortunately, with the recent adoption of laws that severely limit the availability of work visas for non-EU citizens in Italy, au pairing has become less common, especially for stays longer than 3 months (the maximum visa-free visiting period). The Italian government will not grant au pair-specific visas so it is imperative that au pairs take necessary steps with prospective employers to obtain work permits and visas (see **More Visa Information, p. 71**). In Italy, average weekly pay for au pair work is about €65. Much of the au pair experience depends on the family with which you are placed.

Childcare International, Trafalgar House, Grenville Pl., London NW7 3SA, UK (☎+44 20 8906 3116; www.childint.co.uk).

InterExchange, 161 6th Ave., New York City, NY 10013, USA (☎+1-212-924-0446 or 800-AU-PAIRS/287-2477; www.interexchange.org).

Roma Au Pair, V. Pietro Mascagni 138, 00199 Rome (☎33 97 79 41 26; www.romaaupair.it). Provides information on au pair placement throughout Italy.

SHORT-TERM WORK

Romantic images of cultivating the land in a sun-soaked vineyard may dance in your head, but in reality, casual agricultural jobs are hard to find in Italy due to the prevalence of foreign migrant workers who are often willing to work for minimal pay. Those looking for agricultural jobs will have the best luck looking in the northwest during the annual fall harvest or volunteer with **WWOOF** (p. 65). Another popular option is to work several hours a day at a hostel in exchange for free or discounted room and/or board. Most often, these short-term jobs are found by word of mouth or by expressing interest to the owner of a hostel or restaurant. Due to high turnover in the tourism industry, many places are eager for help, even if it is only temporary. *Let's Go* lists temporary jobs of this nature whenever possible; look in the Practical Information sections of larger cities.

ROME (ROMA)

In the books you'll read, the pictures you'll see, and the pithy sayings you'll hear, Rome is the idealized city, an eternal metropolis that seamlessly transitions from history to the present in a matter of city blocks. It has been canonized for its invaluable cultural treasures, from ancient temples to Michelangelo's *Pietà*. Rome is the capital of kingdoms and republics, its genesis the empire that defined the Western world in antiquity. Its system of government is still imitated today, its architecture has laid the course for modern building techniques, and its most recent contribution to world culture, its cinema, is revered. These claims are not exaggerations; the city will live up to its reputation. Expect no excuse for how overwhelming it can be.

This city of 2.7 million people isn't a dreamy idyll, though—or at least, it's more than one. Not as pretty as Paris, not as efficient as Berlin, Rome is a thrumming modern metropolis, a commercial and cultural hub. It is also a city of contradictions. The quiet and respectable neighborhoods around the Vatican rub up against buzzy Trastevere. A 10min. walk takes you from the designer stores around the Spanish Steps to the bargain basements near Termini station. Everywhere you turn, the Holy See has renovated a crumbling pagan building and repurposed it as a Catholic church. Nightclubs and chic hotels pop up in the ruins of the Ancient City. If all this pull between the past and the future gets overwhelming, just take a break and settle right back into the present.

Visitors to Rome often try to do too much—they rush through every cathedral and by every painting. Sometimes, it's worth kicking back with a *caffè* and watching the city march past. In these moments of reflection, you'll see the city's separate identities—romantic shrine, modern metropolis, living archaeological site, and place to build a home—all twirled together like pasta around a fork. Enjoy your newfound understanding of this singular city. You'll realize how much you're going to miss it, and you'll know you can always come back. This stuff has been around a while; it's not going anywhere.

HIGHLIGHTS OF ROME

CHANNEL Rome's Golden Age with a trip to the Ancient City (p. 124).

SURVEY Rome's art scene, and let collections from the Vatican Museums (p. 115) to the Galleria Borghese (p. 116) prove the city deserving of its reputation.

TOSS a coin into the Trevi Fountain for a speedy return to the Eternal City (p. 104).

EVADE the temptations of Circe on the Pontine Islands (p. 129), where the likes of Mussolini, Nero, and even Odysseus were reputedly held captive.

✈ INTERCITY TRANSPORTATION

Flights: Most international flights arrive at **Da Vinci International Airport,** known as **Fiumicino (FCO;** ☎06 65 951). After exiting customs, follow the signs for **Stazione Trenitalia/Railway Station.** The **Termini line** (the colorful Leonardo Express) runs nonstop to Rome's main train station, **Termini** (30min., 2 per hr. 6:35am-11:35pm, €11). Buy a ticket at the Trenitalia ticket counter, the *tabaccheria* on the right, or from one of the machines in the station. Beware of scam artists attempting to sell fake tickets. A train leaves Termini for Fiumicino every 30min. (30min., 5:50am-10:50pm; €11); the very first train of the morning leaves from track 23 and all others leave from track 25. Buy your tickets at the Leonardo Express kiosk on track 25 or from one of the machines in the station. Be warned: track 25 is quite a walk from the entrance to the station on P. dei Cinquecento; try to leave a good 10min. just to get to the departure point. Failure to validate your ticket before boarding could lead to a €50-100 fine. Insert it into one of the little yellow boxes you see near the tracks to get that crucial stamp of approval.

Early And Late Flights: For flights that arrive after 10:30pm or leave before 8am, the most reliable option is to go between Rome and the airport is a **taxi.** (Request one at the kiosk in the airport or call ☎06 49 94 or 66 45.) **Agree on a price with the driver before getting into the cab—**it should be around €40. Factors such as the amount of luggage and the time of day will affect the price. The cheapest option is to take the blue **COTRAL bus** (☎800 17 4471) outside the main exit doors after customs to Tiburtina (1:15, 2:15, 3:30, 5am; €5 onboard). From Tiburtina, take bus N2 to Termini. To get to Fiumicino from Rome late at night or early in the morning, take bus N2 from Termini to Tiburtina (every 20-30min.), then catch the blue COTRAL bus to Fiumicino from the *piazza* (12:30, 1:15, 2:30, 3:45am; €5). The **24hr. airport shuttle service** (☎06 47 40 451 or 42 01 34 69; www.airportshuttle.it) is a good deal for two or more.

Ciampino Airport: Most charter flights and a few international ones, including **Ryanair,** arrive at **Ciampino Airport (CIA;** ☎06 65 951). To get to Rome from Ciampino, take the **COTRAL bus** (every 30min. 6:10am-11:40pm, €1) to Anagnina station on Ⓜ︎A. The public shuttle buses (☎06 59 16 826; www.sitbusshuttle.com) or the **Terravision Shuttle** (☎06 79 34 17 22; www.terravision.it) are slightly more convenient options, especially for late or early flights.

Trains: Stazione Termini is the train and subway hub, though it's closed between midnight and 5:30am. During this time trains usually arrive at Stazione Tiburtina or Stazione Ostiense; both connect to Termini at night by bus #175. Station services include: shopping, **ATMs,** hotel reservations across from track #13, **luggage storage** underneath track #24, and **police** at track #13. Termini's **bathrooms** (€0.70) beneath track #1 are a surreal black-lit wonderland. Trains (Direct, or D, is the slowest; IC is the intercity train; ES, or Eurostar, is the fastest and most expensive) leave Termini for: **Bologna** (IC 3hr., €33; ES 2hr., €42); **Florence** (D 3hr., €14; IC 2hr., €24; ES 1hr., €33); **Milan** (D 8hr., €30; IC 6hr., €41; ES 4hr., €50); **Naples** (D 2hr., €10; IC 2hr., €19; ES 1hr., €25); **Venice** (D overnight, €33; IC 5hr., €39; ES 4hr., €50). Hours and prices are updated every six months; check **www.trenitalia.it** for the most up-to-date schedules and prices.

▣ ORIENTATION

Rome's size and narrow, winding streets can make it difficult to navigate, so it's helpful to orient yourself by using major landmarks and main streets. The **Tiber River,** which snakes north-south through the city, is also a useful reference point. Most trains arrive at **Stazione Termini** east of Rome's historical center. The neighborhood surrounding **Termini** and **San Lorenzo** to the east is home to the city's largest university and most of its budget accommodations. **Via Nazionale** originates two blocks northwest of Termini Station in **Piazza della Repubblica** and leads to **Piazza Venezia,** the city's focal point, recognizable by the immense white **Vittorio Emanuele II monument.** From P. Venezia, **Via dei Fori Imperiali** runs southeast to the Ancient City, where you can find the **Colosseum** and the **Roman Forum. Via del Corso** stretches north from P. Venezia to **Piazza del Popolo,** which has an obelisk in its center that is visible all the way from P. Venezia. The **Trevi Fountain, Piazza Barberini,** and the fashionable streets around **Piazza di Spagna** and the **Spanish Steps** lie to the east of V. del Corso. **Villa Borghese,** home to impressive gardens and museums, is northeast of the Spanish Steps. West of V. del Corso is the **centro storico** (historical town center), the tangle of streets around the **Pantheon, Piazza Navona, Campo dei Fiori,** and the old **Jewish Ghetto. Largo Argentina,** west

ROME

A   B   C

Via S. Nicolò
da Tolentino
Via Barberini
Wic. S. N. da Tolentino
Via L. Bissolati
Via S. Nicolò da Tolentino
V. Flavia
V. XX Settembre
Via Palestro
Via Montebello
PIAZZ
D. CRO
ROSS
V. Sapri

Palazzo
Barberini
S. Susanna
PIAZZA DI S.
BERNARDO
S. Maria
della Vittoria
Ministeri del
Bilancio e del Tesoro
Via Carnaia
Via Mentana

Ministero
Difesa
Esercito
Via XX Settembre
Via d. Quattro Fontane
Via Firenze
Rotonda Museum
Via Montebello
Via Goito
Via Castelfidardo
Via Gaeta

REPUBLICA
PIAZZA D.
REPUBBLICA
Terme di
Diocleziano
Via Calatafimi
Via Gaeta

Via S. Vitale
Via Modena
S. M. d. Angeli
Via Volturno

Via A. de Pretis
Via Nazionale
Via Firenze
Via Torino
Economy
Book and
Video
Center
Via L. Einaudi
Via di Terme Diocleziano
Viminale
PIAZZA D.
CINQUECENTO
PIAZZA
INDIPENDENZA

Via Palermo
Via Venezia
Via A. de Pretis
Teatro
dell'Opera
Museo
Nazionale
Romano
TERMINI
Via Vicenza
Via Magenta
Via Marghera
V. Palestr

Ministero
d. Interno
Via Cesare Balbo
Via Nazionale
Via G. Amendola
Via Principe Amedeo
TERMINI
Station
Via Marsala
Via Milazzo
Via Castro Pretorio

S. Prudenziana
Via Urbana
PIAZZA
ESQUILINO
Via Daniele Manin
Via Marsala

Via Panisperna
Via Cavour
Via d. S. Maria
Maggiore
S. Maria
Maggiore
Via Gioberti

Via Cavour
Via Sforza
Via Paolina
Via della Olmata
Via Carlo Cattaneo
Via Filippo Turati
Via Giovanni Giolitti

CAVOUR
Via Giovanni Lanza
Via S. Martino
ai Monti
Via d. Ste
Prassede
S. Prassede
Via Merulana
Via Carlo Alberto
Via di S. Vito
PIAZZA
M. FANTI
Via Rattazzi
Via Principe Amedeo
Via T. Mamiani
Via B. Ricasoli

Parco
di Traiano
Via Domenichino
Auditorium of
Maecenas
Museo Nazionale
d'Arte Orientale
Via Leopardi
PIAZZA
VITTORIO
EMANUELE
VITTORIO
EMANUELE
Via G. Pepe
S. Biblana
Via Bibia

TO COLOSSEUM
(100m)
Via Merulana
Via Michelangelo
Buonarroti
Via Giusti
Via Ferruccio
Via Foscolo
Via Lamarmora
Via Principe Eugenio
Via Cairoli
Via Conte Verde
Via Principe
Umberto

Via Mecenate
Via Ruggero Bonghi
Via Guicciardini
Via A. Poliziano
Via Macchiavelli
Via Alfieri
Via Tasso
Via Nino Bixio
Via Pianciani
Via Alessandro Manzoni

Via
Normannia
Via
Calmantana
Via S. Giovanni in Laterano
V. dei SS. Quattro Coronati
Via Galilei
Via Ariosto
Viale Alessandro Manzoni
Via Emanuele Filiberto
Viale Alessandro Manzoni
Via di S. Croce in Gerusalemme
Via S. Croce in Gerusalemme

Via dei Querceti
Viale Labicana
MANZONI
Via S. Quintino
Via V. Vittorio
Via Statilia

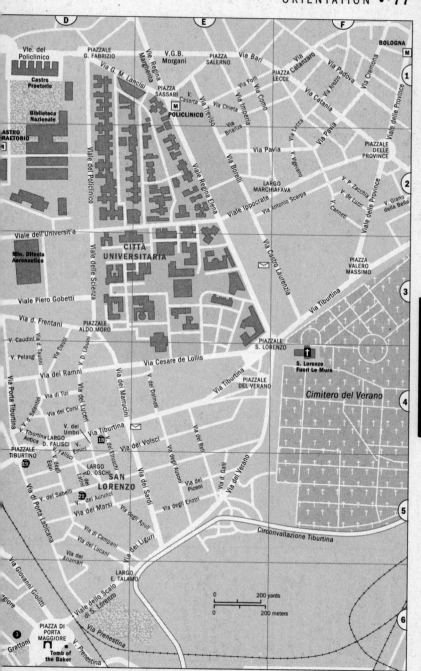

ROME

ROME

Centro Storico & Trastevere

ACCOMMODATIONS

Albergo Pomezia, 68
Albergo del Sole, 75
Casa Banzo, 61
Due Torri, 116
Hotel Fontanella Borghese, 118
Hotel Navona, 88
Hotel Rinascimento, 83
Hotel Smeraldo, 65
Relais Palazzo Taverna, 109
TeatroPace33, 97

FOOD

Ai Spaghettari, 12
Bar della Pace, 101
Biscottificio Artigiano Innocenti, 22
Caffè Tazza d'Oro, 105
Corsetti Il Galeone, 9
Cul de Sac, 85
Da Enzo, 16
Da Paolo, 4
Da Simone, 3
Giolitti, 112
Giorgiagel, 7
Il Capriccio, 6
Il Fornaio, 81
Il Gelato di San Crispino, 106
L'Angolo dell'Artista, 64
L'Insalata Ricca, 80
La Pollarola, 76
La Taverna del Ghetto, 53
La Torre, 10
Miscellanea, 92
Mo' Stò, 32
Panificio Arnese, 39
Pasticceria Ebraico Boccione, 55
Pizza Art, 54

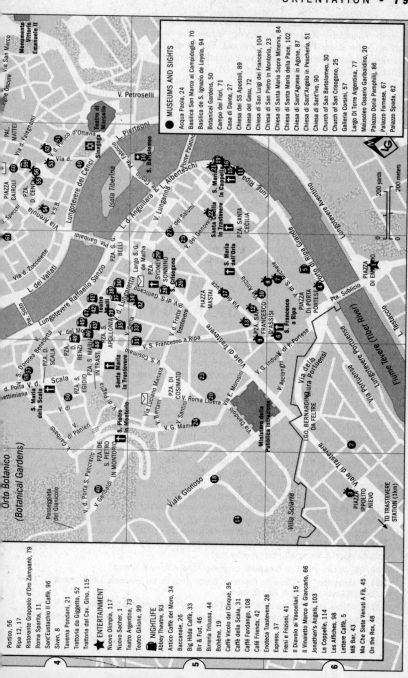

ROME

MUSEUMS AND SIGHTS
- Acqua Paola, 24
- Basilica San Marco al Campidoglio, 70
- Basilica de S. Ignazio di Loyola, 94
- Botanical Gardens, 50
- Campo dei Fiori, 71
- Casa di Dante, 27
- Chiesa dei SS Apostoli, 89
- Chiesa del Gesù, 72
- Chiesa di San Luigi dei Francesi, 104
- Chiesa di San Pietro in Montorio, 23
- Chiesa di Santa Maria Sopra Minerva, 84
- Chiesa di Santa Maria della Pace, 102
- Chiesa di Sant'Agnese in Agone, 87
- Chiesa di Sant'Angelo in Pescheria, 51
- Chiesa di Sant'Ivo, 77
- Church of San Bartolomeo, 30
- Church of San Crisogono, 25
- Galleria Corsini, 57
- Largo Di Torre Argentina, 77
- Mausoleo Ossario Garibaldino, 20
- Palazzo Doria Pamphilj, 86
- Palazzo Farnese, 67
- Palazzo Spada, 62

ENTERTAINMENT
- Nuovo Olimpia, 117
- Nuovo Sacher, 1
- Teatro Argentina, 73
- Teatro Ghione, 99

NIGHTLIFE
- Abbey Theatre, 93
- Antico Caffè del Moro, 34
- Baccanale, 26
- Big Hilda Caffè, 33
- Bir & Fud, 46
- Birreria Trilussa, 44
- Bohème, 19
- Caffè Vicolo del Cinque, 35
- Caffè della Scala, 31
- Caffè Fandango, 108
- Café Friends, 42
- Enoteca Trastevere, 28
- Express, 37
- Freni e Frizioni, 41
- Il Diavolo ai Vascellari, 15
- Il Vinaletto Marco & Giancarlo, 66
- Jonathan's Angels, 103
- Le Coppelle, 114
- Les Affiches, 98
- Lettere Caffè, 5
- M8 Bar, 43
- Ma Che Siete Venuti A Fà, 45
- On the Rox, 48

- Portico, 56
- Ripa 12, 17
- Ristorante Grappolo d'Oro Zampanò, 79
- Roma Sparita, 11
- Sant'Eustachio Il Caffè, 96
- Siven, 8
- Taverna Ponziani, 21
- Trattoria da Giggetto, 52
- Trattoria dal Cav. Gino, 115

of P. Venezia, marks the start of **Corso Vittorio Emanuele II**, which runs through the *centro storico* to the Tiber River. Across the river to the northwest is **Vatican City** and the **Borgo-Prati** neighborhood. South of the Vatican are **Trastevere** and residential **Testaccio**. Be sure to pick up a free color map in English at the tourist office (see Practical Information, p. 81).

Once you've wrapped your head around the center city, it's easier to think about other neighborhoods. Immediately east of the diamond is **Stazione Termini**. If you arrived in the city in any sort of train or on one of the many buses, you've been here. The major street in this area is **Via Nazionale**, which features shopping and touristy cafes; it originates just near P. Venezia and ends two blocks northwest of the station. Reach still further east and you'll start hitting residential neighborhoods, including some hip ones like **Pigneto**. Immediately to the north of the central diamond is **Villa Borghese**, a big, beautiful green space with some impressive museums. North and northeast of the Villa is the upscale residential neighborhood of **Parioli**; west and northwest is the mostly middle-class **Flaminio** area. Major roads here are **Viale dei Parioli** and **Via Flaminia**, respectively. Drift further south and you'll run into the **Aventine** and newly trendy residential areas like **Ostiense** and **Garbatella**, as well as club-filled **Testaccio**. Finally, if you hop west across the Tiber you'll find a series of increasingly gritty neighborhoods running top to bottom along the city's left bank. From north to south, there's **Vatican City** and the quiet, well-to-do **Borgo-Prati** neighborhood; trendy but increasingly touristy **Trastevere**; and the rather scruffy residential neighborhood of **Marconi**.

⌐ LOCAL TRANSPORTATION

Metro: Rome's subway, the **Metropolitana** (www.metroroma.it), has two lines, A and B, which intersect only at Termini. Station entrances are marked by poles with a white "M" on a red square. The subway usually runs daily 5:30am-1:30am, but due to construction of the forthcoming C line, the subway occasionally closes at 10pm. At night, bus N1 replaces Ⓜ️A and N2 replaces Ⓜ️B.

Buses: The network of routes may seem daunting, but Rome's buses are an efficient means of getting around the city, especially since the Metro doesn't serve the *centro storico*. The **ATAC** transportation company has booths throughout the city, including one in Termini. (☎06 80 04 31 784; www.atac.roma.it. Open M-Sa 7am-8pm, Su 8am-7pm.) At any of these *biglietterie*, you can grab a map (€1) or purchase monthly, yearly, or discounted Metro passes. Single-use ATAC tickets (€1) are valid for the Metro and buses, and are sold at *tabaccherie*, newsstands, vending machines, and some bars. Vending machines are in metro stations, on street corners, and at major bus stops; look for ATAC labels. Tickets are valid for one Metro ride or 75 minutes of unlimited bus travel. A **biglietto integrato giornalero,** or daily ticket (€4), covers unlimited bus or train travel in the metropolitan area (including Ostia but not Fiumicino) until midnight the day of purchase; a **carta integrale settimanale** (€16) is good for a week; a 3-day tourist ticket is €11. Enter buses through the front and back doors; exit through the middle door. A few useful bus routes are:

#40/64, Vatican area, C. V. Emanuele, Largo Argentina, P. Venezia, Termini.

#81, P. Malatesta, San Giovanni, Colosseo, Bocca della Verità, P. Venezia, Largo Argentina, V. del Corso, P. Cavour, V. Cola di Rienzo, Vatican.

#116T, Vatican area, Via Giulia, Campo dei Fiori area, Piazza Navona area, V. del Corso, V. Veneto.

#170, Termini, V. Nazionale, P. Venezia, Bocca della Verità, Testaccio, Stazione Trastevere, V. Marconi, P. Agricoltura.

#492, Tiburtina, Termini, P. Barberini, P. Venezia, C. Rinascimento, P. Cavour, P. Risorgimento.

#175, Termini, P. Barberini, V. del Corso, P. Venezia; **Linea H,** Termini to Trastevere.

#910, Termini to Villa Borghese.

Some helpful tram routes:

Tram 8, Largo di Torre d'Argentina to Trastevere.

Tram 3, Trastevere, Colosseo, San Lorenzo, Villa Borghese.

Tram 9, P. Risorgamento, Villa Borghese, San Lorenzo. Note: some trams (the 3, for example) run as buses for significant parts of the day.

Taxis: Ride only in yellow or white taxis and make sure the taxi has a meter. If it doesn't, settle on a price before getting in the car. Expect to pay around €10-12 for a ride from Termini to the Vatican during the day; prices rise significantly at night. The meter starts at €2.33 (M-Sa 7am-10pm), €3.36 (Su and holidays 7am-10pm), or €4.91 (daily 10pm-7am). Surcharges are levied when heading to or from Fiumicino (€7.23) and Ciampino (€5.50), with a €1 charge per suitcase larger than 35cm by 25cm by 50cm. Standard tip is 10%. **RadioTaxi** (☎06 35 70) responds to calls, but be aware that the meter starts the moment the taxi is dispatched.

Bike Rental: ATAC (06 57 003; www.atac-bikesharing.it) has a new bike rental service. Purchase a reloadable bike-sharing card at Ⓜ A-Lepanto, Ⓜ A-Spagna, or Ⓜ-Termini. The spiffy green bikes—with baskets, naturally—can be found at 19 stations around the center. €0.50 per 30min. Bikes can be returned to any rack and are available 24hr.

Scooter Rental: Around €35-55 per day. Helmets, included with rental, are strictly required by law. 16+. **Treno e Scooter** (☎06 48 90 58 23; www.trenoescooter.191.it), on the right-hand side of P. dei Cinquecento from Termini. Open daily 9am-2pm and 4-7pm. AmEx/MC/V. **Bici & Baci,** V. del Viminale 5, (☎06 48 28 443 or 48 98 61 62; www.bicibaci.com), in front of Termini. Open daily 8am-7pm. AmEx/MC/V.

⁊ PRACTICAL INFORMATION

TOURIST AND FINANCIAL SERVICES

Tourist Offices: Enjoy Rome, V. Marghera 8/A (☎06 44 56 890; www.enjoyrome.com). From the middle concourse of the Termini between the trains and the ticket booths, exit right. Cross V. Marsala. The office is 3 blocks down V. Marghera on the left. Helpful, English-speaking staff makes reservations at museums and shows, books accommodations, orients travelers in the city, and leads walking tours of all the city's major areas of the city (€27; under 26 €22). Along with info on excursions and bus lines, the office also provides 2 useful publications: a free map and an *Enjoy Rome* city guide, with practical info and insider tips for making the most of a trip to Rome. Open Apr.-Oct. M-F 8:30am-7pm, Sa 8:30am-2pm; Nov.-Mar. M-F 9am-6pm, Sa 9am-2pm. **PIT Info Points** (☎06 48 90 63 00). Run by the city, these round green kiosks have multilingual staff and provide limited info on events, hotels, restaurants, and transportation, as well as brochures and a basic map of sights. Most open daily 9:30am-7pm.

Embassies and Consulates: See **Essentials,** p. 8.

Currency Exchange and Banks: Banca di Roma and **BNP Paribas** have good rates. **ATMs** are readily available all over town; they are especially concentrated in Termini and P. Venezia. BNP branches open daily 8:30am-1:30pm and 2:45-4:15pm.

LOCAL SERVICES

Luggage Storage: Splashnet, V. Varese 33 (☎06 49 38 04 50; www.splashnetrome.com). €2 per day. Open daily in summer 8:30am-1am, in winter 8:30am-11pm. In **Ter-**

mini (☎06 47 44 777), below track 24. 1st 5hr. €4, €0.60 per hr. up to 12hr., €0.20 per hr. thereafter. Open daily 6am-midnight.

Lost Property: Oggetti Smarriti, Comune di Roma: Circonvallazione Ostiense 191 (☎06 67 69 32 14). Open M-F 8am-6:30pm. **On bus:** ☎06 58 16 040. **On Ⓜ A:** P. dei Cinquecento (☎06 48 74 309). Open M, W, and F 9am-12:30pm. **On Ⓜ B:** Circonvallazione Ostiense 191 (☎06 67 69 32 14). Open M-F 8am-6:30pm. **ATAC:** (☎06 57 003; www.atac.roma.it). Open M-Sa 8am-8pm. **Credit cards:** American Express (☎06 72 90 03 47), MasterCard (☎80 08 70 866), Visa (☎80 08 19 014).

Bookstores: ▧**The Lion Bookshop and Café,** V. dei Greci 33-36 (☎06 32 65 40 07 or 65 04 37; www.thelionbookshop.com), off V. del Corso. Open M 3:30-7:30pm, Tu-Su 10am-7:30pm. **Libreria Feltrinelli International,** V. Emanuele Orlando 84/86 (☎06 48 27 878 or 06 48 70 999; www.lafeltrinelli.it), near P. della Repubblica. Open Sept.-July M-Sa 9am-8pm, Su 10:30am-1:30pm and 4-8pm; Aug. M-Sa 9am-8pm.

GLBT Resources:

ARCI-GAY, V. Zabaglia 14 (☎06 64 50 11 02, helpline 800 713 713; www.arcigayroma.it). Ⓜ B-Piramide. Holds discussions, dances, and special events. Provides psychological and legal counseling, and information on HIV testing, and other services. Welcome group W 7-9pm. Open M-F 4-8pm.

Circolo Mario Mieli di Cultura Omosessuale, V. Efeso 2/A (☎06 54 13 985; www.mariomieli. org). Ⓜ B-San Paolo. From the stop, walk to Largo Beato Placido Riccardi, turn right on V. Corinto. Promotes GLBT rights and holds cultural activities. AIDS activists offer psychological and legal assistance. Welcome group Su 3pm. Open M-Th 10am-7pm, F 10am-6pm.

Libreria Babele, V. dei Banchi Vecchi 116 (☎06 68 76 628; www.libreriababeleroma.it), across from Castel Sant'Angelo. Library focusing on gay literature. Open M 3-7pm, Tu-Sa 11am-7pm.

Laundromats: ▧**Splashnet,** V. Varese 33 (☎06 49 38 04 50; www.splashnetrome.com), 3 blocks from Termini. Internet €1.50 per hr. Free maps. Helpful, English-speaking staff. Wash €3 per 6kg. Dry €3 per 7kg. Ask for the *Let's Go* discount. Open daily in summer 8:30am-1am, in winter 8:30am-11pm.

Supermarkets: Standa: V. Cola di Rienzo 173, Ⓜ A-Lepanto or Ottaviano, inside the COIN department store. Open daily 9am-8pm. Also at V. di Trastevere 60, Tram 8 from Largo Argentina, inside the Oviesse department store. Open M-Sa 9am-8pm, Su 8:30am-1:30pm and 4-8pm. Primarily within department stores. **DiperDì:** V. del Gesu 58/59 (☎06 69 38 08 75; www.diperdi.it), in the *centro storico*. Open M-Sa 8am-9pm, Su 9am-8pm.

EMERGENCY AND COMMUNICATIONS

Emergency Phone Numbers:

Pan-European Emergency Line (Police, Fire, Medical): ☎112.

General Emergency: ☎113.

Fire: ☎115.

Medical: ☎118.

Red Cross Ambulance Service: ☎5510.

Car Breakdown Assistance: ☎116.

Poison Control: ☎06 49 06 63.

Veterinary Emergency: ☎06 66 21 686.

Directory Assistance: ☎12. International operator (English-speaking) ☎170.

Police: Central police station ☎06 46 86. Rome city police ☎06 67 691. Highway police ☎06 22 101.

Crisis and Counseling Lines:

Rape Crisis Line: Centro Anti-Violenza, V. di Torre Spaccata 157 (☎06 23 26 90 49; www.differenzadonna.it) and V. di Villa Pamphili 100 (☎06 58 10 926). Open 24hr.

Samaritans, V. San Giovanni 250 (☎800 86 00 22; www.samaritansonlus.org), in Laterano. English spoken. Counseling available; call ahead. Open daily 1-10pm. For additional resources consult www.controviolenzadonne.org.

Pharmacies: Farmacia Internazionale, P. Barberini 49 (☎06 48 25 456 or 71 195; www.farmint.it). ⓂA-Barberini. Open 24hr. **Farmacia Piram,** V. Nazionale 228 (☎06 48 80 754; www.piram.it). Open daily 8:30am-11:30pm. AmEx/MC/V.

Hospitals: Italy's medical system is socialized, so all public hospitals offer free emergency care (including ambulance service) and may only charge a minimal amount for non-emergency treatment, regardless of citizenship. However, this also means that they tend to be crowded, slow, often without English-speaking doctors, and may require extended waits for appropriate treatment. They also do not allow choice of physician or facilities. Consult your insurance company for accepted private hospitals. 2 private clinics and 1 public hospital are listed below.

International Medical Center, V. Firenze 47 (24hr. ☎06 48 82 371; www.imc84.com). Private hospital and clinic. Prescriptions filled. Paramedic crew on call. Referral service to English-speaking doctors. General visit €110, house visits at night and on weekends €150. Call ahead. Open M-F 9am-8pm; house calls after hours and on weekends.

Policlinico Umberto I, Vle. del Policlinico 155 (emergency ☎06 49 97 70 25, first aid and appointments 06 49 971; www.policlinicoumberto1.it), north of Termini. ⓂB-Policlinico or bus #649. English spoken. Largest public hospital in Rome. No cost for emergency treatment; approximately €25 for treatment of non-emergencies. Open 24hr.

Rome-American Hospital, V. Emilio Longoni 69 (24hr. ☎06 22 551, appointments 06 22 55 290; www.rah.it). English spoken. Private emergency and laboratory services, HIV tests, and pregnancy tests. Visits average €100-200, but prices vary based on required treatment. Reception and appointments open 9am-2pm. Doctors on call 24hr.

Internet Access: Internet Cafe, V. Cavour 213 (☎06 47 82 30 51). Internet €0.50 1st 5min., €0.10-0.20 per min. thereafter. Printing €0.20 per page. €0.50 for CDs/DVDs. Open M-F 11am-1am, Sa-Su 3pm-1am. Cash only. **Yex Internet Points,** www.yex.it. 3 locations between P. Navona and Campo dei Fiori at C. V. Emmanuele 106 (☎06 47 45 98 18; open daily 10am-7pm), P. Sant'Andrea della Valle 3 (☎06 97 84 42 46; open daily 10am-10pm), and V. dei Pastini 22 (☎06 67 94 423; open daily 10am-10:30pm). About €6 per hr. Also offer wire transfer and currency exchange.

Post Offices: V. Giolitti 14, in Termini, and P. San Silvestro 19 (☎06 69 73 72 13). Both open M-F 8am-7pm, Sa 8am-1:15pm. Additional locations throughout the city, each with different hours; see www.poste.it/online/cercaup (in Italian) for a full listing. Stamps available at more numerous *tabacchi*. Postcards cost between €0.40-0.80 to send internationally; all mail can be dropped in red post boxes mounted on walls throughout Rome. **Postal Codes:** 00100 to 00200; V. Giolotti 00185; P. San Silvestro 00187. Code finder: www.poste.it/en/postali/cap/index.shtml.

◪ ACCOMMODATIONS

Rome swells with tourists around Easter, from May to July, and in September; be sure to book well in advance for those times. Most establishments also raise their prices during long weekends and holidays, and also throughout the high season. In general, prices vary widely with the time of year, and a proprietor's willingness to negotiate increases with length of stay, number of vacancies, and group size. Some hotels and hostels list such discounts on their websites, but the best way to get a price that's tailored to your stay is to call or email proprietors directly. As a general rule, independent establishments are more flexible than chains. Also be sure you're booking into a reputable place, and be careful about who you get advice from. Termini is swarming with hotel scouts. Many are legitimate and have IDs issued by tourist offices. However, some impostors

have fake badges and direct travelers to run-down locations with exorbitant rates, especially at night. It's better to book a stay by going to a tourist office yourself. Better still, book in advance and know what you're getting. It may be necessary just to find a bed: some hostels, for instance, require 48hr. notice.

ANCIENT CITY

Pensione Rosetta, V. Cavour 295 (☎06 47 82 30 69; www.rosettahotel.com), past the Fori Imperiali. Buzz at the large, wooden front doors and walk through the Vespa and palm-filled courtyard. Affordable for the location. Spacious rooms have baths, TVs, phones, and fans. A/C €5-10. Free Wi-Fi in lounge. Singles €50-60; doubles €85; triples €95; quads €120. AmEx/MC/V. ❸

Rome Student House, V. Merulana 117. From the Colosseum, walk down V. Labicana and make a left at V. Merulana. Buzz at the front and take Scala II to the 3rd floor. Make reservations beforehand so the owner, who occasionally cooks guests dinner, is not out when you arrive. Colorful rooms with fans, linens, and Wi-Fi. Check-out 10:30am. Reserve online (www.hostelworld.com). 4- to 6-person dorms €20-25. Cash only. ❷

Sandy Hostel, V. Cavour 136 (☎06 48 84 585; www.sandyhostel.com). Near the main ancient sights. Try to ignore the key-operated elevator as you hike up 6 flights of stairs—low prices, attentive staff, and close proximity to the Ancient City will be your reward. Bare-bones backpacker accommodations. Computer with internet in lounge. Linens included. Lock-out 11:30am-2:30pm. Online reservations required. 6-person dorms €15-25; quads with private bath €20-30. Cash only. ❷

Cesare Balbo Inn, V. Cesare Balbo 43 (☎06 98 38 60 81 or 32 72 06 25 59; www. cesarebalbosuite.com). From V. Cavour, make a right on V. Panisperna; walk 2 blocks and make a right on V. Cesare Balbo. The owner, Glenn, lives on site and caters to your every need. Neat, spacious rooms with private bath. A/C and cable TV. Breakfast in room. Free Wi-Fi. Doubles €80; triples €90. AmEx/D/MC/V. ❺

CENTRO STORICO

TeatroPace33, V. Teatro della Pace 33 (☎06 68 61 371; www.hotelteatropace.com), off V. dei Giubbonari. Tucked away in a quiet corner near P. Navona, this hotel in a converted 17th-century *palazzo* is a great value. All rooms come with A/C, TVs, internet, minibars, and safes. Be prepared to carry your bags up the dramatic central staircase. Breakfast included. Singles €100-120; doubles €150-210. AmEx/MC/V. ❺

Relais Palazzo Taverna, V. dei Gabrielli 92 (☎06 20 39 80 64; www.relaispalazzotaverna. com). From P. Navona, take V. Agonale north and make a left onto V. dei Coppelle/V. dei Coronari and another left onto V. dei Gabrielli. Renovated 15th-century building with lots of charm. Each spacious room with A/C, TV, and safe. Wi-Fi. Singles €100-140; doubles €140-210; triples €160-240. AmEx/MC/V. ❺

Due Torri, V. del Leonetto 23 (☎06 68 80 69 56; www.hotelduetorriroma.com). Make a right onto V. della Campana from V. di Monte Brianzo and take the first right onto V. del Leonetto. Difficult to find, but worth the effort. Renaissance-era building with clean, comfortable rooms. Each room with A/C, TV, and internet. Breakfast included. Wheelchair-accessible. Book well in advance. Singles €110-130; doubles €150-195; apartment-style quad €220-260. AmEx/MC/V. ❺

PIAZZA DI SPAGNA

Daphne Inn Veneto, V. di San Basilio 55 (☎06 47 82 35 29; www.daphne-rome. com). Ⓜ A-Barberini. Daphne has just what a top-notch, urban B&B ought to have: spotless rooms with A/C and comfortable beds in an unbeatable location minutes away from the Trevi Fountain. Brand-new furniture, mini-fridges, tea service, and safes. Internet access. A 2nd location at V. degli Avignonesi 20. Singles €100-160; doubles €140-220; triples €210-300. AmEx/MC/V. ❺

Hotel Suisse, V. Gregoriana 54, 3rd fl. (☎06 67 83 649 or 67 86 172; www.hotelsuisserome.com). ⓂA-Spagna/Barberini. From the Spanish Steps, veer right facing away from P. di Spagna. Close to the Steps, but away from the hubbub; at night you'll think you're in another city. This small hotel with impeccable service, sleek, old-fashioned furniture, and an inviting lounge extends over the 3rd floor of a former *palazzo*. All 12 rooms come with comfortable beds, phones, fans, and baths. English-speaking staff. Continental breakfast included. A/C €10. Free Wi-Fi; computer available. Singles €90-110; doubles €140-170; triples €190-220; quads €200-250. MC/V. ❻

Pensione Panda, V. della Croce 35, 2nd fl. (☎06 67 80 179; www.hotelpanda.it). ⓂA-Spagna. Between P. di Spagna and V. del Corso. Situated in a 19th-century building, Hotel Panda is one of the oldest hotels in the historical center of Rome. Immaculate, elegantly-furnished rooms with arched ceilings (some with Italian frescoes). A/C €6. Free Wi-Fi. Reservations recommended. Singles €65-68, with bath €75-80; doubles €75-78/98-108; triples €130-140; quads €180. Rooms sleep a flexible number of occupants; ask for details when booking. AmEx/MC/V. ❹

Hotel Boccaccio, V. del Boccaccio 25, 1st fl. (☎06 48 85 962; www.hotelboccaccio. com). ⓂA-Barberini. Off V. del Tritone near P. Barberini. This quiet, eco-friendly hotel is a renovated 1937 flat in the Trevi area, offering 8 elegant rooms with high ceilings and a breezy terrace. Each room has a fan, but no A/C. Singles €45; doubles €80, with bath €100. Ask about low-season discounts. AmEx/MC/V. ❸

VATICAN CITY

Hardcore party-fiends beware: as you might imagine, most of your nightlife options lie outside this quiet, affl uent area.

🅱 **Colors,** V. Boezio 31 (☎06 68 74 030; www.colorshotel.com). ⓂA-Ottaviano. Take a right on V. Terenzio, off V. Cola di Rienzo, then left on V. Boezio. True to its name, Colors offers 18 beds in rooms painted with a verve that would put Raphael to shame. 2 hostel floors and a 3rd floor with private rooms. A/C. Kitchens and tranquil terraces on all floors. Breakfast included. Internet access €2 per hr. Reserve dorms by 9pm the night before; wise to book earlier. Dorms €27; singles €90, with bath €105; doubles €100/130; triples €120. Low season discount up to 30%. Cash only. ❷

Orange Hotel, V. Crescenzio 86 (☎06 68 68 969; www.orangehotelrome.com). Stylish, eco-friendly boutique hotel offers a lovely terrace with a solarium and a panoramic view over the cupola of San Pietro. Points for guessing the color scheme. Delightful amenities include a rooftop restaurant, parking garage, terrace hot tub, and in-hotel laundromat. All rooms with bathtubs, A/C, TVs, internet, safes, and minibars. Breakfast included. Doubles €93-174, junior suites 154-214; triples 158-218; extra beds available. AmEx/MC/V. ❺

Hotel San Pietrino, V. Giovanni Bettolo 43, 3rd fl. (☎06 37 00 132; www.sanpietrino.it). ⓂA-Ottaviano. Exit on V. Barletta and turn left on V. Bettolo. A quirky amphibian motif manifests itself in frog paintings, frog statues, and stuffed frogs in the hallways. Spacious rooms are comfortable and clean with A/C, TVs, and (sometimes) DVD players. Laundry €8. Internet access. Reserve months ahead in high season. Singles €32-92; doubles €48-118; triples €72-148; family quad €92-168. Discounts negotiable for longer stays or larger groups. MC/V. ❹

MO' MONEY, NO PROBLEMS. Most independently-run hostels and hotels will offer discounts if you pay in cash in order to avoid a 10% tax from credit companies. Put your credit card away and hit up the ATMs.

TERMINI AND ENVIRONS

Welcome to budget traveler central. The accommodations around the **Termini station** are some of the least expensive and most centrally located in Rome. They also play host to the most backpackers and students, so look no further if a fun atmosphere is what you crave.

LET'S NOT GO. Don't have so much fun that you completely let your guard down, though—Termini can be a sketchy area, especially at night, and you can't rely only on your kung fu skills to deter pickpockets.

SAN LORENZO AND NORTHEAST OF TERMINI

Alessandro Palace, V. Vicenza 42 (☎06 44 61 958; www.hostelalessandropalace.com). From Termini's track 1, turn left on V. Marsala and right on V. Vicenza. Renovated dorms with baths and A/C. Fun bar with flatscreen TV and cheap drinks—happy hour (daily 10-11pm) includes €3 beers. Fantastic English-speaking staff. Breakfast and pizza dinners included. Lockers free; supply your own lock. Towels €2; included with doubles, triples, and quads. Internet (computer lounge and Wi-Fi) free 30min. per day; €1 per hr. thereafter. Check-in 3pm. Check-out 10am. 4- to 8-person dorms €25-35; doubles €110; triples and quads €44 per person. MC/V. ❷

Hotel Papa Germano, V. Calatafimi 14/A (☎39 06 48 69 19; www.hotelpapagermano.com). From Termini, turn left on V. Marsala, which becomes V. Volturno, and take 4th right on V. Calatafimi. Clean, simple rooms with TVs. Helpful, English-speaking staff. Continental breakfast included. A/C €5; free fans. Free internet on 3 computers. Reception 24hr. Check-in noon. Check-out 10am. 4-bed dorms €21-28; singles €35-50; doubles €50-80, with bath €60-105; triples €60-90/80-120; quads €85-120/95-140. AmEx/D/MC/V. ❷

Hotel Scott House, V. Gioberti 30 (☎06 44 65 379; www.scotthouse.com). Exit Termini on V. Giolitti and turn left. Cross the street and take a right on V. Gioberti. Modern rooms painted in soothing colors, each with bath, A/C, phone, safe, and TV. English spoken. Breakfast included. Free luggage storage. 1 computer. Free Wi-Fi. Reception 24hr. Check-in 2pm. Check-out 11am. Singles €36-68; doubles €63-98; triples €75-122; quads €88-132. Discount for cash payments. AmEx/MC/V. ❹

Alessandro Downtown, V. Carlo Cattaneo 23 (☎06 44 34 01 47; www.hostelalessandrodowntown.com). From Termini's track #22, take a left on V. Giolitti and a right on V. C. Cattaneo. Worthwhile alternative to the Palace with the same social environment; head to the Palace to use the in-house bar. Dining room, sitting room with satellite TV, and new kitchen open 1pm-midnight. Breakfast included. Free pasta party M-F nights. Lockers, ceiling fans, and Wi-Fi in rooms. Towels €2. Internet 30min. free per day, €1 per hr. thereafter. Check-out 10am. Lockout 11am-2pm. 6- and 8-bed mixed or female dorms €17-25; doubles €70, with bath €90; quads €120/140. AmEx/MC/V. ❶

The Yellow, V. Palestro 44 (☎06 49 38 26 82; www.the-yellow.com). From Termini, exit on V. Marsala, head down V. Marghera, and take the 4th left. Look no farther if you want to party hearty with people from all over the world. Huge rooms with stenciled *Blues Brothers* and *Pussy Wagon* logos accent this modern, chic youth hostel. Rocking hostel bar next door caters to guests. Lockers, linens, luggage storage, and fans included. A/C in rooms with bath. Breakfast €2. Free Wi-Fi in lounge; rent a laptop for 30min. for free or €1 per hr. Check-in 1:30pm. Check-out 10am. 4- to 12- person dorms with shared bath €10-30; 4- and 6-person dorms with private bath €10-34. €5 cash discount. AmEx/D/MC/V. ❶

Fawlty Towers Hotel and Hostel, V. Magenta 39, 5th fl. (☎06 44 50 374; www.fawltytowers.org). From Termini, cross V. Marsala onto V. Marghera and turn right on V. Magenta.

Relaxed, bohemian feel. Brightly colored rooms. Comfortable common room with stained glass, TV, A/C, DVD player, book exchange, and free internet on 1 computer. Most rooms have A/C—ask for it when reserving, at no extra cost. Free lockers, linens, and towels. Kitchen with stocked fridge available for snacking. Free BBQs 2-3 Fridays per month in summer on the sweet outdoor terrace. Check-out 10:30am for dorms, 11am for private rooms. Reception 24hr. 3-bed dorms €25-30; 4-bed dorms €18-25; singles €30-55, with shower or full bath €35-60; doubles €45-70/50-85; triples €70-95/75-99; quads €80-100/80-110. Cash only; pay in advance. ❷

Hostel Funny, V. Varese 31/33 (☎06 44 70 35 23, cell 39 34 07 88 00 60; www.hostelfunny.com). From Termini's track 1, turn right on V. Marsala, left on V. Milazzo, and right on V. Varese. Owner Mabri will leave you laughing with his welcoming nature. He also owns **Splashnet** laundromat-internet cafe (p. 82; reception in same location), where you can kill 3 birds with 1 stone by using the free internet while washing and drying your clothes for €5. Breakfast included; any time of day. Free bottle of wine upon arrival. Free pasta party M-F nights. Dining room, sitting room with TV, and new kitchen. TVs and lockers in rooms. Free fans for rooms without A/C. Check-out 10am. Reception 8:30am-midnight. 4-bed dorms €15-30; doubles €50-90, with bath and A/C €50-100; triples €60-110/60-120. Ask about the *Let's Go* discount. Cash only. ❶

Yes Hotel, V. Magenta 15 (☎06 44 36 38 29; www.yeshotelrome.com). From Termini, cross V. Marsala onto V. Marghera and turn left on V. Magenta. Brand-new hotel with ultra-modern facilities, including a shockingly spacious elevator, lounge covered in black leather and metal, and flatscreen TVs in every room. All rooms have baths, A/C, mini-fridges, phones, hair dryers, and safes. Breakfast included. Doubles €50-150; triples €70-170; quads €90-190. Check for discounts online. AmEx/MC/V. ❹

M&J Place Hostel, V. Solferino 9 (☎06 44 62 802; www.mejplacehostel.com). From Termini's track 1, turn left on V. Marsala and right on V. Solferino. Large party hostel is great if you can get over the dirty communal bathrooms. Luxurious private rooms. Common room, lively bar, and restaurant downstairs. PCs with internet, TVs, and baths with waterfall-flow shower heads in private rooms. Kitchen open 3-10pm. Breakfast included; served at bar. Small lockers at reception. Free fans, linens, and luggage storage. Wi-Fi, computers, and laptop rental. Check-in 3pm. Check-out 10am. Reception 24hr. 4-, 6-, 8-, 10-bed mixed dorms and 6-bed female dorms €12-32, with bath €15-35; singles, doubles, triples, and quads with bath €40-140; doubles with communal bath €40-60. Subtract €2.50-10 per person if you don't want internet and breakfast. Cash only. ❶

Affittacamere Aries, V. XX Settembre 58/A (☎06 42 02 71 61; www.affittacamerearies.com). From Termini, turn left onto V. Marsala, which becomes V. Volturno, and right onto V. Cernia. Make a left on V. Goito and follow it to V. XX Settembre. Comfy rooms with fridges, TVs, towels, free Wi-Fi, and A/C. English spoken. Breakfast €3. Check-in noon. Check-out 11am. Singles €35-80; doubles €45-100, with bath €50-120; triples €70-150. Ask about the *Let's Go* discount; make sure to have your book with you. D/MC/V. ❸

Hotel Bolognese, V. Palestro 15, 2nd fl. (☎/fax 06 49 00 45; www.hotelbologneseinrome.com). From Termini, exit right; walk down V. Marghera and take the 4th left onto V. Palestro. The proud artist-owner's impressive paintings and the cleanliness and comfort of the newly renovated rooms set this hotel apart. Private baths and TVs. Rooms with A/C cost extra. Request a room with a balcony at no extra cost. Breakfast included. Free fans and luggage storage. Check-out 11am. Singles €35-60; doubles €60-100; triples €80-120. AmEx/MC/V. ❸

◘ FOOD

Romans love to eat, and eat often. Whether it's a multi-course meal or an afternoon gelato, Romans settle for nothing but the best—so should you. Don't fall

into the tourist traps around major sights; you'll miss out on authentic Roman cuisine and find yourself paying high prices for mediocre food. Popular Roman dishes include *spaghetti alla carbonara* (egg and cream sauce sprinkled with bacon), *spaghetti all'amatriciana* (spicy thin tomato sauce with chili peppers and bacon), *carciofi alla giudia*(deep-fried artichokes common in the Jewish quarter), and *fiori di zucca* (stuffed, fried zucchini flowers). Pizza—eaten with fork and knife, of course—is unsurprisingly popular in Rome. Rome's proximity to the sea makes *pesce* (fish) popular as well. Expect to pay an extra €1-1.50 for *coperto* (service) and bread—whether or not you eat it.

ANCIENT CITY

☒ I Buoni Amici, V. Aleardo Aleardi 4 (☎06 70 49 19 93). ⓂB-Colosseo. From the Colosseum, take V. Labicana, then take a right on V. Merulana and a left on V. Aleardo Aleardi. Look for a blue *osteria* sign. You'll hear the languages of Italian and mathematics spoken in this local favorite near an engineering school. Try the popular *linguine alle vongole* (pasta with clams; €8). Self-serve antipasto bar €12. Primi and secondi €7-14. Wine €8-35 per bottle. Dessert €4. Cover €1. Open M-Sa 12:30-3pm and 7:30-11pm. AmEx/D/MC/V. ❷

☒ L'Antica Birreria Peroni, V. San Marcello 19 (☎06 67 95 310; www.anticabirreriaperoni.it). From the Vittorio Emmanuele monument, turn right on V. Cesare Battisti and left into P. dei Santissimi Apostoli. 2 blocks down on the left. Energetic *enoteca* with a German twist and backlit beers tempting you from a ledge on the wall. Wash down a *wurstel* (€6-7) with 1 of 4 delicious Peroni beers on tap (€2-5). Fantastic *fiori di zucca* €1. Primi €6-7. Cover €1. Open M-Sa noon-midnight. AmEx/D/MC/V. ❷

Hostaria Nerone, V. delle Terme di Tito 96 (☎06 48 17 952), between the Colosseum and the Domus Aurea. ⓂB-Colosseo. Take V. Nicola Salvi and turn right on V. delle Terme di Tito. Built on the ruins of Nero's Golden House, offering spectacular views of the Colosseum and the Trajan Forum. Traditional Roman menu, featuring homemade gnocchi and ox tail. House wine €2 per ¼ L. Primi €9-10.Secondi €9-15. Cover €1.50. Open Sept.-July M-Sa noon-3pm and 7-11pm. AmEx/MC/V. ❷

Luzzi, V. San Giovanni in Laterano 88 (☎06 70 96 332), just down V. dei Fori Imperiali from the Colosseum. No-fuss *osteria* packed with locals. Specials like *pennette al salmone* (€7) will leave you wanting more. Enjoy inexpensive seafood (shrimp and prawns €10) and enough cheap wine to scuttle a liner (€4 per L). Primi €5-7. Secondi €7-11. Dessert €4. Open M-Tu and Th-Su noon-3pm and 7pm-midnight. AmEx/MC/V. ❷

CENTRO STORICO

☒ Cul de Sac, P. Pasquino 73 (☎06 68 80 10 94), off P. Navona. One of Rome's first wine bars. Substantial list of reasonably priced wines by the glass (from €2.50). At aperitif time, pair your pick with a snack like tuna, tomato and green bean salad, or the tasty baba ghanoush. Primi €7-8. Secondi €7-9. Open daily noon-4pm and 6pm-12:30am. AmEx/MC/V. ❷

Pizzeria da Baffetto, V. del Governo Vecchio 114. Street runs parallel to Corso V. Emanuele II. This neighborhood trattoria quickly fills up with a local crowd. Thin crust pizzas €4.50-10. Open daily 6:30pm-1am. ❶

Pizza Art, V. Arenula 76 (☎06 68 73 16 03 78). From C. V. Emanuele II, cut through Largo di Torre Argentina and walk toward the river. Counter seating only. Thick focaccia pizza topped with arugula, goat cheese, and fried treats including *suppli* (fried rice balls) and *crochette.* Most pizza €11-13 per kg; average slice €2.50. Open daily 8am-10pm. Cash only. ❶

Sant'Eustachio Il Caffè, P. de Sant'Eustachio 82 (☎06 68 80 20 48). Turn right on V. Palombella behind the Pantheon. Muscle your way to the front of the line for the *gran caffè speciale* (double espresso with sugar; €2.20 standing, €4.20 table service).

Ground coffee €22 per kg. Open M-Th and Su 8:30am-1am, F 8:30am-1:30am, Sa 8:30am-2am. Cash only. ❶

Enoteca Cavour 313, V. Cavour 313 (☎06 67 85 496). ⓂB-Cavour. Sip a glass of *grappa* in one of this French-style bar's intimate booths. Organic and locally produced ingredients. *Misto di formaggi* (mixed cheese plate) €8-12. Organic mixed vegetables in oil €10. Mixed plate of meat €7-14. Wine €3-8 per glass; bottles from €13. Open Sept.-July M-Sa 12:30am-2:45pm and 7:30pm-12:30am, Su 7:30pm-12:30am. AmEx/MC/V. ❷

PIAZZA DI SPAGNA

🗹 **Babette,** V. Angelo Brunetti 6 (☎06 32 00 407; www.babetteristorante.it). ⓂA-Flaminio. Dining à la carte can be expensive at this stylish, French-Italian brasserie, but the week-day lunch buffet (daily 1-3pm €10 for the 1st plate, €3.50 for subsequent) is one of the best deals in the area. The price spikes on weekends and holidays (€25 per person; €15 for children), but "Babette's feast" includes wine, coffee, and sweets. Restaurant open daily 1-3pm and 8-11pm. Bar open daily 9am-8pm. AmEx/MC/V. ❷

🗹 **Vladimiro Ristorante Marcello,** V. Aurora 37 (☎06 48 19 467; www.vladimiroristorante. com). ⓂA-Barberini. From V. Veneto, take V. Liguria and make a left onto V. Aurora. Yes, you're surrounded by Americans, but they're onto something. Vladimiro serves some of the best antipasti in the city. €10 sounds pricey, but ordering the *antipasti misti* gets you a big-boy portion of fresh cheese, meats, and vegetables. Primi €8-12. Secondi €8-16. Open M-Sa noon-3pm and 7:30-11pm. AmEx/MC/V. ❷

Zi' Fenizia da Michele, V. dell' Umiltà 31 (☎349 25 25 347). ⓂA-Barberini. From the Trevi Fountain, walk 1 block down V. San Vincenzo and make a right. Michele's kosher pizza is some of the best in Rome and certainly better than the other options around the Fontana. A substantial slice from this storefront—topped with eggplant, potatoes, zucchini, or other goodies—will run you about €2.50. Open M-Th and Su 8am-8pm, F 8am-3:30pm. Closed on Jewish holidays. Cash only. ❶

JEWISH GHETTO

The Jewish Ghetto, about 10min. south of Campo dei Fiori and near the Tiber, serves tempting kosher and traditional Jewish specialties with an Italian twist—a welcome break from pasta and pizza. Keep in mind that much of the Ghetto is closed on Saturdays for Shabbat.

🗹 **Pasticceria Ebraico Boccione,** V. del Portico d'Ottavia 1 (☎06 68 78 637), on the cor-ner of P. Costaguti. The unmarked storefront is difficult to find; keep an eye on the street numbers. Tiny, family-run bakery serves only about 8 specialties, including delicious custard-filled *challah* (€0.60) and sugar-dusted *ciambelle* (doughnuts; €0.80). Open in summer M-Th 8am-7:30pm, F 8am-3:30 pm, Su 8am-2pm and 4-7:30pm; in winter M-Th and Su 8am-7:30pm, F 8am-3:30pm. ❶

🗹 **La Taverna del Ghetto,** V. del Portico d'Ottavia 8 (☎06 68 80 97 71; www.latavern-adelghetto.com). Popular kosher *taverna* prides itself on homemade pasta and deli-cacies like *lingua all'ebraica* (veal tongue). The *carciofo* (artichoke; €5) is exception-ally well-prepared. Primi €11.50. Secondi €13.50-25. Desserts €5.50-6.50. Cover €1.50. Open M-Th and Sa-Su noon-3pm and 6:30-11pm, F noon-3pm. Reservations recommended. AmEx/MC/V. ❸

VATICAN CITY

Cacio e Pepe, V. Giuseppe Avezzana 11 (☎06 32 17 268). From ⓂA-Ottaviano, take the V. Barletta exit; right onto V. de Milizie, then left onto V. Avezzana. Worth the walk. In summer, rub elbows with locals at the close-packed tables outside. Namesake specialty is perfectly al dente, topped with olive oil, grated cheese, and fresh-ground pepper (€6). Open M-F 12:30-3pm and 7:30-11pm, Sa 12:30-3pm. Cash only. ❷

La Tradizione, V. Cipro 8/e (☎06 39 72 03 49; www.latradizione.it). This gourmet store, steps from ⓂA-Cipro, has been educating palates for nearly 3 decades with a broad selection of fine meats, wines, and over 300 cheeses. Beautifully-prepared foods (including regional specialties) sold by the kg. A large meal €15. Open M 3-8:15pm, Tu-Sa 8am-2pm and 4:30-8:15pm. AmEx/MC/V. ❷

TRASTEVERE

▨ **Giorgiagel,** V. di San Francesco a Ripa 130 (☎32 01 65 02 66 or 33 32 70 59 18). Turn right on V. de San Francesco a Ripa from Vle. Trastevere. Large portions of amazing Sicilian pastries and gelato that is right up there with the best in Rome. Unbelievably decadent cioccolato fondente (dark chocolate) and intense frutti di bosco (forest fruit) make a great pair. Ingredients listed. Gelato €1.50-3. Frappè €2.50. Open daily 1pm-9pm. Cash only. ❶

▨ **Da Simone,** V. Giacinto Carini 50 (☎06 58 14 980). From Acqua Paola on the Gianicolo hill, walk behind the fountain and down V. Giacomo Medici to the end of the street. Turn right, walk under the arches to V. Carini; it's behind the bus stop to the left. Treats you to fantastic pizza and prepared foods with only the best ingredients—fine extra virgin olive oil, buffalo mozzarella, and no animal fat. The pizza with 'nduja (spicy Calabrian sausage) is especially great. Reasonably priced by weight (a large slice of margherita around €2-3). Open M-Sa 7:30am-8:15pm. Cash only. ❶

Siven, V. di San Francesco a Ripa 137 (☎06 58 97 110). Northwest on V. de San Francesco a Ripa from Vle. Trastevere. A hole in the wall that sells tasty pizza and prepared pastas and meats (priced by weight) to a constant stream of locals, all of whom treat the chefs like old friends. When you taste their concoctions, you'll understand why. Amazing spicy chicken and lasagna. Cod filets on F. Take your sizeable portion (around €4) and eat in the scenic piazza next door—there's no seating. Open M-Sa 9am-10pm. Cash only. ❶

Biscottificio Artigiano Innocenti, V. della Luce 21 (☎06 58 03 926). From P. Sonnino, take V. Giulio Cesare Santini and turn left on V. della Luce. This haven of baked goodness sells a dizzying variety of cookies and biscuits featured in countless international culinary magazines. Stock up on hazelnut, almond, chocolate, and jam cookies (€10-15 per kg; about €2.50 for 10). Open M-Sa 8am-8pm, Su 9:30am-2pm. Cash only. ❶

Da Enzo, V. dei Vascellari 29 (☎06 58 18 355 or 32 72 09 25 90). East of Vle. Trastevere, near the river. Turn right on V. dei Vascellari from Lungotevere Ripa. Children's drawings of animals cover the canary yellow walls of this local Roman trattoria, where every dish is made with family love. Primi €6.80-9.80. Secondi €7.80-14. House wine €6.50-7.50 per L. Open M-Sa 1-3:30pm and 7-10pm. AmEx/D/MC/V. ❷

VILLA BORGHESE, PARIOLI, AND FLAMINIO

Tree Bar, V. Flaminia 226 (☎06 32 65 27 54). ⓂA-Flaminio. Tram 2 runs up V. Flaminia; otherwise, prepare for a substantial walk from the Metro. This mod wooden restaurant looks like it's been kidnapped from California and plopped in Roman park. Wrap-around windows give patrons a view of the neighborhood—when the glass is opened, it feels like you're dining outside. Fills up with a neighborhood crowd ordering pastas (€9) and salads (€5-8) from the short but appealing daily menu. Bar kicks up at night. Secondi €7-13. Open M-Sa. Cash only. ❷

Bla Kongo, V. Ofanto 6/8 (☎06 85 46 705). This sunny little bistro off V. Po serves delicious Swedish and Swedish-ish food to a crowd of Parioli locals and professionals from the neighborhood's many office buildings. The baked potatoes (€7), topped with treats like yogurt and smoked salmon, make for a great light lunch. Appetizers €3-7. Salads €3-6. Secondi €8.50-18. Open in summer Tu-Sa 12:30-4pm and 7:30pm-midnight., Su 7:30-midnight; in winter Tu-Su 12:30-4pm and 7:30pm-midnight. Cash only. ❸

Allo Specchio, V. Ofanto 35 (☎06 96 03 77 42; www.allospecchio.it). From Corso d'Italia, make a left onto V. Po and then a right. This little trattoria just opened May 2009. For now, at least, it charges eminently reasonable prices for modern Italian fare. The lunch *menùs* (around €10-12), which include a main dish, a side or dessert, water, and bread, are especially good deals. The light, flavorful apple cake is a winner. Primi €7-11. Secondi €11-15. Open M-Sa noon-3pm and 8pm-1am. Cash only. ❸

TERMINI AND ENVIRONS

San Lorenzo offers inexpensive food with local character to the budget-conscious student with a discriminating palate. There's a **Conad** supermarket on the lower floor of Termini Station (open daily 6am-midnight).

>
> **LET'S NOT GO.** Termini and the surrounding areas are unsafe at night. Stay alert and avoid walking alone in the neighborhood after dark.

Hostaria da Bruno, V. Varese 29 (☎06 49 04 03). Take V. Milazzo from V. Marsala and turn right on V. Varese. A bastion of authenticity in a sea of tourist traps. Try *tortellini al sugo* (meat tortellini) or *fettucine alla gricia* (white amatriciana; €7) as you check out the pictures of founder Bruno with Pope John Paul II hanging on the wall. Open M-F noon-3pm and 7-10pm, Sa 7-10pm. AmEx/MC/V.

Hostaria Romana da Dino, V. dei Mille 10 (☎06 49 14 25). From Termini's track 1, turn left on V. Marsala, right on V. Vicenza, and left on V. dei Mille. Delicious dishes for dirt-cheap prices. Loyal local following. Delectable pizza €5-7. Pasta €5-5.50. House wine €1.50 per ¼L. Open M-Tu and Th-Su 11:30am-3pm and 6:30-11pm. MC/V. ❶

Arancia Blu, V. Prenestina 396 (☎34 91 21 51 80), in San Lorenzo, southeast of Termini. Popular restaurant and *enoteca* surrounds diners with wine and makes vegetarian cuisine exciting with adventurous dishes like mint and potato tortellini with pecorino cheese (€8.50). Ask owner and chef Fabio for the refreshing *Moscato Giallo*, a tasty, unlisted Tirolean white wine (€15 per bottle). *Piatti* €8.50-10. Wine €4.50 per glass. Open Sept.-July daily noon-3pm and 8pm-midnight; Aug. 8pm-midnight. AmEx/MC/V. ❷

La Famiglia, V. Calatafimi 11 (☎06 47 28 24). From Termini's track 1, turn left on V. Marsala, continue on V. Volturno, and make a right on V. Calatafimi. 40+ year history of elegant dining on the cheap will make you feel like part of the family. Suited waiters bring the homemade *tortellini famiglia* (meat tortellini in a mushroom, ham, and pea cream sauce; €7) to you indoors or out. Pizza €5-7. Large antipasto buffet €6-8. House wine €6 per L. Primi €5-8. Secondi €6-12. Cover €1.30. Open daily 12:15pm--3:30pm and 6-10:45pm. AmEx/MC/V. ❷

AVENTINE AND TESTACCIO

P. Testaccio is just past V. Luca della Robbia. In the *piazza*, you will find **Testaccio Market,** a small market set up in metal huts. Numerous vendors offer fresh fruit, vegetables, meat, fish, pasta, candy, nuts, and a variety of prepared foods. (Prices vary, most by weight. Open M-Sa 6am-2pm. Cash only.)

🔲 **Il Volpetti Più,** V. Alessandro Volta 8 (☎06 57 44 306; www.volpetti.com). Turn left on V. A. Volta, off V. Marmorata. Relive high school as you slide down the lunch line at this *tavola calda* (cafeteria)—but replace day-old sloppy joes with authentic Italian fare. Primi €6-7.50. Secondi €4-7.50. Fresh fish F €6-8. Desserts €4. Open M-Sa 10:30am-3:30pm and 5:30-9:30pm. AmEx/D/MC/V. ❷

Giacomini, V. Aventino 104-106 (☎06 57 43 645). From ⓂB-Circo Massimo, go south on V. Aventino past V. Licinia. Inside this *alimentari*, owner Claudio, certified *Maestro Salumiere Gastronomio*, prepares indescribably wonderful *panini* to order (€4-8) with the highest quality ingredients, as he has done for over 50 years. Wide selection of hand-picked meats and cheeses from only the best producers, priced by weight. Next door, his wife and daughter create similarly wonderful pizza. Open M-Sa 7:30am-2pm and 4:45-6:30pm. AmEx/MC/V. ❶

Felice a Testaccio, V. Mastro Giorgio 29 (☎06 57 46 800; www.feliceatestaccio. com). ⓂB-Piramide. Turn left on V. Galvani off V. Marmorata and right on V. M. Giorgio. Black squares of foam hang just below the ceiling in the dining room, probably to dampen the cheers of patrons who have just tasted their food. Feast on *spaghetti alla Felice* (cherry tomatoes, basil, mint, oregano, thyme, marjoram, and ricotta; €10) in front of post-Impressionist paintings strung up in a line on the wall. Special *menús* for each day of the week. Famed *tonnarelli cacio e pepe* (pasta with cheese and pepper) €10. Primi €8-10. Secondi €13-22. Cover €1. Open M-Sa 12:30-2:45pm and 8-11:15pm. AmEx/MC/V. ❸

👁 SIGHTS

ANCIENT CITY

PALATINE HILL

South of the Roman Forum, this hill was home to the Roman emperors. Open daily from last Su of Mar. to Aug. 8:30am-6:15pm; Sept. 8:30am-6pm; from Oct. 1 to last Sa of Oct. 8:30am-5:30pm; from last Su of Oct. to Dec. 8:30am-3:30pm; from Jan. 2 to Feb. 15 8:30am-4pm; from Feb. 16 to Mar. 15 8:30am-4pm; from Mar. 16 to last Sa of Mar. 8:30am-4:30pm. Last entry 1hr. before closing. Only combination tickets for the Colosseum, Palatine Hill, and Roman Forum can be purchased; the Forum and the Hill are treated as one. Purchase tickets at any entrance to any sight, though the biglietteria 100m down V. di San Gregorio from the Colosseum (behind the Arch of Constantine) tends to be the least crowded. €12, EU citizens ages 18-24 €7.50, EU citizens over 65 free or under 18. Ticket requires you to see both sights in 2 days, with only 1 entrance to each. Audio tours for the Palatine Hill (€4) available in English, Italian, French, German, Spanish, Russian, Chinese, Arabic, and Japanese. Combined audio tour with the Roman Forum €6. Italian-only tours on weekends at 10am (Forum) and noon (Palatine Hill). Cash only.

Legend has it that the Palatine Hill, a plateau between the Tiber River and the Roman Forum, was home to *la lupa*, the she-wolf that suckled Romulus and Remus. During the Republic, the Palatine was the most fashionable residential quarter, where aristocrats and statesmen, including Cicero and Marc Antony, built their homes. Augustus lived here in a modest house, but later emperors capitalized on the hill's prestige and built gargantuan quarters. By the end of the AD first century, the imperial residence covered the entire hill, whose Latin name, *Palatium*, became synonymous with the palace.

The best way to approach the Palatine is from the northeast by the stairs near the **Arch of Titus.** The path ascends to the 17th-century **Farnese Gardens (Orti Farnesiani),** the world's oldest botanical gardens. Views of the Roman Forum make the gardens perfect for a picnic; *"Affacciata sul Foro"* (Facing the Forum) signs point to a lookout over reflecting pools at the **House of Vestal Virgins.**

On the southwest side of the hill directly below the Farnese Gardens, the remains of an ancient village feature the **Casa di Romulo,** alleged home of Romulus, as well as the **Temple of Cybele.** These remains can be dated to roughly the same period as the Forum's Archaic necropolis, which supports the theory that

Palatine Hill

Rome was founded in the eighth century BC. To the left of Casa di Romulo is the **Casa di Livia,** where Augustus's wife Livia resided. The house used to connect to the **Casa di Augusto** (not to be confused with Domus Augustana) next door. Around the corner to the left, stretching along the Farnese Gardens, is the mosaic-tiled **Cryptoporticus,** a tunnel which connected Tiberius's palace with nearby buildings and was used by slaves and couriers as a secret passage.

To the left of the Casa di Livia at the center of the hill is the sprawling **Domus Flavia,** the site of an octagonal fountain that occupied almost the entire courtyard. Romans have traditionally associated octagons with power; you will see many octagonal rooms in places of important significance, such as the Vatican and at the bases of important statues. To the left of the Domus Flavia stands the solemn **Domus Augustana,** the emperor's private space. Visitors are only allowed on the upper level, from which they can make out the shape of two courtyards down below. The palace's east wing contains the curious **Stadium Palatinum,** a sunken oval space used as a riding school.

Visitors can also see the **Circus Maximus,** which lies right behind the hippodrome. The fire of AD 64 started from there and spread to the Palatine, causing everything in the residences, except for the marble and stone constructions, to burn. The **Museo Palatino,** between the Domus Flavia and the Domus Augustana, displays archaeological artifacts from the early Archaic period on the lower level. The upper floor of the museum displays sculptures of well-to-do Romans and their deities. (Open daily 9:10am-6:20pm. Visiting slots every 20min.; only 30 people per fl. per slot. Free with admission to the Palatine.)

COLOSSEUM

☎06 70 05 469. Ⓜ️B-Colosseo or bus 75 from Termini. Open daily 8:30am-7:15pm. Last entry 6:15pm. **▤Tour with archaeologists** in Italian Sa-Su, English and Spanish daily every 30 min.-1 hr. 9:45am-5:15pm. Tours €4. Audio tour in Arabic, Chinese, English, French, German, Italian, Russian, and Spanish €4.50. Video tour €5.50. Combined tickets with Palatine Hill and Roman Forum €12, EU citizens 18-24 €7.50, EU citizens over 65 or under 18 free. Cash only.

WHOSE LINE IS IT ANYWAY? To avoid waiting for tickets to the Colosseum, purchase from the less-crowded biglietteria on V. di San Gregorio.

The Colosseum—a hollowed-out ghost of Travertine marble that once held more than 50,000 bloodthirsty spectators and now dwarfs every other ruin in Rome—stands as an enduring symbol of the Eternal City. The arena's name comes from the legendary 35m statue of Nero that used to stand beside it. The gilded bronze statue was referred to as "The Colossus," and hence the building became known as the Colosseum. The gaping holes in the bricks are the only signs left of where the brilliant marble ornamentation used to lie. Romans repeatedly stripped monuments of their marble to re-use in new monuments, a process called spoilage. You can see signs of spoilage throughout the ancient city's ruins—look for the holes where iron hooks were ripped out of the wall.

Within 100 days of the Colosseum's AD 80 opening, some 5000 wild beasts perished in its bloody arena, and the slaughter continued for three more centuries. The labyrinth of cells, ramps, and elevators used to transport exotic animals from cages to arena level was once covered by a wooden floor and layers of sand. Upon release, the beasts would suddenly emerge into the arena, surprising spectators and hunters alike. Animals weren't the only beings killed for sport; men were also pitted against men. Though these gladiators were often slaves and prisoners, if they won their fights, they were idolized like modern athletes—at least until the next fight. Contrary to popular belief, not all gladiator matches ended in death. Some fights stopped after the first knockdown, or the loser could ask the emperor—who would defer to the crowd—for mercy.

A section of seating has been reconstructed using original Roman marble to represent what the stands used to look like. Spectators sat according to a hierarchy of class and gender, with senators, knights, and vestal virgins closest to the arena and women of lower classes on the highest tier.

Next to the Colosseum, on the corner of V. di San Gregorio, stands the **Arco di Costantino,** one of the area's best preserved Imperial monuments. The arch commemorates Constantine's bold victory at the Battle of the Milvian Bridge in AD 312, using fragments from monuments to Trajan, Hadrian, and Marcus Aurelius.

ROMAN FORUM

Main entrance on V. dei Fori Imperiali, at Largo Corrado Ricci, halfway between P. Venezia and the Colosseum. Other entrances are opposite the Colosseum, at the start of Via Sacra, and at the Clivus Capitolinus, near P. del Campidoglio. The Forum can also be accessed via the Palatine Hill. ⓂB-Colosseo or bus to P. Venezia. Access to the Forum is unpredictable, as areas are sometimes fenced off for excavation or restoration. Open daily from last Su of Mar. to Aug. 8:30am-6:15pm; Sept. 8:30am-6pm; from Oct. 1 to last Sa of Oct. 8:30am-5:30pm; from last Su of Oct. to Dec. 8:30am-3:30pm; from Jan. 2 to Feb. 15 8:30am-4pm; from Feb. 16 to Mar. 15 8:30am-4pm; from Mar. 16 to last Sa of Mar. 8:30am-4:30pm. Audio tour in Arabic, Chinese, English, French, German, Italian, Japanese, Russian, and Spanish €4. Combined audio tour with the Palatine Hill €6. Cash only.

Because this valley between two of Rome's most famous hills—the Palatine and Capitoline—was originally a marshland prone to flooding, Rome's Iron Age inhabitants (1000-900 BC) avoided it in favor of the Palatine Hill, descending only to bury their dead. In the eighth and seventh centuries BC, Etruscans and Greeks used the Forum as a marketplace. The Romans founded a thatched-hut shantytown here in 753 BC, when Romulus and Sabine leader Titus Tatius joined forces to end the war triggered by the infamous rape of the Sabine women. Today, the Forum bears witness to centuries of civic building.

From the Arch of Constantine by the Colosseum, take V. Sacra, the oldest street in Rome, to the **Arch of Titus.** On the left as you approach the arch lie the **Thermae** (Baths) and the **Temple of Jupiter Stator.** On the right is a series of 10 columns, all that remain of Hadrian's **Temple of Venus and Rome.** Built in AD 81 by Domitian, the Arch of Titus stands in the area of the Forum called the **Velia** and celebrates Jerusalem's sack by Domitian's brother Titus. The right panel shows a triumphal Titus on a quadriga chariot, while his soldiers carry back the spoils of war on the left panel. It is missing the two-sided arches typical of a triumphal arch (2 lower arches flanking a taller middle arch) because they were damaged when it was removed from its original location.

Turn right to face the Baroque facade of the **Chiesa della Santa Francesca Romana** (or **Santa Maria Nova**), which was built over Hadrian's Temple of Venus and Rome. It hides the entrance to the **Antiquarium Forense,** a museum displaying necropolis urns and skeletons (open daily 9:30am-noon and 4:30-7pm). Turn left, and as you pass the Upper Forum, check out the colossal ruins of the **Basilica of Maxentius and Constantine** on the right. Emperor Maxentius began construction in AD 308, but Constantine deposed him and completed the project himself. Farther down you pass the **Temple of Romulus,** named for the son of Maxentius (not the legendary founder of Rome), on the right. The original bronze doors have a AD fourth-century working lock.

Just after the Temple of Romulus is the **Archaic Necropolis,** a flat platform where Iron Age graves lend credibility to Rome's legendary eighth-century BC founding. Farther down on the right, the columns and rigid lattice ceiling help preserve the **Temple of Antoninus and Faustina.** In the AD seventh and eighth centuries, after numerous unsuccessful attempts to demolish it, confirmed by gashes near the at the top, the **Chiesa di San Lorenzo in Miranda** was built in the temple's interior. The church is an example of the medieval approach to the pagan ruins—either tear down the temples or convert them to churches.

Continuing down V. Sacra's right fork, on the left lie the remains of the **Regia,** which once served as the office of the Pontifex Maximus, Rome's high priest and the titular ancestor of the pope. Next on the left is the **Temple of the Deified Julius,** a shrine built by Augustus in 29 BC to honor the great leader and proclaim himself the inheritor of Julius Caesar's divine spirit. This is believed to be the site of Caesar's cremation, where he was burned in a funeral pyre with a piece of wood, flowers, and a cage with an eagle over his body. As the fire was started, the eagle was released from the cage, a symbol of the soul of the dead emperor flying away towards the heavens. Every year on July 12, Caesar's alleged birthday, people bring flowers to the shrine.

Back on V. Sacra, the **Basilica Aemilia** is on the right as you enter the **Civic Forum.** Built in 179 BC, the Basilica housed the guild of the *argentari* (money changers). It was rebuilt several times after fires until one started by Alaric and his merry band of Goths in AD 410 left it in its current state. Melted coins are now shiny studs in the pavement. On the left you'll see the Forum's central section, **Market Square.** The **Column of Phocas** in the square was erected in AD 608 for the

ROME

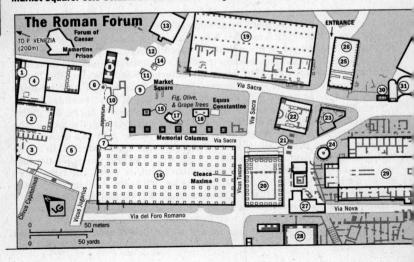

visiting Byzantine emperor, Phocas, and was the last monument erected in the Forum. The **Lacus Curtius** to its left is marked by concentric marble semicircles in the ground and a small frieze of a man on horseback; it commemorates the heroism of the legendary Roman warrior Marcus Curtius, who threw himself into a deep chasm in 362 BC to save the city from collapse. In the center of the square, **Three Sacred Trees of Rome**—olive, fig, and grape—were planted by the Italian state in honor of Curtius' remarkable heroism. Off V. Sacra to the right is one of the Forum's oldest buildings, the **Curia** (Senate House). Contrary to popular belief, it was not in the square outside the Curia where the group of (literally) back-stabbing senators murdered Julius Caesar in 44 BC. Caesar was actually murdered in the Theater of Pompey in the Campus Martius.

The area in front of the Curia holds several noteworthy ruins. The **Imperial Rostra,** now a single, right angle of stone, was once a speaker's platform erected by Julius Caesar just before his death. The **Comitium,** now a marble semicircle in the ground, was the assembly place where citizens voted, where representatives gathered for public discussion, and where Rome's first laws, the Twelve Tables, were first inscribed on bronze tablets. The **Lapis Niger** (Black Stone) is the volcanic rock that marks the location of the underground sixth-century BC altar to the god Vulcan, where archaeologists discovered the oldest-known Latin inscription, which warns against defiling the shrine.

Back on V. Sacra, the **Arch of Septimius Severus** is straight ahead, built in AD 203 to celebrate Septimus's victories in the Middle East. Next to it stands the **Umbilicus Romae,** a circular solid brick structure marking the mythological center of Rome. Turn left to reach the **Temple of Saturn** in the **Lower Forum.** Though built in the early fifth century BC, the Temple of Saturn achieved larger-than-life status during the Golden Age of Rome (AD 1st-3rd centuries). The temple became the site of **Saturnalia,** a raucous Roman winter party where class and social distinctions were forgotten and anything was permitted. The **Tabularium** is the structure built into the rock face which forms the base of the **Campidoglio.** Turn left in front of the Temple of Saturn on the other branch of V. Sacra. To the right is the large **Basilica Julia,** where the well-preserved floor plan supports the intact bases of the columns of the former courthouse. To appreciate the luxury

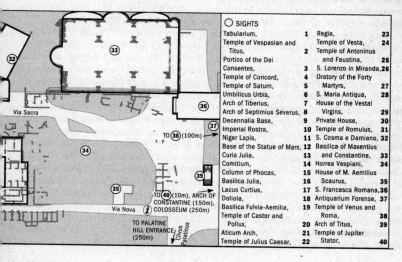

Via Sacra

TO (38) (100m)

TO (40) (10m), ARCH OF CONSTANTINE (150m), COLOSSEUM (250m)

Via Nova

TO PALATINE HILL ENTRANCE (250m)

Clivus Palatino

ROME

that is modern plumbing, take a right on Vicus Tuscus and look right; you'll see the remnants of **Cloaca Maxima,** Rome's first sewer. Check out the remains of the **Temple of Castor and Pollux** at the end of Vicus Tuscus, on the right when facing the Basilica Aemilia. According to legend, the twin gods Castor and Pollux helped Romans defeat the Etruscans at the Battle of Lake Regillus in 499 BC. Immediately after the battle, the twins appeared in the Forum to water their horses at the nearby **Basin of Juturna,** one of the only springs in ancient Rome.

Once again on V. Sacra, in the middle of the path stands the column base of the former **Arch of Augustus,** built by the emperor in his own honor. Uphill from the arch, the **Temple of Vesta,** once circular, is now just a vaguely curved wall next to the **House of the Vestal Virgins.** Among the most respected individuals in ancient Rome, the Vestal Virgins were female priests. The six women were chosen from the most important families by the Pontifex Maximus; they had to be between the ages of six and ten and without physical imperfections. A virgin served 30 years, after which she could choose whether to continue in the priesthood or leave, but as the average lifespan was around 35 years, few made it to the end of their term. The Virgins could walk unaccompanied in the Forum, pardon prisoners, travel in private chariots, and sit in special reserved seats at gladiatorial games and theatrical shows. They were responsible for the city's sacred eternal flame, keeping it lit for over 1000 years. A small statue of Minerva, which Aeneas took from Troy, occupies the **Palladium,** a secret room accessible only to the Virgins. This esteem had its price: a virgin who strayed from celibacy was buried alive (so that no sacred blood would be spilled).

FORI IMPERIALI. The sprawling Imperial Forums lie along V. dei Fori Imperiali, a boulevard Mussolini paved to connect the old empire to his own in P. Venezia, destroying a third of the ruins in the process. The temples, basilicas, and public squares that make up the Imperial Forums were constructed between the first century BC and AD second century in response to increasing congestion in the old Forum. Much of the area is currently being excavated and is closed to the public, but visitors can peer over the railing along the sidewalk on the east side of V. dei Fori Imperiali and side street V. Alessandrina, or take a 🔲**guided archaeological tour** to get closer to the ruins. *(Reservations ☎ 06 67 97 702. English tour given Su at 4:30pm. €7. Inquire within the visitor's information center on V. dei Fori Imperiali.)*

Built between AD 107-113, the **Forum of Trajan** celebrated Trajan's victorious campaign in Dacia (mostly present-day Romania). Its creation rendered the older Roman Forum a tourist attraction of sorts. The complex served practical functions, housing two important libraries of Latin and Greek documents, as well as a colossal equestrian statue of Trajan and a triumphal arch. At one end stands **Trajan's Column,** an extraordinary specimen of Roman relief-sculpture depicting 2500 legionnaires. In 1588, Pope Sextus V replaced Trajan's statue with one of St. Peter. Nearby, the three-floor, semicircular **Market of Trajan** is essentially Rome's first shopping mall, featuring an impressive—albeit crumbling—display of sculpture. A bit farther down V. Alessandrina, the **Forum of Augustus** commemorates Augustus's victory over Caesar's murderers at the Battle of Philippi in 42 BC. The nearby **Forum Transitorium** (also called the **Forum of Nerva**) was a narrow, rectangular space connecting the Forum of Augustus with the Republican Forum. Emperor Nerva dedicated the temple in 97 BC to the goddess Minerva. In the shade of the Vittorio Emanuele II monument, the paltry remains of the **Forum of Caesar** hold the ruins of Julius Caesar's **Temple to Venus Genetrix** (Mother Venus, to whom he claimed ancestry). In **Vespatian's Forum,** the mosaic-filled **Chiesa della Santi Cosma e Damiano** is across V. Cavour, near the Roman Forum. *(Closed for excavations. Tourist office on V. dei Fori Imperiali has maps, guidebooks, and an exhibition about the Imperial Forum. Free.)*

OTHER SIGHTS

DOMUS AUREA. Take a break from the relentless sun and enjoy the cacophony of chirping birds in the shade. Joggers, wildflowers, and ruins now occupy the Oppian Hill. The park houses part of Nero's "Golden House," a 35 hectare palace, which covered much of Ancient Rome. An enclosed lake used to be at the base of the hill, and the hill itself was a private garden. The Forum was reduced to a vestibule of the palace; Nero crowned it with a colossal statue of himself as the sun. He also pillaged all of Greece to find works of art worthy of his abode, including the famous *Laocoön* now held in the Vatican's collections. Apparently, decadence didn't buy happiness: the megalomaniacal Nero committed suicide five years after building his hedonistic pad. *(From P. Venezia, follow V. dei Fori Imperiale past the Colosseum; the park is on the left. Open daily 6:30am-9pm. Free.)*

CHIESA DI SAN PIETRO IN VINCOLI. This fourth-century church is named for the sacred *vincoli* (chains) that bound St. Peter in prison. The two chains were separated for more than a century in Rome and Constantinople, brought back together in the fifth century, and now lie beneath the altar. Michelangelo's ☒**statue of Moses** is tucked in the back right corner. The two horns on his head are actually supposed to be beams of light, indications of wisdom. *(Ⓜ B-Cavour. Walk along V. Cavour toward the Forum and take the seemingly endless stairs on the left to P. San Pietro in Vincoli. Open daily 8am-12:30pm and 3-6pm. Fully covered shoulders and legs required.)*

CIRCUS MAXIMUS AND BATHS OF CARACALLA. Today's Circus Maximus is only a grassy shadow of its former glory as Rome's largest stadium. After its construction in 600 BC, the circus held more than 300,000 Romans who came to watch chariots careen around the track. Today the ruins are all but gone, and the Circus is mainly a concert venue. The mosaic-coated Baths of Caracalla, about a 10min. walk down V. dei Terme di Caracalla, are the largest and best-preserved in Rome. *(Ⓜ B-Circo Massimo, bus #118, or walk down V. di San Gregorio from the Colosseum. ☎ 06 39 96 77 00. Open 24hr.)*

CAPITOLINE HILL. Home to the original "capital," the Monte Capitolino still houses the city's government, topped by Michelangelo's spacious **Piazza di Campidoglio.** *(To get to the Campidoglio, take bus to P. Venezia, face the Vittorio Emanuele II monument, and walk around to the right to P. d'Aracoeli. Take the stairs up the hill.)* At the far end of the *piazza*, the turreted **Palazzo dei Senatori** houses the Roman mayor's offices. Pope Paul III moved the famous **statue of Marcus Aurelius** here from the Palazzo dei Conservatori and then asked Michelangelo to fashion the imposing statues of Castor and Pollux. Framing the *piazza* are the twin Palazzo dei Conservatori to the right and Palazzo Nuovo on the left, home of the **Capitoline Museums** (p. 117). From the Palazzo Nuovo, stairs lead up to the rear entrance of the seventh-century **Chiesa di Santa Maria in Aracoeli.** Its stunning **Cappella del San Bambino** to the left of the altar is home to the *Santo Bambino*, a cherubic statue that receives letters from sick children. *(Santa Maria open daily 9am-12:30pm and 3-6:30pm. Donation requested.)* The gloomy **Mamertine Prison**, consecrated as the **Chiesa di San Pietro in Carcere,** lies downhill from the back of the Aracoeli. St. Peter baptized his captors here with water that flooded his cell. *(Adjacent to Teatro di Marcello at V. dei Teatro di Marcello and V. dei Foro Olitorio. ☎ 39 32 89 02 69 24; www.rome-underground.com. Open Sept.-July M-Sa 4-7pm.)*

THE VELABRUM. The Velabrum lies in a flat, flood plain of the Tiber, south of the Jewish Ghetto. At the bend of V. del Portico d'Ottavia, a shattered pedi-

ROME IS FALLING (APART)

Over the years, sites like Ostia, Nero's Golden Palace, and the Palatine Hill, which together bring the country revenues heftier than a hunk of marble, have slowly degraded. The culprits: water damage, lack of funding, and natural decay. Now, Italian officials fear the worst for Roman landmarks. Millennia of decay have suddenly become an emergency.

Like any state emergency, the decomposition of Rome's ruins call for a small government committee with special disaster-worthy powers. In March 2009, Guido Bertolaso joined the ranks of an elite group (think Caesar, Vespasian, St. Leo) who have been charged throughout history with preventing the fall of Rome. As the new special commissioner for Italian treasures in Rome and Ostia, Bertolaso will, hopefully, carpe the diem and halt the destruction. His position, among other things, will allow him to circumvent the notorious Italian bureaucracy to give Rome's past a viable future.

The task may seem epic, but Bertolaso has dealt with more dire emergencies. Two years ago, when a waste-collection crisis filled the streets of Naples with piles of trash, he was able to clean the mess. His solution—a trash train from Naples to Germany, where the garbage was incinerated. Here's to hoping he doesn't employ the same remedy for the Coliseum.

ment and a few columns are all that remain of the once magnificent **Portico d'Ottavia**. The 11 BC **Teatro di Marcello** next door bears the name of Augustus's nephew; the Colosseum was modeled after its facade. One block south along V. Luigi Petroselli is the P. della Bocca della Verità, the site of the ancient Foro Boario (Cattle Market). Across the street, the **Chiesa di Santa Maria in Cosmedin** harbors lovely medieval decor. The portico's **Bocca della Verità**, a drain cover with a river god's face, was made famous by Audrey Hepburn in 1953's *Roman Holiday*. But beware, medieval legend has it that the "mouth of truth" bites any liar's hand. Inside, perhaps St. Valentine's skull and bones will ignite your romantic side. Nothing says *amore* like centuries-old relics. *(2 blocks south of the Theater of Marcellus along V. Luigi Petroselli. ☎ 06 67 81 419. Portico and church open daily 9:30am-5:50pm. Byzantine mass Su 10:30am.)*

CENTRO STORICO

VIA DEL CORSO AND PIAZZA VENEZIA. Following the ancient V. Lata, V. del Corso began as Rome's premier race course and now plays host to many parades, including **Carnevale**. Running between P. del Popolo and P. Venezia, it is full of restaurants, hotels, *gelaterie*, and affordable boutiques (see **Shopping**, p. 122). From P. del Popolo, take V. del Corso to **Piazza di Colonna Romana** where **Palazzo Wedekind**, home to the newspaper *Il Tempo*, was built in 1838 with columns from the Etruscan city of Veio. Running south from P. del Popolo, V. del Corso ends at P. Venezia, home to the massive white marble **Vittorio Emanuele II monument**. Lovingly referred to as "the wedding cake" or "Mussolini's typewriter," the monolithic monument makes a good reference point. At the top of the exterior staircase is the **Altare della Patria**, which has two eternal flames guarded night and day by the Italian Navy in remembrance of the Unknown Soldier. Walk upstairs to the **Museo Centrale del Risorgimento** for a comprehensive exhibit on Italian unification. *(Open daily 9:30am-6:30pm. Free.)* The **Palazzo Venezia**, right off P. Venezia, once used by Mussolini as both an office and a soapbox, is one of Rome's earliest Renaissance structures.

PANTHEON AND PIAZZA DELLA ROTONDA. The granite columns, bronze doors, and soaring dome of the Pantheon's still, cool interior have changed little over the building's 2000 years. Architects still puzzle over the engineering; its dome, a perfect half-sphere constructed from poured concrete without the support of vaults, arches, or ribs, is the largest of its kind. It was built under Hadrian from

AD 118 to 125 over the site of an earlier Pantheon destroyed in AD 80. In AD 608 the Pantheon was consecrated as the **Chiesa di Santa Maria ad Martyres.** Several noteworthy figures are buried within: Renaissance painter Raphael; King Vittorio Emanuele II, the first king of united Italy; his son, Umberto I, second king of Italy; and finally, Umberto's wife, Queen Margherita, after whom the *pizza margherita* was named in the 19th century. *(Open M-Sa 8:30am-7:30pm, Su 9am-6pm, holidays 9am-1pm. Closed Jan. 1, May 1, Dec. 25. Free. 20min. audio tour €3.)*

In front of the Pantheon, an **Egyptian obelisk** dominates the ever-crowded P. della Rotonda. Around the Pantheon's left side and down the street, another obelisk, supported by Bernini's curious **elephant statue,** marks the center of tiny P. Minerva. Behind the obelisk is Rome's only Gothic church: **Chiesa di Santa Maria Sopra Minerva.** Built on the site of an ancient Roman temple, the unassuming exterior of this hidden gem hides some Renaissance masterpieces, including Michelangelo's *Christ Bearing the Cross*, Antoniazzo Romano's *Annunciation*, and a statue of St. Sebastian recently attributed to Michelangelo. The **Cappella Carafa** in the southern transept boasts a brilliant series of Fra Filippo Lippi frescoes. A decapitated St. Catherine of Siena is reportedly buried under the altar; her head rests in Siena's *duomo*. *(Open daily 7am-1pm and 3-7pm.)* From the upper left corner of P. della Rotonda, V. Giustiniani heads north to V. della Scrofa and V. della Dogana Vecchia, where you'll find **Chiesa di San Luigi dei Francesi,** France's national church in Rome, and home to three of Caravaggio's most famous paintings: *The Calling of St. Matthew, St. Matthew and the Angel,* and *The Crucifixion*. *(P. San Luigi dei Francesi 5. 1 block down V. di Salvatore from C. del Rinascimento, opposite P. Navona. Open daily 10am-12:30pm and 4-7pm.)*

IMBIBE THIS! Remember that Rome's water is *potabile* (drinkable), and many fountains or spigots run throughout the city. Take a drink, or fill up your water bottle from these free sources of cold, refreshing *acqua naturale.*

PIAZZA NAVONA. Originally a stadium built by Domitian in AD 86, P. Navona is now filled with artists, puppeteers, and mimes. Bernini's **Fontana dei Quattro Fiumi** (Fountain of the Four Rivers) commands the *piazza*. Each river god represents a continent: the Ganges for Asia, the Danube for Europe, the Nile for Africa (veiled because the river's source was at the time of construction), and Rio de la Plata for the Americas. Giacomo della Porta's 16th-century **Fontana del Moro** and the **Fontana di Nettuno** stand at opposite ends of the *piazza*. The **Chiesa di Sant'Agnese** in Agone holds the tiny skull of its namesake saint. Legend has it that Agnes was condemned to death for refusing to marry the son of a Roman prefect. To circumvent the law against executing virgins, she was dragged naked to a brothel, but her hair miraculously grew to cover her body. Then, when they tried to burn her alive, she would not light, so one indefatigable Roman soldier swiftly chopped off her head. *(West side of P. Navona, opposite Fontana dei Quattro Fiumi. Open daily 9am-noon and 4-7pm.)* West of P. Navona, at the intersection of V. di Tor Millina and V. della Pace, the **Chiesa di Santa Maria della Pace** houses Raphael's *Sibyls* in its Chigi Chapel. *(Open M-F 10am-noon and 3-6pm, Sa 10am-10pm, Su 10am-1pm.)* On nearby C. del Rinascimento, the **Chiesa di Sant'Ivo's** **corkscrew cupola** hovers over the Palazzo della Sapienza, originally home to the University of Rome before it was enlarged under Mussolini. *(Open M-Sa 9am-6pm. Service Su 9am-noon.)* Down C. V. Emanuele II, Jesuit church **Il Gesu** houses Andrea Pozzo's masterful *Chapel of S. Ignazio* and Bernini's *Monument to S. Bellarmino*. *(Open daily 6:45am-12:45pm and 4-7:45pm.)*

CAMPO DEI FIORI. Campo dei Fiori is across C. V. Emanuele I from P. Navona. By day, the *piazza*'s fountain and colorful, peeling facades play host to a bustling **market.** *(Open daily 9am-1:30pm.)* By night, the Campo transforms into a hip young person's magnet. Under papal rule, the area was a popular execution site; an eerie statue pays tribute to Giordano Bruno, one of the deceased. The English and Irish pubs that dominate today's Campo create an odd juxtaposition between traditional, laid-back Italy and the inescapable Anglo influence that dominates much of the peninsula. South of the Campo, the **Palazzo Farnese** dominates P. Farnese. **Palazzo Spada** and its **art gallery** are to the east.

LARGO DI TORRE ARGENTINA. This busy square is named for the **Torre Argentina** that dominates its southeast corner. The sunken area in the center of the Largo is a complex of four Republican temples unearthed in 1926 during Mussolini's project for demolishing the medieval city. The site is now a cat shelter, and dozens of felines patrol its grounds, providing photo opportunities for cat calendar photographers everywhere. The shelter welcomes donations and volunteers to help take care of the cats. The *piazza* also serves as a handy point of orientation, as it lies along C. V. Emanuele between the P. Navona area and the area surrounding C. dei Fiori and the Jewish Ghetto. *(At the intersection of C. V. Emanuele II and V. di Torre Argentina. Shelter ☎ 06 45 42 52 40; www.romancats.com.)*

MUSEI NAZIONALI ROMANI. The **Museo Nazionale Romano Palazzo Massimo alle Terme** is devoted to art from the Roman Empire, including the Lancellotti *Discus Thrower*, a rare mosaic of Nero's time, as well as ancient coins and jewelry. *(Largo di Villa Peretti 1. In the left corner of P. dei Cinquecento. www.roma2000.it/zmunaro.html. Open Tu-Sa 9am-2pm, Su 9am-1pm. €15, includes admission to Baths of Diocletian. Cash only.)* Nearby, **the Museo Nazionale Romano Terme di Diocleziano,** a beautifully renovated complex partly housed in the huge **Baths of Diocletian,** has exhibits devoted to ancient writing and Latin history as well as a cloister by Michelangelo. *(Vle. Enrico de Nicola 78. Open Tu-Sa 9am-2pm, Su 9am-1pm. €15. Cash only.)* The **Aula Ottogonale,** in another wing, holds Classical sculptures in a gorgeous octagonal space. *(V. Romita. Open daily 9am-1pm and 3-6pm. Included with Baths of Diocletian admission.)*

PIAZZA DI SPAGNA AND ENVIRONS

🔳**FONTANA DI TREVI.** Nicolo Salvi's bombastic Fontana di Trevi has enough presence and grace to turn even the most jaded jerk into a sighing, romantic mush. The fountain's name refers to its location at the intersection of three streets *(tre vie)*, perpetually crowded with people wanting to catch a glimpse of the fountain and tenacious vendors taking advantage of the masses of potential customers. Neptune, in the center, stands in front of the goddesses of abundance and good health; the two horsemen in the water represent the mercurial sea, either covered by rough waves or in placid ripples. Although you should hold back to avoid a steep fine, actress Anita Ekberg couldn't resist taking a dip in the fountain's cool waters in Fellini's famous scene in *La Dolce Vita*. Legend has it that a traveler who throws a coin into the fountain is ensured a speedy return to Rome, and one who tosses two will fall in love there. Three coins ensure that wedding bells soon will ring. For a less crowded view, head to the fountain in the late evening. The water flows all night, even after most tourists have gone to bed. On a less poetic note, the crypt of the **Chiesa dei Santi Vincenzo e Anastasio,** opposite the fountain, preserves the hearts and lungs of popes from 1590 to 1903. Fortunately or unfortunately, depending on your preference, the crypt is not open for public viewing. *(Church open daily 7am-noon and 4-7pm.)*

SPANISH STEPS. Designed by an Italian, paid for by the French, named for the Spaniards, occupied by the British, and currently featuring American greats like Ronald McDonald, the **Scalinata di Spagna** is, to say the least, multicultural. Piazza di Spagna is also home to designer boutiques like Gucci, Prada, and Valentino, and thousands of tourists and Romans alike flock here daily to shop, people-watch, and socialize. John Keats died in 1821 in the pink-orange house by the Steps; it's now the small **Keats-Shelley Memorial Museum,** displaying several documents of the Romantic poet and his contemporaries, including Lord Byron, Percy Bysshe Shelley, and his wife Mary Shelley. (☎06 67 84 235; www. keats-shelley-house.org. Open M-F 9am-1pm and 3-6pm, Sa 11am-2pm and 3-6pm. €3.50.)

PIAZZA DEL POPOLO. Once a favorite venue for the execution of heretics, this is now the "people's square." In the center is the 3200-year-old Obelisk of Pharaoh Ramses II, which Augustus brought from Egypt in AD 10. Climb the hill on the east side of the *piazza* for a spectacular view. **Santa Maria del Popolo** holds Renaissance and Baroque masterpieces. Two exquisite Caravaggios, *The Conversion of St. Paul* and *Crucifixion of St. Peter*, are in the **Cappella Cerasi,** next to the altar. Raphael's **Cappella Chigi** was designed for the Sienese banker Agostino Chigi, reputedly once the world's richest man. Niches on either side of the altar house sculptures by Bernini and Lorenzetin. With so much artwork, an exquisite portrait of the late Pope John Paul II seems orphaned, leaning against a chapel wall. (☎06 36 10 836. Open M-Sa 7am-noon and 4-7pm, Su and holidays 8am-1:30pm and 4:30-7:30pm.) At the southern end of the *piazza* are Carlo Rinaldi's 17th-century twin churches, **Santa Maria di Montesano** and **Santa Maria dei Miracoli.** (☎06 36 10 836. Open M-Sa 7am-noon and 4-7pm, Su and holidays 8am-1:30pm and 4:30-7:30pm.)

VATICAN CITY

The official Comune di Roma tourism kiosk has helpful English-speaking staff who will provide free maps, brochures, hours, location, and ticket info for any of the sites related to the Vatican or Rome. (Castel Sant'Angelo, P. Pia. ☎06 58 33 34 57. Open daily 8:30am-7pm. 10 other locations in the city around the major tourist sites.)

The administrative and spiritual center of the Roman Catholic Church, once the mightiest power in Europe, occupies 108 independent acres within Rome. The Lateran Treaty of 1929 allows the Pope to maintain legislative, judicial, and executive powers over this tiny theocracy, but also requires the Church to remain neutral in national politics and municipal affairs. The Vatican has historically and symbolically preserved its independence by minting coins (Italian *lire* and euros with the Pope's face), running a separate press and postal system, maintaining an army of Swiss Guards, and hoarding some of the world's finest art in the **Musei Vaticani.** Devout pilgrims and atheists alike are awed by the stunning grace and beauty of its two famous churches, the Sistine Chapel and St. Peter's Basilica, and the Vatican Museums are some of Italy's best.

BASILICA DI SAN PIETRO (SAINT PETER'S BASILICA)

The multilingual staff of the Pilgrim Tourist Information Center, located on the left between the rounded colonnade and the basilica, provides Vatican postage, brochures, and currency exchange. A first-aid station and free bathrooms are next to the tourist office. Open daily Apr.-Sept. 7am-7pm; Oct.-Mar. 7am-6pm. Mass M-Sa 8:30, 9, 10, 11am, noon, 5pm; Su and holidays 9, 10:30, 11:30am, 12:15, 1, 4, 5, 5:30pm. Vespers 5pm. Modest attire strictly enforced: no shorts, short skirts, or exposed shoulders allowed. Guided tours Tu and Th 9:45am and W 3pm; meet at Info Center. Free.

PIAZZA AND FACADE. The famous artist Bernini's colonnade around **Piazza San Pietro,** lined with the statues of 140 saints perched around the perimeter, was designed to provide a long, impressive vista to pilgrims after their tiring journey through the tiny, winding streets of Borgo and the *centro storico*. The open circle created by the two sides of the colonnade leading away from San Pietro are said to represent the welcoming arms of the Church, embracing its followers as they enter the *piazza*. Mussolini's broad V. della Conciliazione, built in the 30s to connect the Vatican to the rest of the city, opened a broader view of the church than Bernini ever intended. Round disks mark where to stand so that the quadruple rows of colonnades seem to merge into one perfectly aligned row. Statues of Christ, John the Baptist, and all the apostles except Peter are on top of the basilica. In warm months, the Pope holds papal audiences on a platform in the *piazza* on Wednesday mornings. *(To attend an audience, contact the Prefettura della Casa Pontificia ☎ 06 69 88 46 31 or stop by the Bronze Door, located on the right after you pass through security. Ascend the steps and ask the Swiss Guard for a ticket.)*

 COLOR-CODED. The Virgin Mary can usually be recognized in art by her red dress and bright blue mantle. Blue became her trademark color because the pigment was made from *lapis lazuli*, the most expensive of all paint.

INTERIOR. The iconic basilica rests on the reputed site of St. Peter's tomb. In Holy Years the Pope opens the **Porta Sancta** (Holy Door)—the last door on the right side of the entrance porch—by knocking in the bricks with a silver hammer. The interior of St. Peter's Cathedral measures 187m by 137m along the transepts. Metal lines on the marble floor mark the lengths of other major world churches. To the right of the entrance, Michelangelo's glowing *Pietà* has been encased in bullet-proof glass since 1972, when an axe-wielding fanatic attacked it, smashing Christ's nose and breaking Mary's hand

Bernini's **baldacchino** (canopy) rises on spiraling columns over the marble altar, reserved for the Pope's use. The Baroque structure, cast in bronze pillaged from the Pantheon, was unveiled on June 28, 1633, by Pope Urban VIII, a member of the wealthy Barberini family. Bees, the family symbol, buzz whimsically around the canopy, and vines climb toward Michelangelo's cavernous **cupola**. Seventy oil lamps glow in front of the *baldacchino* and illuminate Maderno's sunken *Confessio*, a 17th-century chapel. Two staircases directly beneath the papal altar descend to St. Peter's tomb. The staircases are closed to the public, but the underground grottoes offer a better view of the tomb, as well as the tombs of countless other popes, including John Paul II. *(Open daily Apr.-Sept. 7am-6pm; Oct.-Mar. 7am-5pm. Free.)*

High above the *baldacchino* and the altar rises **Michelangelo's dome,** designed as a circular dome like that of the Pantheon (p. 102). Out of reverence for that ancient architectural wonder, Michelangelo is said to have made this *cupola* a meter shorter in diameter than the Pantheon's; the difference is not noticeable, however, as the dome towers 120m high and 42.3m across. When Michelangelo died in 1564, only the drum of the dome had been completed. Work remained at a standstill until 1588, when 800 laborers were hired to complete it. Toiling round the clock, they finished the dome on May 21, 1590.

BASILICA ENVIRONS

To the left of the basilica is a courtyard protected by Swiss Guards. The **Ufficio Scavi,** administrative center for the Pre-Constantinian Necropolis, is here. Ask Swiss Guards for permission to enter. To the right of the basilica, at the end of the colonnade, the **Prefettura della Casa Pontifica** gives free tickets to papal audiences in the morning on Wednesdays when the Pope is speaking.

CUPOLA. The cupola entrance is near the Porta Sancta. Ascend 551 stairs to the top or take an elevator to the walkway around the dome's interior. Beware:

even using the elevator, you'll still have to climb 320 steps to see the top ledge's panorama. *(Open daily Apr.-Sept. 8am-5pm; Oct.-Mar. 8am-4pm. By stairs €4, by elevator €7.)*

TREASURY OF SAINT PETER. The Treasury contains gifts bestowed upon St. Peter's tomb. At the entrance, look for a list of all the popes. Highlights include the dalmatic of Charlemagne (the Holy Roman Emperor's intricately designed robe), a Bernini angel, and the magnificent bronze tomb of Sixtus IV. *(Inside the basilica on the left. Open daily Apr.-Sept. 9am-6:15pm; Oct.-Mar. 9am-5:15pm. Last entry 30min. before close. Closed when the Pope is celebrating mass in the basilica and on Christmas and Easter. Wheelchair-accessible. Photographs forbidden. €6, under 13 €4.)*

TOMB OF SAINT PETER AND PRE-CONSTANTINIAN NECROPOLIS. After converting to Christianity, Constantine built his first basilica directly over St. Peter's tomb. In order to build on that exact spot, the emperor had to level a hill and destroy a necropolis that once stood on the site. The basilica's history was mere legend until 1939, when workers came across ancient ruins underneath. Unsure of finding anything, the Church secretly set about looking for St. Peter's tomb. More than 20 years later, the tomb was identified under a small temple beneath the altars of Constantine's basilica. The saint's bones, however, were not found. A hollow wall nearby held what the church later claimed to be the holy remains. Some believe that the bones were displaced from the tomb during the Saracens' sack of Rome in AD 849. Multilingual tour guides will take you around the streets of the necropolis, which hold several well-preserved pagan and Christian mausolea, funerary inscriptions, mosaics, and sarcophagi. *(Entrance to the necropolis is on the left side of P. San Pietro, beyond the info office. ☎06 69 88 53 18; scavi@fsp.va. Office open M-Sa 9am-5pm. To request a tour, arrange in person or write to: The Delegate of the Fabbrica di San Pietro, Excavations Office, 00120 Vatican City. Give a preferred range of times and languages. Phone calls only accepted for confirmations. Reserve as far ahead as possible. Instructions available on website. €10.)*

CASTEL SANT'ANGELO

☎06 68 19 111, reservations 39 96 76 00. Bus #40, 62, 64, 271, 280 to Ponte V. Emanuele or P. Pia. Dungeon. Along the Tiber River on the Vatican side when going from St. Peter's toward the Tiber River. From the centro storico, cross Ponte Sant'Angelo. Open in summer Tu-Su 9am-7pm; in winter daily 9am-7pm. Last entry 1hr. before close. Tours Su 12:30pm in Italian, 11:30am in English. €8, EU students 18-25 €5.50, EU citizens under 18 or over 65 free. Audio tour €4.

LOCAL LEGEND

POPE FICTION

One fine ninth-century day, as the Pope was riding by procession along Via Sacra, he asked to stop by the side of the road. His companions then watched in horror as the Pope, standing on the street, gave birth to a child. The Pope, it seemed, had a surprise hidden under his holy robes.

Vehemently denied by papal scholars (and most reputable historians) but eagerly endorsed by feminist revisionists, the story of Pope Joan has endured as too good to be true, but also too good to forget. According to legend, Pope Joan disguised herself as a man to rise through the ranks of the Catholic hierarchy and ultimately reign as pope for three years around 850. Joan's jig was up when she gave birth to her lover's child in the middle of a papal procession.

Conspiracy theorists find proof of Joan's existence in some bizarre practices of the Catholic Papacy. For example, the fact that Popes often sit on pierced chairs is seen as a vestige of the "physical inspections" that became routine after Joan's charade. Supposedly, the newly-elected Pope sat on "holey" chairs, while cardinals placed below would peep at the Pope's privates. Also, papal processions mysteriously avoid Via Sacra in favor of far less convenient routes, perhaps due to superstitions stemming back to the legend of Popess Joan.

Built by Hadrian (AD 76-138) as a mausoleum for himself and his family, this gigantic brick-and-stone mass overlooking the Tiber has served as a fortress, prison, and palace. When a plague struck in AD 590, Pope Gregory the Great saw an angel sheathing his sword at the top of the complex; the plague abated soon thereafter, and the building was rededicated to the angel. Military aficionados will relish the armory, located on one of the top floors and offering an incomparable view of Rome and the Vatican. Outside, the marble **Ponte Sant'Angelo,** lined with statues by Bernini, is the beginning of the traditional pilgrimage route from St. Peter's to **San Giovanni in Laterano** (p. 112).

VILLA BORGHESE

VILLA BORGHESE. Imagine NYC's Central Park, but a little less central, a little more Mediterranean, and of course, with a little more marble sculpture and Roman grace. To celebrate becoming a cardinal, Scipione Borghese financed construction of the **Villa Borghese,** a stunning park northeast of the *centro storico,* replete with hidden fountains and meandering paths, and home to three art museums—the **Galleria Borghese** (p. 116), **Museo Nazionale Etrusco di Villa Giulia** (p. 118), and the **Galleria Nazionale d'Arte Moderna,** which is actually a Vatican Museum located in the park. *(Get off at ⓂA-Spagna and follow the signs. Or, from the ⓂA-Flaminio stop, take V. Washington under the archway. From P. del Popolo, climb the stairs to the right of Santa Maria del Popolo, cross the street, and climb the small path. ☎ 06 32 16 564. Free.)*

QUIRINAL HILL. At the southeast end of V. del Quirinale, the ◪**Piazza del Quirinale** occupies the summit of the tallest of Rome's seven hills. In the center, the statues of Castor and Pollux (Roman copies of the Greek originals) stand on either side of an obelisk from the Mausoleum of Augustus. The president of the Republic resides in the Palazzo del Quirinale, a Baroque architectural collaboration by Bernini, Maderno, and Fontana. Farther along the street lies the facade of Borromini's **Chiesa di San Carlo alle Quattro Fontane.** Bernini's ◪**Four Fountains** are built into the corners of the intersection of V. delle Quattro Fontane and V. del Quirinale. Be careful when viewing the fountain; sidewalks are nonexistent. *(Palazzo closed to the public. Chiesa open daily 8:30am-12:30pm and 3:30-6pm.)*

PIAZZA BARBERINI. Though the busy traffic circle at V. del Tritone feels more like a modern thoroughfare than a Baroque square, P. Barberini features two Bernini fountains, **Fontana Tritone** and **Fontana delle Api.** Maderno, Bernini, and rival Borromini are responsible for the **Palazzo Barberini,** home to the Galleria Nazionale d'Arte Antica. The severe **Chiesa della Immacolata Consezione** houses the morbidly fascinating ◪**Capuchin Crypt,** decorated with hundreds of human skulls and bones, in themed rooms. *(Church at V. V. Veneto 27. www.cappucciniviaveneto. it. Open M-W and F-Su 9am-noon and 3--6pm. Church free; cash donation requested.)*

TERMINI AND ENVIRONS

◪**BASILICA DI SANTA MARIA MAGGIORE.** One of the four "Patriarchal" churches in Rome granted extraterritoriality, this basilica crowns the **Esquiline Hill** and is officially part of Vatican City. In AD 352, Pope Sixtus III commissioned it when he noticed that Roman women were still visiting a temple dedicated to the pagan mother-goddess, Juno Lucina. He tore down the pagan temple and built a basilica in celebration of the Council of Ephesus's recent ruling that Mary was the mother of God. This gigantic basilica is home to a wealth of holy and artistic wonders. Upon entering, marvel at the beautiful coffered ceiling in the nave and the statues, mosaics, and frescoes that decorate the adjourning chapels. Set in the floor to the right of the altar, a marble slab marks **Bernini's tomb.** Don't miss the **baptistery,** featuring a magnificent statue of St. John the Baptist covered with animal skins and holding a clam shell. The glorious 14th-century mosaics in the church's **loggia** recount the story of the August snowfall that showed the Pope, who had dreamed of snow brought by the Virgin Mary, where to build the church; every mid-August, this miracle is re-enacted as priests sprinkle white petals from the top of the church. Below the altar are what some believe to be relics from Jesus's manger. Since 2001, Santa Maria Maggiore has hosted a museum containing art and papal artifacts significant to the history of the basilica. *(From Termini, exit right onto V. Giolitti, and walk down V. Cavour. At P. dell' Esquilino, walk around to southeastern side of the basilica to enter. Reservations: ☎06 69 88 68 02. Open daily 7am-7pm. Museum and loggia open daily 9am-6pm. Daily tours of the archaeological area. Modest dress required. Museum €4, reduced €2. Loggia €5, reduced €3.)*

BATHS OF DIOCLETIAN. From AD 298 to 306, 40,000 Christian slaves built these 3000-person-capacity public baths, the largest and most lavishly appointed in Rome. They contained a marble public toilet with seats for 30 people, several pools, gymnasiums, art galleries, gardens, brothels, sports facilities, libraries, and concert halls. The AD fourth-century rotunda displays statues from the baths, and the entrance holds gorgeous, stained-glass windows. In 1561, in keeping with the grand tradition of converting pagan structures into centers of Christianity, Michelangelo undertook his last architectural work and converted the ruins into a church, **Chiesa di Santa Maria degli Angeli.** On the bronze door to the left, a startling cross cuts deeply into Christ's body, symbolizing his resurrection. *(P. dei Cinquecento, across the street from Termini. Enter on V. Volturno. ☎06 47 82 61 52. Open Tu-Sa 9am-7:45pm. Free. Museum at opposite end of baths' entrance courtyard. See p. XX for details.)*

VIA XX SETTEMBRE. V. del Quirinale becomes V. XX ("VEN-tee") Settembre at its intersection with V. delle Quattro Fontane, where a spectacular Bernini fountain sits on each of the four corners. A few blocks down, the colossal **Fontana dell'Acqua Felice** graces P. S. Bernardo. Opposite, **Chiesa di Santa Maria della Vittoria** houses an icon of Mary that accompanied the Catholics to victory in a 1620 battle near Prague. Bernini's fantastically controversial ▩**Ecstasy of Saint Theresa of Ávila** continues to amaze and bemuse visitors in the Cornaro Chapel. At the time of its creation, people were outraged by the depiction of the saint in a pose resembling sexual climax; today, many viewers don't notice the innuendo until told of the controversy. The statue illustrates St. Theresa's heart being pierced by an arrow wielded by an angel, filling her with ardent love for God. *(Open daily 6:30am-noon and 4:30-6pm. Modest dress required.)*

VIA NOMENTANA. This road runs northeast from Michelangelo's **Porta Pia** out of the city. Hop on bus #36 in front of Termini or head back to V. XX Settembre and catch bus #60. A 2km walk or bus ride from Pta. Pia past villas, embassies, and parks leads to **Chiesa di Sant'Agnese Fuori le Mura** on the left. Its apse displays a Byzantine-style mosaic of St. Agnes. Underneath the church wind some of Rome's most impressive **catacombs.** While St. Agnes's body is buried here, her head resides in the church bearing her name in P. Navona, the location of her beheading. *(West side of P. Navona, opposite Fontana dei Quattro Fiumi. Open daily 9:30am-12:30pm and 4-7pm.)*

TRASTEVERE

Take bus #75 or 170 or tram #8 to V. Trastevere to reach these sights.

ISOLA TIBERINA. According to Roman legend, Isola Tiberina emerged with the Roman Republic. After the Etruscan tyrant Tarquin raped the virtuous Lucretia, her outraged family killed him and then tossed his body into the Tiber; so much muck and silt collected around his corpse that an island eventually formed. For centuries the river's fast-flowing water was harnessed by mills, which were destroyed by the great flood of 1870. Home to the Fatebenefratelli Hospital since AD 154, the island has long been associated with health and cures. The Greek god of healing, Aesclepius, notoriously appeared to the Romans as a snake and slithered from the river. The eclectic 10th-century **Basilica di San Bartolomeo** has a Baroque facade, a Romanesque tower, and 14 antique columns. (☎06 68 77 973. Open M-Sa 9am-12:30pm and 3:30-6:30pm. Free.) The **Ponte Fabricio**, known as the **Ponte dei Quattro Capi** (Bridge of Four Heads), was built in 62 BC, making it the oldest in the city.

CENTRAL TRASTEVERE. Off Ponte Garibaldi stands the statue of poet G. G. Belli in his own *piazza*, which borders P. Sonnino and marks the beginning of Vle. di Trastevere. Follow V. Giulio Cesane Santina, which turns into V. dei Genovesi, and take a right on V. di S. Cecilia. Beyond the courtyard is the **Basilica di Santa Cecilia** in Trastevere and its fantastic mosaic above the altar. (*P. San Bartolomeo all'Isola 22.* ☎06 68 77 973. Open M-F 9:30am-1pm and 3:30-7pm, Sa 9:30am-1pm and 3:30-5:30pm, Su 9:30am-1pm and 7-8pm.) From P. Sonnino, V. della Lungaretta leads west to P. di S. Maria in Trastevere, home to the Chiesa di Santa Maria in Trastevere, built in the AD fourth century by Pope Julius II. The mosaics and the chancel arch are quite impressive. What appears to be a trash heap around the statue of the friar and the infant at the entrance is actually a pile of prayers written on anything from Metro tickets to napkins. (Open M-Sa 9am-5:30pm, Su 8:30-10:30am and noon-5:30pm.)

GIANICOLO HILL. At the top of the hill, the **Chiesa di San Pietro** in Montorio stands on what is believed to be the site of St. Peter's upside-down crucifixion. The church contains del Piombo's *Flagellation*, from designs by Michelangelo. (Open daily May-Oct. Tu-Su 9:30am-12:30pm and 4-6pm; Nov.-Apr. 9:30am-12:30pm and 2-4pm. Free.) Next door in a small courtyard behind locked gates is Bramante's tiny ▨**Tempietto.** A combination of ancient and Renaissance architecture, the Tempietto was constructed to commemorate the site of St. Peter's martyrdom, and it provided the inspiration for the dome of St. Peter's in Vatican City. (Courtyard open Tu-Sa in summer 9:30am-12:30pm and 4-6pm; in winter 9:30am-12:30pm and 2-4pm. Free.) Check out an aerial view of Rome from a viewing spot in front of **Acqua Paolo.** The sprawling public **gardens** behind Acqua Paolo continue up V. Garibaldi. Rome's botanical gardens lie at the bottom of Gianicolo and contain a garden for the blind as well as a rose garden that holds the bush from which all the world's roses are supposedly descended. (Reach the summit on bus #41 from the Vatican, 115 from Trastevere, 870 from P. Fiorentini, where C. V. Emanuele meets the Tiber, or walk up the medieval V. Garibaldi, from V. della Scala in Trastevere for 10min. Botanical Gardens, Largo Cristina di Svezia 24, at the end of V. Corsini, off V. della Lungara. ☎49 91 71 06. Open M-Sa Apr.-Oct. 9:30am-6:30pm; Nov.-Mar. 9:30am-5:30pm. Closed holidays. Guided tours Sa 10:30am-noon. Comes with leaflet and audio tour in Italian, English, or French. Call for reservations and more info. €5, ages 6-11 and over 60 €3, under 6 free.)

THE JEWISH GHETTO

Rome's Jewish community is the oldest in Western Europe—Israelites came in 161 BC as ambassadors of Judas Maccabee, asking for Imperial help against invaders. The Ghetto, the tiny area to which Pope Paul IV confined the Jews in 1555, was dissolved in 1870, but it is still the center of Rome's Jewish population of 15,000. Take bus #64; the Ghetto is across V. Arenula from Campo dei Fiori. Alternatively, walk down V. Arenula from C. V. Emanuele and make a left at the river. The Ghetto will be on your left. The neighborhood's main attractions and eateries are located on and around V. del Portico d'Ottavia.

PIAZZA MATTEI. This square, site of Taddeo Landini's 16th-century **Fontana delle Tartarughe,** marks the Ghetto's center. Nearby in the Portico d'Ottavia, the AD eighth-century **Chiesa di Sant'Angelo in Pescheria** was named for the fish market that once flourished there. Jews were once forced to attend mass here, an act of evangelism that they quietly resisted by stuffing their ears with wax. *(V. dei Funari. Heading toward the Theater of Marcellus on V. del Teatro Marcello, go right on V. Montavara, which becomes V. dei Funari after P. Campitelli. The church is under restoration indefinitely.)*

SINAGOGA ASHKENAZITA. Built between 1901 and 1904 at the corner of Lungotevere dei Cenci and V. Catalana, this temple incorporates Persian and Babylonian architectural techniques and features a rainbow-colored dome intended to symbolize peace. Take note of the stained glass high up on the right hand side of the synagogue, commemorative of a tragic terrorist bombing in 1982, which killed a small child. The broken glass was replaced by clear glass, in honor of the victim. In response to the attacks, guards now search all visitors, and *carabinieri* patrol the vicinity. In 1986 Pope John Paul II made the first-ever papal visit to a Jewish synagogue here, declaring that Jews are the oldest brothers of Christians. The synagogue houses the **Jewish Museum,** a collection of ancient Torahs and Holocaust artifacts that document the community's history. *(☎06 68 40 06 61. At the corner of Lungotevere dei Cenci and V. Catalana. Open for services only. Museum open June-Sept. M-Th and Su 10am-7pm, F 9am-4pm; Oct.-May M-Th and Su 10am-10pm, F 10am-4pm. Last entry 45min. before closing. Closed Jewish holidays from 1pm the day before and Catholic holidays, after 1pm. €7.50, groups €6.50, students €3, under 10 free. Reservations required. Cash only.)*

TESTACCIO AND OSTIENSE

Take ⓜB to Piramide, Garbatella, or San Paolo.

South of the Aventine Hill, the working-class neighborhood of Testaccio is known for its cheap trattorie and raucous nightclubs. The area centers around the castle-like **Porta San Paolo,** a remnant of the Aurelian walls built in the AD third century to protect Rome from barbarians. Another attraction is the colossal **Piramide di Gaius Cestius,** built in 330 days by Gaius Cestius's slaves under Augustus at the height of Roman Egyptophilia, and the namesake of the Metro stop/train station. Piramide also shuttles droves of sun-loving Romans to the beach on the weekends, so don't be surprised if you're sitting next to bathing-suit-clad *signore* on the Metro. Ostiense is the district south of Testaccio, and is made up of mostly apartment buildings and industrial complexes.

BASILICA DI SAN PAOLO FUORI LE MURA. The massive Basilica di San Paolo Fuori le Mura is the Rome's second-largest church after St. Peter's Basilica. St. Paul's body, after his beheading at the Tre Fontane, is said to have been buried beneath the altar, while his head remained with St. Peter's at the **Arcibasilica of San Giovanni.** The exact point above the body's resting place is marked by a tiny red light on the front of the altar. San Paolo is also home to many less-significant relics; they are held in the **Capella delle Reliquie,** which you can access through the cloister. In addition to an impressive candelabrum, the basilica also displays the likenesses of every pope since the beginning of the church, with a light shining on face of the current pope, Benedict XVI. Before leaving, pick up a bottle of monk-made Benedictine liqueur (€5-15) in the gift shop. If you have the time, stick around for the daily Gregorian chants sung by the monks at vespers at 5pm. *(ⓜB-Basilica San Paolo, or take bus #23 or 769 from Testaccio, at the corner of V. Ostiense and P. Ostiense. ☎06 45 43 41 85; www.basilicasanpaolo.org. Basilica* *open daily in summer 7am-6:30pm; in winter 7am-6pm. Cloister open daily 8am-6:15pm. Mass daily 7, 8, 9, 10:30am, and 6pm. Modest dress required. Donation requested. Cloister €3, reduced €1.50. Audio booths for short history of basilica €1. Audio tour €5. Gift shop cash only.)*

CIMITERO ACATTOLICO PER GLI STRANIERI. This peaceful Protestant cemetery, the Non-Catholic Cemetery for Foreigners, is one of the only burial grounds in Rome for those who don't belong to the Roman Catholic Church. Notable non-Catholics, including Keats, Shelley, von Goethe, and Antonio Gramsci, rest here. Keats's grave, in his typically self-effacing style, is dedicated to "A Young Poet." *(From Piramide, walk in between the pyramid and the castle. Once on V. Marmorata, turn left on V. Caio Cestio. Ring the bell. www.protestantcemetery.it. Open M-Sa 9am-5pm, Su 9am-1pm. Last entry 30min. before closing. €2 donation requested.)*

ABBAZIA DELLE TRE FONTANE (ABBEY OF THE THREE FOUNTAINS). Legend has it that when St. Paul was beheaded here in AD 67, his head bounced on the ground three times and created a fountain at each bounce. The supposed column upon which Paul was decapitated lies in the back-right corner of the chapel. Far from the busiest streets of the city, and heavy with spiritual significance, the chapels have a serenity entirely distinct from the dramatic exuberance of Rome's Baroque churches; visit the Abbey for an hour of quiet contemplation. *(⑫B-Laurentina. Walk straight and take a right on V. Laurentina; proceed about 1km north and turn right on V. delle Acque Salve. About a 15min. walk, or take bus #761 from Laurentina, get off after 2 stops, and walk the rest of the way. The abbey is at the bottom of the hill. ☎06 54 60 23 47. Open daily in summer 8am-1pm and 3-7pm, in winter 8am-1pm and 3-6pm. Trappist shop: www.labottegadeitrappisti.it. MC/V.)*

SOUTHERN ROME

◼SAN GIOVANNI IN LATERANO. The immense **Arcibasilica of San Giovanni in Laterano,** the cathedral of the diocese of Rome, was home to the Papacy until the 14th century. Founded by Constantine in AD 314, it is the city's oldest Christian basilica. The golden *baldacchino* (canopy) rests over two golden reliquaries with the skulls of St. Peter and St. Paul. Note the immense statue of Constantine, the fresco by **Giotto,** the octagonal **Battistero,** and the intimate **cloister.** A museum of Vatican history is on the right when facing the church. *(⑫A-San Giovanni or bus #16 from Termini. ☎06 69 88 64 33. Call ahead to reserve spots on tours of the Lateran complex and excavations under the basilica. Cathedral open daily 7am-6:30pm. Sacristy open daily 8am-noon, 4-6pm. Cloister open daily 9am-6pm. Museum open daily 9am-6pm. Cloister €2, students €1. Museum €1. Audio tour available in Italian, English, French, Spanish, and German €5, students €4; includes entrance into cloister. Last audio tour at 4:45pm. Cash only. Just west of the church on the southwest end of P. di San Giovanni in Laterano lies the baptistry. Open daily 7am-12:30pm and 4-7:30pm. Modest dress required. Free.)*

The **Scala Santa,** outside the church and to the left facing out of the front doors, are revered as the marble steps used by Jesus outside Pontius Pilate's home in Jerusalem. Indulgences are still granted to pilgrims if they ascend the steps on their knees, reciting prayers on each step. Martin Luther took a break from Catholicism here when he was unable to experience true piety in the act and left without finishing. The steps lead to the chapel of the **Sancta Sanctorium,** which houses the Acheiropoieton, or "picture painted without hands," said to be the work of St. Luke assisted by an angel. *(⑫A-San Giovanni or bus #16 from Termini. Across from the main entrance of the church, on the east side of P. di San Giovanni in Laterano. ☎06 77 26 641. Open Apr.-Sept. M-Sa 6:15am-noon and 3-6:15pm, Su 3:30-6:45pm; Oct.-Mar. M-Sa 6:15am-noon and 3-6:15pm, Su 3:30-6:45pm. Donation requested.)*

CAELIAN HILL. The Caelian and the Esquiline are the biggest of Rome's seven original hills. In ancient times Nero built his decadent Domus Aurea (p. 101) between them. **San Clemente** consists of a 12th-century addition on top of an AD fourth-century church, with an ancient **mithraeum** and sewers at the bottom. The upper church holds mosaics of the Crucifixion, saints, and apostles, and a 13th-century Masolino fresco cycle graces the **Chapel of Santa Caterina.** The fourth-century level contains the tomb of St. Cyril, a pagan sarcophagus, and a series of frescoes depicting Roman generals. Farther underground is a dank second-century *mithraeum,* below which is the **insulae,** a series of brick and stone rooms where Nero is said to have played his lyre while Rome burned in AD 64. In summer, the **New Opera Festival of Rome** performs abridged productions in the church's outdoor courtyard. (*⑩B-Colosseo. Bus #85, 87, 810. Tram #3. Turn left down V. Labicana, away from the Forum; then turn right into P. San Clemente. From ⑩A-Manzoni, walk west on V. A. Manzoni; turn left into P. San Clemente. ☎06 77 40 021. San Clemente open M-F 8am-6:30pm, Sa-Su and holidays 9-11am and 3-6:30pm. Lower basilica and mithraeum open M-Sa 9am-12:30pm and 3-6pm; Su and holidays noon-6pm. Last entry 20min. before closing. €5, students under 26 €3.50. Cash only.*)

PORTA SAN GIOVANNI. The **Chiesa della Santa Croce in Gerusalemme** holds the Fascist-era **Chapel of the Relics,** with fragments of the "true cross" as well as other relics purportedly from the Crucifixion. Perhaps the most intriguing of the relics is St. Thomas's dismembered finger, which, when still attached, was used to probe Christ's wounds. On a lighter note, the building's bright, sweeping frescoes seem to leap off the ceiling. (*P. S. Paolo della Croce in Gerusalemme ⑩A-S. Giovanni. From Pta. S. Giovanni north of the stop, go east on Vle. Carlo Felice; church is on the right. Or, from P.V. Emanuele II, take V. Conte Verde. ☎06 70 14 769; www.basilicasantacroce.com. Open daily 7am-12:45pm and 2:30-6pm. Modest dress required. Donation requested.*)

AVENTINE HILL. Enjoy awe-inspiring and sparsely traversed vistas from this exclusive area of town. V. di Valle Murcia climbs past some of Rome's swankiest homes and the **Roseto Comunale,** a beautiful public rose garden. Formerly a Jewish cemetery, the gardens are now marked by commemorative pillars at each entrance that contain the Tablets of Moses. Up the hill, along the left side of the gardens, the street turns into V. di S. Sabina. On the right side of V. di S. Sabina, just before the hill's crest, a park with orange trees and offers sweeping views of southern Rome. Nearby the **Chiesa di Santa Sabina** has a wooden portal that dates to AD 450. The top, left-hand panel contains one of the earliest-known Crucifixion images. V. di Sabina continues along the crest of the hill to **Piazza dei Cavalieri di Malta,** home of the once-crusading order of the Knights of Malta. On the right as you approach the *piazza* is a large, cream-colored, arched gate; peer through its tiny, circular ▩keyhole for a hedge-framed view of the dome of St. Peter's Cathedral. (*At the end of V. Santa Sabina, past the Church dei Santi Bonifacio e Alessio. Entrance to grounds at P. Cavalierie, 4. ☎06 67 58 12 34 for information. Open Sept.-June Sa 10 and 11am; call ahead to confirm hours, as they are subject to change. €5 donation requested.*)

▩THE APPIAN WAY

⑩A-San Giovanni. Exit onto P. Appio and follow the signs back through the brick archways to P. San Giovanni, where you will see the giant basilica. Then take bus #218 to V. Appia Antica; get off at the info office, just before Domine Quo Vadis; hit the button to stop after you turn left onto V. Appia Antica. Or, ⑩B-Circo Massimo or Piramide, then take bus #118 to the catacombs; ⑩A-Colli Albani, then bus #660 to Cecilia Metella. Info office of the Parco dell'Appia Antica, V. Appia Antica 42. ☎06 51 26 314; www.parcoappiaantica.org. Provides maps and pamphlets about the ancient road and its history, excavations, and recreational opportunities. Also rents bikes €3 per hr., €10 per day. Open M-Th 9:30am-1:30pm and 2:30-5:30pm, F

R O M E

9:30am-1:30pm. Free. Archeobus ☎06 68 40 901; single ticket is valid all day. €15. Reduced for ages 6-12 and over 65, holders of Metrebus and Roma Pass cards, €10. Under 5 free.

About 30min. outside the city center, V. Appia Antica, also known as the Appian Way, was the most important thoroughfare of Ancient Rome. In its heyday it stretched from Campania to the Adriatic Coast and rightfully gained the nickname "The Queen of Roads." Marcus Linius Crassus, a first-century BC tycoon and sometime general, crucified 6000 slaves along this road as punishment for joining the rebellion of the legendary gladiator Spartacus. Today, all remnants of such macabre displays are ancient history, leaving a perfect oasis away from the grind of Rome's streets, vendors, and Vespas. Third-century catacombs, medieval and Baroque churches, and a wealth of ancient Roman ruins remain on the Appian Way. On Sundays, when the street is closed to vehicles, take the opportunity to bike through the countryside.

BASILICA OF SAN SEBASTIANO. Perhaps second only to St. Peter's in overall quality, this basilica should not be missed. Originally dedicated to St. Peter and St. Paul, it now honors St. Sebastian. When Sebastian, a captain in the Roman army, was discovered to be a Christian, he was shot with arrows and left for dead. Miraculously, he was nursed back to health and continued to practice his faith, but was eventually executed. He is the patron saint of athletes because of this remarkable endurance, of soldiers due to his profession and perseverance, and of archers—despite his vested interest in their doing poorly. His likeness is reproduced on the gorgeous ceiling, the work of a Flemish artist. In 2000, the magnificent statue of Jesus Christ the Redeemer was attributed to Bernini as his final masterpiece, completed at age 81. However, the oldest but most recently discovered of the church's relics are the snail fossils. Allegedly 120 million years old, the fossils are visible in the marble floor, which sports the fitting nickname *lumacella*, or "little snails," though the snails seem gigantic by today's standards. (*V. Appia Antica 136.* ☎06 78 08 847. Open daily 8:30am-6pm. Free.)

CHIESA DELLA SANTA MARIA IN PALMIS. On the site of this church, also called **Domine Quo Vadis,** St. Peter had a vision of Christ. Allegedly, he asked Jesus, *"Domine, quo vadis?"* ("Lord, where are you going?"). When Christ replied that he was going to Rome to be crucified again because Peter had abandoned him, Peter returned to Rome to suffer his own martyrdom: he was crucified upside down. In the middle of the aisle, just inside the door, Christ's alleged footprints are set in stone. (*At the intersection of V. Appia Antica and V. Ardeatina. Open daily in summer 8am-12:30pm and 2:30-7:45pm; in winter 8am-12:30pm and 2:30-6:45pm. Free.*)

CATACOMBS. Since burial inside the city walls was forbidden during ancient times, fashionable Romans buried their beloved along Appian Way, while early Christians dug maze-like catacombs—an economic solution for pricey land. **San Callisto** is the largest catacomb in Rome, with nearly 22km of subterranean paths. Its four levels once held 16 popes, seven bishops, St. Cecilia, and 500,000 other Christians. (*V. Appia Antica 126, entrance on road parallel to V. Appia.* ☎06 51 30 15 80; www.catacombe.roma.it. Open an-Nov. M-Sa. 8:30am-6pm. Church open daily 8:30am-6pm.) **Santa Domitilla** holds a third-century portrait of Christ and the Apostles, along with other colorful frescoes. (*V. delle Sette Chiese 282. Facing V. Ardeatina from San Callisto exit, cross street, and walk right up V. Sette Chiese.* ☎06 51 10 342; www.catacombe. domitilla.it. Open Feb.-Dec. M and W-Su 9am-noon and 2-5pm. €5, ages 6-15 €3. Cash only.) **San Sebastiano** houses the massive underground tomb of St. Sebastian himself, and was reputedly the home to the bodies of Peter and Paul before their relocation to their final resting places. San Sebastiano also contains three impressive stucco-ceiling tombs from the pre-Christian period. Visit the info office for maps, booklets, and advice. (*V. Appia Antica 136.* ☎06 78 50 350. www.fratilazio.it. Open

M-Sa 9am-noon and 2-5pm. €5, ages 6-15 €3. MC/V. All catacombs accessible only with guided tours in English, Italian, and Spanish, which run every 20min.)

VILLA AND CIRCUS OF MAXENTIUS. Emperor Maxentius built this complex, which contains a villa and a 10,000-spectator chariot racetrack. *(V. Appia Antica 153. Near the Mausoleum of Cecilia Metella. ☎06 78 01 324; www.villadimassenzio.it. Open Tu-Su 9am-1:30pm. Last entry 1pm. €3, reduced €1.50, EU residents under 18 and over 65 and all residents of Paris free. Cash only.)*

MUSEUMS

Rome is home to some of the world's most renowned museums. Though contemporary exhibits do occasionally pass through the city, permanent masterpieces have been secured through the wealth and influence of prominent Roman families and the Vatican. Reserving or buying tickets in advance saves time. Keep your eyes on the ceilings—in many museums they are covered in frescoes. For more info on Rome's museums, visit www.beniculturali.it.

VATICAN MUSEUMS (MUSEI VATICANI)

☎06 69 88 49 47; www.vatican.va. From P. San Pietro, walk 10 blocks north along the Vatican City wall. From ⓂOttaviano, turn left on V. Ottaviano to reach the Vatican City wall; turn right and follow the wall to the museum's entrance. Several signs along the wall point to the entrance. Major galleries open Mar.-Oct. M-Sa 8:30am-6pm. Last entry 2hr. before closing. Closed on major religious holidays. Snack bar between the collection of modern religious art and the Sistine Chapel; full cafeteria near main entrance pavilion. Most of the museums are wheelchair-accessible, though less visited parts, such as the upper level of the Etruscan Museum, are not. €14, ISIC members €8; with guided tour €30, reduced €25; children under 1m tall and last Su of the month 8:30am-12:30pm free. Info and gift shop sell a useful guidebook (€7.50) on ground level past the entrance. Audio tour €6.

The Vatican Museums hold one of the world's greatest collections of art, with ancient, Renaissance, and modern paintings, sculptures, and of course papal odds and ends. After a day of art overload, be sure to admire the famous **bronze double-helix ramp** as you ramble down it towards the exit.

> **⚡TIP** **ARE WE THERE YET?** Lines for the Vatican Museums, which begin forming around 6:30am, only become more unbearable. It's not a bad idea to drag yourself out of that rock-hard hostel bed at an ungodly hour.

SISTINE CHAPEL. Since its completion in the 16th century, the Sistine Chapel, named for its founder, Pope Sixtus IV, has been the site of the College of Cardinals' election of new popes, most recently **Pope Benedict XVI** in April 2005. Michelangelo's **ceiling,** the pinnacle of artistic creation, gleams from its 20-year restoration, which ended in 1999. The simple compositions and vibrant colors hover above, each section depicting a story from Genesis. The scenes are framed by the famous *ignudi* (young nude males). Michelangelo painted the masterpiece by standing on a platform and craning backward—he never recovered from the strain to his neck and eyes. *The Last Judgement* fills the altar wall; the figure of Christ as judge lingers in the upper center, surrounded by his saintly entourage and the supplicant Mary. Michelangelo painted himself as a flayed human skin that hangs symbolically between the realms of heaven and hell. The frescoes on the side walls predate Michelangelo's ceiling; they were completed between 1481 and 1483 by a team of artists under Perugino including Botticelli, Ghirlandaio, Roselli, Signorelli, and della Gatta. On one side, scenes from the life of Moses complement parallel scenes of Christ's life on the other. Sitting is only allowed on the benches along the side. Guards will ask you to be silent, as the chapel is a holy place.

OTHER VATICAN GALLERIES. The **Museo Pio-Clementino** houses the world's greatest collection of antique sculpture. The world-famous statue of **Laocoön,** who was strangled by Neptune's sea serpents for being suspicious of the Greek's gift of the wooden horse, is located in the octagonal courtyard. Proceeding through the courtyard, two slobbering hounds guard the entrance to the **Stanza degli Animali,** a marble menagerie highlighting Roman brutality. The statues of ⬛**Apollo Belvedere** and **Hercules** are both masterful works. The last room of the gallery has the red sarcophagus of Sant'Elena, Constantine's mother. From here, the Simonetti Stairway climbs to the **Museo Etrusco,** filled with artifacts from Tuscany and northern Lazio. Back on the landing of the Simonetti Staircase is the **Stanza della Biga** (room of an ancient marble chariot) and the **Galleria della Candelabra,** which contains over 500 smaller statues. The route to the Sistine Chapel begins here, passing through the dimly lit **Galleria degli Arazzi** (tapestries), the **Galleria delle Mappe** (maps), the **Apartamento di Pio V** (where there is a shortcut to the Sistine Chapel), the **Stanza Sobieski,** and the **Stanza dell'Immacolata Concezione.** From the Stanza dell'Immacolata Concezione, a door leads into the first of the four ⬛**Stanze di Rafaele,** apartments built for Pope Julius II in the 1510s. A door at the back of the second room, originally called the **Room of the Parrot,** depicts St. John the Baptist with parrots on either side of him. The door below leads to the Room of the Swiss Guard and is closed to the public. Another room features Raphael's ⬛**School of Athens,** painted as a trial piece for Julius, who was so impressed that he fired his other painters, destroyed their frescoes, and commissioned Raphael to decorate the entire room. From here, there are two paths: one to the Sistine Chapel, and the other a staircase to the frescoed Borgia apartments and the **Museum of Modern Religious Art.**

PINACOTECA. This collection, one of Rome's best, includes Filippo Lippi's *Coronation of the Virgin,* Perugino's *Madonna and Child,* Titian's *Madonna of San Nicoletta dei Frari,* and Raphael's ⬛**Transfiguration.** On the way out of the Sistine Chapel, take a look at the **Room of the Aldobrandini Marriage,** which contains a series of rare, ancient Roman frescoes.

OTHER MUSEUMS

⬛**GALLERIA BORGHESE.** The crown jewel of the beautiful Villa Borghese, the Galleria Borghese may be Rome's most enjoyable museum. The spellbinding collection, housed in the Villa Borghese, was begun by Cardinal Scipione Borghese in the 1600s. It includes some of the greatest masterpieces by Bernini, Titian, Raphael, Caravaggio, and Rubens—and can be appreciated in one unforgettable afternoon. Without a doubt, a visit to the Galleria Borghese should be a part of any Roman itinerary. Reservations are required, however, as tickets sometimes sell out one month in advance.

Upon entering, don't miss Mark Antonio's **ceiling,** depicting the Roman conquest of Gaul. After perusing the Roman mosaics on the floor, check out the dragon and eagle statues, symbols of the Borghese family, on opposite ends of the room. **Room I** houses Canova's steamy statue of Paolina Borghese portrayed as a reclining Venus triumphant, holding the golden apple given to her by Paris. The myth is also depicted in elaborate frescoes on the ceiling. The next rooms display two of Bernini's most momentous works: the breathtaking ⬛**Apollo and Daphne,** in which Daphne's hands and feet appear to be sprouting leaves and roots as she begins her mythical transformation into a laurel tree, and a magnificent and thought-provoking *David* crouching with his slingshot.

Feel free to marvel at more of Bernini's splendor while taking in Pluto and Prosperina's seemingly weightless bodies in *The Rape of Proserpina*. A trip to the Galleria is not complete without a visit to the renowned ⧉**Caravaggio Room**, featuring six staggeringly impressive works, including his self-portrait, **The Sick Bacchus**, which he painted during a stay in the hospital (supposedly recuperating from either depression or a horse kick to the head). *The Sick Bacchus* bears a striking resemblance to *Young Boy with Basket of Fruit*, as it is more commonly referred to, but the Galleria has it labeled as *Young Girl*. The questionable gender of the main subject and his/her pose of nonchalant suggestiveness (slightly parted lips, tenderly revealed shoulder) has led some art historians to psychoanalyze Caravaggio's sexuality. The stark ⧉**David and Goliath** is another self-portrait, one that epitomizes the artist's tragic reputation.

The collection continues in the *pinacoteca* upstairs, accessible from the gardens around the back by a staircase. **Room IX** holds Raphael's *Deposition*, a masterpiece showing the midpoint between the traditional moments of the Pietà and the Entombment, while Sodoma's *Pietà* graces **Room XII**. Look for self portraits by Bernini, del Conte's *Cleopatra and Lucrezia*, Rubens's *Pianto sul Cristo Morto*, and Titian's famous *Amor Sacro e Amor Profano*. *Ple. Scipione Borghese 5. ⓂA-Spagna; take exit labeled "Villa Borghese," walk to the right past the Metro stop to V. Muro Torto, and then to P. Pta. Pinciana; Vle. del Museo Borghese is ahead and leads to the museum. Or take bus #116 or 910 to V. Pinciana. ☎06 84 13 979; www.galleriaborghese.it/borghese/it/default. htm. Open Tu-Su 8:30am-7:30pm. Entry every 2hr.; last entry 5pm. Limited capacity; reservation required. Guided tours in English at 9:10 and 11:10am. Tickets for high season may be booked a month in advance. Reservations ☎32 810, group reservations ☎06 32 65 13 29 M-F 9am-6pm, Sa 9am-1pm; easiest to book through www.ticketeria.it. The ticket office and a bookshop share the villa's basement. Also go there for the mandatory bag check; it's best to get it over with 10-15min. before your shift. €8.50, including reservation and bag charge; EU citizens ages 18-25 €5.25; EU citizens under 18, over 65, and art students €2. Ticket prices increase dramatically when a special exhibition is up; check before you book. Audio tour €5. Tours €5. MC/V.*

MUSEI CAPITOLINI. This collection of ancient sculptures is the world's oldest public museum of ancient art, and one of its largest. Pope Clement XII Corsini bought the *palazzo* to exhibit Cardinal Alessandro Albani's ancient sculptures in 1733. The *palazzo*'s courtyard contains fragments of the somewhat frightening **Colossus of Constantine**, whose muscular right arm measures almost two meters. The original statue of **Marcus Aurelius**, Bernini's **Head of Medusa**, and the famous **Capitoline Wolf**, which has symbolized the city of Rome since antiquity, occupy the first floor. At the top of the stairs, the **pinacoteca** houses the museum's non-sculpture masterpieces, including Bellini's *Portrait of a Young Man*, Titian's *Baptism of Christ*, Rubens's *Romulus and Remus Fed by the Wolf*, and Caravaggio's *St. John the Baptist* and *Gypsy Fortune-Teller*. The collection continues in the Palazzo Nuovo, which can be accessed through the **Tabularium**, a hall of ancient Rome built in 79 BC. The entryway patio holds **Maforio**, one of Rome's five original "talking statues," to which people would give messages for the public. This gallery also holds the **Galata**, one of the oldest specimens of Roman sculpture. ☎06 82 05 91 27; www.museicapitolini.org. Open Tu-Su 9am-8pm. Last entry 1 hr. before closing. Musei Capitolini's wheelchair-accessible entrance at V. del Tempio di Giove; Tabularium's wheelchair entrance at Palazzo Nuovo. Reservations necessary for groups (12+ people) Sa and holidays €25. Tickets €6.50, EU residents 18-25 €4.50, EU residents under 18 and over 65 free; with temporary exhibition €9; combined Musei Capitolini

PLACES TO SMOOCH IN ROMA

While you may be close enough to pucker up with strangers on the subway, save your saliva for these dreamy destinations.

1. Stroll through **Villa Borghese** (p. 93), find a secluded, shaded spot, and go in for the kill.

2. Bottle of red. Bottle of white. **Trevi Fountain** (p. 104) at night.

3. With the sun setting behind St. Peter's and the swirling Tiber beneath you, **Ponte Sisto** is the perfect place to lay it on. Hard.

4. St. Peter's Square (p. 107). Just try and keep it PG—his Holiness may be watching.

5. Look out over **Circus Maximus** (p. 101) from Palatine Hill and imagine thousands of fans cheering on you and your sweetie.

6. The terrace of the **Vittorio Emanuele II monument** (p. 101). There's a reason people call this spot the "wedding cake."

7. Top of the **Spanish Steps** (p. 104). If it fails, you can always push the person down them.

8. Waiting for the **Metro.** You'd be surprised—it can get pretty steamy. Plus you'll make a stranger's day.

9. Chiesa di Santa Maria in Cosmedin (p. 101). Forget chocolates and roses; the skull and relics of St. Valentine are the key ingredient in any love potion.

10. Over a shared bowl of spaghetti, *Lady and the Tramp* style.

and Centrale Montemartini valid for 7 days €11, ISIC & EU students €9. Audio tour €5.

MUSEO NAZIONALE ETRUSCO DI VILLA GIULIA. This 16th-century villa was built under Pope Julius III. Today, it houses one of the most extensive collections of Etruscan artifacts in the world. Highlights include the noted sarcophagus of a married couple in **Room 9.** Upstairs, archaeologists have put together fragments of a facade of an Etruscan temple, complete with terra-cotta gargoyles, chips of paint, and a relief of the warrior Tydaeus biting into the brain of a wounded adversary. The museum is also home to a chaotic collection of Greek artifacts found in the region, evidence of the extensive trade relationships that once existed between the Etruscans and the Greeks. More interesting than the jewelry, ceramics, and other artifacts is the villa itself. Make sure to stroll around the well-manicured grounds and check out the lily pads and goldfish in the discreetly hidden pond in the center courtyard. *(P. Villa Giulia 9, just north of Villa Borghese, near P. Thorvaldsen.* Ⓜ*A-Flaminio; then tram #30 or 225, or bus #19 from P. Risorgimento or 52 from P. San Silvestro. From Galleria Borghese, follow V. dell'Uccelliera to the zoo and then take V. del Giardino to V. delle Belle Arti. Museum is on the left after Galleria d'Arte Moderna.* ☎ *06 32 26 571, reservations 82 45 29. Open Tu-Su 8:30am-7:30pm. €4, EU citizens ages 18-25 €2, EU citizens under 18 and over 65 free. Mandatory bag check. English audio tour €4.)*

VILLA FARNESINA. The villa belonged to Agostino "Il Magnifico" Chigi, once Europe's wealthiest man. For show, Chigi had his banquet guests toss gold and silver dishes into the Tiber River after every course; ever the miser, he secretly hid nets under water to recover his treasures. To the right of the entrance lies the breathtaking **Sala di Galatea,** mostly painted by the villa's architect, Baldassare Peruzzi, in 1511. The vault displays symbols of astrological signs that represent 9:30pm on November 29, 1466, the moment of Agostino's birth. The room's masterpiece is Raphael's **Triumph of Galatea.** The ceiling of the Loggia di Psiche depicts the marriage of Cupid and Psyche. Returning to the entrance, a stunningly detailed stairway ascends to the **Salone delle Prospettive.** This room, decorated by Peruzzi, incorporates five different colored marbles in the floor design and offers views of Rome between fictive columns. The adjacent bedroom, known as the **Stanza delle Nozze** (Marriage Room), is the real reason for coming here. Il Sodoma, who had previously been busy painting the pope's rooms in the Vatican, frescoed the chamber until Raphael showed up and took over. Il Sodoma bounced back, creating this masterful fresco of Alexander the Great's marriage to the beautiful Roxanne. *(V. della Lungara 230, just across from Palazzo Corsini. Bus #23; get off between Ponte Mazinni and Ponte Sisto.* ☎ *06 680 272 68; www.villafarnesina.it. Open M-Sa 9am-1pm. Last entry 12:40pm.* €5, reduced €4.)

MUSEO NAZIONALE D'ARTE ANTICA. This collection of 12th- to 18th-century art is split between Palazzo Barberini and Palazzo Corsini. Barberini contains paintings from the medieval through Baroque periods. Don't miss Rafael's lover delicately cradling her exposed breast in *La Fornarina. (V. Barberini 18.* ⓂA-Barberini. *Bus #492 or 62.* ☎ *06 48 14 591. For tours call* ☎ *06 85 55 952. Open Tu-Su 8:30am-7:30pm.* €5; *EU citizens ages 18-24* €2; *EU citizens under 18, over 65, and EU students free. Cash only.)* Galleria Corsini's 17th- to 18th-century collection includes works by Rubens, Caravaggio, Bernini, and Brueghel. *(Galleria Barberini: V. Barberini 18.* ⓂA-Barberini. *Bus #492 or 62.* ☎ *06 48 14 591, tours* ☎ *85 55 952. Open Tu-Su 8:30am-7:30pm.* €5; *EU citizens ages 18-24* €2; *EU citizens under 18, over 65, and EU students free. Cash only. Galleria Corsini: V. della Lungara 10. Opposite Villa Farnesina in Trastevere. Take bus #23; get off between Ponte Mazzini and Ponte Sisto.* ☎ *06 22 58 24 93. Open Tu-Su 8:30am-7:30pm. Wheelchair-accessible.* €4, *EU students* €2, *Italian art students and EU citizens over 65 free. Guidebooks in Italian* €10.50. *Cash only.)*

GALLERIA SPADA. Cardinal Bernardino Spada bought a large assortment of paintings and sculptures, and commissioned an even more opulent set of great rooms to house them. Time and good luck have left the palatial seventh-century apartments nearly intact—a visit to the gallery offers a glimpse of the luxury of Baroque courtly life. Before heading into the gallery rooms upstairs, check out Borromini's fantastic example of ▓**3D perspective** in the courtyard. Watch in awe as the seemingly distant, life-size statue through the corridor is revealed to be only three feet tall and less than 35 ft. away. In **Room 1** of the gallery's four rooms, the modest cardinal hung portraits of himself by Guercino, Guido Reni, and Cerini. In **Room 2,** look for paintings by the Venetians Tintoretto and Titian and a frieze by Vaga, originally intended for the Sistine Chapel. In **Room 4** are three canvases by the father-daughter team of Orazio and Artemisia Gentileschi. *(P. Capo di Ferro 13, in the Palazzo Spada. Bus #64. From Campo dei Fiori, take any of the small streets leading to P. Farnese. Facing away from Campo dei Fiori, turn left on Capo di Ferro.* ☎ *06 68 32 409. Open Tu-Su 8:30am-7:30pm. Last entry 7pm. Guided tour Su 10:45am from museum book shop. Pamphlet guides in English available for each room of the exhibit.* €5, *EU citizens 18-25* €2.50, *EU citizens under 18 or over 65 free. Guidebooks* €10.50. *Cash only.)*

GALLERIA DORIA PAMPHILI. The Doria Pamphili family, whose illustrious kin include Pope Innocent X, maintain this stunning private collection in their palatial home. The Classical art is organized by size and theme, and Renaissance and Baroque masterpieces include Caravaggio's *Rest During the Flight in Egypt*, Raphael's *Double Portrait*, and Velasquez's portrait of Pope Innocent X, generally considered to be one of the most outstanding papal portraits of all time. The pope was shocked by the depiction, exclaiming, "It's too real!" The back gallery's mirrors and windows evoke the feeling of a miniature Versailles. *(V. del Corso 305. Bus #40 express or 64 to P. Venezia. From P. Venezia, walk up V. del Corso and take the 2nd left.* ☎ *06 67 97 323; www.doriapamphilj.it. Open M-W and F-Su 10am-5pm. Last entry at about 4pm.* €9, *students* €6. *Informative audio tour in English, French, or Italian included. Cash only.)*

MUSEO CENTRALE MONTEMARTINI. The building, a former turn-of-the-century electrical plant, has a striking collection of Classical art. Highlights include *Hercules's Presentation at Mount Olympus*, a huge well-preserved floor mosaic of a hunt, and a statue of Dionysus, the god of wine and revelry, whose hair is interwoven with grapes. *(V. Ostiense 106.* ⓂB-Garbatella. *Follow signs in the station to V. Ostiense; the museum is directly across the street. Or take bus #702 or #23 three stops from* ⓂB-Piramide. ☎ *06 82 05 91 27; www.centralemontemartini.org. Open*

Tu-Su 9am-7pm. Last entry 30min. before closing. €4.50, reduced €2.50. With entry to the Capitoline Museums (good for 1 week) €8.50, reduced €6.50. Reservations required for tours in Italian, English, French, German, and Spanish. Cash only.)

MUSEO NAZIONALE D'ARTE MODERNA E CONTEMPORANEA. This museum holds a splendid collection of 19th- and 20th-century art, ranging from nationalistic Italian paintings and pastoral scenes to abstract works. In **la sala giardiniere** (the gardener's room), Van Gogh's *L'Arlesiana* and Edgar Degas's *Dopo il bagno* hang among works completed by Italians in Paris. The museum's soaring galleries also house an impressive array of sculptures and temporary traveling exhibitions. *(Vle. delle Belle Arti 131, in Villa Borghese, near Museo Nazionale Etrusco. ⓂA-Flaminio; then tram 30 or 225, bus 19 from P. Risorgimento, or bus 52 from P. San Silvestro. From Galleria Borghese, follow V. dell'Uccelliera to the zoo and take V. del Giardino to V. delle Belle Arti. ☎06 32 29 82 21; www.gnam.arti.beniculturali.it. Open Tu-Su 8:30am-7:30pm. Last entry 6:45pm. €10, EU citizens ages 18-25 €8, EU citizens under 18 or over 65 free. Ticket prices include special exhibitions. Cash only.)*

MUSEO DELL'ARA PACIS. Right beside Augustus's Mausoleum, this museum highlights the art of the restored first-century BC Ara Pacis (Altar of Peace), a temple built to celebrate Augustus's return from Spain and Gaul. Check out the impressive floral frieze on its lower half and noteworthy Romans on top. *(Lungotevere in Augusta. From P. Popolo, walk down V. di Ripetta. The museum is the white building on the right. ☎06 82 05 91 27; http://en.arapacis.it. Open Tu-Su 9am-7pm. €6.50, EU citizens ages 18-25 €4.50, under 18 and over 65 free. Audio tour €3.50. AmEx/MC/V.)*

🎭 ENTERTAINMENT

Roman entertainment just isn't what it used to be. Back in the day, you could swing by the Colosseum to watch a man viciously clawed to death by a bear. Now, Romans seeking diversion are far more likely to go to the opera, a soccer game, or the latest Hollywood flick. Is this progress? Perhaps. But this is no reason for you, bloodthirsty traveler, to content your restless heart with eating *gelato* next to a monument or people-watching in a *piazza*. Rome is full of more entertaining entertainment options.

Weekly *Roma C'è* (www.romace.it; with an English section) and *Time Out* (www.timeout.com/rome), both available at newsstands, have up-to-date club, movie, and event listings. The city of Rome also has a comprehensive website that lists all goings-on in the city (www.comune.roma.it), including a section specifically for summer events (http://en.estateromana.comune.roma.it/; in English). Of course, the city's walls are plastered with advertisements for upcoming concerts, plays, operas, parties, and circuses.

JAZZ

Alexanderplatz Jazz Club, V. Ostia 9 (☎06 58 33 57 81 from 9:30am-6pm for information, 06 39 74 21 71 from 6pm on to book a table; www.alexanderplatz.it). ⓂA-Ottaviano. Head left on V. G. Cesare, take 2nd right on V. Leone IV and 1st left on V. Ostia. Night buses to P. Venezia and Termini leave from P. Clodio. Italy's oldest jazz club, considered Europe's best. Doors open at 8pm, shows start at 10pm. Check website for schedule (also available in English). Open Sept.-May daily 8pm-2am. Moves outside to Villa Celimontana (www.villacelimontanajazz.com) in summer. Most tickets €10 or less.

Big Mama, Vco San Francesco a Ripa (☎06 58 12 552; www.bigmama.it). From V. di Trastevere with your back to the river, make a left on to V. San Francesco a Ripa and then a right onto the Vicolostet. Blues, blues, and more blues. A *tessera* (€8 for 1 month, €13 for 1 year) allows you into the club's many free concerts. Occasional cover for big-name groups. Open late Sept. to June daily 8pm-1:30am; sometimes closed Su and M.

Fonclea, V. Crescenzio 82a (☎06 68 96 302; www.fonclea.it), near P. Risorgimento. ⓂA-Ottaviano. Pub and restaurant with live music. In the summer, moves outside for music and movies. Cover F-Sa €6. Shows generally start at 9:30pm. Open daily 7pm-2am. MC/V.

CLASSICAL MUSIC AND OPERA

Accademia Nazionale di Santa Cecilia, V. Vittoria 6 (☎06 361 10 64; www.santace-cilia.it). This conservatory, named for the martyred patron saint of music, was founded by Palestrina in the 16th century and is home to Rome's official symphony orchestra. Orchestra, chamber, and choral concerts are held at the Parco della Musica, V. Pietro di Coubertin 30, near P. del Popolo. Regular season runs Oct.-June (though still some concerts in the summer), covering the classics and occasional special presentations, such as Jimi Hendrix played by a string quartet and the works of Ennio Morricone.

Teatro Ghione, V. delle Fornaci 37 (☎06 63 72 294; www.teatroghione.it; info@teatroghione.it), near the Vatican. This red velvet theater hosts Euromusica's classical concerts. Box office open Oct.-Apr. Tu-Sa 10:30am-1pm and 4-8pm. Performances Tu-W and F-Sa 9pm, Th-Sa 5pm. Tickets €16-22, students €10-12. Call for occasional discounts. MC/V.

ROCK AND POP

Unfortunately, most internationally-renowed bands bypass Rome in favor of Milan or Turin to the north. However, some do deign to make it down to the capital. Big-name shows (which usually play at the **Palazzo dello Sport** in EUR or at the **Foro Italico** north of Flaminino) will invariably have massive poster campaigns. Some notable concerts are also held in the **Circus Maximus,** generally for free. If you still feel out of touch with the local music scene, ticket agencies and tourist offices have information on upcoming shows. You can also try **www.biglietto.it** for upcoming concerts and tickets. The more popular festivals and performances include:

Roma Incontra il Mondo, Laghetto di Villa Ada, V.de Ponte Salario (☎06 41 73 47 12 or 46 48; www.villaada.org), north of Villa Borghese. A festival of world music and "musica etnica," plus some well-renowned international acts, liven up the lake in Villa Ada. Performers have included the late Nusrat Fateh Ali Khan, Gogol Bordello, Nouvelle Vague, and Patti Smith. Tickets from €8. Concerts mid-June to early Aug.

Fiesta, Ippodrome delle Capanelle, V. Appia Nuova 1245 (☎333 77 51 851; www.fiesta. it), ⓂA-Colli Albani and bus #664. An extremely popular festival running all summer, featuring all things Latin American (food, music, the works). Performers have included Cesaria Evora, Jose Feliciano, and Burning Spear. Don't know how to salsa? Don't worry, you too will be assimilated. Attendance can swell to over 30,000 on weekends. Most tickets €10-20. Concerts at 8pm.

SPECTATOR SPORTS

While other spectator sports may exist in Rome (and the key word is "may"), the only one that matters is *calcio*—soccer. Rome has two teams in Italy's A League: A. S. Roma and S. S. Lazio. Traditionally, Lazio's fans come from the suburbs and countryside around Rome (and tend to be more right-wing politically), while Roma fans are from the city itself, especially the Centro Storico, Trastevere, Testaccio, and the Jewish Ghetto. The two annual Roma-Lazio games often prove decisive in the championship race.

Matches are held at the **Stadio Olimpico** (☎06 32 37 333), in Foro Italico, almost every Sunday from September to June. European cup matches are often played mid-week. *Tifosi*, as hardcore fans are called, show up hours before each game to drink, sing team songs, and taunt rivals. Unfortunately, the festivities sometimes turn ugly, with fans displaying offensive banners and shouting obscenities at the visiting team. For the most part, though, the celebrations are cheerful and melodious: fans wave flags to strains of the "Macarena," while Queen's "We Are the Champions" blends imperceptibly into the background of tens of thousands of fans reciting fight songs to the tune of the "Battle Hymn of the Republic" and in recent years, the White Stripes' "Seven Nation Army" (not kidding, it is *the* tune of Italian soccer). Buy tickets (€11-80; discounts for women) at the stadium or at team stores like **A.S. Roma**, P. Colonna 360 (☎06 69 20 06 42; www.asroma.it. Open daily 10am-6pm.), and **Lazio Point**, V. Farini 34, near Termini (☎06 48 26 688; www.sslazio.it; open daily 9am-7pm.) They are also available at **Orbis**, P. dell'Esquilino 37 (☎06 48 27 403; www.cdflash.com; open M-Sa 9:30am-1:30pm and 4-7:30pm).

🛍 SHOPPING

Rome is a shopper's paradise, versatile enough to accommodate a wide range of tastes and budgets. First, there are the ubiquitous chain stores like **Motivi, Mango, Stefanel, Intimissimi, Zara,** and **United Colors of Benetton.** Then there are the coronary arrest-inducing prices of designer shrines like **Cavalli, Dolce & Gabbana,** and **Prada,** followed by the techno-blasting teen stores that dominate central thoroughfares. Finally, tiny boutiques in the *centro storico*, including **Ethic** and **Havana,** often have locations throughout the city. Below is a list of notable boutiques, budget stores, and fashionable streets. After all, in the public imagination at least, no trip to Italy is complete without a bit of shopping. (You may feel otherwise after you see the prices at Prada, but that's your problem.)

Some advice before setting out with credit card in hand: sales in Italy happen twice a year, in mid-January and mid-July. Don't be surprised if you can't try on everything in all stores. Finally, be clear about exchanges and returns before giving a store your money; Italy is not exactly known for its customer service.

DESIGNER STORES

Time was, the strength of the dollar and relative weakness of Italy's lira made boutique shopping in Rome a bargain-hunter's dream. Now Italy's in on the euro and the dollar has tanked, so those days of massive savings are past. Still, if you're yearning to kill a couple credit cards with some shopping at Rome's chicest boutiques, **Via del Corso, Via dei Condotti,** and the streets that surround them are lined with name-brand stores. More daring—and unique—shops can be found on **Via del Governo Vecchio.** Slightly less pricey stores can be found along **Via Nazionale** and around the **Campo dei Fiori. Via Cola di Rienzo,** near the Vatican, has most of the same stores as the Corso with far fewer shoppers. There is the Roman equivalent of a shopping mall (a few stores in a beautiful *palazzo* with a coffee bar) on the Corso across from P. Colonna: the **Galleria Alberto Sordi** (open daily 10am-10pm). Opening hours in July and August are much less reliable, with a number of shops closing on Saturday morning and reopening only on Tuesday. Most stores, though, will be open continuously, at least on weekdays. If you happen to spend over €155 at one store, you are eligible for a tax refund (see **Essentials,** p. 11).

DEPARTMENT STORES

La Rinascente, P. Colonna (☎06 67 97 691), just past the Galleria Alberto Sordi. The mother of all Roman department stores; it has something for everyone, though it primarily caters to a middle-aged crowd. Wide selection of lingerie in basement; also a decent stock of perfume, makeup, sunglasses, and other accessories. Open M-Sa 9:30am-9:30pm, Su 10am-9pm. AmEx/MC/V.

Coin, P. Appio 7 (☎06 70 80 00 20), near San Giovanni in Laterano. 2nd location on V. Cola di Rienzo. Similar selection and prices as at La Rinascente. Open M-Sa 10am-8pm, Su 10:30am-1pm and 4-8pm. AmEx/MC/V.

Oviesse, Vle. Trastevere 62 (☎06 58 33 36 33). Smaller than the above, but good selection of reasonably-priced basic pieces. Also has some awesomely Italian teenager-focused collections. The Trastevere location is right above the cheap Standa supermarket and has a *profumeria* inside. Open M-Sa 8:30am-8pm, Su 9:30am-1:30pm and 4-8pm. AmEx/MC/V.

UPIM, V. Tritone 172 (☎06 67 83 336). The bargain basement of department stores in Rome; a cheap, solid option for basics and essentials. Open daily 9am-8pm. AmEx/MC/V.

OUTDOOR MARKETS

Street vendors will often try to sell fake Prada bags for exorbitant prices, insisting they're from the hands of Miuccia herself. Seemingly miraculous bargains can end up costing you dearly in the end: a 2005 Italian law stipulates that buyers of fake designer items can be fined €10,000.

Mercato Andrea Doria, on V. Andrea Doria, northwest of the Vatican Museums. A few blocks away from Ⓜ Cipro, or take bus #23 or 70. Caters to the local population, so don't expect to find many English-speaking folks here. Fruits, vegetables, fish, groceries, and clothes sold in a huge open square and in permanent vendor stalls all along the street. By far busiest in the morning, so get there early. Open M-Sa 7am-1:30pm.

Campo dei Fiori, in the *centro storico*. Tram #8 or bus #64. Transformed daily by stalls of fruits and vegetables, meat, poultry, and fish as well as inedible goods. Some of the merchandise is tourist junk, but a few of the produce vendors sell a genuinely good product—prices are a bit high, however. Open M-Sa from 7am until the individual vendors decide their food has run out—usually around 1:30pm.

Porta Portese, in Trastevere. Tram #8 from Largo di Torre Argentina. This gigantic flea market is a surreal experience, with booths selling clothing, shoes, jewelry, bags, toilets, and millions of other items you never knew you needed. Keep your friends close and your money closer, as the place swarms with pickpockets. Open Su 5am-1:30pm.

Mercato delle Stampe, Largo della Fontanella di Borghese. Bus #81, 116, 117, or 492. A bookworm's haven specializing in old books, antiquarian magazines, and pieces of art. Open M-Sa 9:30am-about 2pm.

▨ NIGHTLIFE

Romans find nighttime diversion at the pubs of San Lorenzo, the clubs of Testaccio, and everywhere in between. Pick up *Roma C'è* for updates on clubs' openings and closings. *Time Out* covers Rome's sparse but solid collection of gay nightlife listings, many of which require an **ARCI-GAY pass** (1 year, €10). Also check with **Circolo di Cultura Omosessuale Mario Mieli** (☎06 54 13 985).

ANCIENT CITY

Oppio Caffè, V. delle Terme de Tito 72 (☎06 47 45 262; www.oppiocaffe.it). ⓂB-Colosseo. From the Colosseum, walk up V. Nicola Salvi to the corner of V. delle Terme de Tito. Step through the automatic sliding glass doors into a neon paradise. Color-changing lights and funky art surround a pit with translucent tables in this hip bar overlooking one of history's bloodiest arenas. Check out your dreads in the reflective metal ceiling and get your thump on as DJs pump out indie-electronic beats. Mixed drinks €7. Beer €6-7. Wine €5-6. M, W, F-Su DJs. Live music 1 Th per month. Happy hour daily 5-10pm; buffet and 1 drink €10. Wheelchair-accessible. Open daily 7am-2am. AmEx/D/MC/V over €15.

Tree Folk's, V. Capo d'Africa 29 (☎ 06 97 61 52 72). ⓂB-Colosseo. Walk around the Colosseum and make a left on V. Capo d'Africa. The music and decor is a cocktail of American, German, and British classics in this creative pub that caters to your inner beer connoisseur with 10 delectable taps (€5). You'll have to be drunk to understand why the special Summer Lightning beer is only imported during the winter. Mutton €7-12. Massively delicious salads €7-10. Wine €5 per glass. Wheelchair-accessible. Open daily 7pm-2am. D/MC/V.

Ice Club, V. della Madonna dei Monti 18/19 (☎06 97 84 55 81; www.iceclub-broma.it). From V. Cavour, walk up V. dei Serpenti and make a left on V. della Madonna dei Monti. Ditch your shorts and head into the only bar in Rome made completely of ice—glasses included. The €15 cover includes a coat, gloves, and drink. Down a bunch of vodka (€7) or mixed drinks (€8) quickly, or the -5°C temperature will start to get to you. Weekly special nights (check the website for dates). Wheelchair-accessible. Open daily 6pm-2am. AmEx/D/MC/V.

ComingOut, V. di San Giovanni In Laterano 8 (☎06 70 09 871; www.comingout. it). ⓂB-Colosseo. Walk around the Colosseum and make a left on V. di San Giovanni In Laterano. Look for a backlit rainbow facade and come out to this trendy GLBT bar overlooking the Ancient City's most famous monuments. White leather upholstery, bleached walls and floor, and funkadelic music. 40+ imaginative mixed drinks €5-6. Beer €3-5. Tu 11pm in winter live drag shows. Wheelchair-accessible. Open daily 10am-2am. AmEx/D/MC/V.

CENTRO STORICO

Société Lutèce, Vco. di Montevecchio 17 (☎06 68 30 14 72). Take V. di Parione from V. del Governo Vecchio; bear straight and then make a left onto Vco. di Montevecchio. Effortlessly hip. The perfect place for a pre- or post-dinner drink. Wine €6 per glass. Mixed drinks €7-8. The vaguely Middle Eastern apertif buffet is fresh, yummy, substantial, and included. Wheelchair accessible. Open daily 6pm-2am. MC/V.

Caffé Fandango, P. di Pietra 32/33 (☎06 45 47 29 13; www.caffefandango.net). Off V. dei Pastini. Bar and cultural space attracts a young crowd for live music and other performances. Wine €5-7. Mixed drinks €7-8. *Aperitivo con buffet* (7-10pm) €10, including drink. Wheelchair accessible. Open Tu-Su noon-2am. MC/V.

Sloppy Sam's, P. Campo dei Fiori 9 (☎06 68 80 26 37). This popular pub is packed with visiting students even on a Tuesday. Numerous drink specials and a window on the action on Campo dei Fiori. Wheelchair accessible. Happy hour M-F 4pm-8pm; bottled beer and pints €4, mixed drinks €6.50, house win €3 per glass. Other specials nightly, some requiring student ID. Open daily 4pm-2am. AmEx/MC/V.

Rialto Santambrogio, V. de Sant' Ambrogio 4 (☎06 68 13 36 40; www.rialto.roma.it). Easiest to approach from V. del Portico. Tucked away in the Jewish Ghetto in a more or less unmarked building; pay close attention to the street numbers. Rialto isn't a bar, pub, club, or *discotheque:* it's a *centro sociale,* where serious scenesters meet to hear music, dance to visiting DJs, see art, and talk left politics. No such thing as regular hours—your best bet's to check the website for a schedule of events.

TRASTEVERE

This medieval neighborhood is home to the highest concentration of bars popular among Rome's young residents, visitors, and students. Hop on the H bus from Termini or take tram #8 from Largo Argentina to reach **Viale Trastevere,** the main thoroughfare. The epicenter of nightlife is P. Trilussa, west of Vle. Trastevere, just across from Ponte Sisto. In the summer, many bars set up outposts along the Tiber River, from P. Trilussa to Isola Tiberina, the island in the middle of the river (which also hosts free outdoor movie screenings on a massive display).

- 🏴 **Bir & Fud,** V. Benedetta 23 (☎06 58 94 016; www.birefud.it), behind the P. Trilussa fountain. Delicious, frequently changing Italian craft beers flow from about 20 taps and all organic food graces plates in this taste bud heaven. Co-owner and brewmaster Leonardo takes a break from perfecting his own highly original and uniformly amazing beers at the Birra del Borgo brewery (birradelborgo.it) to come by and engage other beer connoisseurs on weekends. Try the Ke-To Re-Porter (a lighter porter spiced with fermented Kentucky tobacco), the My Antonia (a savory brew originating from a partnership between Leonardo and the Dogfish Head brewmaster), the Rubus (a refreshing raspberry beer with all the fruit but none of the heaviness of a lambic), or the Opperbacco TripIIpa (a cross between a Belgian triple and an IPA with amarillo accents). Beer €5-70. Pizza €5-12. *Fritti* €3-9. Open daily 7pm-2am. AmEx/D/MC/V.

- **Ma Che Siete Venuti A Fà,** V. Benedetta 25 (☎06 97 27 52 18; www.football-pub. com), behind the P. Trilussa fountain. Owned by the same beer luminaries as Bir & Fud, this smaller counterpart across the street specializes in unpasteurized, unfiltered beers hand-picked from international breweries on beer scouting trips. If you want a Coke, go to Applebees; there is absolutely nothing but the 16 taps, 100+ bottled beers, and their fans in the tiny wooden shack of an interior, filled with soccer memorabilia and kegs, and no loud music to take the focus off of malt beverages and good conversation. Try the Montegioco Makkestout, a dry stout with excellent mouth feel brewed especially for the bar. Pints and 33cl bottles €5, 75cl bottles €15. Open daily 3pm-2am. The website lists the new beers you can expect each week. Cash only.

- **On the Rox,** P. San Giovanni della Malva 14 (☎06 81 10 857 or 34 09 05 19 92; www.ontherox.com). In the *piazza* near the back right corner of P. Trilussa as you face the fountain. Owned and staffed by foreign nationals, this second iteration of On the Rox maintains the international student focus of the original in Testaccio. Beer pong and American breakfast (bacon, eggs and pancakes or bust) cure the homesick, while pump-up music and student discounts (Carlsberg pints €3.50, shots €2.50, mixed drinks €5) really broaden the scholar patrons' smiles. All major sports shown until 2am, at which point you can transfer to the Testaccio location and watch until 5am. Mixed drinks €6-8. Beer €6. Daily *aperitivo* from 6-9pm delivers a free buffet with drink purchase. Open daily 9am-2am. AmEx/MC/V.

- **Baccanale,** V. della Lungaretta 81 (☎06 45 44 82 68), 1 block off P. Santa Maria. The hundreds of bottles of Bacardi rum that surround you are needed to produce massive quantities of mojito (€15 per L) for the mixed-age crowd that gathers to watch live matches on the exaggerated number of TVs lining the small interior (great viewing angle guaranteed). Latin and pop music. Full kitchen open until 1am. Pints €5. Bottled beer €3.50. Mixed drinks €5-7. 1L drinks €20-25. Happy hour 4-7pm; beer and mixed drinks €4. Get a drink, bruschetta, primo, and coffee for €10. Open daily 11am-2am. AmEx/D/MC/V.

Café Friends, P. Trilussa 34 (☎06 58 16 111; www.cafefriends.it), to the left as you face the fountain. Lights speckling the dark walls like stars and minimalist chic furniture add to the ambience as loud pop energizes the stylish clientele. Full kitchen open until 1am. Free Wi-Fi. Every Tu in winter live jazz and weekly DJ nights (check website for schedule). Beer €5-6. Mixed drinks €6-7.50. Wine €5-6. Happy hour daily 7-10pm; beer and wine €5, mixed drinks €6. Open M-Sa 7:30am-2am, Su 6pm-2am. AmEx/D/MC/V.

Caffè della Scala, V. della Scala 4 (☎06 58 03 610), before the street intersects with P. San Egidio. Proprietress-bartender extraordinaire Frances offers creative drinks with unusual ingredients that are only served when she is tending bar. Try the potent Christian Alexander (Canadian whiskey, *creme de cacao,* and cardamom pods; €7.50) and the Black Velvet (Guinness and *prosecco;* €6) in the dim, sexy interior as classic pop selections fill the air. *Aperitivo* 7-9pm. Mixed drinks €6-8. Beer mixed drinks €4.50-6. Shots €3. Beer €4.50-5. Wine €3.50-5. Spirits €4-7. Snacks €1.50. Open daily 5pm-2am. Cash only.

TERMINI

Twin's Bar, V. Giolitti 67 (☎06 48 24 932; www.twinbar.com). Directly across from Termini. Bar, restaurant, lounge, and disco bathed in red offers free Wi-Fi, multiple bars, lively indoor and outdoor dancefloors, and live sports on many TVs. DJs pump out diverse beats Th-Su, based on the night's theme (check the website for details). Downstairs, the private room is decked out in armor suits. Wine €4. Beer €4.50. Mixed drinks €7-8. Happy hour 4-7pm: 20% discount on everything and 2-for-1 mixed drinks. Open daily 7pm-2am. AmEx/D/MC/V.

Old Station Club and Pub, P. Santa Maria Maggiore (☎06 47 46 612; www.oldstationmusicpub.it). To the left when facing the eastern entrance of the church. Noise-isolating speakers allow the 3 rooms in this basement club-pub to have their own music and volume level. Daily DJs spin hip-hop, R&B, and techno while people mingle at the bar and lounge in the chill room. In good pub form, the versatile venue shows all major sports. Beer and wine €5. Mixed drinks €8. Shots €3. Every F beer €3, mixed drinks €5, and 1 free shot every hr. Students get €1 off beer and €3 off mixed drinks with ID. Cover during private parties only, max €10, including 1 drink. Open daily 8pm-4am. AmEx/D/MC/V.

Libreria Caffé Bohèmien, V. degli Zingari 36 (☎33 97 22 46 22; margherita-cirillo@libero.it). From V. Cavour, turn onto V. Serpenti and make a right at the fountain to get to V. degli Zingari. Grab a book off the wall below a rotating painting by a young, local artist and dive into your crepe or gulash (€6) as you enjoy piano or classic pop music. Live professional piano performances every weekend; amateur performances at will. Head down the candle-lit stairs to stretch out on a couch in the basement, or sink into the plush, Victorian-style seats upstairs. *Aperitivi* 7-9pm: food and a drink €8. Wine, mixed drinks, organic beer, teas with wine or spirits €5. Open in summer M-Sa 11am-3pm and 7pm-2am, in winter M and W-Su 11am-3pm and 7pm-2am. Cash only.

NOMENTANA

Alien, V. Velletri 13/19 (☎06 84 12 212; www.aliendisco.it; www.myspace.com/aliendisco). Take bus #38 from Termini to Fiume. One of Rome's biggest and most famous discos, it is a scene for those wanting to be seen. Green laser light accompanies beats pumped out by internationally renowned DJs. Attracts a well-dressed, happenin' crowd that packs it every night. Mostly get-up-and-dance house music on weekends and more eclectic fare during the week. Theme nights are frequent, but vary. Cover about €15-20, including 1 drink. Drinks around €10. Open Tu-Su midnight-4:30am. MC/V.

TESTACCIO AND OSTIENSE

▨ **L'Oasi della Birra,** P. Testaccio 38/41 (☎06 57 46 122; www.ristorantidiroma.com/oasi.htm). From V. Marmorata, turn left on V. A. Manuzio and right on P. Testaccio. You'll think it's a mirage in the middle of the club desert until you actually pay the bill. Enjoy affordable, incredibly delicious drinks and food before getting sloshed on expensive, bad selections on the dance floors in the area. The beer catalog boasts over 500 types from all over the world, arranged by region and type (most bottles €4.50), and there is a selection of wines (€10+ per bottle) and grappa in the quadruple digits. Gourmet meats and cheeses are similarly numerous and delectable (try 6 types for €15.50, 8 for €18.50). Happy hour daily 5-8:15pm; food and a drink €10. Open daily 5pm-midnight. AmEx/D/MC/V.

▨ **Akab,** V. di Monte Testaccio 69 (☎06 57 25 05 85; www.akabcave.com). One of Rome's most famous clubs has the potential for entirely different scenes every night on each of 3 dance floors. Advanced ventilation and an expensive permit allow smoking on the primary floor, a large area covered by a metal roof and flanked by a blue-lit bar on one side and a red-lit private table area on the other. On the main floor: Tu techno; Th hiphop, R&B, and rap; F-Sa pop and mix. If you get in, get ready to rub elbows with tons of Rome's hippest club-goers doing their thing and possibly some famous musical talents (50 Cent and Fabolous performed here in 2009). Drinks €10. Cover €10-15 includes 1 drink; more expensive during special performances (check website). Open Tu and Th-Sa 10:30pm-4:30am. AmEx/D/MC/V.

Conte Staccio, V. di Monte Testaccio 65/b (☎06 57 28 97 12; www.myspace.com/contestaccio). Good genes and a slightly alternative style will get you into this club, atypical for V. di Monte Testaccio in that it replaces dancing with live bands (2-3 per night), most blasting indie rock, with reggae and pop-electro thrown in. Head inside to view the performances, or stick around the outdoor bar and watch it go down on the massive projection screen. Reasonably-priced drinks (relative to the surrounding clubs) made with flair by experienced bartenders; orange peels are set ablaze and used to sweeten glass rims before being corkscrewed into garnish strips for cosmos. Music midnight-3:30am. Kitchen serves typical Roman pasta dishes (€8-10). Mixed drinks €8. Beer €6. Wine €5. Open Tu-Su 8pm-5am. Kitchen open 8pm-3am. AmEx/D/MC/V.

Coyote, V. di Monte Testaccio 48B, (☎34 02 41 20 74; www.coyotebar.it). Reserved for the hip-conscious: there's no Ugly involved with this Coyote. The line outside is as long as the one at the Vatican, but it leads to blaring music and an energetic young crowd on a rooftop dancefloor built onto Monte Testaccio instead of a bunch of old art. Color-changing, moving LED lamps around the bar provide an update to the disco ball and induce stage-dancing in front of the projection screen. DJs playing different music throughout the week; check website for details. Cover F-Sa after 2am €5, includes 1 beer. Beer €5. Champagne cocktails €5. Mixed drinks €8. Open daily 10pm-5am. AmEx/D/MC/V.

ROME

OSTIA

In the summer, many Roman clubs shut down operations in the city and head out to the beach. Most are in Ostia, the closest beach to the center, with some notable others in Fregene and elsewhere. For example, **Gilda on the Beach** is the summer version of one of Rome's most famous, upscale discos is at Lungomare di Ponente 11, in Fregene, 40km from city center. (Take the Fregene bus #1 from ⓂA-Lepanto. ☎06 66 56 06 49; www.gildabar.it. Open daily 11pm-4am. Cover €20.). To get to Ostia, head to ⓂB-Piramide. At the top of the stairs, turn left and follow signs to Ferrovia Roma-Lido. Your Metro ticket includes the train ride to Ostia Lido Centro (30min., every 15min. daily 5:40am-11:30pm). Beginning at 11:30pm, the **N3 bus** runs every 30-45min. from P. Venezia to Ostia and back. The train from Piramide and the N3 run along the beach to Ple. Cristoforo Colombo, and buses #06, 061, and 062 traverse the seaside until midnight. After that, be prepared for long walks between the bar clusters near different train stops if you have to hoof it; call a cab if you don't feel like walking the 5km length of Ostia's shore.

🏨 **Open Bar,** Lungomare Lutazio Catulo 6 (☎33 84 59 77 28; www.open-bar.it). Ⓜ️Lido Castelfusano. Take a dip in one of 2 large pools (open M-Th and Su) or relax on the patio overlooking the ocean to cool off, after kicking it to tunes blasted by nightly DJs inside, which resembles a ski lodge with glass walls. Tu electronica, F house, Su "happy" oldies and classics, other days pop mix. Drinks €5-10. Happy hour Sa-Su 9-11:30pm satiates your hunger and cocktail thirst for €10. Eponymous F feature an open bar from 11pm-close: men €20, women €10. Check the website for special performances and events. Open in summer M, F, Sa 9pm-4:30am; Tu-Th and Su 8pm-2am. Open in winter F-Sa 9pm-4:30am. AmEx/D/MC/V.

🏨 **Faber Beach,** Lungomare Paolo Toscanelli 191 (☎06 56 13 849; www.faberbeach.com). Ⓜ️Lido Centro. Walk 15min. or take a bus west, down the beach. Young, pretty people populate this wild and crazy private beach-cum-club, where nightly DJs throw down tracks from a guard tower-inspired booth high above the beach dance floor. Check up on the party or the object of your stalking before you get there via live webcam. Mix of rock, reggae, hip hop, and house; W and some Sa "happy revival" from 70s and 80s. Every F in summer live Italian bands. Australian beers, mixed drinks, and spirits €5-10. Open M-W and Su until 2am, Th-Sa until 3 or 4am. MC/V.

Shilling, Ple. Cristoforo Colombo 25 (☎06 56 47 07 28; www.larotonda.it). Ⓜ️Lido Cristoforo Colombo. Massive hanging paper lanterns and shapely wooden furniture add to the stylish edge of this island resort-themed restaurant and disco. Slightly dressier than your average club, it caters to a classy and slightly older (but still very drunk) clientele. Disco open Th-Sa from about 11pm until 4:30am. Th pop mix, F-Sa rap, R&B, and hip-hop. Drinks €5-10. Tea time and aperitif until 11pm, 8pm in winter. Restaurant open daily in summer from Apr. 7 to Sept. 30 12:30-3:30pm and 8pm-midnight, rest of year 12:30-4pm. Cover €15. AmEx/MC/V.

▶ DAYTRIPS FROM ROME

SPERLONGA

Trains run daily from Rome to the Formia station (1¼-1½hr., 2-3 per hr., €7.40). From the station, take the blue COTRAL bus (30min., 7-11 per day, €1) to Sperlonga. Purchase tickets at the station's tabaccheria. Get off at P. Europa at the top of hill, or, for those wishing to hit the beach, at any of the stops along Vle. Cristoforo Colombo. In P. Repubblica, there is a tabaccheria that sells tickets for COTRAL buses. Facing the tabaccheria, the street to the right of the piazza, V. Ottaviano, winds its way down to the sea and to Vle. Cristoforo Colombo. There are also several burrow-like paths and stairways that lead down the hill to the shore. Note that because Sperlonga's main road is so long, addresses are identified using km rather than plain numbers. However, since the main attractions are fairly close together, you won't really be walking that far.

Sperlonga (spehr-LON-ga; pop. 3102) served as Emperor Tiberius' imperial getaway until he moved to Capri in AD 26. Well worth the trip from Rome, Sperlonga's curving, whitewashed streets lead through cobblestoned *piazze* to sparkling sands and sapphire waters. While *stabilimenti* control some of the town's beach, there's little reason to pay their fees unless you must have color-coordinated beach chairs and umbrellas. The public shore, which is free, is just as spectacular.

Be proud: you're now part of a long and illustrious tradition of daytrippers to Sperlonga. Tiberius used to invite his wealthy Roman friends to enjoy a Tyrrhenian vacation with him. The Emperor and his pals would chill inside his seaside **speluncae** (grottoes), which gave the town its name, and which you're more than welcome to inspect today. A few feet away from the grottoes is the modern and well-exhibited **Museo Archeologico**, V. Flacca 16,600km, where you can see the statuary ruins of Tiberius' villa. The nautically-themed collection represents scenes from Homer's *Odyssey* including the blinding of Polyphemus the cyclops and the attack on Ulysses's boat by the monster Scylla. (10-15min. walk from P. Europa. ☎07 71 54 80 28. Open daily 9:30am-7:30pm. €2, under 18 and over 65 free.)

Sperlonga also served as a refuge for those fleeing barbarian attacks on Rome in the AD sixth century—watchtowers along the coast remain from this period of unrest. In 1534, the town was destroyed by Barbarossa, and it wasn't until the 18th and 19th centuries that Sperlonga regained its popularity as a vacation spot. At its mid-20th century peak, it attracted guests like Albert Camus, Marlene Dietrich, and Andy Warhol. While some of the glitter has faded, Emperor Tiberius's villa and fish-filled grottoes remain popular sights for all who visit this beach getaway.

Facing the cliffside view, hang a left from P. Europa and walk about 30m to get to the Tourist Info Center at C. San Leone 23. There will be a decrepit church to the left and a restaurant to the right. (☎0771 55 70 00; www.comunedisperlonga.it. Open daily 8am-8pm.)

PONTINE ISLANDS

The Pontine Islands are accessible by aliscafi (hydrofoils) or slower, cheaper traghetti (ferries). The closest port to Rome with service to the islands is Anzio. Take the Termini-Nettuno train to Anzio (1hr., every hr. 6am-11pm, €3.20). From the station, head downhill on V. Paolina, then go through P. Battisti onto V. dei Fabbri, and through the next piazza to C. del Popolo. Or take a taxi from the station to the quay (€10). From the port, take the CAREMAR ferry to Ponza (2hr.; M-F 8:45am, Sa 8:30am, Su 8:30am and 3pm; Ponza to Anzio M-Sa 5:15pm, Su and holidays 11am and 5:15pm; €23.40). The CAREMAR ticket office is in the white booth labeled "traghetto" on the quay (☎06 98 60 00 83; www.caremar.it) and in Ponza (☎07 71 80 565). The Linee Vetor hydrofoils are smaller, faster, and leave more frequently. If you take one, however, you'll miss the glorious views that the ferry affords you (1hr. 20min, 2-6 per day, €27-35). The Linee Vetor ticket office is on the quay in Anzio, at no. 40 (☎06 98 45 083; www.vetor.it; open 1hr. before departure) and on the dock in Ponza (☎07 71 80 549).

The Pontine Islands (pop. 4000), a stunning archipelago 40km off the coast of Anzio, offer both striking beauty and intriguing history and lore. These small islands were once believed to be home of the sorceress Circe, who captured and seduced the Greek hero Odysseus and transformed his crew into pigs. Nero was exiled here and Mussolini cast enemies of the state into the 30 million-year-old volcanic residuum, only to be imprisoned here himself. The cliff-sheltered beaches, turquoise waters, coves, tunnels, and grottoes have also provided pirates a place to unwind after pillaging and plundering. You'll be hard-pressed to find an English speaker in this isolated area.

The most accessible and well-supplied island is **Ponza,** with superb beaches and cheerfully colored cliffside residences. As of this writing, **Chiaia,** a beautiful beach 10min. walk from the port, was closed. Ask if it's reopened; if not, locals recommend **Spiaggia di Frontone** as a substitute; it's about a 20min. walk. A beautiful if slightly pulse-quickening ▧**bus ride** (€2.40; buy onboard) around hairpin turns and blind drives leads to what is perhaps the island's most appealing feature, the glorious **Piscine Naturali.** Take the bus to Le Foma and ask to be let off at the *piscine*, or just follow the throngs of people who get off there. Facing the water, the bus stop is to your left, along V. Carlo Pisacane, just past the San Antonio Tunnel, about 3-5min. from the quay; look for the blue buses. Once you exit the bus at the Piscine stop, go down the long, steep path—it's marked by signs. It takes approximately 5-10min. to get to the bottom of the hill. Cliffs crumbling into the ocean create a series of deep, crystal-clear natural pools separated by smooth rock outcroppings perfect for sunbathing. Snorkeling, exploring the rocks, and jumping off the cliffs will make you feel like a modern-day Jacques Cousteau. (The last of these activities is somewhat dangerous—exercise caution and good judgment.)

The western-most Pontine island is **Palmarola;** it features irregular volcanic rock formations and steep, white cliffs. To get to Palmarola, rent a boat (from €45 per day), or take one of the boat tours advertised at the port. The tiny island of **Zannone** is home to a wildlife preserve. Try **Cooperativa Barcaioli Ponzesi,** in the San Antonio tunnel off V. Carlo Pisacane, for boat tours. (☎07 71 80 99 29. Open 9am-midnight. Tours vary in length and price; first leaves 9am, and last returns at 8pm. Reservations necessary.) Tours of Zannone, which is part of the **Circeo National Park,** take visitors around the coast, with time for walks through forests filled with wild sheep and excursions to the medieval, legend-filled **San Spirito monastery.**

OSTIA ANTICA

From Rome, take Ⓜ️B to Piramide (€1). At the top of the stairs, turn left and follow signs to Ferrovia Roma-Lido. Your Metro ticket includes the train ride to Ostia Antica (30min., every 15min. daily 5:40am-11:30pm). After disembarking at Ostia Antica, exit the station and cross the road using the blue pedestrian footbridge. Walk down V. della Stazione di Ostia Antica and cross Vle. dei Romagnoli; entrance is on the left at the end of V. degli Scavi di Ostia Antica. Ticket booth is on the right, after the parking lot. Museum ☎ 06 56 35 02 15. Ruins open daily Apr.-Oct. 8:30am--7pm, Oct.-Nov. 8:30am-6pm, Nov.-Feb. 8:30am--5pm; Mar. 8:30am-6pm. Parking €2.50. Maps €2 at ticket booth. Museum open Tu-Sa 9am-1:15pm and 2:15-6:30pm and Su 9am-1:15pm. Last entry 1hr. before closing. Ruins and museum €6.50, EU citizens ages 18-25 €3.25, under 18 and over 65 free.

An immense archaeological park, Ostia Antica is an ideal environment to experience ancient Roman life away from the crowds in the Roman Forum. According to legend, Ostia was founded in the seventh century BC by King Ancus Martius to protect the *ostium* (mouth) of the Tiber River from would-be invaders. As the years progressed, Ostia blossomed into Rome's busiest commercial port. The Tiber's sedimentary deposits have pushed this former seaside spot 4km from the coast. Nevertheless, Ostia continues to awe travelers with its extensive and intimate **ruins**—an unparalleled glimpse into Roman life.

The **necropolis,** located on V. Ostiense outside of the city walls, greets visitors upon entering the ruins. Tombs vary in size and simplicity, depending on the economic standing of the deceased. V. Ostiense ends at the **Porta Romana,** the entrance to the ancient city, which was once guarded by two towers. From here, **Decumanus Maximus,** the city's main road, leads to the **forum.** As you walk down Decumanus Maximus, an amazing AD first-century statue of Minerva graces the left side, followed by the *horrea* (warehouses), where everything from grain to perfume was stored. Farther down on the right lie the **Terme di Nettuno** (Baths of Neptune). Walk up the steep stairs to see the magnificent black and white **mosaic** of Neptune riding a *quadriga* of *hippocampi*, mythical creatures with the heads of horses and bodies of fish. Continuing down the main road, an ancient *enoteca*, as well as the **teatro,** built by Agrippa and enlarged by Commodus and Septimus Severus. Inside, 4000 Romans would enjoy lewd plays filled with obscene puns, performed strictly by men wearing brown masks for male roles and white masks for female roles. Two millennia later, the theater continues to entertain Romans during the summer.

The forum lies at the center of the city, with the imposing **Capitolium** dominating the *piazza*. Merchants, politicians, and travelers used to flood this formidable center of global commerce in its glory days. In addition to baths, a 20-person **foriza** (latrine) remains well preserved. Make a right on V. dei Mollini to reach a small **museum** containing sarcophagi, busts, and Roman copies of Greek statues found among the ruins. Besides being a great place for a game of hide and seek, Ostia Antica offers a personal, engaging look into Rome's history, away from the mobs of tourists and honking horns of the Fori Romani and Imperiali. Wear sturdy, comfortable shoes, as the ancient streets are often uneven and rocky.

TIVOLI

From ⓂB-Rebibbia, exit the station, turn right, and follow signs for Tivoli through an underpass to reach the other side of V. Tiburtina. Take the blue COTRAL bus to Tivoli (35-45min., €2). Tickets are sold at the tabaccheria right next to the bus stop. Disembark at Ple. delle Nazioni Unite. The return bus to Rome stops across Vle. Arnaldi from the Ple. delle Nazioni Unite stop; it's right in front of the Giardino Garibaldi, recognizable by its playground and children's activities. Tivoli is perhaps more easily accessible by rail (1hr., €2.30). Exit the train station and make a right, heading down the hill. Cross the roundabout at the bottom of the hill to reach the entrance of Villa Gregoriana.

Tivoli (TEE-vo-lee; pop. 49,342) is an awe-inspiring hilltop town poised 120m above the Aniene River where poets Horace, Catullus, and Propertius all once had homes along the rocky cliffs. Today, Tivoli is a beautifully preserved medieval city, with narrow, winding streets and panoramic views of surrounding valleys. Though the three main villas listed below are Tivoli's chief attractions, the tourist office provides a fantastic 🖼map detailing lesser known sites, including a 15th-century castle, an ancient Roman amphitheater, several churches, and Gothic-style houses, all within walking distance of the bus stop.

Villa d'Este, a castle and garden, was laid out by Cardinal Ercole d'Este (the son of Lucrezia Borgia) and his architect Piero Ligorio in 1550 to recreate an ancient Roman pleasure palace. The villa is known for the ingenious and abundant **fountains,** particularly the hydraulic organ. Beneath these famed bubblers lie dank grottoes and three reflecting pools filled with fish. The **Fontana di Diana Efesia,** a statue of a decaying multi-breasted goddess, lies behind the sprinkler-infested gardens. Additionally, the villa itself has a fantastic collection of frescoes and some modern art. One room tells the tale of Hercules, legendary founder of the house of Este. (Walk through the P. Trento's souvenir stands to reach Villa d'Este. ☎07 74 31 20 70; www.villadestetivoli.info. Open Tu-Su May-Aug. 8:30am-6:45pm; Sept. 8:30am-6:15pm; Oct. 8:30am-5:30pm; Nov.-Jan. 8:30am-4pm; Feb. 8:30am-4:30pm; Mar. 8:30am-5:15pm; Apr. 8:30am-6:30pm. €9, EU citizens 18-24 €6, EU citizens under 18 or over 65 free. Audio tour €4.)

🖼**Villa Gregoriana,** at the other end of town, is a park with hiking trails that wind over majestic waterfalls and the alleged caves of Neptune and the Sirens. Tivoli's **Temple of Vesta,** a better-preserved version of the one in the Roman Forum, can be admired from lookouts. The trail winds down the cliffs to the base of the waterfalls and up across the Valley of Hell, ending at the Temple of Vesta. A nice respite from crowded Rome, the villa has many benches and grottoes for reading and relaxing. Give yourself at least an hour to explore, and wear comfortable shoes. (From P. Garibaldi, walk down V. Pacifici, which becomes V. del Trevio; turn left on V. Palatina and left again on V. di Ponte Gregoriano. Cross the bridge; the entrance to Villa Gregoriana is on the left. ☎39 96 77 61. Open daily from Apr. to mid-Oct. 10am-6:30pm; from mid-Oct. to Nov. and Mar. 10am-2:30pm; Dec.-Feb. by reservation only. €4, ISIC holders €3.20, ages 4-12 €2, EU citizens under 18 or over 65 free. Audio tour €4.)

Return to the square and catch bus #4 (€1) by the playground in P. Garibaldi to reach the remains of **Villa Adriana,** the largest and most expensive villa built under the Roman Empire. Ask the bus driver to let you off close to the entrance. Emperor Hadrian, inspired by his travels, designed its AD second-century buildings with an international flair. He often retired here to escape bad moods and pursue artistic endeavors. Look for the *pecile*, built to recall the famous *Stoa Poikile* (Painted Porch) of Athens, and the *canopus*, a statue-lined expanse of water built to replicate a canal in Alexandria, Egypt. (6km from Tivoli proper; take the orange bus #4 from P. Garibaldi's tabaccheria, which sells bus tickets. From the parking lot, head uphill away from the villa until you reach a small COTRAL bus sign. ☎07 74 38 27 33. Open daily 9am-7:30pm. Last entry 1hr. before closing. Parking €2. €6.50, EU citizens 18-24 €3.25, EU citizens under 18 or over 65 free. Archaeological tour €3.50. Audio tour €4.)

There is a helpful **tourist kiosk** in Ple. delle Nazione Unite that offers maps, bus schedules, and info on the villas. (Open Tu-Su 10am-1pm and 4-6pm.)

PIEDMONT (PIEMONTE) AND VALLE D'AOSTA

PIEDMONT (PIEMONTE)

More than just the source of the Po River, Piedmont (pee-yeh-MON-tay) is a fountainhead of nobility and fine cuisine. The area rose to prominence in 1861 when the Savoys selected Turin as capital of their reunified Italy in 1861. The capital relocated only four years later, and Piedmont fell back into obscurity. Today, European tourists escape whirl-wind urban pace on the banks of Lake Maggiore, while outdoor enthusiasts and expert skiers conquer Alpine mountains to the northeast. Sometimes called the "Prussia of Italy," Piedmont is renowned for its high standard of living and modern, well-organized infrastructure. Since Turin hosted the Winter Olympics in 2006, the region's profile has only continued to rise.

HIGHLIGHTS OF PIEDMONT AND VALLE D'AOSTA

EAT at Turin's enormous Eataly, a combination restaurant, cooking school, museum, and fresh food market (p. 139).

CONQUER the glacial slopes beneath the great Matterhorn (p. 151).

TURIN (TORINO)   ☎011

A century and a half before Turin (toh-REE-no; pop. 910,000) hosted the 2006 Winter Olympics, it served as the first capital of unified Italy. The city is characterized by contemporary art masterpieces, and some of Italy's best nightlife. Though Turin's cultural offerings rival Milan's, it manages to avoid pollution and crime problems that plague larger cities. One of the greenest Italian metropolises, Turin is a pedestrian dream: numerous parks and charming Po River treat visitors to everything from boating tours to outdoor nightlife.

▛ TRANSPORTATION

Flights: Caselle Airport (www.aeroportoditorino.it) services European destinations. From Pta. Nuova, take blue Sadem buses to "Caselle Airport," via Pta. Susa (☎011 30 00 611; 40min., €5.50). Buses run regularly to the airport (5:15am-11:15pm) and to the city (6:05am-12:05am). Buy tickets at Bar Cervino, C. V. Emanuele II 57; Bar Mille Luci, P. XVIII Dicembre 5, at newsstand on corner of Corso V. Emanuele II and P. Felice, on left when exiting station, or onboard (€0.50 surcharge). Airport train goes from Torino Dora to airport (20min., every 30min., €3.40). To get to Torino Dora station, take tram #10 from Torino Porta Susa, or buses #46 or 49.

Trains: Stazione Porta Nuova (☎011 66 53 098), on C. V. Emanuele II. The station has a **post office,** luggage storage. To: **Genoa** (2hr., every hr. 5:20am-11:50pm, €8.80); **Milan Centrale** (2hr., every hr. 4:50am-10:50pm, €9); **Rome Termini** (6-7hr., 25 per day 4:50am-11:50pm, from €64); **Venice Santa Lucia** (5hr., 20 per day 4:50am-10:50pm, from €22). Turin's **Stazione Porta Susa** is one stop toward Milan and runs TGV trains to **Paris** via **Lyon, France** (5-6hr.; 8:11, 9:40am, 5:35, 7:05, 9:18pm; around €95).

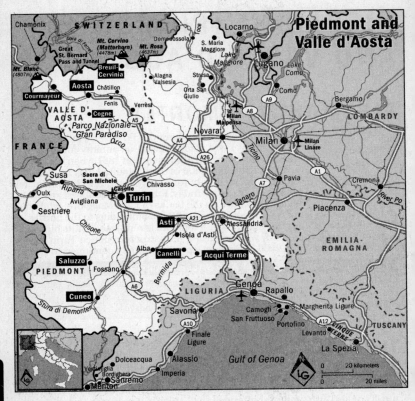

Piedmont and Valle d'Aosta

Buses: Autostazione Terminal Bus, C. V. Emanuele II 131/H in front of the Court (☎011 43 38 100). From Pta. Nuova, take tram #9 or 15 (5 stops). Ticket office open daily 6:30am-1:15pm and 2-8:30pm. Serves ski resorts, the Riviera, and the valleys of Susa and Pinerolo. To **Aosta** (2hr., M-F 3 per day, €7.50), **Courmayeur** via Aosta (4hr., €8.40), and **Milan** (2hr., every hr., €8.70).

Public Transportation: Buy tickets at *tabaccherie*, newsstands, or bars. Buses run daily 5am-1am, some routes stop at midnight. 70min. ticket to **city buses** and **trams** €1; 1-day ticket €3. Metro tickets single-use only, but valid for 70min. for other modes of transport. Get public transport map with buses and trams from tourist office.

Taxis: ☎011 57 37, 57 30, or 33 99.

Car Rental: in Stazione Porta Nuova, on the right side by the platforms. **Avis,** C. Turati 37 (☎011 50 11 07). Open M-F 8:30am-noon and 2:30-6:30pm, Sa 8:30am-noon. **Europcar,** V. Nizza 346 (☎011 69 60 284). Open daily 7am-11pm. C. Grosetto 152 (☎011 22 29 802). Open daily 8:30am-1pm and 2:30-6:30pm.

Bike Rental: Club Amici della Bicicletta, V. S. Domenico 28 (☎011 56 13 059; clubamicidellabici@email.it) and **Bici & Dintorni,** Vle. Bistolfi 20/a (☎011 339 582 9332 and 44 23 014; www.biciedintorni.org). Both €4 per 6hr., €8 per day.

🔳 🔢 ORIENTATION AND PRACTICAL INFORMATION

Stazione Porta Nuova, in the heart of the city, is the usual place of arrival. The city itself is an Italian rarity: its pre-designed streets meet at right angles, making it easy to navigate by bus and foot. **Corso Vittorio Emanuele II** runs east past the station to the **Po River,** where it intersects **Parco del Valentino** on the south and the **Murazzi** district on the north. **Via Roma,** the major north-south thoroughfare, houses many banks and the principal sights and shops. North of the station, it heads through **Piazza Carlo Felice, Piazza San Carlo,** and **Piazza Castello.** From P. Castello, **Via Pietro Micca** extends southwest to **Piazza Solferino** where the tourist office is located, while **Via Po** veers southeast to **Piazza Vittorio Veneto** and the University district, intersecting the river above the Murazzi. **Via Giuseppe Garibaldi** stretches west from P. Castello to **Piazza Statuto** and **Stazione Porta Susa,** a launching point for international trains and the metro to the suburbs. Above P. Castello, the **Palazzo Reale** and **Giardini Reali** lie below the **Corso Regina Margherita,** which connects **Piazza della Repubblica** west to the **Docks Dora** district north of the Giardini Reali. **Via Nizza** heads south from Stazione Pta. Nuova to the **Lingotto** area which housed the former Olympic district.

Tourist Office: Turismo Torino, P. Castello 161 (☎011 53 51 81; www.turismotorino. org), at the intersection of P. Castello and V. Garibaldi. English, French, German, and Spanish spoken. Excellent map of Turin. Info on museums, cafes, hotel booking, and tour reservations. Open daily 9:30am-7pm. **Info booth** at Pta. Nuova, opposite platform 17. Open daily 10am-7pm. Volunteer-run info points near main attractions.

Currency Exchange: In Pta. Nuova. Open M and W-Sa 8am-8pm, Tu and Su 10am-5:30pm. MC/V. Otherwise try the **banks,** most with **24hr. ATMs** along V. Roma and V. Alfieri. Generally open M-F 8:20am-1:20pm and 2:20-4:20pm.

Beyond Tourism: Informagiovani, V. delle Orfane 20 (☎011 800 998 500 or 44 24 977; www.comune.torino.it/infogio). Provides info on jobs, volunteering, and enterprises for young people. Internet access. Open Tu-Sa 9:30am-6:30pm.

English-Language Bookstore: Libreria Internazionale Luxembourg, V. Accademia delle Scienze 3 (☎011 56 13 896), across from P. Carignano. Staff helps navigate 3 floors of English, French, German, and Spanish books, papers, and magazines. Open M-Sa 8am-7:30pm, Su 10am-1pm and 3-7pm.

Laundromat: "Lavasciuga" **Laundrettes and Internet Points** (www.lavasciuga.torino.it) are located throughout the city. Check website for complete list.

Pharmacy: Farmacia Boniscontro, C. V. Emanuele 66 (☎011 54 12 71). 3 blocks east of Pta. Nuova. Open 9am-12:30pm and 3pm-9am. Posts after-hours rotations. MC/V.

Hospital: San Giovanni Battista, C. Bramante 88-90 (☎011 63 31 633; molinette. piemonte.it), commonly known as Molinette. **Maria Adelaide,** V. Zuretti 29 (☎011 69 33 111; www.cto.to.it). **Mauriziano Umberto I,** Largo Turati 62 (☎011 50 81 111).

Internet Access: 1pc4you, V. Verdi 20/G (☎011 81 22 179; www.1pc4you.com), in front of the Mole, €4 per hr.; €2 per hr. with purchased card (€5, includes €3 of use). Open M-Sa 9am-10pm, Su noon-10pm. **Telecom Italia Internet Corners,** V. Roma 18, just off P. Castello. **Branch** inside the Pta. Nuova station. Both have phone card web stations. €3 per hr. Open M and W-Su 8am-10pm.

Post Office: V. Alfieri 10 (☎011 50 60 260), off P. S. Carlo. Facing north (toward P. Reale), head left 2 blocks down on the right. Fax and telegram service. Grab ticket slip by door. Open M-F 8:30am-7pm, Sa 8:30am-1pm. **Postal Code:** 10100.

PIEDMONT AND
VALLE D'AOSTA

Turin

▲ ACCOMMODATIONS

Albergo Azalea,	1 C3
Campeggio Villa Rey,	2 F2
La Foresteria degli Artisti,	3 E2
Nicosia Schaya,	4 E2
Open 011,	5 A2
Ostello Torino (HI),	6 F5

♦ FOOD

Caffè Cioccolateria al Bicerin,	
Caffè Gelateria Florio,	
Eataly,	
Hafa Café,	

Il Punto Verde,	7	B2
Le Vitel Etonné,	8	D3
Spaccanapoli,	9	D6
Stars & Roses,	10	B2
Angoletti & Friends,		

11	E3
12	D3
14	D4
15	C4
28	C2

500 meters
500 yards

Via Bezzecca
Via Crimea
Corso Fiume
Via Gatti
Via Alby
Via G. Cutreno
Via L. Cibrario
Corso C. Lanza
Viale G. Cutreno
Via S. Fermo
Corso Moncalieri
Corso Monc
Lungo Po Sardegna
Ponte Umberto I
PIAZZA CRIMEA
Corso Carolli
Viale Virgilio
Borgo e Rocca Medioevale
Parco del Valentino
Orto Botanico
Castello del Valentino
rat. Calandra
Dipendi
Corso Massimo D'Azeglio
Bike Rentals
Via San Massimo
Via Ormea
Via G. Mazzini
PIAZZA MADAMA CRISTINA
Via Baretti
Via Madama Cristina
an F. da Paola
Corso Vittorio Emanuele II
Via San Pio IV
Via Principe Tommaso
Via Caluso Valperga
TO SAN GIOVANNI BATTISTA (1km)
PINACOTECA GIOVANNI E MARELLA AGNELLI (1.5km), Via Donizetti
MUSEO NAZIONALE DELL'AUTOMOBILE (2km), LINGOTTO, 8 GALLERY & OLYMPIC VENUES (2km), Via Nizza
PIAZZA BODONI
Via B. Galliari
Via Sant'Anselmo
Via Belfore
Via Bel ore
Via Saluzzo
PIAZZA NIZZA
Via Goito
Via Belfore
Corso Guglielmo Marconi
Via Saluzzo
Via Nizza
Lagrange
Airport Bus Tickets (Newstand)
PIAZZA C. FELICE
Stazione Porta Nuova
Via Bertholiet
Via Gramsci
Settembre
Via Sacchi
Telecom Italia
Via Camerana
PIAZZA PALEOCAPA
Via San Secondo
Corso Sommeiller
Via Volta
Via Vincenzo Glioberti
TO OSPEDALE MAURIZIANO UMBERTO I (50m)
dell'Arsenale
Via Massena
C.F.Turati
Corso Re Umberto
enza
Corso Vittorio Emanuele II
Via Magenta
Via Lamarmora
Via Legnano
Via Pastrengo
Via Valeggio
Galleria Civica d'Arte Moderna
Corso Luigi Einaudi
Via Colombo
Via San Quintino
Corso Galileo Ferraris
Corso Stati Uniti
Via M. Fanti
Via Amerigo Vespucci
Corso Giacomo Matteotti
TO CASTELLO DI RIVOLI MUSEO D'ARTE CONTEMPORANEA (15km)
Via C. B. Bricherasio
Via Montevecchio
Corso Duca d'Aosta
Corso Trento
Via Magenta
Via V. Veia
Corso Filleale
Corso Duca Degli Abruzzi

NIGHTLIFE

Arancia di Mezzanotte,	**16 B2**
The Beach,	**17 F3**
Fluido,	**18 E4**
Giancarlo,	**19 E4**
Pier 7-9-11,	**23 E4**
Shore,	**24 B2**
Six Nations Murphy's Pub,	**25 D4**
Sieperotto,	**26 B2**

ACCOMMODATIONS AND CAMPING

Turin's budget accommodations are not clustered together, but several are located near Stazione Pta. Nuova. Many new hotels and residences were built to accommodate Olympic crowds. Family-run B&Bs are in some of the city's best areas, though they're required by law to close for two months each year. Many take this time in July and August, but call ahead to verify exact dates.

> **TIP**
> **WEEKEND OF TOURIN'.** The embodiment of Turin's warm welcome to visitors, the **Turin Week-End offer** includes a 2-night stay (F-Sa or Sa-Su nights) with a hotel breakfast as well as a **Torino Card** with wide access and discounts. Prices start at €59 per person; 4- to 5-star hotels cost about €89-150. Considering the hotels involved and the long list of benefits, this is a steal. All hotels bestow guests with special offers and welcome gifts. Check www.turismotorino.org for a list of hotels and offers. Reserve directly through the hotel; be sure to specify that you want the Turin Week-End offer.

Open 011, C. Venezia 11 (☎011 25 05 35; www.openzero11.it). To reach this brand-new hostel, take bus #52 (#64 on Su) from Pta. Nuova to V. Chiesa della Salute. 5min. walk from Stazione Dora. 34 gleaming rooms (2-4 beds with bathroom). Services include restaurant, bar, TV, terrace, Wi-Fi, and library. Check-in until 10pm. Reception 24hr. Dorms €16.50; singles €30; doubles €42. Reserve ahead. Cash only. ●

Ostello Torino (HI), V. Alby 1 (☎011 66 02 939; www.ostellotorino.it). Bus #52 (#64 on Su) from Pta. Nuova to the Lanza stop at V. Crimea and follow the "Ostello" signs to C. Giovanni Lanza. Turn left at V. Luigi Gatti. Breakfast included; dinner €10. Laundry €4. Reception M-Sa 7am-12:30pm and 3-11pm, Su 7-10am. Lockout 10am-3pm. Curfew 11pm; ask for key if staying out later. Closed Dec. 21-Jan. 14. Single-sex and co-ed 3- to 8-bed dorms €15; doubles €35, with bath €40; triples €51; quads €68. MC/V. ●

La Foresteria degli Artisti, V. degli Artisti 15 (☎011 83 77 85; www.foresteriadegliartisti.it). Ring bell for Coss F&G, then walk to 2nd door on left and ring again. La Foresteria is a furnished apartment with wood floors, antique furniture, DVD player, library, laundry, and kitchen. Breakfast included. Reservations required. Closed Aug. Singles €50; doubles €80. Extra bed €20. Cash only. ●

Albergo Azalea, V. Mercanti 16, 3rd fl. (☎011 53 81 15 or 333 24 67 449; albergo.azalea@virgilio.it). Exit Pta. Nuova. Take bus #58, 72 to V. Garibaldi. Turn left on V. Garibaldi, away from P. Castello, and left on V. Mercanti. If you take bus #52, turn right from the stop. 10 spic-and-span rooms with floral wallpaper and white furniture in central location. No reception; call ahead. Singles €40, with bath €50; doubles €55/65. MC/V. ●

Nicosia Schaya, Largo Montebello 33, top fl. (☎011 19 71 28 73 or 347 00 21 184; www.bedandbnicosia.it). Take bus #3, 68, 13, 16 or 18; get off near Largo Montebello. Sliding-glass door leads to the privacy of comfortable rooms with framed family pictures, phone, fridge, balcony, and bath. Breakfast included. No reception; call ahead. Singles €50; doubles €70. Cash only. ●

Campeggio Villa Rey, Strada Superiore Val San Martino 27 (☎/fax 011 81 90 117). From Pta. Nuova take the #72 or 63 bus to Pta. Palazzo, change to tram #3 on C. Regina, and ride to the end of the line (stop: Hermada). From there, walk 500m uphill or take bus #54. Quiet hillside location with views of the Basilica Superga has caravans and tent campers. Bar, small market, and restaurant. 2-course meal €15. Laundry €3. Office open daily 8am-10pm. €6 per person, €4 per child; €4-7 per tent; €10-11 per car; €11 per site. Electricity €1. Shower €0.80. MC/V. ●

FOOD

Ever since the Savoys started drinking an evening cup of *cioccolato* in 1678, Turin has grown into one of the great international centers of chocolate production. Ferrero Rocher and Nutella are its most famous products. Napoleonic restrictions on buying chocolate brought the hazelnut substitute *gianduiotto*, now the key ingredient in a distinctly *torinese* ice-cream flavor known as *gianduia*, available at cafes around P. Castello. On the savory side, *Piemontese* cuisine is a blend of northern Italian peasant staples and elegant French garnishes. Butter replaces olive oil, while cheese and mushrooms, occasionally served with white truffles, are used more than vegetables or spices. *Agnolotti*, ravioli stuffed with lamb and cabbage, is the local pasta specialty, but polenta, warm cornmeal often topped with fontina cheese, is the more common starch. The three most outstanding red wines in Italy—*Barolo, Barbaresco, and Barbera*, in descending price order—are available in markets and restaurants. To sample the true flavors of *Piemontese* cuisine, be ready to pay—restaurants that specialize in regional dishes are expensive. Self-caterers can head to **DiperDì** supermarket, all over the *centro*. (V. S. Massimo 43. Open M-Tu and Th-Sa 8:30am-1:30pm and 3:30-7:30pm, W 8:30am-1pm. MC/V.) Find food at **Porta Palazzo** in P. della Repubblica, in what claims to be Europe's largest **open-air market** (M-F 7:30am-2pm, Sa until sunset). Many restaurants participate in **Torino Gourmet,** offering fixed-price *menù* for cheap (€22-30).

> **TIP** **CHOCOHOLICS UNITE.** Sample Turin's best with a **ChocoPass** (www.turismotorino.org), offering tastings of chocolate products, including *gianduiotti*, pralines, and ice cream. Buy a coupon book for €15 (3 days; 23 tastings) at any tourist office. This is the pass for the truly dedicated chocoholic.

Eataly, V. Nizza 224 (☎011 19 50 68 11; www.eataly.it). Take bus #1, 18 or 35 to the "Biglieri" stop, near Lingotto Expo Center. Turin's new culinary amusement park is a 10,000 sq. ft. facility that could realistically take at least a half day of sightseeing on its own. Tastings of wine and beer are just the beginning; classrooms feature scheduled cooking classes by famous guest chefs (in English by group reservation), meat and cheese lockers, and museum-quality exhibits demonstrate various foods and preparation techniques. Browse the restaurants, each with its own daily specialty. Open daily 10am-10:30pm; meat and fish restaurants daily 10am-3:30pm and 5:30-10pm. ❷

Agnoletti and Friends, P. Corpus Domini 18/b (☎011 43 38 792; www.agnoletti-andfriends.it). Blends time-honored traditions with cutting edge decor. Perfect location in a quiet square lets patrons relax and focus on the food, from the *agnolotti* (€10-12) to the adventurous meat offerings. Open M-F 6-8pm, Sa-Su noon-3pm and 6-8pm. ❷

Hafa Café, V. Sant'Agostino 23/C (☎011 43 67 091; www.hafa.it). Sit among Moroccan decor and sip creamy *Hafa Café* (tea with spices, milk, and *amaretto;* €5) or Moroccan mint tea (€3). Mixed drinks €7. Open Tu-Sa 1pm-2:30am, Su 5pm-1am. MC/V. ❷

Stars & Roses, P. Paleocapa 2 (☎011 51 62 052), near P. Carlo Felicehead. Head upstairs and pick a room to match your mood: the color scheme, lighting, and furniture change through each doorway. Celebrity photos decorate the walls. Takeout available. Calzones €7-10. Pizza €6.50-15.50. Primi €5-7. Secondi €8-15. Cover €2. Open M and Su 7:30pm-12:30am, Tu-Sa noon-3pm and 7:30pm-12:30am. AmEx/MC/V. ❷

Il Punto Verde, V. S. Massimo 17 (☎011 88 55 43), off V. Po, near P. Carlo Emanuele II. California juice bar meets traditional Italian trattoria. Vegan options. Student lunch *menù* €5, 3-course *menù* €9; dinner *menù monopiatti* (3 courses plus wine, dessert, and coffee) €12, lunch €6. Primi €6.50-11. Secondi €5-11. Dinner cover €1.80. Open M-F

EAT. SHOP. LEARN.

In January 2007, a new restaurant opened in Turin. Actually, 10 of them did, all under one roof. More than just a food court, **Eataly** (see previous page) is a culinary theme park.

Each of Eataly's restaurants specializes in a different food group and prepares your meal in front of you. Including the €1 cover, dishes generally cost €8-15 at each station, a bargain for their high quality. Splitting meals is highly recommended in order to taste from more stations. The daily menus of meat, seafood, vegetables, deli meat, cheese, pizza, and pasta are only the beginning. A coffee shop and gelato stand are also on the ground floor, while the basement has meat and cheese selections. The basement also has two more restaurants, one dedicated to wine and the other to beer. The bottled wine selection is overwhelming but, if you are the mood for something simple, you can fill up your own liter of wine from the tap for €1.30-4 per L.

You can take the cooking into your own hands at the expansive organic food store or at the learning center, which offer varied and valuable cooking lessons from world-famous guest chefs (€20-100). While the calendar of classes is in Italian, many of the cooking lessons are also available in English for groups. (*V. Nizza 224. Take bus #1, 18, or 35 to the Biglieri stop. Reservations ☎011 19 50 68; www.eataly.com.*)

12:30-2:30pm and 7:30-10:30pm, Sa 7-10:30pm. Closed Aug. MC/V. ❷

Caffè Gelateria Fiorio, V. Po 8 (☎011 81 73 225 or 81 70 612; www.fioriocaffegelateria.com), just off P. Castello. Famous for lunch buffet (€14-15). Hangout for the student movement. Fiorio is frequented by artists and noblemen alike. Cones from €1.50. Sundaes €4.50-9. Open M-Th and Su 7am-1am, F-Sa 7am-2am. AmEx/MC/V. ❸

Le Vitel Etonné, V. S. Francesco da Paola 4 (☎011 81 24 621; www.leviteletonne.com). A popular spot for Turin's casual professionals, Le Vitel Etonné has a wine cellar in the basement (€3-5 per glass) and an artisan cafe upstairs, with a menu that changes depending on what's fresh. Primi €9-11. Secondi €13-15. Open Tu-Sa 10:30am-1am, Su 10:30am-3:30pm. Closed 1 week in Aug. MC/V. ❹

Spaccanapoli, V. Mazzini 19 (☎011 81 26 694). Pizza by the meter (€20-36); try gorgonzola or the special *"spaccanapoli"* pizza, large enough to feed an army. Worth the trip for groups of 4 or more people. Delicious desserts. Primi €6-10. Secondi €10-15. Cover €2. Open daily noon-2:30pm and 7pm-midnight. AmEx/MC/V. ❸

Caffè Cioccolateria al Bicerin, P. della Consolata 5 (☎011 43 69 325; www.bicerin.it). The cafe has sold its namesake drink (€4), a hot mixture of coffee, chocolate, and cream since 1763 to such notables as Nietzsche, Dumas, and Puccini. Open M-Tu and Th-F 8:30am-7:30pm, Sa-Su 8:30am-1pm and 3:30-7:30pm. ❶

▣ SIGHTS

▦**MOLE ANTONELLIANA.** Once the largest structure in the world built using traditional masonry (a title sadly lost in the 1900s with the addition of some concrete), and still the world's tallest museum, the Mole dominates Turin's skyline. The towering spire is gloriously reproduced today on the euro two-cent coin. Begun as a synagogue in 1863, it ended as an architectural eccentricity. The glass elevator that leads through the middle of the building goes to the observation deck. Today, the Mole houses the **Museo Nazionale del Cinema.** The ground floor has a mod bar with color-changing tables and movie screens. Interactive exhibits chronicle the history of cinema. At the center of the museum on the second floor, **Temple Hall** holds a field of red velvet chairs for visitors to watch Italian films projected on screens high above. A variety of movies screen in wild settings, like a 60s living room, a Neolithic cave, and a giant fridge with toilets for seats. A suspended staircase nearby winds to hundreds of movie posters. Every hour, images on the dome disappear and music plays, while the Mole's walls are drawn up to reveal the building's skeleton beneath. (*V. Montebello 20, east of P. Castello.* ☎*011 81 25 658; www.museonazionaledelcin-ema.org. Open Tu-F and Su 9am-8pm, Sa 9am-11pm. Last entry 1hr. before closing. Museum €5.20, students €4.20. Elevator €3.62/2.58; combined ticket €6.80/5.20.*)

CATTEDRALE DI SAN GIOVANNI (DUOMO) AND CHIESA DI SAN LORENZO. The **Holy Shroud of Turin,** one of the most enigmatic relics in Christendom, has been housed in the Cappella della Santa Sindone of the **Cattedrale di San Giovanni Battista** since 1694. Said to be Jesus's burial cloth, the 3 ft. by 14 ft. cloth first entered official accounts when the Crusaders brought it back from Jerusalem in the 13th century. Transferred to Turin from Chambéry, France, by the Savoys in 1578, today the shroud rests in a climate-controlled case. With rare exceptions, a photograph of the unfolded shroud to the left of the cathedral's entrance is as close as visitors will get to the real thing. A negative below the photograph of the shroud reveals more detail, including the countenance of a man with a fractured nose and bruised cheek. It was initially carbon-dated to 1350, but recent studies have suggested that a newer, repaired piece of the shroud from the Middle Ages may in fact be 2500 years old. (*Behind Palazzo Reale where V. XX Set-tembre crosses P. S. Giovanni.* ☎*011 43 61 540. Open daily 7am-noon and 3-7pm. Modest dress required. Free.*) Nearby, to the left of the Palazzo Reale, the 16th-century **Chiesa di San Lorenzo** served as temporary home to the shroud before completion of San Giovanni in the 15th century. Its soaring dome was designed by Guarino Guarini, and its ribs form an overlapping, eight-pointed star reminiscent of the Islamic architecture that influenced Guarini on his travels. In the sacristy to the right hangs an exact-size replica of the shroud. (*V. Palazzo di Città 4, at the corner with P. Castello.* ☎*011 43 61 527; www.sanlorenzo.torino.it. Open daily 8am-noon and 3-6pm. Free.*)

TOURIN' CARD. The best deal in the city the **Torino Card** (48hr. €18, 72hr. €21), provides free entrance to all museums and monuments in Turin and throughout Piedmont; access to the **TurismoBus Torino,** the panoramic lift in the Mole, the Sassi-Superga cable car, and the boats for river naviga-tion on the Po; and discounts on guided tours, transportation, and shows. The card is available at any Turismo Torino info point and at most hotels.

CASTELLO DI RIVOLI MUSEO D'ARTE CONTEMPORANEA. This museum houses one of Europe's most impressive contemporary art collections in a 14th-century Savoy residence. The sleek venue holds works from the 50s onward, and many exhibits, including Sol Lewitt's 1992 *Panels and Towers*, were designed specifically for the *castello*'s cavernous spaces. Other featured artists include Bruce Nauman, Claes Oldenburg, and Michelangelo Pistoletto. (*P. Mafalda di Savoia in Rivoli, 22km outside Turin. Take bus #36 or 66 from Turin, or subway from Pta. Susa to Fermi Station and then bus #36 to Rivoli. Inquire at the bus station about the direct shuttle bus.* ☎*011 95 65 222; www.castellodirivoli.org. Open Tu-Th 10am-5pm, F-Su 10am-9pm. €6.50, students €3.50. Under 11 free.*)

PALAZZO DELL'ACCADEMIA DELLE SCIENZE. The *palazzo* houses two of Turin's best museums—the **Museo Egizio** and the **Galleria Sabauda.** From 1903-37, the Italian Archaeological Mission brought thousands of artifacts home to Turin, making Museo Egizio the second largest Egyptian collection outside Cairo. Museum highlights include both wrapped and unwrapped mummies, life-size wooden Nubian statues, the massive Ellesiya temple, and the well-furnished tomb of Kha, a 14th-century BC architect; Kha's tomb was one of the few Egyp-tian tombs spared by grave robbers. The ground floor also holds a cast of the Rosetta Stone. (*V. Accademia delle Scienze 6. 2 blocks from P. Castello.* ☎*011 56 17 776; www.museoegizio.it. Open Tu-Su 8:30am-7:30pm. €6.50, ages 18-25 €3, under 18 or over 65* free.) On the third floor, the **Galleria Sabauda** houses art collections from Palazzo Reale and Palazzo Carignano, and is renowned for its 14th- to 18th-century Flemish and Dutch paintings, including Van Eyck's *St. Francis Receiving the Stigmata* (1427), Memling's *Passion* (1470), and Rembrandt's *Old Man Sleeping* (1629), among others. (V. Accademia delle Scienze 6. ☎011 54 74 40; www.museitorino.it/galleriasabauda. Open Nov.-May Tu and F-Su 8:30am-2pm, W 2-7:30pm, Th 10am-7:30pm; June-Oct. Tu and F-Su 8:30am-2pm, W 2-7:30pm, Th 2-7:30pm. €4, 18-25 €2, under 18 or over 65 free. Combined ticket for both museums €8.)

PINACOTECA GIOVANNI E MARELLA AGNELLI. This tiny museum atop a former Fiat factory holds 26 pieces from the last 300 years. The collection features Venetian landscape works by Il Canaletto, Impressionist works by Matisse and Renoir, and pieces by Tiepolo, Picasso, and Modigliani. (V. Nizza 230. ☎011 00 62 713. Open Tu-Su 9am-7pm. €4, students €2.50. Special exhibits €6.)

GALLERIA CIVICA D'ARTE MODERNA E CONTEMPORANEA (GAM). The city's premiere modern and contemporary art museum devotes four floors to 19th- and 20th-century works made mostly by Italians, including some Modiglianis and de Chiricos. Though its collection is not the most representative of the diverse styles of these periods, it does contain Andy Warhol's gruesome *Orange Car Crash* and a few works by Picasso, Chagall, Klee, and Renoir. (V. Magenta 31. On the corner of C. Galileo Ferraris, off Largo V. Emanuele. Take tram #1, 9, or 15. ☎011 44 29 610; www.gamtorino.it. Open Tu-Su 9am-7pm. €7.50, under 26 or over 65 €6, Tu free.)

BASILICA DI SUPERGA. When the French siege on Turin culminated in the attack on September 6, 1706, King Vittorio Amedeo II made a promise to the Virgin Mary to build a basilica in her honor should the city withstand the invasion. Turin stood unconquered, and famous architect Juvarra helped fulfill the vow, erecting a Neoclassical portico and high drum to support the basilica's spectacular dome. The church houses the tombs of the Savoys. In 1949, a plane carrying the entire Turin soccer team crashed into the basilica; a memorial stands at the accident site today, listing the names of the victims. The basilica is built on a 640m summit outside Turin, once described by Le Corbusier as "the most enchanting position in the world." It offers panoramic views of the city, the Po Valley below, and the Alps beyond. (Tram #15 from V. XX Settembre to Stazione Sassi, then bus #79 or a small cable railway for an 18min. ride uphill. Cable Car ☎011 57 64 733; www.gtt.to.it. Every hr. M and W-F 9am-noon and 2-8pm, Sa-Su 9am-8pm. Round-trip €3, Su and holidays €4. Basilica ☎011 89 97 456; www.basilicadisuperga.com. Open daily Apr.-Oct. M-F 9am-noon and 3-6pm, Sa-Su 9am-noon and 3-6:45pm; Nov.-Mar. M-F 9am-noon and 3-5pm, Sa-Su 9am-noon and 3-5:45pm. Dome of basilica and Savoy tombs each €3, students €2.)

PALAZZO REALE. The Palazzo Reale forms part of the *"Corona di Delitie,"* a ring of Savoy royal residences that came under the UNESCO's protection as a World Heritage site in 1997. Home to the Princes of Savoy from 1645 to 1865, the ornate *palazzo* contains over 300 rooms. Thirty of the rooms, mostly unfurnished, are covered on the long Italian-language tour. Those with short attention spans beware, as there is no leaving or separating from the group once this one-hour tour has begun. André le Nôtre, famous for his work on the gardens of Versailles, designed the grounds in 1697, but the gardens have since been deeply reduced. (In Piazzetta Reale, at the end of P. Castello. ☎011 43 61 455; www.ambienteto.arti.beniculturali.it. Palazzo Reale open Tu-Su 8:30am-7:30pm. Visit only with mandatory guided tour. €6.50, students €3.25. Gardens open 9am-1hr. before sunset. Free.) In the right wing of the Royal Palace lies the **Armeria Reale** (Royal Armory), with medieval and Renaissance war tools. (P. Castello 191. ☎011 54 38 89. Open Tu-F 9am-2pm, Sa-Su 1-7pm. €4, under 18 or over 65 free.)

PARCO DEL VALENTINO. One of Italy's largest parks and the country's first public park, the designer Valentino's lush grounds on the banks of the Po provide a safe haven for whispering lovers and children. Upon entering the park from C. V. Emanuele, **Castello del Valentino** is on the left. Its distinctly French air honors the royal lady Christina of France, who made the castle her favorite residence. It now houses the University's Facoltà di Architettura and is open to the public only by appointment (☎ 011 66 94 592). Nearby, a fake *rocca* (castle) is open to the public. Located in the nearby **Borgo e Rocca Medievale,** it was built for the Italian Industry and Crafts Exhibition of 1884, and today has a shop-filled village attached. *(Park and castle at Vle. Virgilio 107, along the Po. ☎ 011 44 31 701; www.borgomedievaletorino.it. Castle open Tu-Su 9am-7pm. €5, students €4. Village open daily 9am-7pm. Free.)*

SANTUARIO DELLA CONSOLATA. This ornate Baroque church belongs to Turin's cult of the Virgin, with gold and jeweled offerings of gratitude from the wealthy in glass boxes by the entrance. The room to the right is a collection of ex-voto paintings. Reminiscent of children's drawings, they depict catastrophes averted across the decades, as well as scenes from WWI and WWII. *(P. della Consolata. ☎ 011 43 63 235; www.laconsolata.org. Open daily 6:30am-12:30pm and 3-7:30pm. Free.)*

PALAZZO AND TEATRO CARIGNANO. This *palazzo* designed by the Guarini family in 1679 to house the Princes of Savoy was also the seat of the first Italian parliament. The building contains the **Museo Nazionale del Risorgimento Italiano,** which commemorates Italy's unification between 1706 and 1946. *(V. Accademia delle Scienze 5. ☎ 011 56 21 147.)* Across from the *palazzo* is the Baroque **Teatro Carignano,** where Italian poet Vittorio Alfieri premiered his tragedies. *(☎ 011 54 70 54. Call for info on tours. Free.)*

PALAZZO MADAMA. On the site of the ancient Roman military camp, this palace was converted to a castle in the Middle Ages. It lost its defensive function in the 17th century, became a museum in 1934, and today houses an enormous Baroque collection of paintings and artifacts from churches. Highlights include the view from the castle's tower and a small circular room on the ground floor with four medieval marble carvings. *(P. Castello. ☎ 011 44 33 501; www.palazzomadamatorino.it. Open Tu-F and Su 10am-6pm, Sa 10am-8pm. €7.50, over 65 and students under 25 €6.)*

MUSEO DELL'AUTOMOBILE. With an emphasis on Italian cars and racing, this museum documents

LOCAL LEGEND

THE AXIS OF...MAGIC?

Those who refer to Turin as a "magical" destination aren't always talking about its enchanting green riverbank or renowned museums. According to legend, the city is actually a hub of supernatural activity: a rare locus of both white and black magic.

Staunch believers insist that Turin forms one point of a white magic triangle with Lyon and Prague. The black magic triangle is more obtuse, extending to London and San Francisco. These conflicting forces create an exponentially higher mystical charge than cities containing white or black magic alone.

To explore the darker side, begin at **Piazza Statuto,** a former Roman burial ground and site of public hangings and medieval massacres. Today's dark power is limited to a monument honoring the death of railway workers and a statue held to be Lucifer himself. Below, a manhole cover is said to lead to the gates of hell.

Cheer up with a trek to Turin's center of white magic, **Piazza Castello,** which lies directly between two of the most powerful forces of good in the city: the Holy Shroud and the **Chiesa della Gran Madre di Dio,** allegedly built above the Holy Grail. Turin, a city divided against itself.

*For more on Turin's magical side(s), take the **Magic Turin Tour,** a 2½hr. odyssey. (€20. Begins at Piazza Statuto Th and Sa 9pm.)*

the automobile's evolution through prints, drawings, more than 150 original cars, and first models by Ford, Benz, Peugeot, Oldsmobile, and Fiat. *(C. Unità d'Italia 40. Head south 20min. along V. Nizza from Stazione Porta Nuova. ☎011 67 76 66; www. museoauto.it. Open Tu-Su 10am-6:30pm. €7.)*

🎵 ENTERTAINMENT

For the most updated calendar of Turin's yearly events, visit www.torinocultura.it (mostly in Italian) or www.turismotorino.org (in English). If you want the news in print, Turin's daily newspaper, *La Stampa*, publishes *Torino Sette*, a thorough Friday section on cultural events. Turin's **Teatro Regio**, in P. Castello, is home to the city's beloved **opera, ballet**, and **orchestra**, which showcase a combined 130 events a year. (☎011 88 15 557; www.teatroregio.torino.it. Ticket office open Tu-F 10:30am-6pm, Sa 10:30am-4pm, and 1hr. before shows.) Eclectic music, theater, and cinema events enliven Turin between June and August, when **Torino d'Estate** draws many local and international acts to the city. Included in the summer festivities are **Torino Puntiverdi**, 19 July nights of dance and music from tango to orchestra in the Giardini Reali and other venues. (☎011 50 69 967 or 80 00 15 457. Tickets €10-15, available from ticket office at V. S. Francesco da Paola 6. Open M-Sa 10:30am-6:30pm.) Head to the turn-of-the-century glamour of **Cinema Romano**, Galleria Subalpina, P. Castello 9, near the beginning of V. Po. (☎011 56 20 145. Movies daily, usually 4-10:30pm. Tickets €6-10.)

🛍 SHOPPING

One of Turin's unique events is the **Gran Balon flea market**, held every second Sunday of the month behind Porta Palazzo. A smaller-scale **Mercato del Balon** (www.balon.it) occurs every Saturday. The biggest **open-air market** in Europe takes place under Porta Palazzo in P. della Repubblica. (M-F 8:30am-1:30pm, Sa 8:30am-6:30pm.) Over 600 vendors sell food, clothing, and odds and ends. Though clothing stores line Turin's streets, the big-name designer shops on **Via Roma** are more conducive to window-shopping. Turin's student population has attracted trendy and affordable clothing shops to **Via Garibaldi** and **Via Po**; the latter is also home to antique bookshops and record stores. In the **Quadrilatero Romano**, up-and-coming designers have set up shop on the renovated streets within the rectangle outlined by V. Bligny, V. G. Garibaldi, V. XX Settembre, and P. della Repubblica. **8 Gallery**, V. Nizza 262 (www.8gallery.it), is housed inside Lingotto's former Fiat factory in Turin's future cultural center, and features over 100 shops, restaurants, bars, and movie theaters.

🎷 NIGHTLIFE

Turin's raging options are impressive in scope and variety, with something to offer all ages, ranging from good wine and grooving background music to vodka and tonics in a packed club. Clubs are less pretentious, covers are cheap, and choices are conveniently concentrated—mostly along the Po River. Especially in summer, Turin's social scene centers on **I Murazzi**, two stretches of boardwalk, one between Ponte V. Emanuele I and Ponte Umberto I and another smaller stretch downstream from the Ponte V. Emanuele I. Some establishments charge covers late at night, but free bars or clubs can be easily found (many distribute consumption cards at the door that must be stamped, paid for, and returned upon departure; lost card fee €30). **Quadrilatero Romano**, the recently renovated collection of buildings between P. della Repubblica and V. Garibaldi, attracts partygoers who would rather sit and chat than dance to techno music. English and Irish pubs line C. V. Emanuele II from Stazione Porta Nuova to the Po, attracting an English-speaking student crowd. Head south on the I Murazzi side of the river for a few blocks to reach the growing Valentino Park riverfront nightlife, near the Valentino castle.

■ **The Beach,** V. Murazzi del Po 18-22 (☎011 88 87 77). With strobe lights and an energetic crowd, this club easily has the best dance floor in Turin. By 1am, this large, modern club fills with the young trendsetters, electronica music, and Redbull and vodkas. During the week, it hosts occasional performance-art pieces, film openings, and book signings. Mixed drinks €6-7. Open W and Su 5-11pm, Th-Sa 11pm-5am. MC/V.

Giancarlo, V. Murazzi del Po 47 (www.arcitorino.it), closest to Ponte V. Emanuele. 1st bar to invade I Murazzi. Rock and punk music draws an alternative crowd to its cavernous dance floor, and after 4am almost everyone who is not sitting by the river will be here. Beer €3-4. Mixed drinks €5-7. Student night Tu. Open M-Sa 10pm-6am. Cash only.

Pier 7-9-11, V. Murazzi del Po 7-11 (☎011 83 53 56). Flashy dance club. The most outdoor seating in I Murazzi. Shots €3. Beer €4. Mixed drinks €8. Cover with 1 drink included €8. F-Sa every drink €8. Open M-Sa midnight-6am.

Fluido, Vle. Umberto Cagni 7 (☎011 66 94 557; www.fluido.to). Riverside wine bar and restaurant, with a dance club downstairs. On warm evenings, the young clientele spread out in the grassy expanse surrounding the club. Shots €3. Mixed drinks €6. Open Tu-W 10am-2am, Th 10am-3am, F-Sa 10am-4:30am, Su 10am-1am.

Six Nations Murphy's Pub, C. V. Emanuele 28 (☎011 88 72 55). Exit Pta. Nuova, and turn right; the pub is a few blocks down on the left. Beer taps glow in the dim interior, filled with British expats, TVs, darts, and billiards. Sept.-May weekly Erasmus party for international students on W nights. Beer €3-4.50. Open daily 6pm-3am. MC/V.

Seiperotto, V. delle Orfane 17 (☎011 43 38 738; www.seiperotto.com). Specializing, as it claims, in "art, food, and drink," any trip to Seiperotto will inspire through tasty wines and rotating art exhibits. In addition to the photographs and paintings on display, don't neglect the giant bottom half of a stuffed ballerina hanging from the ceiling, tutu and all. Wine €3-4 per glass. Dinner €25. Open Tu-Su 7pm-2am. MC/V.

Shore, P. Emanuele Filiberto 10/G (☎011 43 63 495; www.shorecocktailclub.it). Serves large mixed drinks until the wee hours. Chill-out fusion music completes the mood. Mixed drinks €7. Open daily 6:30pm-2:30am. Cash only.

Arancia di Mezzanotte, P. E. Filiberto 11/I (☎011 52 11 338; www.aranciadimezzanotte.it). Set in a quaint interior, this is a popular place for an aperitif away from the noisy and hectic river area. Beer €4-5. Mixed drinks €8. Open daily 6pm-4am. MC/V.

🎬 FESTIVALS

During the 20s, Turin was home to over 100 movie production companies, and its love affair with cinema still lives on today. During the academic year, Turin's university organizes screenings of **foreign films** in their original languages. Two prestigious film festivals take place annually. The **Turin Film Festival** in November (www.torinofilmfest.org) is one of the liveliest festivals of contemporary cinema in Italy, paying particular attention to up-and-coming cinema auteurs. The various categories explore the many diverse aspects of contemporary cinema: feature films by famous directors, experimental cinema, and documentaries and retrospectives. In addition, **Da Sodoma ad Hollywood** is Turin's GLBT Film Festival held in April (www.tglff.com), one of the most important queer festivals in the world. In the fall, the tourist office organizes guided city tours with a cinematic bent. The **☎TRAFFIC Turin Free Festival,** during early July, attracts international acts to the free celebration of contemporary youth culture (www.trafficfestival.com). Previous performers include Franz Ferdinand and The Strokes. Last but not least, chocoholics venture to Turin every year at the end of February for the **Chocolate Fair** (www.cioccola-to.it).

📌 DAYTRIPS FROM TURIN

📖 SACRA DI SAN MICHELE

From Turin, take a train to Sant'Ambrogio (30min.; 8 per day, last return 7:10pm; €2.50) to tackle the scenic 1½hr. climb from the village of Sant'Ambrogio to the monastery. Exiting the station, walk straight up V. Caduti per la Patria, and turn right on V. Umberto. Continue straight until Chiesa Parrocchiale. Behind the church on the right is a "Sacra di San Michele Mulattiera" sign. The rest of the hike is clearly marked. Do not hike alone, as the unpaved path can be difficult and slippery. Wear sturdy shoes and bring water. Alternatively, take the train to Avigliana (30min., 15 per day, €2.20). From there, either take a taxi (☎011 93 02 18; around €30) or tackle the 14km, 3hr. hike.

On a bluff above the town of Avigliana, the Sacra di San Michele (sa-cra dee san mee-KEH-leh) grows from the very rock on which it was built. *The Name of the Rose*, a movie based on a novel by Umberto Eco, was not filmed at this megalithic stone monastery, but it probably should have been. Eco based his book's plot on the Sacra's history, and even in full summer sunshine, there is an ominous air about the place. Ugo di Montboissier, an Alevernian pilgrim, founded it in 1000, and the **Scalone dei Morti** (Stairway of the Dead), a set of steps chiseled from the mountainside, helps to buttress the structure. Monks' corpses were once draped across the staircase for the faithful to pay their last respects; today, their skeletons are tactfully concealed in the cavities on the side. The stairs ascend to the **Porta dello Zodiaco** (Door of the Zodiac), a door sculpted by 11th-century artist Nicolao with zodiac signs and symbols. Steps in the middle of the nave descend into the shrine of St. Michael and three tiny **chapels.** The oldest dates to the time of St. Michael's earliest known veneration. In 966, St. John Vincent built the largest chapel; today, it holds the medieval members of the Savoy family. (☎011 93 91 30; www.sacradisanmichele.com. Open Mar. 16-Oct. 15 Tu-Sa 9:30am-12:30pm and 2:30-6pm, Su 9:30am-noon and 2:40-6:30pm; Oct. 16-Mar. 15 Tu-Sa 9:30am-12:30pm and 2:30-5pm, Su 9:30am-12:30pm and 2:40-6pm. Last entry 30min. before closing. €4, children and over 65 €3.) For a map of the arduous trek, head to Avigliana's **Informazione Turistica,** C. Torino 6/d, a 5-10min. walk straight ahead from the train station. (☎011 93 66 037. Open M-F 9am-noon and 3-6pm.)

PARCO DELLA MANDRIA AND VENARIA CASTLE

By car: from the by-pass in Turin, take the Venaria Reale exit. By train: take the Torino-Ceres (Airport) line from Stazione Dora to Venaria. By bus: take the blue GTT line #11, 72, or 72b from the centro to Venaria. Ask at tourist office or nearby tabaccherie for the most convenient bus stop. Alternatively, a shuttle bus conveniently runs between C. Stati Uniti, Porta Nuova, Porta Susa, and the palace. (45min.; 14 departures per day 8:05am-6:55pm, 16 returns per day 9am-7:50pm; round-trip €5. Info: ☎011 800 329 329; www.parks.it/parco. mandria or www.lavenariareale.it.)

An immense project mostly constructed by a single architect during the 17th and 18th centuries, this newly restored royal palace has an immaculate contemporary garden and over 5000 sq. m of frescoes and decorations. Parco Della Mandria is a rural, historical park characterized by alluvial terraces where woods alternate with pastures, lakes, and fields. The variable countryside landscape invites you to relax and enjoy the ancient churches and royal residences, which date back to the times of King Vittorio Emanuele II. The area's vegetation includes an ancient forest rich in oaks and ash trees that shelters many animal species. Many activities, such as horseback riding, trekking, and cycling are available. The plan for the building of the castle was begun in 1659 at the request of Duke Carlo Emanuele II. The layout by Amedeo di Castellamonte was finished in 1675, and consists of a village, a palace, and gardens. (La Venaria Reale, P. della Republica 4. ☎011 45 93 675; www.reggiavenariareale. it. Open Tu, Th, and Sa-Su 9:30-11:30am and 2:30-5:30pm.)

VALLE D'AOSTA

Stunning peaks, pine forests, waterfalls, and tiny villages color Italy's least-populated and most-elevated region, Valle d'Aosta (VA-leh da-OS-ta). The valley is a key transportation hub; Hannibal and his elephants once traversed Aosta's St. Bernard Pass, and today an even greater stampede of heavy-goods vehicles barrel through the Monte Bianco tunnel. Some locals fear that Aosta's status as a trade gateway damages the natural splendor and destabilizes the tourist economy. Before the tractor trailers and even before the skiers, Aosta welcomed elites seeking hot springs and alpine freshness. Living so close to their Swiss and French neighbors, *valdostani* take on much of their continental cousins' cultural character, evident at intersections of a *via* with a *rue* or *Strasse*. Though not the Italy of the popular imagination, Valle d'Aosta's unique setting and culture, its relative seclusion from the masses, and the stunning Alps make it the perfect destination to taste Alpine glory.

AOSTA   ☎0165

Aosta (ah-OS-ta; pop. 37,000) straddles the line between Italian and French *valdostana* cultures. For many years, Aosta was ancient Rome's launching point for military expeditions. Boutiques and food shops now pack the *centro storico*, but even here you can admire the jagged peaks and their frosty caps. Within the walls that once defended the imperial Alpine outpost.

TRANSPORTATION

Trains: In P. Manzetti. Ticket window open M-Th 7:20am-2pm and 2:15-5:25pm, F-Sa 6:15am-7:40pm, Su 11:30am-6:10pm. MC/V.) Trains run to: **Turin** (2hr., 14 per day 5:10am-9:41pm, €7.35) via **Châtillon** (20min., €2.10); **Chivasso** (2hr., 5 trains per day, €5.10); **Ivrea** (1hr., 5 per day 6:12am-5:12pm, €4.10); **Milan Centrale** via **Chivasso** (4hr., 12 per day 5:10am-8:40pm, €11.20); **Pré-Saint-Didier** (1hr., 14 per day 6:41am-7:46pm, €2.70); **Verrès** (30min., €3).

Buses: (☎0165 26 20 27; www.savda.it), on V. Carrel off P. Manzetti, to the right exiting the train station. Office open daily 6:40am-7:20pm. Tickets also available on bus. To: **Chamonix** (1hr., 6 per day 8:15am-4:45pm, €14.40); **Châtillon** (30min.; 5:30am, 1:35, 3:15, 5:40, and 8pm; €2.60); **Courmayeur** (1hr., every hr. 6:45am-9:45pm, €3); **Great St. Bernard Pass** (1hr., in summer 2 per day, €3); **Turin** (2-3 per day, €80). Regional buses serve **Cogne** (1hr., 7 per day 8:05am-7:45pm, €3) and **Fenis** (1hr.; 12 per day 6:20am-8pm, reduced service Su; €2.70). Buses also leave from the Châtillon train station for **Breuil-Cervinia** and **Valtournenche**. Local buses are orange and are operated by **SVAP** (www.svap.it). Tickets can be purchased onboard.

Taxis: P. Manzetti (☎0165 36 36 23 or 31 831).

Car Rental: Europcar, P. Manzetti 3 (☎0165 41 432), to the left of the train station. 18+. Open M-F 8:30am-12:30pm and 3-7pm, Sa 8:30am-12:30am. AmEx/MC/V.

Bike and Ski Rental: Gal Sport Shop, V. Paravera 6/B, 3rd fl. (☎0165 23 61 34; shop@galsport.com), past the funicular base. Open M-Sa 9am-12:30pm and 3-7pm. MC/V.

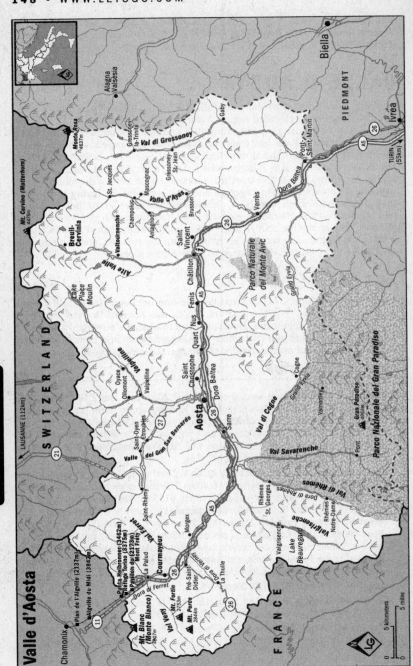

Valle d'Aosta

CONNECTION PERFECTION. Aosta makes a good base for exploring the Italian Alps, but be aware that daytrips to surrounding valleys often require tricky train and bus connections, so plan carefully.

Taxis: P. Manzetti (☎0165 36 36 23 or 31 831).

Car Rental: Europcar, P. Manzetti 3 (☎0165 41 432), to the left of the train station. 18+. Open M-F 8:30am-12:30pm and 3-7pm, Sa 8:30am-12:30am. AmEx/MC/V.

Bike and Ski Rental: Gal Sport Shop, V. Paravera 6/B, 3rd fl. (☎0165 23 61 34; shop@galsport.com), past the funicular base station. Offers bike rentals and sells equipment. Open M-Sa 9am-12:30pm and 3-7pm. MC/V.

ORIENTATION AND PRACTICAL INFORMATION

Trains stop at **Piazza Manzetti.** From there, take **Avenue du Conseil des Commis** past the ruins of the Roman wall until it ends in the enormous **Piazza Chanoux,** Aosta's *centro.* The main street runs east-west through P. Chanoux. Running east it changes its name from **Via de Tillier** to **Via Aubert;** running west, **Via Porta Praetoria** leads to the historical gate, **Porta Praetoria** (and becomes **Via Sant'Anselmo**).

Tourist Office: P. Chanoux 2 (☎0165 23 66 27; www.aiataosta.com), down Ave. du Conseil des Commis from train station. Provides town maps, maps of the valley, accommodations booking, and art guides. English spoken. Open July-Sept. daily 9am-1pm and 2:30-8pm; Oct.-June M-Sa 9:30am-1pm and 3-6:30pm, Su 9am-1pm. **Branch:** P. Arco d'Augusto, across from the Roman arch, offering info only on the city of Aosta itself. In winter, a tourist office opens in **Pila,** at 11020 Gressan, near the top of the funicular.

Alpine Information: Club Alpino Italiano, C. Battaglione Aosta 81, 3rd fl. (☎/fax 0165 40 194; www.caivda.it), off P. della Repubblica. Open Tu 7-8:30pm, F 8-10pm. **Interguide,** V. Monte Emilius 13 (☎0165 40 939; www.interguide.it).

Tours: Associazione Guide Turistiche (☎0165 338 695 1558; www.guideturistichevaldostane.it). Guided group tours.

Currency Exchange: Monte dei Paschi di Siena, P. Chanoux 51 (☎0165 27 68 88). **ATM** outside. Open M-F 8:30am-1:30pm and 2:40-4:10pm. Another ATM at post office.

Laundromat: Onda Blu, V. Chambéry 60. Wash and dry €8. Detergent €1, softener €0.50. Snack machines on premises. Open daily 8am-10pm.

Police: at C. Battaglione Aosta (☎0165 27 91 11).

Pharmacy: Farmacia Chenal, V. Croix-de-Ville 1 (☎0165 26 21 33), near V. Aubert. Posts after-hours rotations. MC/V.

Hospital: Vle. Ginevra 3 (☎0165 54 31).

Internet: Public Library, V. Torre del Lebroso 2 (☎0165 27 48 43). Reserve ahead. Open M 2-7pm, Tu-Sa 9am-7pm. **Aosta Web Service Internet Point** (☎0165 06 00 15), at C. Padre Lorenzo and C. XXVI Febbraio. Open M-Sa 9am-10pm and Su 2-10pm.

Post Office: P. Narbonne 1a (☎0165 27 62 11), in the huge semi-circular building. Open M-F 8am-6:30pm, Sa 8am-1pm. **Postal Code:** 11100.

ACCOMMODATIONS AND CAMPING

Prices vary seasonally in Aosta. Rates are lowest from January to April and from October to mid-December, and highest in early August and around Christmas. The **Valle d'Aosta Pass,** managed by the Association of Hoteliers of Aosta Valley, allows you to book hotels online or by phone for free with at least two days advance notice. (☎0165 23 00 15; www.valledaostapass.com.)

Bed & Breakfast Nabuisson, V. Aubert 50 (☎0165 36 30 06 or 339 609 0332; www. bedbreakfastaosta.it). In a building through the iron gate under the arch between the *tabaccheria* and *libreria.* Near the *centro.* 2 large, rustic-themed rooms have wooden floors, antique furniture, TV, and bath. 1 has kitchen. Breakfast €4. Reservations recommended. Doubles €50-65. Extra bed €10-15. Cash only. ❹

Belle Époque, V. d'Avise 18 (☎0165 26 22 76; fax 26 11 56). Central location and affordable price partially compensate for small rooms. Breakfast €6.50. Singles €22-26; doubles €50-60; triples €65-85. MC/V. ❸

Hotel Mancuso, V. Voison 32 (☎0165 34 526; www.albergomancuso.com). 15min. walk from P. Chanoux. Affordable, clean rooms have great views, bathroom, TV, and hair dryer; some with balcony. Free parking. Singles €30-40; doubles €38-48; triples €55-60; quads €65-70. Let's Go discount 10%. ❷

Hotel Roma, V. Torino 7 (☎0165 41 000; hroma@libero.it), close to the train station and *centro,* around the corner from Hotel Turin (enter off Rue Vevey). Large, recently renovated rooms; all have bath, phone, and TV. Breakfast €6. Parking €6. Singles €40-54; doubles €68-76. Extra bed 30% surcharge. AmEx/MC/V. ❹

Camping Milleluci, Località Roppoz 15 (☎0165 23 52 78; www.campingmilleluci.com), a 1km hike from station. Reception in Hotel Milleluci. Each site has a cabin connected to a trailer. Quiet location with great views. Most crowded June-Sept. Laundry €5. €8-10 per person, €5-7 per child under 10; €15 per tent; €15 per RV. Showers free. Free access to swimming pool. Free electricity. AmEx/MC/V. ❶

🍴 FOOD

Aosta's cold climate and predominantly agricultural lifestyle have created unique cuisine. *Fonduta,* a cheese sauce made from the local *fontina,* usually served with toast, is a local specialty. Regional wines include *blanc de morgex* and *pinot gris.* Pick up local varieties of *fontina* and groceries at **STANDA,** on V. Festaz 10. (☎0165 35 757. Open M-Sa 8am-8pm, Su 9am-1pm and 3:30-7:30pm. AmEx/D/MC/V.) A Tuesday **market** is in P. Cavalieri di V. Veneto.

Pam Pam Trattoria, V. Maillet 5/7 (☎0165 40 960). Romantic trattoria tucked in a centrally located ivy-festooned lane. Rustic fare presented with elegance. Try the *polenta grassa* (polenta with butter and *fontina;* €7.50). Primi €7.50-9. Secondi €8-18. Open Tu-Sa 12:30-2pm and 7:30-10pm. AmEx/MC/V. ❸

Trattoria Praetoria, V. Sant'Anselmo 9 (☎0165 44 356), past Pta. Praetoria. A calm trattoria with a rotating menu that frequently includes the delicious *fonduta valdostana* (cheese fondue with toast; €10) or the *crespelle alla valdostana* (French crepe layered with cured ham and baked cheese; €7.50). Primi €7-10. Secondi €6.50-15. Cover €1.50. Open in summer daily 12:15-2:30pm and 7:15-9:30pm; in winter M-Tu and Sa-Su 12:15-2:30pm and 7:15-9:30pm, W and F 12:15-2:30pm. AmEx/MC/V. ❷

Ristorante la Muscadin, V. Torino 23 (☎0165 363 119). For one of the best values in town, opt for their special *menù,* which includes 2 courses, wine, coffee, and dessert (€10). Open M-F noon-2:30pm, Sa noon-2:30pm and 8-10pm. ❷

La Rotonda, Vle. dei Partigiani 30 (☎0165 43 927). Overwhelmingly large portions at low prices keep the large restaurant full and lively. Beer and wine from €2. Pizza €4.50-6. Primi €5-6.50. Secondi €5.50-11. Cover €1.10. Open M-Tu and Th-Su noon-2:30pm and 6:30pm-midnight. AmEx/MC/V. ❷

👁 SIGHTS

Vestiges of the Roman Empire are thoroughly integrated with modern Aosta; a partially intact, 2000-year-old wall surrounds the *centro,* and modern streets run neatly through its gaps. The **Porta Praetoria,** on the street bearing its name, once served as a guard house. To its left lie the remains of the massive **Teatro Romano.** (Open daily Apr.-Aug. 9am-8pm; Sept. and Mar. 9am-7pm; Oct. and Feb. 9am-6:30pm; Nov.-Jan. 9am-5pm. Free.) Through Pta. Praetoria, V. Sant'Anselmo leads to the **Arco d'Augusto**, built in 25 BC. The monument has sported a hanging Christian cross inside the arch since the Middle Ages. Between Pta. Praetoria and Arco d'Augusto, the renowned **Complex of Sant'Orso** includes the Collegiate Church of Saints Pietro and Orso, the *campanile*, and the cloister. (Open daily July-Aug. 9am-8pm; Oct.-Feb. 10am-12:30pm and 1:30-5pm; Mar.-June 9am-7pm. Free.) **Museo Archeologico**, P. Roncas, has a model of the old town and info on its history. (☎0165 27 59 02. Open daily 9am-7pm. Free.) The ruins of the ancient forum, **Criptoportico Forense,** are off P. Papa Giovanni XXIII. Because the forum has not been excavated, there is not actually much to tour here. (☎0165 27 59 11. Open Apr.-Sept. 2-6pm; Nov.-Feb. 2-5pm upon request. Free.)

◪ NIGHTLIFE

▨ **Gekoo,** P. Chanoux 28 (☎0165 36 14 45; www.myspace.com/gekooaosta). Picnic tables, ski lift benches, and an old Volkswagen van compete for prominence in the quirky but somehow gimmick-free interior. Frequent parties and concerts in the *piazza.* Try their signature drink, a *caipiroska* with violet syrup (€4). Open Tu-Su 4pm-1am.

▨ **Bataclan,** P. Arco d'Augusto 40 (☎0165 36 39 21; www.bataclan.it). One of the town's newest and most popular nightlife establishments. Lounge upstairs beneath the stars, or order a bottle of wine from a candlelit table while listening to live jazz in a grass courtyard. Staff all play instruments and keep them around, so live music may break out at any time. Primi €7-9. Secondi €12-16. Open Tu-Su 12:30-3pm and 7:15pm-12:30am. Kitchen open 12:30-3pm and 7:15-11pm; pizza available until closing. MC/V.

Old Distillery Pub, V. des Prés Fossés 7 (☎0165 23 95 11; www.olddistillerypub.com). From Pta. Praetoria, walk down V. S. Anselmo and turn right on V. des Prés Fossés. A Scottish-themed local favorite. Beamish €5 per pint. Open daily 6pm-2am.

❄ FESTIVALS

The **Fiera di Sant'Orso,** the region's 2000-year-old craft fair, takes place January 30-31 and the second weekend of August in the *centro storico* between P. Arco d'Augusto and P. della Repubblica (open 8am-6pm). The heart of the fair is **L'Atelier,** P. Chanoux, where local craftsmen typically offer demonstrations. The schedule changes annually, so ask at the tourist office.

▶ DAYTRIPS FROM AOSTA

VALTOURNENCHE: THE MATTERHORN AND BREUIL-CERVINIA

SAVDA buses (☎0166 94 90 54, www.savda.it) run to Breuil-Cervinia (1hr., 9 per day 6:10am-7:25pm, €2.60) from Châtillon, on the Aosta-Turin line. Once in Chatillon, exit the train station and walk up the road for 15min. until you come to the circular building that marks the bus stop. Buses run daily from Milan's P. Castello (5hr.) and from Breuil-Cervina to Turin (4hr.; M-Sa 3 per day, Su 1 per day; €7.80).

The most famous mountain in Switzerland, the **Matterhorn (Il Cervino)** looms majestically over the Italian town of **Breuil-Cervinia** in Valtournenche. Despite high costs in this heavily touristed area, fresh-air fiends consider it a small price for the chance to climb up the glaciers of one of the world's most spectacular mountains. A funicular services **Plateau Rosà**, where die-hard skiers tackle the slopes in bathing suits for ◪**summer skiing.** (July-Sept. 7-11am. €24 per day, students and children €18; 2-day pass €40/25. Combo pass with slopes in Zermatt, Switzerland €38/19 per day, 2-day €71/36.) Most hiking trails start near the funicular. Follow **Trail 15** for a day hike with breathtaking views between two waterfalls beneath the Matterhorn (1-2hr.; follow Trail 13 when the trails part). Hikers can also attempt the 3hr. ascent to **Colle Superiore delle Cime Bianche** on Trail 16 (2982m), with views of Val d'Ayas to the east and the Cervino glacier to the west. A shorter trek (1hr.) on the same trail leads to **Lake Goillet**. In Breuil-Cervinia, the Monte Cervino **tourist office**, V. Carrel 29, is off highway A5 next to a Total gas station by the Châtillon Exit; follow signs for the Info Exit. The English-speaking staff has detailed maps and itineraries, as well as info on the winter *Settimana Bianca* (White Week) packages and *Settimane Estive*, the summer equivalent. (☎0166 94 91 36 or 94 44 11; www.cervinia.it. Open high season daily 9am-6pm; low season 9am-12:30pm and 2-5:30pm.) The **Società Guide** (☎0166 94 81 69), across from the tourist office, arranges outings.

> ! **HIKE SMART.** Don't forget your passport on hiking excursions; many trails enter Switzerland.

VAL D'AYAS

Trains run from Aosta to Verrès (30min.; 6:20am, 2:20, 10:15pm; €2.45). SAVDA buses run from the train station at Verrès to Champoluc (1hr.; 6 per day 8:55am-12:25am, 6 returns per day 6:50am-5:30pm; €2.10), as do VITA buses (☎0125 96 65 46; 1hr., 9 per day 7:12am-9:22pm). VITA also runs between Val d'Ayas towns (6:27am-11:04pm). When entering Champoluc, look for the tourist office, V. Varase 16, on the right side of the main road. It may be difficult to identify with signs; look for 5 flags flying above the wooden lodge. It has accommodations info and trail maps. (☎0125 30 71 13; infoayas@ aiatmonterosa.com. Open daily 9am-12:30pm and 3-6pm.)

Budget-minded sports enthusiasts should visit the gently sloping Val d'Ayas, which offers the cheapest **skiing** in the region at **Monterosa Ski Resort.** (☎0125 30 31 68; www.monterosa-ski.com. Open M-F 8:30am-noon and 1-5:30pm. Dec. 19-Apr. 2 €33 per day, children €24; start of season to Dec. 18 and Apr. 3-19 €27/20.) The small town of **Saint Jacques** is the last along the valley road and offers the most **hiking** trails. This should be your departure point if you plan to stay in one of the many *refugi*. The town of **Champoluc** offers the most tourist amenities; the tourist office here should be your stop to plan out any excursions from the valley. An easy hike is the 45min. **Trail #14** from Champoluc to the hamlet of **Mascognaz,** home to a farming population of 10, the charming **Capella di San Grato,** and an excellent restaurant. **Trail #105** wanders over rocks and through pastures to the impressive **Mount Zerbion** (2700m). A 360° panorama displays the soaring Five Giants: the **Matterhorn, Mont Blanc, Monte Rosa, Grand Combin,** and **Gran Paradiso.** Expert hikers may try the **Walser Trail,** staying overnight in tents and following the path of the Germanic migration through Champoluc, Gressoney, St. Jacques, and Valtournenche. For the best views of the valley, turn left after Champoluc and follow the road up the hill to **Antagnod,** which has numerous B&Bs along the steep slope and its own ski lift. **Rafting** is a great way to enjoy the scenery. **Totem Adventure,** Route Mont Blanc 4, has €40-60 packages. (☎0165 87 677; www.totemadventure.com. Reservations recommended. Open July-Aug. daily 8:30am-7:30pm. Cash only.)

COURMAYEUR ☎0165

Italy's oldest Alpine resort lures tourists to the spectacular shadows of Europe's highest peak. French Mt. Blanc (known in Italy as Monte Bianco), with its jagged ridges and snowy fields, is perfect for hiking and skiing. Unfortunately, attractions often cater to the elegant vacationing styles of Europe's rich. However, in May and June, when the snow has melted, quiet descends upon Courmayeur (coor-ma-YUHR; pop. 2800), leaving a sleepy little town surrounded by the beautiful peaks that provide its raison d'être.

▉▉ TRANSPORTATION AND PRACTICAL INFORMATION. A single large complex, the **Centro Congressi Courmayeur,** in **Piazzale Monte Bianco,** houses most travel services, including the **bus station. Buses** run to Aosta (1hr.; every hr. 6:45-9:55pm; €3.10, round-trip €5.30), Milan (4hr.; 3-4 per day; €16, round-trip €29), and Turin (3hr.; M-F 6:45 and 9:45am, Sa-Su 6:45am; €9.30, round-trip €15.80). SAVDA and SADAEM buses, Ple. Monte Bianco 3, buses have frequent service to larger towns. (☎0165 84 20 31 or 84 13 97. Office open daily July-Aug. 8am-7:30pm; Sept.-June 8:45am-12:30pm and 2-7pm. Tickets also sold onboard.) **Taxis** (☎0165 84 29 60) are available 24hr. at Ple. M. Bianco. Pick up a map from the multilingual staff at the **AIAT tourist office,** Ple. M. Bianco 13 (☎0165 84 20 60; www.aiat-monte-bianco.com. Open M-Sa 9am-12:30pm and 3-6:30pm, Su 9am-noon and 3-6pm.) An accommodations board, next to the office, can also help you find a room. (Open Tu-Sa 9am-12:30pm and 3-6:30pm, Su 9am-noon and 3-6pm.). Free **Wi-Fi** is available at the **Cafe des Guides,** though in order to use it, you must be able to register a mobile number; you will receive your access code via text message. The bus station ticket office has currency exchange, as does the **San Paolo Istituto Bancario di Torino,** P. Brocherel 1, which also has an **ATM.** (☎0165 84 20 23. Open M-F 8:25am-1:25pm and 2:40-4:10pm.) In case of **emergency,** go to the **police,** Strada della Margherita 8. A **pharmacy,** V. Circonvallazione 69, posts after-hours rotations. (Open M-F 9am-12:30pm and 3-7:30pm, Sa 9am-12:30pm and 3:30-7:30pm. MC/V.) The **post office** is at Ple. M. Bianco 5, behind the main complex. It also offers currency exchange. (☎0165 84 08 11. Open M-F 8am-1:30pm, Sa 8am-12:30pm.**Postal Code:** 11013.

▉▉ ACCOMMODATIONS AND FOOD. You can't book accommodations far enough ahead, especially if you are hoping to be in Courmayeur for snow season. While hotels abound in Courmayeur, most are expensive without being luxurious. **Pensione Venezia ❸,** Strada delle Villete 2, is by far the best deal in town. From Ple. M. Bianco, head uphill, then left on V. Circonvallazione. This centrally located chalet with rustic rooms, shared bathroom, and TV lounge. (☎/fax 0165 84 24 61. Breakfast included. Singles €35; doubles €46; triples €69. Cash only.) For slightly pricier digs, try the **Hotel Croux ❺,** V. Croux 8, with a convenient location and flowered window-boxes that make it a stand-out. (☎0165 846 735; www.hotelcroux.it. Singles €68-88; doubles €108-135. AmEx/MC/V.)

🍴**Pastificio Gabriella ❶,** Passaggio dell'Angelo 2, at the end of V. Roma, has freshly made sides, breads, pastries, pasta, and sauces. It's the perfect place to pack for a picnic in the shadow of Mt. Bianco. (☎0165 84 33 59. Open July-Aug. daily 8am-12:45pm and 4-7:30pm; Sept.-June M-Tu and Th-Su 8am-12:45pm and 4-7:30pm. MC/V.) Off-piste skiers recharge in the center of town at **Cafe des Guides ❶,** Vle. Monte Bianco 2, below the Società delle Guide. (☎0165 84 24 35. Panini €4-5. Beer €5-6. Mixed drinks €6-8. Cover €1. Free Wi-Fi for those with text messaging services. Open daily 7:30am-2:30am. Cash only.) **Petit Bistrot ❶,** V. Marconi 6, whips up cheap crepes in a city with few budget eateries. (☎0165 347 508 4158. Crepes €4 for takeout, €6.50 inside. Open 11:30am-midnight. Cash only.) Many restaurants close in summer, but **La Terraza ❺,** V. Circonvallazione 73, stays open year-round. Uphill from Ple. Monte Bianco, it specializes in *valdostano* cuisine, like fondue with chestnuts and honey. (☎0165 84 33 30; www.ristorantelaterrazza.com. Pizza €7-12. Primi €12-14. Secondi €17-30. Cover €3. Open daily noon-2:15pm and 7pm-late. MC/V.)

PIEDMONT AND VALLE D'AOSTA

⚠️⛷️ OUTDOOR ACTIVITIES AND SKIING. Courmayeur Ski Resort is famous for its scenic downhill runs, off-piste itineraries, and cross-country offerings (info ☎0165 84 20 60, downhill tickets ☎0165 84 66 58, cross country tickets ☎0165 86 98 12. High season is Dec. 19-Apr. 2. In high season ski passes €41 per day, €224 per week; inquire at the tourist office for the most up-to-date prices.) The brochure Settimane Bianche lists rental prices and often offers discounts. **Buses** also run to **Pré-Saint-Didier** (15min., 8 per day 7:55am-7:15pm, €1.20), which has thermal baths. Pré-Saint-Didier then connects to **La Thuile** (20min., 11 per day 7:55am-8:40pm, €1.20), another ski resort with 150km of intermediate and expert downhill trails and five cross-country skiing tracks.

Buses run from Courmayeur to the trailheads in **Val Veny** and **Val Ferret,** which branch in opposite directions along the base of Monte Bianco. Inquire at the tourist office for a *Valdigne Mont-Blanc: Les Sentiers* map and the brochure *Seven Itineraries around Mont Blanc, Val Veny, and Val Ferret.* The most popular hike in Val Veny is the 1hr. path past the Lac du Miage to **Refuge Elisabetta** (2197m). In Val Ferret, the two short hikes to the **Refuge Bonatti** (2150m) from Lavachey (45min.) and to the **Refuge Elena** (2055m) from Arp Nouva (40min.) make for a relaxing trip. Several trailheads can be accessed directly from Courmayeur. An excellent place to ask questions is **Società delle Guide di Courmayeur,** Strada Villair 2, to the left behind the church. Since 1850, the office has been providing free advice to hikers and finding guides for all major treks and climbs. This headquarters also houses a small museum with photos and exhibits of the original society of mountain guides, established in 1850. (☎0165 84 20 64; guidecourmayeur@tiscali.it. Open in summer M-Tu and Th-Su 9am-noon and 4-7pm, W 4-7pm; in winter Tu-Su 9am-7pm. Museum €3, children €1.50.) A number of excellent **biking** trails traverse Monte Bianco. **Scott Center,** Ple. M. Bianco 15 (☎0165 84 82 54), runs a ski-school and ski-rentals during the winter. During the summer, it becomes **Sirdar** (☎0165 346 578 9776; www.sirdar-montagne.com), and organizes hiking and biking trips.

To explore Monte Bianco, use the 🚠**Funivie Monte Bianco** (☎0165 89 925; www.montebianco.com). *Funivie* depart from **La Palud,** which is accessible by bus from Courmayeur's Ple. Monte Bianco (10min., 8:30am-4:20pm, €1). Head first to the glacier terrace at **Punta Helbronner** (3462m), then across the border to **Aiguille du Midi** (3842m), then to **Chamonix** (1030m). You can take the funicular to La Palud and then to Punta Helbronner, Italy's highest point (round-trip €36; €17 surcharge to continue to Chamonix in summer). In winter, Chamonix is reachable by skiing with a guide. Punta Helbronner affords views of Monte Bianco and the **Matterhorn, Monte Rosa,** and **Gran Paradiso National Park.**

LIGURIA

Liguria (lih-GOO-ree-ah), which stretches along 350km of the Italian Riviera, is home to terraced hillsides, the Apennine Mountains, vineyards, and lush olive groves. Every restaurant boasts the best *frutti di mare* (seafood) and *pesto alla Genovese* (sauce made of basil, pine nuts, and garlic), and rarely do they exaggerate. With trains chugging along the coast, Liguria is easy to explore. Stroll through winding streets lined with colorful houses and elaborately painted architectural in Portofino, trek the coastal cliffs of Cinque Terre, and gaze at Caravaggio masterpieces in Genoa's *Palazzo Bianco*. No matter your destination in Liguria, trade that pair of Italian leather shoes for flip flops and follow the locals' lead through this laid-back vacation oasis.

HIGHLIGHTS OF LIGURIA

TRAIPSE among the villas of Genoa's Via Garibaldi, the "Golden Street" (p. 160).

BEACH BUM with classy Italians on the sandy shores of the Alassio coast (p. 170).

DOUBLE your money in San Remo's casino, a turn-of-the-century gem (p. 175).

GENOA (GENOVA)   ☎010

As any Genovese will proclaim, *"Si deve conoscerla per amarla"*—you have to know Genoa to love her. A city of grit and grandeur, Genoa (JEH-no-va; pop. 600,000) has little in common with neighboring beach towns, except of course impeccable focaccia and pesto. The ugly port and large monuments are the most apparent features of the city, but much of central Genoa is a hidden maze—the narrow, tangled *vicoli* by the port are full of stores, churches, and charm. The world-famous aquarium and the nearby miniscule fishing village of Boccadasse (where people still speak *zenese*, an Italian dialect) attract travelers in the know, but truth be told, most Italians will look at you funny if you say you spent time in Genoa on purpose. Like, for fun. So most travelers just pass through, using the city as a base for exploring the spectacular Ligurian coast. Those who do stick around come to appreciate Genoa as the historic port whose rich intellectual history, financial success, and distinctive culture may just have the rest of Italy a little bit jealous. And we're not just saying that. This place has class.

⌸ TRANSPORTATION

Flights: Cristoforo Colombo Internazionale (☎010 60 151), in Sesti Ponente, sends flights to European destinations. **Volabus #100** runs to the airport from Stazione Principe (every hr. 5:40am-10:40pm, €4.50).

Trains: Stazione Principe, in P. Acquaverde, and **Stazione Brignole,** in P. Verdi. Trains (5min., every 15min., €1.40) and buses #18, 19, 20, 33, and 37 (25min., €1.20) connect the 2 stations. Both offer **luggage storage** (☎010 27 43 4 63). €3.80 for 1st hr., €0.60 per additional hr. for 12hr., €0.20 per hr. thereafter. Open 7am-11pm. Cash only. Ticket validation good for 1hr. Open daily 7am-11pm. Trains run from stations to points along the Riviera and major Italian cities including **Rome** (5-6hr., 10 per day, €27.50) and **Turin** (2hr., every 20-30min., €8-12).

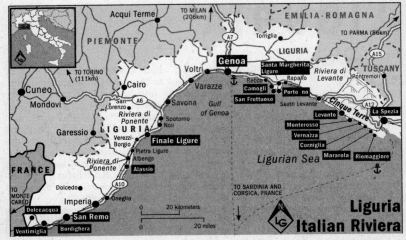

Liguria
Italian Riviera

Ferries: At Ponte Assereto arm of the port. Take bus #20 from Stazione Principe or bus #1 from the aquarium. Purchase tickets at travel agency or Stazione Marittima. Arrive at Terminal Traghetti Ponte Assereto at least 1hr. before departure. Tirrenia (☎010 08 13 17 29 99; www.tirrenia.it) runs ferries to **Sardinia.** Grandi Navi Veloci (☎010 20 94 591; www.gnv.it) heads to **Sardinia, Sicily, Spain,** and **Tunisia.** EneRmaR (☎010 11 97 60 003) goes to **Olbia** and **Palau.** Moby lines (☎010 19 93 03 040; www.moby.it) runs to **Olbia, Bastia,** and **Porto Torres.**

Public Transport: AMT (☎010 80 00 85 311) buses leave from V. Gramsci, in front of the aquarium, or Stazione Brignole. 1-way tickets within the city €1.60. Day passes €4. Passport required for foreigners. Tickets also valid for funicular and elevator rides.

Taxis: (☎010 59 66). From P. de Ferrari.

> **BUS IT.** Though the *centro* is compact, many of Genoa's sights are just beyond a comfortable walking distance. City buses are a frequent and convenient alternative. A 24hr. pass with unlimited rides is just €3.50; if you're traveling with friends, pick up a 24hr. pass for 3 for just €7. Longer stays merit the €12 week long pass with unlimited rides.

ORIENTATION AND PRACTICAL INFORMATION

Genoa has two train stations: **Stazione Principe**, in P. Acquaverde, and **Stazione Brignole**, in P. Verdi. From Stazione Principe take bus #18, 19, or 30, and from Stazione Brignole take bus #19 or 40 to **Piazza de Ferrari** in the center of town. To walk to P. de Ferrari from Stazione Principe, take **Via Balbi** to **Via Cairoli**, which becomes **Via Garibaldi**, and at **Piazza delle Fontane Marose** turn right on **Via XXV Aprile**. From Stazione Brignole, turn right out of the station, left on **Via Fiume**, and right onto **Via XX Settembre**, ending in P. de Ferrari. To get to the **Porto Antico** from P. de Ferrari, take V. Boetto to **Piazza Giacomo Matteoti**, and follow **Via di San Lorenzo** to the water. Genoa's streets stump even natives, so pick up a map.

Tourist Offices: GenovaInforma, Palazzo Ducale, P. G. Matteoti (☎010 86 87 452). Open daily 9am-1pm and 2-6pm. **Kiosks** in Stazione Principe (☎010 24 62 633), and airport (☎010 60 15 247). Both open M-Sa 9:30am-1pm and 2:30-6pm.

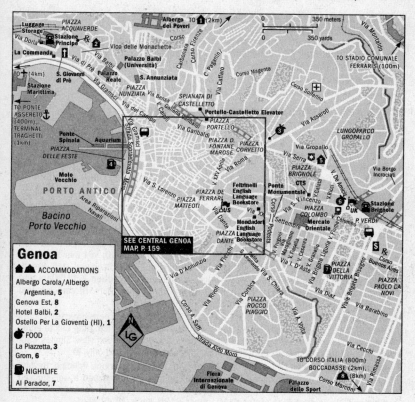

Genoa

♠▲ ACCOMMODATIONS

Albergo Carola/Albergo
Argentina, **5**
Genova Est, **8**
Hotel Balbi, **2**
Ostello Per La Gioventù (HI) **1**

🍴 FOOD

La Piazzetta, **3**
Grom, **6**

🌃 NIGHTLIFE

Al Parador, **7**

Budget Travel: CTS, V. S. Vincenzo 117r (☎010 56 43 66 or 53 27 48), off V. XX Settembre, near Ponte Monumentale. Walk up 1 flight of stairs at the shopping complex to the left. Student fares available. Open M-F 9:30am-6:15pm. MC/V.

Consulates: UK, P. Giuseppe Verdi 6/A (☎010 57 40 071; fax 53 04 096). Take bus #30 (dir.: Sampierdarena) from Stazione Principe to last stop. Open M-Th 9:30am-12:30pm. **US,** V. Dante 2, 3rd fl., 43 (☎010 58 44 92). Open M-Th 11am-3pm.

Beyond Tourism: Informagiovani, Palazzo Ducale, P. G. Matteotti 24r (☎010 55 73 952 or 55 73 965; www.informagiovani.comune.genova.it). Youth center offers info on apartment rentals, jobs, volunteer opportunities, and concerts. Free **Internet** access (1hr. limit). Open M-F 9am-1pm and Tu-Th 2-5:30pm.

English-Language Bookstore: Mondadori, V. XX Settembre 210r (☎010 58 41 40). Huge, with a full wall of classics and some bestsellers. Open M-Sa 9am-8pm, Su 10:30am-1pm and 4:30-8pm. AmEx/MC/V. For a larger selection, check out **Feltrinelli,** V. XX Settembre 231. (Open M-Sa 9:30am-8pm, Su 10am-1pm and 4-8pm. MC/V.)

Pharmacy: Pescetto, V. Balbi 185r (☎010 26 16 09), near Stazione Principe. After-hours rotation posted outside. Open M-F 7:30am-12:30pm and 3:30pm-midnight, Sa-Su 8pm-midnight. AmEx/MC/V. **Farmacia Ghersi,** C. Buenos Aires 18r, across town. Open M-F midnight-12:30pm and 3:30pm-midnight, Sa-Su 7:30pm-midnight. MC/V.

Hospital: Ospedale Evangelico, C. Solferino 1a (☎010 55 221).

Internet Access: Free at **Informagiovani** (see **Beyond Tourism** above). **Number One Bar/Cafe,** P. Verdi 21r (☎010 54 18 85), near Stazione Brignole. €4 per hr. Open M-Sa 7:30am-11:30pm. MC/V. **In-Centro.it Agenzia Viaggi,** V. Roccatagliata Ceccardi 14r, between V. Dante and V. XX Settembre. €3 per hr., students €2.50. Also a bookstore and travel agency. Open M 3-7:30pm, Tu-Sa 9:15am-7:30pm. MC/V.

Post Office: P. Dante 4/6r (☎010 25 94 687). 2 blocks from P. de Ferrari. *Fermoposta* available. Open M-F 8am-6:30pm, Sa 8am-1:30pm. **Postal Code:** 16121.

ACCOMMODATIONS AND CAMPING

Rooms are scarce in October, when the city hosts a wave of nautical conventions. Some budget lodgings in the *centro storico* and near the port rent rooms by the hour for reasons best left uninvestigated. Establishments are more refined around Stazione Brignole and P. Corvetto. The area around Genoa offers plenty of campgrounds, but they fill up in summer, so book ahead.

Albergo Argentina, V. Gropallo 4 (☎/fax 010 83 93 722), near Stazione Brignole, 2 flights down from Albergo Carola. 9 large, clean, comfortable rooms. Singles €30-40; doubles €50-65, with bath €60-75; triples €75-90; quads €85-100. MC/V. ❷

Ostello Per La Gioventù (HI), V. Costanzi 120 (☎/fax 010 24 22 457; www.geocities. com/hostelge). From Stazione Principe, take bus #35; transfer to #40 at the 1st stop on V. Napoli. From Stazione Brignole, take bus #40 (evening #640; last bus 12:50am) 30min. all the way up the hill. Cafeteria, free lockers, and TV. Multilingual staff. Breakfast included. Laundry €7 per 5kg. Wheelchair-accessible. Reception 7-11:30am and 3pm-12:30am. Check-out 10am. Lock-out 10am-3pm. Curfew 2am. HI card required (sold at hostel). Dorms €16; family rooms €16-20 per person. ❶

Albergo Carola, V. Gropallo 4/12, 3rd fl. (☎010 83 91 340; www.pensionecarola.com), near Stazione Brignole. Look for big doors with lion heads on the left. Ring bell to enter. English-speaking staff and 9 rooms with soft beds, some with garden view. Singles €30; doubles €50-65, with bath €60-75; triples €80; quads €90. Cash only. ❸

Hotel Balbi, V. Balbi 21/3 (☎/fax 010 27 59 288), close to Stazione Principe. Beyond the unpromising exterior stairwell lie spacious, comfortable rooms and a well-stocked bar and TV area. All rooms with bath. Breakfast included. Internet access €4 per hr. Singles €65; doubles €80; triples €110; quads €125. AmEx/MC/V. ❺

Genova Est (☎010 34 72 053; www.camping-genova-est.it), on V. Marconi, Località Cassa. Take the train from Stazione Brignole to the suburb of Bogliasco (10min., 6 per day, €1.70); from here, take the free van (5min., every 2hr. 8am-7:50pm) to the campground. While getting there may seem daunting, the campground's website provides train and bus schedules. Shaded sites overlook the sea, with clean bathroom facilities. Laundry €3.50 per load. €6 per person; €5.60-8.60 per tent. Electricity €2.20. ❶

JESUS! THOSE PRICES ARE HIGH. For travelers visiting Genoa during Easter, be aware: prices jump for most accommodations.

FOOD

A dish prepared *alla Genovese* is served with Genoa's pride and joy—pesto. The *genovesi* put it on just about everything and claim that Ligurian water is why true pesto can only be made from basil in this region of Italy. Other delectables include *farinata* (a fried, chickpea flour pancake), focaccia filled with cheese, and *pansotti* (ravioli stuffed with spinach and ricotta in a creamy walnut sauce). To sample a slice of Genoa's famous salami or pick up a jar of pesto, stop by **Salvi Salumeria,** V. di S. Lorenzo 2, near Porto Antico. Also, don't

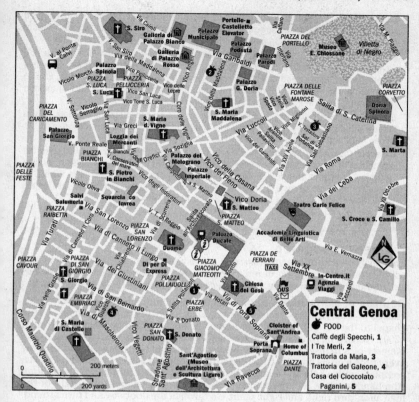

Central Genoa

🍎 FOOD

Caffè degli Specchi, 1
I Tre Merli, 2
Trattoria da Maria, 3
Trattoria del Galeone, 4
Casa del Cioccolato
Paganini, 5

forget to sample the fresh seafood sold along the port-side arcade. For groceries, head to **DìperDì Express**, V. di Canneto Il Lungo 108-112. From P. Matteotti go down Salita Pollaioli, take a right onto V. di Canneto Il Lungo; the supermarket is on the right. (Open M-Sa 8am-7:45pm, Su 9am-1pm and 4-7pm. MC/V.)

🍴 **Trattoria da Maria**, V. Testadoro 14r (☎010 58 10 80), near P. delle Fontane Marose, off V. XXV Aprile. Typical Italian restaurant with checkered tablecloths and a faithful lunch crowd. Outgoing staff serves fresh, delicious dishes of the day. *Menù* includes primo, and secondo, and drink (€9). Open M-Sa 11:45am-3pm. MC/V. ②

🍴 **I Tre Merli**, V. della Maddalena 26r (☎010 24 74 095), on a narrow street off V. Garibaldi. A hidden gem with soft music and a mellow atmosphere. Impeccable service and delicious food make the price well worth it. Wine connoisseurs take note—the list is 16 pages long and very well compiled. Primi €10-12. Secondi €14-16. Open M-F 12:30-3pm and 7:30-11pm, Sa 7:30-11pm. AmEx/MC/V. ④

Trattoria del Galeone, V. di S. Bernardo 55r (☎010 24 68 422). From P. G. Matteoti, take Salita Pollaiuoli, and turn right on V. di S. Bernardo. Galeone is 100m up on the left. Nautically themed dining rooms are crowded with lively yet somewhat older locals. Primi €5-6. Secondi €7-11. Open M-Sa 12:30-2:30pm and 7:30-10pm. Cash only. ②

La Piazzetta, V. Calatafimi 9 (☎010 87 70 28), off P. Marsala. Convenient location in a quiet *piazza* offers Ligurian specials on an outdoor wooden deck. Primi €8-15. Secondi €11-15. Open M-F 12:30-3pm and 7:30-11pm, Sa 7:30pm-midnight. MC/V. ❸

Caffè degli Specchi, Salita Pollaiuoli 43r (☎24 68 193), on the left, down Salita Pollaiuoli from P. G. Matteotti. *Specchio* means mirror, and narcissists will surely enjoy this sophisticated, mirror-lined cafe. The crowds enjoy *bicchierini* (glasses of wine; €3.60) or mixed drinks (€5-5.50) at pleasant outdoor seating. Mini *panini* (€1.50-3) make a tasty snack. Open M-F 7am-9pm, Sa 8am-9pm. AmEx/MC/V. ❶

Grom, V. S. Vincenzo 53r (☎010 56 54 20; www.grom.it), near Stazione Brignole. All you ever wanted gelato to be, made daily with fresh ingredients. Cups and cones from €2. Open M-Th and Su 10am-10pm, F-Sa 10am-midnight. Cash only. ❶

Casa del Cioccolato Paganini, V. di Porta Soprana 45r (☎010 25 13 662). Like the composer of its namesake, the chocolate here just might draw tears of passion. Indulge in unique homemade sweets, from Niccolo Paganini chocolate (boxes from €6.50) to signature *sciroppo di rosa,* a sublime liquid made from sugar, water, and rose petals (€7.30 per bottle). Open M-Sa 12:30-7:30pm. AmEx/V/MC. ❶

◉ SIGHTS

THE CENTRO STORICO

The eerily beautiful *centro storico* is a mass of narrow, winding streets and cobblestone alleyways bordered by **Porto Antico, Via Garibaldi,** and **Piazza de Ferrari.** Remember that walking alone after hours in the *centro storico* is unsafe.

▧CHIESA DI SANTA MARIA DI CASTELLO. With foundations from 500 BC, this church is a labyrinth of chapels, courtyards, cloisters, and crucifixes. In the chapel to the left of the high altar looms the spooky **Crocifisso Miracoloso** (circa 1200). According to legend, the wooden Jesus moved his head to attest to the honesty of a damsel betrayed by her lover, and his beard is still said to grow every time a crisis hits the city. To see the painting of **San Pietro Martire di Verona,** complete with a halo and a large cleaver conspicuously thrust into his cranium (the handiwork of incensed adversaries), go up the stairs to the right of the high altar, turn right, and right again. Go through the doorway and turn around. The painting is above the door. After walking through the door, check out the famous **L'Annunciazione** by Jost di Favensburg (circa 1400) on the right. The real beauty of this sight, though, comes with wandering up stairwells, down porticoes, and through courtyard gardens; there is far more to this church than initially meets the eye. *(From P. G. Matteotti, head up V. di S. Lorenzo toward the water and turn left on V. Chiabrera. A left on serpentine V. di Mascherona leads to the church in P. Caricamento. Open daily 9am-noon and 3:30-6:30pm. Closed Su during masses. Free.)*

▧PALAZZO SPINOLA DI PELLICCERIA. Built at the end of the 16th century, this *palazzo* once hosted Peter Paul Rubens, who described it warmly in a 1622 book on pleasing palaces. Today it houses the **Galleria Nazionale,** a collection of art and furnishings, most donated by the family of Maddalena Doria Spinola. The building tells its own compelling history, as different sections represent architectural styles from throughout the ages. The 18th-century kitchen simulation is particularly intriguing, with a lit stove and flour on the countertop. The museum also contains enormous maps of the world drawn during different eras of exploration, highlighting Genoa's importance in seafaring and cartography of the past. The fourth floor displays Antonello da Messina's 1460 masterpiece *Ecce Homo,* and Van Dyck's portraits of the evangelists reside on the second floor. *(P. di Pelliccera 1, between V. Maddalena and P. S. Luca. ☎010 27 05 300. Open Tu-Sa 8:30am-7:30pm, Su 1:30-7:30pm. €4, ages 18-25 €2.)*

> **TROUBLE IN PARADISE.** Though most of Genoa's crime problems are a thing of the past, travelers should avoid **Via di Prè** entirely and be especially cautious in the area around **Via della Maddalena.** At night, or on weekends when stores are closed, the **centro storico** is also dangerous.

 PORTA SOPRANA. The city's gate was built in 1115 to intimidate Genoa's enemies. The Porta is both the historical centerpiece of P. Dante and the passageway from the modern *piazza* into the *centro storico*. Would-be assailant Emperor Federico Barbarossa took one look at the arch, whose Latin inscription welcomes all coming in peace but proclaims doom to enemy armies, and abandoned his attack. Christopher Columbus's boyhood **home** lies nearby, alongside the remains of the Cloister of St. Andrew's Church. *(From P. G. Matteotti, head down V. di Porta Soprana. ☎ 010 25 16 714. Porta and Columbus's home open daily 10am-6pm. Porta €4, home €4; both €7. Cash only.)*

DUOMO (SAN LORENZO). The *duomo* was reconstructed between the 12th and 16th centuries after religious authorities deemed it "imperfect and deformed." The result may have been an improvement, but it sure wasn't symmetrical; because only one of the two planned bell towers was completed, the church has a lopsided appearance. Climb the completed *campanile* (bell tower) for dizzying city views. On the left in the church, the golden **Cappella di San Giovanni** houses a relic from St. John the Baptist. *(In P. S. Lorenzo, off V. di S. Lorenzo. Open daily 9am-noon and 3-6pm. Guided tour every 30min. Modest dress required. Tickets for campanile sold M-Sa in Museo del Tesoro on left side of church. Campanile €5.50, duomo free. Cash only.)*

CHIESA DEL GESÙ. Also known as **Sant'Andrea e Ambrogio,** this former Jesuit church, completed in 1606, houses two Rubens canvases: *The Circumcision* over the altar and *The Miracle of St. Ignatius* in the third alcove on the left. *(From P. de Ferrari, take V. Boetto to P. G. Matteotti. Open M-Sa 7am-12:45pm and 4-7:30pm, Su 8am-12:45pm and 5-9:45pm. Closed Su during masses 7:15, 10, 11am, noon, 6:30pm. Free.)*

PALAZZO DUCALE. The majestic centerpiece of the *centro storico*, this *palazzo* was constructed in 1290 as the seat of Genoa's government. The neoclassical facade was completed a few years before the end of the Republic of Genoa in 1797 by architect Simone Cantoni, while the interior is done up in Rococo decor. Visit the **museum** on the second floor for rotating exhibits of international artwork. *(P. G. Matteotti 9. ☎ 010 55 74 000; www.palazzoducale.genova.it. Museum open Tu-Su 9am-7pm. Ticket office closes at 6:30pm. €7, students €6. AmEx/MC/V.)*

FROM STAZIONE PRINCIPE TO THE CENTRO STORICO

Outside the winding alleys of the *centro storico*, Genoa boasts a multitude of *palazzi*, many of which have been converted to museums that showcase 16th- and 17th-century Flemish and Italian art. **Via Garibaldi**, which skirts the edge of the *centro storico*, and **Via Balbi**, which runs through the university quarter from Stazione Principe to P. Nunziata, offer the best city views.

PALAZZO REALE. Built in the 15th century, this *palazzo* was originally home to the Balbi family. It became the Royal Palace in 1823. The *piemontese* Rococo throne room, covered in red velvet, remains untouched, along with the royal waiting room and sleeping quarters. The resplendent **Galleria degli Specchi** is modeled after the Hall of Mirrors at Versailles. In the queen's bedroom, the **queen's clock** is really a *notturlabio*, a clock with stenciled numbers lit from behind by a candle. Don't miss the spectacular view from the *palazzo*'s terrace, off Room 22. To see paintings by Tintoretto, Van Dyck, and Bassano, ascend the red-carpeted stairs on the left after purchasing a ticket. *(V. Balbi 10. 5min. walk west of V. Garibaldi. ☎ 010 27 10 236; www.palazzorealegenova.it. Open Tu-W 9am-1:30pm, Th-Su 9am-7pm. Entrances on the ½hr. €4, ages 18-25 €2, under 18 or over 65 free. Cash only.)*

AQUARIUM. Genoa's most elaborate tourist attraction has the most water of any European aquarium. Wander the exhibits, then board **Grande Nave Blu,** a huge barge filled with habitat recreations, from the forests of Madagascar to the Caribbean reefs. There's also a touch tank with sea rays. Guides offer multilingual "Behind the Scenes" tours. *(On Porto Antico, across from tourist kiosk. ☎ 010 23 45 666; www.acquariodigenova.it. Open July-Aug. daily 9am-11pm; Mar.-June and Sept.-Oct. M-F 9:30am-7:30pm, Sa-Su 9am-8:30pm; Nov.-Feb. daily 9:30am-7:30pm. Last entry 1hr. before closing. Various entrance packages, starting at €20. Discounts for groups and children. AmEx/MC/V.)*

VIA GARIBALDI. The most impressive street in Genoa, V. Garibaldi deserves its nickname, *Via Aurea* (Golden Street). In the 17th century, wealthy families lined the way with elegant palaces. Today, the **Palazzi** have been converted into a series of museums that give the paintings center stage. **Galleria di Palazzo Rosso,** built in the 16th century, earned its name when it was painted red a century later. Red carpets cover the floors of exhibit halls that feature several hundred years' worth of *genovese* ceramics. The second floor now holds several Van Dyck portraits of nobility. Across the street, the **Galleria di Palazzo Bianco** exhibits a large collection of Ligurian art. The third floor contains Van Dyck's *Red-Eyed Christ,* as well as works by Caravaggio, Rubens, and Vasari. Several doors down lies **Palazzo Tursi** (also known as the **Palazzo Municipale**). The former home of the Savoy monarchy built between 1565 and 1579, now serves as the city hall and showcases a courtyard and Niccolo Paganini's violin, *Il Cannone,* made by the legendary Giuseppe Guarneri. This instrument is still played by the winner of Premio Paganini, an international violin competition held annually on October 12. *(Galleria di Palazzo Rosso: V. Garibaldi 18. Galleria di Palazzo Bianco: V. Garibaldi 11. Palazzo Tursi: V. Garibaldi 9. All 3 sights ☎ 010 27 59 185. Open Tu-F 9am-7pm, Sa-Su 10am-7pm. Ticket office, V. Garibaldi 9, open daily 9am-8pm. Admission to all 3 museums covered by single ticket. €8, €6 students and seniors, under 18 free. AmEx/MC/V.)*

PORTELLO-CASTELLETTO ELEVATOR. Walk down the tunnel in P. Portello to ride this elevator with locals, who take it as regularly as the bus. A plaque in the entrance tunnel quotes Giorgio Caproni: *"Quando mi sarò deciso d'andarci, in paradiso ci andrò con l'ascensore di Castelletto."* ("When I have decided to go there, in paradise I will go with the elevator of Castelletto.") The 30-second ride, which connects the *centro storico* with neighborhoods in surrounding hills, leads commuters to perfect panoramas one step closer to paradise. *(Through the tunnel entrance in P. Portello. Open daily 6:40am-midnight. Single-use tickets can be purchased for €0.50 from machines at the entrance to the elevator or from newsstands nearby.)*

ART-STARVED? If you plan on visiting many museums, invest in a museum pass. The 24hr. pass (€9), covers Palazzo Reale and Palazzo Spinola, while the 2-day pass (€16, €20 including bus fare) covers every museum in Genoa. Purchase passes at the tourist office or participating museums.

🎵 🎭 ENTERTAINMENT AND NIGHTLIFE

Genoa's new **Cineplex,** V. Magazzini de' Cotone, at Molo Vecchio, shows American movies dubbed in Italian. *(☎ 010 89 90 30 820; www.cineplex.it. Box office open M-F 4-10:30pm, Sa 2:15pm-1am, Su 2-11:30pm. Tickets €7.30, matinees €5.)* A walk farther down the port, to the end of the pier, reveals myriad wine bars which offer views of the highly commercial port and surprisingly cheap glasses of wine. As with most bars, to get the cheapest price, order at the bar rather than sitting at a table. **Corso Italia** is a trendy promenade, home to much of Genoa's nightlife. A 20min. ride down the long boulevard on bus #31 leads to **Boccadasse,** a fishing village and seaside playground for wealthy *genovesi*. Unfortunately for tourists, many clubs are difficult to reach on foot, so travelers in Genoa often drive to reach their nightlife destinations. Local university students flock to bars in **Piazza delle Erbe** and along **Via San Bernardo.** Closer to Stazione Bringole, **Al Parador,** P. della Vittoria 49r, is located in the northeast corner of P. Vittoria, near the intersection of V. Cadorna and V. B. Liguria. Upscale bar by day, by night this watering hole is frequented by both real celebrities like Uma Thurman and Claudia Schiffer and the wannabes who idolize them. (☎010 58 17 71. Mixed drinks €4.50. Open M-Sa 24hr. Cash only.)

RIVIERA DI LEVANTE

CAMOGLI   ☎0185

Lounge, eat, and hike your way to happiness in the postcard-perfect town of Camogli (ca-MOL-yee; pop. 5516). A warm breeze rises off the sea, diffusing the tempting smells of fried fresh seafood from the restaurants that line the promenade. Waitresses at beachside cafes wear bikinis and aprons. Less ritzy and more youth-friendly than nearby Portofino and Santa Margherita, Camogli is a gem in Liguria's aptly named Golfo Paradiso (Gulf of Paradise).

☐ TRANSPORTATION. Camogli is on the Genoa-La Spezia train line. (Ticket office open M-Sa 6:15am-3pm, Su 10am-7pm.) **Trains** run to Genoa (40min., 2 per hr., €1.90); La Spezia (1hr., 1-2 per hr., €4.20) via Santa Margherita; (5min., every 30min., €1.40); and Sestri Levante (30min., every 30min., €3). Tigullio **buses** leave from P. Schiaffino for nearby towns. Buy tickets at the tourist office or at *tabaccherie*. Buses go to Santa Margherita (20min., 20 per day, €1.10), Rapallo, Ruta, and San Lorenzo. For Golfo Paradiso **ferries,** V. Scalo 2 (☎0185 77 20 91; www.golfoparadiso.it), look for the *"Servizio Batelli"* sign near P. Colombo by the water. Buy tickets at dock or on the ferry (cash only). Round-trip ferries go to Monterosso (July and Aug. Su, check at office for more info and summer specials; €20), Portofino (June 10-Sept. 5 Tu-Su depart morning, return late afternoon; €13), and San Fruttuoso (June-Sept. every hr. 8am-7pm, €9).

◼🛈 ORIENTATION AND PRACTICAL INFORMATION. Camogli extends uphill from the sea to pine and olive groves and downhill from the train station to the beach. To get to the **centro,** turn right out of the **train station** on **Via XX Settembre,** walk 100m, and turn left down the stairs to **Via Garibaldi.** Walk down a second flight, marked by the sign: "Scalinata Martiri delle Forbe" to reach the beach. Services include: the **tourist office,** V. XX Settembre 33 (☎0185 77 10 66; Internet access €1.50 per 30min; open in summer M-Sa 9am-12:30pm and 3-6:30pm, Su 9am-12:30pm); *Banco di Chiavari della Riviera Ligure,* V. XX Settembre 19 (☎0185 77 51 13; open M-Sa 8:20am-1:20pm and 2:30-4pm); **police,** G. B. Ferrari (☎0185 77 07 25); **carabinieri,** V. Cuneo 30/F (☎0185 77 00 00); a **pharmacy,** V. Repubblica 4-6 (☎0185 77 10 81; open daily July-Aug. 8:30am-12:30pm and 4-8pm; Sept.-June 3:30-7:30pm; MC/V); and the **post office,** V. Cuneo 4. (☎0185 77 68 31. Open M-F 8am-6:30, Sa 8am-12:30pm. Cash only.) **Postal Code:** 16032.

LIGURIA

ACCOMMODATIONS. Prices and availability vary greatly according to season and day of the week. Though the tourist office can help with last-minute rooms, reserve ahead and be prepared to pay a higher price in summer. Renovated ◼Hotel Augusta ❸, V. Piero Schiaffino 100, has 14 blue and yellow rooms; all have bath, TV, A/C, and phone. Some overlook the harbor from private balconies. From the train station, turn right and keep walking until V. Repubblica turns into V. P. Schiaffino. (☎0185 77 05 92; www.htlaugusta.com. Breakfast included. Internet access free; limit 15min. Singles €40-78; doubles €55-115. AmEx/MC/V.) The ◼Albergo La Camogliese ❹, V. Garibaldi 55, is just steps from the beach. Exit train station, walk down the long stairway to the right, and look for the blue sign. Large rooms are as comfortable as the English-speaking staff is helpful. All have bath, TV, safe, and phone. (☎0185 77 14 02; www.lacamogliese.it. Breakfast included. Internet access available. Singles €50-90; doubles €70-110; triples €95-120. Extra bed €10. 10% discount with cash payment. AmEx/MC/V.) The Pensione Faro ❹, V. Schiaffino 116-118, above a restaurant of the same name, offers quiet rooms with bath, TV, and some sea views. (☎/fax 0185 77 14 00. Breakfast €4. Singles €40-50; doubles €60-80. AmEx/MC/V.)

FOOD. Focaccia is the specialty in Camogli, as is fresh seafood caught by local fishermen. ◼Focacceria Pasticceria Revello ❶, V. Garibaldi 183, is famous in the region for fresh, crispy flatbreads and delectable pastries. This shop invented the town's beloved *camogliesi* (dense and crumbly cookies; €21 per kg). Make like the locals and lunch on focaccia with onions or *formaggio*. (☎0185 77 07 77; www.revellocamogli.com. Focaccia €8.50 per kg. Open daily 8am-2pm and 4-8pm. MC/V.) Il Portico Spaghetteria ❷, V. Garibaldi 197A, offers creative pastas (€6.50-9.50) at excellent values that will satisfy every craving; try the *spaghetti alla carbonara*. (☎0185 77 02 54; www.ilporticodicamogli.it. Cover €1.50. Open daily 12:30-3pm; 8-11pm. Cash only.) The creamy gelato at Gelato e Dintorni ❶, V. Garibaldi 104/105, puts national rivals to shame. They specialize in parfaits made with creamy homemade yogurt and fresh fruit. (☎0185 77 43 53. 2 scoops €1.70. Sicilian *granita* €2. Open daily 11:30am-11pm. Cash only.) Find groceries and picnic supplies at shops on V. Repubblica (one block from the harbor) or at the Picasso supermarket, V. XX Settembre 35. Walk down the stairs immediately past the tourist office. (Open M-Sa 8:15am-12:30pm and 4:30-7:30pm, Su 8:30am-12:30pm. MC/V.) On Wednesdays, an open-air market fills P. del Teatro with local produce and cheap clothing. (Open 8am-noon.)

OUTDOOR ACTIVITIES AND NIGHTLIFE. The Camogli tourist office has a useful trail map. Painted red shapes mark the paths, which start at the end of V. Cuneo near the *carabinieri* station. Bike paths line the city and rentals are available through the tourist office. Ferry or snorkeling trips also make interesting—if more costly—diversions. B&B Diving Center, V. S. Fortunato 11/13, off V. Schiaffino, offers scuba diving. (☎/fax 0185 77 27 51; www.bbdiving.it. Open daily June 15-Sept. 15 9am-1pm and 2:30-7:30pm; Sept. 16-June 14 9am-1pm and 3:30-7pm. 1-person canoe €17 per ½-day, 2-person €30 per ½-day. Scuba tours with guide and equipment Sa-Su 4 per day, €39; equipment only €18-23. 10-person boat capacity. Cash only.) The Sagra del Pesce, an enormous fish fry, is held annually on the second Sunday in May. The night before the big fry, the town gathers for a procession honoring the patron saint of fishermen, followed by a fireworks display and a bonfire-building contest on the beach. The next day the fryers cook in a gargantuan frying pan, which measures 4m in diameter and holds 2000 fish to feed the jolly crowd. After the sardine rush, the colossal pan hangs on a city wall along the stairs to the beach.

Spend nights in peaceful Camogli with a cool drink and a sea view. Order a mojito (€5.50) or sangria loaded with pineapple chunks (€4.50) to cap off the day at upscale **Il Barcollo**, V. Garibaldi 92. (☎0185 77 33 22. Open M-F 4pm-3am, Sa-Su 11am-3am. Cash only.) Down the boulevard is the pirate-themed **Hook**, V. al Porto 4, decorated like a ship's cabin and offering over 60 types of rum (€3.50-20) to wash down the good food. (☎0185 77 07 11. Panini €3-4. Happy hour 6-9pm; drinks €6. Open M, W, Su 8am-3am, Tu 6pm-3am. AmEx/MC/V.)

▶ **DAYTRIP FROM CAMOGLI: SAN FRUTTUOSO.** The hikes from Camogli to tiny San Fruttuoso (san FROO-too-OH-so; pop. 8, 10 including dogs) follow two labeled trails that wind through Portofino's nature reserve. The easier 2hr. hike along **Trail #1**, marked by a red circle, climbs up and around Mt. Portofino through ancient forests and olive groves, with a descent to the harbor on a stone path that can be very slippery when wet. Only experts should venture out on the 2hr. **Trail #2.** Marked by two red dots, Trail #2 winds along the coast past Nazi anti-aircraft bunkers and through forests to sea vistas before it descends into town. Proper footwear is essential.

San Fruttuoso is named for its abbey, the Benedictine **Abbazia di San Fruttuoso di Capodimonte**, constructed during the 10th through 13th centuries. The monastery and tower rotate archaeological exhibits. (*☎0185 77 27 03. Abbazia open daily 10am-6:30pm. Tower open daily 10am-1pm and 2-5:30pm. Last entry 30min. before closing. €7, children €4.*) Fifteen meters offshore and 17m underwater, the bronze *Christ of the Depths* stands with arms upraised in memory of the sea's casualties. The statue now protects scuba divers, and a replica stands in **Chiesa di San Fruttuoso**, enticing visitors to make an offering to the *Sacrario dei Morti in Mare* (Sanctuary for the Dead at Sea). Friendly locals with small boats offer rides to the underwater statue from the docks for €2.50. (*San Fruttuoso is accessible by trails from Portofino Mare 1hr., Portofino Vetta 1hr., or Camogli 2hr. Golfo Paradiso (☎0185 77 20 91; www.golfoparadiso.it) runs boats from Camogli to San Fruttuoso in summer; Tu and Th-Sa every hr. 8am-5pm, last return 6-7pm; round-trip €9.*)

SANTA MARGHERITA LIGURE   ☎0185

For the most part, Santa Margherita Ligure (SAN-ta Mar-ge-REE-ta LEE-gooreh; pop. 10,210) leads a calm existence as a fishing village far from the Levante limelight. The little popularity it has stems from a *National Geographic* feature in the 50s, while the beachfront and palm-tree-lined harbor provides plenty of photo ops. As a resort town, every inch of the manicured coast boasts scenes of natural beauty situated between big-name fashion outlets.

▐ TRANSPORTATION

Trains: on the Genoa-La Spezia line. To: **Genoa** (50min., €2.30) and **Monterosso** (1hr., €3.90). Ticket office is inside the station. Open daily 6am-7pm. MC/V.

Buses: Tigullio (☎0185 28 88 34) departs from the small green kiosk in P. Vittorio Veneto. To: **Camogli** (30min., every 45min., €1.30) and **Portofino** (20min., 3 per hr., €1). Ticket office open daily 7am-7pm. Tickets available after hours at the *tabaccheria*.

Ferries: Servizio Marittimo del Tigullio, V. Palestro 8/1B (☎0185 28 46 70; www.traghettiportofino.it). Docks at P. Martiri della Libertà. To: **Cinque Terre** (1st Su of May through last Su of Sept. 9am, round-trip €23) and **Portofino** (M-F every hour 10:15am-4:15pm, Sa-Su every hour 9:15am-5:15pm; €5, round-trip €8.50).

Taxis: in P. Stazione (☎0185 28 65 08) and on V. Pescino (☎0185 28 79 98).

✛ 🛈 ORIENTATION AND PRACTICAL INFORMATION

From the **train station,** turn right on **Via Roma,** and follow it along the water. At the end of the road turn left on **Corso E. Rainuso** to reach **Piazza Vittorio Veneto.** Turn right on V. Pescino, which winds around **Piazza Martiri della Libertà. Piazza Caprera** is between them set back from the water. From P. V. Veneto, V. Guglielmo Marconi winds around the port and V. XXV Aprile leads to the tourist office, becoming **Corso Matteotti** near the town's main square, **Piazza Mazzini.**

Tourist Office: Pro Loco tourist office, V. XXV Aprile 2/B (☎0185 28 78 17; www.santamargheritaturismo.it). Open M-Sa 9:30am-12:30pm and 3-7:30pm, Su 9:30am-12:30pm and 4:30-7:30pm. **info point,** P. Veneto. Open 10am-12:30pm and 3-5pm.

Police: P. Mazzini 46. ☎0185 20 54 50.

Pharmacy: Farmacia Dr Machi, V. Palestro 44 (☎0185 28 70 02), off P. Caprera. Posts after-hours rotation. Open M-W and F-Su 8:30am-12:30pm and 4-8pm. MC/V.

Hospital: V. Fratelli Arpe. ☎0185 68 31.

Internet Access: The Internet Point, V. Giuncheto 39 (☎0185 29 30 92; liguriacom@ tigullio.it). Follow V. Dogali from P. Mazzini; it's on the left. €2.50 per 20min. Open M-Sa 10am-1pm and 3-7:30pm. Cash only.

Post Office: V. Roma 36 (☎0185 29 47 51). Offers currency exchange, *fermoposta*, and an **ATM.** Open M-F 8am-6:30pm, Sa 8am-12:30pm. Cash only. **Postal Code:** 16038.

🛏 ACCOMMODATIONS

Ritzy waterfront accommodations are by no means the only options, but be prepared to shell out a few more euro than usual in Santa Margherita. Luckily nothing is far from the beach.

🏨 Hotel Conte Verde, V. Zara 1 (☎0185 28 71 39; www.hotelconteverde.it), off V. Roma. From train station turn left down V. Trieste, which becomes V. Roma. Cozy beds and private showers make for a truly heavenly stay. Gold tasseled pillows and other indulgent luxuries. Breakfast included. Singles €50-60, with bath €65-120; doubles €65-90/70-150; triples €90-120; quads €100-230. AmEx/MC/V. ❹

Hotel Nuova Riviera, V. Belvedere 10 (☎0185 28 74 03; www.nuovariviera.com). Run by an English-speaking family. Large, bright rooms decorated in the Victorian style all have private bath. Breakfast included for hotel rooms, €5 for annex rooms. Internet access €5 per 30min. Hotel singles €65-105; doubles €85-110, annex doubles €60-90; triples €75-110. Cash only for annex rooms; MC/V for hotel rooms. ❺

Albergo Annabella, V. Costasecca 10/1 (☎0185 28 65 31), behind P. Mazzini. Kind owner makes guests feel at home in comfortable rooms, some with bath. Breakfast €4. Singles €40-45; doubles €60; triples €80-90; quads €100-120. Cash only. ❹

Hotel Metropole, V. Pagana 2. Recently renovated, this 57-room hotel is located in a beautiful private garden. Rooms with A/C, TV, bath, safe, and minibar. Some rooms have balconies overlooking the water. Doubles €90-160. AmEx/MC/V. ❹

🍴 FOOD

Markets and bakeries line **Corso Matteotti;** pick up some focaccia for a cheap picnic lunch. Buy essentials at the **Coop,** C. Matteotti 8, off P. Mazzini. (☎0185 28 43 15. Open M-Sa 8:30am-1pm and 3:30-8pm, Su 8:30am-1pm. AmEx/MC/V.)

🍴 Trattoria Da Pezzi, V. Cavour 21 (☎0185 28 53 03). Locals descend on the famous trattoria for its home-style cuisine and jovial atmosphere. *Farinata* (€4.50) and *torta* *pasquelina* (pork quiche; €5.20-6) are great choices. Takeout available. Primi €4-7.50. Secondi €6-15. Cover €1. Open M-F and Su 10am-2:15pm and 5-9:15pm. MC/V. ❶

▧ **Trattoria Baicin,** V. Algeria 5 (☎0185 28 67 63), is off P. Martiri della Libertà. Mama Carmela serves glorious plates of *spaghetti carbonara* (pasta in a cream sauce with chopped eggplant, peppers, capers, and garlic; €6.50). Primi €5.50-7.50. Secondi €9.50-16.50. Cover €1.50. Open Tu-Su noon-3pm and 7-11:30pm. AmEx/MC/V. ❸

La Locanda Azzura, V. S. Bernardo 3 (☎0185 28 53 94). From the shore, turn right off C. Matteotti. The *pansotti alla salsa di noci* (vegetable-filled pasta in walnut cream sauce; €7) is tough to beat. Primi €6-10. Secondi €8.50-18.50. Cover €2. Open M-Tu and Th-Su 12:10-2pm and 7:10-10:30pm. MC/V. ❸

L'Approdo, V. Cairoli 26 (☎0185 28 17 89). This place is worth the extra expense for its exquisite presentation and succulent dishes like shrimp scampi with peas (€28). Primi €12-17. Secondi €18-42. Cover €3. Open Tu 7:30pm-midnight, W-Su 12:30-2pm and 7:30pm-midnight. AmEx/MC/V. ❺

Gelateria Centrale, Largo Giusti 14 (☎0185 28 74 80). Crowds gather nightly for *pinguini* (€2.50), chocolate-dipped gelato cones. Open daily 9am-midnight. Cash only. ❶

◨ ◧ SIGHTS AND NIGHTLIFE

If lapping waves at the pebbly public **beach** across from the main promenade, C. Doria, aren't sufficiently invigorating, visit the Rococo **Basilica di Santa Margherita,** in P. Caprera, dripping with gold and crystal chandeliers. The church also contains fine Flemish and Italian artwork commissioned by the Catholic Church. (☎0185 28 65 55. Open daily 7:30am-noon and 3-6:30pm.) Off V. della Vittoria, paths wind uphill to the pink-and-white **Villa Durazzo,** which is surrounded by gardens and holds 16th-century paintings. (Basilica open daily July-Aug. 9am-8pm; Sept. and May-June 9am-7pm; Oct. and Apr. 9am-6pm; Nov.-Dec. 9am-5pm. Villa open daily 9am-1pm and 2:30-6pm. Both free.) **Chiesa di San Francesco,** at the end of Salata al Castello off P. Martiri della Libertà, holds the monument of St. Francis. (Open daily 8:30am-noon and 3:30-5:30pm. Free.)

Come nightfall, youthful crowds claim the multi-colored tables at **Sabot American Bar,** P. Martiri della Libertà 32, which offers appetizers, drinks, sushi platters, and a nightly DJ. (☎0185 28 07 47. Beer €4.50-7. Mixed drinks €8-9. Open daily 5pm-4am. MC/V.) Mingle with the *fashionistas* a few doors down at **Miami,** P. Martiri della Libertà 29, amid with neon lights and vinyl booths. (☎0185 28 34 24. Primi €7-12. Secondi €10-20. Open daily 5pm-3am. AmEx/MC/V.) Next door, **Soleado Cafe** is another stop on the P. Martiri della Libertà bar hop. Cheap drinks draw in a large crowd throughout the week. (Open M-F 5pm-2am and Sa-Su midnight-2am. AmEx/MC/V.)

◪ DAYTRIP FROM SANTA MARGHERITA

PORTOFINO

Take bus #82 to Portofino Mare from green kiosk in P. Martiri della Libertà in Santa Margherita, where tickets are sold behind the train station. From Portofino's P. Martiri della Libertà, Tigullio buses run to Santa Margherita (3 per hr., €1.10). Portofino is also accessible by ferry from Santa Margherita (every hr. 10:30am-4pm, €4.70), and Camogli (2 per day, €11.70).

Portofino (POR-toh-FEE-no; pop. 529) is a perfect half-day outing from Santa Margherita. Yachts fill the harbor, chic designer boutiques and art galleries line cobblestone streets, and luxury cars crowd parking lots. Nevertheless, the tiny bay of this fine port can be enjoyed by the glamorous and the budget-minded alike. The nature reserve that surrounds Portofino and nearby resort village Paraggi boasts a small but beautiful public beach. Treks through the hilly terrain past ruined churches and stately villas lead to Rapallo (2hr.), Santa Margherita (1hr.), and San Fruttuoso (2hr.). Information regarding hikes and necessary trail maps are available at the tourist office. Facing the water, head right, around the port, and climb hundreds of steep stone stairs for 10min. to reach the cool, stark interior of the **Chiesa di San Giorgio.** Don't forget your camera for the views of the port from the nearby lookout. Another 10min. up the hill you'll find the 16th-century **Castello Brown,** V. alla Penisola 13/A. The castle was once a fortress, but the wealthy Brown family converted it into a summer home after Consul Montague Yeats Brown bought it in 1867 from the Kingdom of Sardinia for 7000 lire. (☎0185 26 71 01 or 26 90 46. Open daily 10am-6pm. €4.50.)

Back in town, **Alimentari Repetto ❷,** P. Martiri dell'Olivetta 30, in the main square in front of the harbor, sells sandwiches (from €3) like the special prosciutto *panini,* as well as regional goods like *limoncello* for around €10. (Open daily in summer 8am-10pm; in winter 9am-6pm. Cash only.) **Trattoria Concordia ❸,** V. del Fondaco 5, behind P. della Libertà, serves authentic Ligurian cuisine in a small, nautical-themed dining room. Local favorites are cheaper here than at many other harbor haunts. (☎0185 26 92 07. Primi €10-26. Secondi €14-32. Service 10%. Open M and W-Su noon-3pm and 7:30-10pm. AmEx/MC/V.) The English-speaking staff at the **APT tourist office,** at V. Roma 35, distributes trail maps. (☎0185 26 90 24. Open daily 10:30am-1:30pm and 2:30-6:30pm.)

> **TIP**
>
> **A FERRY TALE.** Though the hikes and train rides through Portofino's nature reserve are gorgeous, the real charm of the small coastal towns is best experienced from the sea. Hop on one of the many ferries between Camogli, San Fruttuoso, Portofino, and Santa Margherita for incomparable panoramas of colorful buildings nestled in the mountains.

RIVIERA DI PONENTE

FINALE LIGURE ☎019

A plaque at the base of a statue along the promenade claims that Finale Ligure (fee-NA-leh LEE-goo-reh; pop. 11,845) is the place for *"il riposo del popolo,"* or "the people's rest." Whether *riposo* involves bodysurfing in the choppy waves, browsing chic boutiques, or sipping coffee in Finalborgo's medieval *piazze,* there are countless ways to pass the time in this sleepy town.

TRANSPORTATION

The **train station** (☎019 27 58 777 or 89 20 21) is in P. Vittorio Veneto. The ticket office is open daily 6am-7pm. Trains run to Genoa (1hr., every 30min 7:53am-10:55pm, €14.50.) via Savona, and Ventimiglia (30min., every 30min. 7:12am-11:46pm, €5.50) via San Remo. ACTS **buses** depart from a side street left of the train station to Finalborgo (5min., every 30min., €1.40) and Savona (45min, every 30min., €2.20). Buy tickets at the bar in the train station. For **taxis,** call Radio Taxi ☎019 69 23 33, or 69 23 34.

🔅 🛈 ORIENTATION AND PRACTICAL INFORMATION

The city is divided into three sections: **Finalpia** to the east, **Finalmarina** in the center, and **Finalborgo,** the *centro storico,* to the northwest. The train station and most services are in Finalmarina. The area's main street winds through the town between the station and **Piazza Vittorio Emanuele II,** whose name changes from **Via di Raimondi** to **Via Pertica** to **Via Garibaldi.** From P. V. Emanuele II, **Via della Concezione** runs parallel to the shore. To reach Finalborgo, turn left from the station, go under the tracks, and keep left on **Via Domenico Bruneghi** for 10min.

The **IAT tourist office** is at V. della Concezione 27. From the station, walk to the water, and then take the only left; signs lead the way. (☎019 68 10 19; www. inforiviera.it. Open M-Tu and Th-Su 7am-7pm. Closed Su in winter.) Currency exchange and an **ATM** are available at **Banca Carige,** V. Garibaldi 4. (Open M-F 8:20am-1:20pm and 2:30-4pm.) In an emergency, call the **police,** V. Brunenghi 67 (☎019 69 26 66). **Farmacia della Marina,** V. Ghiglieri 2, at the intersection where V. Raimondi becomes V. Pertica, lists after-hours rotations. (☎019 69 26 70. Open M-Sa 8:30am-12:30pm and 4-8pm. Ring bell for emergencies.) **Internet** access is available at **Net Village Internet Cafe,** V. di Raimondi 21, across from the train station. (☎019 68 16 283. €5 per hr. Open daily 8am-10pm.) For rock climbing in the area, the **Mountain Shop,** V. Nicotera 4, in Finalborgo, provides maps and the necessary gear. (☎019 68 16 230. Open M and W-Su 9:30am-1pm, 5-8pm, and 9pm-midnight. MC/V.) The **post office** is at V. della Concezione 29. (☎019 69 04 79. Open M-F 8:15am-6:30pm, Sa 8:15am-12:30pm.) **Postal Code:** 17024.

ACCOMMODATIONS AND CAMPING

The youth hostel has the best prices—not to mention the best view. While it may also have the only available rooms, especially in July and August, it's still best to call ahead. The tourist office can help find *affitacamere.*

Castello Wuillerman (HI), V. Generale Caviglia 46 (☎/fax 019 69 05 15). From the station, turn left on V. Raimondo Pertica (just after the intersection), and continue straight. Turn left at the corner of V. Pertica and V. Alonzo, and climb the thigh-burning stairs to the top. The cliffside castle-turned-hostel has locking cabinets in rooms, a beautiful courtyard, and a good restaurant. Breakfast included. Laundry €4 per load. Reception 7-10am and 5-10pm. Curfew midnight. Dorms €14. HI members only. Cash only. ❶

Albergo Carla, V. Colombo 44 (☎019 69 22 85; fax 68 19 65). Across from the seaside walkway. All rooms with bath and phone; some with sea view. Restaurant downstairs. Breakfast €4. Reservations recommended. Singles €28-40; doubles €48-60. MC/V. ❸

Alba Chiara, Vico Tubino 5 (☎019 69 34 18; fax 019 69 07 02). 1-star hotel with long rooms that have blue comforters and white-lace curtains. All rooms have TV and phone. English spoken. Doubles €55-90. AmEx/MC/V. ❸

Petit Hotel, Corso Europa 83 (☎019 60 17 50; fax 019 60 31 30). Modern, colorful rooms have phone, TV, and safe. English spoken. Doubles €60-88. AmEx/MC/V. ❹

Del Mulino (☎019 60 16 69; www.campingmulino.it), on V. Castelli, 15min. from the center of town. From the station, take the Calvisio bus to Boncardo Hotel, then turn left at P. Oberdan and right on V. Porro. Follow signs uphill. Tents pitched on cement on a hill overlooking water and vegetation. Bar, pizzeria, and mini-market. Hot showers. Laundry €5. Reception 8am-8pm. Open Apr.-Sept. €6-7 per person; €5-7 per tent. MC/V. ❶

FOOD

Reservations are helpful for dinner; restaurants fill up quickly. Get basics at **DìperDì Express,** V. Alonzo 10. (Open M-Sa 8:15am-1pm and 4:30-7:30pm. MC/V.)

NO FOOD FOR YOU. During the high season in towns along the Riviera, dinner reservations are harder to come by than a hostel bed. Make reservations a few nights in advance if you're set on a restaurant, otherwise you might find yourself staring at a *completo* sign on the door instead of a menu.

LIGURIA

Spaghetteria Il Post, V. Porro 21 (☎019 60 00 95). Follow V. Colombo from the beach-front past P. Cavour. Turn left onto V. Genova, which becomes V. Porro. Try *formaggi*, including Ligurian specialty *pecorino*, made from sheep's milk (€6.50). Lots of vegetarian options. Bring a few friends, as each dish is made for 2. Cover €1. Open Tu-Su 7:30-11pm. Closed 1st 2 weeks of Mar. Cash only. ❶

Farinata Vini, V. Roma 25 (☎019 69 25 62). Small, popular trattoria serves fresh seafood and pasta. Enjoy yellow *farinata* (pie made from chickpeas, sometimes filled with meat and vegetables) on the table at every meal. Menu changes daily. Primi €8-11. Secondi €10-16. Open M and W-Su 12:30-2pm and 7:30-9pm. MC/V. ❸

Sole Luna, V. Barrili 31 (☎019 68 16 160). A distance from the beach for those who need relief from the sun. *Farinata* €1.50. Pizza €2-2.50 per slice. Grilled focaccia *panini* €2-3.50. Savory crepes €3-4. Open daily 10am-8pm. Cash only. ❶

La Taverna dei Brontoloni, V. della Concezione 7. Considering the beachfront seating overlooking water and palm trees, these prices can't be beat. Try the *trofie alla gevonese* (€9). *Menù turistico* (primo, secondo, and contorno) €15. Pizza €4-8. Primi €7-10. Secondi €8-18. Open M-Tu and Th-Su noon-2:30pm and 6-10:30pm. AmEx/MC/V. ❷

👁 🎵 SIGHTS AND ENTERTAINMENT

Finalmarina is best known for its sandy **beaches**. The free beach is perfect: small and well-populated, but not crowded, the strip of yellow sand is caressed by sparkling waters. For more seclusion but less ready access to snack bars, walk 15min. east along V. Aurelia and through the first short tunnel to another beach, cradled by overhanging cliffs. **Finalborgo**, Finale Ligure's historical district, is a 1km walk or 2min. bus ride up V. Bruneghi from the station. Past the **Porta Reale** (its main entrance), the Chiostro di Santa Caterina houses the **Museo Archeologico del Finale**, dedicated to Ligurian history with displays ranging from Paleolithic artifacts to Roman and Byzantine finds. (☎019 69 00 20. Open Tu-Su Sept.-June 9am-noon and 2:30-5pm; July-Aug. 10am-noon and 4-7pm. Free.) Enjoy the town's medieval architecture and quiet ambience while sipping a *caffè* in one of many small *piazze*. If you crave the small-town charm of narrow streets and ancient churches, consider making a short bus trip to nearby villages of **Borgio** and **Verezzi** (every 15min. 6:15am-10:30pm, round-trip €2.20). Consider visiting during July and August, when the annual **Festival Teatrale** holds live theater performances by national touring companies. (V. IV Novembre. ☎019 61 29 73; www.festivalverezzi.it. Tickets €23, reduced €20.)

In Finalmarina, late summer nights are the norm, and bars, *gelaterie*, and even restaurants are packed until the wee hours. A few blocks from the shore is **Pilade**, V. Garibaldi 67, with live music ranging from blues to soul on some Friday nights and rock and techno during the week. Posters of jazz legends fill the walls and an older crowd fills the tables, ordering mixed drinks (€5) or beer (from €3). Pizza (€2 per slice) and delicious *panini* (€2.60-3) are available for a sit-down meal or takeout. (☎019 69 22 20. Open daily 10am-2am. Closed Th in winter.) Each Saturday night, locals pile into **El Trucadero Cocktail Bar**, V. della Concezione 13, for DJ-hosted "Palm Beach Parties," beginning at 10pm. (Mixed drinks €5-8. Open W-Sa 10pm-3am.) As the sun sets, it's easy to find more nightlife—just follow the crowds to the waterfront, where bathhouses host dance parties and bars fill up with sunbathers along **Via della Concezione**.

ALASSIO ☎0182

Sun-splashed Alassio (ah-LA-see-yo) has attracted high-class Italians and dedicated beachgoers to its sparkling seas for over a century. Though its residential population is only about 13,000, this number seems to triple in summer thanks to sun-worshipping resort-frequenters. Vacationers come for the white-sand beaches, excellent cuisine and nightlife, or a case of the town's signature Baci chocolate pastries (see next page). Even with these luxuries, Alassio maintains a cheery, unpretentious character that makes it perfect for young travelers.

TRANSPORTATION

Trains: between V. Michelangelo and V. Giuseppe Mazzini (☎0182 89 20 21). Ticket office open daily 6am-7pm. 24hr. self-service ticket machines available. To: **Finale Ligure** (20min., every 30min., €3.30); **Genoa** (2hr., every 2hr., €6.40); **Milan** (3hr., every 3hr., €14); **Ventimiglia** (1hr., every 30min., €4.90).

Buses: SAR buses run along V. Aurelia, connecting Alassio to nearby towns.

Bike Rental: Ricciardi, C. Dante Alighieri 144 (☎0182 64 05 55). €5 per hr., €15 per day. Open M-Sa 9am-7pm, Su 10am-12:30pm and 4:30-7pm. AmEx/MC/V.

ORIENTATION AND PRACTICAL INFORMATION

Alassio is a small, navigable town with activity centering around the boardwalk. Head straight out of the **train station** and turn right on **Via Giuseppe Mazzini** in front of the park. V. G. Mazzini forms one part of the city's main street, **Via Aurelia.** Three streets, V. Aurelia, **Corso Dante Alighieri,** and **Via Vittorio Veneto,** run parallel to the sea. Head straight from the train station to hit the shore.

Tourist Office: APT tourist office, V. G. Mazzini 68 (☎0182 64 70 27; alassio@inforiviera.it). Open M-Sa 9am-12:30pm and 3-6:30pm, Su 9am-noon.

Banks: Unicredit Banca, V. Gibb 14, 2 blocks from the train station on V. Aurelia. Open M-F 8:20am-1:20pm and 2:20-4:20pm, Sa-Su 10am-12:30pm and 4:30-7pm.

Luggage storage is available to the left of the train station's main exit. Open daily 7am-noon and 2:15-6:30pm. €3.50 per day.

Farmacia Nazionale is at V. V. Veneto 3. (☎0182 64 06 06). Open daily 8:30am-12:30pm and 3:30-7:30pm. MC/V.

Internet Access: Punto.It, V. Torino 30 (☎0182 47 01 24). Open M 4-7:30pm, Tu-Sa 9:30am-12:30pm and 4-7:30pm. MC/V.

Post Office: P. Airaldi Durante (☎0182 66 091). Open M-F 8am-6pm, Su 8am-1:15pm. Cash only. **Postal Code:** 17021.

ACCOMMODATIONS AND CAMPING

Hotel Fiorenza & Banksia, V. Privata Marconi 11-13 (☎0182 64 05 04; www.alassio.it/banksia). From the station, walk along V. Hanbury and turn right on V. P. Marconi. Welcoming staff provide rooms with TV, phone, and private bath. Breakfast included. Parking €5 per day. Doubles €60-90. Extra bed 25% of room price. Cash only. ❸

Hotel Panama, V. Brennero 27 (☎0182 64 59 16; www.panamavacanze.com). From the station, turn right on V. G. Mazzini and left on V. Torino. Follow to the sea, and then turn right on V. V. Veneto, which becomes V. Brennero. Private beach and cheery dining room with beachwood cabinets. Rooms have flatscreen TV, A/C, and phone. Breakfast included. Lockers and Internet access available. Doubles €80-180. Weekly rates available. Extra bed €20. Full-pension €50-115. AmEx/MC/V. ❸

Hotel Rosa, V. Maddalena Conti 10. Family-run. Rooms with have embroidered duvets. Private garden, 2 terraces, 3 common rooms, and bar. Doubles €75-110. ❸

Camping La Vedetta Est, V. Giancardi 11 (☎0182 64 24 07; fax 64 24 27), 1.5km from Alassio. From V. G. Mazzini, take bus toward Albenga. Bus stops in front on the highway, so be careful. Bungalows and tent sites overlook the sea. Open daily 8:30am-12:30pm and 3-10pm. Campsites €7-8 per person; 2-person bungalows with car and tent €24-35; bungalows €30-145. Cash only. ❶

🍴 FOOD

Alassio is overrun with pizzerias and *gelaterie*. Don't leave without sampling the famed *Baci di Alassio* (fudge pastry) at **Balzola**, P. Matteotti 26. (☎0182 64 02 09. Open daily in summer 9am-4am; in winter 9am-2am.) Buy basics from the **STANDA** supermarket at V. S. Giovanni Bosco 36/66, part of V. Aurelia. (Open daily 8am-8:30pm. AmEx/MC/V.)

▨ **Osteria Mezzaluna**, V. Vico Berno 6 (☎0182 64 03 87; www.mezzaluna.it), on the waterfront. Intimate, Spanish-influenced atmosphere and delectable Mediterranean cuisine. Large platters of meats and cheeses served family-style. Salads €6.50-8.50. Secondi €7.50-10. Live music nightly. Open daily 7:30pm-2am. AmEx/MC/V. ❸

Pizzeria Italia, Passeggiata Toti 19 (☎0182 64 40 95). Ultra-thin-crust pizza just steps from the beach. The *boscaiola* (grilled eggplant, prosciutto, and fresh mozzarella; €7.50) packs a flavorful punch. Primi €8-10. Secondi €10-16. Cover €1. Open daily May-Aug. noon-3:30pm and 7pm-4am. Cash only. ❷

Ristorante Sail Inn, V. Brennero 34-38 (☎0182 64 02 32). Attentive waiters and a waterfront patio make this *ristorante* a classy choice for a fishy feast. Primi €12-24. Secondi €15-40. Open Tu-Su for lunch and dinner. AmEx/MC/V. ❹

Gelateria Acuvea, P. Matteotti 3 (☎0182 66 00 60). After 25 years in business, the Sicilian wizards at Gelateria Acuvea have the whole town in their power, scooping out fresh, whipped gelato. Watch flavors being hand-churned while you wait. 2 scoops €1.70 Open daily in summer 10am-2am; in winter 10am-midnight. Cash only. ❶

👁️ 🍸 SIGHTS AND NIGHTLIFE

Kilometers of pristine, sandy **beaches** stretch in both directions along the coast, leaving little reason to venture inland. There are a few **free** public beaches about a 15min. walk down the shore, but if central location and lively activity are a priority, then a private beach may be worth the price of admission. Most entries requires a €12-20 fee for two to four chairs and umbrella. Take a short stroll down the beach to the east to join the throng of older fishermen at the **pier,** a favorite spot for loafing, line-casting, and relaxed sea-gazing. If you need a beach break, the fishing village of **Laigueglia** offers colorful houses, tiny *piazze*, and twisting stone streets. (30min. coastal walk or 5min. bus ride toward Andorra. SAR buses leave from points on V. Aurelia every 20 min., buy tickets for €1.40 at nearby *tabaccherie*.)

Stoked by tourists and youth from nearby towns, Alassio comes to life at night. Decorated with red lanterns, **Tokai Bar,** V. V. Veneto 151, draws an international crowd for beachfront refreshments and animated conversation. (Mixed drinks and sangria from €5.50. Open M-W and F-Su 10:30am-3am. Cash only.) Local favorite **Bar Cabaret,** V. Hanbury 58, has live music on weekends and a raucous crowd that sings along. Grab a pint (€3-7) and one of many *panini* named after classic rock legends. (☎0182 347 961 5372. Open daily 9:30pm-3am. Cash only.) Trendy **Caffe Roma,** V. Dante 308-310, is the new place to see and be seen among the Euro-chic. All-white decor adorns the two-story lounge, and a young and hip crowd flirts on red-and-black polka-dotted plush couches. (☎0182 64 03 78. Panini €3-5. Mixed drinks €5-9. Open Tu-Su noon-4am.)

LIGURIA

SAN REMO
☎**0184**

With all the cheapness and tacky glamor of a casino town, and yet the tranquility of a resort refuge, this former Russian-elite retreat now hosts a medley of international tourists seeking unadulterated freedom. Despite the crowds that converge to play slots in the largest casino resort town on the Italian Riviera, San Remo (san RAY-mo; pop. 50,608) offers a plethora of urban comforts and entertainment opportunities. The city's many boutiques and upscale shops help winners and indulgent losers alike live like big spenders. Upholding the reputation of the *Riviera dei Fiori* (Riviera of Flowers), San Remo blooms with colorful carnations year-round. Adding to the musical click of poker chips, the town resounds with an international jazz competition each summer.

▐ TRANSPORTATION

Trains: Stazione F.S., V. Carlo Pisacane, facing C. Felice Cavalotti. Ticket office open daily 6:30am-8pm. To: **Genoa** (2-3hr., every hr. 5:24am-10:24pm, €7.90), **Milan** (4hr., 7 per day 5:22am-5:15pm, €15), and **Ventimiglia** (20min., 1-2 per hr. 7:25am-12:55am, €1.90). 5min. walk from ticket booth to train. Prices listed vary seasonally.

Buses: Stazione Autolinee, P. Colombo (☎0184 59 27 06). To: **Ventimiglia** (30min., every 15-30min. 5am-12:55am, €2) via **Bordighera** (20min., €1.40).

Taxis: Radio Taxi, ☎0184 54 14 54.

◀▶ ▐ ORIENTATION AND PRACTICAL INFORMATION

The city is comprised of three main streets that run east-west, parallel to the beach. The train station faces the northern-most of the three, **Corso Felice Cavalotti,** which becomes **Corso Giuseppe Garibaldi** and then **Corso Giacomo Matteotti** on its way west through the *centro*. To the south is **Via Roma,** followed by **Via Nino Bixio** closest to the water. To get to the *centro* from the station, turn right on C. F. Cavalotti, cross the roundabout **Rondo Giuseppe Garibaldi,** and veer left down C. G. Garibaldi. At **Piazza Colombo,** continue straight, bearing left while crossing the *piazza* to reach swanky C. G. Matteotti, which leads to the *lungomare* and the sea. The tourist-free old town, **La Pigna,** is uphill from P. Colombo.

Tourist Office: APT, V. Nuvoloni 1 (☎0184 59 059; www.rivieradeifiori.travel). From P. Colombo, go left onto C. G. Matteotti and follow it to the end. The office is slightly up the hill on the corner on the right. Open M-Sa 8am-7pm, Su 9am-1pm.

Bank: There are plenty of banks for the high rollers in San Remo. **Banca Intesa,** V. Roma 62 (☎0184 59 23 11), offers currency exchange and **ATM.** Open M-F 8:30am-1:30pm and 2:45-5pm, Sa 8:30am-noon.

Bookstore: Libreria Mondadori, V. Roma 91 (☎0184 50 57 12). Large English selection. English-speaking staff. Open 9am-8pm daily.

Laundromat: Blu Acquazzura, V. Alessandro Volta 131 (☎0184 340 417 8480), off Rondo Garibaldi. Wash and dry €3.50 each. Open daily 8:30am-7:30pm.

Pharmacy: Farmacia Centrale, C. G. Matteotti 190 (☎0184 50 90 65). After-hours rotation posted outside. Open M-Sa 8:30am-8:30pm.

Hospital: Ospedale Civile, V. Giovanni Borea 56 (☎0184 53 61).

Internet: Mailboxes, Etc., C. Cavallotti 86 (☎0184 59 16 73). €2.50 per 30min., €4 per hr. Photocopies and fax available. Open M-F 9am-6:30pm. AmEx/MC/V.

Post Office: V. Roma 156. Open M-F 8:15am-6:30pm, Sa 8:15am-1pm. **Postal Code:** 18038.

ACCOMMODATIONS AND CAMPING

San Remo enjoys a high standard of accommodations. Though this means high prices, it also means that even one-star hotels are clean and comfortable.

Albergo Al Dom, C. Mombello 13, 2nd fl. (☎0184 50 14 60). From the train station, turn right onto C. F. Cavallotti and pass through Rondo G. Garibaldi. Follow C. G. Garibaldi and turn left on C. G. Matteotti to reach C. Mombello. Buzz to enter. Welcoming owners tend rooms with full bath, fans, and TV. Breakfast €5. Singles €30; doubles €60. ❷

Hotel Graziella, Rondo Garibaldi 2 (☎0184 57 10 31; fax 57 00 43), 2min. from the train station. Turn right on C. F. Cavalotti, then right around Rondo G. Garibaldi. Hotel is in a villa set back from the road. Elegant rooms with high ceilings, stone balconies, TV, fridge, and phone; most with A/C. Breakfast €5. Singles €65; doubles €85. Prices jump €10-15 per person in August. MC/V. ❹

Hotel Sorriso, C. Raimondo 73 (☎0184 50 03 56; www.soloalberghi.com/hotelsorriso). From the train station, turn right on C. F. Cavalotti, left on V. Fiume, and right on C. Orazio Raimondo. Plush crimson carpeting, in-room TVs, A/C, and showers. English-speaking staff happily points the way to nearby dining and entertainment. Breakfast included. Singles €40-60; doubles €60-120. Prices soar in summer. AmEx/MC/V. ❸

Camping Villaggio dei Fiori, V. Tiro a Volo 3. (☎0184 66 06 35; info@villaggiodeifiori. it). A 10min. bus ride west of town. Take bus from station in P. Colombo to Villa Elios (every 20min., €1) or any bus to Ventimiglia and stop at Villa Elios. The shaded sites and relaxed atmosphere, combined with on-site pool and restaurant, make this a solid option. 2-person tent pitch €20-32; 4-person €29-53. High season 3- to 5-person bungalows €99-128, low season €64-120. Electricity €2. Cash only. ❶

FOOD

Some unique and affordable dining options exist among the pizzerias and pricey restaurants. Try *sardinara*, a local focaccia-like specialty topped with tomato sauce, herbs, and olives. Buy basics at **Casitalia** supermarket in P. Eroi 44. (Open M-F 8:15am-12:45pm and 2-7:30pm, Sa 8:15am-1pm and 4-7:45pm. Closed W afternoon. MC/V.) **Mercato Ortofruitticolo,** in neighboring P. Mercato, sells fresh produce, meat, and bread. (Open M-Sa 6am-1:30pm, Sa 4-7:30pm.)

Vin D'Italia, C. Mombello 5 (☎0184 59 17 47). Upscale restaurant accented with modern vases. Down-to-earth staff. Local food is their middle name; be sure to try *sardinara* (€0.80), hot from a wood-burning oven. Primi and secondi €9-16. Open M-Sa 11am-3pm and 7-10pm. AmEx/MC/V. ❸

Urbicia Vivas, P. dei Dolori 5/6 (☎0184 75 55 66; www.urbiciavivas.com), in a charming *piazza* in the old city. From V. Palazzo, turn left on V. Cavour, and walk through the archway, turn left onto V. S. Sebastiano and continue straight until you reach the 1st *piazza*. Join locals for generous helpings of *ravioli di erbette* (with herbs). Primi €10-14. Secondi €10-17. Open daily 8am-3pm and 7pm-midnight. AmEx/MC/V. ❸

Liberty, V. Imperatrice 70 (☎0184 53 14 96; fax 0184 50 15 74). Traditional Ligurian fare and 90 wines. Elegant dining room overlooks the water. Primi and secondi €22-42. Cover €2.70. Open Dec. 22-Nov. 2, Tu-Su 12-2:30pm and 7-10:30pm. AmEx/MC/V. ❺

Trattoria A Cuvea, C. G. Garibaldi 110 (☎0184 50 34 98). Follow C. F. Cavallotti away from the train station. Tasty cuisine served in this hole-in-the-wall favored by locals. Primi €5.70-7.60. Secondi €7.30-8.75. Open M-Sa noon-3pm and 7:30-10pm, Su 7:30-10:30pm. Cash only. ❷

🔵 🔚 SIGHTS AND BEACHES

San Remo has many historical treasures. Across from the tourist office stands the Byzantine-style, onion-domed Russian Orthodox **Chiesa di Cristo Salvatore**, V. Nuvoloni 2. The intricate exterior is the highlight; the simple interior has a few gleaming icons and plain walls. (Open daily 9:30am-12:30pm and 3-6:30pm. Suggested donation €1.) Leaving the church, follow C. G. Matteotti away from the sea. Turn left onto V. Pietro Calvi, which leads to P. S. Siro, where you'll find the city's most sacred monument, the 13th-century **Basilica di San Siro.** (Open M-Sa 8:30am-noon and 3-6pm, Su 8:30am-noon and 3-8pm. Free.) From the basilica, steer through the vendors along the *gelateria*-lined V. Palazzo and turn left on V. Cavour to **La Pigna**, San Remo's *centro storico*, which most tourists miss. Narrow streets are crowded with tiny medieval churches connected by private secret underground passageways. The streets can be confusing; be sure to ask for a map that includes La Pigna when you stop by the Tourist Office. From La Pigna, follow the tree-lined road upward to P. Assunta, to the elaborate **Il Santuario della Madonna della Costa.** This 17th-century monument features a high dome covered in frescoes and twisting rose marble columns. The *Madonna and Child* painting above the altar, attributed to Fra Nicoló of Voltri, dates to the late 14th century. (☎0184 50 30 00. Open daily 9am-noon and 3-6pm. Modest dress required. Free; donations welcome.)

In the daytime, Speedo- and bikini-clad crowds pack the beach and numerous *bagni* that line the water, so get there early to snag a patch of sand. Most commercial beaches are open from 8:30am to 7:30pm, while the public beach closes at 7pm. Lounge chair and umbrella rental run around €12 per day. Most public beaches require rentals for entrance. Penny-pinchers can head to the end of V. Roma for a well-kept public beach.

🎵 🎭 ENTERTAINMENT AND NIGHTLIFE

When darkness hits in San Remo, so do the gamblers who frequent the enormous **Casino Municipale**, C. Inglesi 18, at the end of C. G. Matteoti. Built in 1905, the casino is a dazzling example of *Belle Époque* architecture. No sandals or shorts are allowed upstairs, and a coat and tie for men and formal wear for women are required in winter. Five hundred slot machines clang away on the lower floors, while the swanky rooms upstairs host the Riviera's most dapper, sipping mixed drinks and hoping to win the famed "Mystery Jackpot." (☎0184 59 51; www.casinosanremo.it. 18+. Passport required. Cover F-Su €7.50. Open M-F 2:30pm-2am, Sa-Su 2:30pm-4am.) After dark, couples meander along the swanky **Corso Matteotti** for gelato and liqueurs. **Mellow Sax Pub,** V. Roma 160, has a sports- and jazz-inspired decor and outdoor seating to attract an all-ages crowd. Drinks run €3-7 and come with *torta di verde* and focaccia. (☎0184 50 37 43; www.saxpub.it. Open M and W-Su 8pm-4am. AmEx/MC/V.) Ten minutes from the casino is **Pico de Gallo,** Lungomare V. Emanuele 11/13, where the liquor starts flowing long before sundown. Sip a Caribbean-inspired drink (€5) as you sit on the beach. The *bagni* (beach area) is open daily 9:30am-7:30pm. (☎0184 57 43 45; www.picosanremo.com. Cash only. Bar open 24hr. Restaurant open 12:30-3pm. MC/V.) On a side street off C. G. Matteotti, **Zoo Bizarre,** V. Gaudio 10, is a small, trendy spot with electric-green tables and a ceiling plastered with movie posters. The hip, though unpretentious, crowd kicks off its weekend evenings here around 9pm with drinks (€4.50-7) and free munchies. (☎0184 50 57 74. Open M-F 5:30pm-2am, Sa-Su 5:30pm-3am. Cash only.)

Alternatives to dice and drinking are harder to find. At the end of January, a float parade livens up the city streets for the annual festival **San Remo in Fiore.**

The **Jazz and Blues Festival,** held in late July and early August, draws international artists to soothe the sunburned crowds.

BORDIGHERA
☎ 0184

A seaside residential locale dominated by middle-class Italian vacationers, Bordighera (bor-dee-GEH-ra; pop. 10,292) first hit the tourist spotlight in the early 20th century, with high profile guests like Claude Monet and Louis Pasteur. Its outer edges are busy with traffic and cheap shops, though the humble *centro storico* offers quiet, palm-tree lined routes for a *passeggiata* (stroll). For those seeking sun, Bordighera also offers small gray stretches of beach, though they pale in comparison to the French Riviera just minutes away.

⬛ TRANSPORTATION. The **train station** is in P. Eroi Libertà. **Trains** run to: Genoa (3hr., 6 per day 4:53am-10:23pm, €7.35); Milan (4hr., 4 per day 6:25am-7:05pm, €24.70); San Remo (15min., every hr. 4:53am-10:23pm, €1.70); Ventimiglia (5min., every hr. 7:35am-12:57am, €1). The ticket office is open daily 6:15am-7:35pm. Riviera Transporti **buses** stop every 300m on V. V. Emanuele and run to San Remo (25min., every 15min. 5:42am-1:22am, €1.20) and Ventimiglia (15min., every 15min. 5:42am-1:22am, €1.20). Buy tickets at *tabaccherie* on V. V. Emanuele or at the post office. Tourist office provides more detailed bus schedules. **Taxis** available outside train station.

⬛🛈 ORIENTATION AND PRACTICAL INFORMATION. The bus from Ventimiglia stops on the main street in the busy, modern city, **Via Vittorio Emanuele,** which runs parallel to the sea and the scenic **Lungomare Argentina.** To get to the *lungomare,* walk down V. Agostino Noaro or V. Generale Luigi Cadorna, and go through the tunnels under the train tracks. The **train station** is located between V. V. Emanuele and the sea, at **Piazza Eroi della Libertà.** To reach the **centro storico,** follow V. V. Emanuele to P. Ruffini. Bear left across the *piazza* and continue straight. This road changes names to V. Libertà, V. Matteotti, and V. Arziglia. Turn left and walk uphill on V. Botafogu Rossi and follow it to the top. **Via Roma,** which becomes **Corso Italia,** runs straight from the station.

For extensive info on all Riviera towns, head to the **tourist office,** V. V. Emanuele 172. From the train station, walk left and turn right onto **Via Sant'Antonio.** (☎0184 26 23 22; fax 26 44 55. Open in summer M-Sa 9am-12:30pm and 3:30-7pm, Su 9am-12:30pm.) **Currency exchange** and **ATM** are available at **Banca Intesa,** V. Roma 4. (☎0184 26 67 77. Open M-F 8:30am-1:30pm and 2:45-4:15pm, Sa 8:30am-noon.) In case of emergency, call the **police,** V. Primo Maggio 49 (☎0184 26 26 26). **Farmacia Centrale,** V. V. Emanuele 145, posts a list of after-hours service. (☎0184 26 12 46. Open M-F and Su 8:30am-12:30pm and 3:30-7:30pm.) The **post office,** P. Eroi della Libertà 5/6, has an ATM outside. (☎0184 26 91 51 or 26 91 31. Open M-F 8:15am-6:30pm, Sa 8:15am-12:30pm.) **Postal Code:** 18012.

⬛⬛ ACCOMMODATIONS AND FOOD. In the high season, many hotels in Bordighera require that clients accept full or half-pension. It is also standard practice to raise prices for guests staying under three days, usually by €5-10. The city's few hotels tend to charge upwards of €125 a night for a double with simple furnishings. Across from the train station, on the left, **Albergo Nagos ❷,** P. Eroi della Libertà 7, third fl., has nine small rooms with long beds; three have private showers. The shared bath is clean and well-stocked. (☎0184 26 04 57. Singles €32; doubles €45. Half-pension €36; full-pension €45. MC/V.)

To escape the beach crowds, head to ⬛**Ristorante la Piazzetta ❷,** P. del Popolo 13, in the *centro.* Savor the specialty wood-fired pizza (€5-8.50) and other

Ligurian fare in bountiful portions. (Primi €7-9.50. Secondi €10-16. Cover €1.20. Open M-Tu and Th-Su noon-2:30pm and 6:30-11pm. AmEx/MC/V.) Locals crowd the marble tables of **Creperie-Caffè Giglio ❷**, V. V. Emanuele 158. A dizzying selection of creative dinner crepes with many vegetarian options complement the seven-page drink menu. Dessert crepes (€3.50-6) are sweet and satisfying. (☎0184 26 15 30. Open Tu-Su 5:30pm-3am. Cash only.) The lively, beach-themed **La Reserve ❸**, V. Arziglia 20, at the eastern end of the *lungomare*, is a great place to grab a seaside drink—follow the blaring island music. (☎0184 26 13 22. Primi €10-16. Secondi €15-30. Bar open 24hr. Kitchen open 8-10am, 12:30-2:30pm, and 8-10pm.) **Osteria La Sfusa**, 144 V. Emanuele (☎0184 345 348 0650), bottles award-winning olive oil (½ liter €7.50; 1 liter €12.50) and uses it in its daily specials. *Giovedi gnocchi* and *sabato trippa* are excellent local draws. (Daily specials and primi €8. Secondi €12. Open Tu-Su noon-2:30pm and 7-10pm.) An outdoor **market** on the *lungomare* sells produce. (Th from early morning to 1pm. There is also a **STANDA** at V. della Libertà 32. (Open M-Sa 8am-8pm, Su 9am-8:30 pm. AmEx/MC/V.)

◫◪ SIGHTS AND BEACHES. Bordighera's **beach** is crammed with locals and tourists who arrive early to rent lounge chairs, umbrellas, and cabanas from one of the many *bagni* (each around €5 per day). A popular free beach is accessed through the subway beneath the train station. To rent jet skis, windsurf boards, or motorboats, call ☎0184 348 518 3835. For sailing, windsurfing, kayaking, or canoeing, contact the **Nautical Club of Bordighera** (☎0184 26 00 94; www.clubnauticobordighera.it). The tourist office also has windsurfing info. Follow V. Arziglia for 20min. to reach the **Giardino Esotico Pallanca**. It's on the left past the tunnel. Buses from V. V. Emanuele heading in the direction of San Remo also stop at the *Giardino* upon request. The exotic garden, once open only to scientists, contains over 3000 species of cacti and flora. The walking tour (1hr.) leads along meandering terraces. (☎0184 26 63 47; www.pallanca. it. Open Tu-Su 9am-12:30pm and 2:30-7pm. €6, under 13 free, groups more than 8 €5.) Returning to town, the **Giardini del Capo** offer spectacular sea views and a glimpse of the statue of Queen Margherita Di Saviolo, one of Italy's first queens. The park leads to the town's **centro storico,** established in 1471, which is too narrow for cars. Walk through the parking lot at the top of the park and through the archway at the end of V. del Campo to explore the narrow stone streets.

▨▨ NIGHTLIFE AND FESTIVALS. Il Barretto is Bordighera's most renowned spot for beachside nightlife—you'll know it when you see it. A town staple since 1960, it has a spring break vibe and no-frills attitude. Come for cheap eats, packed dance floors, and ample amounts of liquor. (☎0184 26 25 66. Pizza €1.50. Shots €3.50. Open daily 9am-4am. Cash only.) A raucous, mostly male crowd fills the dim interior and outdoor tables under an arched arcade at **Graffiti Pub/Risto House,** V. V. Emanuele 122. Along with a wide choice of liquor (€3.50-5), beer on tap (€2.50-4), and wine (€11-15), they also serve cheap meals, including *panini* for €3.50-4. (☎0184 26 15 90. Open M-Sa 5:30pm-3am. Cash only.) A classier, more upscale *discoteca*, the **Kursaal Club,** Lungomare Argentina 7, has both live and recorded underground, house, and industrial music (☎0184 26 46 85. 25+ on F and Su. Open Sept.-July F-Su 7pm-midnight; Aug. daily 11pm-5am. AmEx/MC/V.)

LIGURIA

LOMBARDY
(LOMBARDIA)

Lombardy ("lom-bar-DEE-ah") specializes in the finer things in life. Though coveted by the Romans, Goths, French, Spaniards, Austrians, and Corsicans, the disputing European powers failed to rob Lombardy of its prosperity. The region is filled with ornate art and architecture; from Milan's fashion runways to Cremona's Stradivari violin shops, cultural sophistication permeates the region.

HIGHLIGHTS OF LOMBARDY

DAYTRIP to Certosa di Pavia, where the monastery stands as a monument to the evolution of northern Italian art from early Gothic to Baroque (p. 196).

SPOT the *moda* of the moment in Milan, as stylish *Milanesi* show off Europe's latest cutting-edge fashion (p. 192).

WANDER the streets of Mantua, where Renaissance artists Verdi and Mantegna got their inspiration (p. 196).

MILAN (MILANO)   ☎02

Milan ("mee-LA-no"; pop. 1,200,000) is a proud modern metropolis. Tire giant Pirelli, fashion master Armani, and various executive banks make it Italy's economic powerhouse. Rushed, refined, and unapologetically cosmopolitan, Milan has its share of problems, including traffic congestion and a high cost of living. But its beautifully ornate *duomo* and stunning La Scala theater, thriving alongside big designer shopping and even bigger spenders, attract throngs of visitors. Generally overlooked as a center of commerce, this Italian urban center also hides artistic treasures: Leonardo's *Last Supper*, the Pinacoteca di Brera, and the Pinacoteca Ambrosiana. Today, the city flourishes as Italy's leading producer of cutting-edge style, hearty risotto, and die-hard soccer fans. The city's pace quickens twice a year when local soccer teams AC Milan and Inter Milan face off in matches with fanfare that rivals many religious festivals. Milan's bustling lifestyle has established it as a northern capital.

✈ INTERCITY TRANSPORTATION

Flights: 24hr. flight info (☎02 74 85 22 00; www.sea-aeroportimilano.it).

Malpensa Airport (MXP), 48km from the city. Intercontinental flights. **Luggage storage** and lost-and-found available. Shuttles run to and from right side of Stazione Centrale (1hr.; every 20min. to airport 5am-9:30pm, to Stazione Centrale 6:20am-12:15am; €4.50). Malpensa Express **train** departs Cadorna Metro station and Stazione Nord (40min.; every 30min. to airport 5:50am-8:20pm, to Stazione Centrale 6:45am-9:45pm; onboard €11/13, round-trip €15/17).

Linate Airport (LIN), 7km from town. Domestic, European, and intercontinental flights with European transfers. Starfly **buses** (☎02 58 58 72 37) run to Stazione Centrale (20min.; every 30min. to airport 5:40am-9:35pm, to Stazione Centrale 6:05am-11:35pm; €2.50). City bus #73 runs to Milan's San Babila Metro station (€1), even though it's less convenient than Starfly.

Bergamo Orio al Serio Airport (☎035 32 63 23; www.orioaeroporto.it), 58km from town, serves some budget airlines including **RyanAir.** Shuttle runs to Stazione Centrale (1hr.; to airport 4:15am-10pm, to Milan 8am-1am; €6.70).

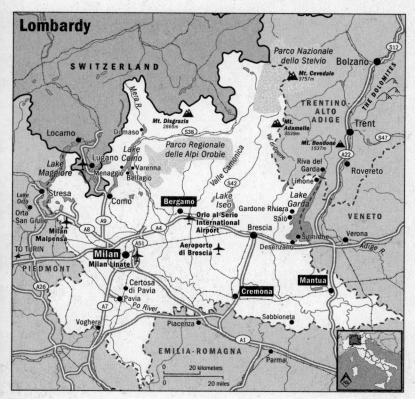

Lombardy

SWITZERLAND

Parco Nazionale
dello Stelvio — Bolzano

Mt. Cevedale
3757m

Locarno

Mt. Disgrazia
2865m

Domaso

Lake Como

Lugano

Mt. Adamello
3539m

TRENTINO-
ALTO
ADIGE — Trent

Mt. Bondone
1537m

Parco Regionale
delle Alpi Orobie

Lake
Maggiore

Lake Lugano

Menaggio
Bellagio

Varenna

Stresa

Lake
Orta

Orta
San Giulio

Como

Valle Camonica

Val di Chiese

Riva del
Garda

Limone

Rovereto

Lake
Iseo

Lake
Garda

VENETO

Bergamo

Gardone Riviera

Salò

Milan
Malpensa

Orio al Serio
International
Airport

Brescia

Verona

Milan

Milan Linate

Aeroporto
di Brescia

Desenzano

Sirmione

Adige R.

TO TURIN

PIEDMONT

Certosa
di Pavia

Mantua

Po River

Pavia

Cremona

TO TURIN

Voghera

Piacenza

Sabbioneta

EMILIA-ROMAGNA

Parma

0   20 kilometers

0   20 miles

Trains:

Stazione Centrale (☎02 89 20 21), in P. Duca d'Aosta. Ticket office open daily 6am-8:40pm. To: **Bergamo** (1hr., every hr. 7:20am-11:37pm, €4.10); **Florence** (3hr., every 1-2hr. 5:30am-8pm, €37); **Rome** (Eurostar 5hr., €56; TBIZ 5hr., €62; sleeper car 8hr., €73); **Turin** (2hr., every hr. 5:18am-12:30am, €8.75); **Venice** (2hr., every hr. 6:05am-9:05pm, €30).

Stazione Cadorna (☎199 15 11 52). Part of Ferrovia Nord, the local rail system that connects to **Como** (1hr., every 30min. 6:12am-9:12pm, €3.70) and **Varese** (1hr., every 30min. 7:06am-1:03am, €4). Malpensa Express runs from the station to the airport (40min., every 30min. 4:20am-11:27pm, €11). **Lockers** available at the station to the left of the Express Cafe (small bag €3.50 per 2hr., medium €4.50, large €6.50).

Stazione Porta Genova, in P. Stazione di Pta. Genova, is on the western line to **Alessandria** (1hr., every hr. 5:10am-8:09pm) and **Mortara** (1hr., every hr. 5:57am-10:42pm).

Stazione Porta Garibaldi (☎02 65 52 078; ticket office open daily 6:30am-9:30pm). Runs to: **Bergamo** (1hr., every hr. 4:50am-6:45pm); **Domodossola** (2hr., every 1hr. 5:05am-8:47pm); **Lecco** (1hr., every hr. 5:35am-9:41pm); **Piacenza** (1hr., every hr. 8:26am-11:04pm).

Buses: At Stazione Centrale. Signs for destinations, times, and prices posted outside. Ticket office open 6:30am-8:10pm. Shuttle bus tickets also available from the *tabaccherie* outside the station on V. Vitruvio. **Intercity** buses depart from locations on the periphery of town. **Autostradale** departs from P. Garibaldi; **SAL, SIA,** and many others

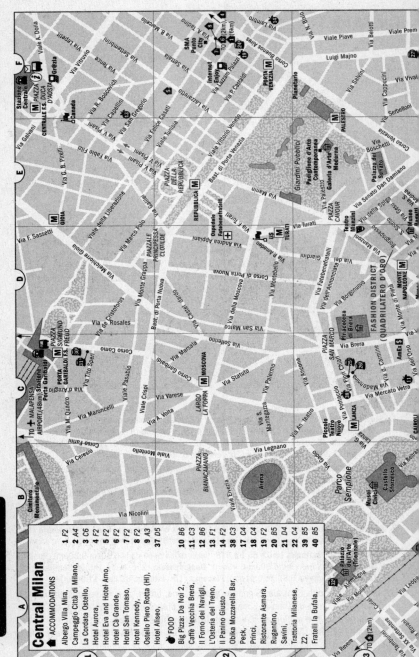

Central Milan

LOMBARDY

▲ ACCOMMODATIONS

Albergo Villa Mira,	1 F2
Campeggio Città di Milano,	2 A4
La Cordata Ostello,	3 C6
Hotel Aurora,	4 F2
Hotel Eva and Hotel Arno,	5 F2
Hotel Cà Grande,	6 F2
Hotel San Tomaso,	7 F2
Hotel Kennedy,	8 F2
Ostello Piero Rotta (HI),	9 A3
Hotel Aliseo,	37 D5

● FOOD

Big Pizza: Da Noi 2,	10 B6
Caffè Vecchia Brera,	11 C3
Il Forno dei Navigli,	12 B6
L'Osteria del Treno,	13 F1
Il Panino Giusto ,	14 F2
Obika Mozzarella Bar,	38 C3
Peck,	17 C4
Princi,	18 C4
Ristorante Asmara,	19 F2
Rugantino,	20 B5
Savini,	21 D4
Trattoria Milanese,	22 C4
Z2,	39 B5
Fratelli la Bufala,	40 B5

NIGHTLIFE	
Bar Magenta	23 B4
Café Capoverde	24 F2
Cave Montmarte	25 C3
Club 2	26 C3
L'elephant	27 C4
Exploit	28 B5
Flying Circus	29 C5
Hollywood	30 C1
Loolapaloosa	31 C1
Old Fashion Café	32 A3
Scimmie	33 B6
Spazio Movida Cocktail Bar	34 B6
Le Trottoir	35 B6
Yguana Café Restaurant	36 C5
La Hora Feliz	41 C5

LOMBARDY

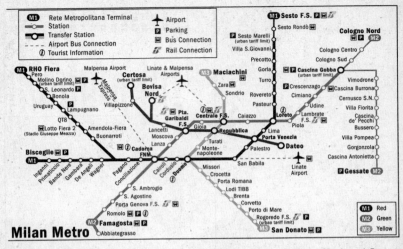

Milan Metro

depart from P. Castello (M1: Cairoli) around V. Jacini near Stazione Nord, and Porta Garibaldi for **Bergamo, Certosa di Pavia,** the **Lake Country, Rimini, Trieste,** and **Turin.**

✳ ORIENTATION

Milan's layout is a series of concentric squares. There are four central squares: **Piazza del Duomo,** where **Via Orefici, Via Mazzini,** and **Corso Vittorio Emanuele II** meet; **Piazza Castello** and the attached **Largo Cairoli,** near Castello Sforzesco; **Piazza Cordusio,** connected to Largo Cairoli by V. Dante and P. del Duomo by V. Orefici; and **Piazza San Babila,** the entrance to the business and fashion district. The **duomo** and **Galleria Vittorio Emanuele II** are at the center of town. Two parks, the **Giardini Pubblici,** with several museums, and **Parco Sempione,** home to the Castello Sforzesco and its **Musei Civici,** sit to the northeast and northwest respectively. **Stazione Centrale,** Milan's transportation hub, lies northeast of the *centro* in a commercial district above the Giardini Pubblici. To reach P. del Duomo, take M3 to the Duomo stop. From there, head through the station's main entrance into **Piazza Duca d'Aosta.** Follow **Via Pisani** as it becomes **Via Turati** and veers into **Via Manzoni,** which leads to **Piazza della Scala,** home to Milan's opera house, and through the Galleria Vittorio Emanuele II to P. del Duomo. From V. Manzoni, turn on **Via della Spiga** to the **fashion district.** From P. S. Babila take **Corso Venezia** north, which will become **Corso Buenos Aires,** and leads to the *pensioni* (budget hotels) district by **Piazzale Loreto. Via Torino,** going away from P. del Duomo, runs to **Corso Porta Ticinese** and the **Navigli Canal District.**

> ❗ **ATTENTION!** Avoid walking alone after dark in the areas east of Stazione Centrale, north of Porta Garibaldi, and below the Navigli.

▣ LOCAL TRANSPORTATION

The layout of Milan's streets makes it difficult to navigate by car. Pick up a map with a street index at the tourist office or any bookstore, or a public transit map at the **ATM Point** (☎800 80 81 81; www.atm-mi.it; open M-Sa 7:45am-8:15pm) in the Metro station under Stazione Centrale or P. del Duomo.

Public Transportation: The **Metropolitana Milanese,** the city subway, operates 6am-midnight and is by far the most useful branch of Milan's transportation network. **Line #1** (red; M1) stretches east to west from the *pensioni* district east of Stazione Centrale (M1: Sesto FS) through the *centro* and west to the youth hostel (**Molino Dorino** northwestern end; **Bisceglie** at the southwestern end). **Line #2** (green; M2) links Milan's 3 train stations from Cologno Nord and Gessate in the east to **Abbiategrasso (Famagosta)** in the west, and crosses M1 at **Cadorna** and **Loreto. Line #3** (yellow; M3) runs south from the area north of Stazione Centrale at **Comasina** to **San Donato,** crossing M2 at **Stazione Centrale** and M1 at the **duomo.** Use the **bus system** for trips outside the city. **Trams #29** and **30** travel the city's outer road; **buses #94** and **61** traverse the inner road. **Azienda Trasporti Milanese (ATM)** tickets (€1) are good for buses, trams, and Metro for 1hr. Tickets €1.30 per night; 10 tickets €9.50; 24hr. pass €3. Metro tickets can be purchased at station machines.

Taxis: White taxis are omnipresent in the city. Call **RadioTaxi** (☎85 85 or 02 40 40).

Car Rental: Both have offices in **Stazione Centrale** facing P. Duca d'Aosta.

Avis (☎02 66 90 280 or 67 01 654). Open M-F 8am-8pm, Sa 8am-2pm.

Europcar(☎02 66 98 78 26). Open daily 7am-midnight. AmEx/MC/V.

Bike Rental: Companies require €100 security deposit and ID. **Rossignoli,** C. Garibaldi 65/71 (☎02 80 49 60). €6 per ½-day, €10 per day, €18 per weekend, €35 per week. Open M 2:30-7:30pm, Tu-Sa 9am-12:30pm and 2:30-7:30pm. **AWS,** V. Ponte Seveso 33 (☎02 67 07 21 45). €5.50 per ½-day. Open Th-Su 9am-1pm and 3-7pm.

▼ PRACTICAL INFORMATION

TOURIST AND FINANCIAL SERVICES

Tourist Office: IAT (Informazioni Accoglienza Turistica), P. Duomo 19A (☎02 77 40 43 43; www.visitamilano.it). Next to the *farmacia* and down the stairs. *Hello Milano* has info in English on events and nightlife. Walking tours depart the tourist office every hr. M-Sa 10am-3pm; €10-20. Office open M-Sa 8:45am-1pm and 2-6pm, Su 9am-1pm and 2-5pm. **Branch:** Stazione Centrale (☎02 77 40 43 18/19), on ground fl. Smaller venue with shorter lines. Open M-Sa 9am-6pm, Su 9am-1pm and 2-5pm.

Tours: Autostradale (☎02 33 91 07 94; www.autostradale.it). Offers hop-on-hop-off sightseeing tours that circle the *centro*. Taped commentary in 8 languages. Buy tickets by phone, at the tourist office, online, or at M2: Garibaldi. Tours (from €40) depart P. del Duomo, usually at 9:30am. Some tours (€55) include admission to all the stops, including La Scala Theater and Leonardo's *Last Supper*.

Consulates: Australia, V. Borgogna 2 (☎02 77 70 41). M1: S. Babila. Open M-Th 8:30am-1pm and 1:30-5pm, F 8:30am-1pm. Appointments recommended. **Canada,** V. Vittor Pisani 19 (☎02 67 58 34 20; www.canada.it). M2/3: Centrale FS. Open M-F 9am-noon. **New Zealand,** V. Guido d'Arezzo 6 (☎02 49 90 201). M1: Pagano. Open M-Sa 8:30am-noon and 1:30-5:30pm. **UK,** V. S. Paolo 7 (☎02 72 30 00 08; emergency 03 35 81 06 857; www.britain.it). M1/3: Duomo. Open daily 9am-1pm and 2-5pm. **US,** V. Principe Amedeo 2/10 (☎02 29 03 51; www.milan.usconsulate.gov). M3: Turati. Open M-F 8:30am-noon.

Banks and Currency Exchange: Most banks open M-F 8:30am-1:30pm and 3-4pm. **ATMs** abound; some with automated currency exchange. **Western Union:** In Stazione Centrale. Open daily 9am-7:45pm. Also at **Money Transfer Point,** V. Porpora 12 (☎02 20 40 07 63). Open M-Sa 9:30am-9pm.

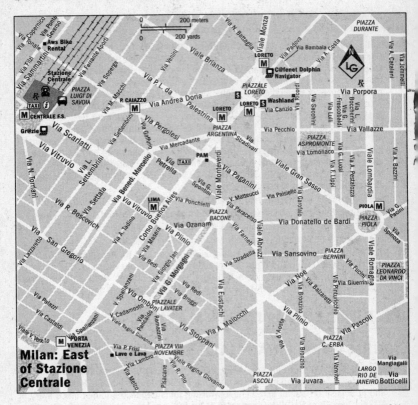

Milan: East of Stazione Centrale

American Express: V. Larga 4 (☎02 72 10 41). Near the *duomo*, at the corner of V. Larga and V. S. Clemente. Holds cardholder mail for up to 1 month for free. Moneygram international money transfer. Also **exchanges currency**. Open M-F 9am-5:30pm, Sa 9am-12:30pm. Also at corner of V. dell'Orso and V. Brera. Open M-F 9am-5:30pm.

Beyond Tourism: InformaGiovani, Vco. Calusca 10 (☎02 88 46 57 60; www.comune. milano.it/giovani), enter at C. Porta Ticinese 106. Take trams #3, 15, 9, 29, 30 or bus #59 or 94. Info for young people looking to work, volunteer, study, or tutor. Also has resources on social events and professional associations, as well as apartment listings. Open M-W 10am-6pm, Th-F 2-6pm. Also at V. Laghetto 2. Open M-F 2-6pm. **Easy Milano** (www.easymilano.it), a biweekly publication for Milan's English-speaking community. Lists work opportunities including childcare and tutoring.

LOCAL SERVICES

Luggage Storage: Malpensa Airport (☎02 58 58 02 98), ground fl. €3.50-4 per bag per day. Open daily 6am-10pm. **Linate Airport** (☎02 71 66 59), ground fl. €3.50-4 per bag per day. Open daily 7am-9:30pm.

Lost Property: Ufficio Oggetti Smarriti Comune, V. Friuli 30 (☎02 88 45 39 00). Open M-F 8:30am-4pm. **Malpensa Airport** (☎02 74 86 83 31; lostpropertymalpensa@sea-aeroportimilano.it). Open M-F 10am-noon. **Linate Airport** (☎02 70 12 44 51). **Stazione Centrale** (☎02 63 71 22 12). Open daily 7am-1pm and 2-8pm.

English-Language Bookstore: The American Bookstore, V. Camperio 16 (☎02 87 89 20), at Largo Cairoli. Open M 1-7pm, Tu-Sa 10am-7pm. AmEx/MC/V. **English Bookshop,** V. Ariosto 12 (☎02 46 94 468). Open M-Sa 10am-7pm.

GLBT Resource: ARCI-GAY "Centro D'iniziativa Gay," V. Bezzeca 3 (☎02 54 12 22 25; www.arcigaymilano.org). Open M-F 3-8pm.

Handicapped/Disabled Services: AIAS Milano Onlus, V. Paolo Mantegazza 10 (☎02 33 02 021; www.milanopertutti.it).

Laundromat: Washland, V. Porpora 14 (☎02 34 00 81 44 77). Wash €3.50 per 7kg, dry €3.50 per 18min. Open daily 8am-10pm. **Lavanderia Self-Service ad Acqua,** V. Vigevano 20 (☎02 49 83 902). Wash €3.50 per 7kg, dry €3.50. Detergent €0.60. Open daily 8am-10pm. **Lava e Lava,** V. Melzo 17 (☎02 34 71 40 42 37). Wash €2, dry €3. Detergent €0.75. Open daily 8am-9:30pm.

EMERGENCY AND COMMUNICATIONS

Police: in P. Beccaria, ☎02 77 271.

Pharmacy: Farmacia Stazione Centrale (☎02 66 90 735). In Stazione Centrale's ground fl. galleria across from the tracks. Open 24hr. **Farmacia Carlo Erba,** P. del Duomo 21 (☎02 86 46 48 32), next to tourist office. Open M 2-7pm, Tu-F 9:30am-1:45pm and 3-7pm. **Farmacia Lombardia,** V. Porpora 65. Open M-F 8:30am-12:30pm and 3:30-7:30pm, Sa 8:30am-12:30pm. **Farmacia Stazione Porta Genova** (☎02 58 10 16 34), Ple. Stazione Porta Genova 5. Open M-F midnight-12:45pm and 3:30pm-midnight, Sa 3:30pm-8:30am, Su 8pm-midnight. AmEx/MC/V. All post after-hours rotations.

Hospital: Ospedale Maggiore di Milano, V. Francesco Sforza 35 (☎02 55 031), 5min. from *duomo* on inner ring road. **Ospedale Niguarda Ca'Granda,** in P. Ospedale Maggiore, is north of the city. **Ospedale Fatebenefratelli,** in C. Pta. Nuova.

Internet Access:

Gr@zia, P. Duca d'Aosta 14 (☎02 89 69 57 33; www.grazianet.com). M2/M3: Centrale FS. To the left and across the street from Stazione Centrale's main door. Wi-Fi and free webcam. €2.80 per 30min., €4 per 1hr., €8 per 3hr. Open daily 8am-midnight.

C@fenet Dolphin Navigator, V. Padova 2 (☎02 28 47 209). M1/M2: Loreto. Frappes, *panini*, and focaccia €3. Fast connection. €1.30 per 15min., €5 per hr. Open M-Sa 6:30am-7pm.

Post Office: P. Cordusio 4 (☎02 72 48 21 26), near P. del Duomo. Offers currency exchange and **ATM.** Open M-F 8am-7pm, Sa 8:30am-noon. **Postal Code: 20100.**

ACCOMMODATIONS AND CAMPING

Milan is a wealthy city with a high standard of living, and its accommodations tend to be priced accordingly. Booking two weeks to one month in advance is strongly advised for most hotels, especially during summer and theater seasons. Prices vary considerably from low season (Dec. and July-Aug.) to high season (Sept.-Nov. and Mar.-May), when room prices often triple. The tourist office assists travelers booking accommodations.

EAST OF STAZIONE CENTRALE

Unless stated otherwise, all hotels are easily accessible from Ⓜ1 or Ⓜ2: Loreto, or by tram #33 from Stazione Centrale. Women should exercise caution when traveling alone at night in this area.

Hotel Cà Grande, V. Porpora 87 (☎02 26 14 52 95; www.hotelcagrande.it), 7 blocks from Ple. Loreto. Tram #33 stops 50m from the hotel. Though a bit far, it is a pleasant option with English-speaking owners and a pleasant garden. All rooms have A/C, TV, sink, and phone. Breakfast included. Singles €40-65, with bath €45-80; doubles €55-85/60-110. AmEx/D/MC/V. ❹

Albergo Villa Mira, V. Sacchini 19 (☎02 29 52 56 18). Despite the barbed wire over the entrance, the small rooms in this family-run hostel are colorful. A few of the rooms overlook the garden patio. Singles €26-35; doubles €45-62; triples €70-85. Cash only. ❷

NEAR GIARDINI PUBBLICI

▦ **Hotel Eva and Hotel Arno,** V. Lazzaretto 17, 4th fl. (☎02 67 06 093; www.hotelevamilano.com or www.hotelarno.com). ⓜ1: Pta. Venezia. Follow V. Felice Casati, then take a right on V. Lazzaretto. Ring bell. Quirky, mirrored decor and spiral staircases make for an intriguing and inviting atmosphere. Note the life-size porcelain snow leopard. 18 large rooms with wood floors, TV, and phone. Shared bathroom. Free luggage storage. Free Internet. Singles €30-45; doubles €50-100; triples €65-90. AmEx/MC/V. ❸

Hotel San Tomaso, Vle. Tunisia 6, 3rd fl. (☎02 29 51 47 47; www.hotelsantomaso.com). ⓜ1: Porta Venezia. Exit at C. Buenos Aires; turn left on Vle. Tunisia. Rooms with TV and phone. Elevator. Singles €30-65; doubles €50-100; triples €70-150. AmEx/MC/V. ❸

Hotel Kennedy, Vle. Tunisia 6, 6th fl. (☎02 29 40 09 34; www.kennedyhotel.it). ⓜ1: Pta. Venezia. Exit at C. Buenos Aires, turn left on Vle. Tunisia. Simple rooms with clean bathrooms. Elevator. Singles €36-75; doubles €55-80, with bath €70-120; triples €90-120; quads €100-160. AmEx/D/MC/V. ❸

Hotel Aurora, C. Buenos Aires 18 (☎02 20 47 960; www.hotelaurorasrl.com). ⓜ1: Pta. Venezia. On the right side of hectic C. Buenos Aires after V. Felice Casati. Offers rooms with new furniture, large beds, A/C, TV, and thick blackout curtains. Reservations recommended. Singles €50-90; doubles €70-130; triples €90-160. AmEx/MC/V. ❹

Hotel Aliseo, C. Italia 6 (☎02 86 45 01 56). Located near the city center and convenient to the metro, this hotel is on the top floor of a building with a small, quiet courtyard. Red lobby is lushly decorated. Rooms available with shared or private bath. Singles €45-60; doubles €60-75. AmEx/MC/V. ❹

ON THE CITY PERIPHERY

▦ **La Cordata Ostello,** V. Burigozzo 11 (☎02 58 31 46 75; www.ostellimilano.it). ⓜ3: Missori. From P. Missori, take tram #15 2 stops to Italia San Luca; continue in the same direction for 1 block and turn right on V. Burigozzo. Entrance around the corner on V. Aurispa. Close to the Navigli area, a lively crash pad for a young, international crowd ready to party. Colorful, plant-filled common rooms with TV and large kitchens. Laundry €3. Free Internet and Wi-Fi. 7-night max. stay. Reception 24hr. except 1-2:30pm. Check-out 11am. Closed Aug. 10-20 and Dec. 23-Jan 2. Single-sex dorms €21-25; doubles €70-100; triples €90-110; quads €100-140. MC/V. ❷

Ostello per la Gioventù AIG Piero Rotta (HI), at the corner of V. Salmoraghi and V. Calliano (☎02 39 26 70 95; www.ostellomilano.it). ⓜ1: QT8. Facing Santa Maria Nascente, turn right on V. Salmoiraghi. Though slightly far from the metro and most sights, this enormous hostel has 400 beds. Breakfast included. Laundry €5.50. 3-night max. stay. 24hr. reception. Check-out 10am. Lockout 10am-2pm. Reserve online 1 day in advance; book well ahead for Apr.-Oct. Closed Dec. 24-Jan. 12. 6-bed dorms €22; private rooms €25 per person. HI-member discount €3. MC/V. ❷

Campeggio Città di Milano, V. Gaetano Airaghi 61 (☎48 20 01 34). M1: De Angeli. From metro, take bus #72 to San Romanello Togni. Backtrack 10m and turn right on V. Togni. Campground is a 20min. walk straight ahead. Enter at Aquatica water park.

Modern facilities, volleyball, and barbecue. Laundry €5. Reservations recommended. Closed Dec.-Jan. €7.50 per person; €11 per tent; €6.50 per car. 2- to 6-person cabins €37-88; bungalows with bath and A/C €80-120. Electricity free. MC/V. ❶

◘ FOOD

Choose between chowing down on focaccia with the lunch-break crowd, clinking crystal glasses, or taking your palate on a world tour through the city's ethnic neighborhoods. Old-style trattorie still follow Milanese culinary traditions with *risotto alla milanese* (rice with saffron), *cotoletta alla milanese* (breaded veal cutlet with lemon), and *osso buco* (lamb, beef, or veal shank). Many local bars offer happy-hour buffets of focaccia, pasta, and risotto that come free with drink purchase. In the *centro*, weary tourists near the *duomo* often succumb to P. del Duomo's pricey and mediocre offerings, but cheap and delicious rewards await those who look a little harder.

◪ **Princi,** V. Speronari 6 (☎02 87 47 97; www.princi.it), off P. del Duomo. Take V. Torino and make 1st left. Stone walls and glass countertops make this more zen than you imagined an Italian bakery could be. Local favorite for authentic food on-the-go. Pastries €1-4. Pizza €3.50-5. Primi and secondi €5. Open M-Sa 7am-8pm. Cash only. ❶

Z2, Corso di Porta Ticinese 32 (☎02 89 42 02 41). Savvy, minimalist decor contributes to a relaxing and elegant atmosphere. Watch chefs in glassed-in kitchen prepare dishes such as *gnocchi agli spinaci* (€10). Primi €9-10. Secondi €10-19. Dessert €7-8. ❸

Fratelli la Bufala, Corso di Porta Ticinese 16 (☎02 83 76 529; www.fratellilabufala. com). Relax in the lively atmosphere of this buffalo-meat inspired pizzeria. Don't miss out on the lunch *menù*, with 2 courses, 1 side, and water (€10). Pizza €5.50-9.50. ❷

Trattoria Milanese, V. S. Marta 11 (☎02 86 45 19 91). M1/3: Duomo. From P. del Duomo, take V. Torino; turn right on V. Maurilio and again on V. S. Marta. Serves *costolette alla milanese* (breaded veal; €18) and *mondeghili milanesi* (breaded meatballs; €14) under brick arches. Primi €6-11. Secondi €8-23. Cover €2. Open M-F noon-3pm and 7-11:30pm. Closed last 2 weeks of July. AmEx/MC/V. ❸

Peck, V. Spadari 9 (☎02 80 23 161; www.peck.it). Aromas from the ground floor spread from the wine cellar in the basement to the deli and cafe above. Open M 3:30-7:30pm, Tu-F 9:15am-7:30pm, Sa 8:45am-7:30pm. AmEx/MC/V. ❷

Savini, Galleria V. Emanuele II (☎02 72 00 34 33; www.savinimilano.it). This world-famous restaurant keeps its decor extravagant and attracts a clientele that matches. Exquisite food, like raw umbrine fish with sherbet of *vermentino di Gallura*. Primi €25-30. Secondi €35-45. Cover €7. Open M-Sa noon-3:30pm and 7:30-10:30pm. AmEx/MC/V. ❺

Caffè Vecchia Brera, V. dell'Orso 20 (☎02 86 46 16 95; www.vecchiabrera.it). M1: Cairoli. Take V. Cusani, which becomes V. dell'Orso, out of P. Cairoli for 2 blocks. Sweet, meaty, or liqueur-soaked crepes €4-8. Primi €7.50-9. Secondi €12-14. Cover €1. Service 10%. Happy hour 5-8:30pm; drinks €5. Open M-Sa 7am-2am. AmEx/MC/V. ❸

Obika Mozzarella Bar, intersection of V. Mercato and V. dei Fiori Chiari (☎02 86 45 05 68; www.obika.it). Sleek, cosmopolitan establishment has a relaxed atmosphere. Don't pass up a slice of one of the several offered mozzarella rolls (like a jelly roll, filled with various savory Italian fillings), €4-6. At night, morphs seamlessly into a classy bar. Open M-F noon-3:30pm and 6-11:30pm, Sa-Su noon-3pm and 6-11:30pm. AmEx/MC/V. ❶

NAVIGLI AND ENVIRONS

An area packed with students means cheap grub. Many bars serve dinner or offer happy-hour buffets with the purchase of mixed drinks, and some happy-hour benefits apply to wine or soda. The **Fiera di Sinigallia,** a bargaining extravaganza, occurs Saturdays on Darsena Banks, a canal around V. d'Annunzio. **PAM** supermarket, Vle. Olona 1/3, is by the Museo "da Vinci." (M2: Sant'Ambrogio. Open M-Sa 8am-9pm, Su 9am-7:30pm.) A **DìperDì Express** supermarket is located at Vigevano 22. (M2: Porta Genova F. S. ☎02 58 10 00 20. Open M-Sa 8:30am-1pm and 3:45-8:15pm. Closed M morning in late July and Aug. MC/V over €15.)

- ▨ **Big Pizza: Da Noi 2,** V. Giosué Borsi 1 (☎02 83 96 77). Takes its name seriously. Beer and house wine flow liberally at this riverfront location, which has a restaurant feel but the prices of a small pizza joint. The *pizza della casa* is topped with pasta (€8). If not in the mood for pizza, try the crab pasta (€5). Calzoni €5-7. Pizza €4-8.50. Cover €1. Open M-Sa 10am-2:30pm and 7pm-midnight. MC/V. ❶

- ▨ **Il Forno dei Navigli,** Alzaia Naviglio Pavese 2 (☎02 83 23 372). Some of the most delicious pastries in the city, fresh out of "the oven of Navigli." The *cestini* (pear tart with Nutella; €2.25) defines decadence. Pastries and breads €0.50-6. Open M-Sa 7am-2pm and 6pm-1am, Su 6pm-1am. Cash only. ❶

- **Rugantino,** V. Fabbri 1 (☎02 89 42 14 04), between the Chiesa di San Lorenzo and the Roman pillars of C. Porta Ticinese. From M2: Sant'Ambrogio, walk down V. Edmondo De Amicis. Savor famous oven-baked dishes. Beer €4. Pizza €7-10. Primi and secondi €9-18. Open daily 12:30-3pm and 7:30pm-midnight. AmEx/MC/V. ❸

NEAR GIARDINI PUBBLICI AND STAZIONE CENTRALE

Avoid the *menù turistico* at a typical trattoria in favor of foods from the neighborhood's immigrant populations. **Unes** supermarket is on V. Melzo, just off C. Buenos Aires (open M-Sa 8am-8:30pm). A **PAM** supermarket, V. Piccinni 2, is just off C. Buenos Aires. (M1: Loreto. ☎02 29 51 27 15. Open M-Sa 8am-9pm.) **Punto SMA** is on V. Noe between P. Piola and P. Bernini. (Open M-F 8:30am-1:30pm and 3:30-7:45pm, Sa 8:30am-7:45pm.)

- **Ristorante Asmara,** V. Lazzaro Palazzi 5 (☎02 89 07 37 98; www.ristoranteasmara.it). M1: Pta. Venezia. Eat spicy Eritrean food, including a *zighini* platter with flavorful meat and vegetables served on *injera* (thin flatbread; €10) with your hands. Vegetarian options available. Antipasti €4-5.50. Entrees €8-11.50. Cover €1.60 Open M-Tu and Th-Su 10am-4pm and 6pm-midnight. AmEx/MC/V. ❸

- **Il Panino Giusto,** V. Malpighi 3 (☎02 29 40 92 97). M1: Pta. Venezia. From the *piazza,* head down Vle. Piave and turn left on V. Malpighi. If you believe sandwiches should contain goat cheese, truffled olive oil, or veal pâté for under €8, welcome home. Beer €4-5. Artisan panini €5-8. Open daily noon-1am. AmEx/MC/V. ❷

- **Shun Feelin' Sushi,** Vle. Tunisia 6 (☎02 29 40 30 96). The fountains and bamboo at this modern sushi restaurant come as a welcome surprise amid the hubbub of nearby C. Buenos Aires. Try *gunkan* (1 piece) from €1.70-3.50 or 8 pieces from €7-10. ❸

- **L'Osteria del Treno,** V. S. Gregorio 46/48 (☎02 67 00 479). M2/3: Centrale F. S. From P. Duca d'Aosta, take V. Pisani; turn left on V. S. Gregorio. Primi €8-9. Secondi €12-14. Cover €2.20. Open M-F 11am-7pm and 8:30pm-12:30am, Sa 7pm-1am, Su 10am-1pm and 3pm-12:30am. AmEx/MC/V. ❹

◉ SIGHTS

NEAR THE DUOMO

▨**DUOMO.** As Milan's geographical and spiritual center, the *duomo* is a good starting point for any walking tour. Built over the remains of three other basilicas, it is Italy's second-largest church. The structure is home to more than 3400 statues, 135 spires, and 96 gargoyles. The newly renovated facade juxtaposes Italian Gothic with later Baroque elements that Archbishop Borromeo commissioned to show allegiance to Rome during the Protestant Revolution. The imposing 16th-century marble tomb of **Giacomo dei Medici** in the southern transept was inspired by the work of Michelangelo. Climb (or ride) to the top of the cathedral from outside the northern transept to the ⌷**roof walkway** for prime views of the city. The rooftop statue of the *Madonnina* has become the symbol of Milan. (Ⓜ*1/3: Duomo.* ☎ *02 72 02 33 75; www.duomomilano.com. Cathedral open daily 7am-7pm. Modest dress strictly enforced. Roof open daily Feb. 16-Nov. 14 9:30am-9:30pm. Stairs €5, elevator €7.)* The **Museo del Duomo** is currently closed for restoration, but normally displays paintings, tapestries, jewels, and stained glass related to the *duomo*'s construction. *(P. del Duomo 14, next to the Palazzo Reale.)*

⌷**PINACOTECA AMBROSIANA.** The 23 palatial rooms of the Ambrosiana display exquisite works from the 14th to 19th centuries, including Botticelli's *Madonna of the Canopy*, Leonardo's *Portrait of a Musician*, Caravaggio's *Basket of Fruit* (the first Italian still-life), Titian's *Adoration of the Magi*, and works by Flemish landscape painters Brueghel and Bril. Raphael's immense ⌷**School of Athens** sketch is dramatically displayed in a darkened room where the life-like nuances of its professors and students as they engaged in lively discussion are plainly visible. The courtyard's statues, fountains, and staircase are also enchanting, as is Bertini's 1867 two-story *Vetrata Dantesca*, a stained-glass window with allusions to Dante's *Inferno*. (Ⓜ*1/3: Duomo. P. Pio XI 2. Follow V. Spadari off V. Torino, and turn left on V. Cantù.* ☎ *02 80 69 21; www.ambrosiana.it. Open Tu-Su 10am-5:30pm. Last entry 30min. before closing. €8, under 18 or over 65 €5.)*

TEATRO ALLA SCALA. Founded in 1778, La Scala has established Milan as the opera capital of the world. Its understated Neoclassical facade and lavish interior set the stage for works by Rossini, Puccini, Mascagni, and Verdi, performed by virtuosos like Maria Callas and Enrico Caruso. Visitors can peek into the theater's interior and soak up La Scala's history at the **Museo Teatrale alla Scala.** Replete with portraits, pianos, and porcelain figurines, the most compelling exhibit is the highly personal account of Maria Callas' contribution to modern opera. From poster art to a plaster cast of Toscanini's hand, the museum offers a glimpse into the operatic past. (Ⓜ*1/3: Duomo. Largo Ghiringhelli 1 or P. della Scala. From P. del Duomo, walk through the Galleria Vittorio Emanuele II. Museum on left side of building.* ☎ *02 88 79 24 73; www.teatroallascala.org. Open daily 9am-12:30pm and 1:30-5:30pm. Last entry 30min. before closing. See Entertainment, p. 191, for info about performances. €5, students €4.)*

MUSEO POLDI PEZZOLI. Poldi Pezzoli, an 18th-century nobleman and art collector, bequeathed his house and art to the city "for the enjoyment of the people." Wind past the 19th-century fountain with bronze cherubs to famous paintings that include Mantegna's *Virgin and Child*, Botticelli's *Madonna and Child of Mary Teaching Christ to Read*, and the signature piece, Pollaiuolo's *Portrait of a Young Woman*. The house itself is a treat, as are the smaller collections of china, marble busts, ancient Roman jewelry, Tiepolo oil sketches, and 18th-century clocks that fill Pezzoli's museum. (Ⓜ*3: Montenapoleone. V. Manzoni 12, near La Scala.* ☎ *02 79 48 89; www.museopoldipezzoli.it. Open Tu-Su 10am-6pm. €8, students and seniors €5.50, under 10 free. English-language audio tour free.)*

GALLERIA VITTORIO EMANUELE II. A 48m glass-and-iron cupola, groundbreaking at the time of construction both in its concept and in the combination of materials, towers over a five-story arcade of offices, overpriced shops, and cafes. Intricate mosaics representing the continents sieged by the Romans adorn the floors and walls. In the years before electricity, a miniature train circled the top of the arcade, keeping the candles lit along the glass. Once known as "Milan's Living Room," this 1870s gallery is now a tourist hub, connecting P. del Duomo to P. della Scala. Spin on the mosaic bull clockwise three times for good luck. *(To the right of the duomo. Free.)*

PALAZZO REALE. This *palazzo* served as the town hall before becoming the residence of Milanese royalty until the 19th century. Giuseppe Piermarini, architect of La Scala, designed its facade. *(To the left of the duomo. P. del Duomo 12. ☎02 88 451. Only open during exhibitions. Prices vary; usually €8, students €6.)*

NEAR CASTELLO SFORZESCO

◼**CASTELLO SFORZESCO.** Restored after WWII damage in 1943, the Castello Sforzesco is one of Milan's best-known monuments. Its towers and courtyard were constructed in 1368 by the Visconti to defend against the Venetians, and Leonardo had his studio here before invaders used the grounds as army barracks and horse stalls. Inside are the ten **Musei Civici** (Civic Museums). Highlights include the ◼**Museum of Ancient Art,** which is housed in rooms and quiet courtyards just as awe-inspiring as the artifacts they contain, among them Michelangelo's unfinished **Pietà Rondanini** (1564), and Leonardo's frescoes on the ceiling of the **Sala delle Asse;** his design was once considered so insignificant it was whitewashed over, actually protecting the original colors. The **Museum of Decorative Art** showcases furnishings, Murano glass, and a giant porcelain crab. At the superb **Museum of Musical Instruments,** check out the amusing display on the history of the glass harmonica, and don't miss the African harps made from rattlesnake heads. (Ⓜ1: Cairoli or Ⓜ2: Lanza. ☎02 88 46 37 03; www.milanocastello.it. Castello grounds open daily Apr.-Oct. 7am-7pm; Nov.-Mar. 7am-6pm. Free. Museums open Tu-Su 9am-5:30pm. Combined admission €3, students and over 65 €1.50. 3-day pass for Castello, Museo Archeologico, Museo di Storia Naturale e Museo del Risorgimento €7/3.50. F 2-5:30pm free.)

CHIESA DI SANTA MARIA DELLE GRAZIE. The church's elaborately frescoed Gothic nave contrasts with the airy Renaissance tribune added by Bramante in 1497. Observe the intricate blue and red geometric drawings on the white walls and the gold sunbursts in the middle of each arch on the ceiling. *(P. S. Maria delle Grazie 2. M1: Conciliazione or M2: Cadorna. From P. Conciliazione, take V. Boccaccio and then right onto V. Ruffini for 2 blocks. Open M-Sa 7am-noon and 3-7pm, Su 7:30am-12:15pm and 3:30-9pm. Modest dress required. Free.)* To the left of the church entrance is the Cenacolo Vinciano (Vinciano Refectory, the convent dining hall), home to one of the best-known pieces of art in the world: Leonardo da Vinci's ◼**Last Supper.** Following a 20-year restoration effort, the painting was re-opened to the public in 1999; pieces have been flaking off almost since the day it was finished in 1498. As a result, only groups of 25 or fewer are allowed in the refractory for no more than 15min. Reservations are mandatory; book at least a month ahead in summer. At the tourist office, some tours with same-day booking include admission to the *Last Supper.* *(Reservations ☎02 89 42 11 46; www.cenacolovinciano.org. Refectory open Tu-Su 8:15am-6:45pm. Wheelchair-accessible. €6.50, EU residents 18-25 €3.25, EU residents under 18 or over 65 free. Reservation fee €1.50. Tours €3.25. Audio tour €2.50.)*

PINACOTECA DI BRERA. The Brera Art Gallery presents a superb collection of 14th- to 20th-century paintings, with an emphasis on the Lombard School. Works include Bellini's *Madonna col Bambino* and *Pietà*, Mantegna's innovative *Dead Christ,* Raphael's *Marriage of the Virgin,* Caravaggio's *Supper at Emmaus,* and Francesco Hayez's *The Kiss.* A small collection of modernist works includes pieces by Modigliani and Picasso. A glass-enclosed chamber in **Gallery 14** allows visitors to watch conservationists at work on the aged canvases. *(V. Brera 28. Ⓜ2: Lanza or Ⓜ3: Montenapoleone. Walk down V. Pontaccio, and turn right* on V. Brera. Or from La Scala, walk up V. Verdi until it becomes V. Brera. ☎02 72 26 31; www. brera.beniculturali.it. Open Tu-Su 8:30am-7:15pm. Last entry 30min. before closing. Wheelchair-accessible. €5, EU citizens 18-25 €2.50, under 18 or over 65 free. Audio tour €3.50.)

MUSEO NAZIONALE DELLA SCIENZA E DELLA TECNOLOGIA "DA VINCI". This family-friendly museum traces the development of science and technology from Leonardo's age to the present. The hall of computer technology features a piano converted into a typewriter. Don't miss the **da Vinci room**, which contains wooden mock-ups of his flying machines, cranes, and bridges. (V. S. Vittore 21, off V. Carducci. Ⓜ2: Sant'Ambrogio. ☎02 48 55 51; www.museoscienza.org. Open Tu-F 9:30am-5pm, Sa-Su 9:30am-6:30pm. Last entry 30min. before closing. €8, students €6.)

BASILICA DI SANT'AMBROGIO. A prototype for Lombard-Romanesque churches throughout Italy, Sant'Ambrogio is the most influential medieval building in Milan. The AD fourth-century **Cappella di San Vittore** in Ciel d'Oro is through the chapel on the right, and the asymmetrical **campanili** are the result of an intense eighth-century feud between Benedictine monks and priests, each of whom owned one tower. (P. Sant'Ambrogio 15. Ⓜ2: Sant'Ambrogio. Walk up V. Giosuè Carducci; the church bulwark rises up to the right. ☎02 86 45 08 95. Open M-Sa 7:15am-noon and 2:30-7pm, Su 7:15am-1pm and 3-8pm. Free. Mosaics ☎86 45 08 95. Open Tu-Su 9:30am-11:45am and 2:30-7pm. €2, students €1.)

🎦 ENTERTAINMENT

Milan sponsors many free events, all of which are detailed in the free, monthly **Milano Mese,** distributed at the tourist office. *Hello Milano* (www.hellomilano. it), an English monthly publication, can also be found at the tourist office.

OPERA AND BALLET

Milan's operatic tradition and unparalleled audience enthusiasm make ◪**La Scala** one of the best places in the world to see opera. The theater's acoustics are phenomenal; even those in the cheap seats appreciate a glorious sensory experience. Opera season runs from December to July and September to November, overlapping the **ballet** season. In December and March, La Scala hosts **symphony concerts.** (Infotel Scala ☎02 72 00 37 44; www.teatroallascala.org. Open daily noon-6pm. Closed Aug. Ticket office at theater, V. Filodrammatici 2. Opens 3hr. before performances and closes 15min. after performance begins. Remaining tickets sold at a discount 2hr. before a show. Ticket prices vary widely, but many options are quite affordable; ask for student discounts.) **Teatro degli Arcimboldi,** Vle. dell'Innovazione 1, has modern concert performances. (☎02 80 01 21 121; www.teatroarcimboldi.org. Open M-Sa 8am-6:45pm, Su 1-6:30pm.)

THEATER, MUSIC, AND FILM

Founded after WWII as a socialist theater, the **Piccolo Teatro,** V. Rovello 2, near V. Dante, specializes in small-scale classics and off-beat productions. (☎02 72 33 32 22. Performances Tu-Sa 8:30pm, Su 4pm. €20-28 student rush tickets €13.) **Teatro delle Erbe,** V. Mercato 3, hosts lyrical opera from October to April. (M1: Cairoli or M2: Lanza. www.felixcompany.it.) Teatri d'Italia sponsors **Milano Oltre,** a drama, dance, and music festival (June-July). Call the **Ufficio Informazione del Comune** for the latest updates (☎02 86 46 40 94; www.comune.milano.it). In July the **Brianza Open Jazz Festival** (☎02 23 72 236; www.brianzaopen.com) draws jazz fans. Brianza is accessible by car from Milan. The **Milan Symphony Orchestra** season runs from September to May. Concerts are primarily at **Auditorium di Milano** at Largo Gustav Mahler. (☎02 83 38 92 01, reservations 89 40 89 16; www.

orchestrasinfonica.milano.it. Ticket office open daily 10am-7pm. Tickets are also sold at the tourist office. Tickets €13-50, students €10-25.) Concerts also held at the **Conservatorio,** V. Conservatorio 12 (☎02 76 21 20), and **Dal Verme,** V. S. Giovanni sul Muro 2 (☎02 87 90 52 01). For concert listings look under *"Spetta-coli"* in the *'Tempo Libero"* section of the daily papers. Movie listings are also in every major paper (check Th editions). Many cinemas screen English-language films, listed on the back cover of *Hello Milano.*

⬚ SHOPPING

Milan is a city where clothes really do make the man (or woman): fashion pilgrims arrive in spring and summer to watch the newest styles take their first steps down the runway. Shows are generally by invitation only, but once designers take their bows, window displays and world-renowned biannual *saldi* (sales) in July and January usher new collections into the real world at more reasonable prices. With so many fashion disciples in the city, the fashion district known as the **Quadrilatero d'Oro** has become a sanctuary in its own right. This posh land—where denim jackets can sell for €2000 and Bentley limos transport poodles dressed-to-impress—is the block formed by V. Monte Napo-leone, Borgospresso, V. della Spiga, and V. Gesu. Giorgio and Donatella live in the suites above the stores that sell their designs. Although most stores close at 7:30pm, have no fear. You can shop 24/7 at the touchscreens outside Ralph Lauren, so long as you don't mind waiting for delivery until the morning.

Designer creations are available to mere mortals at the trendy boutiques along **Corso di Porta Ticinese,** which extends from **Piazza XXIV Maggio** in the **Navigli district** toward the *duomo,* and its offshoot **Via Molino delle Armi.** Trendsetters and savvy shoppers flock to the affordable mix of shops along **Via Torino** near the *duomo* and the stores along **Corso Buenos Aires.** Another option is the depart-ment store **La Rinascente,** V. S. Radegonda 3, where Giorgio Armani began his illustrious fashion career. (☎02 88 52; www.rinascenteshopping.com. Open M-Sa 10am-10pm, Su 10am-8pm.)

Fashionistas who are fine with being a season behind can buy discounted top names from *blochisti* (wholesale clothing outlets). The well-known **Il Sal-vagente,** V. Fratelli Bronzetti 16, is off C. XXII Marzo. (☎02 76 11 03 28. M1: San Babila. Walk up C. Monforte across P. Tricolore to C. Concordia, which becomes C. Indipendenza. Turn right on V. F. Bronzetti. Open M-Tu 3-7pm, W-Sa 10am-7pm.) **Gruppo Italia Grandi Firme,** V. Montegani #7/A, stocks popular brand names at 70% off regular price. (☎02 89 51 39 51; www.gruppoitaliagrandi-firme.it. M2: Famagosta. Head along Vle. Famagosta, then Cavalcavia Schia-voni, under the overpasses and across the river to V. Montegani; turn right. Open M 3:30-7:30pm, Tu-F 10am-1pm and 3:30-7:30pm, Sa 10:30am-7:30pm.) For those who want to stay in the famous fashion center, **DMAGAZINE Outlet,** V. Monte Napoleone 26, sells big names for more reasonable prices. Just don't be surprised when you see that the 90% discounts still leave €300 price tags. (☎02 76 00 60 27. Open daily 9:30am-7:45pm.)

There are also markets and secondhand stores located around C. Porta Tici-nese, the Navigli district, and C. Garibaldi. True bargain hunters attack the bazaars on Tuesday mornings and all day Saturday on **Via Fauché** (M2: Garib-aldi). Also on Saturday, **Viale Papinian** (M2: Agostino) and the 400-year-old **Fiera di Sinigallia,** on V. Valencia (M2: Porto Genova), have a mix of junk and deals.

NIGHTLIFE

Milan is known internationally for its too-cool nightlife. Each of the town's neighborhoods has its own personality. To make the most of a night out, choose a district and wander the streets. The **Brera district** calls to those with creative flair, inviting tourists and *milanesi* alike to test their vocal skills at one of its piano bars. In the nearby **Porta Ticinese**, the young and beautiful meet after a long workday to sip fancy concoctions in the shadow of ancient ruins. Students descend upon the **Navigli canal district's** endless stream of cafes, pizzerias, pubs, bars, barges, and bars on barges. A single block of **Corso Como** near Stazione Garibaldi is home to Milan's most exclusive clubs, where bouncers reject the underdressed. Bars and clubs dot the rest of the city, especially around **Largo Cairoli,** home to Milan's hottest outdoor dance floor, as well the areas southeast of **Stazione Centrale** and east of **Corso Buenos Aires,** which features a mix of bars along with much of Milan's gay and lesbian scene. The best jazz clubs are on the town's periphery.

> **TIP**
> **GET BUZZED IN BARS, NOT BY BUGS.** Before heading out, don't underestimate Milan's sizable mosquito population, especially around the Navigli, where insect repellent is the cologne of choice.

Check any paper on Wednesday or Thursday for info on clubs and events. *Corriere Della Sera* publishes an insert called **Vivi Milano** on Wednesday, and La *Repubblica* produces **Tutto Milano** every Thursday. The best guide to nightlife is **Pass Milano,** published in Italian every two months and available in bookstores (€12.50). **Easy Milano** (www.easymilano.it), published biweekly by the city's English-speaking community, contains the latest on hot night spots and is free in many bars and restaurants. Free booklets listing bars and club venues, as well as calendars of performances, are available at almost any club or bar: look through **2night** (www.2night.it), a guide to the city's top bars, and **Zero2,** the Milanese edition of an Italian biweekly guide to music, disco, and bar acts.

BRERA DISTRICT

You won't find any clubbing here; instead, mostly older couples stroll the pedestrian thoroughfares between V. Brera and V. Mercado Vetero. Karaoke is one of the main highlights of an exciting evening in the Brera district. To reach the heart of the district from Ⓜ2: Lanza, head to V. Pontaccio, turn right on V. Mercato and then left on V. Fiori Chiari.

Club 2, V. Formentini 2 (☎02 86 46 48 07), down V. Madonnina from V. Fiori Chiari. This bar sets the mood with red lights and a grand piano on the ground floor and a maze of cushions in its dark downstairs "discopub." Loud bass downstairs. F-Sa DJ and karaoke. Basement open daily in winter. Beer €6. Mixed drinks €10. Open daily 8:30pm-3am.

Cave Montmartre, V. Madonnina 27 (☎02 86 46 11 86). With dozens of outdoor tables at a perfect people-watching corner, Cave Montmartre serves gelato and mixed drinks to help the weary partygoer enjoy the catwalk of Milan locals. Gelato cones and cups €1.50-2.60, sundaes €3.70-7.80. Beer €3.50-5. Mixed drinks €6.50-7. Open Apr.-Sept. M-Sa 7am-2am, Su 5pm-2am. Oct.-Mar. M-Sa 7am-2am.

CORSO DI PORTA TICINESE AND PIAZZA VETRA

Welcome to the land of the nightly happy hour buffet—one mixed drink buys you dinner. Chilled-out, well-dressed crowds of locals come to socialize at bars that charge no cover. This area is accessible by Ⓜ2 stop Sant'Ambrogio.

▨ **Yguana Café Restaurant,** V. Papa Gregorio XIV 16 (☎89 40 41 95), just off P. Vetra, a short walk down V. E. de Amicis and V. Molino delle Armi. Beautiful people sip fruity mixed drinks (€8-10). Lounge on a couch outside, or groove to hip hop downstairs. Su brunch noon-4pm. Happy-hour buffet (M-Sa 5:30-9:30pm, Su 5:30-10pm) with 50 rotating dishes makes other bars' offerings look downright pedestrian. Open M-Th and Su 5:30pm-2am, F-Sa 5:30pm-3am. Kitchen open M-F 12:30-3pm.

Flying Circus, P. Vetra 21 (☎02 58 31 35 77; www.flyingcircusmilano.com). Walk down V. E. de Amicis and V. M. delle Armi to P. Vetra. A relaxed lounge welcomes guests to this airplane-themed, red-walled, glass-encased wine bar. Mixed drinks and wine €7-8. W night €3 beers 9pm-2am. Happy-hour buffet daily 6-9:30pm. Open M-Sa 6pm-2am.

Exploit, V. Pioppette 3 (☎02 89 40 86 75; www.exploitmilano.com), on C. Porta Ticinese near Chiesa di San Lorenzo Maggiore down V. E. de Amicis. Where the old meets the new: a chic bar-restaurant next to Roman ruins. Free Wi-Fi. Mixed drinks €7-9. Wine €6 per glass, €18-20 per bottle. Primi €10. Secondi €18-25. Diverse happy-hour buffet daily 6-9:30pm. Open daily noon-3pm and 6pm-2am.

▨THE NAVIGLI

On summer nights Navigli's sidewalks fill with outdoor vendors, and students flock to its bars for their wallet-friendly prices. From Ⓜ2: Pta. Genova, walk along V. Vigevano until it ends, and turn right on V. Naviglio Pavese. After you see the canals, look for ▨**Via Sforza,** which has countless bars and cafes, most with outdoor seating. Less refined and younger than the other neighborhoods, Navigli lets you have fun in Milan and still afford a plane ticket home.

▨ **Le Trottoir,** P. XXIV Maggio 1 (☎/fax 02 83 78 166; www.letrottoir.it). Located in the center of P. XXIV Maggio as its own island in a sea of roads. This self-proclaimed *"Ritrovo d'Arte, Cultura, e Divertimento"* (House of Art, Culture, and Diversions) may be the Navigli's loudest, most crowded bar and club. A young, alternative crowd comes nightly to get down to live underground music 10:30pm-3am on ground fl., while upstairs features a DJ or jazz (M and W). Check schedule for weekly roster and other music nights. Mixed drinks €6-9. Pizza and sandwiches €8. Cover depends on act; usually €8, includes 1 drink. Happy hour daily 6-8pm with beer €4. Open daily 11am-3am. AmEx/MC/V.

Scimmie, V. Sforza 49 (☎02 89 40 28 74; www.scimmie.it). Near the end of a street filled with nightlife choices is a nightclub in 3-part harmony: pub on a river barge, polished *ristorante,* and cool bar with nightly performances. Talented underground musicians play fusion, jazz, blues, Italian swing, and reggae. Concert schedule online. Mixed drinks €4-9. Primi €8-10. Secondi €18-20. Open daily 8pm-2am.

Spazio Movida Cocktail Bar, V. Sforza 41 (☎02 58 10 20 43; www.spaziomovida.it). Like its namesake Spanish cultural movement, Movida changes the tone of the social scene, spilling Latin music out onto the street from the sleek, colorful indoors. Free Wi-Fi. Mixed drinks €7. Happy hour 6-9pm; mixed drinks €6. Open daily 6pm-2am.

La Hora Feliz, V. S. Vito 5 (☎02 837 6587; www.lahorafeliz.com). For those looking for a Cuban feel, this "rumeria" is the place for you. With festive Latino flair and a wide selection of drinks, including their famous mango daiquiri (€6), it's a little different from your average Italian bar. Happy hour 6-9pm. Open daily 1pm-2am. MC/V.

AROUND CORSO COMO

While models mingle with movie stars over €15 mojitos inside the clubs, crowds of people are served curbside drinks and share a smoke along C. Como and C. Garibaldi. Many clubs close in August. Take the Ⓜ2 line to Garibaldi FS, and go one block south on C. Como.

Loolapaloosa, C. Como 15 (☎02 65 55 693). Guests are invited to dance on the bar while the bartenders entertain by swinging lamps and ringing bells. Mixed drinks €6-8. Cover from €6. Buffet 6:30-10:30pm. Open M-Sa noon-4am, Su 2pm-4am.

Hollywood, C. Como 15 (☎02 65 98 996; www.discotecahollywood.com). Slip into something stunning and pout for the bouncer: this club selects revelers with discretion. Mixed drinks from €10. Tu hip hop. W house. Th-Sa mixed music by resident DJs. Su tends to be invite-only party for celebs. Cover €12-30. Open Tu-Su 11pm-5am.

AROUND LARGO CAIROLI

Take the metro to Ⓜ2: Cairoli. While the bars don't exactly cluster into one scene, it's one of the few places west of the Castello Sforzesco worth the trip.

☒ **Old Fashion Café,** Vle. Emilio Alemagna 6 (☎02 80 56 231; www.oldfashion.it). M1/2: Cadorna F. N. Walk up V. Paleocapa next to the station, and turn right on Vle. Alemagna before the bridge. Club is to left of Palazzo dell'Arte along a dirt path. Summer brings stylish clubgoers to couches encircling an outdoor dance floor and stage, with live music and DJ. Tu is the most popular night, with mixed music. Su brunch noon-6pm; €20. Appetizer buffet 7:30-10pm; €13. Open M-Tu and Th-Sa 10:30pm-4:30am, W 10:30pm-4am, Su 11am-4pm and 7:30pm-midnight.

Bar Magenta, V. Carducci 13 (☎02 80 53 808; www.barmagenta.it). M1/M2: Cardona. A short walk down V. G. Carducci to C. Magenta. More masculine than the name would imply. A popular music- and sports-filled institution that dates back to 1807. Free Wi-Fi. Pints €5.50. Happy-hour buffet 6-9pm €6 with 1 drink. Open daily 2pm-3am.

EAST OF CORSO BUENOS AIRES

The establishments southeast of Stazione Centrale are mostly frequented by locals. Most are accessible from Ⓜ1/2: Loreto or M1: Pta. Venezia.

☒ **L'elephant,** V. Melzo 22 (☎02 29 51 87 68; www.lelephant.it). M2: Pta. Venezia. From C. Buenos Aires turn right on V. Melzo and walk 5 blocks. An almost entirely male crowd socializes at tables under chandeliers, and on the street corner. Gay- and lesbian-friendly. Mixed drinks €7-8. Happy hour 6:30-9:30pm; €6. Open Tu-Su 6:30pm-2am.

Café Capoverde, V. Leoncavallo 16 (☎02 26 82 04 30; www.capoverde.com). M1/M2: Loreto. A long 30min. walk along V. Costa, which becomes V. Leoncavallo. Greenhouse/bar/restaurant. Pick a cactus for mom; grab a strawberry daiquiri for yourself. Mixed drinks €8. Organic happy-hour buffet 6:30-9:30pm with a drink. Large, tasty assortment of gluten-free dishes. Open M-Sa noon-3pm and 6pm-2am, Su 6pm-2am.

❀ FESTIVALS

Rival to Venice's famed festivities, Milan's increasingly popular **Carnevale** is Italy's oldest. The masked mystique and medieval revelry radiates from the *duomo* and spreads through the city annually during the days that precede Ash Wednesday. The **Mercatone dell'Antiquariato sul Naviglio Grande** (☎02 89 40 99 71; www.navigliogrande.mi.it), a giant antiques extravaganza, takes place the last Sunday of each month, except July. Experience true flower power during the **Fiori sul Naviglio,** the first Sunday of April, when flowers fill the district. **Festa di Naviglio** is usually the first Sunday of June, and is accompanied by another special market. The second week of May, don't miss **Arte sul Naviglio Grande,** when the Naviglio plays host to the creativity of over 300 young Italian artists whose work takes over a 10,000m long area. **La Notte Bianca** (White Night) occurs annually one night in June when the Metro, theater, shops, and restaurants stay open all night from 3pm-6am. The *Assessorato alla Cultura* publishes a special

LOMBARDY

summer edition (in Italian) of **Milano Cultura,** found at the tourist office, high-lighting all summer events. The **Feast of Sant'Ambrogio,** the patron saint of Milan, is December 7. During the first weeks of December, a special market named **Oh Bej** sets up around the basilica. The **Serate al Museo** celebration with free concerts (both classical and contemporary) spreads throughout Milan's museum courtyards and great halls; check the schedule at the tourist office.

▣ DAYTRIPS FROM MILAN

▧ CERTOSA DI PAVIA

SILA buses F5 or F6 from ⓜ2: Milan-Famagosta serve Certosa (30min.; €2.40). In Certosa, return tickets to Milan are sold at Il Giornale newsstand in the bus lot. Bus to Milan stops next to the stand. Exiting the bus in Certosa, go to the traffic light, and turn right; continue straight for a few blocks on the road, which becomes the long, tree-lined V. Certosa. The monastery is at the end. Trains also run from the Milano Rogoredo station to Certosa (dir: Voghera, via Certosa; 20min., every hr. 5:44am-10:37pm, €2.65), and arrive quite a distance behind the walled city. From the train station, head through the parking lot and turn left in front of the wall, right at the cross street at the end, then right at the 1st street after the wall (500m). Continue 400m, and go through the portal on the right.

Seven kilometers north of Pavia stands the ▧**Monastero della Certosa di Pavia** (chehr-TOH-zah dee pa-VEE-ya). Gian Galeazzo Visconti founded it in 1396 as a mausoleum for the Visconti clan, who ruled the area from the 12th to 15th centuries. Consecrated as a monastery in 1497, the building testifies to the evolution of Italian art. Inlaid marble, bas-reliefs, and sculptures embellish every available surface. Completion of the work required over 250 craftsmen during the 15th-century Lombard Renaissance. Statues of biblical figures, carvings of narratives, and 61 medallions adorn the base, while the upper half relies more on geometric patterns formed by the contrasting colors of marble for embellishment. Today, the Cistercians oversee the monastery in place of the Carthusian monks. Past the gate in the left apse, note the figures of Ludovico il More and Beatrice d'Este. On Beatrice's feet, note the oldest artistic rendition of platform shoes, which she wore to match her husband's height. The old **sacristy** houses a Florentine triptych carved in ivory; 99 sculptures and 66 bas-reliefs depict the lives of St. Mary and Jesus. Encircling the **choir** are 42 intricate wood inlay representations of saints, prophets, and apostles. Beyond Gian Galeazzo's mausoleum, walk through an unoccupied monk's quarters and its peaceful courtyard. Worlds away from Milan's sleek, modern style, visiting the Monastero is a deeply moving experience not to be missed. (☎*02 92 56 13; www.comune.pv.it/certosadipavia. Open Tu-Su Apr. 9-11:30am and 2:30-5:30pm; May-Aug. 9-11:30am and 2:30-6pm; Sept.-Oct. and Mar. 9-11:30am and 2:30-5pm; Nov.-Feb. 9-11:30am and 2:30-4:30pm. Modest dress required. Free.)*

MANTUA (MANTOVA)   ☎ 0376

Although Mantua (in Italian, "MAHN-toh-vah"; pop. 46,372) did not become a bustling cultural haven until the Renaissance, art and culture have shaped the city's history since the birth of the poet Virgil in 70 BC. Having provided inspiration for native and foreign artists alike including Verdi (1813-1901), the Renaissance writer Castiglioni (1478-1529), and artist Pisanello (1380-1456), the town is brimming with art. Mantova has a quiet energy, but an energy nonetheless —with great shopping along Corso Vittorio Emanuele II and small personable restaurants tucked in side streets around the sprawling *centro,* the town is constantly active. Surrounding towns like Castellaro, Cavriana, and Solferino house scenic vineyards with Lombardy's greatest gem, sparkling red wine.

E TRANSPORTATION. The **train station** is in P. Don Leoni, at the end of V. Solferino. (☎32 16 47. Ticket office open M-Sa 5:40am-7:45pm, Su 6am-7:45pm.) **Trains** run to Cremona (1hr., 8 per day 5:20am-8:50pm, €4.50); Milan (2hr., 9 per day 5:20am-7:43pm, €8.55); Modena (1hr., 5:57am-8:49pm, €3.70); Verona (40min., 20 per day 6am-10:41pm, €2.55). APAM **buses** (☎0376 23 01; www. apam.it) run locally and to nearby towns, including the village of Sabbioneta. Check the *biglietteria* to the left of the train station for schedule booklets of urban and interurban buses. There are two stations: one directly in front of the train station and the other at Stazione Risorgimento, in front of Palazzo Te. **Taxis** (☎0372 32 53 51, 36 88 44, or 32 44 08) are available 5am-1am. For **bike rentals** try La Rigola, on V. Trieste, next to Antica Osteria ai Ranari. (☎0376 36 66 77 or 335 60 54 958. €2.50 per hr., €10 per day. Open daily 9:30am-8pm. Cash only.)

⬛🅷 ORIENTATION AND PRACTICAL INFORMATION. Getting to most of the city's sights and shops from the train station takes 10-15min. From **Piazza Don Leoni,** turn left on **Via Solferino,** then right on **Via Bonomi** to the main street, **Corso Vittorio Emanuele II.** Follow it to **Piazza Cavallotti,** crossing the **Sottoriva River,** to get to **Corso Umberto I.** This leads to **Piazza Marconi, Piazza Mantegna,** and the main **Piazze d'Erbe** and **Sordello.** Find a helpful, English-speaking staff at the **tourist office,** P. Mantegna 6. (☎0376 43 24 32; www.aptmantova.it. Open daily 9:30am-6:30pm.) Check out the **museum tourist office,** P. Sordello 23, located in the Casa di Rigoletto. (☎0372 36 89 17. Open Tu-Su 9am-noon and 3-6pm.) C. V. Emanuele II is lined with **banks,** most with **ATMs,** including **UniCredit Banca,** C. V. Emanuele II 26. (Open M-F 8:20am-1:20pm and 2:35-4:05pm.) In an emergency, call the **carabinieri** (☎0376 32 88 88) or the **police,** P. Sordello 46 (☎0376 20 51). Call the **Ospedale Carlo** (☎0376 28 61 11 or 28 60 11), V. Albertoni, for medical assistance. **Farmacia Silvestri** (☎0376 32 13 56), V. Roma 24 (open Tu-Sa 8:30am-12:30pm and 4-8pm; MC/V), is one of many **pharmacies. Bit and Phone,** V. Bertinelli 21, across from the train station, offers **Internet** access and Western Union. (☎0376 22 05 94; www.bitandphone.it. Open M-Tu and Th-Sa 10am-10pm, Su noon-10pm. €2 per hr.) For English-language books, check out **Librogusteria il Pensatoio,** V. Accademia 56. (☎0376 618 107 88; www.pensatoio-inrete.it. Open Tu-Su 10am-9pm. MC/V.) The **post office,** P. Martiri Belfiore 15, up V. Roma from the tourist office, has currency exchange. (☎0376 31 77 11; fax 32 53 04. Open M-F 8:30am-7pm, Sa 8:30am-12:30pm.) **Postal Code:** 46100.

🛏 ACCOMMODATIONS. Accommodations in neighboring towns like Castellaro and Monzambano are less expensive than Mantua itself. In Mantua, accommodations near the train station and main *piazze* are pricey and hard to find. B&Bs as well as *affittacamere* are the least expensive options, though prices everywhere skyrocket in early September during Festivaletteratura. At **B&B La Zucca ❷,** V. Giovanni Battista Spagnoli 10, you won't have to sacrifice location for price. (☎339 61 89 870. Call ahead. Double €20-60, with bath €30-120.) Hotel **ABC ❹,** P. Don Eugenio Leoni 25, across from train station, is a modern hotel with comfortable rooms and an outdoor patio. All rooms have TV, A/C, and new bathrooms. Ring bell to enter after 11pm. (☎/fax 32 23 29; www.hotelabcmantova.it. Breakfast included. Luggage storage free for guests, €5 for others. Parking €12-20. Singles €44-165; doubles €66-165; triples €77-222; quads €88-250.) **Ostello del Mincio ❶,** V. Porto 23/25, is 15km away from Mantua. To the left of the train station, buy a ticket for bus #1; take it to Stazione Risorgimento. Find bus #13 (last departure at 7:40pm) to Rivalta. Though far, it is the only youth hostel in the area. Bear in mind that the bus does not run on Sundays. (☎0376 65 39 24; www.ostellodelmincio.org. Free Wi-Fi. Dorms €16-18.)

📗 **FOOD.** Mantuan cuisine is known for its *tortelli di zucca* (pumpkin-filled ravioli). Specialties include parmesan cheese, risotto, Mantuan salami (identifiable by its light color due to the proportion of quality meat) and *sbrisolona*, a crumbly almond cake. In July and August many small restaurants and bars close for anywhere from a week to two months, but you can generally rely on the series of nearly indistinguishable outdoor restaurants lining **Piazza delle Erbe** and **Piazza Sordello,** whose popularity with tourists ensures they seldom close. For tasty and reasonably priced local cuisine, head to **Hosteria Leon D'oro,** V. Leon D'oro 6, where the candlelit interior is dappled with partially revealed frescoes. (☎338 124 21 11; www.hosterialeondoro.net. Primi €8.50-13. Secondi €14-18.50. Open daily noon-3pm and 8pm-midnight.) To get to **Trattoria con Pizza da Chiara ❸,** V. Corridoni 44/A, from P. Cavallotti, follow C. Libertà and turn left on V. Roma, then right on V. Corridoni. Young professionals dine in this chic but unpretentious restaurant. Try the delicious *tortelli di zucca* for €8. (☎0376 22 35 68. Pizza and primi €4.50-9. Secondi €9-14.50. Cover €2. Open M and W-Su noon-2:30pm and 7-10:30pm. MC/V.) For a sleek and metropolitan cafe, check out **Undici Calvi Caffe ❷,** V. Calvi 11. Go for a cappuccino (€1.30) or a mixed drink (€3.50) while listening to the jazzy soundtrack. (☎0376 355 036. Open M-F 7:30am-8:30pm, Sa 8am-8:30pm, Su 9am-9pm. Cash only.) A **market** is held every Thursday morning in P. delle Erbe. **GS Supermarket** is on P. Cavallotti. (Open M-Sa 8am-8pm, Su 9am-7pm. AmEx/MC/V.)

🅖 SIGHTS

PALAZZO DUCALE. The behemoth Palazzo Ducale, home of the Gonzaga family since the start of the 14th century, dominates the Mantuan skyline. In medieval times, this was the largest palace in Europe, with 500 rooms and 15 courtyards constructed by the best architects and artists of the 14th to 17th centuries. Originally many separate buildings, the *palazzo* expanded as the Gonzagas annexed surrounding structures, the most prominent being the **Castello di San Giorgio.** This four-towered castle once served as a fortress and boasts an elaborate 17th century ceiling in its **Hall of Mirrors,** modified to suit Neoclassical tastes by Giocondo Albertoli a century later. In the Pisanello Room, the recent removal of a painted plaster frieze revealed a heroic cycle of frescoes depicting the knights of King Arthur. The **New Gallery** houses dozens of locally produced altarpieces from the 16th-18th centuries, removed from monasteries during the Hapsburg and Napoleonic eras. *(P. Sordello 40. ☎0372 22 48 32; www.mantovaducale.it. Open Tu-Su 8:45am-7:15pm. Last entry 45min. before closing. Ticket office under porticos facing the piazza. €6.50, EU students €3.25, EU citizens under 18 or over 65 free. Audio tour €4.)*

TEATRO BIBIENA. Commissioned by Maria Theresa of the Hapsburgs to serve as a venue for cultural events and scientific expositions, this theater resembles a miniature fairy-tale castle and is one of few in northern Italy not modeled after Milan's La Scala. Four tiers of stone balconies with intricately painted wood rise to the ceiling, illuminated by soft lantern light. Music lovers first filled the velvet couches when a 14-year-old Mozart inaugurated the building in 1769. Patrons continue to pour in today to attend musical and theatrical performances. *(V. Accademia 47, at the corner with V. Pomponazzo. ☎32 76 53. Open Tu-Su 9:30am-12:30pm and 3-6pm. Last entry 30min. before closing. €2.50, under 18 and over 60 €1.20.)*

PALAZZO TE. Built by Giulio Romano in 1534 for state guests of Federico II Gonzaga, who seldom stayed there himself, this opulent *palazzo* combines the layout of a Roman villa with the flamboyant ceiling frescoes that range in theme from the mythological to the Biblical. Pause in the **Sala dei Cavalli** (Room of Horses) to ponder the Gonzaga family's passion for animals, then continue past racy murals of **Cupid and Psyche.** The ▓**Room of Giants** is adorned with a fresco that depicts the demise of the Titans at the hands of Jupiter. In summer, concerts are often held in the courtyard. Meanwhile, the oft-overlooked **hidden garden** of the *palazzo* and **grotto** at the far end are not to be missed. *(At the southern end of the city through P. Veneto and down Largo Parri. ☎ 32 32 66. Open M 1-6pm, Tu-Su 9am-6pm. Last entry 30min. before closing. €8, over 60 €5.50, ages 12-18 and students €2.50.)*

CHIESA DI SANT'ANDREA. Passed on to the Pope by Matilde di Canossa, a powerful countess of Mantua, the oldest church in Mantua (built in the 11th century) is dwarfed by the surrounding buildings, including the **Palazzo della Ragione** (Palace of Justice) next door. *(☎ 0376 22 38 10 or 22 00 97. Open only during exhibitions Tu-Su 10am-1pm and 4-7pm. €3.)* Opposite the **Rotunda di San Lorenzo,** Mantua's most important Renaissance creation, Leon Battista Alberti's **Chiesa di Sant'Andrea** (1472-1594), was the first monumental space constructed in the Classical style since the days of imperial Rome. The church's plan served as a prototype for ecclesiastical architecture for the next 200 years. Giorgio Anselmi painted the dome's frescoes in muted colors. Mantegna's (1431-1506) tomb rests in the first chapel on the left after the entrance. The church's **sacri vasi del preziosissimo sangue** (sacred vases of the precious blood), a piece of earth believed to be in Christ's blood, parades through the streets in two intricate gold vessels during the annual Good Friday procession. The rest of the year, this relic is kept in a crypt under the nave. To view the relic, ask a *chiesa* volunteer, to the right of the entrance. *(Open daily 7:30am-noon and 3-7pm. Free.)*

▐▌ ▓ **ENTERTAINMENT AND FESTIVALS.** Located in the park near the monument to Virgil, the popular outdoor bar ▓**Tre60,** P. Virgiliana 17, has raised outdoor patios scattered with lounge-style furniture. Bartenders experiment with a few new drinks (€5-6) every summer. *(☎ 0376 22 36 05. Wine €5. Open Apr.-Oct. daily 5:30pm-1am. MC/V.)* Irish pub **Doolin,** V. Zambelli 8, near P. Virgiliana, is a hidden bar popular with the locals. *(☎ 36 25 63. Open Tu-Sa 6:30pm-2am, Su 6pm-1am. Cash only.)* New pubs in P. Mantegna that have recently grown in popularity are **La Cantina** and **Cafe degli Artisti** (V. Galana 19). Both are small, and their central location make them easily accessible at night from all over the city. A more traditional night spot is **Enoteca Buca Della Gabbia,** V. Cavour 98, a semi-underground restaurant in a wine cellar with over 650 vintages. *(☎ 36 69 01. Open M-F 10:30am-3pm and 6:30pm-1am, Sa 10:30am-3pm and 5:30pm-2am, Su 10:30am-1pm. Cash only.)* The **Teatro Bibiena** *(☎ 0376 32 76 53),* V. Accademia 4, hosts countless events, including the **Concerti di Fine Settimana,** a series of operettas and recitals every Sunday, and the similar **Concerti della Domenica** series from November to February. Between October and April, enjoy the first classical concert season, while April to June hosts round two of classical concerts as well as the jazz season. In early September, Italian scholars pack Mantua for the five-day **Festivaletteratura,** which attracts literary buffs from around the world. (Office at V. Accademia 47. ☎ 0376 36 70 47; www.festivaletteratura.it.)

THE LAKE COUNTRY

Travelers who need some serious rejuvenation should follow the example of artistic visionaries like List, Longfellow, and Wordsworth: retreat to the serene shores of the northern lakes, Italy's pocket of paradise. Summer attracts droves of foreign and Italian visitors, and each gorgeous lake has its own vibe. A young, mostly-German crowd descends upon the more affordable Lake Garda, enjoying aquatic sports by day and bars by night. The mansion-spotted coast of Lake Como fills its abundant hotels year-round with visitors seeking Kodak moments and a resort getaway. A playground for the rich and famous, Lake Como's shoreline harbors a couple well-run and inexpensive hostels in addition to its famous villas, including George Clooney's. In the neighboring province of Piedmont, palatial hotels dot Lake Maggiore's sleepy shores.

HIGHLIGHTS OF THE LAKE COUNTRY

BASK in the sun along the grass "beaches" in Riva del Garda (p. 203).

DE-STRESS in Stresa, a resort town that draws visitors from all over (p. 215).

LAKE GARDA (LAGO DI GARDA)

Lake Garda, the largest lake in Northern Italy offers freshness and energy thanks to the youthful tourists and sports enthusiasts that flock to its striking blue-green waters and rocky shores. Stretching 52km into the regions of the Veneto, Lombardy, and Trent, Lake Garda's shores are popular with Europeans seeking aquatic sports on the breezy beaches or hiking in the gorgeous Dolomite mountains. In the south, the more crowded cities emphasize the good life that comes from quality food and wine.

SIRMIONE ☎ 030

Isolated on a peninsula from the surrounding lakeside towns, tiny Sirmione (seer-mee-OH-neh; pop. 7000) retains some of the old-world charm that once moved the poet Catullus to praise the beauty of his home here. Among the town's attractions are the healing powers of its spa waters, which have been renowned since ancient times. The *centro storico* is a pedestrian-only zone; nevertheless, the heavy tourist traffic gives Sirmione the feel of a bustling resort. Trendy boutiques, restaurants, and hotels line the sidewalks, sharing the space with traces of Sirmione's Roman history and medieval architecture. Despite all of the class, Sirmione remains the beachiest of the lake towns, with scads of people soaking up sun or splashing in its aquamarine waters.

TRANSPORTATION AND PRACTICAL INFORMATION. SAIA **buses** run from the station, V. Marconi 26, to all stops along the Brescia-Verona

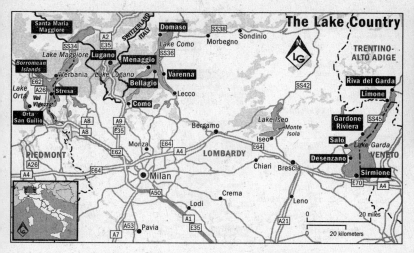

The Lake Country

line, including Desenzano, the nearest **train station.** (Ticket office open M-Tu 9am-1pm and 2-6pm, W-Su 7am-1pm and 2-8pm. After hours, purchase bus tickets from the *tabaccheria* on Vle. Marconi, about 200m from the ticket counter.) Navigazione Lago di Garda (☎030 91 49 511; www.navigazionelaghi.it), at the end of P. Carducci, runs **ferries** to Desenzano (15min.; 17 per day 10am-8pm; €3, express €5.10), Gardone via Salò (1-2hr.; 11 per day 8:27am-5:41pm; €6.90, express €9.80), and Riva del Garda via Limone (2-3hr.; 9:46, 10:20, 10:28am, 2:15, 3:00, 4:55pm; €9.70, express €13.10). Schedules are sold in the tourist office and at the ferry ticket offices. For a **taxi,** call ☎030 91 60 82. Rent **bikes, scooters,** and **motorbikes** at Adventure Sprint, P. Virgilio 31 (☎030 91 90 00). (Bikes €12 per day; scooters €50-75; motorbikes €110-140. Open daily 9am-6:30pm. MC/V.)

The **tourist office,** V. Guglielmo Marconi 8 (☎030 91 61 14; www.comune.sirmione.bs.it), is in the circular building in front of the SAIA station. (Open Apr.-Oct. daily 8am-8pm; Nov.-Mar. M-F 9am-1pm and 2-6pm, Sa 9am-12:30pm.) Other services include: **Banca Popolare di Verona,** P. Castello 3/4 (open M-F 9am-1:20pm and 2:35-3:35pm, Sa-Su 9-11:20am); the **police** (☎030 99 05 772); the **Tourist Medical Clinic,** P. Virgilio 35 (☎347 97 16 620); and **Farmacia di Turno,** V. S. Maria Maggiore (open M-W and F-Su 9:45am-12:15pm and 4:30-7pm, Th 9:45am-12:15pm), in the *centro storico.* The **post office,** V. G. Marconi 28, is behind the SAIA station (open M-F 8:30am-2pm, Sa 8:30am-12:30pm). **Postal Code:** 25019.

⌂⌂ ACCOMMODATIONS AND FOOD. A thorough exploration of Sirmione takes only an afternoon, but those looking for prolonged relaxation can choose from among a number of fairly pricey hotels or slightly cheaper accommodations in Colombare. Reserve early in summer, when rates are steeper. Closer to the end of the island by Grotte di Catullo, lovely host Sordelli's ▓**Villa Paradiso ❸**, V. Arici 7, offers accommodations inside a privately-owned, almost regal house. Rooms provide nearly 360-degree views of the lake from atop Sirmione. (☎030 91 61 49. Doubles €66. Cash only.) **Albergo Grifone ❸**, V. Bocchio 4, off V. Dante to the right of V. Vittorio Emanuele II past the *castello,* has country-style rooms all with small bathrooms and lake views. (☎030 91 60 14; fax 91 65 48. Doubles

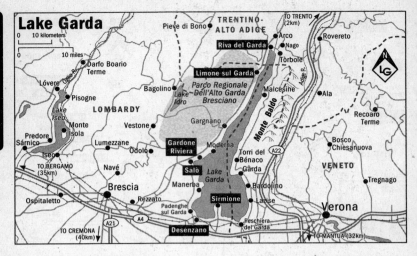

€67. Extra bed €23. Cash only.) Closer to the *centro storico*, **Hotel Speranza ④**, V. Castello 2, feels brand-new and has a breakfast room that would make Martha Stewart proud. Though still expensive, it is one of the more reasonable options in the older part of the town. (☎030 91 61 16; www.hotelsperanza.sitonline.it. Breakfast included. Open late Feb. to mid-Nov. Singles €50-60; doubles €85-100; triples €90; quads €105. AmEx/MC/V.) **Campeggio Sirmione ①**, V. Sirmioncino 9, in Colombare, offers some of the least expensive accommodations on the peninsula for two or more people. It boasts a swimming pool and beach access as well as a small market and cafe. (☎030 99 05 089; www.camping-sirmione.it. Open late Mar.-Oct. €6-9 per person, €6-16 per tent. 2-person cabins €48-78; for a third person, add €7-11; 4-person cabins €63-113. MC/V.)

Sirmione's restaurants are numerous, but there are few that fit well in a budget. **Ristorante Pizzeria Valentino ②**, P. Porto Valentino 10, off V. V. Emanuele II, is one of the more affordable establishments. It offers delicious fare, including homemade gnocchi and trout with Garda sauce and *polenta* (€14). (☎030 61 13 14. Pizza €4.50-9.50. Primi €8-19. Secondi €10-20. Cover €1.50. Open daily 11:15am-4pm and 6:30-10:30pm. AmEx/MC/V.) The gelato is piled high at **Master del Gelato Artigianale ①**, near P. Castello. **Ristorante-Pizzeria Roberto ②**, on V. Garibaldi 6, specializes in shrimp pizza (€8.70), *tagliolini* in cream sauce, and mushroom ravioli (both €7). After getting off the Colombare bus stop, walk 5min down V. Colombare. (☎030 919 359; www.ingarda.com/roberto. *Bruschetta* €2. Pizza €5-83.50-8.70. Antipasti €5-11.50. Primi €5-9.50. Secondi €8-22. Service 10%. Open Tu-Su 11:45am-2:30pm and 5:30-11pm.)

🔘 **SIGHTS.** At the far end of the peninsula along V. Catullo is the **Grotte di Catullo,** perhaps the best-preserved and most impressive aristocratic Roman villa in northern Italy, spread over five acres of olive groves, it offers some of the most spectacular panoramas of Lake Garda. Although named for the poet Catullus, the ruins appear to date from the late first century BC, after the poet's death. Artifacts in the **archaeological museum** inside the grotto have English explanations. (☎030 91 61 57. Ruins and museum open Tu-Su Mar.-Oct. 8:30am-7pm;

Nov.-Feb. 8:30am-5pm. €4, EU students 18-25 €2.) A small train runs between Sirmione and the grotto (€1, 8:30am-6:30pm). The 13th-century **Castello Scaligero** sits in the center of town as a testament to the power of the della Scala family who controlled the Veronese region from 1260 to 1387. Completely surrounded by water, the *castello*'s commanding views are its main attraction. Except for some dirt and cannonballs, the interior is empty. (☎030 91 64 68. Open Tu-Su 8:30am-7pm. €4, EU students 18-25 €2.) Ruins of the city's **fortified walls** lie above Lido delle Bionde, near the ruins of a Lombardian church. **Chiesa di San Pietro in Mavino,** Sirmione's oldest church, dating to the AD 8th century, lies just off V. Catullo but is temporarily closed, due to newly discovered artifacts during excavation. Sixteenth-century frescoes decorate the church's interior.

🔳🔳 ENTERTAINMENT AND NIGHTLIFE. Sirmione's renowned thermal waters and mud baths at **Terme di Sirmione,** V. Punto Staffalo 1, are available only for those with prescriptions from a doctor. However, even the young and healthy can take advantage of the wellness packages (starting at €28) at the attached **Aquaria Spa,** which offers a range of services including thermal water soaks, massages, mud baths, and more. (☎030 91 60 44. Open Mar.-Oct. M 1-10pm, Tu-Su 10am-10pm; Nov.-Mar. M-F 4-10pm, Sa-Su 10am-10pm. AmEx/ MC/V.) Though slightly rocky, the free **public beach,** Lido delle Bionde, on Sirmione's east shore may be a better choice. **Canoes** and **paddleboats** are available for rent just below the **Lido delle Bionde** bar, off V. Catullo. (☎333 54 05 622. €6 per 30min., €8 per hr.; beach chair with umbrella €7 per day. Open daily Apr.- Sept. 8:30am-7pm. Cash only.) Walk around the tip of the peninsula to reach the **Punta Grotte,** a striking line of jagged cliffs slicing through the water. The town also has summer events, which generally include musical and dance performances, art exhibits, and fish tastings. Ask at the tourist office or look for Sirmione d'Estate flyers (www.commune.sirmione.bs.it).

A few bars and *enoteche* can be found on V. S. Maria Maggiore, off V. V. Emanuele II, the most scenic place to have a drink at night may be the beachside **Bar La Torre,** off V. Antiche Mura, behind the *castello*. (Drinks €3-8. Food €4-5. Open daily 10am-8pm, Sa until 2am. MC/V.) There is live jazz in P. Carducci on Friday evenings during the summer.

RIVA DEL GARDA ☎0464

With aquamarine lake waters lapping at the foot of the Brenta Dolomites, Riva del Garda (REE-va del GAR-da; pop. 14,500) is a spot for budget travelers looking to experience the Lake Country's beautiful views. Gentle mountain winds make Riva del Garda ideal for windsurfing, and its aquatic sports schools are world-renowned. The area is also a prime location for hiking, canoeing, whitewater rafting, kayaking, bicycling, swimming, and, above all else, relaxing on its extensive beaches—all made accessible and affordable by the attractive youth hostel. A walk or swim along the coast offers a view of the most stunning portion of the lake, where cliffs crash dramatically into the sea.

🔲 TRANSPORTATION

Buses: Vle. Trento 5 (☎0464 55 23 23). Ticket office open M-Sa 6:30am-7:15pm, Su 9:05am-noon and 3:35-7:05pm. Local tickets available at dispenser in station. Buses run to: **Brescia** (2hr., 4 per day 7:45am-7:35pm, €5.30); **Desenzano** (6 per day 5:40am-5:10pm); **Limone** (20min., 6 per day 5:40am-5:10pm, €1.55); **Milan** (3hr.,

7:45am and 3:45pm, €8.60); **Rovereto** (1hr., 15 per day 5:50am-7:05pm, €2.45); **Salò** (6 per day 5:40am-5:10pm, €3.35); **Verona** (every hr. 5am-8pm).

Ferries: Navigazione Lago di Garda (☎0464 91 49 511; www.navigazionelaghi.it) in P. Catena, next to an information booth. Pick up a schedule in the tourist office or at the ferry ticket offices. To **Limone** (30min.; 17 per day 8am-6:05pm; €3.40, express €5.20); **Sirmione** (2-4hr.; 5 per day 8:35am-5pm; €9.70, express €14) via **Gardone Riviera** (1-3hr.; 5 per day 8:35am-5pm; €8.60, express €12); **Salò** (€8.60, express €12). Ticket office open 20min. before each departure.

Taxi: ☎848 80 07 79.

Bike Rental: Cicli Pederzolli, Vle. dei Tigli 24 (☎/fax 0464 55 18 30). Bikes €8-15 per day. **Bike Shop Girelli,** Vle. Damiano Chiesa 15/17 (☎0464 55 66 02). €15 per day. Both open M-Sa 9am-noon and 3-7pm. MC/V.

Scooter Rental: Sembenini Moto, Vle. Dante 3 (☎0464 55 45 48). €19 per 2hr., €49 per day. Open Tu-Su 9:30am-12:30pm and 4-7pm. MC/V.

▚ ▟ ORIENTATION AND PRACTICAL INFORMATION

To reach the **centro** from the bus station, head down **Viale Trento,** then cross the traffic circle. Go behind the church on **Via Roma** to reach **Piazza Cavour.**

Tourist Office "Ingarda Trentino": Largo Medaglie d'Oro 5 (☎0464 55 44 44; www.gardatrentino.it), at the old bus station at the end of V. della Liberazione. Lists hotel vacancies and offers a variety of cheap regional tours. Ask for a city map and hiking routes. City tour Sa 9:30am (3hr., €3); book 1 day in advance. English spoken. Wheelchair-accessible. Open M-Sa 9am-noon and 3-6:30pm, Su 9am-noon and 3:30-6:30pm.

Laundry: Vle. Rovereto 74. Take V. D. Alighieri, which becomes V. Giosuè Carducci and then Vle. Rovereto.

Internet Access: Internet Point, V. Dante Alighieri 70/B, has individual hookups for laptops. €3 per 30 min., Open M-Sa 10am-12:30pm and 3:30-10pm, Su 3:30-10pm.

English language books: Giunti, just outside the arched gate of P. Cavour. Open M-W 9am-8pm, Th 9am-10pm, F-Sa 9am-midnight, Su 10am-8pm.

Police: V. Brione 5 (☎0464 57 80 11).

Pharmacy: V. D. Alighieri 12/B (☎0464 55 25 08). Open M-F 8:45am-12:30pm and 3:30-7:30pm.

Post Office: V. S. Francesco 26 (☎0464 57 87 00). Open M-F 8am-6:30pm, Sa 8am-12:30pm. Also has ATM. **Postal Code:** 38066.

▛ ▜ ACCOMMODATIONS AND CAMPING

▨ **Ostello Benacus (HI),** P. Cavour 10 (☎0464 55 49 11). From bus station, head right down V. Trento; cross through the traffic circle to V. Roma, turn left after the arch, and cross left through P. Cavour. Central location and clean facilities. Breakfast included; dinner €10. Laundry €4. Internet €2 per hr. Reception 7-9am and 3-11pm. Check-out 9am. Bathrooms closed 10am-3pm. Curfew 11pm; ask for key if returning after 11pm. Reservations recommended. Dorms €16. HI-member discount €3. MC/V. ❶

Albergo Garni Rita, V. Brione 19 (☎0464 55 17 98; www.garnirita.com). B&B located in a quiet area 25min. outside the *centro* within a cluster of similarly priced accommodations. Breakfast included. Reservations recommended. Located in a cluster of hotels and B&Bs with similar prices. Open Mar. 10-Nov. 3. €38 per person. Cash only. ❸

Bavaria, V. Rovereto 100 (☎0464 55 25 24), on the road toward Torbole. Pizzeria and *gelateria* in front of campground. Take lessons in windsurfing and sailing right behind the campground at Surfsegnana. Hot shower €1. Reception 9am-1pm and 3-6pm. Quiet hours 3-5pm and 11pm-8am. No entry by car 11pm-7am. Open Apr.-Oct. €8 per person, €6 per child. Site €10. AmEx/MC/V for €100 or more. ❶

Camping Monte Brione, V. Brione 32 (☎0464 52 08 85; www.campingbrione.com). Offers a pool, bar, laundry services, and minimarket situated 800m from the lake, next to biking trails. Free hot showers. Internet €4 per hr. Reception 8am-1pm and 3-7pm. Reservations recommended. €6.50-8.50 per person. Small site without electricity €7-9; large site with electricity and parking €9.50-12. MC/V. ❶

🄵 FOOD

An **open-air market** sells produce in P. delle Erbe. (Open M-Sa mornings.) A **Despar** supermarket sells groceries just outside the *centro* at V. Roma 19. (Open M-Sa 8:30am-1pm and 3:30-7:30pm, Su 9am-12:30pm. Cash only.)

▧ **La Casa del Pane,** V. Disciplini, 3 (☎0464 5508 39). Outside of P. Cavour. Look no further for a delicious and cheap breakfast or lunch. Pizza cut by the slice will fill you up on the go (priced by weight, most slices €2-3.50). Absolutely don't miss one of their fantastic *brioche con cioccolato* (€1); baked fresh every morning, these warm and flaky beauties are the perfect way to start the day. Friendly owners will occasionally slip an additional cookie or slice of foccacia in with your order. ❶

Leon d'Oro, V. Fiume 28 (☎0464 55 23 41). A general openness allows this energetic and traditional restaurant to spill pleasantly out onto the bustling street. Try the *risotto mantecato alle code di gambero* (with lemon-marinated prawns; €12) with local wine. Primi €7.50-13. Secondi €8.50-17. Cover €1.50. Open daily mid-March to mid-Nov. 11am-3:30pm and 5pm-11pm. AmEx/MC/V. ❸

Ristorante Ancora, V. Montanara 2 (☎0464 52 21 31). Maritime decor and sun-kissed rooftop terrace. Pizza €3-8. Salads €4-6. Primi €8-13. Secondi €9-19. Open daily noon-midnight. AmEx/MC/V. ❸

👁 🄰 SIGHTS AND OUTDOOR ACTIVITIES

Take local bus #1, 2, or 6 from V. Martiri to reach **Cascata Varone,** which has a waterfall, stunning views, swimming, and sunbathing on amazing ▧**grass beaches.** Follow the lakeside path behind the tourist office and head away from the mountains to **Lungolago dei Sabbioni** and **Lungolago dei Pini.** Three kilometers outside town, the 20,000-year-old waterfall **Cascata Varone** has shaped a huge 110m gorge in the mountain. Foliage arches over surrounding mountain paths, making them ideal for easy strolls. (☎0464 52 14 21; www.cascata-varone.com. Open May-Aug. daily 9am-7pm; Sept. daily 9am-6pm; Oct. daily 9am-5pm; Nov.-Feb. Su 10am-5pm; Mar. daily 9am-5pm; Apr. daily 9am-6pm. €5. Cash only.) The **Ponale,** a road previously used by the military to connect Riva del Garda with Valle di Ledro during WWI, begins south of the city, a few hundred meters down the western shore, just before tunnel leading to Limone. The road boasts impressive views, tunnels, and mountain bike paths. For fun in the water, **Noleggio Rudderboat Rental,** in front of P. Battisti, by the castle, rents paddleboats. (☎0464 55 44 75. Rental for 2 people €7 per hr., €8 per 4hr., €9 per 5hr. Pay 2hr., get 1 free. Open daily 8:30am-7pm. Cash only.) **Surfsegnana,** behind campground Bavaria, offers windsurfing, sailing, and canoeing lessons. (☎0464 50 59 63; www.surfsegnana.it. Open daily 8am-6pm.) The cliffs above the lake draw hikers out of the city *centro*. Follow V. D. Alighieri to the mountains as it changes to V. Bastione; then, take a left up the ramp and follow the winding cobblestone path for 20min. to the 15th-century **Bastione** (the white building seen from below), a circular fortress that survived Napoleon's onslaught in 1796 but lost its upper half in the process. Today, hikers can explore the edges of the historical treasure or admire the aerial view of the vibrantly blue Lake Garda.

speckled with tiny boats. Farther up, a steep 1hr. ■hike leads to **Chiesetta Santa Barbara,** a tiny chapel poised over misty mountains and the valley below. Just look into the mountains for the white speck to locate it. There are numerous well-regarded **mountain biking** paths; for details, go to the tourist office.

NIGHTLIFE

The *centro* is peppered with English-style pubs that cater to a large German tourist contingent. The tourist office keeps a schedule of free beach parties during the summer that offer lakeside fireworks.

■ **Pub All'Oca,** V. S. Maria 9 (☎0464 55 34 57; www.puballoca.com). Jazz and more upstairs, in an old leather booth or around the horseshoe bar. Downstairs is more fashionable, with black modern furniture. Young, international clientele and English-speaking staff. Mixed drinks €6. Open daily 6pm-2am. Cash only.

Nuovo 900, V. Gazzoletti 6 (☎0464 030 900; www.nuovo900.it). This jazzy, relaxing wine bar features surprisingly colorful futuristic decor and a candle-lit deck on the street. Wine starting at €3 per glass; ask about regional specialties. Open 6pm-2am. MC/V.

J24, P. Catena 7a (☎0464 55 31 73). J24 has plenty of seats that look out onto the lake and one of the more youthful clienteles along the *piazza*. Offers fresh fruity concoctions as well as a wide selection of rum and whiskey (€3.50-7 per glass). Open daily in summer 10am-1am; in winter 6pm-1am. MC/V.

DESENZANO   ☎030

As the only town with train access and home to the largest port in the region, Desenzano (deh-sen-ZA-no; pop. 23,000) is the gateway to Lake Garda. It also holds extensive shopping and nightlife that is unavailable in most of its quieter neighboring towns. With lovely pedestrian streets, good restaurants, and a weekly lakeside open-air market, this town never lets a traveler down.

⊞⚆ TRANSPORTATION AND PRACTICAL INFORMATION. Trains, on the corner of V. da Vinci and Vle. Cavour, serve Milan (24 per day 6:33am-10:16pm; €6.80), Venice (22 per day 6:30am-10:13pm; €8.40), and Verona (14 per day 6:09am-11:39pm, €2.60). **Buses** leave across the street from the train station and stop by the port (tickets sold in a yellow newsstand there), serving Gardone (45min., 6 per day 6am-6pm, €2.80); Limone (1hr., 6 per day 6am-6:30pm, €4.90); Riva (2hr., 6 per day 6am-6:30pm, €5.60); Salò (30min., 6 per day 6am-6:30pm, €2.60); Sirmione (19 per day 5:40am-7:05pm, €1.60-4). The tourist office provides bus schedules. From the port in P. Matteotti on V. Anelli, Navigazione sul Lago di Garda runs **ferries** to Garda (8 per day 10:15am-5:40pm; €6.90, express €9.80) and Riva del Garda (4 per day 10am-4:55pm; €11, express €15). (☎030 91 49 511 or 800 55 18 01; www.navigazionelaghi.it. Ticket office open 20min. before departure time.) For **taxis,** call ☎030 91 41 527.

The **tourist office** is at V. Porto Vecchio 34. (☎030 91 41 510. Open M-Tu and Th 9am-12:30pm and 3-6pm.) Other services include: **Banco di Brescia,** V. Guglielmo Marconi 18, with **ATM** (open M-F 8:25am-1:25pm and 2:40-4:10pm); **police** (☎030 91 43 572); **medical emergency** (☎030 91 20 393); **pharmacy,** V. S. Maria 1, off P. Matteotti (open 9am-12:30pm and 3:30-7:30pm; MC/V); **Internet** and **Western Union,** V. Mazzini 3 (€1 per 15min., €3 per hr.; open daily 9am-10pm); **post office,** V. Crocefisso 27-29, near Villa Romana (open M-F 8:30am-7pm, Sa 8:30am-12:30pm). **Postal Code:** 25015.

ACCOMMODATIONS AND FOOD. Accommodations are plentiful in Desenzano, though they can be expensive, especially compared to those in nearby towns. **Hotel Flora ❸,** V. Guglielmo Marconi 22, on the main road entering the city, and walking distance from the water, has spacious rooms in addition to free parking, Wi-Fi, and fax. Rooms include TV, telephone, A/C, and a small safe. From the train station, take V. Cavour until V. G. Marconi, then make a right. (☎030 99 12 547; www.hotelflora.org. Breakfast included. Singles €40-60; doubles €60-80; triples €80-100. AmEx/MC/V.) **Hotel Trattoria Alessi ❸,** V. Castello 3, (not to be confused with the connecting V. Stretta Castello) boasts an ideal location, right beneath the *castello*. (☎030 91 41 980; www.hotelalessidesenzano.com. Breakfast included. Singles €40-50; doubles €60-70. AmEx/MC/V.) Another conveniently located hotel is **Albergo Moniga ❹,** V. Canonica 16, which overlooks a quiet street. (Singles €50; doubles €70. Breakfast included. MC/V.)

Restaurants line P. Giacomo Matteotti, as well as the pedestrian streets parallel to the waterfront, V. S. Maria, V. Papa, and V. Roma. Walk a while west on V. Roma until it becomes V. Cesare Battisti to get to Spiaggia Desenzanino, the home of **Ristorante-Pizzeria Desenzanino ❷,** C. Battisti. (☎030 91 28 096. Pizza €3-10. Open Tu-Su noon-2:15pm and 7-10:30pm. MC/V.) On the east end of town, **La Briciola ❶,** V. Tommaso dal Molin 5, offers inexpensive self-service food. Menu changes daily; most items under €7. (Open M-Sa noon-4:20pm. AmEx/MC/V.) To escape the heavy tourist feel of the center, make the short uphill trip to P. Garibaldi and try **La Frasca Osteria ❸,** which combines high-end cuisine with a homey yet sophisticated atmosphere. (030 991 27 98; www.osterialafrasca.com. Primi €8-9.50. Secondi €9-15. Open daily 12:15-2:30pm and 6:30-117-10:30pm. Cash only.) Discounts fall like manna from heaven upon the extremely cheap **Supermercato,** V. G. Marconi 17. (Open M-Sa 8:30am-12:30pm and 3:30-7:30pm, Su 9am-1pm.)

SIGHTS. Beaches, Desenzano's chief appeal, are on the far west end of town (Desenzanino), as well as some cultural attractions. **Pedal-boats** run €6 per 30min. and €15 per 2hr., and kayaks cost €6-10 per hr. Views from the **Castello,** in the center of town, are striking. Inquire at the tourist office about free performances inside the castle. (Open Tu-Su 10:30am-12:30pm and 4-7pm. €1. Th free.) The **Villa Romana,** constructed before the AD first century, offers some of the most important remnants of Roman villas in northern Italy built during

VON-TRAPPED IN DESANZANO

Every year in mid-July, residents of Desenzano and the tourists who flock to its shores welcome a group of very special guests—a troupe of all ages from Tyrole, a state in western Austria. While world-famous for its unsurpassed skiing, the remote Austrian region deflates in size when the snow melts and the crowds of visitors go with it. The tourism agency has thus elected to send emissaries of Tyrolean goodwill to its Italian sister city. For three nights, these men and women in traditional costume descend on Desenzano's castle, serving up fragrant, hearty messes of Wurst and Weizenbier, piping hot slices of strudel, and an extra helping of alpine spirit. Aside from sampling the delicious food—a welcome respite from the ubiquitous risotto—visitors and Desenzano residents can gawk at the hard-at-work Tyrolean blacksmiths forging their wares.

As a symbol of peace, the northern visitors bring with them the accordions of love and understanding. Not only do they come yodeling in five-part harmony bearing jovial oompa bands, but as the night wears on, dancers emerge—breeches, dirndls, and all—and make their way from the stage to the town's central square.

If you want to see just how alive these hills really are, look no further to this soulful Italo-Austrian meeting of the minds!

the demise of the Empire. Don't expect imposing columns or domed ceilings, however—the site brings to mind the word ruins, consisting mostly of low stone walls and mosaic-covered floors. For a more impressive set of debris, head to nearby Sirmione for the Grotte di Catullo. (☎030 91 43 547. Open daily Mar.-Oct. 8:30am-6:30pm; Nov.-Feb. 8:30am-5pm. €2.) The **Galleria Civica di Palazzo Todescini,** around the corner from the tourist office, has rotating art exhibits. (Open M-F 10:30am-12:30pm and 5pm-8pm, Sa-Su 10:30am-12:30pm, and 5-10pm. Hours depend on exhibition. Some exhibits free; for others prices vary.)

⬛🟦 **FESTIVALS AND NIGHTLIFE.** From the end of June to the first days of July, Desenzano celebrates its revered saint, **San Luigi**. Check www.commune. desenzano.brescia.it for more festivals. Many of the restaurants along P. Matteotti and P. Capelletti double as bars; check out the (relatively) hip offerings along P. Matteoti. For youthful glamour, check out **Circus**, P. Matteotti 23, where the sleek, vaguely circus-themed decor is more sexy than goofy. (☎030 25 015. Open daily in summer 7pm-3am, winter closes at 2am.) The area on V. Castello is less mainstream, but is home to unique establishments like the Irish pub **Fiddler of Dooney**, V. Castello 36. (☎030 91 42 262. Pints €3.50. Pizza €2.50. F and Sa live music. Open M-F 6pm-2am, Sa 5:30pm-2am, Su 4pm-2am.)

LAKE COMO (LAGO DI COMO)

As indicated by the luxurious villas lining its shores, Lake Como has been a refuge for the well-to-do since before the Roman Empire. But the area is not all about glitz and glamor: the stately beauty surrounding one of Europe's deepest lakes (410m) has provided inspiration for revered artists like Rossini, Bellini, and Shelley alike. Bellagio, Menaggio, and Varenna, the three central lake towns, make for a more relaxing stay than Como, holding peaceful villages quietly tucked into the densely green slopes.

COMO ☎031

Situated on the southwestern tip of Lake Como, closest to Milan, Como (CO-mo; pop. 86,000) is the lake region's comparative metropolis, where physicist Alessandro Volta (who brought us the battery) was born and where Giuseppe Terragni immortalized his fascist architectural designs. Como is a livelier, more youthful city than others on the lake, with visitors coming for the cutting edge shopping, eateries, and nightlife. For those interested in nature, Como's nearby hiking is more than enough to entertain those passing through.

⬅ TRANSPORTATION

Trains: Stazione San Giovanni (☎031 89 20 21). Open daily 6:40am-8:25pm. Ticket office open daily 6:40am-8:25pm. To: **Chiasso** (10min., every hr. 6:29am-1:29am, €1); **Milan Centrale** (1hr., 15 per day 6:25am-11:08pm, €3.50); **Milan Porta Garibaldi** (1hr., 21 per day 5:08am-10:20pm, €3.50); **Basel, Switzerland** (5hr., 9 per day 6:29am-7:59pm, €58); **Zurich, Switzerland** (4hr., 10 per day 7:43am-8pm, €46). **Ferrovia Nord** runs trains from **Stazione Ferrovia Nord** (☎031 30 48 00), near P. Matteotti, to **Cadorna Stazione Nord** and **Milan** (1hr., 32 per day 5:46am-9:16pm, €3.45).

Buses: SPT (☎031 24 71 11; www.sptlinea.it) in P. Matteotti runs buses to nearby lake towns. Ticket office open M-Sa 6:15am-8:15pm, Su 8:10am-12:25pm and 1:25-7:40pm. Info booth open M-F 8am-noon and 2-6pm, Sa 8am-noon. **C30** to Bel-

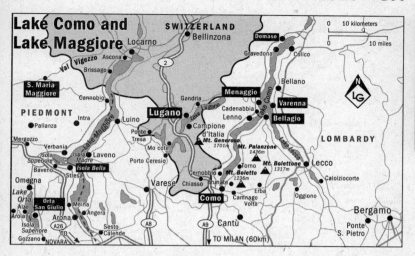

Lake Como and Lake Maggiore

lagio departs from Station San Giovanni. (1hr.; M-Sa 16 per day 6:25am-8:14pm, Su 8 per day 8:45am-8:14pm; €2.40). **C46** to **Bergamo** departs from P. Matteotti (2hr.; M-Sa 6:45, 9:30am, 12:10, 3:45, 6:30pm; Su 9:10am, 1:10, 4, 6:20pm; €4.60). **C10** to **Domaso** departs from P. Matteotti (dir.: Colico), but some end in **Menaggio** (2hr.; M-Sa 12 per day 7:10am-8:35pm, Su 9 per day 8:20am-8:15pm; €4).

Ferries: Navigazione Lago di Como (☎031 57 92 11; www.navigazionelaghi.it). Ticket office open 8:10am-6:50pm. Ferries depart daily to all lake towns from piers along Lungo Lario Trieste in front of P. Cavour. Ferries run to: **Bellagio** (1-2hr.; 21 per day 7:33am-7:10pm; €7.90, express €11); **Domaso** (1-4hr.; 11 per day 8:45am-7:10pm; €9, express €13); **Menaggio** (1-2hr.; 20 per day 7:33am-7:10pm; €7.90, express €11); **Varenna** (1-2hr.; 13 per day 8:45am-7:10pm; €7.90, express €11). Day-passes €20. Pick up the booklet *Orario* for a schedule, including summer night service.

Public Transportation: Buy bus tickets (€1) at *tabaccherie,* bus station, or hostels.

Taxis: RadioTaxi (☎031 26 15 15) in front of both train stations.

Car Rental: Europcar, Vle. Innocenzo XI 14. (☎031 24 16 43).

🏳 🛈 ORIENTATION AND PRACTICAL INFORMATION

From Como's **Stazione San Giovanni,** head down the stairs, and then straight ahead through the park. At **Piazzale San Rocchetto,** take V. Fratelli Recchi on the left, and then turn right on Vle. Fratelli Rosselli, which becomes **Lungo Lario Trento** and leads to **Piazza Cavour.** The **bus station** and **Stazione Ferrovia Nord** are in **Piazza Matteotti,** 2min. farther down the lake along **Lungo Lario Trieste.**

Tourist Office: ATC, P. Cavour 17 (☎031 26 97 12; www.lakecomo.it), on the right when facing the *piazza.* Open M-Sa 9am-1pm and 2:30-6pm, Su 9:30am-12:30pm. **Como Viva,** a booth on V. Comacini next to the *duomo,* also offers info. Open Su 10am-6pm.

Currency Exchange: Banca Nazionale del Lavoro, P. Cavour 32 (☎031 31 31), near tourist office, has a **24hr. ATM.** Open M-F 8:30am-1pm and 2:30-4pm.

Carabinieri: V. Borgo Vico 171. (☎112).

Pharmacy: Farmacia Centrale, V. Caio Plinio Secondo 1, off P. Cavour. Posts after-hours rotations. Open M 3:30-7:30pm, Tu-Su 8:30am-12:30pm and 3:30-7:30pm.

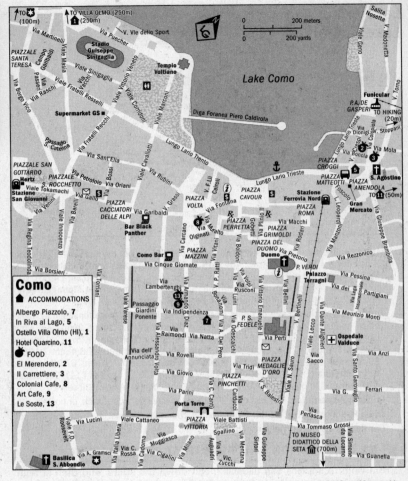

Como

ACCOMMODATIONS

Albergo Piazzolo, **7**
In Riva al Lago, **5**
Ostello Villa Olmo (HI), **1**
Hotel Quarcino, **11**

FOOD

El Merendero, **2**
Il Carrettiere, **3**
Colonial Cafe, **8**
Art Cafe, **9**
Le Soste, **13**

Hospitals: Ospedale Valduce, V. Dante 11 (☎031 32 41 11). **Ospedale Sant'Anna,** V. Napoleana 60 (☎031 58 51 11).

Internet Access: Bar Black Panther, V. Garibaldi 59 (☎031 24 30 05). €3 per hr. Open Tu-Su 7am-midnight. **Como Bar,** V. Alessandro Volta 51 (☎031 26 20 52). Free drink with 2hr. Internet use. €1.40 per 30min., €3 per hr. Open M-Sa 8am-9pm. Cash only.

Post Office: V. V. Emanuele II 99 (☎031 27 63), in the *centro.* Open M-F 8:30am-7pm, Sa 8:10am-12:30pm. Branch on V. Gallio. **Postal Code:** 22100.

ACCOMMODATIONS

In Riva al Lago, P. Matteotti 4 (☎031 30 23 33; www.inriva.info), near the bus station. Soothingly airy new rooms with attractive architectural touches, bath, TV, and A/C. Some have minifridge. Internet €1.50 per 30min. Wi-Fi €3 per day, €5 per 2 days. Free luggage storage. Bustling restaurant-pub on ground fl. Reception 8am-11:30pm. Reservations recommended. Singles €35-45, with bath €40-53; doubles €40-63; triples €58-80; quads €68-98; 4- to 6-person apartments €95-115. AmEx/MC/V over €110. ❸

Ostello Villa Olmo (HI), V. Bellinzona 2 (☎031 57 38 00; ostellocomo@tin.it). From Stazione San Giovanni, turn left and walk 20min. down V. Borgo Vico to V. Bellinzona. Or take bus #1, 6, or 11 to Villa Olmo (€1). Summer-camp feel. Single-sex rooms. Ask about discounts for local attractions. Breakfast included; dinner €12. Laundry €4, dry €3; ironing €1. Parking available. Bike rental €12.50 per day. Reception 7-10am and 4pm-midnight. Check-out 10am. Lockout 10am-4pm. Curfew midnight. Reservations recommended. Open Mar. 1-Nov.15. Dorms €18; family room €16.50 per person (only for families with children). HI-member discount €3. Cash only. ❶

Hotel Quarcino, Salita Quarcino 4 (☎031 30 39 34; www.hotelquarcino.it), offers spacious and calming rooms, some with terraces overlooking the nearby Chiesa di San Agostino. Pleasant garden. Free private parking. Singles €50, with breakfast €52; doubles €75/82; triples €100/110; quads €110/120. AmEx/MC/V. ❹

Albergo Piazzolo, V. Indipendenza 65 (☎/fax 031 27 21 86). From P. Cavour, take V. Bonta, which becomes V. Boldini, then V. Luni. V. Indipendenza is on the right. Tastefully decorated rooms above restaurant, all with bath, TV, and phone. Breakfast €6.50. Closed Nov. Doubles €60; triples €90; quad €110. AmEx/MC/V. ❹

🍴 FOOD

Piazza Mazzini and the streets branching out from it are a veritable Mecca of trendy, modern cafes and art galleries. *Resta* (sweet bread with dried fruit) is a Como specialty sold at **Beretta Il Fornaio,** Vle. Fratelli Rosselli 26/A. (Open Sept.-June M 7:30am-1:30pm, Tu-Sa 7:30am-1:30pm and 4-7pm; July-Aug. M-Sa 7:30am-1:30pm.) Local cheeses, like the pungent *semuda* and *robiola*, are available at supermarkets. Try **GS,** on the corner of V. Fratelli Recchi and V. Fratelli Roselli. (☎031 57 08 95. Open M 9am-8pm, Tu-Sa 8am-8pm, Su 9am-1pm. AmEx/MC/V.) **Gran Mercato** is by the bus station in P. Matteotti. (Open M and Su 8:30am-1pm, Tu-F 8:30am-1:30pm and 3:30-7:30pm, Sa 8am-7:30pm.) An **open-air market** is held in P. Vittoria (Tu and Th mornings, all day Sa).

Le Soste, V. Diaz 52/A (☎031 266 024; www.lesoste.biz), is a small, youthful restaurant for those tired of the traditional *ristorante/pizzerie* combination. Try the Nettle dumplings with melted butter and poppy seeds (€10). Open M-Th noon-2:30pm and 6:30-10:30pm, F-Sa noon-2:30pm and 6:30pm-11:30pm. ❸

Art Cafe, V. Diaz 56 (☎031 268 013; www.i5sensi.it) operates not only as a cafe with a tasty array of wines and *aperitivi*, but also as an art gallery, with exhibits changing monthly and ranging from photos and paintings to multimedia sculptures and woven tapestries. Wine €4. Mixed drinks €5. Open daily noon-3pm and 6pm-2am. ❷

Colonial Cafe, V. Olginati 14 (☎031 449 1535; www.colonial-cafe.com), near P. Mazzini. A lush fusion of decor from various colonized nations around the world serving over-the-top tea and coffee creations. Specializes in countless varieties of profoundly sweetened espresso drinks, spiked with liqueurs and topped with a mountain of fresh whipped cream. Open daily 8am-midnight. ❷

Il Carrettiere, V. Coloniola 18 (☎031 30 34 78), off P. Alcide de Gasperi, near P. Matteotti. Draws crowds with Sicilian cuisine like *risotto con filote di pesce persico*. Pizza €5-8. Primi €8.50-10. Secondi €8.50-19.50. Cover €1.30. Open Tu-F 7pm-1am, Sa-Su noon-2:30pm and 7pm-2am. Reservations recommended. AmEx/MC/V. ❸

El Merendero, V. Crespi 4 (☎031 30 44 77). A lively hangout for nearly 30 years, offering 75 different types of beer to all types of locals. Try the potent Devil's Kiss (€2).

Beer €3.50-6. Mixed drinks €4. Panini €4. Secondi €6-8. Open daily noon-3pm and 7:30pm-2am. Closed May-Sept. all day W and Su afternoon. Cash only. ❷

👁 SIGHTS

DUOMO. A gleaming white beacon in the center of the city, Como's recently restored octagonal *duomo* dates from 1396 and harmoniously combines Romanesque, Gothic, Renaissance, and Baroque elements. The Rodari brothers' life-like sculptures of the Exodus from Egypt animate the exterior, while a collection of 16th-century tapestries brighten the cavernous interior. Statues of Pliny the Elder and Pliny the Younger, long-past Como residents, flank the main door; inside, each massive column hosts its own illuminated statue. (From P. Cavour, take V. Caio Plinio II to P. Duomo. Open daily 7am-noon and 3-7pm.)

TEMPIO VOLTIANO. The Neoclassical structure was dedicated to Como's native son Alessandro Volta, inventor of the battery. The collection includes early attempts at wet-cell batteries the size of a kitchen table, and apparatuses used for experimenting on frog muscles. (From P. Cavour, walk left along the waterfront, and turn onto Lungolago Mafalda di Savoia; look for the small building with a dome. ☎ 031 57 47 05 and 27 13 43. Open Tu-Su Apr.-Sept. 10am-noon and 3-6pm; Oct.-Mar. 10am-noon and 2-4pm. €3.)

VILLA OLMO. Around the western edge of the lake right next to the youth hostel, the light yellow ambassadorial Villa Olmo, built in Lombard style, sits in a spacious, statue-lined waterfront park of the same name. It hosts one art exhibit a year, from March to July. Last year's focus was Viennese painters Klimt, Schiele, and Kokoschka. (On V. Cantoni. ☎ 031 25 24 43. Gardens open daily Apr.-Sept. 8am-11pm; Oct.-Mar. 9am-7pm. Exhibit prices vary.)

MUSEO DIDATTICO DELLA SETA. The worms and silk looms that put Como on the textile map are now displayed in all their finery at this museum just outside of town. (V. Vallegio 3. Entrance at V. Castelnuovo 1. ☎ 031 30 31 80; www.museosetacomo.com. Open Tu-F 9am-noon and 3-6pm. Wheelchair-accessible. €8.)

🎒 DAYTRIPS FROM COMO

DOMASO

Domaso lies 50km away from Como and can be reached by hydrofoil (1hr.; €11.50) or bus (2hr.; €4). Contact the tourist office in Como for more info.

The breezes in Domaso (doh-MA-zoh; pop. 1500), located at the top of the lake, create perfect **windsurfing** conditions. **Windsurfcenter Domaso,** V. Case Sparse 24, at Camping Paradiso, outfits sailors and windsurfers and offers classes from May 1 to October 14. (☎380 70 00 010; www.windsurfcenter-domaso.com. Board and sail rental €37 per half-day, €45 per day. Private lessons €55 per hr. not including equipment rental. Bikes €16 per half-day. Cash only.) If the wind isn't cooperating, travel 30min. farther along the main road to **Canottieri Domaso,** V. Antica Regina 36, where waves take out **wakeboarders.** (☎034 497 462; www.canottieridomaso.it. Wakeboarding €108 per hr., water skiing €120 per hr. Open daily 9am-noon and 1-6pm. AmEx/MC/V.) The **tourist office,** in Ple. Madonnina, has maps and info on aquatic sports. (☎031 96 322; www.comune-domaso.it. Open June-Sept. daily 10am-1pm and 3:30-6pm.)

BELLAGIO ☎031

Once favored by the upper-crust of *milanese* society, Bellagio (beh-LA-jee-yo; pop. 3000, in summer 6000) is one of the loveliest—and certainly the most heavily visited—of the central lake towns. While the tiny town center is generally crowded with tourists, a trip to the grounds of the Villa Melzi allows visitors to stretch their legs in the peaceful splendor of carefully manicured nature. Its name is a compound of *bello* (beautiful) and *agio* (comfort); fittingly, the town is filled with lakeside promenades, sidewalk cafes, and shaded streets.

🖪🏧 TRANSPORTATION AND PRACTICAL INFORMATION. The best way to reach Bellagio is by **ferry.** The ferry next to the *biglietteria* in P. Mazzini serves people, while the one across the port also serves cars. Ferries depart to most lake towns, including Menaggio (10-15min., 8:36am-7:53pm, €3.50), Varenna (10-15min., 9:08am-10:20pm, €3.50), and Como (45min.-2hr., 6:47am-8:34pm, €7.90). SPT C30 **buses** run to Como (1hr., 19 per day 5:55am-6:55pm, €2.65). Lecco Trasporti runs buses to Lecco (1hr., 4-6 per day 6:30am-7:50pm, €2.10.). Ferries dock at **Piazza Mazzini,** which becomes **Via Roma** to the left and **Lungo Lario Manzoni** to the right. The English-speaking staff at the **tourist office,** in P. Mazzini, gives detailed daytrip info. (☎031 95 02 04; www.bellagiolakecomo.com. Open M-Sa 9am-12:30pm and 3-6:30pm, Su 9am-2:30pm.) In case of emergency, call the **carabinieri** (☎112) or the 24hr. **doctor** on-call (☎031 84 00 06 61). A **pharmacy** is at V. Roma 12. (☎031 95 06 23. Open June-Sept. M-Sa 8:30am-12:30pm and 3:30-7:30pm, Su 9am-12:30pm; Sept.-June M-Tu and Th-Sa 8:30am-12:30pm and 3:30-7:30pm.) **Banks** with **ATMs** are on Lungo Lario Manzoni, including **Banco San Paolo,** Lungo L. Manzoni 32. (Open M-F 8:20am-1:20pm and 2:35-4pm.) Use the **Internet** or taste wine at **bellagiopoint.com,** Salita Plinio 8/10/12, off V. Garibaldi. (☎031 95 04 37. €2 per 15min., €6 per hr. Open daily 10am-10pm. AmEx/MC/V.) The **post office,** Lungo L. Manzoni 10, also offers currency exchange. (☎031 95 19 42. Open M-F 8:30am-2pm, Sa 8:30am-12:30pm.) **Postal Code:** 22021.

🖪🍴 ACCOMMODATIONS AND FOOD. Expect higher rates in Bellagio than in other lake towns. **⊠Albergo Giardinetto ❹,** V. Roncati 12, off P. della Chiesa, is by far the best deal in town, with simple rooms overlooking beautiful gardens and grape arbors. (☎031 95 01 68; tczgne@tiscali.it. Breakfast €6. Open Easter-Nov., weather permitting. Singles €45; doubles with bath €60, with balcony €65; triples with bath €75. Cash or traveler's checks only.) **Hotel Suisse ❺,** P. Mazzini 8/10, is the only other choice for less expensive accommodations in the city, even though it is a bit pricey. (☎031 95 03 35; www.bellagio.co.nz/suisse. Breakfast €10. Doubles €85, with lake view €100; triples €125. AmEx/MC.) Another option is the **Albergo Europa ❸,** V. Roma 21, with a cheery restaurant and lobby. (☎031 950 471; www.hoteleuropabellagio.it. Doubles €78-90.)

⊠Baba Yaga ❶, V. Eugenio Vitali 8, serves huge pizzas until late at night. For those not eagerly anticipating a walk to get their food, Baba Yaga also offers a free taxi service for customers. Call them and they will dispatch a cab to pick you up. (☎031 95 19 15. Takeout available. Primi and secondi until 10:30pm, pizza until 11pm.) Walk down a winding street away from the *centro,* starting from P. della Chiesa, to reach **Ristorante La Punta ❹,** V. Vitali 19. The cheese-and-walnut ravioli in cream sauce (€13) is a dream. (☎031 95 18 88. Primi €9-13. Secondi €12-14. Cover €2.50. Open daily noon-2:30pm and 7-10pm. AmEx/MC/V over €50.) **Ristorante Barchetta ❺,** Salita Mella 13, is on a shaded second-floor terrace in the heart of the old town and has featured Lombard cuisine since 1887. Try the gnocchi with shrimp and asparagus tips for €14.50. (☎031 95 13 89. Primi €14.50-17. Secondi €14-23. Cover €4. Open M and W-Su noon-2:30pm and 7-10:30pm. AmEx/MC/V.) The **Gelateria del Borgo,** V. Garibaldi 48, is said to have the creamiest and lightest gelato in Bellagio.

NIGHTLIFE. Far Out, Salita Mella 4, has live jazz every night at 9pm. Well-dressed couples come here for their mixed-drink fix. (☎031 95 17 43; www. farout.it. Primi €6-12. Secondi €10-17.50. Cover €2. Open noon-3pm and 7pm-midnight. Kitchen open noon-3pm and 7-10pm.) **La Divina Commedia "Spiritual Cafe" ❷,** near Far Out on Salita Mella, is one of the town's few nightlife options, with quirky decor and a devoted clientele. (Mixed drinks €7. Open 9pm-2am.)

SIGHTS. The 17th-century **Villa Serbelloni** (not to be confused with the stately, five-star Grand Hotel Villa Serbelloni down the hill) offers spectacular views from the fortifications on the promontory and a lovely, cypress-lined garden with artificial grottoes. Today, it is home to the Rockefeller Foundation and can be toured (except for the interior) twice daily in a guided group. (☎/fax 031 95 15 55. 1hr. tours Apr.-Oct. Tu-Su 11am and 3:30pm. Purchase tickets ¾-1hr. before at P. Chiesa 14. Small info office only open 1hr. before tours. €7, children €3.50.) From the ferry dock, 800m along Lungo Largo Europa, down Lungo Largo Manzoni to reach **Villa Melzi.** The lakeside gardens here, constructed by famous architect Albertolli at the beginning of the 19th century, are perhaps the most sublime place in the north country to take in the lake view while strolling or lounging. The villa is still a private residence, but the grounds are open to the public. (Open daily Mar.-Oct. 9am-6pm. €6.) The **Basilica di San Giacomo,** namesake of the P. della Chiesa, is an excellent example of 10th- to 12th-century Lombard Romanesque architecture—worth a stop for the glittering mosaic scenes in the cupolas of the chapels on either side of the main altar and the life-like wooden carving of Jesus, encased in glass along the left wall. (Open daily 8am-6pm.) While many simply stroll Bellagio's streets, most aquatic sports and organized recreation activities are based in the town. **Sports and Adventures-Cavalcalario Club,** Località Gallasco 1, offers sailing, motorboats, lake fishing, rock climbing, kayaking, canyoning, horseback riding, mountain biking, and paragliding. (☎031 33 95 308 138; www.bellagio-mountains.it.)

DAYTRIP FROM BELLAGIO: VILLA DEL BALBIANELLO. Central Lake Como is known for its grandiose villas, a testament to the luxurious Como of days past. Reputed to be the lake's most gorgeous, **Villa del Balbianello** in Lenno, originally a Franciscan convent, was rebuilt in 1787 by Cardinal Durini as a "splendid palace of delights." The motto, "Do what you would like," welcomes visitors at the entrance. More recently, it was featured as the other-worldly site of the wedding in *Star Wars II: Attack of the Clones* (2002). The highlight of the villa's peninsula is a panoramic, terraced garden dominated by an elegant loggia. *(Lenno is accessible by ferry. 20-40min., 18 per day 6:37am-6:28pm, €3-4.60. From ferry, go left on the Lungolago Lomazzi all the way to the end. From there, villa is accessible by 1km walk, or by taxi boat Th-F only. ☎031 333 410 3854. 10min. ride every 30min.; round-trip €5. Villa ☎034 456 110. Open Mar. 17-Oct. 31 Tu and Th-Su 10am-6pm. Last entry 5:30pm. Garden €5, ages 4-12 €2.50. Guided tour of villa €11/6, with reservation €8/4.)*

LAKE MAGGIORE AND LAKE ORTA

Steep green hills punctuate the dark blue shoreline, and to the west, the glaciated outline of Monte Rosa (4634m) peers across the temperate mountain waters of Lake Maggiore, also known as Lake Verbano. Though many writers and artists have been seduced by the lake's beauty—Byron, Stendhal, Flaubert, Dickens, Hemingway, and da Vinci have all spent time here—today, Lake Maggiore, provides an alternative to the getaway cities along Lake Como. Stresa and Verbania serve as convenient bases for exploring the Borromean Islands and nearby Lake Orta, while secluded Santa Maria Maggiore in Valle Vigezzo offers hiking trails and inexpensive skiing.

STRESA   ☎0323

Stresa (STREH-zah; pop. 5000) retains much of the manicured charm that lured visitors like Queen Victoria, in the 19th and early 20th centuries. Hydrangeas and Art Nouveau hotels line the waterfront, giving the small town a romantic, old-fashioned feel. Stresa is very much a resort town, albeit one that caters emphatically to those in their silver years. Those looking for bronzed and uninhibited coeds playing beach volleyball or doing tequila shots late into the night should look elsewhere. Families and the elderly come here for a trip to the Borromean Islands or for a ride up the funicular with options to bike or hike back down. The real draw, however, is in an evening walk along the lake.

TRANSPORTATION AND PRACTICAL INFORMATION. Stresa lies 1hr. from Milan on the Milan-Domodossola train line. (Ticket office in lobby open M-Sa 6:10-10:45am, 11am-4:15pm, and 4:30-7:20pm; Su 7-10:45am, 11am-4:15pm, and 4:30-8:10pm.) **Trains** run to Milan (1hr., every 30min. 5:23am-10:32pm, €4.60) and Domodossola (40min., 14 per day 6:37am-10:46pm, €3). **Buses** going to Orta (1hr.; 10am, 2, 5pm; €2.45) and Verbania-Pallanza depart from the lakeside church. The best way to see the region's scenery is to make the complete circuit through Lake Maggiore to Switzerland by **ferry** and return through Valle Vigezzo on rail, connecting from Locarno-Domodossola-Stresa. This loop can be easily done by Lago Maggiore Express. (☎0323 23 32 00 or 091 75 18 731. Ferries run Apr.-May Th-Su; June 1-Sept. 23 daily. Departures from Stresa 10:50am and 11:30am. Last connection between Locarno to Domodossola 7:25pm, connection from Domodossola to Stresa 9:55pm. 1-day round-trip €28, children €14; 2-day round-trip €34/17. Bring passport.) **Bikes** can be rented from Sapori d'Italia, V. de Martini 35. (☎0323 93 46 42. €10 per half-day, €18 per day, €45 per 3 days. Insurance €4.) For mountain biking, try Bici Co, at the base of the funicular. (☎0323 30 399; www.bicico.it. €21 per half day, €26 per day. Includes helmet and lock. Ask for detailed trail map. Open daily Apr.-Sept. 9:30am-5:30pm; funicular stops 12:30-1:30pm. Cash only.)

Most of Stresa's services line the water on **Corso Umberto, Piazza Marconi, Corso Italia** or the major north-south thoroughfares, **Via Principe Tomaso** and **Via Roma,** which run uphill from the water. To reach the *centro* and the **IAT tourist office,** P. Marconi 16, on the ferry dock, exit the train station, turn right on V. Principe di Piemonte, take a left on V. Duchessa di Genova, walk downhill toward the waterfront, and turn right. (☎0323 30 150. Open Mar.-Oct. daily 10am-12:30pm and 3-6:30pm; Nov.-Feb. M-F 10am-12:30pm and 3-6:30pm, Sa 10am-12:30pm.) For currency exchange and **ATM,** try **Banca Popolare di Intra,** C. Umberto 1, just off P. Marconi. (☎0323 30 330. Open M-F 8:20am-1:20pm and 2:35-4pm, Sa 8:20am-12:15pm.) In case of emergency, call the **carabinieri,** on Vle. D. di Genova, at ☎0323 30 118, or an **ambulance** (☎0323 33 360). **Farmacia Dott. Polisseni,** V. Cavour 16, posts after-hours rotations. (Open M-W and F-Sa 8:30am-1pm and 3:30-8pm, Th 8:30am-1pm.) **New Data,** V. De Vit 15/A, off P. Cadorna, provides **Internet** access, including connections for personal laptops. (☎0323 30 323. €3 per 30min. Open daily 9:30am-12:30pm and 3:30-10pm.) **Lidrovolante Internet Cafe,** Ple. Lido 6 (☎0323 31 384; www.lidrovolante.com), offers Internet access near the funicular. The **post office** is at V. Anna Maria Bolongaro 44. (☎0323 30 065. Open M-F 8:30am-7pm, Sa 8:30am-1pm.) **Postal Code:** 28838.

◼◻ ACCOMMODATIONS AND FOOD. The pristine ◼**Albergo Luina ❸**, V. Garibaldi 21, centrally located and on the water, has vast, welcoming rooms with TV, bath, and phone. From the train station, walk to the waterfront and head right until you pass the ferry dock. Multilingual proprietress Renata makes guests feel at home and offers extensive advice on travel options. (☎0323 30 285; luinastresa@yahoo.it. Breakfast €3.50. Reservations recommended in summer. Singles €35-52; doubles €55-80; triples €56-80. *Let's Go* discount. MC/V.) With a prime location on the coveted waterfront, **Gigi Meuble ❹**, P. S. Michele 1, has seven rooms with bath and some with balconies. Don't miss the fantastic panoramic view of the lake from the breakfast room. (☎0323 30 225; gigihotel@email.it. Singles €50; doubles €60. AmEx/MC/V.) With numerous four-person rooms, **Hotel Meeting ❺**, V. Bonghi 9, is a popular choice for groups and families. Don't leave without experiencing the stellar panoramic view of the city, lake, and islands from the large rooftop sundeck. (☎0323 32 741; hotelmeeting@stresa.it. Singles €50-90; doubles €70-100; quads €90-120. AmEx/MC/V.)

Popular **Taverna del Pappagallo ❷**, V. Principessa Margherita 46, serves great brick-oven pizza (€4.50-10) and various pastas in a lively indoor seating or in the grapevine-covered courtyard. Greet the embalmed parrot on your way in. (☎0323 30 411. Primi €6.50-13. Secondi €7.50-14. Cover €1.30. Open M-Tu and Th-Su noon-2:30pm and 6:30-11pm. AmEx/MC/V.) Lounge bar **El Gato Negro Café ❷**, V. Principessa Margherita 52, is the most youthful hangout in this heavily silver-lined town. (☎0323 33 621. Mixed drinks €5. Panini €3.50. Salads €6. Primi €5.50. Secondi €6-9. Cover €0.50. Open daily 8:30am-midnight. AmEx/MC/V.) For refuge from the more expensive restaurants, **Il Capriccio ❶**, V. de Vit 15, offers creative pizza slices for only €2-2.20. (☎0323 31 687. Open Tu-Su 10:30am-2pm and 4:30-9pm. Cash only.) **Lago Maggiore ❷**, V. Cavour 34-36, is tucked behind the lakeside church. (☎0323 32 746. Primi €6-10. Secondi €7-15. Lake fish €9-21. Open daily 11:30am-3pm and 6:30pm-11:30pm. AmEx/MC/V.) Food in Stresa can be overpriced and often unsatisfying; a great option is to stock up on groceries at **GS**, V. Roma 11, and eat by the water or on the mountain. (Open M-Sa 8:30am-1pm and 3-8pm, Su 8:30am-12:30pm. AmEx/MC/V.)

◼◻ SIGHTS AND ENTERTAINMENT. Turn right out of the tourist office and follow the waterfront all the way to Vle. Lido to reach the **Stresa-Alpino-Mottarone Funivia**, P. Lido 8, which allows visitors to explore Mottarone's (1491m) extensive hiking and mountain biking trails. (☎0323 30 295; www.stresa-mottarone. it. Open daily 9:30am-12:30pm and 1:50-5:30pm; often closed Nov. for repairs. 20min.; every 20min., last return 5:40pm; €5-7.50.) Close to the water, **Villa Pallavicino**, down C. Italia, boasts 50 acres of gardens filled with over 40 species of exotic animals such as flamingoes and zebras. (☎0323 31 533; www.parcozoopallavicino.it. Open Mar.-Oct. daily 9am-6pm. €9, children €5.) From the last week in July to the second week in September, classical musicians and fans gather for the **Settimane Musicali di Stresa e del Lago Maggiore,** a celebration of the full canon of classical music. Performances crowd Stresa's Palazzo dei Congressi or Isola Bella. Contact the ticket office at V. Carducci 38. (☎0323 31 095 or 30 459; www.settimanemusicali.net. Open daily 9:30am-12:30pm and 3-6pm. Tickets €20-100, under 26 half-price, limited number of tickets €10. Package tickets available.) Stresa's new and only nightclub, **Loco Beach Club**, P. Lido, is next to the funicular. The rooftop bar, swanky beachside patio, and modern dining room draws a crowd of older tourists after 9pm. (☎0323 93 47 40. Mixed drinks €5-6. Primi €11. Secondi €15-18. Open daily 9pm-3am.)

THE BORROMEAN ISLANDS (ISOLE BORROMEE) ☎0323

Beckoning visitors with dense greenery and stately villas, the lush beauty of the Borromean Islands (in Italian "EE-so-leh bo-ro-MEY") is one of the lake's major attractions. Situated between Stresa and Pallanza, the islands are easily accessible by ferry. The opulent ■**Palazzo e Giardini Borromeo** is set on the pearl of Maggiore, **Isola Bella**. This Baroque palace, built in 1670 by Count Vitaliano Borromeo, features meticulously designed rooms constructed over 300 years, with priceless tapestries and Van Dyck paintings. Napoleon and Josephine slept in the alcove of the grand **Napoleon Room** during his first Italian campaign in 1797. The **Sala della Musica** hosted Mussolini, Laval, and MacDonald at the 1935 **Conference of Stresa**, the last attempt to stave off WWII. Six underground man-made **grottoes** are covered in mosaics; for years, peasants collected black stones to complete the masterpieces. Ten terraced gardens rise up like a wedding cake, punctuated by statues of gods and topped with a unicorn, the symbol of the Borromeo family, whose motto, *Humilitas* (humility), is not so apparent here. (☎0323 30 556; www.grandigiardini.it. Open daily Mar. 21-Oct. 21 9am-6pm, garden until 6:15pm. Last entry 30min. before closing. Tours for 2-50 people can be arranged at least one day in advance by phone or at info@borromeoturismo.it. €11, ages 6-15 €5. Combined ticket for the *palazzo* and the Villa Taranto on Isola Madre €16, children €7. Audio tour €2.50. €35 per group.)

From Isola Bella, a short ferry ride leads to **Isola Superiore dei Pescatori,** a quaint fishing village full of souvenir vendors and cats, who come for the daily catch. There's a little-used rocky swimming beach on the west end of the island, but keep in mind this is an alpine lake; the water may be more chilling than refreshing. On top of the hill in the village, the only other attraction is the **Chiesa di San Vitore,** dedicated to a martyred second-century *borromese* native who later became a saint. While most of the church dates from 1638, portions of the altar date from the first century. (Open daily 9am-6pm. Free.) There is no such thing as a non-touristy restaurant on these popular islands, but head left when exiting ferry to reach **Ristorante Italia ❸,** V. Ugo Ara 58, which specializes in local fish and serves it in a charming blue-and-white house overlooking the lake. (☎0323 30 456; www.stresaonline.com/italia. Primi €7-10. Secondi €10-15. Cover €1.50. Open daily noon-3pm and 7-10pm. AmEx/MC/V.)

Isola Madre, almost entirely covered by its garden, is the largest and most tranquil of the islands, and thus predictably the local favorite—perhaps because it also feels like a step back in time. Its elegant **Villa Taranto** was started in 1502 by Lancelotto Borromeo and finished by Count Renato 100 years later, after Lancelotto reputedly met his end in the mouth of a ■**dragon.** A far cry from many stuffy residences of European nobility, the villa has a number of room-sized puppet theaters, set with scenery and marionettes ranging from whimsical to creepy. The villa's gardens have exotic flora and fauna—a flock of white peacocks and various other flamboyantly plumed birds guard the 200-year-old Cashmir Cyprus. Visit in July to see the rare lotus blossoms in bloom. (☎/fax 0323 31 261. Open daily Mar.-Sept. 9am-noon and 1:30-8:30pm; Oct.-Feb. 9:30am-12:30pm and 1:30-5pm. €10, ages 6-15 €5. Combined ticket with the Palazzo e Giardini Borromeo €16.50, children €7.50. Audio tour €2.50.)

If you've budgeted a day for island hopping, stop across the lake from Stresa at the small monastery ■**Santa Caterina del Sasso.** Tucked along the coast, a few miles away from Baveno, the monastery is difficult to reach other than by boat; the complete isolation is worth exploring for the amount of late-Renaissance artwork inside, the highlight being a 17th-century fresco *God the Father.* Boats depart from Stresa (7-8 per day from 9:20am-4:35pm) for the monastery. (www.provincia.va.it/preziosita/ukvarese/itin/maggiore/gemonio.htm. Open daily Apr.-Oct. 8:30am-noon and 2:30-6pm; Nov.-Mar. 9am-noon and 2-5pm. Free.)

THE LAKE COUNTRY

Ferries (☎0323 800 551 801; www.navigazionelaghi.it) run from Stresa to Carciano, Isola Bella, Isola Superiore, Baveno, Isola Madre, then Pallanza, and ending in Intra. Ferries leave Stresa every 15-30min. from 7:10am to 7:10pm and return from Intra until 6pm. A one-day ticket for unlimited travel between Stresa, Pallanza, and the three islands costs €11.50. Individual tickets from Stresa to Isola Bella or Superiore cost €6.60, and to Isola Madre €8.40. All tickets are valid until returning to departure point. A single day combined ride to Isola Bella, Isola Superiore, and Isola Madre with ferry ride costs €28.

SANTA MARIA MAGGIORE ☎0324

Carved out by the same glaciers that melted to Lake Maggiore and Lake Orta, Valle Vigezzo (VAL-lay vee-JET-soh) is a gorgeous valley with few tourists. The area has sparked artistic inspiration so often that it is now known as "Painter's Valley." Santa Maria Maggiore (SAN-ta ma-REE-ah ma-JO-reh; pop. 1280), the lake's largest town, is bordered by the smaller towns of Arvogno, Craveggia, Re, and Toceno. Perhaps the biggest highlight, however, is journeying through the valley to witness its stunning landscape, resplendent with enormous mountains, fields, villages, waterfalls, and streams.

🚉🚌 TRANSPORTATION AND PRACTICAL INFORMATION. From Stresa, take the **train** to Domodossola (☎0324 24 20 55; 40min., 20 per day 6:37am-10:34pm, €3), then transfer to the SSIF (or Centovalli) line by turning left out of the train, walking underground, taking the train toward Locarno, and getting off at Santa Maria Maggiore (40min.; 17 per day 5:30am-7:58pm, last return 8:15pm; €2.60.) The ticket office (☎0324 24 20 55) is open 20min. before departures. For a **taxi**, call ☎0324 92 405 or 98 045.

From the train station on **Piazzale Diaz**, cross **Via Luigi Cadorna** to **Via Dante**, which ends at **Via Antonio Rosmini**. Turn right to reach **Piazza Risorgimento**, the *centro*. The **Ufficio Turistico Pro Loco**, P. Risorgimento 4, offers free maps of the town and valley, and **Internet** access. (☎0324 94 565. Internet €3 per 30min. Open in summer M-Sa 10am-noon and 4-6pm, Su 10am-noon; in winter Sa 10am-noon and 4-6pm, Su 10am-noon.) Follow V. Cavalli from P. Risorgimento until it becomes V. Rossetti Valentini to reach **Banca Popolare di Novara**. (☎0324 95 002. Open M-F 8:20am-1:20pm and 2:35-3:35pm.) In case of emergency, call the **carabinieri** (☎0324 95 007) or the **guardia medica turistica**, V. Guglielmo Marconi 4. (☎0324 94 360. Open daily July-Aug. 2-6pm.) A **pharmacy** is on V. Matteotti 5. (☎0324 95 018. Open M-Sa 9am-12:30pm and 3:30-7:30pm, Su 9am-12:30pm.) The **post office** is at V. R. Valentini 26. (☎0324 90 53 87. Open M-F 8:30am-2pm, Sa 8:30am-1pm.) **Postal Code:** 28857.

🛏️🍴 ACCOMMODATIONS AND FOOD. There are few budget accommodations in Santa Maria Maggiore. **Albergo Oscella ❸**, V. Matteotti 84, offers the best value in town, located just outside of the *centro*. (☎0324 951 70. Singles €35; doubles €65; triples €75.) For delicious and conscientiously prepared local food, head to **Osteria Bar Al Cortiletto ❸**, V. Cavalli 20. Save room for the homemade desserts. (☎0324 90 56 78. Pizza €4-7.50. Primi €6.50-8. Secondi €8.50-14. Cover €1.80. Open daily Dec.-Oct. 9am-10pm. AmEx/MC/V.)

📷🏔️ SIGHTS AND OUTDOOR ACTIVITIES. One of the main attractions in Santa Maria Maggiore is the **Museo dello Spazzacamino (Chimney Sweep Museum)** in the Parco Villa Antonia, which has a collection of equipment, and sends visitors through a tunnel of pictures, sounds, and smells. As the land was unsuitable for farming, young Vigezzo inhabitants, emigrated en masse to cities throughout

Europe as chimney sweeps; the museum is a dedication to those who returned and used their earnings to boost the valley's economy. (☎0324 90 56 75; www. museospazzacamino.it. Open June-Sept. Tu-Su 10am-noon and 3-6pm; Oct.-May Sa-Su 10am-noon and 3-6pm. €2.) The **▧Santuario della Madonna del Sangue** houses the painting *Madonna del Sangue* (Madonna of the Blood), which is said to have bled for 20 days in 1494 after being hit with a stone. To get to the sanctuary, take the Piana di Vigezzo Funivia (see below) to the stop in the town of Re. (☎0324 97 016. Open daily 8am-9pm. Free.) The best outdoor excursions in the area are in the **▧Parco Nazionale Val Grande,** created in 1992. The 15,000 hectare park is less than 100km from Milan; it can be accessed only by car from the A8 motorway from Milan or the A26 from Genoa/Turin. Exit at "Gravellona Toce" and take Ossola highway toward the Simplon Pass. The park is not only known for its wilderness but also its relics of a once-major alpine civilization. Ask the tourist office for park info, and acquire hiking itineraries and maps at the office inside the park entrance. (☎0323 55 79 60; www.parcovalgrande.it.) **Arvogno** (1260m), starts hiking paths toward high peaks, and the **La Cima chair lift** takes visitors ever higher on summer weekends (8:30, 11:30am, 2:30, 5pm). In winter, it becomes part of the Valle Vigezzo ski ticket, which includes the **Piana di Vigezzo Funivia** (cable car) that mounts to **Colma Trubbio** (2064m) from **Prestinone.** (Ascents daily 8am-5:30pm. 1-way €7, children €4; round-trip €10/6. Full-day ski pass M-F €20, Sa-Su €24; ages 4-12 €15/18. Half-day pass €13/15, ages 4-12 €10/13. Equipment rental available at top of *funivia.* AmEx/MC/V.)

ORTA SAN GIULIO   ☎0322

Orta San Giulio (OR-ta san JOO-lee-oh; pop. 1120) is the gateway to Lake Orta—by far the smallest and least touristed of the lakes—though just as striking as any of them. The 19th-century villas that line the narrow, cobblestone streets evoke the very best of old Italy. Though difficult to reach without a car, the town has drawn many to its secluded location. In fact, the privacy is precisely what drew Friedrich Nietzsche here in 1882 with his young love, Lou Salome, in order to escape the watchful eye of her mother. Nietzsche claimed he couldn't remember whether or not the two had kissed because the views had sent him into a state of grace.

◨ TRANSPORTATION. If coming by train from Stresa, switch lines at Premosello (1hr.; 4 per day 6:37am-6:47pm, return 6:28am-8:17pm; €3), getting off at Orta-Miasino. In Orta, buy train tickets at the nearby bar. (Open M-F 6:30am-midnight, Sa 7:30pm-midnight.) You can also access Orta-Miasino from Domodossola, north of Stresa on the Milan-Domodossola line. If coming or going to Milano Centrale, switch trains at Novara to the line ending in Domodossola (9 per day 6:39am-7:20pm, €4.70). Down the hill from the train station, a small red train-shaped vehicle, Il Trenino di Orta, shuttles passengers between the intersection of V. Panoramica and V. Giuseppe Fava (in front of the tourist office that is halfway on the walk) and the *centro;* the train also stops in front of Sacro Monte. (☎0322 347 488 3509. 5min.; Apr. 15-Oct. 15 M-Tu and Th-Su every 15-30min. 9am-8pm, Oct. 16-Apr. 14 Su; €4, children €2; round-trip €5/3.) **Bus 30** (or Nerini Mini-Bus; ☎0323 55 21 72; €3) runs to Orta from Stresa. In Stresa the bus departs from in front of the church near the ferry station (5 per day 7:40am-5pm, 1hr.). In Orta the bus departs from Ple. Prarondo (1hr., 3 per day 11am-6pm). Be early and stand in a visible location in the parking lot; as the bus doesn't stop if no one appears to be waiting for it. Small **motoscafi** (motorboats) in P. Motta weave back and forth from Isola di San Giulio to the mainland during the summer upon request. (☎0323 333

THE LAKE COUNTRY

605 0288; www.motoscafipubbliciorta.it. 10min.; daily Apr.-Oct. every 15min. 9am-6:30pm; Nov.-Mar. every 40min. 9am-5pm; €4). Navigazione Lago d'Orta runs larger boats between the island and the mainland. (☎0323 84 48 62. 5min.; Apr.-Sept. daily every 30min. 9:55am-7:10pm, Oct. Sa-Su, Nov. Su; €4.) On the mainland call a **taxi** (☎0323 328 391 1670 or 335 65 56 340).

🛈 PRACTICAL INFORMATION. The *centro* is **Piazza Motta.** Amble along **Via Olina,** which becomes **Via Bossi,** then **Via Gippini** to reach **Via Motta** and the footpath, Strada del Movero, and ultimately **🏖Lungo Lario 11 Settembre,** a sublime path hugging the shore where you can sunbathe on the docks or jump off them into the clear blue water. There are two **tourist offices** in Orta. The primary one is on V. Panoramica, across the street and downhill from Villa Crespi. To reach the office from the train station, exit left from the station, make the first left downhill, and continue through the rotunda straight ahead. (☎0323 90 56 14 or 90 51 63; inforta@distrettolaghi.it. Open W-Su 9am-1pm and 2-6pm.) The second office is in the Palazzo Comunale, V. Bossi 11, straight past P. Motta. (☎0323 90 155; www.ortainfo.com. Open Apr.-Oct. M and W-F 11am-1pm and 2-6pm, Sa-Su 10am-1pm and 2-6pm.) **Banca Popolare di Novara** is at P. Ragazzoni 16. (☎0323 90 57 01. Open M-F 8:20am-1:30pm and 2:35-3:35pm, Sa 8:20-11:20am.) A **pharmacy,** V. Albertolletti 10, is off P. Motta. (☎0323 90 117. Open M-W and F-Sa 9am-12:30pm and 3:30-7:30pm. MC/V.) In case of emergency, call the **carabinieri,** V. Circonvallazione 4 (☎0323 90 114), in nearby Omegna or an **ambulance** (☎0323 81 500). The only **Internet** access inside the city is at the hotel booking center on V. Poli 13. (☎0323 90 55 32. €4 per 5min., €10 per 30min. Open daily 9am-7pm. Cash only.) They also rent bikes. **Il Cantuccio,** across from the train station, also has InternetThe **post office,** P. Ragazzoni 5, offers currency exchange. (☎0323 90 157. Open M-F 8:30am-2pm, Sa 8:30am-1pm.) **Postal Code:** 28016.

🛏 ACCOMMODATIONS. Orta's relative seclusion means high accommodation prices. Down the street from Villa Crespi, **B&B Villa Pinin ❸,** on V. Fava, is one of the best deals in town. Admire a gorgeous view of the lake from any spot in the spacious yard. (☎0323 90 55 05 or 340 00 69 323. Reservations required. High-season doubles €80, low-season €60. Cash only.) The enormous **Villa Francesco ❸,** V. Prisciola 6, has huge, bountiful rooms opening onto a spectacular terrace, as well as a breakfast room, restaurant, bar, garden, and chapel, all just a few short minutes from the station. Facing the train station, go left and continue 300m down the road. (☎0323 90 258; www.hotelsanfrancesco.it. Breakfast included. Singles €34; doubles €56. MC/V.) **Hotel Santa Caterina ❺,** V. Marconi 10, has what are undoubtedly the hippest Scandanavian-themed lodgings in Orta. The included buffet breakfast is an impressive value. Walk from the train station toward town, and the hotel is on the left several minutes before passing the tourist office. (☎0323 915 865 75; www.ortainfo.com. Singles €70-80; doubles €95-105. AmEx/MC/V.) The lakeside **🏖Camping Orta ❶,** V. Domodossola 28, welcomes campers with a private beach and Internet access. (☎0323 90 267; www.campingorta.it. Wash €3, dry €3. Internet €3 per 30min. Reception open 8:30am-12:30pm, and 2-7:30pm. €5-7 per person, €3.50-4.50 per child under 12; €8-15 per tent; €5-6 per car. Bungalows €65-90. Electricity €2. Showers €0.20 for 4 min. Cash only.)

🍴 FOOD. Local cuisine is known for *tapulon* (spiced, minced donkey and horse meat cooked in red wine) eaten with cornmeal polenta, typically only served in winter. There isn't a better place to try the locally produced wine, *Ghemme,* or the native cheese, *Tomo di Motarone,* than at **🏖Al Boeuc ❷,** V. Bersani 28, a tiny, dimly lit wine bar one street inland from P. Motta. Large *bruschette* (€10) or mixed *salame* plates go well with wine. While *Ghemme* is only available by the bottle, other local wines come by the glass, such as *Traversa*, made from the same grapes. (☎0323 339 584 0039. Open M and W-Su 11am-3pm and 6:30pm-1am. Cash only.) Though most restaurants in the town center are quite touristy, **Ristorante Edera ❷**, V. Bersani 15, off the main square, is slightly less so. Primi €6-8. Secondi €8-13. (☎0322 9055 34. Open for dinner F-Sa.) At night, the mature crowd heads to classy **Caffè and Jazz ❷**, V. Olina 13, where Thursday (July-Sept.) means live jazz at 10pm. (☎0323 333 923 2522. Wine €4-5 per glass. Bruschette €7. Salads €8-9. Open Tu-Su 11am-3pm and 6pm-1am. Cash only.) Since 1228, P. Motta has had a weekly Wednesday **market.** The food market **La Dispensa,** V. Bersani 38, off P. Motta, and the fruit market next door offer *panini* (€2.30-4) and picnic basics. (Open M-Tu and Th-Sa 9am-6:30pm, W 9am-2pm, Su 10am-6:30pm.)

◙ SIGHTS. At the intersection of V. Panoramica and V. G. Fava, the ornate **Villa Crespi,** which now houses a hotel, was built in 1873 in an Arabian style to satisfy cotton pioneer Cristoforo Crespi's nostalgia for his trips to the Orient. The large stone columns of the ground floor portico of the beautiful city hall, also known as the **"Palazzoto,"** dominate P. Motta. Right up V. Albertoletti is the **Chiesa Santa Maria Assunta,** a church built to celebrate the end of the 1485 plague. (Open daily 9am-6pm.) On the lake across from Orta lies the **Isola di San Giulio.** According to legend, the island was inhabited by ◙dragons and serpents until they were destroyed by Julius, a traveler from Greece, in the AD fourth century. Today, it is inhabited by three families as well as a convent of 72 nuns who have taken a vow of seclusion. While the convent is not open to the public, the island can be visited by ferry or motorboat. Pedestrians cover the tiny island on a cobblestone path (10min.), known as **The Way of Meditation,** where periodic multilingual markers offer sage advice on the art of introspection. Walking the path in reverse will take you on **The Way of Silence,** where signs comment on the beauty of silence. The 12th-century Romanesque **Basilica di San Giulio,** built on fourth-century foundations, is filled with Baroque ornamentation and adorned with pink cloud frescoes. The true masterpiece is the **pulpit,** carved from black *oira* stone. Downstairs, the skeleton of San Giulio, dressed in brocade robes and mask, rests in a gold and glass sarcophagus. (Open daily 9:30am-12:15pm and 2-6:30pm. Modest dress required. Free.) A short 15min. hike off V. Panoramica onto V. della Cappelletta leads to the **Sacro Monte** monastic complex, a UNESCO World Heritage site. The complex holds 20 chapels filled with life-size, terra-cotta statues and frescoes that chart the life of St. Francis of Assisi. (☎0323 91 19 60; www.sacromonteorta.it. Open daily in summer 9am-5pm; in winter 9am-7pm. Free guided tours with reservations. Park open 24hr. Free.)

THE VENETO

From the rocky Dolomite foothills to the fertile Po valleys, the diversity of the Veneto (VEH-neh-toh) begins with its dramatic topography. Once loosely united under the Venetian Empire, the Veneto's towns and cities have retained their cultural independence; today, visitors are more likely to hear regional dialects than standard Italian. The region's marine supremacy, enviable location near the center of the peninsula, and heavy international and inter-provincial traffic have brought a variety of cuisines and cultural traditions. The influx of Austrian and Slovenian cultures in the mountain villages in the North creates a pleasant surprise for visitors expecting to find only gondolas and mandolins.

HIGHLIGHTS OF THE VENETO

BEHOLD St. Mark's remains at Venice's Basilica di San Marco (p. 238).

SERENADE your loved one during a gondola ride on Venice's Grand Canal (p. 239).

WANDER the hallowed halls of the Università di Padova, where luminaries such as Dante, Galileo, and Copernicus set the academic world on fire.

VENICE (VENEZIA)   ☎ 041

From its hedonistic, devil-may-care Carnevale, to the repentant God-may-care-too services in its soaring marble cathedrals, Venice (in Italian, "ve-NET-see-ah"; pop. 60,000) is a mystical, waterlogged city. Founded by Roman fishermen in the 11th century, the city soon became the major meeting point between East and West. Global commerce depended on Venetian merchants to supply silks, spices, and coffee for over a century before the city's trade dominance diminished. Since then, sea-bound ships have been replaced with gondolas as Venice trades naval prowess for a booming tourist industry and scores of gondoliers in silly hats. Though the busiest *piazze* and major sights may be overrun with visitors, Venice's beauty remains intact, and continues to defy guidebook descriptions. The awe of its seemingly untouched artistic masterpieces, the serene quiet of its hidden *piazze*, and the size and strength of its mighty canals will overtake you. Venice is impossible to master, but the reward of discovering an authentic *enoteca* or a tiny residential neighborhood will lure you back again and again.

✈ INTERCITY TRANSPORTATION

Flights: Aeroporto Marco Polo (☎041 26 09 260; www.veniceairport.it), 10km north of the city. **ATVO shuttle** (☎042 13 83 671) links the airport to P. Roma on the main island (30min., every hr. 8am-12:30am, €3). ATVO ticket office open daily 5am-8:40pm.

Trains: Stazione Santa Lucia (☎041 89 20 21), the main station, is in the northwestern corner of the city. Upon arrival, disembark at S. Lucia, not Mestre on the mainland. Info office open daily 7am-9pm. Ticket windows open M-F 8:30am-7:30pm, Sa-Su 9am-1:30pm and 2-5:30pm. AmEx/MC/V. To: **Bologna** (2hr., 32 per day 3:11am-11:30pm, €8.20); **Florence**

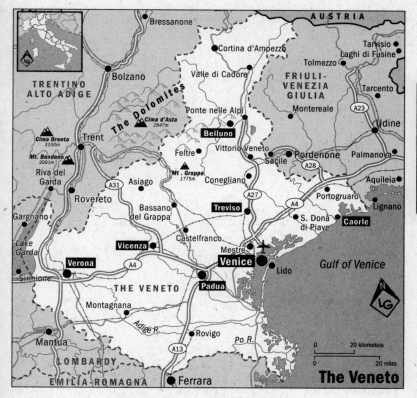

The Veneto

(3hr., 19 per day 3:11am-7:57pm, €23.50); **Milan** (3hr., 26 per day 3:11am-8:03pm, €13.75); **Padua** (45min., 83 per day 12:17am-11:34pm, €2.90); **Rome** (4hr., 23 per day 12:17am-11:30pm, €41.50); **Trieste** (2hr., 32 per day 12:10am-10:47pm, €8.75). Reservations often required; check info booth. Prices, frequency, and travel time vary by company. **Lost and found** (*oggetti rinvenuti*) near track 5 (☎041 78 56 70; open daily for luggage retrieval 8am-noon; open for info 7am-9pm) and **luggage storage** by track #14 (see **Practical Information,** p. 19).

Buses: ACTV (☎041 24 24; www.hellovenezia.it), in Ple. Roma. Office open daily 7am-8pm. Ticket window open daily 6am-11:30pm. **ACTV long-distance carrier** runs buses to **Padua** (1hr., every 15-30min. 4:45am-12:45am, €4.50) and **Treviso** (1hr., every 15-30min. 4:55am-8:55pm, €3). Cash only.

🔶 ORIENTATION

Venice comprises 118 islands in a lagoon, connected to the mainland city of Mestre by a thin causeway. With the **Canale Grande** snaking throughout, the city is divided into seven *sestieri* (sections): **San Marco** in the center, encircled by **Cannaregio** to the north, **San Polo** and **Santa Croce** to the west, **Dorsoduro** along the southwestern shore, **Castello** along the eastern shore, and **Giudecca** to the south,

Venice

ACCOMMODATIONS

Alloggi Gerotto Calderan, **5**
Camping Miramare, **16**
Casa Peron, **17**
Domus Civica (ACISJF), **14**
Foresteria Valdese, **15**
Hotel Arcadda, **4**
Hotel Bernardi-Semenzato, **12**
Hotel Marie & Biasin, **6**
Ostello di Venezia (HI), **30**
Pensione Seguso, **29**
La Residenza, **25**

FOOD

Gam Gam, **2**
Pizzeria/Trattoria
  Al Vecio Canton, **21**
Osteria da Rioba, **1**
Pleasure Cafe, **7**
Al Giardinetto, **8**
Pizza and Kebab Toletta, **9**

NIGHTLIFE

Café Blue, **18**
Bistrot ai Do Draghi, **20**
Café Noir, **19**
Impronta Cafe, **10**
Orange, **27**
Paradiso Perduto, **3**

Vaporetti Stops

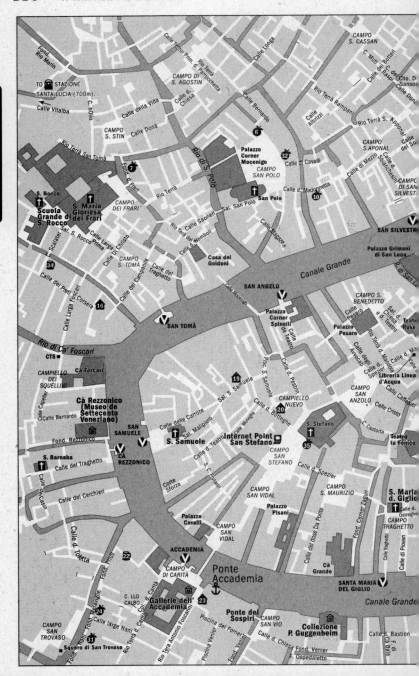

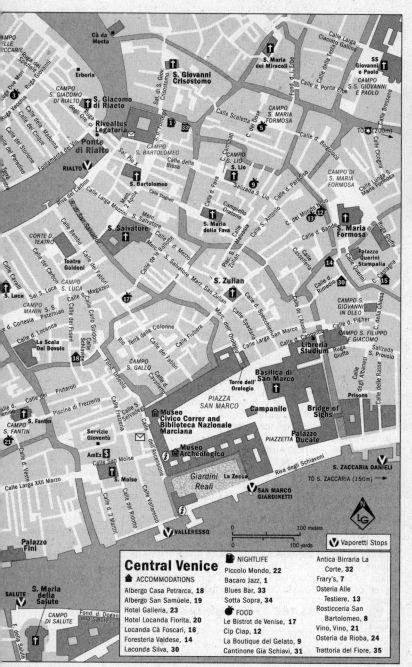

Central Venice

🏠 **ACCOMMODATIONS**
Albergo Casa Petrarca, **18**
Albergo San Samüele, **19**
Hotel Galleria, **23**
Hotel Locanda Fiorita, **20**
Locanda Cà Foscari, **16**
Foresteria Valdese, **14**
Laconda Silva, **30**

🍸 **NIGHTLIFE**
Piccolo Mondo, **22**
Bacaro Jazz, **1**
Blues Bar, **33**
Sotta Sopra, **34**

🍴 **FOOD**
Le Bistrot de Venise, **17**
Cip Ciap, **12**
La Boutique del Gelato, **9**
Cantinone Gia Schiavi, **31**

Antica Birraria La
Corte, **32**
Frary's, **7**
Osteria Alle
Testiere, **13**
Rosticceria San
Bartolomeo, **8**
Vino, Vino, **21**
Osteria da Rioba, **24**
Trattoria del Fiore, **35**

🚤 Vaporetti Stops

THE VENETO

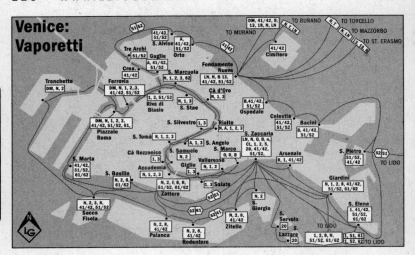

Venice: Vaporetti

separated from Venice proper by the large Giudecca canal. *Sestieri* boundaries are vague but should be of some use in navigating the city's narrow alleys.

Venice's layout consists of a labyrinth of *calli* (narrow streets), *campi* (squares), *liste* (large streets), and *ponti* (bridges). Abandon all hope, ye who enter. It's practically impossible to avoid getting lost—maps are of little use, as many streets are either too narrow to be plotted, lack street signs, or have erratic street numbers. To get by, simply learn to navigate like a true Venetian and look to your hotel for a detailed map of the area you are staying in. Locate the following sights on the map: **Ponte di Rialto** (in the center), **Piazza San Marco** (central south), **Ponte Accademia** (southwest), **Ferrovia** (or Stazione Santa Lucia, the train station; northwest), **Ponte Scalzi** (in front of the station), and **Piazzale Roma** (southwest of the station). These are Venice's main orientation points. A plethora of yellow signs posted throughout the city point the way to major landmarks and bridges.

When trying to find a place, locate the *sestiere*, then find a nearby landmark (often a major *campo*), and follow signs in that general direction. As you get closer, use the address numbers and busier streets to work your way toward the destination. As a general rule, follow the arrows on the yellow signs as precisely as possible. If a street suddenly leads into a *campo* and branches in five different directions, pick the street that follows the original direction of the arrow as closely as possible until reaching the next sign. Note that in Venice, addresses are not specific to a particular street, and every building in a *sestiere* is given a number ("San Marco 3434" is a typical address). Buildings are generally numbered consecutively, but there are also often large jumps, so the next number could be one block away or down an alleyway.

To get to **Piazza San Marco** or the **Rialto Bridge** from the train station, take V#1 (15min. to Rialto, 35min. to San Marco, every 10min.) or V#2 (10min. to Rialto, 25min. to San Marco, every 10min.). On foot, follow signs to P. S. Marco, starting left of the station on Lista de Spagna.

V MARKS THE SPOT. *Vaporetti* stops appear in the text as V.

⧉ LOCAL TRANSPORTATION

The cheapest—and often the fastest—way to see the city is to walk through it. Pedestrians can cross the Grand Canal at the *ponti* Calatrava, Scalzi, Rialto, and Accademia. **Traghetti** (gondola ferry boats) traverse the canal at seven locations, including Ferrovia, San Marcuola, Cà d'Oro, and Rialto (€0.50). *Vaporetti* (water buses) provide 24hr. service around the city, with reduced service after midnight. Tickets vary in price based on the duration of their validity. 1-way *traghetti* tickets cost €6.50. Longer-term **travel cards** allow unlimited access to both *traghetti* and buses running to Mestre and Lido. (12hr. €16, 24hr. €18, 36hr. €21, 2 day €28, 7 day €50.) Students aged 14-29 may purchase a 3-day pass (€22) that includes the perks of the Rolling Venice card and unlimited access to *traghetti* and buses. Travel cards can also be a time-saver; they come pre-validated whereas single fare tickets must be validated at the yellow boxes at each stop. Unvalidated tickets risk a fine; the "confused foreigner" act won't work in a town where tourists often outnumber residents two to one. Schedules, route maps, and tickets are available at tourist offices (**Practical Information,** p. 312). Tickets are also sold in front of all *vaporetti* stops.

MAIN VAPORETTO LINES
V #2, 4: Run from P. S. Marco, up the Giudecca Canal, to the station, down the Grand Canal, back to P. S. Marco, and then to Lido. Always crowded, with long lines.
V #1: Has a similar route to #2, but stays on the Grand Canal, skips Giudecca, and makes more local stops. Also 10min. slower than #2 but less crowded.
V #41, 42, 51, 52: Circumnavigates Venice. #41 and 51 run from the station to San Michele, Murano and Giudecca, ending up back at the station. #42 and 52 follow the same route in the opposite direction.
V #LN: Runs from F. Nove to Murano, Burano, and Lido with connections to Torcello.

Car Rental: Expressway, P. Roma 496/N (☎041 52 23 000; www.expressway.it). From €65 per day (€45 for smaller cars), €285 per week. Free car delivery to and from airport. 18+, with added insurance charge for those under 21. Open daily 8am-7pm. *Let's Go* discount 15%. AmEx/MC/V. **Hertz,** P. Roma 496/F (☎041 52 84 091; fax 52 00 614). From €93 per day (€72 without insurance). Credit card required. 25+. Open M-F 8am-6pm, Sa-Su 8am-1pm. AmEx/MC/V.

Parking: P. Roma (☎041 27 27 301) and island of Tronchetto (☎041 52 07 555; asm@asmvenezia.it). €30 per day. 24hr. Parking is considerably cheaper on the mainland. Consider parking in Mestre (1st train stop out of Venice).

⧉ PRACTICAL INFORMATION

TOURIST AND FINANCIAL SERVICES

Tourist Services:

APT Tourist Offices are located all over the city. Avoid the train station office, as it is always packed. If you do use it, prepare for long lines at peak hours. Branches: P. Roma (☎041 24 11 499; open daily 9:30am-1pm and 1:30-4:30pm; AmEx/MC/V); P. S. Marco 71/F, directly opposite the Basilica (☎/fax 041 52 98 711; open daily 9am-3:30pm; AmEx/MC/V); Lido, Gran Viale 6/A (☎041 52 65 721; open daily June-Sept. 9am-noon and 3-6pm). Every location offers pricey city tours, *vaporetto* tickets, the **Rolling Venice Card** (see next page), city maps and guides (€2.50), and theater and concert tickets. Ask for the magazine *Leo* or visit www.turismovenezia.com for info on history, sights, and activities.

VeneziaSi (☎041 522 2264; www.veneziasi.it), in the train station, right of the tourist office. Finds available hotel rooms and makes same-day reservations in Venice and Rome (€2). Open daily 8am-9pm. Branches at P. Roma (☎041 52 28 640) and airport (☎041 54 15 133). Also books rooms (€2); call (instead of going in person) to avoid a charge for booking.

Rolling Venice Card: Provides discounts at over 200 restaurants, cafes, hotels, museums, and shops for those aged 14-29. Tourist offices have a list of participating vendors. Card costs €4; valid for 1 year. A 3-day *vaporetto* pass with card discount saves €9. Purchase it at the **ACTV VeLa** office (☎041 27 47 650), in P. Roma, at all APT tourist offices, and at ACTV VeLa kiosks next to the Ferrovia, Rialto, S. Marco, and Vallaresso *vaporetto* stops. Open daily 7am-8pm.

Budget Travel: CTS, Fondamenta Tagliapietra, Dorsoduro 3252 (☎041 52 05 660; www.cts.it). From Campo S. Barnaba, cross the bridge closest to the church and follow the road through the small *piazza*, then turn left at the foot of the large bridge. Sells ISICs (€10) and discounted plane tickets. Open M-F 9:30am-1:30pm and 2:30-6pm. MC/V.

Consulates: UK, Mestre, Ple. Donatori di Sangue 2 (☎041 50 55 990). Closest **US** (☎02 29 03 51) and **Australian** (☎02 77 70 41) consulates in Milan; **Canadian** consulate (☎049 87 64 33) in Padua.

Currency Exchange: Use banks whenever possible for best rates, and inquire about additional fees beforehand. The streets around San Marco, San Polo, and the train station are full of banks and **ATMs.** Note that banks close Sa-Su in Venice.

American Express: Calle San Moisè, San Marco 1471 (toll free ☎800 87 2000 for lost or stolen checks). Exit P. S. Marco facing away from the basilica and walk 2min. Currency exchange available. Open M-F 9am-1pm and 2-5pm.

LOCAL SERVICES

Luggage Storage: At the train station. €4 for up to 5hr., €0.60 per hr. up to 12hr., €0.20 per hr. thereafter. Open daily 6am-midnight. Cash only. Maximum of 5 days and 20kg weight limit. **Deposito Pullman Bar,** P. Roma 497/M (☎041 52 31 107). €3.50 per day. Open daily 6am-9pm. Cash only.

English-Language Bookstore: Libreria Studium, San Marco 337/C (☎/fax 041 52 22 382). From P. S. Marco, turn left on Calle delle Canonico between the basilica and the clock tower; it's the last shop on the right. Rolling Venice cardholders get 10% discount. Open M-Sa 9am-8pm, Su 9:30am-1:30pm. MC/V.

Laundromats: Speedy Wash, Calle dei Colori, Cannaregio 1520. Wash €6-8, dry €3 per 15min. Detergent €1. Purchase a key next door at **Planet Internet** for a 30% discount. Open daily 8am-10pm.

Public Toilets: AMAV W.C., under white and blue signs. €1.50. Open daily 8:30am-8:45pm.

Disabled travelers: Informa Handicap (☎041 27 48 144) offers assistance to physically disabled and hearing-impaired travelers in Italy. Free Braille maps. Open Th 9am-1pm and 3-5pm. APT tourist office provides a list of wheelchair-accessible lodgings in Venice. Pick up a free map of the city outlining wheelchair-friendly routes in each *sestiere* and keys for wheelchair lifts at the bridges. V#1 is wheelchair-accessible.

EMERGENCY AND COMMUNICATIONS

Carabinieri: 112 Campo San Zaccaria, Castello 4693/A. **Questura,** Fondamenta S. Lorenzo, Castello 5056.

Pharmacy: Farmacia Italo-Inglese, Calle della Mandola, San Marco 3717 (☎041 52 24 837). Follow Calle Cortesia out of Campo Manin. There are no 24hr. pharmacies in Venice, but late-night and weekend pharmacies rotate hours. After-hours rotations posted. Open M-Sa 9am-1:30pm and 2:30-7:30pm. AmEx/MC/V.

Hospital: Ospedale Civile, Campo Giovanni e Paolo Santissimi, Castello (☎041 52 94 111).

Internet Access: Wi-Fi is notoriously absent in Venice. Although a few restaurants offer complimentary internet to their patrons, the best bet might be to seek out one of the several McDonald's in the city, which offer free Wi-Fi. The most accessible is on C. Larga S. Marco just 2 streets north of P. San Marco.

ABColor, Lista di Spagna, Cannaregio 220 (☎041 52 44 380; www.abcolor.it). Look for the "@" symbol on a yellow sign, left off the main street heading from train station. €6 per hr.; students €4 per hr. For longer than 5hr., purchase an internet card for €3 per hr. Printing €0.20 per page. Open daily 10am-10pm. Cash only.

Internet Station, Cannaregio 5641. Just over the bridge from C. Apostoli. €4 per 30min., €7 per hr. 20% with student ID. Open M-F and Su 10am-10pm, Sa 10am-8pm. Cash only.

VeNice, Lista di Spagna, Cannaregio 149 (☎041 27 58 217; www.ve-nice.com). €4.50 per 30min., €8 per hr. Printing €0.35 per page. Open daily 9am-11pm. MC/V over €10.

Internet Point San Stefano, Campo San Stefano, San Marco 2967 and 2958 (☎041 52 20 402). €8 per hr., 33% discount with ISIC or Rolling Venice card. Open daily 10am-midnight. MC/V.

Post Office: Poste Venezia Centrale, Salizada Fontego dei Tedeschi, San Marco 5554 (☎041 24 04 158), off Campo S. Bartolomeo. *Fermoposta* at window #16. Open M-F 8:30am-6:30pm, Sa 8:30am-1pm. **Postal Codes:** 30121 (Cannaregio); 30122 (Castello); 30123 (Dorsoduro); 30124 (San Marco); 30125 (San Polo); 30135 (Santa Croce).

ACCOMMODATIONS AND CAMPING

Unsurprisingly, Venetian hotels can break the bank as swarms of tourists descend like locusts during the high season. That said, savvy travelers can find cheap alternatives, especially during the winter months. Agree on a price before booking and reserve at least one month ahead, especially in summer.

SAN MARCO

Surrounded by designer boutiques, souvenir stands, scores of restaurants, practically domesticated pigeons, and many of Venice's most popular sights, these lodgings are pricey options for those in search of Venice's showy side.

Albergo San Samuele, Salizada S. Samuele, San Marco 3358 (☎041 52 28 045; www.albergosansamuele.it). Follow C. delle Botteghe from Campo Santo Stefano and turn left on Salizada San Samuele. Spacious and simple rooms on a quiet street 10min. from P. S. Marco, including several family suites with kitchens. Smaller rooms only have fan. Breakfast (€5) served 5min. away at Ribo Restaurant. Free Wi-Fi. 24hr. reception. Reserve 1-2 months ahead. Singles with shared bath €45-65; doubles €65-85, with bath €85-120. Check website as prices change often. AmEx/MC/V. ❹

Albergo Casa Petrarca, C. Schiavine, San Marco 4386 (☎041 52 00 430; www.casapetrarca.com). From Campo San Luca, follow C. Fuseri; take the 2nd left and then turn right. Look for the vine-covered sign at the end of the street. Cheerful, English-speaking owner keeps 7 sunny rooms, most with bath and A/C. Try to score one with a view of the canal. Breakfast included. Singles €95; doubles €125-135. Extra bed €35. Cash only. ❺

Hotel Locanda Fiorita, Campiello Nuovo, San Marco 3457/A (☎041 52 34 754; www.locandafiorita.com). From Campo S. Stefano, take C. del Pestrin and walk across the raised *campiello*. Elegant rooms with flatscreen TV, phone, bath or shower, free Wi-Fi, and A/C in a quiet courtyard with a small garden. Breakfast included. Reception 24hr. Singles €130-150; doubles €145-170; extra bed €20. MC/V. ❺

CANNAREGIO

The area around the Lista de Spagna has excellent budget options for weary travelers arriving late by bus, train, or plane. Though it requires a 20min. *vaporetto* ride or a 15-25min. walk to most sights, the proximity to the train station and bustling nightlife make it a good home base.

☒ **Alloggi Gerotto Calderan,** Campo San Geremia, Cannaregio 283 (☎041 71 55 62 or 041 71 53 61; www.283.it). From the train station, turn left on Lista di Spagna; continue for 5min. until you reach C.S. Geremia. Half hostel, half hotel in a great location. All rooms have bath. Internet €4 per hr. Wi-Fi available, 1st 15min. free. Check-in 2pm. Lockout for dorms 10:30am-2pm. Curfew 1am. 4- to 6-person dorms €23-25; singles €35-60; doubles €50-90; triples €75-105. Rolling Venice discount 10%; discounts for longer stays. Cash only. ❷

Hotel Arcadia, Cannaregio 1333/D (☎041 717 355 www.hotelarcadia.net). From Campo Geremia, cross Ponte delle Guglie and follow the road. Look for the sign on the left. Housed in a 17th-century palace, this hotel offers luxurious rooms 5min. from the train station. Rooms are equipped with private baths, TV, and safe, but (sigh) no A/C. Breakfast included. Free Wi-Fi. Singles €45-80; doubles €80-120; triples €80-150; quads €90-160. MC/V. ❹

Hotel Bernardi-Semenzato, C. dell'Oca, Cannaregio 4366 (☎041 52 27 257; www.hotelbernardi.com). From Campo SS. Apostoli head North on Salizada Pistor and take the 1st left. Sunny hallways and elegantly furnished rooms with TV; some have private baths. Lack of A/C can be a killer. Breakfast included. Free Wi-Fi. Reception open 7am-midnight. Singles €35; doubles with bath €80-95; quads €120-130. Rolling Venice discount 10% on larger rooms. AmEx/MC/V. ❸

SAN POLO AND SANTA CROCE

In the heart of western Venice, these neighborhoods hug the city's winding river, providing easy *vaporetto* access to the city's sights.

Best B&B, Calle del Capeler, S. Polo 1575 (☎349 00 70 508). From Ponte Rialto walk northwest on Ruga D. Oresi, turn left on Calle D. Boteri and left again on Calle Del Capeler. Simple B&B in the center of the city with dorm-style rooms and a very friendly owner. Breakfast included. Reservations required. Dorms €18-28 per person; doubles €60-80; triples €100-120. Cash only. ❷

Domus Civica (ACISJF), Campiello Chiovere Frari, San Polo 3082 (☎041 72 11 03; www.domuscivica.com). From the train station, cross Ponte Scalzi and turn right. Turn left on Fondamenta dei Tolentini and left through the courtyard on Corte Amai; the hostel is to the right after the bridge. Primarily student housing in the winter, in the summer it offers simple rooms. Common TV room and social 4th floor terrace. Free internet. Reception open 7am-12:30am. Strict curfew 12:30am. Open June-Sept. 25. Singles €38, with Rolling Venice €31.50, with ISIC and for students under 26 €29; doubles €30/27/24 per person. AmEx/MC/V. ❸

Casa Peron, Salizada S. Pantalon, Santa Croce 84 (☎041 71 00 21 or 041 71 10 38; www.casaperon.com). From the train station, cross Ponte Scalzi, turn right, and then turn left on Fondamenta dei Tolentini; after a while turn left down Fondamente Minotto. Casa Peron is on the left. Lace-accented lobby leads to modest but cozy rooms; watch the low ceilings. Some have bath and A/C. Breakfast included. Reception open until 1am. Singles with shared bath €50; doubles €85, with bath €100; triples €100/120. MC/V. ❹

DORSODURO

Situated near the Grand Canal between Chiesa dei Frari and Ponte Accademia, this *sestiere* is home to many pricey hotels. Spartan facades line the canals that trace Dorsoduro's quiet streets. Art museums here draw visitors to canal-front real estate, while the interior remains a little-visited residential quarter surrounding Campo Santa Margherita, the city's most vibrant student hub.

Pensione Seguso, Fondamente Zattere ai Saloni, Dorsoduro 779 (☎041 52 86 858; www.pensioneseguso.com). From V: Zattere, walk right. Great real estate right on the canal. Antique decor. Breakfast included; ½- and full-pension available. Reception open 8am-9pm. Open Jan. and Mar.-Nov. Singles €40-122, with bath €50-160; doubles €65-180/70-190; triples €150-235/160-245; quads €190-255. Prices vary seasonally. AmEx/MC/V. ⑤

Locanda Cà Foscari, Calle della Frescada, Dorsoduro 3887/B (☎041 71 04 01; www. locandacafoscari.com). From V: San Tomà, turn left at the dead end, cross Ponte de la Frescade, turn right, then turn left at the alley. Carnevale masks embellish this tidy hotel, which offers basic rooms, some with private bath. No A/C. Breakfast included. 3-night min. stay on weekends. Reception 24hr. Reserve 2-3 months ahead. Singles €60-85; doubles €70-105; triples €110-130; quads €140. Prices vary greatly with season, length of stay, and availability. AmEx/MC/V. ⑥

Hotel Galleria, Rio Terrà Antonio Foscarini, Dorsoduro 878/A (☎041 52 32 489; www. hotelgalleria.it), on the left of the Ponte Accademia facing the Accademia museum. Hardwood floors and stunning Grand Canal views lend an aura of elegance. Interior filled with velvet and other funky curios. Carved headboards are a nice touch. Breakfast included. Reception 24hr. Singles €85; doubles €120-135, with bath €150; large doubles €180-195. Extra bed 30% surcharge. MC/V. ⑤

CASTELLO

Castello, where most Venetians live, is arguably the prettiest part of the city. A second- or third-floor room with a view of the sculpted skyline is worth the confusion of navigating some of the city's narrowest and most tightly clustered streets.

Foresteria Valdese, Castello 5170 (☎041 52 86 797; www.diaconiavaldese.org/venezia). From Campo Santa Maria Formosa, take Calle Lunga Santa Maria Formosa; it's over the 1st bridge. An 18th-century house run by a Protestant church. Ornately decorated with a gorgeous fresco on the ceiling and river views to match. Breakfast included. Reception 8:30am-8pm. Lockout 10am-1pm. Reservations required for bedrooms, though not possible for dorms. Dorms €27 for 1-night stays, €24 otherwise; doubles €78-88, with kitchen €85-91; triples €90-99, with bath €96-102; quads with bath €114-126; quints with bath €132-147. Rolling Venice discount €1. MC/V. ⑤

La Residenza, Campo Bandiera e Moro, Castello 3608 (☎041 52 85 315; www. venicelaresidenza.com). From V: Arsenal, turn left on Riva degli Schiavoni and right on C. del Dose into the *campo*. Live like a prince: lavish carpets and paintings and a sunny terrace overlooking the *campo* greet guests in this renovated 15th-century *palazzo*. Spacious and elegantly furnished rooms with TV, A/C, private bathroom, safe, and minibar. Breakfast included. Free Wi-Fi. Reception 24hr. Singles €50-100; doubles €80-180. Extra bed €35. MC/V. ④

Hotel Doni, C. del Vin, Castello 4656 (☎041 52 24 267; www.albergodoni.it). From P. San Marco, turn left immediately after the 2nd bridge on C. del Vin and stay left when the street splits. Cheery staff, headed by owner Annabella, and proximity to P. San Marco make this hotel an amazing deal. A rickety staircase leads to lovely rooms with antique decor and furnishing. Many come with private bathroom and fan or A/C. Breakfast included. Reception 24hr. Singles €45-65; doubles €70-95, with bath €80-120. MC/V. ④

Locanda Silva, Fondamenta del Rimedio, Castello 4423 (☎041 52 27 643 or 52 37 892; www.locandasilva.it). From P. San Marco, walk under clock tower, turn right on C. Larga San Marco, and left on C. de l'Anzolo before the bridge. Head right on Ramo de l'Anzolo, turn left, and follow to the end. Rustic rooms with a sunny 18th-century breakfast room overlooking the canal. Internet €3 per hour. Reception 24hr. Singles €45-65, with bath €55-80; doubles €60-85, with bath €70-100, with shower €80-130; triples €110-150; quads €130-170. MC/V. ⑤

Hotel Casa Linger, Salizada Sant'Antonin, Castello 3541 (☎041 52 85 920; www.hotel-casalinger.com). From P. San Marco, follow Riva degli Schiavoni until you reach C. del Dose; turn left and continue until you reach C. Bandiera e Moro. Walk until you hit S. Sant'Antonin; the hotel is on the right. Large, simple rooms are sunny and clean, and come with great views. Some have TV and private bath, but no A/C might be a deal-breaker. Reception 24hr. Singles €40-90, with bath €40-110; doubles €60-90/80-100; rooms with kitchen and bathroom (max. 7 people) €25-35 per person. MC/V. ❸

Hotel Casa Verardo, Castello 4765 (☎041 52 86 127; www.casaverardo.it). From P. San Marco, follow Riva degli Schiavoni until you reach C. de le Rasse. Turn left and follow it to Campo SS. Filippo e Giacomo. Take Callede la Sacrestia and turn right at Cale Rimpeto. Housed in a national monument, this 16th-century hotel's mosaic floors and fancy stucco make travelers feel like Venetian royalty. Private courtyard, lounge, bar, and terraces overlook the canal. Rooms with A/C, safe, minibar, and TV. Buffet breakfast and internet included. Singles €60-180; doubles €90-390; junior suites €110-650. Extra bed €30-60. Discount for web reservations or cash payment. AmEx/MC/V. ❹

CAMPING

While the low cost of camping is appealing, take into account that you'll be paying for pricey transportation to and from Venice (about €13-16 per day, €31 for 3 days), which may cost more than just staying in the city. Plan on at least a 40min. commute to Venice. In addition to this campground, the Litorale del Cavallino, on the Lido's Adriatic side, has multiple beach campsites.

Camping Miramare, Lungomare Dante Alighieri 29 (☎041 96 61 50; www.camping-miramare.it). A 40min. ride on V: #LN from P. S. Marco to Punta Sabbioni. 700m along the beach on the right. Wheelchair-accessible. During high season, 2-night min. stay in campground, 5-night for bungalows. Reception open 8am-9pm. Check-out 10am. Open Mar.-Nov. Camping €4.70-7.20 per person, €9.60-15 per tent; bungalows €30-70 plus camping charge per person. Rolling Venice discount 15% with cash payment. MC/V. ❶

🗋 FOOD

In Venice, authentic dining may require extensive exploration, since many of the best restaurants lie in less-traveled areas. Avoid restaurants near major sights; they're typically overpriced and inauthentic. Naturally, Venetian cuisine is dominated by fish. *Sarde in saor* (sardines in vinegar and onions) and other *cicchetti* (Venetian appetizers similar to tapas), available only in Venice, can be sampled at most bars and *enoteche*. The Veneto and Friuli regions produce many wines. Local whites include *prosecco della marca*, the dry *tocai*, and *bianco di custoza*. For a red, try *valpolicella*. The least expensive option is by no means inferior: a simple *vino della casa* (house wine) is usually a fine local merlot or chardonnay. For informal alternatives to traditional dining, visit an *osteria* or *bacaro* for pastries, seafood, or *tramezzini* (bread with any delicious filling).

Venice's Rialto **markets,** once the center of trade for the Venetian Republic, spread between the Grand Canal and the San Polo foot of the Rialto every morning from Monday to Saturday. Smaller produce markets are set up in Cannaregio, on Rio Terà San Leonardo by Ponte delle Guglie, and in many of the city's *campi*. The **BILLA** supermarket, Strada Nuova, Cannaregio 5660, has groceries and a small bakery and deli near Campo San Fosca. (Open M-Sa 8:30am-8:30pm, Su 9am-8:30pm. AmEx/MC/V.) A **Punto** supermarket is at Campo Santa Margherita 5017 (☎041 52 26 780; open M-Sa 7:30am-8pm; MC/V.)

SAN MARCO

▨ **Le Bistrot de Venise,** C. dei Fabbri, San Marco 4685 (☎041 52 36 651; www.bistrotdevenise.com). From P. San Marco, head through 2nd Sottoportego dei Dai under the awning. Follow road over two bridges and turn right. Scrumptious Venetian dishes and over 50 wines, based on medieval and Renaissance recipes. Only restaurant with an in-house librarian scouring for *renascimento* delicacies. Share the tasting *menù* (€45) or try dishes like marinated *umbrine* in black grape sauce with yellow garlic and almond pudding (€28). Check the website for cultural events and wine tastings on the schedule. *Enoteca: cicchetti* €3-4, meat/cheese plates €12-24. Restaurant: primi €12-24; secondi €18-32. Wine from €5 per glass. Open daily 10:30am-midnight. Rolling Venice discount 10%. AmEx/MC/V. ❶

▨ **Trattoria da Fiore,** Santo Stefano 3461 (☎041 52 35 310; www.trattoriadafiore. com). Take Calle de le Boteghe from Campiello San Stefano. Neighbors claim this is the only true *bacaro* left in San Marco. Serves a simple menu with wine (from €2 per glass) and tasty *cicchetti* (from €0.50). Try *spaghetti pinoli* with fresh tomatoes and basil (€10). Brush up on your Italian; this place is filled with locals. Plates €9-15. Open M and W-Su 8:30am-12:30am. Cash only. ❷

CANNAREGIO

▨ **Gam Gam,** Canale di Cannaregio, Cannaregio 1122 (☎041 71 52 84). From Campo S. Geremia, cross the bridge and turn left. Canal-side tables, friendly owners, and a unique mix of Italian and Jewish cuisines. Bars from the old Jewish ghetto preserved for all to see. Try their *Pasticcio Gam Gam* (vegetable lasagna; €9) or their special Israeli appetizer plates (€9.80). Main courses €7.50-15. Kosher. Open M-Th and Su noon-10pm, F noon-4pm. *Let's Go* discount 10%. Cash only. ❶

Osteria da Rioba, Fondamenta della Misericordia, Cannaregio 2553 (☎041 52 44 379, www.doriba.com). From Campo S. Fosca, head north across two bridges and then turn west. Paintings of distant mountains on the walls give this canal-side eatery a far-away feel. Enjoy dishes like eggplant stuffed with ricotta and toasted pine nuts. All the pasta is homemade. Salads €8-9. Primi €8-13. Secondi €15-20. Cover €1.50. Open Tu-Su 12:30-2:30pm and 7:30-10:30pm. Call ahead on summer weekends to reserve outdoor seating. AmEx/MC/V. ❹

Frulala, Campo Ricardo Selvatico, Cannaregio 5620 (☎392 92 08 537). From Campo SS. Apostoli walk south following the signs for S. Marco until you reach Campo R. Selvatico. This hip juice bar offers smoothies (€3.50-5.50), fruit salads, and drinks (€5-7) along with eclectic music and fresh fruit right on the walls. Open daily 8am-1am. Cash only. ❶

Trattoria da Bepi, Cannaregio 4550 (☎/fax 041 52 85 031). From Campo S. S. Apostoli, turn left on Salizada del Pistor. Staples like potato *tortelli* with ricotta and spinach (€9). Don't let the accordion distract from enjoying the art on the walls. Primi €7-12. Secondi €12.50-17. Cover €1.50. Open M-W and F-Su noon-3pm and 7-11pm. Reservations recommended. MC/V. ❸

SAN POLO AND SANTA CROCE

▨ **Antica Birraria La Corte,** Campo S. Polo, San Polo 2168 (☎041 27 50 570; www.birrarialacorte.it). The expansive interior of this former brewery houses a large restaurant and bar as well as outdoor tables on the large peaceful *campo*. Head inside for a fun beer-hall atmosphere. Filling salads (€10) hit the spot in the summer heat. Pizza

€5.50-9. Primi €11-15. Secondi €13.50-19. Cover €2. Restaurant open daily noon-2:30pm and 7-10:30pm. Pizzeria open summer 10am-midnight. AmEx/MC/V. ❸

Frary's, Fondamenta dei Frari, San Polo 2559 (☎041 72 00 50). Across from entrance to S. Maria Gloriosa dei Frari. Right on the river. Serves Greek and Arab cuisine with many vegetarian options. Try the lunch *menù* (€12), which includes 1 appetizer and 1 main course, or the tasting *menù* (€9). Appetizers €4-6. Main courses €8.50-14. Cover €1.50. Open M and W-Su noon-3:15pm and 6-10:30pm. AmEx/MC/V. ❷

Al Giardinetto, San Toma, 2910 Rio della Frescada (☎ 041 52 24 100; www.algiardinetto.it). From Campo S. Rocco, follow Salizada S. Rocco until Campo S. Toma then cross bridge. Smells of tasty grilled meat waft from the kitchen as the sound of caged birds chirping overhead mingles with Italian music. Meat *menù* €6-18. Seafood €12-16. Open daily 11am-3pm and 7:30pm-12:30am. AmEx/MC/V. ❸

Al Nono Risorto, Sotoportego de Siora Bettina, Santa Croce 2338 (☎041 52 41 169). From Ponte Rialto, follow yellow signs for Ple. Roma until you reach Campo S. Cassiano; restaurant is under the bridge. Serves hearty dishes in its casual interior and sunny garden. Oddly conscientious *menù* changes weekly to reflect social issues; past themes have included a "*menù* of women" and "*menù* of the refugees." Pizza €5-9. Primi €8-9. Secondi €10-15. Cover €1.70. Open M-Tu and Th-Su noon-2:30pm and 7-11pm. Cash only. ❸

DORSODURO

🏶 **Cantinone Gia Schiavi,** Fondamenta Meraviglie, Dorsoduro 992 (☎041 52 30 034). From the Frari, follow signs for the Accademia bridge. Just before Ponte Meraviglie, turn toward the Chiesa di San Trovaso. Cross the 1st bridge. Choose from hundreds of wines (€2-5) and dozens of fresh *cicchetti* (€1) with toppings like pumpkin cream in this old *enoteca*. Standing room only. Open M-Sa 8am-11pm, Su 8am-noon. Cash only. ❶

Gelati Nico, Zattere, Dorsoduro 922 (☎041 52 25 293). From V: Zattere, walk west along the waterfront. Grab a quick, freshly made gelato (€1.20) before a long walk along the waterfront. Open M-Sa 6:45am-12pm and 7:30-11:30pm. Cash only. ❶

Pizza and Kebab Toletta, Dorsoduro 1215 (☎041 24 13 324). From Ponte Accademia head west on C. Contarini Corfu, cross the bridge and follow C. Tolleta. Skip overpriced restaurants next to the museums and grab a huge slice of pizza (€1.80) or falafel sandwich (€3) at this simple pizzeria just a few blocks away. Pies €3.50-7. Open daily 11am-4pm and 5:30pm-midnight. Cash only. ❶

CASTELLO

🏶 **Cip Ciap,** C. del Mondo Novo, Castello 5799/A (☎041 52 36 621). From Campo S. Maria Formosa, follow C. del Mondo Novo. Perhaps Venice's best value pizzeria. Uses fresh ingredients on Sicilian slices sold by weight (€1.20 per 100g). Their best deals are the huge prosciutto-filled calzones and margherita pies (€2.50). No seating; nab a bench in the nearby *campo*. Open M and W-Su 9am-9pm. Cash only. ❶

La Boutique del Gelato, Salizada S. Lio, Castello 5727 (☎041 52 23 283). From Campo Bartolomeo, walk under Sottoportego de la Bissa, then cross the bridge into Campo S. Lio. Follow Salizada S. Lio; it's on the left. This tiny *gelateria* dishes up gigantic scoops acclaimed by locals and tourists as Venice's best. 1 scoop €1.20; 2 scoops €2. Open M 10:30am-8pm, T-Su 10:30am-11pm. Cash only. ❶

SIGHTS

THE VENETO

AROUND PIAZZA SAN MARCO

▓ BASILICA DI SAN MARCO. The **basilica** is the city's most popular tourist attraction—and rightly so. Venice's crown jewel is a spectacular fusion of gold mosaics, marble walls, and rooftop balconies, graced with ultra-realistic mosaic portals and guarded by winged lions on the rooftop. The long lines move surprisingly quickly; unfortunately, this makes for crowded walkways inside. Visit in the early morning for the shortest wait or in late afternoon for the best natural illumination. Construction of the basilica began in the AD ninth century, when two Venetian merchants stole St. Mark's remains from Alexandria and packed them in pork meat to smuggle them past Arab officials. After the first church dedicated to St. Mark burned down in the 11th century, Venice designed a new basilica, choosing a Greek-cross plan with four arms and five domes instead of the Church's standard cross-shaped layout. A cavernous, eerily quiet interior sparkles with Byzantine and Renaissance mosaics and elaborate gold ornaments. The blue-robed **Christ Pantocrator** (Ruler of All) sits above the high altar. The floor, covered in colorful geometric 12th-century stone mosaics, is a sight unto itself. Behind the altar screen, the rectangular **Pala d'Oro** relief frames a parade of saints in gem-encrusted gold. Within the altar rests the tomb of St. Mark, adorned with a single gold-stemmed rose. Steep stairs lead to the **Galleria della Basilica,** which offers an eye-level view of the tiny golden tiles of the ceiling mosaics, a balcony overlooking the *piazza* below, and an intimate view of the bronze **Cavalli di San Marco** (Horses of St. Mark). Nearby, the **Cassine** displays mosaic heads (the most valuable and artistically challenging section of any masterpiece) removed during renovations in 1881. *(Basilica open M-Sa 9:45am-5pm, Su 2-4pm; illuminated 11:30am-12:30pm. Modest dress required—no bare shoulders or revealing skirts or shorts. Baggage prohibited; follow signs to free storage at nearby Ateno San Basso on Calle San Basso; open daily 9:30am-5:30pm. Pala d'Oro and Treasury open in summer M-F 9:45am-5pm, Sa-Su 2-4:30pm, €3; in winter M-F 9:45am-4pm, Sa-Su 2-4pm, €2. Galleria open daily 9:45am-4:45pm, €4.)*

▓PALAZZO DUCALE (DOGE'S PALACE). Home for eight centuries to the Doge, Venice's mayor, the Palazzo Ducale displays spectacular artwork, including Veronese's *Rape of Europa*. In the courtyard, Sansovino's enormous sculptures, *Mars* and *Neptune*, flank the **Scala dei Giganti** (Stairs of the Giants), upon which new Doges were crowned. On the balcony stands the **Bocca di Leone** (Lion's Mouth), into which the Council of Ten, the Doge's assistants, who also acted as judges and administrators, would drop the names of criminal suspects. Admire the sculptures of Hercules slaying the Hydra and Atlas bearing a brilliant blue, starry world on either side of the elaborate **Scala D'Oro**. From there, climb up to the **Sala delle Quattro Porte** (Room of the Four Doors), whose ceiling is covered in biblical judgments and representations of mythological tales related to events in Venetian history. More doors lead through the courtrooms of the much-feared Council of Ten, the even-more-feared Council of Three, and the **Sala del Maggior Consiglio** (Great Council Room), dominated by Tintoretto's harrowing *Paradise*, the largest oil painting in the world. Near the end, thick stone lattices line the covered **Ponte dei Sospiri** (Bridge of Sighs) and continue into the prisons. The bridge gets its name from 19th-century Romantic writers' references to the mournful groans of prisoners descending into the small, damp cells. The rest of the palace is best enjoyed by getting lost in the endless maze of tunnels. (☎ 041 52 09 070; www.museivenezia.it. Open daily Nov.-Mar. 10am-5pm; Apr.-Oct. 10:30am-5:30pm. Last entry 1hr. before closing. Wheelchair-accessible. €16, students and Rolling Venice cardholders €10, ages 6-14 €3. Includes entrance to P. San Marco museums. Audio tours in multiple languages €5, 2 for €8. Special English tours offered daily every 50min. 9:55am-12:25pm. Book 2 days in advance. MC/V.)

CHIESA DI SAN ZACCARIA. Dedicated to the father of John the Baptist and designed in the late 1400s by Coducci, the Gothic-Renaissance church holds S. Zaccaria's corpse in an elevated, glass-windowed sarcophagus along the nave's right wall. Nearby, watch for Bellini's *Virgin and Child Enthroned with Four Saints*, one of the masterpieces of the Venetian Renaissance. Ask the custodian for entrance into the 10th-century crypt, which features paintings by Tintoretto and others. (V: S. Zaccaria. From P. San Marco, turn left along the water, cross 2 bridges, and turn left through the tunnel marked "San Zaccaria." ☎ 041 52 21 257. Open daily 10am-noon and 4-6pm. Church free. Crypt entrance €1.)

PIAZZA SAN MARCO. Unlike the rest of Venice's labyrinthine streets, P. San Marco, Venice's only official *piazza*, is a magnificent expanse of light, space, architectural harmony, and pigeons. Although mobs of photo-snapping tourists jostling each other may be annoying, the *piazza* is certainly worth it. Enclosing the *piazza* are rows of cafes and expensive glass and jewelry shops along the ground floors of the Renaissance **Procuratie Vecchie** (Old Treasury Offices), the Baroque **Procuratie Nuove** (New Treasury Offices), and the Neoclassical **Ala Napoleonica** (more Treasury Offices). At the end of the *piazza*, near the shoreline of the lagoon, sits the **Basilica di San Marco,** where mosaics and marble horses overlook the chaos below. Some nights the *piazza* floods as tidal waters come rushing in, making for bathtime for kids (and the exasperation of onlooking parents). Between the basilica and the Procuratie Vecchie perches the **Torre dell'Orologio** (Clock Tower), constructed according to Coducci's design between 1496 and 1499. The 24hr. clock indicates the hour, lunar phase, and ascending constellation. A 96m brick **campanile** provides one of the best elevated views of the city. Though it originally served as a watchtower and lighthouse, Venice took advantage of its location to create medieval entertainment by dangling state prisoners in cages from its top. The practice ceased in the 18th century, but the tower is still worth a visit. (☎ 041 52 25 205. Campanile open daily May-Oct. 9am-9pm; Nov.-Apr. 9:30am-4:15pm. €8; roups of 20 or larger €4 per person. Audio tour €3.)

MUSEUMS OF PIAZZA SAN MARCO. The **Museo Civico Correr,** a Venetian history museum, fills most of the two-story complex with curiosities from the city's imperial past, including naval maps and models, ornate Neoclassical artwork, and weapons like a 16th-century key that fires poison darts. Highlights of the collection include Antonio Canova's sculptures *Winged Cupid* and *Daedalus and Icarus* in the first room. Near the end of the first floor, the **Museo Archeologico** houses a sizable collection of ancient pieces, from first-century Egyptian funeral parchment to Greek and Roman sculptures. A series of ceiling paintings by seven artists, including some from Verona, adorn the dark gilded reading room of the **Biblioteca Nazionale Marciana,** built between 1537 and 1560. *(Beneath the arcade at the short end of P. San Marco. ☎041 52 24 951. Museums open daily Apr.-Oct. 10am-6pm; Nov.-Mar. 10am-5pm. Last entry 1hr. before closing. Either purchase museum pass (€18, students €12) or a single ticket (€12). Ticket also includes entrance to the Doge's Palace and all 3 museums. €10 for school groups. Call ahead to make arrangements.)*

LA SCALA DEL BOVOLO. This marble "staircase of the snails" takes guests up five stories of tightly spiraling marble *loggia* to a circular portico at the top. Legend has it the staircase was designed by Leonardo da Vinci. Once leading to a now-destroyed palace, today the top affords views of the green courtyard below as well as an eye-level panorama of red rooftops and the distant domes of San Marco. *(From the Campo Manin facing the bridge, turn left down the alley, and look for the signs. ☎041 53 22 920.)*

AROUND THE RIALTO BRIDGE

◪**THE GRAND CANAL.** Over 3km long, the Grand Canal loops through the city and passes under four bridges: **Ponte di Calatrava, Ponte Scalzi, Ponte Rialto,** and **Ponte Accademia.** Coursing past the facades of cheek-to-cheek palaces that crown their banks, the blue-green waters are a constant reminder of Venice's history and immense wealth. Although each *palazzo* displays its own unique architectural blend of *loggia*, canal-side balconies, and marble sculptures, most share the same basic structural design. The most decorated floors, called *piani nobili* (noble floors, or 2nd and 3rd stories), housed luxurious salons and bedrooms. Rich merchant families stored their goods on the ground floor, and servants slept in tiny chambers below the roof. At night the facades are illuminated, producing a dazzling display of reflections. The candy-cane *bricole* posts used for mooring boats on the *canalare* are

IN RECENT NEWS

VENICE: IN HOT WATER?

It's hard to picture Venice without water. Images of drifting gondolas, glistening canals, and apartments on stilts lend as much flavor to the city as do its history and cuisine. But ironically, Venice's most essential element has recently become the bane of its existence, causing flooding and pollution in the now "sinking city."

While *la acqua alta* has always been a subject of Venetian concern, debate over how best to handle the situation erupted after a storm left parts of the city under six feet of water, permanently damaging historic buildings and priceless works of art.

The most significant preventative effort currently underway is the MOSE project (Experimental Electromechanical Module), a $5 billion endeavor to protect the city from tides higher than 50 in. By 2012, MOSE hopes to resolve water-related concerns. Meanwhile, it has created a controversy among Venetians, many of whom claim that the issue of flooding is greatly exaggerated. MOSE poses its own consequences for the city as well. The cost of the project has forced many to move out and has halted business growth, and MOSE may cause pollution, damage to biodiversity, and dangerous changes in tidal patterns.

Should the topic arise, try to keep your head above water and remain respectful; you will likely face a cascade of debate.

painted with the family colors of the adjoining *palazzo. (For great facade views, ride V#2 or the slower #1 from the train station to P. S. Marco. For the best canal views open to the public, visit Collezione Peggy Guggenheim or Ca Rezzonico.)*

RIALTO BRIDGE. Named after Rivo Alto, the first Venetian colony, the original wooden bridge collapsed in the 1500s. Antonio da Ponte designed the present-day stone structure, where strips of boutiques separate a wide central lane from two side passages. Don't expect to see much during the day, however, as camera-toting, souvenir-happy tourists will do everything in their power to stand between you and the picture-perfect views. Expensive stores also dominate the bridge, but unauthorized vendors selling overpriced, cheaply made goods manage to find their way onto the thoroughfare as well.

CANNAREGIO

CÀ D'ORO. Built between 1421 and 1440, this "Golden House" houses the **Galleria Giorgio Franchetti.** Highlights include Andrea Mantegna's *Saint Sebastian* (temporarily out for restoration) in the small chapel on the first floor, Bonaccio's *Apollo Belvedere* (one of the 15th century's most important bronzes), several Bernini sculptures and Titian frescoes on the second floor, and two balconies above the Grand Canal. Don't miss the back courtyard, which contains a stunning mosaic floor designed by Baron Giorgio Franchetti. Take in the best view of the balconies and Cà d'Oro's tiered wedding cake facade from a *traghetto* crossing the canal toward the Rialto Markets. *(V: Cà d'Oro. ☎041 52 00 345; www.cadoro.org. Open M 8:15am-2pm, Tu-Su 8:15am-7:15pm. Last entry 30min. before closing. Closed Dec. 25, Jan. 1, and May 1. €5, EU students and EU citizens age 18-25 €2.50, EU citizens under 18 and over 65 and art students free. Audio tour €4, 2 for €6. Cash only.)*

JEWISH GHETTO. In 1516, the Doge forced Venice's Jewish population into the old cannon-foundry area, creating the first Jewish ghetto in Europe. (*Ghetto* is the Venetian word for foundry.) At its peak, the ghetto housed 5000 people in buildings up to seven stories high, making them among the tallest European tenements at the time. Now, locals gather in this sequestered spot for the tranquility of the **Campo del Ghetto Nuovo,** where delicious smells from nearby local bakeries inevitably waft. In the *campo*, the **Schola Grande Tedesca** (German Synagogue), the oldest synagogue in the area, now houses the **Museo Ebraica di Venezia** (Hebrew Museum of Venice). In the adjacent Campiello delle Scuole stand the opulent **Schola Levantina** (Levantine Synagogue) and **Schola Spagnola** (Spanish Synagogue), both designed at least in part by Longhena. The Canton and Italian synagogues also occupy the area. *(Cannaregio 2899/B. V: Santa Marcuola. Follow signs straight, then turn left into Campo del Ghetto Nuovo. ☎041 71 53 59. Hebrew Museum open M-F and Su June-Sept. 10am-7pm. Last entrance 5pm; Oct.-May 10am-4:30pm. 40min. English and Italian tours leave from the museum every hr. June-Sept. 10:30am-5:30pm; Oct.-May 10:30am-4:30pm. €3, students €2. Museum and tour €8.50, students €7. MC/V.)*

SAN POLO

▧BASILICA DI SANTA MARIA GLORIOSA DEI FRARI. Even if churches aren't your thing, this Venetian marvel is worth it. The all-star collection of paintings, looming sculptures, and dangling chandeliers will awe any visitor. Franciscans began construction on the Gothic church, also known as *I Frari*, in 1340. Today, the gray interior boasts two Titian paintings as well as the corpse of the Renaissance master himself, who is entombed within the cathedral's cavernous terra-cotta walls. His ▧Assumption (1516-18), on the high altar, marks the height of the Venetian Renaissance. Titian's other work, *The Madonna and Child with Saints and Members of the Pesaro Family* (1547), is on the left from the entrance. Titian's elaborate tomb, a lion-topped triumphal arch with bas-relief scenes of Paradise, lies directly across from the enormous pyramid where the sculptor Canova (1757-1822) rests. Donatello's gaunt wooden sculpture, ⬛St. John the Baptist (1438), stands framed in gold in the Florentine chapel to the right of the high altar. *(V: S. Tomà. Follow signs back to Campo dei Frari. ☎041 27 28 618; www.basilicadeifrari.it. Open M-Sa 9am-6pm, Su 1-6pm. Last entry 30min. before closing. Included in the Chorus Pass. €3. Audio guide €3. Cash only.)*

CHIESA DI SAN GIACOMO DI RIALTO (SAN POLO). Smack in the middle of the chaos between the Rialto and the surrounding markets, Venice's first church, diminutively called "San Giacometto," is remarkably peaceful. An ornate clock-face adorns its *campanile*. Across the *piazza*, a statue called *Il Gobbo* (The Hunchback) supports the steps, once used for public announcements. It was at the foot of this sculpture that convicted thieves could finally collapse after being forced to run naked—chased by spectators along the way—from P. San Marco. *(V: Rialto. Cross bridge and turn right. Church open M-Sa 10am-5pm. Free.)*

DORSODURO

⬛**COLLEZIONE PEGGY GUGGENHEIM.** Guggenheim's elegant waterfront **Palazzo Venier dei Leoni,** once home to and social haven for the world's artistic elite, now displays a private modern collection maintained by the Solomon Guggenheim Foundation. The museum holds works by Duchamp, Klee, Kandinsky, Picasso, Magritte, Pollock, Dalí, and Guggenheim's confidante, Max Ernst. Especially stunning are Constantine's blue glass figurines in the window, watching over the canal below, each modeled after Picasso sketches from 1964. Ms. Guggenheim and her beloved pet shih tzus are buried in the peaceful garden. The Marini sculpture *Angel in the City*, which sits (apparently aroused) on horseback on the terrace, was designed with a detachable penis so Peggy could make emergency alterations if church groups happened to be riding by on the Canal. The ivy-lined marble terrace offers a rare unobstructed view of the Grand Canal. See **Beyond Tourism** (p. 70) for internship opportunities. *(Fondamenta Venier dei Leoni, Dorsoduro 701. V: Accademia. Turn left and follow the yellow signs. ☎041 24 05 411; www.guggenheim-venice.it. Open M and W-Su 10am-6pm. Last entry 15min. before closing. €12; seniors €10; students, ISIC, and Rolling Venice cardholders €7; under 10 free. Audio tour €7. AmEx/MC/V.)*

⬛**GALLERIE DELL'ACCADEMIA.** This colossal gallery boasts the most extensive collection of Venetian art in the world. Start at the top of the stairs in **Room I,** then continue behind Veneziano's ornate *Lion Polyptych with the Annunciation*. Giovanni Bellini's *Madonna Enthroned with Child, Saints, and Angels* stands in **Room II. Rooms IV** and **V** display more works by Bellini, including the magnificent *Madonna and Child with Magdalene and Saint Catherine*, and two works by Giorgione, who defied contemporary convention by creating works with no apparent narrative. *The Tempest*, for instance, continues to foil even today's art historians; an x-ray has revealed that Giorgione originally painted a bathing woman where the young man now stands. In **Room VI,** three paintings by Tintoretto—*The Creation of the Animals, The Temptation of Adam and Eve*, and *Cain and Abel*—lend a progressively darker feel. Venetian Renaissance works line the rooms leading to **Room X,** home to Veronese's colossal *Supper in the House of Levi*. Originally painted as a *Last Supper*, the infuriated Inquisition council tried to force Veronese to modify his unorthodox interpretation of the memorable event, which depicts a Protestant German, a midget, dogs, and fat men. Instead, Veronese cleverly changed the title, saving his artistic license and his life. On the opposite wall is Titian's last painting, a *Pietà* he intended specifically for his tomb, a request that was apparently ignored. Art historians speculate that this final painting was an autobiographical statement, and that the luminous figure is Titian suffering from the raging plague. In **Room XX,** works by Bellini and Carpaccio display Venetian cityscapes so accurately that scholars use them as "photos" of Venice's past. *(V: Accademia.* ☎ *041 52 00 345. To pre-order tickets, call Teleart M-F ☎ 041 52 22 247. Open M 8:15am-2pm, Tu-Su 8:15am-7:15pm. Last entry 45min. before closing. €6.50, EU students age 18-25 €3.25, EU citizens under 18 or over 65 free. Guided tours in English Tu-Su 11am-noon €5. Audio tour €4. Combined ticket to with Cà d'Oro and Museo Oriental €11. Cash only.)*

CHIESA DI SANTA MARIA DELLA SALUTE. The *salute* (Italian for "health") is a hallmark of the Venetian skyline; perched on Dorsoduro's peninsula just southwest of San Marco, the church and its domes are visible from anywhere in the city and afford a spectacular view. Inside, the central area is roped off, so stroll its circumference for a glimpse of its paintings, including one by Titian near the sacristy entrance. In 1631, the city commissioned Longhena to build the church for the Virgin, whom they believed would end the plague. These days, Venice celebrates the plague's end on the third Sunday of November by building a pontoon bridge across the Canal and lighting candles in the church (see **Festivals,** p. 245). Next to the *salute* stands the *dogana*, the old customs house, where ships sailing into Venice were required to stop and pay appropriate duties. *(V: Salute.* ☎ *041 52 25 558. Open daily 9am-noon and 3-5:30pm. The inside of the dogana is closed to the public. Church free. Entrance to sacristy €2, students €1.)*

ISLANDS OF THE LAGOON

> **🟊 TIP:** **ISLAND HOPPING.** *Vaporetto* ticket prices border on extortionate. The best way to visit all the islands is the 12 or 24hr. *vaporetto* pass for €14 and 16, respectively—hop between islands as often as you'd like for a full day!

■ LIDO. The breezy resort island of Lido provided the tragic setting for *Death in Venice*, Thomas Mann's haunting novella of love and lust. Visconti's film version was also shot here at the famous Hotel des Bains, Lungomare Marconi 17. Tree-lined streets, crashing blue waves, and the popular public beach seem miles away from Venice's mobbed urban seafront. An impressive shipwreck looms at one end. The island also offers a casino, horseback riding, and one of Italy's finest golf courses. *(V #1: Lido. From the vaporetto stop, cross the street, and continue until you reach Gran Viale, which traverses the island to the beach. Beach open daily 9am-8pm. Free. Lockable changing rooms €16 per day, €8 after 2:30pm. Beach umbrella and chair €23; long deck chair €10; small safe free. AmEx/MC/V.)*

■ MURANO. Famous since 1292 when glass artisans were forced off Venice proper because their kilns started fires, the six-island cluster of Murano affords visitors the opportunity to witness resident artisans blowing and spinning crystalline creations free of charge. Quiet streets are lined with tiny shops and glass boutiques with jewelry, vases, and delicate figurines for a range of prices; for demonstrations, check signs directing to the *fornace*, concentrated around the Colona, Faro, and Navagero *vaporetto* stops. The speed and grace of these artisans are stunning, and some studios let visitors blow their own glass creations. The **Museo Vetrario** (Glass Museum) houses a collection that begins with funeral urns from the AD first century and ends with pieces like an ornate model garden made entirely of glass and a cartoonish, sea-green octopus presumably designed by Carlo Scarpa in 1930. *(Fondamenta Giustianian 8. V #DM, LN, 5, 13, 41, 42: Faro from either Santa Zaccaria or Fondamenta Nuove.* ☎ */fax 041 73 95 86. Open Apr.-Oct. M-Tu*

and Th-Su 10am-6pm; Nov.-Mar. M-Tu and Th-Su 10am-5pm. €6; EU students, EU residents age 6-14 and over 65, and Rolling Venice cardholders €3.)

Down the street, a marble *loggia* lines the second story of the 12th-century **Basilica di Santa Maria e San Donato,** which features hundreds of mosaics on the church floor, blue chandeliers in the side apses, and a holy waterfront with fused pieces of bright yellow, red, green, and blue glass. A huge crucifix, blown from a single piece of glass, hangs to the right of the altar. *(☎041 73 90 56. Open daily 8am-7pm. Modest dress required. Free.)*

BURANO. As you approach Burano, the lagoon's most postcard-worthy island, you'll immediately notice the brightly colored houses that distinguish this destination. Handmade lace has become the art form of choice for this traditional fishing village. The small and somewhat dull **Scuola di Merletti di Burano** (Lace Museum), once the home of the island's professional lace-making school, features 16th-century lace strips and yellowing lace-maker diplomas. **Chiesa di San Martino** sits across from the museum, and its altar features gorgeous blue stained-glass windows as bright as Burano's pastel buildings. *(40min. by boat from Venice. V #LN: Burano from Fondamenta Nuove. Museum in P. Galuppi. ☎041 73 00 34. Church open daily 8am-noon and 4-7pm. Free.)*

⊞ ENTERTAINMENT

The weekly guide *A Guest in Venice* (free in hotels, tourist offices, and at www.unospitedivenezia.it) lists current festivals, concerts, and gallery exhibits.

GONDOLAS

Gondolas were once displays of multicolored brilliance. Winding slowly through the city's tiny canals, gondolas have become the emblem of Venetian beauty and culture. Legend has it that their lavish reds and purples turned to black when the Plague struck: wooden boats were supposedly coated with tar and pitch to stop further contamination from spreading throughout the disease-infested canals. The morbid color was also a sign of respect for the dead and dying. A more likely story, however, is that a 17th-century city ordinance ordered all boats painted black to prevent noble families from launching gondola-decorating feuds. Certain dignitaries, of course, were exempt. These days the boats are mainly filled with tourists seeking up-close views of Venetian houses and palaces from the original canal pathways. Rides are most romantic about 50min. before sunset and most affordable if shared by six people. Gondolas are a private service; the rate that a gondolier quotes is negotiable, but expect to pay €80-100 for 40min. (and don't pay more). The most bargain-friendly gondoliers are those standing by themselves, rather than those in the groups at "taxi stands" throughout the city.

ORCHESTRAL MUSIC

Venice swoons for orchestral music, from the outdoor chamber orchestras in P. San Marco to costumed concerts. **Vivaldi** (p. 54), the priest and choirmaster of the Chiesa di Santa Maria della Pietà (a few blocks along the waterfront from P. San Marco), was forgotten for centuries after his death. Today, his compositions, particularly *The Four Seasons*, can be heard regularly in the summer and during the winter. The **Chiesa di San Vidal,** next to Campo San Samuele in San Marco, hosts performances using period instruments. *(☎041 27 70 561. Open daily 9am-5pm. Concerts M-Sa 9pm. €23, students €18. Purchase tickets at the church or visit www.interpreteveneziani.com.)*

THEATER, CINEMA, AND ART EXHIBITIONS

Teatro Goldoni, C. del Teatro, San Marco 4650/B, showcases varying types of live productions, often with a seasonal theme. Check with the theater for upcoming listings. (☎041 24 02 011; teatrogoldini@libero.it. Rolling Venice discount 10%. AmEx/MC/V.) The **Mostra Internazionale di Cinema** (Venice International Film Festival), held annually from late August to early September, is a worldwide affair, drawing both rising talents and more established names like Steven Spielberg. Movies are shown in their original languages. (☎041 52 18 878. Tickets €20, students €10, available for purchase throughout city. Some late-night outdoor showings free.) Venice's main cinemas include the **Giorgione,** Campo S. Apostoli, Cannaregio (☎041 52 26 298), and the **Rossini,** San Marco 3988 (☎041 52 30 322), off Campo Manin, which generally shows films in Italian. The famed **Biennale di Venezia,** an international contemporary art exhibition with musical and dance performances, takes over the Giardini Pubblici and the Arsenal with provocative art in odd-numbered years and contemporary architecture exhibits in even ones. Check the website for exact dates. (☎041 52 18 898; for tickets, HelloVenezia ☎041 24 24; www.labiennale.org. Open daily 10am-6pm. Reservations required for dance performances; call ☎041 21 88 28 M-F 10am-5pm. Tickets €15, reduced €12, students and under 26 years €8. Consider buying a 6-performance pass for €75, students €48.)

⬚ SHOPPING

Venice offers the dedicated shopper everything from international designer chains to authentic, family-run holes in the wall. Be wary of shopping in the touristy P. San Marco or around the Rialto; shops in other areas often have better selection and quality for about half the price. Most Italian designer stores can be found in the area to the west of P. San Marco and offer the latest Italian fashion for those rolling deep in euro. Boutiques selling clothing, glass, and masks line the streets leading from the Rialto to Campo S. Polo and Strada Nuova and from the Rialto toward the station, but even these are mobbed with visitors in summer and on weekends. The map accompanying the Rolling Venice Card lists many shops that offer cardholder discounts. The most concentrated and varied selections of Venetian glass and lace require trips to the nearby islands of Murano and Burano, respectively.

▨ NIGHTLIFE

While pubs and bars are not uncommon in Venice, most residents agree that a vibrant nightlife is virtually nonexistent. The majority of locals prefer an evening spent sipping wine in a *piazza* to grinding in a disco, but the island's fluctuating population means that new establishments spring up (and wither and die) regularly. Student nightlife is concentrated around **Campo Santa Margherita** in Dorsoduro, and tourists swarm **Lista di Spagna** in Cannaregio.

▨ **Café Blue,** Campo S. Pantalon, Dorsoduro 3778 (☎041 52 27 613, www.cafebluevenezia.com). Popular, laid-back local hangout that is busy any time of day. Grab a glass of wine (€1.50-3.20) or a distinctly Venetian "sex on the bridge" (€6). F live jazz and blues. Free Wi-Fi. Open M-F 10am-2am, Sa-Su 6pm-2am. Cash only.

▨ **Orange,** Campo S. Margherita, Dorsoduro 3054/A (☎041 52 34 740; www.orangebar. it). The painted bar seems to be on fire at this crowded spot, where an attentive staff serves everything from *panini* (€4) to mixed drinks (€3.50-7). Humming during the day and hopping later. For a break from the orange, retreat to the quiet garden out back or the white umbrella seats in front. Beer €3-6. Wine from €2.50. Open daily 9am-2am. Cash only.

■ **Bistrot ai Do Draghi,** Campo S. Margherita 3665 (☎041 52 89 731). Maybe not as fierce as the name implies ("Bistro of the Two ■Dragons" in Venetian dialect), but certainly more artsy than its neighbors. A cozy spot for a late night drink with old-fashioned, wood decor and dim lighting. Extensive wine list (€1.20-1.80). Famous spritz €1.20. Open daily 8am-2am. Cash only.

Sotto Sopra, Dorsoduro 3740/1 (☎041 52 42 177). From C. Santa Margherita, follow C. della Chiesa, cross bridge and continue towards the right until you reach C. San Pantalon. Keep going until you hear the music. Funky bar features 2 fl. of stained-glass windows, Pop art, and rock music near student nightlife. Bar downstairs. Cozy upstairs seating. Beers €2-5.50. Mixed drinks €5. Wine €1.20. Open M-Sa 10am-2am. MC/V.

Impronta Cafe, Dorsoduro 3815/17 (☎041 27 50 386). Cool murals and fancy blackboard drawings distinguish this cafe from its neighbors. A sleek restaurant by day (pasta from €10), the bar is just as lively at night. Pricey, but still draws Euro-boppers living it up on papa's euro. Frozen drinks €5. Beer €3-5. Wine €2.50-3.50. Primi €6.50-12. Secondi €9-18. Open M-Sa 7am-2am. AmEx/MC/V.

Blues Bar, Campo S. Stin 2532 (☎041 347 575 5566). From the Frari, head north to the next *campo*. With the quiet *campo* all to themselves, customers sit leisurely under white umbrellas, enjoying cold drinks and *panini*. Inside, lively music, exposed brick walls, and hanging instruments add flavor to this eclectic bar. Live jazz and blues F night. Wine €3-7. Beer €3-6. Mixed drinks €4.50-7. Open daily 7am-midnight. Cash only.

❊ FESTIVALS

Banned by the church for several centuries, Venice's famous **Carnevale** was successfully reinstated in the early 70s. During the 10 days preceding Ash Wednesday, masked figures jam the *piazze* and street performances spring up throughout the city. On Mardi Gras, the city's population doubles. Contact the tourist office (see **Practical information,** p. 9) in December or January for details and make lodging arrangements far in advance. Venice's second most colorful festival is the **Festa del Redentore** (third Saturday in July), originally held to celebrate the end of a 16th-century plague. It kicks off on Saturday night with a fireworks display at 11:30pm. On Sunday, craftsmen build a pontoon bridge across the Giudecca Canal, connecting Il Redentore to the Zattere. On the first Sunday in September, Venice stages its classic **regata storica,** a gondola race down the Grand Canal. During the religious **Festa della Salute** (Nov. 21), the city celebrates with another pontoon bridge, this time over the Grand Canal.

PADUA (PADOVA)   ☎049

It is the oldest institutions of Padua (PA-do-va; pop. 215,000) that still draw visitors: pilgrims flock to San Antonio's tomb, athletes skate around peaceful picnickers along the looping Prato della Valle, and lecturers and academics frequent the hallowed university halls. Dante, Petrarch, Galileo, Copernicus, and Donatello built the city's long-standing reputation as an intellectual center. Home to Italy's second oldest university, Padua brings scores of 20-somethings into its busy *piazze*, where crowds linger late into the night.

▌ TRANSPORTATION

Trains: In P. Stazione, at the northern end of C. del Popolo, the continuation of C. Garibaldi. Station open daily 5am-midnight. Ticket office open daily 6am-9pm. Info booth open

THE VENETO

Padua

🏠 **ACCOMMODATIONS**
Hotel Al Santo, **11**
Locanda la Perla, **10**
Ostello Città di
  Padova (HI), **13**
Hotel Mignon, **1**
Al Giardinetto, **2**
Belludi 37, **3**

🍴 **FOOD**
Antica Trattoria
  Paccagnella, **9**
Lunanuova, **7**
Il Grottino, **4**
Pizza Shop di Andrea
  Bettini, **5**
Osteria all'Antica
  Colonna, **6**

🍷 **NIGHTLIFE**
Fly, **8**
Da Tempo, **12**
Via Roma, **16**
Il Gottino, **14**
Osteria l'Anfora, **15**

daily 7am-9pm (☎049 89 20 21). To: **Bologna** (1hr., 32 per day 12:41am-8:33pm, €6.40); **Milan** (2hr., 25 per day 5:51am-8:24pm, €12.20); **Venice** (30min., 82 per day 12:41am-11:07pm, €2.90); **Verona** (1hr., 44 per day 5:51am-11:28pm, €5).

Buses: SITA (☎049 82 06 834), in P. Boschetti. From the train station, walk down C. del Popolo, turn left on V. Trieste, and bear right at V. Vecchio. Ticket office open M-Sa 5:30am-8:30pm, Su 6:20am-8:40pm. To: **Venice** (45min., 30 per day, every 15-30min 5:25am-10:25pm, €3.10) and **Vicenza** (1hr., 31 per day 5:50am-8:15pm, €3.20). Reduced service Sa-Su. Cash only.

Public Transportation: APS (☎049 82 41 111), at the train station, runs local buses. Ticket office open daily 6am-midnight. To get downtown, take buses #8, 12, or 18 M-F and #8 and 32 Sa-Su. 1hr. pass €1; purchase tickets at the *tabaccheria*.

Taxis: RadioTaxi (☎049 65 13 33).

Car Rental: Europcar, P. Stazione 6 (☎049 65 78 77), across parking lot from the station. 19+. Open M-F 8:30am-noon and 3-7pm, Sa 8:30am-12:30pm. AmEx/MC/V.
Maggiore National, P. Stazione 15 (☎049 87 58 605; fax 87 56 223). Open M-F 8:30am-12:30pm and 2:30-7pm, Sa 9am-noon. AmEx/MC/V.

✈ 🛈 ORIENTATION AND PRACTICAL INFORMATION

The train station is on the northern edge of town, outside the 16th-century walls. A 10min. walk down **Corso del Popolo,** which becomes **Corso Garibaldi,** leads to the heart of town and main area of the **Università degli Studi di Padova.**

Tourist Office: Vco. Cappellato Pedrocchi 7 (☎049 87 67 927; info@turismopadova.it), off P. Cavour. Free Internet with 15min. limit. Open M-Sa 9am-1:30pm and 3-6:50pm. Branches: P. del Santo (☎049 87 53 087), across from the basilica. Open Mar.-Oct. M-Sa 9am-1:30pm and 3-6pm, Su 10am-1pm and 3-6pm. In the train station (☎87 52 077). Open M-Sa 9:15am-7pm, Su 9am-noon.

Budget Travel: CTS, V. S. Sofia 96. (☎049 87 51 719). Sells ISICs and train tickets. Open M-F 9am-12:30pm and 3-6:30pm, Sa 9am-noon. Cash only.

English-Language Bookstore: Feltrinelli International, V. S. Francesco 14 (☎049 87 50 792). From the train station, turn left off V. Cavour. Wide selection of magazines, novels, and travel guides. Open M-Sa 9am-1pm and 3:30-7:30pm. AmEx/MC/V.

Hospital: Ospedale Civile, V. Giustiniani 1 (☎049 82 11 111), off V. Ospedale.

Internet Access: Free at the main tourist office (see above). **Internet Point Padova,** V. Altinate 145 (☎049 65 92 92). Printing, fax, and photocopy. €1 per 20min., €3 per hr. Open M-Sa 10am-midnight, Su 4pm-midnight. MC/V.

Post Office: C. Garibaldi 25 (☎049 87 72 111). Open M-Sa 8:30am-6:30pm. **Postal Code:** 35100.

🏠 ACCOMMODATIONS

🏨 **Belludi 37,** V. Luca Belludi 37 (☎049 66 56 33; www.belludi37.it). Too good to be true. Modern decor with simple stone steps, smooth hardwood floors, and glass tables in the heart of the city. Huge rooms have AC, cordless phones, orthopedic beds, LCD TVs, free DSL Internet, and private baths. Buffet breakfast or breakfast in bed at no extra cost. Parking €10. Singles €50-70; doubles €90-110. Extra bed €30. AmEx/MC/V. ❹

Ostello Città di Padova (HI), V. Aleardi 30 (☎049 87 52 219; www.ostellopadova. it). From station, take bus #12 or 18 to Prato della Valle, or walk 25min. Large, efficiently run hostel rents 6-bed dorms. TV room and good location 10min. from *centro.* Breakfast included. Laundry wash €3, dry €2.50. Internet €5 per hr. €3 key deposit for locker in room. Wheelchair-accessible. 5-night max. stay. Reception 7:15-9:30am and 4:30-11pm. Lockout 9:30am-4:30pm. Curfew 11:30pm. Call ahead. 6-bed dorms €18; 4-person family rooms €64, with private bath €84. MC/V. ❶

Al Giardinetto, Prato della Valle 54 (☎049 65 67 66; www.hotelalgiardinetto.it). Impeccable service, a lovely garden, and a great location overlooking the majestic *piazza.* Red-carpeted hallways and pink walls lead to large rooms adorned with coordinating flowers. All rooms have TV, phone, A/C, fridge, and private bath. Free Wi-Fi. Breakfast included. Singles €40, with bath €60; doubles €90. AmEx/MC/ V. ❸

Hotel Mignon, V. Luca Belludi 22 (☎049 66 17 22; www.hotelmignonpadova.it). Sunny rooms and a cheery staff, just 5min. from Basilica di San Antonio. Humbly furnished but comfortable and spacious rooms have private bath, TV, AC, and phone; some have balconies. Breakfast €2.50. Singles €52; doubles €67; triples €82; quads €97. MC/V. ❹

Hotel Al Santo, V. del Santo 147 (☎049 87 52 131; www.alsanto.it), near the basilica. Recently renovated, spacious rooms with modern decor, TV, A/C, Wi-Fi, phone, and bath.

Breakfast included. Lunch or dinner *menù* €16. Restaurant downstairs. Singles €65; doubles €80-100; triples €120. Prices may drop with longer stays. AmEx/MC/V. ❺

Locanda la Perla, V. Cesarotti 67 (☎049 87 58 939), a 5min. walk from the Basilica di San Antonio. Friendly owner Paolo rents clean, fairly large rooms with comfortable beds, simple decor, phone, and shared bath on each floor. Fan and TV provided upon request. Closed last 2 weeks of Aug. Singles €35; doubles €45, triples €60. Cash only. ❸

🗂 FOOD

Morning **markets** are held in P. delle Erbe and P. della Frutta where sidewalk vendors also sell fresh produce, meats, and cheeses. (M-F 7am-1:30pm, Sa 7am-8pm). There's a **PAM** supermarket downtown in Piazzetta della Garzeria 3, past Palazzo Bo to the right of Caffè Pedrocchi. (Open M-Tu and Th-Sa 8am-8:30pm, W 8am-2pm. MC/V.) For an inexpensive taste of the gourmet, visit the specialty store, **Franchin,** V. del Santo 95. (☎049 87 50 532. Open M-Tu and Th-Su 8:30am-1:30pm and 4:30-8pm, W 8:30am-1:30pm. MC/V.) Wine lovers should sample a glass from the nearby **Colli Euganei** district. Visitors to the **Basilica di Sant'Antonio** can nibble on *dolci del santo* (saint's sweets), a flaky, powdered cake with creamy nut and fig filling, in nearby *pasticcerie.*

🍴 **Il Grottino,** V. del Santo 21. (☎049 66 41 76). Locals crowd this casual spot where simple dishes like *tortellini in brodo* (€5) are served in an unimposing, warmly lit interior. Menu changes daily. Primi €5-7. Secondi €10-18. Open in winter M-Tu and Th-Sa 8:30am-3:30pm and 7pm-12:30am, Su 9am-3:30pm and 7pm-12:30am; in summer M-Tu and Th-Su 9am-3:30pm and 7pm-12:30am. MC/V. ❹

🍴 **Pizza Shop di Andrea Bettini,** V. G. Morgagni 48/B (☎049 87 51 648). Friendly owner Andrea has been making the best-priced and tastiest pizza in town for ages. Small interior, so take your slice to the nearby *piazza* or park. Marinara pies (€2.60) with toppings up to €6. Slices €1-1.30. Open Tu-Sa 11am-2:45pm and 6-10:45pm. Cash only. ❶

Osteria all'Antica Colonna, V. Altinate 127 (☎049 65 50 85). Colorful flags, clocks displaying world times, and overflowing wine bottles line the walls of this old trattoria, which specializes in Tuscan cuisine. Long wine list. Primi €6.50-9. Secondi €7-17. Wine from €2.50. Open M 6pm-midnight, Tu-Sa 10am-3pm and 6pm-midnight. MC/V. ❸

Lunanuova, V. S. Gregorio Barbarigo 12 (☎049 87 58 907), heading off P. Duomo. Buzz at stained-glass doors for entrance. Mix of healthy Middle Eastern and vegetarian cuisine. Handwritten daily menu with dishes like creamed fennel in sesame sauce (€4.50). Individual plates €4.50-5.30, 2 plates €8.80, 3 plates €9.80, 5 plates €11. Open Tu-Sa 12:30-2:30pm and 7:30pm-midnight. Cash only. ❷

Antica Trattoria Paccagnella, V. del Santo 113 (☎/fax 049 87 50 549). The place to go for authentic Paduan cuisine. Regional favorites like *cappellaci with rucola* and smoked *provola* (€9) in a relaxed atmosphere. Primi €7-11. Secondi €12-17. Cover €2.50. Open M-Sa 8am-4pm and 6:30pm-midnight. AmEx/MC/V. ❹

GIMME TEN. Padua's sights are best visited with either the 48hr. or 72hr. **Padova Card** (€15/20), which covers all major sights in Padua, excluding the *duomo.* The card also provides free transport on local buses and discounts from participating merchants. Visit the tourist office for more info.

🔲 SIGHTS

🏛**CAPPELLA DEGLI SCROVEGNI (ARENA CHAPEL).** Enrico Scrovegni dedicated this tall brick chapel to the Virgin Mary in an attempt to save the soul of his father Reginald, a usurer famously lambasted in the 17th canto of Dante's *Inferno*. Pisano carved the chapel's statues and Giotto covered the walls with frescoed scenes from the lives of Jesus, Mary, and her parents, Saints Joachim and Anne. Completed between 1305 and 1306, this 38-panel cycle is one of the earliest examples of depth and realism in Italian Renaissance painting. A brilliant blue ceiling is adorned with bright gold stars and images of Jesus and Mary, each surrounded by prophets. Across the top panel, the marriage of Joachim and Anne is depicted with startlingly crisp lines and vibrant hues. The next two rows depict the life of Jesus, the players in the story portrayed with unprecedented emotion and realism. Note that the chapel has two entrances; one belonged to the citizens of the city, while the other, which is now the visitor entrance, was reserved for the Scrovegni family. Down a short gravel path from the museum, there is a multimedia room, featuring a short multilingual video on the chapel's history (narrated amusingly from Scrovegni's perspective) and an in-depth explanation of the fresco-painting technique. Additionally, the Musei Civici Eremitani has assembled an art collection including ancient Roman inscriptions and a beautiful crucifix by Giotto that once adorned the Scrovegni Chapel. (*P. Eremitani 8. ☎ 049 20 10 020; www.cappelladegliscrovegni.it. Reservations by phone or website required. Call M-F between 9am-7pm and Sa 9am-6pm. Museum and chapel open M-F 9am-7pm. Museum €10; combined ticket €12, students €8, disabled €1. Evening visits to chapel €8, reduced €6. AmEx/MC/V.*)

> **GIOTTO'S JUDGMENT.** In the **Last Judgment,** Giotto painted himself among the blessed as a signature and perhaps a self-assessment. Check him out: he's fourth from the left, with the pink robe and yellow hat.

BASILICA DI SANT'ANTONIO (IL SANTO). An array of rounded gray domes and conical spires caps Padua's enormous brick basilica. Bronze sculptures by Donatello grace the high altar, which is surrounded by the artist's *Crucifixion* and several Gothic frescoes. Upon entering, walk along the left side to reach the **Tomba di Sant'Antonio,** which sits on a platform underneath a huge marble arch. Each year, thousands of pilgrims crowd the marble bas-reliefs to cover the black stone of the sepulcher with framed photographs and prayers. Along the right side, the **Cappella di San Giacomo** is marked by a luminous blue ceiling with gold stars that recall Giotto's signature chapel. Along the pane of glass that now protects the frescoed wall, scratched-in and graffiti-written names can be detected by past couples and visitors. Behind the main altar in the apse sits the **Cappella delle Reliquie,** where ornately carved sculptures look down on shrines containing everything from St. Anthony's tunic to his jawbone and tongue; frightening cupids holding skulls line the way. A multimedia show in the courtyard (follow "Mostra" signs) details St. Anthony's life. To the right on the way out of the basilica, the tiny **Oratorio di San Giorgio,** which briefly served as a prison under Napoleon, displays Giotto-inspired frescoes. (*P. del Santo. ☎ 049 82 42 811; www.basilicadelsanto.org. Basilica open daily Apr.-Sept. 6:15am-7:45pm; Nov.-Mar. 6:15am-6:45pm. Modest dress strictly enforced. Free. Capella delle Relinque open daily 8am-12:45pm and 2:30-7:30pm. Mostra open daily 9am-6pm. Free multilingual audio tour available at front desk. Oratorio and Scuola ☎/fax 049 82 42 831. Oratorio open daily Apr.-Oct. 9am-12:30pm and 2:30-7pm; Nov.-Mar. 9am-12:30pm and 2:30-5pm. Scuola open daily 10-11am and 3-4pm. Wheelchair-accessible. €2.50, Padova Card €2. Cash only.*)

ORTO BOTANICO (BOTANICAL GARDEN). Leafy trees and high stone walls surround a circular grid of iron fences, gravel walkways, and low fountains in Europe's oldest university botanical garden, recognized as a UNESCO World Heritage site. Take your time wandering through the oasis of water lilies, cacti, and medicinal herbs, or inhale the fresh scents from one of the many benches. **"Goethe's palm,"** planted in 1585, was given the name after the poet visited and developed his own pre-Darwinian theory of evolution based on the garden's leaves. (*V. Orto Botanico 15. Follow signs from basilica.* ☎049 82 72 119. *Open Apr.-Oct. daily 9am-1pm and 3-7pm; Nov.-Mar. M-F 9am-1pm. €4, over 65 €3, students €1. Cash only.*)

NIGHTLIFE AND FESTIVALS

Pilgrims pack the city on June 13, as Padua commemorates the death of its patron saint, Saint Anthony, with a procession bearing his statue and jawbone. An **antique market** is held in the Prato della Valle on the third Sunday of the month. The area holds a **clothing market** on Saturdays. As the sun sets on summer evenings, Padua's *piazzas* fill with crowds spilling out from nearby bars and cafes. Nightlife rages during the school year, but dies down in summer.

Il Gottino, V. S. Martino e Solferino 29 (☎049 87 74 647). Students liven up this nearly bare room. Funky floral wallpaper, rustic wood floors, dim lighting, and techno. Free *cicchetti.* Wine €2-4. Mixed drinks €5. Open M-Sa 10am-midnight. AmEx/MC/V.

Da Tempo, V. S. Sofia 70 (☎049 87 60 319; www.datempo.it). Bohemian bar with ample seating, a cool garden, and reasonable prices. An ideal student hangout. Flatscreen TV. Beer €2-4.50. Wine €1.50-3. Mixed drinks €3-5. Open M-T and Th 6:30am-8pm; W and F 6:30am-midnight; Su 4pm-midnight. Cash only.

Via Roma, V. Roma 96 (☎049 87 52 712). Upscale mix of modern and antique with funky mirrors and glittering chandeliers, complemented by fluorescent blue lighting, leopard print seating, and **Klimt posters.** A lively crowd lounges outside under white umbrellas. Mixed drinks €6. Wine €3-7. Open daily 7am-2am. AmEx/MC/V.

Osteria l'Anfora, V. dei Soncin 13 (☎049 65 66 29). Great for both a hearty meal or an evening drink. Large wood tables among brick columns and bookshelves seat large groups, while the bar is ideal for traditional *sarde in saor* (€6) and wine (€1.50-5). Beer €3-4.50. Food €5.50-15. Open M-Sa 8am-midnight. AmEx/MC/V.

Fly, Galleria Tito Livio 4/6, (☎049 87 52 892) between V. Roma and Riviera Tito Livio. Fly is a pedestrian cafe by day and a swinging hot spot by night. This bar's great location near V. Roma and student nightlife make it a great choice for an evening out. Wine €2-3.50. Mixed drinks €3.50-4.50. Open daily 8am-1am.

VERONA   ☎045

Verona (veh-RO-nah; pop. 4000) offers visitors much more than a Romeo and Juliet gimmick. From the winding river Adige to the city's dizzying towers, Verona offers the perks of a large city while maintaining a reputation for authentic local cuisine, rich wines, and an internationally renowned opera.

TRANSPORTATION

Flights: Aeroporto Valerio Catullo (☎045 80 95 666; www.aeroportoverona.it), 16km from *centro.* For shuttles from train station (☎045 80 57 911; www.atv.verona.it; 5:40am, then every 20min. 6:10am-11:10pm; €4.50), buy tickets on the bus.

Trains: In Verona Porta Nuova P. XXV Aprile (☎045 89 20 21). Ticket office open daily 6am-9pm. To: **Bologna** (2hr., 22 per day 3:05am-10:38pm, €7.50); **Milan** (2hr., 34 per day 4:05am-10:42pm, €7); **Rome** (7hr., 4 per day 5:30am-11pm, €45); **Trent** (1hr., 25 per day 12:46am-10:48pm, €4.65); **Venice** (1hr., 41 per day 5:52am-10:43pm, €8); **Vicenza** (45min., 55 per day 5:52am-10:42pm, €3.40).

Buses: ATV, P. XXV Aprile (☎045 88 71 111; www.atv.verona.it), in the gray building in front of the train station. Station open M-Sa 6am-8pm, Su 6:30am-8pm. Buses run to **Brescia**

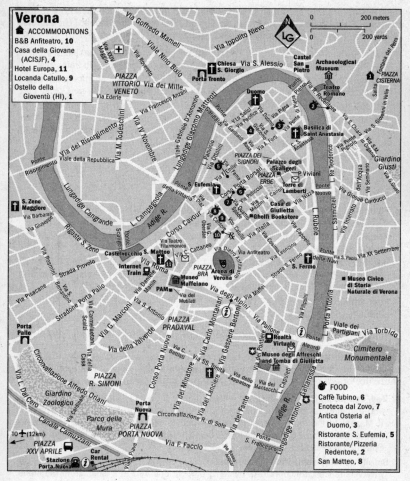

Verona

🏠 ACCOMMODATIONS

B&B Anfiteatro, **10**
Casa della Giovane
(ACISJF), **4**
Hotel Europa, **11**
Locanda Catullo, **9**
Ostello della
Gioventù (HI), **1**

THE VENETO

🍴 FOOD

Caffè Tubino, **6**
Enoteca dal Zovo, **7**
Antica Osteria al
Duomo, **3**
Ristorante S. Eufemia, **5**
Ristorante/Pizzeria
Redentore, **2**
San Matteo, **8**

(2hr., every hr. 6:40am-6:10pm, €5.30), **Riva del Garda** (2hr., 15 per day 6:40am-6:45pm, €5.20), and **Sirmione** (1hr., 17 per day 6:40am-10pm. Reduced service Sa-Su).

Taxis: RadioTaxi (☎045 53 26 66; www.radiotaxiverona.it). 24hr.

Car Rental: Avis (☎045 80 06 636). Open M-F 8am-noon and 3-7pm, Sa 8am-noon. **Europcar** (☎045 92 73 161). Open M-F 8:30am-noon and 2:30-7pm, Sa 8:30am-noon. **Hertz** (☎045 80 00 832). 21+. Open M-F 8am-noon and 2:30-7pm, Sa 8am-noon. All 4 have offices at the train station. AmEx/MC/V.

🗺️ ORIENTATION AND PRACTICAL INFORMATION

From the **train station**, in P. XXV Aprile, walk 20min. up **Corso Porta Nuova,** or take bus #11, 12, 13, 51, 72, or 73 (weekends take #91, 92, or 93; tickets €1, full day €3.50) to Verona's *centro*, the **Arena di Verona**, in **Piazza Brà.** Most sights lie between P. Brà and the **Adige River. Via Mazzini** connects the Arena to the monuments of **Piazza delle Erbe** and **Piazza dei Signori.** The **Teatro Romano** and the **Giardino Giusti** lie across the bridges **Pietra, Navi,** and **Nuovo** on the Adige.

Tourist Office: At V. degli Alpini 9 (☎045 80 68 680; www.tourism.verona.it). From C. Pta. Nuova, enter P. Brà; office is on the right. Open M-Sa 9am-7pm, Su 9am-3pm.

Luggage Storage: At the train station (☎045 80 23 827; info@grandistazioni.it). €3.80 for 1st 5hr., €0.60 per hr. for 6-12hr., €0.20 per hr. thereafter; 5-day max. 20kg max. per bag. Open daily 6am-10pm. Cash only.

English-Language Bookstore: Ghelfi & Barbato, V. Mazzini 21 (☎045 80 02 306), at the intersection with V. Quattro Spade. Small, yet balanced English section with cafe upstairs. Open M-Sa 9am-12:30pm and 3:30-7pm. MC/V.

Beyond Tourism: Informagiovani, V. Ponte Aleardi 15 (☎045 80 78 770; www.informagiovani.comune.verona.it), helps find work or study opportunities in Verona. Open M and F 9am-1pm, Tu and Th 3-6:30pm, W 9am-1pm and 3-6:30pm.

Police: V. del Pontiere 32/a (☎045 80 78 411).

Pharmacy: Farmacia Due Campane, V. Mazzini 52 (☎045 80 06 660). Open M-F 9:10am-12:30pm and 3:30-7:30pm, Sa 9:10am-12:30pm. MC/V.

Hospital: Ospedale Civile Maggiore (☎045 80 71 111), on Borgo Trento in P. Stefani in the north part of town.

Internet Access: Internet Train, V. Roma 17/A (☎045 80 13 394). From P. Brà, turn right on V. Roma; 2 blocks down on left. High-speed PCs, color printers, photocopiers, and scanners. €3.50 per hr. Open M-F 10am-11pm, Sa-Su 2-8pm. MC/V.

Post Office: V. Cattaneo 23 (☎045 80 03 998). Open M-F 8:30am-6:30pm, Sa 8:30am-1pm. **Postal Code:** 37100.

ACCOMMODATIONS

Budget hotels are sparse in Verona; those that do exist fill up quickly. Make reservations ahead, especially during opera season (June-Sept.). Prices rise when there are opera performances, and drop precipitously in the low season.

Bed and Breakfast Anfiteatro, V. Alberto Mario 5 (☎347 24 88 462; www.anfiteatro-bedandbreakfast.com). Walking toward P. Brà, V. Alberto Mario branches off from V. Mazzini to the right. Its central location and romantic rooms with TV and Internet access make this B&B one of the town's best options. Breakfast buffet included. Singles €60-90; doubles €80-130; triples €100-150. ❹

Ostello della Gioventù Villa Francescatti, Salita Fontana del Ferro 15 (☎045 59 03 60; www.villafrancescatti.com). Take bus #73 or night bus #90 to P. Isolo. From the Arena, turn on V. Anfiteatro, cross Ponte Nuovo on V. Carducci, turn left on V. Giusti, then right on V. San Giovanni in Valle. Follow yellow signs uphill. Quiet, out-of-the-way. Breakfast included; dinner €8, with vegetarian options. Laundry €2.50. Check-in by 5pm. Check-out 9am. Curfew midnight, extended for opera-goers. Reservations accepted for family rooms (€19 per person per night). Dorms €17. Cash and traveler's checks only. ❶

FOOD

Verona is famous for its wines, among them the dry white *Soave* and the red *Valpolicella, Bardolino, Recioto,* and *Amarone.*

Enoteca dal Zovo, Vco. San Marco in Foro 7 (☎045 80 34 369; www.enotecadalzovo.it), off C. Pta. Borsari. This small winery occupies a converted chapel with original frescoes still adorning the ceiling, though cluttered shelves of bottles make the space seem more like an apothecary. Owner Oreste dal Zovo serves impressive wines, welcoming visitors like old friends. Open daily 8am-8pm. Cash only. ❶

Antica Osteria al Duomo, V. Duomo 7/a (☎045 80 04 505), on the way to the *duomo*. Small, laid-back restaurant with dark wood interior has a few cozy tables and a bar, and serves excellent, simple cuisine like *tagliatelle* with shrimp and zucchini. Customers enjoy drinks outside on the quiet street when the interior gets too crowded. Primi €6.50-7. Secondi €7-15. Cover €1.50. Open M-Sa 11am-3pm and 7-11pm. MC/V ❶

San Matteo, Vco. del Guasto 4 (☎045 80 04 538; fax 59 39 38), from P. delle Erbe on C. Pta. Borsari, walk 5min., and turn left. Housed in a beautiful, centrally located former church with simple, elegant interior. Primi €7.50-11. Secondi €9-17. Cover €1.50. Open daily noon-2:30pm and 6pm-12:30am. AmEx/MC/V. ❸

🔆 SIGHTS

SHAKESPEAREAN HUBRIS. Shakespeare buffs still flock to Verona for its role as the setting of *Romeo and Juliet*, hoping to absorb some love from the Bard's ill-fated couple. At the **Casa di Giulietta,** tourists pose on the stone balcony, but the house is best admired from the outside, where vastly more entertaining lovers' graffiti has built up. The Veronese authorities have protected the building from further poetic injury by slyly installing plastic sheets where people write, replacing them every two months with no young Romeo the wiser. Contrary to popular belief, the Capulet family never lived here, so save your money and skip the inside. (*V. Cappello 23. ☎045 80 34 303. Open M 1:30-7:30pm, Tu-Su 8:30am-7:30pm. Ticket office closes 6:45pm. €4, students and seniors €3. Cash only.*) A canopy shades the walkway into the **Museo Degli Affreschi,** which displays Veronese artwork, including an excellent collection of Italian frescoes from the 10th to 16th centuries. The museum's garden houses the faux **Tomba di Giulietta,** a cave with a single window illuminating the sepulcher. It will take only a moment to mourn at the *tomba*—which like the Capulet house is lined with lovers graffiti—but stay a minute longer in the atrium courtyard, a quiet place to rest your feet after touring the art inside. (*V. del Pontiere 35. ☎045 80 00 361. Open M 1:30-7:30pm, Tu-Su 8:30am-7:30pm. Ticket office closes 6:45pm. €3, students and seniors €2.*) The **Casa di Romeo,** reportedly once home to the Montecchi (Montague) family, sits around the corner from P. dei Signori at V. Arche Scaligeri 2. The villa is privately owned and closed to the public.

ROMEO, ROMEO, WHEREFORE ART THOU ROMEO? Juliet & Co. provides excellent full- and half-day walking tours of Verona for groups (€105-210, up to 30 people). Individuals may join alternative walking tours (1¼hr), which run daily from Apr. 1 to Nov. 5 and depart from P. Brà at 5:30pm. (☎045 81 03 173; www.julietandco.com. €10; no booking required.)

PIAZZA ERBE AND PIAZZA DEI SIGNORI. Tourists and school groups swarm to P. Erbe, which features a market selling fruit and tacky souvenirs. Shops and restaurants line the *piazza;* in its center, pigeons hop around tiers of the **Madonna Verona's Fountain.** The nearby **Berlina**—a platform on which medieval convicts were punished by being pelted with produce—is also a crowd pleaser. P. delle Erbe lies near **Via Mazzini,** where pink marble leads local glitterati to Gucci and Louis Vuitton along the city's fashion row. The **Arco della Costa** (Arch of the Rib) connects P. delle Erbe to **Piazza dei Signori.** A whale rib, prophesied to fall on the first passing person who has never told a lie, still dangles from the arch, and a statue of Dante stands in the center of the *piazza*. The 15th-century

Loggia del Consiglio sits in the *piazza* just behind Dante's back. The della Scala family lived in the **Palazzo degli Scaligeri,** and the medieval **Tombs of the Scaligeri,** on V. Arche Scaligeri, are through the arch in P. dei Signori.

THE ARENA. Red velvet curtains and an eroding stone archway welcome visitors to this AD first-century Roman amphitheater, home to the annual **Verona Opera Festival.** For the best view and the lowest price, opt for original stone slab seating above. The age and authenticity of the arena is slightly thrown off by the concession stands and souvenir tables that draw hoards of tourists, especially during opera season. *(In P. Brà.* ☎ *045 80 03 204. Open M 1:30-7:30pm, Tu-Su 8:30am-7:30pm. Closes 4:30pm on opera nights. Ticket sales end 1hr. before closing. Wheelchair-accessible. €4, students and seniors €3, children 8-13 €1.)*

MY FAIR VERONA. The **Verona Card** (day pass €8, 3 days €12) is an excellent money saver, which includes free ATV bus rides and entry to most of the city's museums, churches, and sights. Purchase it at participating museums, churches, or *tabaccherie.* Churches also offer their own pass (€5, students and seniors €4), permitting entrance to the basilica, *duomo,* S. Fermo, S. Zeno, and S. Lorenzo. For more information, visit www.comune.verona.it.

🎵 ENTERTAINMENT

The Arena di Verona is the venue for the world-famous ▣**Verona Opera Festival,** which attracts opera enthusiasts in droves every year from June to August. The 2009 opera season runs from June 19 to Aug. 30. (Tickets and info at V. Dietro Anfiteatro 6/B, along the side of the Arena. ☎ 045 80 05 151; www.arena.it. Open M-F 9am-noon and 3:15-5:45pm, Sa 9am-noon. Open on performance days and Sundays during opera season 10am-9pm. Admission €19-198; seats range from general admission on stone steps to reserved "gold" membership seating. AmEx/MC/V.) Also in summer, the **Teatro Romano,** V. Regaste Redentore 2, close to the Ponte Pietà, stages dance performances and Shakespearean plays performed in Italian. June brings the **Verona Jazz Festival.** (Info ☎ 045 80 66 485 or 045 80 66 488; www.estateteatraleveronese.it. Ticket office at Palazzo Barbieri, V. Leoncino 61. Open M-Sa 10:30am-1pm and 4-7pm. Tickets €11-21.)

TRENTINO-ALTO ADIGE

The Mediterranean feel of Italy's southern and eastern regions fades under Germanic influences in the jagged peaks of the Dolomites in Trentino-Alto Adige (tren-TEE-noh AL-toh ah-DEE-jay). One glance at the conifers and snow-covered peaks of *Le Dolomiti* (leh doh-loh-MEE-tee) explains why backpackers and skiers still swarm the area.

At the onset of the 19th century, Napoleon conquered this part of the Holy Roman Empire, but eventually relinquished it to the Austro-Hungarian Empire. Trentino and the Südtirol (South Tyrol) came under Italian control at the end of WWI, a transition that created hybridized linguistic patterns and cultural traditions. Though Germany thwarted Mussolini's brutal efforts to Italianize the region, Benito did manage to give every German name an Italian equivalent, which explains the dual street and town names used today. From *wurst* stands in Bolzano's *piazze* to the German-speaking locals in Bressanone, Trentino-Alto Adige's Germanic aura bears witness to a deep-rooted Austrian culture, which still thrives today.

HIGHLIGHTS OF TRENTINO-ALTO ADIGE

CHILL OUT with Bolzano's Ötzi the Iceman from the 4th millennium BC (p. 261).

BE BOLD and try some violet gelato in Trent (p. 257).

TRENT (TRENTO, TRIENT)   ☎ 0461

Pedestrian-friendly streets and an idyllic mountain location give Trent (TREN-toh; pop. 111,000) a small-town feel. The city represents a historical intersection between Italian and Nordic cultures. While the delicious strudel in Trent's bakeries attests to the town's proximity to Austria, the colorful buildings and *piazze* are quintessentially Italian. Named "Alpine City of the Year" in 2004 for its local pride and carefully preserved culture, Trent is growing in prominence in contemporary culture and hosts annual festivals and events. Easily explorable, it combines a vibrant student life with excellent nearby hiking options.

⬛ TRANSPORTATION

Trains: V. Dogana (☎0461 89 20 21). Ticket office open daily 5:40am-8:30pm. Info office open M-F 8:30am-12:15pm and 1:15-4:30pm. To: **Bologna** (3hr., 12 per day 1am-9:27pm, €15); **Bolzano** (45min., 33 per day 1:55am-10:59pm, €2.89); **Venice** (3-4hr., 12 per day 7:05am-5pm, €10); **Verona** (1hr., 2 per hr. 4am-9:48pm, €4.65).

Buses: **Atesina** and **Trentino Transporti** (☎0461 82 10 00; www.ttspa.it), on V. Pozzo next to the train station. Info office open M-Sa 7am-7:30pm. Bulletin board at the back of the station posts line suspension alerts. Buses run to **Riva del Garda** (1hr., every 2hr. 5:57am-7:50pm, €3.20) and **Rovereto** (50min., every hr. 5:57am-7:50pm, €2.70).

Public Transportation: Atesina runs local buses. Tickets (€0.90 for 70min. ticket; €2.30 for 24hr. ticket) available at the bus station, train station, or *tabaccherie.*

Cableways: Funivia Trento-Sardagna (☎0461 23 21 54), on Lung'Adige Monte Grappa. From bus station, turn right on V. Pozzo; take 1st right on Cavalcavia di San Lorenzo. Cross bridge over train tracks, and cross the intersection to the red-and-yellow building to the right of the tracks. To ◼Sardagna on Mt. Bondone (4min.; every 15-30min.; €0.90 for a 70min. ticket; €1.20 for 2 hr. ticket; €2.30 for 24hr. ticket.) May bring up to 3 bikes per person, €0.90 per bike. Open daily 6:35am-10:30pm. Cash only.

Taxi: RadioTaxi (☎0461 93 00 02).

🔧🛈 ORIENTATION AND PRACTICAL INFORMATION

The **bus** and **train** stations are on the same street, between the gardens next to the Adige River and the circles-of-hell statue of **Piazza Dante.** The *centro* lies east of the Adige. From the stations, walk right to the intersection of **Via Pozzo** with **Via Torre Vanga.** V. Pozzo becomes **Via delle Orfane** and then the curving **Via Cavour** before it reaches **Piazza del Duomo** in the *centro.* **ATMs** are nearby.

Tourist Office: APT, V. Manci 2 (☎0461 21 60 00; www.apt.trento.it). Turn right from the train station and left on V. Roma, which becomes V. Manci as it intersects V. Alfieri. **Tours** leave from the office. No reservation required. Limited to groups of 10 or fewer. Tours July-Aug. Th and Sa 3pm, Sept.-June Sa 3pm; €3. Castle tours July-Aug. Th and Sa 10am; Sept.-June Sa 10am; €3. Open daily 9am-7pm.

Bookstore: Libreria Disertori, V. Diaz 11 (☎0461 98 14 55), near V. Battisti. A slim selection of mostly classic English books, including Shakespeare. Open M 3-7pm, Tu-Su 9am-noon and 3-7pm. AmEx/MC/V.

Police: Vle. Verona, outside the *centro* to the south.

Pharmacy: Farmacia dall'Armi, P. Duomo 10 (☎0461 23 61 39). Serving the city since 1490. After-hours rotation posted in window. Open July-Aug. M-Sa 8:30am-12:30pm and 3-7pm; Sept.-June M-Sa 8:30am-7pm. Cash only.

Hospital: Ospedale Santa Chiara, Largo Medaglie d'Oro 9 (☎0461 90 31 11 or 91 43 09), up V. Orsi. From the bus stand directly in front of train station, take bus #2.

Internet Access: The city of Trent provides free Wi-Fi through **WilmaNet.** Sign up at one of 2 registration offices: **ITAL GM,** 15 V. del Suffragio (☎0461 19 20 141; trento@wilmanet.it) or **URP,** 3 V. Belenzani and 2 Via Manci (☎0461 88 44 53; comurp@comune.trento.it). Anyone with valid ID may register. Most of the city is connected.

Post Office: V. Calepina 16 (☎0461 98 47 15), offers fax services and money exchange just off P. Vittoria. Open M-F 8am-6:30pm, Sa 8am-12:30pm. **Postal Code:** 38100.

🏠 ACCOMMODATIONS

◼ **Ostello Giovane Europa,** V. Torre Vanga 11 (☎0461 26 34 84; www.gayaproject.org). Exit train station and turn right; hostel is the white building on the corner of V. Pozzo and V. Torre Vanga. Centrally located clean dorms offer private bath, sunny terraces, desks, and phones. €10 deposit gains access to games and a foosball table. Library study area stocked with a multitude of books and brochures. Breakfast included. 3-course dinner €9. Laundry €4.50; dry €2.50; soap €1. Reception 7:30am-11pm. Check-out 10am. Curfew 11:30pm; ask for door code to return later. Reservations recommended. Dorms €14-16; singles €25; doubles €42; triples €54. AmEx/MC/V. ❶

Hotel America, V. Torre Verde 52 (☎0461 98 30 10; www.hotelamerica.it). Located 5-10min. from both the train station and the town center. Cozy, well-furnished rooms with bath, TV, A/C, and minibar. Balconies with hanging plants offer beautiful views of Trent and Castello del Buonconsiglio to the east. Breakfast included. Attached restaurant with a daily *menù* for €20. Wi-Fi €2 per 30min., €3.50 per hr., €9 for 4hr. Singles €70; doubles €108; triples €120. AmEx/MC/V. ❺

Aquila d'Oro, V. Belezani 76 (☎0461 98 62 82; www.aquiladoro.it). Provides luxurious bedrooms with free Wi-Fi, private bath, parking, and breakfast in its spacious restaurant downstairs. Though the price is high, the central location and palatial feel may be worth the splurge. Singles €77-85; doubles €153-170. ❺

🍴 FOOD

Trentino cuisine owes much to the local production of sterling cheeses like *nostrano, tosela,* and the highly prized *vezzena. Piatti del malgaro* (herdsman's plates) include cheeses, polenta, mushrooms, and sausage. A Germanic undercurrent surfaces in the exceptional local version of *apfelstrudel.* **Supermercati Trentini** lies across P. Pasi from the *duomo* at P. Lodron 28. (☎0461 22 01 96. Open Tu-Su 9am-8pm, M 2:30-8pm. MC/V.)

▨ Osteria Il Cappello, P. Lunelli 5 (☎0461 23 58 50). From the station, turn right, then left on V. Roma. After 4 blocks, turn right on V. San Pietro, then take the tunnel near #27 into P. Lunelli. This classy restaurant overlooking a private courtyard serves traditional Trentino cuisine like cream of asparagus with crisp *sfogliatine* (€8.50). Delicious assortment of breads and a good selection of wines (€3-5.50 per glass). Primi €8.50-9.50. Secondi €14-17. Cover €2. Open Tu-Su noon-2pm and 7:30-10pm. AmEx/MC/V. ❹

▨ Alla Grotta, Vco. San Marco 6 (☎0461 98 71 97). Huge pizzas heaped with toppings make this busy spot perfect for those in search of a filling meal or late-night drink. Pizza and primi €4.10-7.20. Open Tu-Su noon-3pm and 6:30-11:30pm. MC/V. ❷

Ristorante Al Vò, Vco. del Vò 11 (☎0461 98 53 74; www.ristorantealvo.it). From the station, turn right and walk to V. Torre Vanga. Turn left and continue for 200m; Ristorante Al Vò is on the right. Outdoor seating, friendly staff, and a brightly lit interior complete this casual dining experience. Try the *spaghettini* with mushrooms for a taste of traditional Trentino cuisine. *Menù del giorno* €15. Primi €6.50. Secondi €8.50. Cover €1.20. Open M-Sa 11:30am-2:30pm and 7-9:30pm. AmEx/D/MC/V. ❸

La Cantinota, V. San Marco 22/24 (☎0461 23 85 27). From the station, turn right and then left on V. Roma, which becomes V. San Marco. Sip sparkling wine in the elegant upstairs dining room or indulge in traditional gnocchi with pesto, arugula, and green beans in the trattoria downstairs. Primi €7-12. Secondi €12-14. Restaurant open Sept.-July M-W and Su noon-3pm and 7:30-11pm, F 7:30-11pm. MC/V. ❹

La Gelateria, V. Belanzani 50, near P. del Duomo. This colorful *gelateria* serves up intimidatingly large scoops of rich gelato—exotic flavors include violet and 2 different types of pistachio. 3 huge scoops €2.40. Open daily 11:30am-11:30pm. Cash only. ❶

📷 SIGHTS

PIAZZA DEL DUOMO. Trent's P. del Duomo offers everything from religious history to modern shops and services. At the **Fontana del Nettuno** in the center of the *piazza*, a majestic Neptune waves his trident as merpeople spit incessantly at his feet. Nearby stands the **Cattedrale di San Vigilio.** Its majestic interior housed the historical Council of Trent (1545-1563), which standardized Catholic traditions during the Counter-Reformation. Dark, rich art adorns the massive incense-filled building, illuminated by sunlight and clusters of votive candles. *(Open daily 7-11:45am and 2:45-7pm. Free.)* Underneath, the **Basilica Paleocristiana di San Vigilio,** entered from the left of the altar, displays religious artifacts and statues uncovered in excavations near the *duomo. (Open M-Sa 10am-noon and 2:30-5:30pm. €1.50, ages 12-18 €1. Free admission with ticket to Museo Diocesano.)*

MUSEO DIOCESANO TRIDENTINO. The **Museo Diocesano** was officially reopened by Pope John Paul II in 1995 after renovations were made to the tapestries, paintings, and illuminated manuscripts from regional churches. The museum offers insight into the importance of the diocese, local history, and politics. The eight elaborate Flemish tapestries on the museum's second floor that depict the Passion of Christ once decorated the hall where sessions of the Council of Trent were held. *(P. del Duomo 18. ☎0461 23 44 19; www.museodiocesanotridentino. it. Open M and W-Su 9:30am-12:30pm and 2-5:30pm. Hours extended during exhibitions. Ticket counter closes 15min. before museum. €4, groups of 20 or more €2.50. Entrance includes access to Basilica Sotterranea di San Vigilio. Free audio tours in English, French, German, and Italian.)*

FREE TRENTO. Consider buying the Trento Card for free access to all museums (including special exhibitions), guided tours of wine cellars, public transportation, bike rental, discounts in fitness and wellness centers, and tours of the city. €10 for 24 hours; €15 for 48 hours. Available at the tourist office. Call ☎0461 21 60 00 for more information.

🎵 🎭 ENTERTAINMENT AND NIGHTLIFE

While Trent is fairly quiet at night, local bars and lively restaurants provide visitors with some action. At **Osteria Trentina,** V. Roma 48, cozy seating and live jazz keeps a hip young crowd happy. (☎0461 23 88 41. Wine €2-3.50. Open M-Th 10am-10pm, F 10am-2:30pm and 6pm-2am, Sa 6pm-2am. Cash only.) **Supercinema Vittoria,** 72 V. G. Manci, screens the latest hits and offers deals on Monday. (☎0461 23 52 84; www.cineworld.info. Tickets €7.50.)

BOLZANO (BOZEN) ☎0471

Bolzano (bohl-ZAH-no; pop. 100,000) is most famous for 5000-year-old Ötzi the Iceman, a partially decayed body found frozen in 1991, held in the South Tyrol Museum of Archaeology. The best sights in the city, however, don't charge admission. Winter hikers climb to the snowy peaks, while summer visitors bike along the crystal-green Talvera River, wander up the stone pathway to Castel Roncolo, or gaze at the steep hills, resplendent with rows of grape vines. Whether it is the *duomo*'s mixed architecture or the city's two languages, Italian and German, Bolzano seems to rise above national borders.

🚉 TRANSPORTATION

Trains: in P. Stazione (☎0471 48 89 93). Ticket office open daily 6am-8:50pm. Info office open M-Sa 8am-7pm, Su 9am-1pm and 2-5pm. Customer service open daily 7am-9pm. To: **Bologna** (3hr., 16 per day 5:11am-3:36am, €20); **Bressanone** (30min., 33 per day 4:32am-10:40pm, €3.25); **Trent** (45min., 36 per day 1am-10:49pm, €3);

Venice (3hr., 1 per day, €16); **Verona** (1hr., 31 per day 3:36am-9:31pm, €10); **Munich, DEU** (4hr., 8 per day 2:25am-6:32pm).

Buses: SAD, V. Perathoner 4 (☎0471 45 01 11), between train station and P. Walther. Bus station and tourist office distribute bus schedules for travel to the western Dolomites. **Luggage storage** available. MC/V. Office open M-Sa 7am-7:25pm, Su 7am-1:15pm.

Funiculars: 3 cableways, located at the edges of Bolzano, carry visitors to nearby mountain towns. For info, visit either the tourist office or the alpine info office.

Funivia del Colle, V. Campiglio 7 (☎0471 97 85 45). The world's oldest cableway leads from V. Campiglio to **Colle** or **Kohlern** (9min., every 30-60min., daily June-Sept. 7am-noon and 1-7:30pm, Oct.-May 7am-noon and 1-7pm. €3, round-trip €4; children under 14 and adults over 65, €1.50; bikes €2.) No baggage or dogs allowed.

Funivia San Genesio, V. Rafenstein 15 (☎0471 97 84 36), off V. Sarentino, across the Talvera River, near Ponte Sant'Antonio. Connects Bolzano to **Salto's** high plateaus (8min., every 30 minutes, daily from mid-June to mid-Sept. 10am-12:30pm and 2:30-7pm, from mid-Sept. to mid-June 9am-12:30pm and 2:30-6pm. €3.50; €2 per bike.)

Public Transportation: SASA (☎0471 45 01 11). All lines stop in P. Walther or the station at V. Perathoner 4. Buy tickets (€1) at *tabaccherie* or from machines near stops.

Taxi: Radiofunk Taxi, V. Perathoner 4 (☎0471 98 11 11; www.ratabz.it.) 24hr.

Bike Rental: Run by the **Cooperativa Sociale** (☎0471 97 55 92), on Vle. Stazione, right off P. Walther. Main office at V. Carduci 9. 1st 6hr. €1, over 7hr. €2. Whole day €5. Deposit required. Open M-Sa Apr.-Oct. 7:30am-7:50pm. Cash only.

🔲 7 ORIENTATION AND PRACTICAL INFORMATION

The *centro storico* lies between the **train station** and the **Talvera River** (*Talfer Fluss*). All major *piazze* are within walking distance. Visitors should consider renting bikes, Bolzano's transportation of choice. Street and *piazze* names appear in Italian and German, and most maps mark both. From the bus stop, follow **Via Alto Adige** (*Südtirolerstrasse*) to **Piazza Walther** (*Waltherplatz*) and the *duomo*. Farther along, **Piazza del Grano** leads directly to **Via Portici** (*Laubenstrasse*). Here, German and Italian merchants set up shop on opposite sides of the arcade. To reach **Ponte Talvera,** take V. Portici past **Piazza delle Erbe.**

Tourist Office: AST, P. Walther 8 (☎0471 30 70 00; www.bolzano-bozen.it). Offers 2hr. guided tours of the city's museums and churches (M and Sa 10:30am, €5), and horseback-riding trips. Also publishes *Bolzano a Passeggio,* a guide to 14 walks in the surrounding hills. Open M-F 9am-1pm and 2-7pm, Sa 9am-2pm. **Alpine Info: Club Alpino Italiano (CAI),** P. delle Erbe 46, 2nd fl. (☎0471 97 81 72). Ring bell. Info on hiking, climbing, and tours. Open Tu, Th, F 1-5pm, W 11am-1pm, 5-7pm.

Currency Exchange: Banca Nazionale del Lavoro, P. Walther 10, next to tourist office. Good rates. Open M-F 8:20am-1:20pm and 2:30-4pm.

Bookstore: Athesiabuch, 41 V. Portici (☎0471 92 72 85). Well-stocked bookstore also carries CDs, software videogames, and magazines. English section is limited to mostly classics. Open M-F 9am-7pm, Sa 9am-6pm.

Laundromat: Lava e Asciuga, V. Rosmini 81, near Ponte Talvera. Wash €3 (€5 for 2 loads), dry €3. Detergent €1. Open daily 7:30am-10:30pm.

Pharmacy: Farmacia all'Aquila Nera, V. Portici 46/B. Open M-F 8:30am-12:30pm and 3-7pm, Sa 8:30am-12:30pm. After-hours rotation posted outside.

Hospital: Ospedale Regionale San Maurizio (☎0471 90 81 11), on V. Lorenz Böhler.

Internet Access: MultiKulti, V. Dott Streiter 9 (☎0471 05 60 56; www.multikulti.info), 1 street past V. Portici. €3 per hr. Also offers international calling, money transfer, and fax. Open M-Sa 10am-10pm, Su noon-10pm. Cash only. **Caffè Brennpunkt,** V. Brennero

7 (☎0471 98 29 53), is a slick bar with 2 even slicker flat-screen computers. €1 per 15min. Open M-W and Su 7:30am-8pm, Th-F 7:30am-1am, Sa 7:30am-2pm.

Post Office: Palazzo della Posta 13 (☎0471 32 22 81), by the *duomo*. Open M-F 8am-6:30pm, Sa 8am-12:30pm. **Postal Code:** 39100.

> **TIP**
>
> **RIDOTTO!** Bolzano offers two Museum Cards, which grant holders the *ridotto* price of entry to the city's museums and sights. With the purchase of any museum ticket, you receive a booklet of one-time use cards for many of the city's important museums. Alternatively, pay €2.50 for a card and receive a 20% discount every time you visit one of the city's surrounding museums and castles. Check the tourist office or participating museums for details.

 ACCOMMODATIONS AND CAMPING

The tourist office lists affordable *agriturismi* options, but most require private transportation—rent a bicycle and enjoy the countryside or reserve ahead for the inexpensive accommodations in the *centro*.

Youth Hostel Bolzano, V. Renon 23 (☎0471 30 08 65; www.ostello.bz). From train station, turn right onto V. Renon. Squeaky clean rooms, friendly staff, and bountiful amenities make this new hostel a great deal. Kitchen access until 10pm. Excellent breakfast buffet included. Showers in the room, lockers, and linens free. Laundry €2 wash, €2 dry. Internet access €2 per hr. Reception 8am-4am. Check-in 1pm. Check-out 9am. Dorms €19.50; singles €22. €2 surcharge for 1-night stay. AmEx/MC/V. ❶

Garni Eisenhut-Cappello di Ferro, V. Bottai 21 (☎0471 97 83 97; www.cappellodiferro.com). 1 block north of P. Walther, follow V. Bottai out of P. Municipio. Accommodating, English spoken. Small, comfortable rooms with bath and TV. Breakfast included; ½- and full pension options available. Singles €50; doubles €80. Extra bed €25. MC/V. ❸

Hotel Regina, V. Renon 1 (☎0471 97 21 95; www.hotelreginabz.it), 5min. from P. Walther. From the train station, take a right; hotel is across the street. Snug rooms mostly overlook a busy street, which makes for a noisy stay, though some have views of the green mountains that loom over Bolzano. All rooms have private bath, TV, and phone. Breakfast and linens included. Internet access €1.50 per 30 min. Parking €1.50 per hr. Singles €55-65; doubles €83-100; triples €108-120. MC/V. ❹

Schwarze Katz, Stazione Magdalena di Sotto 2 (☎0471 97 54 17; schwarze.katz@virgilio.it), near V. Brennero, 20min. from the city center. From the train station, turn right at V. Renon; keep left as you pass the cable car station, and look for signs; walk uphill into the steep driveway. Simple, spacious rooms in this family-run hostel have TV and free Internet access. Most rooms use shared bathrooms. Breakfast included. Reception open in summer M-Sa 7am-10pm; in winter M-F 7am-midnight, Sa 7am-9pm. Reservations recommended. Singles €25-30; doubles €60. AmEx/MC/V. ❷

Moosbauer, V. San Maurizio 83 (☎0471 91 84 92; www.moosbauer.com). Take SAD bus toward Merano; ask driver to stop at Moosbauer. Beautifully tended, off-the-beaten-path campground has pool, bar, restaurant, Internet cafe (€0.10 per min.), market, and playground. Friendly English-speaking staff has brochures on local activities. Convenient to nearby trails for hikers looking for a relaxing stay. Showers included. Laundry €3, dry €3. Reception open 8am-9pm daily. Reservations require a €50 down payment and 3-night min. stay. Entrance fee €5.50-6 per car. Tent/RV sites €12.50-16, includes water and electricity. €7.50-8.50 per adult, €5-6 per child, €3.50-4 per dog, €5.50-6 per tent. No tent rentals. 10% discount for those staying 10 days with cash payment. MC/V. ❶

Hotel Luna (Mondschein), V. Piave 15 (☎0471 97 56 42 www.hotel-luna.it info@hotel-luna.it). From P. Walther, walk to V. Portici. Turn right until it becomes V. Piave; Hotel Luna is on the left. Elegant garden terrace provides a peaceful refuge from the bustle of the *piazza*. Spacious rooms with TV, minibars, private bath, and Internet. Breakfast €11; half and full board available. Singles €95; doubles €142. ❺

⌨ FOOD

For a full smorgasbord of Bolzano's hybrid cuisine, start with a bowl of *rindgu- lasch* (beef stew); then try *wurst* (spicy sausage), *speck* (smoked bacon that tops pizzas and breads across mainland Italy), and Hearty *knödel* (dumplings). For dessert, chose from three types of flaky strudel: *apfel* (apple), *topfen* (soft cheese), and *mohn* (poppyseed). An all-day **market** in P. delle Erbe and along V. della Roggia has sold fine produce, cheese, baked goods, and meats since 1295. (Open M-F 7am-7pm, Sa 7am-1pm.) A **Despar** supermarket, is on the corner of V. della Rena. (☎0471 97 07 46. Open M-F 8:15am-7:15pm, Sa 8am-6pm.)

▨ **Hopfen & Co.,** P. delle Erbe 17 (☎0471 30 07 88, www.boznerbier.it). Housed in an 800-year-old building. No-frills pub, perfect for beer lovers and carnivores. Hearty Bavar- ian menu. At night, a young clientele spills out onto the street, gathering in nearby vacated vendor stands. Beer from €1.90-4.50. Specialty plates for 2 (€12-23) leave customers satisfied. Cover €1. Open M-Sa 9:30am-1am. MC/V. ❷

Exil Lounge, P. del Grano 2 (☎0471 97 18 14). To the *wurst*-intolerant traveler's delight, this colorful cafe in the heart of town offers a diverse selection of healthy salads and sandwiches. Perfect lunch treats include baguettes with grilled vegetables, mozzarella, and pesto as well as yogurt bowls with granola and seasonal fruit. Extensive tea, wine, and drink list. Open M-W 10am-midnight, Th-Sa 10am-1am. Cash only. ❷

Lowengrube, P. Dogana 3 (☎0471 97 68 48). The name of this Bolzano favorite, which opened in 1543, translates from German to "the place of the lion." Cheerful Austrian decor surrounds crowds of locals who attest to its popularity as a lunch spot. Primi €6.50-8.50. Secondi €12-19.50. Beer €1.60. Open daily 8am-1am. MC/V. ❸

Hostaria Argentieri, V. Argentieri 14 (☎0471 98 17 18). Flower-lined patio and quiet, candlelit tables provide a romantic evening at this upscale fish restaurant. Customers choose from a limited but tasty, handwritten menu. Primi €3.50-10. Secondi €7.50-30. Cover €1.50. Open M-Sa noon-2:30pm and 7-10:30pm. AmEx/MC/V. ❹

Trattoria Bar Nadamas, P. delle Erbe 44. What little nightlife Bolzano has to offer is cen- tered around P. delle Erbe, mostly due to its cheap drinks. A slightly more mature crowd of locals and tourists fill the spacious, wood-furnished interior before gathering outside, drinks in hand. At lunch, enjoy bruschetta (€4.70), salads (€4-10.50) and a wide selec- tion of *antipasti* (€4-8.20). Glasses of wine and beer from €1. Open M-Sa 9am-1am. Kitchen open noon-2:30pm and 7-10:30pm. ❷

⊙ SIGHTS

DUOMO. The bell tower's spined hollow spire and the ornate masonry around its eaves demonstrate Bolzano's transition from Romanesque to Gothic reli- gious architecture, while paintings, frescoes and statues line the walkways inside. (*P. Walther. Open M-F 10am-noon and 2-5pm. Free.*)

SOUTH TYROL MUSEUM OF ARCHAEOLOGY. Tourists at this museum file by the giant refrigerator that houses **Ötzi,** the 5000-year-old Neanderthal discov- ered by hikers in the Alps in 1991. Ötzi has his own floor, where English-lan- guage displays chart the extensive investigations archeologists have made of his daily life. (*V. Museo 43, near Ponte Talvera. ☎0471 32 01 00; www.iceman.it. Open Tu-Su 10am-5:30pm; July-Aug. and Dec. also open M. Wheelchair-accessible. €8, students and seniors €6, under 6 free. Multilingual audio tours €2.*)

CASTEL RONCOLO. This medieval fortress looks more like a Disney wonderland. Lavish wall frescoes narrate the legend of Tristan and Isolde. The winding stone path to the castle and the connector between the museum's two wings offer spectacular views of the mountains and city below. *(V. Sant'Antonio 15. Take city bus #12 from P. Walther to the Funivia stop, then go up V. Weggerstein to V. San Antonio. Ask at the ticket desk about the free bus for tourists back to P. Walther. ☎ 0471 32 98 08; www.roncolo. info. Open Tu-Su 10am-6pm. Gates for frescoes close 5:30pm. €8; groups of 10 or more, students, and seniors €5.50. Guided tour supplement €2.70.)*

⊂ NIGHTLIFE

While most of Bolzano's activities center on hiking, camping, and bicycle trips through the city and surrounding mountains, those seeking a fun evening should head to **Piazza Erbe**, where hordes of young people gather on the street. With beer from **Hopfen & Co.**, a lively crowd, and an informal atmosphere, visitors are sure to enjoy themselves on a warm summer evening.

FRIULI-VENEZIA GIULIA

Bounded by the Veneto to the west and Slovenia to the east, Friuli-Venezia Giulia (free-OO-lee veh-NETS-ya JOOL-ya) was once several distinct provinces united only by a common clergy in the sixth through 15th centuries. The Hapsburgs claimed the area in the early 1700s as an economic stronghold for Austria and Hungary. Since then, the region has changed hands multiple times, with each new occupant leaving its mark on local cuisine, culture, and architecture. Its natural beauty also draws from varied sources; serene lakes and jagged peaks characterize the north, while dramatic views of the Adriatic Sea shape the coastal regions. James Joyce wrote the bulk of *Ulysses* in the coffeehouses that still dot Trieste, while Ernest Hemingway found inspiration for *A Farewell to Arms* in the region's Carso cliffs. Although smaller towns retain their idyllic charm, Friuli-Venezia Giulia's cultural mixing pot and growing metropolises are what make it one of Italy's most cosmopolitan provinces.

HIGHLIGHTS OF FRIULI-VENEZIA GIULIA

INDULGE in the cuisine of Trieste, Italy's gateway to central Europe (p. 266).

RUMMAGE through ruins at Aquileia, a former Roman city on the Adriatic.

SUNBATHE on the beautiful beaches of Lignano.

TRIESTE ☎040

After volleying between Italian, Austrian, and Slavic allegiances for hundreds of years, Trieste (tree-YE-steh; pop. 241,000) has finally settled down, celebrating its 50th anniversary as an Italian city in 2004. Yet subtle reminders of Trieste's Central European past remain in its architecture, cuisine, and artwork. Locals strut along bustling waterfront *piazze*, while the natural beauty of the Carso cliffs and the Adriatic Sea complement Trieste's constant excitement.

⌐ TRANSPORTATION

Flights: Aeroporto Internazionale di Ronchi dei Legionari (Gorizia) V. Aquileia 46 (☎0481 77 32 24; www.aeroporto.fvg.it. Ticket office: 04 81 77 32 32), 20km from the centro. **Bus-Navetta** runs from the city to the airport (☎340 230 6444) and also has an outer city bus (☎040 42 50 20).

Trains: P. della Libertà 8 (☎040 89 20 21). Ticket counter open daily 6:05am-7:50pm. Info office open daily 7am-9pm. Trains run to **Udine** (1-2hr., 32 per day 5:02am-9:16pm, €6.70) and **Venice** (2hr., 29 per day 4:30am-9:25pm, €8.20).

Buses: P. della Libertà 11 (☎040 42 50 20), next to train station. Ticket office open M-Sa 6:25am-7:40pm, Su 6:30-11:05am. Buses depart for **Udine** as well as destinations in Croatia, Serbia, and Slovenia.

Ferries: Depart on a number of lines for **Albania.** Schedules and tickets can be found at Agemar Viaggi, P. Duca degli Abruzzi 1/A (☎040 36 37 37; fax 63 81 72; albania.bk@agemar.it), on the east side of C. Cavour. Open M-F 8:30am-1pm and 3-6:30pm.

Friuli-Venezia Giulia

Public Transportation: ACT buses travel to **Carso, Miramare,** and **Opicina.** Trieste Trasporti office located at V. d'Alviano. (www.triestetrasporti.it. Open M-Th 8:30am-3:30pm, F 8:30am-1pm. Purchase tickets at *tabaccherie.* €1 per hr., €3.30 per 24hr.)

Taxis: RadioTaxi (☎040 30 77 30).

⚡ 🚆 ORIENTATION AND PRACTICAL INFORMATION

The center of Trieste is a grid, bounded on the east by **Via Carducci,** which stretches south from **Piazza Oberdan** toward the historical Capitoline Hill. To the west, **Corso Italia** runs from the spectacular **Piazza dell'Unità d'Italia,** a vast square beside the harbor. The two streets intersect at busy **Piazza Goldoni.** Along C. Italia, just steps from P. dell'Unità d'Italia, lies **Piazza della Borsa,** the place where *triestini* come to see and be seen.

Tourist Office: APT, P. dell'Unità d'Italia 4/B (☎040 34 78 312; fax 34 78 320), has great info and lists of *manifestazioni* (artistic events). Open daily 9am-7pm. Audio tours (€4, 2 for €7; free with the FVG card) of the city available.

Luggage Storage: At the train station (☎040 83 06 68). 1st 12hr. €3, each 12hr. thereafter €2. Max. 2 bags. Open 7am-9pm. Storage also available at the bus station. €2.50 for 24hr. below 0.75 cubic meters, €3 for 24 hr. above 0.75 cubic meters.

Currency Exchange: Deutsche Bank, V. Roma 7 (☎040 63 19 25). Open M-F 8:20am-1:20pm and 2:35-3:35pm.

Pharmacy: Farmacia alla Borsa, P. della Borsa 12/A (☎040 36 83 56). Open M-F 8:30am-1pm and 4-7:30pm, Sa 8:30am-1pm. Posts after-hours rotations.

Internet Access: Bar Unità, Capo di P. Monsignor Antonio Santin 1/B (☎040 36 80 33). €4 per hr. Open M-Th and Su 6am-midnight, F-Sa 6am-3am. **Maranzina Service,** V. Milano 22/C (☎040 34 78 246; lucamaranzina@libero.it), off V. Carducci. €2 per hr. Offers fax, photocopy, and money transfer. Open M-Sa 9am-9pm. Cash only.

Post Office: P. Vittorio Veneto 1 (☎040 67 64 282), along V. Roma. From the train station, take 3rd right off V. Ghega. Open M-Sa 8:30am-7pm. **Postal Code:** 34100.

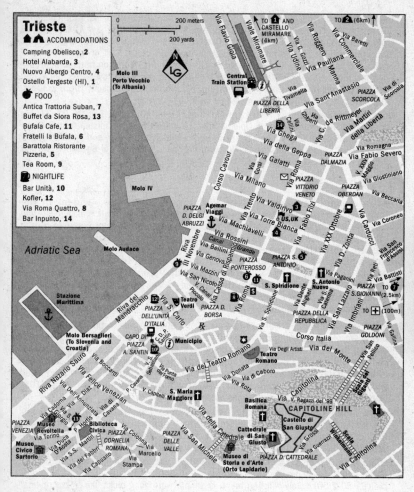

Trieste

🏨🏠 ACCOMMODATIONS

Camping Obelisco, **2**
Hotel Alabarda, **3**
Nuovo Albergo Centro, **4**
Ostello Tergeste (HI), **1**

🍴 FOOD

Antica Trattoria Suban, **7**
Buffet da Siora Rosa, **13**
Bufala Cafe, **11**
Fratelli la Bufala, **6**
Barattola Ristorante
  Pizzeria, **5**
Tea Room, **9**

🎵 NIGHTLIFE

Bar Unità, **10**
Kofler, **12**
Via Roma Quattro, **8**
Bar Inpunto, **14**

Adriatic Sea

FRIULI-VENEZIA GIULIA

🏨🏠 ACCOMMODATIONS AND CAMPING

Nuovo Albergo Centro, V. Roma 13 (☎040 34 78 790; www.hotelcentrotrieste.it). Centrally located hotel with sunny, spacious rooms with minibar, phone, fan or A/C, and satellite TV. Breakfast included. Internet access €4 per hr. Parking €14. Reception open 7:30am-midnight. Reservations require a deposit and are recommended for summer and weekend stays. Singles €37, with bath €52; doubles €54/72. AmEx/MC/V. ●

Hotel Alabarda, V. Valdirivo 22, 3rd fl. (☎040 63 02 69; www.hotelalabarda.it). From the station, head down C. Cavour and turn left on V. Valdirivo. Cheerful staff offers simple, clean rooms with satellite TVs. Breakfast included. Internet access free for 1st 30min., €2.50 per hr. thereafter. Singles €35, with bath €55; doubles €55-75. AmEx/MC/V. ●

Ostello Tergeste (HI), V. Miramare 331 (☎040 22 41 02; ostellotrieste@hotmail.com), 4km from the *centro*. Cross V. Miramare from the station to take bus #36 (every 10 min., last bus at 9pm, €1); ask for the Ostello stop and then walk 7min. to the hostel. Despite small rooms without locks, breathtaking views of the Gulf of Trieste from the patio and balcony make for a pleasant stay. Guests share a common bathroom. Breakfast included; dinner €9.50 on a lovely vine-covered patio that overlooks the water. Lockers €10 deposit. Reception 8-10am and 3:30pm-midnight. Lockout 10am-3:30pm. Midnight curfew. Dorms €16. HI members only. Cash only. ❶

Camping Obelisco, Strada Nuova per Opicina 37 (☎040 21 16 55; fax 21 27 44; campeggioclubtrieste@tin.it), in Opicina. Take Capolinea Tram di Opicina from P. Oberdan to Obelisco stop and follow the signs up the hill. Showers, bar, and parking. Sporting activities organized for guests. No tents provided. Reception Tu-Sa 9am-1pm and 2-6pm. €3.70-4.50 per person; €2.50-3 per tent. MC/V. ❶

🔆 FOOD

Trieste's cuisine has distinct Central European overtones, evident in the region's *sauerkraut*, strudel, and *iota* (sauerkraut, bean, and sausage stew). There's no shortage of quality seafood restaurants along Riva Nazario Sauro and Riva Gulli. The *alimentari* on V. Carducci provide an ideal place to eat on the cheap, while the hundreds of city cafes offer a chance to people-watch. There's a giant **PAM** supermarket, V. Miramare, across from the train station. (☎040 42 61 004. Open M-Sa 8am-8pm, Su 9am-9pm. MC/V.) At Trieste's covered **market,** V. Carducci 36/D, on the corner of Vle. della Majolica, dishware booths and magazine vendors peddle their wares amid vendors hawking fruits and cheeses. (Open M 8am-2pm, Tu-Sa 8am-5pm.)

🔲 **Buffet da Siora Rosa,** P. Hortis 3 (☎040 30 14 60). This family-run joint has served *triestini* favorites since it opened over 50 years ago. Try their porcini mushroom and pork sausage doused in *senape, kren,* and *crauti* (mustard, horseradish, and sauerkraut with cumin and juniper; €12.80). Other regional specialties prepared in their open kitchen include *jota* (bean soup with onions and turnips marinated in wine), goulash, and bread gnocchi. *Panini* €2.90-4.50. Cover €1. May-Sept. *piazza* seating service charge 10%. Open M-F 8am-9:30pm. Reservations recommended. MC/V. ❷

🔲 **Antica Trattoria Suban,** V. Comici 2 (☎040 54 368). Take bus #35 from P. Oberdan. Austro-Hungarian and Italian dishes are heavenly. Try the house specialty of crepes with basil (€7). Primi €6-8. Secondi €11-16. Cover €2.50. Open M 7-10:30pm, W-Su noon-3pm and 7-10:30pm. Closed Aug. Reservations recommended. AmEx/MC/V. ❸

Bufala Cafe, V. Roma 14 (☎040 06 44 208). If the dark lighting and loud tropical music don't hold allure, then the thick *panini* (€2.50-6), pizza (€2), and fresh focaccia (€1.80-2.50) surely will. The menu is simple with filling picks like *"Pizza ripiena"* (pizza stuffed with tomatoes and veggies; €3.50). Friendly service accompanies cheerful decor, making for a great lunch spot. Open M-Sa 7:30am-11pm. Cash only. ❶

🔘 SIGHTS

THE CENTRO

🔲**MUSEO REVOLTELLA.** Also known as the **Galleria d'Arte Moderna,** this museum displays temporary modern art exhibits and an extensive permanent collection that includes the work of Italian artists Francesco Hayez, Domenico Morelli, and Giacomo Favretto. The Revoltella Palace, built in 1858 under the direction of Friedrich Hitzig, is an ornate building with an older collection of Neoclassical works, while the more stark Brunner Palace holds modern works by artists such as still life painter Giorgio Morandi and proto-surrealist Giorgio De Chirico. Don't miss Magni's **Fontana della Ninfa Aurisiana,** a marble fountain of a woman representing Trieste. *(V. Diaz 21. ☎ 67 54 350; www.museorevoltella.it. Open M and W-Sa 9am-1pm and 4-7pm, Su 10am-7pm. Ticket sales end at 6:15pm. Guided tours Su 11am. Special tours of 20 or more people, €2. €5, students €3.)*

 TRIESTE FOR VIPS. A great way to experience Trieste is the **T For You Card.** The card (€10) is valid for 48 hours, and allows free admission to all civic museums, use of special motor ships, "Trieste by Bus" tours, and admission to the race-course, lighthouse, and beach resort at Grignano. Discounts are also offered at hotels, restaurants, shops, and theaters. Purchase one at the Central Travel Office, P. Unita d'Italia 6, or consult the tourist office.

CITTÀ NUOVA. The oldest areas in southern Trieste (the *Castelvecchia,* or "Old City") sport a tangle of roads in no discernible pattern. In the 1700s, Empress Maria Theresa of Austria commissioned a *città nuova* plan, which 19th-century Viennese urban planners implemented between the waterfront and the **Castello di San Giusto.** The resulting grid, lined with Neoclassical palaces, centers around the **Canale Grande,** where colorful rowboats bob past the pedestrian-only paths. Facing the canal from the south is the majestic Serbian Orthodox **Chiesa di San Spiridione,** an AD ninth-century church with blue domes and frescoes of biblical characters. *(Open Tu-Sa 9am-noon and 5-8pm, Su 9am-noon. Modest dress required.)* The vast **Piazza dell'Unità d'Italia,** Italy's largest waterfront square, provides a full view of the Adriatic coastline. On the eastern side of the *piazza,* the Municipio (Town Hall) faces the **Mazzoleni Fountain of the Four Continents,** which represents the world as it was known at the time of the fountain's completion in 1750.

PIAZZA DELLA CATTEDRALE. Climb to this hilltop *piazza* for a spectacular view of downtown Trieste and the Adriatic. At the edge of the *piazza,* a majestic statue covered in flowers and ribbons commemorates Trieste's fall in the War of Liberation. Across the street is the restored **Cattedrale di San Giusto,** created in the 14th century from two parallel churches: the original *Cattedrale* and **Santa Maria Assunta.** Inside, gray walls and humble archways are set off against glittering blue and gold mosaics at the main altar. Climb the *campanile* next door for a nice breeze and views of the city and Gulf. *(The site is reached by bus #24. ☎ 040 30 93 62. Open M-Sa 8am-noon and 2:30-6:30pm, Su 8am-8pm; closed to tourists Su mornings for mass. Cathedral free. Campanile €1.50, children under 6 years free. Printed guides €7.)*

CITY ENVIRONS

CASTELLO MIRAMARE. Archduke Maximilian of Austria commissioned this luxurious castle in the mid-19th century, intending its carefully tended flowers and lush greenery as a meditative respite from the bustle of the city. Each of the castle's carefully preserved rooms contains explanatory panels in English. Miramare's towers are easily visible from the Capitoline Hill in Trieste and most points along the **Barcola,** a boardwalk extending 7km between the Castello and Trieste. *(Take bus #36 to Ostello Tergeste and walk along the water for 15min. ☎ 040 22 41 43. Open M-Sa 9am-7pm, Su 8:30am-7pm. Ticket office open daily 9am-6:30pm. €4, EU citizens ages 18-25 €2, EU citizens under 18 or over 65 free. Guided tours in English €3.50; audio tours in multiple languages, including English €3.50, 2 for €5. Gardens open daily Apr.-Sept. 8am-7pm; Mar.-Oct. 8am-6pm; Nov.-Feb. 8am-5pm. Free.)*

FRIULI-VENEZIA GIULIA

♪ 🎭 ENTERTAINMENT AND NIGHTLIFE

On the second Sunday in October, Trieste stages the annual **Barcolana,** a regatta that blankets the harbor with thousands of billowing sails. The acclaimed **Teatro Verdi** hosts opera and ballet for six weeks from July to mid-August. Buy tickets or make reservations at the **box office,** Riva III Novembre 1. Enter on the P. Giuseppe Verdi side of the building. (☎040 67 22 298; www.teatroverdi-trieste. com. Open Tu-Su 9am-noon and 4-7pm. Tickets €8-40. AmEx/MC/V.)

The night heats up early at ⬛**Via Roma Quattro,** whose name is also its address. Funky orange decor, lively music, and comfy outdoor seating distinguish this central spot, where young trendsetters come for drinks. Thick *panini* (€3.50) stuffed with veggies and sliced meat also make it a great lunch spot. (☎040 63 46 33. Beer €2-4.10. Mixed drinks €3.50-6.20. Open M-Sa 7:30am-11pm. AmEx/ MC/V.) Trieste's *glitterati* are out in full force along the bars of **Capo di Piazza Monsignor Antonio Santin,** part of the pedestrian district that connects P. della Borsa and P. dell'Unità d'Italia. On summer evenings, the crowd gravitates toward fresh mixed drinks (€2.50-8), beer (€2-5), and *piazza* seating at **Bar Unità,** Capo di P. M. A. Santin 1/B, on the southwestern corner of P. dell'Unità d'Italia. (☎040 36 80 33. Internet access €4 per hour. Open M-Th and Su 6am-midnight, F-Sa 6am-3am. Cash only.) **Bar Inpunto,** V. Ghega 6, sports a dark interior with hanging plants, loud music, and sleek booths. (☎36 47 56; www.inpuntomu-sicbar.com. Beer €2.40-5. Mixed drinks €3-5.50. Open M-Sa 6am-2am. Cash only.) At **Kofler,** Riva del Mondracchio 14, Paulaner signs and a lion emblem adorn the walls. Huge interior accommodates a crowd at night and the bar up front serves an extensive menu of beer (€3-8), wine (€2.80-5), and hard liquor (€2.80-6.20). What's more, the view of the Adriatic can't be beat. (☎040 37 912. Open M-Th 7pm-2am, F-Sa 7pm-2:30am, Su 6:30pm-1:30am. MC/V.)

CIVIDALE DEL FRIULI   ☎0432

On the banks of the Natisone River, tiny Cividale (chee-vee-DAH-leh; pop. 11,000) is perhaps the most enchanting town in Friuli. Founded by Julius Caesar as Forum Iulii, Cividale eventually became the capital of the first Lombard duchy in AD 568 and later flourished as a meeting point for artists and nobility during the Middle Ages. Cividale, a mere 20min. train ride from Udine, draws visitors with its well-preserved medieval monuments and natural beauty.

🚉🛈 TRANSPORTATION AND PRACTICAL INFORMATION. Cividale is best reached by **train** from Udine (20min., 25 per day 6:33am-11:33pm, €2.10). Buy tickets in the Udine train station. The train station, Vle. Libertà 43, is near the *centro.* (☎0432 73 37 16.) For a **taxi,** call ☎3396 59 10 14. To reach the *centro* from the station, take **Via Guglielmo Marconi.** Turn left through the stone gate, **Porta Arsenale Veneto,** when Vle. G. Marconi ends. Cross **Piazza Dante** and turn right on **Via San Pellico,** then left on **Largo Boiani;** the *duomo* is straight ahead. To reach the **tourist office,** P. Paolo Diacono 10, take C. Giuseppe Mazzini from P. Duomo to its end. The office offers free **Internet** access and serves as an **Infor-magiovani** to help young people find work. (☎0432 71 04 60; www.cividale.net. Open daily 9:30am-noon and 3:30-6pm.) In case of emergency, contact the **police,** P. Armando Diaz 1 (☎0432 70 61 11). Services include: **Farmacia Minisini,** Largo Boiani 11 (open M 3:30-7:30pm, Tu-F and Su 8:30am-12:30pm and 3:30-7:30pm, Sa 8:30am-12:30pm; MC/V); **Ospedale Cividale,** P. dell'Ospedale, south of the Nati-sone river (☎0432 70 81); and the **post office,** Largo Boiani 37-39 (☎0432 70 57 11; open M-F 8:30am-7pm, Sa 8:30am-1pm). **Postal Code:** 33043.

C **ACCOMMODATIONS AND FOOD.** Quiet Cividale lacks a wide variety of budget accommodations, but the tourist office lists available *affittacamere* (rooms for rent). **Casa Franca,** V. Alto Adige 15, is a 10 minute walk from the train station. Turn left from the station, then left on V. Bottego and follow it until it becomes V. San Moro; V. Alto Adige is the first street on the left. This large accommodation has two doubles, one single, a shared bathroom, kitchen, and lounge. (☎0432 73 40 55. Breakfast €5. Price upon request; call ahead. Cash only.) Find warm service at the family-run **Locanda Al Pomo d'Oro ➍,** P. San Giovanni 20, a restored medieval inn from the sixth century. Though close to the *centro*, the secluded atmosphere makes for a quiet, cozy stay. Rooms have TV, fridge, safe, and private bath. (☎0432 73 14 89; www.alpomodoro.com. Breakfast included. Wheelchair-accessible. Check-in by 6pm. Singles €60; doubles €80. AmEx/MC/V.) The few rooms at **B&B La Casa Dai Toscans ➌,** C. Mazzini 15, are spacious, sunny, and elegantly furnished with private bath and TV. Traditional or American breakfast served in a cozy breakfast nook. (☎3490 76 52 88; www.lacjasedaitoscans.it. Singles €40; doubles €70. Cash only.)

Regional culinary specialties include *stakanje* (a puree of potatoes and seasonal vegetables) and *gubana* (a large fig- and prune-filled pastry laced with *grappa*). Try the flaky *gubana* (€0.75) at **Cattarossi V. di Blasutig Alberto ➊,** C. Paolino d'Aquileia 10, where owner Alberto has amassed a loyal following over the last few decades with his consistently mouth-watering pastries. (☎0432 73 21 52. Open M-Sa 7:30am-11pm and 3:30-8pm, Su 8:30am-1pm and 2:30-8pm. Cash only.) **Antica Osteria alla Speranza ➌,** P. Foro Giulio Cesare 15, across from the post office, offers delicious plates like *linguine al pesto di Rucola* (€7) under frescoed ceilings or among hanging plants in its back courtyard. (☎0432 73 11 31. Primi €7. Secondi €9-12. Cover €1.20. Open M, W-F, and Su 10am-2:30pm and 5pm-midnight, Sa 9am-2:30pm and 5pm-midnight. MC/V.) For more upscale dining, **Alla Frasca ➌,** V. Stretta de Rubeis 11, serves traditional pasta in elegant booths or at outside tables under a leafy canopy. (☎0432 73 12 70; www.allafrasca.it. Primi €7-8. Secondi €12-19. Cover €2. Open Tu-Su 10:30am-3pm and 6:30pm-midnight. AmEx/MC/V.) **Coopca,** V. Adelaide Ristori 15, sells groceries. (☎0432 73 11 05. Open M and W 8:30am-12:45pm, Tu and Th-Su 8:30am-12:45pm and 4-7:30pm. Cash only.)

S **SIGHTS.** The dark, gray-stone interior of the *centro*'s 15th- and 16th-century **duomo** houses the Renaissance sarcophagus of Patriarch Nicolò Donato, left of the entrance. Five stained-glass windows at the apse illuminate the dim church and the magnificent silver altarpiece of Pellegrino II dating from 1194-1204. Annexed to the *duomo* is the **Museo Cristiano,** displaying the *Battistero di Callisto*, commissioned by the first Aquileian patriarch in Cividale, and the *Altar of Ratchis*, a Lombard sculpture from AD 740. (☎0432 70 12 11. *Duomo* and museum open M-Sa 9:30am-noon and 3-6pm, Su 3-6pm. Free.) Circle around the right side to the back of the *duomo* and follow Riva Pozzo di Callisto to the bottom of the stairs where signs point to **Tempietto Longobardo,** an AD 8th-century sanctuary whose original purpose remains a mystery. Built on the remains of a Benedictine convent, it houses a remarkable collection of frescoes and stucco figures. *The Procession of Virgins and Martyrs*, which stares down from a high perch, is rumored to have been painted by a Muslim who fled westward to avoid persecution for his religious art. Follow the rocky ledge overlooking the emerald green Natisone River to the museum's entrance. (☎0432 70 08 67. Open Apr.-Sept. M-F 9:30am-12:30pm and 3-6:30pm, Sa-Su 9:30am-1pm and

3-7:30pm; Oct.-Mar. M-F 9:30am-12:30pm and 3-5pm, Sa-Su 9:30am-12:30pm and 2:30-6pm. €2.50, students €1.) The elegant Venetian **Superintendent's Palace,** P. Duomo 13, designed by Andrea Palladio, houses the **Museo Archaelogico Nazionale.** Recovered mosaics from Roman and Early Christian times, tombstones of Jewish residents, and Romanesque reliefs occupy the ground floor, while the extensive collection of jewelry found at Longobard funerary sites occupies the first. English and Italian explanations trace the Longobard rule in Cividale up to the Carolingian period in the AD ninth century. (☎0432 70 07 00. Open M 9am-2pm, Tu-Su 8:30am-7:30pm. Last entry 30min. before closing. Tickets €2, ages 18-25 €1, under 18 and over 65 free.) From the *duomo,* follow C. Paolino d'Aquileia to **Ponte del Diavolo,** a 15th-century stone bridge set between cliffs 22m above the **Natisone River.** The bridge, now a symbol for the city itself, was named for Lucifer, who allegedly allowed the bridge to stand in exchange for the first soul to cross. The tricky townspeople got the better of Lucifer by sending an unsuspecting cat across first. Head behind the Chiesa San Martino for another lookout point on the river from the balcony along the steep banks. From there, turn off C. P. d'Aquileia on Vle. Monastero Maggiore right before the bridge to explore the dim, steep stone tunnels of **Ipogeo Celtico,** Monastero Maggiore 10, an ancient Roman prison with open-jawed skulls engraved in the walls, remnants of its former use as a graveyard. (Open Tu-Su 7am-3pm. Free.) For the key, visit **Bar all'Ipogeo,** Monastero Maggiore 2, or call the **Informagiovani** (☎0432 71 04 60).

█ NIGHTLIFE. Cividale doesn't offer much in the way of nightlife, but the town's center is the place to find what little there is. By night, █**Caffe San Marco** attracts a youthful yet refined clientele with its swanky red-and-silver lounge, live jazz, and late hours. (☎0432 73 10 01. Beer €2.30-4.30. Wine €1.50-3. Open M-Th 7:30am-1am, F 7:30am-3am, Sa-Su 8:30am-3am. Cash only.) **Bea Caffe,** 16 V. Alessandro Manzoni, is an eclectic hub with hanging lanterns, American rock music, *calcio* paraphernalia, and posters of Mt. Rushmore. Although the eye-catching interior is tough to turn down, small tables are also available outside. (Beer €2. Open daily 7am-2am. Cash only.)

EMILIA-ROMAGNA

Italy's wealthiest wheat- and dairy-producing region, Emilia-Romagna (eh-MEE-lya ro-MAN-ya) spans the Po River Valley's fertile plains and is home to some of the peninsula's finest culinary traditions. Gorge on Parma's famous *parmigiano-reggiano* and prosciutto, Bologna's fresh *spaghetti alla bolognese* and *mortadella*, and Ferrara's *grana* cheese and *salama*. Complement the local specialties with regional wines like the sparkling red *Lambrusco*. Although the Romans originally settled this region, most of the visible ruins are medieval, and today's travelers find urban scenes that have escaped the oppressive tourism of other major Italian cities. Visitors will enjoy enough peace and quiet to contemplate Emilia-Romagna's art and natural beauty.

HIGHLIGHTS OF EMILIA-ROMAGNA

ABSORB the Byzantine influence through Ravenna's world-famous mosaics (p. 283).

PARTY with students and backpackers at the notorious clubs in Rimini (p. 292).

BOLOGNA ☎ 051

Affectionately referred to as the *grassa* (fat) and *dotta* (learned) city, Bologna (bo-LOHN-ya; pop. 370,000) has a legacy of excellent food, education, and art. While the Po Valley provides tables with hearty egg pasta and savory local wines, Bologna's museums and churches house priceless artistic treasures. The city is also home to Europe's oldest university—a law school founded in 1088 to settle disputes between the Holy Roman Empire and the Papacy. After taking in free sights, unbelievable food, and the lively student-based nightlife, travelers leave Bologna more than satisfied with their taste of *la dolce vita*.

⬛ TRANSPORTATION

Flights: Aeroporto Guglielmo Marconi (☎051 64 79 615; www.bologna-airport.it), at Borgo Panigale, northwest of the *centro*. The Aerobus (☎051 29 02 90) runs to the airport from Track D outside the train station and makes stops at several locations in the *centro* (every 15min. 5:20am-11:40pm, €5).

Trains: Ticket office open 5:30am-11:30pm. Info office (☎051 89 20 21). Open daily 7am-9pm. West platform disability assistance (☎199 30 30 60) is open daily 7am-9pm. To: **Florence** (1hr., 38 per day 5:15am-10:08pm, €5.10); **Milan** (3hr., 40 per day 4:12am-10:16pm, €19); **Rome** (3hr., 46 per day 12:44am-8:46pm, €32); **Venice** (2hr., 30 per day 3:18am-11:20pm, €8.20).

Buses: Terminal Bus (☎051 24 21 50), next to ATC ticket counter, provides Eurolines bus service. Open M-F 9am-6:30pm, Sa 8:30am-6pm, Su 3-6:30pm. Cash only.

Public Transportation: ATC (☎051 29 02 90) runs efficient buses that get crowded in the early afternoon and evening. Intra-city tickets (€1) are good 1hr. after onboard vali-

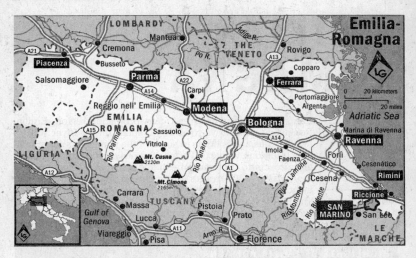

dation; 24hr. tickets €3. Purchase at newsstands, self-service machines, or *tabaccherie.* Buses #11, 20, and 27 run from the train station, up V. Indipendenza and down V. Rizzoli and from there, along V. S. Stefano, V. Barberia and Strada Maggiore, respectively.

Car Rental: Hertz, V. Amendola 16/A (☎051 25 48 30). Turn right from the train station, and left on V. Amendola. 25+. Open M-F 8am-8pm, Sa 8am-1pm. AmEx/MC/V.

Taxis: C.A.T. ☎051 53 41 41. **RadioTaxi** ☎051 37 27 27. 24hr.

✦ 🗹 ORIENTATION AND PRACTICAL INFORMATION

From the train station, turn left on **Viale Pietro Pietramellara,** and head to **Piazza XX Settembre.** From there, take **Via dell'Indipendenza,** which leads to **Piazza del Nettuno;** behind it is **Piazza Maggiore,** the *centro.* At P. del Nettuno, V. dell'Indipendenza intersects **Via Ugo Bassi,** which runs west, and **Via Rizzoli,** which runs east to **Piazza Porta Ravegnana. Via Zamboni** and **Strada Maggiore** lead out of this *piazza.*

> **❗ NO BOLOGNA.** Treat Bologna like a big city—use caution, and hold onto your wallet. At night, solo travelers should avoid the train station, the northern part of V. dell'Indipendenza, and the areas surrounding the university.

Tourist Office: P. Maggiore 1/e (☎051 23 96 60), in Palazzo del Podestà. Offers free accommodation booking through **CST** (☎800 85 60 65 or 23 47 35; www.cst.bo.it), guided city **tours,** and a list of Internet access points. Open daily 9:30am-7:30pm.

Budget Travel: CTS, Vle. Filopanti 4/M (☎051 23 73 07 or 23 75 01). Resources include ISICs (€10), train tickets, tour packages, and discounts on air and sea travel. Open M-F 9am-12:30pm and 2:30-6pm. MC/V.

Luggage Storage: At the train station. Max. bag weight 20kg. €3.80 for 1st 5hr., €0.60 per hr. up to 12hr., €0.20 per hr. thereafter. Open daily 6am-10pm. Cash only.

English-Language Bookstore: Feltrinelli International, V. Zamboni 7/B (☎051 26 80 70). Wide selection. Open M-Sa 9am-7:30pm. AmEx/MC/V.

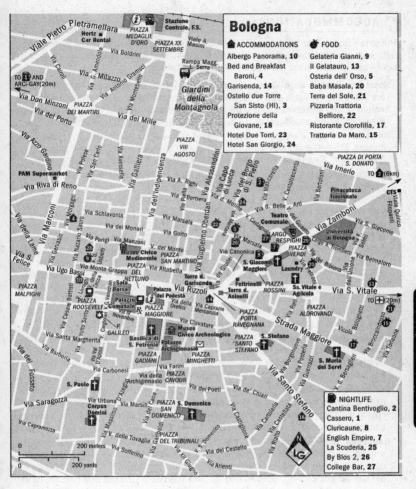

Bologna

ACCOMMODATIONS

Albergo Panorama, 10
Bed and Breakfast
Baroni, 4
Garisenda, 14
Ostello due Torre
San Sisto (HI), 3
Protezione della
Giovane, 18
Hotel Due Torri, 23
Hotel San Giorgio, 24

FOOD

Gelateria Gianni, 9
Il Gelatauro, 13
Osteria dell' Orso, 5
Baba Masala, 20
Terra del Sole, 21
Pizzeria Trattoria
Belfiore, 22
Ristorante Clorofilla, 17
Trattoria Da Maro, 15

NIGHTLIFE

Cantina Bentivoglio, 2
Cassero, 1
Cluricaune, 8
English Empire, 7
La Scuderia, 25
By Blos 2, 26
College Bar, 27

GLBT Resources: ARCI-GAY, V. Don Minzoni 18 (☎051 64 94 416; www.cassero.it). Library and counseling center. Open M-F 9am-7pm. **Cassero** nightclub downstairs (p. 279).

Laundromat: Lavarapido, V. Petroni 38/B, off P. Verdi, near V. Zamboni. Wash €3.40 per 8kg. Detergent €0.60. Open M-Sa 9am-9pm, Su 10:30am-9pm. Cash only.

Police: P. Galileo 7 (☎051 16 40 11 11).

24hr. Pharmacy: Farmacia Comunali AFM Bologna, P. Maggiore 6 (☎051 23 85 09).

Internet Access: Sportello Iperbole, P. Maggiore 6 (☎051 20 31 84). Wi-Fi, limit 3 hr. per day. Reserve a few days ahead for free Internet on public computers, limit 2hr. per week. Open M-F 8:30am-7pm, Sa 8:30am-2pm, 3-7pm; last use at 5:30pm.

Post Office: P. Minghetti 4 (☎051 80 31 60), southeast of P. Maggiore, off V. Farini. Exchanges currency. Open M-F 8am-6:30pm, Sa 8am-12:30pm. **Postal Code:** 40100.

ACCOMMODATIONS

Bologna's hotels are pricey and fill up quickly, especially during the September high season; reservations are recommended. The most affordable establishments are located near **Via Ugo Bassi** and **Via Marconi**.

Hotel Due Torri, V. degli Usberti 4 (☎/fax: 051 26 98 26 or 23 99 44). White flowers and glittering lights adorn the lobby of this charming hotel. Slightly cramped but well-furnished and quiet rooms have minibar, TV, phone, A/C, and free Internet access. Breakfast served amid floral decor. Singles €60-79; doubles €80-90. AmEx/MC/V. ❹

Hotel San Giorgio, V. Moline 17 (☎051 24 86 59; www.sangiorgiohotel.it). Conveniently located. Elegant, gold lobby. Spacious rooms with bath. Satellite TV. Breakfast included. Free Internet. Singles €55-60; doubles €85-90; triples €100-110. AmEx/MC/V. ❹

Albergo Panorama, V. Livraghi 1, 4th fl. (☎051 22 18 02; www.hotelpanoramabologna. it). From P. del Nettuno, take V. Ugo Bassi; take the 3rd left. Large rooms have TV. Breakfast included. Reception 7am-10pm. Check-in by 6pm. Singles €50; doubles €60-70, with private bath 80; triples €80-85/120; quads €90-95/140. MC/V. ❹

Ostello due Torre San Sisto (HI), V. Viadagola 5 (☎/fax 051 50 18 10), off V S. Donato, in Località di S. Sisto. Take bus #93 from V. Marconi 69 (15min., M-Sa every 30min. 6:05am-8:20pm). For late night service take 21B from in front of the train station (M-Sa every hr. 8:44pm-12:44am). On Su, take #301 from bus station (6 per day 7:30am-8pm). Exit at S. Sisto. Comfortable, but out-of-the-way hostel with basketball court, satellite TV, and DVDs. Breakfast included. Free lockers in room. Laundry €2.60 per load. Internet access €3.50 per hr. Wheelchair-accessible. Reception 7:30-10am and 3:30-11:30pm. Lockout 10am-2pm. Dorms €16; singles €23, with bath €25; doubles €38; family rooms €18 per person. HI-member discount €3. AmEx/MC/V. ❶

Bed and Breakfast Baroni, V. Morgagni 9 (☎340 29 41 752; www.bedandbreakfast-baroni.it). From V. Marconi, take a left onto V. Riva di Reno then a right onto V. Morgani. Centrally located B&B offers 3 colorful rooms in quiet area near the *centro.* Breakfast €5. Singles €35-45; doubles €55-65. AmEx/MC/V. ❹

Protezione della Giovane, V. S. Stefano 45 (☎051 22 55 73). Past the church, on the right. Buzz and climb the large staircase at the end of the hall. Frescoed ceilings and French windows. Check-in or call between 10am and 5pm. Curfew 10:30pm. Reservations recommended. 2- to 3-bed dorms €15. Women only. MC/V. ❶

Garisenda, Galleria Leone 1, 3rd fl. (☎051 22 43 69; www.albergogarisenda.com). Take V. Rizzoli and turn right into the gallery. A hallway lined with antiques leads to 7 spacious rooms with basic furnishings. Unbeatable location. Breakfast €5. Reserved parking €7 per day. Singles €45-55; doubles €65-85, with bath 85-110. Extra bed €30. MC/V. ❸

FOOD

Bologna is known for its stuffed pastas, such as tortellini in meat sauce or with ricotta and spinach, and for its salamis and hams, which include *mortadella,* a sausage-like creation that bears little resemblance to American bologna. Restaurants cluster on side streets near the *centro;* circle by **Via Augusto Righi, Via Piella,** and **Via Saragozza.** The area around **Via Petroni** has smaller, cheaper joints that cater mostly to students. Indoor **Mercato delle Erbe,** V. Ugo Bassi 27, sells produce, cheese, meat, and bread. (Open in summer M-W 7am-1:15pm and 5-7:30pm, Th and Sa 7am-1:15pm, F 7am-1:15pm and 4:30-7:30pm; in winter M-W and F 4:30-7:30pm. Cash only.) Buy essentials at **PAM** supermarket, V. Marconi 28/A. (Open M-Sa 7:45am-8pm, Su 9am-8pm. AmEx/MC/V.)

▨ **Osteria dell'Orsa,** V. Mentana 1/F (☎051 23 15 76; www.osteriadellorsa.com). Serves simple, fresh cuisine like homemade pasta (€6), panini (€5), *piadine* (round flatbread; €4-5), and big salads (€7). Try healthy, veggie-filled options like the "Macro" with brie, mushroom, arugula, corn, and artichoke (€5). Communal seating perfect for students before a night on the town. Wine €4 per 0.5L. Open daily noon-1am. MC/V. ❶

▨ **Terra del Sole,** V. Petroni 3/B (☎051 26 26 08). Small and student-friendly. Delicious Bolognese cuisine with a healthy twist. Daily menu of fresh pasta (€4.50), calzones (€2.20), and salads (€3.80). Try the *sformato pitta,* a savory baked gratin made from potatoes, onions, olives, capers, tomatoes, and ricotta (€3). Limited seating—try the nearby Piazza Verdi. Open M-F 11am-8pm. Cash only. ❶

Pizzeria Trattoria Belfiore, V. Marsala 11/A (☎051 22 66 41). Traditional Bolognese pasta and pizza (€2.60-6) served on a quiet street beneath soft, yellow arches and bamboo curtains. Try savory classics like tortelloni with ricotta, spinach, and tomatoes (€7) or *garganelli* with cream, prosciutto, and peas (€6.50). Primi €6-7.50. Secondi €7-9. Cover €2. Open M, W-Su 12:30-2:30pm and 7:30-12:30am. AmEx/MC/V. ❸

Ristorante Clorofilla, Strada Maggiore 64/C (☎051 23 53 43). "Eat your way to good health" is the motto at this wholesome organic eatery. The signature is couscous with tofu, vegetables, and tomato sauce (€6.50). Hot entrees €6-7.50. Salads from €4.50. Fresh juices €2.30. Cover €1. Organic beer and wine from €2.80. Open Jan.-July and Sept.-Dec. M-Sa noon-3pm and 7:30-11pm. AmEx/MC/V. ❷

Gelateria Gianni, V. Montegrappa 11 (☎051 23 30 08), at the corner of V. degli Usberti. Madly popular chain with 99 unthinkably decadent flavors, which include the "Samurai" (mascarpone, ricotta, and powdered cocoa). 1 scoop €1.80-2.20; 3 scoops €2.80-3.30. Open M-Tu and Th-Su noon-midnight. Cash only. ❶

Il Gelatauro, V. S. Vitale 98/B (☎051 23 00 49). This upscale *gelateria* churns out classics like *stracciatella* (vanilla with a chocolate swirl) as well as a large selection of creamy nut flavors like pistachio, almond, and pine nut (2 flavors €2.10; 3 flavors €2.40). Also has gourmet chocolates, truffles, and pastries. Open Jan.-July and Sept.-Dec. M 8am-7pm, Tu-Th 8am-11:30pm, F-Su 8am-11pm. Cash only. ❶

◉ SIGHTS

▨**PIAZZA MAGGIORE.** Aristotle Fioravanti, designer of Moscow's Kremlin, remodeled the Romanesque Palazzo del Podestà, now the boxy, brick home of varied cafes and shops that line its loggia. The 15th-century building is a feat of engineering: the weight of the palace rests entirely on columns. Directly across the *piazza* sits the **Basilica di San Petronio,** designed by Antonio da Vincenzo in 1390. The *bolognesi* originally plotted to make their basilica larger than St. Peter's in Rome, but the Vatican ordered that the funds be used to build the nearby Palazzo Archiginnasio. The cavernous Gothic interior hosted both the Council of Trent and ceremony where Pope Clement VII gave Italy to German Kaiser Karl V in 1530. Golden panels and cherubs fill the **Cappella di San Petronio,** left of the entrance, where opulence contrasts the basilica's predominantly bare walls. From the base of the nave nearby, a marble track dotted with constellation symbols and a single gold line extends across the church's floor to create the ▨**world's largest zodiac sundial.** Don't miss the main altar, which elevates ornate stone statues toward the arches above. The tiny museum contains models of the basilica, beautiful chalices, and illuminated books. (*P. Maggiore 3.* ☎*051 22 54 42. Open daily 7:45am-12:30pm and 3-6pm. Modest dress required. No bags or backpacks. Museum open M 9:30am-12:30pm and 3:30-6:30pm. Free.*)

EMILIA-ROMAGNA

ᵈ YOU CAN'T TAKE THE EAT, GET OUT OF THE KITCHEN

ᵗo take a little of the "fat" city ᵐome with you, try a class at any ᵒf Bologna's short-term culinary ᵍchools. Consult the tourist office ᵒr a complete listing.

La Vecchia Scuola Bolognese ᵗ051 64 93 627; www.lavec-ᵗhiascuola.com), the mother of ᵒcal cooking schools, offers a 4hr. ᵗourse topped off by a fabulous ᵐeal. Master the art of fresh pasta ᵂith help from a professional, ᴱnglish-speaking staff. When all ᵍ said and done, you'll get to eat ᵞour own pasta creations; if your ᵃttempts don't quite succeed, ᵞou'll still be served the school's ᵐenu of *bolognese* specialties.

La Cucina di Petronilla, V. ᵍan Vitale 53 (ᵗ051 22 40 11), ᵒffers group classes or one-on-one ᵉssons upon request. The courses ᵗocus on wine pairing with food ᵃnd cooking regional dishes. The ᵗhef believes in healthy organic ᵗuisine, but fear not: it's still ᵐearty *bolognese* fare.

La Cantina Bentivoglio (ᵗ051 ᵗ6 54 16; www.affari.com/ben-ivoglio), a classy restaurant offer-ᵗng delicious local cuisine and live ᵃzz as well as demonstrations ᵗhough not lessons) of the pasta-ᵐaking process. The price and ᵉngth of demonstrations vary, ᵍo call ahead to book a custom ᵍemo with the restaurant.

PALAZZO ARCHIGINNASIO. This *palazzo*, the first seat of the city's university, features thousands of names and coats-of-arms of past students. The building, constructed to consolidate the schools of the university, now houses the **Biblio-teca dell'Archiginnasio**, the university's main reading room and a city library with over 800,000 texts. Above the central courtyard's 30 arches sits the **Teatro Anatomico**, a lecture hall where bronze statues of famous doctors blend into the woodwork. A marble table marks where dissections took place beneath the starry ceiling decorations. *(V. Archiginnasio 1, next to the Museo Archeologico. Follow signs from P. Maggiore. ☎ 051 27 68 11. Palazzo open M-F 9am-6:45pm, Sa 9am-1:45pm. Closed 1st 2 weeks of Aug. Free.)*

PIAZZA DEL NETTUNO. This *piazza* contains Giam-bologna's 16th-century stone-and-bronze fountain *Neptune and Attendants*. Affectionately called "The Giant," a nude Neptune reigns over a collec-tion of water-babies and sirens spraying water from every bodily orifice. According to local legend, Pope Pious IV, who commissioned the statue, was disturbed by the large original size of Neptune's manhood and ordered Giambologna to change it. Giambologna, who agreed to alter the actual mem-ber, had the last laugh: standing near the steps of Sala Borsa, it appears as if Neptune is at his orig-inal—ahem—grandeur. Nearby, a wall of portrait tiles commemorates the Bolognese resistance to Nazi occupation, while a Plexiglas plaque lists the names and ages of the more recent victims of the 1974, 1980, and 1984 Bologna train bombings.

PINACOTECA NAZIONALE. The Pinacoteca displays religious artwork dating from the Ancient Roman era to the 18th century, with pieces by Giotto, Titian, and Giovanni Battista. **Gallery 15** contains works by Raphael and his Florentine followers, while **Gallery 24** has *Sampson Victorious* by Bolo-gna's own Guido Reni, and floor-to-ceiling *Pietà detta dei Mendicanti*. **Gallery 26** displays Fran-cesco Albani's beautiful *Madonna e Bambino*, and **Gallery 22** holds several large canvases, including Vasari's *Christ in Casa di Marta*. *(V. delle Belle Arti 56, off V. Zamboni. ☎ 051 42 09 411; www.pinacotecabologna.it. Open Tu-Su 9am-7pm. Last entry 30min. before closing. €4, EU students €2, under 18 and over 65 free. Cash only.)*

PALAZZO COMUNALE. Nicolò dell'Arca's terra-cotta *Madonna* and Alessandro Menganti's bronze statue of Pope Gregory XIV adorn the outside of this *palazzo*. The **Collezioni Comunali d'Arte** houses regional art from the 13th to the 20th century. The Rusconi wing displays furnishings from ornate

Bolognan homes, to the gorgeous **Sala Boschereccia,** where walls painted with serene landscapes and playful winged angels surround Baruzzi's 19th-century statue of Apollo. *(P. Maggiore 6. Office ☎ 051 21 93 526 or 21 93 629. Open Tu-F 9am-3pm, Sa-Su 10am-6:30pm. Free.)* If you're looking for secular art, don't miss the **Museo Morandi,** which displays luminous oil paintings and watercolors. It also features the reconstructed V. Fondazza studio of early 20th-century painter, Giorgio Morandi, along with his landscapes and muted oil still-lifes of jugs, cups, and bottles. *(P. Maggiore 6. ☎ 051 219 33 32 or 219 36 29; www.museomorandi.it. Wheelchair-accessible. Open Tu-F 9am-3pm, Sa-Su 10am-6:30pm. Free.)*

MUSEO CIVICO MEDIOEVALE. This collection contains all things *bolognese,* including images of its patron saints, wax seals of local nobility, an impressive set of sepulcher lids, and weaponry. Watch for a 17th-century dagger that shatters after stabbing its victims and the 17th-century Roman *Sileno con Otre,* a rare example of an obese antique marble statue. In the basement, funerary slabs depicting classroom scenes immortalize celebrated Bolognese professors. *(V. Manzoni 4. Off V. dell'Indipendenza, near P. Maggiore. ☎ 051 219 39 30; www.comune. bologna.it/iperbole/MuseiCivici. Open Tu-F 9am-3pm, Sa-Su 10am-6:30pm. Free. Audio tour €4.)*

THE TWO TOWERS. After seismic shifts left Bologna with an unexpectedly tilted **Torre degli Garisenda,** the city strove for new heights with the 97.2m **Torre degli Asinelli.** Visible from all over the city, the towers have become Bologna's architectural symbols. Climbers mount 498 narrow wooden steps past four landings to a breezy perch where a sea of red rooftops, Gothic church spires, yellow villages, and miles of uninterrupted horizon sit stories below. *(P. Pta. Ravegana, at the end of V. Rizzoli. Open daily 9am-6pm. Last ticket sale 5:40pm. €3. Cash only.)*

MUSEO CIVICO ARCHEOLOGICO. This museum of local artifacts brims with Roman inscriptions, red-and-black Greek pottery, and two dirt-covered, mummified Etruscans. The enormous Etruscan section is filled with jewelry and other tiny ornaments. The basement's Egyptian collection has items from 2640 BC, including stone reliefs from the tomb of Pharaoh Horemheb. *(V. Archiginnasio 2. Follow signs from P. Maggiore. ☎ 27 57 211; www.comune.bologna.it/Musei/ Archeologico. Open Tu-F 9am-3pm, Sa-Su 10am-6:30pm. Free. Audio tour €4.)*

CHURCHES

CHIESA SANTO STEFANO. This cluster of buildings and courtyards was shaped from remains of Egyptian temples honoring the goddess Isis. Four of the seven churches of the original Romanesque basilica, known collectively as "Holy Jerusalem," remain. Built to hold the relics of Saints Vitalis and Agricola, the **Cripta** now contains the tomb of Martin the Abbot. In the small **Chiesa di San Sepolcro,** another of Bologna's patron saints, St. Petronio, is entombed in the towering **Edicola del Santo Sepolcro,** supposedly modeled from Christ's sepulcher in Jerusalem. In the rear courtyard is the **Cortile di Pilato** (Basin of Pilate), where the governor reportedly absolved himself of responsibility for Christ's death. *(In P. S. Stefano. Follow V. S. Stefano from V. Rizzoli. ☎ 051 22 32 56. San Stefano open daily 7am-noon and 3:30-6:45pm. Santo Sepolcro open M-F 9am-noon and 3:30-6pm, Sa-Su 9am-1pm and 3:30-6:30pm. Modest dress required. Both churches free.)*

CHIESA DI SANTA MARI DEI SERVI. Glittering red votives and faded patches of fresco conceal the bottom half of this soaring basilica from street-level view. Inside the well-preserved Gothic structure, octagonal columns support an unusual blend of arches and ribbed vaulting. Cimabue's *Maestà* hangs in a dimly lit chapel behind an exquisite altar that was sculpted by Giovanni Antonio Montorsoli, a pupil of Michelangelo. *(Take Strada Maggiore to P. Aldrovandi. ☎ 051 22 68 07. Open daily 7:30am-12:30pm and 3:30-7:45pm. Free.)*

EMILIA-ROMAGNA

CHIESA DI SAN DOMENICO. Tall marble columns line San Domenico's clean interior, but its signature minimalism stops at the two transept chapels. In the Cappella di San Domenico, St. Dominic's body lies in a marble tomb sculpted by Nicolò Pisano and Michelangelo. Across the nave in the Cappella del Rosario, 15 small paintings by Fontana, Carracci, and others depict the mysteries of the rosary and frame a statue of the Virgin beneath a painted ceiling of playful angels. Because St. Dominic is largely credited with institutionalizing the rosary as a conventional form of prayer, this chapel is especially notable. *(From P. Maggiore, follow V. Archiginnasio to V. Farini. Turn right on V. Garibaldi. ☎051 64 00 411. Open daily 9:30am-12:30pm and 3:30-5:30pm. Free. English tours daily upon request.)*

CHIESA DELLE SANTISSIME VITALE E AGRICOLA. With its polygonal brick spire jutting over the walls of local homes, this small church incorporates shards of capitals and columns into its facade. A lavish gold altar illuminates the otherwise dimly lit interior, and underneath the building, an 11th-century crypt holds paintings by Francia and Sano di Pietro. Look for a sculpture of Christ based on the **Shroud of Turin's** (p. 141) anatomical clues. *(V. S. Vitale 50. ☎051 22 05 70. Open daily 8am-noon and 4-7:30pm. Chapel free. Crypt €1.)*

CHIESA DI SAN GIACOMO MAGGIORE. This church's exterior blends Romanesque and Gothic styles, but it's the artwork inside that makes it worth a visit. Next door, the **Oratorio di Santa Cecilia** contains a fresco cycle depicting St. Cecilia's marriage and martyrdom. *(Follow V. Zamboni to P. Rossini. ☎051 22 59 70. Church open daily 7am-noon and 3:30-6pm. Enter Oratorio from V. Zamboni 15. Oratorio open daily in summer 10am-1pm and 3-7pm; in winter 10am-1pm and 2-6pm. Both free.)*

♪ ▓ ENTERTAINMENT AND NIGHTLIFE

Every year from June to September, Bologna sponsors an ▓**entertainment festival** of dance, music, cinema, and art. Many events are free; some cost €5. The tourist office has programs. The **Teatro Comunale**, Largo Respighi 1, hosts world-class operas, symphonies, and ballets. To order tickets ahead, call or sign up outside the ticket office two days before performances. In summer, the theater hosts free concerts at 9pm. Pick up a schedule at the tourist office. *(☎051 52 99 99; www.comunalebologna.it. Box office open Tu-F 3-7pm, Sa 10am-noon and 3-7pm. 10% surcharge for pre-order. AmEx/MC/V.)*

Bologna's student population accounts for the city's large number of bars, pubs, and nightclubs. A mass of them are on **Via Zamboni,** near the university. Call ahead for hours and cover; info changes frequently. In June and July, clubs close and the party scene moves outdoors. The tourist office has a list of outdoor music venues. Don't expect much activity in August—even the outdoor *discoteche* close as locals head to the beach.

▓ **College Bar,** Largo Resphigi 6/D (☎051 349 003 7366). From the music to the inexpensive drinks to the Carl Jung books placed inconspicuously above the bar, this place screams college. Live music ranging from jazz to techno performed daily by students. From 10am-5pm choose any 2 drinks for €3.50, or at 5pm try their special "4x3" shot deal: 4 shots made from 3 liquors, all for €2.50. Open daily 10am-3am. Cash only.

   Cluricaune, V. Zamboni 18/B (☎051 26 34 19). Huge, multi-level Irish pub adorned with old bicycles attracts local students with extensive beer selection. Beer from €2. Mixed drinks €4.50. Happy hour 7:30-8:30pm; W 7:30-10:30pm. Open June-Aug. M-Th noon-2am, F-Sa noon-2:30am; Sept.-May daily 4pm-2am. MC/V.

   La Scuderia, P. Verdi 2 (☎051 65 69 619; www.lascuderia.bo.it). A large fresco of the deposition graces the entrance to this huge student hangout. Live music. Free Wi-Fi. Nightly buffet 6-8pm. Beer €2.70. Mixed drinks €6. Spritz €4. Student discount 30%. Open M-Th 8am-8pm, F-Sa 6pm-3am. AmEx/MC/V.

Cassero, V. Don Minzoni 18 (☎051 64 94 416; www.cassero.it). Take V. Marconi to P. dei Martiri and turn left on V. Don Minzoni. This popular club draws chatty crowds of students and locals into cavernous dance hall. Popular with the gay community. Arcigay card required for entrance (€15 per year; tourists can purchase a 1-month card for €8 (see **Practical Information,** p. 272). Beer €3. Mixed drinks €7. W night free and features pop music. F and Sa feature techno. Cover €10; join the guest list online for €5 discount. Open in summer daily 9pm-6am; in winter W-Su 9pm-6am. Cash only.

English Empire, V. Zamboni 24, near the University. Drawing crowds of loyal patrons, this bar mixes old-world pub with bumping club music and flashing lights. Under the motto of "one day of pleasure is worth two of sorrow," enjoy *piadine* and crepes (€4.50) or hamburgers, fries, and pizza with a variety of drinks. Great Tu deal: 2 drinks for €5. Mixed drinks €5, after 6:30pm €6. Beer €3.50/4.50. Open daily noon-3am. Cash only.

By Bios 2, V. Marsala 17/19 (☎051 22 63 86). Pink lights, a bubbling fish tank, cow-print columns, and flatscreen TVs decorate the otherwise modern decor of this spacious restaurant/bar. Enjoy pizza (€3.50-6) by day and stick around for a night of *aperitivi,* mixed drinks, beer, and wine (€3.50-7). Live music daily Sept.-May. Open M-Th 8am-1am, F 8am-3am, Sa 5pm-3am, Su 3pm-1am. AmEx/MC/V.

Cantina Bentivoglio, V. Mascarella 4/B (☎051 26 54 16), near Largo Respighi and the Teatro Comunale. Caters to a classier crowd with pricey food and cheap drinks. Relaxed atmosphere. Umbrella-covered patio. Extensive wine list (glasses from €8). Live jazz nightly Sept.-May; outdoors Th-F. Cover €1.20. Open daily 8pm-2am.

PARMA   ☎0521

Although a trip to Parma (PAR-ma; pop. 180,000)—where platters overflow with aged parmesan cheese and rosy-pink prosciutto—will certainly never leave the taste buds unsatisfied, Parma's artistic excellence is not confined to the kitchen. In the 16th century, Mannerist painting flourished under native artists Parmigianino and Correggio. The city was also the birthplace of composer Giuseppe Verdi, who resided in Parma while writing some of his greatest works. Pervasive French influences inspired Stendhal to choose the picturesque town as the setting for his 1839 novel *The Charterhouse of Parma.* If your tastes are less literary, have no fear—Parma's nightlife, though confined to a few central streets, rivals that of much larger cities. Summer nights find students and travelers alike enjoying the bars, live music, and theatre.

▐▀ TRANSPORTATION

Flights depart from **Giuseppe Verdi Airport,** V. dell'Aeroporto 44/A (☎98 26 26; fax 99 20 28). Parma lies on the Bologna-Milan line. **Trains** leave the station in Ple. Carlo Alberto della Chiesa (☎0521 89 20 21 or 77 14 26; ticket office open daily 5:55am-12:05am) to: Bologna (1hr., 3 per hr. 4:11am-12:18am, €5); Florence (2hr., 6:46am-9:24pm, €10); Milan (1hr., 3-5 per hr. 5:14am-10:36pm, €7.40); Modena (30min., 4 per hr. 5:46am-11:51pm, €3.50); Rome (4hr., 6:46am-11:51pm); Turin (3hr., 5 per day 5:53am-10:36pm, €11.70). **Buses** to nearby towns including Bardi, Busseto, and Colorno stop at P. Carlo Alberto della Chiesa 7/B, at the InfoBus booth. (☎0521 27 32 51. Ticket office open M-Sa 6am-7:15pm, Su 7am-1pm.) **Intra-city buses** run throughout Parma, and stop in front of the train station. For bus rides between 8pm and 1am, reserve a ride with ProntoBus (☎800 977 900; www.tep.pr.it; around €3). Call a **taxi** (☎0521 25 25 62) for 24hr. service. **Rent a car** at the airport from Avis (☎0521 29 12 38). For **bike rental,** check out Parma PuntoBici, Vle. P. Toschi 2. (☎0521 28 19 79; www.parmapuntobici.it. Bikes €0.70 per hr.; €10 for 1st day, €5 each day thereafter. Electric bikes €1/20/10. Open M-Sa 9am-1pm and 3-7pm, Su 10am-1pm and 3-7pm.)

🔁 ℹ️ ORIENTATION AND PRACTICAL INFORMATION

To get to the city, exit the station with the fountain on your right. Turn left on **Viale Bottego** and right on **Strada Garibaldi**. Follow it 1km into town. Turn left on **Strada Mazzini** to reach **Piazza Garibaldi**, the *centro*. **Strada della Repubblica**, **Strada Cavour**, and **Strada Farini**, Parma's main streets, branch out from this *piazza*.

Tourist Office: Strada Melloni 11/A (☎0521 21 88 89; www.turismo.comune.parma.it). From train station, walk left on Vle. Bottego, turn right on Strada Garibaldi, then left on Strada Melloni. Open M 9am-1pm and 3-7pm, Tu-Sa 9am-7pm, Su 9am-1pm.

Beyond Tourism: Informagiovani, Strada Melloni 1 (☎0521 21 87 49; http://informagiovani.comune.parma.it), next to the tourist office. Posts jobs, volunteer work, and apartment listings. English spoken. Free **Internet** access and study room. Open M-Tu and F-Sa 9am-1pm and 3-7pm, W 9am-1pm, Th 9am-7pm.

Bank: Banca Antonveneta, Strada dell'Università 2, just off P. Garibaldi. Open M-F 8:20am-1:20pm and 3-4pm, Sa 8:20-11:50am. Also has **24hr. ATM.**

Western Union: Infinitho, Strada M. D'Azeglio 23/A (☎0521 23 45 55; www.hopera.net), just across the river over Ponte di Mezzo from V. Mazzini. Internet access €1.10 per 15min., students €0.90; €4/3 per hr. Skype and webcam access also available. Open M-W and F-Sa 8:30am-9pm, Th 8:30am-2pm. AmEx/MC/V. .

Laundromat: WashingPoint, Strada Massimo D'Azeglio 108a. Wash and dry €2. Detergent €1. Open daily 8-10pm.

Police: Vle. Villetta 12/A (☎0521 21 87 40).

Pharmacy: Farmacia Guareschi, Strada Farini 5/C (☎0521 28 22 40). Open M-F 8:30am-12:30pm and 3:30-7:30pm. After-hours rotation posted outside.

Hospital: Ospedale Maggiore, V. Gramsci 14 (☎0521 70 21 11 or 70 31 11), over the river past the Parco Ducale. For emergencies go to entrance on V. Abbeveratoria.

Internet: Free at **Informagiovani** (see **Beyond Tourism**, above). **Web'n'Wine,** Strada M. D'Azeglio 72/D (☎0521 03 08 93; www.webnwine.it), across the river. €2.50 per 30min. English spoken. Open M-Th 9am-8pm, F 9am-9pm, Sa 10am-8pm.

Post Office: On Strada Melloni across from the tourist office. Open M-F 8:30am-5pm, Sa 8:30am-12:30pm. Currency exchange also available. **Postal Code:** 43100.

🏠 ACCOMMODATIONS

🏨 **Ostello della Gioventù (HI),** V. San Leonardo 86 (☎0521 19 17 547; www.ostelloparma.it). From the train station, turn left onto V. Bottego. Make a right onto Strada G. Garibaldi. The bus stops on the other side of the street, in front of the fountains. Take bus 2, 2N, or 13 (until 8pm; if later, use ProntoBus). Or, to walk, turn left onto Strada G. Garibaldi, which becomes V. S. Leonardo. Hostel on left immediately after highway overpass. Beautiful, new, and easily accessible. Young, English-speaking staff, large common areas, laundry (€6), and Internet (€3.50 per hr.). Dorms €19; doubles €41. ❶

Albergo Leon d'Oro, Vle. Fratti 4a (☎0521 77 31 82; www.leondoroparma.com), 1 block from the train station, just after the intersection with Strada Garibaldi. Required advance payment may seem unorthodox, but guests will find elegant rooms with large windows and big beds. Shared modern bath. Restaurant downstairs. Singles €35-60; doubles €60, with private bath €80; triples €105. AmEx/MC/V. ❸

Casa della Giovane, Strada del Conservatorio 11 (☎0521 28 32 29; www.casadellagiovane.it). From Strada Mazzini, turn left on V. Oberdan; hotel is on the right. Only accepts female guests aged 14-26. Religious community. 2 beds per room and shared bath. Fridge access. Breakfast and lunch or dinner included. Free laundry. Check-out 10am. Curfew M-Tu, Th-F, and Su 10pm; W and Sa 11pm. €25 per person. Cash only. ❷

FOOD

Parma's cuisine is rich, delicious, affordable, and renowned throughout Italy. Aged parmesan cheese and *prosciutto crudo* fill the windows of the *salumerie* (delicatessens) along V. Garibaldi. Local *Malvasia* is the wine of choice. When exported, this sparkling white loses its natural fizz, so carbon dioxide is usually added to compensate—sip a glass here to sample the real thing. An **open-air market** displays its goods at P. Ghiaia every Wednesday and Saturday morning, and Wednesday and Friday nights during summer. It offers local varieties of cheese, meats, and vinegar. **Dimeglio** supermarket is located at S. XXII Luglio 27/C. (☎0521 28 13 82. Open daily 8:30am-1:30pm and 4:30-8pm.) **ECU Convenience** market is on V. San Leonardo 17. (Open daily 8:30am-1pm and 4pm-7:30pm. Closed Th afternoon. AmEx/MC/V.)

Trattoria Sorelle Picchi, Strada Farini 27 (☎0521 23 35 28), several blocks from P. Garibaldi. Food served out of a *salumeria* of the same name. This local secret cooks traditional dishes including roasted pheasant, homemade lasagna, and sweet-and-sour onions. Let the waitstaff advise on specialties and starters, like the mixed prosciutto plate (€9). Primi €8-9. Secondi €10-15. Cover €2. *Salumeria* open 8:30am-7pm. *Trattoria* open M-Sa noon-3pm. AmEx/MC/V. ❸

Trattoria Corrieri, Strada del Conservatorio 1 (☎0521 23 44 26; www.trattoriacorrieri. it). Rustic decorations surround a narrow ivy-draped courtyard. Vibrant atmosphere and modest prices keep tables full. Majestic pasta is made fresh daily. Primi €7.50-9. Secondi €7.50-10. Open noon-2:30pm and 7:30-10:30pm. AmEx/MC/V. ❸

SIGHTS

PALAZZO DELLA PILOTTA. Built in 1602, the *palazzo*'s grandeur suggests the ambitions of the Farnese dukes; today, the *palazzo* houses several museums, accessible through the courtyard. Though there have been no actual performances in the theater since the curtain last fell in 1732, the elegant, wooden **Teatro Farnese,** completed in 1618, underwent restorations in the 50s to repair damage inflicted by WWII bombs. Beyond the theater, the **Galleria Nazionale** contains numerous medieval polyptychs and portraits, including Leonardo da Vinci's *Testa d'una Fanciulla* (Head of a Young Girl), as well as a gallery devoted to Parmigianino and Correggio. The **Museo Archeologico Nazionale** displays bronzes, and sculptures of ancient origin. *(From Strada Cavour, turn left on Strada Pisacane and cut across P. della Pace to P. Pilotta. ☎0521 23 37 18. Open June-Sept. Su 9:30am-12:30pm and 4-7pm. Closed in afternoon Aug. €2.)*

DUOMO, BATTISTERO, AND MUSEO DIOCESANO. Parma's 11th-century Romanesque *duomo* balances paintings of clouds with austere masterpieces like the Episcopal throne and Benedetto Antelami's bas-relief *Descent from the Cross* (1178). The stunning *duomo* features Correggio's Virgin ascending to heaven. *(In P. Duomo. From P. Garibaldi, follow Strada Cavour, and turn right on Strada al Duomo. ☎23 58 8. Open daily 9am-12:30pm and 3-7pm. Free.)* The pink-and-white *battistero* (baptistry) displays medieval frescoes of enthroned saints and apostles some represented with animal heads that rise from each of the dome's 16 sides. *(☎0521 23 58 86. Open daily 9am-12:30pm and 3-6:30pm. €4, with Museo Diocesano €5.)* Diagonally across the *piazza*, the Museo Diocesano holds examples of 12th- and 13th-century sculpture while preserving Roman ruins in the basement. *(In P. Duomo. ☎20 86 99; www.cattedrale.parma.it. Open daily 9am-12:30pm and 3-6:30pm. €3.)*

IL MONASTERIO DI SAN PAOLO. This aged monastery holds an impressive fresco above the **Camera di San Paolo,** which depicts the coat of arms of the

Abbess, under whose direction the monastery prospered. Don't miss the ceiling frescoes of what seem to be heavily muscled babies cavorting with decapitated animals. *(V. Melloni 3. From P. Garibaldi, head up Strada Cavour, turn left on Strada Melloni, and follow the signs. ☎53 32 21. Open Tu-Su 8:30am-1:30pm. Last entry 1pm. €2, ages 18-25 €1, under 18 or over 65 free.)* The complex of St. Paul also houses **Il Castello dei Burattini** (Puppet Castle), densely showcasing a collection of over 1500 puppets in a few small but well-arranged rooms. *(☎0521 031 631; fax 0521 218 876; www.castello-deiburattini.it. Open Tu-Su Apr.-Oct. 9am-7pm; Nov.-Mar. 9am-5pm. €2.50, students €1.50.)* Just around the corner, the **Pinacoteca Stuard** holds 270 paintings from the 14th-19th centuries. Near the entrance you'll see the prized *Madonna in trono con Bambino* by Maestro della Misericordia (c. 1350-75). *(Borgo Parmigianino 2. ☎0521 50 81 84. Open M and W-Sa 9am-6:30pm, Su 9am-6pm. €4, under 25 and over 65 €2.)*

CHIESA DI SAN GIOVANNI EVANGELISTA.
This 10th-century church is a long-standing Italian classic. The dome was famously frescoed by Correggio, while frescoes by Parmigianino run along the left nave and over the first, second, and fourth chapels. The belltower was constructed in 1613. *(In P. San Giovanni, behind the duomo. ☎0521 23 53 11. Open daily 8am-noon and 3-7:45pm. Monastery closes 6pm. Reservations recommended for guided tours. Free.)*

CHIESA MAGISTRALE DI SANTA MARIA DELLA STECCATA.
Built in 1521 to house a miraculous picture of the Virgin Mary, the church now frames the icon with red marble columns. This Renaissance church also features impressive frescoes by Parmigianino. Call ahead to see the **Crypt of the Farnese Dukes** and pay respect to the famous Alexander, whose helmet and sword still sit above his tomb, and Antonio Farnese, the last Duke of Parma. *(P. Steccata 9, up V. Garibaldi. ☎0521 23 49 37. Open daily 9am-noon and 3-6pm. Free.)*

TEATRO REGIO.
Commissioned by Marie Louise in 1821, the Teatro Regio is known worldwide. Its Neoclassical facade is complemented by Borghesi's decorations inside. The four-tiered Baroque balconies feature red velvet seats interrupted only by the large crowned ducal box that faces the stage. *(V. Garibaldi 16, next to P. della Pace. ☎0521 03 93 93; www.teatroregioparma.org. Open M-Sa 10:30am-noon. Guided tours in Italian every 30min. Advance booking recommended. €2, students €1.)*

PARMIGIANO AND PROSCIUTTO FACTORIES.
Cheese enthusiasts interested in seeing the origin of 38kg blocks of Parmigiano should contact the **Consorzio del Parmigiano-Reggiano** to arrange a 2hr. tour of factories around Parma. Tours are offered infrequently and only on weekdays, are inaccessible by public transportation, and must be booked in advance. *(Strada dei Mercati 9. ☎0521 29 27 00; sezionepr@parmigiano-reggiano.it.)* Visits to a prosciutto factory are usually available only during the **Prosciutto Festival** in the first week of September. *(For more info, call the Consorzio del Prosciutto di Parma. ☎24 39 87; fax 24 39 83.)* A somewhat more feasible and satisfying option is the **Museo del Prosciutto di Parma.** *(V. Bocchialini 7. 23km outside Parma in Langhirano, accessible by bus #12. ☎0521 85 83 47 and ☎33 56 66 4220. Open Sa-Su 10am-6pm. €3; Parma ham tasting €3; "typical products tasting" €9.)* The **Parmigiano-Reggiano Museum** is in Soragna. *(☎22 81 52. Open Mar.-Oct. M-F only by reservation, Sa-Su 9:30am-12:30pm and 3-6pm; Nov.-Feb. only by reservation. €5, includes tasting.)*

OTHER SIGHTS.
Although many French palaces were destroyed during WWII, Marie Louise's gardens remain by the Baroque **Palazzo Ducale** in Parco Ducale. *(West of Palazzo della Pilotta, across Ponte Verdi. Park open daily in summer 6am-midnight; in winter 7am-8pm. Free. Palazzo ☎53 76 78; call in morning. Open M-Sa 9:30am-noon. €3, students and under 25 €2.)* Across the river, the **Palazzo Cusani,** or Casa della Musica, first served as the seat of the University of Parma and later as the Mint of the Duchy of Parma. Today, it houses a museum. *(Ple. San Francesco 1. Follow Borgo del*

Parmigianino from the tourist office, then turn right on V. Daimazia. ☎ *0521 03 11 70. Open July to mid-Aug. M-Sa 9am-1pm and 3-7pm; Sept.-June Tu-Sa 9am-6pm, Su 9am-1pm.)*

🎭 🎵 NIGHTLIFE AND ENTERTAINMENT

At night, *parmigiani* stroll along Strada Farini, or the intersection of Strada Maestri and V. Nazario Sauro, where the truly vibrant nightlife rivals that of a much larger city. Bars and street performers densely pack along this central strip. A gaggle of merrymakers spill out of **Tabarro,** Strada Farini 5/B, where glasses of wine (€2.50-5) are served along with the vegetable bowls. (☎0521 200 223; www.tabarro.net. Open Tu 6:30pm-1am, W-Th noon-3pm and 6:30pm-1am, F-Sa noon-3pm and 6:30pm-2am, Su 6pm-midnight. Cash only.) For a chilled-out vibe and a mostly white decor, head to **Mood Cafe,** P.le S. Apollonia 3/A. (☎0521 181 3841. Mixed drinks €6. Open M 8:30am-9pm, Tu 8:30am-3pm, W-Th 7am-3pm and 6pm-midnight, F 7am-3pm and 6pm-2am, Sa 6pm-2am. Cash only.) For even more casual revelry, enjoy the balmy nights and cool green grass in front of P. Pilotta.

The **Teatro Regio** is one of Italy's premier opera houses, hosting operatic, cultural, and theatrical extravaganzas throughout the year. (Strada Garibaldi 16/A, next to P. della Pace. ☎0521 03 93 93; www.teatroregioparma.org.) The opera season runs from November to April, while the popular **Verdi Festival,** honoring the native composer with local concerts and operas, takes place each year usually in October at the *teatro*. The **Parma Poesia Festival,** debuted in 2005, organizes a week of poetry readings, lectures, and slams throughout the city in June. In May, the city hosts **Parma Danza,** an international festival of ballet and modern dance. **Grande Estate** brings classical music, opera, jazz, and tango concerts to Ple. della Pilotta in July. (☎0521 21 86 78. Tickets €10-35.) Info for all events may be obtained at the *teatro*'s ticket office. The **Cinema Astra,** V. Rondizzoni 1 (☎0521 96 05 54; www.cinema-astra.it), also hosts the summer movie festival Estive Astra in June and July. (All movies begin at 9:30pm. €5-6, students €4.) Last but not least, the annual **Prosciutto Festival** takes over the city and the surrounding area during the first two weekends in September; contact the Consorzio del Prosciutto di Parma for annual scheduled events. (☎0521 24 39 87; www.festivaldelprosciutto.it or www.finestreaperte.it.)

RAVENNA   ☎0544

Ravenna's (ra-VEH-na; pop. 150,000) mosaics appear everywhere, from under your drink at the bar to behind the glass windows of tourist shops, and, of course, at every major sight. The streets paved with colored stones are almost entirely car-free, and travelers walk past monuments like Dante's tomb (to the chagrin of the Florentines, who maintain an empty sepulcher for their exiled son). For the artistically and academically inclined, Ravenna is filled with churches and historic monuments that date from its Byzantine glory under Justinian and Theodora, all within walking distance from the compact *centro*. Yet Ravenna knows how to kick back and relax—its proximity to the shore also attracts plenty of vacationers who want nothing more than a spot in the sun.

🚗 TRANSPORTATION

Trains: Station in P. Farini. Open daily 3:50am-12:35am. Ticket counter open daily 6:05am-8:35pm. AmEx/MC/V. To: **Bologna** (1hr., 13 per day 5:05am-8:35pm, €5),

Ferrara (1hr., 11 per day 4:13am-9:33pm, €4.50) with connections to **Florence** and **Venice,** and **Rimini** (1hr., 22 per day 12:31am-9:35pm, €3).

Buses: ATR (regional) and **ATM** (municipal) depart from outside the train station. Office (☎0544 68 99 00) open in summer M-Sa 6:30am-8:30pm, Su 7am-8:30pm; during school year M-Sa 6:30am-7:30pm, Su 7:30am-7:30pm. AmEx/MC/V. To: **Lido Adriano** (Line 80, 20min.; every 30min.; 5:40am-8:10pm; for evening service take Line 75: 8:40pm-midnight, every 30 min.; €1) and **Marina di Ravenna.** (Line 60 and 70. 20-30min.; every 30min. 5:40am-7:55pm; €1.) Tickets (1-day pass €3 valid for all buses) are sold at the booth marked "PUNTO" to the right when you exit the station. Return tickets can be bought on board with a surcharge.

Taxis: RadioTaxi (☎0544 33 888), in P. Farini.

✈ ℹ ORIENTATION AND PRACTICAL INFORMATION

The train station is in **Piazza Farini** at the eastern end of town. **Viale Farini** leads from the station to **Via Diaz,** which runs to **Piazza del Popolo,** the *centro.*

Tourist Office: V. Salara 8 (☎0544 35 404; www.turismo.ravenna.it). Walk to the end of P. del Popolo, turn right on V. Matteotti, and follow the signs. Free bike rental; ID required. Office open M-Th 8:30am-7pm, F 8:30am-11pm, Su 10am-6pm.

Youth Center: Informagiovani, V. Massimo D'Azeglio, 2nd floor (☎0544 48 24 56; www. racine.ra.it/informagiovani/ravenna). Work, volunteer, travel info, and free Internet (max. 30min.) for students. Open Tu and Th 10am-1pm and 2-6pm, W and F-Sa 10am-1pm.

Luggage storage: left of the station. Lockers €2-5. 24hr. max. Open M-Sa 7am-7:30pm.

Laundry: Fast Clean Laundry, V. Candiano 16. Open daily 7am-10pm.

Police: P. Mameli (☎0544 48 29 99).

Hospital: Santa Maria delle Croci, Vle. Randi 5 (☎0544 28 51 11).

Internet: free for students at **Informagiovani** (above). **Internet and Phone Center,** V. Rocca Brancaleone 4/6, (☎0544 33 744). €2 per hr. Open daily 9am-9pm.

Post office: P. Garibaldi 1 (☎0544 24 33 11), off V. Diaz before P. del Popolo. Offers currency exchange. Open M-F 8am-6:30pm, Sa 8am-12:30pm. **Postal Code:** 48100.

🏠 ⛺ ACCOMMODATIONS AND CAMPING

▨ **Ostello Dante (HI),** V. Nicolodi 12 (☎0544 42 11 64; hostelravenna@hotmail.com). Take bus #70 (every 20-30min. 5:40am-7:55pm; get off at stop 249), 80 (every 30-40min. 5:40am-8:10pm; get off at stop 121), or the red or yellow line from V. Pallavicini, across from the station. This hostel offers foosball tables, a lounge area, books, board games, and bike and cooler rental. Rooms are named after cantos from Dante's *Inferno.* Kitchen access and safes available. Breakfast included. Laundry wash €2.50, dry €2.50. Internet access 1st 15min. free, €3 per hr. thereafter. Wheelchair-accessible. Reception 7-11am and 2:30-11:30pm. Lockout 11am-2:30pm. Curfew 11:30pm; €1 key card to enter later. Dorms €14; singles €24; doubles €21; family rooms €16 per person. HI-member discount €3. MC/V. ❶

La Rocca B&B, V. Rocca Brancaleone 116 (☎0544 45 34 88), across from beautiful Rocca Park. From the station, turn left onto V. Maroncelli, then left again until you reach V. Rocca Brancaleone. Accommodating owner offers 3 quiet rooms with A/C, fan, TV, and balcony. Breakfast included. Singles €30; doubles with bath €50. Cash only. ❷

A Casa di Pino, V. Baccarini 37 (☎0544 38 524; www.acasadipino.it). Take bus #3 to Borgo San Rocco, or any other bus to Piazza Caduti. Cheerful former hotel owner. Sunny apartment stocked with classic American movies. Guests have their own bathroom, access to TV (until 10pm), and fan. Breakfast included. Curfew around 11pm; arrange ahead of time. Singles €34; doubles €54. Cash only. ❸

Camping Adriano, (☎0544 43 72 30; www.campingadriano.com). From the train station, take bus #80 (every 30-40min. 5:40am-8:10pm) to V. dei Campeggi 7, in Punta Marina Terme, 8km from the *centro*. 4-star, family-friendly facilities with bocce courts and a pool and soccer field. Near public beach. Reception daily 8:30am-1pm and 3-9pm. Reservation required for bungalows. Camping open mid-Apr. to late Aug., bungalows open until mid-Sept. €5.10-10.30; per person, €7.50-17.50 per tent. MC/V. ❶

🍴 FOOD

The distinctive flavors of *ravennese* salt, extra-virgin olive oil, and chestnuts characterize Ravenna's cuisine. Accompany a filling meal with a full-bodied *Albana* or *Trebbiano* wine. For dessert, try *zuppa inglese*, a combination of biscuits and custard with a splash of cordial. There's a **Coop** across the street at V. Aquileia 110, near the hostel. (Open M-Sa 8am-8pm. AmEx/MC/V.) In the *centro*, there's a **Plenty Market,** V. Roma 150. (Open M-Sa 7:30am-8:30pm, Su 10am-1:30pm. ☎0544 21 71 16. MC/V.) Fruit, meat, and cheese stands fill the covered **market** at P. Andrea Costa 2, up V. IV Novembre from P. del Popolo. (Open M-Th and Sa 7am-2pm, F 7am-2pm and 4:30-7:30pm. Cash only.)

🍝 Cupido, V. Cavour 43/A (☎0544 37 529). Hearty plates of freshly made pasta and sandwiches near local sights. Warm *piadine* (€3.20-4.50) filled with both sweet and savory; try the ricotta mousse with balsamic strawberry vinagrette (€4.30). Pizza €2.70-6.30. Primi €5.50. Open Tu-F 11am-8pm, Sa 7am-8pm, Su 7am-3pm. AmEx/MC/V. ❶

La Piadina del Melarancio, V. IV Novembre 31 (☎0544 21 20 71). Sells hot *piadine* (€4), fresh milk, and local wine. Classics like *parma* and *squaquerone* cheese (€4.50) hit the spot. Panini €2.50-4. Open M-T and Th-Su 10:45am-8:30pm. AmEx/MC/V. ❶

Verderame, V. Cavour 82 (☎/fax 0544 32 248). Dried flowers, hand-painted menus, and mosaic tabletops complement famous hot chocolate. Try invigorating blends like "Chocolate Pick Me Up" (liquor, chocolate, whipped cream, and *nocciolo;* €6). Open in summer M-Sa 8:30am-8pm, Su 2-8pm; in winter M-Th 8:30am-8pm, F-Sa 8:30am-midnight, Su 10am-8pm. Cash only. ❶

Ristoro Sant'Apollinare Nuovo, V. di Roma 53 (☎0544 35 679), turn right by the basilica entrance. Grab lunch at the self-service counter for a cheap meal. Daily menu with traditional pastas like gnocchi with 4 cheeses. 4-course lunch *menù* €8. Primi €4-5.50. Secondi €4-6. Open M-F noon-2:30pm. AmEx/MC/V. ❷

Ristorante Gallo d'Oro, Borgo della Salina 3 (☎0521 20 88 46). From P. Garibaldi, take Strada Farini and turn left. Eat in a 16th-century stone building. Wines €3 per ¼-bottle, €4 per ½-bottle, €7-11 per bottle. Primi €6.50-9. Secondi €6.50-9.50. Cover €2. Open M-Sa noon-2:30pm and 7:30-11pm. AmEx/MC/V. ❷

Ristorante Leon d'Oro, V. Fratti 4a (☎0521 77 31 82; www.leondoroparma.com), off Strada Garibaldi. Features platters of colorful antipasto, typical *parmigiano* meals, and desserts. Primi €8. Secondi €18. Cover €2. Open daily May-Sept. 12:30-2pm and 8-10pm. Reservations recommended Sa-Su. AmEx/MC/V. ❸

👁 SIGHTS

🏛 BASILICA DI SAN VITALE. The glimmering jewel in mosaic-crazy Ravenna, this remarkable basilica overwhelms viewers with its ornate tile work and the dusty warmth that seems to float on the earth-colored frescoes. Peer up at the colorful mosaics that decorate the apse; at the center, Christ Pantocrator is depicted in lush blue and gold, while to the side a scene with Theodora and

Justinian is rendered in bright aqua, scarlet, and green. At the center, rosy paintings grace the walls as warm light streams through the quartz windows. *(V. S. Vitale 17. From tourist office, turn right on V. Cavour, then again on V. Argentario. ☎ 0544 21 62 92. Open daily Apr.-Sept. 9am-7pm; Mar. and Oct. 9am-5:30pm; Nov.-Feb. 9:30am-5pm. Individual ticket not available; included in the Ravenna Card pass.)* Mosaics cover the interior of the tiny **Mausoleo di Galla Placidia,** where a single lamp illuminates 570 gold stars set against a night sky, arranged in concentric circles around a cross. Three stone sarcophagi are said to contain the remains of Costanzo III, Empress Galla Placida, and Valentiniano III. *(Behind S. Vitale. Same hours as basilica.)*

DAY AND NIGHT, NIGHT AND DAY. American jazz musician Cole Porter, after having toured Ravenna by night in 1920, was allegedly so struck by the beautiful light in the Mausoleo di Galla Placida that he composed the song "Night and Day" with the structure's starry ceiling in mind.

BASILICA DI SANT'APOLLINARE IN CLASSE. A bus ride from the town center, this church at first seems simple, with dark wood beams and unlabeled marble columns. But keep exploring: the real draw is the massive mosaic above the apse, where Sant'Apollinare and flocks of sheep fill the enormous half-dome. *(In Classe, south of the city. Take bus #4 or 44; both stop across from the train station. ☎ 0544 34 424. Open daily 8:30am-7:30pm. Last entry 30min. before closing. €3, EU students 18-25 €2, under 18 and over 65 free. Free entry Su mornings. Cash only.)*

DANTE'S TOMB AND THE DANTE MUSEUM. Ravenna's most popular monument is the unassuming, green-domed tomb of Dante Alighieri, who died in Ravenna in 1321 after being exiled from his native Florence. A suspended lamp that has burned with Florentine oil since 1908 illuminates a relief of Dante leafing through books. The nearby Dante Museum contains Wostry Carlo's illustrations of Dante's works, the poet's bones in a fir chest, 18,000 scholarly volumes on his works, and the trowel and hammer that laid the cornerstone of Rio de Janeiro's *Dante Monument.* However, the peaceful garden outside provides a nice respite from the city streets. *(V. D. Alighieri. From P. del Popolo, cut through P. Garibaldi to V. D. Alighieri. Museum ☎ 0544 33 667. Tomb open daily Apr.-Sept. 9:30am-6:30pm. Free.)*

RAVENOUS FOR ART. Individual tickets to 5 of Ravenna's monuments are not available, but the **Ravenna Card** (€8.50, students €7.50) provides admission to 5 museums and monuments for 7 days: the Basilica di San Vitale, Basilica di Sant'Apollinare Nuovo, Battistero Neoniano, Mausoleo di Galla Placidia, and Museo Arcivescovile. From Mar. 1 to June 15, Mausoleo di Galla Placidia costs an extra €2. A group ticket to Basilica di Sant'Apollinare in Classe, Mausoleo di Teodorico, and the Museo Nazionale costs €8. For info on the churches, contact the **Ufficio Informazioni e Prenotazioni dell'Opera di Religione della Diocesi di Ravenna,** V. Canneti 3. (☎ 0544 54 16 88; fax 54 16 80. Open M-F 9am-12:30pm and 3:30-6pm.)

MUSEO NAZIONALE. This former Benedictine monastery features Roman, early Christian, Byzantine, and medieval works, like the sixth-century bronze cross from the roof of San Vitale's cupola and the original apse vault of Sant'Apollinare in Classe. Discovered in the 70s during excavations, the original vault featured peacocks, doves, and fruit trees, but the renovators eventually went with the existing design of herds of lambs instead. *(On V. Fiandrin Ticket booth to the right of Basilica di San Vitale's entrance. Museum is through courtyard. ☎ 0544 34*

EMILIA-ROMAGNA

424. Open Tu-Su 8:30am-7:30pm. Last entry 30min. before closing. €4, EU students ages 18-25 €2, under 18 and over 65 free. Cumulative tickets with Basilica di Sant'Apollinare in Classe and Mausoleo di Teodorico €8, reduced €4. Cash only.)

BASILICA DI SANT'APOLLINARE NUOVO. This sixth-century basilica makes quite an impression with white tile floors, graceful columns, crushed seashell mortar, and gilded coffers. A dynamic procession of white-robed mosaic figures leads to the apse where a soft gray-green ceiling houses beautiful sculptures. Beside the rustic exterior of chipping brick, a tall, circular *campanile* spirals up six stories over the church's sloping, red-tiled roof. (On V. di Roma. ☎0544 21 95 18. Open daily Apr.-Sept. 9am-7pm; Mar. and Oct. 9:30am-5:30pm; Nov.-Feb. 10am-5pm.)

BATTISTERO NEONIANO. Originally a Roman bath, today, this pint-sized baptistry welcomes visitors into a deep blue interior decked out in gold floral designs. The 12 apostles, rendered in blue and yellow, circle the domed ceiling while good luck coins litter the bottom of the baptismal font in the center. Seating along the sides allows visitors to gawk for the five brief minutes they are allowed inside. (From P. del Popolo, follow V. Cairoli, turn right on V. Gessi, and head toward P. Arcivescovado. Duomo open daily 7am-noon and 2:30-6:30pm. Baptistry open daily Apr.-Sept. 9am-7pm; Mar. and Oct. 9:30am-5:30pm; Nov.-Feb. 10am-5pm.)

MUSEO ARCIVESCOVILE. This one-room museum offers an up-close look at the city's most celebrated art form, displaying detailed religious mosaics that were rescued from the now-destroyed Ursian Basilica. To the left of the entrance, the eyes of four mosaic faces look in different directions. At the center, an ivory throne given to Justinian by Maximilian impresses all with its exceedingly ornate carvings. (To the right of the Battistero Neoniano. ☎0544 21 52 01. Open daily Apr.-Sept. 9am-7pm; Mar. and Oct. 9:30am-5:30pm; Nov.-Feb. 10am-5pm.)

🎭 🎆 ENTERTAINMENT AND FESTIVALS

Many bars and cafes stay open late around P. del Popolo. Watch for the **Organ Music Festival,** held annually in late July in the basilica, and the **Ravenna Festival,** which brings together some of the world's most famous classical performers each June and July. (Info office at V. D. Alighieri 1. ☎0544 24 92 11; www.ravennafestival.org. Open M-W and F-Sa 10am-1pm, Th 4-6pm; during festival. M-Sa 10am-1pm and 4-6pm, Su 10am-1pm. Box Office Ravenna Live at G. Raspni 9. ☎0544 24 92 44. Tickets from €10. Reserve ahead for popular events.) In the second week of September, Dante's legacy comes to life with the exhibits and theatrical performances of the **Dante Festival** (☎0544 30 252).

Vin Vita, V. Monfalcone 10 (☎0544 47 14 18). Funky leopard seats, a shiny bar, and spacious seating. F and Sa *discoteca* nights with live music in the laid-back lounge. Every Su, starting at 6pm, *aperitivi* (€2.50-4) served with live house music. Beer €2. Wine €3-4. Open daily 6pm-2am. AmEx/MC/V.

Caffe Grand Italia, in P. Popolo (☎0544 217 529). Classy, silver bar with soft lighting and great mixed drinks. Live music. Dishes like ricotta ravioli with braised endive and *bruciatini* in cheese fondue (€8.50) by day. Primi €8. Secondi €11-15. Mixed drinks €6. Wine €4-6. Open in summer M-Th and Su 6:30am-midnight, F-Sa 6:30am-3am; in winter M-Tu, Th and Su 6:30am-midnight, F-Sa 6:30am-3am. AmEx/MC/V.

RIMINI ☎ 0541

Given the lack of surprise on doormen's faces when they let in mojito-stained lodgers at 3am, Rimini (REE-mee-nee; pop. 136,000) is clearly a city that's used to playing fast and loose. Inland, the *centro storico* preserves its Roman heritage with *piazze* overshadowed by immense monuments. But the town shows its true colors on buses crammed with rowdy drunk teens and during colorful midnight explosions of impromptu fireworks. Beaches, pastel-colored hotels, and wide boardwalks filled with clothing vendors and fortune-tellers all contribute to an atmosphere in which it's perfectly acceptable—and even admirable—to collapse into bed and wish the rising sun "good night."

▐ TRANSPORTATION

Flights: Miramare Civil Airport (☎0541 71 57 11; www.riminiairport.com), V. Flaminia 409. Mostly charter flights. Serves many European cities. Bus #9, across from the train station, goes to the airport (every 30min. 6:09-1:01am-10:52pm and 1:02am, €1).

Trains: P. Cesare Battisti and V. Dante Alighieri (☎0541 89 20 21). Info office open daily 7:30am-8:30pm. Ticket office open daily 5:15am-10:15pm. To: **Ancona** (1hr., 44 per day 12:14am-11:02pm, €5); **Bologna** (1hr., 44 per day 2:30am-10pm, €7); **Milan** (3hr., 23 per day 2:56am-10:22pm, €28); **Ravenna** (1hr., 23 per day 3:33am-10:58pm, €4); **Riccione** (10min., 37 per day 12:30am-11:03pm, €1.10). AmEx/MC/V.

Buses: Buy both intercity and municipal tickets at ticket booth across from train station. Open daily 5:50am-12:20am. Municipal bus tickets available (90min. pass €1, purchased onboard €1.50; 24hr. pass €3; 72hr. pass €5.50; 7-day pass €11). 24hr. service to many inland towns (€1.03-3.36). Local bus #11 travels to Riccione. **TRAM intercity bus station** (☎0541 30 05 11 ; www.tram.rimini.it), at V. Roma in P. Clementini, near the station. From the train station, follow V. D. Alighieri, and take 1st left.

Taxis: RadioTaxi (☎0541 50 020). Available 24hr.

Car Rental: Avis, Vle. Trieste 16/D (☎0541 51 256; fax 56 176), off V. Amerigo Vespucci. Bus #11: stop 12. 21+. Prices starting at €66 per day. Open M-F 8:30am-1pm and 3-7:30pm, Sa 8:30am-1pm and 4-7pm. AmEx/MC/V.

Bike/Scooter Rental: P. Kennedy 6 (☎0541 27 016). Bikes €3 per hr., €10 per day; pedal-powered cars €30 per hr.; scooters from €20 per hr.; €60 per day. Open Apr.-Sept. daily 9am-midnight. AmEx/MC/V.

▐ ORIENTATION AND PRACTICAL INFORMATION

To reach the beach from the train station in **Piazzale Cesare Battisti**, turn right from the station, take another right into the tunnel at the yellow arrow indicating *"al mare,"* and follow **Viale Principe Amedeo**. To the right, **Viale Amerigo Vespucci**, the hub of Rimini activity, runs one block inland along the beach. **Bus #11** runs from the train station to the beach and continues along Vle. Vespucci and V. Regina Elena (every 15min. 5:22am-2am). Buy tickets at the kiosk in front of the station or at *tabaccherie*. To reach the **centro storico**, follow **Via Dante Alighieri** from the station to **Piazza Tre Martiri**. The center of Rimini is **Marina Centro** with **Rivabella** to the northwest and **Bellariva** to the southeast. **Rimini Sud** (south) branches out from the main city along the coast and comprises the neighborhoods of Marebello, Rivazzurra, and Miramare. **Rimini Nord** (north) goes toward the less-visited Viserba, Viserbella, and Tre Pedrera.

Tourist Offices: IAT, P. Fellini 3 (☎0541 56 902; www.riminiturismo.it), at the beginning of V. Vespucci. Bus #11: stop 10. Open in summer M-Sa 8:30am-7:15pm, Su 8:30am-2:15pm; in winter M-F 9am-1pm and 3:30-7pm, Sa 9am-1pm. Branch: Ple. Cesare Battisti 1 (☎0541 53 399), on the left after the train station. Open in summer M-Sa 8:15am-7:15pm; in winter M-Sa 8:30am-6:30pm.

Budget Travel: CTS/Grantour Viaggi, V. Matteucci 2/4 (☎0541 51 001 or 55 525). Open M-W and F 9am-12:30pm and 3:30-7pm, Th 9am-4pm, Sa 9am-12:30pm.

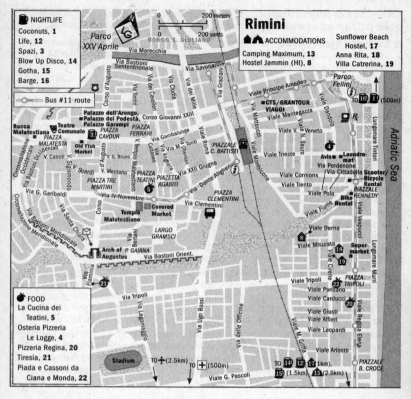

Luggage Storage: Self-service lockers in train station. €3-5 for 1st 6hr., €1 per hr. thereafter. Coins only. Call ☎0541 23 428 for problems.

Laundromat: Lavanderia Trieste Express, Vle. Trieste 16 (☎0541 26 764). 5 kg wash €10, dry €10. No self-service. Open M-Sa 8:30am-12:30pm and 3-7:30pm.

Police: C. d'Augusto 192.

Pharmacy: Farmacia del Kursaal, V. Vespucci 12/E (☎0541 21 711). Open daily 8:30am-1pm and 4-10pm. AmEx/MC/V.

Hospital: Ospedale Infermi, V. Settembrini 2 (☎0541 70 51 11 or 78 74 61).

Internet: Central Park, Vle. Vespucci 21 (☎0541 27 550). €1 per 10min., €2 per 30min., €5 per 80min. Open daily 9am-2am. MC/V.

Post Office: C. d'Augusto 8 (☎0541 78 16 73), off P. Tre Martiri, near the Arch of Augustus. Currency exchange available. Open M-F 8am-6:30pm, Sa 8am-12:30pm. Branch at P. Marvelli 3. Open M-F 8am-1:30pm, Sa 8am-12:30pm. **Postal Code: 47900.**

ACCOMMODATIONS AND CAMPING

With 1146 hotels and 62,000 beds, Rimini overwhelms visitors with its array of cookie-cutter accommodations. The smaller streets off Vle. Vespucci and Vle. Regina Elena between bus #11 stops 12 and 20 are filled with more hotels than homes. Prices peak in August, and reservations are necessary far in advance. If plans fall through, however, the tourist office provides booking services.

Sunflower Beach Hostel, Vle. Siracusa 25 (☎0541 37 34 32; www.sunflowerhostel. com), 20min. from the station and 15min. from Marino Centro. Bus #11, stop 24. Funky hostel in the heart of the party scene. Fully equipped kitchen, laundry, bar, garden, and common room. Weekly pizza and pasta parties. Breakfast included. Free lockers, Wi-Fi, and bike rental. Check-in after 2pm. Check-out 11am. Open Mar.-Oct. Dorms €14-23, with bath €16-24; singles €24-44/26-47; doubles with bath €42-60. AmEx/MC/V. ❶

Anna Rita, V. Misurata 24 (☎0541 39 10 44; www.hotelannarita.it). Bus #11, stop 13. A cut above its neighbors, this family-oriented hotel just steps from the beach offers top-notch services including free Wi-Fi, beach umbrellas, bicycle rentals, and parking. Comfortable rooms with bath, phone, TV, safe, and A/C. Buffet breakfast, takeout lunch, and dinner included. €31-53 per person during the summer (€10 surcharge for singles); in winter €20 (only bed and breakfast). Reservations recommended. AmEx/MC/V. ❸

Hostel Jammin (HI), Vle. Derna 22 (☎0541 39 08 00; www.hosteljammin.it). Bus #11, stop 13. Ideal place for beachgoers and party-seekers, just minutes from the action. Boasts excellent amenities. Central lounge features perpetually playing music videos, a well-stocked bar, and an outdoor patio. Breakfast included. Free bike rental for 1st 4hr., €1 per hr. thereafter. €10 key deposit. Lockers €1 per 24hr. Internet access €1 for 1st 15min., €3 per hr. thereafter. Reception 24hr. Closed Jan. Dorms €21; singles €33; doubles €29 per person; triples €28; quads €24, with bath €26. AmEx/MC/V. ❷

Villa Caterina, V. Cirene 21 (☎0541 30 78 50; www.villacaterina.it). Newly renovated hotel on a quiet street near the beach. Snug and simple rooms have TV, phone, safe, A/C, and private bath; some have balconies. Breakfast in an elegant dining room. Private garden. Free bike rental. Open Apr.-Sept. €28-42 per person, full pension €36-60. Stays shorter than 3 days 20% surcharge; single rooms €8 extra. AmEx/MC/V. ❷

Camping Maximum, Vle. Principe di Piemonte 57 (☎0541 37 26 02; www.camping-maximum.com). Bus #11, stop 33. Across from the beach on the way to Riccione, this lively campground is sandwiched between seaside hotels. Showers and electricity free. Wi-Fi €4 per hr. Reception 7am-10pm. Open May 20-Sept. 20. €7-10 per person, €4-5 per child; €8.50-12 per tent; €2.50-4 per car; bungalows €60-130. AmEx/MC/V. ❶

🗋 FOOD

Rimini's covered **market** between V. Castelfidardo and the **Tempio** sells fresh produce, fish, meat, bread, and cheese. (Open M-Sa 7:30am-7:30pm.) If you don't see what you're looking for, check out **STANDA** supermarket, Vle. Vespucci 133, between P. Kennedy and P. Tripoli. (Open daily 8am-10:30pm. AmEx/MC/V.) On Saturday nights, reservations are advisable at nicer, popular restaurants. For a quick lunch or late-night snack, grab a *piada*, a typical Emilia-Romagna dish of pita-like bread topped with ingredients like *prosciutto crudo*, arugula, and *squacerone* (a soft, regional cheese); or a *cassoni*, similar but sealed like a quesadilla and stuffed with cheese, meat or vegetables.

Piada e Cassoni da Ciana e Monda, Vle. Don Giovanni Bosco (☎348 563 2992). From P. Tripoli, walk down Vle. Tripoli and turn left on V. D. G. Bosco. The beach is littered with *cassoni* and *piade* joints, but this humble, family-owned spot is the real thing. Try classics like sausage, smoked bacon, and mozzarella or a vegetarian option with tomatoes, mushrooms, artichokes, and mozzarella. *Cassone* €2.50-5. *Piade* €0.70-4.50. Open June-Sept. Tu-Su 11:30am-2pm and 4-11pm. Cash only. ❶

La Cucina dei Teatini, P. Teatini 3 (☎0541 28 008, reservations 340 12 41 107), just off V. IV Novembre, near the temple. This romantic restaurant in the *centro* serves Italian plates with a healthy twist. Enjoy dishes like baked lamb with potato *pâté*, yogurt, and cucumbers (€18) or one of the *"energia"* plates (€9.50). Pasta €9-9.50. Meat €15-22. Open M-Sa 12:30-2:30pm and 7:30-11pm, Sa 7:30-10:30pm. MC/V. ❸

Pizzeria Regina, Vle. Regina Elena 37 (☎0541 38 85 96). Big helpings of dishes like sliced beef with *rucola* and balsamic vinaigrette (€12). Great late-night stop. Pizza €3-8. Primi €6. Secondi €5.50-12. Meat or fish *menù* with primo, secondo, contorno and bread €13-15. Cover €0.50. Open in summer daily 11am-5am. AmEx/MC/V. ❷

Tiresia, V. XX Settembre 41 (☎0541 78 18 96; www.osteriatiresia.it). From the Arch of Augustus, walk 5min. down V. XX Settembre. Dim lighting, cobblestone floors, rustic exposed beam ceilings, and a quiet garden out back set the tone for a laid-back, romantic night in the *centro storico.* Homemade pasta €9.50-11. Secondi €11-20. Contorni €4.50-10. Open Tu-Su 6pm-2am. AmEx/MC/V. ❸

Osteria Pizzeria Le Logge, Vle. Trieste 5 (☎0541 55 978). On a shady street off the crowded beachfront. Tasty pizza (€2-11) and seafood dishes like *strozzapretti* (gnocchi) with prawns, mushrooms, onions, and a brandy cream sauce (€8.70). Grapevines and palm awnings on the deck generate a romantic, slightly upscale feel. Primi €6.70-11. Secondi €7.50-15. Cover €1.50. Open M-Tu and Th-Su 7pm-1am. AmEx/MC/V. ❶

👁 🔍 SIGHTS AND BEACHES

TEMPIO MALATESTIANO. Rimini's cultural life once relied largely on Sigismondo Malatesta, a 15th-century lord who refurbished the *tempio* with funereal chapels for himself and his fourth wife. The simple white interior with a dark, wood ceiling houses beautiful frescoes. To the right of the apse, Piero della Francesca's *Sigismondo Pandolfo Malatesta in preghiera davanti a San Sigismondo* shows Malatesta kneeling in front of his Rimini castle, the family dog lying dutifully behind. In the first chapel, a statue of the ruler sits atop two elephants—the family emblem. The apse holds a painted crucifix by Giotto, Rimini's only work by the artist. The small brick protrusion on the exterior was added by Leon Battista Alberti to resemble the Arch of Augustus (below) as per Malatesta's orders. *(On V. IV Novembre. Follow V. D. Alighieri from the train station. ☎0541 51 130. Open M-Sa 8:30am-1pm and 3:30-7pm, Su 8:30am-1pm. Modest dress required. Free.)*

ARCH OF AUGUSTUS. Built in 27 BC to celebrate Caesar Octavian Augustus's recent completion of the Via Flaminia, this impressive arch now triumphantly marks the entrance to Rimini's *centro storico.* The top of the arch, probably destroyed in an earthquake, was refinished with medieval brick ramparts, while marble pillars depicting the gods and an inscription honoring Augustus survive today. *(Follow V. IV Novembre to P. Tre Martiri, and turn left on C. d'Augusto.)*

PIAZZE. Shops and bars surround the 18th-century *pescheria* (fish market) under the brick arches in **Piazza Cavour.** The four stone fish in the corners of the arcade once spouted water used to clean the daily catch. Perpendicular to the municipal building lies the modern **Teatro Comunale,** whose auditorium was destroyed in WWII. In the center of the *piazza,* the 1543 **Fontana della Pigna** contains an inscription by Leonardo da Vinci. In the center of the square, a militant Pope Paul V sits on his throne, his fierce gaze doing little to ward off pigeon admirers. Farther south lies **Piazza Tre Martiri.** Once a medieval jousting venue, the *piazza* now houses outdoor cafes, an 18th-century bell tower, and the mint-green domes of the **Chiesa di Sant'Antonio di Padova.**

BEACHES. Though hotels own most of the shore, a minimum charge of about €3.50 will buy a lounge chair and use of whirlpools, volleyball courts, lockers, and other facilities. The fun continues into the night with bars and live music. Vendors by the beach offer watersports equipment. A **free beach,** located at the top of the shore, is less picturesque and has no storage or lounge amenities, but the price is right and the waves are huge.

NIGHTLIFE

Rimini is notorious for the nonstop partying at clubs near the *lungomare* in Rimini Sud. A bustling nightlife scene lights up the *centro storico* by the old fish market. From P. Cavour, follow **Via Pescheria**, where pubs and bars stay open until 3am—but the real action that attracts a younger crowd of vacationers is outside the *centro storico*, near the port, where *discoteche*, pubs, and clubs glitter. Many clubs offer free bus service (check the travel agency in P. Tripoli at stop 14 for schedules; ☎0541 39 11 72; open M-Sa 8:30am-7pm, Su 9am-noon), but there is also a **Blue Line bus** (☎0541 74 35 94; www.bluelinenus.com; from June to early Sept. every 20min. 2:20am-5:40am; 1-night pass €4, 1-week €14) for late-night discogoers. It has color-coded lines depending on the *discoteca* destination and travels up the coast hitting **Miramare, Rivazzurra, Bellaria, Rivabella, Marebello, Cattolic,** and **Riccione.** Buy tickets onboard. The last bus leaves at 5:40am, after which bus #11 resumes service. During the high season, **bus #11** is an institution—by midnight, expect a crowd of strangers singing drinking songs, comparing outfits, and cheering. The route runs from Rimini to the bus station in Riccione, where Blue Line buses allow easy access to seven more nightclubs grouped together in a valley. Clubs change their hours and prices frequently, and many close in winter.

CLUB HOPPING. Nightlife in Rimini has a quick turnover rate, so it's tough to stay on top of what's popular. Ask around (especially on bus #11), follow the crowds, and if a venue is not to your liking upon arrival, just hop back on the bus—there is a world of Rimini still to discover.

Life, Vle. Regina Margherita 11 (☎0541 37 34 73), in Bellariva. Bus #11, stop 22; offers a free bus service. One of the busiest night spots, this *discoteca* draws partygoers to its movie-poster strewn bar upstairs and expansive dance floor below. DJs play American and foreign hits popular with the international crowd. Mixed drinks €5-7.50. Shots €3-4. Cover €7-12 and includes 1 drink. Open daily 11pm-4am. Cash only.

Blow up Disco, Vle. Regina Elena 209 (☎0541 38 60 60 or 335 706 3445; www.blowupdisco.it). Bus #11 to stop 21; offers a free shuttle service. Covered walkway and an upstairs lounge lead to a pulsing dance floor with lit floors, marble columns, mirrors, and neon couches. R&B, house, and Top 40 play late into the night. Partygoers tend to be young tourists, ready to experience the best of Rimini nightlife. W night guest DJ. Mixed drinks €7. Cover €10, includes 1 drink. Open daily 9:30pm-4am. Cash only.

Coconuts, Lungomare Tintorin 5 (☎0541 52 325 or 339 658 5135; www.coconuts.it). Bus #11, stop 10. Walk through Parco Fellini and 5-10min. down Lungomare Tintori. Expansive interior surrounded by comfy lounge seating, dancing platforms, and scattered bars. Attracts a young, classy crowd. Leafy plants, hardwood floors, and colorful lighting generate a tropical vibe as chic male dancers and bikini-clad women strut the dance floor. Street bar opens at 8pm, but don't expect things to start up before 9:30pm. Su features pop music. W, F and Sa have live house music. *Aperitivo* buffet at 6pm. Mixed drinks €4-8. Open daily 6pm-4:30am. MC/V.

Barge, Lungomare Tintori 13 (☎0541 70 98 45,; www.thebarge.eu). Laid-back spot near the water with a friendly, young staff. Live music. The outside enclave off the main street attracts a crowd of varied musical tastes: classic rock, jazz, and blues performed on the stage in front W, F, and Sa nights. Beer €4.50. Mixed drinks €6. Shots €4. Open M-F 7pm-4am, Sa-Su noon-3pm and 7pm-4am. AmEx/MC/V.

Gotha, Vle. Regina Margherita 52 (☎0541 47 87 39; www.gotha-rimini.com). Bus #11 to stop 28. Laid-back yet social alternative to busy neighboring *discoteche*. Large lounge surrounded by palm leaves, exotic cloths, and colored lights. R&B, pop, and Latin music. Slightly more mature crowd. From mid-July to late Aug., crowds pack the dance floor Th nights. Mixed drinks €7. Shots €4. Open daily 9pm-4am. AmEx/MC/V.

Spazi, (☎0541 23 439), in P. Cavour. More traditional spot perfect for a relaxed drink before hitting the *discoteche*. Attracts a slightly older clientele with an extensive wine list, trendy bar, and patio. Wine €3-6 per glass. €10 special includes 1 chalice of wine and 1 plate of sushi. Open M-Sa 7am-1am, Su 4pm-1am. AmEx/MC/V.

SAN MARINO   ☎0549

San Marino (san ma-REE-no; pop. 30,000) is one of two independent states inside Italy—the other is the Vatican. Officially titled the Serenissima Repubblica di San Marino ("The Most Serene Republic of San Marino"), it was founded in AD 301 by Marinus, a pious stone cutter who fled to Mt. Titano to escape the advances of an overly affectionate girl. The winding cobblestone streets of San Marino may be wrought with jewelry shops and *piadinerie* aimed at roping in the busloads of daily tourists, but this stifling commercialism is more than made up for by stunning views of rolling hills and the patchwork countryside.

STAYING IN TOUCH WITH SAN MARINO. San Marino's country code is ☎328. It is necessary to dial it only when calling from outside Italy. Within Italy and San Marino, just dial the city code (☎0549).

TRANSPORTATION

Trains: The closest train station is in Rimini (p. 287).

Buses: Fratelli Benedettini (☎0549 90 38 54) and Bonelli (☎0541 66 20 69) companies run from San Marino's *centro* to Rimini's train station (45min., 12 per day 6:30am-7pm, €3.70) and from Rimini to San Marino (11 per day 7:30am-7pm).

Funicular: connects Borgo Maggiore to the *centro storico* (☎0549 88 35 90). Every 15min. July to mid-Sept. 7:50am-1am; from mid-Sep. to Oct. 8am-7pm; Nov.-Dec. 8am-6:30pm; Jan.-Feb. 7:50am-6:30pm; Mar.-Apr. 7am-5:30pm; May-June 8am-8:30pm. €2.80, round-trip €4.54, 12 rides €8.

Taxis: in P. Lo Stradone. ☎0549 99 14 41.

ORIENTATION AND PRACTICAL INFORMATION

San Marino consists mostly of long streets that zig-zag up a steep hill; walk up any stretch to reach one of the many *piazze*, where stunning views of the countryside await. Street signs direct you to hotels, restaurants, and sights. From the bus, exit to the left, climb the staircase, and pass through the **Porta San Francesco** to begin the ascent. **Via Basilicus** leads to **Piazza Titano**. From there, turn right to **Piazza Garibaldi,** then follow **Contrada del Collegio** to **Piazza della Libertà.**

Tourist Office: Contrada del Collegio 40. (☎0549 88 29 14; www.visitsanmarino.com. Open M-F 8:30am-6:30pm, Sa 9am-1pm and 1:30-6:30pm. Cash only.)

Currency Exchange: San Marino mints coins interchangeable with the euro, though they're more collector's items than anything else. Pick them up at the **Coin and Stamp Office,** P. Garibaldi 5. (☎0549 88 23 70. Open July-Aug. daily 8:15am-6pm; Sept.-June M and Th 8:15am-6pm, Tu-W, and F 8:15am-2:15pm. MC/V.)

EMILIA-ROMAGNA

Police: ☎0549 88 77 77.

Internet Access: Caffè del Titano, Piazzetta del Titano 4 (☎0549 99 24 73). €1 per 15min. Open daily Apr.-July 7am-7pm; Aug. and Nov.-Mar. 7am-6pm. AmEx/MC/V.

Post Office: Vle. Onofri 87 (☎0549 88 29 07). Open M-F 8:15am-4:45pm, Sa 8:15-11:45am. Cash only. **Postal Code:** 47890.

ACCOMMODATIONS

Hotel Rosa, V. Lapicidi Marini 23 (☎0549 99 19 61; www.hotelrosasanmarino.com). From Salsita alla Rocca, follow signs for the Museo delle Cere. Excellent services in a prime location. Rooms have TV, phone, minibar, A/C, private bath, safe, and radio. Breakfast included. Internet access available in the bar. Reception 9am-11pm. Singles €45-55; doubles €65-110. AmEx/MC/V. ❸

Hotel Joli, Vle. Federico d'Urbino 36/B (☎0549 99 10 09), 5min. from the bus station. From P. Calcigni, climb the stairs, turn right onto Ple. lo Stradone and continue until it becomes Vle. Federico Durbino. Professional service. Elegant, sunny rooms with TV, radio, phone, shower, A/C or fan, and minibar. Restaurant downstairs. Breakfast included. Free Wi-Fi. Singles €42-75; doubles €68-110. AmEx/MC/V. ❸

Bellavista, Contrada del Pianello 42/44 (☎0549 99 12 12). Bellavista offers simple rooms with private bathroom and TV, and—as the name suggests—great views of the mountains nearby. Reception 8am-8pm. Singles €40; doubles €60. AmEx/MC/V. ❸

Hotel La Rocca, Salita alla Rocca 33 (☎0549 99 11 66; fax 99 24 30), down the street from the *castello.* Kind staff offers 10 spacious rooms with TV, private bath, phone, and fantastic views. There's also a restaurant downstairs. Breakfast included. Reception daily 9am-4pm. Singles €50-59; doubles €65-79; triples €85-100. AmEx/MC/V. ❹

FOOD

Find basics at **Alimentari Chiaruzzi,** Contra del Collegio 13, between P. Titano and P. Garibaldi. (☎0549 99 12 22. Open daily Aug. 7:30am-midnight; Sept.-July 7:30am-7:30pm. AmEx/MC/V.)

Buca San Francesco, Piazzetta Placido Feretrano 3 (☎0549 99 14 62) past Porta San Francesco. Sample regional pasta like the *Tris della Buca* (ravioli, *tagliatelle,* and cheesy lasagna in a light *ragù*) for €8. Primi €5-8. Secondi €6-9. Offerta Buca includes *lasagne, escalope* of veal, and fries €10. Bar open daily 8am-6pm. Restaurant open daily noon-3:30pm; closed Tu in winter. AmEx/MC/V. ❷

La Capanna, V. Salita alla Rocca 47 (☎0549 99 05 44). Reward yourself for the steep climb to the castles with a well-priced meal and spectacular views of the hills. Pizza heaped with toppings and classic pasta. Pizza €4.40-7. Primi €5.50. Cover and service included. Open Apr.-Oct. daily 9am-1am. AmEx/MC/V. ❶

Da Pier, Contrada S. Croce 5 (☎0549 99 03 76). Scrumptious dishes at surprisingly low prices. *Menù* of the day includes ravioli, gnocchi, or lasagna, roast or cutlet, 2 contorni, fruit salad, and wine (€16). For the less hungry, there's pizza (€3.60-7.25) or home-made pasta (€5.20-6.20). Open daily 8:30am-10pm. V. ❷

Il Loco, V. Basilicius 8 (☎0549 99 05 98). Before hopping on the bus, grab a bite at this self-service restaurant, which offers a 3-course meal for €8.30. Individual plates like *cannelloni* with ricotta and vegetables or baked lasagna €4.30-7. Open daily Aug. 9am-10pm; Sept.-July 9am-6pm. Cash only. ❶

EMILIA-ROMAGNA

🌀 🌺 SIGHTS AND FESTIVALS

Guards clad in festive red-and-green uniforms stand outside the late 19th-century **Palazzo Pubblico,** which serves as the seat of San Marino's parliament. The marble interior features the **Sala del Consiglio** (Hall of the Council), from which the city is still run amid a depiction of Justice (holding a broadsword) and Peace (at a slight disadvantage, holding an olive branch). The changing of the guard takes place in front of the *palazzo* from April to September at half past the hour from 8:30am to 6:30pm. (P. della Libertà. ☎0549 88 31 52, museum 88 26 74. Open daily June-Sept. 8am-8pm; Oct.-May. 9am-12:30pm and 2-5:15pm. Last entry 30min. before closing. €3. Cash only.) Two of the three points along San Marino's defensive network are open to the public, but just traveling between them offers many of the same views for free. The first tower is the **Castello della Guaita,** which offers stunning views of the country's hills and cypress trees from atop winding pathways. Climb to the tower, where lovers have scratched their names into the rafters. Be careful as you ascend the steep staircase. (Follow signs from P. della Libertà. ☎0549 99 13 69. Open from Apr. to mid-Sept. daily 8am-8pm; from mid-Sept. to Oct. M-F 9am-5pm, Sa-Su 9am-6pm; Nov.-Mar. daily 9am-5pm. Last entry 30min. before closing. €3, combined with Castello della Cesta and Museum of Ancient Arms €4.50. AmEx/MC/V.) Follow signs along the trail to the highest peak of Mt. Titano, where the **Castello della Cesta** offers the best views of the distant Adriatic and the Castello della Guaita. Inside, the **Museo delle Armi Antiche,** an arms museum, displays a selection of fierce weapons ranging from 15th-century tridents to medieval helmets. (☎0549 99 12 95. Same hours as Castello della Guaita. €3, with Castello della Guaita €4.50. Cash only.) Castle fanatics can follow the trail to the third tower, **Torre del Montale,** a squat, mossy turret closed to the public. Nearby, stone outcroppings offer quiet views of the hills and ocean.

In late summer, a **medieval festival** brings parades, food, musicians, and jugglers to San Marino. September 3 is San Marino's day of independence; the **Palio delle Balestre,** or crossbowman's show, commemorates this event; increased bus service makes daytripping easy. (Early Sept.; for specific dates and info, call☎0549 88 29 98 or the tourist office, p. 293)

EMILIA-ROMAGNA

TUSCANY (TOSCANA)

Tuscany is the stuff of Italian dreams—and more than one romantic Brits-in-Italy movie. Gazing out over rolling hills, fields of sunflowers, and inviting cobblestone streets, it's hard not to wax poetic. Tuscany's Renaissance culture became Italy's heritage, and its regional dialect—the language of Dante, Petrarch, and Machiavelli—became today's textbook Italian. The subtle variations in Tuscan cuisine give you an excuse to have a meal and a bottle of wine in every single town.

Though cut from similar cloth, each Tuscan city has its own fierce heritage and unique characteristics; after all, they did spend centuries trying to conquer each other. The land from Chianti's vineyards to Viareggio's beaches has something for everyone, served with a dose of quaint small-town Italian charm..

HIGHLIGHTS OF TUSCANY

ADMIRE the towering marble statues in Florence's Piazza della Signoria (p. 317).

TASTE local reds and whites in the vineyards of Tuscan wine country (p. 324).

SIGH as the sun sets gloriously over the Ponte Vecchio in Florence (p. 318).

FLORENCE (FIRENZE)   ☎ 055

Thanks to the floods, wars, famine, and Black Death that haunted Europe during the early Renaissance period, sopping-wet, battle-weary, emaciated, and plagued Florence—or Firenze (Fee-REN-zeh; pop. 400,000)—was not a pleasant sight. In the late 14th century, however, Florence was able to etch itself into the history books. Florentines Boccaccio, Dante, and Giotto created trend-setting masterpieces and, in the 15th century, Florence had gained further artistic distinction as the Medici family amassed a priceless collection, supporting masters like Botticelli, Brunelleschi, Donatello, and Michelangelo, among other ninja turtles. Rivalries between families, political factions, neighboring towns, and artists led to increasingly impressive shows of power—now yours to enjoy in the resulting art and architecture.

Today, you can't turn a corner in Florence without finding a famous church, museum, or building designed by Arnolfo di Cambio—and the attendant tour groups. The historical center must be one of the most crowded squares in Europe, but venture just a few blocks outside of P. della Signoria and you'll find homey trattorie, artisanal shops, and the block parties that comprise local Florentine nightlife. Nowhere else is there so much concentrated beauty, whether man-made or soil-born. There's definitely something in the water.

✈ INTERCITY TRANSPORTATION

Flights: Aeroporto Amerigo Vespucci (FLR; main line ☎055 30 615, 24hr. automated flight info line 30 61 700; www.aeroporto.firenze.it) in the suburb of Peretola. Mostly

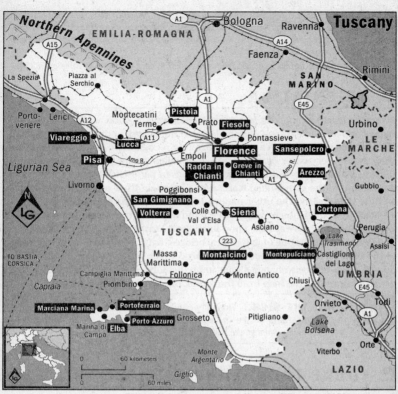

domestic and charter flights. **Volainbus,** a join effort by SITA and ATAF&Linea, runs buses (25min., every 30min., 5:30am-11pm, €4.50) between the Departures side of the Florence airport and Santa Maria Novella Station. Tickets can be purchased in the airport area at the bar, in any SITA or ATAF ticket office, or onboard. As with ATAF tickets, Volainbus tickets must be validated on board in an automated machine. **Taxis** mill around the arrivals area of the airport; a ride to the city center costs €20-27.

Trains: Stazione Santa Maria Novella, just north of Santa Maria Novella. Ticket station (*biglietteria*) open daily 6am-9pm; after-hours, purchase tickets at self-service machines located throughout the station. Info office open daily 7am-9pm, next to track 5 (after-hours ☎055 89 20 21). Luggage storage (6am-11:50pm; €4 for the first 5hr., €0.60 per hr. for the next 6-12, €0.20 per hr. for 13 or more) and lost property services available. Trains to: **Bologna** (1hr., every hr. 4:35am-11:40am, €20); **Milan** (2½hr., every hr. 7:10am-9:20pm, €47); **Rome** (3hr., every hr. 5:50am-9:49pm, €44); **Siena** (1½hr., every hr. 5:35am-11:10pm, €14); **Venice** (3hr., every hr. 5:45am-1:45am, €44).

Buses: 3 major bus companies run out of Florence; their offices are near P. della Stazione. Intercity buses depart from P. della Stazione, P. Adua, or in front of the train station.

SITA, V. Santa Caterina de Siena (☎055 80 03 73 760). Station and ticket office open M-Sa 5:50am-8:30pm, Su 6:15am-7:55pm. MC/V. Information office open M-Sa 8:30am-12:30pm and 3pm-6pm, Su 8:30am-12:30pm. To: **Arezzo** (2hr., 3 per day, €4.30); **San Gimignano** (1hr., 12 per day, €6); **Siena** (1-1½hr., 15 per day, €6.80); **Volterra** (2hr., 6 per day, €7.40) via Colle Val D'Elsa.

LAZZI, P. Adua 2 (☎055 35 10 61; www.lazzi.it). Depart from P. Adua. Office open M-Sa 6:10am-8:15pm, Su 7am-7:20pm. Cash only. To: **Lucca** (1hr., every hr. 6:45am-8:15pm, €5.10); **Pisa** (3hr., every hr. 6am-8:15pm, €6.10); **Pistoia** (1hr., every hr. 7am-6pm, €3); **Prato** (45min., every hr. 6am-11pm, €2.30).

CAP, Largo Alinari 10 (☎055 21 46 37). Office open M-F 6:40-8pm. To **Prato** (1hr., 6am-8pm, €2.30).

◆ ORIENTATION

From the front steps of **Stazione Santa Maria Novella,** a short walk down **Via de' Panzani** and a left on **Via de Cerrentari** leads to the **Duomo,** in the heart of the city. Most streets in Florence lead to this instantly recognizable dome, which soars high above every other city structure and makes getting lost a little easier to remedy. **Via de Calzaiuoli,** dominated by throngs of pedestrians, leads south from the Duomo to the statue-filled **Piazza della Signoria,** in front of the **Palazzo Vecchio** and the **Uffizi Gallery.** The other major *piazza* is the **Piazza della Republica,** down **Via Roma** from the Duomo. Major streets run north from this *piazza* toward the Duomo and south toward the shop-lined **Ponte Vecchio** (literally, "Old Bridge"). The Ponte Vecchio is one of five central bridges that cross from central Florence to the **Oltrarno,** the district south of the Arno River. When navigating Florence, note that most streets change names unpredictably, often every flew blocks. To get around, grab a free map from the tourist office (see opposite page).

I SAW THE SIGN. Florentine street signs are not on signposts, and they're not always on the corner. Instead, they're located on the buildings themselves. So when you're lost, be sure to look up!

◆ LOCAL TRANSPORTATION

Buses: Orange **ATAF** and **Linea buses** run 6am-1am. Buy tickets at any newsstand, *tabaccheria,* or coin-operated ticket dispenser. €1.20 for 70min. (€2 onboard), €4.50 for 4 tickets, €5 for 1 day. Only ask to buy a ticket on board while at a red light or while the bus is picking up passengers. Validate all tickets onboard using the orange machine or risk a €50 fine. The ATAF ticket booth is located on an island directly across from the pharmacy end of Santa Maria Novella Station, and employees can usually tell you which line to board for particular destinations. However, for more extensive route maps and to avoid clogging the ticket line, turn to the ATAF info office (☎055 80 04 24 500; www.ataf.net), which is in the cement building to the left of the ticket booth. Open M-F 7:30am-7:30pm, Sa 7:30am-1:30pm. Most ATAF bus routes begin or pick up right outside of Santa Maria Novella station at one of four pick-up points, and many of them pass through the Duomo. There are a few **night buses** that run until approximately 3am; these routes are written on the bus signs in a black background with white or orange lettering. However, after midnight they only arrive once every 40min.-1hr., so if you're counting on them for transit, pay attention to the scheduled arrival time and get there 10min. early to be safe. The **#70** runs through most of the central stops, including Santa Maria Novella, San Marco, and the Duomo.

Taxis: ☎055 43 90, 47 98, 90 44 99, or 90 42 42.

🔃 PRACTICAL INFORMATION

TOURIST AND FINANCIAL SERVICES

Tourist Offices: Informazione Turistica provides info in major foreign languages on tourist attractions, events, directions, available tours, and general emergency information. Offices are run through the **City of Florence, the Comune di Firenze,** and the **Agenzia per il Turismo di Firenze.** At P. Della Stazione 4 (☎055 21 22 45; turismo3@comune. fi.it), across the *piazza* from the station's main exit. Open M-Sa 8:30-7pm, Su and holidays 8:30am-2pm. At Borgo Santa Croce 29r (☎055 23 40 444; turismo2@comune. fi.it). Open Mar.-Oct. M-Sa 9am-7pm, Su and holidays 9am-2pm; Nov.-Feb. M-Sa 9am-5pm, Su and holidays 9am-2pm. At V. Cavour 1r (☎055 29 08 32; infoturismo@provincia.fi.it). At Amerigo Vespucci Airport (☎055 31 58 74). Open daily 8:30am-8:30pm. At V. Manzoni 16 (☎055 23 320; info@firenzeturismo.it). Open M-F 9am-1pm.

Budget Travel: Centro Turistico Student and Youth, V. Borgo La Croce 42r (☎055 28 95 70; www.cts.it). Transalpino tickets and ISICs available. Open M-F 9:30am-1pm and 2:30-6pm, Sa 9:30am-12:30pm. MC/V. Branch at V. Maragliano 86 (☎055 33 41 64). Open M-F 9-1pm and 3-7pm, Sa 10am-1pm.

Consulates: UK, Lungarno Corsini 2 (☎055 28 41 33; www.ukinitaly.fco.gov.uk). Open M-F 9:30am-12:30pm and 2:30-4:30pm. **US,** Lungarno Amerigo Vespucci 38 (☎055 26 69 51; www.florence.usconsulate.gov). For more info, see **Essentials,** p. 8.

LOCAL SERVICES

Luggage Storage: (☎055 23 52 190). At the far end of the train station, beside platform 16, toward the bus depot. €4 for 1st 5hr., €0.60 per hr. 6-12hr., €0.20 per hr. thereafter; max. 5 days. Must present identification. Open daily 6am-midnight. Cash only.

Lost Property: Ufficio Oggetti Rinvenuti (☎055 23 56 120), next to the baggage deposit in train station. **City Council Lost Property Office,** V. Circondaria 19 (☎055 32 83 942 or 32 83 943), holds all property handed in at Police Headquarters, Carabinieri, and Railway Police Offices. Inquiries about property left in taxis should first be made at the urban police offices and then at the City Council Offices.

English-Language Bookstores: Feltrinelli International Bookstore, V. Cavour 12 (☎055 29 21 96). Open M-Sa 9am-7:30pm. Via de'Cerretani 30/32r (☎055 23 82 652). Open M-F 9:30am-8pm, Sa 10am-8pm, Su 10:30am-1:30pm and 3-6:30pm. A large chain with an equally large selection. MC/V. **Mel Bookstore,** V. de'Cerretani 16r (☎055 28 73 39). The English language selection and the long hours make this location one of your best bets for finding something other than our travel guide to read on the train. Open M-F 9am-midnight and Su 10am-midnight. **Paperback Exchange,** V. delle Oche 4r (☎055 28 73 39; www.papex.it). Probably the best selection of children's books in English. In addition to both fiction and nonfiction bestsellers, the store also has an eclectic, ever-changing selection of used books fun to hunt through. Trade-ins welcome. Open M-F 9am-7:30pm and Sa 10:30am-7:30pm.

Laundromats: Wash and Dry (☎055 58 04 480; www.washedry.it). Self-service locations throughout the city. Wash and dry €3.50 each. Detergent €1. **Branches:** V. dei Servi 105r , V. della Scala 52/54r, V. del Sole 29r, Borgo San Frediano 39r, Via dei Serragli 87r, V. Nazionale 129r, V. Ghibellina 143r, V. Dell'Agnolo 21r.

EMERGENCY AND COMMUNICATIONS

Emergency: ☎113 or ☎055 31 80 00

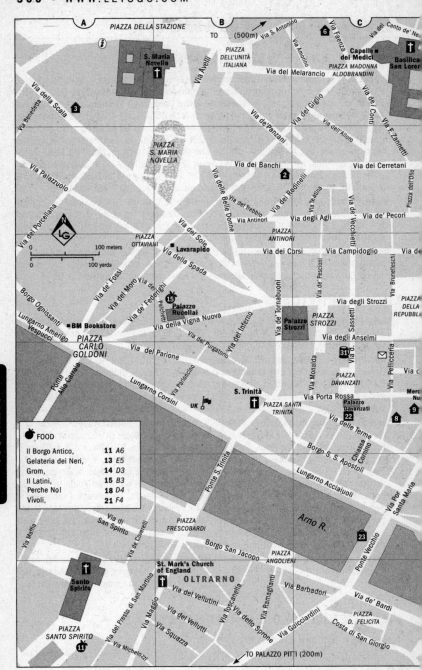

PIAZZA DELLA STAZIONE

TO (500m) Via S. Antonino

Via S. Antonino

PIAZZA DELL'UNITÀ ITALIANA

S. Maria Novella

Via del Canto de' Nel

Via Faenta

Capelle dei Medici

Basilica San Lorer

PIAZZA MADONNA ALDOBRANDINI

Via del Melarancio

Via Avelli

Via Amorino

Via del Giglio

Via dell'Alloro

Via de' Conti

Via F. Zannetti

Via della Scala

Via Benedetta

PIAZZA S. MARIA NOVELLA

Via dei Banchi

Via dei Cerretani

Piazza dell'Olio

Via Palazzuolo

Via delle Belle Donne

Via del Trebbio

Via dei Rondinelli

Via Teatina

Via de' Vecchietti

Via de' Pecori

Via Antinori

PIAZZA ANTINORI

Via del Porcellana

Via dei Corsi

Via Campidoglio

Via de

Lavarapido

PIAZZA OTTAVIANI

Via della Spada

Via de Pescioni

Via Brunelleschi

PIAZZA DELLA REPUBBL

Via de Fossi

Via del Sole

Via de Federighi

Via del Moro

Palchetti

Palazzo Rucellai

Via degli Strozzi

PIAZZA SASSETTI

BM Bookstore

Via della Vigna Nuova

Via dell'Inferno

Via de' Purgatorio

Via de Tornabuoni

Palazzo Strozzi

PIAZZA STROZZI

Via degli Anselmi

Via Sassetti

Borgo Ognissanti

Lungarno Amerigo Vespucci

PIAZZA CARLO GOLDONI

Via del Parione

Via Parioncino

PIAZZA DAVANZATI

Via Pellicceria

Via c

Ponte Alla Carraia

Lungarno Corsini

UK

S. Trinità

PIAZZA SANTA TRINITA

Via Porta Rossa

Via Monalda

Palazzo Davanzati

Via delle Terme

Merc Nu

Borgo S. S. Apostoli

Chiassa Comino

Lungarno Acciaiuoli

Via di San Spirito

PIAZZA FRESCOBARDI

St. Mark's Church of England

OLTRARNO

Via del Vellutini

Borgo San Jacopo

PIAZZA ANGOLIERI

Arno R.

Ponte S. Trinita

Ponte Vecchio

Via Por Santa Maria

Via Maffia

Via di Coverelli

Via del Presto di San Martino

Via Maggio

Via del Vellutti

Via Squazza

Via Michelozzi

Via Toscanella

Via dello Sprone

Via Ramaglianti

Via Barbadori

Via Guicciardini

Via de' Bardi

Costa di San Giorgio

PIAZZA D. FELICITA

Santo Spirito

PIAZZA SANTO SPIRITO

TO PALAZZO PITTI (200m)

TUSCANY

100 meters

100 yards

PIAZZA
AN LORENZO
Palazzo
Medici
Riccardi
Via dei Ginori
Via dei Gori
Via Cavour
■ Galleria Michelangelo

Mercato di
San Lorenzo

Borgo San Lorenzo
Via de' Martelli
Via Ricasoli

Via dei Pucci
Palazzo
Pucci
Via del Castelaccio

Libreria
Martelli

Via dei Servi

Battistero

Duomo ✝

Museo dell'Opera
del Duomo

Via Bufalini

Via della Pergola

PIAZZA
S. MARIA
NUOVA ✚

PIAZZA
S. GIOVANNI
Campanile
PIAZZA
DEL DUOMO

Via dell'Oriuolo

Via Porta Rossa

Via San Egidio

Via di Roma

Tosinghi
Via de' Medici
Paperback
Exchange
14
26
Via delle Oche
Via dello Studio
Via del Proconsolo
Via San Elisabetta

Via Speziali
Via del Corso
Borgo degli Albizi

Via del Calzaioli
Via dei Cerchi
Casa di
Dante
AmEx
S
Via S. Margherita
Via Dante Alighieri
Via de' Giraldi
Via de' Seggiole
Via de' Pandolfini
V. d. Crocifisso
Via Palmieri
7

Arte d. Lana
Via
Lamberti
18
Orsanmichele
Via dei
Tavolini
Via del Cimatori
Badia ✝
Lavarapido
Bargello
Via Ghibellina
Via della Vigna Vecchia
Via Giuseppe Verdi

Via della Condotta
Via Acqua
Via A. Burella
21

Rₓ
Via Calimaruzza
30
Via del Vacchereccia
PIAZZA DELLA
SIGNORIA
Neptune's
Fountain
Via Gondi
PIAZZA
SAN
FIRENZE
Via dell'Anguillara
Via Bentaccordi
V. Isole delle Stinche
Via Torta
Via de Verzano

Chiasso del Buco

Via de' Baroncelli
Loggia
dei Lanzi
Palazzo
Vecchio
Via di
Ninna
Via d. Corno
Borgo de' Greci
Via de' Pepi
PIAZZA
PERUZZI
PIAZZA
SANTA
CROCE

Via Lambertesca
The Uffizi
PIAZZA DEGLI UFFIZI
Via de' Castellani
Via Vinegia
Via de' Magalotti
Via de' Rustici
Via Canto Rivolo
Via de' Brache
Via de' Benci
Santa
Croce ✝

Itada
olami

Museo di Storia
della Scienza
PIAZZA
DEI GUIDICI
Casalito d'Altrafronte
Osteria del Guanto
Corso dei Tintori
Via della Mosca
Via de' Saponai
13
Via dei Neri
29
i
Borgo S. Croce

PIAZZA
MENTANA
Via de' Vagellai
Via Malenchini

Lungarno Generale Diaz

PIAZZA
S. MARIA
SOPR' ARNO
Lungarno Torrigiani
Ponte alle
Grazie

TUSCANY

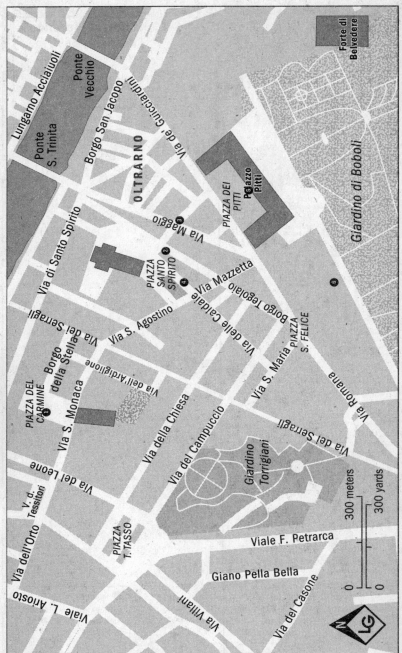

Police: Tourist Police, Ufficio Stranieri,V. Zara 2 (☎055 49 771). For visa or work-permit problems. Open M-F 9:30am-1pm. To report lost or stolen items, go around the corner to **Ufficio Denunce,** V. Duca d'Aosta 3 (☎055 49 771). Open M-Sa 8am-8pm.

Municipal Police: ☎055 32 831, in emergency ☎055 32 85.

Fire Station: ☎115 or 055 24 18 41.

Pharmacies: Farmacia Comunale (☎055 28 94 35), by track 16 at the train station. **Molteni,** V. dei Calzaiuoli 7r (☎055 28 94 90). **All'Insegna del Moro,** P. San Giovanni 20r. All open 24hr. AmEx/MC/V.

Medical Services: Tourist Medical Services, V. Lorenzo il Magnifico 59 (☎055 47 54 11). English-, German-, and French-speaking doctors with 70 specialists. In P. Duomo (☎055 21 22 21). Open M-F 8am-8pm, doctors on-call 24hr. **Ospedale Santa Maria Nuova,** P. Santa Maria Nuova 1 (☎055 27 581), near the Duomo.

Internet Access: Internet Train, V. Guelfa 54/56 (☎055 26 45 146), V. dell'Oriolo 40r (☎055 26 38 968), Borgo San Jacopo 30r (☎055 265 7935), V. Giacomini 9 (☎055 50 31 647), V. de'Benci 36r (☎055 26 38 555), V. Alamanni 5a (☎055 28 69 92), V. Porta Rossa 38r (☎055 27 41 037), Lungarno B. Cellini 43r (☎055 38 30 921). Internet €3.20-4.30 per hr. Wi-Fi €2.50 per hr. Open daily 10am-10:30pm.

Post Office: V. Pellicceria 3 (☎055 27 36 480), off P. della Repubblica. Open M-F 8:15am-7pm, Sa 8:15am-12:30pm. **Postal Code:** 50100.

▯ ACCOMMODATIONS

▨ **Locanda Orchidea,** Borgo degli Albizi 11 (☎055 24 80 346; www.hotelorchideaflorence. it). Turn left off V. Proconsolo from the Duomo. Dante's wife was born in this 12th-century *palazzo.* Rooms have marble floors and famous Renaissance prints. Clean shared baths. Singles €55; doubles €75; triples with shower €90-100; quads €120. Cash only. ❸

▨ **Hotel Medici,** V. dei Medici 6 (☎055 28 48 18). A 6-story student favorite. Top-floor terrace looks out over unbelievable views of the Duomo and Campanile. Breakfast included; we recommend dining on the aforementioned terrace. No A/C. Singles €50; doubles €75; quads €100. MC/V. ❸

▨ **Hotel Bretagna,** Lungarno Corsini 6 (☎055 28 96 18; www.hotelbretagna.net). Gilded common rooms with 200-year-old porcelain plates, spacious breakfast hall, elegant bar, and a small balcony with an incredible view of the river. Doubles €110, with river view and jacuzzi €140-150. Prices 35% lower Nov.-Mar. AmEx/MC/V. ❺

▨ **Relais Cavalcanti,** V. Pellicceria 2 (☎055 21 09 62). From P. della Repubblica walk down V. Pellicceria toward the Arno past the Central Poste. Wake up to the scent of roses in a room with antique furniture and gold-trimmed headboards. All rooms with satellite TVs, A/C, and Wi-Fi. Complimentary coffee, tea, and sweets in a shared kitchen. Singles €70-80; doubles €90-120; triples 130-150. MC/V. ❺

▨ **Hotel Abaco,** V. dei Banchi 1 (☎055 23 81 919; www.abaco-hotel.it). Convenient location, helpful staff, and extravagant rooms. Each room is a masterpiece named after a Renaissance great. Each with phone and TV. Breakfast included. Wi-Fi. Singles €60; doubles €70-95; triples €110. MC/V. ❸

▨ **Hotel Consigli,** Lungarno Amerigo Vespucci 50 (☎055 21 41 72; www.hotelconsigli. com). Once the playground of a Renaissance prince, this riverside palace is a sunlit sanctum of vaulted ceilings, sweeping frescoes, and marble stairs. The rooms are enormous, cool, and quiet, and the balcony and breakfast room look out over postcard-perfect views of the Arno. A/C. Breakfast included. Wi-Fi €3 per hr., €5 per 2hr., €7 per 3hr. Parking €15 per day. Singles €60-90; doubles €60-150. AmEx/MC/V. ❸

TUSCANY

- ▣ **Ostello Archi Rossi**, V. Faenza 94r (☎055 29 08 04; www.hostelarchirossi.com). You'll feel the Florentine creative vibe as soon as you see the frescoes painted in the reception by local art students. Each of the 30 spotless rooms comes with a PC, locker, and shared bathroom. Archi Rossi boasts a romantic garden, free Wi-Fi, computer use, and a free walking tour every morning with an English-speaking guide. Breakfast included; features bacon and eggs. Complimentary pasta dinners also occasionally served. Luggage storage available. Reception 24hr. Dorms €18-25; singles €25-35. MC/V. ❶
- ▣ **Holiday Rooms**, V. Nazionale 22 (☎055 28 50 84; www.marcosplaces.com). Owner Marco has been known to meet guests at the train station to help them with their baggage—a small taste of the conveniences and perks to come. Hardwood beds and satin curtains adorn 8 quiet rooms equipped with satellite flatscreen TVs, computers, Wi-Fi, and laundry access. Kitchen available. Rooms €25-40 per person. Discounts at some local restaurants. ❶
- ▣ **Soggiorno Luna Rossa**, V. Nazionale 7, 3rd fl. (☎055 29 23 04; www.marcosplaces.com). From the Piazza Stazione near Santa Maria Novella Station, walk to V. Nazionale until you reach Marco's other place. Wake up in a brightly-decorated room to the morning sun streaming through the spectacular stained-glass windows of this centrally located hostel. 18 private rooms available, 3 with shared bathrooms. Each with Wi-Fi, computer, satellite flatscreen TV, and free international calls. Kitchen available. Rooms €25-40 per person. ❷
- **Hotel Bigallo**, Vicolo degli Adimari 2 (☎055 21 60 86; www.hotelbigallo.it). Sumptuous furnishings and an unbeatable location beside the Baptistery make this the Hotel Savoy of the budget-savvy. Each room equipped with satellite TV, mini-bar, and A/C. Some rooms have views of the Duomo. Breakfast included. Internet €5 per hr. Doubles €60. Cash only. ❸

Hostel AF19, V. Ricasoli 9 (☎055 23 98 665; www.academyhostels.com). A bright and spacious hostel with multi-floor suites and a location literally steps from the Duomo. A/C. Safety lockers. Laundry €5. Free Wi-Fi in the lobby. Lockout 11am-2pm. 2- to 6-bed dorms €28-36. Cash preferred. AmEx/MC/V. ❶

Pensione Ferretti, V. delle Belle Donne 17 (☎055 23 81 328; www.hotelferretti.com). Dainty and affordable rooms on the edge of Santa Maria Novella. The helpful manager stores luggage for guests after check-out. Breakfast included. Free Wi-Fi. Singles with shared bath €40; doubles €50; triples €90; quads €110. Cash only. ❷

Hotel Crocini, Corso Italia 28 (☎055 21 29 05; www.hotelcrocini.com), next door to the Teatro Comunale, 15min. from Santa Maria Novella station. Family-run establishment outfits its classic rooms with satellite TV and spacious showers. No A/C. Free Wi-Fi. Reception 24hr. Singles €39; doubles €49. AmEx/MC/V. ❷

Hotel Tina, V. San Gallo 31 (☎055 48 35 19; www.hoteltina.it). Family-run pension with pleasant blue decor welcomes guests into large carpeted rooms with comfortable plush furniture. Breakfast included. Free Wi-Fi. Singles €30-40; doubles with shower €45-75, with bath €70-80; triples €65-90; quads €80-120. MC/V. ❷

Hotel San Marco, V. Cavour 50 (☎055 28 18 51; www.hotelsanmarcofirenze.it), just a few feet away from P. San Marco. Sunlit white walls and bright bedspreads. Quiet rooms away from the street available on request. Breakfast included; enjoy it while watching *calcio* on the communal TV. A/C and Wi-Fi. Singles €35-50; doubles €65; quads €108. Cash only. ❷

Hotel Gioia, V. Cavour 25 (☎055 28 28 04; www.hotelgioia.it). A professional establishment with classy rooms. Frequented by both businessmen and tourists. Each room has satellite TV, mini-bar, A/C, and safe. Breakfast included; room service available. Wi-Fi. Singles €80; doubles €89; quads €130. MC/V. ❺

Hotel Benvenuti, V. Cavour 112 (☎055 57 39 09; www.benvenutihotel.it). Friendly staff and a quiet, relaxing atmosphere make up for the minimal decor and slightly inconvenient location. A/C available. Breakfast included. Free Wi-Fi. Singles €20-30, with private bath €33-35; doubles €55; quads €72. AmEx/MC/V. ❶

Ostello Santa Monaca, V. Santa Monaca 6 (☎055 26 83 38; www.ostello.it). Basic rooms on the cheap. Enjoy a discounted meal at a local restaurant or wash-and-dry laundry service for €6.50 per load. Fans of late-night showers, hope you like them cold: hot water shuts off midnight-6am every night. Common room open 7am-1am. Microwave and stove-top available. Free internet. Check-in 6am-2am. Lockout 10am-2pm. Curfew 2am. 16- to 22-bed dorms €17; 10-bed dorms €18; 8-bed dorms €18.50; 6-bed dorms €19; 4-bed dorms €20. AmEx/MC/V. ❶

Campeggio Michelangelo, V. Michelangelo 80 (☎055 68 11 977; www.ecvacanze. it), beyond Ple. Michelangelo. Take bus #13 from the station to the Camping 1 stop (15min., last bus 11:25pm). Chain campground is family-geared and very crowded, but offers good (if distant) views of the city and a shaded olive grove. Market and bar available. Towels €1.50. Laundry €7. Internet €3 per hr. Reception daily 7am-11pm. €9.30-11 per person. April-Nov. 2-person tent €36. MC/V over €100. ❶

Sognando Firenze Bed and Breakfast, V. Giampaolo Orsini 115 (☎055 68 32 78; www. sognandofirenze.it). Boasts a bright breakfast room overlooking the street, neat yellow rooms with A/C, and private bathrooms. Breakfast included. Free Wi-Fi. Singles €60; doubles €70; triples €85; quads €105. MC/V. ❸

◨ FOOD

▧ **Grom,** V. del Campanile (☎055 21 61 58), off P. del Duomo to the left of the Campanile. The kind of gelato you'll be talking about in 50 years. As fresh as it gets; sublimely balanced texture. Large store is standing-room only and flooded with tourists and locals. Cups €2-5, cones €2-4. Open daily Apr.-Sept. 10:30am-midnight, Oct.-Mar. 10:30am-11pm. ❶

Trattoria Le Mossacce, V. del Proconsolo 55r (☎055 29 43 61; www.trattorialemossacce.it). The sort of place that you just don't expect near the Duomo, Mossace seats strangers shoulder-to-shoulder and whips out Tuscan specialties. Primi €5-8.50. Secondi €5.50-10. Cover €1. Open daily noon-2:30pm and 7-9:30pm. ❷

Gelateria del Neri, V. dei Neri 20-22r (☎055 21 00 34). Follow the street between Uffizi and Palazzo Vecchio. Just big enough for a counter and the waiting line, this gelateria is the locals' favorite. Serves generous scoops of creative flavors like *crema giotto* (a blend of coconut, almond, and hazelnut) and equally delicious classics like pistachio. Cones and cups from €1.50. Open daily 11am-midnight. Cash only. ❶

Teatro del Sale, V. dei Macci 111r (☎055 20 01 492). It's "members only" at this private club, but the slight fee and mission statement ensure that the pretensions end here. In a high-arched, hardwood theatre, Fabio Picchi picks the freshest ingredients and announces each delicious course from his open kitchen. Once the last piece of mouthwatering dessert has been snatched off the plate, the entertainment begins, ranging from music lessons to theatrical performances—but many shows are in Italian, so plan ahead. Breakfast €7; lunch €20. Membership fee €5. Open Tu-Sa 9-11am, noon-2:15pm, and from 7:30pm until the end of the show. Reservations required. AmEx/MC/V. ❹

Ruth's Kosher Vegetarian Restaurant, V. Luigi Carlo Farini 2A (☎055 24 80 888). Carnivorous Christians, be not afraid! There are plenty options for you, as well. Photos of Woody Allen and Kafka look on as wise owner Simcha makes everyone feel part of the community, serving hummus (€6), pasta (€7), and couscous (€13-15). Students enjoy special dinners W nights for €10. Free Wi-Fi. Open M-Th and Su noon-2:30pm and 7:30-10:30pm, F noon-2:30pm. AmEx/MC/V. ❷

Ok Bar, V. de Servi 97r (☎055 21 71 49). A one-stop shop for any dish that your stomach could demand, this all-purpose bar serves up everything from American breakfast (toast and omelette €6) to four-cheese and shrimp risotto (€8.50). The to-go display is filled with pizza (€3), *panini* (€2.50-5), and pastries (€4-8). Primi €6-9.50. Secondi €6-14. Open daily 7am-midnight. MC/V. ❷

Antico Noe, Volta di San Piero 6r (☎055 23 40 838). When you're sick of reheated *rosticceria panini*, head to Antico Noe for freshly crafted sandwiches. Flavorful combinations like stuffed chicken, peppers, and mozzarella (€4) and roast pork, pecorino, and eggplant (€4). Popular vegetarian plates €3.80. Open Ma-Sa noon-midnight. Cash only. ❶

Buongustai, V. dei Cerchi 15 (☎055 29 13 04). Walk north from Palazzo Vecchio . After a day at the nearby Duomo, Bargello, and P. della Signoria, relax at this quirky and casual spot. Make sure to try the house special *Piatto del Buongustai* (Tuscan salami, cheese, and pickled vegetables; €10). Primi €4.50-6.50. Secondi €6.50-10. Open M-Th 9:30am-3:30pm, F-Sa 8:30-11pm. Cash only. ❷

Il Latini, V. dei Palchetti 6r (☎055 21 09 16; www.illatini.com). Waiting in line has never been so pleasant. Il Latini's host offers complimentary glasses of white wine and cheese to those waiting outside. Primi €5-10. Secondi €14-23. Open Tu-Su noon-2:30pm and 7:30-10:30pm. AmEx/MC/V. ❹

Vivoli, V. Dell' Isola Del Stinche 7r (☎055 29 23 34, www.vivoli.it). From Palazzo Vecchio, take Borgo dei Greci and turn left on V. Bentaccordia. Delicious treats. Coneheads take heed: the spoonfuls of sugar only come in cups here. Cups from €1.70. Open Tu-F 7:30am-midnight, Su 9:30am-midnight. Cash only. ❶

Trattoria Contadino, V. Palazzuolo 69-71r (☎055 23 82 673). Casual, homestyle meals in a dining room with black and white decor and a relaxed atmosphere. You're sure to leave feeling stuffed—the only option is a multi-course *menù* that includes primo, secondo, a vegetable dish, bread, and house wine. Lunch €10. Dinner €11.50. ❷

Ristorante La Spada, V. della Spada 62r (☎055 21 87 57; www.laspadaitalia.com). This classic *cucina* serves Tuscan dishes ranging from the familiar (ravioli €9) to the uniquely Florentine (rabbit on a spit €10.50). Take a peek into the attached *rosticceria* (deli-kitchen) to watch the chef grilling your dishes in the open-air flame oven. The lunch *menù* (€11) includes primo, secondo, fruit salad, and drink. Check for nightly dinner deals. Cover €2.50. ❸

Rosticceria Gastronomia II, Il Pirata, V. dei Ginori 56. Heaping helpings of hit-the-spot comfort food. As you chow down on your cheesy, meaty medley, check out the multilingual array of messages that guests have left on the wall and consider adding your own. The all-you-can-eat dinner buffet (with beer €8, with wine €9.50) is unbeatable. Buffet 6-9:30pm. Open M-Sa 11am-10pm. Cash only. ❷

Pizzeria and Ostaria Centopoveri, V. Palazzuolo 31r (☎055 21 88 46; www.icentopoveri.it). Deliciously gooey pizza you'll need a knife and fork to tackle. The lunch special (€8) includes a pizza, bread, and *caffè*. Or check out the Ostaria for the special *menù* (€10) that includes primo, secondo, water, and *caffè*. Both open daily noon-3pm and 7pm-midnight. ❷

Amon Specialità e Panini Egiziani, V. Palazzuolo 26-28r (☎055 29 31 46). This Egyptian alleyway take-out whips up kebabs (€3.50-3.90), falafel (€3), hummus (€2.80), and kofta for hungry Florentines on the go. Kebab sandwiches are stuffed with generous heaps of juicy shaved meat. Open daily noon-3pm and 6-11pm. Cash only. ❶

Trattoria Mario, V. Rosina 2r, near P. del Mercato Centrale. Despite the 45min. wait, this family-run restaurant has proven its worth. Be prepared to share tables with other parties. ½ portions are available on select dishes, and all courses are created with entirely

TUSCANY

fresh ingredients; there isn't a freezer in the whole place. Try the *ribollita* (soup with beans, bread, vegetables; €4.50), the *pollo fritto* (fried chicken) on M, or come for fish F. Be sure to arrive early in the afternoon before ingredients run out and some dishes stop being served. Open M-Sa 12-3:30pm. Cover €0.50. Cash only. ❷

Trattoria Zàzà, P. del Mercato Centrale 16r (☎055 21 54 11). 3 outdoor areas and 4 themed indoor rooms set the scene for a delicious meal of fresh pasta at this 30-year-old favorite—but they still don't provide enough seating for all the hungry visitors—so be prepared to wait in line. Specializes in traditional Tuscan grilled meats. Primi €8-10. Secondi €11-22. Open daily 11am-11pm. AmEx/MC/V. ❹

Antica Gelateria Florentina, V. Faenza 2A. Every day, some of the best gelato in the Duomo area is prepared at this *gelateria* using fresh milk and fruit. The painted walls and the knowledgeable staff impart some of the treat's rich history. Enjoy nearly 30 flavors like *nocciola* (hazelnut) and *napole*, a fruit native to Italy. Cones and cups €1.60-4. Open daily noon-1am. Cash only. ❶

Bar Cabras, V. Dei Panzani 12r (☎055 21 20 32). For coffee and pastries near Santa Maria Novella, there's no better place. The older couple that has owned the small cafe for nearly half a century serves you sweets to the melody of classic rock. Enjoy custard-filled *torta della nonna* (€0.90), cannoli (€2.5), waffles (€3), and sandwiches (€3.5). ❶

La Mescita, V. degli Alfani 70r, near the intersection with V. dei Servi. Look for the "Vino" sign above the door. La Mescita is a wonderful hole in the wall that posts its prices on construction paper and writes the daily menu in marker. They'll quickly heat up your choice of the day's offerings and bring it to your table, but if you're aiming to save money, take it to go, because there's a €1 table service charge. *Panini* €1.60-3.50. Primi €4-5. Secondi €3-6. Open M-Sa 8am-9pm. ❶

VinOlio, V. San Zanobi 126r (☎055 48 99 57). On the corner with V. delle Ruote. Locals on lunch break dive into the chairs for hearty primi (€5.50-7) like pasta in ragu (€5.50) and roast beef with potatoes (€6). While the black-and-white photos and profusion of wine bottles may suggest a lazy, epicurean style, the incredibly speedy service at this restaurant caters to a crowd that has to be back at work soon. Open M-Sa 7:30am-1am. AmEx/MC/V. ❶

Ristorante Dioniso, V. San Gallo 16r (☎055 21 78 82). This blue-and-white Greek gem has won the local lunch crowd with its outgoing, energetic waiters and welcoming atmosphere. Lunch specials (€9) include fish, meat, and vegetarian options, all of which come with an extensive accompaniment of side dishes. Cover €1.50. Open M-Sa noon-3pm and 7:30pm-midnight, Su 7:30pm-midnight. AmEx/MC/V. ❷

A Casamia, P. de Ghiberti 5r (☎055 26 38 223). Crisp, clean decor means that eating so cheap never looked so good. Each weekday, choose from 3 different primo, secondo, and *contorno* offerings, have some bottled water, and enjoy a *caffè* for just €6, including cover. Primo and beverage €3.30. Open Tu-Su 11:30am-3pm and 6:30pm-2am. ❶

Acquacotta, V. dei Pilastri 51r (☎055 24 29 07). Sweet and simple, with flowered ceramic ware on the shelves and cream-colored walls, this Tuscan trattoria serves fresh pasta and seasonal dishes. Stop in for lunch when you can choose a primo, like ravioli stuffed with pheasant and truffle cream sauce, and a secondo, like beef filet with *Chianti Classico* sauce, for €12.50. Reservations recommended for weekend dinner. Primi €7-11. Secondi €12-20. Open Tu-Su noon-2:30pm and 7-11pm. AmEx/MC/V. ❹

Il Giova, Borgo la Croce 73r. Colorful tables and amphibian designs on the counter tiles create a tropical vibe in this gourmet restaurant. The highlights are duck breast with red onion and figs (€15) and sliced steak with truffle (€16). Primi €7-8.50. Secondi €11-18. Open M-Sa 12:30-3pm and 7:30-11pm. AmEx/MC/V. ❹

Dante, P. Nazario Sauro 12r (☎055 21 92 19; www.ristorantedante.net). Let the doorman welcome you in and enjoy a comfortable meal surrounded by the restaurant's own brand of wine, bottled by a local winery. Students can enjoy it for free with a special deal that includes a free drink and no cover charge. Primi €6-18. Secondi €10-22. Cover €2. Open daily 12pm-1am. AmEx/MC/V. ❹

Cammillo, Borgo San Jacopo 57r (☎055 21 24 27). Bow-tied and mustachioed, the experienced waiters will make you feel at home in this trattoria. The Impressionist artwork give it the air of a true Italian restaurant from the date scene in a black-and-white movie. Primi €10-15. Secondi €16-25. MC/V. ❹

Seme d'uva, V. dell'Orto 25r (☎055 22 86 471). The friendly staff provides a relaxed and intimate dining experience focused around a seasonally changing menu. The large, colorful paintings on the walls were made by local, amateur artists. Try the meat ravioli with cream sauce (€7.50) and *crespelle alla fiorentina* (pasta envelopes filled with asparagus and cheese, €8). Primi €7-9. Secondi €12-16. Open M-Sa 7-10:30pm. Cash only. ❸

👁 🏛 SIGHTS AND MUSEUMS

◼UFFIZI GALLERY. Giorgio Vasari designed this palace for Duke Cosimo in 1554 and called it the "Uffizi" because it housed the Medici's administrative offices (*uffizi*). An impressive walkway between the two branches of the building, full of street performers, human statues, and vendors hawking trinkets and prints, leads from P. della Signoria to the Arno River; the street is surrounded every morning by art-hungry tourists waiting to enter the museum. Beautiful statues overlook the walkway from niches in the columns; play spot-the-Renaissance-man and try to find da Vinci, Machiavelli, Petrarch, and Vespucci.

Before visiting the main gallery on the second floor, stop to see the **Cabinet of Drawings and Prints** on the first floor. This exhibit includes rare sketches by Botticelli, Leonardo, Raphael, and Michelangelo. Upstairs, in a U-shaped corridor, is a collection of Hellenistic and Roman marble statues. Arranged chronologically in rooms off the corridor, the collection promises a thorough education on the Florentine Renaissance, as well as a sampling of German and Venetian art. Framing the entrance to **Room 2** are three magnificent Madonnas by Renaissance forefathers Cimabue, Duccio di Buoninsegna, and Giotto. **Room 3** features art from 14th-century Siena, including works by the Lorenzetti brothers and Simone Martini's *Annunciation*. **Room 4** contains several works from Bernardo Daddi, including *Madonna with Child and Saints*. **Rooms 5** and **6** hold examples of International Gothic art, popular in European royal courts. Check out the rounded war-horses in the *The Battle of San Romano*, Paolo Uccello's noble but slightly jumbled effort to conquer the problem of perspective. **Room 7** houses two paintings by Fra Angelico (also called Beato Angelico) and a *Madonna and Child* (1426) by Masaccio. Domenico Veneziano's *Sacra Conversazione* (1445) is one of the first paintings of Mary surrounded by the saints. Piero della Francesca's double portrait of Duke Federico and his wife, Battista Sforza, stands out for its translucent color and honest detail. (A jousting accident gave the Duke's nose its unusual hooked shape.) **Room 8** has Filippo Lippi's *Madonna and Child with Two Angels* (1440). **Room 9** includes works by Botticelli and Pollaiolo.

MAKE FRIENDS WITH THE UFFIZI. If you plan on visiting 3 or more museums in Florence, consider obtaining an **Amici degli Uffizi card.** Students under 26 pay €25 for the card (regularly €60) and receive free admission to the Uffizi and all state museums in Florence (including the Accademia and Bargello). It includes one visit to each of the museums and gets you to the front of the line. For more information, call Amici degli Uffizi, V. Lorenzo il Magnifico 1, ☎055 47 94 422, or email amicidegliuffizi@waf.it.

Rooms 10-14 are a shrine to Botticelli—the resplendent *Primavera* (1478), *Pallas and the Centaur* (1482), *Birth of Venus* (1485), and *Madonna della Melagrana* (1487) glow from recent restorations. **Room 15** moves into the High Renaissance with Leonardo da Vinci's *Annunciation* (1480) and the remarkable, unfinished *Adoration of the Magi* (1481). **Room 18,** the tribune designed by Buontalenti to hold the Medici treasures, has a mother-of-pearl dome and a collection of portraits, most notably Bronzino's *Bia dei Medici* (1542), Vasari's *Lorenzo il Magnifico* (1485), and del Sarto's *Woman with the Petrarchino* (1528). Also note Rosso Fiorentino's oft-duplicated *Musician Angel* (1515). **Room 19** features Piero della Francesca's pupils, Perugino and Signorelli. **Rooms 20** and **22** detour into Northern European art. Note the contrast between Albrecht Dürer's lifelike *Adam and Eve* (1504) and Lucas Cranach's haunting, more surreal treatment of the same subject. Bellini's *Sacred Allegory* (1490) and Mantegna's *Adoration of the Magi* (1495) highlight **Room 23.**

Room 25 showcases Florentine works, including Michelangelo's only oil painting in Florence, *Doni Tondo* (1503). Raphael's *Madonna of the Goldfinch* (1505) and Andrea del Sarto's *Madonna of the Harpies* (1517) rest in **Room 26. Room 27** holds the incredible art of Jacopo Pontormo, including the moving *Portrait of a Musician* (1518). **Room 28** displays Titian's sensual *Venus of Urbino* (1538). Parmigianino's Mannerist-style, eerily lovely, and regal *Madonna of the Long Neck* (1534), now in **Room 29,** was discovered unfinished in the artist's studio following his death. Works by Paolo Veronese and Tintoretto dominate **Rooms 31** and **32. Room 33,** in fact a corridor, holds Vasari's *Vulcan's Forge* (1545). **Room 34** is dedicated to Paolo Veronese, and **Room 35** to Tintoretto. The staircase vestibule, **Rooms 36-40,** contains an ancient Roman marble boar, inspiration for the brass Porcellino in Florence's Mercato Nuovo. **Rooms 41** and **43-45** house works by Rembrandt, Goya, Rubens, and Caravaggio, currently on display after lengthy restorations. The Uffizi architect, Vasari, designed a **secret corridor** running between the Palazzo Vecchio and the Medici's Palazzo Pitti. The corridor runs through the Uffizi and over the Ponte Vecchio, housing more art, including a special collection of artists' self-portraits. The corridor is opened sporadically and requires both a separate entrance fee and advance booking. *(Off P. della Signoria. ☎055 29 48 83; www.polomuseale.firenze.it. Open Tu-Su 8:15am-6:35pm. €10; EU citizens 18-25 €5; EU citizens under 18 or over 65, EU student groups, and archaeology students in American programs free. Visit website for details. Proof of eligibility required. Reserve a ticket ahead of time and avoid lines with an extra €4 fee. Audio tours (1½hr.) €5.50.)*

DUOMO (CATTEDRALE DI SANTA MARIA DEL FIORE). In 1296 the city fathers commissioned Arnolfo di Cambio to erect a cathedral so magnificent that it would be "impossible to make it either better or more beautiful with the industry and power of man." Arnolfo succeeded, designing a massive nave with the confidence that by the time it was completed (1418), technology would have advanced enough to provide a solution to erect a dome. It was Filippo Brunelleschi, after studying Classical methods of sculpture, who devised the ingenious techniques needed to construct a dome large enough for the nave. For the *duomo*'s sublime crown, now known simply as **Brunelleschi's Dome,** the architect designed a revolutionary, double-shelled structure that incorporated self-supporting, interlocking bricks. During construction, Brunelleschi built kitchens, sleeping rooms, and lavatories between the two walls of the cupola so the masons would never have to descend. The **Museo dell'Opera del Duomo** chronicles Brunelleschi's engineering feats in an in-depth exhibit. A 16th-century Medici rebuilding campaign removed the *duomo*'s incomplete Gothic-Renaissance facade. The walls remained naked until 1871, when Florentine architect Emilio de Fabris won the commission to create a facade in the Neo-Gothic style. Especially when viewed from the southern side, the patterned green-white-and-red marble walls are impressively grand.

Today, the *duomo* claims the world's third-longest nave, after St. Peter's in Rome and St. Paul's in London. It rises 100m into the air, making it as high as the surrounding Tuscan hills and visible from nearly every corner of the city. Though ornately decorated on the outside, the church's interior is rather chilly and stark; unadorned dark stone was believed to encourage humble devotion. One notable exception to this sober style is the extravagant frescoes on the dome's ceiling, where visions of the apocalypse glare down at visitors in a stunning display of color and light. Notice, too, Paolo Uccello's celebrated monument to the mercenary captain Sir John Hawkwood on the cathedral's left wall and his *trompe l'oeil* clock on the back wall. This 24hr. timepiece runs backward, starting its cycle at sunset, when the *Ave Maria* is traditionally sung. *(Open M,W, F 10am-5pm; Th 10am-4:30pm; Sa 10am-4:45pm; Su 1:30-4:45pm. Shortest wait just before opening. Mass daily 7:30, 8:30, 9:30am, and 6pm. Su Mass 7:30, 9, 10:30am, and 12:30pm. English Mass Sa 5pm. Free. Ask inside the entrance to the left about free guided tours in English.)* Climb the 463 steps inside the dome to Michelangelo's lantern for an expansive view of the city from the external gallery. Halfway up, visitors can enjoy a view of the dome's frescoed interior from just inches away. *(Entrance on southern side of the duomo. ☎ 055 23 02 885. Open M-F 8:30am-7pm, Sa 8:30am-5:40pm. €6.)*

▧PALAZZO PITTI. Luca Pitti, a 15th-century banker, built his *palazzo* east of Santo Spirito against the Boboli hill. The Medici family acquired the *palazzo* and the hill in 1550 and enlarged everything they could. During Italy's brief experiment with monarchy, the structure served as a royal residence. Today, the **Palazzo Pitti** is fronted with a vast, uninhabited *piazza* and houses a gallery and four museums, providing enough diversions for a lengthy and unhurried visit. *(Ticket office is on the right before the palazzo. ☎ 055 29 48 83. 3-day ticket €12.50.)*

The **▧Galleria Palatina** was one of only a few public galleries when it opened in 1833. Today, it houses Florence's second most important collection (after the Uffizi). Its artistic smorgasbord includes works by Botticelli, Canova, Caravaggio, del Sarto, Perugino, Raphael, Rubens, Tintoretto, Titian, Vasari, Velasquez, and Veronese. The **Appartamenti Reali** (Royal Apartments), at the end of the *galleria*, are lavish reminders of the time when the *palazzo* served as the Royal House of Savoy's living quarters. The apartments hold a few Renaissance and Baroque greats. For a change of pace, check out the early 19th-century proto-Impressionist works of the Macchiaioli group in the **Galleria d'Arte Moderna.** *(☎055 29 48 83. Gardens ☎055 29 48 83. Galleria d'Arte Moderna ☎055 23 88 616. Gallerie and Appartamenti open Tu-Su 8:15am-6:50pm. Combined ticket for Palatine Gallery, Royal Apartments, and Modern Art Gallery €8.50, EU students €4.25. Combined ticket for all 5 sights €10, EU students €4. Cash only.)*

Find out if the clothes make the Medici in the **Galleria del Costume,** a decadent display of the family's finery. The **Museo degli Argenti** on the ground floor exhibits Medici family treasures, including cases of precious gems, ivories, silver, and Lorenzo the Magnificent's famous vase collection. The *salone* depicts a floor-to-ceiling fresco of blind Homer and the nine Muses leaving Mount Parnassus, alluding to scholars who fled to Tuscany from Greece after the Turkish invasion of 1453. An elaborately landscaped park, the ▓**Boboli Gardens** is an exquisite example of a stylized Renaissance garden and provides open spaces with beautifully groomed lawns and impressive marble statues. A large oval lawn sits just up the hill behind the palace, marked by an Egyptian obelisk. Labyrinthine avenues of cypress trees lead eager wanderers to bubbling fountains with graceful nudes. Be sure to see the fountain of a portly Bàcchus, sitting astride a very strained turtle. While the gardens seem like the perfect picnic spot, visitors are unfortunately prohibited from bringing in outside food. The **Museo della Porcellana,** hidden behind the gardens, exhibits fine porcelain from the Medici collection. (☎ *055 23 88 709. G Gardens open daily Oct. 8:15am-5:30pm; Nov.-Feb. 8:15am-4:30pm; Mar.-May 8:15am-6:30pm; June-Aug. 8:15am-7:30pm. Museo degli Argenti and Museo della Porcellana open daily 8:15am-6:50pm. Museo degli Argenti and Museo della Porcellana open daily 8:15am-7:30pm. Closed 2nd and 4th M and 1st, 3rd, and 5th Su of each month. Combined ticket for all 4 sights €10, EU students €4. Cash only.)*

▓**PALAZZO DAVANZATI.** The 14th-century palace fell into the hands of the merchant and scholar Bernardo Davanzati in 1578 and belonged to his family until the early 20th century; it was eventually purchased by the Italian state in 1951 and turned into a museum designed to showcase the life of a Florentine merchant in the 15th-17th centuries. Renaissance furniture adorns the rooms,

TUSCANY

and the painted walls are the highlights. Check out the bedroom on the second floor with the 17th-century bed and the painting *Madonna Adoring the Christ Child with Young Saint John,* from Filippino Lippi's workshop of the late 15th century. Also of particular interest are the vibrant wall paintings in the **Sala dei Pappagalli** (Room of the Parrots). *(V. Porta Rossa 13. ☎ 055 23 88 610. Open daily 8:50am-1:50pm. Closed 1st, 3rd, 5th M and 2nd and 4th Su of each month. Free.)*

☒BASILICA DI SANTA CROCE. Ascetic as they may have been, the Franciscans produced what is arguably the city's most magnificent church with a unique Egyptian cross layout, far to the east of their Dominican rivals at Santa Maria Novella. Architect Arnolfo di Cambio decided to change things up a bit, designing the splendid Basilica that was established in 1294. Breathtaking marble sculptures adorn the grand tombs of Florentine luminaries on both sides of the main aisle, frozen in expressions of grief and mourning. The Renaissance greats buried here include Michelangelo, who rests near the beginning of the right aisle; Galileo, directly opposite in the left aisle; and Machiavelli, farther down and on the right. Michelangelo chose his final resting spot with the hope that he would rise out of his tomb on Judgment Day to view the great Duomo through Santa Croce's front entrance; he'll have to take a glance at the grave Vasari built for him first, though, since his body is actually buried under the floor and slightly to the left of his monument. Beside him, the empty tomb of Italy's greatest poet stands as an attribute to Dante Alighieri, who was banished from the city in 1321. Although Dante was forgiven posthumously, his body never made it out of the hands of the literary necrophiles in Ravenna, where he died.

In the **Cappella Bardi di Vernio,** the first to the left of the transept, is Donatello's *Crucifix* (1412-13). The frescoes that adorn the chapels also showcase the work of some of the great precursors to the Renaissance. In the central **Cappella Maggiore,** the frescoes of Agnolo Gaddi are undergoing restoration, while next door once can still pick out the work of Giotto's school. **Cappella Peruzzi** features scenes from the life of St. John the Baptist, while **Cappella Bardi** has six scenes from the life of St. Francis,. Once you enter the courtyard, run the gauntlet past the tombs and busts of those long dead through the barely lit **Galleria dei Monumenti Funebri,** to the right of the bottom of the stairs. At the end of the cloister next to the church is Brunelleschi's **Cappella Pazzi,** a modest marvel of perfect proportions. Construction continued after his death in 1446, but work on the nearly-completed chapel halted in 1478, when Pazzi's involvement in the assassination of Lorenzo the Magnificent's brother Giuliano led to the family's ruin. Luca della Robbia created the glazed terra-cotta medallions depicting the *Twelve Apostles,* and the four medallions showing the *Four Evangelists* are attributed to Brunelleschi himself. **The Museo dell'Opera** contains a collection of fresco remnants and artwork either removed from the church during renovations or relocated after the Napoleonic invasions. While wandering the church and the museum, note the water mark about eight feet up the walls—an enduring reminder of the devastating effects of the flood of 1966. Santa Croce is located in a dip below the level of the Arno River, and during the flood, the waters rose to over 13 ft at some points. *(☎ 055 24 66 105 or 055 23 02 885. Open M-Sa 9:30am-5:30pm, Su and holidays 1-5:30pm. Last entrance at 5pm. €5, ages 11-17 €3. Cash only.)*

ACCADEMIA. In 1784, Pietro Leopoldo I gave a group of paintings to the Academy of Fine Arts (Accademia di Belle Arti) for study purposes, and in 1873 the **David** and other statues by Michelangelo wended their way into the collection, solidifying its eternal fame. No matter how many pictures of Michelangelo's triumphant sculpture you've seen, seeing *David* in the marble flesh will blow you away. From five feet away, Michelangelo's painstaking attention to detail—

like the veins in David's hands and at the backs of his knees—bring the statue to life. The sheer size of the work, and the fact that Michelangelo used a 4.1m block of marble from the Museo dell'Opera del Duomo that was discarded by artists including Leonardo da Vinci, give new appreciation to Michelangelo's genius. He carved it when he was 29. The statue's base was struck by lighting in 1512, damaged by anti-Medici riots in 1527, and finally moved here from P. della Signoria after a stone hurled during a riot broke David's wrist in two places. However, even the move couldn't save David from accidents: in 1991, a vandal splintered his left foot with a stone, though the damage has now been undone with restoration. If this real David seems a bit different from the copy in front of the Palazzo Vecchio, there's a reason: Michelangelo intended him to be positioned on a high pedestal and therefore exaggerated his head and torso to correct for distortion from viewing far below; in the Accademia, the statue stands on a relatively high pedestal and appears less top-heavy. Here, the statue is housed in a special room built for it in 1882.

If you can manage to pull your eyes from David, look for Michelangelo's four **Slaves** (1520), also called *Prisoners*, lining the hall. Even today, it is hotly debated whether the statues were meant to appear unfinished. Chipping away only enough to show the figures emerging from the marble, Michelangelo left his cramped, struggling subjects half-lodged in their stone prisons, creating an effect that truly embodied his theories on "releasing" statues from the living stone. Also worth a look are Botticelli's paintings of the Madonna as well as works by Uccello. Two panel paintings, Lippi's *Deposition* (1504) and Perugino's *Assumption* (1504), sit in the room just in front of the rotunda. The Serviti family, who commissioned the two-sided panel, disliked Perugino's depiction so much that they only displayed Lippi's portion in their church.

Past the rotunda, down the corridor to the left, you can get a glimpse of what they learned back when the Accademia was actually an academy. This room, the **Gallery of Plaster Casts,** is literally stacked with plaster models made by two of the Accademia's master teachers, Lorenzo Bartolini and Luigi Pampaloni. You'll notice that all the molds are dotted with what appear to be black freckles. These are actually from iron staples, which were inserted into the molds as reference points of distance and height so that the assistants could do a better job in transferring the mold to marble. Upstairs, in the **Sala del Tardo Trecento,** there is an extraordinary piece of Florentine textile work from 1336. *The Coronation of the Virgin Among Eight Angels and Fourteen Saints*, embroidered by Jacopo di Cambio, is so intricately sewn that you'll think it's a painting at first glance. In the **stairwell,** the museum houses the highlights of its Russian icons collection, the oldest in the world outside of Eastern Europe. *(V. Ricasoli 60, between the churches of San Marco and the Santa Annunziata. Line for entrance without reservation begins at V. Ricasoli 58. The line is shortest early in the day. ☎055 23 88 609. Open June-Aug. Tu-Th and Sa-Su 8:15am-6:50pm, F 8:15am-10pm; Sept.-May Tu-Su 8:15am-6:50pm. Last entry 45min. before close. Most areas wheelchair-accessible. €10, with reservation €14. Audio guide €5.50.)*

BASILICA DI SAN LORENZO. Built on the site of an early church consecrated in 393 by St. Ambrose of Milan, the Basilica di San Lorenzo claims to be Florence's first cathedral. In 1418, leading Renaissance architect Filippo Brunelleschi redesigned the original Romanesque building. The financial burden for the project was shared by the Church and the Medici family who wished to turn the basilica into their familial crypt. Changes were slow, and by 1440 only the Old Sacristy had been done. Brunelleschi soon died and the basilica was "completed" in 1461 by Antonio Manetti, though many portions still remained unfinished. Michelangelo designed the church's exterior, but, disgusted by the corruption of Florentine politics, he abandoned the project to study architecture in Rome, which accounts for the basilica's still unadorned brown-stone facade. Today, the church continues to hold a regular mass every morning at 9:30am with additional services on Sunday at 11am and 6:30pm.

The family cleverly placed **Cosimo de' Medici's grave** in front of the high altar (underneath the dome, marked by grilles in the floor and the Medici arms), making the entire church his personal mausoleum. The church also houses the craftsmanship of some of the greatest Renaissance masters. Donatello created two bronze pulpits, one for each aisle; they were completed c.1460 and are his last works. Their fine engravings depict the last days of Christ, including scenes such as the *Agony in the Garden, Christ Before Pilate, the Crucifixion* (north pulpit), *the Marys at the Sepulchre,* and *the Resurrection* (south pulpit). Also by Donatello, the *Martelli Sarcophagus* in the left transept takes the form of a wicker basket woven in marble.

The **Old Sacristy,** to the left when facing the altar, was the first part of the church to be rebuilt (1420-29). Decorative details on the vault are by Donatello; the sarcophagus in the center is by Buggiano and holds Giovanni Bicci de' Medici and Piccarda Bueri (parents of Cosimo il Vecchio). The porphyry and bronze sarcophagus placed on the wall is that of Giovanni and Piero de'Medici (Cosimo il Vecchio's sons), commissioned from Verocchio by Lorenzo il Magnifico in 1472.

A small **chapel** near the entrance to the cloister has an *Annunciation* by Filippo Lippi; the beautiful cloister is by Manetti (1457-62). *(☎055 26 45 184. Open Mar.-Oct. M-Sa 10am-5pm, Su 1:30-5pm; Nov.-Feb. M-Sa 10am-5pm. €3.50. Basilica and the Laurentian Library €6.)*

THE CAPPELLE DEI MEDICI (MEDICI CHAPELS). These chapels consist of dual design contributions by Matteo Nigetti and Michelangelo. Michelangelo created and sculpted the entire **New Sacristy**—architecture, tombs, and statues—in a mature, careful style that reflects his study of Brunelleschi. Designed to house the bodies of four of the Medicis, the room contains two impressive tombs for Medici Dukes Lorenzo of Urbino and Giuliano of Nemours. Lounging on the tomb of the military-minded Lorenzo are the smooth, minutely rendered female *Night* and the muscle-bound male *Day,* both left provocatively "unfinished," but considered to be among his greatest works. Michelangelo rendered the hazier *Dawn* and *Dusk* with more androgynous figures for the milder-mannered Giuliano's tomb, which is closer to the entrance. Some of the artist's sketches can be found in the basement. Plans for even more statues by Michelangelo had been made, but the only other one by the master in this chapel is the Madonna and Child, the last Madonna Michelangelo sculpted.

The large **Cappella dei Principi** (Chapel of the Princes) was designed by Giovanni de'Medici, Cosimo I's illegitimate son, and exhibits some stunning pietre dure craftsmanship. Buried here are (right to left): Ferdinando II, Cosimo II, Ferdinando I, Cosimo I, Francesco I, and Cosimo III. *(Walk around to the back entrance in P. Madonna degli Aldobrandini, behind the Basilica di San Lorenzo. ☎055 23 88 602. Open daily 8:15am-5pm. Closed 1st, 2nd, and 5th M and 2nd and 4th Su of each month. €9).*

LAURENTIAN LIBRARY. This adjacent building was built to signify the Medici entrance into intellectual society and now contains over 11,000 manuscripts, including those from the private library of the Medici family. Construction began in 1525, but the library did not open until 1571. Michelangelo's famous entrance **portico** confirms his virtuosity; the *pietra serena* sandstone staircase is one of his most innovative architectural designs. *(☎055 21 07 60. Open daily 8:30am-1:30pm. Free with entrance to San Lorenzo.)*

BATTISTERO. Though built between the fifth and ninth centuries, the octagonal *battistero* was believed in Dante's time to have been a Roman temple. The building's exterior has the same green- and white-marble patterning as the *duomo*, and the interior contains magnificent 13th-century, Byzantine-style mosaics. Dante was christened here, and later gained inspiration for his *Inferno* from the murals of damnation. Florentine artists competed fiercely for the commission to create the famous **bronze doors,** which depict scenes from the Bible in exquisite detail. In 1330 the winner, Andrea Pisano, left Pisa to cast the first set of doors, which now guard the southern entrance (facing the river). In 1401 the cloth guild announced a competition to choose an artist for the remaining two sets. Two young artists, Brunelleschi and Ghiberti, were asked to work in partnership to enter the competition, but the uncompromising Brunelleschi left in an arrogant huff, allowing Ghiberti to complete the project alone. Their separate entries into the competition are displayed side by side in the **Bargello** (p. 318). Ghiberti's project, completed in 1425, was so admired that he immediately received the commission to forge the final set of doors. The ◼**Gates of Paradise,** as Michelangelo reportedly called them, are nothing like Pisano's earlier portals. Originally intended for the northern side, they so impressed the Florentines that they were moved to their current eastern position facing the *duomo*. Best admired in the morning or late evening after the tourist crowds have thinned, the doors are truly a masterpiece, each panel a work of art itself. Even Leonardo da Vinci assumed a role in the structure's execution, finishing the terra-cotta models. *(Opposite the duomo. ☎055 23 02 885. Open M-Sa noon-7pm, Su and 1st Sa of the month 8:30am-2pm. Mass M-F 10:30 and 11:30am. €3. Audio tour €2.)*

CAMPANILE. Also called "Giotto's Tower," the 82m bell tower next to the *duomo* has a marble exterior that matches neighboring monuments. Three great Renaissance minds contributed to its construction: Giotto drew the design and laid the foundation in 1334, Andrea Pisano added two stories, and Francesco Talenti completed construction in 1359. The 414 steps to the top offer stunning views of the *duomo*, baptistry, and city. The best time to make the trek is in the early morning, to avoid the smog. *(☎055 23 02 885. Open Nov.-May daily 8:30am-6:50pm; June-Oct. 1st M-Th and Su 8:30am-6:50pm, F-Sa 8:30am-10:20pm. €6.)*

MUSEO DELL' OPERA DEL DUOMO. Most of the original art from the Duomo and Baptistery resides in this less crowded, modern museum. The pieces have been moved here to preserve them: the three statues whose replicas are now over the Baptistery were damaged by acid rain, and the Gates of Paradise, torn off their door by the Flood of 1966, have to be kept in a nitrogen environment to prevent further damage. However, Arnolfo di Cambio's statue **Madonna with the Glass Eyes,** on the ground floor, was put into the Opera's storage room because the popular devotion to it was so intense that Church leaders feared they were encouraging superstition by keeping it in the cathedral. The museum's most famous work is a late **Pietà** by Michelangelo, up the first flight of stairs. He began working on it in his early 70s, and the soft curves and flowing lines of the marble and the limpness of Christ's body are said to reflect the artist's conception of his own mortality. He also used his own face as the model for the man cradling Christ, the biblical figure of Nicodemus. Despite his personal investment in the statue, Michelangelo smashed the statue's left arm with a hammer in a fit of frustration with the marble's imperfections. An over-eager apprentice touched up the work soon after, leaving lines visible on Mary Magdalene's head. Also in the museum's collection are Donatello's achingly realistic *St. Mary Magdalene* (1455) and his beardless *Prophet* (supposedly based on Brunelleschi's face), Donatello and Luca della Robbia's *cantorie* (choir balconies with bas-reliefs of cavorting children), and the gold frames from the baptistery's original Gates of

Paradise. The statues that remain from Arnolfo di Cambio's original facade are also here, along with a wooden model of what it probably looked like. A huge wall displays on the first floor all of the paintings submitted by architects in the 1870 competition for the Duomo's facade. *(P. del Duomo 9, behind the Duomo. ☎055 23 02 885. Open M-Sa 9am-6:50pm, Su 9am-1pm. €6. Audio tour €4. Cash only.)*

ORSANMICHELE. A grain market was built here in 1284 over the site of the ninth-century church of **San Michele ad Hortum.** In the early 14th century, after a great fire convinced city officials to move grain operations outside of the city, the building was transformed into a church. Florence's powerful craft and trade guilds used the chapel and, late in the 14th century, the city told these groups to ornament the facades of the church with statues of their patron saints. Naturally, the guilds fought it out to get the best artists of the day to represent their standing. Of the statues lining the church walls, many are those of Ghiberti: *St. John the Baptist* (1412-16), for the cloth merchants, on V. dei Calzaiuoli; *St. Matthew* (1419-22), for the banking guild, on V. Arte della Lana; and *St. Stephen* (1428), for the wool guild, on the same street. On V. Orsanmichele are Donatello's *St. George* (a copy—the original is in the **Bargello,** (see next page) for the armory guild and Brunelleschi's *St. Peter* for the butchers' guild. The interior of the church contains 14th-century frescoes and the magnificent tabernacle by Andrea Orcagna (1355-59), which depicts tales from the life of the Virgin Mary with marble, colored glass, and reliefs. *(V. Arte della Lana, off V. de Calzaiuoli, between the Duomo and P. della Signoria. ☎055 28 49 44. Open Tu-Su 10am-5pm. Free.)*

PIAZZA DELLA SIGNORIA. With the turreted **Palazzo Vecchio** to the west and the Uffizi Gallery to the south, this 13th-century *piazza* is now one of the city's most touristed areas. You can enjoy the statues outside of Palazzo Vecchio, like the copy of Michelangelo's **David,** and the 14th-century stone **Loggia della Signoria** with gelato in hand, outside the confines of a traditional museum. The palace's location, said to have been chosen to avoid the "damned" house of the Ghibellines, made the *piazza* into an L shape and encouraged the square to blossom into Florence's cultural and political center. In 1497, religious zealot Girolamo Savonarola convinced Florentines to light the Bonfire of the Vanities in the *piazza*, barbecuing some of Florence's best art, including (according to legend) all of Botticelli's secular works held in public collections. A year later, disillusioned citizens

LOCAL LEGEND

MEDICI DRUG LORDS

Ever wonder about the polka-dotted Medici crest plastered on nearly every building in Florence? Although scholars offer various explanations for the six buttons adorning the city's most famous dynastic emblem, some speculate that the dots are actually pills, alluding to some pharmaceutical family lore. Like most stories about pill-pushing, this one puts the illustrious Medici family in a sketchy breach of medical ethics.

Back in the day before the MCATs or modern skepticism, an enterprising Medici ancestor was in the business of selling pills he promised could cure any ailment. A farmer who lost his donkey came to this crafty "doctor" and asked him for help. The doctor sold him six pills and told the farmer to take them while wandering around looking in places a donkey might be tempted to go. After three days of popping pills and roaming the back roads of Tuscany screaming his donkey's name, this intelligent fellow finally stumbled upon his pet eating some delicious thistle. The farmer widely proclaimed this discovery a miracle, and the story of the six "magical" pills catapulted the doctor to great fame and fortune. The doctor capitalized on his placebo success and founded the Medici family, whose name means "doctors" in Italian.

At the time of printing, none of the famous Medicis have a medical degree, nor has anyone been convicted of prescription fraud.

sent Savonarola up in smoke on the same spot, marked today by a comparatively discreet commemorative disc near the **Fountain of Neptune.** The fountain, to the left of the Palazzo Vecchio, so revolted Michelangelo that he decried the artist: "Oh, Ammanato, Ammanato, what lovely marble you have ruined!" The Loggia, once used for civic orators, is now one of the best places in Florence to see world-class sculpture for free, including Giambologna's spiraling composition of ◨**The Rape of the Sabines.**

THE PONTE VECCHIO. Built in 1345, Florence's oldest bridge played host in the 1500s to butchers and tanners, a group that lined the bridge to dump pig's blood and intestines into the river Arno. The resulting smell understandably offended the powerful bankers who crossed the Arno on the way to the office. In an effort improve the area, the Medici clan—themselves originally bankers—kicked out the lower-class shopkeepers, making room for goldsmiths and diamond-cutters. Today, their descendants line the street in medieval-looking boutiques and the bridge glitters with rows of gold necklaces, brooches, and charms. While technically open to vehicles, it is chiefly pedestrians who swamp the roadway. The historical position of the bridge has helped preserve it throughout the years. During WWII, Ponte Vecchio was the only Florentine bridge to escape the German bombs. A German commander who led his retreating army across the river in 1944 couldn't bear to destroy it, choosing instead to make it impassable by toppling nearby buildings. From the neighboring **Ponte alle Grazie,** the heart-melting ◨**sunset view** of Ponte Vecchio showcases its glowing buildings and the shimmering Arno River beneath.

THE BARGELLO. In the heart of medieval Florence, this 13th-century brick fortress was once the residence of Florence's chief magistrate. Later, it became a brutal prison with public executions held in its courtyard, but when the death sentence was abolished in 1786 the torture materials were burned in the same space. In the 19th century, Bargello's former elegance was restored, and it now gracefully hosts the quiet **Museo Nazionale,** a treasury of Florentine sculpture and the "minor arts" gathered from the Medici collection and other generous donors. On the ground floor, a room displays the work of Michelangelo and his students. Michelangelo created *Bacchus* on his first visit to Rome in 1497 for banker Jacopo Galli, and it was later bought by the Medici. Other works on display by the hometown hero are the *Tondo of Madonna and Child* (1503-05) and the intense bust of *Brutus* (1539), the only bust Michelangelo ever made— it was supposedly sculpted after the murder of Duke Alessandro de' Medici, in honor of the Republican victory over Medici tyranny. In the second part of the room, a group of works by Cellini attract particular attention. On the same floor, the gothic cortile is lined with 16th-century sculpture; off the courtyard is the **Sala del Trecento** with 14th-century statues, many from Orsanmichele and the Badia. Works by Donatello and his contemporaries occupy the rooms on the first floor, the most famous being his bronze *David* (c. 1430) in the **Salone del Consiglio Generale,** the first free-standing nude since antiquity. This "nude" still poses in hat and boots. David's playful expression and youthful posture contrast with Michelangelo's perfectly chiseled David in the Accademia Gallery. On the right, two bronze panels of the *Sacrifice of Isaac* submitted by Ghiberti and Brunelleschi to the Duomo's baptistery door contest compete for attention. Also of note are the works by Luca della Robbia and his students, who carefully guarded their secret method of enameled terra cotta sculptures. Other rooms on the floor house collections of Islamic art and Byzantine jewelry. Make a stop in the old **armory,** which has a collection of arms and armor, some used by the Medicis themselves. *(V. del Proconsolo 4, between the Duomo and P. della Signoria. ☎ 055 23 88 606. Open daily 8:15am-6pm. Closed 2nd and 4th M of each month. €7. Audio tour €5.50.)*

BADIA. Founded in AD 978, the Badia was the site of medieval Florence's richest monastery and the parish church of Dante's love, Beatrice Portinari; in fact, it is supposedly where he saw her for the first time. The building was so much a part of daily Florentine life that the bell's tolling set time for the city and is mentioned in the Divine Comedy (*Paradiso*, XV). The church's simple facade belies the treasures within. Filippino Lippi's stunning *Apparition of the Virgin to St. Bernard*, one of the most acclaimed paintings of the late 15th century, hangs in eerie gloom to the left of the church. Note the beautiful frescoes and Corinthian pilasters, and be sure to glance at the intricately carved dark wood ceiling by Felice Gamberai. Visitors are asked to walk silently among the white-robed monks. *(Entrance on V. Dante Alighieri, off V. Proconsolo. ☎ 055 26 44 02. Officially open to tourists M 3-6pm, but respectful visitors can walk through the church at any time.)*

PALAZZO VECCHIO. The "Old" Palace was constructed in 1299 from a design attributed to Arnolfo di Cambio, but after the election of Cosimo I de' Medici as Duke in 1537, the palace underwent a complete overhaul, leaving only the structure as a reminder of its medieval design in favor of a more resplendent interior. During the republican era of the 15th century when the Medici were expelled, the interior was altered to create, among other things, the **Sala dei Cinquecento** to house the new regime's legislative body. Once the Medici made a comeback, the inside was redone again—although the Medicis did not enjoy it for long, leaving this side of the river for the **Palazzo Pitti** (p. 311). The asymmetrical structure of the building is a result of the medieval ban on building on the land belonging to the treasonous Uberti family. Today, housing the mayor's office and administrative office, the palace has preserved its original grandeur. Much of the palace was dedicated to proclaiming the glory of Florence; the entrance wall of the Sala dei Cinquecento portrays the Florentine conquest of Pisa, while the opposing side shows the conquest of Siena. On the ceiling, the center fresco depicts Cosimo I being crowned by the city of Florence in honor of his wedding to Joanna of Austria. Leonardo da Vinci and Michelangelo were both commissioned to do frescoes for the room, but both left before the works were anywhere near done. The current incarnation was designed by Vasari. Upstairs, wander through the various rooms once occupied by the early Medici rulers, including the **Green Room,** named for the landscape scenes that once covered the walls in the room adjacent to the chapel of Eleonora of Toledo, wife of Cosimo I. Eleonora so wanted a garden that Palazzo Pitti was built outside of the city walls to create her desired haven, and a door from her Green Room opens to the palace across the Arno. In the **Room of the Maps,** giant cabinets once held clothes, tapestries, and detailed ancient maps. The **Sala dei Gigli** has a fresco by Ghirlandaio of St. Zenobius and lunettes depicting the heroes of ancient Rome. The rooms on the second floor also offer beautiful views of the city from their windows. *(☎ 055 27 68 465. Open M-W and F-Su 9am-7pm, Th 9am-2pm. Palazzo €6, ages 18-25 €4.50. Courtyard free. Combined ticket with Cappella Brancacci €8/6.)*

CASA DI DANTE. This residence, reputedly identical to Dante's original home, traces the poet's life from youth to exile in its displays and pays homage to the *Divine Comedy* that immortalized him. Wooden representations of Florentine family crests line the hallway and stairwell accompanied by English descriptions. Unfortunately, the more interesting objects in this small museum, like the replicas of medical instruments that may have been used by Dante, remain without English explanations. *(Corner of V. Dante Alighieri and V. Santa Margherita, 1 block from the Bargello. ☎ 055 21 94 16. Open Tu-Su 10am-5pm. €4, groups over 15 €2 per person.)*

SYNAGOGUE OF FLORENCE. The relationship between the Jewish community of Florence and the rest of the city was tense in the centuries before the Synagogue's construction. The area around Piazza della Repubblica marks the location of the old Jewish ghetto, where Jews had been required to live since 1570, at the command of Cosimo I. The community was finally permitted to live and work outside of the ghetto in 1848, and when wealthy Jewish businessman and president of the Hebrew University David Levi died in 1870, he left his fortune for the construction of "a monumental temple worthy of Florence." The main design, created by architect Marco Treves with the assistance of Mariano Falcini and Vincenzo Micheli, is now situated behind a hefty iron gate among the Renaissance creations that dominate the city. During WWII, the Nazis used the Synagogue as a parking garage when they occupied Florence in 1943. Before leaving, they planted bombs throughout the Synagogue, but only destroyed the upper left women's gallery. The only temple in Florence also houses the **Museo del Tempio Israelitico,** which showcases a small collection of Jewish ritualistic items, like a beautiful 19th-century circumcision dress. (☎ 055 23 46 654. Open M-Th and Su 10am-6pm, F 10am-1:30pm. Cash only.)

CASA BUONARROTI. Once Michelangelo made it big, he decided to celebrate and bought three houses, including this one, on the same street. Though the master never actually lived here, it is now a small museum and holds selections from the collection of the Buonarroti family: Michelangelo's sketches and early work as well as examples of art directly influenced by him. On the ground floor, check out the exhibit of tiny first-century statuettes in the **Archeological Room** and then find Da Vinci's studies of horses in movement. Upstairs, two of Michelangelo's earliest works from when he was just 16 years old, hold the museum's place of honor. The first, *Madonna of the Steps*, is a carved panel that demonstrates the artist's study of Donatello, while *The Battle of the Centaurs*, a subject said to have been suggested to Michelangelo in the court of Lorenzo the Magnificent by poet Agnolo Firenzuola, shows the artist's passion for ancient art. Another room is covered floor to ceiling with paintings dedicated to scenes from Michelangelo's own life. (V. Ghibellina 70. ☎ 055 25 17 52. From P. Santa Croce, follow V. dei Pepi and turn right on V. Ghibellina. Open M-Th and Su 9:30am-4pm. €6.50, students and groups over 10 people €4.50.)

MUSEO ARCHEOLOGICO. The unassuming archaeological museum holds a surprisingly diverse collection behind its bland plaster facade. Its rooms teem with the statues, sarcophagi, and bronzes of the ancient Greeks, Etruscans, and Egyptians. As the home of both the **Florence Egyptian Museum** and Italy's most important collection of Etruscan bronzes, this museum would be a major cultural highlight in almost any other city in the world—but in Florence it is uncrowded and unfortunately understaffed. The Egyptian collection is especially extensive, spanning eleven rooms and containing some 15,000 objects; **Room 13** alone has four mummies. Since a large portion of the collection was retrieved during a joint French-Italian expedition to Egypt, many of the pieces have a twin in the Louvre. The second-floor exhibits—focused on Etruscan bronzes, Greco-Roman sculpture, and Greek attic pottery—are usually open to explore, but when the museum is understaffed for the day (a particular problem in the summer), they are only accessible through a guided visit every hour or so. Don't miss the *Chimera d'Arezzo*, a bronze sculpture from the late fifth century BC in **Room 14.** One of the most interesting and least accessible areas of the museum is the **Monumental Garden,** where visitors can wander among Etruscan tombs rebuilt here with their original materials. It is usually open on Saturday mornings, but call ahead to be sure that you won't miss out on this unique open-air museum. (V. della Colonna 38. The museum is located in the P. della Santis-

sima Annunziata, at the corner of V. Gino Capponi and V. della Colonna. ☎055 23 57 50. *Open M 2-7pm, Tu and Th 8:30am-7pm, W and F-Su 8:30am-2pm. €4, EU citizens under 26 €2.)*

🎭 NIGHTLIFE

In summer, the **Europa dei Sensi** program hosts **Rime Rampanti** (☎055 34 85 80 48 12), a series of nightly cultural shows featuring music, poetry, and food from a chosen European country. Call the info office for reservations. The same company also hosts **Le Pavoniere** (☎055 30 81 60), a pseudo beach party with live music, pool, bar, and pizzeria, in the **Ippodromo delle Cascine** (along the river and past the train station). The **Festa del Grillo** (Festival of the Cricket) is held the first Sunday after Ascension Day, which is 40 days after Easter. Crickets in wooden cages are sold in the Cascine Park to be released into the grass— Florentines believe a cricket's song brings good luck.

◼ **Mago Merlino Tea House,** V. Pilastri 31r (☎055 24 29 70). Always ready to share his wisdom, expert Rocco serves steaming cups of sophisticated tea in his Moroccan-inspired cafe. Choose from a variety of specialty brews (€7-9 a pot) containing everything from amber and saffron to homemade orange water and fresh mint. Take your shoes off and lounge among the floor pillows in the back room, or hit the hookah (€15 per group) in the small courtyard. Come during Happy hour (6:30-9pm) and have organic vegetarian food as you sip on a tea cocktail (€5); Rocco will make it with absinthe if you ask. Open daily 6:30pm-2am. Cash only.

Angie's Pub, V. de Neri 33 (☎055 28 37 64). 4 nights a week, a DJ brings a mix of European and American music to this anime-inspired bar, but you likely won't find much dancing. The crowd here mingles to a different drum than those of many other nightclubs in the area. Beer €3-5. Sangria €3. Open daily 4pm-2am. Cash only.

Twice, V. Giuseppe Verdi 57r (☎055 24 76 356). Glittering white walls give the impression that this club is made of ice. Populated by students and older couples alike. Trendy bar, smoking lounge, and dance floor are definite pluses. Come early (7-11pm) for the happy hour and *aperitivo* buffet (€5), or dance late to the daily disco theme, like Tu International Students Night. Beer €6. Mixed drinks €8. Shots €4. Open daily 7pm-4am. AmEx/MC/V.

Antico Caffè del Moro (Café des Artistes), V. del Moro 4r (☎055 28 76 61). A classy, candlelit place that specializes in coffee-based mixed drinks (€8.50) and fresh fruity beverages. Squeeze into a table or just lean on the bar during their crowded happy hour (6:30-9pm). Open daily 6:30pm-2am.

Central, V. del Fosso Macinante 2 (☎055 35 35 05), in Parco delle Cascine. Four open-air dance floors pulse with hip-hop, reggae, and Italian "dance rock." Favored by teens and university students. Well-dressed bouncers and management keep things under control. All drinks €10. Cover €20, foreign students €3 until 1am. Open in summer Tu-Su 8pm-3am. AmEx/MC/V.

Aquarama Meccanò, Vle. degli Olmi 1 (☎055 33 13 71), near Parco delle Cascine. One of Florence's most popular discos; caters to a slightly older crowd than Central. Open-air dance floors and sparkling grounds make for sophisticated fun. Drinks €10. Cover €10-16; includes 1 drink. Open Tu-Sa 11pm-4am. AmEx/MC/V.

Space Club Electronic V. Palazzuolo 37 (☎055 29 30 82; www.spaceelectronic.net). Conveniently closer to the *centro* than Central and Meccanò, Space Club rocks out in a shamelessly themed, space-age atmosphere. Pleather, fog machines, orgies of neon—it's all here. Drunk Americans and Italian men cover the dancefloor on weekends. Mixed drinks and beer €6.50. Cover €16, €10 for foreign students; includes 1 drink. Open daily 10pm-4am.

Shot Café, V. De' Pucci 5A (☎055 28 20 93). Just 1 block from the Duomo, Shot Café has it all. The quirky wallpaper and leather couches match the whimsical decor, which includes brightly-painted windows and Cabbage Patch Dolls on the lamps. The staff will dish on the best places to visit in Florence. Enjoy a delicious coffee break during the day or drink mixed drink specials (€4) with locals and students at night. Free Wi-Fi. Open daily noon-2am. AmEx/MC/V.

Café Deluxée, V. XXVII Aprile 65r (☎055 48 57 49; www.cafedeluxee.com). Cafe by day and bar by night, Deluxée boasts a diverse mix of locals and students. Hip bartender Alessandro will engage in friendly conversation with you, while either a DJ or a live band plays. Free appetizer buffet with drink purchase. Wine €3.50-4. Beer on tap €3.50-5.50. Mixed drinks €7. Buy 3 shots for €2.50 and get 1 free. Open daily 6pm-4am. V.

Kitsch Pub, V. San Gallo 20r. Decorated with stained-glass windows, leather booths, and velvet paneling, this tavern playfully embraces medieval kitsch. With 4 rooms, shots like Orgasmo and Tequila bum bum (€3), and a dinner menu until 10 pm, Kitsch is a merry place to start your evening with friends. Beer on tap and mixed drinks €7. *Aperitivi* €7. Open daily 6:30pm-2:30am. Cash only.

Las Palmas, P. Ghiberti (☎347 27 60 033). Each summer, P. Ghiberti is transformed into a neighborhood block party with the help of Las Palmas. Drinks, live music, and an outdoor dance floor ensure fun-filled nights. Serves tasty dishes. Tables fill quickly, so make reservations. Happy hour 6:30-9pm; drinks €4. Beer €4. Mixed drinks €7. Shots €3. Open daily from the 2nd week of May to the 2nd week of Aug. 6:30pm-1:30am.

Moyo, V. de' Benci 23r (☎055 24 79 738; www.moyo.it). With a vibe like a classy terra cotta cafe, this restaurant becomes a hip spot at night. Outdoor seating, yummy *aperitivi,* and W night sushi draw crowds. Order a fruity Striptease (€7), sit back, and enjoy. Happy hour daily 6-10pm; free *aperitivi.* Open daily 8:30am-2am. AmEx/MC/V.

Caffè Sant'Ambrogio, P. Sant'Ambrogio 7 (☎055 24 10 35). Hip red lights and pulsating techno pop. People begin pouring in for *aperitivi* 6-9pm, but during the rest of the night, most just come in to buy their drinks before heading back into the warm night air of the *piazza.* Wine €4-6. Beer €2.50-5. Open M-Sa 10am-2am, Su 6pm-2am. MC/V.

Kitsch the Bar, Vle. Gramsci 1-5r (☎055 23 43 890; www.kitsch-bar.com), in P. Beccaria. Despite its location in the outskirts, this popular companion to the *centro* pub overflows with young Italians chatting in leopard-print booths. A great spot on the north side of the river to stop for drinks on your way to the nightlife near Ponte San Niccolò. *Aperitivo con buffet* daily 6:30-10pm. Beer €4-6. Mixed drinks €7. Open daily 6pm-2am. Cash only.

James Joyce Pub, Lungarno B. Cellini 1r (☎055 65 80 856). A warm, literary vibe saturates the old-fashioned interior of this "Books and Beer" pub while the huge outdoor patio hosts chain-smoking Italians and foosball. A window on the back wall of the bar opens onto the outdoor area, so you can enjoy the night air without even moving. ½-pints €3.50, pints €5. Mixed drinks €7-8. Open daily 4pm-2:30am. AmEx/MC/V.

Flò, Ple. Michelangelo 84 (☎055 65 07 91; www.flofirenze.com). "Standing room only" would be an exaggeration of the space available in this insanely popular open-air lounge bar. Locals of all ages are willing to wait in a quick-moving but winding line for their chance to chat beneath the green-lit greenery of Vle. Michelangelo. Pay for drinks at the cash register by the door 1st and use your receipt to order at the bar. Beer €6. Mixed drinks €8. Open daily 7pm-late. V.

⚡ DAYTRIPS FROM FLORENCE

FIESOLE

A 30min. bus ride from Florence. Catch the ATAF city bus #7 from the train station every 30 min.; it stops in the centro at P. Mino da Fiesole. Return tickets can be purchased at the newsstand beside the bus stop for €1.20. The tourist office, V. Portigiani 3 (☎055 59 87 20; www.comune.fiesole.fi.it), is next to the Teatro Romano. Cross the street from the bus stop, go down V. Giovanni Dupre, and take the first right; the office is on the left. The office provides a free map with museum and sights listings. Open Easter-Oct. M-F 9:30am-6:30pm, Sa-Su 10am-1pm and 2-6pm; Nov.-Easter M-F 10am-6pm, Sa-Su 10am-4pm.

Fiesole (FEE-yeh-SOH leh; pop. 14,000) is the site of the ancient Etruscan settlement that later extended down the hill to become Florence. Fiesole's clean, cool breezes have long been a welcome escape from the sweltering summer heat of the Arno Valley and this spot on the hill, with its awesome views of the city below, has been a source of inspiration for many a famous figure: Alexandre Dumas, Anatole France, Paul Klee, Marcel Proust, Frank Lloyd Wright, and Gertrude Stein. Leonardo da Vinci once used the town as a testing ground for his famed flying machine.

Begin your exploration by facing away from the bus stop, walking across P. Mino da Fiesole, and down V. Dupre to the entrance of the Teatro Romano, V. Portigiani 1. One ticket provides admission to three associated attractions: Museo Civico Archeologico, Museo Bandini, and the Teatro Romano within the **archeological area.** The archeological area includes the perfectly rectangular foundations of Etruscan thermal baths and the toppled columns and sturdy archways of temple ruins. The well-preserved **Teatro Romano** still retains the components of an ancient Roman amphitheater, though it is now occasionally gussied up with modern sound equipment and spotlights for summer concerts. On the right, after entering the archeological grounds, the **Museo Civico Archeologico** houses an extensive collection of Etruscan artifacts (most gathered from Fiesole and its territory), well-preserved Grecian urns, a reconstructed tomb with a skeleton, and vases from Magna Graecia (southern Italy, once part of the Greek Empire). Cross the street to breeze through **Museo Bandini,** V. Dupre 1, which holds the collection of 18th century intellectual Canonical Angelo Maria Bandini. Within the museum, you'll find Italian works from the 13th through 15th centuries, including works by Cortona's Signorelli, Giotto, the della Robbias, Gaddi, and Botticelli. (☎055 59 61 293. Open Apr.-Sept. M and W-Su 10am-7pm.; Oct. M and W-F 10am-6pm; Nov.-Feb. M and Th-Su 10am-4pm; Mar. M and W-Su 10am-6pm. Last entry 30min. before close. €12, students and over 65 €8, family groups up to 2 adults and 4 children €24. MC/V).

A short, steep walk uphill to the left of the bus stop takes you past the **public gardens.** The entrance to the gardens is on the left side of the path. These small areas provide stunning views of Florence. The panorama of the valley below is perhaps the only context in which Florence's massive duomo appears small. At the end of the path is the **Chiesa di San Francesco.** Take the stairs through the door to the right of the main entrance to experience the eerie quiet of the small rooms of study. The church itself contains 15th and 16th century Tuscan paintings, such as Piero di Cosimo's *Immaculate Conception.* Go through the door on the right side of the church to check out the **Museo Etnografico.** Housing Etruscan and Roman archeological findings and materials gathered by Franciscan missionaries in ancient China and Egypt, the museum's collection features Chinese pottery, jade figurines, and even an Egyptian mummy.

(Open T-F 10am-noon and 3-7pm. Free). Live performances bring new life to the Roman theater from June through September, when **Estate Fiesolana** (www. estatefiesolana.it) sponsors concerts, opera, theater, and film. Accommodations in Fiesole are expensive, so a daytrip can be more budget-friendly. Take in Arno Valley views over coffee (from €0.80) or gelato (from €1.60) at **Blu Bar ①**, P. Mino 39. (☎055 59 363. Pizza €3.50. Crepes €6. Mixed drinks €10.50. Open daily Feb.-Dec. 9am-11pm. AmEx/MC/V.)

GREVE IN CHIANTI

SITA buses run to Greve from Florence (1hr., every hr. 7am-8pm, €3.10; reduced service Su and holidays). There are 2 stops in Greve; get off at the first at P. Trento. P. Trento is not clearly labeled, so be sure to ask the bus driver to alert you when the bus arrives there. From P. Trento, continue to walk in the direction of the bus on Vle. Vittorio Veneto, turning right at the first stop light on V. Battisti, leading to the main square, P. Matteotti.

Welcome to Chianti country, where the cheese and olive oil are exquisite and the wine is even better. The tiny town of Greve (GREV-ay; pop. 12,855), is the hub of it all. To find out what that *Chianti Classico* (key-AN-tee CLAS-see-ko) is all about, get your taste buds ready and sip with the best.

Just down Vle. Vittorio Veneto and on the right in P. delle Cantine, a wine lover's paradise awaits at **⬛Le Cantine di Greve in Chianti**, P. delle Cantine 2, which is part wine museum, part *enoteca.* Opened in 2000, the Cantine use a new technology for wine tasting where the bottles rest in vacuum-valves that enable over 150 bottles to be tasted at once, including a wide range of local *Chianti Classico* and *Supertuscan.* They also stock *Nobile, Brunello,* and *Bolgheri,* wines from other Tuscan towns. Grab a tasting card in denominations of €10, €15, €20, or €25, and insert the card above the wine you wish to taste; tastes start around €0.60, depending on the type of wine. Helpful staff will help you navigate the stands that pack the brick-arched, stone-walled basement. (☎055 85 46 404; www.lecantine.it. Open daily 10am-7pm. Free. AmEx/MC/V.) Many other *enoteche* in town offer free wine tastings of 3-5 wines in the hopes that you'll whip out the wallet. The selection at **Enoteca del Chianti Classico**, P. San Croce 8, is especially impressive. (☎055 85 32 97; www. chianticlassico.it Open daily in summer 9:30am-7:30pm, in winter 9:30am-12:30pm and 3:30-7:30pm. AmEx/MC/V.)

Accommodations in the *centro* are scarce and many nearby villas are not easily accessible by public transportation. However, **Albergo del Chianti ④**, P. Matteotti 86, belies this generalization at a price. Located in the main *piazza,* the hotel offers 16 clean, comfortable rooms, each with bath, mini-bar, phone, A/C, and TV. The rustic lobby and adjoining bar open onto an outdoor oasis: a lovely patio, garden, and swimming pool. (☎055 85 37 63; www.albergodelchianti.it. Breakfast included. Singles €75; doubles €100.) For a truly Tuscan meal, the well-known **Mangiando, Mangiando ③**, P. Matteotti 80, will do the job with traditional plates such as *cinta senese* (a type of pig native to Tuscany) under a wood-beamed ceiling or under outdoor umbrellas. (☎055 85 46 372. Primi €6.50-11. Secondi €12-25. Open Tu-Su in summer 11am-11pm, in winter noon-3pm and 7-10:30pm. MC/V.) For fresh, local goods, **Macelleria,** P. Matteotti 69-71, is as authentic as it gets. Choose from the wide array of meats and cheeses or pop into the back room to taste several varieties for free. Wine tastings start at €10.20. (Open M-Sa 8am-1pm and 3:30-7:30pm, Su 10am-1pm and 3-7:15pm. AmEx/MC/V.) Pick up fresh bread and sweets (from €1.50) at **Forno**, P. Matteotti 89. (Open daily in summer 7am-1pm and 5-8pm, in winter 5-8pm. Cash only.)

For a list of local vineyards and help booking accommodations, head to the building shared by the **tourist office** and **Chianti Slow Travel Agency**, P. Matteotti 11. (☎055 85 46 299. Open M-F 9:30am-1pm and 2-6pm, Sa 2pm-6pm.) **Officina Marco Ramuzzi**, V. Italo Stecchi 23 (☎055 85 30 37; www.ramuzzi. com), offers scooter and mountain bike rentals. (Bikes €20 per day, €120 per week. Scooters €30-55 per day, €175-290 per week.)

SIENA ☎05 77

Siena's (see-EH-na; pop. 50,000) vibrant character and local energy make it a distinctly Tuscan city. Locals are fiercely proud of their town's history, which dates back to the 13th century. The city's vehement (and still palpable) rivalry with Florence resulted in grandiose Gothic architecture and soaring towers, though the arrival of the Black Death briefly put a halt to the architectural one-upmanship. These days, the Sienese celebrate their heritage with festivals like the semi-annual *Palio*, a riotous display of pageantry in which jockeys race bareback horses around the central square. In the heart of the Tuscan wine country, Siena is also an ideal base for exploring local vineyards and vintages.

▐ TRANSPORTATION

Trains: P. Rosselli, 15min. from the *centro* by bus #3, 4, 7, 9, 10, 17, or 77. Buy tickets from vending machines by the station entrance or at the ticket office (€1). Ticket office open daily 6:30am-1:10pm and 1:40-8:10pm. To **Florence** (1¼hr., 21 per day 5:50am-9:18pm, €6.10) and **Rome** (3hr., 19 per day 5:45am-8:19pm, €13) via **Chiusi. Buses:** **TRA-IN/SITA** (☎05 77 20 42 46; www.trainspa.it). Some intercity buses leave from P. Gramsci, but most leave from the train station. Ticket offices in the underground terminal in P. Gramsci (open daily 7am-7pm) and at the train station (open M-Sa 6:15am-8:15pm, Su 7:30am-12:30pm and 2:30-6:30pm). To reach the train station from P. Gramsci, take bus 3, 9, or 10 to Ferrovia. Tickets can be purchased at the underground ticket office or at the local *tabaccheria* (€0.95). To: **Arezzo** (7 per day, €5.20); **Florence** (every hr., €6.80); **Montalcino** (7 per day, €3.30); **Montepulciano** (4 per day, €4.70) via **Buonconvento** or **Torrenieri**; **San Gimignano** (31 per day, €5.30) via **Poggibonsi**. TRA-IN also runs buses within Siena.

Taxis: RadioTaxi (☎05 77 49 222), in P. Indipendenza and P. Matteotti.

Car Rental: Siena Perozzi Rental, V. dei Gazzani 16 (☎05 77 28 83 87) and V. del Romitorio 5 (☎05 77 28 08 39; www.perozzi.it), off P. la Lizza. Cars €50-115 per day. Open M-Sa 9am-7pm and Su 9am-1pm. AmEx/MC/V.

▓ ▐ ORIENTATION AND PRACTICAL INFORMATION

From **Piazza Gramsci**, the main bus stop, follow **Via Malavolti** into **Piazza Matteotti**. Cross the *piazza* and continue straight on **Via Banchi di Sopra**, heading through the heart of town. Continuing downhill, pass through one of the several archways that lead to **Piazza del Campo**, Siena's *centro storico*, also known as **Il Campo**. The **Palazzo Pubblico**, the tourist office, and the best people-watching in the town are located here. To get to the *centro* from the **train station**, cross the street to the mall and take one of the buses listed above from the underground terminal. These buses stop in **Piazza del Sale** or P. Gramsci. Some buses stop just before P. Gramsci, which makes it difficult to know where to get off; ask the bus driver. From either *piazza*, follow the signs to Il Campo. From the bus station in **Piazza San Domenico**, follow the signs to P. del Campo. **Piazza del Duomo** lies 100m west of Il Campo.

Tourist Office: APT, P. del Campo 56 (☎05 77 28 05 51; www.terresiena.it). Knowledge-able staff offers brochures, some at a nominal fee. Open daily 9am-7pm. **Prenotazioni Alberghi e Ristoranti** (☎05 77 28 80 84 or 84 80), in P. San Domenico, makes hotel reservations (€2). Books reservations for 2hr. walking tours of Siena (M-F 11am, reserve by 10am; €20) and San Gimignano. Open M-Sa 9am-7pm, Su 9am-noon.

Budget Travel: CTS, V. Sallustio Bandini 21 (☎05 77 28 50 08). Student travel services. Open M-F and Su 9am-12:30pm and 3:30-7pm. MC/V.

Laundromat: Express Wash, V. Pantaneto 38. Self-service. Wash €3.50. Dry €3.50. **Onda Blu,** V. Casato di Sotto 17. Wash €3 per 7kg, dry €3. Both open daily 8am-10pm.

Police: (☎112), on V. del Castoro near the *duomo.*

Pharmacy: Farmacia del Campo, P. del Campo 26. Open M-F 9am-7:30pm. Posts late-night rotations. AmEx/MC/V.

Hospital: V. Le Scotte 14 (☎05 77 58 51 11). Take bus #3 or 77 from P. Gramsci.

Internet Access: Cafe Internet/International Call Center, V. Cecco Angiolieri 16 (☎05 77 41 521). €2 per hr. Open M-Sa 8:30am-11pm, Su 9am-11pm. Cash only.

Post Office: P. Matteotti 36. Open M-F 8:15am-7pm, Sa 8:15am-1:30pm. **Postal Code:** 53100.

ACCOMMODATIONS

Casa Laura, V. Roma 3 (☎05 77 22 60 61), 10min. from Il Campo in the university area. Ring 3rd doorbell down, labeled *"Bencini Valentini."* Sacrifice immediate access to downtown Siena for spacious, well-priced rooms with TVs, some with baths. Kitchen available. Singles €55; doubles €70; triples €70; quads €90. MC/V. ❸

Piccolo Hotel Etruria, V. Donzelle 3 (☎05 77 28 80 88; www.hoteletruria.com). A stone's throw from Il Campo. Small, family-run establishment maintains 20 immaculate rooms, each with phone, TV, telephone, safe box, and hair dryer. Breakfast €6. Curfew 1am. Singles €50, with bath €55; doubles €90-110; triples €117. Extra bed €28. AmEx/MC/V. ❸

Ostello della Gioventù "Guidoriccio" (HI), V. Fiorentina 89 (☎05 77 52 212), in Local-ità Lo Stellino, a 10-20min. bus ride from town. Take bus #10, 17, 15, or 36 from P. Gramsci. Buses #15 and #36 stop at front door. For buses #10 and 17, continue from the stop in the bus's direction and take the 1st right; it's another 50m down. Mostly 2- to 4-person rooms in this 100-bed hostel. Breakfast included; dinner €10. Wi-Fi €3 per day. Lockout 9:30am-3pm. Reservations recommended. Dorms €20. Cash only. ❶

FOOD

Siena specializes in rich pastries. The most famous is *panforte,* a concoction of honey, almonds, and citron that was once baked as a trail mix for the Crusad-ers. For something a little less military and little more sugary, try *ricciarelli,* soft almond cookies topped with a thick coating of powdered sugar. Sample either (€2.20 per 100g) at the **Bar/Pasticceria Nannini,** V. Banchi di Sopra 22-24, Siena's oldest *pasticceria,* now a chain. (Open M-Sa 7:30am-9pm, Su 8am-9pm. AmEx/MC/V.) The local meat specialty, *cinta senese,* and the region's trade-mark thick spaghetti, *pici,* are also popular. Siena's **open-air market** fills P. La Lizza each Wednesday (8am-1pm). For groceries, head to **Conad,** in the Gal-leria Metropolitan in P. Matteotti (open M-Sa 8:30am-8:30pm, Su 9am-1pm and 4-8pm; MC/V), or **Pam,** in the mall across from the train station. (Open M-Sa 8:30am-9:30pm, Su 9am-9pm. AmEx/MC/V.)

Trattoria Papei, P. del Mercato 6 (☎05 77 28 08 94), on the far side of Palazzo Pub-blico from Il Campo. Despite the large capacity, the outdoor tables and stone-arched dining room at this popular trattoria can get crowded and noisy, but the company's

TUSCANY

always cheerful. Vast range of homemade pasta dishes, including scrumptious *pici alla cardinale* (spaghetti with tomato-pepper sauce and pancetta; €7), and traditional meat dishes. Cover €2. Open Tu-Su noon-3pm and 7-10:30pm. AmEx/MC/V. ❷

Osteria La Chiacchera, Costa di San Antonio 4 (☎05 77 28 06 31), next to Santuario di Santa Caterina. Frequented by young Italians and savvy tourists. Delicious Italian staples at low prices in a casual and lively atmosphere. Primi €5.50-6.50. Secondi €6.50-12. Open M and W-Su noon-3pm and 7-10pm. MC/V. ❷

Nonno Mede, V. Camporeggio 21 (☎05 77 24 79 66), down the hill to the left of Chiesa San Domenico. Expansive outdoor seating area with great views of the *duomo* and picturesque Siena rooftops. Extensive pizza menu, along with everything from mixed vegetables to stuffed rabbit. Pizza €4.50-7. Primi €6-7.50. Secondi €10-15. Cover €1.60. Open daily noon-3:30pm and 7pm-1:30am. MC/V. ❶

🎧 SIGHTS

The "My name is Duccio" all-inclusive ticket (€10) includes the Duomo, the Museo dell'Opera and *facciatone*, the Cripta, the Battistero, and the Oratorio di San Bernardino. It can be purchased from the ticket office of any of the participating sights.

◼IL CAMPO. Siena radiates from the **Piazza del Campo**, a shell-shaped square designed for civic events and affectionately referred to as "Il Campo." The *piazza's* brick paving is divided into nine sections, representing the city's medieval Council of Nine. Dante's *Inferno* referred to the square in the account of the real-life drama of Provenzan Salvani, a heroic Sienese merchant who panhandled in Il Campo to pay a friend's ransom. Later Sienese mystics used the *piazza* as a public auditorium. Today, Il Campo is framed by restaurants and cafes overlooking the monstrous clock tower, and it provides a perfect hangout. Twice each summer, the **Palio** (p. 329) morphs the mellow Campo into a chaotic arena as horses race around its edge. At the top of the slope is the **Fonte Gaia**, a rectangular marble fountain nestled into the slanted *piazza*. The water here emerges from the same 25km aqueduct that has refreshed Siena since the 14th century. Standing at the bottom of the *piazza* is the imposing **Palazzo Pubblico** and its looming *campanile*, the **Torre del Mangia**. In front of the *palazzo* is the **Cappella di Piazza**, which was started in 1348 but took 100 years to complete due to the arrival of the Black Death.

PALAZZO PUBBLICO. This impressive medieval building was home to Siena's Council of Nine in the Middle Ages, and it still houses city government offices today. However, the main draw is its **Museo Civico.** While the Sienese art pieces here range from medieval triptychs to 18th-century landscapes, the greatest treasure is the collection of late-medieval to early-Renaissance painting from the distinctive Sienese school. The large and airy **Sala del Mappamondo,** named for a lost series of astronomical frescoes, displays Simone Martini's *Maestà*, which combines religious overtones with civic and literary awareness. The Christ child is depicted holding a parchment inscribed with the city's Horatian motto, *"Expertus fidelem"* ("having found him faithful"), and the steps of the canopied throne are engraved with two stanzas from Dante's *Divine Comedy*. In the next room, the **Sala dei Nove** holds Ambrogio Lorenzetti's famous frescoes, the *Allegories of Good and Bad Government and their Effects on Town and Country*, with opposing visions of Hell on Earth and utopia on the right and left walls. (☎05 77 29 26 14. Open daily from mid-Mar. to Oct. 10am-7pm; from Nov. to mid-Mar. 10am-6pm. Last entry 45min. before closing. €7.50, students €4.50, under 11 free. Combined ticket for tower and Museo €12. Cash only.)

The Palazzo Pubblico's other star attraction is the **Torre del Mangia,** named for the gluttonous bell-ringer Giovanni di Duccio, also called *"Mangiaguadagni"* ("Eat-the-profits"). At 102m, Italy's tallest secular medieval monument is Siena's equivalent of the North Star. Lost tourists need only search for the tower's ornate top to orient themselves. After 500 dizzying and narrow steps, persistence pays off underneath the tower's highest bell: from the top, Siena's tiled rooftops, farmlands, and vineyard hills form an enchanting mosaic. Arrive early, as it gets crowded in the afternoon. *(Open daily from mid-Mar. to Oct. 10am-7pm; from Nov. to mid-Mar. 10am-6pm. €7.50, students €4.50. Cash only.)*

DUOMO. Atop one of the city's seven hills, the *duomo* is one of few completely Gothic cathedrals south of the Alps. Construction began in 1229 and the entire structure was completed over a hundred years later. The dome was built in 1263, the bell tower by 1313. The huge arch of the *facciatone*, part of a striped wall facing the front of the cathedral, is the sole remnant of Siena's 1339 plan to construct a new nave, which would have made this *duomo* the largest church in all Christendom. The effort ended when the Black Plague decimated the working population in 1348. One of the *duomo's* side aisles has been enclosed and turned into the **Museo dell'Opera Metropolitana.** Statues of philosophers, sibyls, and prophets by Giovanni Pisano stand guard beneath impressive spires.

The bronze sun on the *duomo's* facade was the creation of San Bernardino of Siena, who wanted the feuding Sienese to relinquish their emblems of nobility and unite under this symbol of the risen Christ. Alas, his efforts were in vain—the Sienese continue to identify with the animal symbols of their *contrade* (districts). The marble floor, like the rest of the *duomo*, is ornate, depicting diverse and often violent themes like the *Slaughter of the Innocents.* Michelangelo, Donatello, Pinturicchio, and Bernini are just a few of the many renowned artists who worked on the floor, called "the Unveiled Floor" because it is only open to the public from mid-August to October. Halfway up the left aisle is the **Piccolomini Altar,** designed by Andrea Bregno in 1503. The statue was built to host a very special holy relic: St. John's right arm. The lavish **Libreria Piccolomini,** commissioned by Pope Pius III in 1492, houses elaborately illustrated books of his uncle, Pius II. On the right, the **Papal Chapel of Madonna del Voto** houses two Bernini statues. *(Open daily from mid-Mar. to Sept. 10:30am-8pm; Oct. and 1st 2 weeks of Mar. 10:30am-7:30pm; Nov.-Feb. 10:30am-6:30pm. Open holidays Mar.-Sept. 1:30-6pm and Nov.-Feb. 1:30-5:30pm. Modest dress required. €4-5.50. Cash only.)*

Outside and downhill lies the 14th-century **baptistery.** Inside, lavish fifteenth-century frescoes depict the lives of Christ and St. Anthony. The central part of the ceiling, painted by Vecchietta, illustrates the ideas and important events from the Apostles' Creed . The baptistery's centerpiece is the hexagonal Renaissance baptismal font, made of marble, bronze, and enamel. Panels include Ghiberti's *Baptism of Christ* and Donatello's *Il Battista davanti a Erode. (Open daily from mid-Mar. to Sept. 9:30am-7:30pm; 1st 2 weeks in Mar. and all of Oct. 9:30am-7:30pm; Nov.-Feb. 10am-5pm. Modest dress required. €3. Cash only.)*

X MARKS THE SPOT. If you look closely, you'll notice a small cross two-thirds of the way up the stairs that lead from P. San Giovanni to the entrance of the *duomo*. This mark is neither a trick of the pavement nor graffiti. Legend has it that this step is where St. Catherine of Siena tripped and fell down the stairs in the 14th century, supposedly pushed by the devil. Despite the steepness and severity of the marble steps, she walked away without a scratch—*un miracolo* worthy only of a saint, as any Sienese will tell you.

CRIPTA. Recently rediscovered in 1999, the 700-year-old "crypt" was actually a series of underground rooms where pilgrims would prepare themselves for entering the *duomo*; they're called the *cripta* only because that's what the archaeologists who discovered them originally thought they were. The 13th-century depictions of the Old and New Testament episodes are attributed to the pre-Duccio Sienese painters, including Diotisalvi di Speme, Guido da Siena, and Guido di Graziano. Due to the absence of light, climactic instability, or human intervention, the colors remain vibrant and detailed. (*In P. del Duomo. Entrance halfway down the stairs, to the left of the baptistery. Open daily from mid-Mar. to Sept. 9:30am-8pm; Nov.-Feb. 10am-5pm; Oct. and 1st 2 weeks of Mar. 9am-7:30pm. €6. Audio guide in English, French, German, or Italian included. Cash only.*)

MUSEO DELL'OPERA METROPOLITANA. This museum, feeling spurned, holds all the art that won't fit in the *duomo*. It shouldn't: the first floor contains some of the foremost Gothic statuary in Italy, all of it by Giovanni Pisano. Upstairs, the 700-year-old *Maestà*, by Duccio di Buoninsegna, originally served as a screen for the cathedral's altar. Other notable works are the Byzantine *Madonna dagli Occhi Grossi*, paintings by Lorenzetti, and two altarpieces by Matteo di Giovanni. Follow signs for the **Panorama dal Facciatone**, in Room 4, to a balcony over the nave. A very narrow spiral staircase leads to a tiny tower for a beautiful, unadvertised view of the entire city. (*Entrance outside of duomo; exit portals and turn left. Open daily from mid-Mar. to Sept. 9:30am-7:30pm; Oct. and 1st 2 weeks of Mar. 9:30am-7pm; Nov.-Feb. 10am-5pm. €6. Cash only.*)

OSPEDALE DI SANTA MARIA DELLA SCALA. Built as a hospital in the 13th century, the *ospedale* is now a museum displaying its original frescoes, chapels, and vaults. The **Sala del Pellegrinaio**, or the Pilgrims' Hall, used as a ward until the late 20th century, contains an expressive fresco cycle by Vecchietta that tells the history of the hospital's construction. The **Sagrestia Vecchia**, or *Cappello del Sacro Chiodo*, houses masterful 15th-century Sienese frescoes. On the way downstairs, duck into the dim underground chapels and vaults, sites of rituals and "acts of piety for the dead" performed by various *contrade*. One level down is the entrance to the **Museo Archeologico**, included in admission to the *ospedale*. Established in 1933 to preserve Etruscan artifacts from the Siena area, the museum is now almost entirely housed in the eerie, medieval, underground waterworks of the city. Signs point the way through dank, labyrinthine passageways before emerging into rooms with well-lit displays of Etruscan pottery and coins. (*Opposite the duomo. Open daily 10:30am-6:30pm. Last entry 30min. before closing. €6, students €3.50, under 11 free. Cash only.*)

PINACOTECA NAZIONALE. Siena's superb art gallery displays works by every major artist of the highly stylized Sienese school. Masters represented include seven followers of Duccio—Simone Martini, the Lorenzetti brothers, Bartolo di Fredi, Bartolomeo Bulgarini, Sano di Pietro, and Il Sodoma. The museum is refreshingly free of tourist crowds, though the collection is geared toward artlovers. (*V. San Pietro 29, in the Palazzo Buonsignori, down V. del Capitano from the duomo. Open M 8:30am-1:30pm, Tu-Sa 8:15am-7:15pm, Su 8:15am-1:15pm. €4, EU citizens and students 18-26 €2, EU citizens under 18 or over 65 free. Cash only.*)

ENTERTAINMENT AND NIGHTLIFE

Siena's **Palio**, hands-down the highlight of the town's entertainment, overtakes the city twice each summer, transforming Siena into an exciting frenzy as people pack Il Campo to watch the bareback horse race. Even when it isn't fueled by primitive racing, Siena's nightlife keeps booming, thanks to the large population of local and foreign students. A great place to sample regional wines is **Enoteca Italiana,** in the Fortezza Medicea near the entrance off Vle. Cesare Maccari, where fine wines are sold by the bottle or by the glass. (☎05 77 22 88

TUSCANY

13. Wine from €3.50. Open Apr.-Sept. M noon-8pm; Tu-Sa noon-1am; Oct.-Mar. M-W noon-8pm, Th-Sa noon-1am. AmEx/MC/V.)

▣ **Caffè del Corso,** V. Bancha di Sopra 25 (☎0566 22 66 56; www.caffedelcor sosiena.it.) Cheap eats like pizza upstairs; bar downstairs that doubles as an outdoor dance floor in summer. Beer €3-4.50. Mixed drinks €5. 3-shot specials €5. Open daily 8am-3am.

▣ **Gallery,** V. Pantaneto 16-22 (☎05 77 34 05 73 16 32). A centrally-located bar serving a variety of drink specials. Pounding music, fluorescent lights, and a young crowd make this bar popular. The crowd is best after midnight. Beer €4.50. Mixed drinks €5-6. Open Tu and Th-Sa 11pm-3am.

Barone Rosso, V. dei Termini 9 (☎05 77 28 66 86; www.barone-rosso.com). A study-abroad crowd sprinkled with locals. Lively themed parties. F-Sa live music. W reduced prices for international students W. Open daily 9pm-3am. AmEx/MC/V.

▶ DAYTRIPS FROM SIENA

RADDA IN CHIANTI

Buses connect Siena to Radda in Chianti (1hr., 4 per day, round-trip €5.80). Buses leave from Siena's train station. Take bus 9 to the station from P. Gramsci. Buses also connect Radda to Florence (1hr., 3 per day), though schedules are sporadic; call ☎800 37 37 60 for info. In the morning, buses arrive at and depart from V. XX Settembre. In the afternoon, return buses to Florence and Siena usually leave from a stop across the street about 100m down, but sometimes don't, so ask at the tourist office. Stand in front of the orange sign and flag down the bus as it approaches.

Siena lies within easy reach of the Chianti region, a harmonious landscape of green hills, ancient castles, tiny villages, and of course, uninterrupted expanses of vineyards. In the Middle Ages, the small countryside towns of Castellina, Radda, and Gaiole formed a military alliance against French and Spanish invaders, adopting the black rooster as their symbol. Today, the rooster adorns bottles of Chianti, which are famous throughout the world. Peaceful **Radda in Chianti** (RAD-da; pop. 1668), just 30km from Siena, makes a great base for exploring the surrounding countryside. Every year on the 2nd of June, the town comes together for **Radda in the Glass.** For this one-day event, the *enoteche* provide ample bottles of Chianti on outdoor tables along V. Roma as rosy-cheeked citizens and lucky visitors make frequent stops with glasses in hand. If you can get out of town, most wineries in the area give free tastings, though a stroll down V. Roma also reveals numerous *enoteche* willing to let you try free samples. Cellar tours often require reservations—tourist offices provide bookings.

Located in the center of town, the outgoing staff at **La Bottega di Giovannino ❷,** V. Roma 37, serves filling plates on a breezy outdoor patio or in a wine-bottle laden dining room. Pair pasta with a glass of *Chianti classico* (from €3). The Bernardoni family lovingly maintains their restaurant and also offers transportation and tours for groups of seven or fewer to local wineries. (☎05 77 73 80 56; www.labottegadigiovannino.it. Primi €6. Secondi €6-9. Open M and W-Sa 8:32am-10:03pm, Su 11:30am-8:03pm. MC/V.) After a rigorous day of wine-tasting, relax in the public gardens outside the city walls, near P. IV Novembre. Inside the reputable **Porciatti Alimentari,** P. IV Novembre 1-3, master butchers sell handmade salami, pork sausages, and cheese that are available for tastings or as fillings for a delicious *panino.* They also sell bus tickets. (☎05 77 73 80 55; www.casaporciatti.it. Open in summer M-Sa 8am-1pm and 4-8pm, Su 8am-1pm, in winter M-Tu and Th-Sa 8am-1pm and 4-8pm, W and Su 8am-1pm. AmEx/MC/V.) Across the street and down Camminamento Medievale, a medieval passageway from the 14th century, is **Casa Porciatti,** run by the same owners.

Savor the free samples of wine, *grappa*, and olive oil, or schedule a tasting with a larger group (6-8 people) for €8-12. (☎05 77 73 80 55; www.casaporciatti. it. Open from mid-Mar. to Oct. M-Sa 10:30am-7pm, Su 10:30am-12:30pm and 3-7pm. MC/V.) The cheapest place to pick up wine is the **Coop** supermarket, V. Primo Maggio 32, which stocks bottles from €1.50. (www.e-coop.it. Open M-Sa 8:30am-1pm and 4-8pm. AmEx/MC/V.)

Check at the **tourist office** for bus and train information, directions, free brochures, or help scheduling wine tastings and tours. The office is located in P. Castello, off V. Roma. Turn off V. Roma onto Sdrucciolo di Castello. Follow the street to P. Castello, and the office will be on your left. (☎05 77 73 84 94. Open M-Sa 10am-1pm and 3:15-7pm, Su 10:30am-12:30pm.) For maps, and for more info on touring nearby wineries, vacation rentals, and excursions to the countryside, inquire at **A Bit of Tuscany,** V. Roma 39, next to Camere di Giovannino and housed in a real estate office. Private tours begin at €60 for 5hr. Larger, public tours are more economical, if slightly less revealing. (☎05 77 73 89 48. Open M-F 10am-1pm and 2:30-6pm.)

 VINTAGE TIMING. Many hotels in the Tuscan wine country consider September and October to be their high season (instead of the typical July and August tourist peak in Italy) because of the grape harvest. Prices can jump to €10-30 per night.

AREZZO   ☎05 75

Michelangelo once said, "Any talent I have is a result of the fine air of your town, Arezzo." Indeed, for its size, Arezzo (ah-RET-so; pop. 92,000) has seen a parade of influential artists and thinkers pass through. In addition to Michelangelo, the town was home to Renaissance titan Piero della Francesca, the poet Petrarch, the humanist Leonardo Bruni, and the artist and historian Giorgio Vasari. It's also the hometown of Roberto Benigni, director and star of the Oscar-winning *La Vita è Bella* (*Life is Beautiful*; 1997), who shot much of the film in the surrounding countryside. Escape the busy *centro* with a stroll outside the eastern portion of the medieval city walls, where you can catch striking views of the countryside and glimpses of backyard olive trees, vegetable gardens, and flowerbeds.

⊏ TRANSPORTATION

Trains: In P. della Repubblica. Ticket booth open M-Sa 5:50am-8:50pm; self-service ticket machines open 24hr. To **Florence** (1hr., 2 per hr. 4:30am-9:50pm, €5.70) and **Rome** (2hr., every 1-2hr. 6:30am-10:10pm, €11.50-11.70).

Buses: ATAM ticket office (☎0575 800 38 17 30), in front and to the left of train station exit across from the bus depot. Open daily 5:50am-8:50pm. **TRA-IN, SITA,** and **LFI** run to **Sansepolcro** (1hr., every hr., €3.50) and **Siena** (1hr., 4 per day, €5.20). Call ☎0575 38 26 51 for more info.

Taxis: RadioTaxi (☎0575 38 26 26). 24hr.

Car Rental: Autonoleggi Royal, V. Marco Perrenio 21 (☎05 75 35 35 70). 21+. Manual and automatic available. Open M-F 8:30am-12:30pm and 3:30-7:30pm, Sa 8:30am-12:30pm.

TUSCANY

⊕ 🔒 ORIENTATION AND PRACTICAL INFORMATION

Via Guido Monaco, which begins directly across from the **train station** at **Piazza della Repubblica,** parallels **Corso Italia;** together they form the backbone of the commercial district. To get to the *centro storico,* follow V. G. Monaco from the station to the traffic circle at **Piazza Guido Monaco.** Turn right on **Via Roma** and then turn left on the pedestrian walkway C. Italia, which leads to the old city. **Piazza Grande** lies to the right, 250m up C. Italia.

Tourist Office: Centro Servizi Turistici, P. Emiciclo Giovanni Paolo II (☎05 75 18 22 770; www.arezzoturismo.it) is located on the opposite side of town from the train station. Facing the entrance to the *duomo,* turn left and enter the adjacent building. Walk through the short hallway to the right, down the escalator, and the office is on the right. Services include hotel, airline and tour bookings, free **luggage storage,** and **Internet** access (€1.50 per 15min.). Open daily 9am-7pm. **APT,** P. della Repubblica 28 (☎05 75 20 839; www.apt.arezzo.it). Turn right after exiting the train station. Free maps and brochures of the town and nearby valleys. Open in summer daily 9am-1pm and 3-7pm; in winter M-Sa and the 1st Su of the month 10am-1pm and 3-6pm, other Su 9am-1pm.

Budget Travel: CTS, V. V. Veneto 18 (☎05 75 90 78 08). Sells Eurail passes and plane tickets. Open M-F 9am-7:30pm, Sa 9am-1pm.

Bank: Line V. G. Monaco between the train station and P. G. Monaco. **Banca Nazionale del Lavoro,** V. G. Monaco 74. **Currency exchange** and **24hr. ATM.** Open M-F 8:20am-1:35pm and 2:50-4:05pm.

Police: V. Leone Leoni 16 (☎05 75 90 66 67).

Pharmacy: Farmacia Comunale, Campo di Marte 7 (☎05 75 90 24 66), next to Conad supermarket on V. V. Veneto. Front doors open daily 8am-11pm. For 24hr. service, ring the bell outside of the "Servizio notturno" at Campo di Marte 6.

Hospital: Ospedale Civico, V. Pietronenni (☎05 75 25 51).

Internet: InformaGiovani, P. G. Monaco 2 (☎05 75 37 78 68). 30min. free for customers living in Arezzo (including students studying abroad). Otherwise, €1 per 30min. Open M-F 10:30am-7:30pm, Sa 10:30am-12:30pm.

Post Office: V. G. Monaco 34 (☎05 75 33 24 11). **Currency exchange;** €0.50 commission. Open M-F 8:15am-7pm, Sa 8:15am-1:30pm. **Postal Code:** 52100.

🏠 ACCOMMODATIONS

Hotels fill to capacity the first weekend of every month due to the **Fiera Antiquaria** (Antique Fair). Finding a cheap room can pose a challenge given the expensive chain hotels that crowd Arezzo.

Foresteria San Pier Piccolo, V. Bicchieraja 32 (☎05 75 32 42 19). In the old city, a short walk from Arezzo's main sights. Rooms in this 14th-century Benedictine convent have changed little over the years. Thankfully, spartan stone walls and wooden furniture have been supplemented with electricity, renovated baths, and TVs. Breakfast €3. Reception 7am-11pm. Curfew 11pm. Singles €24, with bath €35; doubles with bath €75; triples with bath €95. Cash only. ❶

Albergo Cecco, C. Italia 215 (☎05 75 20 986). Follow V. G. Monaco from the train station, turn right on V. Roma, and right again on C. Italia. The no-frills rooms are great for the budget-minded who care about location. Breakfast €3. Singles €32, with bath €42; doubles €64-70; triples €80; quads €95. AmEx/MC/V. ❷

FOOD

An open-air **market** takes place in P. Sant'Agostino on weekdays until 1pm. Head to **La Mozzarella**, V. Spinello 25, to the right and across the street from the train station, for a great variety of cheeses. (Open M-F 8am-1pm and 4-8pm, Sa 8am-1pm. Cash only.) **Eurospar**, V. G. Monaco 82, carries basic groceries. (Open M-Sa 8am-10pm, 1st Su of the month 9am-1pm. MC/V.)

Antica Osteria L'Agania, V. Mazzini 10 (☎05 75 29 53 81; www.agania.com). Sample wine from local vineyards (€4 per bottle) in an *osteria* that feels like a family kitchen. Primi and secondi €5-7. Open Tu-Su noon-3pm and 7-11pm. AmEx/MC/V. ❶

Trattoria Il Saraceno, V. Mazzini 6/a (☎05 75 27 644; www.ilsaraceno.com), off C. Italia. *Arezzese* specialties like duck and *pecorino* cheese in honey (€10). Pizza €6-8. Primi €7-8. Secondi €8-12. Cover €2. Open M-Tu and Th-Su noon-3:10pm and 7-9:30pm. AmEx/MC/V. ❷

Osteria del Borghicciolo, Corso Italia 34/35 (☎05 75 24 488). The staff swears the only secret to its great-tasting eats is authentic Italian extra virgin olive oil. 4-course meal for 2 €18. Cover €2. Open daily noon-3:30pm and from 7pm-late. ❷

Paradiso di Stelle, V. G. Monaco 58c (☎05 75 27 048). Great homemade gelato (from €1.70) and even better crepes (from €2). Open daily 11am-11pm. Cash only. ❶

◎ SIGHTS

BASILICA DI SAN FRANCESCO. This extraordinary 13th-century basilica houses elaborate 15th-century frescoes like Piero della Francesca's **Leggenda della Vera Croce** (*Legend of the True Cross*) in the *Bacci* chapel behind the main altar. It tells the story of the first crucifix and its role in early Christianity. The narrative begins with the death of Adam and proceeds to major events such as Emperor Constantine's conversion in the fourth century. St. Francis kneels at the foot of the cross. (*Walk up V. G. Monaco from train station and turn right into P. San Francesco. Basilica open daily 8:30am-noon and 2-7pm. Chapel containing della Francesca's frescoes open Apr.-Oct. M-F 9am6:30pm, Sa 9am-5:30pm, Su 1-5:30pm; Nov.-Mar. M-F 9am-5:30pm, Sa 9am-5pm, Su 1-5pm. Groups of 25 admitted every 30min. Last entry 30min. before closing. Reservation required. Call ☎05 75 29 90 71 or 35 27 27, or visit the office to the right of the church. Basilica free. Church €6, EU students 18-25 €4, art history students or EU citizens under 18 €2. Cash only.*)

CASA VASARI. Colors swirl on the elaborate ceilings of the Casa Vasari, built by the artist and historian himself. Vibrant portrait-frescoes by Michelangelo and del Sarto cover the walls. In one room, Vasari's depictions of the Muses crown the ceiling; one is a likeness of his fiancée, Niccolosa. He even painted himself taking in the view from one of the *casa*'s windows. (*V. XX Settembre 55, just off V. San Domenico. Ring bell to enter. ☎05 75 40 90 40. Open M and W-Sa 8:30am-7:30pm, Su 8:30am-1:30pm. Last entry 30min. before closing. €2, EU students €1. Cash only.*)

PIAZZA GRANDE (PIAZZA VASARI). This *piazza*, which surrounds a small fountain decorated by the garden club of Arezzo, contains the **Chiesa di Santa Maria della Pieve,** a spectacular Romanesque church built in the 12th century. Elegant columns and rounded arches frame a 13th-century portico. On the elevated presbytery sits Pietro Lorenzetti's brilliantly restored *Annunciation* and *Madonna and Child*. Below lies the 11th-century church upon which the Pieve was built. The adjoining pock-marked **tower** is known appropriately as the "Tower of 100 Holes." Surrounding *palazzi* enclose P. Grande with pleasing proportionality. The 14th-century Romanesque **Palazzo della Fraternità** and

16th-century Baroque **Palazzo delle Logge Vasariane** recall past eras. For a livelier version of history, attend the monthly **antique fair** or the semi-annual **Giostra del Saracino** each summer. To reach **Parco "Il Prato,"** a grassy retreat of flowers, picnic areas, and ancient statues, follow C. Italia to V. dei Pileati. *(Tower open M-Sa 8am-noon and 3-7pm, SU 8:30am-noon and 4-7pm. Park open daily until dusk. Free.)*

DUOMO. The massive 13th-century *duomo* sits high on the hill of Arezzo. Built in the Tuscan Gothic style, the cathedral houses Arezzo native Piero della Francesca's *Maddalena* and Bishop Guido Tarlati's tomb on the left side of the nave near the altar. Carved reliefs relate stories of the iconoclastic bishop's unconventional life. The seven elaborate stained-glass windows were designed by French artist Guillaume de Marcillat. The *Cappella della Madonna del Conforto*, off the austere nave, holds a notable terra-cotta *Crucifixion* by Andrea della Robbia. *(Up V. Andrea Cesalpino from P. San Francesco. ☎05 75 23 991. Open daily 7am-12:30pm and 3-6:30pm. Modest dress required. Free.)*

CHIESA DI SAN DOMENICO. The church's true gem is Cimabue's ▨**crucifix** (1265-70), which hangs over the main altar. It is the artist's oldest and best preserved work. Other significant pieces in the simple, wood-timbered interior include Spinello Aretino's *Annunciation* and a Marcillat rose window depicting St. Augustine. *(Take V. A. Celaspino from P. San Francesco, turn left at P. Libertà on V. Ricasorli, then right on V. di Sassoverde. Open daily 8:30am-1pm and 3:30-7pm. Hours may vary. Closed to public during mass. Free.)*

PISA ☎050

Millions of tourists arrive in Pisa (PEE-zah; pop. 85,379) each year to marvel at the famous "Leaning Tower," forming a photo-snapping mire of awkward poses. Though worn around the edges, the heart of Pisa is still alive as a haven for the exuberant, opinionated students that attend the city's three universities. After that inevitable Kodak moment, take some time to wander through the alleys of P. dei Cavalieri and P. Dante, decorated with impassioned political graffiti in the sprawling university neighborhood, or along the Arno in the evening to take in the lively local nightlife.

▐ TRANSPORTATION

Flights: Galileo Galilei Airport (☎050 84 93 00; www.pisa-airport.com). Trains make the 5min. trip (€1.10) between the train station and the airport every 30 min., departing from track 14 (find access at the end of platform 1). Not a major Italian airport. Bus **LAM ROSSA** (red line) runs between the airport, train station, the Tower, and other points in Pisa and its environs (every 20min., €1.10).

Trains: Pisa Centrale, P. della Stazione (☎050 413 85), at the southern end of town. Ticket booth open 6am-9pm; self-service ticket machines available 24hr. MC/V. To **Florence** (1hr., every 30min. 4:15am-10:30pm, €5.60); **Livorno** (15min., every 30min., €1.80); **Rome** (4hr., every 2hr. 5:45am-7pm, €18-36). Regional trains to **Lucca** (30min., 2 per hr. 6:20am-9:50pm, €2.40) also stop at Pisa's **San Rossore** (€1.10), close to the *duomo* and Tower. If leaving from San Rossore, buy tickets from *tabaccherie*.

Buses: Lazzi (☎058 358 48 76; www.lazzi.it) and **CPT** (☎050 50 55 11; www.cpt.pisa) in P. Sant'Antonio. Ticket office open daily 7am-8:15pm. To: **Florence** (2hr., every hr., €6.10) via **Lucca** (every 40min., €2); **Livorno** (every hr., €2); **Volterra** (1hr., €5.20) via **Pondeterra.**

Taxis: RadioTaxi (☎050 54 16 00).

Car Rental: A number of companies have rentals available at the airport. **Avis** (☎050 42 028). **Budget** (☎050 50 37 56). **Europcar** (☎050 41 081). **Hertz** (☎050 43 220). **Thrifty** (☎050 45 490). Book in advance to ensure availability.

■✶ 🛈 ORIENTATION AND PRACTICAL INFORMATION

Pisa lies near the mouth of the **Arno River**, which splits the town. Most sights lie to the north of the Arno; the main **train station** is to the south. To reach **Piazza Duomo** from the station, take the bus marked LAM ROSSA going toward San Jacopo; it leaves from across the station, in front of Hotel Cavalieri. The plaza can also be reached by foot in 30min.—head straight from the station down **Viale Gramsci** to **Piazza Vittorio Emanuele II.** From there you can take the more direct route by walking around the plaza on the left, taking the first left into **P. Sant'Antonio,** near the bus station, and then heading right up **V. Francesco Crispi,** which will lead you over **Ponte Solferino** onto **Via Roma** and straight to P. Duomo. Alternatively, from P. Emanuele take the store-lined **Corso Italia** and once across **Ponte Mezzo,** walk along the river until you reach Ponte Solferino and turn right onto V. Roma.

Tourist Office: P. V. Emanuele II 13 (☎050 42 291). Open M-F 9am-7pm, Sa 9am-1:30pm. At P. Duomo in Museo dell'Opera del Duomo on the Arno side of the tower. (☎050 56 04 64). Open daily in summer 10am-7pm, in winter 10am-5pm. At the airport (☎050 50 37 00). Open daily 11am-11pm.

Budget Travel:New Taurus Viaggi, V. Francesco Crispi 25/27 (☎050 50 20 90), sells international tickets. Open M-F 9am-12:30pm and 3:30-7:30pm, Sa 9am-12:30pm. AmEx/MC/V.

Banks: Deutsche Bank, on the corner of V. Giusue Carducci and V. San Lorenzo, between P. Cavalieri and P. Martiri della Libertà. **24hr. ATMs.**

Laundromat: Lavenderia, V. Carmine 20. Wash €4, dry €4. Includes detergent. Open daily 7am-11pm.

Police: (☎050 58 35 11). For emergencies ☎113.

Pharmacy: Farmacia, Lugarno Mediceo 51 (☎050 54 40 02). Open 24hr.

Hospital: Santa Chiara (☎050 99 21 11) on V. Bonanno near P. del Duomo.

Internet Access: Internet Surf, V. Giusue Carducci 5. €2.50 per hr. Students €2 per hr. Open daily 9am-10pm.

Post Office: P.V. Emanuele II 8 (☎050 51 95 15), near the station on the right of the *piazza.* Open M-F 8:15am-7pm, Sa 8:15am-1:30pm. **Postal Code:** 56125.

🏠🏠 ACCOMMODATIONS AND CAMPING

Albergo Helvetia, V. Don G. Boschi 31 (☎050 55 30 84), off P. Arcivescovado. These rooms offer little in the way of style, but their location near major sights is convenient. Equipped with TV, fans, and phones. Shared and private baths available. Reception 8am-midnight. Breakfast €5. Singles €35, with bath €50; doubles €45/60. Extra bed €15. Cash only. ❷

Hotel Galileo, V. Santa Maria 12 (☎050 40 621; hotelgalileo@pisaonline.it). Stellar rooms in the university district, all with frescoed ceilings, minifridges, and TV. Shared bath is well-kept. Single €40, with bath €45; doubles €48/60; triples €63/75. MC/V. ❷

Pisa Tower Hostel, P. Garibaldi 9 (☎331 788 68 59). Taking a cue from the *gelateria* next door, these sherbet-colored rooms come with a few sweet deals, including free drop-off at the airport, internet, and kitchen facilities. Female-only dorms €25; private rooms available. ❶

Camping Village Torre Pendente, V. delle Cascine (☎050 56 17 04; www.campingtor-rependente.it). From P. del Duomo, go through the arch on the west side into P. Manin. Take V. Pisano right to the intersection next to the Pam Supermarket, take a left onto V. Cascine, and go all the way through the underpass tunnel; at the end campsite will be about 200m on the right. An easy walk to the towers, this campsite provides dorm beds in close quarters, bungalow rental, and sites for campers and tents. On-site market, bar, and outdoor swimming pool. Dorms in bungalows offer bathrooms and kitchen facilities. April-June €8, tent €7.50, dorms €20. July-Aug. €9.50/14/25. MC/V over €10. ❶

🅵 FOOD

Il Paiolo, V. Curtatone e Montanara 9 (☎050 42 528). Great music and original artwork hanging on the yolk-yellow walls set the mood for this popular university neighborhood restaurant where students fill the benches and the waitstaff adds friendly service to the fun atmosphere. Primi and secondi €6-9. Cover €1. Open M-F 12:30-3pm and 8pm-2am, Sa-Su 8pm-2am. MC/V. ❷

Ristoro al Vecchio Teatro, P. Dante (☎050 202 10). Enjoy fresh Pisan cuisine *al fresco* or in the dining room of one of the city's oldest buildings. Try the *risotto di verdure miste*, a butter dish with artichoke, garlic, and peppers. Primi and secondi €8. Cover €1.50. Open M-Sa noon-3pm and 7:30-10pm. AmEx/MC/V. ❷

Osteria dei Cavalieri, V. San Frediano 16 (☎050 58 08 58; www.osteriacavalieri.pisa.it). Relax after a busy day and sample traditional *spaghetti all'arrabbiata* (spicy pasta with tomato and herbs). Primi €8-9. Secondi €11-15. Open M-F 12:30-4pm and 7:45-10pm, Sa 7:45-10pm. MC/V. ❷

Galileo, V. San Martino 6 (☎050 28 287; www.ristorantegalileo.com). Crisp, white decor dominates this classy yet family-friendly dinner spot. Sit under the cover of the outdoor seating or inside beneath the chandeliers. Primi €7-10. Secondi €12-18. Cover €2. Open daily 12:30-2:30pm and 7:30-11pm. MC/V. ❷

🅾 SIGHTS

◼LEANING TOWER. The white stone buildings of the **Piazza del Duomo**, aptly renamed Campo dei Miracoli (Field of Miracles) by poet Gabriele d'Annunzio, stretch across the well-maintained greens of the *piazza*, which houses the Leaning Tower, *duomo*, baptistery, and *Camposanto* (cemetery). Look closely: all of the buildings lean at different angles, thanks to the mischievous, shifty soil. No matter how many postcards you see of the Tower, nothing quite compares to witnessing the 5.5° tilt in person. Bonanno Pisano began building the tower in 1173, and construction was repeatedly delayed as the soil shifted and the building began to lean. The tilt intensified after WWII, and thanks to tourist traffic, it continues to slip 1-2mm every year. In June 2001, the steel safety cables and iron girdles that imprisoned the Tower during years of stabilization efforts were finally removed. One year later, the Tower reopened, albeit on a tightly regulated schedule: once every 30min., guided groups of 30 visitors are permitted to ascend. (*Make reservations at the ticket offices in the Museo del Duomo, online, or next to the tourist info office. Tours depart daily June-Aug. 8:30am-10pm; Sept.-May 8:30am-8:30pm. Groups meet beside the tower 10min. before scheduled entry. Bags not allowed. Free storage for small bags, but not backpacks, so plan accordingly. Children under 8 not permitted, under 18 must be accompanied by an adult. €15. MC/V.*)

◼BATTISTERO. The baptistery, an enormous barrel of a building unfairly overshadowed by the all-too-famous leaning legend, was begun in 1153 by a man known as Diotisalvi ("God save you"), its design inspired by the church of the Holy Sepulchre in Jerusalem. Blending architectural styles, it incorporates

Tuscan-Romanesque stripes with a multi-tiered Gothic ensemble of gables, pinnacles, and statues. Guido Bigarelli's **fountain** (1246) dominates the center of the ground floor. Nicola Pisano's **pulpit** (1260) recaptures the dignity of classical antiquity and is one of the harbingers of Renaissance art in Italy. Each of the building's four portals face one of the cardinal directions. The dome's acoustics are astounding: a choir singing in the baptistery can be heard 2km away. A staircase embedded in the wall leads to a balcony just below the dome; farther up, a space between the interior and exterior of the dome yields views of the surrounding *piazza. (Open daily Apr.-Sept. 8am-8pm; Oct. 9am-7pm; Nov.-Feb 10am-5pm; Mar. 9am-6pm. Last entry 30min. before close. €5; combined ticket with 1 other Piazza del Duomo sight €6; with 4 other sights, excluding the tower, €10.)*

CAMPOSANTO. Built in 1277, this cloistered courtyard cemetery greets visitors with over 600 tombstones, covered with earth that Crusaders brought back from Golgotha, and Roman sarcophagi that date from the AD third century. The sarcophagi reliefs inspired Pisano's pulpit in the baptistery. Fragments of enormous frescoes shattered by WWII Allied bombs line the galleries. The **Cappella Ammannati** contains haunting frescoes of Florence succumbing to the plague; its unidentified, 14th-century creator is known as the "Master of the Triumph of Death." *(Next to the duomo. Open daily Apr.-Sept. 8am-8pm; Oct. 9am-7pm; Nov.-Feb 10am-5pm; Mar. 9am-6pm. Last entry 30min. before close. €5; combined ticket with 1 other Piazza del Duomo sight €6; with 4 other sights, excluding the tower, €10.)*

DUOMO. The *duomo*'s dark green-and-white facade is the archetype of the Pisan-Romanesque style. Begun in 1064 by Buscheto (who is now entombed in the wall), the cathedral is the *campo*'s oldest structure. Enter the five-aisled nave through Bonanno Pisano's richly decorated bronze doors. Although a 1595 fire destroyed most of the interior, the cathedral was masterfully restored; original paintings by Ghirlandaio hang on the right wall, Cimabue's spectacular gilded mosaic **Christ Pantocrator** graces the apse, and bits of intricately patterned marble Cosmati pavement remain. Giovanni Pisano's last and greatest **pulpit** (1311), designed to outdo his father's in the baptistery, sits regally in the center. *(Open Apr.-Sept. M-Sa 10am-7:30pm, Su 1-7:30pm; Oct. M-Sa 10am-5:30pm, Su 1-5:30; Nov.-Feb. M-Sa 10am-12:30pm and 3-4:30pm, Su 3-4:30pm; Mar. M-Sa 10-5:30pm, Su 1-5:30pm. Closed for religious ceremonies. €2; combined ticket with 1 other Piazza del Duomo sight €6; with 4 other sights, excluding the tower, €10.)*

LUCCA
☎ 05 83

Lucca (LOO-ka; pop. 9000) is a pleasant retreat from the sight-seeing frenzy of other Tuscan destinations, successfully dabbling in nearly every area of tourist activity. Bikers rattle through the town and along the 4km tree-lined promenade that runs atop the city's encircling medieval walls; the well-heeled take on the trendy boutiques along the main streets; and art lovers admire the Romanesque churches and elegant architecture of the *centro*. Picturesque *piazze* appear every few blocks, along with notice boards advertising concerts, often related in some way to the operas by Lucca's own Giacomo Puccini. Tranquil and compelling, Lucca is no party spot, but it is the ideal location if you're looking to get away from it all.

▐ TRANSPORTATION

Trains: Station in Ple. Ricasoli. Ticket office open daily 6:30am-8:10pm. To **Florence** (1½hr., every hr., €5); **Pisa** (30min.; 2 per hr. M-Sa 5:40am-9:30pm, Su 7:42am-

9:30pm; €2.40); and **Viareggio** (16min.; every hr. M-Sa 6:19am-11:30pm, Su 7:59am-11:30pm). For other major cities, change in Pisa. For **Cinque Terre,** change in Viareggio.

Buses: Lazzi (☎0583 587 897; www.valibus.it), in Ple. Verdi. To **Florence** (1hr. 10min.; M-Sa 1-2 per hr. 6:25am-6:55pm, Su every 2hr. via Montecatini 9:45am-7:45pm; €5.10) and **Pisa** (50min.; M-Sa 1-2 per hr., Su every 2hr. 8am-8pm; €2.80).

Taxis: RadioTaxi (☎0583 333 434). Taxis pick up at 4 stands around the city. To call a taxi, enter the appropriate code for your desired pick-up point when prompted. For pick up at the train station 01, in P. Napoleone 02, in P. Santa Maria 03, in Ple. Verdi 04.

Bike Rental: Most rental locations have comparable fares and hours of operation. In general, basic bicycles are €2.50 per hr., €12.50 per day; mountain and racing bikes €3.50/17.50; tandem bikes €5.50 per hr. Most rental places are open daily 9am-7:30pm. **Chronò,** Corso Garibaldi 93 (☎0583 490 591). **Cicli Bizzarri,** P. Santa Maria 32 (☎0583 49 66 82; www.ciclibizzarri.net). **Cicli Rai,** V. San Nicolao 66 (☎348 893 7119). **Poli Antonio Biciclette,** P. Santa Maria 42 (☎0583 493 787; www.biciclette-poli.com). **Promo Tourist,** Porta San Pietro (☎348 380 0126). Or from the **tourist office** in Ple. Verdi (☎0583 583 150; www.luccaitinera.it).

Car Rental: Autonoleggio Giglio, V. Orzali 391 (☎058 349 2698). **Avis,** in Ple. Italia (☎0583 317 283; www.avisautonoleggio.it). **Europe Car,** Vle. Castracani 110 (☎058 39 56 058; www.europecar.it). **Hertz,** V. Catalani 59 (☎058 350 5472; www.hertz.it). **Pittore,** P. Santa Maria 34 (☎058 34 67 960). **Travel Car,** Vle. Puccini 82 (☎058 35 82 284).

✦ 🔢 ORIENTATION AND PRACTICAL INFORMATION

To reach the *centro storico* from the **train station,** cross the street and walk forward past **Piazza Ricasole** to take a left on **Viale Regina Margherita.** Enter the city through the arches to the right to of **Porta San Pietro.** Walk forward one block to take a left onto **Corso Garibaldi.** Turn right onto **Via Vittorio Veneto** and follow it one block to reach **Piazza Napoleone** (also called Piazza Grande). Continue walking on V. Veneto to reach to reach **Piazza San Michele** in the center of town. If arriving by bus, walk to the right through **Piazza Verdi,** follow **Via San Paolino** toward the center of town and P. San Michele, and turn right on V. Veneto to reach P. Napoleone.

Tourist Offices: Ufficio Regionale, P. Santa Maria 35 (☎0583 919931; www.luccaturismo.it). Includes an internet point, currency exchange, hotel booking, and tickets for Trenitalia. Open daily in winter 9am-1pm and 3-6pm, in summer 9am-8pm. **Ufficio Provinciale** (☎0583 91994) in Corile Carrara beside P. Napoleone. Open daily 10am-1pm and 2-6pm. **Centro Accoglienza Turistica** (☎0583 583150; www.luccaitinera.it), in Ple. Verdi, offers Wi-Fi for €2, scheduled guided tours (Sa 3pm, 2-3 hr., meets in P. San Michele under the Loggia of Palazzo Pretorio, €10), and self-guided audio tours (€9, €6 for every additional tour). Open daily 9am-6pm. 2nd branch near the train station in P. Curtatone on Vle. Guisti (☎0583 495 730). Open daily 10am-1:30pm and 2:30-5:30pm.

Currency Exchange: Ufficio Regionale, tourist office, in P. Santa Maria. Open daily in winter 9am-1pm and 3-6pm, in summer 9am-8pm.

24hr ATM: On corner of V. San Paolino, 50m away from the UniCredit Banca. Also on the corner of V. Fillungo and V. Mordini, beside Deutschebank.

Laundry: Lavanderia Niagara, V. Michele Rosi 26 (☎349 164 5084 or 328 675 4181). €4 per 7 kg. Open daily 7am-11pm.

Pharmacy: Farmacia Comunale, in P. Curtatone. Open 24hr.

Hospital: Campo di Marte (☎058 39 55 791), outside the wall in the Northeast corner on V. dell'Ospedale.

Police: ☎112 Carabinieri, ☎113 Police.

TUSCANY

Internet: The tourist office in P. Verdi has Wi-Fi for €2 per hr. The other three have computers with internet. **Copesteria Paolini**, V. Paolini 63, has both. Internet €3 per hr.; Wi-Fi €2 per hr. Open M-F 8:30am-7:30pm, Sa 9am-1pm and 3:30-7:30pm.

Post Office: V. Vallisneri (☎058 34 34 51). Open M-F 8:15am-7pm, Sa 8:15am-1:30pm. **Postal Code:** 55100.

▛ ACCOMMODATIONS

La Gemma di Elena Bed and Breakfast, V. della Zecca 33 (☎058 34 96 65; www.virtualica.it/gemma). Though the building is 450 years old, this B&B radiates with energy. The laid-back, friendly staff help make your stay even more comfortable in 1 of 6 plush and pretty rooms full of personality, some with fireplace and terrace. Shared and private baths. Common room and private parking available. Pets welcome. Breakfast included, served 8:30-10:30am. Check-out 11am. Singles €35; doubles €55, with bath €65. Extra bed €15, in room with bath €20. AmEx/MC/V. ❷

Ostello San Frediano (HI), V. della Cavallerizza 12 (☎058 34 69 957; www.ostellolucca. it), 15min. from P. Napoleone. Walk along V. Beccheria past P. San Michele as the street becomes V. Santa Lucia and then V. del Moro. At the road's end, turn left on V. San Giorgio and make an immediate right onto V. C. Battisti. When you reach the Basilica San Frediano, go right around the church, along the front, and straight onto V. Cavallerizza. Spacious rooms with hardwood bunk beds. Common spaces with high ceilings and plenty of couches. Internal and external baths, private and shared rooms available. Breakfast €3-5, lunch or dinner €11. Towels €1.50. Linens included. Reception 7:30am-10am and 1:30pm-midnight. Check-out 10am. Lockout 10am-3:30pm. 6- to 8- person dorms €18-20; 2- to 6-person rooms with bath €55-135. HI discount. Cash only. ❶

Bed and Breakfast La Torre, V. del Carmine 11 (☎058 39 57 044; www.roomlatorre. com). This family-run rest stop actually has 2 locations within a ½ a block of each other. At the reception portion, rooms are homey, with colorful bedspreads and family portraits on the walls. Though this 1st set of rooms is perfectly nice, ask to be placed in **Torre 3** when booking. These doubles come with private bathrooms, kitchenettes, high ceilings, and antique furniture. Breakfast included. Free internet. Free pickup available; call ahead. Singles €35, with bath €50; doubles €50/80. Apartments with kitchen, parlor, and TVs for 2 people €80 per night, for 4 people €120 per night. MC/V. ❷

Zimmer La Colonna, V. dell'Angelo Custode 16 (☎058 34 40 170), off P. Maria Foris Portam. Colonnaded hallways lead to spacious rooms with TV and antique decor. Clean shared baths. Doubles €45, with bath €65. AmEx/MC/V. ❷

Da Elisa Alle Sette Arti, V. Elisa 25 (☎058 349 45 39). Antique beds and Art Deco furnishings in ornately-tiled *affitacamere*. Shared and private bath. Kitchen. Breakfast €6. Bike rental €2 per hr. June-Sept. singles €47, with bath €65; doubles €52/70, triples €67/77. Oct.-May singles €42/52; doubles €45/55; triples €57/62. ❸

Residence Santa Chiara, V. Santa Chiara 12 (☎058 34 91 349; www.residencesantachiara.com). Spacious rooms with tiled floors in a 16th-century building. Take breakfast in summer in the outdoor terrace; in the winter, have it brought to your room. Jan-Mar singles €50; doubles €65. Apr.-Dec. singles €65, doubles €90. AmEx/MC/V. ❹

Piccolo Hotel Puccini, V. di Poggio 9 (☎058 35 54 21; www.hotelpuccini.com). Named for the famous Luccan, the rooms of this 3-star hotel are decorated with framed playbills from Puccini's operas. Bath, TV with English channels, phone, and safe. Breakfast €3.50. Wi-Fi available. Singles €70; doubles €95; triples €115. AmEx/MC/V. ❹

▟ FOOD

On Wednesday and Saturday mornings from 8am-1pm, an **open-air market** overtakes V. dei Bacchettoni on the east end of town. Within the city walls, **SIDIS,**

P. del Carmine 2, stocks basic groceries. (Open M-Tu and Th-Su 8am-8pm, W 8am-1pm. MC/V.) Outside the north side of the city walls, **Esselunga** stocks a more extensive variety of supermarket goods.

Ristorante da Francesco, Corte Portici 13 (☎058 34 18 049), off V. Calderia between P. San Salvatore and P. San Michele. Ample patio seating. Ideal for a light but filling meal. Try the *zuppa di verdure* (vegetable soup; €6). Primi €6-7. Secondi €8-12. *Menù turistico* for lunch (primo, secondo, a glass of wine, and coffee) €15. Cover €1.50. Open Tu-Su noon-2:30pm and 7-10pm. MC/V. ❷

Da Leo, V. Tegrimi 1 (☎058 34 92 236; www.trattoriadaleo.it). Have a casual pasta meal at this local favorite. Reservations needed for outdoor seating. Primi €6-6.50. Secondi €9-11.50. Cover €1. ❷

Caffè Di Simo, V. Fillungo 58 (☎058 34 96 234; www.anticocaffedisimo.it). Amid a row of designer boutiques, the hardwood of this restaurant shines while mellow music plays in the background. Lunch buffet €10. Primi €7-9. Secondi €8.50-11. Open daily 12:30-3pm and 8-11:30pm. MC/V. ❷

Pizzeria da Felice, V. Buia 12 (☎058 34 94 986). Pizza *al taglio* (slices from €1.30) is a cheap and delicious meal option for hungry locals and tourists. Open M-Sa 10am-8:30pm. ❶

Gelateria Santini Sergio, P. Cittadella 1 (☎058 35 52 95). Has been wowing sweet-toothed passers-by since 1916 with flavors like *paciugo* (nougat, chocolate, cookies, and rum) and standard favorites. Cups and cones €1.50-3. Open daily July-Sept. 9am-midnight, Oct.-June 10am-8pm. AmEx/MC/V. ❶

👁 SIGHTS

▨BALUARDI. No tour of Lucca is complete and no journey into the city possible without passing the perfectly intact medieval city walls, or *baluardi* (battlements). The shaded 4km pedestrian path along the walls, which passes grassy parks and cool fountains, is perfect for a breezy, afternoon picnic or a sunset view. Rent a bike and try to master the Luccan art of simultaneously biking and chatting on your cell phone, or simply admire the city's layout as you stroll.

DUOMO DI SAN MARTINO. Though supposedly begun in the AD sixth century and rebuilt in 1070 by Pope Alexander II, the majority of the building that stands today is the result of another reconstruction, which took place between the 12th and 15th centuries. The multi-layered, arched facade of this asymmetrical *duomo* is the oldest feature of the present structure. The 13th-century reliefs that decorate the exterior of the *duomo* include Nicola Pisano's *Journey of the Magi and Deposition.* Matteo Civitali, Lucca's famous sculptor, designed the floor and contributed the San Martino statue to the right of the door. His prized *Colobium,* in the left aisle, houses the 11th-century **Volto Santo** (Holy Face). Reputedly carved by Nicodemus at Calvary, this wooden crucifix is said to depict a from-life image of Christ. Other highlights include Tintoretto's *Last Supper* (1590), the third painting on the right, and *Holy Conversation* by Ghirlandaio, in the sacristy off the right aisle. The **Museo della Cattedrale,** left of the *duomo,* houses religious objects from the *duomo.* (*P. San Martino. From P. Napoleone, take V. del Duomo past P. Giglio and P. San Giovanni. Duomo and sacristy open daily Apr.-Oct. 9:30am-5:45 pm; Nov-March 9:30am-5pm. Closed for Su mass 11am-noon. Duomo free. Sacristy €2. Museo della Cattedrale open from mid-March to Oct. daily 10am-6pm; from Nov. to mid-Mar. M-F 10:30am-2pm and Sa-Su 10am-5pm. €4; combined ticket for duomo, Sacristy, Museo della Cattedrale, and Chiesa di San Giovanni €6. Audio tour €1. Cash only.*)

CHIESA DI SAN MICHELE IN FORO. Given its current setting in a busy *piazza,* it's hard to tell that construction on this church actually began in the AD eighth century on the site of a Roman forum. Once inside, the church's large, stone interior holds beautiful and dramatic oil paintings, such as Lippi's bold *Saints Helen, Roch, Sebastian, and Jerome* toward the end of the right aisle, and Luca della Robbia's *Madonna and Child* near the front. Original religious statues were replaced in the 19th century with likenesses of prominent political figures: Cavour, Garibaldi, and Napoleon III. *(Open daily 8am-noon and 3-6pm. Closed during Su mass. Free.)*

CHIESA DI SAN GIOVANNI. The simple plaster dome of this unassuming church holds a recently excavated AD second-century Roman complex, complete with mosaic pavement, the ruins of a private house and bath (the church's foundations), a Longobard burial site, and a Paleochristian chapel, as well as a 10th- to 11th-century crypt. *(From P. Napoleone, follow V. del Duomo. Open from mid-Mar. to Oct. daily 10am-6pm; from Nov. to mid-Mar. Sa-Su 10am-5pm. Combined ticket with archeological area and baptistery €2.50; combined ticket valid for complete cathedral complex, including Museo della Cattedrale and Sacristy €6. Cash only.)*

TORRE GUINIGI AND TORRE DELL'ORE. These are two of the 15 remaining towers from medieval Lucca's original 250. Narrow **Torre Guinigi** rises above Lucca from the stone mass of Palazzo Guinigi, which is closed to the public. Crouch through a small door to reach a set of 227 stairs; seven little oak trees, called *"lecci,"* provide a shaded view of the city and the hills beyond. *(V. Sant'Andrea 41. From P. San Michele follow V. Roma 1 block, turn left on V. Fillungo and right on V. Sant'Andrea. ☎ 058 331 68 46. Open daily June-Sept. 9:30am-7:30pm; Oct.-May 9:30am-6:30pm. Last entry 20min. before close. €3.50, students and over 65 €2.50. Combined ticket for both towers €5/4. Cash only.)* For some more exercise, climb the 207 steps of the **Torre delle Ore** (Hour Towers/Clock Towers), where you can see the inner workings of the city's tallest timepiece. *(V. Fillungo 24. Open daily June-Sept. 9:30am-7:30pm; Oct.-May 9:30am-6:30pm. Last entry 20min. before close. €3.50, students and over 65 €2.50. Combined ticket for both towers €5/4. Cash only.)*

PIAZZA NAPOLEONE. Also called "Piazza Grande" by locals, this *piazza* is the town's administrative center. The 16th-century **Palazzo Ducale** now houses government offices. At night, *lucchese* pack the *piazza* for *passeggiate* (strolls).

PIAZZA ANFITEATRO. Closely packed buildings, three-star hotels, and upscale restaurants create a nearly seamless, oval wall around this *piazza*, originally an ancient Roman amphitheater. Though the ruins are now nearly 3m below the ground, some of the original arches are visible on the outer walls of the buildings. Locals and tourists mingle over coffee and conversation close to but free of the hyperactivity of Piazza Napoleone.

BASILICA DI SAN FREDIANO. Multiple additions led to San Frediano's proud, Romanesque structure. Originally constructed in the AD sixth century with the facade facing west, it was rebuilt in the first half of the 12th century with an eastward orientation. The gleaming Byzantine mosaic atop the facade is striking. *(Open M-Sa 9am-noon and 2:30pm-6pm, Su 9-noon and 2:30pm-5:30pm. Free.)*

PALAZZO PFANNER. Palazzo Pfanner's sumptuous garden oasis, complete with an octagonal fountain and statuary of mythical figures, was designed by Filippo Juvarra in the 18th century. While the view from the wall is free, sitting in the garden makes you feel like royalty. The *palazzo* now serves as a museum that showcases 18th- and 19th-century costumes and old medical instruments belonging to Dr. Pietro Pfanner, the surgeon who owned the *palazzo* and gave it his name. *(V. degli Asili 33. From the Basilica di San Frediano, take V. San Frediano to V. Cesare Battisti and turn left. Take a right onto V. degli Angeli to reach V. degli Asili. ☎ 340 923 30 85. Open daily Apr.-Oct. 10am-6pm. Palazzo €3.50, students €3; garden €3.50/3; both €5/4. €0.50 discount on all tickets in Apr. and Oct.)*

ORTO BOTANICO. For a change of pace, retreat to the calming paths of Lucca's botanical gardens. Created in 1820 by duchess Maria Luisa of Bourbon, the garden was originally linked to the Royal University of Lucca for scientific study. A broad main avenue leads to a pond and marshy plants before branching off into smaller, more isolated trails. *(In the southeast corner of the city. ☎058 344 21 60. Open daily from July to mid-Sept. 10am-7pm; from mid-Sept. to Oct. 10am-5pm; Nov-Dec. by reservation only M-Sa 9:30am-12:30pm; Mar. 20 to Apr. 30 10am-5pm; May-June 10am-6pm. Last entry 30min. before closing. €3.)*

🎵 🎭 ENTERTAINMENT AND NIGHTLIFE

Teatro Comunale del Giglio, Piazza del Giglio 13/15 (☎058 34 65 31; www.teatrodelgiglio.it), provides theater, opera, and dance performances year round.

Gelateria Veneta, V. V. Veneta 74 (☎058 34 70 37; www.gelateriaveneta.net.). For evidence that Lucca is a sleepy Tuscan town at its heart, look no further than the epicenter of its nighttime activity. Delicious all-natural homemade flavors and outdoor seating. The whipped mousse flavors are sensational. Cones €1.90-3. Granita €1.90-2.70. Open daily Mar.-Oct. 10:30am-1am. MC/V over €10.

Betty Blue, V. del Gonfalone 16 (www.betty-blue.eu), slightly away from the *centro*. Internet cafe by day and buzzing bar by night, this mod-styled spot attracts a hip and friendly crowd. Wine €4. Beer €3-5. Long drinks €7 at table or €5 at the bar. Open M-Tu and Th-Su 11am-1am.

ELBA

According to legend, the enchanting island of Elba (EL-ba; pop. 28,000) grew from a precious stone that slipped from Venus's neck into the Tyrrhenian Sea. Since then, Elba's extensive 150km coastline has seen its share of visitors. Renowned since Hellenic times for its mineral wealth, the island also derived considerable fame for its association with Napoleon. The "Little Emperor" was sent into his first exile here in 1814, creating both a temporarily war-free Europe and the famous palindrome: "Able was I ere I saw Elba." The island's turquoise waters, dramatic peaks, and rich vegetation can take the breath away of conqueror and commoner alike. Pebble beaches, fashion boutiques, and amateur moped riders dot this Italian retreat, from the justifiably touristed Portoferraio, to the clear waters of Marciana Marina. Make like the Italians and trade city dirt for Elba's sweet, salty air—a bit of Tuscany, untamed.

PORTOFERRAIO ☎0565

As the island's main port, Portoferraio (por-TOH-feh-RYE-oh; pop. 11,000) is Elba's liveliest city and contains most of its essential services. Visitors and locals alike spill from the pink, peach, and yellow buildings of the *centro* that seem to carpet the steep hillsides. Lively, restaurant-inundated *piazze* overlook the nearby harbor, filling the air with the smell of local cuisine and the sound of Italian conversation at all hours of the day.

🚌 TRANSPORTATION

Ferry service is at Toremar, Calata Italia 32 (☎0565 96 01 31; portoferraio@toremar.it), and Moby Lines, V. Elba 12 (☎0565 91 41 33; moby.portoferraio@moby.it). Buy tickets at the travel agency, Calata Italia 22, across from the docks, in order to compare prices and schedules. Portoferraio is accessible by bus from Elba's other towns. ATL, V. Elba 22, across from the Toremar landing, runs **buses** to Marciana Marina (every hr., 7:15am-8pm) and Porto Azzuro (every hr., 5:10am-8pm). For other schedules, ask the office. (☎0565 91 43 92. Open June-Sept. daily 8am-8pm; Oct.-May M-Sa 8am-1:20pm and 4-6:30pm, Su 9am-12:30pm and 2-6:30pm. Tickets €2-2.50. Day pass €7, 6-day pass €19.) For **taxis** call ☎0565 91 51 12. Rent Chiappi, Calata Italia 38, rents **cars** (€45-65 per day). (☎0565 91 66 87; www.rentchiappi.it. Open daily 9am-7:30pm. MC/V.)

▓▓ ⚑ ORIENTATION AND PRACTICAL INFORMATION

Though it's Elba's largest city, Portoferraio has a tiny *centro*. **Calata Italia** runs parallel to the harbor and **Via Manzoni** runs perpendicular. The first right off V. Manzoni is **Via Vittorio Emanuele**. From Calata Italia, a right turn on **Viale Elba** goes further inland toward services like banks and grocery stores. V. V. Emanuele turns into **Calata Mazzini,** which curves with the borders of the harbor; follow street signs and turn left through a brick arch, **Porta Medicea,** to **Piazza Cavour.** Cut through the *piazza* to reach **Piazza della Repubblica,** the center of town.

Tourist Offices: APT, Calata Italia 43 (☎0565 91 46 71; www.aptelba.it). From the Toremar docks facing away from the water, proceed left on Calata Italia. Open in summer M-Sa 9am-7pm, Su 9am-noon and 3-7pm; in winter daily 8am-1pm and 4-6:30pm.

Boat Excursions: Visione Sottomarina (☎0565 32 87 09 54 70) runs trips along the coast (€18) in glass-bottomed boats for prime views of the seafloor. Arrive 20min. early for decent seats. Tickets sold onboard or through tourist office. Morning tours depart from Portoferraio, afternoon tours from Marciana Marina.

Parks and Nature: Parco Nazionale Arcipelago Toscano, Vle. Elba 8 (☎0565 91 94 94). Has maps and info on hikes. Office open Tu-Th 9am-noon, Sa-Su 9am-2:30pm.

Internet Access: Da Ciro Bar, V. V. Emanuele 14 (☎0565 91 90 00), across from the Toremar dock. €3 per 30min., €5 per hr. Open daily 9am-10pm. AmEx/MC/V.

Post Office: V. Manganaro 7M (☎0565 93 47 31), around the left side of the building. Open M-F 8:15am-7pm, Sa 8:15am-12:30pm. **Postal Code:** 57037.

⌂ ACCOMMODATIONS

Uphill from a heavenly beach, ▨**Albergo Le Ghiaie ❸**, Località Le Ghiaie, has comfortable rooms with bath. Great common areas foster a sense of community. Mornings start with coffee on the wooden terrace. From the harbor, take V. Manzoni and bear left on V. Cairoli. (☎0565 91 51 78. Breakfast included. Private parking. Singles €40-45; doubles €80-85; triples €110; quads €125. AmEx/MC/V.) The small, no-frills rooms at **Hotel Nobel ❷**, V. Manganaro 72, are a decent option for a tight budget in high season. Follow V. Elba from the port for 10min. until it merges with V. Manganaro; the hotel is on the right. (☎0565 91 52 17; fax 91 54 15. Singles €20-34, with bath €42; doubles €44/62; triples with bath €78. AmEx/MC/V.) **Acquaviva ❶**, Località Acquaviva, has good camping on a picturesque site roughly 4km west of the *centro*. Take the bus toward Viticcio (8am, 12:30, 3, 6pm; €1) from Portoferraio and ask the driver to stop at the campground *(campeggio)*. Located on the beach, the site has a bar, restaurant, and grocery store. (☎0565 91 91 03; fax 91 55 92; www.campingacquaviva.it. Reserve via fax. €7.30-14 per person, €6-15 per tent, €2-3.50 per car. MC/V.)

◪ FOOD

Two Elban specialties of note are *schiaccia*, a flat sandwich bread cooked in olive oil and studded with onions or black olives, and *aleatico*, a sweet

TUSCANY

liqueur. Elba as a whole suffers from an infestation of overpriced, tourist-trap restaurants, but Portoferraio has options for value-conscious diners. Dwarfed by ships, **Ristorante Stella Marina** ❸, V. Vittorio Emanuele 1, in a parking lot across from the Toremar dock, offers courteous service and fabulous seafood dishes at busy tables. Try some *tagliolini ai frutti di mare* (pasta with mussels, clams, shrimp, and octopus; €10), or splurge on Elban lobster (€14). The pasta-dominated vegetarian menu is reasonably priced (€6.50-9). (☎0565 91 59 83. Primi €9-12. Secondi by weight. Cover €2.50. Open May to mid-Nov. Tu-Su noon-2:30pm and 7:20-10:30pm. AmEx/MC/V.) **Il Garibaldino** ❷, Calata Mazzini 1, is a popular find right on the waterfront. (☎0565 91 47 51. Pizza €3.50-5. Primi €5.50-8.50. Secondi €6.50-18. Open daily 12:30-2:30pm and 7-10:30pm. AmEx/MC/V.) **Trattoria-Pizzeria Napoletana da Zucchetta** ❸, P. della Repubblica 40, is a casual spot in the *centro storico* with outdoor seating and affordable pizza. (☎0565 91 53 31. Pizza €3-8. Primi €7-11. Secondi €9-25. Open M-Tu and Th-Su 11:30am-3pm and 6-11:30pm, W 6-11:30pm. MC/V.) For groceries, head to the centrally located **Conad**, P. Pietri 2/4, off Vle. Elba, next to the Banca di Roma. (Open from M-Sa 7:30am-9pm, Su 8am-1:30pm and 4:30-8:30pm. AmEx/MC/V.)

🔲 🔲 SIGHTS AND BEACHES

Inside Emperor Napoleon's one-time residence, the **Villa dei Mulini,** rest his personal library, letters, several silk chairs once graced by his imperial derriere, and the sovereign Elban flag that he designed. (☎0565 91 58 46. Ticket office open July-Aug. M-Sa 9am-7pm, Su 9am-1pm; Sept.-June closed Tu. €5; 3-day combined ticket with Villa Napoleonica €9. Cash only.) Monogrammatic Ns emblazon the **Villa Napoleonica di San Martino,** placed there after Napoleon's death. Note especially the Sala Egizia, with friezes depicting his Egyptian campaign. (Take bus #1 5km out of Portoferraio. ☎0565 91 46 88. Ticket office open July-Aug. M-Sa 9am-7pm, Su 9am-1pm; Sept.-June Tu-Sa 9am-7pm, Su 9am-1pm.) The **Museo Archeologico della Linguella** glorifies Elba's seafaring history, displaying finds from ancient trading boat wrecks dating back to the AD 5th century. (In the Fortezza del Lingrella, up the hill from the Villa dei Mulini in the *centro storico.* ☎0565 91 73 38. Open daily Sept.-June 10am-1pm and 3-7pm; July-Aug. 9am-2:25pm and 6pm-midnight. €3, children and individuals in large groups €2. Cash only.) The **Medici Fortress**, looming over the port, is worth a quick peek. Cosimo dei Medici, Grand Duke of Tuscany, founded the complex in 1548. The structure was so imposing that the dreaded Turkish pirate Dracut declared the building impenetrable and called off his planned attack in 1553. (Open Tu and Th-Su 10am-1pm and 3:30-7:10pm. €3, children €2. Cash only.)

Many large signs from the harbor point to **Spiaggia delle Ghiaie,** so, unsurprisingly, every day its shores are quickly covered with the chairs and towels of the masses grabbing their piece of the precious rocky, white beach. Bring a towel and claim a spot to avoid roped-off areas and their corresponding fees. Come for sun, not serenity: music-blasting restaurants and a kiddie park in the vicinity make this a beach exclusively for jamming tanners. For those who wish to tan in tranquility, farther east and down a long flight of stairs from the Villa dei Mulini is the sandy and more secluded ■**Spiaggia delle Viste.** Appropriately named for its views, this beach is framed with cliffs and is the perfect spot to take a dip in the crystal-blue water.

UMBRIA

Because of its wild woods and fertile plains, craggy gorges and gentle hills, Umbria (OOM-bree-ah) is known as the "green heart of Italy." Cobblestone villages and lively international universities are scattered throughout the region, bringing a distinct vitality to the land. Three thousand years ago, Etruscans settled this regional crossroads between the Adriatic and Tyrrhenian coasts. One thousand years later, Christianity transformed Umbria's architecture and regional identity. St. Francis shamed the increasingly extravagant Church with his legacy of humility, pacifism, and charity that persists in Assisi to this day. The region also produced medieval masters Perugino and Pinturicchio and holds Giotto's greatest masterpieces. Umbria's artistic spirit gives life today to the internationally acclaimed Umbria Jazz Festival and Spoleto Festival.

HIGHLIGHTS OF UMBRIA

EAT GELATO with locals on the steps of Cattedrale di San Lorenzo (p. 350).

WATCH a performance at the historic Teatro Romane in medieval Gubbio (p. 354).

PERUGIA   ☎ 075

The citizens of Perugia (peh-ROO-ja; pop. 162,000) rose to political prominence after chasing the *Umbri* tribe into surrounding valleys. Wars with neighboring cities dominate Perugia's history, but periods of peace and prosperity led to the stunning artistic achievements for which the city is known today. The city's own Pietro Vannucci, a painter and mentor to Raphael, is known as "Perugino" because of his association with the town. While not as pristine as neighboring cities, well-worn Perugia is loved by visitors and locals for its convenient big-city amenities and easily navigable small-town layout. Whether through the renowned jazz festival, the decadent chocolate, the religious art, or the student-driven university atmosphere, Perugia displays its character with pride.

⬛ TRANSPORTATION

Trains: Perugia lies on the Foligno-Terontola line. It is serviced by 2 stations.

Stazione Fontiveggio, in P. Vittorio Veneto. Info booth open daily 7am-8pm. Ticket window open daily 6:10am-8pm. To: **Arezzo** (1hr., every hr., €4); **Assisi** (25min., every hr., €2.05); **Florence** (2hr., 6 per day, from €8); **Foligno** (40min., every hr., €3); **Orvieto** (1hr., 11 per day, €7) via **Terontola** (40min., €6); **Rome** (2hr., 7 per day 6am-6pm, €11); **Spoleto** (1hr., every hr., €4.50); Terni (1hr., 19 per day 7:31am-12:30am, €4.85).

Perugia Sant'Anna, in Ple. Bellucci. Commuter rail runs to **Sansepolcro** (1hr., 18 per day 6:18am-7:40pm, €4.50), **Terni** (1hr., 14 per day 6:06am-6:58pm, €4.40), and **Todi** (1hr., 5 per day 6:53am-7:41pm, €3.05).

Buses: APM (☎80 05 12 141; www.apmperugia.it), in P. dei Partigiani. To: **Assisi** (1hr., 7 per day 6:40am-7.05pm, €3); **Chiusi** (1hr., 8 per day 6:20am-6:35pm, €5.40); **Gubbio** (1hr., 16 per day 6:40am-8:08pm, €4.50); **Siena** (1hr., M-F 8:30am and 5:30pm, €11); **Todi** (1hr., 10 per day 6:30am-7:30pm, €5.40). Reduced service Su. Additional buses leave from the train station. Tickets at Radio Taxi Perugia (☎075 50 04 888), to

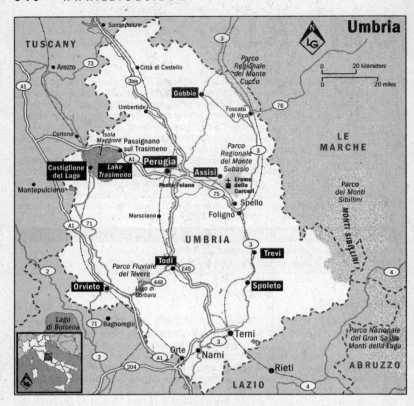

the right of the train station. **City buses** in P. dei Partigiani, down a series of escalators through Rocca Paolina from P. Italia. Bus #6 (€1) runs to the train station.

Taxis: In P. Italia and P. Vittorio Veneto or call **Radio Taxi** (☎075 50 04 888).

Car Rental: Hertz, P. Vittorio Veneto 2 (☎075 50 02 439; hertzperugia@tiscali.it), in the train station. Open M-F 8:30am-12:30pm and 3-7pm, Sa 8:30am-1pm. AmEx/MC/V.

ORIENTATION AND PRACTICAL INFORMATION

From Fontiveggio train station, buses #6, 7, 9, 11, 13, and 15 run to **Piazza Italia** (€1). The **Minimetro** (E1) is a fun alternative and goes to Pincetto, near Piazza Matteotti. Otherwise, it's a 2km trek uphill to the *centro*. To get to P. Italia from the **bus station** in **Piazza dei Partigiani** or from the nearby **Perugia Sant'Anna** train station at **Piazzale Belucci,** follow the signs to the **escalators** (open 6:15am-1:45am; free) that run beneath the old city and through the *Rocca Paolina*. From P. Italia, **Corso Vannucci,** the main shopping thoroughfare, leads to **Piazza IV Novembre** and the *duomo*. Behind the *duomo*, Via Rocchi winds downhill to **Piazza Braccio Fortebraccio** and the university district. Just off C. Vannucci is Via Baglioni, which leads to **Piazza Matteotti,** the municipal center.

Tourist Office: IAT di Perugia, P. Matteotti 18 (☎075 57 36 458; fax 57 20 988). The office offers free maps and pamphlets on accommodations, restaurants, and cultural events. If in stock, a free 📕**Perugia Little Blue** guide in English is especially helpful for long-term stays and exploration. Open daily 8:30am-6:30pm. **Info Umbria,** Largo Cacciatori delle Alpi 3/B (☎075 57 57; www.infoumbria.com), next to the bus station in P. dei Partigiani; provides free maps and free bookings for many hotels, as well as tickets for the **"Perugia City Tour."** On-board tour audio guide provides info on sites in English, French, German, and Italian. Open M-F 9am-1pm and 2:30-6:30pm, Sa 9am-1pm. Tour €13. Check www.umbriabest.com for information on the town and events.

Budget Travel: CTS, V. del Roscetto 21 (☎075 57 20 284; www.cts.it), off V. Pinturicchio toward the bottom of the street. Offers vacation deals to ISIC cardholders. Open M-F 9:30am-1pm and 3-6:30pm. AmEx/MC/V.

Currency Exchange: Banks have the best rates; those in P. Italia and P. dei Partigiani have 24hr. **ATMs.**

Luggage Storage: In Stazione Fontiveggio. €3 for 1st 12hr., €2 for each additional 12hr. Open daily 8am-7:30pm. Cash only.

English-Language Bookstore: L'Altra Libreria, V. Rocchi 3 (☎075 57 36 104). Small selection of classics, travel guides, and, in the summer months, trendy titles. Open M-Sa 9am-1pm and 3:30-8:30pm, Su 10:30am-1pm. AmEx/MC/V.

Laundromat: 67 Laundry, V. Fabretti 7/A. Wash €3.50 per 8kg, dry €2 per 20kg. Open daily 8am-9pm. **Bolle Blu,** C. Garibaldi 43. Wash €3.50 per 8kg, dry €3. Open daily 8am-10pm.

Police: V. Cortonese 157 (☎075 50 621).

Pharmacy: Farmacia San Martino, P. Matteotti 26 (☎075 57 22 335).

Hospital: (☎075 57 81) for specific concerns. **Ospedale Silvestrini** (☎075 57 86 400) for emergencies.

Internet: Coffee Break, V. Danzetta 22, off V. Baglioni near P. Matteotti. Free Wi-Fi. Internet €1 per hr. Open M-Sa 8am-11:30pm, Su 11am-11pm. AmEx/MC/V.

Post Office: P. Matteotti 1. Open M-Sa 8am-6:30pm. **Postal Code:** 06110.

🏠 🏕 ACCOMMODATIONS AND CAMPING

Reserve ahead when crowds descend on Perugia for the Umbria Jazz Festival in July and the Eurochocolate Festival in late October.

🏠 **Ostello Ponte Felcino,** V. Maniconi 97 (☎075 59 13 991; www.ostellopontefelcino.com). Settled in the gardens of Ponte Felcino just outside of Perugia, this well-kept hostel gives its guests a taste of authentic small town Umbrian life. Bus service is frequent into P. dei Partigiani. Clean rooms, complimentary breakfast, and spacious common areas. Internet access available. Dinner €10. Dorms €16; singles €22; doubles €36. ❷

Ostello della Gioventù/Centro Internazionale di Accoglienza per la Gioventù, V. Bontempi 13 (☎075 57 22 880; www.ostello.perugia.it). 300-year-old frescoes and helpful staff adjacent to lively P. IV Novembre in downtown Perugia. Kitchen, library, lockers, spacious showers, lobby phone, and TV room. Linens €2. 2-week max. stay. Check-in 4-11:30pm. Check-out 7:30-9:30am. Lockout 9:30am-4pm. Curfew midnight, in summer 1am. Open Jan. 16-Dec. 14. Dorms €15. AmEx/MC/V. ❶

Hotel Priori, V. Vermiglioli 3 (☎075 57 23 378; www.hotelpriori.it), located directly off V. dei Priori. 55 large rooms centrally located near historic street. Private terrace is ideal for relaxing and lounging. Take advantage of off-season prices. Singles €45-70; doubles €65-95; triples €85-125; quads €100-145. ❹

Albergo Anna, V. dei Priori 48 (☎/fax 075 57 36 304; www.albergoanna.it), off C. Vannucci. Ornate 17th-century rooms, some with ceramic fireplaces and views of city rooftops. Breakfast €2. Singles €40-50; doubles €65-80; triples €70-90. MC/V. ❹

Hotel Umbria, V. Boncambi 37 (☎075 57 21 203; www.hotel-umbria.com), off P. della Repubblica. 17 rooms with small beds, high ceilings, and standard hotel furnishings,

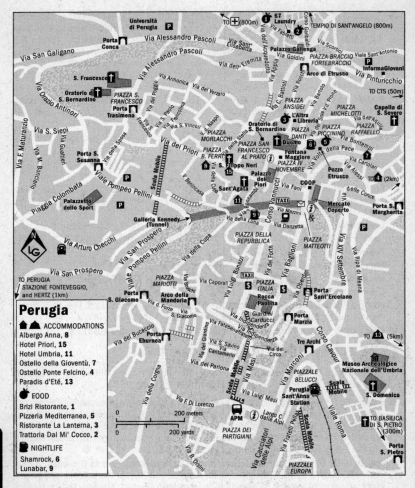

Perugia

🏠🏔 ACCOMMODATIONS
Albergo Anna, **8**
Hotel Priori, **15**
Hotel Umbria, **11**
Ostello della Gioventù, **7**
Ostello Ponte Felcino, **4**
Paradis d'Eté, **13**

🍴 FOOD
Brizi Ristorante, **1**
Pizzeria Mediterranea, **5**
Ristorante La Lanterna, **3**
Trattoria Dal Mi' Cocco, **2**

🌙 NIGHTLIFE
Shamrock, **6**
Lunabar, **9**

UMBRIA

including TV, phone, and bath. Reservations recommended, especially in summer. Singles €40-50; doubles €75; triples €90; quads €120. AmEx/MC/V. ❸

Paradis d'Eté, Strada Fontana 29H (☎/fax 075 51 73 121), 8km from the city, in Colle della Trinità. Take a city bus from P. Italia (dir.: Colle della Trinità. 30min.. every 2hr.), and ask the driver to stop at the campground. Free hot showers and pool access in summer. €7 per person; €5.50 per tent; €3 per car. AmEx/MC/V. ❶

🍴 FOOD

No visit to Perugia is complete without a taste of the world-famous chocolate at **Perugina**, C. Vannucci 101. (Open M 2:30-7:45pm, Tu-Sa 9:30am-7:45pm, Su and holidays 10:30am-1:30pm and 3-8pm.) While you're at it, try the *torta di formaggio* (cheese torte) or *mele al cartoccio* (apple pie) at sweet-smelling **Ceccarani**, P. Matteotti 16. (☎075 57 21 960. Open M-Sa 7am-8pm, Su 9am-1:30pm.) Check out the **covered market** in P. Matteotti. Entrance is below street level, to the right of the post office off Via Baglioni. (Open M-Sa 7am-7:30pm.) The Italian chain, **Coop**, P. Matteotti 15, stocks essentials. (Open M-Sa 9am-8pm. MC/V/AmEx.) Complement meals with one of the region's native wines: *Sagrantino Secco*, a dry red, or *Grechetto*, a light white.

Trattoria Dai Mi' Cocco, C. Garibaldi 12 (☎075 57 32 511). Secluded local favorite. Leaves diners happily stuffed. Full course meal (€15) includes antipasti, primi, secondi, daily special, bread, dessert, and a glass of liqueur. Open Tu-Su 11am-2pm and 8:15-10pm. Reservations recommended. MC/V. ❷

Pizzeria Mediterranea, P. Piccinino 11/12 (☎075 57 21 322). From P. IV Novembre, walk to the right of the *duomo*, and turn right shortly before Ostello della Gioventù. A college crowd descends by night for typical pizza at reasonable prices (€4-12). Cover €1.10. Open daily 12:30-2:30pm and 7:30-11pm. MC/V. ❶

Brizi Ristorante, V. Fabretti 75 (☎075 57 21 386). From P. IV Novembre, walk right of the *duomo*, veer left through P. Danti, and right down V. Rocchi to P. Braccio Fortebraccio. On far side of *piazza*, turn left on V. Fabretti. Skip the *menù* and order well presented pasta and carnivorous offerings, like the delicious lamb (€6-7.50). Cover €1.50. Open M and W-Su noon-3pm and 7:30-10pm. MC/V. ❷

Ristorante La Lanterna, V. Rocchi 6 (☎075 57 26 397), near the *duomo*. Enjoy pizza (€7) baked *forno a legna* (wood oven), as well as rich pasta (€8-11) and meat dishes (€10-16). A romantic setting with elegant, brick-vaulted rooms managed by accommodating waiters. Cover €2. Open M-W and F-Su noon-3pm and 7-10pm. AmEx/MC/V. ❸

 SIGHTS

PIAZZA IV NOVEMBRE AND ENVIRONS

PIAZZA IV NOVEMBRE. The social center of Perugian life, P. IV Novembre presents a pageant of young, lively locals, students, tourists, and resident internationals against a backdrop of monuments. Perugia's most popular sights frame the *piazza*; the **Duomo**, the **Galleria Nazionale Dell'Umbria**, and most other monuments lie no more than a 15min. walk away. The **Fontana Maggiore** (1278-80), designed by Fra' Bevignate and decorated by Nicola and Giovanni Pisano, sits in the center of the *piazza*. Bas-reliefs depicting both religious and Roman history cover the double-basin fountain. Beginning at dusk, the *piazza* plays hosts to a diverse assortment of people enjoying the summer night air, savoring gelato, and conversing on the ancient city steps.

PALAZZO DEI PRIORI AND GALLERIA NAZIONALE DELL'UMBRIA. The 13th-century windows and turrets of this *palazzo*, on the left when facing the Fontana Maggiore, are remnants of an embattled era. This building, one of the finest examples of Gothic communal architecture, shelters the grandiose **Galleria Nazionale dell'Umbria**. The collection contains a number of 13th- and 14th-century religious works by Duccio, Fra Angelico, Taddeo di Bartolo, Guido da Siena, and Piero della Francesca. Among these early masterpieces, Duccio's skillful rendering of delicately translucent garments in his *Virgin and Child and Six Angels* in **Room 2** is worth a closer look. Another highlight is della Francesca's detailed *Polyptych of Saint Anthony* in **Room 11**. Native sons Pinturicchio and Perugino share **Room 15**. The two right panels of *Miracles of San Bernardino of Siena* are Pinturicchio's. Note his rich tones that contrast with Perugino's characteristic soft pastels of the two panels on the right. Downstairs, three rooms display Baroque and Neoclassical works as well as a collection of jewelry and

UMBRIA

textiles. *(In P. IV Novembre at C. Vannucci 19. ☎ 075 57 21 009; www.gallerianazionaleumbria. it. Open Tu-Su 8:30am-7:30pm. Last entry 1hr. before closing. Closed Jan. 1 and Dec. 25. €6.50; reduced €3.25. Cash only.)* To the right of the Galleria sits the **Sala dei Notari**, once the citizens' assembly chamber. Thirteenth-century frescoes adorn the eight Romanesque arches, which support the vault. Note the scene on the fourth arch on the left of the crow and the fox from Aesop's fables. *(Up the steps. Sometimes closed for public performances. Open June-Sept. Tu-Su 9am-1pm and 3-7pm. Free.)*

DUOMO (CATTEDRALE DI SAN LORENZO). The rugged facade of Perugia's imposing Gothic *duomo* was begun in the 14th century, but builders never completed it. Though not as ornate as other cathedrals in Tuscany and Umbria, the groin-vaulted interior and 15th- to 18th-century embellishments, lit by small chandeliers, are quite elegant. The church is also said to hold the Virgin Mary's wedding ring, snagged from Chiusi in the Middle Ages, though the average visitor is unlikely to catch a glimpse of the guarded treasure. *(P. IV Novembre. Open M-Sa 8am-1pm and 4-8pm, Su 4-5:45pm. Modest dress required. Free.)*

COLLEGIO DELLA MERCANZIA AND COLLEGIO DEL CAMBIO. The walls of the audience chambers on either side of Palazzo dei Priori are covered in magnificent wood paneling and elaborate frescoes. The elegantly carved bench in the *Collegio della Mercanzia* (Merchants' Guild) is a tribute to the Republic of Perugia, marking an advancement from the previous feudal system. In the *Collegio del Cambio* (Exchange Guild), the **Sala dell'Udienza** (audience chamber) holds Perugino's frescoes, which portray heroes, prophets, and even the artist himself. The members of Perugia's merchant guild have met in this wood-paneled structure since the 14th century. *(Collegio della Mercanzia: C. Vannucci 15, adjacent to the police station. ☎ 075 57 30 366. Open daily Mar.-Oct. and Dec. 18-Jan. 3 Tu-Sa 9am-1pm and 2:30-5:30pm, Su and holidays 9am-1pm; Nov.-Dec. 17 and Jan. 4-Feb. Tu and Th-F 8am-2pm, W and Sa 8am-4:30pm, Su 9am-1pm. €1. Collegio del Cambio: C. Vannucci 25. ☎ 075 57 28 599. Open M-Sa 9am-12:30pm and 2:30-5:30pm, Su 9am-1pm. €4.50. Cash only.)*

VIA DEI PRIORI. Don't be fooled by the street's present-day calm and stone-like serenity. Via dei Priori, which begins under the arch at Palazzo dei Priori, was once one of medieval Perugia's goriest streets: the spikes on the lower walls of the street were once used to impale the rotting heads of executed criminals. The Neoclassical **Chiesa di San Filippo Neri,** begun in 1627 and built in the form of a Latin cross, resides solemnly in P. Ferri; Santa Maria di Vallicella's heart is kept to the right of the altar. *(Open daily in summer 7am-noon and 4:30-7:30pm; in winter 8am-noon and 4-6pm. Free.)* **Piazza San Francesco al Prato** is a grassy square used for lounging and strolling. At its edge the 15th-century **Oratorio di San Bernardino** serves as a retreat from urban commotion. *(Next to Chiesa di San Francesco, down V. San Francesco. Open daily 8am-12:30pm and 3:30-6pm. Free.)*

THE NORTHEAST

VIA ROCCHI. From behind the *duomo*, medieval V. Rocchi, both the city's oldest street and a former aqueduct, winds through the northern city and straight underneath the impressive **Arco di Etrusco**, a perfectly preserved Roman arch built on Etruscan pedestals. Walk straight through P. Braccio Fortebraccio, the youth hang-out where V. Rocchi turns to C. Guiseppe Garibaldi, and follow it for 10min. toward the humbling **Tempio di Sant'Angelo** (also known as **Chiesa di San Michele Arcangelo**), a fifth-century circular church constructed with stone and wood taken from ancient pagan buildings. The **Porta Sant'Angelo,** an arch and tower that welcomes visitors to the city, stands nearby, its top level offering a view of all of Perugia. *(Past Palazzo Gallenga, to the right near the end of C. Garibaldi. ☎ 075 57 22 624. Open daily 10am-noon and 4-6pm.)*

CAPPELLA DI SAN SEVERO. San Severo is home to *The Holy Trinity and Saints*, one of many collaborations by Perugia's favorite mentor-student tag team, Perugino and Raphael, who painted the lower and upper sections, respectively. Opposite the chapel, a *piazza* wall holds a plaque with a quote from Dante's *Paradiso* praising the city. (*In P. Rafaello.* ☎ *075 57 33 864. Open Apr.-Oct. M and W-Su 10am-1:30pm and 2:30-6pm; Nov.-Mar. 10:30am-1:30pm and 2:30-5pm. €2.50.*)

POZZO ETRUSCO. With a depth of 36m, the Etruscan Well dates to the third century BC and was once Perugia's main water source. Perugians were forced to use the well again during WWII, when bombs destroyed outside water lines to the city. Descend damp stairs to the footbridge spanning the well just meters above the water. (*P. Danti 18, across from the duomo. Look for the "Pozzo Etrusco" sign above a small alleyway and follow the cobblestone alley down to the left.* ☎ *075 57 33 669. Open Apr.-Oct. Tu-Su 10am-1:30pm and 2:30-6:30pm; Nov.-Mar. Tu-Su 11am-1:30pm and 2:30-5pm. Free.*)

THE EAST SIDE

BASILICA DI SAN PIETRO. This 10th-century church consists of a double arcade of closely spaced columns that lead to a choir. Its art-filled interior contains solemn, majestic paintings and frescoes depicting saints and soldiers, all in brilliant color on a dramatic scale. Look for Perugino's *Pietà* along the northern aisle. At the far end through the arch is a small garden; its lower section offers a must-see view of the surrounding countryside. (*V. Borgo XX Giugno, past P. San Pietro. Entrance to church is on the far left side of the courtyard; garden is through courtyard on right. Open daily 7:30am-12:30pm and 3-6pm. Free.*)

CHIESA DI SAN DOMENICO. This cathedral, though a relatively unremarkable example of Italian architecture, is Umbria's largest. The Gothic rose window brightens the otherwise simple, cream-colored interior, rebuilt in 1632. The intricately carved **Tomb of Pope Benedict XI** (1325) rests in the Capella del Santissimo Sacramento to the right of the high altar. (*From P. Giordano Bruno, follow the main road, C. Cavour. Open daily 7am-noon and 4-7:30pm. Free.*)

GIARDINI CARDUCCI. These romantic public gardens are named after the 19th-century poet Giosuè Carducci. From the garden wall, enjoy a splendid panorama of the Umbrian countryside; a castle or an ancient church crowns every hill. (*Behind P. Italia at the far end of C. Vannucci, off P. IV Novembre. Free.*)

ROCCA PAOLINA. The underground remains of a grandiose fortress, the *Rocca* was built by the architect Antonio Sangallo il Giovane on the order of Pope Paolo III Farnese. Several escalators descend through the brick structure, connecting the upper (P. Italia) and lower (P. dei Partigiani) parts of the city. Nearby, the **Museo della Rocca Paolina** offers information and exhibits illuminating the Rocca's history. (*Entrances beneath P. Italia and across from bus station in P. dei Partigiani. Open daily 6:15am-1:45am. Free. Museum open daily 10am-1:30pm and 2:30-6pm. €1*)

⚡ 🌺 NIGHTLIFE AND FESTIVALS

Perugia provides more nightlife opportunities than any other city in Umbria, and its large student population keeps clubs packed nearly every night of the week from September to May. Unfortunately, in summer many nightlife establishments shut down, and most are reachable only by car or bus. During the academic year, join the nightly bandwagon at **Piazza Braccio Fortebraccio,** known as **Piazza Grimana** to locals, where free buses depart for several nearby clubs (starting at midnight). In the city, students congregate at all hours on the steps of **Piazza IV Novembre** to people-watch or chat over pizza and wine. Bottles aren't allowed on the steps after 8pm and on-site police enforce this rule, but never fear—neighboring cafes happily dole out drinks in plastic cups.

To find **Lunabar/Ferrari**, V. Scura 1/6, follow the loud music emanating from an entrance under the neon "Hotel Umbria" sign off C. Vannucci. In a city where traditional nightlife is a bit hard to find, Lunabar is a rowdy yet sophisticated relief for anyone looking to drink, dance, and mingle with the college population. (☎075 57 22 966; www.lunabarferrari.it) **Shamrock**, P. Danti 18, is down a small side street on the way to the Pozzo Etrusco. Bite into juicy bacon burgers (€3.50) at this Irish pub. (☎075 57 36 625. Drinks €3.50. Happy hour 6-9pm. Open daily 6pm-2am). Late-night cafes along **Via Mazzini**, **Corso Vannucci**, and **Piazza Matteotti** are a popular alternative to bar-hopping.

Every July, the 10-day ◪**Umbria Jazz Festival** draws world-class performers like B.B. King, Herbie Hancock, James Brown, and Alicia Keys. Grab a snack and a bottle of wine and head to one of the free outdoor concerts, or dance all night by the stage in P. IV Novembre. (Info ☎800 46 23 11; www.umbriajazz.com. Ticket office, C. Vannucci 39. Open M-F 10am-1pm and 3-7pm, Sa 10am-1pm. During festival, open daily 10am-7pm. Tickets €17-68, some events free.) In September, the **Sagra Musicale Umbra** occurs in many Umbrian cities and fills Perugia's churches with religious and classical music. Check Palazzo Gallenga or www.sagramusicaleumbra.com for event listings. During the 10-day **Eurochocolate Festival** (www.eurochocolate.perugia.it) at the end of October, chocolate becomes the focus of fanciful creations, and throngs of chocolate devotees wait for their free samples. On the first Sunday of the festival, throughout Perugia sculptors hack away at huge blocks of chocolate to make *Pietà*, the face of Berlusconi, or animals of every kind—stand close and grab the shavings.

▶ DAYTRIPS FROM PERUGIA

LAKE TRASIMENO AND CASTIGLIONE DEL LAGO

The easiest way to Castiglione del Lago from Perugia is by bus (1hr., 6 per day, €4.80) from P. dei Partigiani. Buses stop in P. Guglielmo Marconi. From there, walk up the stairs into P. Dante Alighieri, which leads up to the city entrance. The tourist office, P. Mazzini 10, is in the only square in town. (☎075 96 52 484. Open M-Sa 9am-1pm and 3:30-7pm, Su 9am-1pm and 4-7pm.) To exchange currency or for an ATM, head to bank Monte dei Paschi di Siena, V. Vittorio Emanuele 57-61. (Open daily 8:20am-1:40pm and 2:20-3:30pm.)

LOVE THE LAKE? If you plan to spend a long time exploring Lake Trasimeno, consider participating in the **Museo Aperto** museum tour, sponsored by the region's tourist offices. One ticket costs €5 and includes admission to attractions in Castiglione del Lago, Città della Pieve, Pacicino, and Panicale. A €3 supplement includes a tour on Isola Maggiore. Inquire at the tourist office in any of the four towns to buy tickets or book tours.

Thirty kilometers west of Perugia, Lake Trasimeno (trah-see-MEH-no) is a refreshing oasis. After advancing down the Alps in 217 BC during the Second Punic War, Hannibal's elephant-riding army routed the Romans just north of the lake, killing 16,000 soldiers. Sadly, neither elephants nor bloodshed can be found in Castiglione del Lago today. A system of ferries connects the main town with Passignano sul Trasimeno, Tuero, San Feliciano, and Lake Trasimeno's two largest islands—Isola Maggiore and Isola Polvese.

Castiglione del Lago (ca-steel-YON-ay del LA-go; pop. 14,500) is now a much quieter town than in past centuries, when it was conquered by Arezzo, Cortona, and finally Perugia in 1184. Clinging to a limestone promontory covered in olive groves, its medieval walls enclose two main streets and a single *piazza*. At the end of V. Vittorio Emanuele, next to the hospital, stand the **Palazzo della Corgna** and the medieval **Rocca del Leone**. The 16th-century *palazzo* is notable for its frescoes, particularly those in **Sala delle Gesta d'Ascanio** by Niccolò Circignani, the Italian painter known as Pomarancio. Follow a dark passageway to view the Lake from the *Rocca*. The courtyard of the crumbling *Rocca* is free and open to the public, and its grass lawn sometimes serves as a venue for open-air concerts during the summer. (☎96 58 210. Open daily Mar. 21.-Apr. 9:30am-1pm and 3:30-7pm; May-June 10am-1:30pm and 4-7:30pm; July-Aug. 10am-1:30pm and 4:30-7pm; Sept.-Oct. 10am-1:30pm and 3:30-7pm; Nov.-Mar. 20 9:30am-4:30pm. Combined ticket €3.) Visitors can also catch a ferry to nearby **Isola Maggiore**, one of Lake Trasimeno's only inhabited islands. From V. Belvedere, take V. Giovanni Pascoli to Vle. Garibaldi. Tickets can be purchased on board.

Budget lodgings are scarce in Castiglione del Lago's immediate vicinity, but **Il Torrione ❹,** V. delle Mura 2/4, right on V. Battisti just inside the gates, is a worthy option. The large garden overlooking the lake leads to four rooms and two apartments with bath and fridge. (☎ 075 95 32 36; www.trasinet.com/iltorrione. Reserve ahead in summer. Singles €65; doubles €80. Cash only.) **La Torre ❹**, V. Vittorio Emanuele 50, offers nine well furnished rooms with bath, TV, A/C, and fridge in the heart of the old town. (☎075 95 16 66; www.trasinet.com/latorre. Breakfast €5. Singles €50; doubles €65-75; triples €80. AmEx/MC/V.) Gourmet food shops line the busier streets, while cheap pizzerias, where prices average €3-8 per person, crowd V. Vittorio Emanuele. With beautiful views and an attentive waitstaff, **La Cantina ❷**, V. V. Emanuele 93, offers a fancier dining experience full of Umbrian cuisine and seafood specialties from the Lake. (Pizza €4-8. Primi €6-9. Secondi €10-18. *Menù* €12.50. Cover €1.80. Open June-Sept. W-Su 12:30-3pm and 7pm-1am; Oct.-May W-Su 12:30-3pm and 7-10:30pm. AmEx/MC/V.) With prices typical of this ritzy retreat, **Ristorante L'Acquario ❸**, V. V. Emanuele 69, offers a variety of lunch *menù* for €30. Try a Trasimeno original: pasta with black truffles or *tagliatelle* with lake fish eggs and perch fillets. (☎075 96 52 432. Primi €8-12. Secondi €9-16. Open M-Tu and Th-Su noon-2:30pm and 7-10:30pm; Nov.-Feb. closed M. MC/V.)

TODI

APM (☎075 89 42 939 or 800 51 21 41) runs buses to and from Perugia (1hr.; M-Sa 10 per day; last bus from Todi 4:58pm, last bus from Perugia 7:30pm; €5.40). The bus station is in P. della Consolazione, near Tempio di Santa Maria della Consolazione. Todi is also accessible by train from Ponte Rio (45min., 7 per day 6:30am-1pm and 3:30-8pm, €2.70). Last train leaves from Terni at 8:10pm and from Perugia 8:50pm; city bus C runs to the station at P. Jacopone until 7:45pm. (€1, €1.50 on board.) The IAT Tourist Office, P. del Popolo 38, has free maps, schedules, and info on history, restaurants and lodgings. (☎075 89 42 526. Open M-Sa 9:30am-1pm and 3:30-6:30pm, Su 10am-1:30pm.)

At the foot of Todi's (TO-dee) lush hills sits the Renaissance **Tempio di Santa Maria della Consolazione,** whose elegant domes are thought to have been based on architectural genius Bramante's early draft for St. Peter's Basilica in Rome. The orderly geometric shapes of the central dome are pleasing alone, and even more impressive when seen alongside the Baroque altarpiece and the 12 surrounding statues. (Open daily Apr.-Oct. 9am-12:30pm and 2:30-6:30pm; Nov.-Mar. 9:30am-12:30pm and 2:30-5pm. Free.) From P. della Consolazione, follow a sinuous, cypress-lined dirt path (Serpentina della Viale) to V. della Vittoria or the less curvy V. della Consolazione to reach **La Rocca**, a ruined 14th-century castle that fronts a large, but generic public **park** with picnic tables and a basketball court. (Open daily Apr.-Oct. 6:30am-10pm; Nov.-Mar. 7am-7pm.) From the park, enter Piazza IV Novembre and follow V. della Rocca to the towering

Tempio di San Fortunato. Built by the Franciscans between the 13th and 15th centuries, the church, dedicated to Todi's patron saint, features a high vaulted ceiling with decorative medallions and aged frescoes like *The Madonna and Jesus With Angels* by Masolino da Panciale in the fourth chapel on the right. Peek into the sixth chapel on the right and the fifth chapel on the left to see of vestiges of magnificent frescoes from the 14th century. Part of the original church is currently used as a school, but ask the guardian for permission to view the cloisters for unobstructed **360 degree views of Todi.** (Open Tu-Su 9am-1pm and 3-7pm. Free.) From San Fortunato, follow P. Jacopone to the **Piazza del Popolo,** encircled by three palaces-turned-municipal-centers, two souvenir shops, two *gelaterie,* and a 900-year-old church. The 12th-century **duomo** is at the far end of P. del Popolo atop a flight of broad stone steps. The 16th-century rose window at the rear brightens up the interior. (Open daily 8:30am-12:30pm and 2:30-7pm. Mass daily in summer 11:30am and 6pm; in winter 6pm. Free.)

Staying in Todi is an unnecessary expense, as cheaper accommodations are easily found in nearby Perugia. ⧉**Crispolti Holiday House** ❸, V. Santa Prassede 36, near P. del Popolo. Walking down V. del Duomo, turn right on V. S. Prassede, and wind to the right until you reach V. Cesia; the Holiday House is ahead on the left. This hostel-style accommodation provides private and dormitory rooms in an old monastery. Crispolti offers a bar, inexpensive restaurant, meeting room, terrace overlooking the Umbrian countryside, TV room, and Internet access. (☎075 89 44 827; www.crispoltiholidayhouse.com. Breakfast included. Dorms €25-40; singles €35-60; doubles €70-90; triples €90-120; quads €120-160. Group discounts available. MC/V.) You'll find **Pizzeria al Vicoletto** ❷, V. Vicoletto 11, on the sidestreet between P. Garibaldi and P. Jacopone. This small pizzeria provides a relief from tourist-infested *gelaterrie* that double as souvenir-shops. Italian radio soothes local patrons as they munch on pizza by the slice (€1.20) in the stone alleyway. (Open M and W-Su 8:35am-2:30pm and 4-9pm.) **Antica Hosteria de la Valle** ❷, V. Ciuffelli 17-21, serves meals in a stately dining room of brick and wood. The menu, as well as the local art displayed on the walls, changes bi-weekly. (☎075 89 44 848. Primi €8-14. Secondi €10-16. *Menù* €20-22. Cover €1. Open Tu-Su 12:30-2:30pm and 7:30-10pm. MC/V.)

GUBBIO   ☎075

Roman remains, a thriving ceramics trade, historical festivals and the artistic feats of a local painting school all find themselves packed together in the medieval alleyways of Gubbio (GOO-bee-yo; pop. 32,000). The town's famous 300-100BC Eugubine Tablets, one of the only existing records of the ancient Umbrian language, offer a glimpse into Umbria's history and provide important evidence of an Umbrian and Roman alliance against invading Etruscans. The town's mountain backdrop offer unrivaled views, and serves as a convenient daytrip from Perugia for travelers who wish to avoid the high prices.

◨ ⒉ TRANSPORTATION AND PRACTICAL INFORMATION

The nearest **train station** is in **Fossato di Vico,** 15km away and on the Rome-Ancona line. Trains run to Ancona (1hr., 14 per day, from €4.30), Rome (2hr., 12 per day, €10.12), and Spoleto (1hr., 10 per day, €3.36). **APM buses** (☎075 50 67 81) run to and from Perugia (1hr.; M-F 9 per day, Sa-Su 4 per day; €4.50) and are much more convenient than the train. The bus is the easiest way to reach Gubbio from Fossato (M-Sa 11 per day, Su 5 per day; €2). Tickets are sold at the newsstand in P. Quaranta Martiri, at the Perugia bus stop, and at the newsstand in Fossato's train station. If stranded in Fossato without bus service, call a **taxi**

(☎075 91 92 02 or 033 53 37 48 71; €28 per 20min.). In Gubbio, **taxis** (☎075 92 73 800) are available in P. Quaranta Martiri.

Tiny Gubbio's medieval streets are easily navigable. Buses stop in **Piazza Quaranta Martiri,** where you can find a 24hr. **ATM.** A short walk up **V. della Repubblica,** on the far right of P. Quaranta Martiri from the bus stop, is the **ITA Tourist Office,** V. della Repubblica 15, which offers bus schedules and maps. (☎075 92 20 790; www.gubbio-altochiascio.umbria2000.it. Open Mar.-Oct. M-F 8:30am-1:45pm and 3:30-6:30pm, Sa 9am-1pm and 3:30-6:30pm, Su 9:30am-12:30pm and 3:30-6:30pm; Oct.-Mar. M-F 8:30am-1:45pm and 3-6pm, Sa 9am-1pm and 3-6pm, Su 9:30am-12:30pm and 3-6pm.) V. della Repubblica crosses **Corso Garibaldi,** the second major street on the right. **Farmacia Luconi** is at C. Garibaldi 12. (☎075 92 73 783. Open M-Sa Apr.-Sept. 9am-1pm and 4:30-8pm; Oct.-Mar. 9am-1pm and 4-7:30pm.) Signs point uphill to **Piazza Grande,** the civic headquarters. The **hospital** can be reached at ☎075 92 391. The **post office** is at V. Cairoli 11. (☎075 92 73 925. Open M-F 8am-1:30pm, Sa 8am-12:30pm.) **Postal Code:** 06024.

◤◖ ACCOMMODATIONS AND FOOD

A private garden and enthusiastic staff make ◼**Residenza di Via Piccardi ❸,** V. Piccardi 12, an ideal place to relax. Six comfortable rooms each have bath and TV. (☎075 92 76 108; e.biagiotti@tiscali.it. Breakfast included. Check-in before 8pm. Singles €35; doubles €50; triples €60. Extra bed €10. Cash only.) Directly across the street is another option, **Residenza Le Logge ❹,** V. Piccardi 7/9, where rooms feature religious art and small bath. For a splurge, ask for the huge suite with a whirlpool tub. (☎075 92 77 574; www.paginegialle.it/residenzalelogge. Singles €35-45; doubles €52-80, with bath €65-100. AmEx/MC/V.) Walk up from P. Quaranta Martiri on V. della Repubblica, and turn right on V. Gioia to reach **Hotel Grotta dell'Angelo ❸,** V. Gioia 47. Bright, large, and cheery rooms make this an ideal stay that's worth the extra penny. (☎075 92 71 747; www.grottadellangelo.it. Breakfast €5. Singles €38-42; doubles €55-60. AmEx/MC/V.)

Sample local delicacies at **Prodotti Tipici e Tartufati Eugubini ❶,** V. Piccardi 17, including *salumi di cinghiale o cervo* (boar or deer sausage), cheese, and the region's white-truffle oil. (☎075 92 71 751. Open Apr.-Jan. 7 daily 10am-1:30pm and 3:30-8pm. MC/V/AmEx.) Take advantage of the chance to interact and learn from friendly locals at the **outdoor market** in P. Quaranta Martiri. Purchase homegrown seasonal produce and other *prodotti tipici* of Gubbio. (Open M-Sa 7am-1pm.) Enjoy regional truffles and other specialties amidst 14th-century decor at **La Cantina Ristorante/Pizzeria ❸,** V. Francesco Piccotti 3, off V. della Repubblica. (☎075 92 20 583. Pizza €4.50-7. Primi €6.50-12. Secondi €7-14. 4-course meal €14. Cover €1. Restaurant open Tu-Su noon-2:30pm and 7-10pm. Pizzeria open noon-3pm. MC/V.) The stone dining room of **San Francesco e il Lupo ❹,** V. Cairoli 24, serves homemade pizza and has a wine cellar with over 200 labels. (☎075 92 72 344. Pizza €4-7.50. Primi €8-13. Secondi €8-24. Cover €2. Open M and W-Su noon-2pm and 7-10pm. AmEx/MC/V.) The health conscious **Bar Jolly ❷,** V. della Repubblica 4, comes as close to a night scene as can be found in medieval Gubbio with its midnight closing time. The menu includes a variety of sandwiches, pasta, and creative salads (€5.50-7). Try the *Insalatone Esotica,* which comes with mozzarella, pineapple, olives, nuts, and kiwi. (Open daily noon-midnight.) Dine under elegant stone vaulted ceilings in the dining room of **Ristorante La Lanterna ❸,** V. Gioia 2. The menu selections offer staples of Eugubine fare such as mushrooms and truffles. (☎075 92 76 694. Primi €7-10. Secondi €8-14. Open M-W and F-Su noon-3pm and 7:30-10:30pm. MC/V.)

👁 SIGHTS

PIAZZA QUARANTA MARTIRI. In the middle of the *piazza* stretches the **Giardino dei Quaranta Martiri** (Garden of the 40 Martyrs), a memorial to those slain by the Nazis in reprisal for the assassination of two German officials. Across the *piazza* from the bus stop stands the **Chiesa di San Francesco,** which was completed in 1256 and is one of the places rumored to be the site where St. Francis experienced his conversion. The left-hand apse holds the *Vita della Madonna,* a partially destroyed, 15th-century fresco series by Ottaviano Nelli, Gubbio's most famous painter. The frescoes are skillfully rendered and the 15th-century *campanile* rises gracefully outside. *(Church open daily 7:15am-noon and 3:30-7:30pm. Free.)* Via Matteotti runs from P. Quaranta Martiri, outside the city walls, to the **Teatro Romano,** built at the end of the first century BC. While restorations are a modern addition, a sense of power and stability still seems to emanate from the semi-circular stone tiers. Productions are staged in July and August. *(Vle. del Teatro Romano. Tickets €15.)* The nearby **Antiquarium** displays impressive Roman mosaics found in the city and preserved foundations beneath your feet.

PALAZZO DEI CONSOLI. This white stone palace (1321-1330) was built for Gubbio's high magistrate. Inside, the **Museo Civico** displays a collection of Eugubinian and Roman artifacts. In a room upstairs, the ▨**Tavole Eugubine** (Eugubine Tablets), are comparable to the Rosetta Stone for their linguistic significance. Five of these seven bronze tablets, dating from 300 to 100 BC, are showcased as rare proof of the ancient Umbrian language, as well as an Umbrian and Roman alliance against the Etruscans. The last two tablets are in Latin. An illiterate farmer discovered them in 1444 in an underground chamber of the Roman theater just outside the city walls; he was subsequently tricked into swapping them for a worthless piece of land. The texts spell out the social, religious, and political organization of early Umbria, and they describe how to read religious omens from animal livers. *(P. Grande. ☎ 075 92 74 298. Open daily Apr.-Oct. 10am-1pm and 3-6pm; Nov. to mid-Mar. 10am-1pm and 2-5pm. €5, ages 7-25 €3, under 7 free.)*

DUOMO. The pink Gothic *duomo,* sitting up on a hill from P. Grande, was built in the 13th and 14th centuries on the site of a Romanesque church. The interior is simple, with a single pitched-roof nave. Notable are the 12th-century stained-glass windows, art by Perugino's student Dono Doni, and Antonio Tatoti's *Adoration of the Magi. (Open daily Apr.-Sept. 9am-6pm; Oct.-Mar. 10am-5pm. Free.)*

MONTE INGINO. See the sights from a new perspective by hopping into the shaky cages of the ▨**funivia,** a standing chairlift, which, in six short minutes, climbs to an unparalleled view of Gubbio's medieval rooftops and the Umbrian hills. Climb the hill behind the *funivia*'s drop-off point to reach the **Basilica and Monastery of Sant'Ubaldo,** which houses the saint's preserved body in a glass case above the altar. The stained glass at the entrance tells the story of his life; the three *ceri,* large wooden candles carried in the **Corsa dei Ceri** procession each May, are also on display. Each December, lights transform the entire hill into the world's largest Christmas tree (documented in the Guinness Book of World Records). Follow the dirt trail behind the basilica up to the scaffolding where the star is placed atop the "tree," and then continue up to an ancient but well-preserved tower for spectacular 360-degree vistas of the Umbrian mountains and valleys. *(To reach the funivia, exit Pta. Romana to the left. From the uphill entrance to the basilica, bear left and continue upward on a dirt path to the top of the mountain. Chairlift open June M-Sa 9:30am-1:30pm and 2:30-7pm, Su 9am-7:30pm; July-Aug. daily 9am-8pm; Sept. M-Sa 9:30am-1:30pm and 2:30-7pm, Su 9:30am-1:30pm and 2:30-7:30pm; Mar. M-Sa 10am-1:30pm and 2:30-5:30pm, Su 9:30am-1:30pm and 2:30-6pm; Apr.-May M-Sa 10am-1:30pm and*

2:30-6:30pm, Su 9:30am-1:30pm and 2:30-7pm; Oct. daily 10am-1:30pm and 2:30-6pm; Nov.-Feb. M-Tu and Th-Su 10am-1:30pm and 2:30-5pm. €5, round-trip €6. Cash only.)

▓ FESTIVALS

The annual **Corsa dei Ceri,** 900 years old and still going strong, takes place every May 15, the day of patron Saint Ubaldo's death. Three *ceri* (candles) are carved like hourglasses and topped with little statues of saints. Each one corresponds to a distinct section of the populace: the masons (Sant'Ubaldo), the farmers (Sant'Antonio Abate), and the artisans (San Giorgio). After 12hr. of furious preparation and frenetic flag-twirling, squads of *ceraioli* (candle runners) clad in Renaissance-style tights lift the heavy objects onto their shoulders and run a wild relay race up Monte Ingino. This raucous festival turns Gubbio's quiet streets into a chaotic stomping ground bristling with intense ritual fervor. Visitors will be entranced; locals will almost certainly be drunk. During the **Palio della Balestra,** held in P. Grande on the last Sunday in May, archers from Gubbio and nearby Sansepolcro have gathered for a fierce crossbow contest since 1139. The contest provides an excellent excuse for Gubbio to throw a huge party every year and maintain an industry in medieval-weaponry toys.

SPOLETO ☎ 0743

The magnificent gorge and medieval walls that surround Spoleto (spo-LEH-toh; pop. 38,000) shelter a town full of Roman ruins and friendly locals. Travelers have always admired Spoleto's dramatic gorge, spanned by the 14th-century Ponte delle Torri, but it wasn't until 1958 that Spoleto's tourist industry took off. In that year, the Italian composer Giancarlo Menotti selected the city as the trial site for a summer arts festival, and his *Festival dei Due Mondi* (Festival of Two Worlds) has attracted summer visitors there ever since.

▐ TRANSPORTATION

Trains: The station (☎0743 48 516) is in P. Polvani. Ticket window open M-F 7:10-11am and 2-5pm. To: **Ancona** (2hr., 12 per day 6:16am-10:09pm, €8.20); **Assisi** (40-60min., 19 per day 5:40am-10:09pm, €3.30); **Orte** (1hr., 15 per day 5:06am-9:23pm, €3.90); **Perugia** (2hr., 19 per day 5:40am-10:09pm, €4.20); **Rome** (1hr., 18 per day 5:06am-9:23pm, €7.50). Trains to Assisi and Perugia often run via **Foligno.**

Buses: SSIT (☎0743 21 22 09; www.spoletina.com). Departs P. della Vittoria for **Foligno** (40min., M-F 5 per day 7:04am-7:40pm, €3.10), **Monteluco** (6 per day 8:45am-6:20pm mid-June to early-Sept., €1.40), and **Perugia** (1½hr., 3 per day 6:20am-2:05pm €5.80). Schedule and tickets available at *tabaccherie* around the *piazza.*

Taxis: P. della Libertà (☎0743 22 58 09) and at the train station (☎0743 22 04 89).

▓ ▐ ORIENTATION AND PRACTICAL INFORMATION

Piazza della Libertà is most easily accessible from the train station. Take a white and orange SITA bus (direct to *centro*, €0.90). Buy tickets in the station at the newsstand, marked with a yellow "Lotto" sign. From **Corso Mazzini,** turn left up **Via del Mercato** to **Piazza del Mercato,** a cafe-laden marketplace. **Via del Municipio** runs from P. del Mercato to **Piazza del Municipio** and **Piazza Campello,** and **Via Saffi** leads to **Piazza del Duomo.** Most of the city sights are in these *piazze.*

Tourist Office: P. della Libertà 7 (☎0743 23 89 20 or 22 07 73; www.comune.spoleto. pg.it). Open Apr.-Oct. M-F 8:30am-1:30pm and 4-7pm, Sa-Su 9:30am-12:30pm and

4-7pm; Nov.-Mar. M-Sa 9:30am-1:30pm and 3:30-6:30pm, Su 9:30am-12:30pm; during Spoleto Festival daily 8:30am-1:30pm and 4-8pm.

Luggage storage: in the train station. €3 per 12hr. per bag. Open daily 5:30am-11pm.

Police: V. dei Filosofi 57 (☎0743 23 22 00).

Pharmacy: Farmacia Betti, V. Trento e Trieste 63 (☎0743 22 31 74), on the way to town from the train station. Open M-F 9am-1pm and 4-8pm.

Hospital: V. Madonna di Loreto, outside the southwestern walls of the *centro*.

Internet Access: Spider Service, V. Porta Fuga 11 (☎0743 22 51 65). €0.80 per 10min. With card, €2 per hr.; inquire at desk. Open M-Sa 9am-10pm.

Post Office: Vle. Giacomo Matteotti 2 (☎0743 40 373). Open M-F 8am-6:30pm, Sa 8am-12:30pm. **Postal Code:** 06049.

🏠 ACCOMMODATIONS

Well-priced options clutter the *centro*'s periphery, but finding accommodations during the summer music festival may be more trying. Contact **Conspoleto**, P. della Libertà 7, for help finding a room. (☎/fax 0743 22 07 73; www.conspoleto. com. Charges commission. Open M-Sa 8:30am-1:30pm and 4-7pm.)

☒ Ostello di Villa Redenta, Villa Redenta 1 (☎0743 22 49 36; www.villaredenta.com). From the train station, walk up Vle. Trento e Trieste and make the 1st left at the parking lot; veer left onto V. San Tommaso, then right onto V. delle Tre Madonne. With its expansive garden, feels like a country residence. Spacious rooms have private bath and TV. Breakfast included. Free laundry and Internet access. Wheelchair-accessible. Reception 8am-1pm and 3:30-8pm. Singles €25-30; doubles €60; triples €68-80; quads €78-90. 6-bed dorms in winter, €22. Cash only. ❷

Istituto Bambin Gesu, V. Montrone/Via S. Angelo 4 (☎0743 40 232). From P. della Liberta, take Vle. G. Matteotti just past the post office. Turn left on V. B. Egio. Veer left onto V. degli Abeti, descend the stairs, and turn right onto V. Monterone. Spacious and peaceful rooms in a 16th-century monastery. Breakfast included. Call ahead to check availability and arrange arrival. Singles €25; doubles €30, with bath €35. Cash only. ❷

Hotel Clarici, P. della Vittoria 32 (☎0743 22 33 11; www.hotelclarifici.com). From the station walk 10min. up Vle. Trento e Trieste and turn into P. Garibaldi; hotel is to the right. Modestly furnished rooms in a central location with balconies, phone, TV, A/C, and private bath. Breakfast included. Free Wi-Fi. Singles €45-65; doubles €70-120. MC/V. ❸

Albergo Due Porte, P. della Vittoria 5 (☎0743 22 36 66), just outside the city walls, 10min. from the train station toward the *centro*. Head down Vle. Trento e Trieste, and bear right into P. della Vittoria. Large rooms with bath, TV, A/C, and phone. Breakfast included. Free parking. Wheelchair-accessible. Singles €35; doubles €60; triples €85; quads €100. Discount with longer stays. AmEx/MC/V. ❸

🍴 FOOD

Rare is the Spoleto restaurant that doesn't boast its own version of the town's signature dish: *strengozzi alla spoletina*, a zesty take on pasta with tomato sauce. Other specialties include the same pasta garnished with a generous portion of flavorful shaved truffles. An **outdoor market** runs along V. Cacciatori delle Alpi, which stretches south from Ponte G. Garibaldi on Friday mornings. For groceries, head to **Vega Sigma Supermarket**, V. Cesare Micheli 1, off P. Garibaldi. (Open M-W and F-Su 8am-1pm and 4:45-7:45pm, Th 8am-1pm. MC/V.)

Ristoritrovo ConTe, V. Porta Fuga 43 (☎0743 22 52 21). If the strains of karaoke or the squawking parrot outside don't draw you in, then surely the magenta walls and 1m tall pink wine bottles will. This wacky restaurant dishes up the famous *strengozzi* with mush-

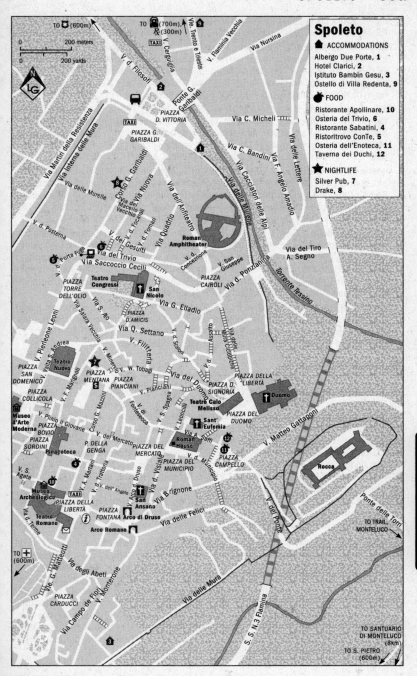

Spoleto

🏠 ACCOMMODATIONS

Albergo Due Porte, 1
Hotel Clarici, 2
Istituto Bambin Gesu, 3
Ostello di Villa Redenta, 9

🍎 FOOD

Ristorante Apollinare, 10
Osteria del Trivio, 6
Ristorante Sabatini, 4
Ristoritrovo ConTe, 5
Osteria dell'Enoteca, 11
Taverna dei Duchi, 12

⭐ NIGHTLIFE

Silver Pub, 7
Drake, 8

UMBRIA

rooms, garlic, chili pepper, and tomatoes (€7.50). Pizza €4.30-7. Primi €6-15. Secondi €8-16. Open Tu-Su 11am-2:30pm and 7-11pm. Cash only. ❸

Ristorante Apollinare, V. Sant'Agata 14 (☎0743 22 32 56; www.ristoranteapollinare. it). Former 10th-century convent serves fresh local cuisine. 3- and 5-course *menùs* (€25-35) are some of Umbria's best. Try mouthwatering roasted, stuffed rabbit with olive sauce and grilled raddichio (€13). Primi €8-20. Secondi €10-24. Desserts €5-7. Open daily noon-2:30pm and 7-10:30pm. Closed Tu in winter. AmEx/MC/V. ❸

Ristorante Sabatini, C. Mazzini 52-54 (☎0743 22 18 31). Photos of famous past customers line the otherwise simple walls of this expansive restaurant. Look for shots of Niki Lauda or Scalfaro as you enjoy dishes like pork fillet soaked in red wine, rosemary, and wild juniper berry sauce (€11). Excellent vegetable contorni €4. Primi €8-12. Secondi €8-13. Open Tu-Su 12:30-2:30pm and 7-10pm. AmEx/MC/V. ❸

Osteria del Trivio, V. del Trivio 16 (☎0743 44 349; www.osteriadeltrivio.it). From V. Garibaldi, turn left on V. del Trivio. Festively decorated with paintings and musical instruments. Some of the best food in town. Menu features traditional *strengozzi* with fava beans, bacon, and *pecorino* cheese (€9) and beef fillet in Sagranino wine (€15). Primi €8-13. Secondi €8-15. Open daily 12:30-2:30pm and 7-10pm. AmEx/MC/V. ❸

Taverna dei Duchi, V. Saffi 1 (☎0743 44 088). The restaurant is unmarked, so look for green walls with stone arches. All manner of Umbrian specialities, most often including truffles. Don't fill up on the focaccia before trying the *strengozzi al rancetto* (with onion, bacon, and pecorino cheese; €6), a tomato-less take on the local favorite. 3-course *menù* (€16) is a good deal. Pizza €5.50-11; dinner only. Primi €5.50-11. Secondi €7-11. Open M-Th, Sa-Su noon-3pm and 7-10pm. MC/V. ❸

Osteria dell'Enoteca, V. Saffi 7 (☎0743 22 04 84). At this stylish *osteria,* diners enjoy traditional *strengozzi* (€9) or richer dishes like *tortellini alla montanara* with meat, truffle sauce, gorgonzola, and bacon (€9). Primi €6.50-12. Secondi €6.50-13. Cover €1. Open M and W-Su 11:15am-3pm and 7-11pm. AmEx/MC/V. ❷

🧭 SIGHTS

ROCCA ALBORNOZIANA AND PONTE DELLE TORRI. The Rocca, a papal fortress up V. Saffi from P. del Duomo, was a high-security prison until 1982. During WWII, 94 Italian and Slovenian prisoners staged an escape to join partisans in the Umbrian hills. The complex's only drama now is in the restored 15th-century frescoes of the **Camera Pinta.** *(☎0743 46 434. Museum open Tu-W and Su 9am-1:30pm, Th-Sa 9am-7:30pm. €6, ages 18-25 €3, under 18 and over 65 free. Rocca open M 10am-6pm, Tu-W and Su 9am-6pm, Th-Sa 9am-3:30pm. €6, ages 15-25 and over 60 €5, ages 7-14 €2.50, under 6 free. Combined ticket €7.50/6.50/3.50/free. Tower €2. Guided tours in Italian offered Sa-Su 11am and 3pm; call to reserve.)* On the far side of the Rocca is the massive **Ponte delle Torri,** a stunning 14th-century engineering feat on an ancient Roman aqueduct. Ten 80m arches support the bridge, and the view across the Tessino Gorge is riveting. Several hikes start at the end of the bridge. *(Free.)*

MONTELUCO. The 800m trail along Spoleto's steep "mountain of the sacred grove" begins across Ponte delle Torri and winds through a canopied forest, passing abandoned mountain shrines and the churches of **San Giuliano** and **San Pietro.** At the peak of Monteluco, you'll find hotel-restaurants, a flat grassy picnic-ready clearing, and the tiny, 13th-century **Santuario di San Francesco di Monteluco,** once the refuge of St. Francis of Assisi and St. Bernadine of Siena. *(Open 9am-noon and 3-6pm. Free.)* Rain can turn the path into a rocky stream; to avoid slippery terrain, it's best to hike there on a sunny day or take a bus. Wear proper footwear and get a trail map from the tourist office before leaving.

DUOMO. Spoleto's Romanesque cathedral was built in the 12th century and later expanded by a 1491 portico and 17th-century interior redecoration. Inside, brilliantly colored scenes by Fra Filippo Lippi fill the domed apse, such as *The Coronation* in the half-dome of the main apse and a nativity scene on the lower right side. The 15th-century *Cappella dell'Assunta* is covered in eroding frescoes, while the more lavish 17th-century *Cappella della Santa Icone* stands to the right of the main apse. Lorenzo dei Medici commissioned Lippi's tomb, which was decorated by the artist's son, Filippino, and is now in the right transept. The soaring *campanile* features a mixture of styles and materials: stone blocks, fragments of inscriptions, friezes, and other remnants of the Roman era combine to form this structure. *(Down the steps from Casa Romana. Open daily 8:30am-12:30pm and 3:30-7pm. No visits during Mass M-Sa 9am and 6pm; Su 9, 11:30am, 6pm.)*

CASA ROMANA. This small AD first-century Roman house, once home to Emperor Vespasian's mother Vespasia Polla, features well-preserved mosaic floors and other artifacts. *(V. di Visiale 9. Beneath city hall. From P. del Duomo, take stairs opposite duomo entrance, then take a right and follow the yellow sign. ☎0743 23 42 50. Open daily Mar. 16-Oct. 14 10am-8pm; Oct. 15-Mar. 15 daily 10am-6pm. €2.50, ages 15-25 and over 65 €2, ages 7-14 €1; with Museum of Modern Art and Pinacoteca €6/4/1.50, valid for 3 days.)*

CHIESA DI SANT'ANSANO AND CRIPTA DI SAN ISAACO. Built on the ruins of a Roman temple dating to the first century BC, Sant'Ansano has a Renaissance facade and interior. Haunting frescoes detail scenes from the life of St. Isaac, who lives in an AD sixth-century sarcophagus at the center of the room. *(Heading away from P. Mercato on V. dell'Arco di Druso, the church is on the left hand corner. ☎0743 40 305. Open daily Apr.-Oct. 9am-noon and 3-7pm; Nov.-Mar. 9am-noon and 3-6pm.)*

MUSEUM OF MODERN ART. A refreshing alternative to ancient ruins and holy frescoes, this collection includes early works by Moore, Consagra, Pomodoro, and Leoncillo. The museum's first room is dedicated to American artist Alexander Calder, whose *Teodelapio* now stands in Spoleto's P. della Stazione. *(Follow V. Mercato as it turns into V. Giovane, and go downstairs; the museum lies straight ahead. ☎0743 46 434. Open Mar. 16-Oct. 14 daily 10:30am-1pm and 3:30-7pm; Oct. 15-Mar. 15 M and W-Su 10:30am-1pm and 3-5:30pm. €4, ages 15-25 and over 65 €3, ages 7-14 €1.50.)*

🎎 FESTIVALS

▦ **Spoleto Festival (Festival dei Due Mondi)** (☎800 56 56 00; www.spoletofestival.it.), 2 weeks in late June and early July. One of the world's most prestigious international arts events with concerts, operas, ballets, films, modern art shows, and craft fairs. Purchase tickets beginning in late April by contacting the box office, P. della Libertà 10 (☎0743 89 21 01; www.ticketone.it Open daily from April 22 to June 26 W and F 10:30am-1:30pm and 4-7pm, Sa 10:30am-12:30pm and 4-7pm. During the festival M-F 10:30am-1:30pm and 4-7pm, Sa-Su 10:30am-12:30pm and 4-7pm. Call center open M-F 9am-8pm, Sa 9am-5:30pm). Ages 25 and under or over 60, 20% discount.

Vini nel Mondo, during the last weekend of June. Citywide wine tastings and musical and theatrical performances.

Spoleto Estate, throughout Aug. and Sept. Cultural events pick up where the Spoleto Festival leaves off. Schedules available at the tourist office.

Stagione del Teatro Lirico Sperimentale A. Belli di Spoleto, P. Bovio 1 (☎0743 22 16 45), from late Aug. to Sept. Renowned experimental opera season.

NIGHTLIFE

Down **Corso Garibaldi,** crowds gather in the early evening in the busy **Piazza Vittoria** where cafes serve *aperitivo* buffets and dish up creamy gelato. Young people and couples hang out on the *piazza*'s central fountain.

Drake, C. Garibaldi 92 (☎0743 49 311). Serves hot pizza and cold drinks, or cold *panini* and hot drinks. The Dark Violet is a hot mix of absinthe, sambuca, blue curacào, and orange juice (€6). During winter, *discobar* downstairs opens with a DJ on Su, live music on Sa, and Latin W. Mixed drinks €4-6. Beer €2.50-5. Open Tu-Su 11:30am-3:30pm and 6:30pm-3am. AmEx/MC/V.

Silver Pub, V. Felice Cavalloti (☎0743 22 10 00). From P. della Liberta, follow V. Mazzini to the left. Imposing wood doors open up to an off-beat bar with a huge selection of mixed drinks (€5-6) and beer. Yellow walls, a steep spiral staircase, live music, and an even livelier crowd make this one of Spoleto's most popular spots. Happy hour daily 8-10pm. Karaoke F. Open M-Tu and Th-Su 8pm-3am. Cash only.

DAYTRIP FROM SPOLETO

TREVI

From Spoleto, take a train to Trevi. Dir: Perugia or Ancona, 10min., 17 per day 12:10am-10:09pm, €1.75. From the station, take an orange municipal bus to town. Buses run to P. Mazzini, the main piazza at the top of the hill. M-Sa 6 per day 7:30am-6:15pm, return buses M-Sa 5 per day 6:55am-5:40pm; €0.70.

Removed and unhurried compared to the more trafficked Umbrian towns, Trevi (TREH-vee; pop. 7800) rests among sloping olive groves atop a hill. Most sights are easily reached from **Piazza Mazzini,** the *centro.* The **Pinacoteca Raccolta d'Arte di San Francesco** houses a collection of Renaissance religious art. The unique **Museo della Civiltà Dell'Ulivo** offers a history of the city's staple olive oil industry as well as samples and recipes. Follow V. San Francesco from P. Mazzini to reach the museums, both at Lungo Don Bosco 5. (☎0742 38 16 28; www.sistemamuseo.it. Open June-July Tu-Su 10am-12:30pm and 3:30-7pm; Aug. daily 10am-12:30pm and 3-7:30pm; Sept. and Apr.-May Tu-Su 10am-12:30pm and 2:30-6pm; Oct.-Mar. F-Su 10am-12:30pm and 2:30-5pm. €4, students €2.50.) The **Flash Art Museum,** V. Placido Riccardi 4, showcases avant-garde art in a 15th-century *palazzo.* The small museum, which is associated with the contemporary Italian art magazine, *Flash,* hosts rotating exhibits of modern art. (☎0742 38 10 21; www.treviflashartmuseum.org. Open Tu-Su 4-7pm.) The **Illumination Procession,** one of Umbria's oldest religious festivals, takes place on January 28.

Ristorante Maggiolini ❷, V. San Francesco 20, near the museums off P. Mazzini, has an intimate interior and a bar for sampling Trevi's olive oil. (☎0742 38 15 34. Primi €6-8. Secondi €6-12. Open M and W-Su noon-3pm and 7-10:30pm. MC/V.) The Pro Loco **tourist office,** P. Mazzini 5, offers assistance in renting one of the abundant *affitacamere,* a better deal than any of Trevi's expensive hotels. (☎0742 78 11 50; www.protrevi.it. Open daily 9am-1pm and 3:30-7:30pm.) To reach the office from P. Garibaldi, take V. Roma to P. Mazzini.

UMBRIA

LE MARCHE

Green foothills separate the umbrella-laden beaches along the Adriatic from the craggy inland Apennines in Le Marche (LAY MAR-kay), one of Italy's most under appreciated regions. In its rural towns, remains of the Gauls, Picenes, and Romans hint at a fascinating past, but the present is alive and well among friendly locals and picturesque side streets. The legacy of Raphael and Donato Bramante in Urbino, the palm-lined boardwalk of San Benedetto del Tronto, the winding streets of Ascoli Piceno, and the hidden beauty of Ancona are just a few of the highlights of this geographically and historically diverse region. Just as it has charmed the knickers off artists in the past, it'll charm the sleek, white capris off you and your fellow stylin' travelin' band members.

> ## HIGHLIGHTS OF LE MARCHE
>
> **BAKE** on the untouristed beaches of the sleepy town of Fano (p. 367).
>
> **CLIMB** up to the grand hilltop Palazzo Ducale in Urbino (p. 369).
>
> **STROLL** along Pesaro's promenade for some of Italy's best Adriatic views (p. 363).

PESARO ☎ 0721

Pesaro (PEZ-ah-ro; pop. 92,000) strikes a balance between its neighbors—hip Rimini and laid-back Fano—offering a blend of culture, couture, and seaside serenity. While the bright blue Adriatic delights beachgoers, the *centro* charms visitors with street concerts and back-alley shops. Come here to buy a smokin' bikini, then stake your claim on the sandy shores to justify your purchase.

◪ TRANSPORTATION

Trains: at the end of V. Risorgimento and Vle. della Liberazione. Ticket counter open daily 6:10am-8:30pm. AmEx/MC/V. To: **Ancona** (1hr., 31 per day 12:59am-11:46pm, €3.25); **Bologna** (2hr., 34 per day 4:43am-11:18pm, €7.90); **Fano** (10min., 22 per day 6:27am-11:13pm, €1.35); **Rimini** (30min., 41 per day 4:43am-11:18pm, €2.70).

Buses: 50 ft. from the train station (☎0721 32 401). Open M-Sa 7:30am-1pm. Buses #10, 11, 14, 20, 30, 40, 50, 60, 70, 130, and C/S stop at Ple. Giacomo Matteotti and run to **Fano** (25min., every 15-30min. 6:35am-9:05pm, €1.40) and **Gradara** (55min., M-F 6:05am-7:05pm every hr., Su every 2hr.; €1.60). ADRIABUS (☎0721 54 96 20) runs to **Urbino** from the train station (55min.; M-Sa 20 per day 6:15am-8:15pm, Su 9 per day 8:15am-8:15pm; €2.75). **Bucci**

runs to **Rome's** Tiburtina station from Ple. G. Matteotti (4hr., 6am and 2pm, €22). Buy tickets on board. Cash only.

Taxis: Available 24hr. at the train station (☎0721 31 111 or 45 44 25), P. del Popolo (☎0721 31 430), and Ple. G. Matteotti (☎0721 34 053).

Bike Rental: in Ple. d'Annunzio, at the intersection of Vle. Trieste and Vle. G. Verdi (☎347 75 29 634). €3 per hr., €9 per day. Open May to Sept. 8:30am-midnight. Cash only.

🔢 ORIENTATION AND PRACTICAL INFORMATION

From the train station, take **Via Risorgimento** and walk straight through P. Garibaldi and up V. Branca to reach **Piazza del Popolo**, the relaxed *centro storico*. **Corso XI Settembre** runs west toward Chiesa di Sant'Agostino, while **Via San Francesco** runs east toward **Piazzale Giacomo Matteotti** and the bus station. **Via Rossini** runs straight toward **Largo Aldo Moro**, which leads to **Viale della Repubblica, Piazzale Libertà**, and the sea. **Viale Trieste** runs along the beach.

Tourist Offices: IAT, V. Rossini 41 (☎0721 69 341; iat.pesaro@regione.marche.it). Open M-Sa 9am-1pm and 3-6pm, Su 9am-1pm. **Provincial tourist office** (☎800 56 38 00; www.comune.pesaro.it), off Largo Aldo Moro. Open M-Sa 9am-1pm and 4-7pm, Su 9am-1pm.

Luggage storage: near the "Taxis" sign outside the station. 1st 12hr. €3, each additional 12hr. €2. Open daily 6am-11pm.

Police: ☎0721 42 551.

Hospital: Ospedale San Salvatore, Ple. Cinelli 4 (☎0721 36 11).

Pharmacy: V. Rossini 42 (☎0721 67 121), right off Largo Aldo Moro. Open daily 8:30am-12:30pm and 4pm-8pm. MC/V.

Internet: Max3D, V. Passeri 54/56. (☎0721 35 122). €3 per hr. Open M 3:30-8pm, Tu-Sa 9:30am-1pm and 3:30-8pm. Cash only.

Laundry: New Blue City, Vle. Fiume 10 (☎0721 87 47 408). Wash €2, dry €3. Open daily 7:30am-midnight.

Post Office: P. del Popolo 28 (☎0721 43 22 85). Open M-F 8am-6:30pm, Sa 8am-12:30pm. **Postal Code:** 61100.

🏠 ACCOMMODATIONS AND CAMPING

Pesaro is a low-season steal, but bargains are harder to find come summer.

Hotel Holiday, Vle. Trento 159/161 (☎0721 34 851), on a quiet street minutes from the beach. Rooms have floral ceilings, sunny balconies, phone, private bath, minibar, safe, TV, and fan. Breakfast, lunch, and dinner included. 3-night min. stay. Reception 7am-10pm. €38-58 per person; €6 surcharge for singles. AmEx/MC/V. ❸

Hotel Continental, Vle. Trieste 70 (☎0721 31 808; www.hotelcontinental.it). Colorful flags greet guests at this cheery hotel, practically on the sand. Sunny rooms with private bath, phone, TV, and balcony. Great services include buffet breakfast, communal TV rooms, free beach umbrellas, and daily *aperitivo* buffet. €41-62 per person; €6 surcharge for singles. MC/V. ❸

San Marco, Vle. XI Febbraio 32 (☎0721 31 396; www.hotelsanmarcopu.it). From the station follow V. Risorgimento, bear right into Ple. Garibaldi, and turn right onto Vle. XI Febbraio. Eager staff offers sparse but spacious rooms with Internet access, phone, and TV. A/C €6 about extra. Breakfast included. Wheelchair-accessible. Singles €42-55; doubles €68-83; triples €84-103; quads €100-115. AmEx/MC/V. ❸

Camping Panorama, (☎0721 20 81 45; www.campingpanorama.it), is near a national park and a beach, 7km north of Pesaro on Strada Panoramica S. Bartolo toward Gabicce Mare. Take bus #14 (M-Sa 5 per day, Su 2 per day) from the train station or Ple. Mat-

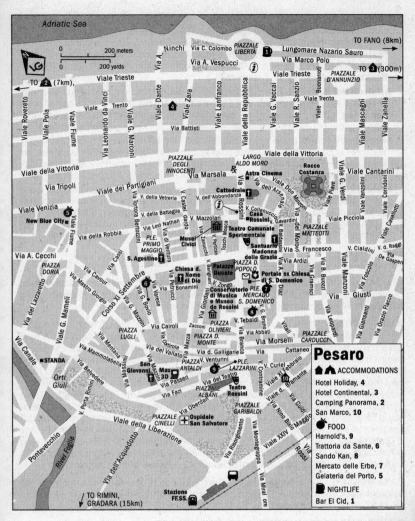

Pesaro

▲▲ ACCOMMODATIONS

Hotel Holiday, 4
Hotel Continental, 3
Camping Panorama, 2
San Marco, 10

● FOOD

Harnold's, 9
Trattoria da Sante, 6
Sando Kan, 8
Mercato delle Erbe, 7
Gelateria del Porto, 5

▮ NIGHTLIFE

Bar El Cid, 1

teotti and ask for Camping Panorama. On-site pool, market, and laundry. Hot showers free. Open May-Sept. €6-9 per person; €16 per tent. Electricity €2.50. Cash only. ❶

▶ FOOD

There's a **Standa** supermarket at V. Canale 41. (Open M-Sa 7:30am-8:30pm, Su 8am-1:30pm. AmEx/MC/V.) **Mercato delle Erbe,** at the San Domenico Convent off V. Branca, sells flowers, bread, meat, fruit, and *piadine*. (Flower and bread stands open M-Sa 7am-8:30pm; *piadine* and food open M and W-Su 5-8:30pm.)

Trattoria da Sante, V. Bovio 27 (☎0721 33 676.www.trattoriadasante.com). Follow C. XI Settembre north from P. del Popolo, and turn left on V. Bovio. Heaping portions of delicious seafood pasta on a quiet side street off the *centro.* Try the filling *menù* of grilled fish, antipasto, primo, contorno, coffee, wine, and dessert (€30). Primi €6-8. Secondi €8-11. Cover €1. Service 15%. Open Tu-Su noon-2:30pm and 7-10:30pm. Reservations recommended Sa-Su. Cash only. ❸

Gelateria del Porto, Vle. Fiume 12 (☎0721 35 350). Retreat into the acqua blue interior after a hot day on the sand. Sorbets like *azzurro* (to match the bright walls) or richer flavors like "*scrok!*" (vanilla, *pinoli,* and caramel) are served in homemade chocolate-dipped cones (€1.50-4). Open M-Sa 7am-midnight, Su 7am-5pm. AmEx/MC/V. ❶

Sando Kan, V. Tebaldi 14 (☎339 830 4045), just off V. Branca coming from P. del Popolo. Warm red lights and intimate tables provide a cozy setting for classic Indian plates like *kukar daal* (lentils with chicken and basmati rice; €9), or *malaee kofta* (ground pork with cream and lemon; €13). Open Tu-Su 12:30-2:30pm and 7-11pm. Cash only. ❷

Harnold's, Ple. Lazzarini 34 (☎0721 65 155), 3 doors down from Teatro Rossini. From P. del Popolo, follow V. Branca away from the sea. Affordable fare ranges from extra thick *panini* and salads to the "Big Ben" (double-decker cheeseburger; €4.80). The food, prices, and feel-good atmosphere are worth the wait at the busy outdoor tables on summer nights. Panini €2-4.80. Open daily 8am-3am. Closed Su Oct.-Mar. MC/V. ❶

👁 SIGHTS

PIAZZA DEL POPOLO. Pesaro's main square holds the massive **Palazzo Ducale,** commissioned in the 15th century by Alessandro Sforza. *(Open to visitors during exhibitions only. Ask the tourist office about scheduled events.)*

MUSEI CIVICI. Rich clay deposits from the nearby Folgia River have made the crafting of ceramics a long-standing tradition in Pesaro. Within the Musei Civici, the **Museo delle Ceramiche** showcases centuries of local ceramics, which range from prehistoric artifacts to colorful contemporary works. In the same building, Pesaro's **Pinacoteca** holds the fiery *Fall of the Giants* by Guido Reni and four still-lifes by Benedetto Sartori. Don't miss Bellini's remarkable *Incoronazione della Vergine,* surrounded by 15 panels depicting scenes ranging from Christ's Nativity to St. George's somewhat unimpressive slaying of an iguana-sized 🐉dragon. *(V. Toschi Mosca 29. From P. del Popolo, head down C. XI Settembre with Palazzo Ducale on your left, and turn right on V. Toschi Mosca. ☎0721 38 75 41; www.museicivicipesaro. it. Open July-Aug. Tu and Th 9:30am-12:30pm and 4-10:30pm, W and F-Su 9:30am-12:30pm and 4-7pm; Sept.-June Tu-W 9:30am-12:30pm, Th-Su 9:30am-12:30pm and 4-7pm. €4, ages 15-25 and over 65 €2, under 15 free. Combined ticket with Casa Rossini €7/€3. Cash only.)*

CASA ROSSINI. Gioachino Rossini's birthplace is now a museum with his old photographs, theatrical and opera memorabilia, and piano. *(V. Rossini 34. ☎0721 38 73 57. Same hours as Musei Civici. €4, under 26 or over 65 €2, under 15 free. Cash only.)*

🎵 🎭 ENTERTAINMENT AND NIGHTLIFE

Pesaro hosts the **Mostra Internazionale del Nuovo Cinema** (The International Festival of New Films) from late June to July (☎0721 44 56 643; www.pesarofilmfest. it). Live theater and movie screenings are held in buildings along V. Rossini and at the **Teatro Comunale Sperimentale** (☎0721 38 75 48), an experimental theater on V. Rossini. Native composer Rossini founded the Conservatorio di Musica G. Rossini, P. Olivieri 5, which sponsors artistic events year-round. Contact **Teatro Rossini,** Ple. Lazzarini 29 (☎0721 38 76 21), off V. Branca, for show times and prices. The annual **Rossini Opera Festival** runs from early August through September. Reserve tickets at Teatro Rossini's box office starting April 18. (☎0721

38 001; www.rossinioperafestival.it. Info line open M-F 10am-1pm and 3-6pm. Theater open M, W, and F 8:30am-1:30pm and 3:30-5:30pm. Ticket office open 9:30am-12:30pm and 4:30-7:30pm and 1hr. before performances.)

The perfect spot for a light lunch during a day of beaching, **Bar El Cid,** Ple. della Libertà, offers a great summer salad buffet from noon-3pm and breezy beachside seating. Try the packed Nizzarda salad with tuna, tomato, mozzarella, olives, mushrooms, eggs, and radicchio (€6). Return at night to sample the extensive drink list. (☎0721 31 891. Salad buffet and bread €5. Mixed drinks €5.50. Beer €3-4. Open daily Mar.-Oct. 7am-2am. Cash only.)

◤ DAYTRIPS FROM PESARO

FANO

Fano is accessible from Pesaro by train (10min., 22 per day 6:27amm-11:13pm, €1.35) and by bus (every 15min.-hr., €1.40). To get to the beach, exit the train station right on V. Cavallotti and turn right on V. Cesare Battisti. To reach P. XX Settembre, the centro, turn left on V. Garibaldi from V. Cavallotti then right on C. Giacomo Matteotti.

Fano (FA-no; pop. 62,000) is a sleepy town stretching 20km along the coast from Pesaro to some of Italy's quietest seaside retreats. Even in summer, vacationers are scarce on the northern beaches; farther inland, a quiet *centro* offers relatively untouristed churches and restaurants serving seafood specialties. Marking the western entrance to these streets is the **Arco d'Augusto,** named for the city's founder, Augustus. Nearby stands a larger-than-life bronze statue of the man himself and the crumbling brick walls he built to protect his small city. Hotels reserve most of the private shoreline for their guests, but there is a rocky **public beach;** the first entrance sits across from Vle. Adriatico 150. Though this beach is convenient, you'll need some padding to sunbathe comfortably. (Open daily 5am-11pm. Free.) If you schedule your trip well, you might find yourself at the **July Jazz by the Sea,** which in the past has hosted artists like Wynton Marsalis. At **Al Pesce Azzuro ❷,** Vle. Adriatico 48/A, a brightly painted ship's hull welcomes visitors to this funky, self-service restaurant on the beach's northern end. (☎0721 80 31 65. *Menù* €10. Open Apr.-Oct. Tu-Su noon-2pm and 7:30-10pm.) Inland, **La Vecchia Fano ❸,** V. Vecchia 8, serves authentic *fanese* plates like *tagliolini al farro* (wheat pasta; €6.50). From V. Garibaldi, turn left through P. Costanzi on V. Cavour, then right on V. Vecchia. (☎/fax 0721 80 34 93. Primi €6.50-11. Secondi €6.50-20. Cover €2. Open Tu-Su noon-2:30pm and 7:30-10:30pm. AmEx/MC/V.) A **PuntoSMA** supermarket is at V. Garibaldi 53. (Open M-Sa 8am-8pm. MC/V.) The **tourist office** is at Vle. Battisti 10. (☎0721 80 35 34; www.turismofano.com. Open M, W, and F-Sa 9am-1pm, Tu and Th 3-6pm.)

URBINO ☎0722

With picturesque stone dwellings scattered along steep city streets and a turreted palace ornamenting its skyline, Urbino (oor-BEE-no; pop. 15,500) encompasses all that is classically Italian. The cobblestone streets and *piazze* lead to many artistic treasures and Renaissance monuments, including Piero della Francesca's *Ideal City* and Raphael's childhood home. This cultural beauty within the city walls is rivaled only by the magnificence of surrounding mountains and valleys. A huge university population and stream of international visitors continually bolster Urbino's vitality: when classes are in session, the town's population swells from 9,000 to nearly 30,000.

LE MARCHE

▐ TRANSPORTATION

Buses stop in Borgo Mercatale and serve train stations in Pesaro and Fano. ADRIABUS (☎0722 37 67 11) runs to P. Matteotti and the depot outside the train station in Pesaro (45min.-1hr.; M-Sa 20 per day 6:20am-8:35pm, Su 9 per day 7:35am-8:35pm; €2.75) and Fano Pincio (1½hr.; 18 per day 5:40am-8:10pm, service reduced on Su). Buy tickets onboard. Bucci (☎0722 32 401; www.autolineebucci.it) runs buses to Rome (4hr., 6:15am and 3pm, €25). **Taxis** are in P. della Repubblica (☎0722 25 50) and at the bus stop (☎0722 32 79 49).

✦ ▐ ORIENTATION AND PRACTICAL INFORMATION

A short walk up **Via Mazzini** from **Borgo Mercatale** leads to **Piazza della Repubblica,** the city's hub, from which **Via Raffaello, Via Cesare Battisti, Via Vittorio Veneto,** and **Corso Garibaldi** radiate. Another walk uphill on V. V. Veneto leads to **Piazza Rinascimento** and the **Palazzo Ducale.**

Tourist Office: V. Puccinotti 35 (☎0722 26 13; www.marcheturismo.it), across from Palazzo Ducale. Free guided **tours** Mar.-Sept. Sa-Su 10:30am; Aug. Sa-Su 10:30am and 3:30pm. Open M and Sa 9am-1pm, Tu-F 9am-1pm and 3-6pm. Info booth (☎0722 26 31) in Borgo Mercatale. Open M-Sa 9am-6pm, Su 9am-1pm.

Laundromat: Powders, V. Battisti 35 (☎0722 21 96). Wash €3.75 per kg. Dry €2. Open M-Sa 9am-8pm. Cash only.

Police: V. S. Provinciale Feltresca 9. ☎0722 37 89 00.

Hospital: V. Bonconte da Montefeltro, off V. Comandino (☎0722 30 11).

Internet Access: Due Mila Net, V. Mazzini 17 (☎/fax 0722 37 81 95). €4 per hr., students €2.50 per hr.; min. 3hr. Open M-Sa 9am-10pm. Cash only.

Post Office: V. Bramante 28 (☎0722 37 791), off V. Raffaello. Currency exchange and **ATM** available. Open M-F 8am-6:30pm, Sa 8am-12:30pm. **Postal Code:** 61029.

▐ ▐ ACCOMMODATIONS AND CAMPING

Pensionato Maria Immacolata, V. Mazzini 30 (☎0722 28 53), steps from the bus station and P. della Repubblica. High ceilings, a peaceful inner courtyard, and beautiful stone floors. Shared baths. Reception 7am-10pm. Curfew 10pm. Singles €18; doubles €32. Women only. Cash only. ❶

Pensione Fosca, V. Raffaello 67 (☎0722 32 96 22 or 339 54 05 640), on the top floor. From P. della Repubblica, turn left onto V. Raffaello and climb hill. Central location, kind proprietress, and unbeatable value. Shared bath. Call ahead to arrange check-in time. Singles €21; doubles €35; triples €45. Cash only. ❷

Albergo Italia, C. Garibaldi 32 (☎0722 27 01; www.albergo-italia-urbino.it), just off P. della Repubblica. A charming staff welcomes you to spotless modern rooms with wood floors and furniture, beautiful countryside views, and excellent services. Rooms have private bath, minibar, TV, and A/C. Breakfast included. Free Wi-Fi; computer with Internet access €1 per 15min. Wheelchair-accessible. Singles €47-70; doubles €70-120; triples €120-145; quads €160. Discounts with longer stays. AmEx/MC/V. ❹

Hotel Raffaello, Vicolino S. Margherita 40 (☎0722 47 84 or 48 96; www.albergorafello. com). From P. della Repubblica, turn left on V. Raffaello, left on V. S. Margherita, and right on the 1st side street. Tall blue ceilings, checkered marble floors, and bright decor give this hotel an eclectic feel. Historic location near the House of Raphael. Snug rooms have minibar, A/C, TV, phone, private bath, radio, and views of the hills. Breakfast included. Internet. Reception 7:30am-midnight. Singles €50-70; doubles €90-115. MC/V. ❹

Piero della Francesca, V. Comandino 53 (☎0722 32 84 28; fax 32 84 27), in front of the hospital. Bus #1 from Borgo Mercatale or a 15min. walk from P. della Repubblica. Modern rooms have bath, TV, phone, and balconies with views of the misty hills. Reception 24hr. Singles €31; doubles €52; triples €68. AmEx/MC/V. ❸

Camping Pineta, Località San Donato (☎0722 47 10; www.camping-pineta-urbino.it), 2km from Urbino. Take bus #4 or 7 from Borgo Mercatale; request to stop at camping. Private sites with city views. Open from 1 week before Easter to Sept. Reception 9am-10pm. €8-9 per person; €14-16 per tent. Electricity €2. Showers free. Cash only. ❶

▣ FOOD

Urbino's *caciotta* is a delicate cheese that pairs well with a glass of *Bianchello del Metauro*. **Supermarket Margherita,** V. Raffaello 37, has meats and cheeses. (☎0722 32 97 71. Open M-Sa 7:30am-1:55pm and 4:30-8pm. MC/V.)

▩ **Il Portico,** V. Mazzini 7 (☎0722 43 29; www.porticourbino.it). A maze of exposed brick leads to the warm interior of this family-run restaurant, which serves Mediterranean food and wine. Try the especially popular *fiori di zucchine ripieni* (stuffed zucchini; €4.50), or a hearty portion of spaghetti with mussels and pecorino cheese (€8). Live music Tu and Sa-Su. Open Tu-Su noon-3pm and 7-11pm. Cover €2. AmEx/MC/V. ❷

▩ **Pizzeria Le Tre Piante,** V. Voltaccia della Vecchia 1 (☎0722 48 63). From P. della Repubblica, take V. Veneto, turn left on V. Nazario Sauro, right on V. Budassi, and left down the stairs onto V. Foro Posterula. Join locals on the terrace for fine fish and pasta. Try the *tagliatelle* with beans, rucola, and *pendoini* (€6.80), while watching the sun set over the Apennines. Pizza €3.50-6.50. Primi €6.80-7.50. Secondi €8-15. Cover €1.50. Open Tu-Su noon-3pm and 7-11:30pm. Cash only. ❸

La Trattoria del Leone, V. Battisti 5 (☎0722 32 98 94). Brick archways and simple yellow walls provide a cozy space to enjoy regional dishes liked salted beef with orange, walnuts, and parmesan (€7.50). Vegetarian dishes include spaghetti with eggs, breadcrumbs, and parmesan in vegetable broth (€7.50). Primi €7. Secondi €6.50-12. Cover €2. Open M-F 6:30-11:30pm, Sa-Su 12:30-2:30pm. AmEx/MC/V. ❷

Ristorante Ragno d'Oro, Vle. Don Minzoni 2/4 (☎0722 32 77 05). Follow Vle. Raffaello to the statue at the top of the hill and turn right on Vle. Don Minzoni. Students and locals hike to the top of the hill, where the town's best pizza and *piadine* awaits. Try the signature Ragno d'Oro, with mozzarella, spinach, ricotta, and speck ham (€7); wash it down with the German beer on tap. Pizza €3.50-7.50. Primi €6-8. Secondi €7-17. Cover €1.50. Open Apr.-Oct. daily 9am-2:30pm and 7:30-midnight. AmEx/MC/V. ❸

Un Punto Macrobiotico, V. Pozzo Nuovo 4 (☎0722 32 97 90). From P. della Repubblica, take C. Battisti and then 1st right. Small, community-minded socially conscious market. Serves delicious organic food. Prices vary with the daily menu. Rice dishes €3-8. Open M-Sa 12:30-2:30pm and 7:30-9pm. Students eat ½-price. Cash only. ❶

Caffè del Sole, V. Mazzini 34 (☎0722 26 19). Popular student hangout serves *panini,* drinks, and hearty helpings of local personality. Walls decorated with sun motifs, a mural of clinking wine glasses, and a giant mouth on the back wall. Sept.-May W nights jazz concerts. Open M-Sa 7am-2am. AmEx/MC/V. ❶

▣ SIGHTS

▩**PALAZZO DUCALE.** The turreted silhouette of the Renaissance *palazzo* in P. Rinascimento dominates Urbino's skyline. A stairway inside leads to the **Galleria Nazionale delle Marche,** in the former residence of Duke Frederico da Montefeltro. The gallery contains an extensive Italian art collection, including works like Piero della Francesca's *The Ideal City.* In the last rooms, Berruguete's

Portrait of Duke Federico with a Young Guidubaldo, Raphael's *Portrait of a Lady*, and Paolo Uccello's narrative panel *The Profanation of the Host* are on display. The building also contains the **Museo Archeologico's** collection of Roman art and artifacts. (☎0722 32 26 25. *Open M 8:30am-2pm, Tu-Su 8:30am-7:15pm. Last entry 1hr. before closing. €8, EU students 18-25 €4, under 18 and over 65 free.*)

CASA NATALE DI RAFFAELLO. Raphael's birthplace is now filled with period furnishings and paintings. The only piece in the museum attributed to Raphael himself is a fresco of the Virgin and Child in the room where the artist was born. Within these walls, Raphael began learning the trade from his father, Giovanni Santi. A celebrated painter in his own right, Santi's *Annunciation* hangs in the next room. (*V. Raffaello 57.* ☎0722 32 01 05. *Open M-Sa 9am-1pm and 3-7pm, Su 10am-1pm. Last entry 20min. before closing. €3. Cash only.*)

DUOMO. Beside Palazzo Ducale sits the stark facade of the *duomo*. White and mint-green walls, as well as paintings like Veronese's fantastic *Translazione della Santa Casa e Sant'Andrea*, decorate the interior. Next door, the **Sale del Castellare** has free art exhibits. (*Open daily 9:30am-1pm and 2:30-6:30pm. Free.*)

ORATORIO DI SAN GIOVANNI BATTISTA. From P. della Repubblica, take V. Mazzini and turn right up the small path on the right, following the sign. The 1416 Gothic frescoes that decorate the oratory on V. Barocci, include a gorgeous floor-to-ceiling Crucifixion and panels depicting events from the life of St. John. Its painters, the Salimbeni brothers Giacomo and Lorenzo, are said to have drawn their sketches with lamb's blood. (☎347 67 11 181. *Open M-Sa 10am-12:30pm and 3-5:30pm, Su 10am-12:30pm. €2. Cash only.*)

NIGHTLIFE

The main *piazze* stay lit well into the night, when people head to cafes for one last shot of espresso (or tequila, as the case may be). Students keep the party scene going strong until well after 3am during the school year, but come summer, Urbino slows down as its median age rises drastically. Bars are stocked with German beers, hard liquor, and even the occasional bottle of absinthe.

Daunbailo, V. Posta Vecchia 7. An artsy spot with checkered ceiling, red and turquoise walls, and snapshots from Audrey Hepburn's days in *Roman Holiday*. Live music Tu nights. Monthly photo exhibits. Beer €3.50. Wine €2.50. Mixed drinks €4.50. Open Tu-Sa 6pm-2am, Su 6pm-1am. Cash only.

The Bosom Pub, V. Budassi 24 (☎0722 47 83). Dark wood paneling and beer paraphernalia. Beer from €2.50. Wine €5 per bottle. Mixed drinks €2-6. Happy hour Tu and F-Sa from 10pm-midnight, with beer as cheap as €1 and 2 sangrias for €3. Open daily June-July 8pm-2am; Aug.-May 6pm-2am. Cash only.

Caffè del Corso, C. Garibaldi 3 (☎0722 24 77). Fuschia walls and brick archways lead to comfy modern seating. Creative drinks like hot China martinis (€2.50) and Jamaican coffee (espresso, rum, sugar, and cream; €3.50). Meals during the day €3.50-6.50. Mixed drinks €4.50. Beer €3-4.50. Open daily 6am-2am. Cash only.

Tanto Piacere, V. V. Veneto 29 (☎347 75 64 292). Draws a genial crowd to a simple, jazz-filled, white-brick interior. Appetizer buffet 6:30pm. Beer €2.50-3.50. Wine €2-4. *Bruschette* €3-6. *Crescia* €2-6. Open Tu-Su 10am-2am. Cash only.

FESTIVALS

In July the town resounds with Renaissance music during the **Antique Music Festival.** Saturdays are amateur nights—bring your ancient lute and rock out. The third Sunday of August brings the **Ceremony of the Revocation of the Duke's Court.**

Jousting matches erupt on the eve of the festival. The **Festa dell'Aquilone,** held on the first Sunday in September, is a fierce kite-flying competition between different cities. (The rain date is the 2nd Su of Sept.)

ANCONA ☎071

Midway down the boot, Ancona (an-CO-na; pop. 102,000) is still kickin' as Northern Italy's major transportation hub for boats to Croatia, Greece, and Slovenia. Though most travelers only pass through on their way to more exotic locales, those who choose to linger will enjoy the centuries-old *duomo*, a lively *centro storico*, and the sparkling water along Ancona's concrete beach.

TRANSPORTATION

Trains: P. Rosselli. To: **Bologna** (2hr., 36 per day 1:26am-8:40pm, €11); **Milan** (3-5hr., 18 per day 1:59am-7:13pm, €34); Pesaro (45min., 38 per day 4:27am-10:35pm, €3.25); **Rimini** (1hr., 44 per day 1:32am-10:35pm, €4.80); **Rome** (3-4hr., 11 per day 3:36am-7:05pm, €13.80); **Venice** (5hr., 22 per day 2:34am-8:40pm, €27.50). Ticket office open daily 5:55am-8pm. AmEx/MC/V.

Ferries: Stazione Marittima (☎071 20 78 91). Call the day before departure to confirm; cancellations can occur. Reserve ahead in July and Aug., when prices jump by up to 30%. The following companies all accept AmEx, MC, and Visa:

Adria (☎50 21 16 21; www.adriaferries.com). To: **Durazzo, Albania** (18 hr., €70).

ANEK (☎071 20 72 346; www.anekitalia.com). To: **Igoumenitsa, GRC** (16hr.) and **Patras, GRC** (22hr., €60). 20% youth discount, 10% for families and those over 60; 30% for round-trips.

Jadrolinija (☎071 20 43 05; www.traghetti.amatori.com) To: **Split, HRV** (10hr.; €48).

SEM Maritime Co (SMC) (☎071 20 40 41; www.marittimamauro.it). To: **Split, HRV** (9hr.; €38-44).

SNAV (☎071 20 76 116; www.snav.it) To: **Spalato, HRV** (4hr.; €63).

 THE FERRY FAIRY. To find all of the most up-to-date info on ferries from Ancona, check out www.doricaportservices.it.

ORIENTATION AND PRACTICAL INFORMATION

The train station is a 25min. walk from **Stazione Marittima.** Buses #1, 1/3, and 1/4 head along the port toward Stazione Marittima and up **Corso Stamira** to **Piazza Cavour,** the *centro.* Buy tickets (€1) at *tabaccherie.* For Stazione Marittima, disembark at **Piazza della Repubblica,** walk back toward the water, and turn right on the waterfront. Ancona has no central tourist office, but city info, maps, accommodation listings, and brochures can be found at V. Gramsci 2/A. (☎320 01 96 321. Open May-Oct. daily 10am-1pm and 4-8pm.)

Youth Center: InformaGiovani, C. Garibaldi 111 (☎071 54 958, ext. 8; www.anconagiovane.it). Offers 1hr. free Internet access. No Internet within 30min. of closing. Open M, W, and Sa 10am-12:30pm, Tu and Th-F 10am-12:30pm and 4:30-6:30pm.

Luggage storage: Stazione Marittima. Open daily 8am-8:30pm. €1 per bag per day for 1st 2 days; €2 per bag each day thereafter. Cash only.

Pharmacy: Farmacia Central, C. Mazzini 1 (☎071 20 27 46). Open daily 7:45am-12:30pm and 4:30-11pm. AmEx/MC/V.

Police: ☎071 22 881.

Hospital: Ospedale Regionale Umberto I, V. Conca-Torrette (☎071 59 61).

LE MARCHE

Internet: Informagiovani (see above). Internet cafes crowd the *centro*, charging around €1.50 per 2hr.

Post office: P. XXIV Maggio 2, off P. Cavour (☎071 50 12 260). Open M-F 8am-6:30pm and Sa 8am-12:30pm. **Postal Code:** 60100.

ACCOMMODATIONS

Ostello della Gioventù (HI), V. Lamaticci 7 (☎/fax 071 42 257), from the train station, cross the *piazza* and turn left. Quiet with convenient access to the train station. Clean, spacious rooms with wooden bunk beds. Kind, welcoming staff. Reception 6:30-11am and 4:30pm-midnight. Check-out 9:30am. Lockout 11am-4:30pm, but owner is occasionally flexible. Curfew midnight. Dorms €17. AmEx/MC/V. ❶

Albergo Gino, V. Flaminia 4 (☎/fax 071 42 179, 42 562, or 41 157), on the right side of the *piazza*. Simple, sunny rooms with private bath and TV. Breakfast included. Singles €35; doubles €47; triples €60; quads €80. AmEx/MC/V. ❸

Pensione Euro, C. Mazzini 142 (☎/fax 071 20 34 22). Central location. A cheery hallway leads to modestly furnished but spacious rooms with TV and large windows; most have private bath. Reception 5:30am-midnight. Singles €25; doubles €40-50; triples €60-69. Discount for longer stays. Cash only. ❷

Hotel Roma & Pace, V. G. Leopardi 1 (☎071 20 20 07 or 20 73 743). From P. Roma, turn left onto C. Garibaldi and take the 1st left onto V. Leopardi. With elegant, old-fashioned decor and modern comforts, this 19th-century building contains grandly furnished rooms, all with private bath, TV, A/C, and phone. Breakfast included. Internet access €6 per hr. Singles €59; doubles €95; triples €112; quads €124. AmEx/MC/V. ❹

FOOD

For groceries, hit up **DìperDì,** V. Matteotti 115 (open M-W and F 8:15am-1:30pm and 5-7:35pm, Th 8:15am-1:30pm, Sa 8:15am-1pm and 5-7:40pm. Cash only) or **STANDA,** C. C. Alberto 2, near the station (open daily 8am-9pm).

🍽 **La Cantineta,** V. Gramsci 1 (☎071 20 11 07). Locals crowd tightly packed tables. Don't be deceived by the average-looking exterior—a genial, welcoming staff offers large portions of regional cuisine like *stoccafisso* (cod; €14) or *tacchino* (turkey) *alla milanese* (€5) at reasonable prices. At least among locals, this secret is out—come early or be prepared to wait. Open M and W-Su noon-2:40pm and 7:30pm-midnight, Tu and Th noon-2:40pm. Primi €4-13. Secondi €5-15. Cover €1.50. AmEx/MC/V. ❷

🍽 **Pizzeria Papa,** C. Mazzini 60 (☎339 75 72 238). Smells of baking bread waft from this tiny pizzeria near the water. Pizza (€0.50-1.20; pies €4-5) comes loaded with toppings. A fresh, warm, and cheap favorite among locals. Calzones €1.50. Open daily in summer 9am-2pm and 5-9pm; in winter 10am-2pm and 4-8pm. Cash only. ❶

Roma & Pace, V. G. Leopardi 1 (☎071 52 278). Relaxed but social self-service restaurant. More extensive dinner menu has dishes liked grilled *sardoncini* on a bed of arugula (€9). Pizza €4-7.50. Primi €7. Secondi €9-13. AmEx/MC/V. ❸

Enopolis, C. Mazzini 7 (☎071 20 71 505; www.enopolis.it). Genial staff. Extensive regional and foreign wine selection. Downstairs, a labyrinth of stone hallways houses live music and rotating art exhibits. Organic *menù* features *spaghetti al farro con Adriatic Sarde, brodetto di pesce,* apple tart, and wine (€35). Primi €11. Secondi €16. Cover €2. Wine €5 per glass. Open Tu-Su 9:30am-midnight. AmEx/MC/V. ❹

LE MARCHE

SIGHTS AND BEACHES

Above the city in Piazzale del Duomo stands the ■**Cattedrale di San Ciriaco,** a Romanesque church built above the remains of an early Christian basilica and an even earlier Roman temple to Venus. From P. Cavour, follow C. Mazzini to the port and turn right on V. Gramsci at P. Repubblica. Continue to P. del Senato and climb 247 steps to the cathedral. Look in the basement on the left for the tomb of S. Ciriaco and a rather gruesome view of the body; don't miss the fantastic views of Ancona and the Adriatic. (☎071 52 688. Open daily in summer 8am-noon and 3-7pm; in winter 8am-noon and 3-6pm. Free.) The 16th-century **Palazzo Ferretti** houses Le Marche's foremost archaeological museum, the **Museo Archeologico Nazionale delle Marche,** V. Ferretti 6, an impressive collection including the Ionian Dinos of Amandola, Greek pottery, and jewelry unearthed in the 1900s. From Palazzo Bosdari, continue toward the *duomo*. (☎071 20 26 02. Open Tu-Su 8:30am-7:30pm. €4, ages 18-25 €2, under 18 and over 65 free. Cash only.) From P. Roma, head down C. Garibaldi toward the port. Turn right at P. Repubblica onto V. Gramsci and go straight until you reach Ancona's art gallery, the **Pinacoteca Comunale Francesco Podesti,** in the Palazzo Bosdari, V. Pizzecolli 17. The gallery features works by the Camerte school including Crivelli's *Madonna con Bambino* and Titian's *Apparition of the Virgin*. The top floor features contemporary and 18th- and 19th-century paintings. (☎071 22 25 041. Open in winter Tu-F 9am-7pm, Sa 8:30am-6:30pm, Su 10am-1pm and 4-7pm; from mid-June to mid-Sept. M 9:30am-noon, Tu-Sa 9am-7pm, Su 10am-1pm and 4-7pm.€4.60, ages 16-25 €3.50, under 16 free. Cash only.)

Far from the port's industrial clutter, cool off at the unorthodox **Passetto Beach.** Sunbathers relax on the concrete sidewalk near ladders that drop directly into the sapphire waters. Above the beach, hundreds of stairs lead to the WWII memorial, **Monumento ai Caduti.** (P. IV Novembre. Take bus #1/4 from the station or from P. Cavour along Vle. della Vittoria to the shore. Free.)

> **FIND PASSETTO PASSÉ?** If Passetto Beach doesn't satisfy your cravings for sand, the towns north and south of Ancona have excellent beaches. Ask at the tourist office. Keep in mind that the beaches to the north of Ancona are sandy but have murky water (still clean; just the effect of sand mixing with the water), while beaches to the south are rocky with clear water.

■ NIGHTLIFE

Crowds head to **Piazza Roma** for drinks and many bars and cafes have *aperitivo* buffets in the early evening.

■ **Osteria Teatro Strabacco's,** V. Oberdan 2/2A (☎071 56 748; www.strabacco.it). Since 1978, its motto has been *"fino all'ora del cappucino"*—finish at the cappucino hour—in other words, at breakfast. Eclectic restaurant lined with murals and twinkling lights. With 873 vintages, the snug *osteria* houses an alleged 10,000 bottles. Primi €7-10. Wine €5 per glass. Open Tu-Su noon-3pm and 7:15pm-3am. AmEx/MC/V.

Note di Vino, C. Mazzini 106 (☎393 05 99 972). Extensive wine list. Upbeat music plays at outdoor white tables that overlook a marble fountain. Wine €4-10 per glass. *Aperitivo* buffet starts at 6pm. Open Tu-Su 6pm-midnight. Cash only.

Classi Cafe, C. Mazzini 19 (☎071 20 30 00). Funky music and a hip crowd. Buffet at 6pm. Mixed drinks €6. Beer €3.50-4.50. Open daily 8am-late. Cash only.

ABRUZZO AND MOLISE

The foothills of the Apennine mountains are home to medieval fortresses, Roman rubble, and sprawling wilderness. The people of this region have been shepherds since the Bronze Age, and only in the last half-century has their way of life begun to transform. Millennia-old shepherds' paths weave through the countryside, and the villages sustain a sleepy lifestyle largely similar to that of their ancestors. About two hours from the Eternal City and still predominantly untouched by tourism, these highlands offer natural beauty and a unique retreat from bustling urban life. A single region until they split in 1963, Abruzzo (ah-BROOTS-oh) and Molise (mo-LEEZ-eh) lie at the juncture of Northern and Southern Italy. Abruzzo offers crystal lakes, lush pines, and unique wildlife, especially in its national park. The smaller Molise, inhabited long ago by Samnite highlanders, is home to wondrous ruins, medieval festivals, and especially flavorful food. These regions may not fit in with the stereotypical image of Italy, but if you seek an unexpected twist on *la dolce vita*, look no farther.

HIGHLIGHTS OF ABRUZZO AND MOLISE

GLIMPSE herds of wild horses on the Gran Sasso d'Italia (p. 377).

EXPLORE Ovid's homeland of Sulmona (p. 378).

SET UP CAMP in Abruzzo National Park after an arduous day of hiking (p. 380).

L'AQUILA ☎0862

As the story goes, in 1254, 99 lords from 99 castles banded together to erect L'Aquila ("The Eagle"; LA-kwee-la; pop. 65,000), Abruzzo's capital. Some historians claim the city plan mimics that of Jerusalem, perhaps a result of Frederick II's desire to create a new seat for Catholic Christianity following the decline of Rome. Dubbed the "Salzburg of the South," this city has rediscovered its charm, echoing its glory days now that over 40,000 students crowd its streets and hikers ascend its nearby mountains.

TRANSPORTATION

The train station (☎0862 41 92 90) is on the outskirts of town. (Ticket office ☎0862 41 28 08. Open M-Sa 6:15am-8:15pm, Su 7am-2pm.) **Trains** go to Sulmona (1hr., 11 per day 6:23am-8:47pm, €4.50) and Terni (2hr., 11 per day 6:15am-8:04pm, €6). L'Aquila has two **bus** systems: blue ARPA regional buses and orange municipal buses. ARPA buses (☎0862 199 166 952) stop at the station near P. Duomo and go to: Avezzano (50min., M-Sa 38 per day 5:50am-8:30pm, €4.90); Pescara (1hr., M-Sa 20 per day 6am-9:10pm, €7.50); Rome (1hr., M-Sa 33 per day 4:40am-8pm, €9.10); Sulmona (40min., M-Sa 6 per day 6:20am-7:15pm, €4.50). The yellow **municipal buses** stop at AMA markers and serve surrounding towns and sights. (☎0862 31 98 57; www.ama.laquila.

ABRUZZO AND MOLISE

it. One-way €0.90, 1hr. €1.10, 1-day pass €2.10.) Tickets are available at *tabaccherie*, newsstands, bars, and the bus station, past P. del Collemaggio on V. Giacomo Caldora. A subway runs from the station to P. del Duomo. Find **taxis** (☎0862 22 115) at the bus station.

⬥ 🔃 ORIENTATION AND PRACTICAL INFORMATION

Take bus #M11, 5, or 8 from the train station to **Via XX Settembre** to reach the *centro*. On foot, follow signs to *"Fontana delle 99 Cannelle"* to the right and hike 2km uphill. C. Federico II becomes **Corso Vittorio Emanuele II**, the main street which stretches between **Piazza del Duomo**, the heart of L'Aquila's *centro storico*, in the south, and the **Castello Cinquecentesco** and the **Fontana Luminosa** in the north. Beyond P. del Duomo, the street continues as Corso Federico II until reaching the gardens of the **Villa Comunale** and **Via XX Settembre**. Pick up a map at the tourist office; L'Aquila's often unlabeled streets are difficult to navigate.

Tourist Office: APT, V. XX Settembre 8 (☎0862 22 306). Stocks free maps. Open M-Sa 9am-1pm and 3-6pm, Su 9am-1pm. There is also an office in the front of P. del Duomo, (☎0862 23 021; www.centrostorico.laquila.it). Open daily 10am-9pm.

Police: at V. del Beato Cesidio.

Pharmacy: right next to the *duomo*. Open 9am-1pm and 4:30-8pm.

Internet Access: Duomo.net, V. Cimino 25. Opposite the *duomo* on the *piazza*. Open M-Sa 9am-10pm, Su 4pm-10pm. Internet €3 per hr., students and over 65 €2.50.

Post Office: in P. del Duomo (☎0862 63 71). Exchanges currency. Open M-F 8am-6:30pm, Sa 8am-12:30pm. **Postal Code:** 67100.

ACCOMMODATIONS

Centro Spiritualita Sant'Agostino, V. Tre Spighe 9 (☎347 490 5672). From P. Duomo, take C. V. Emanuele to the Fontana Luminosa, and turn left on V. Tre Spighe. The monastery was built in 1375, but guests stay in a modern building with a garden, TV and reading room, and communal kitchen. Breakfast included. €25 per person. Cash only. ❷

Casa Ospitalita' San Giuseppe, P. Pasquale Paoli 12 (☎0862 42 05 66 or 41 07 55). Offers similar accommodations to the Centro Spiritualita Sant'Agostino. €25-30 per person. Reservations required. Cash only. ❷

Porto Rivera Hostel, Ple. della Stazione 27 (☎0862 29 56 85; www.portariverahostel. it). Clean, well-lit rooms have full bath, phone, TV, and minibar. Wheelchair-accessible. Breakfast included. Singles €40; doubles €55; triples €74; quads €87. MC/V. ❸

Bed and Breakfast "da Charlie," V. Monte Brancastello 22 (☎347 85 97 938). A 10min. ride on bus #79 or 81 from La Fontana Luminosa to "Cianfrano". Named after the owner's dog. Offers clean rooms and cheap food with a great city view. Breakfast included. Reservations required. Singles €25; doubles €40-45. ❷

FOOD

Find everything from fresh fruit and cured meats to clothes at the busy **market** in P. del Duomo. (Open M-Sa 8am-noon.) A **STANDA supermarket,** C. Federico II 1, is two blocks from V. XX Settembre. Enter at the corner of V. Monteguelfi and V. Sant'Agostino. (☎0862 26 482. Open M-Sa 8am-9pm. AmEx/MC/V.)

La Stella Alpina, V. Crispomonti 19 (☎0862 41 31 90). 2nd to none. Lunch special (€7) buys pizza and a drink. Primi €5-7. Open Tu-Su noon-3pm and 7:30-midnight. ❶

Darkover, V. dell'Arcivescovado 17 (☎0862 40 60 20). The cool, maze-like interior is decorated with mythical Chinese characters, but Darkover maintains its Italian flavor. Try the specialty, *arrosticini* (lamb kebab; €5). Pizza €4-8. Open daily 7:30-midnight. ❷

L'Insalata Ricca, C.V. Emanuele 81 (☎0862 26 642; www.linsalataricca.it). Nearly 50 fresh, unique salads (€4-7.50). A nightly grand buffet (€7) is serves typical *abruzzese* produce. Antipasti €3-7. Primi €5.50-7. Secondi €8-16. MC/V. ❶

SIGHTS

BASILICA DI SANTA MARIA DI COLLEMAGGIO. At the request of Pietro da Marrone (later Pope and Saint Celestine V), L'Aquila began constructing this church in 1287. The pink-and-white checkered facade is the symbol of the Knights Templar, a group with origins in medieval times that is now linked to the Freemasons. Notice the number eight and the serpent made by circles on the floor design, both Templar symbols. Despite its controversial cross, the basilica's claim to fame is its **Holy Door**—the first of only seven in the world. The door is opened only once a year on August 28th; those who walk through it are said to have their sins absolved. *(From P. del Duomo, take C. Federico I past V. XX Settembre or the tram to the bus station and turn left onto V. di Collemaggio after Villa Comunale. Open in summer daily 8am-12:30pm and 3-8pm; in winter hours vary. Modest dress required. Free.)*

CHIESA DI SAN BERNARDINO. Built in 1454 and restored after an earthquake in 1703, San Bernardino peers over the mountains south of L'Aquila. The interior boasts four beautiful ceiling paintings and the tomb of San Bernardino, complete with a Templar cross. Years ago, schoolchildren from the saint's hometown of Siena would make a pilgrimage to L'Aquila on May 20 to bring oil to light the lamp in front of the church's mausoleum for the rest of the year. *(To reach both the stairway and the church, walk down V. S. Bernardino from C. V. Emanuele II. Open daily 7:30am-noon and 3:30-8pm. Modest dress required. Free.)*

CASTELLO CINQUECENTESCO. In the 16th century, Spanish viceroy Don Pedro da Toledo built the castle at the end of C. V. Emanuele II, to defend himself against the rebelling *aquilesi*. Never attacked, the *castello* is more active today in its role as the **Museo Nazionale di Abruzzo,** showcasing Roman sarcophagi, Renaissance tapestries, and a million-year-old mammoth skeleton, discovered locally in 1954. *(Located at V. Colecchi 1. ☎0862 63 31; www.psaelaquila.it. Open Tu-Su 8:30am-7:30pm. €4; ages 18-25 €2; EU university students, under 18, and over 65 free.)*

🏞 DAYTRIPS FROM L'AQUILA

GRAN SASSO D'ITALIA. The snow-capped Gran Sasso d'Italia ("The Rock of Italy"), the highest mountain ridge within Italy's borders, looms 12km north of L'Aquila. Take a funicular midway up the Sasso (and above the tree line) to a flat plain, **Campo Imperatore,** home to herds of wild horses, shepherds, never-ending landscapes, and a hotel built to imprison Mussolini. On a clear day, you can see both of Italy's coasts from the **Corno Grande,** the highest peak in the range at 2912m. The trail map (€8), available at the Club Alpino Italiano, newsstands in town, and at the base of the mountain, is useful for planning hikes. *Sentieri* (paths) are marked by difficulty, and only the more taxing routes reach the top. The peaks are snowy from September to June, when only experienced mountaineers should venture all the way up. In winter, Gran Sasso teems with **skiers.** The trails around the funicular are among the most difficult, offering one 4000m and several 1000m drops. Ten trails descend from the funicular and the two lifts. Purchase a weekly pass at the *biglietteria* at the base of the funicular. **Campo Felice,** at nearby Monte Rotondo, has 16 lifts, numerous trails of varying difficulty, and a ski school. *(In summer a funicular ascends the 1008m to Campo Imperatore, making Sasso an easy afternoon excursion from L'Aquila, although driving offers a far more picturesque ride than the 10min. funicular. The funicular is closed during parts of June and Oct. ☎0862 60 61 43. Every hr. 8:30am-5pm, €7. Trails start at the upper funicular station. Contact Club Alpino Italiano at ☎0862 24 342 or www.cai.it for current conditions. For info on mountain guides, inquire at the tourist office or Club Alpino Italiano. To reach Campo Felice from L'Aquila, take yellow bus #76 or blue shuttle M6 from the bus station. 30min., 12 per day, €1. Buy tickets at tabaccherie or the station. For ski info, contact Campo Felice at ☎0862 60 61 43. Lift tickets €14-25. Ski rentals around €10.)*

OTHER DAYTRIPS. If skiing is not on your itinerary, **ARPA buses** run to centuries-old towns within 50km of L'Aquila. Ask at the bus station for the most up-to-date schedules. Buses to Castel del Monte (40km, €3.50) stop in medieval towns like Santo Steffano di Sessanio (25km), where the Medici family built an economic stronghold for wool trade in the 15th century. Their legacy is manifested in the grand **Torre Medicea** that still stands today in Santo Steffano. The same bus also stops in Calascio (30km), where the millenary Norman castle **La Rocca Calascio** stands at an altitude of 1500m. Take AMA buses to the town of Stiffe and gaze at the stalactite-filled **Grotte di Stiffe.** *(☎0862 86 142; www.grottestiffe. it. Open 10am-1pm and 3-6pm. Complex has two museums, picnic grounds, and a bathing area on Lago di Sinizzo.)* Buses to San Vittorino (7km west) take you near the **Sitio Amiternum,** an archaeological site with a first-century Roman theatre. AMA Bus #16 goes to Fossa, where you can walk through a necropolis. Near Campo Felice is

ABRUZZO
AND MOLISE

Rocca di Mezzo, the town with the greatest number of hotels and restaurants in the **Sirente Velino Regional Park**. A park information office is found here at the Piazza dell'Oratorio. (*☎0862 91 61 25; www.parcosirentevelino.it.*)

SULMONA ☎0864

Hidden deep in Abruzzo's Peligna Valley, medieval Sulmona (sool-MO-nah; pop. 26,000) is encircled by the hulking Apennines. The charming inhabitants of this small town churn out *confetti* (Sulmona's signature candy) and profess pride in their famous native son, the poet Ovid (43 BC-AD 17). The letters "SMPE," adorned on Sulmona's streets and inscribed on its buildings, are shorthand for the poet's famous proclamation, *"Sulmo mihi patria est"* ("Sulmona is my homeland"). A stroll around the public gardens, a hike in the surrounding mountains, or an amble through nearby hamlets are excellent afternoon diversions when the town shuts down for *siesta*.

▐ TRANSPORTATION

Trains: Station (☎0864 34 293), 2km outside the city, 30min. by foot from the *centro*. Serves Rome-Pescara and Carpione-L'Aquila-Terni lines. To: **Avezzano** (1hr., 3 per day 6:30am-2:03pm, €3.50); **L'Aquila** (1hr., 7 per day 6:54am-8:45pm, €3.40); **Naples** (4hr., 4 per day 6:32am-3:44pm, €14-16); **Pescara** (1hr., 15 per day 6:23am-9:30pm, €3.40); **Rome** (1-2hr., 7 per day 5:55am-8:10pm, €7-12). Bus A (5:30am-9:30pm, €0.70) runs from the *centro*. Return bus departs from the public gardens.

Buses: ARPA (☎0864 20 91 33) runs from its main stop at the hospital past Porta Napoli to Castel di Sangro in Abruzzo National Park (1hr.; 10 per day 6:40am-6:10pm, reduced service Su; €4, buy ticket on bus).

Taxis: ☎0864 31 747 from the *centro* or ☎0864 31 446 from the train station.

✈ 🛈 ORIENTATION AND PRACTICAL INFORMATION

Viale Stazione runs from the train station to Sulmona proper (2km). In town, it becomes **Viale Roosevelt** and continues past the public gardens where it becomes **Corso Ovidio**, the main thoroughfare. C. Ovidio runs past **Piazza XX Settembre** (with the statue of Ovid), and **Piazza Garibaldi** (with the medieval aqueduct), and then exits the *centro storico* through **Porta Napoli**. From P. XX Settembre, the northbound **Via de Nino** becomes **Via Giovanni Pansa** as it reaches the **Ponte Capograssi**.

Tourist Office: APT tourist office, C. Ovidio 208 (☎/fax 0864 53 276). Multilingual staff. Free city maps and hotel, B&B, and restaurant listings. Club Italiano Alpino maps (€5-7) and guided **tours** of the countryside. Open M-Sa 9am-1pm and 4-7pm, Su 9am-1pm. **UST tourist office**, across the street in Palazzo dell'Annunziata (☎0864 21 02 16; www.comune.sulmona.aq.it). Helpful English-speaking staff. Detailed hiking info, train and bus schedules, Club Alpino Italiano maps, free city maps, and references for local mountain guides. Open daily 9am-1:30pm and 4-8pm.

Police: ☎0864 35 661.

Internet: .COM, C. Ovidio 90 (☎0864 56 491). €3 per hr. Open daily 9am-1pm and 4-8pm.

Post Office: in P. Brigata Maiella (☎0864 62 47 292). **ATM** available. Open M-F 8am-6:30pm, Sa 8am-12:30pm. **Postal Code:** 67039.

🎿 ACCOMMODATIONS

Hotel Italia, P. Salvatore Tommasi 3 (☎0864 52 308). Family-run, vine-covered former *palazzo*. Medieval-inspired ambiance. 27 antique-filled rooms, some with balconies and mountain views. Singles €25, with bath €33; doubles €43/54. Cash only. ❷

Bed and Breakfast "La Dimora", C. Ovidio 238 (☎0864 95 02 98; www.bandbladimora.com). Well located 15th-century *palazzo*. 4 rooms on 3rd floor come with A/C, free Wi-Fi, and breakfast. Owner Oscar is eager to help trekkers arrange tours or plan excursions in Abruzzo. One of Sulmona's best. Singles €30-40; doubles €60-90; triples €80-110. Cash only. ❸

Albergo Stella, V. Panfilo Mazara 18 (☎0864 52 653; www.hasr.it), off C. Ovidio. Service-oriented staff and spacious, pleasantly decorated rooms with bath, phone, and TV. *Enoteca* connected to the restaurant. Breakfast included. Free Internet access. Singles €40-50; doubles €70-80. AmEx/MC/V. ❹

🍴 FOOD

Before the *confetti* after party, you'll need something substantive; don't worry, Sulmona doesn't disappoint in this area either. A morning **market** takes place in P. Garibaldi (W and Sa). Buy basics at the **CONAD supermarket** on V. Papa Giovanni XXIII, 22. (Turn right after crossing Ponte Capograssi. Open 8am-8:30pm. MC/V.)

Ristorante Al Quadrivio, V. Odorisio 4 (☎0864 55 533), off V. Panfilo Mazara. The best-kept secret for traditional *Abruzzese* cuisine. Try the *budino ubriaco* (bread pudding soaked in *ratafia* liqueur; €2.50). Handmade pasta €6. Primi €6. Secondi from €7. Open M-Sa 7:30-11pm, Su noon-3pm and 7:30-11pm. MC/V. ❷

Hostaria dell'Arco, V. D'Eramo, 58 (☎0864 21 05 53). For a relaxed, intimate experience, head to the cheapest restaurant in town that still offers quality, traditional dishes. The lamb (€7) is delicious. Vegetable antipasti buffet €8. Dessert €2-3. Open M-Sa 1-2:30pm and 8-11:30pm, Su 1-2:30pm. AmEx/MC/V. ❷

👁 SIGHTS

CATTEDRALE DI SAN PANFILO. The center of this Romanesque-Gothic church was built 1000 years ago on the ruins of a temple dedicated to Apollo and Vesta. Its crypt contains 14th-century frescoes. *(At the end of the Villa Communale.)*

CHIESA DELLA SANTISSIMA ANNUNZIATA. Adjacent to the cherub-decorated church, a 15th-cen-

NO WORK, ALL PLAY

ONE INDULGENT KNIGHT

While the Giostra Cavalleresca (see next page) is easily Sulmona's claim to fame, the weeks leading up to the joust have their "fare" share of traditional treats as well. The weekend before, the town celebrates La Panarda, a 24-course feast featuring typical *abbruzese* cuisine and an endless flow of local wine.

When the sun sets over a decorated *piazza*, guests are invited to unbuckle their belts and enjoy their *portate* (dishes), surrounded by Renaissance entertainment. Flag shows, dances, and live music accompany the seemingly interminable banquet. As the night progresses, waiters in costume serve a bounty of seasonal fruits, cold cuts, Pecorino cheese, hearty soups, handmade pastas, and succulent roasted lamb.

In antiquity, such joyous feasts were held in honor of good harvests and weddings. Recently, Panarde-goers have indulged in as many as 77 *portate*. The eating pace is always slow and each dish is more delectable than the previous. Skip lunch and bring the whole family—this feast typically lasts from 8pm-2am and is enough to feed an entire cavalry.

Contact Associazione Cultural Sestiere Porta Manaresca (☎ 348 92 36 896) or the Sulmona UST tourist office (☎/fax 0864 53 276). Reservations recommended 1 month ahead. Banquet €45.

tury Gothic *palazzo* houses the UST tourist office (p. 378) and a very small **museum** presenting rare local Renaissance goldwork. There is also a collection of wood statues from local churches. *(From the public gardens, follow C. Ovidio to the church.* ☎ *0864 21 27 11. Open July-Aug. Tu-F 9am-1pm, Sa-Su 6-8:30pm and 9:30-11pm; Sept.-June Tu-Sa 9am-1pm. €1.)*

PIAZZA GARIBALDI. The colossal *piazza* surrounds Renaissance-era **Fontana del Vecchio**, which flows with mountain water channeled from a nearby **medieval aqueduct** that is still intact. With the towering Apennines as its backdrop, P. Garibaldi is a favorite hangout, particularly in the evening.

PELINO FACTORY. When you feel the *confetti*-induced sugar-high start to wear off, replenish your supply of these colored, sugar-coated almonds right from the source. The Pelino family has been making *confetti* since 1783 with traditional machinery; some of it is displayed in the free museum. The candy's universal appeal is evident in pictures of St. Pio and prior popes eating *confetti* shaped like religious icons. *(V. Stazione Introdaqua 55. Turn right after Porta Napoli onto V. Trieste, continue 1km down the hill as it becomes V. Stazione Introdaqua, and enter the Pelino building on the left.* ☎ *0864 21 00 47; www.pelino.it. Open M-Sa 8am-12:15pm and 3-6:30pm.)*

🎇 FESTIVALS

The city itself dons medieval garb during the last week of July for the **Giostra Cavalleresca di Sulmona,** when beacon-bearing knights ride figure-eights around P. Garibaldi. Each knight's crest represents one of the seven *borghi* (neighborhoods) of medieval Sulmona. Purchase a seated ticket (€5-12) from the ticket office (☎0864 340 51 846 26; open daily 10am-12:30pm and 5-8pm) in the Rotunda San Francesco, off P. Garibaldi, or stand on tip-toe in the crowd to watch for free. In preparation for the big event, the *borghi* host public festivals on June weekends. The first weekend of August brings the **Giostra Cavalleresca di Europa,** which features international knights (tickets €3-8).

🏔 HIKING

The mountains of **Majella National Park** (also spelled "Maiella") tower over Sulmona. The park's headquarters (☎0871 40 851) are in **Guardiagrele.** From the *centro,* several trails are easily accessible by ARPA bus or on foot. The Sulmona tourist offices have info on the capricious bus schedules; keep mid-afternoon service gaps in mind. High on the cliffs, visit the cave retreat of the saintly hermit who became Pope Celestine V, the only pope to renounce his post. It's a fairly easy hike (round-trip 1hr.) from the town of Badia, which is accessible by bus from Sulmona's public gardens (20min.; 11 per day 7:35am-7:40pm, reduced service Sa-Su; €1, purchase tickets at *tabaccherie*). Several longer routes can be reached from Campo di Giove, accessible by bus from Sulmona (25min.; 4 per day 6:30am-6pm, reduced service Sa-Su; €2.20). For hiking info, consult the UST tourist office (p. 378) and the **Club Alpino Italiano** (☎0842 10 635) for maps (€5-7). The difficulty levels in the Club Alpino Italiano guide refer to mountaineering experience, not hiking experience—so hikes of "moderate difficulty" may be challenging for those not used to mountain climbing. Take advantage of buses since trailheads are tough to find on foot; ask the driver to let you off directly at the trailhead.

ABRUZZO NATIONAL PARK

Parco Nazionale d'Abruzzo, Lazio, e Molise contains the highest peaks in the Apennines, which provide spectacular views of lush woodlands and crystal-clear lakes as frigid as they are pristine. The park's 44,000 hectares bristle with wildlife. Grazing horses, white *abruzzese* sheep-dog packs, herds of *chamois* (hoofed, goat-like animals with horns), and aloof *marsicano* brown bears are the current proprietors of abandoned castles and pre-Roman ruins. This immaculate refuge is interrupted by only five towns: Barrea, Civitella Alfedena, Opi, Pescasseroli, and Villetta Barrea. Enter the park from Castel di Sangro in the south, or from Avezzano in the northeast. Pescasseroli, the park's administrative center and largest town, provides the best base for exploration. The other four towns are tiny and a bit uneventful—especially Barrea and Civitella Alfedena—but this does not detract from their beauty. Though the wild creatures and landscapes are diverse, the park's human inhabitants are unified in their unfailing warmth and generosity.

TRANSPORTATION AND PRACTICAL INFORMATION

Trains run from Avezzano to Pescara (2-3hr., 7 per day 6:13am-8:10pm, €6.90), Rome (2hr., 13 per day 4am-8:50pm, €6), and Sulmona (1hr., 10 per day 6:13am-8:10pm, €3.90). An ARPA **bus** (☎0863 26 561 or 0863 22 921) runs from Avezzano through the park to Castel di Sangro on the other side (2hr., M-Sa 5 per day 6:40am- 7pm, €5.20), making five stops en route: Pescasseroli (1hr., €3.90); Opi (1hr., €4.20); Villetta Barrea (2hr., €4.20); Civitella Alfedena (2hr., €4.20); Barrea (2hr., €4.40). Buses also run to Pescasseroli from Rome (3hr., 7:45am, one-way €14). All services are reduced or nonexistent on Sunday.

AVEZZANO
Conveniently located on the edge of the park, Avezzano is well-positioned near train stations serving other regions and bus stations serving the park. The **post office** is next to the train station. (Open M-F 8am-1:30pm, Sa 8:30am-12:30pm.)

PESCASSEROLI

Tourist Office: Centro Accoglienza Turistici, Vico Consultore 1 (☎0863 91 13 242; www.parcoabruzzo.it). Essential park map €6. Open daily 10am-1pm and 3-7pm.

Police: ☎0863 91 07 16.

State Forest Division: Call ☎1515 in case of an environmental emergency.

Bank: next to IAT (☎0863 91 951). Open M-F 8:25am-1:25pm and 2:40-4:10pm.

Pharmacy: Farmacia del Parco, P. V. Emanuele 12 (☎0863 91 07 53). Posts a 24hr. rotation. Open M-W and F-Su 9am-1pm and 4:30-8pm.

Guardia Medica: ☎0863 91 06 75.

Internet Access: Punto Internet is at I Traversa di Fiume Sangro 6 (☎0863 91 10 64). €2.50 per 30min., €4 per hr. Open daily 9:30am-1pm and 4-8pm.

Post Office: V. Piave 1/A (☎0863 91 07 31), in front of the IAT office. Open M-F 8am-1:30pm, Sa 8am-noon. **Postal Code:** 67032.

ACCOMMODATIONS AND CAMPING

PESCASSEROLI
Abruzzo National Park's largest and most popular town, tranquil Pescasseroli (PES-ca-SE-ro-lee; pop. 2212) is a convenient base for exploring the rest of the park. Solo travelers may have a hard time finding a single, as establishments generally only offer double rooms, especially in August; bring friends or come ready to camp. Inquire at the IAT office about *affittacamere* (rooms for rent).

▨ **Di Clemente Elena,** V. Isonzo 2 (☎0863 91 05 06). Welcoming Elena offers blonde wood rooms with bath, TV, and hand-stitched quilts. Singles €20-30; doubles €36-60; triples €50-80; quads €55-90. Cash only. ❷

Il Piccolo Principe, Vle. Principe di Napoli 43/a (☎0863 91 753), visible from the IAT office. Family-run. 10 clean, simple rooms with TV. Terrace is perfect for sunbathing. Singles €35; doubles €45-70; triples €60-90. No singles in Aug. Cash only. ❸

Campeggio dell'Orso, (☎0863 91 95 or 339 76 43 656), 1km from Pescasseroli on the road to Opi. Friendly, English-speaking Geraldo maintains quiet, family-oriented grounds. A good base for hikes. Some houses with hostel beads and kitchen available. Bring linens. €8.50 per person, €4 per child ages 5-10. Hostel bed €12. Cash only. ❶

BARREA

Entering from the south makes Barrea (bah-REH-ah; pop. 769) the first breath-taking highlight of Abruzzo National Park. Known as "the pearl" of the Park for its picturesque location on **Lago di Barrea,** its historic streets meander down the steep mountainside before slowly giving way to forest in the valleys below.

Ostello dagli Elfi, V. Leonardo di Loreto 54 (☎0864 88 408; www.albergodaglielfi.it). Breakfast area overlooks Lago di Barrea at the cheapest option in town. Staff organizes excursions in the park. Internet access available. Open year-round. Dorms €15, with breakfast €18; singles €25/27; doubles €40/45; triples €55/65; quads €70/80. ❶

Camping "La Genziana", (☎0864 88 101; www.pasetta.it), less than 1km from Ostello dagli Elfi, on the way to Castel di Sangro. Within sight of the K trailhead. Owned and operated by famous K2-Pakistan climber T.D. Pasetta. €7.20 per person, €3 per child; €8 per tent; €3 per car. Hot showers €1. Open year-round. ❶

◪ FOOD

PESCASSEROLI

Though small, the town of Pescasseroli packs a culinary punch. Be sure to sample assorted sweets in the town's many excellent pastry shops. A **supermarket** is at the start of Vle. San Lucia, to the left when walking into the city. (Open daily noon-2pm and 4-8pm.)

▨ **La Dolceria dell'Orso,** V. Valle Cicala 5c (☎340 14 34 303). Sample a boundless supply of free almond-, chocolate-, and honey-laden samples from the tiny shop's friendly owner. Open M, W, and F-Su 9am-1pm and 3-8pm; Tu and Th 3-8pm. Cash only. ❶

da Giuseppe, IX Traversa Sangro 3 (☎0863 91 22 05). Always packed. Primi €5-7. Open M-W and F-Su 12:30-2:30pm and 7:30-9:30pm. ❷

Picchio, V. Lungo Sangro. Walk from P. Vittorio Emanuele through V. Traversa Sangro. to this spacious pizzeria. Meat is cooked on a traditional log grill. Pizza €3-6. Primi €6-8. Secondi €5-14. Open M, Tu and Th-Su 12:15-3pm and 7-10pm. MC/V. ❷

BARREA

Al Borgo Antico, V. Stratta (☎338 947 0784). Follow your nose to the fully-loaded pizzas (€3-6) and attentive servers at this small local establishment. Primi €6. Secondi €3.50-7. Open Tu-Su 12:30-3pm and 7:30pm-midnight. Cash only. ❶

Ristorante Tana dell'Orso, V. Duca degli Abruzzo 66 (☎0864 88 125). A town staple since 1962. Serves fair portions of house-made *gnocchetti* (€6) in a quiet setting. Primi €6. Secondi €5-9. Open daily 12:30-2:30pm and 8-10:30pm. AmEx/MC/V. ❷

Bar Centrale, V. Duca degli Abruzzo 23 (☎0864 88 405). Local crowds and late-night fun. Beer €2. Mixed drinks €3-4. Open daily 7am-midnight. Cash only. ❶

NOT TO BE CONFUSED WITH. Remember that Barrea and Villetta Barrea are 2 different locations separated by 10km; Civitella Alfedena and Alfedena are also different. Before setting out from Pescasseroli, verify with the bus driver the correct stop for your intended destination. From Avezzano, Civitella comes before Alfedena, just 10min. after Villetta Barrea.

HIKING, SIGHTS, AND OUTDOOR ACTIVITIES

The ascent from Avezzano to Pescasseroli is breathtaking; this trail, which marks the beginning of the park, passes by fields of poppies, fertile valleys, and rocky outcrops. The indispensable trail map (€6) from the **Centro Accoglienza Turistici** in Pescasseroli (see **Practical Information,** p. 381) indicates prime stakeout points for catching a glimpse of bears, deer, wolves, and eagles. The park teems with trails, but bear in mind that due to the sheer number of paths, even a map can't always keep you from getting lost. This overview of hikes should not be counted as a map substitute. Be sure to consult professionals who know the area before setting off. Clever coordination of hikes with the ARPA bus schedule can enable hikers to embark from any of the park's major towns.

From Pescasseroli, the short trail **BN1** passes castle ruins at **Monte Ceraso** (50min.; moderate difficulty), or the 5hr. round-trip **C3** takes you on a hike of medium-difficulty to the beautiful **Valico di Monte Tranquillo** (1673m). From Opi, the **FN1** trail (50min.) takes you through the highly-praised **Val del Fondillo.** True adventurers starting from Opi can take on one of the park's highest peaks, **Monte Marsicano** (2245m), with the steep and arduous **E6** trail (7-8hr. round-trip). From Civitella Alfedena, explore the **G** trails (about 1hr.; varying difficulties), which pass by **Camosciara,** or take the **I1** (3hr.; difficult) to **K6** (3hr.; difficult) through the beautiful **Valle di Rose** to see the park's largest herd of chamois. K6 is one of the more difficult trails deep into the Valle di Rose, yet it makes for a leisurely hike from Barrea to the Valle Iannanghera (1hr.; easy), where it meets trails **J2** to return by the lakeshore to Barrea (1hr.; easy) and **I4** (1hr.; easy) to hike to Civitella Alfedena. From June to early September, this area can only be explored with a guide (€8-10 per person). Go to an *ufficio di zona* the day before a planned excursion for more info about the trails or to obtain a permit and reserve a guide. From Barrea, the **K5** trail (4hr. round-trip) runs through a forested valley to the **Lago Vivo,** which dries up from June to October.

If the park's creatures prove elusive, check out Pescasseroli's family-friendly **Centro di Visita,** Vle. Colle dell'Orso 2, off V. S. Lucia, heading toward Opi, which has a museum and a small zoo. (☎0863 91 131. Open daily 10am-1pm and 3-7pm. €6, children €4.) **Ecotur,** V. Piave 7, second floor., in Pescasseroli, offers organized excursions throughout the park, many of which include wildlife viewing. (☎0863 91 27 60; www.ecotur.org. Hikes €10. Wolf-watching €20. Bear-watching €50. Open daily 9am-1pm and 4-7:30pm; closed Su in winter.) Antonucci in Civitella Alfedena, organizes hikes of the G trails, mountain bike trips, and horseback rides. (☎0864 89 01 35;www.camosciara.com). Fishing in Lago di Barrea is restricted. Obtain a license (€10 per day) or inquire about seasonal subscriptions at the **Centro Operativo Servizio Educazione** in Villetta Barrea (☎0864 89 102. Open M-Sa.) In winter, this area offers excellent downhill skiing and snowboarding, with challenging slopes and heavy snowfall. Package deals called *Settimane Bianche* (White Weeks) provide accommodations, lift tickets, and half pension. For ticket info, call **Gestione Impianti Sportivi Pescasseroli** (☎0863 91 11 18). For the snow bulletin, call ☎0862 66 510. Pescasseroli's website (www.pescasseroli.net) has winter sports info.

Award Winning Hostel in the center of Naples

hostelofthesun
napolinaplesitaly

beds from € 16.00

Hostel of the Sun offer:
Full kitchen - Free breakfast
24hrs reception - No curfew - Free lockers
Hot showers - English speaking staff
Free luggage storage - Tourist information
Free Internet - Free wifi - Lounge room
Free maps - Satellite tv - Dvd room
Laundry service

Hostel of the Sun is perfectly located in the center of Naples. It is in a safe area of the city and is a comfortable, clean and very welcoming base for your stay in Naples. Just across the street from the bus stop to **Pompeii**, **Amalfi** coast and the ferry port to the islands of **Capri** and **Ischia**, HOTS is conveniently located for day trips as well as visits to some of the main sights in the city itself, and of course to try the famous Napoletan pizza!

for info: **Hostel of the Sun**
via Melisurgo, 15
80133 Napoli - Italy
phone and fax:
081 420 63 93
(from anywhere in Italy)
0039 081 420 63 93
(from anywhere outside Italy)

for reservation and info:
www.hostelnapoli.com

How to get to Hostel of the Sun:

If you're coming in on the train, either refer to the map and walk (20 minutes) or catch the bus. Take the R2 bus from Piazza Garibaldi just outside the train station. The bus leaves from the middle of the square, and you can buy tickets from any Tabacchi shop. Once on board the bus, get off at the 7th stop, which is the second stop on 'Via Depretis'. Cross the street and take the street just to the left of the Hotel Mercure, 'Via Melisurgo'. We are number 15, on your left, just give us a buzz and come up!

VIA DUOMO
R2 BUS
PZZA N. AMORE
CORSO UMBERTO
PIAZZA GARIBALDI
C.SO GARIBALDI
R2 BUS
VIA SANFELICE
PZZA BOVIO
CORSO UMBERTO
R2 BUS
DE PRETIS
VIA DE GASPERI
BUS R2 STOP HERE
PIAZZA MUNICIPIO
VIA MELISURGO
SITA BUS TO POMPEII AND AMALFI COAST
VIA C. COLOMBO
Alibus
ALIBUS TO THE AIRPORT
PORT FOR FERRIES TO CAPRI, ISCHIA, AMALFI SORRENTO, SICILY
CASTEL NUOVO
2009

CAMPANIA

Campania (cam-PAH-nee-ah) is a land of contrasts, where a chaotic, modern city, a wealth of remarkably preserved Roman ruins, and a coastline of peaceful villages all coexist. The beautiful *centro storico* in Naples draws visitors to the area, and the nearby islands' emerald waters embrace them when the city's frenetic disorder overwhelms. Nearby, the preserved ancient cities of Pompeii and Herculaneum attest to the destructive power of Mt. Vesuvius, which remains a constant—and yes, very active—threat. One of Italy's poorest regions, Campania has withstood natural disasters and foreign invasions, but its people have managed to cultivate and sustain a unique, carefree attitude—the region's true treasure.

HIGHLIGHTS OF CAMPANIA

DESCEND underneath the city of Naples to tour catacombs and aqueducts (p. 397).

PEER into the crater of Mt. Vesuvius, mainland Europe's only active volcano (p. 402).

SIP *granita* or *limoncello* in the shade of Amalfi's lemon groves (p. 414).

NAPLES (NAPOLI) ☎081

From zipping Vespas to bustling crowds, Naples (NAH-po-lee; pop. 1,000,000) rarely rests. Neapolitans spend every waking moment out on the town, eating, drinking, carousing, and laughing. Surrounded by the ancient ruins of Pompeii and the gorgeous Amalfi Coast, Naples—Italy's third-largest city—is the anchor of Campania. The city has a reputation for crime and grime, but on the bright side, UNESCO recently declared its historical center the most architecturally varied in the world. As the birthplace of pizza and home of tantalizing seafood and pasta, Naples is world-renowned for culinary delights. Whereas Milan flaunts sophistication and Venice emanates mystique, Naples wallows in cheerful chaos. This is a city with personality that doesn't tolerate ambivalence—either you can't stand it or you can't get enough.

☒ INTERCITY TRANSPORTATION

To get to Naples from Rome, hop on a Trenitalia train. Departures from Stazione Termini in Rome from about 5am-10pm take between 1¼-1¾hr.. (ES, ES/Av, and Ex trains; €30-40) or 2-3 hours (Ic, Icn, and R trains; €10-20); tickets can be booked at the station or online (www.ferroviedellostato.it)

Flights: Aeroporto Capodichino (NAP), Vle. Ruffo Fulco di Calabria (☎081 84 88 88 77, info line 78 96 259; www.gesac.it), northeast of the city. Open daily 5:30am-11:30pm. A white **Alibus** travels between the port near P. Municipio, Stazione Centrale, and the airport (15-20min., 6:30am-11:30pm, €3.10). City bus **3S** runs from P. Garibaldi to the airport arrivals terminal (every 30min., €1.10). Buy tickets at any newsstand or *tabaccheria.* Cheaper than the Alibus and with many more stops, the city bus is a target for pickpockets. **Taxis** run to and from the airport to Stazione Centrale for the *tariffa predeterminata* of €19 (make sure to confirm with the driver before embarking). **Alitalia**

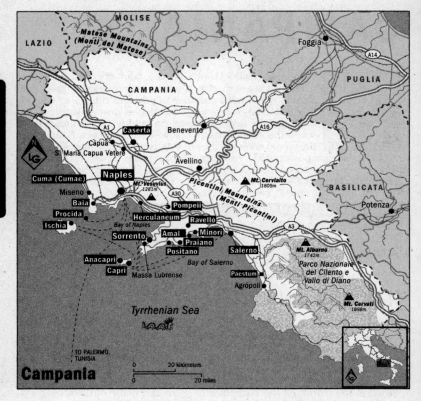

Campania

(☎081 06 22 22), **British Airways** (☎081 199 71 22 66), **Lufthansa** (☎081 199 40 00 44), and **Easy Jet** (☎081 848 88 77 66) fly to Naples.

Trains: Naples is served by 3 train companies from **Stazione Centrale,** P. Garibaldi (www. napolipiazzagaribaldi.it). **Luggage storage** is available but not secure.

Circumvesuviana (☎800 053 939; www.vesuviana.it). To **Herculaneum** (€1.80), **Pompeii** (€2.40), and **Sorrento** (€3.30). Trains depart every 30min. 5:09am-10:42pm.

Ferrovia Cumana and **Ferrovia Circumflegrea** (☎081 800 00 16 16). Trains from Montesanto to **Cumae** and **Puzzuoli** (every 20min.). Info booth in the station open daily 7am-9pm.

Trenitalia (☎081 56 72 430 or 89 20 21; www.trenitalia.it). Ticket office open daily 6am-9:40pm.

Ferries: The daily newspaper *Il Mattino* (€1) has up-to-date ferry schedules. Port taxes may apply. Hydrofoils depart from **Mergellina, Molo Beverello,** and **Pozzuoli,** and ferries from **Stazione Marittima** (on **Molo Angioino**) and **Molo Beverello.** Molo Angioino is for longer trips to **Sicily** and **Sardinia.** Molo Beverello is at the base of P. Municipio. Take the R2, 152, 3S, or Alibus from P. Garibaldi to P. Municipio.

Alilauro (☎081 49 72 238; www.alilauro.it). Ticket offices at Molo Beverello and Mergellina. Open daily 6am-7pm. Ferries to **Ischia** (23 per day 7:10am-8:15pm, €16-18; last return 6:50pm).

Caremar (☎081 83 70 700; www.caremar.it). Ticket office on Molo Beverello. Open daily 6am-10pm. Ferries and hydrofoils to **Capri** (ferry 1¼hr., 3 per day 7:35am-6:40pm, €11; hydrofoil 50min., 4 per day 5:40am-9:10pm, €16), **Ischia** (ferry: 1¼hr., 8 per day 6:25am-9:55pm, €10; hydrofoil:

1hr., 5 per day 7:50am-6:15pm, €16), and **Procida** (ferry 1hr., 5 per day 6:25am-9:55pm, €9.90; hydrofoil 40min., 6 per day 7:40am-8:30pm, €13).

Metro del Mare (☎081 199 600 700; www.metrodelmare.com). Ticket office at Molo Beverello and Mergellina. 3 Lines run between **Bacoli** and **Salerno** (€17), Bacoli and **Sorrento** (€6), and **Monte di Procida** and Salerno (€18). Stops at Pozzouli, Napoli Mergellina, Napoli Beverello, Ercolano, Torre del Greco, Torre A. Pompeii, Sorrento, Capri, Positano, and Amalfi, among others.

SNAV (☎081 42 85 555; www.snav.it). Ticket office at Molo Beverello and Mergellina. Open daily 9am-7pm. Hydrofoils Apr.-Oct. go to **Capri** (45min., 6 per day 7:10am-5:35pm, €19; last return 6:35pm), **Ischia-Casamicciola Terme** (1hr., 4 per day 8:20am-6:45pm, €16; last return 5:40pm), and **Procida** (40min., 4 per day 8:20am-6:45pm, €14; last return 6pm).

⚡ ORIENTATION

In Naples, hectic modern grime rubs shoulders with historic architectural gems. To the east, the area around **Stazione Centrale** is dangerous; beware of pickpockets and exercise extra caution at night. From **Piazza Garibaldi** (right outside the station), take a left on C. Garibaldi and walk until it ends at the water in P. Guglielmo Pepe. With the water on your left, V. Nuova Marina turns into V. Cristoforo Colombo and later V. Ferdinando Acton, which leads to **Piazza del Plebiscito,** the historic and social center of Naples. From here, turn away from the water onto **Via Toledo,** the town's shop- and restaurant-lined main drag. This street passes through the disordered **Spanish Quarter,** the northern half of which is unsafe, on its way to **Piazza Dante** and **Piazza Salvo D'Aquisto** (also known as **Piazza Carità**), which lie on the western extreme of the **centro storico (Spaccanapoli).** A right off V. Toledo on V. Maddaloni (which later becomes V. Capitelli, V. Benedetto Croce, and V. San Biagio dei Librai) leads through the central *piazze* of the historical district, **Piazza Gesù Nuovo** and **Piazza San Domenico Maggiore.** Lots of hip, unique restaurants and hangouts are found around the university in **Piazza Ruggero Bonghi.** A short funicular ride from V. Toledo will take you to the **Vomero** district, away from the chaos of central Naples. Returning back down V. Toledo to P. del Plebiscito, turn right at the water to reach upscale boutique restaurants and shops tucked away on the side streets off **Riviera di Chiaia** in the **Chiaia** district. The nearby **Piazza dei Martiri** offers good nightlife. **Mergellina,** the beautiful and relaxed waterfront district, is accessible by foot along V. Caracciolo or by Metro line #2. **Posillipo** is also pleasant and even farther along the wild, wild west.

⛟ LOCAL TRANSPORTATION

One **UnicoNapoliticket** (☎081 55 13 109; www.napolipass.it) is valid for all modes of transportation in Naples: **bus, metro, train,** and **funicular.** Tickets are available at *tabaccherie* in three varieties: 1½hr. (€1.10), full day (€3.10), and weekend (€2.60). The buses and Metro stop running shortly before midnight, and the *notturno* (nighttime) buses require extra caution and sometimes long waits. The main bus stop is on the opposite end of P. Garibaldi from Stazione Centrale. Transportation in Naples' environs includes the **Metro del Mare** (see **Intercity Transportation,** p. 563), the **Circumvesuviana** train to the areas around Mt. Vesuvius and the **Metro** to Pozzuoli. All buses and trains in Campania are on the **UnicoCampania** system (www.unicocampania.it). Ticket costs depend on the *fascia* (zone) of your destination (€1.70-8.20, daily tickets €3.50-16.40). The daily newspaper, *Il Mattino*, has schedules, which change constantly.

CAMPANIA

Public Transportation:

Buses: Public buses are orange. Stops have signs indicating routes and destinations. **R1** travels from P. Bovio to Vomero (P. Medaglie d'Oro), and **R2** runs from P. Garibaldi to P. Municipio. **3S** connects the 3 stations: the airport, Stazione Centrale in P. Garibaldi, and Molo Beverello, where boats leave for islands in the Bay of Naples and other more distant destinations.

Metro: (Info ☎800 56 88 66; www.metro.na.it.) To cover long distances (e.g., from the train station to P. Cavour, Montesanto, P. Amedeo, or Mergellina), use the efficient Metro that runs west to Pozzuoli from P. Garibaldi. Go to platform #4, 1 fl. underground at Stazione Centrale. Line #1 stops at **Piazza Cavour** (Museo Nazionale), **Montesanto** (Cumana, Circumflegrea, funicular to Vomero), **Piazza Amedeo** (funicular to Vomero), **Mergellina,** and **Pozzuoli.** Transfer at P. Cavour for line #2. For **Procida** or **Ischia,** take the Metro to Pozzuoli.

Funiculars (Info: ☎800 56 88 66; www.metro.na.it). 3 connect the lower city to Vomero: **Centrale,** most frequently used, runs from V. Toledo to P. Fuga; **Montesanto** from P. Montesanto to V. Morghen; **Chiaia** from V. del Parco Margherita to C. Cimarosa. Centrale and Chiaia make intermittent stops at C. V. Emanuele. A 4th, **Mergellina,** connects Posillipo to Mergellina. 6 per hr., M-Tu 6:30am-10pm, W-Su 6:30am-1:30am.

Taxis: Consortaxi (☎081 55 13 06; www.consortaxi.it). **Cotana** (☎081 570 70 70; www.la570.it). **Napoli** (☎081 44 44 44; www.consorziotaxinapoli.it). **Partenope** (☎081 55 60 202; www.radiotaxilapartenope.it). Only take official taxis with meters, and inquire about prices up front; even well-known companies have been known to charge suspiciously high rates. For all taxis, the meter starts at €3 M-Sa, €5.50 Su and at night (10pm-7am); each additional 65m costs €0.05. There is also a €0.50-1 surcharge for luggage. Service to and from the airport is set at €19. Other fixed tariffs must be agreed upon before meter starts. Tariffs double for trips beyond the city limits.

Car Rental: Avis (☎081 75 16 052; www.avisautonoleggio.it), in the airport. Open M-F 8am-7:30pm, Sa 8:30am-1pm and 4-6pm, Su 9am-1pm. Extra 12% tax on cars rented at airport. **Hertz,** V. Ricciardi 5 (☎081 20 62 28 or 199 91 12 211). Branch at airport, V. Scarfoglio 1 (☎081 78 02 971; www.hertz.it). Open M-F 8am-1pm and 2-7pm, Sa 8am-noon. **Maggiore** (☎081 19 91 51 120; www.maggiore.it), in Stazione Centrale. Open M-F 8am-1pm and 3-7pm, Sa 8:30am-1:30pm.

⑦ PRACTICAL INFORMATION

TOURIST AND FINANCIAL SERVICES

Tourist Offices:

EPT, P. dei Martiri 58 (☎081 41 07 211; www.eptnapoli.info). Offers booking services, free maps, and the indispensable ▓**Qui Napoli,** a twice-monthly tourist publication with event schedules. Make sure to ask for *Zero 81,* which also lists all cultural, musical, and artistic events happening every night in the city. English spoken. Open M-F 9am-2pm. Branch at Stazione Centrale (☎081 26 87 79). This office is very busy and usually inexplicably closed; go elsewhere for more attentive service. Open M-Sa 9am-7pm, Su 9am-1pm. Branch at Stazione Mergellina (☎081 76 12 102). Open M-Sa 9am-7pm.

AASCT (☎081 25 25 714; www.inaples.it), at Galleria Umberto in P. del Plebiscito. Friendly info on accommodations and sights. English spoken. Open M-Sa 9:30am-1:30pm and 2:30-6:30pm, Su 9:30am-1:30pm. Branch at P. Gesù Nuovo (☎081 55 12 701). Open M-Sa 9:30am-1:30pm and 2:30-6:30pm, Su 9am-1:30pm.

Budget Travel: CTS, V. Mezzocannone 25 (☎081 55 27 960; www.cts.it), off C. Umberto on the R2 line. Student travel info, ISIC and FIYTO cards, and booking services. Open M-F 9:30am-1:30pm and 2:30-6pm, Sa 9:30am-12:30pm. Branch at V. Cinthia 36 (☎081 76 77 877.) Open May-Sept. M-F 9:30am-1pm and 4-7pm, Sa 9:30am-1pm; Oct.-Apr. M-F 9:30am-12:30pm.

Consulates: Canada, V. Carducci 29 (☎081 40 13 38). Open M-F 9am-1pm. **UK,** V. dei Mille 40 (☎081 42 38 911). Open in summer M-F 9am-12:30pm and 2-4pm.

CAMPANIA

US, P. della Repubblica 2 (☎081 58 38 111, 24hr. emergency 033 79 45 083), at the western end of Villa Comunale. Open M-F 8am-1pm and 2-5pm. For more info, see **Essentials,** p. 8.

Currency Exchange: Stazione Centrale has expensive 24hr. currency exchange. Smaller offices along C. Umberto I charge more reasonable fees, as do the banks along V. Toledo and in P. Municipio and P. Garibaldi. Decent rates at **Thomas Cook** in the airport. Open M-F 9:30am-1pm and 3-7pm. Branch at P. Municipio 70 (☎081 55 18 399).

LOCAL SERVICES

English-Language Bookstores: Feltrinelli, V. San Tommaso d'Aquino 70/76 (☎081 55 21 436; www.lafeltrinelli.it), just north of the Municipio. Open M-F 9am-8pm, Sa 9am-2pm and 4-8:30pm. AmEx/D/MC/V.

LUG YOUR LUGGAGE. The luggage storage in Stazione Centrale is extremely unsafe; bring your bags to your hostel locker or hold onto them!

EMERGENCY AND COMMUNICATIONS

Police: ☎112 or 113.

Tourist Police: Ufficio Stranieri, V. G. Ferrairis 131 (☎081 60 64 111), near Stazione Centrale. Helps tourist who have been victims of crime. Assists with passport problems. **Ambulance:**☎118.

Passenger Information: ☎081 89 20 21.

Pharmacy: (☎081 26 88 81), at Stazione Centrale by Trenitalia ticket windows. Open 24hr. Closed some Sa and holidays.

Hospital: Incurabili (☎081 25 49 422), near the Museo Archeologico Nazionale. ⓂCavour (Museo). From the metro, the emergency ward is directly up V. Maria Longo.

Internet: Internet points cluster around V. Mezzocannone and P. Bellini. **Lemme Lemme By Internet Bar,** P. Bellini 74 (See **Nightlife,** p. 401). Internet €0.05 per min. Free Wi-Fi. Open daily in summer 6pm-2am, in winter 9am-2am.

Post Office: P. Matteotti (☎081 55 24 233), at V. Diaz. Take the R2 line, a view into true Neapolitan life like nothing else. Notoriously unreliable *fermoposta*. Branches in Galleria Umberto I (☎081 55 23 467) and outside Stazione Centrale. Open M-F 8:15am-6pm, Sa 8:15am-noon.**Postal Code:** 80100.

ACCOMMODATIONS

Hotels litter the seedy, hectic area around **Stazione Centrale.** Don't trust anyone who approaches you in the station—people working on commission are happy to lead naïve foreigners to unlicensed, overpriced hotels. Stazione Centrale has several comfortable and inexpensive options that are quiet despite their bustling surroundings, but be especially careful when returning at night. The **centro storico** and **Piazza del Plebiscito** areas are more expensive but also more relaxed. **Vomero,** albeit farther from the sights, provides tranquility and views. **Mergellina,** even farther from the hub, is even calmer. Be cautious when selecting a place to stay, and if possible, make reservations in advance. Don't surrender documents or passports before seeing a room, always agree on the price in writing before unpacking, and look for an intercom system or night attendants. Keep in mind that rooms with views of the city are rarely insulated from the

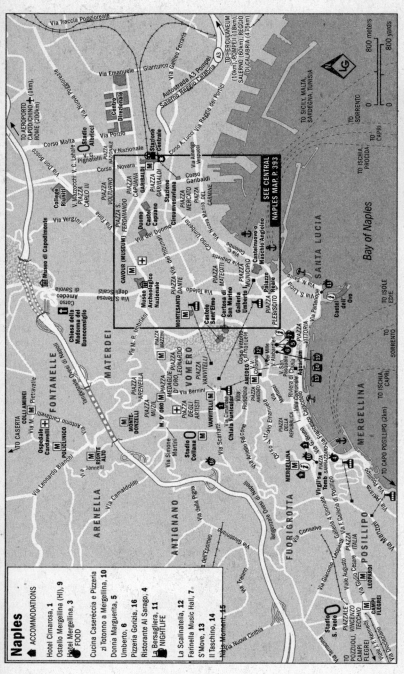

Naples

ACCOMMODATIONS

Hotel Cimarosa, 1
Ostello Mergellina (HI), 9
Hotel Mergellina, 3

FOOD

Cucina Casereccia e Pizzeria
zi Totonno a Mergellina, 10
Donna Marguerita, 5
Umberto, 6
Pizzeria Gorizia, 16
Ristorante Al Sarago, 4
La Bersagliera, 11

NIGHTLIFE

La Scalinatella, 12
Farinella Music Hall, 7
S'Move, 13
Il Taschino, 14
Nia Moment, 15

SEE CENTRAL
NAPLES MAP, P. 393

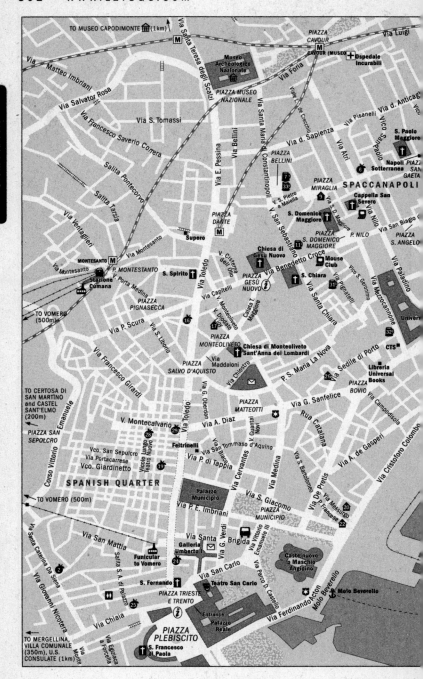

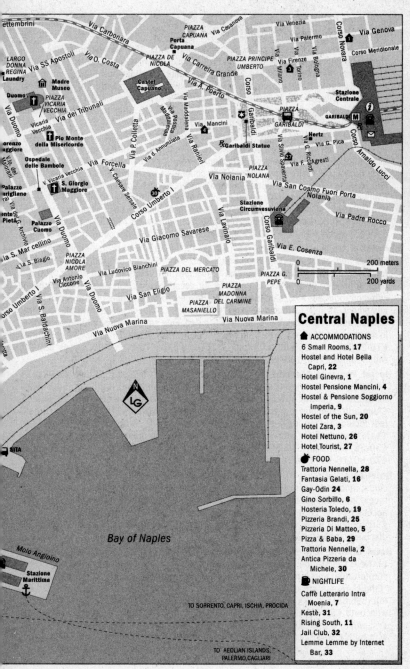

Central Naples

ACCOMMODATIONS
6 Small Rooms, **17**
Hostel and Hotel Bella
  Capri, **22**
Hotel Ginevra, **1**
Hostel Pensione Mancini, **4**
Hostel & Pensione Soggiorno
  Imperia, **9**
Hostel of the Sun, **20**
Hotel Zara, **3**
Hotel Nettuno, **26**
Hotel Tourist, **27**

FOOD
Trattoria Nennella, **28**
Fantasia Gelati, **16**
Gay-Odin **24**
Gino Sorbillo, **6**
Hosteria Toledo, **19**
Pizzeria Brandi, **25**
Pizzeria Di Matteo, **5**
Pizza & Baba, **29**
Trattoria Nennella, **2**
Antica Pizzeria da
  Michele, **30**

NIGHTLIFE
Caffè Letterario Intra
  Moenia, **7**
Kestè, **31**
Rising South, **11**
Jail Club, **32**
Lemme Lemme by Internet
  Bar, **33**

noisy streets below. The tourist office has a pamphlet of accommodations. For camping, check out the towns on the Bay of Naples.

6 Small Rooms, V. Diodato Lioy 18, 3rd fl. (☎081 79 01 378; www.6smallrooms.com). From P. Dante, turn left on V. Toledo, left on V. Senise, and right on V. Lioy. Huge, beautiful rooms defy the name. Frescoed kitchen open until 10:30pm and English video collection available. Resident cat and dogs. Breakfast included. Wash and dry €5. Free lockers, internet, and Wi-Fi. Some private rooms have A/C. Dorms €18-20; small singles or doubles with bath and A/C €25-45; doubles €50-55, with bath €55-65; triples €60-75; quad 80-95. 10% *Let's Go* discount. MC/V. ●

Hostel and Hotel Bella Capri, V. Melisurgo 4 (☎081 55 29 494; www.bellacapri.it). Take R2 bus from station, exit at V. De Pretis. Top-notch hostel offers clean, safe, and fun accommodations for all. Laid-back atmosphere and helpful owner who likes to organize pizza outings. All rooms have A/C and TVs; some have bay views. Flatscreen satellite TV and DVDs in the common room. Common kitchen. English spoken. Breakfast included. Free lockers, luggage storage, and high-speed Internet access. Wash and dry €4. Reception 24hr. Mixed and all-female dorms €15-20; singles €40-50, with bath €50-70; doubles €50-60/60-80; triples €70-80/80-100; quads €80-90/90-110; quints and 6-person rooms with bath €20-29 per person. 10% *Let's Go* discount. AmEx/MC/V. ●

Hostel of the Sun, V. Melisurgo 15 (☎081 42 06 393; www.hostelnapoli.com). Take R2 bus from station, exit at V. De Pretis. Buzz #51. Surefire entertainment and comfort are provided by the exuberant staff, who give out free maps and advice, organize outings once or twice a week, and cook for guests one night a week. Colorful, bright common room has A/C, satellite TV, DVDs, Skype phone, and tons of pictures of happy customers. All private rooms have TV, DVD, and A/C. Wheelchair accessible facilities. Kitchen and fridge available. Breakfast included. Free small lockers, internet, and Wi-Fi in most rooms. Wash €3, dry €3; free with 3 nights' stay. Reception 24hr. 5-7 bed dorms €16-20; doubles €55-60, with bath €60-70; triples €75-80/70-90; quads €80-90, with bath €85-100. 10% *Let's Go* discount. D/MC/V. ❷

Hostel Pensione Mancini, V. Pasquale Stanislao Mancini 33, 2nd fl. (☎081 55 36 731; www.hostelpensionemancini.com), off far end of P. Garibaldi, 5min. walk to Stazione Central. Attentive owners share their extensive knowledge of Naples. Clean and spacious rooms. New common room and kitchen. English spoken. Breakfast included. Free luggage storage, lockers, and Wi-Fi. Reception 24hr. Check-out 11am. Excellent for late-night arrivals. Co-ed and female dorms €14-18; singles €30-35, with bath €40-50; doubles €40-50/50-60; triples €60-75/70-80; quads €70-80/76-90. 10% *Let's Go* discount. AmEx/MC/V. ●

Hotel Zara, V. Firenze 81 (☎081 28 71 25; www.hotelzara.it; info@hotelzara.it). Spacious, renovated rooms near the station, all with TVs, A/C, and baths; most with terraces. International book library and exchange. Breakfast €5. No Wi-Fi, but internet access free for *Let's Go* users. 24h. reception. Reservations recommended. Singles €35; doubles €45, with bath €50-70; triples €75-80; quads €100. 5% *Let's Go* discount. AmEx/D/MC/V. ❷

Hotel Ginevra, 2nd fl., V. Genova 116 (☎/fax 081 28 32 10; www.hotelginevra. it). Near the station. Exit P. Garibaldi on C. Novara, turn right on V. Genova. Clean, comfortable, and family-run. Owners can reserve private tours of Naples for guests. "Ethnic" rooms are chock full of faux-bamboo and rainforest kitsch. Breakfast €5. Internet €5 per 40min. Free Wi-Fi. Reservations recommended. Singles €25-35, with bath €35-50; doubles €35-50; superior doubles, with minibars, safes, baths, TVs, and A/C €45-70; "ethnic" doubles with fans and baths €40-65; triples €45-65, with bath €50-75. 10% *Let's Go* discount. AmEx/D/MC/V. ❷

▐ FOOD

PIZZERIE

If you ever doubted the legendary Neapolitan pizza, the city's pizzerie will take that doubt, beat it into a ball, throw it in the air, spin it on their collective finger, punch it down, cover it with sauce and mozzarella, and serve it *alla margherita*. The *centro storico* is full of excellent choices.

▓ **Antica Pizzeria da Michele,** V. Caesare Sersale 1/3 (☎081 55 39 204; www.damichele.net; info@damichele.net), at the corner of V. Colletta. From P. Garibaldi, take C. Umberto I and turn right. Huge line outside is an even better indication of quality than the legion of reviews, which are correct in proclaiming da Michele's the best pizza in the world. Serves only marinara and margherita, the perfect formula for which has been refined and practiced since shortly after the shop opened in 1870. Walk in and get a number from a pizza chefs or order your pie to go and watch them work their magic at the wood-fired oven. Pizza €4-5. Open M-Sa 10am-11pm. Cash only. ❶

▓ **Gino Sorbillo,** V. dei Tribunali 35 (☎081 44 66 43; www.sorbillo.eu), in the *centro storico* near Vco. San Paolo. The original owner created both the *ripieno al forno* (calzone) and 21 pizza-making children, 3 of whom (Gino, Antonio, and Esterina) have "Sorbillo" restaurants near each other along V. dei Tribunali. Reservation may reduce your wait time. Both floors are always abuzz with customers. Basic marinara (€3) and margherita (€3.50) never tasted so good, yet this is the one place to feast on a calzone *fritto al forno* (literally "fried in the oven"; €6.50). Pizza €3-7. Cover €1. Open M-Sa noon-3:30pm and 7pm-11:30pm. Closed 3 weeks in Aug. MC/V. ❶

▓ **Pizzeria Di Matteo,** V. dei Tribunali 94 (☎081 45 52 62), near V. Duomo. A brick oven churns out some of the best marinara around (€2.50). Pizzas burst with flavor and the building bursts with Neapolitans—get on the waiting list and try some of the fried zucchini while you wait. Pizza €2.50-6. Open M-Sa 9am-midnight. Cash only. ❶

Pizzeria Brandi, Salita Sant'Anna di Palazzo 1/2 (☎081 41 69 28; www.brandi.it), off V. Chiaia. In 1889, Raffaele Esposito invented the *margherita* for Queen Margherita in Brandi's oven to symbolize Italy's flag with green basil, red tomato sauce, and white mozzarella. Famous patrons include Luciano Pavarotti and Gérard Depardieu. Margherita €6.90, with *mozzarella di bufala* €9.40. Other pizzas, dedicated to kings and celebrities like Sofia Loren, up to €10.50. Cover €1.80. Service 15%. Open Aug.-June daily 12:30pm-3:30pm and 7:30pm-midnight, July Tu-Su12:30pm-3:30pm and 7:30pm-midnight. Reservations recommended. AmEx/D/MC/V. ❷

RESTAURANTS AND TRATTORIE

Local seafood enjoys an exalted place in Neapolitan dishes. Devour plentiful *cozze* (mussels) with lemon or in soup. Savor *vongole* (clams) in all their glory, and don't miss their more expensive cousin, the *ostrica* (oyster). Try not to gawk as true Neapolitans suck the juices from the heads of *aragosta* (lobster) or devour *polipo* (octopus). For fresh fruits and seafood, the lively **market** on V. Soprammuro, off P. Garibaldi, is the place to go (open M-Sa 8am-1:30pm). Fruit stands, grocery stores, and pastry shops line V. Tribunali in the *centro storico*. The waterfront offers a combination of traditional Neapolitan fare and a change of culinary pace; take the Metro or C25 bus to P. Amedeo, on the Mergellina waterfront, for informal, hearty seafood. A large supermarket, **Supero,** is on Vco. San Domenico Soriano 20. (Open M-Sa 8:30am-8pm, Su 8:30-1:30pm. MC/V.) When you're sick of pizza, the **Spanish Quarter** is the place to go for a sit-down meal.

CAMPANIA

■ **Trattoria Nennella,** Vco. Lungo Teatro Nuovo 105 (☎081 41 43 38). Family-run trattoria with fantastic daily *menù* (primo, secondo, *contorno*, fruit, and wine; €10). Local cuisine at an unbeatable value attracts hordes of Neapolitans nightly. Don't be surprised if the jovial waiters slam a watermelon down and chop it up in front of you, without warning. Open Sept.-July M-Sa noon-3pm and 7-10:30pm. Cash only. ●

Hosteria Toledo, Vco. Giardinetto 78/A (☎081 42 12 57; www.hosteriatoledo.it; info@hosteriatoledo.it). Neapolitan comfort food. Tons of antipasti, pasta, and seafood options. If you can't decide, try the chef's surprise—it rarely disappoints. Try the fried zucchini with mint and vinegar (€3), a favorite passed down from Mamma Sosora. Primi and secondi €6-18. Pizza from €5. Cover €2; €1 for pizza. Service 10%. Open M and Th-Su 1-4pm and 7pm-midnight, Tu 1pm-4pm. D/MC/V. ●

Pizza e Baba, V. Montecalvario 3 (☎081 41 52 44; www.pizzaebaba.com), off V. Toledo. Fresh fish and Neapolitan fare at fair prices. The cool staff and cooler temperature are a welcome relief from the summer grind. More secluded seating available in renovated basement rooms used as shelters during WWII. Pizza margherita €3.50. Primi €7-15. Secondi €6-14. Cover €1.50. Open daily 11:15am-midnight. AmEx/D/MC/V. ●

GELATERIE AND PASTICCERIE

Naples's most beloved pastry is *sfogliatelle*, filled with sweetened ricotta, orange rind, and candied fruit. It comes in two forms: the popular *riccia*, a flaky-crust variety, and a softer, crumblier *frolla*. Look for creamy textures and muted colors for the most authentic tastes.

■ **Gay-Odin,** V. Toledo 427 (☎081 55 13 491; www.gay-odin.it), in the *centro storico*. Also at V. Vittoria Colonna 15/B (☎081 41 82 82) off P. Amedeo in Chiaia, and V. Benedicto Croce 61 (☎081 55 10 794) near P. Plebiscito. Chocolate treats at this shop include *foresta*, a sweet and crumbly chocolate stalk (from €1 for a small twig to €9 for a trunk best shared with friends). Also offers 12 flavors of gourmet chocolate gelato. Open M-Sa 9:30am-1:30pm and 4:30-8pm, Su 10am-2pm. AmEx/MC/V. ●

■ **Storico Gran Caffè Gambrinus,** V. Chiaia 1/2 (☎081 41 75 82; www.caffegambrinus.com; info@caffegambrinus.com), off P. del Plebiscito. No visit to the impressive *piazza* is complete without a stop at this equally grand coffee spot. Established in 1860 and renovated in the Liberty style in 1890, the *caffè* still prepares hazelnut cream coffee (€2, €4.50 with table service), historically sipped by Ernest Hemingway, Oscar Wilde, Italian presidents, and Neapolitans alike. Frozen desserts from its spectacular *gelateria* start at €5.50. Beware the large differences in price between counter and table service. Open Su-Thu 7am-1am, F 7am-2am, Sa 7am-3am. AmEx/MC/V. ●

Fantasia Gelati, V. Toledo 381 (☎081 55 11 212), in the *centro storico*. Also at P. Vanvitelli 22, V. Gilea 80, L. Lala 30, and V. Fragnito 39. The shop's fruit flavors, including tangy papaya, are made with real juices, yielding tart, refreshing results. Over 25 flavors and generous scoops. Cones €1.50-5; gluten-free €2. Open in summer daily 7am-1am, in winter Tu-Su 7am-11pm. Cash only. ●

Scaturchio, P. San D. Maggiore 19 (☎081 55 16 944; www.scaturchio.it), in the *centro storico*. Tucked quietly into a *piazza*, this is the perfect place to enjoy divine desserts and watch Neapolitans pass. A contender for the city's best *sfogliatelle* (€1.40). The wintertime specialty is *ministeriale*, a chocolate and rum pastry (€1.60). Excellent gelato (cones from €2). Open daily 7:20am-8:40pm. AmEx/D/MC/V. ●

⑤ SIGHTS

The city's exquisite architecture narrates the story of Greek, Roman, and Spanish conquest. The Museo Archeologico Nazionale and the Museo di

Capodimonte have excavations in site. The Palazzo Reale's apartments and the city's castles give a taste of 18th-century royal Neapolitan life.

CENTRO STORICO (SPACCANAPOLI)

Naples's most renowned neighborhood is replete with brilliant architecture. Major sights get lost among ornate banks, *pensioni*, and *pasticcerie*, so watch for shoebox-sized signs on buildings. To get to the *centro storico* from P. Dante, walk through Pta. Alba and past P. Bellini before turning down V. dei Tribunali, the former Roman road that now contains some of Naples's best pizzerie.

BARGAINAPOLI. The **Campania Artecard** is a worthwhile investment for those taking a few days to tour regional sights. It grants free admission to any 2 of 48 participating museums and sites in and around the city (including Pompeii), and half-price admission to the rest. Free public transportation, special weekend transportation, and discounts on audio tours are also included. Artecards are available at the airport, train stations, travel agencies, and all the museums and sites included on the card throughout the region. (☎800 60 06 01; www.campaniartecard.it. Sights and transportation in Naples and Campi Flegrei €13 for 3 days, ages 18-25 €8; in all of Campania €25 for 3 days, €18 reduced; €28/21 for 1 week.)

NAPOLI SOTTERRANEA(CATACOMBS AND UNDERGROUND OF NAPLES). The underground of Naples, started by the Greeks in the seventh century BC, was used until the 1960s; the catacombs of San Gennaro, San Gaudioso, and San Severo provide a glimpse of ancient Neapolis. Fascinating guided tours (1½hr.) of the city's subterranean alleys set visitors crawling through narrow underground passageways, grottoes, and catacombs. On your walk beneath the historic center, you'll explore Roman aqueducts, witness Mussolini-era graffiti from the area's days as a bomb shelter, and enter Neapolitan homes to see how ancient Roman theaters have been incorporated into architecture over the ages. *(P. San Gaetano 68. Take V. Tribunali and turn left right before San Paolo Maggiore. ☎081 29 69 44; www.napolisotterranea.org. Tours in English and Italian every 2hr. M-F noon-4pm, Sa-Su and holidays 10am-6pm. €9.30, students €8. 10% Campania Artecard discount.)*

MUSEO ARCHEOLOGICO NAZIONALE. This former seat of the University of Naples in a 17th-century *palazzo* is one of Europe's oldest museums. A guidebook, audio tour, or guided tour is worth the price. The museum's Farnese Collection displays sculptures from Pompeii and Herculaneum as well as imperial portraits and colossal statues from Rome's Baths of Caracalla. The massive Farnese Hercules depicts the hero after his last labor—another mythical account adds an extra labor to the traditional 12: sleeping with 100 women in one night. Check out the **Farnese Bull,** one of the largest surviving statues from antiquity. Sculpted from a single slab of marble, the figure was reworked by none other than Michelangelo. The mezzanine contains a room of exquisite mosaics from Pompeii, most noticeably some delicious-looking fruits and the **Alexander Mosaic,** which depicts a young, fearless Alexander the Great routing the Persian army. Though most have heard of the lovely Aphrodite, the **Gabinetto Segreto** (Secret Cabinet), introduces her lesser-known counterpart, Hermaphrodite, who was blessed with a curvy feminine form and handy masculine member. The collection specializes in erotic art from Pompeii, which includes everything from images of godly love to phallic good luck charms. *(P. Cavour Maseo. Turn right from station, walk 2 blocks. ☎081 44 22 149; www.pompeiisites.org. Open M and W-Su 9am-7:30pm and on public holidays; when holidays fall on a Tu, it is closed the following*

W. Maps given out at info booth next to ticket office. Some collections closed each day; call ahead for specifics. €10, EU students 18-24 and those with Campania Artecard €5, under 18 or over 65 free. Audio tour in Italian, English, and French €4, with Campania Artecard €2.50. Cash only.)

DUOMO. The modest 19th-century facade of Naples's *duomo* conceals an ornate interior. Inaugurated in 1315 by Robert of Anjou, the *duomo* has been subject to many additions and renovations. Inside to the right, the main attraction is the **Cappella del Tesoro di San Gennaro,** decorated with Baroque paintings. A beautiful 17th-century bronze grill protects the high altar. The reliquary contains the saint's head and two vials of coagulated blood. According to legend, disaster will strike the city if the blood does not liquefy on the day of the Festa di San Gennaro (see **Entertainment and Festivals,** p. 401). Behind the main altar of the church lies the saint's crypt, decorated with Renaissance carvings in white marble. The underground excavation site, also open to visitors, contains an intimate tangle of Greek and Roman roads constructed over several centuries, as well as 4th century Christian mosaics. *(Walk 3 blocks up V. Duomo from C. Umberto I, or take bus #42 from P. Garibaldi. ☎ 081 44 90 97. Open M-F 8:30am-noon and 4:30-6:30pm, Sa-Su 8:30am-1pm and 5pm-7pm. Baptistery and excavation site open M-F 9am-12:30pm and 4:30pm-7pm, Sa-Su 9am-1pm; last entry 30min. before closing. Chapel free. Excavation site €1.50.)*

CAPPELLA SAN SEVERO. The chapel, founded in 1590, is now a private museum. Several remarkable 18th-century statues inhabit its lovely corridors, including the ◪**Veiled Christ** by Giuseppe Sanmartino. Because the chapel's founder, Prince Raimondo of the San Severi, reached Grand Master status in the Free Masons, allusions to Masonry are laced throughout the Christian artwork. These include the swastika labyrinth design, which represents the exploration of universal mysteries. Three major symbols of Masonry can be found at the Veiled Christ's feet: a hammer, a compass, and pliers. Legend claims that the chapel's builder—an alchemist as well as a Grand Master—murdered his wife and her lover by injecting them with a poison that preserved their veins, arteries, and vital organs. *(V. De Sanctis 19, near P. San D. Maggiore. ☎ 081 55 18 470; www.museosansevero.it. Open M and W-Sa 10am-6pm, holidays 10am-1:30pm; last entry 20min. before closing. €6, with Campania Artecard €5, students 10-25 €4, under 10 free.)*

CHIESA DI SANTA CHIARA. The bright and spacious Santa Chiara was built in the 1300s by the rulers of the house of Anjou. Since then, it has been renovated several times, most recently after a WWII bombing, which destroyed the floor on the left side. The church is littered with sarcophagi and tombs from the Middle Ages, including the 14th-century tomb of Robert of Anjou. The first chapel to the left is dedicated to Neapolitan-born Salvo D'Acquisto, who sacrificed his life during WWII. German troops, enraged at losing one of their own, rounded up 26 women and children to pay dearly for it—Salvo offered his life in the place of theirs, and the Germans conceded. Check out the garden, archaeological site, and cloister, adorned with numerous colorful columns, fruit trees, Gothic frescoes, and *majolica* (brightly painted clay) tiles. *(P. Gesù Nuovo. From P. Dante, take V. Toledo and turn left on V. B. Croce. ☎ 081 55 21 597 or 79 71 235; www.santachiara. info. Open M-Sa 7:30am-1pm and 4:30pm-8pm, Su 2pm-8pm. Archaeological site and cloister open M-Sa 9:30am-5:30pm and Su 10am-2:30pm. €5, reduced €3.50.)*

CHIESA DI GESÙ NUOVO. After its 15th-century construction for the Prince of Salerno, the church passed into the hands of the Jesuits. Its simple facade belies the opulent Baroque interior with inlaid marble floors and colorful ceiling frescoes. The magnificent main altar, featuring a triumvirate of marble statues and a towering gold sun, is overwhelming. Outside the church, a soaring spire glorifies the lives of Jesuit saints. *(Across from Chiesa di Santa Chiara. ☎ 081 55 18 613. Open daily 7am-1pm and 4-7:30pm. Modest dress required. Free.)*

PIO MONTE DELLA MISERICORDIA. This chapel was built by a group of nobles to help the sick and needy, house pilgrims, and help ransom Christian slaves held by infidels. The main archway holds Caravaggio's *Seven Works of Mercy.* Outside in the *piazza* stands a spire dedicated to San Gennaro, who saved the city from plague in 1656. *(V. Tribunali 253, 1 block after V. Duomo. ☎081 44 69 44; www.piomontedellamisericordia.it. Open M-Tu and Th-Su 9am-2pm. €5; with Campania Artecard €4; EU students, over 65, and under 14 €3. Call to book a tour Tu, Th, Sa 9:30am-1:30pm.)*

CHIESA DI SAN DOMENICO MAGGIORE. Many renovations to this 13th-century church have resulted in the 19th-century spiked Gothic interior visible today. To the right of the altar in the Chapel of the Crucifix hangs the 13th-century painting that allegedly spoke to St. Thomas Aquinas when he lived in the adjoining monastery. Fine Renaissance sculptures decorate the side chapels, but many have been moved to the Capodimonte museum. *(P. San Domenico Maggiore. ☎081 45 91 88. Open M-F 8:30am-noon and 4pm-7pm, Sa/Su 9am-1pm and 5pm-7pm. Free.)*

PIAZZA DEL PLEBISCITO AND CHIAIA

🔲**PALAZZO REALE.** Statues of Neapolitan rulers decorate this 17th-century *palazzo,* now home to the **Museo di Palazzo Reale.** The museum holds opulent royal apartments with Bourbon furnishings, but its artwork pales in comparison to its views of the Bay of Naples and Vomero, which towers majestically in the distance. The *palazzo* is also an intellectual mecca, housing the 1,500,000-volume **Biblioteca Nazionale,** which contains carbonized scrolls from the Villa dei Papiri (p. 405) in Herculaneum. Also in the *palazzo* is the famous **Teatro San Carlo,** built in 1737 and reputed to have better acoustics than La Scala in Milan. For info on performances, see **Entertainment and Festivals,** p. 580. *(P. Plebiscito 1. Theater entrance on P. Trieste e Trento. Palazzo ☎081 40 05 47; www.pierreci.it. Library ☎081 78 19 231. Theater ☎081 79 72 331; www.itineranapoli.com. Palazzo open M-Tu and Th-Su 9am-7pm. Library open by reservation Tu, Th, Sa 10am-1pm; M-F 3:30pm-7pm. Palazzo exhibitions €3. Palazzo apartments and exhibitions €6; EU students €3; under 18, over 65, and those with Campania Artecard free.)*

CASTELNUOVO O MASCHIO ANGIONO. It's impossible to miss this five-turreted landmark that dominates the Neapolitan skyline. Built in 1284 by Charles II of Anjou as his Naples residence, the fortress's most stunning feature is the soaring triumphal entrance marked by reliefs that com-

TRASH TALK

After nearly a decade of trash problems, Naples may finally be cleaning up its act—and its streets. In 2008, the amount of uncollected garbage exceeded 7,000 tons in the metropolitan region around Naples, enough for the EU to finally put its foot down on the boot. Prime Minister Silvio Berlusconi has made it a priority to rescue Naples's nearly defunct municipal waste disposal system from the hands of the Camorra (the Neapolitan Mafia) and to reverse the dumping trend that health experts warned would breed infectious diseases and rat infestations, and thus an increase in cancer and genetic defects.

As attempts to export the city's trash have yielded no sustainable solution, both citizens and politicians are pushing for the latest but not last resort: a *termovalorizzatore,* or incinerator. The chosen model would be located in a former US military space in Agnano (northwest of Naples). Engineers affirm that the state-of-the-art technology, which can burn up to 250,000 tons per year, would pose low risks for the area—and even produce electricity from the combustion process.

Meanwhile, Naples's tourist industry is less than healthy as a result. World-renowned museums, cathedrals, and pizza pies are often skipped over by tourists who fear contact with the *immondizia* (Italian for the trash problem), and assume trash and pickpockets are all that the city has to offer.

memorate the arrival of Alphonse I of Aragon in 1443. Don't miss WWII bullet holes left on the northern wall. Though actual exhibitions are limited—with the exception of a huge bronze helmet standing about 3m tall—the castle offers wonderful views of Naples. The splendid **Cappella Palatina,** also called the Chapel of St. Barbara, is a cool retreat from the castle's windy open churchyard. *(P. Municipio. Take the R2 bus from P. Garibaldi, or walk from centro storico. ☎081 42 01 241. Open M-Sa 9am-6pm. €5.)*

CASTEL DELL'OVO (EGG CASTLE). This massive, yellow-brick Norman castle was built on a large chunk of tufa rock. Virgil—who was believed in medieval times to possess magical powers—is said to have put an enchanted egg in the foundation. According to legend, if the egg breaks, the city will crumble. Originally a monastery, the structure was converted to a fortress to defend against invaders at the end of the AD fifth century. It offers beautiful views, especially during sunset. *(Borgo Marinari. Take bus #1 from P. Garibaldi or P. Municipio to San Lucia and walk across the jetty. ☎081 24 00 055. Open M-Sa 8:30am-6pm, Su 8am-2pm.)*

GALLERIA UMBERTO I. Though now a shopping mall busy with vendors selling designer knockoffs, this 19th-century building is one of Naples's most beautiful. Designed by Emanuele Rocco and inspired by a similar gallery in Milan, this space became a meeting place for Allied soldiers toward the end of WWII and is now honored in John Horne Burns's *The Gallery* and Norman Lewis' *Naples '44. (P. Trieste e Trento. Most stores open daily 10am-1pm and 4-8pm.)*

SHOPPING

A thriving black market and low prices make Naples an enticing place for shopping—as long as you keep in mind that the street vendor's livelihood depends on his craftiness, so given the chance to outwit you, he will. If a transaction seems too good to be true, it is. **Never buy electronic products from street vendors.** Even brand-name boxes have been known to be filled with newspaper or rocks, and CDs and DVDs are often blank. The same applies to cigarettes—don't go there, or you may be sorry. In the dog-eat-dog world of unregulated transactions, bargaining is the law.

> **! TWO WORDS ABOUT BARGAINING.** Do it.

There is a bustling street market on **Via Pasquale Stanislao Mancini,** across P. Garibaldi from Stazione Centrale (open daily from about 8am to 1pm). **Via Santa Maria di Constantinopoli,** south of the Archaeological Museum, has old books and antique shops. **Spaccanapoli** and its side streets near the Conservatorio house small music shops with inexpensive manuscripts. **Via Toledo, Corso Umberto I,** and **Via Duomo** provide high-class shopping for a lower budget, and the streets south of **San Lorenzo Maggiore** house Neapolitan craftsmen. **Piazza Martiri** offers major Italian designers, and **Galleria Umberto** has plenty of high-end stores. The most expensive shopping district is in the hills of **Vomero** along the perpendicular **Via Scarlatti** and **Via Luca Giordano.** Many artisans' workshops inhabit the streets nearby, hawking everything from wrought iron to delicate cameos. Most markets are open Monday through Saturday from 9am to 2pm. Two weekends of every month (1 per month June-July), the **Fiera Antiquaria Neapolitana,** along V. Francesco Caracciolo on the waterfront, hosts flea markets filled with ancient artifacts. Though such items come with hefty price tags, hundreds of shoppers wander through the stands browsing stamps, books, coins, and art. *(☎081 62 19 51. Open daily 8am-2pm.)* From early December to early January, Neapolitan artisans gather along the Spaccanapoli and surrounding streets to create fine handmade porcelain nativity scenes. Renowned throughout Europe, this spectacle draws a huge international crowd.eZ   Entertainment And Festivals Once famous occasions for revelry, Naples's religious festivals are now excuses for sales and shopping sprees. On September 19 and the first Saturday in May, the city celebrates the **Festa di San Gennaro.** Join the crowd to watch the procession by the *duomo* in May and see the patron saint's blood miraculously liquefy in a vial. In July, P. San Domenico Maggiore holds concerts and the **Neapolis Festival** hosts pop concerts at Arena Flegrea in Campi Flegrei.

Teatro San Carlo (☎081 79 72 331 or 79 72 412), at Palazzo Reale. Hosts symphony (Oct.-May) and opera (Dec.-June) performances. Gallery tickets should be purchased in advance (from €12). Consult the ticket office and *Il Mattino* for schedules.

Stadio San Paolo (☎081 23 95 623), in Fuorigrotta. Ⓜ Campi Flegrei, or buses 152, M1, or SEPSA. Catch a soccer match for an accurate portrait of Neapolitan life. **Napoli,** in Serie A (the 1st division), attracts spectators Sept.-June. Tickets from €15.

◐ NIGHTLIFE

Travelers hoping to dance the night away may be surprised by the lack of discos, but Naples is not without nightlife. Come summer, young Neapolitans pack the *piazze* by the hundreds, especially on Sundays. The ◐evening aperitivo, a predinner drink accompanied by light fare, is an institution among older crowds. To maximize your enjoyment of the city's bustling nocturnal scene, follow this crash course in *piazza* personalities. At night, **Piazza Gesù Nuovo** and **Piazza Duomo** are crammed with university students who firmly believe in the "healing powers" of certain botanicals. **Via Santa Maria La Nova** are also always packed with crowds looking for a late-night hot dog or low-priced liquor (beer usually €1). The area around **Piazza dei Martiri** in Chiaia has the most bars, while the *aperitivo* culture thrives on **Via Giuseppe Ferrigni.** Bars in the quieter **Piazza Bellini** host a relaxed mix of locals and tourists at its *librerie* and Wi-Fi-equipped bars. The *piazza* is also a gathering point for the gay community. The young and chic gather at **Piazza Vanvitelli,** just a short Metro or funicular ride alongside **V. Toledo.** Beware: buses and funiculars may not run past 11pm. *Il Mattino* and *Zero 81* guides print decent club listings. From September through June, **Angels of Love** attracts world-renowned DJs to host parties for upward of 5,000 people in the outskirts of Naples. Grand-scale bashes of this kind are typically accessible only by car or taxi (☎330 86 83 23 or 339 68 23 066; www.angelsoflove.it).

CENTRO STORICO

▨ **Rising South,** V. San Sebastiano 19 (☎081 33 36 53 42 73; www.risingsouth.it), near P. Gesù Nuovo. *Enoteca,* bar, cultural association, cinema—this club does it all. Plush, Oriental carpets, vintage chandeliers, and a soundproof main hall carved from tufa set the scene at this student favorite for term-time fun. Mixed drinks €3-6. Open as a bar Sept.-May Tu-Su 10pm-3am (depending on weather) and for special events in summer.

Caffè Letterario Evaluna, P. Bellini 72 (☎081 29 23 72; www.evaluna.it). Appeals to an intellectual crowd or those who have always wanted to drink in a library (for whatever reason), with books laid out for skimming and rotating photo and painting exhibitions; focus on feminist literature. Secluded outdoor courtyard holds theater performances. Beer from €3. Spirits and mixed drinks €5-7. Wine €4. Open M-Sa in summer 7pm-1am, in winter 5-11pm. AmEx/MC/V.

Lemme Lemme By Internet Bar, P. Bellini 74 (☎081 29 52 37). Located in 1 of Naples's more peaceful *piazze,* this bar has art expos, internet access, and outdoor seating. The music is as soft as the relaxed atmosphere. Internet and Wi-Fi €0.05 per min. Beer €3-5. Mixed drinks €5. *Aperitivo* daily 6pm-7pm. F Oct.-Apr. live jazz and blues. Open daily in summer 9am-2am; in winter 6pm-2am. AmEx/D/MC/V.

OUTDOOR ACTIVITIES

The **waterfront** streets of Naples afford city-dwellers a great opportunity for relaxation. A 4km rocky shoreline stretches from V. Nazaro Sauro in the P. del Plebiscito area through V. Caracciolo in Mergellina. Ignoring the nearby ports, Neapolitans claim these rocks as their escape from the city, bathing in the sun and casually dipping into the bay or swimming around the Castel dell'Ovo. Kiosks at **Piazza Nazaro Sauro** sell refreshing drinks and even lemon-sprayed, salted tripe late into the night. Downstairs in the *piazza*, easygoing locals let **rowboats.** (☎081 33 19 86 98 09. Open daily 7am-9pm. €20 for 2hr., but counter-offers are highly recommended.) Currents are generally mild, and **swimming** in the open water is both refreshing and cleaner than near the shore. Find shade and enjoy a picnic at the **Villa Communale**, a large public park which stretches along V. Caracciolo opposite to the waterfront. (Open daily 7am-midnight. Free.) Waterfront bars abound along V. Partenope. If you're famished after a swim, **Bar dell'Ovo**, V. Partenope 6, outdoes its surrounding competitors with an *aperitivo* hour (7pm), a *discoteca* (Nov.-May Th-Su midnight-5am), an electrifying bar crew, and outdoor seating characteristic of the *lungomare*. (☎081 24 74 653. Beer €3. Wine €4. Mixed drinks €4.50. Open 8am-3am. Cash only.)

POMPEII (POMPEI)

On the morning of August 24, AD 79, a deadly cloud of volcanic ash from the eruption of nearby Mt. Vesuvius overtook Pompeii (pom-PAY), engulfing the city in black clouds. Many fled, but others—including the famous historian Pliny the Elder—unaware of the severity of the eruption or scared their property would be stolen, decided to stay. Mere hours after the eruption, stately buildings, works of art, and human bodies were sealed in casts of ash—natural tombs that went undisturbed for centuries. Today, visitors to the site bear witness to an intimate record of the town's demise. Since excavation efforts began in 1748, archaeologists have continually turned up discoveries in their ongoing mission to understand life in the Roman era. Most of the interesting artifacts from Pompeii are in Naples's Museo Archeologico Nazionale (p. 397) meaning that the site itself consists mostly of buildings and streets. To get more out of your trip to Pompeii, preface it with a visit to the museum's extensive Pompeii collection and listen to the audio tour.

TRANSPORTATION AND PRACTICAL INFORMATION

The quickest route to Pompeii (25km south of Naples) is the Circumvesuviana **train** (☎081 77 22 444). Board at Naples's Stazione Centrale (dir.: Sorrento; 40min., 2 per hr. 5:40am-10:40pm, €2.30) or from Sorrento's station. Get off at "Pompei Scavi." The **Porta Marina** entrance to the city is downhill to the left. Trenitalia trains also leave from the Naples station, stopping at modern Pompeii en route to Salerno (30min., every hr., €2.20). The Trenitalia station is a 10min. walk from the excavations' eastern entrance; to reach it, walk to the end of V. Statale until it becomes V. Sacra and turn left on V. Roma.

The excavations stretch along an east-west axis, with the modern town (and its hotels and restaurants) at the eastern end. Stop by the **tourist office**, V. Sacra 1 (☎081 85 07 255; www.pompeiisites.org), or the info booth at the site for a

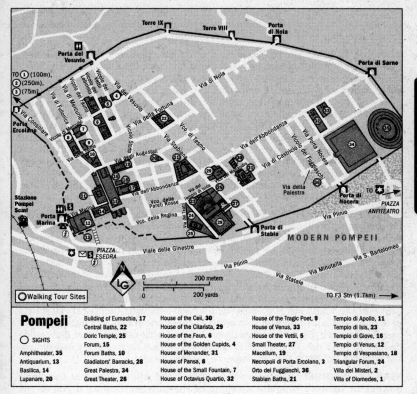

Pompeii

○ SIGHTS

Amphitheater, 35
Antiquarium, 13
Basilica, 14
Lupanare, 20

Building of Eumachia, 17
Central Baths, 22
Doric Temple, 25
Forum, 15
Forum Baths, 10
Gladiators' Barracks, 28
Great Palestra, 34
Great Theater, 26

House of the Ceii, 30
House of the Citarista, 29
House of the Faun, 6
House of the Golden Cupids, 4
House of Menander, 31
House of Pansa, 8
House of the Small Fountain, 7
House of Octavius Quartio, 32

House of the Tragic Poet, 9
House of Venus, 33
House of the Vettii, 5
Small Theater, 27
Macellum, 19
Necropoli di Porta Ercolano, 3
Orto dei Fuggiaschi, 36
Stabian Baths, 21

Tempio di Apollo, 11
Tempio di Isis, 23
Tempio di Giove, 16
Tempio di Venus, 12
Tempio di Vespasiano, 18
Triangular Forum, 24
Villa dei Misteri, 2
Villa of Diomedes, 1

free map. From the Pompei Scavi stop, take a right; follow the road down the hill to the **branch office**, P. Porta Marina Inferiore 12. (☎081 800 013 350. Both offices open M-F 8am-3:30pm, Sa 8am-2pm.) Free **luggage storage** and an **ATM** are available at ruins entrance. There is a **police station** and a **post office** (☎081 85 06 164; open M-F 8:30am-1:30pm and Sa 8:30am-noon) at the entrance, P. Esedra 1. Another police station at P. Bartolo Longo, where V. Roma ends.

SIGHTS

A comprehensive exploration of Pompeii takes all day. A popular tourist attraction year-round, Pompeii's **ruins** are most crowded in the spring when they are visited by throngs of school groups. A trip in early summer or fall is best for avoiding the crowds. (Ruins open daily Apr.-Oct. 8:30am-7:30pm; Nov.-Mar. 8:30am-5pm. Last entry 1hr. before close. Tickets €11, EU students €5.50, EU citizens under 18 or over 65 free. No re-entry. Wheelchair access through the eastern entrance at P. Anfiteatro.) Those planning to visit several sites should consider buying a three-day archeological pass to Pompeii, Herculaneum, Opionti, Stabia, and Boscoreale. (€20, EU citizens €10. Sold at site ticket office.) The budget-conscious in search of an engaging tour should consider the excellent audio tours, available at the site's entrance, to supplement the free map.

(€6.50, 2 tours for €10, children's tour €4.50.) Independent guides gather solo travelers by the ticket office to form tour groups. Informative guided tours are crowded and expensive (2hr., €90 for 3 people).

NEAR THE FORUM. The **basilica** walls are to the right upon entering the ruins. Before the eruption, lawyers and prominent citizens fought battles on this floor. Walk farther down V. Marina to reach the **forum,** ringed by a marble colonnade. Once dotted with statues of emperors and gods, this site was the city's commercial, civic, and religious center. Glass display cases house gruesome body casts of Vesuvius's victims, contorted in shock and agony. The **Tempio di Giove**—largely destroyed by an earthquake 17 years before the eruption—stands at the upper end of the forum and offers a view of Mt. Vesuvius. To the left, the **Tempio di Apollo** contains copies of the statues of Apollo and Diana (originals displayed in the **Museo Archeologico Nazionale,** (p. 397) and a column topped by a sundial. With the Tempio di Giove behind you, the **Tempio di Vespasiano** across the forum retains a delicate frieze depicting preparations for a sacrifice. To the right, the **Building of Eumachia** has a door frame carved with animals and insects.

NEAR THE HOUSE OF THE FAUN. At the **Forum Baths,** notice rooms allotted for servants who accompanied their patrons to watch their belongings. The **House of the Faun** has yielded stunning treasures, among them a dancing bronze faun and the spectacular Alexander Mosaic (originals in the **Museo Archeologico Nazionale,** p. 397). The building's opulence leads archaeologists to believe that it was the dwelling of one of the richest men in town. The **House of the Vettii** was the home of two brothers whose rivalry is apparent on every wall. A famous painting of the fertility god Priapus, flaunting his very ample endowment, is in the vestibule. Phalli were considered lucky and believed to scare off evil spirits in ancient times. Notice the ruts worn in the stone roads by chariot wheels passing through. *(Exit the forum through the upper end by the cafeteria; Forum Baths are on the left. A right on V. della Fortuna leads to the House of the Faun. Continuing on V. della Fortuna, turn left on Vco. dei Vettii to reach the House of the Vettii on the left.)*

NEAR THE BROTHEL. The racier side of Pompeii can be found at the small brothel, or **Lupanare** (literally, dwelling of she-wolves). Beware if you've got young travelers in tow: the brothel is unsurprisingly covered in pornographic imagery. The **Stabian Baths** were privately owned and therefore fancier than the Forum Baths; the women's side has an impressive marine-creature mosaic. More body casts—some of the site's most gruesome and impressive—rest in dusty glass cases. *(From Vco. dei Vettii, cross V. della Fortuna over to Vco. Storto, and turn left on V. degli Augustali to reach Lupanare. Baths are on the main avenue, V. dell'Abbondanza.)*

NEAR THE GREAT THEATER. The **Great Theater,** built during the second century BC, was already somewhat destroyed by the time the volcano erupted. Many stone-walled cells, thought to have been **Gladiators' Barracks,** line the edges of the field in front. The nearby **Small Theater** was used for music and poetry. North of the theaters stands the **Tempio di Isis,** Pompeii's monument to the Egyptian goddess. At the end of the street, take a left to re-connect to the main road. The altar was built to ward off evil spirits, which Romans believed gathered at crossroads. *(Across V dell'Abbondanza from the baths, V. dei Teatri leads to the theaters.)*

SOME DON'T LIKE IT HOT. The sites at Pompeii provide few water fountains and little shade. Bring lots of water to avoid heat stroke. If you need medical attention, flag down a guide or call ☎113. Remember, you are walking a whole city! Don't think that because it's ancient, it's small.

NEAR THE AMPHITHEATER. Red graffiti covers the walls along V. dell'Abbondanza with everything from political slogans to insults to declarations of love. At the end of the street await the **House of Octavius Quartio** and **House of Venus,** where gardens have been replanted according to modern knowledge of ancient horticulture. Nearby is the impeccably preserved **amphitheater** (70 BC), which once held crowds of 20,000. The spectators determined whether a gladiator would live or die during battle with a casual thumbs-down or thumbs-up. In the **Orto dei Fuggiaschi,** some of the body casts of fleeing victims display expressions and individual facial features. Also nearby, the **Great Palestra's** columns still surround a courtyard that once housed exercise sessions for local boys and now offers a great place to rest under the shadows of surrounding trees.

VILLA DEI MISTERI. Outside the city walls, the **Villa dei Misteri** is the best-preserved Pompeiian villa; gape at the extravagant atrium and the varied architecture—all "Four Styles" of Pompeii are displayed. The *Dionysiac Frieze* depicts a bride's initiation into the cult of Dionysus. Nearby, the famed **Cave Canem mosaic** still guards the entry to its master's villa, known as the **House of the Tragic Poet.** Head through the *porta* for a great view of the entire city. *(For the Villa go to western end of V. della Fortuna, turn right on V. Consolare, and walk up Villa delle Tombe.)*

HERCULANEUM (ERCOLANO)

To reach Herculaneum, take a Circumvesuviana train from Naples's Stazione Centrale to "Ercolano Scavi" (dir.: Sorrento; 20min.). Walk 500m downhill to the ticket office. The Municipal Tourist Office, V. IV Novembre 82, is on the way (☎081 78 81 243; open M-Sa 9am-2pm). Archaeological site: ☎081 85 75 347; www.pompeiisites.org. Open Apr.-Oct. daily 8:30am-7:30pm; Nov.-Mar. 8:30am-5pm. Last entry 1hr. before close. €11, EU students €5.50, EU citizens under 18 or over 65 free. Audio tours (in English, French, German, Italian, or Spanish) are especially enlightening. 1-2hr.; €6.50, 2 for €10; under 18 €4/7. Grab an illustrated guidebook (€4-6) at the shops that flank the entrance, or pick up the free Brief Guide to Herculaneum and map at the entrance. Free mandatory bag check.

Neatly excavated and intact, the remains of this prosperous Roman town hardly deserve the term "ruins." Buried in superheated volcanic tuff instead of the ash that covered Pompeii, Herculaneum (in Italian, "ehr-co-LA-no") is much more intact—many buildings still have second stories—and better preserved than its larger and more famous neighbor. Exploring the houses—complete with frescoes, furniture, mosaics, and small sculptures can make a tourist feel more like a house guest; artifacts displayed in their original contexts lend to a very rewarding and informative experience.

Though archaeologists long held the opinion that most of Herculaneum's residents escaped the eruption that destroyed Pompeii, a 1982 discovery of skeletons huddled in a boathouse suggests that a large part of the population was buried while attempting to get away. Much of the city remains un-excavated, and only about a quarter of the city is open to the public. One of the more opulent buildings is the **House of Deer,** named for the grisly statues of deer being mauled by packs of dogs. Here, archaeologists also found the statues *Satyr with a Wineskin* and *Drunken Hercules,* a majestic marble representation of the hero struggling to relieve himself. The **palestra,** a gym and exercise complex, complete with a large vaulted swimming pool, still holds shelves once laden with massage oils and the *strigili* (back scrapers) used to clean skin after a rubdown. The **House of Neptune and Amphitrite** is famous for a stellar mosaic. The house is connected to a remarkably well-preserved **wine shop.** Dating to the second century BC, the **Samnite House** is one of the oldest buildings in Herculaneum. Down the street, the three-floored **House of the Wooden Partition** still has a door in its elegant courtyard and a clothes press around the corner. Outside the site lies the **theater,** perfectly preserved though buried underground. A well dug in 1709 unearthed the theater and catalyzed excavation of the rest of Herculaneum; unfortunately, the theater was soon stripped of its valuable decorations. (☎081 73 24 311. Occasionally open for visits; call to check.) The extravagant 250m-long **Villa dei Papiri**, 500m west of Herculaneum, earned its name in 1752 when papyrus scrolls were found inside; the highly damaged works are still being studied and restored—thus far, no classics have been found. (Rarely open to the public; Campania Artecard holders can view the site by special arrangement. Contact municipal tourist office at ☎081 78 81 243 for details. Scrolls on display at Biblioteca Nazionale, p. 399)

their word. Lacco Ameno and Casamicciola Terme are packed with thermal baths. The springs are often closed due to falling rocks; ask the tourist office before setting out. *(Reach the beach from Panza by a 20min. hike.)*

BAY OF NAPLES

Home to the pleasant islands of Capri, Ischia, and Procida, and the coastal town of Sorrento, the Bay of Naples could hardly seem further away from the city that shares its coast. When in the Bay, the golden rule is to just take it easy.

CAPRI AND ANACAPRI ☎081

Nicknamed "the pearl of the Mediterranean," Capri (CA-pree; pop. 7000) has been a destination of the rich and famous for thousands of years. Augustus fell in love with Capri in 29 BC before trading its rocky cliffs for the fertile, volcanic Ischia. His successor Tiberius passed his last decade here, leaving scattered villas and a legacy of idyllic retirement homes. Today's royalty flits between ritzy boutiques and top-notch restaurants. Perched on the hills above Capri, Anacapri (AH-na-CA-pree; pop. 5000) is a relative oasis of budget hotels, lovely villas, and deserted mountain paths. Take time to revel in the relaxed island life while enjoying a languid stroll along Capri's cobblestone paths, a breezy vista from Monte Solaro, or a dip in the Grotta Azzurra.

FROGGER IT! Keep to the footpaths in Capri if you're planning on walking. The very narrow streets have no sidewalks and vehicles move at high speeds without watching for pedestrians. Walking on the major thoroughfares is strongly discouraged, so take the bus to faraway destinations.

◪ TRANSPORTATION

Ferries and Hydrofoils: Capri's main port is **Marina Grande.** Naples and Sorrento are the main gateways to Capri.

Caremar (☎081 83 70 700) runs to **Naples** (ferries: 1hr., 3 per day 5:45am-2:50pm, €9.60; hydrofoils: 1hr., 4 per day 10:25am-10:20pm, €15) and **Sorrento** (hydrofoils: 25min., 4 per day 7am-6:15pm, €7.10).

SNAV (☎081 83 77 577) runs hydrofoils to **Naples** (45min., 7 per day 8:10am-6:10pm, €17).

Linea Jet (☎081 83 70 819) runs hydrofoils to **Naples** (40-50min., 11 per day 9:35am-7:10pm, €17) and **Sorrento** (25min., 12 per day 9:20am-7pm, €15).

Public Transportation: SIPPIC buses (☎081 83 70 420) depart from V. Roma in Capri for **Anacapri** (every 15min. 6am-2am), Marina Piccola, and points in between. In Anacapri, buses depart from P. Barile, off V. G. Orlandi, for the Grotta Azzurra (Blue Grotto), the *faro* (lighthouse), and more. From Marina Grande to P. Vittoria in **Anacapri** (every hr. 5:45am-10:10pm; €1.40, day pass €6.90). Note that all-day pass is rarely worth it. **Funicular** from Marina Grande to **Capri** (every 10min. 6:30am-1:30am, €1.40).

Taxis: At main bus stop in Marina Grande (☎081 83 70 543), at bus stop in Capri (☎081 83 70 543), or in P. Vittoria, in Anacapri (☎081 83 71 175).

 KEEP THE CHANGE. On Capri, tickets (€1.40) are generally bought onboard the bus. Have exact change on hand to avoid holding up the bus; it won't leave until you pay.

ORIENTATION AND PRACTICAL INFORMATION

There are two towns on the isle of Capri: **Capri** proper, near the ports, and **Anacapri,** higher up. Ferries dock at **Marina Grande,** below the town of Capri. To get to Anacapri, either wait in long lines for the funicular, take the bus, or trek for 1hr. up the steep and winding stairway. Expensive boutiques and bakeries line the streets that radiate from **Piazza Umberto. Via Roma,** to the right exiting the funicular, leads to Anacapri. The bus to Anacapri passes through **Piazza Vittoria,** the main square; Villa San Michele and the Monte Solaro chairlift are nearby.

Tourist Office: AAST (☎081 83 70 634; www.capritourism.com). At Marina Grande. Open daily 9am-1pm and 3:30-6:45pm. Branches: Capri, in P. Umberto (☎081 83 70 686), under the clock. Open M-Sa 8:30am-8:30pm, Su 8:30am-2:30pm. Anacapri, V. G. Orlandi 59 (☎081 83 71 524), right from bus stop. Open M-Sa 9am-3pm. All provide free detailed maps, ferry and bus info, and *Capri è...*, a magazine with detailed info on the island's hotels and restaurants. Multilingual staff. Reduced hours Oct.-May.

Currency Exchange: V. Roma 31 (☎081 83 74 768), across from the main bus stop, and in P. Umberto. Also in Anacapri at P. Vittoria 2 (☎081 83 73 146). Open in summer daily 8am-6pm; winter hours vary.

Luggage Storage: Outside Capri's funicular. €4 per bag per day. Open daily in summer 8:30am-8pm; in winter 8:15am-7pm.

English-Language Bookstore: Librerie Studio La Conchiglia, V. Le Botteghe 12 (☎081 83 76 577; www.laconchigliacapri.com), in Capri, off P. Umberto. Open daily in summer 9am-1:30pm and 3-10:30pm; in winter 9am-1:30pm and 3-9pm.

Emergency: ☎081 83 81 205.

Police: V. Roma 70 (☎081 83 74 211), in Anacapri.

Medical Services: Ospedale Capilupi, V. Provinciale Anacapri 5 (☎081 83 81 111), a few blocks down V. Roma from P. Umberto. **Tourist Medical Clinic,** V. Caprile 30 (☎081 83 81 240), in Anacapri. **Ambulance:** ☎081 83 81 205.

Internet Access: Bar Due Pini, P. Vittoria (☎081 83 78 160), in Anacapri. €7 per hr. Open daily 8:30am-6:30pm.

Post Office: Anacapri, Vle. Tommaso. de Tommaso 8 (☎081 83 71 015). Open M-F 8:30am-1:30pm, Sa 8:30am-noon. **Capri,** V. Roma 50 (☎081 97 85 211). Open M-F 8:30am-7pm, Sa 8:30am-1pm. **Postal Codes:** 80071 (Anacapri), 80073 (Capri).

ACCOMMODATIONS

Lodgings in Capri proper are pricey year-round and become even more expensive in the summer; daytrip from Naples or Sorrento to save money. Though cheaper and more serene than Capri, Anacapri will dent anyone's budget. Camping is a great option as long as you make sure you find a legitimate campground; makeshift camping is illegal and heavily fined.

CAMPANIA

ANACAPRI

Hotel Bussola, V. Traversa La Vigna 14 (☎081 83 82 010; www.bussolahermes.com). Call from P. Vittoria in Anacapri for pickup rather than navigate Anacapri's streets. A new building; imitates the neoclassical style of Pompeii, with statues and mosaics. Mediterranean rooms with flat-screen TV, phone, safe, and bath; some with terrace. A/C €10 per day. Free Wi-Fi. Breakfast included. Singles €70-130; doubles €70-130; triples €85-150; quads €90-180. *Let's Go* discount 8%; reserve via phone or email. MC/V. ●

Villa Mimosa Bed and Breakfast, V. Nuova del Faro 48/A (☎081 83 71 752; www.mimosacapri.com). 100m on the right past the last stop of the Marina Grande-Anacapri bus. Elegant rooms surround a terrace; all come with satellite TV, A/C, safe, and bath. Breakfast included. Doubles €70-110. 10% *Let's Go* discount Oct.-Mar. MC/V. ●

Hotel Loreley, V. G. Orlandi, 16 (☎081 83 71 440; www.loreley.it). Convenient location by the funicular/bus stop in Anacapri. Tranquility and relaxation are the order of the day. Large clean rooms with great vistas. Open Mar. 15-Nov. Singles €60-85; doubles €80-120. Extra bed €30. 10% *Let's Go* discount weekdays Sept.-July. AmEx/MC/V. ●

CAPRI

Villa Palomba, V. Mulo 3 (☎081 83 77 322; www.capri.it/villapalomba), off V. M. Piccola. Friendly owners and great vistas make this relaxed, private spot a nice place even for young travelers. Best deal in Capri. Rooms with TV, minibar, safe, bath, and A/C (€10 per day). Breakfast included. Singles €45-75; doubles €75-125. MC/V. ●

Hotel La Tosca, V. Dalmazio Birago 5 (☎081 83 70 989; www.latoscahotel.com). Take V. Cimino from P. Umberto, then turn left on V. D. Birago. Soothing terrace facing the Faraglioni rocks. Simple rooms with phone, A/C, and bath. Breakfast included. Open Apr.-Oct. Doubles €70-140. Cash only. ●

Vuotto Antonino, V. Campo di Teste 2 (☎/fax 081 83 70 230). Take V. V. Emanuele from P. Umberto, turn left on V. Camerelle, right on V. Cerio, and left. In "Villa Margherita." Antique-filled rooms with terraces. Open Mar.-Nov. Doubles €70-105. Cash only. ●

Albergo 4 Stagioni, V. M. Piccola 1 (☎081 83 70 041; www.hotel4stagionicapri.com). From P. Umberto, walk 5min. down V. Roma. Turn left at the 3-pronged fork in the road; look for green gate on the left. 12 plain and pristine rooms. Pricier doubles enjoy garden access and sea views. Breakfast included. Open Mar.-Nov. Singles €40-70; doubles €70-130. Extra bed €20-25. Ask about *Let's Go* discount. MC/V. ●

▣ FOOD

Savor creamy local mozzarella served with sweet red tomatoes, glistening olive oil, and zesty basil in an *insalata caprese*—the island's trademark, which many consider the *sine qua non* (a must-have) of summer dining. Conclude with the indulgent *torta di mandorle* (chocolate almond cake), also known as *torta caprese*. Be discerning around P. Umberto, where restaurants serve overpriced stale pastries. Fruit stands around the island sell delectable goods at low prices. (Open daily 8am-1pm and 4-8pm.) In Anacapri, find fixings at the well-stocked **supermarket,** V. G. Orlandi 299. (☎081 83 71 119. Open M-Sa 8:30am-1:30pm and 5-8:30pm, Su 8:30am-noon.) Interestingly enough, it is often cheaper to buy *panini* at restaurants than at *salumerie*. **Via Giuseppe Orlandi,** running from P. Vittoria, leads past restaurants on the way.

ANACAPRI

Al Nido D'Oro, Vle. T. de Tommaso 32 (☎081 83 72 148), on the way to the bus stop for the Grotta Azzurra. Probably the cheapest restaurant on the island. Extremely popular with islanders for its high-quality *Caprese* cuisine. Pizza and drink €7. Primi €5-8. Lunch *menù* €12. Open M-Tu and Th-Su 11am-3:30pm and 7pm-midnight. ❶

🏛 **Da Giovanni a Gradola,** Località Gradola 8 (☎081 83 73 673). Though not as elegant as its upscale neighbors, this multi-level trattoria offers the same panoramic view of the Tyrrhenian Sea. Descend its stairs to a free uncrowded beach. *Panini* €5. Primi €8-10. Secondi €10-13. Open from mid-June to Sept. 9:30am-7:30pm. Cash only. ❷

🏛 **Ristorante Il Cucciolo,** V. La Fabbrica 52 (☎081 83 71 917). Try the fresh *ravioli Caprese* (€9). Seaside terrace. With *Let's Go* discount: primi and secondi €6-9. Service 12%. Open daily Mar.-Oct. noon-2:30pm and 7:30-11pm. AmEx/MC/V. ❷

Ristorante Materita, V. G. Orlandi 140 (☎081 83 73 375). Devour delicious pizza (from €6) on a candlelit terrace overlooking Anacapri's most fashionable *piazza,* then linger over house-made *limoncello.* Primi and secondi from €8.50. Cover €2.50. Open Apr.-Oct. daily 11:45am-3:30pm and 6:45-midnight; Nov.-Mar. M and W-Su 11:45am-3:30pm and 6:45pm-midnight. MC/V. ❷

Caffé Orlandi, V. G. Orlandi 83 (☎081 83 82 138). The ideal lunch-spot before a visit to Monte Solaro or a walk around Anacapri's *centro storico.* €10 lunch *menù;* includes salad, primi, and coffee. Open daily Feb.-Dec. 9am-10pm. MC/V. ❷

Vini e Bibite, P. Diaz (☎081 83 73 320). An oasis from the touristy tumult. Primi and secondi €6-13. Service 12%. Open daily noon-3pm and 7pm-midnight. ❸

La Rondinella, V. G. Orlandi 295 (☎081 83 71 223), near P. Vittoria. Enjoy a romantic, candlelit feast under a canopy. Fresh antipasti and seafood offerings, like succulent *gamberoni* (prawns; €21). Dinner reservations suggested. Primi €9-13. Secondi €9-15. Cover €3. Service 10%. Open daily noon-3pm and 7pm-midnight. AmEx/MC/V. ❸

CAPRI

🏛 **Longano da Tarantino,** V. Longano 9 (☎081 83 70 187), just off P. Umberto. Perhaps the best deal in town. Sea view and €18 *menù.* Packed, but service is friendly and efficient. Pizza €4-9. Excellent grilled seafood €10-13. Cover €0.80. Open Mar.-Nov. M-Tu and Th-Su 11:30am-3pm and 7pm-midnight. Reservations recommended. AmEx/MC/V. ❷

Villa Verde, Vico Sella Orta 6/A (☎081 83 77 024; www.villaverde-capri.com). Off V. V. Emanuele, near P. Umberto. Prices reflect the earning power of celeb guests whose pictures adorn the walls. Large portions of fresh fish and lobster. Specialties are *fusilli Villa Verde* (€15) and rich desserts (€5-7). Pizza €5.50-15. Primi €10-25. Secondi €12-25. Service 15%. Open daily noon-4pm and 7pm-1am. AmEx/MC/V. ❸

Aurora Pizzeria, V. Fuorlovado 20-22 (☎081 83 70 181; www.auroracapri.com). Celebs like Michael Douglas and Giorgio Armani come for the *Pizza al Acqua* (€10). Cover €3. Service 15%. Open daily Mar.-Dec. noon-3pm and 7pm-midnight. AmEx/MC/V. ❷

Gelateria Lo Sfizietto, V. Longano 6. Treat yourself to gelato (from €2) made from real fruit for a refreshing break from the Capri sun. Try *Cassatina,* a combo of chocolate chips and dry fruit. Cones from €2. Open daily Mar.-Dec. 10am-11:30pm. Cash only. ❶

👁 🔺 SIGHTS AND OUTDOOR ACTIVITIES

CLIFFS. An exploration of the island's natural beauty can be a much-needed break from crowded *piazze* and commercial streets. For those who prefer land to sea, various trails starting in Capri lead to stunning panoramas. At the island's eastern edge, a 1hr. round-trip walk connects the **Arco Naturale,** a majestic stone arch, and the **Faraglioni,** the three massive rocks featured on countless postcards. Part of the path is unpaved; wear proper footwear. (*V. Tragara goes from Capri Centro to the Faraglioni, while the path to the Arco Naturale connects to the route to Villa Jovis through V. Matermania.*) Hike a steep uphill path 45min. to the ruins of Emperor

CAMPANIA

Tiberius's magnificent **Villa Jovis.** Tiberius lived here, the largest of his 12 Capri villas, during his more eccentric final years. Always the gracious host, he was prone to tossing displeasing guests over the precipice. Sweeping views from the villa's **Cappella di Santa Maria del Soccorso** are unrivaled. (*Take V. Longano from P. Umberto. Don't miss the left on V. Tiberio, and follow the signs. Open daily 9am-6pm. €2.*)

COAST. Daily **boat tours** explore the gorgeous coast, including the Grotta Azzurra. (*Tickets and info at Grotta Azzurra Travel Office, V. Roma 53, across from the bus stop. ☎081 83 70 466; g.azzurra@capri.it. Ticket office open M-Sa 9am-1pm and 3:30-7pm, Su 9am-12:30pm. See below for info on Grotta Azzurra. Departures from Marina Grande at 9:30, 10:30, 11:30am. €13.*) Cavort in the clear water amid immense lava rocks, or rent a **motor boat** from **Banana Sport**, in Marina Grande. (*☎081 83 75 188 or 330 22 70 64. Open daily 9:30am-6:30pm. 2hr.; May-June and Sept.-Oct. €80; July-Aug. €95. AmEx/MC/V.*) Pebbly **beaches** surround the island. Take a Bagni Tiberio boat (€9 round-trip) from the port or walk between vineyards to **Bagni di Tiberio,** a bathing area within ruins of an imperial villa. A walk along **Marina Piccola** is also nice. (*Take V. Roma from P. Umberto to 3-pronged fork in road; take the left-most fork and head down the path to the left.*)

VILLA SAN MICHELE. Henry James once declared this Anacapri enclave a mix of "the most fantastic beauty, poetry, and inutility." The 20th-century estate displays Roman sculptures from a former Tiberian villa and glorious gardens, which host contemporary art shows and Friday night concerts from June to August. (*Upstairs from P. Vittoria and to the left, past Capri Beauty Farm spa. ☎081 83 71 401. Open daily 9am-6pm. Concert info available at ticket desk and tourist offices. Villa €6.*)

LA GROTTA AZZURRA (THE BLUE GROTTO). The walls of this water-filled cave shimmer vivid blue when sunlight radiates from beneath the water's surface (for this reason, the grotto is more impressive on sunnier days). Watch your head when entering. Some who visit find the water amazing; others don't think it's impressive enough to justify spending €9 on a guided tour (even if there *is* singing involved). Despite the narrow cave opening and the sign warning that swimming is "strictly forbidden," some visitors take dips in the grotto for free after boats stop at 5pm. Check with the tourist office to make sure that the grotto isn't closed due to choppy water. If you rent a boat, consider visiting the **Grotta Verde,** on the other side of the island. (*Take the bus marked "Grotta Azzurra" from the intersection of Vle. T. De Tommaso and V. Catena in Anacapri. The grotto is accessible with the island boat tour as well, but the entrance charge still applies.*)

OTHER SIGHTS. Capri's location makes it ideal for surveying southern Italy's topography. Viewed from the peak of ⛰**Monte Solaro,** the Apennines loom ahead to the east and the mountains of Calabria are to the south on the right. The vistas are so stunning that sky and sea actually seem to become one. A 12min. chairlift from P. Vittoria to the summit dangles from precipitous heights. (*☎081 83 71 428. Chairlift open daily July-Sept. 9am-6pm; Mar.-Apr. and Oct. 9:30am-4:45pm. Round-trip €7.*) Alternatively, take the difficult 45min. hike up V. Monte Solaro, which starts from the base near Villa San Michele. A bus from P. Vittoria leads to the **Faro Punta Carena,** Italy's second-tallest lighthouse, and a fairly desolate swimming area. The pedestrian stretch of V. G. Orlandi, off P. Vittoria in Anacapri, leads to the least expensive—yet still pricey—**shopping.**

🎵 NIGHTLIFE

Nocturnal action carries a hefty price tag, though Anacapri's prices are slightly lower. In typical Italian fashion, no one bothers heading out until around midnight. **Underground,** V. G. Orlandi 259, is one of the town's most popular night spots, thanks to no cover and €5 mixed drinks. In Capri try **BaraOnda,** V. Roma

8, which enjoys theme nights on most weekends. (☎081 83 77 147. Drinks €7.) Both Capri clubs are open all night. Those sufficiently self-assured to hang with dressed-to-kill Italians should remember that buses stop running at 1:40am. For a more sophisticated night, attend a Friday night concert at Villa San Michele.

AMALFI COAST

It happens almost imperceptibly: after the exhausting tumult of Naples and the compact grit of Sorrento, the highway narrows to a two-lane road that zigzags down the coastline. Though the effortless simplicity and sophistication of Positano, Amalfi, and Praiano seduced Emperor Augustus, Ernest Hemingway, and Jacqueline Kennedy Onassis, the region's ultimate appeal rests in the tenuous balance it strikes between man and nature. Whitewashed homes cling defiantly to rock and crazy bus drivers tame even crazier roads. The coast's unassuming grandeur is a reminder to simply relax and enjoy life.

POSITANO ☎089

As birthplace of the modern bikini, Positano (po-zee-TA-no; pop. 4000) has quite a reputation to live up to. In the mid-1900s, the town was a posh haven for artists and literati, attracting visitors such as John Steinbeck, Jack Kerouac, and Tennessee Williams. Positano's classy reputation soon drew millionaires in addition to the writers, painters, actors, and filmmakers who made it famous, and today, its beachfront teems with a diverse crowd of vacationers. Though tourism may have changed Positano since Steinbeck sought solitude along its coast, the town remains a playground for the rich, as well as for the not-so-famous—ordinary travelers seeking its tranquility and beauty.

▐ TRANSPORTATION

Over land, Positano is best reached by **bus.** Blue or green-and-white SITA buses run to Amalfi and Sorrento (June-Sept. 25 per day 7am-9pm, €2). There are two stops in Positano along V. G. Marconi, the main coastal road. Walk downhill from either stop to reach the *centro.* Tickets are sold at Bar Internazionale, by the Chiesa Nuova stop on V. G. Marconi, or at *tabaccherie.* Alternatively, catch a **ferry** or **hydrofoil** from Spiaggia Grande. Linee Marittime Partenopee (☎089 81 19 86) runs daily to Amalfi (ferry 25min., 9 per day 10am-6:30pm, €6; hydrofoil 15min., 3 per day 4-7:15pm, €7.50), Capri (ferry 40min., 8:50 and 10am, €14.50; hydrofoil 25min. 4 per day, 9am-6pm, €16.50), Salerno (ferry 1¼hr., 5:45 and 7:15pm, €10; hydrofoil 40min., 3 per day 4-7:15pm, €12), and Ischia (ferry 2hr., 8:50am, €19). Metro del Mare (☎089 199 600 700) runs hydrofoils daily to Amalfi (20min., 6 per day 8:50am-3:55pm, €9), Napoli Molo Beverello (1½hr., 5 per day 10:40am-7pm, €14), and Sorrento (40min., 4 per day 10:40am-7pm, €9).

◼▐ ORIENTATION AND PRACTICAL INFORMATION

Positano clings to two huge cliffs that overlook the Tyrrhenian Sea. Coming from Sorrento, **Chiesa Nuova** is the first SITA stop in town on **Via Guglielmo Marconi,** in front of Bar Internazionale. From here, if you don't mind the steep downhill walk, take **Viale Pasitea,** or wait for one of Positano's frequent **local buses** marked "Positano Interno" (every 15-30min. 7:15am-midnight, €1.50); the bus route ends in **Piazza dei Mulini.** The second SITA stop is at the intersection of V. G. Marconi and **Via Cristoforo Colombo;** internal buses don't run here, so walk 10min. downhill on V. C. Colombo to reach P. dei Mulini, where V. C. Colombo becomes Vle. Pasitea. Also from P. dei Mulini, **Via dei Mulini** winds through town, past the Santa Maria, and to **Spiaggia Grande,** the main beach. Take the footpath from Spiaggia Grande to get to the cozier **Fornillo** beach on the right.

Tourist Office: V. del Saraceno 4 (☎089 87 50 67; www.aziendaturismopositano.it), near the church. Provides a free map, hotel listings, and ferry and bus schedules. English spoken. Open in summer M-Sa 9am-2pm and 3-8pm; in winter M-Sa 9am-3pm.

Currency Exchange: P. dei Mulini 6 (☎089 87 58 64), on the V. Mulini side of the *piazza.* Decent rates; €1 commission per traveler's check. Open daily in summer 9:30am-1:30pm and 4-9:30pm; in winter 9:30am-1pm and 3:30-7:50pm.

English Language Bookstore: La Libreria, V. C. Colombo 165 (☎089 81 10 77). Open daily Apr.-Oct. 10am-1:30pm and 5-8:30pm. AmEx/MC/V.

Carabinieri: (☎089 87 50 11), near top of the cliffs down the steps by Chiesa Nuova.

Hospital: (☎089 081 533 1111), in Sorrento; a tourist medical clinic is in Amalfi.

Pharmacy: Vle. Pasitea 22 (☎089 87 58 63). Open in summer daily 9am-1pm and 5-9pm; in winter M-W and F-Sa 9am-1pm and 4-8pm.

Internet Access: Conwinum, V. Rampa Teglia 12 (☎089 81 16 87; www.positano.conwinum.it), below Buca di Bacco. €6 per hr. Open daily 9am-11pm.

Luggage Storage: Blu Porter, in front of the pharmacy at Vle. Pasitea 22 (☎089 81 14 96). Prices from €5 per day. Night service available.

Post Office: V. Guglielmo Marconi 320. Open M-F 8am-1:30pm, Sa 8am-12:30pm. **Postal code:** 84017.

ACCOMMODATIONS

Budget travelers might want to make Positano a daytrip from Sorrento or Salerno; there are few cheap accommodations. The tourist office helps arrange *affittacamere* for longer stays.

Ostello Brikette, V. G. Marconi 358 (☎089 87 58 57; www.brikette.com). Take an orange Interno bus or SITA bus to "Chiesa Nuova" stop and walk 100m to the left of Bar Internazionale. Rooms with A/C and great terrace views. English-speaking staff provides advice on sights and restaurants. Organic breakfast €1.50-6. Laundry €10. Free Wi-Fi. With *Let's Go* guide, free 30min. Internet access. Lockout 11am-2:30pm. Lights-out M-Th and Su midnight. No curfew for private rooms. Reservation recommended July-Aug. Open from late Mar. to Nov. Dorms €22-25; doubles €65-100. MC/V. ❷

Pensione Villa Verde, Vle. Pasitea 338 (☎089 87 55 06; www.pensionevillaverde.it). Take Interno bus to "Casale." 12 simple rooms overlooking Positano; all with terrace and bath. TV and A/C available upon request. Breakfast included. Open Mar.-Dec. €30-50 per person. Ask for *Let's Go* cash discount. AmEx/MC/V. ❸

Pensione Maria Luisa, V. Fornillo 42 (☎089 87 50 23; www.pensionemarialuisa.com). Take the Interno bus to V. Fornillo. English-speaking owner. Bright, comfortable rooms with bath, fridge, and seaside terrace. Free beach towel rental. Free Internet access with *Let's Go.* Singles €50; doubles €70-80; triples €90-100. Cash only. ❹

Pensione Villa delle Palme, Vle. Pasitea 252 (☎089 87 51 62; www.positanovilladellepalme.com). In the same building as Saraceno d'Oro restaurant, with an easily accessible beach. Rooms full of quirky antiques; all with bath, TV, and balcony or terrace. Breakfast €5. Doubles €75-85; triples €100-110. Cash only. ❹

Casa Guadagno, V. Fornillo 36 (☎089 87 50 42; fax 81 14 07). Take the Interno bus to V. Fornillo. All rooms have bath, minifridge, and terrace with seaside views. Internet access €2 per hr. Free Wi-Fi. Free breakfast on terrace. With *Let's Go* discount, doubles €85-90; triples €110; quads €120. Reservation recommended. Cash only. ❹

FOOD

In Positano, high prices generally reflect high quality: homemade pasta, fresh produce, and excellent seafood are the norm. The **Alimentari de Lucia Giovanni**, V. G. Marconi 512, sells fresh sandwiches, cheese, and produce. (☎089 87 50 99. Open daily M-Sa 7am-2pm and 4-9pm, Su 7am-2pm. Cash only.)

◼ **Da Constantino**, V. Corvo 95 (☎089 87 57 38). From Ostello Brikette, walk upstairs, and turn right when you hit the real road, or take the bus to Nocelle. Amazing views, sea breezes, and occasional live music. Try the specialty *crespolini al formaggio* (cheese crepes; €9). A vegetarian buffet is available (€9.50). Pizza from €4. Primi €5-10. Secondi €8-13. Open in summer daily noon-3:30pm and 7pm-midnight; in winter M-Tu and Th-Su noon-3:30pm and 7pm-midnight; closed Nov.-Jan. AmEx/MC/V. ●

◼ **C'era una volta**, V. G. Marconi 127 (☎089 81 19 30), near Ostello Brikette. Local and backpacker favorite. *Pizza margherita* €4. Live outdoor music F-Su. Primi €6-9. Secondi €5-11. Open daily May-Jan. noon-2:30pm and 7pm-midnight. AmEx/MC/V. ●

Il Grottino Azzurro, V. G. Marconi 304 (☎089 87 54 66), across from the "Chiesa Nuova" bus stop. Excellent fish and seafood priced right. Linger for hours in simple but inviting interior. House-made white wine €2. Fresh seafood from €9; spaghetti with squid €11. Homemade pasta dishes €8-10. Killer tiramisu €3. Cover €2. Open M-Tu and Th-Su 12:30-2:30pm and 7:30-10:30pm. Closed from Dec. to mid-Feb. MC/V. ●

Lo Guarracino, V. Positanesi d'America 12 (☎089 975 794). To avoid over-priced restaurants by Spiaggia Grande, take the stairs on the way to Fornillo Beach; the restaurant is to the right. Pizza €10; takeout €5. Primi and secondi €9-16. Reservations suggested for seaside tables. Open daily noon-3pm and 7pm-midnight. AmEx/MC/V. ●

Da Gabrisa, Vle. Pasitea 219 (☎089 81 14 98). Bright, breezy dining room and great service. Savor the grilled vegetable antipasto with tender pumpkin and plump mozzarella (€8). *Pasta alla norma* (pasta in tomato sauce with eggplant; €8) is a savory treat. Primi €7-16. Secondi €7-15. Open daily 12:30-2:30pm and 6-11pm. AmEx/MC/V. ●

👁 🏖 SIGHTS AND BEACHES

Tourists in Positano often peruse crowded boutiques and sidewalk kiosks, or take boat excursions along the coast and to neighboring islands, as well as the **Emerald** and **Blue Grottoes** (p. 410). For most, Positano's beaches are its main attraction. Your best bet for serene and secluded relaxation, and a waterside post-beach meal, is **Fornillo Beach**, hidden from the docks and downtown chaos by a shady, rocky walkway. Take **Via Positanese d'America**, a footpath that starts from the right side of the port facing the water and winds past **Torre Trasita**. There's a free beach left of La Marinella. Though crowded, the only free area of the expansive **Spiaggia Grande** is next to the docks. Outside the entrance, **Blue Star** (☎089 81 18 88; www.bluestarpositano.it) rents motorboats and rowboats, and provides boat tours of the Blue and Emerald Grottoes. For a short, free boat ride, jump on any of the small, white boats off Spiaggia Grande, which pass restaurants that can only be reached by sea.

Positano offers tremendous **hikes** for those with quads of steel. **Montepertuso**, a high mountain pierced by a large *pertusione* (hole), is one of three perforated mountains in the world (the other two are in India). Hike the 45min. trail or take the bus, which leaves from P. dei Mulini near the port. From Montepertuso, take the **Path of the Gods** (4hr.), which explores the surrounding area. Ask the tourist office for a map. The three **Isole dei Galli**, peeking out of the waters off Positano's coast, were allegedly home to Homer's mythical Sirens, who lured unsuspecting victims with their spellbinding songs. While swimming around these beautiful islands is permitted, setting foot on them is not.

🎵 🎭 ENTERTAINMENT AND NIGHTLIFE

Positano's Art Festival includes fashion shows, art exhibitions, dance, and music concerts at different spots in the city (Apr.-Oct.; contact tourist office for more info). The swanky piano bar and disco, **Music on the Rocks,** on the far left side of the beach facing the water, packs well-dressed locals and visitors into a large cave with one side open to the water. Celebrities like Denzel Washington and Lenny Kravitz have been known to drop in. (☎089 87 58 74. Mixed drinks from €12. Cover varies: M-Th and Su often free, Sa €25.) Catch the sun falling behind the mountains from **Next2,** Vle. Pasitea 242, and then stick around for a drink (€4-8) and lounge music. (☎089 81 23 516. Open daily Apr.-Nov. 8pm-2am.) Watch Positano light up for an enchanting night from **Sunrise Bar,** V. Pasitea 119, with light music and modern lounging over a breathtaking terrace. (☎089 87 50 10. Beer €4. Wine €3. Mixed drinks €8. Open daily 5pm-1am.)

AMALFI   ☎089

Picture-perfect Amalfi (ah-MAL-fee; pop. 5500) lies nestled between the jagged rocks of the Sorrentine peninsula and the azure waters of the Tyrrhenian Sea. Monuments like the fanciful Arab-Norman *duomo* and medieval paper mills are the legacy of a long history of international prominence. Amalfi was the seat of Italy's first sea republic and the preeminent maritime powerhouse of the southern Mediterranean, thanks in part to the compass, invented here by Flavio Gioia. Sadly, Amalfi's universal appeal is also responsible for the throngs of tourists, gaudy souvenir shops that characterize the town today. Consider daytripping from neighboring Atrani (ah-TRAH-nee; pop. 1000) to avoid the exorbitant prices. Southern Italy's smallest town, Atrani is a backpacker haven, offering many budget options.

🚆 TRANSPORTATION

The bus terminal is in P. Flavio Gioia, on the waterfront. SITA **buses** (☎089 26 66 04; www.sitabus.it.) go to Positano (40min., 25 per day 6:30am-11pm, €1.30), Salerno (1hr., 20 per day 6am-10pm, €1.80), and Sorrento (1hr., 29 per day 5:15am-11pm, €2). Salerno- and Ravello-bound buses pass the Atrani bus stop 5min. after leaving Amalfi. Buy tickets from *tabaccherie* (45min., €2; 1½hr., €3; 24hr., €6; 3-day, €15). **Ferries** and **hydrofoils** are at the dock off P. Flavio Gioia. Travelmar (☎089 87 31 90; www.coopsantandrea.it) runs hydrofoils to Minori (5min., 11 per day 7:30am-7:15pm, €2.50), Positano (25min., 7 per day 9:20am-6pm, €6), and Salerno (35min., 6 per day 10:40am-7:10pm, €6). Metro del Mare (☎089 19 96 00 700; www.metrodelmare.com) runs ferries to Sorrento (1hr., 5 per day 10:10am-6:30pm, €11) and Napoli Molo Beverello (2hr., 5 per day 10:10am-6:30pm, €15). For **taxis,** call ☎089 87 22 39.

🧭 🛈 ORIENTATION AND PRACTICAL INFORMATION

Amalfi is in the shape of an upside-down "T;" the top runs along the shore. **Via Lorenzo d'Amalfi,** heads uphill from the shore past the white arch of **Piazza Flavio Gioia** and the town's main square, **Piazza Duomo.** This main street becomes V. Pietro Capuano, V. Marino del Giudice, and V. delle Cartiere as it passes through the *centro.* **Piazza Municipio** is a 100m walk up **Corso Repubbliche Marinare** (on the left when facing the sea). Ferries and buses stop in P. F. Gioia, the intersection of the two roads. Go through the tunnel on C. Repubbliche Marinare to reach Atrani, 250m down the coast, or follow the public path through the restaurant just next to the tunnel, on the side facing the sea. The pleasant, easy walk takes

10min. A stairway connects Atrani's bus stop to P. Umberto I, the main *piazza*.
V. dei Dogi, the city's only street, ends at beautiful **Valle del Dragone.**

The **AAST tourist office,** C. delle Repubbliche Marinare, 27, is through a gate
on the left on the road toward Atrani. Grab a free map along with hotel and
restaurant listings. Ferry and bus timetables are also available. (☎089 87 11
07; www.amalfitouristoffice.it. Open M-F Apr.-Sept. 9am-1pm and 4-7pm; Oct.-
May 10am-6pm.) Other services include: the **carabinieri,** V. Casamare 19 (☎089
87 10 22); the **police,** inside the Municipio building on V. dei Dogi; a **pharmacy,**
Farmacia Del Cervo, P. Duomo 41 (Open daily 9am-1pm and 5-9pm); and **Internet** access at **L'Altra Costiera,** V. L. d'Amalfi 34, which has three computers and
also rents scooters. (☎089 87 36 082; www.altracostiera.com. Internet €5 per
hr. Scooters from €45 per day; insurance included. 18+. Open daily Mar.-Nov.
9am-9:30pm.) The **post office,** C. Repubbliche Marinare 35, next to the tourist
office, offers an **ATM** and currency exchange. (☎089 83 04 811. Commission
€2.58. Open M-F 8am-6:30pm, Su 8am-12:30pm.) **Postal code:** 84011.

ACCOMMODATIONS

Lodgings fill up quickly in August, so reserve far ahead. Those on a budget
should consider staying in Atrani, Salerno, or Naples for the lower prices.

> **NO-TELL MOTEL.** Don't accept tips from English-speaking solicitors at
> the Amalfi bus station waiting for gullible travelers. They hand out info on
> unregistered hostels. Such hostels—though inexpensive—are illegal, unregu-
> lated, often unsanitary, and very unsafe.

ATRANI

A'Scalinatella, P. Umberto 6 (☎089 87 14 92; www.hostelscalinatella.com), 15min.
from Amalfi bus station. Simple, affordable rooms year-round. Breakfast included.
Dorms €21; doubles €50-60, with bath €73-83; quads with bath €120. ●

Vettica House, V. Maestra dei Villaggi 96 (☎089 87 18 14 or 338 47 39 200; www.
hostelscalinatella.com), 2km away in Vettica. A haven of tranquility amid natural beauty.
Bright rooms with bath. Quick access to hiking trails. Kitchen available. Must call ahead;
check-in at A'Scalinatella only. With *Let's Go* discount, singles with bath €35-50; doubles €50-60, with bath €60-83; quads €100. Cash only. ●

L'Argine Fiorito, V. dei Dogi 45 (☎089 87 36 309; www.larginefiorito.it). Built inside a
17th-century pasta factory. Cozy rooms with bath and great balcony views. Pets allowed.
Breakfast included. Doubles €80-95. Extra bed €30-35. Call ahead. AmEx/MC/V. ●

AMALFI

Hotel Lidomare, V. Piccolomini 9 (☎089 87 13 32; www.lidomare.it), through an alley
across from the *duomo.* Cozy rooms have terrace, satellite TV, phone, fridge, A/C, safe,
and fantastic hydromassage bath. Small library and sitting room. Breakfast included. In
summer singles €65; doubles €130. In winter €55/90. Extra bed €20. AmEx/MC/V. ●

Villa Lara, V. delle Cartiere 1 (☎089 87 36 358; www.villalara.it). Climb 200 steps
through a lemon grove, or take the elevator. English-speaking owner. Modern rooms with
TV, minibar, A/C, phone, safe, and hydromassage bath; some with terrace. Free Internet.
Free breakfast on many scenic terraces. Singles €75-145; doubles €90-195. MC/V. ●

Hotel Fontana, P. Duomo 7 (☎089 87 15 30; www.hotel-fontana.it). Comfortable, modern rooms overlooking the *piazza* and harbor. All have bath, satellite TV, A/C, and mini-

fridge. Free Wi-Fi. Breakfast included. May-Sept. singles €75; doubles €130; extra bed €40. Oct.-Apr. €50/100/30. Suites available. AmEx/MC/V. ❺

Apartments in Amalfi, V. Sant'Andrea (☎089 87 28 04; www.amalfiapartments.com), next to the *duomo* at Suportico Sant'Andrea. Rents 2 small apartments with views of the sea and the *piazza*. The double fits 4 and the studio is perfect for a couple; they share a terrace. Reserve 1 mo. ahead. 2-person €65; 4-person €90-110. Cash only. ❺

🏛 FOOD

Indulge in delicious seafood or *scialatelli* (a coarsely cut local pasta). The town's many *paninoteche* are perfect for a tight budget, but so are some of its restaurants. After dining, head to **La Valle dei Mulini,** V. L. d'Amalfi 11, for local *limoncello, meloncello,* and *lemonciok.* (☎089 87 32 88. Bottles €3-9. 10% *Let's Go* discount. Open daily Mar.-Dec. 10am-8:30pm.) Reserve 4 days in advance to visit their museum, garden, and factory.

🏛 **Bar Birecto,** P. Umberto I (☎089 87 10 17; www.ilbirecto.com), in Atrani. Fun-loving bar crew and cheap grub. A popular backpacker hangout. Free snacks and after-meal *limoncello.* Free Internet access and Wi-Fi for clients. €8 *menù.* €6 pizza and drink *menù.* Open Apr.-Oct. daily 7am-3am; Nov.-Mar. M-W and F-Su 7am-9pm. Cash only. ❷

🏛 **Donna Stella Pizzeria,** Salita Rascica 2 (☎089 338 358 8483; www.donnastella. com). From V. Capuano, turn right on Suportico Rua and follow the tunnel on the left to Salita Rascica. The cool hang out for *amalfitani,* with a gorgeous citrus terrace filled with the fruits and herbs. Pizza to rival that of Naples (€5-9). Make reservations or arrive early. Cover €1.50. Open Tu-Su 7-11:30pm. ❶

Il Chiostro, V. dei Prefetturi 2 (☎089 87 33 80). Left of the *duomo,* this is the perfect place for a light lunch or sumptuous dinner. Comfortable and private, the service, food, and ambience are the best Amalfi has to offer. Primi €6-10. Secondi €8-12. Open daily noon-2:30pm and 7-11pm. AmEx/MC/V. ❸

Il Mulino, V. delle Cartiere 36 (☎089 87 22 23; www.ristoranteilmulino.biz). Past the commotion of Amalfi's *centro,* locals know this family-owned restaurant for its spicy, smoked octopus with tomato and *peperoncino* (€7). Worth the wait, all dishes are made from scratch upon ordering. Margherita €5, takeout €3. Primi €5-12. Secondi €7-12. Cover €1.50. Open July-Aug. daily noon-4pm and 7pm-midnight; Sept.-June Tu-Su noon-4pm and 7pm-midnight. AmEx/MC/V. ❸

Trattoria e Pizzeria da Meme', Salita Marino Sebaste 8 (☎089 83 04 549). Inside the 18th-century Chiesa di Santa Nicola. A family-friendly locale; specializes in handmade pasta. Pizza from €4. Primi €5.50-10. Secondi €6-13. Cover €1.50. Open daily Mar.-Oct. noon-3pm and 6:30pm-midnight. AmEx/MC/V. ❷

Al Teatro, V. E. Marini 19 (☎089 87 24 73). From V. L. d'Amalfi, turn left up Salita degli Orafi. Try the *scialatelli al Teatro* (local pasta with tomato and eggplant; €8). Primi and secondi from €6. *Menù* €15. Cover €2. Open from mid-Feb. to early Jan. M-Tu. and Th-Su 11:30am-3pm and 7-11pm. AmEx/MC/V. ❷

Ristorante La Perla, Salita Truglio 5 (☎089 87 14 40), around corner from Hotel Amalfi. Excellent local cuisine in a quiet *piazza.* Homemade pasta with seafood is served in a giant seashell. *Menù* with delightful desserts €20. Primi €6-12. Secondi €8-15. Cover €2. Open Apr.-Oct. daily noon-3pm and 7pm-midnight. MC/V. ❸

Pasticceria Pansa, P. Duomo 40 (☎089 87 10 65; www.pasticceriapansa.it). Enjoy citrus-based pastries like *delizia al limone* (€2) or the Santa Rosa, a cream and ricotta puffs with caramelized orange peel (€1.50). Open daily June-Sept. 8:30am-1am; Oct.-Dec. and Feb.-Apr. 8:30am-10pm. Cash only. ❶

La Risacca, P. Umberto 16 (☎089 87 08 66; www.risacca.com), in Atrani. Caters to older crowds. Free snacks and after-meal coffee. Pizza €4-6. *Panini* €3.50. Free Internet access and Wi-Fi for customers. Open May-Oct. daily 8am-2pm and 4pm-midnight; Nov.-Apr. Tu-Su 8am-2pm and 4pm-midnight. AmEx/MC/V. ❶

Porto Salvo, P. Duomo 8 (☎089 338 188 1800). This is the place for hanging out and eating great pizza and sandwiches (both €3). Thick focaccia with toppings from €4. Order at the counter and enjoy its delicacies out on the beach. Mixed salads and vegetarian *panini* available. Open daily 8:30am-8:30pm. Cash only. ❶

Da Maria, P. Duomo 14 (☎089 87 18 80; www.amalfi-trattoriadamaria.com). Daily seafood specials, with traditional favorites like *scialatelli* and delectable seafood risotto (€13). Live piano music, cooking and *limoncello* production demonstrations in summer weekends. Pizza from €4.50. Primi €9-13. Secondi €10-20. Menù from €20. Wheelchair-accessible. Free Wi-Fi for clients. Open June-Sept. daily noon-3pm and 6-11pm; Oct.-May Tu-Su noon-3pm and 6-11pm. Reservations recommended. AmEx/MC/V. ❸

🅢 SIGHTS

DUOMO DI SANT'ANDREA. This AD ninth-century Cathedral of Amalfi is the small town's dominant feature. Its facade's intricate geometric designs of vividly contrasting colors, typical of the Arab-Norman style, will transport you to southern Spain. The **bronze doors,** crafted in Constantinople in 1066, are so handsomely wrought that they started a bronze door craze throughout Italy. *(Open for prayer daily 7:30-10am and 7pm, for visiting 10am-6pm. Modest dress required. Free.)*

CHIOSTRO DEL PARADISO (CLOISTER OF PARADISE). This 13th-century cemetery, made for Amalfitan nobles, has 120 striking marble columns and an intricate fresco of the Crucifixion. The elegant, interlaced arches of both the cloister and the church reflect a Moorish influence. The modest church **museum** houses mosaics, sculptures, and the church's treasury. Underneath, the newly restored **crypt** contains the body of the church's namesake, St. Andrew the Apostle, whose remains were brought to Amalfi during the Crusades. *(Left of the Duomo di Sant'Andrea. ☎089 87 13 24. Open daily in summer 9am-9pm; in winter 10am-5pm. Free multilingual guides available. Cloister, museum, and crypt €2.50.)*

FONTANA DI SANT'ANDREA. This fountain does its best to counteract the church's stately influence, featuring a marble female nude with water trickling from her nipples. Those who can put their Freudian complexes aside might venture a drink from the fountain, which was rebuilt in the 19th century according to an original medieval plan. The 9th-century waterfront contains relics of Amalfi's former maritime glory, including examples of Amalfitan currency (the *tarì*), and early compasses by Flavio Gioia. *(In P. Umberto I.)*

MUSEO DELLA CARTA (PAPER MUSEUM) This museum was a major paper-producing powerhouse during the Middle Ages. In a 13th-century paper mill, it showcases the history of paper production, including free paper samples made from pressed flowers and the water-powered machines. The ticket covers a 20min. tour with a multilingual guide. *(V. delle Cartiere 24. ☎089 83 04 561; www.museodellacarta.it. Open Mar.-Oct. daily 10am-2pm and 3-6:30pm. €3.50, students €2.60.)*

🅒 🅢 BEACHES AND NIGHTLIFE

Amalfi has two small **beaches;** one sandy, the other rocky. The sandy beach, though not stunning, is a social stretch near the marina. Find better, free options 10min. away in nearby **Atrani** (see **Practical Information,** p. 414). With about 1000 inhabitants today, Atrani is a quiet refuge from Amalfi's crowds during the day. At night, Atrani's P. Umberto offers lively bars and a casual atmosphere just a stumbling distance away from A'Scalinatella. At **La Risacca's (see opposite page),** the "Crazy Hour" features beers (€5) and long drinks (1L,

€6-8), and occasional live music on weekends in summer. Located beside an old paper mill at the end of Amalfi's V. delle Cartiere, *discoteca* **Roccoco** offers DJ and live music, plus free pasta at midnight. (☎089 87 30 80. Beer, wine, and mixed drinks €5. Open F-Su 10pm-3am.)

SALERNO   ☎089

As capital of the Norman Empire from 1077 to 1127 and home to Europe's first medical school, Salerno (sa-LEHR-no; pop. 144,000) once played host to a proud, powerful culture. During WWII, however, the city was blasted by Allied bombs and much of its medieval past was turned to rubble. Unlike the dreamy villages of the Amalfi Coast, Salerno is an urban reality with an industrial core and a famous university. A cheap base for visiting the Amalfi Coast and Paestum's ruins, Salerno is not wholly without charm of its own; side streets in the old city and the sea front promenade offer pleasant walks and views.

⌷ TRANSPORTATION

Trains: (☎089 25 50 05), in P. V. Veneto. To: **Naples** (45min., 37 per day 3:41am-10:21pm, €5-10); **Paestum** (40min., 17 per day 5:52am-9:55pm, €2.70); **Reggia di Calabria** (3-5hr., 16 per day 2:19am-8:19pm, €21-35); **Rome** (2-3hr., 16 per day 3:25am-8:42pm, €23-33).

Buses: SITA buses leave from the train station for **Amalfi** (1hr., 24 per day 6am-10:30pm, €2) and **Naples** (1hr., 38 per day 5:05am-10:10pm, €3). Buy tickets from *tabaccherie*, and ask where your bus leaves from (either P. Veneto or P. della Concordia). CSTP runs buses from P. della Concordia to **Paestum** (1hr., 12 per day 6:30am-7:30pm, €2.70) and from P. Veneto to **Pompeii** (1hr., 14 per day 6:10am-9pm, €3.20).

Ferries and Hydrofoils: Ferries leave from Molo Masuccio, P. della Concordia, 2 blocks from the train station. Travelmar (☎089 87 29 50) runs to **Positano** (1¼hr., 7 per day 8:40am-5:15pm, €10) via **Amalfi** (35min., €6).

Public Transportation: Orange CSTP buses connect the train station to the rest of the city. For schedules, check the ticket booth in P. Veneto. 1hr. tickets €1, day pass €5.

Taxis: ☎089 75 75 75.

Car Rental: Travel Car, P. Veneto 33 (☎089 22 77 22). Cars from €35 per day. 18+. Open daily 8am-1:15pm and 3-8pm. AmEx/MC/V.

✦ ⁊ ORIENTATION AND PRACTICAL INFORMATION

Salerno's **train station** is in **Piazza Vittorio Veneto.** The pedestrian **Corso Vittorio Emanuele** veers right out of the *piazza,* becoming **Via dei Mercanti** upon reaching the old quarter, the liveliest and most historically interesting part of Salerno. **Via Roma,** home to many of the city's best restaurants, runs parallel to C. V. Emanuele, one block toward the waterfront. Along the waterfront in front of the train station is **Piazza della Concordia,** from which many intercity buses depart, and **Lungomare Trieste,** which runs to Salerno's port, **Molo Manfredi.**

Tourist Office: EPT (☎089 23 14 32), in P. V. Veneto 1, to the right when leaving the station. Friendly staff provides free maps, brochures on hotels and restaurants, and bus and train info. Open M-F 9am-2pm and 3-8pm, Sa 9am-1pm and 3:30-7:30pm.

English-Language Bookstore: La Feltrinelli, C. V. Emanuele 230. Decent selection of classics and new fiction. Open M-F 9:30am-2pm and 4-8:30pm, Sa 10am-2pm and 4-10pm, Su 10am-1:30pm and 5-9:30pm. MC/V.

Public restrooms: 2nd fl. of train station in P. Veneto.

Carabinieri: V. Duomo 17 (☎089 22 56 80).

Hospital: G. da Procida, V. S. Calenda (☎089 69 11 11).

Internet Access: PAK, V. Romualdo Guarna 12b, near the *duomo*. €2.50 per hr. Open M-F and Su 9am-1pm and 4-8pm.

Post Office: C. Garibaldi 203 (☎089 25 72 111). Open M-Sa 8:15am-6:15pm. **Branch,** V. Roma 130, has an **ATM.** Open M-F 8am-1:30pm, Sa 8am-12:30pm. Currency exchange at main office only. **Postal Code:** 84100.

ACCOMMODATIONS

■ **Ostello Ave Gratia Plena,** V. Canali (☎089 23 47 76; www.ostellodisalerno.it). Take C. Vittorio Emanuele into the old district, where it becomes V. dei Mercanti; then turn right on V. Canali. Amazing location in a former convent, close to restaurants and nightlife. Clean rooms, large showers, and a great courtyard bar with music and cheap food. Book exchange and tourist information point. Private rooms have bath. Breakfast included. Towels €2. Laundry €3. Internet access €3.50 per hr. Curfew 2am. Single-sex 4- and 8-bed dorms €15; singles €32; doubles €45; triples €67.50. AmEx/MC/V. ●

Albergo Koinè, V. Angelo. Napolitano 10 (☎089 27 51 051; www.hostelkoine.it). 10min. walk from train station and port. Modern and cool, this hostel was recently renovated and even has an infirmary. Dogs welcome. Laundry €5. Internet access €2. Wheelchair-accessible bath available. Reception 24hr. 4-, 6-, and 10-bed dorms €12. MC/V. ●

Albergo Santa Lucia, V. Roma 182 (☎089 22 58 28). Simple rooms with TV, phone, bath, and balcony offer unbeatable proximity to the public beach. For a tranquil stay, ask for air-conditioned rooms not facing the street. Operates the Santa Lucia restaurant below. Singles €35; doubles €55; triples €70. ●

FOOD

■ **Hosteria Il Brigante,** V. Linguiti 4 (☎089 22 65 92). From P. Duomo, head up the ramp, look for sign on the left. Laid-back. Handwritten menu boasts "rigorously homemade" dishes like the *pasta alla sangiovannara* (€3), a hodgepodge of pasta, tomato, cheese, and sausage. Open Tu-Su 1:30-2:30pm and 9-11:30pm. Cash only. ●

Trattoria "da Peppe a Seccia," V. Antica Corte 5 (☎089 22 05 18). Large, yet quaint and intimate restaurant in the heart of the historical center serves cheap, delicious seafood. The fresh squid antipasto (€5) is a must. Pizza €4-6. Primi €5-9. Cover €1.50. Open Tu-Su noon-2:30pm and 8pm-midnight. MC/V. ●

Santa Lucia, V. Roma 182/184 (☎089 22 56 96). Located in the main street of Salerno's historical center, this restaurant offers the same cool breeze, glamor, and laid-back ambience as its neighbors, but at cheaper prices. Try the *spaghetti alle vongole* (with clams; €7), or choose from a large array of cheap entrees €5-8. Cover €1.50. Open Tu-Su noon-2:30pm and 7-11:30pm. AmEx/MC/V. ●

SIGHTS AND ENTERTAINMENT

To take in the evening air, stroll down C. V. Emanuele or sit in the lush gardens of the **Villa Comunale** (open daily 7:30am-midnight). For a bit of history, explore the medieval section, starting at C. V. Emanuele; turn right off V. Mercanti or V. Roma on to V. Duomo, which runs uphill to ■**Duomo San Matteo.** First constructed in AD 845, the *duomo* was destroyed and rebuilt 200 years later by the Norman leader Robert Guiscard. If its beauty isn't enough of a draw, come to see a tooth from Evangelist Matthew, a hair from the Virgin Mary, and a splinter from the True Cross. (☎089 23 13 87. Open M-Sa 10am-6pm, Su 1-6pm. Modest dress required. Free.) To soak up some rays, take the bus along Lungomare

Trieste and head to the beach near the sailboat harbor. Though Salerno is right by the water, its beaches are not the nicest. Instead, you might want to hop on a bus and head to nearby **Vietri sul Mare,** home to hundreds of artisans and a pleasant beach. (Buses #4 and 9; 10min., €0.80.)

The impressive **Teatro Municipale Giuseppe Verdi,** P. Matteo Luciani, hosts concerts as well as theater and ballet performances from October to March. (☎089 66 21 41; www.teatroverdisalerno.it. Concert tickets €10-60; opera and events €17.50-70. Box office open daily 10am-1pm and 5-8pm. MC/V.) Through July, the **Salerno Summer Festival,** at the Arena del Mare near the Molo Manfredi, hosts jazz and blues concerts for all to enjoy. (☎089 66 51 76; www.comune. salerno.it. Concerts usually start 10pm. Prices vary.) At night, younger crowds gather on the seaside promenade near **Bar/Gelateria Nettuno,** Lungomare Trieste 136-138. Purchase a cone (€1.50-2.70) and push up to the counter for some of the most popular flavors in town. (☎089 22 83 75. Beer €1.70. Open July-Sept. daily 7am-2am; Oct.-June M-Tu and Th-Su 7am-2am.) **Galleon,** one of the many pubs along V. Roma, is where yuppie pirates-at-heart come to find their next booty, or at least a cold, €4 beer. (V. Roma 256. Open daily 7pm-3am.) The small bar **Tekabega,** V. Giovanni da Procida 7, packs a nighttime punch with bartender DJs and occasional fanciful feasts at a beach location outside Salerno. Gay-, lesbian-, and transgender-friendly. (www.tekabega.it. Beer €2-4. Mixed drinks €4.50. Wine €3. Open Tu-Su 9pm-4am.)

PUGLIA AND CALABRIA

PUGLIA

The often-overlooked Puglia (POOL-ya) region gives Italy its sun-baked southern kick—after all, what's a boot without a heel? Its ports are as animated and international today as they were hundreds of years ago when the Greeks and Romans used them as trade routes to the East, though now they tend to ferry tourists to Greece instead. Besides serving as a useful launching spot, the region harbors cultural treasures all its own: remote medieval villages, cone-roofed *trulli* houses, and ports with a distinct Middle Eastern flavor. Tourism has only recently begun to materialize in rustic, sunny Puglia, which remains a refreshing pause from Italy's more frequented destinations. Travelers to Puglia will welcome its passionate cultural heritage and distinctly southern zest for life.

BARI   ☎080

Exquisite Puglian cuisine and nightlife, fueled by the city's university population, add to the complexity of Bari (BA-ree; pop. 329,000), the main Italian transportation hub for travel to Greece. On every street, clothing shops and *gelaterie* tempt pedestrians, and the sea is never more than a few blocks away. Amid the commotion, reckless drivers zoom about the modern city's wide avenues and pickpockets dart down alleys in the small medieval section. Although Bari does not figure prominently on most itineraries, its cosmopolitan vibes and urban grit make it a worthwhile divergence from southern Italy's more touristy cities, if only for a brief visit. Just ask the locals, who say Paris could be a *piccolo* Bari (little Bari) if it only had the sea.

⌐ TRANSPORTATION

Ferrotramviaria Nord (☎080 57 89 542; www.ferrovienordbarese.it). Left of Centrale, exit and re-enter the station. To **Ruvo** (45min., 24 per day 6:22am-10:15pm, €2.30). On Su the Ruvo route is served by bus from P. Aldo Moro.

Ferrovie Appulo Lucane (☎080 57 25 229; www.fal-srl.it), next door to Ferrotramviaria Nord station in P. Aldo Moro. Trains depart for **Matera** (1hr., 8 per day 6:48am-9:57pm, €4) via **Altamura.**

Buses: SITA (☎080 52 16 004; www.sitabus.it), behind station, on Viale Unità d'Italia.

Ferries: Obtain info and tickets at **Stazione Marittima** (☎080 52 19 140), individual company offices, or **Porto di Bari** (☎080 52 82 828; www.porto.bari.it). Take bus #20 to and from railway station. Some companies are listed below, but call ahead; schedules and prices vary, especially on weekends. Check-in at least 2hr. before departure. Visit www.greekferries.gr for more info on ferries to Greece. High season from late July-Aug.

Marlines (☎080 52 31 824 or 080 52 75 409, reservations 080 52 10 266; www.marlines.com). To **Durres, Albania** (schedules vary weekly July-Sept., high season €62-130).

Superfast Ferries (☎080 52 41 527; www.superfast.com), offices in front of port terminal. Sails to **Greece.** To **Corfu** (8hr.; odd days July and early Sept., even days in Aug. 8pm), **Igoumenitsa** (8hr., M-Sa 8pm), and **Patras** (14hr., daily 8pm). The line to **Corfu** is operated by partner company **Blue Star Ferries.** High season €95-430, depending on seating. Discount for Eurail pass holders.

Ventouris Ferries, V. Piccinni 133, c/o P. Lorusso & Co. (☎080 52 17 609 to Greece, ☎080 52 75 499 to Albania; www.ventouris.gr). Windows #18-20 in Stazione Marittima. To **Corfu-Igoumenitsa, Greece** (10hr.; 2 per week Feb.-Apr., at least 5 per week May-Dec., daily in high season; shared cabin of four with bath €83-112) and **Durres, Albania** (7hr., €70-87).

Public Transportation: Local AMTAB **buses** leave from P. Aldo Moro, in front of the train station. Tickets sold at *tabaccherie* (€0.80) or on the bus (€1.50). Bus #20/ makes hourly trips between Stazione Marittima and train stations.

Taxis: RadioTaxi ☎080 53 46 666, leave voice message with departure location and destination. Taxi station ☎080 52 10 600.

ORIENTATION AND PRACTICAL INFORMATION

Via Sparano runs from the train station to **Piazza Umberto I,** Bari's main square. The end of V. Sparano intersects **Corso Vittorio Emanuele II** and the edge of the old city. To walk to the port, skirt the old city's winding streets by turning left on C. Vittorio Emanuele II and right at **Piazza della Libertà** onto **Piazza Giuseppe Massari.** Circle the castle, head right, and follow the coast. Otherwise, take the hourly bus #20/ from the station. For a calmer route to the sea (not the port), turn right off V. Sparano on C. Vittorio Emanuele II, continuing past **Corso Cavour** to **Piazza Eroi del Mare.** Then turn right and enjoy a nice stroll down **Lungomare Araldo di Crollalanza.** Above all, make sure to see the beautiful **Piazza del Ferrarese** and **Piazza Mercantile in Il Borgo Antico** (The Old Town) by walking down C. Cavour.

Outside the train station, find the **APT Tourist Office,** P. Aldo Moro 33/A. Inquire about and reserve the free ▓**Flash Tours** of the province here. (☎080 99 09 34; www.pugliaturismoinfopointbari.com. Open M-Sa 9am-7pm, Su 9am-1pm.) Do laundry at **Clean It,** V. Dante Alighieri 260. (☎080 52 37 096. Internet access €3 per hr. Wash €3.50 per 7.5kg; dry €3.50. Open M-F 11am-3:30pm and 6:30-9:30pm, Sa 11am-4pm.) For a **pharmacy,** try **San Nicola,** C. Cavour 53a. (Open M-F 8:30am-1pm and 4:30-8pm.) Get **Internet** access and tourist info at **Netcafe,** V. Andrea da Bari 11. (☎080 52 41 756; www.netcafebari.it. €4 per hr. Open M-Sa 9am-11:30pm, Su 10am-1pm and 5-9:30pm. Cash only.) In case of emergency, dial the **carabinieri** (☎080 52 45 960). **Policlinino,** the local **hospital,** is at Ple. Giulio Cesare 11 (☎080 54 21 854). The **post office** is at P. Umberto I 31, to the right of P. Battisti, facing away from the train station. It has an ATM outside. (☎080 57 57 187. Open M-F 8am-6:30pm, Sa 8am-12:30pm.) **Postal Code:** 70100.

> **! BARESI, BEWARE.** Ancient citizens built the old city as a labyrinth in which to hide from surprise attacks. Today, the old city remains a maze for travelers and is safest when enjoyed in the light of day; turn to one of the many shop owners in P. Perrarese if you get lost. There is no need to venture into the old city at night, but if you do, exercise caution.

Puglia and Calabria

ACCOMMODATIONS AND FOOD

The top-notch hostel ■**La Nuova Arca** ❷, C. Alcide de Gasperi 320, is inside the Parco di Cagno Abbrescia, 6km away. Take bus #4 from C. Benedetto Croce behind the station; ask the driver to stop at the park. Facilities for the single-sex rooms include multiple common rooms with A/C, bath, TV, game console, terrace, pianos, pool tables, bicycle rentals, and a chapel. (☎080 56 48 789; www.lanuovarca.com. Internet €3 per hr. Breakfast, towels, and linen included. Reserve in June for July-Aug. Dorms €24; doubles €79; triples €89. Cash only) A popular choice, **Hotel de Rossi** ❸, V. de Rossi 186, offers clean, bright rooms with TV, phone, A/C, and bath. (☎080 52 45 355. Reserve 1 month ahead. Breakfast included. Singles €35; doubles €60; triples €85. MC/V.)

Eating in the old city's restaurants can feel like a time warp; often restaurants offer neither menus nor itemized checks. The food, however, is inevitably excellent, and the raucous atmosphere, enjoyable. Follow *baresi* students and families to ■**Pizzeria Il Rustico** ❷, V. Quintino Sella 95, a hidden gem for hungry travelers. The €9 *menù* includes an amazing antipasto buffet that piles up on your table, a large pizza, drink, and liqueur to top it off. (Open M-Sa 7:30pm-midnight. Cash only.) For a true Italian experience, head to cozy **Vini e Cucina** ❷, V. Vallisa 23, in a prime spot next to P. del Ferrarese. Squeeze into a free seat, let the waiters tell you which of their daily specials you'll be receiving, then sit back and enjoy the authentic ambience and beauty of this *baresi* favorite. (☎330 43 30 18. Antipasti €3. Primi €4.50. Secondi €6.50. Drinks €1. Open M-Sa noon-3pm and 7pm-midnight. MC/V.) Find groceries at **CONAD market,** V. Crisanzio 20/22. (Open M-Tu and Th-Su 7am-3pm and 5-8pm, W 8am-2pm. MC/V.)

🔵 SIGHTS

Looks like Mom and Dad were wrong—there really is a Santa Claus, and the 🔲**Basilica di San Nicola** proves it. Sixty *baresi* sailors tomb raided St. Nicholas's remains from Turkey in 1087; the sailors initially refused to cede the body to local clergy, they ultimately gave it up when the Church built this spartan basilica as Santa's final resting place. On the back wall, several paintings commemorate the jolly saint's good deeds, including his resurrection of three children who were sliced to bits and plunged into a brine barrel by a nasty butcher. (Open M-Sa 8:30am-noon and 4:30-6:30pm, Su 9:30am-7pm, except during mass. Free.) Just outside the old city, off C. Vittorio Veneto near the water, stands the colossal **Castello Svevo,** P. Federico di Svevia 4, built in the 13th century by Frederick II on Norman and Byzantine foundations. Visitors can't climb the jagged ramparts, but the medieval cellar displays art from the region's cathedrals and castles, and other areas display locally produced modern art. (☎080 52 86 111. Open M-Tu and Th-Su 9am-7pm. €2, ages 18-25 €1, under 18 and over 65 free.) Down Lungomare Nazario Sauro past P. Armando Diaz at V. Spalato 19, on the fourth floor, is the **Pinacoteca Provinciale.** Housed in a beautiful building with a tall clock tower, the gallery displays landscapes and works by Veronese, Tintoretto, Bellini, De Nittis, and Francesco Netti, an acclaimed hometown artist. As well as a vast collection of Greek art from the 1800s. (☎080 54 12 422. Open Tu-Sa 9am-7pm, Su 9am-1pm; Aug. open only in the morning. €2.60, students €0.60.)

🎵 🎭 ENTERTAINMENT AND NIGHTLIFE

Bari is Puglia's cultural nucleus. **Teatro Piccinni,** C. V. Emanuele 86, offers a spring concert season and year-round opera. (☎080 52 10 878; www.fondazion-eliricabari.it. Open M-F 10:30am-12:30pm and 5-8pm.) Consult the ticket office, *La Gazzetta del Mezzogiorno* (the local newspaper), or the free newspapers *Leggo* and *City* for the latest info. From September through June, sports fans can catch **soccer matches** every Sunday. Tickets start at €15 and are available at the stadium or in bars. On May 7-9, *baresi* celebrate their stolen saint in the **Festa di San Nicola,** featuring traditional foods and a parade of children. There's also a huge **Summer Jazz Festival** in mid-July (☎080 45 55 696).

Bari does not have much of a club scene, but its bars are hopping. Most are open nightly from 8pm until 1 or 2am (3am on Sa) and generally close in August, when the town's university is on holiday. V. Sparano and P. Umberto are packed at night, and on weekends students cram into P. del Ferrarese and other *piazze* along the breezy waterfront east of the old city. To avoid expensive drinks, try **El Chiringuito,** Molo San Nicola, next to P. Eroi del Mare, a main hangout for college students. (☎080 52 40 206. Open daily 11pm-4am.)

SALENTO PENINSULA

Tourists often overlook Italy's sun-baked heel, home to hidden grottoes, medieval fortresses, and the beautiful beaches of two seas. With roots stretching back to ancient Greece, the Salento modestly bears the laurels of centuries of history. Its art and architecture are some of the best preserved in Italy, its vistas pristine, and its scuba diving superb. Transportation within the peninsula can sometimes be complicated, but a sojourn along the varied coastline or inland among olive groves and vineyards is well worth the careful planning.

LECCE ☎ 0832

One of Italy's hidden pearls, Lecce (LEH-chay; pop. 90,000) is where Italians go when foreign tourists take over their country. Historical invaders have included Cretans, Romans, Saracens, and Swabians; Spanish Hapsburg influence during the 16th and 17th centuries inspired beautiful Baroque buildings that now line Lecce's streets. Most of the city's churches and palaces are sculpted from *tufigna*—soft, locally quarried "Lecce stone" that hardens when exposed to air. At night, the illuminated buildings make for a memorable *passeggiata* (promenade). The "Florence of the South" and home to some of the country's best beaches, is a great starting point for a tour of the Salento Peninsula.

▐ TRANSPORTATION

Trains: Lecce is the southeastern terminus of the state railway. The **Trenitalia Station** (☎0832 30 10 16) is in P. Massari. Buses #24 and 28 (€0.80) leave from the station on V. Oronzo Quarta. Trains to **Bari** via **Brindisi** (1-2hr., 13 per day 5:30am-8:03pm, €8.60-13) and **Rome** (6-9hr., 5 per day 6am-10:20pm, €30-54). FSE trains (☎0832 66 81 11; www.fseonline.it) cross the Salento Peninsula. The *biglietteria* is on the right end of Binario 1. Trains run M-Sa to **Gallipoli** (1hr., 11 per day 6:56am-8:50pm, €3.40) and **Otranto** (1hr., 11 per day 6:56am-8:50pm, €2.90) via **Maglie**. Schedules are subject to frequent change; consult www.salentointrenoebus.it for detailed schedules.

Buses: The **FSE Station** (☎0832 34 76 34; www.fseonline.it), on V. Boito, is easily accessible by bus #4 (€0.80) from the train station. FSE buses depart daily from the FSE Garage, across from the train station on the left, and stop at the FSE station on their way out of town. Tickets are available in the train station bar. To **Gallipoli** (1hr., 5 per day, €2.90) and **Taranto** (2hr., 5 per day 7am-4pm, €4.58). STP (☎0832 22 84 41), on V. San Nicola, heads to smaller towns of the Salento Peninsula. Pick up a schedule at the tourist office. In July-Aug., Salento in Bus (☎0832 35 03 76; www.salentointrenoebus.it) is the most convenient way to traverse the peninsula, with green-line buses running to **Gallipoli** (1hr., 7 per day 7:05am-9:53pm, €3.50) and red-line buses to **Otranto** (1hr., 9 per day 7:13am-12:23am, €3.50), and other peninsular towns such as Santa Maria di Leuca and Porto Cesareo. Buses stop on V. Pitagora, by the train station. Local buses (€0.80 in *tabaccherie*, €1.50 onboard) service the *centro* and metropolitan area. Line #32 to the coastal town San Cataldo starts at Porta Napoli (every 40min., 6:50am-8:40pm) and makes a stop in front of the Palazzo Uffici Financieri on Viale Gallipoli, the 2nd right off Viale Oronzo Quarta from the train station.

Taxis: (☎0832 24 79 78) at the train station; (☎0832 30 60 45), in P. Sant'Oronzo.

▐ ▐ ORIENTATION AND PRACTICAL INFORMATION

Lecce lies 35km southeast of Brindisi. From the **train station**, take **Viale Oronzo Quarta** until it becomes V. Cairoli. Turn left on V. Paladini, and wind around the **duomo**. To the left, **Via Libertini** passes **Piazza Duomo** and Chiesa di San Giovanni Battista, eventually exiting the old city walls through Porta Rudiae. To the right lies **Via Vittorio Emanuele II**, which passes **Piazza Sant'Oronzo**, Lecce's main square, with the Roman amphitheater and *castello* beyond.

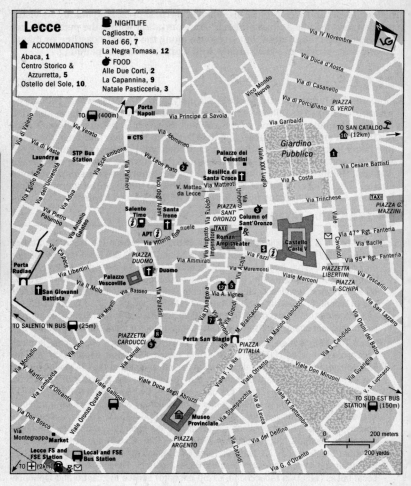

Lecce

ACCOMMODATIONS
Abaca, 1
Centro Storico &
Azzurretta, 5
Ostello del Sole, 10

NIGHTLIFE
Cagliostro, 8
Road 66, 7
La Negra Tomasa, 12

FOOD
Alle Due Corti, 2
La Capannina, 9
Natale Pasticceria, 3

PUGLIA AND CALABRIA

Tourist Office: APT Lecce, V. V. Emanuele 24 (☎0832 24 80 92; www.viaggiareinpuglia. it), near P. Duomo. Free maps and a comprehensive booklet on Lecce's numerous B&Bs. Open in summer daily 9am-1pm; in winter M-Sa 9am-1pm. Dozens of other tourist offices, both public and private, around P. Sant'Oronzo.

Budget Travel: CTS, V. Palmieri 89 (☎0832 30 18 62). From P. Sant'Oronzo, take V. V. Emanuele, and turn right onto V. Palmieri. Provides flight and train info and sells tickets. Open M-F 9am-1pm and 4-8:30pm, Sa 9am-noon.

Laundromat: Lavanderia Self-Service, V. dell'Università 47, between Pta. Rudiae and Pta. Napoli. Wash €3-8, dry €1.50 per 12min. Detergent €1. **Western Union** services. Open M-Sa 8am-8:30pm, Su 8am-1pm.

Public Restrooms: In P. Sant'Oronzo, on the corner with V. Imperatore Augusto.

Carabinieri: V. Calabria (☎0832 27 98 64).

Pharmacy: In train station (☎0832 28 85 52). Open M-Sa 8:30am-1pm and 5-8:30pm.

Farmacia Ferocino, P. Sant'Oronzo 57 (☎0832 30 91 81), posts a 24hr. rotation.

Hospital: Ospedale Vito Fazzi (☎0832 66 11 11), on V. San Cesario.

Internet: Salento Time, V. Regina Isabella 22 (☎0832 30 36 86; www.salentotime. it. €2.50 per hr. Student discount. Also has **bicycle** rentals (€2 per hr., €10 per day); includes info on bike tours of varying difficulty. Open daily 10am-9pm. Info Point at Castello Carlo V is open June-Sept. M-F 9am-9pm, Sa-Su 9:30am-9pm.

Post Office: ☎0832 27 41 11. In Piazzetta Libertini, across from the castello. Open M-F 8am-6:30pm, Sa 8:30am-1:30pm. **Postal Code:** 73100.

ACCOMMODATIONS AND CAMPING

B&Bs offer an alternative to impersonal hotels and the tourist office lists affordable *affittacamere* (rooms for rent). Consider staying in the youth hostel in San Cataldo, whose only drawback is limited night public transporation.

Ostello del Sole, V. Amerigo Vespucci 45 (☎0832 65 08 90; www.ostellodelsole.it), 12km away in San Cataldo. Take bus #32. In a pinewood in front of the public beach, this newly-renovated hostel offers large dorms with A/C, free lockers, and communal baths. The campsites include hot showers and free parking. Bring your own tent. Reception 24hr. Reserve 2 weeks ahead. 4-bed dorms €15-25, 2-bed dorms €20-30; singles €25-30. Campsites €8-18 plus €5-6 per person. MC/V. ❶

Abaca, V. Cavalloti 19 (☎0832 24 05 48 or 338 72 00 435). Buses #24, 27, and 28 from the train station stop 1 block away. The owner's passion for ballet is reflected in the dainty decor. Nice views, a terrace, A/C, fridge, and a large communal kitchen and bathroom add to the appeal. €20-40 per person. Discounts for extended stays. ❸

Centro Storico, V. Andrea Vignes 2/B (☎338 58 81 265; www.bedandbreakfast.lecce. it). From P. S. Oronzo, take V. Augusto Imperatore until it becomes V. Federico D'Aragona; V. A. Vignes is on the left. Centrally located, this charming B&B boasts a sunroof with city views. 5 big rooms all have A/C, TV, and refrigerator. Breakfast included. Free Wi-Fi. Reservations recommended. Singles €35-40, with bath 50-80; doubles €52-57, with bath €70-109. Extra bed €20. AmEx/MC/V. ❸

Azzurretta, V. A. Vignes 2/B (☎338 25 85 958; www.bblecce.it). Shares management and 16th-century building with Centro Storico. 3 spacious rooms and 1 apartment with kitchen have big, sunny windows, A/C, TV, balcony, and shared sunroof. Breakfast included. Free Wi-Fi. Reservations recommended. Singles €33-38; doubles €61-70; apartment €39-70. Extra bed €17-19. Cash only. ❸

FOOD

Leccese food is a delight. Regional specialties range from hearty *cicerietria* (chickpeas and pasta) and *pucce* (sandwiches made with olive-bread rolls) to *confettoni* (traditional chocolate candies).

Alle Due Corti, Corte dei Giugni 1 (☎0832 24 22 23; www.alleduecorti.com), at the corner with V. Prato. Dedicated to the preservation of *leccese* culture through cuisine—it's so authentic, even Italians can't read some of the dialect on the ever-changing menu. The vegetable *antipasti* are excellent (€6-9). Primi €5-8. Secondi €6-10. Cover €1.50. Reservations recommended. Open M-Sa noon-2pm and 8pm-12:30am. MC/V. ❷

La Capannina, V. Cairoli 13 (☎0832 30 41 59), between the train station and P. Duomo. If you've ever dreamed of eating in the Parthenon, this is likely as close as you'll get. Attentive service in a nearly private *piazza* surrounded by columns, which are illuminated at night. Try the pasta specialty *orecchiette alla casereccia* (with meat, tomato, and cheese sauce; €5.20). Pizza €3.50-6.20; dinner only. Primi €5.20-7.50. Secondi €5.85-12. Cover €1.30. Open Tu-Su noon-3pm and 7pm-midnight. MC/V. ❷

Natale Pasticceria, V. Trinchese 7 (☎0832 25 60 60), off P. Sant'Oronzo. This copper-frosted pastry shop is full of so many pastries, candies, flavors of gelato, and eager customers that your head will spin. Take a number and try the pistachio if the crowds haven't already devoured it. Cones and *granita* €1.80-3. Local, cream-filled delights from €0.80. Open daily 8:30am-midnight. MC/V. ❶

👁 SIGHTS

Lecce's close-knit *centro storico* is visually enchanting. Get an education in Baroque architecture by touring its churches and *palazzi*, which are a 10min. walk apart, but can take hours to enjoy.

PUGLIA AND CALABRIA

BASILICA DI SANTA CROCE. Constructed between 1549 and 1695, this church is a masterpiece of *leccese* Baroque. Most of the area's architects contributed their skills to its ▓facade at some point. Inside, the lighting, artwork, and ambience are captivating; look closely to see the profile of Gabriele Riccardi, the basilica's original designer, hidden between the upper window and the column to its left. *(From P. Sant'Oronzo, head down V. Umberto I. Open daily 9am-noon and 5-8pm, except during mass. Modest dress required. Free.)*

DUOMO. Though construction began in 1114, the *duomo* was renovated between 1661 and 1662 by Giuseppe Zimbalo, nicknamed "Lo Zingarello" (The Gypsy) for his tendency to wander aimlessly from one project to another. Except for two *leccese* altars, the stained-glass-bedecked interior dates from the 18th century. At night, when crowds flood the *piazza*, misty streams of light pour out of the *campanile* that rises from the left side of the cathedral. Opposite, the Palazzo Vescovile (Bishop's Palace) has been remodeled several times since its 1632 construction. On the right, with a Baroque well in its center, stands the seminary, designed by Cino in 1709. *(From P. S. Oronzo, take V. V. Emanuele. Duomo open daily 7am-noon and 5-7:30pm. Free.)*

ANCIENT ATTRACTIONS. The **Column of Sant'Oronzo** is one of two that marked the termination of the Appian Way in Brindisi (p. 425). Today, it is topped by a saint, and towers melodramatically over P. Sant'Oronzo. Nearby, the ruins of a second-century **amphitheater** recede into the ground. In its prime, the structure held 20,000 spectators; these days, people gather there on summer nights to flirt or just eat gelato. The **Castello Carlo V,** built on 13th-century foundations, was fortified by King Carlo V in the 16th century. In the midst of heavy archeological excavation and restoration, it only houses small art exhibits for the foreseeable future. (Open M-F 9am-1pm and 4-8:30pm, Sa-Su 9:30am-1pm and 4-8:30pm. Free.) Near the station, the **Museo Provinciale** contains a large collection of Apulian ceramics and figurines from the fifth century BC, as well as rotating art exhibits. *(V. Gallipoli 28. ☎0832 68 35 03. Wheelchair-accessible. Open M-Sa 9am-1:30pm and 2:30-7:30pm, Su 9am-1:30pm. Free.)*

BEACHES. A relaxing daytrip of sand and sun at one of many beaches is just a short trip from Lecce. The nearest access points to the coast are San Cataldo's free beaches, accessible by bus #32. Try the small but beautiful **Torre dell'Orso,** a vacationer's hot spot with many free stretches. *(Blue line #101. 1 hr., 8 per day.)* Popular with locals, **Santa Cesarea Terme** has a wide expanse of clear, pale blue ocean lapping against many caves and coves. *(Blue line, change in Maglie.)* At the tip of the peninsula, the rocky enclaves of **Santa Maria di Leuca** offer small, untouristed beaches and an important lighthouse marking the divide between the Adriatic and the Ionean seas. *(Blue line.)*

◆ ❋ NIGHTLIFE AND FESTIVALS

Don't be fooled by the quiet that takes over Lecce every afternoon; by night, the city wakes from a long *siesta* as people stroll its sidewalks and mingle in its many *piazze*. To join the fun, head to **Via d'Aragona** or **V. Trinchese,** which are crammed with young barhoppers on weekends. Major *piazze*, such as **Piazza Duomo** and **Piazza Sant'Oronzo,** often have live music on weekends. Most night-clubs, especially ones which open only for summer, are on the coast and are thus only accessible by car. For up-to-date info on the hottest nightlife options, consult the publication *Salento in Tasca*, available at local bars. **La Negra Tomasa,** V. d'Aragona 2, is at the core of the street's pub scene, with a definite student following for its Monday-night pizza happy hour and Friday-night live music in winter. (☎0832 33 27 68. Beer €3-4.50. Mixed drinks €6. Open M-Tu and Th-Su 6:30pm-2:30am.) Despite its private, exclusive feel, **Cagliostro,** V. Cairoli 25, has a chill interior and relaxed outdoor seating, making it a favorite for all crowds. (☎083230 18 81. Nov.-May live jazz music Tu and Th 9pm-midnight. Draft beer and mixed drinks from €2.50. Open daily 7pm-3am.) Though lacking authentic Italian charm, **Road 66,** V. dei Perroni 8, near Pta. San Biagio, emulates American bars with its gas-station decor. Try the Road 66 (€3.50), a special fire shot. (☎0832 24 65 68. Beer €2.50-4. Mixed drinks €5. Open daily 6pm-2am.)

The inner courtyard of **Palazzo dei Celestini,** next to Basilica di Santa Croce, hosts rock and classical music concerts in summer. Keep an eye out for posters or ask at the APT office for more info. On the second and third weeks of August, Lecce hosts **La Notte della Taranta,** a festival dedicated to the *pizzica*—Lecce's own *tarantella* dance—which culminates in a grand final concert (☎0832 82 18 27; www.lanottedellataranta.it/eng. Free.)

GALLIPOLI ☎0833

Ideal as a brisk daytrip from Lecce or a prolonged seaside vacation, Gallipoli (ga-LEE-po-lee; pop. 20,000) boasts a wealth of assets: gorgeous beaches, excellent seafood, and a charming maze of historical homes and churches. Gallipoli's old city is perched on a small island that juts into the sparkling Ionian Sea. Throughout its history, outsiders have coveted the island's strategic location; foreign remnants include a Greek fountain and an Aragonese Castle. Today, Gallipoli's residents maintain a carefree island mentality, and the old city has retained an air of authenticity. Despite its growing popularity as a vacation spot, its whitewashed alleys and clear waters remain largely undiscovered.

◢ ⁊ TRANSPORTATION AND PRACTICAL INFORMATION. Gallipoli is south-west of Lecce, and is best reached by **train** from Lecce. FSE trains run M-Sa (1hr., 11 per day 6:56am-8:50pm, €3.40). In July and August, Salento in Bus (☎0832 35 03 76; www.salentointrenoebus.it) runs to the town hall in the *città nuova* (1hr., €2.30 at info points, €3.30 onboard) on the green line; catch it in Lecce on V. Gallipoli, in front of Bar Rossa Nera. The train station is in the *città nuova;* to reach the *città vecchia*'s main *piazza*, **Piazza Imbriani,** from the train station, turn right on C. Roma, cross the bridge, and turn right. From there, the main road, **Via Antonietta de Pace,** runs past the *duomo*, on the left, to the other side of the island. The **IAT Tourist Office,** P. Imbriani 10, offers advice on travel around the Salento Peninsula, and has free maps. (☎0833 26 25 29. Open daily 8:30am-1pm and 4-8:30pm.) In case of emergency, contact the **carabinieri,** P. Malta 2 (☎0833 26 74 00), or the **police** (☎0833 26 77 11). **Farmacia Provenzano** is at V. A. de Pace 59. (☎0833 26 64 12. Open M-Sa 8:30am-12:30pm and 4-8pm.) The **Ospedale Sacro Cuore di Gesù** (☎0833 27 01 11) is at V. Alezio 12. **Internet Café,**

V. Bartolo Ravenna 2/A, is 200m to the immediate right of the train station. (☎0833 26 25 47. €4 per hr. Open M-F and Su 8:30am-1:30pm and 4:30-8:30pm, Sa 8:30am-1:30pm.) The **post office**, V. Quartini 1, is on the first right after crossing the bridge from the *città vecchia* to the *città nuova*. (☎0833 26 75 11. Open M-F 8am-6:30pm, Sa 8am-12:30pm.) **Postal Code:** 73014.

PUGLIA AND CALABRIA

▐▌▐▌ ACCOMMODATIONS AND FOOD. Gallipoli's hotels are expensive, particularly in July and August. The seaside **▐La Riviera Bed and Breakfast ❸**, Riviera Sauro 7, decorated with intricate frescoes, has rooms with A/C, phone, bath, and flat-screen TV, some boasting a terrace with views of the Ionian sea. (☎0833 26 10 96; www.bedandbreakfastlariviera.com. Breakfast included. Free Wi-Fi. Singles €50, only available Sept.-May; doubles €60-80, in Aug. €120; triples €80-110/150; quads €100-130/160. Cash only.) Take the green line minibus (20min., 10 per day 8:31am-10:16, €1) from V. Kennedy in the *città nuova* to **▐Camping Baia di Gallipoli ❶**, Litoranea per Santa Maria di Leuca. With a 2400-person capacity, this large village has a campground, bar, restaurant, pool, private beach, and bungalows. (☎0833 27 32 10; www.baiadigallipoli.com. Free Wi-Fi. Reception 8am-1pm and 4-8pm. €6-18 per person. Bungalows €45-115.)

Escape the crowds and inflated prices of the city center by heading to the family-run **Osteria La Pentola degli Gnomi ❷**, V. Consalvo di Cordoba 8. Enjoy Salentine specialties like *purè di fave e cicorie* (bean and chicory; €7) in a breezy inner courtyard. From the train station, turn left on C. Roma. V. C. di Cordoba is the fourth street on the right. (☎0833 26 41 60. Primi €7-10. Secondi €6-12. Open July-Sept. daily 10:30am-3pm and 7pm-midnight; Oct.-June M-Tu and Th-Su 10:30am-3pm and 7pm-midnight AmEx/MC/V.) **Trattoria L'Angolo Blu ❸**, V. Carlo Muzio 45, offers local seafood specialties. Enjoy perfect *al dente* pasta in the cool, stone-walled interior. (☎0833 26 15 00. Primi €6-8.50. Secondi from €7. Cover €1.50. Open daily noon-3pm and 7pm-1am. MC/V.)

▟ BEACHES. By day, Gallipoli's cobbled streets are a colorful jungle of markets and produce vendors, its walls draped in fishing traps and fresh laundry. By night, the city is set aglow with lights. Residents make their evening *passeggiata* along the promenade encircling the *città vecchia;* the promenade passes by the port as well as the island's small, uncrowded, and completely free beach: **Seno della Purità.** The turquoise waters make for excellent swimming. Three miles down the coast, beaches encircle the emerald **Baia Verde,** with free sandy strips interspersed along private beaches. Three miles from Gallipoli's *città vecchia*, Baia Verde is accessible by bus #5 (€0.70) or by walking along the coastal seawall, bearing right after crossing the bridge. The walk passes many tiny beaches carved into the *tufa,* and offers excellent views of the coastline.

◀▌ SIGHTS AND ENTERTAINMENT. Aside from its beaches, the city contains many layers of historical relics. All the churches in the *città vecchia* are open daily in July and August 10am-noon and 5-9pm, except during mass. Lookout for IAT tour guides inside the main churches who give **▐free tours** daily (info ☎0833 26 42 42). On V. Duomo, find the ornate exterior of the city's 17th-century **Baroque Cattedrale di Sant'Agata.** Its arched walls and ceilings are covered with intricate murals, and the inside boasts 700 square meters of impressive paintings on canvas. (Open daily 8am-noon and 4-9pm. Free.) Just before the *duomo* lies the **Museo Diocesano,** V. A. de Pace 51, containing religious art from the *duomo* and other churches in Gallipoli. Its large terrace offers great views of the *città vecchia* and harbor. (☎0833 51 26 90. Open June-Sept. Tu-Su 5:30-11pm; Oct.-

May Tu-F 9am-12:30pm, Sa-Su 9am-12:30pm and 3:30-6:30pm. €2.50, children and seniors €1.50, under 12 free.) Farther up the street on V. della A. de Pace 108, the **Museo Civico** contains a variety of relics and artwork from the town's past. (Open M-F 10am-1pm and 4-8pm, Sa-Su 10am-1pm and 5-9pm. €1.) Before crossing the 17th-century bridge to the *città vecchia*, find the recently restored Greek fountain, also known as the **Fontana Ellenica**, to the left.

The free publication *Night & Day* lists Gallipoli's restaurants, bars, and distant *discoteche*. In the evening, don't miss the ◼sunset from Riviera Sauro, when the brilliant Salentino sun slips beneath the horizon in a thrilling finale of pink and orange. Continue to the other side of the old city to reach bar **Ritrò**, Riviera Armando Diaz 1/3. Candle-lit and canopied, the daily *aperitivo* hour (6:30-8pm) is the perfect place to try a live *riccio di mare* (sea-urchin) with your drink. (☎0833 26 39 01; www.ritroristobar.com. Beer €3-4. Mixed drinks €5. Wine €3. Open daily in summer 10am-3am; in winter M-Tu and Th-Su 10:30am-3pm and 7pm-midnight.) From July 23-25, the city honors its patron saint with the **Festa di Santa Cristina**. Aside from a sea procession with the saint's statue, locals gather at this time for the traditional challenge of *"la cuccagna"*, which involves grabbing a flag at the end of a greased pole suspended over the port waters. The *Museo Diocesano*, along with museums from Otranto and Lecce, also hosts **Arte Mare**, a series of concerts, art displays, and discussions from the beginning of July to the end of August.

CALABRIA

Sometimes called the last great oasis of the Mediterranean, Calabria (ca-LAH-bree-ah) is an undiscovered land of inspiring history and unspoiled natural beauty. Long stretches of beaches lie on the coast, and untamed mountain wilderness reigns in the interior. As one of Italy's less developed regions, it is one of the few places that has not become completely overrun with camera-toting tourists. Two and a half millennia ago, when the northern cities that now belittle Calabria were but small backwaters, the region was of international importance, home to leading philosophers, artists, and athletes. Fortunately for local pride, traces of this illustrious past remain in abundance, from the castles that dot the coast to the stunningly intact Greek bronze statues still on display in Reggio di Calabria's Museo Nazionale della Magna Graecia. What Calabria lacks in urban bustle, it makes up for in quiet natural beauty and a relaxed attitude that the North simply cannot match—or understand for that matter.

REGGIO DI CALABRIA ☎0965

Though often regarded as a mere departure point for Sicily, Reggio and its environs actually comprise some of the finest landscapes and friendliest people in Italy. The provincial capital of Reggio di Calabria (REH-jo dee Ca-LA-bree-ya; pop. 185,000) was one of the earliest and proudest Greek settlements on the Italian mainland, but it slid into neglect and disarray following centuries of raids and natural disasters. After a devastating 1908 earthquake, a new city arose from the rubble, crowded with designer stores and turn-of-the-century *palazzi*. A vibrant and manageable city, Reggio offers magnificent sunsets, the amazing Riace Bronzes, and a serene evening stroll along the *lungomare*. The nearby towns of Scilla and Locri offer one of Italy's most attractive beaches and finest collections of archaeological treasures.

PUGLIA AND CALABRIA

⬛ TRANSPORTATION

Flights: Aeroporto dello Stretto (☎0965 64 05 17) is 5km south of town. **Orange buses** #113, 114, 115, 125, or 131 run from P. Garibaldi outside Stazione Centrale to the airport (€1). Flights service Bologna, Florence, Milan, Rome, Venice, and Turin.

Trains: Stazione Centrale (☎0965 27 120), on P. Garibaldi at the south end of town. Info office open daily 7am-9pm. Trains run to: **Cosenza** (2hr., 14 per day 5:05am-7:35pm, €13.60); **Naples** (4hr., 12 per day 5:45am-11:40pm, €22); **Rome** (8hr., 14 per day 5:45am-11:40pm, €30); **Scilla** (30min., 20 per day 5:05am-8:35pm, €5.50); **Tropea** (2hr., 10 per day 5:10am-8:35pm, €11).

Buses: Most buses run from P. Garibaldi.

Lirosi: (☎0965 57 552) runs buses to **Florence** (12hr.; M, W-F, and Su 6:45pm; €47) and **Rome** (8hr.; 7am, 11:45am, and 10pm; €35). Buy tickets at Agenzia Viaggi Simonetta, C. Garibaldi 551. (☎0965 81 40 24. Open M-F 9am-8pm, Sa 9am-1pm. AmEx/MC/V.)

Costaviola: (☎0965 75 15 86; www.costaviolabus.it) runs buses to Scilla (45min., 12 per day 7:20am-8:10pm, €3). Buy tickets onboard.

Ferries and hydrofoils: depart from the port at the northern end of the city and serve Messina and the Aeolian Islands.

Trenitalia: (☎0965 81 76 75), to the left of the port. Office open daily 6:30am-8:15pm.

Ustica: (☎090 66 25 06 or 090 36 40 44), to the right of Trenitalia. Office hours vary.

NGI (General Italian Navigation Line): (☎335 84 27 784), across from Onda Marina to the right of the port entrance. Open M-F 12:30-10pm, Sa 12:30-8pm.

⬛ ORIENTATION AND PRACTICAL INFORMATION

Reggio's main thoroughfare is **Corso Garibaldi,** which runs parallel to the sea and to all the major sights. Facing away from **Stazione Centrale,** walk straight through **Piazza Garibaldi** to C. Garibaldi; a left turn leads to the *centro*. At the end of C. Garibaldi and down Vle. Genoese Zerbi is Reggio's **port,** from which hydrofoils and boats depart. One block to the left of the station, the twin roads **Corso Vittorio Emanuele III** and **Viale Matteotti** trace the *lungomare*. City buses run continuously up and down C. Garibaldi and northward along the two roads. At its center, C. Garibaldi becomes a pedestrian route, perfect for an evening *passeggiata* past the many bars and designer outlets that line the street.

Tourist office: APT, V. Roma 3, 1st fl. (☎0965 21 171). Provides info and free maps. Open M-W 7:30am-1:30pm and 2-4pm, Th-F 7:30am-1:30pm. Branches: at Stazione Centrale (☎0965 27 120) and airport (☎0965 64 32 91).

Currency exchange: Banca Nazionale del Lavoro, C. Garibaldi 431 (☎0965 85 11). Open M-F 8:20am-1:20pm and 2:35-4pm.

Police: (☎0965 53 991), near Stazione Centrale.

Hospital: Ospedale Riuniti (☎0965 39 111), on V. Melacrino.

Internet Access: Online Internet Point Multiservices, V. De Nava 142 (☎0965 23 902). €4 per hr., students €3 with student ID. Open daily 9am-1pm and 4-8:30pm.

Post office: V. Miraglia 14 (☎0965 31 52 68). Open M-F 8:30am-6:30pm, Sa 8am-12:30pm. **Postal Code:** 89121.

⬛ ACCOMMODATIONS

Cheap, quality accommodations are difficult to find in Reggio, but they exist.

⬛ **B&B La Pineta,** Vle. G. Zerbi 13/B (☎0965 59 37 13; www.bblapineta.info). A diamond in the rough; simple rooms on the *lungomare*. All have bath and TV; doubles have A/C. Reserve ahead July-Aug. Singles €35; doubles €50; triples €60. Cash only. ❸

B&B Le Stanze di Anna e Catarina, V. Chiesa Pepe, 11/13 (☎333 19 879 25; www. lestanzediannaecaterina.it). Hidden within a maze of curving streets and parked cars. The epitome of budget luxury. Elegant wardrobe, stunning collection of impressionist paintings, and colorful themed rooms. Terrace, TV lounge, reading room and A/C. Free Wi-Fi. Reservations recommended. Singles €35-40; extra bed €10. Cash only. ●

Hotel Mundial, V. Gaeta 9 (☎0965 33 22 55; hotelmundial@virgilio.it). Offers relatively cheap rooms near the train station. All rooms with bath, TV, A/C, and phone. Singles €40; doubles €55; triples €60; quads €80. Cash only. ●

B&B Villa Maria, V. Marina Arenile 3 (☎0965 37 26 33), in Gallico Marina. Take bus #110 from P. Garibaldi, walk to the waterfront (10min.), and turn right, or call to be picked up. The B&B is on V. Marina Arenile behind the "Ottica" shop. Offers rooms near the coast with shared terrace. Singles €30-€40, extra bed €25. Cash only. ●

FOOD

Chefs in Reggio serve spaghetti alla calabrese (pasta with pepper sauce), capocollo (ham spiced with local hot peppers), frittole (pork cooked in a boiler), and pesce spada (swordfish). Bars along C. Garibaldi often offer baked goods, so sweeten the day with a few of the region's beloved *biscotti.* Stock up on groceries at **Dì per Dì** supermarket, past the museum where V. de Nava crosses V. Roma. (☎0965 81 12 79. Open M-Sa 8am-1:30pm and 5-8:30pm. MC/V.)

Cordon Bleu, C. Garibaldi 205 (☎0965 33 24 47). Despite chandelier lighting and a haughty French name, this versatile joint serves cheap tavola calda goodies (from €1.50), as well as more sophisticated meat and vegetable entrees. Primi €5-6. Secondi €6-8. Open daily 6:30am-11pm. Kitchen open 11am-9pm. AmEx/MC/V. ●

Lord Byron, V. del Plebiscito 20 (☎0218 33 908 02). Everything from the *rosticceria* is €1, including *calzoni, arancini, pizza a taglio, schicciate,* and *sfoglie.* Open 24hr. ●

La Taverna dei Templari, V. del Torrione 35 (☎349 16 614 25). A medieval menu and feudal decorations make this pizzeria stand out from all the rest. €16 dinner *menù* would make any knight burst his armor. Enormous pizzas €3.50-6. Open 8pm-4am. ●

SIGHTS

The preeminence Reggio di Calabria enjoyed in antiquity as a great Greek polis may have passed, but the **Museo Nazionale** preserves the city's historical claim to fame with one of the world's finest collections of art and artifacts from Magna Graecia (Greater Greece). In the first floor galleries, a wealth of *amphorae* and *pinakes* (wine jars and votive tablets) depict scenes from mythology and daily life. The floor above the gallery has a large coin collection and a 2300-year-old novelty sarcophagus shaped like a huge, sandaled foot. Downstairs, treasures formerly submerged in the Ionian Sea, such as pottery and broken statues, comprise the **Sezione Subacquea** (Underwater Section). If the Subacquea is the centerpiece, **I Bronzi di Riace** are the crown jewels. Rescued from the sea in 1972, the Riace Bronzes are among the best (and arguably the most valuable) ancient Greek sculptures in the world. Dating from the fifth century BC, they depict nude male warriors in stunning detail. Muscular and assured, the bronzes share gallery space with the realistic **Head of the Philosopher,** which some cite as the Greek tradition's first life-like portrait. A display documents the bronzes' restoration process. (P. de Nava, on C. Garibaldi toward the Stazione Lido. ☎0965 89 69 72 or 0965 31 62 42. Open Tu-Su 9am-8pm. Last entry 30min. before closing. €6, ages 18-25 €3, under 18 or over 65 free.) **Castello Aragonese** is said to date from 536 BC and has provided the city with protection ever since. It was greatly enlarged under the rule of Ferdinand of Aragon and Charles V, who sought to defend the city from Turkish invasions.

Today the castle provides magnificent views of the city and Calabria's neighboring Sicily. (P. Castello; take V. degli Ottimati up from C. Garibaldi. ☎0965 36 21 11. Open daily, hours vary.) For more stunning views, enjoy a stroll through the **Parco della Rotonda,** across from Chiesa San Paolo. (Take either V. del Salvatore or V. E. Cuzzocrea away from the sea, turn right at V. Udine, and then walk until you see the park. Open 10am-12:30pm and 5-8pm. Free.)

🔲 🎵 BEACHES AND ENTERTAINMENT

As the day cools, *reggiani* mingle on the 🔳**lungomare,** a long narrow, botanical garden stretching along the seaside that Italian author Gabriele d'Annunzio immortalized as the "most beautiful kilometer in all of Italy." When they desire a dip, travelers and locals head to the beach near **Lido Comunale.** Playgrounds, an elevated boardwalk, and monuments to the city's more famous citizens dot the *lungomare,* while the quiet beauty of a sunset behind the misty blue mountains of nearby Sicily provides the final natural touch to a pleasant afternoon swim. Private beaches come alive at night and play host to Reggio's youth. Calabrians finish the summer with the humongous **Festival of the Madonna della Consolazione.** This four-day festival, beginning the second Saturday of September, starts with an enormous parade led by men carrying an effigy of the Holy Virgin, and concludes with an elaborate fireworks display over the ocean.

🔳 DAYTRIP FROM REGGIO DI CALABRIA

🔳SCILLA
Scilla is accessible from Reggio by train (30min., 20per day, €5.50) or by bus (45min., 12 per day, €3). Scilla's train station does not sell tickets, so purchase a round-trip ticket from Reggio or ask at nearby bars for regional train tickets.

Walk along the beach and listen for mermaids singing; local legend has it that merfolk still dwell off the Scillan coast. Homer immortalized Scilla's (SHEEL-la; pop. 5134) great cliffs in *The Odyssey* as the home of the menacing Scylla, a terrible monster with six heads, 12 feet, and a fierce temper. Even fiercer was the monster's snare—as ships fled nearby Charybdis, a hazardous whirlpool in the straits where Sicily and Italy meet, Scylla would wait patiently and then devour the vessels as they sailed past. Travelers today are greeted instead by a resort town filled with beach umbrellas and untroubled tourists. Only 23km from Reggio, Scilla's languorous pace and distinctive geography (it is built directly into cliffs which enclose a sandy beach) can make the real world seem far away—especially when the meteorological oddity *Fata Morgana* creates a natural magnifying glass out of the light over the sea, making the Sicilian city of Messina appear to be floating just above the water. Former hippies seeking the good old days should look no further than this oceanic retreat; Dalì City Scilla ❷, V. Porto 6, offers *panini* (€3.50-4), salads (€5), and a variety of drinks (€2-7) in a seaside shack. Electric guitars hang from the ceiling, posters of Jimi Hendrix, Janis Joplin, and the Beatles cover both the inside and outside, and classic rock erupts from the stereo system. (☎0965 79 01 96. Hours vary, so listen for the music.) Zanzibar Gelateria ❶, V. Spirito Santo 1, specializes in *granita* (Italian flavored ice) and old-fashioned gelato. (☎339 33 272 35; open afternoons, hours vary). Those craving seafood should try La Pescatora ❸, V. Cristoforo Colombo 32. (☎0965 17 54 147. Primi €4-7.50. Secondi €7-11.50. Open M-Tu and Th-Su noon-3:30pm, 8-11:30pm. AmEx/MC/V.)

COSENZA ☎0984

One of the most important cultural and industrial centers of Calabria, Cosenza (co-SEN-za; pop. 71,680) is full of intrigue. From the plundered riches that King

Alaric I supposedly buried in the city's Busento River in AD 410 to the Norman-style castle built by the Saracens, Cosenza's treasures mirror its unusual history. Though often ignored by tourists due to its inland location, Cosenza's labyrinthine *centro storico*, massive student population, and thriving nightlife make it worth a stopover. The best time to visit is in spring, when university is in session, Teatro Rendano echoes with plays, and weather is moderate.

> **SUNDAY SERVICES.** Transportation options from Cosenza are severely reduced Su. City buses run less frequently, and Ferrovie della Calabria trains and buses do not run at all. Act like a local and lay low.

TRANSPORTATION. Trains depart from **Stazione Cosenza** (☎0984 39 47 46), on V. Popilia, 4km north of the city center. The ticket office is open daily 6:10am-12:42pm and 1:50-8:22pm. Trains go to Naples (4hr., 13 per day 4:35am-6:25pm, €17.30) and Reggio di Calabria (2hr., 15 per day 4:35am-9:25pm, €13.60). Ferrovie della Calabria sends trains to Camigliatello (1hr., M-Sa 9:18am, €3). It also sends blue **regional buses** to Camigliatello (45min., M-Sa 8 per day 6:50am-7:05pm, €2) and San Giovanni (2hr., M-Sa 10 per day, €3) from the station on V. Autostazione and the Stazione Cosenza. The ticket office is opposite the train ticket window and is open daily 6am-2:20pm and 4-7:30pm. All orange **city buses** stop at P. Matteotti. Tickets (€0.77) are sold at kiosks (main kiosk at V. Trieste with C. Mazzini, near P. dei Bruzi) and at most *tabaccherie*. Buses #4T, 22, and 23 serve the *centro storico*, departing from P. Bruzi and stopping in P. Prefeturra (every 30min. 5:30am-11pm). Buses #17 and 27 run between P. Matteotti and the train station (every 7min. 5am-midnight). Routes are posted on yellow street signs in P. Matteotti and at all bus stops. (Info ☎800 24 24 00.)

ORIENTATION AND PRACTICAL INFORMATION. The Busento River divides the city into two parts: the traffic-heavy new city, north of the Busento, and the relaxed *centro storico*, south of the river. **Corso Mazzini,** the main pedestrian thoroughfare and shopping center, begins near the river at **Piazza dei Bruzi,** continues through **Piazza Kennedy,** and ends in **Piazza Bilotti.** To get to C. Mazzini, hop on any bus to Piazza Matteotti and, facing away from the bus stop, walk one block up Corso Umberto to P. dei Bruzi. The bus station is on **Via Autostazione,** to the right off P. Bilotti at the end of C. Mazzini, where the *corso* splits seven ways. Cosenza's *centro storico* lies across the **Ponte Mario Martiri.** A maze of medieval stone buildings, the old city has winding streets and cobblestone staircases. The only discernible street, the narrow **Corso Telesio,** begins in **Piazza Valdesi,** near the Busento, and climbs to the statue of Telesio in the Piazza XV Marzo (also called Piazza Prefettura).

For tourist info, head either to the **Agenzia Informagiovani,** V. Francesco Acri 1/C-1/E, next to Morrone Park (☎0984 74 044), or the town hall, P. dei Bruzi 1 (☎0984 81 31). Be aware that opening hours are sporadic. In case of emergency, call the **police** in P. dei Bruzi, behind the town hall (☎0984 25 422). **Farmacia Berardelli,** C. Mazzini 40, posts after-hours rotations. (☎0984 26 452. Open M-F 8:30am-1pm and 4:30-8pm.) The **Ospedale Civile dell'Annunziata** (☎0984 68 11) is on V. Felice Migliori. **Libreria Mondadori,** C. Mazzini 156, has a small selection of English-language bestsellers. (☎0983 79 58 14. Open M-F 9am-1pm and 4:30-8:30pm, Sa 9am-1pm. AmEx/MC/V.) For **Internet** access, head to **Web Point,** P. Campanella 32. (€2 per hr. Open daily 9am-1pm and 4:30-9pm.) The **post office,** V. Veneto 41, is at the end of V. Piave, off C. Mazzini. (☎0984 22 162. Open M-F 8am-6:30pm, Sa 8am-12:30pm). **Postal Code:** 87100.

PUGLIA AND CALABRIA

⛄⛄ ACCOMMODATIONS AND FOOD. Ostello Re Alarico ❶, Vico II Giuseppe Marini Serra 10, is the perfect base for exploring the old city and its surroundings. To get there, cross the Crati River from the old city and follow V. G. M. Serra until the brown sign for V. II Giuseppe. The hostel offers ornately furnished eight-bed rooms, a bar, lounge, kitchen, and courtyard. (☎0984 79 25 70; www.ostellorealarico.com. Internet €3 per hr. Light breakfast included. Dorms €17. AmEx/MC/V.) Also located in the historic center, **B&B Confluenze ❶,** Vico IV Santa Lucia 48, boasts four modern rooms with heating and historic feel. (☎320 372 6087. Internet, telephone, and laundry access. Reservations required. Singles €25-35; doubles €50-70. Cash only.) To reach **Hotel Grisaro ❸,** V. Monte Santo 6, walk one block up C. Mazzini from P. dei Bruzi, then turn left on V. Trieste and look for V. Monte Santo. Rooms are spacious and comfortable, with TV, and balcony. (☎0984 27 952; fax 27 838. Wheelchair-accessible. Reservations recommended. Singles with exterior private bath €29, with interior bath €36; doubles €52; triples €67; quads €78. MC/V.)

Cosenza's cuisine is a crossroads of flavor, drawing on fresh prosciutto and rich mushrooms of the Sila forests, plentiful fish from the Tyrrhenian Sea, and the fruit of the region's orchards. For a proper meal, hike up the stone steps next to Teatro Rendano to reach **Taverna L'Arco Vecchio ❷,** P. Archi di Ciaccio 21. Outfitted in elegant wood, this versatile restaurant offers guests a range of salads (€6-8), pizzas (€3-10), and entrees in a garden dining area. Enjoy the large wine selection and the marvelous location by the city's old arch. (☎0984 72 564. Primi €4-8. Secondi €3-6.50. Cover €1.50. Open M-Sa 1-3pm and 8-11pm. Reservations recommended. AmEx/MC/V.) For a cheaper, more filling feast, check out **Fire ❶,** V. degli Alimena 125 (off C. Mazzini), a hybrid pizzeria, *rosticceria,* and *tavola calda* serving up enormous portions at low prices. Order the *"pranzo completo,"* a two-course lunch with sliced bread and a cold drink (€7). Hurried patrons order the *pizza margherita* (€0.70) and a wildberry *granatina* (€0.70) to go. (☎348 08 18 210. Open daily noon-8pm, though hours sometimes vary. Cash only.) Owned and operated by the same family since 1803, **Gran Caffè Renzelli ❶,** C. Telesio 46, specializes in homemade sweets; their *varchiglia alla mocale* is a chocolate-covered almond treat still made by nuns with a recipe from the 1300s. The *gran caffè* is as pretty as it is powerful, with steamed milk, cocoa, and *vov,* an egg liqueur. (☎0984 26 814; www.grancafferenzelli.it. Mini pizza *rustica* €1. Gelato €2.60. Cover €0.50. Open daily 7am-midnight. Closed Tu in winter. Cash only.) For fresh, juicy produce, stop at **Cooper Frutta,** Vle. Trieste 33, a block from C. Mazzini; and for everything else at **Cooperatore Alimentare,** next door at Vle. Trieste 35. (Both open M-F 7am-8pm, Sa 7am-2:30pm.)

◆◆ SIGHTS AND NIGHTLIFE. Via Corso Mazzini, filled with expensive shops and restaurants, is the place to see and be seen. Be sure to stroll through during the late afternoon, when the whole city comes alive. For an older, less crowded sight, cross Ponte Mario Martiri into the old city and head left up C. Telesio to reach the **duomo.** Alternatively, take bus #22 or 23 to P. Prefettura; facing away from P. del Governo, turn right down C. Telesio. Originally erected in 1140 with a Romanesque design, the church had to be entirely rebuilt in 1184 after an earthquake. When the *duomo* was reconsecrated in 1222 after yet another earthquake, Frederick II gave the city a gilt **Byzantine crucifix** containing a splinter allegedly from the True Cross. Now the cross is in the Galleria Nazionale at the Palazzo Arnone; call ahead to see it. Inside the *duomo* is Cosenza's most prized work of art after the famed cross—*La Madonna del Pilerio,* a 12th-century painting in the Byzantine style. It is in a Baroque chapel, the first to the left side of the church entrance. (☎0984 79 56 39. Open daily mornings and late afternoons.) Back in P. Prefettura, the **Teatro Rendano,** Calabria's most prestigious performance venue, was constructed in 1895 and destroyed by WWII bombing. It has since been restored to its former glory, and its plush interior has even showcased the likes of José Carreras. Reservations for non-*calabresi* or unconnected foreigners are extremely difficult to get during opera season (Oct.-Dec.); seats for theater season (Jan.-May) may be somewhat easier to come by. The Rendano also hosts regional performance groups during summer, with readily available tickets. (☎0984 81 32 20. For plays, tickets are sporadically available from 10am-1pm and 5-8pm on performance day. Tickets from €18, student discounts available.)

Revelers from surrounding towns flock to Cosenza, as it is the region's nightlife hub. **Beat Pub**, P. Duomo 4/6, right next to the *duomo*, is huge, with more than 50 Belgian beers. (☎0984 29 548. Beers from €2. Open daily 7:30pm-3am. AmEx/MC/V.) **Planet Alex**, P. XI Settembre 12, off C. Mazzini, is a disco-pub in the new city that blasts dance music. (☎0984 79 53 37. Live music Th-F in winter. Open M-Sa 7am-2am, Su 5pm-2am. AmEx/MC/V.) Get a taste of the Emerald Isle at the **James Joyce Irish Pub**, V. Cafarone 19, a lively bar that's packed on weekends. (☎0984 22 799. Open daily from 8pm. AmEx/MC/V.)

CAMIGLIATELLO AND SILA MASSIF ☎0984

"Its nature will amaze you," states a billboard near the Sila Massif train station. Indeed, the 1850 sq. km plateau is an untainted landscape of fertile green mountains, prismatic lakes, and woods that burst with wildflowers in the spring. Covering the widest part of the Calabrian peninsula, Sila was once a single forest, exploited from its earliest days to provide fuel and material for the buildings of Rome. Today, the area offers some of Italy's most spectacular natural settings and a wealth of activities to satisfy intrepid explorers. Camigliatello (cah-MEE-lyah-TEH-loh; pop. 700), a resort town, offers bus connections and access to hikes and ski slopes, making it the best base for exploring Sila.

TRANSPORTATION AND PRACTICAL INFORMATION. Trains to Sila-Camigliatello run from Cosenza (1hr., 9:18am, €2) but are often erratic; buses from Cosenza are usually more reliable (40min., 9 per day 6:30am-7pm, €2). Find bus schedules at the tourist office and buy tickets at **Bar Pedace**, the bar closest to the bus stop. Info on Sila and surrounding attractions, events, and trails can be found at the **Pro Loco** tourist office, V. Roma 5, uphill from the train station and bus stop. (☎0984 57 81 59. Open Tu-Su 9:30am-1pm and 3:30-7:30pm.) Banca Carime is at V. del Turismo 73. (☎57 80 27. Open M-F 8:30am-1:15pm and 2:30-3:30pm.) In case of emergency, call the guardia medica (☎0984 57 83 28), near the bus stop. The **post office**, on V. Tasso, is at the intersection of V. del Turismo and V. Roma, next to Hotel Tasso. (☎0984 57 80 76. Open M-F 8am-1:30pm, Sa 8am-12:30pm.) **Postal Code:** 87052.

ACCOMMODATIONS AND FOOD. Hotel Meranda ❸, V. del Turismo 29, offers clean modern rooms in a secluded area just off the main road. Facilities include an elegant restaurant and *discoteca*, plus TV, telephone, heating, and A/C in every room. Prices rise during ski season. (☎0984 57 80 22; fax 57 92 93. Breakfast included. Singles €30-60; doubles with half pension €48-65, full pension €53-70. Extra bed €35-52. AmEx/MC/V.) Buses run from Camigliatello to campground **La Fattoria** ❶, 54.5 km from Camigliatello, which boasts a pizzeria, bowling alley, and minigolf course. (☎0984 57 83 64. Tent provided. €5.60 per person. Cash only.) The classy **Hotel Cristallo** ❸, V. Roma 91, has 43 rooms with private bath and seven two-room apartments for families, as well as a large conference room, restaurant, stylish *discoteca*, and games rooms. (☎0984 57 80 13; www.hotelcristallosila.it. Singles €35-55; doubles €55-85. AmEx/MC/V.)

Le Tre Lanterne ❸, V. Roma 142, is a popular spot specializing in Sila's famous porcini mushrooms. (☎0984 57 82 03. Pizza from €3.50. Primi €6-8. Secondi €8-12. Cover €1.50. Open Tu-Su noon-3pm and 7-11pm. AmEx/MC/V.) Dine by lantern light at **Ristorante Hotel Lo Sciatore ❸**, V. Roma 128, where patrons savor creamy mushroom risotto in a dining room with a wooden ski-lodge feel. Starving patrons should ask about the ever-varying but always enormous *pranzo turistico* (€15), and oenophiles should examine the extensive wine list, provided they have some extra money. (☎0984 57 81 05. Wood-oven pizza €3-6.50, Sa and Su only. Primi €6. Secondi €7.50. Cover €1.60. Open daily 12:30-3pm and 7:30-10pm. AmEx/MC/V.) **La Casa del Fungo ❸**, on P. Misasil, just next door to Campanaro, sells locally-grown mushrooms. (Open daily 9am-8:30pm. Closed Tu in winter. Cash only.) Picnic grounds lie 10min. from the *centro*, up V. Tasso. There are a number of *salumerie* overflowing with cheeses, meats, and mushrooms, like **Antica Salumeria Campanaro**, P. Misasi 5, across from the post office (☎0984 57 80 15. Open daily 9am-9pm. MC/V.)

❂ NIGHTLIFE. Bar Le Bistro ❶, V. C. Alvaro 68, off V. Roma and across from the bus stop, has it all. With six virtual slot machines, two driving arcades, billiards, and a foosball table, not to mention a variety of assorted liquors from Italy and abroad (from €2), this bar is your best bet for a good time. *Caffè freddo* (€0.70) is a favorite, as are the sweet and salty snack offerings. (☎0984 06 807 68. Open daily 3pm-midnight. Cash only. A local hot spot known for its subdued atmosphere and mouth-watering *cioccolata bianca* (€0.80), Bar Pantusa ❶, V. Roma 202, also has a large selection of low-priced alcohol, ice cream, and snacks. (☎0984 57 84 59. Open 1-9pm. Cash only.).

> **MENACING MUSHROOMS.** When exploring the Parco Nazionale di Calabria, think twice before taking home any of the region's famous wild mushrooms. While the *funghi porcini* are both edible and delicious, other species range from mildly poisonous to lethally toxic. The safest way to enjoy Silan mushrooms is to purchase them in local shops or restaurants.

▣▣ OUTDOOR ACTIVITIES AND SKIING. Come winter, there's plenty of snow at the **Tasso Monte Curcio Ski Trail**, 2km from town up V. Roma and left at Hotel Tasso. Go right at the fork in the road. In winter, minibuses leave for the trailhead from Camigliatello's bus stop. Buy tickets on board. Though Tasso offers 35km of cross-country skiing, it has only 2km of downhill trails. (☎0984 57 81 36 or 57 80 37. When snow is on the ground, lifts are open daily 9am-4:30pm. Round-trip lift ticket €4, weekends €5; day pass €15/20.) The Sci Club Camigliatello, V. Roma next door to Pro Loco, offers lessons at low prices (www.sciclubcamigliatello.it.) Master skier Fiorino Spizzirri offers both individual and group lessons through his **Scuola Italiana Sci Camigliatello**, V. del Turismo 11 (☎328 95 709 93; www.incamigliatello.it.) Getting to the ▣Parco Nazionale di Calabria (☎0984 57 97 57), 10km northwest, is tricky, but well worth it. Just two Autolinee Scura (☎0984 31 324) buses head into the park daily, so plan your day accordingly and be prepared to wait. **Altipiani,** V. Roma 146 (☎0984 57 81 54 or 0984 339 26 42 365; www.inaltipiani.it), is a tremendous tourist resource that offers outdoor activities for every season. Hike through the park with a knowledgeable guide, mountain bike the trails with a group of riders of similar ability, hunt for edible mushrooms with experts, or study the lifestyle of wolves and other animals in the Sila forest with professional researchers. English-language group tours of the park are available year-round. Arrange times and prices through reservation. Altipani also rents bikes. (Bikes €12 per half-day, €18 per day. Snowshoes €13 per day. Cross-country skis €18 per day. *Let's Go* discount €3 on all full-day rentals. Cash only.) The █**Greenwood Cooperative Society** (Società Cooperativa Greenwood), V. Pozzillo 21, conducts research in the park and urges *"turismo naturalistico,"* or tourism that helps sustain the environment rather than spoil it. Tourist services include guided treks on foot, mountain bike, and horseback, as well as night excursions and birdwatching. In addition, Greenwood uses volunteers to help with ecological studies and research, such as a full week of studying and tracking wolves with GPS devices and topographic maps (€350 to cover food, camping, and research supplies). These studies change every season, so explore the Greenwood website to see what's coming up on the ever-expanding environmentally friendly horizon. (☎0984 44 55 26; www.scgreenwood.it. Reservations required.)

PRAIA A MARE   ☎0985

Although Praia a Mare (PRY-ah A MAR-eh) has only 6280 year-round residents, come summer, vacationing Italians swarm this beach town and cause the population to swell dramatically. Largely undiscovered by foreigners, this peaceful hamlet boasts glistening sands, cliff diving, and a popular philosophy of repose not found in any major northern city. Home to both the natural beauty of Isola Dino and the non-stop parties of the *Festa di Santa Maria della Grotta*, Praia offers something for everyone.

⊡⊞ TRANSPORTATION AND PRACTICAL INFORMATION. The best way to reach Praia is by train. Trains depart from the Praia station for: Cosenza (2hr., 16 per day, €7); Naples (3hr., 14 per day, €9); Reggio di Calabria (3hr., 20 per day, €14); Rome (3-5hr., 12 per day, €30). For taxis, call ☎338 76 49 71. The best way to get around town is by bike: rentals are available at **Bike Motor Points**, P. Italia. (☎0985 72 126. €10 per day.) Praia basically consists of three main streets that run parallel to the ocean. Via Roma is the first street outside the train station; next is Via C. P. Longo, which becomes Via L. Giuguie and the main avenue through town. After that is the lungomare, which follows the ocean all the way to the beautiful beaches of Fiuzzi. For maps and info on events in town head to the **IAT tourist office**, V. Amerigo Vespucci 12. (☎0985 72 322. Open daily 8am-8pm.) For currency exchange and an ATM right off the main street, go to **Banca di Napoli**, V. della Libertà 14. (☎0985 72 071. Open daily 7am-2pm.) In an emergency, call the carabinieri (☎0985 72 020). **Farmacia Nappi** can be found at V. C. P. Longo 51. (☎0985 72 009. Open daily 8am-8pm.) Internet with free Wi-Fi can be found at the Museo Communale on V. Verdi. (☎0985 77 020. Open M-F 8am-noon and 4-10pm, Sa 7pm-midnight.) The post office is located in P. Municipio near the town center. (Open M-Sa 7am-1pm.) **Postal Code:** 87028.

WHAT'S IN A NAME? Praia a Mare also goes by the name Praja; both names show up on maps and train schedules. Trenitalia clumps the Praia a Mare stop with two other towns: look for Praja-Ajeta-Tortora.

▌▐ ACCOMMODATIONS AND FOOD. Although prices in Praia skyrocket in August, a few budget bargains remain. With a fun community atmosphere, █**The Onda Road Beach Hostel ❶**, V. Boccioni 13, is the best bet for backpackers. Martina, Papa, and their dog Sylia welcome foreigners with open arms. The hostel has simple dorms and two doubles. The real deals are their incredible discounts on attractions such as rafting, paragliding, bikes, and the beach clubs. (☎34 70 73 61 69; www.calabriahostel.com. Free pickup from train station. Papa runs Isola di Dino boat tours for about €10 per person. Kitchen available. Breakfast and lunch included. Laundry €3 per load, free for stays longer than 3 nights. Reservations recommended. Dorms €19; doubles €50. Cash only.) For slightly classier digs right in the center of town, head to Le Arcate ❹, V. Filippo Turati 25. This modern hotel has large marble-floored rooms, many with balconies overlooking the main street. All rooms have bath, TV, AC, and phone. (☎0985 72 297. Breakfast included. Reservations recommended in Aug. Singles €45-76; doubles €60-150; triples €75-225. Full pension required in Aug.) For a more intimate experience, the Calabrese hospitality at B&B Al Vecchio Pioppo ❺, V. Turati 77, is sure to charm. Four lavishly-furnished rooms offer private baths, AC, refrigerators, and TV. (☎0985 77 73 52; www.alvecchiopioppo.com. Singles €30-45; doubles €60-90. AmEx/MC/V.) Camping can be found a short walk from town near Fiuzzi at La Mantinera ❶, V. Giovanni Battista Falcone. With a pool, private beach, amphitheater, and restaurant, the campground truly deserves its self-proclaimed title of tourist village. (☎0985 77 90 23; www.lamantinera.it. Reservations recommended Aug. €4.50-14 per person, €14-97 per tent. Bungalows €330-1350 per week. Prices rise during *Ferragosto*. AmEx/MC/V.)

While the eateries in Praia are generally overpriced, the restaurant at Le Arcate ❺, V. Filippo Turati 21, provides affordable upscale dining. Try their drink and pizza special for €5. (☎0985 72 297. Pizza from €3.50; dinner only. Primi €4.55-8. Secondi €6.27-14. Cover €1.50. Open 24hr. in summer. AmEx/MC/V). Also be sure to visit Ciacco Caffè-Gelateria ❷, V. C. P. Longo 1, the favorite spot in town to beat the heat with a rich gelato. Choose from over 20 flavors, including Nutella, (medium cone €1.50), which was voted best in its class for five straight years. (☎275 72 30 780. Open daily 7am-midnight, or whenever people stop coming. Cash only.) If you're being chased by a coyote, or just in a general hurry, grab a hot slice and a cold drink at Road Runner ❶, V. della Libertà. (Pizza from €1. Open daily 5-11pm. Cash only.) There are five supermarkets within the city center, as well as numerous vegetable stands and fish markets. The most convenient is the Sisa supermarket located at V. L. Giugni 37 right in the middle of town. (Open daily 9am-1:30pm and 4:30-8:30pm.)

◢◣ SIGHTS AND BEACHES. Just a few meters from the beaches at Fiuzzi lies the massive, craggy ◼Isola di Dino, owned by the famous Ferrari family. Though a climb to the tiptop of the isle costs €7, the grottoes underneath are easily accessible by kayak, paddle boat, or motorboat. The truly brave can venture to a natural arch 10min. away by boat that accommodates 22m dives. Novices should not attempt this as serious injury can result! Those less inclined for savage leaps should snorkel in the water around the island. (Boat tours and all other rentals can be arranged at most of the beach clubs. Prices vary by season.) Home of the city's patron, the Blessed Madonna, the Santuario Madonna della Grotta is found in a large cave in the cliffs overlooking the city. Follow V. della Grotta up from V. L. Giugni. The cave itself houses an ongoing archaeological dig, a modern church, and, of course, the statue of the Madonna, which sits safely in a plexiglass case. You can only get up close and personal with the Virgin Mary by embarking on a guided tour. Legend claims that a 12th-century Christian sea captain chose this cave as the refuge for the statue after his Muslim shipmates, stuck off the coast of Praia, deemed it a curse. The Madonna was later discovered by sheepherders, who later founded Praia a Mare. The cave has been inhabited for the last 14,000 years and has provided archaeologists with a wealth of information regarding the lives and culture of the ancient settlements of Calabria. (For tours call ☎0985 72 061. Open daily 8am-8pm.)

Beaches run the length of Praia all along the *lungomare*, though the nicest ones are located at Fuizzi nearest to Isola Dino. Chairs (from €5) and umbrellas (from €5) can be rented from any of the beach clubs. Don't feel intimidated; the beaches are free regardless of the club presence. If sunbathing sounds too tame, **FlyTirreno** offers paragliding excursions. After driving 600m up into the nearby mountains, the pilot takes off for a 20min. flight over Praia and land on the beach directly next to Fuizzi. (☎347 55 70 595. Flights €70, Onda Road Hostel guests €40. Reservations required. Cash only.)

🎵🎭 **NIGHTLIFE AND ENTERTAINMENT.** Check out **Bar Perfetti,** next door to Bike Motor Points and directly across from Ciacco. The disco bar is the local hangout year-round, but it really fires up during high season, when the owners place a DJ outside, and revelers dance in the street until the sun comes up. When the music stops, cool off with a refreshing *cedrata* for only €2. (Open 7am-midnight Tu-Su, and until 4am in August. Cash only.) If a quieter drink sounds more appealing, visit **Bar Branca**, V. L. Giugni 48, which offers reasonably cheap prices and an assortment of alcoholic and non-alcoholic drinks. (Open daily 7am-1pm and 4pm-whenever people stop coming. Cash only.) Although Praia fills up during summer, it reaches critical mass on August 15 for the Festa di Santa Maria. Locals bring the Madonna down from the church and parade it by boat through the harbor.

🎒 DAYTRIPS FROM PRAIA A MARE

🚣 **LAO RIVER RAFTING.** The Lao River was once used by the ancient Greeks to send messages quickly from Greece to Sicily. Today, rafters can rush through the very same rapids, pausing only to gape at natural wonders. Located deep within the mountainous interior of Calabria, the Lao River Valley remains untouched by man. Although the river is cold, rafters will be adequately out-fitted with wetsuits and rubber shoes and can jump in and float along for the initial phase of the trip. Rafters will brave a few rapids, but nothing overly strenuous; just make sure to hang on to your paddle! Rafting Yahoooooo, V. Marconi 11, in Scalea, runs 5hr. tours of the river and will drive guests to the valley from anywhere in Scalea or Praia. Feel free to bring along a camera, as tour guides offer waterproof cases. (☎333 72 58 276; www.raftingcalabria.it.) Wetsuits provided. Reservations required. €65 per person, €40 for Onda Road Hostel guests. Group rates available.) While the rafting itself is over an hour by van inland, most of the rafting companies are based in nearby Scalea which can easily be reached by train from Praia. (10min., 15 per day, €1.80.)

SICILY (SICILIA)

An island of contradictions, Sicily's (see-CHEE-lee-ya) complex culture emerges from millennia of diverse influences. Every great Mediterranean empire since the arrival of the Phoenicians in 900 BC has left its mark here. A string of Greek colonies followed Phoenician rule, and even today, the island sports more Greek temples than Greece itself. Roman theaters, Arab mosques, and Norman cathedrals round out the physical remnants of Sicily's past. While Italian culture dominates modern Sicily, the separation with the mainland is far greater than the narrow Strait of Messina suggests. The ancient Greeks lauded the "golden isle" as the second home of the gods, but today it is known to many tourists as the home of The Godfather. The Mafia remains an unspoken presence in Sicilian society, but has lately been largely reduced to mostly petty crime. Regardless of her connotations, Sicily overflows with the rich cultural, culinary, and natural wonders that its position at the center of the Mediterranean truly merits.

HIGHLIGHTS OF SICILY

BASK in the glow of Byzantine gold at Monreale Cathedral near Palermo (p. 449).

SCALE Mt. Etna (p. 470) in the morning and party all night in Syracuse (p. 476).

PALERMO
☎ 091

Both turbulent and exquisite, Italy's fifth largest city is an alluring mix of beauty and decay. A smoggy, gritty metropolis with over 1,000,000 inhabitants, Palermo's (pa-LEHR-mo) pace of life dispels any myth of sleepy Sicily; its racing stream of cars, buses, and scooters set the city's breakneck pace. Those who opt to slow down will be rewarded by Palermo's impressive sights and relics. While poverty, bombings, and centuries of neglect have taken their toll on Palermo, the city is slowly experiencing a revival. The 1993 election of an anti-Mafia mayor brought a temporary end to the Mob's knee-bashing control, and with political reform underway, Palermo is now left at peace, to work on restoring its many architectural treasures.

✈ INTERCITY TRANSPORTATION

Flights: Falcone Borsellino Airport (☎091 70 20 111), at Punta Raisi, 30min. from central Palermo. Prestia & Comande (☎091 58 04 57) runs buses every 30min. from P. Castelnuovo (45min.) and Stazione Centrale (1hr., €4.90). Taxis (☎091 59 16 62) charge at least €40-50 to get to town and are parked outside the airport. For trains, look for the "shuttle to trains" sign. Free shuttles run every 30min. to and from the nearby train station at Punto Raisi. At the station, head left and down the escalator. Trains to Stazione Centrale run every hr. 5:40am-10:40pm (€5).

Trains: Stazione Centrale (☎091 60 31 111; www.palermocentrale.it), in P. Giulio Cesare. Ticket office open daily 5:30am-9pm. Luggage storage available (**Practi-**

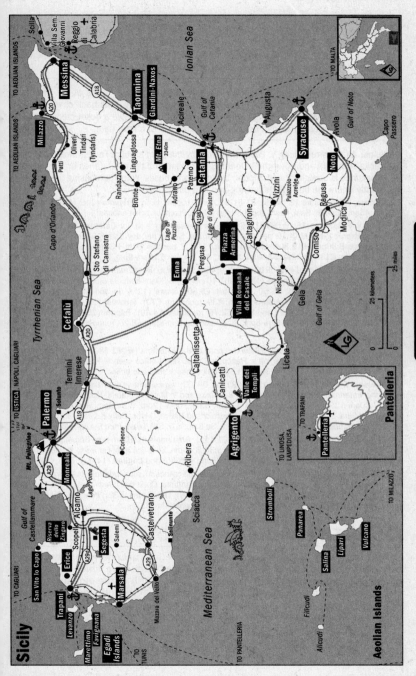

SICILY

cal Information, p. 446). To: **Agrigento** (2hr., 13 per day 7:35am-8:15pm, €7.60); **Catania** (3hr., 2 per day 8:15am, €12); **Messina** (3hr., 11 per day 4:05am-8:30pm, €11); **Milazzo** (3hr., 17 per day 4:05am-8:30pm, €9.50); **Falcone Borsellino Airport** (40min., every hr. 5am-10:10pm, €5); **Rome** (12hr., 3 per day 7:30am-6:40pm, €42); **Trapani** (2hr., 8 per day 6:38am-6:29pm, €7.40)

SPARE SOME CHANGE. When purchasing train tickets at the Stazione Centrale, avoid using large bill; the machine only gives back change up to €4.50. If your change exceeds €4.50, you will receive a ticket credited to that amount that can be used in the machine at a later date.

Buses: All lines run along V. Paolo Balsamo, by the train station. Facing away from the tracks, turn right and exit with McDonald's on the left and the newsstands on the right; V. P. Balsamo is straight ahead, hidden by an army of buses. When purchasing tickets, ask exactly where the bus will be arriving and find out its logo.

Cuffaro, V. P. Balsamo 13 (☎091 61 61 510; www.cuffaro.info). To **Agrigento** (2hr.; M-Sa 9 per day 5:45am-8pm, Su 8am, noon, and 3:30pm; €7.20. Purchase ticket onboard).

SAIS, V. P. Balsamo 16 (☎09161 66 028; www.saisautolinee.it). To: **Catania** (3hr.) and **Catania Airport** (2hr.; M-Th 12 per day, F 14 per day, Sa 11 per day 5am-8:30pm, Su 7 per day 8:30am-8:30pm; €12.80); **Messina** (3hr.; M-F 7 per day 5am-7:30pm, Sa-Su 4 per day 9am-8pm; €13.70); **Piazza Armerina** (2hr., 4-5 per day 6:15am-9pm; €7.30).

Segesta, V. P. Balsamo 14 (☎09161 69 039; www.segesta.it). Buses marked "Sicilbus," "EtnaTransport," or "Interbus" to: **Alcamo** (1hr.; M-F 7-10 per day 6:30am-8pm, Sa 6 per day 6:30am-8pm, Su 11:30am and 8pm; €5.50, round-trip €8.80); **Rome** (12hr.; Th and Su from Politeama 7pm); from **Stazione Centrale** 7:15pm; €39, round-trip €70); **Terrasini** (1hr.; M-Sa 6 per day 6:30am-8pm, Su 11:30am and 8pm; €2.70, round-trip €4.40); **Trapani** (2hr.; M-F 25 per day 6am-9pm, Sa 16 per day 6am-8pm, Su 10 per day 7am-8pm; €8.20, round-trip €13).

Ferries and Hydrofoils:

Grimaldi Group, Calata Marinai d'Italia (seaport) on the waterfront (☎091 58 74 04; www.grimaldi-ferries.com), on V. del Mare, off V. Francesco Crispi. Ticket office open M-F 9am-1pm. Sporadic ferries to **Salerno** (€35) and **Tunisi** (€80). Call or check schedule online.

Siremar, V. Francesco Crispi 118 (☎091 58 24 03; www.siremar.it), on the last street before the waterfront, between V. Principe di Belmonte and V. Mariano Stabile. Ticket office open M-F 7:30am-12:45pm, 3-3:30pm, and 4-7pm; Sa 7:30am-12pm, 3-3:30pm, and 6:30-7pm; Su 7-8:15am, 3-3:30pm, and 6:30-7pm. Hydrofoils to **Ustica** (1¼hr.; daily 8:15am, 3:30pm, 7pm; €24). Ferries to **Ustica** (2¾hr.; M-Sa 9am, Su 8am; €18.35). Leave from Stazione Marittima.

Tirrenia, V. Molo Vittorio Veneto (☎09160 21 111; www.tirrenia.it), 100m from Grimaldi. Open M-F 8:30am-12:30pm and 3:30-8:45pm, Sa 3:30-8:45pm, Su 5-8:45pm. Ferries to **Naples** (10hr.; Oct.-June 8:15pm, July-Aug. 10am and 8:45pm; €35-80) and **Cagliari** (14hr., F 7pm, €30-60).

Ustica, V. Cap. di Bartolo (☎091 84 49 002; www.usticalines.it), runs hydrofoils twice a day to the Aeolian Islands. Open daily 9am-1pm and 5-7pm. All Hydrofoils to: **Alicudi** (2hr., €20); **Filicudi** (3hr., €26); **Lipari** (4hr., €32); **Panarea** (3 hr., €37); **Salina** (3hr., €33); **Stromboli** (4hr., €31.30); **Vulcano** (4hr., €32).

🔲 ORIENTATION

Palermo's newer half follows a grid, but older sections near the **train station** form a tangled knot. The station dominates **Piazza Giulio Cesare,** from which two streets define Palermo's central axis. **Via Roma** runs the length of the old city, ending at V. Emerico Amari, to the right of the **Politeama.** On the left side of P. Giulio Cesare, running parallel to V. Roma, **Via Maqueda** meets **Via Vittorio Emanuele** at the **Quattro Canti;** and this intersection forms the *centro storico.* Continue up V. Maqueda to **Piazza Verdi** and **Teatro Massimo.** Turn right at P. Verdi on **Via Cavour** and go past V. Roma to reach the port. At P. Verdi, V. Maqueda becomes **Via Ruggero**

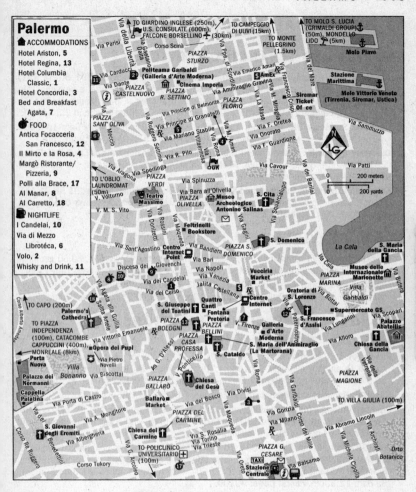

Palermo

🏠 ACCOMMODATIONS
Hotel Ariston, **5**
Hotel Regina, **13**
Hotel Columbia
   Classic, **1**
Hotel Concordia, **3**
Bed and Breakfast
   Agata, **7**

🍎 FOOD
Antica Focacceria
   San Francesco, **12**
Il Mirto e la Rosa, **4**
Margò Ristorante/
   Pizzeria, **9**
Polli alla Brace, **17**
Al Manar, **8**
Al Carretto, **18**

🍷 NIGHTLIFE
I Candelai, **10**
Via di Mezzo
   Libroteca, **6**
Volo, **2**
Whisky and Drink, **11**

SICILY

Settimo, which leads to **Piazza Castelnuovo** and the Politeama. From there V. Ruggero Settimo becomes **Via della Libertà** and leads to the **Giardino Inglese.**

🚌 LOCAL TRANSPORTATION

Public Transportation: AMAT city buses. Main terminal in front of Stazione Centrale, under a green awning. Tickets €1.10 per 90 min., €3.50 per day. Buy tickets from *tabaccherie*, or ticket booths. Pick up a **free transit map** from the tourist office or AMAT info booth. Most bus stops are labeled and have route maps posted. Palermo also has the Metropolitana **subway** system, but it's usually faster to take a bus or walk.

Taxis: Station office ☎091 61 62 001. **Autoradio** ☎091 51 27 27. **RadioTaxi** ☎091 22 54 55, in front of Stazione Centrale next to the bus stop.

⚡ PRACTICAL INFORMATION

TOURIST AND FINANCIAL SERVICES

Tourist Office: P. Castelnuovo 34, at the west end of the *piazza* (☎091 60 58 351; www.palermotourism.com). Maps, informative brochures, and *Agenda,* a seasonal info packet. Open M-F 8:30am-2pm and 2:30-6pm. **Branches** at train station (☎091 61 65 914) and airport (☎091 59 16 98). Both open M-F 8:30am-2pm and 2:30-6pm).

Consular Services: UK, V. Cavour 117 (☎091 32 64 12). Open daily 9am-1pm and 4-7pm. **US,** V. Giovan Battista Vaccarini 1 (☎09130 58 57). Open M-F 9am-1pm.

Currency Exchange: At the central post office. **Banca Nazionale del Lavoro,** V. Roma 201. Open M-F 8:20am-1:20pm. **ATMs** on V. Roma and V. Maqueda; the Bancomat 3-plus ATMs are newer and more reliable.

American Express: G. Ruggieri and Figli Travel, V. Emerico Amari 38 (☎091 58 71 44). From P. Castelnuovo, follow V. E. Amari toward the water. Cashes **Travelers Cheques** for cardholders only. Open M-F 9am-1pm and 4-7pm, Sa 9am-1pm.

LOCAL SERVICES

Luggage Storage: In the train station, track #8. €3.90 per bag for 1st 5hr., €0.60 per each additional hr. up to 12hr., €0.20 per each additional hr. thereafter. Open daily 7am-11pm.

Laundromat: L'Oblio, V. Volturno 62 (☎091 333 80 32 82). 1 block west of Teatro Massimo. Wash and dry €8. Detergent included. Open M-F 9am-7pm, Sa 9am-3pm.

EMERGENCY AND COMMUNICATIONS

Police: V. Dogali 29 (☎091 69 54 111).

Pharmacy: Lo Cascio, V. Roma 1 (☎091 61 62 117). Look for green cross near the train station. Open daily midnight-1pm and 4:30pm-midnight. **Di Naro,** V. Roma 207 (☎091 58 58 69), on the right after V. V. Emanuele. Open M-F 8:30am-1pm and 4:30-8pm.

Hospital: Policlinico Universitario, V. del Vespro 147 (☎091 65 51 111).

Internet: Among a multitude of Internet points scattered around the city, the best is **Centro Internet Point,** V. Maqueda 304 (☎091 61 13 576), with 7 fast computers. €0.50 per 15min., €2 per hr.; 15min. minimum.

Post Office: V. Roma 322 (☎091 75 39 392). Massive white-columned building 5 blocks up V. Roma, past V. V. Emanuele. Open M-F 8am-1:30pm, Sa 8am-12:30pm. Branch at Stazione Centrale (☎09180 31 60), next to track 1. Open M-F 8am-6:30pm, Sa 8am-12:30pm. **Postal Code:** 90100.

🏠 ACCOMMODATIONS

When it comes to finding a place to stay, Palermo is pricey. For the sake of comfort and, more importantly, safety, plan on spending a little more in Palermo.

🏨 **Hotel Regina,** V. V. Emanuele 316 (☎091 61 14 216; www.hotelreginapalermo.it), at the intersection of V. Maqueda and V. V. Emanuele, across from Hotel Centrale. 18 no-frills rooms at the best price in town. All have fan; some have balconies. Beach passes available. Curfew midnight. Credit card required for reservation. Singles €28; doubles €54, with bath €64. AmEx/MC/V. ❷

🏨 **Hotel Ariston,** V. Mariano Stabile 139, 6th fl. (☎091 33 24 34; www.aristonpalermo.it). Walk on V. Roma 4 blocks past V. Cavour, or take bus #122 from the station, and get off before V. E. Amari. Between Teatro Massimo and the Politeama. Bright rooms with modern art. All have bath, A/C, TV, safe, and free Wi-Fi. Book in advance. 1st night paid with reservation. Singles €40-49; doubles €50-69; triples €70-85. AmEx/MC/V. ●

Bed and Breakfast Agata, V. Roma 188 (091 61 16 581 or 347 91 19 815; www.bbagata.it). Hidden B&B offers 20 rooms with high ceilings and original paintings, as well as A/C, TV, phone, and dresser. Breakfast included. Singles €35; doubles €45-50; triples €75-90; quint €100. Student discount 20% for stays longer than 2 nights. MC/V. ●

Hotel Columbia Classic, V. del Celso 31 (☎/fax 091 61 13 777; www.hotelcolumbiapalermo.com). Although it doesn't look like much from the outside, the inside is a different story—white tiles, sparkling chandeliers, marble stairs, and glass countertops make for a fancy abode. Large rooms come with A/C, private bath, TV, free Wi-Fi, phone, minifridge, and safe. Breakfast area, minibar, and panoramic terrace overlooking Palermo's historical center. Singles €35-45; doubles €65-85. MC/V. ●

Hotel Concordia, V. Roma 72, 4th fl. (☎091 62 30 635; www.concordiahotel.info). Midway between the Quattrocanti and the train station on a main shopping thoroughfare, Hotel Concordia offers 13 individually decorated rooms with private bath, A/C, satellite TV, fridge, phone, and desk. Breakfast included. Singles €40-50; doubles €70-90; triples €90-100; quad suite €100-110. AmEx/MC/V. ●

SICILIAN STREET SMARTS. Be careful in Palermo. The city can feel deserted at any time of the day, and some of the streets, particularly in the helter-skelter old city, south of Teatro Massimo, can be hard to navigate. When possible, stay on main streets: Via Roma, Via Maqueda, Via Ruggero Settimo, Via della Libertà, and Via Vittorio Emanuele. These straight thoroughfares will keep you on track, and the steady stream of traffic is reassuring.

◘ FOOD

The best restaurants in town are between Teatro Massimo and the Politeama. Palermo's three bustling food markets provide fresher and more interesting selections than most supermarkets. **Ballarò** dots V. Maqueda and V. V. Emanuele, while **Capo** covers the streets behind Teatro Massimo. **Vucciria,** in the area between V. V. Emanuele and P. San Domenico, completes the trio. All are open Monday through Saturday during daylight hours. Try the *Palermitano* specialty *cassata,* a sweet ricotta pastry. If you don't feel like haggling, head to **Supermercato GS,** Salita Partanna 1. From P. Marina, with Villa Garibaldi on your left, walk straight toward Chiesa di. S. Maria dei Miracoli and turn right when you get there. (Open M-Sa 8:30am-8:30pm. MC/V.)

▨ **Margò Ristorante/Pizzeria,** P. Sant'Onofrio 3 (☎091 61 18 230). Follow Discesa dei Giovenchi, away from the intersection of V. Maqueda and V. Bari. Taste the best pizza in town (€4-8) or the specialty *ravioli di cernia, spada, e crema di asparagi* (with grouper, swordfish, and cream of asparagus; €8.50). Primi €5.50-9. Secondi €7.50-15. Cover €2. Open Tu-Su 8pm-midnight. AmEx/MC/V. ●

Al Carretto, Salita Artele 5 (☎091 58 57 85), behind Palermo's Cathedral. Family-style Sicilian fare reminiscent of the Middle Ages. Diners enjoy plates like spaghetti *Vesuvio* (with swordfish, shrimp, and tomatoes; €9) and specialty *risotto ai frutti di mare* (€10) amidst depictions of battling knights and dragons, or under white umbrellas next to the church. 28 styles of pizza €5-7. Antipasti €2-6. Primi €8-10. Secondi €10-15. Salads €4-6. Cover €2. Open daily 10am-3pm and 7pm-midnight. AmEx/MC/V. ●

Polli alla Brace, C. Tukory 54 (☎091 65 17 023). Follow C. Tukory for 5 minutes from the train station and look to the left. Polli is the best bet in the area for a filling meal at a cheap price. For €5 they offer half of a rotisserie chicken and a heaping selection of Italian sides—more than enough for 2 people. Open daily 5:30-10:30pm. Cash only. ❶

Antica Focacceria San Francesco, V. Alessandro Paternostro 58 (☎09132 02 64). From V. Roma, take V. V. Emanuele toward the port and turn right. This expansive *focacceria* has served delighted patrons in a secluded *piazza* since 1834. Behind the counter sits an infamous vat of *milza* (spleen). While the brave can try it in a *panino* or with *maritata* cheese (€2), the rest can choose from 2 separate menus: 1 features standard Italian fare, the other international cuisine. Complete vegetarian dinner (*panelle, taboulè, involtini di melanzane, cannolo*, drink; €12). 19 salads from €4. Primi €6-12. Secondi €6-18. Cover €1-4. Open daily 12-3:30pm and 6pm-midnight. AmEx/MC/V. ❷

Al Manar, V. S. Isidoro 23 (☎091 32 76 03). Tunisia and Italy unite here, where seafood takes center stage. Try the *couscus con pesce, carne, e verdura* (€8), or go for the swordfish *spiedino manar* (€10). Pizza options include the vegetarian (€5) and the Chef's Specialty (€7), with calamari. Antipasti €3-6. Primi €7-9. Secondi €7-14. Contorni €3-5. Open Tu-Su 11:30am-3pm and 7-11pm. M 11:30am-3pm. AmEx/MC/V. ❷

Il Mirto e la Rosa, V. Principe di Granatelli 30 (☎091 32 43 53; info@ilmirtoelarosa.com). Helpful owner serves traditional fare, including house specialty, *polpette di melanzane* (fried eggplant balls; €5). Primi €7-10. Secondi €6-15. *Menù* €13-21. Open M-Sa 12:30-3pm and 7:30-11pm. AmEx/MC/V. ❷

SIGHTS

Ancient glory, centuries of neglect, and heavy bombing during WWII have made Palermo a city of deteriorated splendor, where ancient and modern ruins stand side-by-side. For much of the 20th century, corrupt politicians and Mafia activity diverted funds and attention from dilapidated landmarks, but recent political changes have made promising strides toward cleaning and rebuilding.

> **PALERMO FOR POCKET CHANGE.** Sightseeing in Palermo can leave you with a bill that makes the Byzantine mosaics look cheap. If you're planning to visit several sights, consider an all-in-one pass from the ticket office of any major museum. Good for 2 days, the passes open the doors to multiple sights at reduced prices. For details on rates and specific deals, go to the tourist office and ask for the free guide, *Palermo e Provincia.*

TEATRO MASSIMO. Constructed between 1875 and 1897, the Neoclassical Teatro Massimo is the second-largest indoor stage in Europe, so big that real horses and elephants were used in a production of *Aida*. After 30 years of renovation, the theater reopened for its 100th birthday in 1997. Rumor has it that the restoration was prolonged by Mafia feuding, not by artistic debates. (Incidentally, it was here that Francis Ford Coppola shot the climactic scene in *The Godfather: Part III*.) Guided tours allow visitors to repose in the VIP guest box and view the beautiful Murano flower light fixtures. Operas, plays, and ballets are performed here all year (student discounts available), while the **Festival della Verdura** brings famous performers in July. For this month only, shows move from the Massimo to nearby Villa Castelnuovo. (*On P. Verdi. From Quattro Canti walk up V. Maqueda. ☎ General info 800 65 58 58, tour info 091 60 90 831, box office 091 60 53 580; www.teatromassimo.it. Open Tu-Su 10am-3pm. No entry during rehearsals. 25 min. tours every 30min. in English, French, and German. €5, under 18 or over 65 €3, under 6 free.*)

⌘MONREALE. Palermo's greatest golden treasure isn't in Palermo, but in little Monreale, 8km from the city. The extraordinary Cattedrale di Monreale is an example of Sicilian Norman architecture, a mixture of Arabic and local styles on the northern template. The interior is a masterpiece of Byzantine design; the mystical flavor of the locale is emphasized by the minimal light from the cathedral's windows. Its walls glisten with 6340 sq. m of gold mosaics, the largest display of Byzantine religious art outside the Hagia Sofia. The series of panels over the main altar depicts the massive Christ Pantocrator. Every few minutes someone pays €1 to activate electric lighting in a portion of the church, and the sudden illumination is startling. The Old Testament narrative begins with Genesis at the upper left of the central aisle and continues clockwise with images of Adam and Eve. The quiet **cloister** offers a contrast to the cathedral's solemn shadows. The interior columns are ringed with 228 paired Sicilian columns, alternating with ones decorated by Arabic tiles. Each capital is constructed in Greco-Roman, Islamic, Norman, Romanesque, and Gothic styles. A balcony along the cathedral's apse looks over the cloisters to all of Palermo. Two doors down from the cloister is the entrance to tranquil **gardens.** *(Bus #389 leaves from Palermo's P. Indipendenza for Monreale's P. Vittorio Emanuele. 30min., 3 per hr., €1.10. To get to P. Indipendenza, take bus #109 or 318 from Palermo's Stazione Centrale. Tourist info (☎09164 04 413) to the left of the church. Cathedral open daily 8am-1pm and 2:30-6:30pm. Reduced hours Nov.-Apr. Modest dress required. Free. Balcony open M-Sa 9-12:30pm and 2:30-5:15pm, Su 2:30-5:15pm. €1.50. Tesoro open M-Sa 9am-12:45pm and 2:30-6:15pm, Su 2:30-6:15pm. €1.50. Cloister open daily 9am-6:30pm. €6. Under 10 and over 65 free.)*

SAVE MONEY. The courtyard adjoining the Cattedrale di Monreale charges a steep €6 entry fee. Unless you're an architecture aficionado or especially interested in Doric, Corinthian, and Ionic columns, consider viewing the garden from the terrace of the cathedral (€1.50).

PALERMO'S CATHEDRAL. As a part of their ongoing rivalry, the leaders of Palermo and Monreale competed to construct the most beautiful church. Although many consider Monreale's mosaics to be superior, Palermo's cathedral is still awe-inspiring. Renovated from the 13th to 18th centuries, this structure's exterior shows various styles butting heads. Arabic columns, Norman turrets, and an 18th-century dome crowd the facade and walls. Note the Qur'an inscription on the first left column before the entrance; in 1185 the *palermitano* archbishop chose to plunk his cathedral down on top of a mosque, and this column was part of its stonework. The interior is dominated by saint-lined arches and carved rock walls. The neighboring **archbishop's palace** now serves as the Diocesan Museum of Palermo, and can be visited on the same ticket. *(On V. V. Emanuele. ☎09133 43 73. Cathedral open M-Sa 7am-7pm, Su 8am-1pm and 4-7pm. Treasury and crypt open M-Sa 9:30am-1:30pm and 2:30-5:30pm. Archbishop's museum open Tu-F 9:30am-1:30pm, Sa 10am-6pm, Su 9:30am-1:30pm. Admission €5, €2.50 treasury and crypt only.)*

CAPPELLA PALATINA. This chapel, in the monstrous **Palazzo dei Normanni,** houses a smaller version of the Monreale mosaics. One corner to the far left of the altar was designed by local artisans; Norman kings imported artists from Constantinople to cover the remaining interior in gold and azure. Locally crafted Arabic mosaics complete the effect. Those who prefer this Christ Pantocrator over that of Monreale claim it is softer and more compassionate. *(Take V. V. Emanuele past the cathedral on the right and through the Porta Nuova; take a left just before P. Indipendenza. ☎091 70 56 001. Chapel open M-Sa 8:30am-12pm and 2-5pm, Su 8:30am-12:30pm. Closed*

Easter M. Tu-Th entire palace €6, chapel €4; Under 18 or over 65 €3; M and F-Su special chapel-only rate not available. Guided tours of upstairs Sala di Ruggero every 20min. in Italian.)

CATACOMBE DEI CAPPUCCINI. Over the course of 350 years, the Cappuchin friars preserved remains of over 8000 men, women, and children. Hanging from niches by wires and nails, and lying in glass-sided caskets, many are dressed in their finest and are in various stages of decay. Several notables are buried here—including several bishops and the painter Velázquez—but the most arresting remains are those of Rosalia, a three-year-old girl who lies in her own tiny glass box. (P. Cappuccini 1. Take bus #109 or #318 from Stazione Centrale to P. Indipendenza. From there, hop on #327. Or, from V. V. Emanuele, pass P. Indipendenza, and turn right on V. Cappuccini, then right again on V. Ippolito Pindemonte. ☎091 21 21 17. From P. Indipendenza, about a 20min. walk. Open daily 9am-noon and 1-5pm. €2.)

THE LEG BONE'S CONNECTED TO THE KNEE BONE. Travelers to Sicily will undoubtedly come across the Trinacria. The island's ancient symbol, an unusual combination of mythological references, consists of 3 legs bent at the knee, that radiate from Medusa's snakey mane. Famous for turning men into stone with her fearsome gaze, Medusa was in charge of protecting the ends of the earth, which in the days of ancient Greece meant Sicily. The sheaves of wheat represent the cultivation of Sicily's fertile soil, and the 3 legs stand for the 3 corners of the triangular island: Capo Pallor at Messina, Capo Passer at Syracuse, and Capo Lille west of Marsala. The leg bent at the knee was a Spartan symbol of power. The Trinacria is most often represented in burnished gold, the color of the sun.

MUSEO ARCHEOLOGICO ANTONINO SALINAS. Hidden in a quiet *palazzo* in the town center, this museum features an impressive collection of Sicilian archaeological treasures. Most impressive are several fine Greek and Roman works, including a large section of the **Punic Temple of Himera,** and the 3rd-century BC Greek **Ram of Syracuse.** Also not to be missed is the recently restored **Mosaico delle Quattro Stagioni,** which depicts the four seasons in a haunting mosaic. Other temple remnants include fantastic renditions of Perseus beheading Medusa and Zeus courting Hera. (P. Olivella 24. From Teatro Massimo, cross V. Maqueda and head down V. Bara all'Olivella. ☎091 61 16 805. Open M, W, Sa 8:30am-1:45pm, Tu and F 8:30am-1:45pm and 3-6:45pm. €4.50, students 18-25 €2, EU residents under 18 or over 65 free.)

QUATTRO CANTI AND LA FONTANA PRETORIA. The intersection of V. Maqueda and V. V. Emanuele forms the center of the old city at the Quattro Canti (Four Screens). Dividing the old city into four districts, each sculpted corner of this 17th-century *piazza* has three levels. The lowest level has statues of the four seasons; on the middle level are the Spanish viceroys who commanded Sicily and Southern Italy, and on the top level are the city's patron saints. P. Pretoria, down V. Maqueda, houses the Fontana della Vergogna (Fountain of Shame; also called Fontana Pretoria) adjacent to Teatro Bellini. The fountain got its name from irate churchgoers who didn't like staring at monsters and nude figures as they left Chiesa di San Giuseppe dei Teatini across the street. An even more shameful story explains its shameless size. In the early 16th century, a rich Florentine commissioned the fountain for his villa and sent his son to the marble quarries to ensure its safe delivery. In need of cash, the son sold the fountain to the senate of Palermo and shipped it to Sicily, bringing Albert Mobilio's words to mind: "Sicily is a world where deception is only frowned upon to the degree it lacks artfulness." (630m down V. Maqueda from the train station.)

CHIESA DEL GESÙ (CASA PROFESSA). Nicknamed "Il Gesù," this green-domed church has a dazzling interior and Surrealist ceiling paintings of the Last Judgment, depicting figures with swords beating the unworthy into Hell and a black-clad man waving a pastel flag with "Jesus" written across it. WWII bombing damaged its courtyard and the Quartiere dell'Albergheria, leaving behind bomb-blackened facades. *(In P. Casa Professa, on V. Ponticello, across V. Maqueda. Open daily Sept.-July 7-11:30am and 5-6:30pm, Aug. 7-11:30am. No visits during mass. Free.)*

GALLERIA D'ARTE MODERNA. Recently moved from the foyer of the Politeama to the newly refurbished Piazza Sant'Anna in the historical center, this gallery showcases much newer art than that found in Palermo's churches and museums. The ground floor is dedicated to the great Exhibitions, with works by Francesco Lojacono portraying a new image of Sicily. Move up a floor to see realism in literary themes, and finish with 20th-century Sicilian works of symbolism and modernism. *(V. Sant'Anna 21. ☎091 84 31 605. Open Tu-Su 9:30am-6:30pm, last ticket sold one hour before closing. €7, students 19-25 €5, over 60 and under 18 free.)*

PUPPETS. There are no small parts, only small wooden actors. For 300 years, Sicilian-made puppets have taken the stage at the **Museo Internazionale delle Marionette**, which showcases over 3000 examples of Sicilian stage culture. Galleries also display puppets from across the globe; it's a small world, after all. *(P. Niscemi 5. Follow signs from P. Marina. ☎091 32 80 60; fax 091 32 82 76. Open M-F 9am-1pm and 4-7pm. Closed 1 week in Aug. 15. €5, under 18 and over 65 €3. Demonstrations on request.)* Catch a puppet show at Vincenzo Argento's **Opera dei Pupi.** Tall, armored puppets reenact the chivalric *Orlando e Ronaldo per la Bella Angelica* and other works. *(V. Pietro Novelli 1. ☎091 61 13 680. Shows Sa-Su 5:30pm. €10, children €3.)*

GARDENS. The city's fresh gardens and parks provide relief from Palermo's smog-filled urban jungle. The large **Giardino Inglese,** off V. della Libertà, is not a stiffly organized British garden as its name might suggest, but a paradise harboring picnickers. In summer, the park hosts concerts and carnival rides for children. Down V. V. Emanuele toward the port, the **Giardino Garibaldi** in P. Marina features enormous banyan trees. The large Parisian-style **Villa Giulia,** at the end of V. A. Lincoln, has flower beds and fountains. *(Open daily 8am-8pm.)*

MONTE PELLEGRINO. Monte Pellegrino, an isolated mass of limestone rising from the sea, is Palermo's principal natural landmark, separating the city from the beach at Mondello. Near its peak, the **Santuario di Santa Rosalia** marks the site where young Rosalia sought refuge from her marriage and wandered into ascetic seclusion. After dying there, she appeared as an apparition to a woodsman and told him to carry her bones in a procession believed to have ended the plague that had been destroying Palermo. The bones of Rosalia, who is now the patron saint of the city, can be found in Palermo's cathedral or on parade display every year on July 15. *(Take bus #812 from P. Castelnuovo. Buses every 1hr. 7am-8pm. Last bus back 7:30pm. ☎091 54 03 26. Open daily 7am-7:30pm.)*

ACQUAPARK MONREALE. Slip and slide at Sicily's biggest water park, enjoying water chutes, fountains, pools, and restaurants. Fun for the whole family, but it's not as cheap as the beach. *(Contrada Fiumelato, V. Pezzingoli 172. ☎091 64 60 246; www.acquaparkmonreale.it. Open daily 9:30am-6pm. €10-18, children 7-13 €7-12; under 7 €2-5.)*

▓ NIGHTLIFE

Palermo's nightlife is as varied as the city's history. For info on cultural events, pick up *Un Mese a Palermo*, available at any APT office and in News-News.

Piazza Olivella, Via dei Candelai, and Via Spinuzza, are popular nightlife hubs where mobs of young *palermitani* flood the outdoor bars and dance floors every night.

I Candelai, V. dei Candelai 65 (☎333 70 02 942; www.candelai.it). Picks up around midnight. Sip Carlsberg *alla spina* and listen to local cover bands do their best Chuck Berry impression. DJs spin Top 40 hits Th-Sa nights. Open daily noon-3:30pm and 7pm-3am. Closed M in winter. Cash only.

Whisky and Drink, V. di Carducci 38 (☎320 14 11 405), 2 blocks west from P. Castelnuovo. Loud rock music and cheap drinks draw a huge crowd nightly to this popular local bar. Beer €1.50-3. Mixed drinks €3.50-4.50. Open M and W-Su 7pm-3am. Cash only.

Via di Mezzo Librotéca, V. Sant'Oliva 20/22 (☎091 60 90 090; viadmezzo@virgilio. it), from P. Sant'Oliva, walk toward Villa Fillipina, and Librotéca will be around the corner. The name stands for book+tea+coffee, and describes the vibe at this caffeteria-pub. Coffee and tea €1-2.50. Beer €3.50-4. Mixed drinks €3.50-5. Wine €3-4. Open daily 12-3pm and 7pm-1:30am. AmEx/MC/V.

Volo, V. della Libertà 12 (☎091 61 21 284). 2 blocks up from P. Castelnuovo, after V. Giosuè Carducci on the left. Dress to impress at Volo, where the Euro-sleek interior and elegant garden exterior are equally perfect settings for young singles to flit about. Mixed drinks €5. Happy hour with free hors d'oeuvres 6-9pm. Open daily June-Oct. 12:30-3pm and 6:30pm-1:30am. Closed M Nov.-May. AmEx/MC/V.

◪ BEACHES

Mondello Lido is a beach for tourists by day and a playground of clubs and bars by night. All registered hotels provide tickets that must be shown at the entrance. Otherwise, beachgoers pay €8 to set up camp in the area near the Charleston—or sit for free directly on the shoreline. Take bus #101 or 102 from the station to reach the Politeama and V. della Libertà, then bus #806 in the same direction to reach Mondello; the beach is beyond a tree-filled area known as *la Favorita*. Watch for the frequent vendors who wander the sand with all types of goodies. *Ciambelle* (donuts caked in sugar; €1) are an essential beach treat. Mondello starts summer a little early each May with the **World Festival** on the Beach, a full week jam-packed with sports, music, and shows right on the water. Call the tourist office for info.

◪ DAYTRIPS FROM PALERMO

USTICA

Accessible by ferry or hydrofoil from Palermo. L'Agenzia Miletello, V. Capitano Vincenzo di Bartolo 15, next to Chiesa S. Fernando Re, is open daily 6:10-6:45am, 9am-1pm and 3:30-6pm (☎091 84 49 002; fax 091 84 49 457). Hydrofoils (1¼hr.; daily 6:45am, 1pm, and 5:15pm; €21.55) and ferries (2¾hr., M-Sa 5pm, €16.35) to Palermo. Orange public minibuses run the perimeter of the island, from P.Vito Longo (every 30min., €1). Many rental shops off P.Umberto I, the centro of Ustica, rent scooters (with helmet and gas) for around €20 per day. Try Servizi Generali di Isidoro, V. Spezeria 3 (☎338 28 45 718; www.servizigeneraliustica.it). Open daily 9am-1pm and 4-8pm. To get to town from the hydrofoil port, turn right, and head up the road until you reach the staircase with an arrow marked "Centro" and follow that to P. Umberto I; with your back to the stairs, P.Capitano Vito Longo will be up and to the right. To reach the town from Cala Cimitero, the ferry port, take the road uphill and turn left at the fork.

The self-proclaimed "diving capital of the world," Ustica (OOS-tee-ca; pop. 1300) has become a bustling tourist port with abundant outdoor and underwater activities. Hiking trails wind around the island's 9km scenic coastline and guided tours explore a prehistoric village and necropolis. The island' spectacular attractions are arguably the ancient artifacts buried just belo water's surface, catalogued and labeled for divers to explore.

Boat tours are a great way to navigate grottoes along the coastline, including the waters of **Grotta delle Barche** and **Grotta Azzurra,** a nautical graveyard filled with ancient vessels. Small boat owners advertise cheap rides that circle the island; find them at P. Umberto I or at the port. Set a price before embarking; women traveling alone should join a larger group. The island's most popular activity, **scuba diving** off rocky coasts, is quite affordable. **Alta Marea,** on V. Cristoforo Colombo, runs dives from May to October. (☎347 17 57 255; www.altamareaustica.it. Boats leave the port daily 9:15am and 3:15pm. Single immersion €35, with full equipment €55; 6 dives €200; 10 dives €300. Diving class €330.) Once submerged, see the **underwater archaeological remains** of Roman anchors and *amphorae* (vases), part of Ustica's underwater archaeology experiment.

If you miss the last hydrofoil back to Palermo, your best bet for a night's accommodation is **Ustica Hotel ❸,** V. Cristoforo Colombo 1. Rooms all come with A/C and private bath; some come with a panoramic view. Breakfast included at the in-house bar. (☎091 84 49 796; www.usticahotelresidence.it. Doubles without view €55-95; with view €65-110. Extra bed €15-25. MC/V.) Satisfy your post-dive hunger at **Ristorante Da Umberto ❸,** P. della Vittoria 7, which serves local dishes like *polpette di finocchio* in *agrodolce* (€9) and "*spaghetti alla Giulietta*" (€8) in an outdoor dining area. (☎ 091 84 49 542; www.isoladiustica.com. Antipasti €7-10. Primi €6-8. Secondi €12-18. Contorni €4-6. Dessert €3. Cover €1.50. Open daily noon-3pm and 8pm-midnight. AmEx/MC/V.)

> **TIP**
>
> **RENAISSANCE MAN.** To experience the best Ustica has to offer, you need to know only one man: Gigi Tranchina. A lifelong resident of Ustica, Gigi is a one-man tourist office who knows everything about the island and will gladly coordinate hikes, scooter rentals, and diving trips. Head to **Trattoria da Umberto** to find Gigi himself, or check him out online at his websites: www.usticatour.it and www.isoladiustica.it.

CEFALÙ ☎0921

The Sicilian proverb "good wine comes in small bottles" captures the timeless nature of Cefalù (che-fa-LOO; pop. 14,000), whose sleepy, seaside qualities were featured in the Academy Award-winning film *Cinema Paradiso*. Dominated by *La Rocca*, the imposing fortification rising 278m above the old town, Cefalù is a labyrinth of cobblestone streets. The city's aging terra-cotta and stone buildings cling to the water's edge, just as tourist crowds congregate along the expansive *lungomare* (seafront). Be aware, however, that Cefalù's charms do not come cheaply: the city's reputation as a beach resort, as well as its proximity to Palermo, allow *pensioni* to charge whatever they please.

 TRANSPORTATION

Cefalù is best accessed by train; call the tourist office for a complete schedule. The **train station,** located in P. Stazione, offers service to: Messina (3hr., 12 per day 5:15am-9:40pm, €8.10), Milazzo (2 hr., 18 per day, €6.55), and Palermo (1hr., 33per day 5:15am-10pm, €4.70). Sommatinese, V. Cavour 2 (☎0921 42 43 01), runs **buses** throughout the city (from €1.70). Schedules are posted at the train station bar's window and are also available in the tourist office. **Taxis** are available in P. Stazione or by calling ☎0921 42 25 54.

⚔ 🛈 ORIENTATION AND PRACTICAL INFORMATION

From the **train station,** head right on **Via Aldo Moro,** which curves up to the city's biggest intersection. To the left, **Via Roma** cuts through the center of the new city. Straight and to the left, **Via Matteotti** leads into the old city, changing at the central **Piazza Garibaldi** into the boutique-lined **Corso Ruggero. Via Cavour,** across the intersection from V. A. Moro, leads directly to the *lungomare.*

Tourist Office: C. Ruggero 77 (☎0921 42 10 50; fax 42 23 86), in the old city. Brochures, maps, hotel listings, and transportation schedules. Open M-Sa 8am-8pm.

Currency Exchange: Credito Siciliano (☎0921 42 39 22), near train station, at the corner of V. Giglio and V. Roma. Open M-F 8:30am-1:30pm and 2:30-4pm. **ATM** at the **Banca di Sicilia** (☎0921 42 11 03 or 0921 42 28 90), in P. Garibaldi.

Police: ☎0921 92 60 11. Guardia Medica: Vle. Mazzini 8 (☎0921 42 36 23).

Pharmacies: Dr. V. Battaglia, V. Roma 13 (☎0921 42 17 89), in the new city. Open M-F 9am-1pm and 4-8pm. AmEx/MC/V. **Dr. Vacanti,** V. Vazzana 6 (☎0921 42 25 66), across the street from the post office. Open M-F 9am-1pm and 4-8pm. AmEx/MC/V.

Hospital: (☎0921 92 01 11), on Contrada Pietra Pollastra, outside city limits.

Internet: Capriccio Siciliano, V. Umberto I 1 (☎0921 42 05 50; capriccios@libero.it). €3 for 30min. Open daily 9am-1pm and 3-9pm. **Kefaonline,** P. San Francesco 1 (☎92 30 91). €5 per hr. Open M-F 9am-1pm and 3:30-7:30pm, Sa 9am-1pm.

Post Office: V. Vazzana 2 (☎0921 92 55 40). On the right off the *lungomare,* 2 blocks off V. Roma. Open M-F 8am-6:30pm, Sa 8am-12:30pm. **Postal Code:** 90015.

🏠 🏕 ACCOMMODATIONS AND CAMPING

If you're planning on staying in one place for a week or more, consider renting an apartment from a local. Sealing the deal might take some haggling (and will often requires a basic knowledge of Italian), but it usually pays off in the long run—especially when hotel rates peak during July and August. Look for *"affittasi"* signs in the desired area of residence.

La Fenice Affittacamere, V. Bagno Cicerone 21, 2nd fl. (☎347 23 76 011), near the water. Recently opened. Bright rooms overlooking the ocean are Cefalù's best-kept secret. All come with private bath, A/C, and view. Communal kitchen and living room with satellite TV. English spoken. Breakfast included. Towel and linens provided. €25-35 per person. Cash only. ❺

Locanda Cangelosi, V. Umberto I 26 (☎092142 15 91), off P. Garibaldi. The private apartments are large, clean, and simply adorned. All come with fan and towel; some come with a balcony. Laundry €5 per load. Reservations recommended. Singles €25-30; doubles €35-40; triples €50-60. Cash only. ❸

Camping Costa Ponente (☎0921 42 00 85; fax 0921 42 44 92), west of Cefalù, on Contrada Ogliastrillo. A 45min. walk or short ride on the Cefalù-Lascari bus (round-trip €2.30) from P. Colombo. Swimming pool and hot showers included. July-Aug. €6.20 per person; €6 per tent; €5 per car. Sept.-June €5.50/5/4. ❶

🍴 FOOD

Seafood is undoubtedly Cefalù's specialty, but delicious, formerly land-dwelling cuisine is also easily found. Just off the *lungomare,* next to the post office on V. Vazzana, an **IperSidis** supermarket sells basics, including bathing suits. (☎0921 42 45 00. Open M-Sa 8:30am-8:30pm, Su 9am-1pm.)

🍨 **Gelateria di Noto,** V. Bagno Cicerone 3 (☎0921 42 26 54; www.gelateriadinoto.it), where the *lungomare* meets the old town. More than 40 flavors of some of Sicily's best gelato. Flavors include black cherry, mint cream, wildberry, *cassata siciliana,* and hazelnut, plus every traditional flavor found in lesser *gelaterie.* Some English spoken. Cones from €1.80. Open daily Apr.-Oct. 7am-1am. Cash only. ❶

Ristorante Trappitu, V. di Bordonaro 96 (☎0921 92 19 72). Offers filling food, including Sicilian sea bass (€14). Seaside seating. Enormous olive press in the middle of the restaurant. Some English spoken. Primi €6-17. Secondi €7-17. Open daily noon-3pm and 7pm-midnight. Cover €1.50. AmEx/MC/V. ❸

CAFFÈ, SICILIAN STYLE. In an attempt to combat the sweltering summer heat, Sicilians have devised a cool alternative to traditional Italian coffee. Called *"caffè freddo"* and available in most cafes, this popular concoction is a mixture of espresso, raw sugar, and ice.

La Brace, V. XXV Novembre 10 (☎0921 42 35 70). Cheap food served in a low-lit setting with jazz. Meat-lovers should go for the *chili con carne* (€8.50), while vegetarians can opt for *rigatoni al rustico* (€6.50). Antipasti €4.50-8.50. Primi €6-9.50. Secondi €6-13. Contorni €2.50-5. Dessert €3-5. Open Tu-Su 1-3:30pm and 7-11pm. MC/V. ❷

Al Vicoletto, P. Duomo (☎0921 42 01 81). Found in an alley next to Il Caffè Duomo, Vicoletto offers respite from the crowds in P. Duomo. Family-style dining, animated staff, and large portions. Sample the *casarecce "Al Vicoletto"* (pasta with tomato, shrimp, and zucchini; €10). 30 styles of pizza €5-10. Antipasti €4-10. Primi €6-10. Secondi €7-15. Service 10%. Open daily 10am-1:30pm and 6pm-11pm. AmEx/MC/V. ❷

SIGHTS

La Rocca stands above Cefalù at the center of the city's history and offers breathtaking views. Take Salità Saraceni to Tempio di Diana, a 20min. uphill hike. From Diana, continue up for another, steeper, 20min. hike to Il Castello. From P. Garibaldi, follow the signs for *Pedonale Rocca* up V. G. Fiore to Vco. Macell between the fountain and Banco di Sicilia. Use caution, as the path is slippery when wet. Medieval fortifications lace the edges, while crumbling cisterns line forgotten avenues. The **Tempio di Diana** first acted as a place of sea worship and later as a defensive outpost. At the top of La Rocca is **Il Castello,** a military fort dating back to the Byzantines. Most remains date from the 12th and 13th centuries AD. (Gates closed 1hr. before sunset.) During the winter months, **Club Alpino Italiano,** Vicolo alle Falde 4 (www.caicefalu.it), coordinates hiking excursions in the area and yoga sessions up on La Rocca.

Tucked away in Cefalù's narrow streets is the city's *duomo.* It was constructed in 1131 after King Ruggero II promised to build a monument to the Savior if he lived through a terrible shipwreck. The dramatic structure combines Arabic, Norman, and Byzantine styles, reflecting the cultures of the craftsmen hired for its construction. Once a potential fortress with towers and firing outposts, it now protects the king's remains and stunning Byzantine mosaics. An enormous Christ Pantocrator mosaic surveys with glistening calm all who enter. The carved pillars of the newly opened cloister depict Biblical stories from Genesis to Revelations. *(Sanctuary open daily in summer 8am-7pm; in winter 8am-5:30pm. Free. Cloister open daily 10am-1pm and 2:30-6pm. €3, €2 per person for groups of 10 or more. Modest dress required.)* Stuffed alligator cases and ancient urns get equal footing in the **Museo Mandralisca,** V. Mandralisca 13. Local 19th-century art connoisseur Baron Mandralisca bequeathed his collection to the city; this included an array of medieval and early Renaissance Sicilian paintings by anonymous artists, including the centerpiece, the *Ritratto di Ignoto,* by 15th-century Sicilian master Antonello da Messina. The image is inescapable in Cefalù—it smirks at tourists from every postcard rack—and the actual painting is surprisingly lively. Upstairs, hundreds of strange shells and old coins shimmer behind glass cases, as well as a half dozen lamps of questionable taste. The lifelike stuffed birds, iguana, and porcupine in the final room will startle any visitor numb from staring at terra-cotta vases and Roman sculptures in the preceding hall. *(Opposite the duomo.* ☎*0921 42 15 47. Open daily 9am-7pm. €5, €3 per person in groups of 10 or more.)* For some maritime adventure, **Hippokampus Pesca Turismo** offers boat excursions off Cefalù's coast. Participants can admire caves, encounter dolphins, and immerse themselves in the job of a fisherman for a half-day. (3 sessions per day €45-50; includes lunch or dinner of fish, fruit, and wine.)

⛱ 🌙 BEACHES AND NIGHTLIFE

Mazzaforno and **Settefrati**, Cefalù's most attractive beaches, lie west of town. Take the Cefalù-Lascari bus (round-trip €3) from the train station or the Cefalù-Mazzaforno bus (round-trip €2.40) from P. Colombo. Settefrati boasts white sand, turquoise shallows, and free showers; it is crowded for good reason. The seven stones jutting out from the waves are said to have been placed in memory of seven brothers who died here while trying to rescue their sister from pirates. All the beaches are free, though renting an umbrella and lounge chair costs around €5. Easily-accessible beaches along Cefalù's lungomare near the city center include **Lido di Apollo, Lido Angeli del Mare,** and **Lido Pura Vida.** They all have soft sand, shallow water, and daytime crowds. To splash without sand, take a trip to **AcquaVerde,** a waterpark in nearby Capo San Nicola, which houses slides, pools, fountains, and a health spa. (☎0921 93 11 33; www.hotel-costaverde.it. Open daily 9am-6:30pm. Full day pass €15; half day €10.)

While nightlife is limited, there are a few good hangouts. Head to the open-air garden at **Be Bop Pub,** V. Nicola Botta 4, and sip on something (€2-5) beneath the oleander trees. From P. Duomo, head down C. Ruggiero, toward P. Garibaldi. V. Botta is two streets down on the right. (☎0921 92 39 72. Karaoke Th and Su. Open daily 7:30pm-3am.) With a great seaside location, **Murphy's Pub,** Lungomare G. Giardina 5, offers draft beers (€2-4) and a big-screen TV. Occasional live music during summer or karaoke depending on the crowd. (☎0921 42 25 88. Mixed drinks €4. *Panini* €3-4. Pizza €3.50-9. Open Tu-Su 7:30pm-3am.)

EASTERN SICILY

MESSINA ☎090

Messina (meh-SEE-na; pop. 240,00) is more than a busy transportation hub. Despite centuries of invasions, plagues, and earthquakes, Messina maintains its immense dignity in points of historical interest and beauty. Those planning to "just pass through" on the way to Sicily should think twice before skipping the sacred *duomo*, the allegorical clock tower, and the Santuario di Montalto.

⮐ TRANSPORTATION

Trains: Stazione Centrale, in P. della Repubblica (☎090 67 97 95 or 147 88 80 88). To: **Milazzo** (30min., 21 per day, €3.10); **Palermo** (3hr., 14 per day, €11); **Rome** (9hr., 7 per day, €45); **Syracuse** (3hr., 14 per day, €9); **Taormina** (40min., 23 per day, €3.30).
Buses: Messina has 4 bus carriers, many of which serve the same routes.

AST, V. I Settembre 156 (☎090 66 22 44, ask for *"informazioni"*). Buy tickets at the orange minibus in P. del Duomo across from the cathedral or onboard. Serves remote areas in southern Italy.

Giuntabus, V. Terranova 8 (☎090 67 37 82 or 67 57 49), 3 blocks up V. I Settembre, left on V. Bruno, right on V. Terranova. To **Milazzo** (45min.; M-Sa 16 per day 6am-8pm, Su 1 per day 7:15am; €3.40, €5.20 round-trip). Purchase tickets on bus.

Interbus, P. della Repubblica 6 (☎090 66 17 54; www.interbus.it), has blue offices next to SAIS. To: **Giardini-Naxos** (1hr., 8 per day, €2.50); **Naples** (1 per week, Su, €22). **Rome** (2 per day, €30); **Taormina** (1hr., 12 per day, €2.50).

SAIS, P. della Repubblica 8 (☎090 77 19 14). Ticket office to the left when exiting the train station. To: **Catania airport** (1-2hr., 17 per day, €7.30); **Catania** (1hr., 23 per day, €6.50); **Florence** (12hr., 1 per week, €50); **Naples** (22hr., 3 per week., €25); **Palermo** (1hr., 6 per day, €13.30).

Speedboats and Hydrofoils: From **BluVia** (☎090 67 86 51 7), the waterfront wing of Stazione Centrale, Trenitalia sends hydrofoils to **Reggio di Calabria** (25min., M-F 13 per day 6:10am-7:40pm, Sa-Su 7 per day 7:30am-7:40pm, €3) and **Villa San Giovanni** (40min., 2 per hr., €1). From the station facing the *piazza,* turn right and walk toward the waterfront, then look for BluVia signs. Ticket office on the docks. MC/V. **Ustica** (☎090 36 40 44; www.usticalines.it), has offices in a blue building on the waterfront side of V. V. Emanuele, 2km north of the train station off C. Garibaldi. Hydrofoils to: **Lipari** (2.5hr., 5 per day 7:10am-6:20pm, €18.50), **Panarea** (2hr., 3 per day 7:10am-3:25pm, €22), and **Salina** (2hr., 6 per day 7:10am-6:20pm, €22). AmEx/MC/V.

Public Transportation: Orange **Azienda Trasporti Milanesi buses** leave either from P. della Repubblica or from the bus station, 2 blocks up V. I Settembre from the station, on the right. **Bus #79** stops at the *duomo,* museum, and aquarium, and only runs from P. della Repubblica. **Trams** run from the station to the museum (10min., every 10min. 5am-10pm). The same ticket (€1, valid for 3hr.), available at any *tabaccheria* or newsstand, is good for both the ATM buses and the tram.

Taxis: Radiotaxi Jolly (☎090 51 513 or 65 01 11), to the right of the *duomo.*

Car rentals: AVIS Autonoleggi, V. Garibaldi 109 (☎090 67 91 50)

ORIENTATION AND PRACTICAL INFORMATION

Messina's transportation center is **Piazza della Repubblica,** in front of the **train station,** home to two tourist offices and several bus lines. The tram leaves from the *piazza,* and ferry and speedboats run from the port right next to the station. **Via Guiseppe la Farina** runs in front of the train station. Beyond the high rises to the left, **Via Tommaso Cannizzaro** leads to the *centro,* meeting palm-lined **Viale San Martino** at **Piazza Cairoli.** At the far right end begins **Via I Settembre,** which intersects **Corso Garibaldi,** which runs along the harbor to both the hydrofoil dock and **Corso Cavour.**

>
>
> **MIDNIGHT MESSINA.** Women should not walk alone in Messina at night, and no one should roam the streets near the train station or the port after 10pm. Stay near the more populated streets around the *duomo* and the university. Be wary of pick-pockets and keep money in a secure place.

Tourist Office: Provincia Regionale, V. Calabria 301 (☎090 67 42 71; aptmeinfoturismo@virgilio.it), immediately to the right when exiting the train station. Well staffed and very helpful, with maps and info on Messina and the Aeolian Islands. Open M-Th 9am-1:30pm and 3-5pm, F 9am-1:30pm.

Currency Exchange: Frattelli Grosso, V. Garibaldi 58 (☎090 77 40 83). Open M-F 8:30am-1pm and 4:30-8pm.

ATMs: Outside the train station and to the right. Also at V. Tommaso Cannizzaro 24, and **Banco di Napoli** on V. V. Emanuele facing the port.

Pharmacy: Farmacia Abate, Vle. San Martino 39 (☎090 63 733, for info on all pharmacies in town 71 75 89). From the train station take V. del Vespro 4 blocks and turn left. All pharmacies open M-F 8:30am-1pm and 4:30-8pm. Posts after-hours rotation.

Hospital: Ospedale Piemonte, Vle. Europa (☎090 22 24 238 or 22 24 347). **Medical Clinic:** V. Garibaldi 242 (☎090 34 54 22). Open M-F 8am-8pm, Sa 10am-Su 8am.

Internet Access: Last Planet Internet and Games, V. Nicola Fabrizi 20, offers 18 computers with fast connections. €2 for 30min. Open M-Th 9am-1:30pm and 3:30pm-midnight, F-Sa 9am-1:30pm and 3:30pm-2:30am, Su 1:30-8:30pm. **Punto Internet,** V. Ghibellina 87, on the small street across V. T. Cannizzaro from Libreria Nunnari e Sfameri. 4 fast computers. €0.05 per min. Open daily 9:30am-1pm and 4-8pm.

Post Office: ☎090 66 86 415. In P. Antonello, off C. Cavour and across from Galleria. Open M-Sa 8:30am-6:30pm. **Postal Code:** 98100.

▌ ACCOMMODATIONS

Although most of Messina's hotels cater to deep-pocketed businessmen, budget accommodations can be found in the neighborhood by the station.

Hotel Mirage, V. Nicola Scotto 3 (☎090 29 38 842). From the train station walk left past the buses and under the overpass and look for the hotel's sign. Simple rooms at an affordable price, perfect for those passing through. Rooms have TV, fan, sink, phone, and shared bath. Singles €21; doubles €37, with private bath €51; triples €41. ❷

Hotel Touring, V. Nicola Scotto 17 (☎090 29 38 851; www.hoteltouring-me.it). Similar to Hotel Mirage, a few doors down. Offers 19 rooms with the added luxuries of AC, heating, and phones. Some of the more expensive rooms come with private bath and TV. Singles €20-40; doubles €40-70; triples €60-90. Prices vary by season. Cash only. ❷

Hotel Cairoli , Vle. San Martino 63 (☎090 67 37 55), off P. Cairoli. Rooms at this older hotel have bath, A/C, TV, and phone. Ask front desk for free breakfast coupon. Singles €45; doubles €80. MC/V. ❸

▌ FOOD

Restaurants and trattorie line V. Risorgimento. To reach this neighborhood, follow V. Tomaso Cannizzaro two blocks past P. Cairoli. Messina is hooked on *pesce spada* (swordfish): baked, fried, or stewed. Another specialty is *caponata*, a dish of fried eggplant, onion, capers, and olives in a red sauce. For dessert, sugary *pignolata* is a decadent treat.

▨ **Osteria Etnea,** Vle. San Martino 38 (☎090 67 260), three blocks east of the intersection between C. Cavour and V. T. Cannizaro. Signature pasta and fish dishes (from €5). Try the *spaghetti etnea* (€5), a house specialty that packs a delicious shrimp-and-calamari one-two punch. Cover €1. Open M-Sa 11am-3:30pm and 8-11:30pm. MC/V. ❶

Happy Island, C. Cavour 122 (☎090 028 7155 0832). Hip local favorite offers over 15 varieties of pizza *a taglio* ("by the slice"; €1-1.50), as well as volcano-shaped *arancini al ragu* (fried rice balls in meat sauce; €1.50), all to a fun soundtrack of Italian rap and rock music. Open M-F 10am-9pm, Sa 10:30am-3pm and 5:30pm-midnight. MC/V. ❶

▌ SIGHTS

Though Messina has lost many of its monuments to both natural and manmade calamities, the town still contains a number of great sights. Churches on the outskirts of the town offer sweeping vistas of the city and port.

PIAZZA DEL DUOMO. Trees provide a shaded, relaxing respite from the city that surrounds this central *piazza*. The great ▨**duomo,** built in Norman times and dedicated to the Virgin Mary in 1197, dominates the square with an enormous marble facade. The long nave stretches past 14 niche sculptures of saints above sweeping tile floors and arrives at a massive altar dedicated to Madonna della Lettera, the city's patron saint. A statue of Archbishop Angelo Paino to the left of the altar commemorates the tireless efforts of the man who twice rebuilt the *duomo*, first after the earthquake of 1908 and again after WWII bombing. **Il Tesoro** (The Treasury) houses the church's most valuable possessions, including gold reliquaries and candlesticks. The *piazza*'s highlight is the ornate **Manta d'Oro** (Golden Mantle), a special cover decorated with precious stones and jewels used to drape the picture of the Madonna and Child in the church's altar. After being locked away for three centuries, it is on display once more and is brought out each year for an annual festival (see **Festivals,** p. 460). Plans for the *campanile* began in the early 16th century, and at 90m, it was intended to be Sicily's highest. After being struck by lightning in 1588, restorations continued until 1933, when the tower acquired its clock. At noon, a mechanized lion lets out a few roars and a creaky recording of the Ave Maria booms. Below the clock tower, ancient myth and local lore meet in stone at the ▨**Fontana di Orione,** designed in 1547 by Angelo Montorsoli, a pupil of Michelangelo. The fountain glorifies Orion, the mythical founder of Messina. *(Duomo open daily 7am-7pm. Treasury open Apr.-Oct. M-Sa 9am-1pm and 3:30-6:30pm; Nov.-Mar. M-Sa 9am-1pm. Duomo free. Treasury €3, under 18 €2. Campanile €3.50/2. Combined ticket for treasury and campanile €5/3.50. Guided tours of treasury in English, French, German, and Spanish.)*

MUSEO REGIONALE. A converted spinning mill houses all that was salvaged from the monastery of St. Gregory and the churches throughout the city after the devastating earthquakes of 1894 and 1908. Galleries around a quiet courtyard display the development of Messina's rich artistic tradition. Among more notable pieces are 15th-century *The Polyptych of the Rosary* by local master Antonello da Messina, Andrea della Robbia's terra-cotta *Virgin and Child*, and Caravaggio's life-sized *Adoration of the Shepherds* and *Resurrection of Lazarus.* Just past the entrance, door panels tell the story of the *Madonna della Lettera. (Take the tram from the station or catch bus #78 or 79 from P. Duomo; look for the museum and walk around to the left to find entrance. ☎ 090 36 12 92. Open June-Sept. M and F 9am-1:30pm, Tu, Th, and Sa 9am-1:30pm and 4-6:30pm, Su 9am-12:30pm; Oct.-May M and F 9am-1:30pm, Tu, Th, and Sa 9am-1:30pm and 3-5pm, Su 9am-12:30pm. Last entry 30min. before closing. €4.50, EU residents 18-25 €1.50, EU residents under 18 or over 65 or students free.)*

PORT. The port is more than a place to catch a hydrofoil; Messina's history and former naval prowess still inform the city's character. The enormous **La Madonnina,** a 6m golden statue, surveys the city from a 60m column across the water in the port's center. On the city side, the gleaming **Fontana di Nettuno** graces the intersection of V. Garibaldi and V. della Libertà. The muscular marble god stands triumphant over the chained, muscle-bound she-beasts, Scylla and Charybdis. Directly behind the fountain lies the impressive **Palazzo del Governo,** and to the left across the street sits the **Chiesa San Giovanni,** which boasts a museum brimming with religious treasures, including the ornate Cappella Palatina. *(Open Tu-Sa 9am-1pm and 4-7pm; closed M and Su. Call ☎ 090 42 877 to reserve a guided tour. €1.50.)* For kids and kids at heart, the **Acquario di Messina** (directly across the street from Chiesa S. Giovanni) holds entire school districts of fish species in colorful tanks, with informative posters along the walls and guides ready to answer any questions. *(Open Tu-Sa 9am-1pm and 3-7pm. €3, students and children €2. Remember that the port can be dangerous after dark, so make this adventure a daytime excursion.)*

FESTIVALS

The **Festa di Madonna della Lettera** on June 3 celebrates Messina's guardian. Parades throughout the city end at the *duomo*, where the sacred *Manta d'Oro* is restored to the altar for one day. Candy and toy vendors flood Piazza Duomo and nearby streets, taking advantage of the business presented by the hordes of tourists who come to photograph the Capello di Maria. If you plan to be in the area on June 3, make hotel reservations well in advance. Later in summer, Messina overflows with approximately 150,000 white-robed pilgrims during the nationally celebrated **Ferragosto Messinese** festival on August 13-15. During the first two days of Ferragosto, two huge human effigies called Mata and Grifone zoom through the city on horseback in the *Processione dei Gianti*.

TAORMINA ☎0942

Legend has it that the sea-god Neptune wrecked a Greek boat off the eastern coast of Sicily in the eighth century BC and that the sole survivor, inspired by the area's beauty, founded Taormina (tah-or-MEE-na; pop. 10,000). Historians tell a different tale: the Carthaginians founded Tauromenium in the fourth century BC, only to have it wrested away by the Greek tyrant Dionysius. Disputed origins aside, Taormina's brilliance is uncontested, with pines and mansions crowning a cliff above the sea. Disoriented, fanny-packed foreigners, hearty backpackers, and elite VIPs all come for a glimpse of what millions of photographic flashes and hyperbolic statements can't seem to dull—a vista that sweeps from boiling Etna to the straits of Messina.

▐ TRANSPORTATION

Taormina is accessible by bus from Messina or Catania. Though trains are more frequent than buses, the train station lies 5km below Taormina, next to neighboring Giardini-Naxos. Buses run from the train station to Taormina and Giardini-Naxos (every 30min., 7:30am-11pm, more frequently in summer).

Trains: ☎0942 89 20 21. To: **Catania** (50min., 25 per day 6:30am-8:25pm, €3.60), **Messina** (1hr., 20 per day 9:50am-8:07pm, €3.60), and **Syracuse** (2hr., 10 per day 7:12am-8:25pm, €10.50).

Buses: Interbus, at the end of V. L. Pirandello (☎0942 62 53 01), off C. Umberto I. (Open daily 6:20am-11:45pm.) To: **Catania** (M-Sa 16 per day 6:30am-7:45pm, Su 12 per day 8:45am-6pm; €4.40, round-trip €6.70); **Isola Bella, Mazzaro,** and **Spisone** (M-Sa 12 per day 6:30am-7:40pm, Su 4 per day 8:40am-5:40pm; €1.70, round-trip €2.20); **Gole Alcantara** (M-Sa 4 per day 9:15am-4:45pm, Su 9:15am; €2.80, round-trip €4.80); **Messina** (M-Sa 5 per day 6:20am-5:40pm, Su 3 per day 8:50am-6pm; €3, round-trip €5.30). Same bus runs to **Giardini-Naxos** and **train station** (dir.: Recanti or Catania; M-F every 30min. 7:30am-11pm; €1.40, round-trip €2.50). The schedule changes monthly, so be sure to grab a copy at the Taormina bus terminal.

Taxis: ☎0942 23 000 or 23 800. From the train station to downtown Taormina €15. Don't pay more than €7 within the city. €3 surcharge 10pm-6am.

Scooter Rental: Cundari Rent, Vle. Apollo Arcageta 12 (☎0942 24 700), around corner from post office at the end of C. Umberto I. Scooters €15-40 per day. 21+.

◼ ◪ ORIENTATION AND PRACTICAL INFORMATION

To reach the city from the **train station,** hop on the blue Interbus that makes the trip uphill (10min., every 30min. 6:50am-11:35pm, €1.40). Cars are not allowed on Taormina's steep, narrow streets; automobiles can park in a small lot at the base of **Via Luigi Pirandello.** From the bus depot, a short walk on V. L. Pirandello leads to the town's main street, **Corso Umberto I.** The boutique-lined road runs left from a stone arch through four principal *piazze:* **Piazza Vittorio Emanuele II, Piazza IX Aprile, Piazza del Duomo,** and **Piazza S. Antonio.** Small stairways and side streets wind downhill to a more affordable part of the city. Accurate and detailed maps are posted on brown signs throughout the city.

Tourist Office: AAST (☎0942 23 243; www.gate2taormina.com), in the courtyard of Palazzo Corvaja, off C. Umberto I across from P. Vittorio Emanuele II. Offers turquoise brochure *SAT Sicilian Airbus Travel.* Open M-F 8am-2:30pm and 4-7pm.

Tours: CST, C. Umberto I 99-101, 1st fl. (☎0942 62 60 88; csttao@tiscalinet.it). Offers Etna Tramonto, a sunset trip up the volcano (June-Oct. F 4pm; €70) and runs treks to 3000m (M and W June-Sept. 3pm, Oct. 2:15pm; €60); and to 2000m (year-round Tu and Th 8am; €30). AmEx/MC/V. **SAT,** C. Umberto I 73 (☎0942 24 653; www.sat-group.it), operates day-long bus excursions to Mt. Etna from €21.

Currency Exchange: Banks and **ATMs** line C. Umberto I and V. L. Pirandello, as do many currency exchange offices, including **Rocco Frisono,** C. Umberto I 224 (☎0942 24 806), between P. Sant'Antonio and P. Duomo. Open M-Sa 9am-1pm and 4-8pm.

American Express: La Duca Viaggi, V. Don Bosco 39, 2nd fl. (☎0942 62 52 55), in P. IX Aprile. Open M-F Apr.-Oct. 9am-1pm and 4-7:30pm; Nov.-Mar. 9am-1pm and 2-6pm.

Police: ☎0942 23 232. **Emergency:** ☎0942 61 11 11.

Pharmacy: Farmacia Ragusa, P. Duomo 9 (☎0942 23 23). Open M-Tu and Th-Su 8:30am-1pm and 5-8:30pm. Posts after-hours rotations. AmEx/MC/V. **First aid:** ☎0942 62 54 19 or 0942 57 92 97.

Hospital: Ospedale San Vincenzo (☎0942 57 91), in P. San Vincenzo.

Internet Access: Net Point, V. Jallia Bassia 34 (☎0942 62 60 80), down V. del Ginnasio from the public gardens. Wi-Fi, Skype, and photocopies. Internet €2 for 1-20min., €0.10 per min. thereafter. Unlimited Wi-Fi €2. Open daily 9am-9pm.

Post Office: ☎0942 73 230. In P. Sant'Antonio at the very top of C. Umberto I. Cashes traveler's checks. Open M-Sa 8am-6:30pm. **Postal Code:** 98039.

⛰ ACCOMMODATIONS

Taormina's popularity as a resort town makes cheap accommodations difficult to find. Those on a tight budget should consider staying in the hostel, or perhaps in nearby Mazzarò, Spisone, or Giardini-Naxos. Hike down steep trails to Mazzarò and Spisone or take the bus or cable cars; service stops around 1am.

▦ **Taormina's Odyssey Youth Hostel,** Traversa A di V. Galiano Martino 2 (☎0942 24 533). A 15min. walk from the intersection of C. Umberto I and V. L. Pirandello. Take V. C. Patrizio to V. Cappuccini. When it forks, turn right onto V. Fontana Vecchia. Follow Greek ship signs. Renowned among backpackers. English-speaking employees. Clean rooms and lockers. Kitchen open 10am-9pm. Towel rental €2. Breakfast included. Luggage storage €1. Reservations recommended. Dorms €18; 1 double €60. Cash only. ❶

Pensione Grazia, V. Iallia Bassia 20 (☎0942 24 776), off V. Giovanni di Giovanni, between the Greek theater and the lush public gardens. 4 cozy doubles (€50-60) with A/C, heating, shared bath, and terraces. Reservations recommended. Cash only. ❷

Inn Piero, V. L. Pirandello 20 (☎0942 23 139; www.hotelinnpiero.com), near base of C. Umberto I. Piero. Rooms have full bath. Breakfast included. Reservations recommended. Singles €50; doubles €70. Sept.-July. student discount 10%. AmEx/MC/V. ❶

SICILY

Hotel Villa Nettuno, V. L. Pirandello 33 (☎0942 23 797; www.hotelvillanettuno.it). Charming inn with stone steps and garden. All rooms with bath. Breakfast €4. Reservations recommended. Singles €40; doubles €70-80. Extra bed €15. Cash only. ❸

Hotel Villa Astoria, V. L. Pirandello 38 (☎0942 23 943; villaastoria@libero.it), across from the bus stop. All rooms come with balcony and private bath. Singles €45; doubles €65-80; triples €85-100. Cash only. ❹

🍴 FOOD

Taormina's restaurants are of consistently high quality; prices vary, though, so shop around. The **SMA supermarket,** V. Apollo Arcageta 21, is at the end of C. Umberto I. (Open M-Sa 8am-9pm, Su 8:30am-12:30pm. Cash and debit only.)

🔲 **La Cisterna del Moro,** V. Bonifacio 1 (☎0942 23 001), off C. Umberto I near P. IX Aprile. Serves incredible food on a secluded terrace with great views. Try the *stuzzichini caserecci* (€12), an antipasto plate of vegetables, meats, and cheese. Cover €1.50. Open daily noon-3pm and 7pm-midnight, closes later in summer. AmEx/MC/V. ❷

Ristorante Il Ciclope, C. Umberto I (☎0942 23 263), 50m past L'Arco dell'Orologio. Locals and tourists alike come to the self-proclaimed "number 1 since 1950" for the "best fish in Taormina." Primi €6.50-9.50. Fish platters €8-15. Cover €2. Open M-Tu and Th-Su 10am-3pm and 7-11pm. AmEx/MC/V. ❸

Granduca, C. Umberto I 172 (☎0942 24 983). According to locals, the views of Etna and the sea from the terrace are the most spectacular in town. Pizza €6-9.50. Primi €9-15. Secondi €16-24. Cover €2. Open 7pm-midnight. AmEx/MC/V. ❸

Pigghia e Potta, V. Giovanni di Giovanni 23 (☎0942 62 62 86), off P. V. Emanuele II. Brightly decorated and friendly hole-in-the-wall serves tasty and cheap takeout. Pizza €2. Pasta €5. Open daily 11am-midnight. Cash only. ❶

Bella Blu, V. L. Pirandello 28 (☎0942 24 239). One of the city's most unique views: cable cars glide down the mountain between clusters of cypress trees that overlook blue water and sandy beaches. Pizza and drink €8.50. Primi €5.50-9. Secondi €4.50-15. Cover €1.50. Open daily 11am-5pm and 6-11pm. AmEx/MC/V. ❷

EAT SHELLFISH WITHOUT SHELLING OUT. For fresh yet cheap seafood, consider taking a short excursion outside the city. In nearby **Forza D'Agro,** a small hillside town 15km from Taormina, locals enjoy excellent fare for a fraction of the price. Though buses stop running early in the evening, a rental scooter or car will get you up the hill and back in under 45min. Ask for directions in the tourist office or at any hotel.

👁 SIGHTS

From P. V. Emanuele II, walk up V. Teatro Greco to Taormina's best treasure: the well-preserved **Greek theater.** Though originally constructed by the Greeks in the third century BC, it was rebuilt and enlarged by Romans in the AD second century. On clear days, it offers an unsurpassed view of Etna, whose sultry smoke and occasional eruptions rival even the greatest Sophoclean tragedies. The cliff-side arena packs 5000 spectators into its seats for annual summer festivals. (☎0942 62 06 66. Open daily May-Aug. 9am-7pm; Apr. and Sept. 9am-6:30pm; Oct. and Mar. 9am-5pm; Nov.-Feb. 9am-4pm. €6, EU residents 18-25 €3, EU residents under 18 or over 65 free.) From P. V. Emanuele II, take C. Umberto I to reach the **duomo.** This 13th-century structure, rebuilt during the Renaissance, now takes center stage. The Gothic interior shelters paintings by Messinese artists and a statue of the Virgin Mary. A two-legged female centaur,

Taormina's mascot, crowns the fountain out front. (Hours vary; inquire at the **Museo Sacra** next door.) Behind the tourist office, the grandiose **Chiesa di Santa Caterina** protects a small theater, the Roman **Odeon**. The short walk down V. Giovanni di Giovanni leads to Taormina's tranquil public gardens, the **Villa Comunale**. Filled with vibrant flowers and people relaxing under palms during summer's greatest heat, the gardens look out over Giardini-Naxos below and Etna in the distance. V. Circonvallazione leads away from the crowds to a small stairway that snakes up the mountainside to the **Piccolo Castello**. The **Galleria Gagliardi**, C. Umberto I 187a, debuts contemporary art. Exhibits change every 15 days. (☎0942 62 89 02. Open daily 10am-1pm and 5:30-10pm.)

◧ NIGHTLIFE

Deja Vu, P. Garibaldi 2 (☎0942 62 86 94), behind the post office. This exotic bar's mixed drinks (from €8) and Turkish coffee (€5-6) seduce partygoers both indoors and out. Open Tu-Su 5pm-3am. MC/V.

O Seven Irish Pub, Largo La Farina 6 (☎0942 24 980), at P. IX Aprile. Massive selection of local and international beer and liquor (from €2), and a nice patio for people-watching on the main thoroughfare. Open Tu-Su 11am-2am. AmEx/MC/V.

Re di Bastoni, C. Umberto I 120 (☎0942 23 037; www.redibastoni.it.). Classy, laid-back vibe goes well with live jazz on F and Su nights. Drinks from €4. Open July-Aug. daily 11am-2am; closed Sept.-June M. AmEx/MC/V.

Morgana Bar and Cocktail Garden, Scesa Morgana 4, off C. Umberto I. Generous staff, purple and white couches inside, and a floral patio out back. Huge assortment of mixed drinks (from €7) and beer (from €2). Open 5pm-1am. MC/V.

La Giara, Vico La Floresta 1 (☎0942 23 360). Turns into Taormina's only dance club every Sa night with Top 40 and techno from 1-5am. Restaurant open M-Tu and Th-Su 7:30pm-midnight, bar open later. Alcohol from €3.50. MC/V.

◧ ◧ BEACHES AND ENTERTAINMENT

Cable cars take a breezy ride along the funivia from V. L. Pirandello to the beach. (☎0942 23 605. Every 15min. M 8am-1:30pm, Tu-Su 8am-1:30am; €2, round-trip €3.) At the popular **Lido Mazzarò**, lounge-chair rentals (€7.50) from Lido La Pigna include shower, parasol, and changing area—or just enjoy the view with your coffee on the terrace upstairs. Five minutes to the right, there is a beautiful beach where sparkling waters surround the ◧**Isola Bella,** a nature preserve 100m offshore. **SAISTours,** Corso Umberto 222 (☎0942 62 06 71), offers daily bus excursions to Etna and the Alcantara Gorges (from €21), Syracuse (€33), Palermo, and Cefalù (€42). Ask for the *Excursions from Taormina* brochure at the tourist office. **Acquaterra,** V. A. Longo 74 (☎0942 50 30 20; www.acquaterra.com), hosts Alcantara canyoning and river trekking adventures geared toward families and groups (½-day €30-50, full-day €50-80).

Every summer brings ◧**Taormina Arte,** a theater, ballet, music, and film extravaganza with performances from June to August. Shows, held in the Greek Theater, have featured Bob Dylan and Ray Charles. (Box office in P. V. Emanuele II. ☎0942 62 87 30; www.taormina-arte.com.)

◧ DAYTRIP FROM TAORMINA: GIARDINI-NAXOS

Now the eastern coast's ultimate beach town and a touristy watering hole, Giardini-Naxos (JAR-dee-nee NAX-ohs; pop. 9150) was the first Greek colony in Sicily in 734 BC. Excavations in the 60s unearthed traces of a Greek city built of lava blocks, founded in the shadow of the volcano. Visit the fortress ruins, now overgrown with wildflowers, for a break from the city. The nearby **Museo Archeologico** records the ancient city's earliest days and includes an inscribed ceramic cup, the colony's earliest surviving writing. (*☎0942 51 001. Open daily 9am-7pm. €2, ages 18-25 €1, EU citizens under 18 or over 65 free.*) While there are some public beaches, private beaches rent umbrellas, lounge chairs, and cabanas, and are much less crowded. **Lido di Naxos,** toward the end of the line of private beach clubs, also rents pedal boats and canoes (*€8 and €6 per hour, respectively*). Restaurants crowd the *lungomare* and offer sunbathers pricey options. **Taverna Naxos da Angelo ❷,** V. Naxos 42, is an exception. The staff, fluent in French, English, and German, serves delicious meals and desserts. Try the special *spaghetti alle vongole* (spaghetti with clams) for €6. (*☎0942 52 251. Primi €4.70-6.30. Secondi €5.50-13.50. Cover €1.40. Open M-Tu and Th-Su 11am-4:30pm and 6:30pm-midnight. MC/V.*) Consider heading off the beach for more budget options. Buy necessities at **Sigma supermarket,** V. Casarsa 15. Look for sign on V. Dalmazia, just off V. Naxos. (*Open M-Sa 8:30am-1:30pm and 4:30-9pm, Su 8:30am-1pm.*) Giardini-Naxos shares a train station with its neighbor, Taormina, which is just 5km away. **Interbus** runs from Giardini to the train station and Taormina's bus station. (*☎0942 62 53 01. 35 per day 7:35am-11:35pm; €1.40, €2.30 round trip.*)

CATANIA
☎ 095

Modern Catania (ca-TA-nee-ya; pop. 500,000) hasn't forgotten its ancient roots. From the stately grace of its *piazze* to its ancient ruins, the city merges tradition with youthful revelry, as university students funnel into its plentiful bars and cafes. Leveled repeatedly, sometimes by invaders but mostly by nearby Mt. Etna, Catania has been rebuilt often since its founding in 729 BC. After the monstrous 1693 earthquake, Giovanni Battista Vaccarini recreated the city with his Baroque *duomo* and *piazze*, which fill daily with eager vendors.

▐ TRANSPORTATION

Flights: Fontanarossa (CTA), C. Sicilia 71 (*☎095 34 05 05 or 800 60 56 56*). Take Alibus #457 from the train station; purchase bus tickets in kiosk outside station or in *tabaccherie.* The 15min. cab ride to the airport costs about €20.

Trains: ☎095 53 27 19. In P. Papa Giovanni XXIII. To: **Agrigento** (3hr., 4 per day 5:45am-7pm, €10.50); **Enna** (1hr., 7 per day 5:45am-7pm, €5.30); **Messina** (2hr., 24 per day 5:15am-8:20pm, €5.50); **Palermo** (3hr., 3 per day 10:45am-7:15pm, €12); **Rome** (10hr., 5 per day 9:10am-10:20pm, €50); **Syracuse** (1hr., 12 per day 5:15am-9pm, €5.50); **Taormina/Giardini-Naxos** (1hr., 30 per day 4am-8:15pm, €4).

Buses: All companies are on V. D'Amico, across the *piazza* in front of the train station. Because service is significantly reduced Su, weekend travelers may want to opt for the train. Info office inside the train station to the left.

SAIS Trasporti (*☎095 53 62 01*). To: **Agrigento** (3hr., 20 per day 6:30am-9pm, €11) and **Rome** (14hr.; 8, 9:15pm; €45) via **Naples.**

SAIS Autolinee (*☎095 53 61 68*) to **Enna** (1hr.; M-Sa 8 per day 6:30am-8pm, Su 3 per day 9am-8pm; €7), **Messina** (1hr.; M-Sa 22 per day 5:15am-8:15pm, Su 5 per day 7am-8:30pm; €7.20), and **Palermo** (3hr., 14 per day 5am-8pm, €13).

Interbus and Etna (*☎095 53 27 16*). Both run to: **Brindisi** (8hr.; 10:15am, 10pm; €40); **Noto** (2hr.; 2, 5:30, 7:15pm; €6.50); **Ragusa** (2hr., 9 per day 6am-8pm, €6.50); **Taormina/Giardini-Naxos** (1hr., 16 per day 7:15am-9:15pm, €4.40).

Ferries: La Duca Viaggi, P. Europa 1 (*☎095 72 22 295*), up Vle. Africa from train station. To **Malta** (€89). Open M-F 9am-1pm and 4:30-7pm, Sa 9am-noon. **Traghetti Caronte**

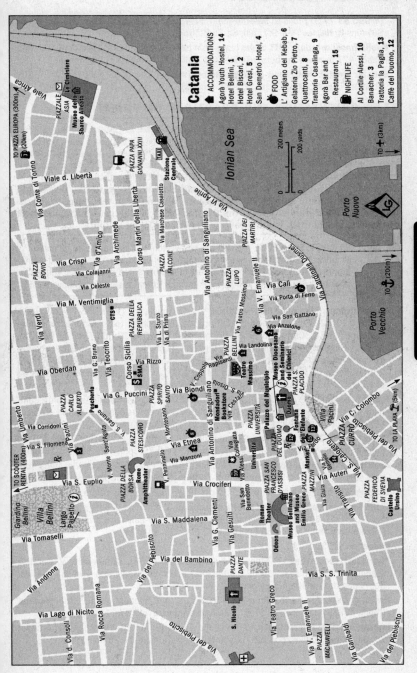

Catania

ACCOMMODATIONS
Agora Youth Hostel, 14
Hotel Bellini, 1
Hotel Biscari, 2
Hotel Gresi, 5
San Demetrio Hotel, 4

FOOD
L' Artigiano del Kebab, 6
Gelateria Zio Pietro, 7
Quattrocanti, 8
Trattoria Casalinga, 9
Agora Bar and
Restaurant, 15

NIGHTLIFE
Al Cortile Alessi, 10
Banacher, 3
Trattoria la Paglia, 13
Caffè del Duomo, 12

(☎095 53 77 97) runs to **Salerno** (daily 11:45pm). **Traghetti TTTLines** (☎095 28 13 88) runs to **Naples** (M-F 9:15pm, Sa-Su 7:30pm).

Public Transportation: AMT buses leave from train station in P. Papa Giovanni XXIII. Take Alibus #27 to reach the beach. Tickets (€1; valid 1hr.) are sold at *tabaccherie.*

Scooter Rental: Hollywood Rent by Motoservice, P. Cavour 12 (☎095 44 27 20). Scooters €16-42. Motorcycles €52-93. Cars €62-130 per day. 21+. AmEx/MC/V.

ORIENTATION AND PRACTICAL INFORMATION

Via Etnea, connecting the *duomo* to the **Giardini Bellini,** is Catania's main street. Several main thoroughfares run perpendicular to V. Etnea. From north to south: **Via Umberto I** runs from Piazza Galatea on the water to Villa Bellini; **Corso Martiri della Libertà** runs from the bus and train stations at Piazza Papa Giovanni XXIII and becomes **Corso Sicilia** at Piazza della Repubblica, bisecting V. Etnea at Piazza Stesicoro; **Via Antonino di Sangiuliano** runs past Piazza Bellini and the Teatro Massimo; and **Via Vittorio Emanuele II** leads from the water to Piazza Duomo. **V. VI Aprile** curves south from the train station and turns into **V. Cardinale Dusmet** at P. dei Martiri, leading to Villa Pacini and P. del Duomo.

> ❗ **STREET SMARTS.** As with any city, visitors to Catania should be careful of petty theft. Know where your things are at all times, don't walk around with a map glued to your face, and be wary of manufactured distractions. At night, stick to the populated, well-lit areas along V. Etnea and other main avenues.

Tourist Offices: Municipal Tourist Office, V. V. Emanuele II 172 (☎095 74 25 573 or 800 84 10 42). English-speaking staff provides self-guided tours and theater schedules. Open M-F 8:30am-7pm. **AAPIT,** V. Cimarosa 10 (☎095 73 06 279 or 73 06 222), near the Giardini Bellini. From V. Etnea, turn on V. Pacini before the post office, and follow signs. Open M-F 8am-8pm, Sa-Su 8am-2pm. Annexes at train station (☎095 73 06 255), V. Etnea 63 (☎095 31 17 78 or 73 06 233), and the airport (☎095 73 06 266 or 73 06 277) have the same hours as the main office.

Tours: Acquaterra, P. della Republica 1 (☎095 50 30 20; www.acquaterra.com). Company picks up clients from hotels and runs daily Jeep excursions up Mt. Etna. Half-day trip €50, full-day €59 (lunch and an excursion to the Alcantara River Gorges included).

Budget Travel: CTS, V. Monsignore Ventimiglia 153 (☎095 53 02 23; fax 53 62 46), off P. della Repubblica. Open M-F 9:30am-1pm and 4:30-7:30pm, Sa 9:30am-12:30pm.

American Express: La Duca Viaggi, P. Europa 1 (☎095 72 22 295), up Vle. Africa from train station. Open M-F 9am-1pm and 4-7:30pm, Sa 9am-12:30pm.

Luggage Storage: In train station. €3.50 per 12hr. Open daily 8am-8pm.

English-Language Bookstore: Libreria Mondadori, V. Antonino di Sangiuliano 223/225 (☎095 31 51 60), just down from Teatro Bellini. Brand-new branch of national chain. In-store cafe. Open M and Sa 5pm-2am, Tu-F and Su 9am-2am.

Police: ☎095 53 13 33.

Pharmacy: Crocerossa, V. Etnea 274 (☎095 31 70 53). **Croceverde,** V. Gabriele D'Annunzio 43 (☎095 44 16 62), at the intersection of C. Italia and C. della Provincia. Both open daily 8:30am-1pm and 4:30-8pm. AmEx/MC/V.

Hospital: Ospedale Garibaldi (☎095 75 91 111), in P. Santa Maria del Gesù. **Medical Clinic,** C. Italia 234 (☎095 37 71 22). **Ambulance:** ☎095 37 71 22.

Internet Access: Internetteria, V. Penninello 44 (☎095 31 01 39). Wi-Fi and Internet access €1 per 30min. Food €2-7. Open M-Sa 10am-midnight, Su hours vary.

Post Office: V. Etnea 215 (☎095 71 55 111), in the big building next to Giardini Bellini. Open M-F 8am-6:30pm, Sa 8am-12:30pm. **Postal Code:** 95125.

ACCOMMODATIONS

The plethora of posh stores that lines the streets suggests high hotel prices, but many *pensione* near V. Etnea are affordable. Reserve early for summer travel.

Agorà Youth Hostel, P. Currò 6 (☎095 72 33 010; www.agorahostel.com). From the train station follow V. Dusmet until you pass the park (Villa Pacini), then walk uphill on V. Pardo until you reach P. Currò. English spoken. On-site grotto restaurant and wine bar serve food. *Piatto unico* (all-in-one course) and drink €6. Happy hour 5-10pm; 2-for-1 beer and mixed drinks €4. Bike rental €8 per day. Towels €2. Laundry €4. Internet access €2 per hr. Breakfast included. Sept.-July dorms €19; Aug. €20. AmEx/MC/V. ❶

Hotel Bellini, V. Landolina 41 (☎095 71 50 969; www.bellinihotel.com). Convenient to Teatro Bellini. Marble stairs lead to 7 rooms with A/C, TV, and phone. Reservations requested. Doubles €50-55. MC/V. ❷

Hotel Gresi, V. Pacini 28 (☎095 32 27 09; www.gresihotel.com), off V. Etnea before Villa Bellini. Inviting salon, breakfast room, and spacious social bar. Spotless rooms have bath, A/C, TV, and phone. Breakfast €5. Singles €55; doubles €80. AmEx/MC/V. ❹

San Demetrio Hotel, V. Etnea 55 (☎095 25 00 237; www.hotelsandemetrio.com), at the intersection of V. Sangiuliano. 6 enormous rooms have private bath, A/C, phone, and TV. Continental breakfast and laundry service available. Singles €30-60; doubles €41-82. Reservations requested. AmEx/MC/V. ❸

Hotel Biscari, V. Anzalone 7 (☎095 25 00 209), off V.V. Emanuele II. Gold statues and smooth stone floors welcome guests. Large rooms with A/C, TV, and phone. Breakfast included. Small bar in common area. Doubles €60-70; triples €85-95. MC/V. ❸

FOOD

When *catanesi* gather at the table, chances are they'll be dining on eggplant- and ricotta-topped *spaghetti alla norma*, named for Bellini's famous opera. Another hit is the fresh *masculini* (anchovies), alleged aphrodisiacs. The expansive **market** off P. del Duomo and V. Garibaldi features fish, fruit, and sweets vendors. (Open M-Sa morning and early afternoon.) An **SMA supermarket** is at C. Sicilia 50. (☎095 32 60 699. Open M-Sa 8:30am-8:30pm, Su 8:30am-1pm.) **Bar Savia**, V. Etnea 304, across from Bellini Gardens, serves the best *granite di gelsi* (mulberry iced drinks; €1.80) in town. (Open M-Sa 8am-9:30pm.) Perhaps the best deal, however, is the catanese *arancino*—a filling fried rice ball stuffed with meat, available for around €1.50 at any bar with a *"tavola calda"* sign.

Trattoria la Paglia, V. Pardo 23 (☎095 34 68 38), near P. Duomo. Share a table with locals and trade tired red sauce for *spaghetti al nero di seppia* (with squid ink; €5). Primi €4-10. Secondi €7-12. Cover €1. Open M-Sa 10am-midnight. AmEx/MC/V. ❷

Trattoria Casalinga, V. Biondi 19 (☎095 31 13 19). Popular with local theater-goers, and *casalinghe* (housewives), serves up traditional cuisine *al fresco*. Primi €6-8. Secondi €8-12. Cover €1.50. Open M-Sa noon-4pm and 8pm-midnight. MC/V. ❸

Quattrocanti, V. Etnea 84 (☎095 71 50 885). Popular, modern restaurant right on the main thoroughfare. F night karaoke. Fried calamari €6.50. Primi €3.50-6. Secondi €4-12. Contorni €1.50-2. Beer €1.50-3.50. Open daily 8pm-12:30am. MC/V. ❷

L'Artigiano del Kebab, V. V. Emanuele II 94 (☎340 35 83 831). Indian flavors meet classic Sicilian cuisine. *Pranzo completo* (primo, secondo, kebab, and drink) €6. Pizza *a taglio* €2. Indian plates from €4. Primi €4-7. Open daily 9am-midnight. Cash only. ❸

Gelateria Zio Pietro, V. Porto di Ferro 47, off V. Cardinale Dusmet. Local favorite since 1964. 35 flavors include Kit Kat and pistachio. The latter, made from locally grown nuts, is reputedly the world's finest. 2 scoops €1. Open Tu-Su 11am-11pm. Cash only. ❸

👁 SIGHTS

PIAZZA DUOMO. Giovanni Battista Vaccarini's little lava ▨**Fontana dell'Elefante** (1736) commands the city's attention. Vaccarini carved his elephant (the symbol of the city) without visible testicles. When the statue was unveiled, horrified *catanesi* men, who construed this omission as an attack on their virility, demanded corrective measures. Vaccarini's acquiescence was, well, monumental. Residents claim that visitors may attain citizenship by smooching the elephant's nether regions, but the height of the pachyderm's backside precludes fulfillment of such aspirations. Other buildings on the *piazza*, including the 18th-century Palazzo del Municipio on the left and the former Seminario dei Chierici on the right, are striped black-and-white to mirror the *duomo*'s side. Pose for a picture at the **Amenano fountain** in the southwest corner of the *piazza*, and then visit the **Museo Diocesano,** V. Etnea 8, to see centuries-old priestly vestments. The 1950 restoration of the *duomo* revealed an interior that predates the Baroque makeover. Restorers discovered stumps of the columns and pointed arches of the original apses. The walls of the Norman **Cappella della Madonna** on the *duomo*'s right side surround a 15th-century statue of the Virgin Mary. The body of Catania's beloved priest, the Beato Cardinal Dusmet, lies nearby. To the right of the main door is Bellini's tomb, guarded by a marble angel. The words and music from his *Sonnambula* are inscribed above the tomb and translate as, "Ah, I didn't think I'd see you wilt so soon, flower." (☎095 28 16 35. Open M-Sa 9am-noon and 4-6pm, Su by appointment. Long pants and sleeves are required for men and no short skirts or bare shoulders for women. Free.)

GIARDINI BELLINI AND ENVIRONS. The centerpiece of Catania's restoration sits on V. Etnea and is marked by a fountain and crooked cypresses. These gardens sprawl across small hills and around tiny ponds. Half the city strolls here, gelato in hand, on Sunday afternoons. Below a Victorian bandstand, a plot displays the day's date in perfect grass figures, replanted daily. A few blocks away in P. Stesicoro, modern streets cradle a sunken pit holding ruins of an AD second-century **Roman amphitheater,** with visible tunnels that gladiators once used to enter the arena. Uphill from P. Duomo, at V. V. Emanuele 260, lies the entrance to the **Roman Theater,** built in the AD second century on the grounds of an earlier Greek theater. Passageways lined with the remains of marble columns spill out into the similar but smaller **Odeon,** with another entrance around the back. Mt. Etna's 1669 eruption coated both theaters in lava. (☎095 71 50 508. Open daily 9am-1pm and 3-7pm. €3, EU residents 18-25 €2, under 18 and over 65 free.)

OTHER SIGHTS. Near the train station on Vle. Africa, **Le Ciminiere,** a rescued factory complex, has been restored as a cultural center with free art exhibits, concerts, and home improvement expositions. In addition, the ▨**Museo Storico dello Sbarco Alleato in Sicilia-Estate 1943** (Historical Museum of the Allied Landing in Sicily—Summer 1943), Ple. Asia, skillfully showcases an oft-ignored event in WWII history. Exhibits highlight the Allied bombing and subsequent invasion of Sicily by American, British, Canadian, and Australian troops, which immediately preceded Mussolini's defeat. The museum depicts a typical Sicilian city square before and after bombing, as well as Axis and Allied propaganda. Also included are wartime Italian postcards of various saints blessing the fascist troops marching under the fascist banner. (☎095 53 35 40. Open Tu-Su 9:30am-12:30pm, Tu and Th also 3-5pm. Guided tours in Italian, English, or French upon request.)

€4, under 18 and over 60 €1). **The Museo del Cinema,** next door, provides a broad education in cinematic techniques, as well as a closer look at the past films of the once-renowned Catania Industry of Cinema. (☎095 40 11 928. Open W, F, Sa, and Su 9am-1:30pm, Tu and Th 9am-5:30pm. Guided tours every hr. €4, under 18 and over 60 €1.)

BEACHES. The crowded **La Playa** offers a charming view of a nearby power plant. (Take Alibus #27.) Farther from the port is the rugged **La Scogliera,** with jutting cliffs and a not-so-jutting bathing area. (Take bus #534 or #535 from P. Borsellino.)

🎵 📷 ENTERTAINMENT AND NIGHTLIFE

During opera season (Jan.-June), the **Teatro Massimo (Bellini),** V. Perrotta 12, off V. Antonino di Sanguiliano, mesmerizes audiences with its sumptuous setting during opera season. (☎095 71 50 921. Student discounts available on all tickets; contact tourist office. Tours in Italian available upon request. Box office open M-F 9:30am-12:30pm.) In cooler months, *catanesi* love their nightly *passeggiate* (stroll), circulating both P. Duomo and P. Bellini. Cafes pulsate with life on weekends, drawing a sometimes raucous crowd. Local university students and urban 30-somethings frequent local watering holes. In the late evening, students pack the streets around P. Duomo. **Piazza Spirito Santo** offers a little sliver of Ireland every night with three neighboring pubs: **Murphy's Irish Stout, Joyce Irish Pub,** and **Waxy O'Connor's.** Catania's biggest feast day honors the city's patron, **Sant'Agata.** Fireworks and non-stop partying in the first five days of February salvage the city from winter gloom. In the summer, most *catanesi* leave town. Summer crowds typically scooter 15min. away to **Banacher** or **Aci Castello** and nearby **Aci Trezza,** nearly identical nightlife hubs with expensive bars and pretty seaside views. AAPIT's free monthly bulletin *Lapis,* available at the tourist office and in bars, details Catania's nightlife, concerts, and festivals.

Banacher, V. XXI Aprile-S.S. 114 (☎095 27 12 57), a 15min. taxi ride from Catania's *centro.* Crowds dance into the wee hours at what is reputedly Europe's largest outdoor disco. Cover €10. Open Tu-Su 10pm-3am.

Agorà Bar and Restaurant, Piazza Currò 6, next to the hostel. Youth swarm this outdoor favorite by the hundreds. Cheap drinks, loud music, and plenty of company combine for a fun experience sure to last into the morning. Open 9pm-late. MC/V.

THE HIDDEN DEAL

SPOILER ALERT!

While it threatens to be just another overpriced tour, the guided visit at the **Museo Storico dello Sbarco** in Sicily is really much more. In a startling way, it recounts "Operation Husky," the Allied landing in Sicily in 1943 that paved the way for Italy's liberation.

The tour begins with a 12min. video in Italian detailing the historical background; forget the language barrier—the often-horrifying images speak for themselves.

In the first room, curators have reconstructed an entire Catania *piazza,* complete with newspapers from the time, Fascist propaganda, and a typical *catanese* kitchen.

As you enter the second room, air-raid sirens begin to blare, and the guide rushes everyone into an anti-aircraft shelter, where special effects bring history to life. Visitors then reenter the *piazza,* now destroyed by bombings, and guests are left to explore alone. After your heart stops pounding, peruse wax depictions of key events, from the meeting between Roosevelt and Churchill to the signing of the 1943 armistice.

The final room is dedicated to the British war cemetery near Catania, which holds soldiers killed in Sicily. Names of the dead flash onto a screen as a poignant final reminder of war's infinite costs.

Sicilia-Estate 1943, V. le Africa (☎095 53 35 40). Open Tu and Th 9:30am-12:30pm and 3-5pm, W, F, and Sa-Su 9:30am-12:30pm. €4, under 18 and over 60 €1.

Al Cortile Alessi, V. Alessi 30, offers courtyard dining under swaying *nespola* trees and a welcome respite from the buzzing nightlife nearby. Open Tu-Su 8pm-late. AmEx/MC/V.

Caffè del Duomo, (☎095 71 50 556), across from the elephant fountain. Offers gelato and coffee for a low-key night in Catania's main *piazza*, where monuments sparkle under the full moon and blazing street lamps. Open daily 6am-3am. Cash only.

DAYTRIP FROM CATANIA

MOUNT ETNA

An AST bus leaves from Catania's central train station at 8am for a 2hr. ride to Rifugio Sapienza. The bus leaves Etna around 4:30pm (schedules vary; round-trip €5). Tours to Mt. Etna by various organizations depart daily from Catania (p. 464) and Taormina (p. 460). From Catania, **Geo Etna Explorer** *(☎349 61 09 957; www.geoetna.it) offers free pick-up from your hotel and a Jeep tour of the volcano (€55, under 18 €35).* **EtnASicilyTouring** *(☎329 09 50 051; www.etnasicilytouring.com) has a half-day excursion to Etna and the Silvestri Mountain craters (€39), a full-day trek up the mountain and through the Alcantara Gorge (€59), and the spectacular Etna by Night (€39). Tours daily, free pick-up from hotel.* **Etna Experience** *(☎349 30 53 021; www.etnaexperience.com) offers a 9hr. Classic Tour that stops at the Bove Valley, the lava caves, the craters and lava flow, and finally the Alcantara Canyons (adults €59, children and students under 26 years old €45). Pick-up from hotel, picnic lunch, and Etna wine included. Reservations required for all tours.*

Mount Etna's lava-seared wilderness is one of Italy's most compelling natural settings. Etna's history of volcanic activity is the longest documented of any volcano—the first recorded eruption was in 1500 BC, though it was probably active long before that. Also Europe's tallest active volcano (3350m), it has long held sway over eastern Sicily's residents: the Greek poet Hesiod envisioned Etna as the home of Typhon, the last monster conceived by Earth to fight the gods before the dawn of the human race. The ancients also claimed its fires were the home of Vulcan, the blacksmith god. Apparently Typhon's aggressions aren't over yet: a 1985 eruption destroyed much of the summit tourist station, and eruptions in 2001 and 2002 sent lava rolling down slopes at 160km per hour. The most recent major eruptions occurred in the fall and winter of 2002-2003 and formed two new craters near the volcano's peak.

DON'T BE A HERO. The trek up Mt. Etna is not for the faint of heart (or the faint of breath). Since you have 6hr. until the bus returns to Catania, you can take your time scaling the volcano. If you decide to bypass the hike for the comforts of the cable car, it's worth it to pay the extra €24 for the shuttle to the *Torre del Filosofo.* The hike to the towers is both steep and dusty.

From the parking lot at Rifugio Sapienza (1900m) where the AST bus stops, you can either hike to the aptly named **Torre del Filosofo** (Philosopher's Tower; 3hr.; 2920m) or take the cable car and an off-road shuttle. (Cable car, off-road shuttle, and guided tour of craters €50; cable car and guided tour only €30). Ask at the information center about times and prices for these excursions, as they vary immensely based on crowds and season. Anyone with sturdy shoes can take a 30min. jaunt to explore the crater in front of the parking area. From the Philosopher's Tower, a 2hr. hike leads to the **craters** themselves. **Valle del Bove,** Etna's first volcanic crater, is on the way down. While the view of the hardened lava, huge boulders, and unearthly craters is incredible, the trail is so difficult and the volcanic activity so unpredictable that sightseers are allowed access only by guided tour. On a certified **tour,** hikers can sometimes hold molten rocks heated by subterranean activity or watch guides burn newspapers on exposed rifts in the rock. Those who brave the trip should take precautions: carry water and bring warm clothing, as winds are ferocious and pockets of snow can linger into mid-July. Windbreakers and hiking boots can be rented at the top of the cable car route for €2 each.

SOUTHERN SICILY

SYRACUSE (SIRACUSA) ☎0931

Syracuse (SEE-ra-COO-sa; pop. 125,000) blends ancient archaeological treasure with extravagant Baroque beauty. In its golden age, Syracuse was home to some of the greatest contributors to Western culture: Theocritus, Archimedes, and the Greek lyric poet Pindar. After many conquests, the city's fortune waned and Syracuse receded from the spotlight. Today, nighttime crowds meander around the lighted ruins of the Temple of Apollo and the ancient *duomo*, and party from dusk to dawn at the nearby Fontane Bianche.

TRANSPORTATION

Trains: V. Francesco Crispi (☎0931 46 44 67). To: **Catania** (1hr., 18 per day 5am-8:25pm, €5.80); **Messina** (3hr., 9 per day 5am-9:30pm, €9.50); **Milan** (18hr., 5:15 and 5:40pm, €50); **Noto** (45min., 10 per day 5:15am-8:05pm, €3.10); **Ragusa** (2-3hr., 4 per day 5:15am-2:50pm, €8.90); **Rome** (10-13hr.; Tu, Th, Sa-Su 8am and 6pm; €44); **Taormina** (2hr., 10 per day 5am-9:30pm, €8.30).

Buses: AST (☎0931 46 27 11 or 44 92 15), on C. Umberto I near the train station. To **Gela** (4hr., 6:50am and 12:30pm, €9) and **Ragusa** (3hr.; M-Sa 8 per day 7:25am-7:15pm, Su 2:10pm and 8:30pm, €8.50). Interbus, V. Trieste 40 (☎0931 66 710), 1 block from P. delle Poste toward center of Ortigia, 2nd street on left after stone bridge. To **Catania** (14 per day M-F 6:15am-8:30pm, Sa and Su 4 per day 6:18am-7:33pm; €4.70) and **Noto** (1hr.; M-Sa 5 per day 7:50am-5:10pm, Su 4:05pm; €2.85).

Public Transportation: Orange AST buses depart from P. delle Poste. Buses #21 and 22 run past Fontane Bianche every 2-3hr.; buses #23 and 24 do so much less frequently. Tickets (€1) sold in *tabaccherie* and bars displaying an AST sticker in the window.

Taxis: ☎0931 69 722 or 60 980. From the train station to Ortigia costs about €8.

ORIENTATION AND PRACTICAL INFORMATION

Ponte Umbertino connects the island of Ortigia to mainland Syracuse. **Ponte Nuovo** (Ponte Santa Lucia), just to the left of Ponte Umbertino facing the mainland, is open even when Umbertino is closed to car traffic. On the mainland, **Corso Umberto I** links the bridge to the train station and passes through **Piazza Marconi,** from which **Corso Gelone** passes through town to the **Archaeological Park.** C. Umberto I continues past **Foro Siracusano** to the train station.

Tourist Office: AAT Office Ortigia, V. Maestranza 33 (☎0931 46 42 55). After crossing Ponte Umbertino, turn right through P. Pancali to uphill C. Matteoti. Turn left on V. Maestranza at the fountain in P. Archimede; office is in the *palazzo*'s courtyard across from the pharmacy. English spoken. Open M-Th 8:30am-1:45pm and 3-5:30pm, F 8:30am-1:45pm. **URP,** V. Malta 106 (☎0931 46 88 69; www.provincia.siracusa.it), has a tourist section, with brochures in many languages, detailed maps of Syracuse and surrounding cities, and guides to the nearby historical sights. Open M-F 9am-1pm.

Luggage Storage: In train station. €4 per hr. Open daily 7:30am-1pm and 3-7pm.

SICILY

SICILY

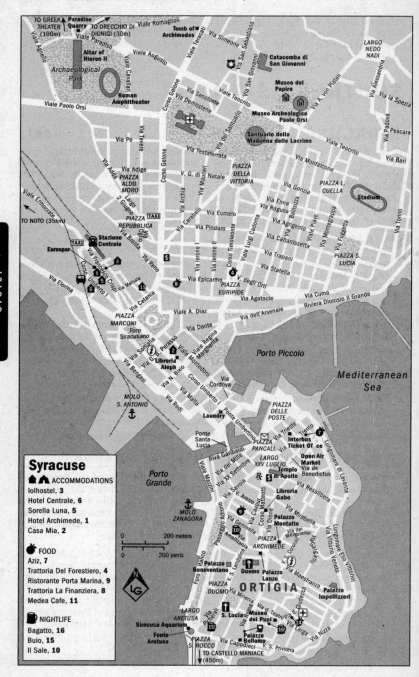

Syracuse

🏠 🏕 ACCOMMODATIONS

lolhostel, 3
Hotel Centrale, 6
Sorella Luna, 5
Hotel Archimede, 1
Casa Mia, 2

🍎 FOOD

Aziz, 7
Trattoria Del Forestiero, 4
Ristorante Porta Marina, 9
Trattoria La Finanziera, 8
Medea Cafe, 11

🍷 NIGHTLIFE

Bagatto, 16
Buio, 15
Il Sale, 10

English-Language Bookstore and Internet Access: Libreria Gabo, C. Matteotti 38 (☎0931 66 255). Internet access €1.50 per 15min. Open M-F and Su 9am-1pm and 4-8:30pm, Sa 5-8:30pm. AmEx/MC/V.

Tours: Ortigia Passengers, V. dei Mille (☎368 31 70 711; www.ortigiatour.com). Captain Emanuele and his fearless crew sail to the sea caves and along Ortigia's coast, providing passengers plenty of photo ops and a truly memorable experience. Every hr. from 9am-8pm. €10 per person, €40 minimum. Cash only.

Laundry: Lavenderia ad Acqua, C. Umberto I 13, near the bridge to Ortigia. Wash €3.50, dry €1 per 6min. Detergent €1. Open M-Sa 8:30am-8pm.

Police: ☎0931 49 51 11. **Carabinieri:** ☎0931 44 13 44.

Pharmacy: Mangiafico Farmacia, C. Matteotti 53 (☎0931 65 643). Open M-Sa 8:30am-1pm and 4:30-8pm. After-hours rotations posted outside. AmEx/MC/V.

Hospital: Ospedale Generale Provinciale, V. Testaferrata (☎0931 68 555), off C. Gelone. **Guardia Medica,** V. della Giudecca (☎0931 48 46 39). Open daily 8am-8pm.

Post Office: P. delle Poste 15, on Ortigia. Turn left crossing the bridge. Currency exchange available. Open M-F 8:15am-6:30pm, Sa 8am-12:30pm. **Postal Code:** 96100.

> **TIP**
>
> **OLD TIME TOURS.** Ask at the APT tourist office about the Val di Noto train tour (€25), an all-day tour of southeastern Sicily with guided stops in either Noto and Modica or Ragusa and Scicli to admire the history, regional cuisine, and Baroque architecture from a historical steam locomotive.

ACCOMMODATIONS

Many budget accommodations have staked out the area between the station and the bridge to Ortigia. While the price is often right, quality is very uneven. Don't be fooled by big signs and a lot of flyers. This area is somewhat run down, and at night, visitors should stick to the well-lit thoroughfares. Ortigia's options are more expensive, but generally of higher quality.

 lolhostel, V. Francesco Crispi 94 (☎0931 46 50 88; www.lolhostel.com). Opened in June 2007, this conveniently located hostel is becoming a true Syracusan legend. ROFL LOLZ! Rooms have A/C. Communal kitchen—I can haz cheezeburger? English spoken. Internet. Free Wi-Fi. Dorms €18-20; singles €35-40; doubles €60-64. Cash only. ❶

Piccolo Hotel B&B "Casa Mia," C. Umberto I 112 (☎0931 46 33 49; www.bbcasamia. it). Former palace in the middle of Syracuse's *centro storico*. Rooms have A/C, bath, TV, and phone. Breakfast included. Free Internet access and bike rentals for guests. Singles €40-50; doubles €60-80; triples €75-90; quads €80-100. AmEx/MC/V. ❸

Sorella Luna, V. Francesco Crispi 23 (☎0931 21 178; www.sorellalunasrl.it). Former convent with exposed-beam ceilings. 12 rooms have phone, A/C, bath, wet bar with minifridge, and TV. Breakfast included. Free Wi-Fi. Singles €45-55; doubles €70-90; triples €85-110; quads €100-125. Extra bed €20. AmEx/MC/V. ❹

Hotel Archimede, V. Francesco Crispi 67 (☎0931 46 20 40; www.archimedehotels. com). Theatrical theme. 14 spacious rooms with A/C, TV, bath, and locker. Continental breakfast included. Wheelchair-accessible. Singles €35-55; doubles €50-85; triples €75-100; quads €100-130. AmEx/MC/V. ❸

Hotel Centrale, C. Umberto I 141 (☎0931 60 528; www.hotelcentralesr.com), near the train station. Recently renovated, modern rooms; some with sea views (€5 extra). Rooms have bath, TV, and A/C. Breakfast included. Wi-Fi in the lobby. Singles €45-60; doubles €70-80; triples €90-110. AmEx/MC/V. ❹

◘ FOOD

Though hotel prices run fairly high, restaurants in Syracuse are affordable. On the mainland, the area around the station and the Archaeological Park offers some of the best deals. Ortigia has an **open-air market** on V. Trento, off P. Pancali, as well as several budget options on V. Savoia and V. Cavour. There is a **Eurospar supermarket** at C. Umberto I 174 (☎0931 44 20 874), just beyond the bus station. (Open M-Sa 8:30am-8:30pm, Su 8:30am-1pm. AmEx/MC/V.)

■ **Ristorante Porta Marina,** V. dei Candelai 35 (☎0931 22 553), off V. Cavour. Elegant and affordable. Great selection of seafood in a sleek modern space. The brave start with the *carpaccio polipo* (octopus salad; €8), and then move to the chef's special *risotto alla marinara* (squid, shrimp, shellfish, and tomatoes; €9). Antipasti €6.50-10. Primi €7-16. Secondi €8-18. Open Tu-Su 12:30-3pm and 8-11:30pm. AmEx/MC/V. ❸

■ **Trattoria Del Forestiero,** C. Timoleonte 2 (☎335 84 30 736), on the mainland, 10min. from Ortigia. A lively favorite. Try swordfish in marinara sauce (€6). 22 styles of pizza from €2.50-4.50 (dinner only). Primi €3.50-6. Secondi €4.50-7. Cover €1.10. Takeout available. Open M and W-Su 12:30-4:20pm and 7-11pm. Cash only. ❷

Medea Cafe, C. Gelone 136/138 (☎0931 74 30 892). The perfect spot to grab a quick, filling meal before exploring nearby sights. Breakfast pastries €1. Primi €3.50. Secondi €3.50-4.50. Open M-Sa 6:30am-11pm. Cash only. ❶

Trattoria La Finanziera, V. Epicarmo 41 (☎0931 46 31 17). Self-proclaimed "Seafood Specialists". Experience authentic local cuisine with the *fettucine alla siracusana* (€9). Primi €7-15. Secondi €8-15. Extensive wine list €8-15. Generous tourist discount with passport. Open M-Sa 9:30am-4pm and 6pm-midnight. MC/V. ❸

Aziz, V. Trento 10 (☎349 59 78 909), off of C. Umberto I right before the Temple of Apollo. A great late-night local hangout with outdoor seating and an upstairs dining room complete with pillows and hookah (€5). Kebabs €3.50. Couscous €7-13. Open Tu-Su noon-3pm and 8:30pm-midnight. Cash only. ❷

◎ SIGHTS

MAINLAND SYRACUSE

■**ARCHAEOLOGICAL PARK.** Three centuries as a strategic city on the Mediterranean left Syracuse with a collection of colossal Greek and Roman monuments. Two theaters, an ancient quarry, and the remains of the world's largest altar share a fenced compound, viewable with a single ticket. The view from the **Greek Theater,** carved into the hillside in 475 BC, competed with the actors for the audience's attention. If the 16,000 spectators watching Aeschylus's original production of *The Persians* got bored, they could look out over the impressive landscape. Greek inscriptions line the walls along the mid-level aisles, and the track for the *deus ex machina*, a large crane that made the gods "fly," is still in place. The **Paradise Quarry** next to the theater derives its name from the gardens that line the base of the chalky cliffs. These quarries provided most of the gray stone that built old Syracuse. Two large caves, the **Orecchio di Dionisio** (Ear of Dionysius) and the **Grotta dei Cordari** (Ropemakers' Cave), were cut in the walls. The latter is closed to the public for safety, but visitors can still hear the famous echoes that ricochet off the Orecchio di Dionisio's walls. Legend claims tyrannical Dionysius held political prisoners here so he could eavesdrop on their conversations. *(Open daily from 9am-6pm. Included in park entrance.)* Outside this area lies the **Ara di Ierone II** (the altar of Hieron II, 241-215 BC). Once used for public sacrifices to Zeus Eleuterio, the altar was torn down in the 16th century by the

Spanish, who used the stone to build the walls of Ortigia. The enormous steps of the altar's base are still intact. Up the hill is an AD third-century Roman **amphitheater.** *(Take C. Gelone to Vle. Teocrito. Park entrance down V. Augusto to the left; follow signs. Walk through the gauntlet of souvenir stands to reach the ticket office. Info ☎ 0931 65 068. Park and ticket office open daily in summer from 9am-6pm; in winter 9am-2pm. Theater open from July to early May. €8, EU residents 18-25 €3, EU residents under 18 or over 65 free.)*

CATACOMBA DI SAN GIOVANNI. Dating from AD 315-360, this subterranean maze has over 20,000 tombs carved into the walls of what used to be a Greek aqueduct. No corpses linger—only ghostly frescoes, an occasional sarcophagus, and a few wall carvings. The adjoining crypt of San Marciano includes the basilica in which Paul the Apostle remained for three days as he preached the gospel throughout Syracuse. *(Across from the tourist office on V. San Giovanni, off Vle. Teocrito from C. Gelone. ☎ 0931 64 694; www.kairos-web.com. Open daily 9:30am-12:30pm and 2:30-5:30pm. Mandatory guided tours every 30min. €5, under 15 and over 65 €3. AmEx/MC/V.)*

DUOMO. The 18th-century exterior of the cathedral looks like the standard Baroque compilation of architectural styles, but the interior holds a secret. A fifth-century BC Temple of Athena first stood on the site, and rather than demolishing the pagan structure, architects incorporated it into their construction. Fluted columns line the interior, recalling the structure's Classical origins. Large, shiny letters proclaim this the **first Christian church** in the West. Legend has it that the temple became a church with the arrival of St. Paul. The first chapel on the right is dedicated to Santa Lucia, the light-bearer and Syracuse's patron saint. Catch a glimpse of her left arm in the elaborate glass reliquary. Hidden from view above the reliquary is a masterpiece of Sicilian silver work, a life-sized statue of Lucia that parades through the streets on her feast day (see **Entertainment,** p. 476). Lest people forget how she died, silversmiths thoughtfully included a dagger protruding from her throat, the punishment dealt the saint by the pagan government of AD 304. *(From P. Archimede, take V. Roma and turn right on V. Minerva. Open daily 8am-7pm. Modest dress required. Free.)*

SANTUARIO DELLA MADONNA DELLE LACRIME. For three days in 1953, a mass-produced statuette of the Madonna reputedly began to weep in the home of the Iannuso family. Since then the number of pilgrims to the site has grown so large that the commanding spire of the **Basilica Madonna delle Lacrime** was built in 1994 according to the plans of Frenchmen Michel Arnault and Pierre Parat. Whether you're a pilgrim or not, the impressive architecture is worth a visit. The **Museum of Lacrymation** and the **Museum of Liturgy** complement the basilica; timetables placed outside the sanctuary tell the statue's tale, from the first teardrop to Pope John Paul's inauguration and papal blessing of the Sanctuary in November 1994. *(On Vle. Teocrito, off V. del Santuario. ☎ 0931 21 446; www.madonnadellelacrime.it. Both museums open daily 9am-12:30pm and 4-6pm. Sanctuary open 8am-noon and 4-7pm; Museum of Lacrymation €1.60, Museum of Liturgy €1, both museums €2. Sanctuary free.)*

MUSEO ARCHEOLOGICO PAOLO ORSI. Named for Sicily's most famous archaeologist, this collection has over 18,000 objects from prehistory through ancient Greece and early Christianity (roughly from 40,000 BC to AD 600). From the introductory room at the museum's core, hallways branch into chronologically arranged galleries. Exquisite kouroi torsos, grimacing Gorgons, elegant vases, and pygmy-elephant skeletons rest in 9000 square meters of dimly lit galleries. *(Vle. Teocrito 66. ☎ 0931 46 40 22. Open Tu-Sa 9am-7pm, Su 9am-2pm. Last entry 1hr. before close. €6, EU residents 18-25 €3, EU residents under 18 and over 65 free.)*

MUSEO ARETUSEO DEI PUPI. The first museum in Italy devoted entirely to puppets focuses on the long, noble tradition of Sicilian puppetry. Visitors make their way through life-like marionettes in traditional Sicilian costume, armed wood soldiers in shining battle gear, and fantastic creatures. Knowledgeable guides offer tours through the museum, around the puppet construction laboratory, and behind the theater facade. An extensive library with books, videos, and audio related to puppetry is available for guests' perusal upon request. When motionless puppets get boring, the **Piccolo Teatro dei Pupi** puts on elaborate puppet shows of traditional Sicilian tales. *(Museum located at P. S. Giuseppe 33.* ☎ *0931 46 55 40; www.pupari.com. Open Mar.-Sept. M-Sa 10:30am-1pm and 4-7pm, Oct.-Dec. M-Sa 11am-1pm and 4-8pm. €2. Theater located at V. della Giudecca 17/19. Performances Jan. and Mar.-Dec. daily at 6:30, 7:30pm. Adults €7, under 18 €5.)*

AQUARIUM. Tucked between Fontana Aretusa and a shady park with a view of the sea, the Siracusa Aquarium is home to an international variety of marine life. Tanks are divided into two sections, the first with freshwater tropical fish and plants, such as those native to African lakes and the Amazon River. The second section houses a mix of the aqarium's strangest, most vibrantly-colored sea-invertebrates and fish. *(Located in Largo Aretusa, directly in front of the fountain.* ☎ *333 16 74 461; www.aquariumsr.it. Open daily 10am-8pm. Adults €4, children €3.)*

TEMPIO DI APOLLO. Standing proudly at the entrance to Ortigia since its construction by the Greeks in the sixth century BC, two intact columns and part of the southern wall of Apollo's Temple are still a sight to behold. Though it is Sicily's oldest Doric temple, it's main role today is to attract tourists to the outdoor markets in the surrounding streets. *(Follow Ponte Umbertino to Ortigia's entrance, walk through P. Pancali, and the temple is visible behind an iron fence from everywhere in Largo XXV Luglio. Oudoor markets begin to the left of the temple and extend nearly to the sea.)*

FONTANE BIANCHE. Like all Italians, *siracusani* fall prey in summer to ancestral instincts that lure them from the cities to beaches like the Fontane Bianche, which offers music on the weekends. *(Take bus #21 or 22. 30min., every 2-3hr., €1.)*

🎵 🎭 ENTERTAINMENT AND NIGHTLIFE

In May and June, the city stages **classical Greek drama** in its ancient amphitheaters. The APT office (see **Practical Information,** p. 471) has details. Tickets for **Istituto Nazionale del Dramma Antico** are available at the theater box office, in the Archaeological Park. (☎0931 48 72 48; www.indafondazione.org. Open M-F 10am-7pm.) During the **Festa di Santa Lucia,** December 13, men clad in green shoulder the silver statue of the city's patron saint in a 6hr. procession from the *duomo* to Santa Lucia al Sepolcro on the mainland.

Piazzetta San Rocco is a nightlife hot spot. The best bar here is the eclectic 🔲**Buio,** V. delle Vergini 16, where the elderly owner blares Tupac and other hip-hop favorites well into the night (☎348 58 54 695). **Il Sale,** hidden away in the courtyard of an old building off V. Amalfitania, hosts live bands and revelers well past 3am (☎339 15 77 381). **Bagatto,** in the small P. S. Giuseppe, often features free, live music and is popular amongst locals for its prime location (☎0931 22 040; show schedule available at www.bagattoilpub.it).

AGRIGENTO ☎0922

Agrigento (AH-gree-JEN-toh; pop. 52,000) is a peculiar mix of old and new, from stunningly intact Greek temples to Armani Emporiums, from winding medieval paths to the shiny Mercedes-Benz sedans that traverse them, and from family-run trattorie to the glittering McDonald's across the street. Home to the father of modern medicine, Empedocle, and Nobel Prize-winning author Luigi Pirandello, the city celebrates its roots year-round with traditional parades and

festivals. Visitors come explicitly for the Valle dei Templi, and end up staying longer to enjoy the beaches, warmth, and an evening gelato on Via Atenea.

TRANSPORTATION

Trains: The **train station** is in P. Marconi, below P. Aldo Moro. Ticket office open daily 6:30am-8pm. Trains go to **Catania** (3hr.; 12:20pm, 6:50pm; €9.80), via **Enna** (2hr., 4 per day 9am-5pm; €6.50), **Caltanissetta** (1hr. 20min.; 8:15am, 1:50pm; €5.10), and **Palermo** (2hr., 112 per day 4:40am-8:05pm, €6.90).

Buses: Just beyond P. V. Emanuele, buses depart from P. Roselli, where the ticket booth is located. Cuffaro, V. Balsamo 13 (☎0922 091 61 61 510; www.cuffaro.info), runs buses to **Palermo** (M-Sa 8 per day 5:15am-6:30pm, Su 8:15am, 4:30, 6:30pm; €7.50); info available at the bar in P. Roselli. SAIS Trasporti, V. Ragazzi del 99 (☎0922 59 59 33), runs buses to **Caltanissetta** (1hr., M-Sa 11 per day 4:45am-6:15pm, €4.60) and **Catania** (2hr., 12 per day, €11.20). Lumia (www.autolineelumia.it), runs buses to **Trapani** (M-Sa 6:30, 8:30am, 1:40pm; €10.50). Reduced service Su.

Public Transportation: Orange TUA buses depart from the train station. Find tickets (€0.90) valid 1hr. in the station. Buses #2 and 2/ run to the beach at **San Leone**; #1, 1/, 2, 2/, 3, and 3/ run to the **Valle dei Templi**; #1 runs to **Pirandello's house.**

Taxis: At train station, in P. Marconi (☎0922 26 670). A trip to the temples (p. 479) should run about €15 on the meter—just make sure it's running.

ORIENTATION AND PRACTICAL INFORMATION

Agrigento's **train station** is in **Piazza Marconi,** the main stop for all city buses. Walk up the stairs to find the town's lively park-like central square, **Piazza Aldo Moro.** From P. Aldo Moro, the posh **Via Atenea** leads to the *centro storico.* At the far side of P. Aldo Moro is **Piazza Vittorio Emanuele,** just beyond which is the **bus station.** The temples are a bus ride or a long walk away.

Tourist Office: AAPIT kiosk in the train station and **AAST** (☎0922 20 454), adjacent to P. Aldo Moro. English-speaking staff, maps, and brochures. AAST open M-Sa 8:30am-1pm and 3:30-7pm. AAPIT kiosk open daily in summer 9am-1pm and 3:30-7pm; in winter 9am-1pm. Another summer office is in **Valle dei Templi,** adjacent to parking lot. English spoken. Open daily 8:30am-1pm and 3pm-sunset.

English-Language Bookstore: Capalunga, V. Atenea 123 (☎0922 22 338; www.capalunga.com). Art shows, hip decor and a modest selection of English books. Curl up in an egg-shaped window seat overlooking the sea. Customers enjoy free Internet access. Open daily 9:30am-1pm and 6-10pm; July-Aug. closed M.

Carabinieri: P. Aldo Moro 2 (☎0922 59 63 22). **First Aid:** ☎0922 40 13 44.

Pharmacy: Farmacia Averna Antonio, V. Atenea 325 (☎0922 26 093) and **Farmacia Dr Patti,** V. Atenea 129 (☎0922 20 591). Both open M-F 9am-1:30pm and 5-8:30pm. Both also post late-night and weekend rotations.

Hospital: Ospedale Civile (☎0922 44 21 11), 6km from town center toward Palermo on Contrada Consolida, off V. San Michele. Take bus #4 from P. Rosselli.

Internet Access: A.M. Servizi Internet Train, Cortile Contarini 7 (☎0922 40 27 83; www.internettrain.it). 1 block before Chiesa del Purgatorio, make a right onto V. Atenea from P. Aldo Moro. 15 high-speed computers. Wi-Fi and Internet access €3.20 per hr. Open M-Sa 9:15am-1:15pm and 3:30-9pm.

Post Office: P. V. Emanuele (☎0922 59 51 50; fax 0922 22 926). Open M-Sa 8am-6:30pm. **Postal Code:** 92100.

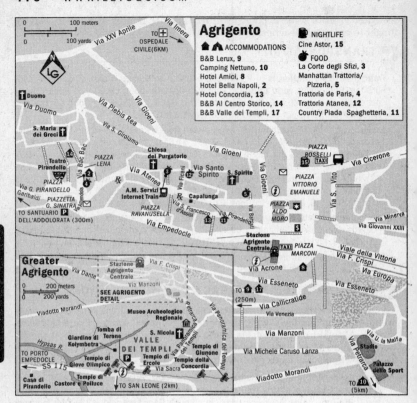

Agrigento

ACCOMMODATIONS

B&B Lerux, **9**
Camping Nettuno, **10**
Hotel Amici, **8**
Hotel Bella Napoli, **2**
Hotel Concordia, **13**
B&B Al Centro Storico, **14**
B&B Valle dei Templi, **17**

NIGHTLIFE
Cine Astor, **15**

FOOD
La Corte degli Sfizi, **3**
Manhattan Trattoria/
  Pizzeria, **5**
Trattoria de Paris, **4**
Trattoria Atenea, **12**
Country Piada Spaghetteria, **11**

ACCOMMODATIONS

Bed and Breakfast Valle dei Templi, V. Callicratide 164, 5th fl. (☎0922 27 912 or 0922 340 54 59 400). 5 brightly decorated rooms come with desks, dressers, TV, and comfortable beds. Shared kitchen with all the necessities, plus 3 large bathrooms in the hallway. 2 rooms come with A/C, and the others with fans. Free Internet access on the 4th fl. Homemade breakfast included. €20-25 per person. Cash only. ❶

Hotel Concordia, P. S. Francesco 11 (☎0922 59 62 66; www.albergo-concordia.it). Ideal location off V. Atenea and near P. Aldo Moro. 30 cozy, clean rooms with comfortable beds and large windows. All with large private bath, phone, TV, and A/C. Breakfast included. Singles €30; doubles €60; triples €75. MC/V. ❷

Bed and Breakfast Al Centro Storico, V. Saponara 19 (☎0922 59 60 57), off P. Lena in the historic center. 3 elegantly furnished rooms come with A/C, satellite TV, large private bath, and free Wi-Fi. Enormous breakfast included. Doubles €60-70; triples €80-90. Reservations recommended. Cash only. ❷

Hotel Bella Napoli, P. Lena 6 (☎/fax 0922 20 435; hotelbellanapoli@tin.it), off V. Bac Bac. Take V. Atenea 500m uphill, and turn right at the sign for Trattoria de Paris. Cheerful, yellow hallways lead to bright rooms with bath, A/C, phone and TV; some with balcony. Breakfast €3. Singles €35; doubles €65; triples €85. AmEx/MC/V. ❸

Bed and Breakfast Lerux, V. Callicratide 164 (☎0922 27 203 or 0922 333 20 59 606). A 5min. walk from the train station down V. Acrone. Cheap apartment rooms in the residential district. Shared bath and communal TV room. Laundry €3. Reservations recommended. Singles €20-25; doubles €40-48; triples €60-75. Cash only. ❷

Hotel Amici, V. Acrone 5 (☎0922 40 28 31; www.hotelamici.com). Down the stairs and next to the bingo parlor in P. Marconi. Offers 20 quiet rooms with bath, TV, and A/C; some with balcony and sea views. Parking and breakfast included. Singles €40-50; doubles €65-80; triples €75-90; quads €90-120. MC/V. ❹

Camping Nettuno, (☎0922 41 62 68), on the beach at V. l'Acquameno, by the bus stop. Take bus #2 or 2/ from the train station. Market, restaurant, bar, and pizzeria on premises. Free showers. €6 per person; €6 per tent; €3 per car. Cash only. ❶

◧ FOOD

Alimentari cluster near P. Aldo Moro, while the small stairways tucked off V. Atenea lead to authentic, inexpensive trattorie. Indulge your sweet tooth at the candy stalls along V. della Vittoria. The *Sette Soli*, a smooth local wine, provides a nice complement to most meals.

▨ **Trattoria Atenea,** V. Ficani 12 (☎0922 20 247), off V. Atenea. This famed family favorite serves up typical Sicilian specialties like *pasta con sarde* (€3.50) and *risotto alla marinara* (€3.50). Hungry patrons can fill up with the *pranzo della casa* (homemade lunch; €14.50), an enormous meal of the house *cavatelli* and grilled seafood, with salad and a choice of white or red wine. Primi €3.50. Secondi €5.50-7.50. Dessert €3. Open M-Sa noon-3pm and 6pm-midnight. Cash only. ❷

▨ **Trattoria de Paris,** P. Lena 7 (☎0922 25 413), beside Hotel Bella Napoli. Supplies locals with fresh pasta at a deliciously low price. Try the *cavatelli al cartoccio* (homemade pasta with eggplant, basil, ricotta cheese, and tomato sauce; €5), or the *scaloppine al vino bianco* (€6). Primi €5.50. Secondi €6-8. Service 15%. Open M-Sa noon-3pm and 7:30-10:30pm. AmEx/MC/V. ❷

▨ **Manhattan Trattoria/Pizzeria,** Salita degli Angeli 9 (☎0922 20 911), off V. Atenea. Sit inside or outside on terraced steps and enjoy regional specialties like *gnocchi al gorgonzola e pistacchio* (€6). The chef's specialty ravioli and tortellini options are excellent (€7-8). Antipasto buffet €6. Dinner pizza from €4-7. Primi €5-8. Secondi €6-15. Dessert €1-4. Cover €1.50. Open M-Sa noon-3pm and 7-11pm. AmEx/MC/V. ❷

Country Piada Spaghetteria, V. Pirandello 21 (☎0922 40 28 59). A little piece of the Wild West right in the heart of Agrigento, Country Piada cooks are quick to draw *panini* (€2.60-3) with fun names like Billy the Kid (€2.60) and Smoking Pistol (€3). Full *panino* or *piadina* plates with drinks and *contorno* (€5.50-6). Antipasti €4.50-5. Primi €4-7. Secondi €6. Open Tu-Su 1-3pm and 8pm-midnight. Cash only. ❷

La Corte degli Sfizi, Cortile Contarini 4 (☎0922 349 57 92 922), off V. Atenea. Classic Sicilian dishes served in a lush bamboo-enclosed garden. Go for the house specialty *spaghetti finocchio e sarde* (€7.50), with some local *panelle* (€3) on the side. Pizza €4-8. Antipasti €3-8. Primi €5-8. Secondi €6-13. Dinner *menù* €18-20. Cover €2, pizzeria service 20%. Open M and W-Su 11am-3pm and 6:30pm-midnight. Cash only. ❷

◔ SIGHTS

▨**VALLE DEI TEMPLI.** Planted on a ridge below Agrigento's hilltop perch, the five temples revere the invincibility of Greek architecture. Having survived the ravages of time, earthquakes, vicious Punic Wars, and the rise of Christianity, the temples are official UNESCO World Heritage Sites. As sunlight transitions to moonlight, the temples cast eerie silhouettes across the countryside; after dark, they're illuminated by concealed lighting. From the ticket booth right off the road leading to Agrigento, an avenue heads uphill along the ridge, passing the **Tempio di Ercole.** You can climb among one row of solid, squat columns, which is all that remains of the earliest of the temples. Farther along, the perfectly intact pediment and columns of the **Tempio della Concordia** are the Valle's star attraction. Erected in the mid-fifth century BC from limestone, it owes its survival to its use by the Archbishop of Agrigento who, after kicking out the demons Eber and Ray, rededicated the temple to Saints Peter and Paul and transformed it into a Christian church. The road through the valley ends at the fifth-century BC **Tempio di Giunone.** During the ascent, hollows in the rock face to the left mark an early Christian burial site. Down the street lies the entrance to the eternally unfinished **Tempio di Giove Olimpico.** Had Carthaginian troops not interrupted its construction in 406 BC, it would have been one of the largest Greek temples ever built. The toppled partitioned columns and walls have challenged archaeologists for years, but the temple's most interesting sights are the gigantic telamones, 8m sculpted male figures meant to encircle the temple. One of these massive men has been reconstructed at the site. At the end of the path stand four columns of the long since destroyed **Tempio di Castore e Polluce,** also known as the Tempio dei Dioscuri, where sailors and athletes would offer sacrifice for good fortune in their endeavors.

The **Museo Archeologico Regionale,** uphill from the parking lot, has an enormous collection of red- and black-figure vases, terra-cotta votive figures, and funerary vessels from the area's necropolis, as well as a large collection of Paolo Orsi's Agrigento discoveries. Check out a upright telamon and a model projections of how a completed Tempio di Giove Olimpico might have looked. Signs in Italian and English explain each item's significance, and audio tours are offered in many languages (€5). The **Chiesa di San Nicola** near the museum displays the sarcophagus of Phaedra, one of the most impressive AD third-century works. *(30min. walk from the train station. Starting on V. F. Crispi, follow signs downhill and left at the lower intersection. Buses #1/, 2, 2/, 3, or 3/ run from the train station and stop in a dirt parking lot with a snack bar. Make sure to bring lots of water, sunscreen, light clothes, and good walking shoes. Visiting when the park opens or right before it closes is a good way to avoid heat and crowds. Agrigento KREA Touristic Service, ☎0922 26 191 or 0922 55 49 18; puntoKREA@libero.it, located at the ticket office, offers guided tours and helpful information in many languages. Temple ☎0922 390 92 22 64 36, Museum ☎0922 290 22 59 54 48. Lower temples open daily in summer 8:30am-7pm; in winter 8:30am-5pm. Upper temples open daily in summer 8:30am-7pm and 9pm-midnight; in winter 8:30am-7pm. Temples €8; museum €8; combined ticket €10; students 18-24 temples €5, museum 4; under 18 or over 65 free. Parking €2 for 3hr., motorcycle €1.50.)*

GIARDINO DELLA KOLYMBETRA. Originally used as a garden and irrigation basin by the Greeks in 500 BC, the Gardens at Kolymbetra, translated roughly as "the place of giving waters," was used continually as an orchard until the 20th century. Given over to the FAI (Italian Environmental Agency) in the 1990s, the garden is now restored to its formal quiet splendor. Take a break from temple-gazing and enjoy a quiet walk through the shade. *(In a valley next to the Tempio di Castore e Polluce; follow signs to the garden. ☎0922 335 12 29 042; www.fondoambiente.it. Open daily July-Sept. 10am-7pm; Apr.-June 10am-6pm; Oct.-Mar. 10am-5pm. €2.)*

CHIESA DI SANTA MARIA DEI GRECI. First constructed by the Normans in the 1100s and remodeled by the Byzantines in the 1300s, Santa Maria dei Greci's real attraction is not what's inside, but what's beneath. Below the pews and through its glass floors, visitors can see a fifth-century BC ancient Greek temple dedicated to Athena and recently excavated ruins of Agrigento's first

Christian church from the AD fifth century. The original Athenian sacrificial altar stands behind the Christian altar in the present church. Down below, pay special attention to the large hole in front of the temple's altar, where the entrance to a tunnel once led all the way to the Valle dei Templi. *(Follow the signs up the hill from V. Bac Bac, off V. Atenea. ☎ 0922 333 87 02 111. Open M-Sa 9am-1pm and 3-6pm, Su upon request. Modest dress requested. Donations requested.)*

CHIESA DEL PURGATORIO (SAN LORENZO). The legendary craftsman Serpotta employed all of his wizardry to make this church's stucco sculptures look like marble. The statues of the Virtues were intended to help parishioners avoid purgatory by reminding them of its unpleasantries. Church elders did a thorough job—it's pretty hard to ignore the reminders of eternal damnation: an abundance of skulls and crossbones adorn each confessional and countless eery depictions of roasted sinners pepper the walls. You may not want to come here unless you're certain you won't end up in a place like this. *(P. Purgatorio, off V. Atenea, in the centro storico. Open M-Sa 9:30am-7:30pm. €1.50.)*

TEATRO PIRANDELLO. Dedicated to Queen Margherita in 1880, the theater was renamed in honor of Agrigento's favorite son, playwright Luigi Pirandello, on the 10th anniversary of his death in 1946. After brief stints as a movie theater, the building now hosts a variety of plays in the winter months, including many works by Pirandello. There are no plays in the summer, but the 19th-century building designed by local architect Dioniso Sciascia is worth a peek. Look for the four names on the dome ceiling of ancient *agrigentini* famous for the arts. *(☎ 0922 59 02 22. Open M-F 8am-1pm, Tu and Th 3-6pm. Plays Nov.-May. Check the schedule posted at the theater or ask at the tourist office. €2.50, includes tour in English.)*

▨ ▣ FESTIVALS AND BEACHES

The hills surrounding the Valle dei Templi come alive with the sound of music every year on the first Sunday in February, when Agrigento hosts the **Almond Blossom Festival,** an international folk-dancing fest that draws eager visitors from around Italy and the globe. Dancing, music, and huge parades take over the city for a week as thousands journey from all over the world to join in the old-time fun. The **Settimana Pirandelliana,** a week-long outdoor festival of plays, operas, and ballets in P. Kaos, pays homage to the town's beloved son in late July and early August. Overlapping with the celebration of the city's patron saint, San Calogero. (Info ☎ 0922 23 561.) During summer months, some *agrigentini* abandon the town in search of the beach and nightlife at San Leone, 4km from Agrigento by bus #2. Just be careful not to tumble down the **Scala dei Turchi,** the beautiful natural steps that descend to Lido Rossello, another popular beach, after a night of carousing.

WESTERN SICILY

TRAPANI ☎ 0923

From the ancient rooftops and buildings adorned with exquisite tilework to the colorful fishing boats and massive ferries just below the horizon, Trapani (TRA-pa-nee; pop. 75,000) is every bit the crossroads between Europe and North Africa it has been for centuries. Reliable transportation and extensive lodgings make Trapani a good base for adventures to Marsala's monuments, Segesta's temple, the Egadi Islands' peaceful nature, Erice's medieval streets, San Vito Lo Capo's beaches, and the natural splendor of Riserva dello Zingaro.

⚏ TRANSPORTATION

Flights: Vincenzo Florio Airport (☎0923 84 25 02), in Birgi en route to Marsala, 16km outside of Trapani. Buses run from P. Malta. Serves **Rome** and **Pantelleria** daily.

Trains: (☎0923 89 20 21), in P. Umberto I. Ticket office open daily 6am-7:45pm. To: **Castelvetrano** (1hr., 10 per day 6:42am-6:40pm, €4.60); **Marsala** (30min., 16 per day 6:42am-9:25pm, €3); **Palermo** (2hr., 11 per day 6am-8pm, €6.90).

Buses: AST, P. Malta (☎0923 23 222) runs to: **Erice** (45min.; M-Sa 8 per day 6:40am-8pm, Su 4 per day 9am-5:30pm; €2.10), **Marsala** (M-Sa 6:50am, 12:50, and 2:10pm; €2.75), and **San Vito Lo Capo** (1hr.; M-Sa 8 per day 6:45am-8pm, Su 4 per day 7:50am-6:45pm; €3.50). **Segesta** (☎0923 21 754) runs to **Rome** (15hr.; Th and Su 5pm, Sa 6am; €49).

DESTINATION	COMPANY	DURATION	FREQUENCY	PRICE
Favignana (Egadi Islands)	Siremar (ferry)	1hr.	3 per day	€3.90
Favignana (E.I.)	Ustica (hydrofoil)	30min.	9 per day	€9.80
Favignana (E.I.)	Siremar (hydrofoil)	30min.	10 per day	€9.80
Levanzo (E.I.)	Siremar (ferry)	1hr.	3 per day	€3.90
Levanzo (E.I.)	Siremar (hydrofoil)	30min.	10 per day	€9.80
Levanzo (E.I.)	Ustica (hydrofoil)	30min.	9 per day	€9.80
Marettimo (E.I.)	Siremar (ferry)	3hr.	1 per day	€8.40
Marettimo (E.I.)	Siremar (hydrofoil)	50min.	3 per day	€18
Marettimo (E.I.)	Ustica (hydrofoil)	50min.	2 per day	€18
Pantelleria	Siremar (ferry)	5hr.	M-F and Su 1 per day	€30
Cagliari (Sardinia)	Tirrenia (ferry)	11hr.	Tu 1 per day	€45
Tunis, Tunisia	Tirrenia (ferry)	8hr.	M, W, F 1 per day	€50
Tunis, Tunisia	Ustica (ferry)	8hr.	M, W, F 1 per day	€44

Ferries: Ferries and hydrofoils to the **Egadi Islands** (Levanzo, Favignana, and Marettimo), **Pantelleria, Sardinia,** and **Tunisia.** Ferries depart Stazione Marittima across from P. Garibaldi; hydrofoils depart farther along V. Ammiraglio Staiti, 150m toward the train station. Buy tickets from travel agents along V. A. Staiti, from ticket booths on the docks, and at Stazione Marittima. The chart above shows high-season (June-Aug.) times and rates; ferries and hydrofoils are less frequent and less expensive in low season.

Ustica: (☎0923 22 200; www.usticalines.it), in a yellow booth at the hydrofoil dock. AmEx/MC/V.

Siremar: (☎0923 54 54 55; www.siremar.it). Ticket offices at a blue-and-white striped waterfront booth, at the hydrofoil dock, and in Stazione Marittima. Open M-F 6:15am-noon, 3-6pm, and 9pm-midnight; Sa 6:15am-noon, 4:15-5:15pm, and 9:30pm-midnight; Su 6-10am, 5-5:45pm, and 9:30pm-midnight. AmEx/MC/V.

Tirrenia: (☎092354 54 33; www.tirrenia.it), in Stazione Marittima. Open M and W-F 9am-1pm and 3-6pm, Tu 9am-1pm and 6-9pm, Sa 9am-noon. AmEx/MC/V.

Public Transportation: Orange **SAU buses** (☎0923 55 95 75). Main terminal at P. Emanuele, 4 blocks from the train station. Tickets (€1) sold at most *tabaccherie.*

Taxis: in P. Umberto I (☎0923 22 808), outside the train station. Near the port in V. Ammiraglio Staiti (☎0923 23 233).

⚏ ⚏ ORIENTATION AND PRACTICAL INFORMATION

Trapani is on a peninsula 2hr. west of Palermo. The *centro storico* begins at the outer tip of the hook, grows backward from the peninsula, and spills new streets and high-rises onto the mainland. The train station is in **Piazza Umberto I;** the bus station is behind and to the left in **Piazza Malta. Via Scontrino** runs past the train station; a right from the station leads to an intersection with **Via Garibaldi** at **Piazza Emanuele**. V. Garibaldi becomes **Via Libertà** on its way into the *centro storico*. **Via Torrearsa** is off V. Libertà. **Via Roma**, also off V. Libertà, leads to the port. V. Libertà merges with **Corso Vittorio Emanuele**, which runs to **Torre di Ligny**.

Tourist Offices: AAPIT (☎0923 29 000; www.apt.trapani.it), off V. Torrearsa. Eager staff. Pick up *Trapani Hotels* for regional accommodations listings. Open M-Sa 8:30am-8pm, Su 9am-noon. **Provincial Tourism Office**, V. San Francesco d'Assisi 27 (☎092354 55 11; www.apt.trapani.it), off V. Verdi. Marked "APT" on maps. Open M-Tu and Th-Sa 8am-1pm, W 8am-1pm and 3-6pm.

Currency Exchange: Banks line many of the city's streets. They generally have better rates than the train station. **ATMs** are at Stazione Marittima in the old city and along V. Scontrino in front of the train station.

Emergency: Police, P. Vittorio Veneto (☎0923 59 02 98). **Carabinieri**, V. Orlandini 19 (☎0923 27 122). **Ambulance:** (☎0923 18 09 450).

Pharmacy: Vle. Margherita 9, next to P. V. Veneto. All pharmacies open M-F 9am-1:30pm and 4:30-8pm. Posts after-hours rotation.

Hospital: Ospedale Sant'Antonio Abate, V. Cosenza 81 (☎0923 80 91 11).

Internet Access: Phone and Internet, V. Regina Elena 26/28 (☎0923 28 866; www. trapaniservice.it), next to P. Garibaldi along the *lungomare*. €5 per hr. International phone services and fax. Open M-Sa 10am-1pm and 4-8:30pm.

Post Office: P. V. Veneto 3 (☎0923 43 41 11), in P. V. Veneto on V. Garibaldi. Currency exchange available. Open M-Sa 8am-6pm. **Postal Code:** 91100.

> **TIP** **KA-CHING!** Before exchanging money, always ask about the commission, which can be as high as €10. No Italian law requires financial institutions to inform clients of exchange fees before finalizing transactions.

ACCOMMODATIONS

▨ **Hotel Moderno,** V. Genovese 20 (☎0923 21 247; hotelmodernotrapani@virgilio.it). From P. Sant'Agostino on C. Vittorio Emanuele, turn right on V. Roma and left on V. Genovese. Accommodating staff and modern, well-kept rooms, all with TV and bath. Reception 24hr. Singles €25; doubles €50; triples €67. AmEx/MC/V. ❷

Albergo Messina, C. V. Emanuele 71, 4th fl. (☎/fax 0923 21 198). Tiny family-run hotel in the *centro storico*. All rooms have balcony and fridge. Shared bath. Breakfast €4. Free Internet access. Singles €20; doubles €40. AmEx/MC/V. ❷

Albergo Maccotta, V. degli Argentieri 4 (☎0923 28 418; fax 0923 43 76 93; www.albergomaccotta.it), near P. S. Agostino. Centrally located. Rooms have private bath, phone, TV, desk, and A/C. Free Wi-Fi. Singles €35-40; doubles €60-75. AmEx/MC/V. ❸

Hotel Vittoria, V. Francesco Crispi 4 (☎0923 87 30 44; www.hotelvittoriatrapani.it), off P. V. Emanuele, near train station. Large, luxurious rooms offer modern comforts, including A/C, free Wi-Fi, and, for some, coastal views. Inviting communal area in the lobby. Breakfast included. Singles €65; doubles €100; triples €130. AmEx/MC/V. ❹

FOOD

Trapani's cuisine is an exotic blend of North African and Italian flavors. Try the specialty couscous with fish or *biscotti con fichi* (moist, fig-filled cookies). The *centro storico* has *alimentari* and a daily **market** at the intersection of V. Maggio and V. Garibaldi. **Supermercato DìperDì**, V. San Pietro 30, is two blocks up from the port between Chiesa Santa Maria del Gesù and Chisa San Pietro. (☎0923 24 620. Open M-Sa 7:30am-1:30pm and 4:30-8:30pm, Su 8:30am-1pm.)

🔲 **Trattoria da Salvatore,** V. Nunzio Nasi 19 (☎0923 54 65 30), 1 block toward the port from C. V. Emanuele. Serves regional pasta (€6.50) and spicy couscous (€8.50) family-style. Primi €4-8.50. Secondi €7-8.50. Cover €1.50. Open daily noon-3:30pm and 6-11pm; closed Su in winter. AmEx/MC/V. ❷

Ristorante Medina, Vle. Regina Margherita 19 (☎0923 29 028), across from the main gate to Villa Margherita. Popular teen hangout. Middle Eastern cuisine and pizza. Pizza from €1.50. Kebabs €3.50. *Panini* €3.50. Open daily noon-3pm and 7pm-midnight. ❶

Cantina Siciliana, V. Giudecca 32 (☎0923 28 673; www.cantinasiciliana.it), 1st left off V. XXX Gennaio from the port. *Trapanese* cuisine. Antipasti €5-10. Primi €6-10. Secondi €9-13. Contorni €3. Dessert €3. Open daily 12:30-4pm and 7:30-11pm. MC/V. ❸

Trattoria Al Solito Posto, V. Orlandini 30 (☎0923 24 545), 3 blocks east from Hotel Vittoria. Renowned for its authentic Trapanese fare, like the *tonno alla Trapanese* (Trapanese tuna; €12). Lavish seaside dining room. Antipasti €3-10. Primi €5-6.50. Secondi €9-14. Contorni €1.50-4.50. Open daily 1-4pm and 8-10pm. AmEx/MC/V. ❸

👁 SIGHTS

CHIESA DEL PURGATORIO. Delicate stone statues blend into the gray exterior of this Baroque church. Inside, 20 nearly life-sized wooden sculptures, known as *i misteri* ("the mysteries"), depict the Passion and the Crucifixion. On Good Friday, the sculptures, each requiring the strength of 14-30 men to move, are dressed up and paraded. The sculptures' 18th-century artists constructed the Roman soldiers to resemble Spanish conquistadors, reflecting Spanish domi-nance in Sicily at the time. Several statues were damaged in WWII but have since been restored. *(1 block from P. Garibaldi. Open daily 9am-noon and 3:30-6pm. Free.)*

SANTUARIO DELL'ANNUNZIATA. The modern city's main attraction is this enor-mous, lavishly decorated church, which houses a 14th-century statue of the Madonna of Trapani. Legend has it that a boat carrying the statue was caught in a storm; the captain promised God that if he survived, he would leave it as a gift to the first port at which he arrived. The **Museo Regionale Pepoli,** which features a collection of local sculpture and painting, coral carvings, and folk-art figurines, is in the same complex. *(2 blocks to the right of the train station or a #24, 25, or 30 SAU bus ride from P.V. Emanuele. Sanctuario ☎0923 53 91 84; museum ☎0923 55 32 69 or 0923 53 12 42. Santuario open M-Sa 8am-noon and 4-7pm, Su 8am-1pm and 4-7pm; museum open Tu-Sa 9am-1:30pm, Su 9am-12:30pm. €4, ages 18-25 €2, EU residents under 18 or over 65 free.)*

TORRE DI LIGNY. At the end of a wide jetty off a promontory, this tower is vis-ible from both of Trapani's ports. By day, the rock walls seem like outcroppings of the rocky surf, as the identically colored brick fortress rises over boulders. By night, the bright lights of the northern coastline reflect off the water. Locals young and old convene on the beaches to either side of the tower to swim and sunbathe from dawn to dusk. The tower houses the **Museo di Preistoria/Museo del Mare,** with shells, artifacts, and underwater excavation pieces. *(☎0923 28 844 or 347 29 60 043. Open M-Sa 9:30am-noon, Su 10:30am-12:30pm. €1.70.)*

VILLA MARGHERITA. At the cusp of the old and new cities, these gardens offer a change of pace from cobblestone and cement. Banyan trees, palms, stat-ues, and fountains surround avenues. Playgrounds and an aviary complete the serene environment. *(Park open July-Aug. 8am-10pm; Apr.-June and Sept.-Oct. 8am-8pm; Jan.-Mar. and Nov.-Dec. 8am-5pm. Free.)*

🔛 DAYTRIPS FROM TRAPANI

SAN VITO LO CAPO

AST buses leave Trapani's P. Malta for San Vito Lo Capo (9 per day 6:45am-8pm, return 8 per day 6:45am-7:40pm; €3.50, round-trip €5.55). AST info ☎ 0923 23 222.

A popular vacation spot for Italians, Germans, and Spaniards, San Vito Lo Capo (sahn vee-TOH lo CAH-poh; pop. 3900) has remained under the radar of the English-speaking world. While sun worshippers flock to San Vito's 3km of flawless beaches in July and August, the annual **Couscous Fest,** held during the third week of September, is the Olympics of multi-ethnic Mediterranean cuisine. For shade and seclusion, escape to the 🖼**Riserva dello Zingaro,** Italy's first nature reserve, to find rare Bonelli's eagles, mountain trails, and prehistoric caves. An unfinished four-lane highway came perilously close to marring the pristine reserve's isolation, but a 1981 environmental rally halted construction. Once in the reserve, follow the road to secluded, pebble beaches that stretch along the coast. The middle two beaches offer the most privacy. Although camping and cars are prohibited on the shore, the hiking is superb. **Bluvacanze,** V. Savoia 166, runs excursions (M-F 9am, return 4pm; €10) and rents **scooters, bikes,** and **cars.** (☎ 0923 62 10 85; www.bluvacanze.net. Bikes €5 per day. Scooters €30-35 per day. Cars €42-54 per day. Office open daily 9:30am-1pm and 4-7:30pm. Cash only.) **Nautisub Diving Center,** V. Faro 24, offers guided diving and snorkling near the Riserva dello Zingaro for groups and individuals. (☎ 348 29 40 610 or 328 81 80 748; www.nautisub.it.) For a **taxi,** call ☎ 328 56 26 098.

Five minutes from the beach, **Eden Camere ②,** V. Mulino 58, provides clean, simply furnished rooms, all with private bath and A/C. Doubles often come with a full and a twin bed, or a full bed and two bunked twins. (☎ 0923 97 24 60. Open Apr.-Oct. Singles €25-35; doubles €45-80. Cash only.) **Hotel Sikania ③,** V. G. Arimondi 128, has colorful rooms near the water with A/C, TV, phone, and minibar. (☎ 0923 85 13 95; www.hotelsikania.com. €30-60 per person; €20-35 surcharge for singles.)

For a taste of authentic Sicilian and Tunisian cuisine, head to the elegant Arabic-tiled dining area of **Tha'am ③,** V. Duca degli Abbruzzi 32, off V. Farina near the waterfront. (Antipasti €7-9. Primi €9-15. Secondi €10-17. Contorni €4-5. Cover €2.50. Open daily 12:30-3pm and 7pm-3am. MC/V.) **U Sfizziusu ②,** V. Lungomare 19, offers dishes like *cuscus con pesce* (couscous with fish; €7.50) on an outdoor patio with great views. (☎ 348 04 23 967. Primi €7-10. Secondi €6-12. Contorni €3.50-5. Open 24hr. Cash only.)

SARDINIA
(SARDEGNA)

An old legend says that when God finished making the world, He had a handful of dirt left over, which He threw into the Mediterranean, stepped on, and—behold—created the island of Sardinia (in Italian, "Sar-DEN-ya"). Another myth claims that Sardinia is truly the land of Atlantis, covered by a tidal wave in the second millennium BC. However Sardinia came to be, control of the island has bounced back and forth between empires for centuries, rendering many of its current inhabitants wary of any type of foreign investment or exploitation. Shuffled between the Phoenicians and the Carthaginians, Sardinia got a slight break when the Romans made it an agricultural colony. But by the 13th century, it was again a theater for conflict among the Pisans, the Aragonese, the newly united Spanish, and the Piemontese. Until just decades ago, *padroni* (landlords) controlled the land, and farmers toiled under a system akin to serfdom. Though agriculture is still a significant economic staple, today the island proudly plays host to tourists that come in droves to bask in the perfection of its beaches and the glory of its mountain vistas and to indulge in its unique and delicious cuisine. The architecture, language, and food of Sardinia render it a cultural anomaly—hybrid of African, Italian, and Spanish influences. Though officially a part of Italy, Sardinia is classified as an autonomous region—an administrative manifestation of the island's strong sense of independence.

HIGHLIGHTS OF SARDINIA

RIDE bus #8 from Nuoro to the top of Monte Ortobene where a statue of Christ the Redeemer seems to leap from the summit (p. 504).

SAIL from Alghero's busy waterfront to the luminescent Grotte di Nettuno (p. 500).

TRANSPORTATION

FLIGHTS. **Alitalia** flights link Alghero, Cagliari, and Olbia to major Italian cities. Though flights are significantly faster than water travel, exorbitant fares discourage most would-be air passengers. Recently, Ryanair and EasyJet have begun to serve Sardinia's airports. **easyJet** (www.easyjet.com) flies from Olbia to Berlin, Bristol, Geneva, London, and Milan, and from Cagliari to Geneva, London, and Milan. **Ryanair** (www.ryanair.com) flies from Cagliari to Barcelona, Madrid, Milan, and Pisa; from Olbia to Birmingham; and from Alghero to Barcelona, Bremen, Dublin, Dusseldorf, East Midlands Frankfurt, Liverpool, London, Madrid, Milan, Pisa, Rome, and Stockholm.

FERRIES. The cheapest way to reach Sardinia is by ferry from **Civitavecchia, Genoa,** or **Livorno** to Olbia. Civitavecchia, the official port of Rome, is easily reached by train from Rome's Termini station (80min., €4.50). The **ticket offices** and ferry info centers are at the dock. Exit the train station and make a right, following the signs leading to the *centro* and the ferry terminal. Expect to pay

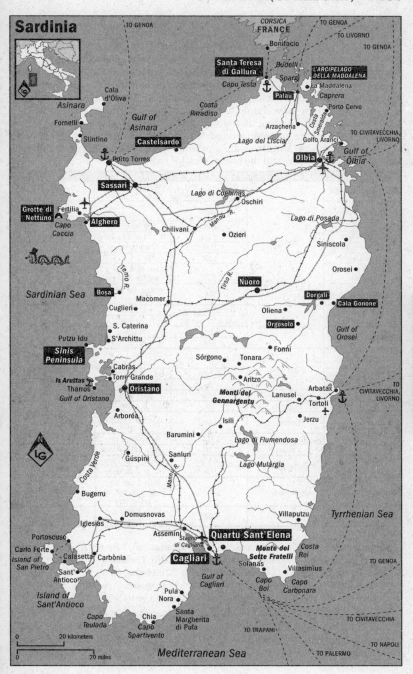

Sardinia

€23-75 each way, depending on the company, season, boat speed, and departure time (night trips, fast ferries, and summer ferries cost more). The cheapest fares are for daytime *posta ponte* (deck class) slots on slow-moving boats, but most ferry companies require that *poltrone* (reserved armchairs) be sold to capacity before they open *posta ponte*. Expect to pay €10-20 more for a *cabina* with a bed, plus €5-15 depending on the season, trip duration, and taxes. Travelers with vehicles, animals, or children should arrive 1hr. before departure; everyone else should arrive 45min. ahead. Transporting vehicles can cost €50-120, depending on the voyage length and the season. The ferry schedule below is for summer service. Winter ferries sell at lower prices and run overnight. Prices and times are extremely variable depending on time of day and the boat speed; call the companies for more info.

ROUTE	COMPANY	DURATION	FREQUENCY	PRICE
Civitavecchia-Olbia	Tirrenia	5-7hr.	M-F 8:30am and 11pm, Sa-Su 3pm	€22-33
Civitavecchia-Cagliari		12hr.	M-Th and Sa 8:30am	€29-43
		14hr.	F and Su 6:30pm	
Genoa-Olbia		13hr	M and W-Su 11pm	€23-50
Genoa-Porto Torres		10hr.	Daily 8:30pm	€30-68
Naples-Cagliari		15hr.	Th 7:15pm	€29-44
Fiumicino-Golfo Aranci		4hr.	M and W 8:30am, Tu and Th-Sa 9am	€32-63
Fiumicino-Arbatax		3hr.	In Aug. M and W 7pm	€38-63
Civitavecchia-Golfo Aranci	Sardinia Ferries	7hr. (C. Shuttle)	8:15am	€17-38
		4hr. (C. Express)	2:15pm	€40-55
Livorno-Golfo Aranci		8hr.	11pm	€24-48
		6hr.	8:15am	€29-55
Livorno-Olbia	Moby Lines	7-11hr.	Daily 8am, 9:30, and 11:30pm	€20-40
Civitavecchia-Olbia		4-10hr.	Daily 3 and 10pm	€20-54
Genoa-Olbia		9hr.	Daily 10pm	€20-59
Genoa-Porto Torres	Moby Lines	10hr	Daily 10pm	€20-59
Bonifacio-S.Teresa	Saremar	1hr.	Daily 8, 11am, 5pm	€8-10
Genoa-Palau	Enermar	11hr.	W and F 7pm	€58-72
			Su 9am	€47
Genoa-Olbia	Grandi Navi	9-10hr.	Daily, times vary	€31-38
Genoa-Porto Torres	Veloci	11hr.	Daily, 2-3 per day	€31-38
Genoa-Palau	Dimaio Lines	12-13hr.	M, W, F-Sa 7pm	€16-70
Salerno-Olbia		15hr.	M, W, F 6:30pm	€20-45
Piombino-Olbia	Linea dei Golfi	6hr.	Aug. 2 per day; Sept.-July days and times vary	€18-23
Civitavecchia-Olbia	SNAV	7-8hr.	Daily 11am and 10pm	€30-40

Tirrenia: (☎89 21 23; www.tirrenia.it). Offices: **Arbatax** (☎07 82 66 78 41); **Cagliari** (☎07 06 66 065); **Civitavecchia** (☎07 66 58 19 25); **Fiumicino** (☎06 65 21 670); **Genoa** (☎01 02 69 81); **Olbia** (☎07 89 20 71 02); **Livorno** (☎05 86 42 47 30), on Calata Addis Abeba-Varco Galvani; **Naples,** Rione Sirignano 2 (☎08 15 51 90 96); **Palermo** (☎09 16 02 11 11); **Porto Torres,** V. Mare 38 (☎07 95 18 10 11).

Sardinia Ferries: (☎19 94 00 500; www.sardiniaferries.com). Offices in: **Livorno** (☎05 86 88 13 80), at the Stazione Marittima; **Civitavecchia** (☎07 66 50 07 14), at Terminal Autostrade del Mare; **Golfo Aranci** (☎07 89 46 780), at the Stazione Marittima.

Moby Lines: (www.moby.it). Offices in: **Olbia** (☎07 89 27 927), Stazione Marittima; **Livorno**, V. Veneto 24 (☎058 68 99 950); **Genoa** (☎01 02 54 15 13), Terminal Traghetti. General help desk (☎19 93 03 040), in English (☎61 11 40 20).

Grandi Navi Veloci: (☎0102 09 45 91). Offices: **Civitavecchia** (☎0766 59 631); **Olbia** (☎0789 20 01 26); **Genoa** (☎0102 54 65); **Porto Torres** (☎0795 16 034).

SNAV: (www.snav.it). Offices in: **Civitavecchia**(☎07 66 36 63 66); **Olbia** (☎07 89 20 00 84); **Naples** (☎08 14 28 55 55).

TICKET FOR TOMORROW. If you buy your ferry ticket from Palau to Maddalena the day before, you can save 20% on **EneRmaR** tickets. So, if you arrive late in Palau and are planning on visiting La Maddalena the following day, be sure to buy your round-trip tickets for the day before.

CAGLIARI ☎070

Since the Phoenicians founded the ancient port town of Korales over two millennia ago, several great civilizations have competed for possession of what is now known as Cagliari (CAL-ya-ree; pop. 158,000), Sardinia's largest city and capital. In the 11th century, after defeating the Genoese, the Pisans built the fortified town of Castrum Kolaris, which became one of the most important artistic and cultural centers on the Mediterranean and was later renamed Cagliari. While the city maintains its rich history through its still-functioning Roman amphitheater, Cagliari also incorporates features of modern urban design like the Bastione di San Remy, which offers panoramic views of the port and surrounding territories. If you tire of the throbbing pulse of city life, a 20min. bus ride will transport you to the green water and beachside nightclubs of Il Poetto, one of the most frequented stretches of beach in Sardinia.

▐ TRANSPORTATION

Flights: In the village of Elmas. ARST buses run the 8km from the airport to the city terminal at P. Matteotti (30min., 32 per day 5:20am-10:30pm, €1).

Trains: (☎070 89 20 21), in P. Matteotti. Ticket office open daily 6:10am-8:45pm. 24hr. ticket machines. To: **Olbia** (4hr., 6:30pm, €14.60) via **Oristano** (1hr., 17 per day 5:33am-10:02pm, €5.15) or **Macomer; Porto Torres** (4hr., 2 per day, €14.60); **Sassari** (4hr., 4 per day 6:39am-4:38pm, €13.65). Other destinations include **San Gavino, Iglesias, Decimomannu,** and **Carbonia.**

EXTRA, EXTRA! Sardinia's daily newspaper, L'Unione Sarda, publishes a page titled "Agenda" which lists departure times and contact info for all bus, airplane, train, and ferry routes serving Cagliari, Alghero, Oristano, Olbia, Arbatax, Porto Torres, Palau, Nuoro, Lanusei, and Sassari. Available at any newsstand on the island.

Buses: 2 major bus companies serve Cagliari.

ARST, P. Matteotti 6 (☎070 40 98 324). Office open M-Sa 8-8:30am, 9am-2:15pm, and 5:30-7pm; Su 1:30-2:15pm and 5:30-7pm. Info in the front entrance area, ticket booth in the ARST station next to the McDonald's. When office is closed, buy tickets onboard. To **Bosa** (3hr., M-F 2 per day, €11:50), **Nuoro** (2hr., 3:30pm, €14.50), and **Oristano** (1hr., M-F 2 per day, €6.50). Also serves local towns, including the beaches of **Chia** (1hr.; 9 per day 6:30am-7:35pm, last return 8pm; round-trip €7), **Villasimius** (5 per day 5am-8:10pm, €3).

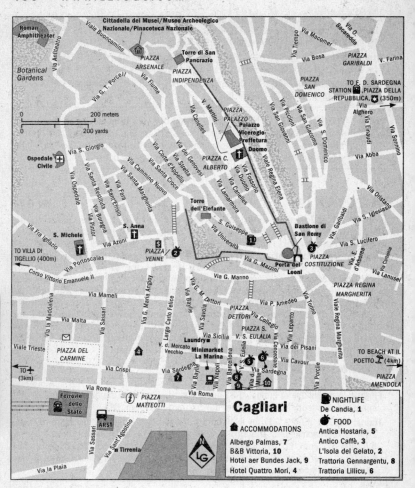

FMS (☎070 80 00 44 553; www.ferroviemeridionalisarde.it). Buses leave from ARST station or P. Matteotti. Buses run to smaller towns. To: **Calasetta, Sant'Antioco-San,** and **Giovanni Suergiu** (6 per day 1:43-7:50pm); **Giba** and **Nuxis Santadi** (4:14, 6:19, 6:38pm); and **Iglesias** (14 per day 5:50am-8:47pm). Buy tickets at newsstand across from Farmacia Spanno on V. Roma or at the ticket booth by McDonald's in the ARST station.

Ferries: Tirrenia (☎070 66 60 65). Buy tickets from red building 1 block behind the ARST station. Ticket office open M-F 8:30am-12:30pm and 3:30-6:50pm, Sa 8:30am-12:20pm and 3:30-6pm, Su 4-6pm. **Linea dei Golfi** (☎070 65 84 13), V. Sonnino. Open daily 8am-7pm. Ferries leave from Stazione Marrittima.

Local Buses: (☎070 20 911 or 20 91 200). Orange **CTM buses** run from P. Matteotti. Tickets sold in various *tabaccherie* and newsstands around P. Matteotti and V. Roma, and at the ticket office by the McDonalds in the ARST station. €1 per 1hr., €1.50 per

2hr., €2.30 per day. **Buses P, PQ,** and **PF** go to Il Poetto 5:20am-10:50pm, last return 11:25pm; in the summer, lines **3/P, 9/P, Yellow,** and **Arancio** run to Il Poetto. Pick up a map of the bus routes at the tourist office.

Taxis: Radiotaxi Quattro Mori (☎070 40 01 01), in front of the train station.

Car Rental: Auto Assistance, V. la Plaia 15 (☎070 68 48 874; www.autoassistance.it), in the garage beneath Iper Pan. 21+. Insurance included. Mountain bikes €10 per day; cars from €60 per day. Open M-F 9am-1pm and 4-7pm. AmEx/MC/V.

▓▓ ✷ ORIENTATION AND PRACTICAL INFORMATION

Via Roma greets new arrivals to Cagliari, with the **harbor** and **Stazione Marittima** on one side and outdoor cafes on the other. **Piazza Matteotti,** between V. Roma, **V. Sassari,** and **Largo Carlo Felice,** contains the **train station,** the **ARST station,** and the **tourist office.** Across from P. Matteotti, **Largo Carlo Felice** climbs the steep hill leading to **Piazza Yenne,** then ascends even farther to the *centro storico,* also known as the **Castello district.**

Tourist Office: (☎070 66 92 55), in P. Matteotti, across from the train stations. Info on local sights and lodgings. Open M-F 8:30am-1:30pm and 2-8pm, Sa-Su 8am-8pm; in winter hours vary. **EPT,** P. Deffenu 9 (☎070 60 42 41; enturismoco@tiscalinet.it). Open in summer M-Sa 9am-1pm and 5-8pm; in winter hours vary.

Currency Exchange: Banca di Roma, P. Yenne 5, at the corner of C. Vittorio Emanuele II. **ATM** outside. Open M-F 8:20am-4pm, Sa 8:30am-noon.

Luggage Storage: At ARST station. €1 per hr.

Laundry: Ghibli Lavanderia Self-Service, V. Sicilia 20 (☎070 56 55 21 or 349 43 31 129), off V. Baylle, near most budget accommodations. Wash €4 per 6kg, €7 per 16kg; dry €4 per 20min. Detergent €1. Open daily 8am-10pm; last wash 9pm.

Police: ☎070 40 40 40.

Hospital: Ospedale San Giovanni di Dio, V. Ospedale 54 (☎070 66 32 37), 5min. walk from Chiesa di San Michele. Open daily 8:30am-12:30pm. **Guardia medica:** V. Talente 6. Nights and weekends ☎070 50 29 31.

Internet: Hay Service, V. Napoli 8 (☎070 32 01 81 97 27), off V. Roma. 5 fast computers; fax, photocopy, and Western Union money transfer also available. €2 per 30min.; €3 per hr. Open M-F and Su 9am-1pm and 4-8pm.

Post Office: V. Carmine 27 (☎070 60 311). Take V. Sassari from P. Matteotti. *Fermoposta* available. Open M-F 8am-6:50pm, Sa 8am-1:15pm. **Postal Code:** 09100.

▟ ACCOMMODATIONS

Budget hotels and B&Bs dot the area just off V. Roma, between Lago Carlo Felice and Vle. Regina Margherita.

Hotel aer Bundes Jack, V. Roma 75 (☎/fax 070 66 79 70; hotel.aerbundesjack@libero. it). Run by the same couple as B&B Vittoria, this hotel's historic past has been documented in hand-written registers since 1938. 14 rooms with Venetian chandeliers, Victorian molding, phone, radio, and A/C. Private or shared bath available. Check-in on 2nd fl. Breakfast €7. Reservations recommended. Singles €48-58; doubles €70-88, with sea view €88; triples €114. *Let's Go* discount 10%. Cash only. ❹

B&B Vittoria, V. Roma 75, 2nd fl. (☎070 64 04 026 or 349 44 73 556). Airy, spacious rooms with antique decor, Murano glass chandeliers, clean bathrooms, A/C, and radio. Some rooms have TV. Be sure to sample the *Vernaccia,* a special, strong white wine produced by owner Luigi's family near Oristano, at the small bar in the breakfast room. Singles €48; doubles €78. *Let's Go* discount 10%. Cash only. ❹

Albergo Palmas, V. Sardegna 14 (☎070 65 16 79). 14 large no-frills rooms with sinks. Shared baths. Single €30; double €38, with shower €45; triples €60. MC/V. ●

⬛ FOOD

Many small shops sell fruit, cheese, and bread along V. Sardegna. Try **Mini Market La Marina,** V. Sardegna 43, which has a great bakery. (Open M-Sa 7am-1:30pm and 4:30-8:30pm. MC/V.) Find groceries at the ⬛**Iper Pan La Plaia** at V. la Plaia 15. (Open M-Sa 9am-9pm, Su 9am-2pm.) On Sunday mornings, there's a **market** on the far side of the stadium in Borgo Sant'Elia for fresh fruit and seafood.

⬛ **L'Isola del Gelato,** P. Yenne 35 (☎070 65 98 24). Friendly owner Giuseppe presides over this lively island-themed *gelateria* right in P. Yenne. A steady stream of customers flows over the artificial river running beneath the transparent floor. 50+ flavors, including low-fat options for those watching their beach figures. Cups from €1. *Granita* €2. Open Mar.-Nov. daily 9am-2am. Cash only. ●

⬛ **Trattoria Gennargentu,** V. Sardegna 60/c (☎070 65 82 47). After exploring the sights along V. Roma, join locals here for the seasonal spaghetti with sea urchin and dried mullet fish (€8) or zesty *salsiccia arrosta* (roasted sausage; €5). Primi €4.50-8. Secondi €5-15. Cover €1.60. Open M-Sa 12:30-3pm and 8-11pm. AmEx/MC/V. ❷

Antico Caffè, P. Costituzione 10/11 (☎070 65 82 06). Walls covered in photo collage of patrons who have come for over 150 years in search of appetizers and delicious desserts. Avoid service charge by ordering your drink inside and drinking at the counter. Crepes €3.40-5.60. Sundaes €3.10-7.20. Service 20%. Open daily 7am-2am. Call to reserve a table outside. AmEx/MC/V. ●

◉ SIGHTS

⬛BASTIONE DI SAN REMY. Approaching **Piazza Costituzione,** an enormous arch encases a staircase that seems carved into the hillside. Climb up the graceful double stairway to the expansive terraces of the 19th-century *bastione* for a spectacular view of Cagliari. Take note of the pink flamingoes, the **Golfo degli Angeli,** and the **Sella del Diavolo** (Devil's Saddle), a massive rock formation. The *bastione* divides the modern city and the medieval Castello district. For a stroll through medieval Cagliari, start at the top of the *bastione* and follow the narrow streets past *aragonese* churches and *piemontese* palaces. *(Take the stairway from P. Costituzione or enter through the elevator on Vle. Regina Elena. Open 24hr. Free.)*

⬛PALAZZO VICEREGIO. Constructed by the Aragonese in 1216 and later used as a seat for Spanish and Savoyard viceroys, this beautiful *palazzo* serves as Cagliari's provincial capital. Portraits inside are by Sardinian masters like Giovanni Marghinotti, and the *palazzo* maintains its original Pisan marble floor and 18th-century furnishings. *(Next to the duomo in P. Palazzo. Open daily 9am-2pm and 3-7pm. Entrance only with tour in English or Italian. Free.)*

DUOMO (CATTEDRALE DI SANTA MARIA). The Pisans constructed this massive Gothic cathedral during the second half of the 13th century, dedicating it to the Virgin Mary and St. Cecilia, whose likenesses can be seen in mosaics above the doors. The *duomo* is modeled after the one in Pisa (p. 337) and filled with art by Pisan masters. Maestro Guglielmo carved the pulpits on either side of the main door in 1162, and Pisano sculpted the four lions at the base of the altarpiece in 1302. The ornate wood balcony to the left, in front of the altar, was constructed for the Piedmontese king, who refused to sit among the people for fear of regicide. Colorful marble inlays conceal 179 niches housing the remains of about 200 martyred saints from Cagliari. *(P. Palazzo 4. ☎070 16 63 837. Open M-F*

8am-12:30pm and 4:30-8pm, Su 8am-1pm and 4-8pm. Altar and some chapels currently under restoration. Modest dress required. Free.)

MUSEUMS. The **Cittadella dei Musei** houses a modern complex of research museums, including the **Museo Archeologico Nazionale.** The extensive collection of Sardinian artifacts from the Nuraghic to Byzantine eras includes Mycenean pottery from 1600 BC; Barumini, jewelry and coins from the times of Punic control, Roman glass works and mosaics, and a 1000-year-old army of tiny bronze figurines. Comprehensive explanations, with wall-text displays in English and Italian, narrate the history of Sardinian occupation. The entire second floor of the museum is devoted to the archaeological history of Cagliari from the Nuraghic to Roman ages. *(P. Arsenale. Take V. Buoncammino to P. Arsenale, go under the arch and turn left. ☎070 68 40 00. Open Tu-Su 9am-8pm. Wheelchair-accessible. €4, students 18-25 €2, under 18 or over 65 free. MC/V.)* The **Pinacoteca Nazionale,** in the same complex as the archaeological museum, displays medieval and Baroque religious paintings and altarpieces, including works by Pietro Cavaro, who is considered as the greatest Sardinian painter of all time. This labyrinthine museum is built around the remains of a 16th-century fortification, discovered during the reconstruction of the Citadel in 1966. The remains are visible on the ground floor. Be sure to visit the anonymously painted █**Madonna con Bambino** on the lower floor, which depicts Baby Jesus with flowing golden locks. For a chronological experience, try to visit this museum after visiting the archaeological museum. *(☎070 68 40 00. Open Tu-Su 9am-8pm. Wheelchair-accessible. €2, students 18-25 €1, under 18 or over 65 free. Both museums €5, students €2.50. Get tickets at the Museo Archeologico Nazionale biglietteria. Ticket office open Tu-Su 8:30am-7:15pm.)*

ROMAN AMPHITHEATER. Constructed after the Carthaginians succumbed to the Roman juggernaut in 238 BC, this amphitheater lost its downhill side to the Pisans, who used the wall as a quarry to build their 13th-century monuments. Underground cages once held ferocious animals during the age of gladiators. Today, much of the original seating along the sides remains, and the venue hosts summer performances that are a bit more civilized than the ancient carnage. *(V. Fra Ignazio. ☎070 65 29 56; www.anfiteatroromano.it. 30min. guided tours Apr.-Sept. Tu-Sa 9:30am-1pm, Su 10am-1pm. €3.30, students €2.20, over 65 free.)*

TORRE DI SAN PANCRAZIO. As Cagliari's highest point, the tower was once used to observe ships and enemies during war, then converted into a medieval prison. Today, visitors can climb the steep stairs, blanketed in pigeon droppings, to the top to view the city below. Despite a great view, it isn't worth the euro. *(€4, students €2.50. Guided visit €0.50. Open Tu-Su 9am-1pm and 3:30-7:30pm.)*

▓ ▓ ENTERTAINMENT AND NIGHTLIFE

The **Roman amphitheater** continues to dazzle spectators with theater, dance performances, opera, and concerts in July and August on its large modern stage. Most shows start at 9:30pm and cost €18-50. Buy tickets at the amphitheater starting at 7pm on performance nights or at the box office, at Vle. Regina Margherita 43. *(☎070 65 74 28. Open M-F 10am-1pm and 5-8pm, Sa 10am-1pm, Su when there's a show.)* **Outdoor movies,** mostly dubbed American films, are screened in July and August around 9pm at the Marina Piccola off Spiaggia del Poetto. Buy tickets (€4) at the Marina. On Sunday mornings, merchants converge for **flea markets** in P. del Carmine and Bastione di San Remy, where visitors hone their haggling skills and find bargain antiques.

Most bars and clubs in the city are open from 9pm to 5am, but they shut down in the summer when students hit the beaches and the dancing moves outdoors. To dance the night away, either find a ride or rent one—most *discoteche* are on the beaches, 15-20km outside of Cagliari. The best night to go out is Friday. For a downtown hot spot that's still parties hard into the summer, check out **De Candia,** V. De Candia 1, and enjoy the DJ or live music and colorful mixed drinks, including *assenzio* (absinthe). The bar is one of several positioned on a terrace on top of the Bastione di San Remy that feature lounging leather couches and hammocks. (☎070 65 58 84. Mixed drinks €6-7. Open daily 7am-4am.) The area around P. Costituzione is usually hopping with street performers and window shoppers. On the first of May, Sardinians flock to Cagliari for the **Festival of Sant'Efisio,** honoring a deserter from Diocletian's army who saved the island from the plague but couldn't save himself from decapitation. A costumed procession escorts his effigy from the capital down the coast to the small church that bears his name.

BEACHES

Il Poetto, Cagliari's most popular stretch of beach, spans 10km from the Devil's Saddle to the Margine Rosso (Red Bluff). The beach was famous for its pure white sands until the government dumped several tons of coarse brown sand on top to prevent erosion. Locals claim it's ugly, but only because the white sands found in the gorgeous nearby beach towns of **Villasimus** and **Chia** allow them to have high standards. The average traveler will be so focused on the crystal-clear waters that he'll hardly notice the slight imperfection. Behind Il Poetto, the salt-water **Stagno di Molentargius** (Pond of Molentargius) provides a habitat for flamingos. (City buses P, PQ, and PF, as well as the yellow and orange buses Arancio run frequently to the beaches. 20min., €1.) Resist jumping off the bus at the first sight of sand; by remaining on the bus for a few extra stops, you'll avoid crowded areas. For a more remote sunning and swimming area, head to **Cala Mosca,** which is smaller and surrounded by dirt paths. Because some parts of the water contain submerged seaweed-covered rocks, water shoes might be a good idea for squeamish swimmers looking to avoid squishy surfaces. Take bus #5 to Stadio Amsicora, then bus #11 to the beach.

SASSARI   ☎079

Sassari (SA-sa-ree; pop. 129,072), the second largest and first independent city in Sardinia, maintained its medieval wall perimeter until the late 1800s, despite constant encroachment by Pisans, Genoese, Aragonese, and Austrians. Sassari is home to the island's first university, the University of Sassari, popularly called "Culleziu." The university's presence has bolstered Sassari's cultural life, crowding its streets with bookstores, museums, tiny restaurants and shops, and plenty of students. Despite its lack of visitor activities, Sassari is quite close to more touristed destinations, such as Castelsardo and Alghero, and is a great place to stay for urban conveniences with easy access to the countryside.

TRANSPORTATION

Trains: In P. Stazione (☎079 89 20 21), 1 block from P. Sant'Antonio. Take bus #8 from P. d'Italia. Buy tickets (€0.80) at *bars.* To: **Alghero** (35min., 11 per day 6am-8:55pm, €2.20); **Cagliari** (3hr., 8 per day 6:36am-6:52pm, €13.65); **Olbia** (2hr., 4 per day 6am-5:08pm, €6.35); **Porto Torres** (20min., 7 per day 7am-6:44pm, €1.40).

Buses:

ARST (☎07 92 63 92 06/03; www.arst.sardegna.it). Buses depart from V. Italia in the public gardens, and the bus station on V. XXV Aprile, in front of the train station. To: **Alghero-Fertilia Airport** (40min.; 9 per day 5am-6:50pm, 5 and 5:30am depart from the bus station at V. Turati; €4); **Castelsardo** (1hr.; 13 per day 7:20am-7:45pm, reduced service Sa-Su; €2.50); **Nuoro** (1hr.,

M-F 2 per day, €8); **Olbia** (1hr., M-F 2:10pm); **Porto Torres** (20min., 1-2 per hr. 5:15am-9:15pm, €1.25); **Santa Teresa di Gallura** (3hr.; 5 per day 7:20am-7:45pm, reduced service Sa-Su; €7.80). Tickets sold at Tonni's Bar, C. Savoia 11, and at the bus station. Cash only.

FDS (☎079 24 13 01; www.ferroviesardegna.it). Buses leave from V. XXV Aprile. Tickets sold at bus stop on C. Vico. To: **Alghero** (50min.; 14 per day 5:50am-8:15pm, reduced service Sa-Su; €3); **Bosa** (2hr., 2 per day); **Castelsardo** (1hr., M-F 11:35am, €1.10); **Fertilia** (1hr.; 10 per day 6:30am-8:15pm, reduced service Sa-Su.)

Taxis: RadioTaxi (☎079 26 00 60). 24hr.

Car Rental: Eurorent, V. Roma 56 (☎079 23 23 35; www.rent.it). Ages 18-20 pay a surcharge. Credit card required. Open M-F 8:30am-7pm, Sa 8:30am-noon. MC/V.

◼◼ 🛈 ORIENTATION AND PRACTICAL INFORMATION

Many buses stop in the **giardini pubblici** (public gardens) before heading to the **bus station**. Since these gardens are close to Sassari's attractions, get off at **Via Italia** in the park. **Emiciclo Garibaldi,** a small, semi-circular *piazza,* lies ahead past **Via Margherita di Savoia.** To reach the *centro,* head straight through Emiciclo Garibaldi to **Via Carlo Alberto,** which spills into **Piazza d'Italia.** To the right, **Via Roma** runs to the tourist office and the Museo Sanna. To the left lies **Piazza Castello,** packed with people and restaurants. Two hundred meters away, **Corso Vittorio Emanuele,** a major thoroughfare, slices through the *centro storico.*

Tourist Office: V. Roma 62 (☎079 23 17 77; aastss@tiscali.it). Facing the provincial administration building, walk a few blocks to the right of P. d'Italia. Go through the gate and the doorway on the right. English-speaking staff provides maps and transportation schedules. Open M-Th 9am-1:30pm and 4-6pm, F 9am-1:30pm.

Currency Exchange: Banca Commerciale D'Italia, P. Italia 22-23, has an **ATM** outside. Open M-F 8:30am-1:30pm and 2:45-4:15pm, Sa 8:30am-noon.

Luggage Storage: In the bus station. €1.50 per bag per day. Open M-Sa 6am-9:15pm, Su 7am-2:15pm and 5:15-9:15pm. Cash only.

Hospital: Ospedale Civile, V. Montegrappa 82/83 (☎079 20 61 000).

Internet Access: Net Gate, P. Università, 4 (☎079 23 78 94). 6 computers. €0.08 cents per min. Open M-F 9am-1pm and 3:30-8pm, Sa 9am-1pm.

Post Office: V. Brigata Sassari 11/13 (☎079 28 21 267), off P. Castello. **Currency exchange,** phone cards, and *fermoposta.* Open M-F 8am-6:50pm, Sa 8am-1:15pm. Branch located across the street from V. XXV Aprile's bus station. **Postal Code:** 07100.

◼ ◻ ACCOMMODATIONS AND FOOD

◼**Casa Chiara ❸,** Vco. Matteo Bertolinis 7, a recently renovated B&B located in the *centro storico,* has three large, tastefully decorated rooms (a single, a double, and a triple) all have a TV as well as two clean, shared bathrooms and a kitchen. (☎079 20 05 052 or 333 69 57 118; www.casachiara.net. Breakfast included. Free Wi-Fi. Reservations recommended. €30 per person. Cash only.) Located close to the train and bus stations and the *centro,* **B&B Quattro Gatti ❸,** V. Sant'Eligio 5, so named for the cats that actually live on the premises, has a kitchen, whimsically decorated modern rooms, and a young, sociable owner. Call to arrange free pickup from station. (☎079 23 78 19 or 349 40 60 481. Breakfast, locker, and use of washing machine included. Free Wi-Fi. Singles €27-35; doubles €55-70; triples €80-100. Discounts for longer stays.)

At **Trattoria La Vela Latina ❸,** Largo Sisini 3, in a *piazza* off V. Arborea, owner Francesco loves his patrons as much as they love his food. Flavorful *cavallo* (horse meat; €9.30) or *asino* (donkey meat; €10) win over even the most timid diners. For something less adventurous, try the fantastic lobster salad or the *riso alla pescatora* for €8. (☎079 23 37 37. Primi €5-7.75. Secondi €7-13. Cover €2. Open M-Sa 1-2:30pm and 8-10:30pm. AmEx/MC/V.) **Il Senato ❹**, V. Alghero 36, is reputedly one of Sardinia's best restaurants and uses only first-rate seasonal ingredients. Don't miss the *dolce della suocera* (the mother-in-law cake; €6) with ricotta, almond, and a caramelized sugar crust. (☎079 27 77 88. Primi €10-15. Fish €8-15 per 100g. Meat €12-17 per 100g. Open M-Sa 1-2:30pm and 8-11pm. AmEx/MC/V.)

👁 🎵 SIGHTS AND ENTERTAINMENT

The **Museo Giovanni Antonio Sanna**, V. Roma 64, is an informative and fascinating archaeological museum. Extensive collections of artifacts dating from the Neolithic Period to the Middle Ages, including arrowheads, tools, ceramics, bronze statuettes, and Roman sculptures, chronologically detail Sardinia's history. The museum also hosts one of the largest collection of ancient Roman lead anchors. (☎079 27 22 03. Open Tu-Su 9am-8pm. €2, ages 18-25 €1, EU citizens under 18 or over 65 free.) From the *centro*, walk down C. V. Emanuele from P. Castello, and turn left on V. al Duomo to P. Duomo to reach Sassari's *duomo*, **Cattedrale di San Nicolò**. Reconstructed in Gothic style in 1480, only the *campanile* remains from the original 13th-century structure. The impressive facade, covered with statues and engravings, conceals a somewhat spartan interior, but you may want to take a peek at some recently uncovered early frescoes that fill the side chapels. (Open daily 8:30am-noon and 4-7:30pm. Mass M-Sa 6pm; Su 9 and 11:30am, 6pm. Modest dress required. Free.)

If it weren't for the **University Pub**, V. Amendola 49/A (☎079 20 04 43), Sassari would be devoid of any kind of youth scene. The subdued, three-tiered pub offers cheap drinks (beer from €2) and overflows with students when school is in session. Try the "Barman" (€5) or the potent, double-malted *biere di demon* for €4.30. (Th karaoke night. Open Sept.-July M and W-Su 8:30pm-1am.) In the third week of May, the lavish **Sardinian Cavalcade** is the island's largest folk festival. The party includes a parade of costumed emissaries from local villages, a horse exhibition, singing, and dancing. On August 14th, **I Candelieri** brings worker's guilds carrying enormous candles through the streets. Each guild has its own costume, and the candles are decked with flowers and streamers.

ALGHERO ☎079

With a vibrant *centro storico* hanging over the sea, Alghero (al-GEH-ro; pop. 45,000) stretches along Sardinia's northwestern coast. Over the centuries, Alghero has swapped hands between native Sardinians, Spanish Aragonese, and the Ligurian Genoese. As a result, a distinctly Spanish vibe can still be felt—along with Italian, a dialect of Catalán chimes in the streets. Visitors to Alghero can explore rich history, beachside nightlife, and natural wonders like the 70 million-year-old Grotte di Nettuno, only a short bus ride away.

🚍 TRANSPORTATION

Flights: Fertilia Civil Airport (☎079 93 52 82), 6km north of the city. Buses run from the *centro* every hr. **Ryanair** (www.ryanair.com) runs domestic flights year-round to **Barcelona, Bremen, Dublin, Dusseldorf, East Midlands, Frankfurt, Liverpool, London, Madrid, Milan, Pisa, Rome,** and **Stockholm.**

Trains: FDS (☎079 95 07 85) on V. Don Minzoni. Take **AP** or **AF bus** from in front of Casa del Caffè in the park (3 per hr.) or walk 1km along port to the station. Taxis €7 from *centro*. Buy tickets at **Trenitalia** stand in the park, and ride the bus to the station for

free, or buy from *biglietteria* in station. **Luggage storage** available (€1 per bag per day).
To **Sassari** (35min.; 11 per day 6:01am-8:47pm; €2.20, round-trip €3.80).

Buses:

ARST (☎079 800 86 50 42) and **FDS** (☎079 24 13 01). Tickets at stand in the public gardens
(☎079 95 01 79). Blue buses depart V. Catalogna, next to park. To: **Bosa** via **Villanova Monteleone,** mountain route (1hr., Sept.-June 2 per day 6:35am and 3:40pm, €4.50); **Bosa** via **Litoranea,**
coastal route (1hr. to *centro* and Bosa Marina, 1hr. to Bosa Stazione FDS; June-Sept. 9:55am and
7:30pm, Oct.-May 9am and 1:50pm; €3); **Porto Torres** (1hr.; up to 8 per day 4:45am-8:45pm,
reduced service Sa-Su; €2.50); **Sassari** (1hr., 1-2 per hr. 5:35am-7:50pm, €3).

FDS also runs orange **city buses** (☎079 95 04 58). Buy tickets (€0.70) at *tabaccherie*. Buses
run from P. della Mercede (in front of the church), stop at V. Cagliari (in front of Casa del Caffè),
and go to the airport (20min., 13 per day 5am-10pm; schedule changes monthly). **Line AF** runs
between Fertilia and V. Cagliari, stopping at the port (40min.; from Alghero 7am, then every hr.
from 8:40am-11:40pm, additional buses M-F between 8:10am and 1:10am; from Fertilia 7:50am
then every hr. 9am-midnight, additional weekday buses between 8:30am and 1:30pm). **AP** buses
run from Vle. della Resistenza to **train station** (every 30-60min. 6:20am-9pm). **AO** goes from V.
Cagliari to the beach and the **hospital** (2 per hr. 7:15am-11:50pm). **AC** runs from V. Liguria to
Carmine (2 per hr. 7:20am-7:50pm). Tourist office provides a complete schedule.

Taxis: V. Vittorio Emanuele (☎079 97 53 96), across from the BNL bank. Private cab
(☎079 98 92 028). From *centro* to airport about €20. Night prices vary..

Car Rental: Avis, P. Sulis 9 (☎079 97 95 77; www.avisautonoleggio.it), or at the airport
(☎079 93 50 64). 25+. Credit card required. Open M-F 8:30am-1pm and 4-7pm, Sa
8:30am-1pm. AmEx/MC/V. **Europcar** (☎079 93 50 32; www.europcar.it), at the airport. Open daily 8am-11pm. AmEx/MC/V.

Bike and Scooter Rental: Cycloexpress di Tomaso Tilocca (☎079 98 69 50; www.
cicloexpress.com), near the port at the intersection of V. Garibaldi and V. Spano. Bikes
€7-13 per day; tandems €15 per day; electric scooters €15 per day; motor scooters
€25-55 per day. Open M-Sa 9am-1pm and 4-8:30pm, Su 9am-1pm. AmEx/MC/V.

⊞ 🛈 ORIENTATION AND PRACTICAL INFORMATION

ARST and FDS buses stop next to the public gardens at the corner of **Via Catalogna** and **Via Cagliari,** on the waterfront one block from the **port.** The tourist
office, in **Piazza Porta Terra,** lies diagonally across the small park, on the right
beyond the towers of the *centro storico.* The **train station** is a hike from the *centro* (about 1km) but accessible by local orange buses (lines AF and AP).

Tourist Office: P. Porta Terra 9 (☎079 97 90 54; infoturismo@comune.alghero.ss.it),
on the right from the bus stop, toward the *centro storico.* Multilingual staff offers an
indexed street map, bus and train schedules, tours of the city, and daytrips to local villages. Open Apr.-Oct. M-Sa 8am-8pm, Su 10am-1pm; Nov.-Mar.

Currency Exchange: Banca Nazionale del Lavoro (BNL), V. V. Emanuele 5 (☎079 98
01 22), across from the tourist office, has a **24hr. ATM.** Open M-F 8:20am-1:20pm and
2:30-4pm, Sa 8:20-11:50am. **Currency exchange** also available at the post office.

English-Language Bookstore: Ex Libris Liberia, V. Carlo Alberto 2a (☎079 98 33 22),
has a selection of English-language paperbacks. Open daily 9am-midnight. MC/V.

Police: P. della Mercede 7 (☎079 97 20 01). **First Aid:** ☎079 99 62 33.

Pharmacy: Farmacia Puliga di Mugoni, V. Sassari 8 (☎079 97 90 26). Posts after-
hours rotations. Open May-Oct. M-Sa 9am-1pm and 5-9pm. AmEx/MC/V.

Hospital: Ospedale Civile (☎079 99 62 33), on V. Don Minzoni in Regione La Pietraia.

Internet Access: Bar Miramar, V. Gramisci 2. 3 computers. €1.60 per 15min., €5 per hr.
Open daily 8am-noon and 3pm-3am. Cash only.

Post Office: V. Carducci 33/35 (☎079 97 20 231), has *fermoposta* and currency exchange. Open M-F 8am-6:50pm, Sa 8am-1:15pm. **Postal Code:** 07041.

ACCOMMODATIONS AND CAMPING

Hotel San Francesco, V. Ambrogio Machin 2/4 (☎079 98 03 30; www.sanfrancesco-hotel.com). This converted 14th-century church cloister and architectural gem in the heart of the *centro storico* offers 20 rooms with stone walls, bath, A/C, and phone. Enjoy a drink in the small bar, which used to be a monk prison. Ask the informative staff about the classical music festival hosted by the cloister. Breakfast included. Reservation required June-Aug. Singles €49-60; doubles €78-96; triples €99-125. MC/V. ●

Bed and Breakfast MamaJuana, Vco. Adami 12 (☎079 33 91 36 97 91; www.mama-juana.it), a cozy B&B in the heart of the *centro storic*. Rooms with wooden ceilings, retro decor, private bath, and TV. Breakfast at nearby bar included. Check-out 10am. Reception 9am-9pm; call ahead. Single €40-60; doubles €60-90. Cash only. ●

FOOD

On Wednesday, there is an **open-air market** on V. Europa and V. Corsica. (Open 8:30am-1pm.) Walk 15min. from the *centro* to check out the wine-lover's paradise that is **Antiche Cantine del Vino Sfuso,** C. V. Emanuele 80. You can sample and purchase local wholesale table wines for a mere €1.50 per L; just bring your own tasting cup. (Open M-Sa 8:30am-1pm and 4:30-8pm. MC/V.) To cool off after a day at the beach, stroll over to **Gelateria Arcobaleno,** P. Civica 33 (☎079 98 71 52), which serves divine homemade gelato that's perfection in a cup. (Cup €1.50-3. Cash only.) A **Sisa** supermarket is at V. Sassari 49. (☎079 97 31 067. Open M-Sa 8am-8:30pm, Su 8am-1:30pm.) Fresh produce market stalls also line the archways beneath V. Sassari 19-23. (Open M-Sa 7am-1:30pm and 4-8pm.)

Osteria Taverna Paradiso, V. Principe Umberto 29 (☎079 97 80 01). Vaulted stone ceilings and fine cuts of meat like the Argentina Angus filet (€6.50 per 100g) make for charming, casual but classy dining in the *centro*. Try the *Maestro Formaggiaio* (Cheese Master), owner Pasquale's renowned cheese platter (€16). Primi €8.30-12. Secondi €13-20. Cover €1.50. Open daily noon-2pm and 8pm-midnight. AmEx/D/MC/V. ●

Al Tuguri, V. Maiorca 113 (☎/fax 079 97 67 72; www.altuguri.it). Delicious variations on traditional cuisine give Al Tuguri its stellar reputation. Well-loved for its distinct personality, innovative approach, and personalized service. Emphasis on local and pure ingredients. Try the *triglie* (red mullet fish; €15.80) or the exceptional 5-course *menù* (€40), with a vegetarian option (€34). Primi €12-15. Mandatory secondi €19-23. Open Mar.-Dec. 20 M-Sa 12:30-2pm and 8-10pm. Reservations recommended. MC/V. ●

Ristorante la Cueva, V. Gioberti 4 (☎079 97 91 83). From P. Porta Terra, take V. Simon, and turn right on V. Gioberti. Housed in an 8th-century building with arched stone ceilings. Savory fare with a distinctly local Catalán twist includes *porcetto sardo* (roast suckling pig; €15), *paella,* and homemade *sebadas* (Sardinian dessert ravioli deep fried and drizzled with honey; €4). Primi €7-20. Secondi €9-20. Open M and W-Su 1-2:30pm and 7:30pm-midnight. AmEx/MC/V. ●

SIGHTS

A leisurely walk through the *centro storico* reveals tiny alleys, half-hidden churches, and ancient town walls. The old city is hard to navigate without a map, so stop by the tourist office first. The **Torre di Porta Terra** near the public gardens dominates the entrance to the *centro*. Financed by the Jewish community in the 15th-century and consequently known as the **Torre degli Ebrei** (Tower of the Jews), it now offers visitors a great place to capture views of

SARDINIA

the town. (Open M-Sa 9:30am-1pm and 5-9pm. €1.50.) Heading down V. Roma, Alghero's *duomo*, **La Cattedrale di Santa Maria**, is at the intersection with V. Principe Umberto. Begun in 1552, it took 178 years to construct, resulting in a unique and stunning Gothic-Catalán-Renaissance facade. Rebuilt in the 19th century, the cathedral has Gothic choirs, a mosaic of John the Baptist, and the original *porta petita* (small door) from the Catalán structure. One block from the *duomo*, down V. P. Umberto, are the 19th-century **Teatro Civico** and **Palazzo Machin**, classic examples of Gothic-Catalán architecture. Backtrack up V. Roma and take a right on V. Carlo Alberto to find **Chiesa di San Francesco.** The simple Neoclassical facade conceals a graceful Gothic interior with beautiful marble altar. (Open M-F 9:30am-noon and 5-6:15pm, Su 5-6:30pm. Modest dress required. Free.) Heading away from the harbor, take V. Carlo Alberto to reach the beautiful **Chiesa di San Michele** at P. Ginnasio, built between 1661 and 1675 and dedicated to the patron saint of Alghero. V. Carlo Alberto ends at P. Sulis and the **Torre dello Sperone**, where French soldiers were imprisoned in 1412 after failing to capture the Catalán fortress. In the 19th century, Sardinian patriot Vincenzo Sulis was a prisoner here, thus giving the *piazza* its name.

▓ OUTDOOR ACTIVITIES

The countryside around Alghero is filled with spectacular nature reserves, inland mountains, and cliffs plunging into the sea, making it a popular destination for **trekking** and **bicycling.** Inquire at the tourist office for a comprehensive list of itineraries. One of the most popular parks, **Le Prigionette Nature Reserve,** lies at **Porto Conte,** off the Fertilia-Porto Conte highway on the road to Capo Caccia. Buses heading toward the Grotte di Nettuno (see next page) pass by the reserve three times daily. Bike and hiking paths wind through mountains, past sloping valleys dotted with wild horses. The forestry house at the park entrance supplies good maps and advice. (☎079 94 90 60. Open daily 9am-5pm.) FDS buses also lead directly to Porto Conte (30min.; 11 per day 7am-11:30pm; returns 11 per day 7:30am-midnight; €1), where a dirt road leads to **Punta Giglio Reserve.** The road is a difficult but popular route for bikers, ending after 3km at a ▓limestone peak on Punta Giglio. This point has the region's most impressive views, as well as several semi-abandoned WWII barracks for war buffs or curious minds. For those not biking, get off at the Porto Conte stop and walk 300m down the road back toward town, and the entrance is on the right (45-60min.). The low-traffic seaside highway that heads away from Alghero to the Porto Conte area is also popular for biking. For the bike ride, follow the beachside road; V. Garibaldi turns into V. Lido, and then Vle. Maggio. Vle. Maggio leads to the dock at the end of Alghero's coast (8km); cross the bridge onto the highway to Fertilia. Continue along the bike path with the forest on one side and the highway on the other (3km). When the bike path ends, continue along highway for another 3km until Porto Conte. The **Nuraghi di Palmavera** is 3km past Fertilia, along the highway from Alghero to Porto Conte/Capo Caccia. Follow the bike path next to the forest to its end and then go another 200m on the highway. A central tower surrounded by 50 huts forms a limestone complex dating from 1500 BC. (☎079 95 32 00; fax 98 87 65. Open daily Apr.-Oct. 9am-7pm; Nov.-Mar. 9:30am-4pm. €3, over 65 and children €2.) The **S.I.L.T. cooperative,** V. Mattei 14, offers tours of Nuraghi in English by request. (☎079 98 00 40; www.coopsilt.it. Tours run every hr. 9:15am-11:15am and 4-6pm. €2, audio tour €3.)

▓ ▓ ENTERTAINMENT AND NIGHTLIFE

Alghero comes alive at night. Crowds stream through the *centro storico*'s cramped streets and pour onto the promenade until the early morning hours.

In summer, locals in search of warm evening breezes and live music head to the beachside bars along **Lungomare Dante** and along the **waterfront** all the way to Fertilia. Both locals and tourists also enjoy **Poco Loco**, V. Gramsci 8, a gnarly pizza place just past P. Sulis, inland from Lungomare Dante. Famed for its pizza-by-the-meter (€17-27 per m; 0.5m also available), Poco has six bowling lanes (€3.50-6 per game) and Internet for €3 per hr. (☎079 97 31 034; www.pocolocoalghero.it). Live music in summer W 10:30pm; in winter F-Sa 11pm. Beer from €2. Mixed drinks €5. Open in summer daily 7:30pm-3am or later. MC/V.)

DAYTRIPS FROM ALGHERO

KILLING TIME. The FDS buses leaving at 9:15am, 3:10, and 5:10pm will arrive at Capo Caccia a few minutes past the hour, meaning you'll have to wait around 45min. until the next hourly tour of the Neptune's Grottoes. Also, if relying on the bus for transpotation, take the 9:15am or 3:10pm buses from Alghero since the 5:10 bus will leave you stranded in Capo Caccia.

GROTTE DI NETTUNO. Booming waves echo amidst ancient stalactites and stalagmites in the wondrous ▧**Grotte di Nettuno** (Neptune's Grottoes). These caves, first discovered by fishermen, have been around for 60 to 70 million years and are one of Sardinia's most frequented tourist destinations. Thanks to modern lighting, the caves come alive when blue, green, and yellow light dances over the rocks. Well-run 45min. tours, conducted in English and Italian, point out whimsical rock formations like Christmas trees, chandeliers, and pipe organs in the bowels of the caves. The caves are in Capo Caccia, a steep promontory that juts out from Porto Conte into a nationally protected marine area. Built in 1954, the steep Escala del Cabirol provides access to the grotto for those adventurous enough to descend the 654 steps that lead to the sea between massive white cliffs. (☎079 94 65 40. Open daily Apr.-Sept. 9am-7pm; Oct. 9am-5pm; Nov.-Mar. 9am-4pm. Groups admitted every hr. for 45 min. tour, €10, children €5. FDS buses run to Capo Caccia. ☎079 95 01 79. 50min.; 3 per day 9:15am-5:10pm, last return 6:05pm; €2. Or take the pleasant Navisarda Grotte di Nettuno ferry tour. ☎079 97 62 02 or 95 06 03; www.navisarda.it. Guide in English and Italian. Boats leave Alghero's Bastione della Maddalena. 2hr. round-trip, with tour of caves; June-Sept. 9 per day 9am-5pm; Apr.-May and Oct. 9, 10am, and 3pm. Round-trip €13, under 13 €7.)

BOSA ☎079

Glowing with cheery pastels, Bosa (BO-sa; pop. 7,935) is half medieval city, half Riviera vacation hot spot. Situated on the banks of the Temo River, the only navigable river in Sardinia, Bosa boasts a trademark castle, situated high up on a hill overlooking palm tree-lined streets and spacious *piazze* on the Temo River Valley. Though the *centro storico* is generally a sleepy place, the newer Bosa Marina, 1km from the old city, boasts beautiful beaches, an assortment of seaside bars, and a hostel. If arriving by bus or car from Oristano, you will be treated to some incredible views from the small hill-towns along the way.

TRANSPORTATION. ARST **buses** run from Bosa to Oristano (2hr., M-Sa 5 per day 5:25am-4:05pm, €5.50). Buy tickets at the bar or *tabaccheria* in P. Zanetti. FDS **buses** run to Alghero via Litoranea, the coastal route (1hr., 3 per day, €3), or via Villanove Monteleone, the mountain route (2 hr., 2 per day, €4.50); Nuoro (1hr.; 6 per day 6:06am-7:41pm, reduced service Sa-Su; €5.10); and Sassari (2hr., 3 per day 8:20am-5:20pm, €5.50). Buy tickets at the FDS office in P. Zanetti.

(Open daily 6:30pm-midnight.) Buses also run from Bosa to Piazza Palmiro Togliatti in Bosa Marina (5min., 22 per day, €1). For a **taxi**, call ☎079 33 68 11 800. To rent **cars, scooters**, or **bikes**, stop by Euroservice, V. Azuni 23. (☎079 37 34 79. 25+ for car or scooter. Bikes €10 per day; scooters €25-50; cars from €65. Open M-F 9am-1pm and 5-8pm.)

▄▌ ORIENTATION AND PRACTICAL INFORMATION. Bosa, the city proper, lies across the **Temo River** from **Bosa Marina.** Buses stop in Bosa's **Piazza Angelico Zanetti,** from which **Via Azuni** leads to **Piazza Gioberti** at the base of the *centro storico.* The **Pro Loco tourist office,** V. Azuni 5, at the intersection with V. Francesco Romagna, provides maps and info on the town and surrounding area. Ask for the brochure, which contains a free map. (☎079 37 61 07; www.info-bosa.it. Open M-Sa 10am-1pm.) The **tourist office** for Bosa Marina, Vle. Colombo, is on the *lungomare* about 5min. after the right turn off the main bridge. (☎079 37 71 08; www.agenziailponte.it or www.bosa.it. Open M-F 8:30am-12:30pm and 3:30-7:30pm.) For currency exchange and an **ATM,** head to **Unicredit Banca,** at the corner of V. Lamarmora and V. Giovanni XXIII. (☎079 37 31 18. Open M-F 8:20am-1:20pm and 2:35-4:05pm, Sa 8:20am-12:45pm.) In case of emergency, call the **carabinieri** (☎079 37 31 16), **Red Cross** (☎079 37 38 18), **hospital** (☎079 37 31 07), or **guardia medica** (☎079 37 46 15). **Internet Web Copy,** V. Gioberti 12, has six computers with fast connections (€0.07 per min.) and fax services. (☎079 37 20 49; web.copy@tiscali.it. Open M-Sa 9am-1pm and 5-9pm.) The **post office,** V. Pischedda 1, also has currency exchange. (☎079 07 85 37 31 39. Open M-F 8:15am-6:50pm, Sa 8:15am-1:15pm.) **Postal Code:** 08013.

▐▐ ACCOMMODATIONS AND FOOD. Located between Bosa *centro* and Bosa Marina, the ▨**Royal Hotel ❸,** Vle. Alghero 27, offers 22 rooms decorated with fresh, Victorian elegance and plenty of flowers. Rooms are equipped with bath, TV, A/C, phone, and balconies. Some even come with hydromassage showers. Breakfast included. (☎079 37 70 37; info@royalhotelbosa.it. €34-44 per person low season, €47-59 high season.) Bosa Marina is home to one of Sardinia's two youth hostels, called simply **Youth Hostel (Ostelle della Gioventú) (HI) ❶,** V. Sardegna 1. After crossing the bridge from the *centro*, take a right on the *lungomare.* V. Sardegna is about 5min. down on the left. Close to the beach, the hostel has clean rooms with large communal bathrooms, and a bar open until midnight. (☎079 37 50 09 or 34 62 36 38 44; valevacanzesardegna@hotmail.com. Breakfast included. A/C €3 per day. Reception 9am-1pm and 4pm-midnight. Curfew midnight. 5-bed dorms €16; doubles €40. Cash only.)

In a medieval building in the *centro storico*, **Ristorante Borgo Sant'Ignazio ❷,** V. S. Ignazio 33, serves marine delicacies like *nido dello chef* (egg pasta with tomato sauce and local lobster; €12 per 100g) and *azadda iscritta* (€10), a relative of shark. Don't miss the house special *zuppo di pesce* ("fish soup"), a savory seaside specialty throughout Italy chock-full of *frutti di mare* and a mind-boggling variety of fish. (☎079 37 41 29. Primi €8-15. Secondi €10-15. Cover €2. Open in summer Tu-Su 1-3pm and 7:30-11pm. AmEx/MC/V.) Across the bridge from P. Duomo, **Sa Pischedda ❷,** V. Roma 8, offers elegant outdoor dining on a garden patio and candlelit tables which are graced by delicious dishes like *razza alla bosana* (garlicky, sautéed flat fish; €7), *alisanzas al ragu di sorfano e basilico* (pasta with local fish, tomato, and basil; €8), and a selection of brick-oven pizzas. (☎079 37 30 65. Pizza €4.50-11, dinner only. Primi €7-11. Secondi €5 per 100g of fish. Open daily 1-2:30pm and 8-10:30pm. MC/V.) Head to **Sisa** supermarket, P. Gioberti 13, for groceries. (☎079 37 34 23. Open M-Sa 8am-1pm and 5:30-8:30pm, Su 9am-12:30pm.)

SARDINIA

SIGHTS AND BEACHES. Bosa's principal museum, **Casa Deriu,** C. Vittorio Emanuele II 59, exhibits furnishings, tapestries, and family portraits from the wealthy Deriu family's 19th-century home. Examples of filet weaving, unique to Bosa, and traditional Sardinian dress and gold jewelry can be seen on the first floor. The third floor holds a collection of ceramics, prints, and paintings by Melkiorre Melis, a leader in the applied and plastic arts. Art lovers will enjoy the landscapes of Bosa, and surrealist works by Antonio Atza are housed in a permanent collection across the street. (Open Tu-Su 10:30-1pm and 8:30-11pm. €4.50, children €2.) The town's signature **Castello Malaspina** is a short hike uphill through the *centro storico;* take the flower-lined staircase or V. del Castello to see the imposing castle that dates from 1112 and is also home to the early 14th-century **Chiesa Nostra Signora Regnos Altos.** The walk uphill and the entrance fee are well worth the experience that waits at the top, with mountain and ocean views available from the castle. On the second weekend of September, residents celebrate the Virgin Mary by adorning their houses with flowers and small altars, dancing, and parading through the streets. The festival culminates with a mass in the courtyard of the castle. (☎079 33 35 44 56 75. Castle and church open daily 9:30am-1:30pm and 5:30-8:30pm. €2, under 12 €1.)

Local families fill a long stretch of sandy beach in Bosa Marina, where bars line the *lungomare* around the **Aragonese Tower.** The **Bosa Diving Center,** V. Colombo 2 (☎079 37 56 49; www.bosadiving.it), offers snorkeling, scuba diving, and boat tours to nearby grottoes and beaches. Call for more info.

NUORO ☎0784

The architecture of this provincial capital, high up in the mountains of central Sardinia, is a mix of the Spanish-influenced buildings and modern block-style apartment complexes. Nuoro (noo-OH-ro; pop. 36,000) is known as a Sardinian center of high culture, home to the island's contemporary art museum, the Museo Arte Nuoro (MAN), and the only government-commissioned ethnographic museum. Locals also proudly tout Nuoro's status as the birthplace and final resting place of Nobel prize-winning author Grazia Deledda. Once you've had your fill of museums, a stomach-churning bus ride or an arduous hike up Monte Ortobene will reveal an imposing statue of Christ the Redeemer and similarly spectacular views of the sea.

S.O.S. At 8:30pm, buses stop running, and taxis are a rarity. If you plan to be out past this time and are staying outside the *centro,* arrange for transportation home in advance to avoid getting stranded. If you need a taxi in the early hours of the morning (before 9am), arrange for pick-up beforehand.

TRANSPORTATION

Trains: FDS station (☎0784 30 115), on V. Lamarmora, in P. Stazione. Ticket office open M-Sa 7:30am-5:15pm. To **Cagliari** (3hr., 5 per day 6:24am-6:51pm, €13.50) via **Macomer.** Important: When switching trains in Macomer, note that the FDS station is across the street from the Trenitalia station, and you'll need to switch from the FDS Nuoro-Macomer train to the Trenitalia Macomer-Cagliari train.

Buses:

ARST (☎0784 29 41 73). Buses stop at the ARST station on V. Toscana between Vle. Sardegna and V. Santa Barbara. Tickets available next door at Il Gusto Macelleria, Vle. Sardegna 21 (☎0784 32 408). To: **Cagliari** (2hr., 2:05pm, €14.50); **Olbia** (stops in port, airport, and city, although not all buses make all 3 stops; 1hr., 7 per day 5:30am-5:40pm, €7.50); **Cala Ganone** (1hr., 7 per day 6:53am-7pm, €3) via **Dorgali** (45min.; 8 per day 6:53am-7pm; reduced service Sa-Su; €2.50); **Orgosolo** (30min.; 9 per day 5:50am-6:30pm, last return 7:05pm, reduced service Sa-Su; round-trip €2.50); **Sassari** (4:20 and 7:10pm, €7.50). **Luggage storage** available.

F. Depiano buses run from Vle. Sardegna, 1 block to the right of the ARST station, to the **Olbia airport** (☎0784 29 50 30; 1hr., 6 per day 4:15am-5:15pm, €10) and the **Alghero airport** (☎0784 30 325; 2hr.; 11:25am, 3:20, 5pm; €18). Buses coincide with plane arrivals and departures.

Public Transportation: Buy tickets (€1.10) for the local buses at newsstands, *tabaccherie*, or in the train station. **Bus #2** runs from P. Vittorio Emanuele through the *centro* to the train station and the hospital. **Bus #8** runs to the top of M. Ortobene. **Buses #3** and **#9** run between P. V. Emanuele and the ARST station.

Taxis: (☎0784 33 53 99 174 or 368 90 94 71). At night it can be a very long wait, so call ahead. Reserve the night before for taxis before 9am.

Car Rental: Autonoleggio Maggiore, Vle. Monastir 116 (☎0784 27 36 92; fax 20 80 536). 23+. Open M-F 8am-1pm and 4-7pm, Sa 8am-1pm and 4-6pm. AmEx/MC/V.

ORIENTATION AND PRACTICAL INFORMATION

From the ARST **bus station,** turn right on Viale Sardegna. When you reach **Piazza Sardegna,** take a right on **Via Lamarmora** and follow it to **Piazza delle Grazie** and the *centro.* To get to the tourist office from P. delle Grazie, turn left and follow Via IV Novembre uphill through **Piazza Dante** to **Piazza Italia.** Brown signs will direct you the rest of the way. **Via Roma** leads from P. Italia to **Piazza San Giovanni** and the town's social hub, **Piazza Vittorio Emanuele. Corso Garibaldi** is a major street with shops and cafes that runs out of P. V. Emanuele.

Tourist office: P. Italia 19, (☎0784 23 88 78. Open in summer daily 9am-7pm.) The enthusiastic, English-speaking staff at **EPT** has brochures, maps, and hiking info. Open in summer daily 9am-7pm. There is another tourist office closer to the *centro* at C. Garibaldi 155 (☎0784 38 777, www.puntoinforma.it.), with an equally enthusiastic and helpful staff. This office also offers a wealth of information on locations of interest in the island's interior. Ask them to help you set up excursions.

Pharmacy: C. Garibaldi 65, (☎0784 30 143).

Hospital: Ospedale San Francesco, V. Mannironi (☎0784 24 02 49), is on the highway to Bitti. The 24hr. **guardia medica** is on V. Deffenu (☎0784 24 08 48).

Internet: Smile Caffè, V. Piemonte 3, off V. Veneto. €3 per hr. Open Jun.-Aug. M-Sa 7am-10pm.

Post Office: P. Crispi 8 (☎0784 24 52 10) off V. Dante. Open M-F 8am-6:50pm, Sa 8am-1:15pm. Another **branch,** V. Santa Barbara 24 (☎0784 23 28 07), is near the ARST station. Open M-F 8am-6:50pm, Sa 8am-1:15pm. **Postal Code:** 08100.

ACCOMMODATIONS AND FOOD

Inexpensive hotels are rare in Nuoro, and campgrounds are in distant towns. If you plan to stay in the area, consider B&Bs close to Nuoro or Monte Ortobene, or head to the smaller hamlets in the hills. **Casa Solotti ❸,** in Località Monte Ortobene, a peaceful location in the countryside, has five large rooms that share two bathrooms and a terrace with a mountain view that extends to the sea on clear days. Take bus #8 (every 50min. 8:15am-8pm) from P. V. Emanuele, which stops in front of the Casa at the "Solotti" stop. Welcoming multilingual owner, **Mario,** serves homemade jam, yogurt, and pastries for breakfast. Mario also sometimes takes travelers on an excursion to his family's farm, where you can see an inhabited natural cave, pet domestic animals, and purchase organic cheese. (☎0784 32 86 02 89 75; www.casasolotti.it. Call for free pickup from town. €26-30 per person, depending on time of year. Cash only.)

For a local favorite, visit ◼**Ristorante Tascusi ❷**, V. Aspromonte 15, just off V. Garibaldi, where high quality cuisine comes at surprisingly low prices. The *menù* includes a primo, secondo, side dish, and 0.25L of wine or 0.5L of water for only €10. Come early to beat the crowds. (☎0784 37 287. Open M-Sa noon-3pm and 8-10:30pm. MC/V.) For classy and relaxing dining while enjoying mountain views from the patio, try **Ristorante Ciusa ❸**, V. Francesco Ciusa 55. Menu offers many seafood dishes, tons of pizza, and a magnificently decadent *seadas* with pistacchio gelato for dessert. (☎0784 25 70 52. Primi €8-10. Secondi €12-22. Dessert €5. AmEx/MC/V.) At **Canne Al Vento ❷**, V. Biasi 123, a half hour outside of town, high class and low prices dominate. Guests dine on classic *culurgiones* (ravioli stuffed with potatoes, cheese, and mint; €7) and sip rich espresso. (☎0784 20 17 62. Primi €5-8.50. Secondi €6.70-12.50. Open M-Sa 12:30-3pm and 8-10:30pm. AmEx/MC/V.) A quality bakery, **Antico Panifico Sardo ❷**, V. Ferraciu 73 (☎0784 36 275), off P. delle Grazie, offers some of the best traditional baked goods in town, including hot rolls, *pane carasau* (€5 per kg), and scrumptious *panzerotti* (from €2) filled with cheese, tomato, and a choice of eggplant, mushroom, or ham. (Open M-F 8am-1:30pm and 4:30-8pm, Sa 8am-1:30pm.) **Pellicano** supermarket in P. Mameli has groceries. (☎0784 23 26 66. Open M-Sa 8:30am-2pm and 5-8pm, Su 5-8pm. AmEx/MC/V.)

👁 SIGHTS

◼**MUSEO DELLA VITA E DELLE TRADIZIONI POPULARI.** Sardinia's largest and highly informative ethnographic museum contains a collection of traditional costumes, hand-woven rugs, musical instruments, and jewelry from around the island. The pieces are arranged in a series of stucco houses circling a flowered courtyard—a reconstruction of a typical Sardinian village. One house contains carnival masks shaped like devils, donkeys, pigs, cows, and goats; don't miss the creepy *Mamuthone* (traditional Sardinian costume masks) or your very own cutout mask in the museum's handout. (V. Antonio Mereu 56. ☎0784 25 70 35. Open daily July-Sept. 9am-8pm; Oct.-June 9am-1pm and 3-7pm. €3, under 18 and over 60 €1.)

◼**MONTE ORTOBENE.** The bronze ◼**Christ the Redeemer,** a 1905 statue of the town's symbol, beckons hikers to the peak of this hill, where a shady park and spellbinding views await. After the hike to the statue, walk 20m down the road from the bus stop on Monte Ortobene to see Monte Corrasi, which dwarfs the neighboring town of Oliena. (Take the sensational bus #8 from P. V. Emanuele 7km to the summit. 14 per day 8:15am-8pm, last return 8:15pm; €1.10. To hike there take the 4.5km trail La Solitudine; start behind Chiesa della Solitudine at the beginning of V. Ortobene, and follow the red-and-white marked "Trail 101." Look for yellow sign saying "Redentore" to reach the statue.)

MUSEO ARTE NUORO. Affectionately termed the "MAN," this striking white building contains a collection of 20th-century Sardinian art that incorporates both traditional and contemporary themes. The middle two floors hold a permanent collection of works by 20th-century Sardinian painters such as Francesco Ciusa and Antonio Ballero, while the first and fourth floors display rotating exhibits by contemporary artists. (V. Satta 27. ☎0784 25 21 10; www.museoman.it. Open Tu-Su 10am-1pm and 4:30-8:30pm. €3, students 18-25 €2, under 18 or over 60 free.)

APPENDIX

CLIMATE

Geographically, Italy lies in a temperate zone and has a predominantly Mediterranean climate. Yet, due to the peninsula's length, temperatures and weather often vary drastically in different parts of the country, based on proximity to the coast or the mountains. Summers in the south near the coast are dry and hot, as the sea and beaches are baked by the warm *sicorro* wind blowing in from North Africa. Moving north and inland, summer temperatures remain hot, but in the absence of a sea breeze, excessive humidity gets added to the mix. Things cool down countrywide in the winter, but to varying degrees, ranging from mild temperatures in the south to freezing fog, frost, and snow in the northern valleys.

AVG. TEMP. (LOW/HIGH), PRECIP.	JANUARY			APRIL			JULY			OCTOBER		
	°C	°F	mm	°C	°F	mm	°C	°F	mm	°C	°F	mm
Florence	1/10	34/50	73	8/19	46/66	78	17/31	63/88	40	10/21	50/70	88
Milan	0/5	32/41	44	10/18	50/64	94	20/29	68/84	64	11/17	52/63	125
Naples	4/12	39/54	116	9/18	48/64	62	18/29	64/84	19	12/22	54/72	107
Palermo	8/16	46/61	71	11/20	52/68	49	21/30	70/86	2	16/25	61/77	77
Rome	5/11	41/52	71	10/19	50/66	51	20/30	68/86	15	13/22	55/72	99
Venice	1/6	34/43	37	10/17	50/63	78	19/27	66/81	52	11/19	52/66	77

To convert from degrees Fahrenheit to degrees Celsius, subtract 32 and multiply by 5/9. To convert from Celsius to Fahrenheit, multiply by 9/5 and add 32.

CELSIUS	-5	0	5	10	15	20	25	30	35	40
FAHRENHEIT	23	32	41	50	59	68	77	86	95	104

MEASUREMENTS

Like the rest of the rational world, Italy uses the metric system. The basic unit of length is the meter (m), which is divided into 100 centimeters (cm) or 1000 millimeters (mm). One thousand meters make up one kilometer (km). Fluids are measured in liters (L), each divided into 1000 milliliters (mL). A liter of pure water weighs one kilogram (kg), the unit of mass that is divided into 1000 grams (g). One metric ton is 1000kg.

MEASUREMENT CONVERSIONS	
1 inch (in.) = 25.4mm	1 millimeter (mm) = 0.039 in.
1 foot (ft.) = 0.305m	1 meter (m) = 3.28 ft.
1 yard (yd.) = 0.914m	1 meter (m) = 1.094 yd.
1 mile (mi.) = 1.609km	1 kilometer (km) = 0.621 mi.
1 ounce (oz.) = 28.35g	1 gram (g) = 0.035 oz.
1 pound (lb.) = 0.454kg	1 kilogram (kg) = 2.205 lb.
1 fluid ounce (fl. oz.) = 29.57mL	1 milliliter (mL) = 0.034 fl. oz.
1 gallon (gal.) = 3.785L	1 liter (L) = 0.264 gal.

LANGUAGE

Italian is the official language of Italy, and if you plan to get anywhere in the country—physically or otherwise—you should brush up on the language before your trip. While the tourism-driven economy of urban areas has instilled locals with some English familiarity—ranging from knowledge of a few words to complete fluency—the likelihood of meeting an English-speaking Italian drops drastically the farther you travel from heavily touristed areas. In the south, on the islands, and in small towns to the north, tourists with no knowledge of Italian may have to rely entirely on hand gestures, a tactic that is naturally vulnerable to awkward misunderstandings. Be aware that spoken dialects vary greatly between different regions. To get in good with the locals wherever you may be, memorize a few Italian phrases to break the ice, and make sure to end any conversation with a polite, "Grazie" (GRAHT-see-yeh).

PRONUNCIATION

VOWELS

There are seven vowel sounds in standard Italian. **A, i,** and **u** each have one pronunciation. **E** and **o** each have two slightly different pronunciations, one open and one closed, depending on the vowel's placement in the word, the stress, and the regional accent. Below are approximate pronunciations.

VOWEL	PRONUNCIATION
a	"a" as in "father" (casa)
e (closed)	"ay" as in "gray" (sera)
e (open)	"eh" as in "wet" (sette)
i	"ee" as in "cheese" (vino)
o (closed)	"o" as in "bone" (sono)
o (open)	"aw" as in "ought" (bocca)
u	"oo" as in "moon" (gusto)

CONSONANTS

C and G: Before a, o, or u, **c** and **g** are hard, as in *candy* and *goose* or as in the Italian *colore* (koh-LOHR-eh; color) and *gatto* (GAHT-toh; cat). Italians soften c and g into **ch** and **j** sounds, respectively, when followed by i or e, as in *cheese* and *jeep* or the Italian *cibo* (CHEE-boh; food) and *gelato* (jeh-LAH-toh; ice cream).

Ch and Gh: H returns c and g to their "hard" sounds in front of i or e (see above): *chianti* (ky-AHN-tee), the Tuscan wine, and *spaghetti* (spah-GEHT-tee), the pasta.

Gn and Gli: Pronounce **gn** like the **ni** in *onion,* or as in the Italian *bagno* (BAHN-yoh; bath). **Gli** is pronounced like the **lli** in *million,* or as in the Italian *sbagliato* (zbal-YAH-toh; wrong).

Sc and Sch: When followed by **a, o,** or **u,** sc is pronounced as **sk.** *Scusi* (excuse me) yields "SKOO-zee." When followed by an **e** or **i,** sc is pronounced **sh** as in *sciopero* (SHOH-pair-oh; strike). The addition of the letter **h** returns c to its hard sound (sk) before **i** or **e,** as in *pesche* (PEHS-keh; peaches).

Double consonants: When you see a double consonant, stress the preceding vowel; failure to do so can lead to confusion. For example, *penne all'arrabbiata* is "short pasta in a spicy, red sauce," whereas *pene all'arrabbiata* means "penis in a spicy, red sauce."

PHRASEBOOK

NUMBERS			
1	uno	8	otto
2	due	9	nove
3	tré	10	dieci
4	quattro	11	undici
5	cinque	12	dodici
6	sei	13	tredici
7	sette	14	quattordici
15	quindici	40	quaranta
16	sedici	50	cinquanta
17	diciassette	60	sessanta
18	diciotto	70	settanta
19	dicianove	80	ottanta
20	venti	90	novanta
30	trenta	100	cento

DAYS	
Monday	lunedí
Tuesday	martedí
Wednesday	mercoledí
Thursday	giovedí
Friday	venerdí
Saturday	sabato
Sunday	domenica

GENERAL		
ENGLISH	ITALIAN	PRONUNCIATION
Hi/Bye (informal)	Ciao	chow
Good day/Hello	Buongiorno	bwohn-JOHR-noh
Good evening	Buonasera	bwoh-nah-SEH-rah
Good night	Buonanotte	bwoh-nah-NOHT-teh
Goodbye	Arrivederci/Arrivederla (formal)	ah-ree-veh-DEHR-chee/ah-ree-veh-DEHR-lah
Please	Per favore/Per piacere	pehr fah-VOH-reh/pehr pyah-CHEH-reh
Thank you	Grazie (formal/polite)	GRAHT-see-yeh
How are you?	Come stai/Come sta (formal)?	COH-meh STA-ee/stah
I am well	Sto bene	stoh BEH-neh
You're welcome /Please	Prego	PREH-goh
Excuse me	Scusa (formal)/Scusi (informal)	SKOO-zee/-zah
I'm sorry	Mi dispiace	mee dees-PYAH-cheh
My name is	Mi chiamo	mee kee-YAH-moh
I'm on vacation	Sono qui in vacanza	SOH-noh qwee een vah-CAHN-zah
I live in	Abito a	AH-bee-toh ah
What's your name?	Come ti chiami? Come si chiama Lei (formal)?	COH-meh tee kee-YAH-mee/COH-meh see kee-YAH-mah lay
Yes/No/Maybe	Sì/No/Forse	see/no/FOHR-seh
I don't know	Non lo so	nohn loh soh
Could you repeat that?	Potrebbe ripetere?	poh-TREHB-beh ree-PEH-teh-reh
I don't understand	Non capisco	nohn kah-PEES-koh
Could you help me?	Potrebbe aiutarmi?	poh-TREHB-beh ah-yoo-TAHR-mee
How do you say?	Come si dice?	KOH-meh see DEE-cheh
this/that	questo/quello	KWEH-sto/KWEHL-loh
more/less	più/meno	pyoo/MEH-noh
What time is it?	Che ore sono?	keh OHR-eh SOH-noh
What time does it open/close?	A che ora apre/chiude?	ah keh OHR-eh AH-preh/kee-OOH-deh

GENERAL		
now	adesso/ora	ah-DEHS-so/OH-rah
let's go	andiamo	ahn-dee-AH-moh
tomorrow	domani	doh-MAH-nee
today	oggi	OHJ-jee
yesterday	ieri	ee-YEH-ree
right away	subito	SU-bee-toh
soon	fra poco/presto	frah POH-koh/PREHS-toh
after	dopo	DOH-poh
before	prima	PREE-mah
late/later	tardi/più tardi	TAHR-dee/pyoo TAHR-dee
early	presto	PREHS-toh
late (after scheduled arrival time)	in ritardo	een ree-TAHR-doh

DIRECTIONS AND TRANSPORTATION		
ENGLISH	**ITALIAN**	**PRONUNCIATION**
there	lì/là	lee/lah
the street address	l'indirizzo	leen-dee-REET-soh
the telephone	il telefono	eel teh-LEH-foh-noh
street	strada, via, viale, vico, vicolo, corso	STRAH-dah, VEE-ah, vee-AH-le, VEE-koh, VEE-koh-loh, KOHR-soh
speed limit	limite di velocità	LEEH-mee-teh dee veh-loh-chee-TAH
slow down	rallentare	rah-lehn-TAH-reh
one-way street	senso unico	SEHN-soh OOH-nee-coh
large, open square	piazzale	pee-yah-TZAH-leh
stairway	scalinata	scah-lee-NAH-tah
beach	spiaggia	spee-YAH-geeah
river	fiume	fee-YOO-meh
toilet, WC	gabinetto	gah-bee-NEHT-toh
What time does the ... leave?	A che ora parte ... ?	ah keh OHR-ah PAHR-teh
From where does the ... leave?	Da dove parte ... ?	dah DOH-veh PAHR-teh
the (city) bus	l'autobus	LAOW-toh-boos
the (intercity) bus	il pullman	eel POOL-mahn
the ferry	il traghetto	eel tra-GHEHT-toh
the hydrofoil	l'aliscafo	LA-lee-scah-foh
the plane	l'aereo	lah-EHR-reh-oh
the train	il treno	eel TREH-noh
the ticket office	la biglietteria	lah beel-yeht-teh-REE-ah
How much does it cost?	Quanto costa?	KWAN-toh CO-stah

DIRECTIONS AND TRANSPORTATION		
I would like to buy ...	Vorrei comprare ...	voh-RAY com-PRAH-reh
... a ticket	... un biglietto	... oon beel-YEHT-toh
... a pass (bus, etc.)	... una tessera	... OO-nah TEHS-seh-rah
one-way	solo andata	SO-lo ahn-DAH-tah
round-trip	andata e ritorno	ahn-DAH-tah eh ree-TOHR-noh
reduced price	ridotto	ree-DOHT-toh
student discount	lo sconto studentesco	loh SKOHN-toh stoo-dehn-TEHS-koh
the track/train platform	il binario	eel bee-NAH-ree-oh
the flight	il volo	eel VOH-loh
the reservation	la prenotazione	la preh-no-taht-see-YOH-neh
the entrance/exit	l'ingresso/l'uscita	leen-GREH-so/loo-SHEE-tah
I need to get off here	Devo scendere qui	DEH-vo SHEN-dehr-eh kwee

EMERGENCY		
I lost my passport/wallet	Ho perso il passaporto/portafoglio	oh PEHR-soh eel pahs-sah-POHR-toh/por-ta-FOH-lee-oh

EMERGENCY		
I've been robbed	Sono stato derubato/a	SOH-noh STAH-toh deh-roo-BAH-toh/tah
Wait!	Aspetta!	ahs-PEHT-tah
Stop!	Ferma!	FEHR-mah
Help!	Aiuto!	ah-YOO-toh
Leave me alone!	Lasciami stare!/Mollami!	LAH-shah-mee STAH-reh/MOH-lah-MEE
I'm calling the police!	Telefono alla polizia!	tehl-LEH-foh-noh ah-lah poh-leet-SEE-ah

MEDICAL		
I have ... allergies	Ho ...delle allergie	OH ... DEHL-leh ahl-lair-JEE-eh
... a cold	... un raffreddore	oon rahf-freh-DOH-reh
... a cough	... una tosse	OO-nah TOHS-seh
... the flu	... l'influenza	linn-floo-ENT-sah
... a fever	... una febbre	OO-nah FEHB-breh
... a headache	... mal di testa	mahl dee TEHS-tah
My foot/arm hurts	Mi fa male il piede/braccio	mee fah MAH-le eel PYEH-deh/BRAH-cho
I'm on the pill	Prendo la pillola	PREHN-doh lah PEE-loh-lah

RESTAURANTS		
food	il cibo	eel CHEE-boh
wine bar	l'enoteca	len-oh-TEK-ah
breakfast	la colazione	lah coh-laht-see-YO-neh
lunch	il pranzo	eel PRAHN-zoh
dinner	la cena	lah CHEH-nah
coffee	il caffè	eel kah-FEH
appetizer	l'antipasto	lahn-tee-PAH-stoh
first course	il primo	eel PREE-moh
second course	il secondo	eel seh-COHN-doh
side dish	il contorno	eel cohn-TOHR-noh
dessert	il dolce	eel DOHL-cheh
bottle	la bottiglia	lah boh-TEEL-yah
waiter/waitress	il/la cameriere/a	eel/lah kah-meh-ree-EH-reh/rah
the bill	il conto	eel COHN-toh
cover charge	il coperto	eel koh-PEHR-toh
tip	la mancia	lah MAHN-chyah

HOTEL AND HOSTEL RESERVATIONS		
hotel/hostel	albergo/ostello	al-BEHR-goh/os-TEHL-loh
I have a reservation	Ho una prenotazione	oh oo-nah preh-no-taht-see-YOH-neh
Could I reserve a single room/double room?	Potrei prenotare una camera singola/doppia?	poh-TREY preh-noh-TAH-reh oo-nah CAH-meh-rah SEEN-goh-lah/DOH-pyah
Is there a bed available tonight?	C'è un posto libero stasera?	cheh oon POHS-toh LEE-ber-oh sta-SAIR-ah
with bath/shower	con bagno/doccia	kohn BAHN-yo/DOH-cha
open/closed	aperto/chiuso	ah-PEHR-toh/KYOO-zoh
sheets/linens	i lenzuoli	ee lehn-SUO-lee
the blanket	la coperta	lah koh-PEHR-tah
the bed	il letto	eel LEHT-toh
Is there heating?	C'è riscaldamento?	cheh ree-skahl-dah-MEHN-toh
Is there air conditioning?	C'è aria condizionata?	che AH-ree-ah con-deet-syon-AH-tah
How much is the room?	Quanto costa la camera?	KWAHN-toh KOHS-ta lah KAM-eh-rah
I will arrive (at 2:30pm)	Arriverò (alle due e mezzo)	ah-ree-veh-ROH (ah-leh DOO-eh MED-zoh)

HOTEL AND HOSTEL RESERVATIONS		
You'll have to send a deposit/check	Bisogna mandare un anticipo/un assegno	bee-ZOHN-yah mahn-DAH-reh oon ahn-TEE-chee-poh/oon ahs-SEHN-yoh
What is that funny smell?	Che cos'è quest'odore strano?	keh kohz-EH kwest-oh-DOHR-eh STRAH-noh

AMORE		
I have a boyfriend/girlfriend	Ho un ragazzo/una ragazza	Oh oon rah-GAHT-soh/oo-nah rah-GAHT-sah
Let's get a room	Prendiamo una camera	prehn-DYAH-moh oo-nah CAH-meh-rah
To be in love with	Essere innamorato/a di	Eh-seh-reh een-am-mo-RAH-to/ta dee
Just a kiss	Solo un bacio	SOH-loh oon BAH-chyoh
Are you single?	Sei nubile?	NOO-bee-leh
You're cute	Sei carino/a (bello/a)	SEY cah-REEN-oh/ah (BEHL-loh/lah)
I love you, I swear	Ti amo, te lo giuro	tee AH-moh, teh loh DJOO-roh
I'm married	Sono sposato/a	SOH-noh spo-ZA-to/ta
I only have safe sex	Pratico solo sesso sicuro	PRAH-tee-coh sohl-oh SEHS-so see-COO-roh
Leave right now!	Vai via subito!	vah-ee VEE-ah SOO-beet-oh
I'll never forget you	Non ti dimenticherò mai	nohn tee dee-men-tee-ker-OH mah-ee
The profound mystery of what you just said sets my soul on fire	Il profondo mistero di ciò che stai dicendo mi infuoca il cuore	eel pro-FOHN-doh mee-STEH-roh dee CHOE keh sty dee-CEN-doh mee een-FWOH-cah eel ku-WOR-eh
Not if you're the last man on earth	Neanche se lei fossi l'unico uomo sulla terra	neh-AHN-keh seh lay FOH-see LOO-nee-koh WOH-moh soo-LAH TEH-rah

AT THE BAR		
May I buy you a drink?	Posso offrirle qualcosa da bere?	POHS-soh ohf-FREER-leh kwahl-COHzah dah BEH-reh
a beer	una birra	oo-nah BEER-rah
glass of wine	bicchiere di vino	bee-KYEH-reh dee VEE-noh
liter of wine	litro di vino	LEE-troh dee VEE-noh
I'm drunk	Sono ubriaco/a	SOH-noh oo-BRYAH-coh/cah
I don't drink	Non bevo	nohn BEH-voh
Cheers!	Cin cin!	cheen cheen
No thank you, I don't smoke	No grazie, non fumo	noh GRAH-zyeh, nohn FOO-moh

MENU READER

PRIMI (FIRST COURSE)	
gnocchi	potato dumplings
ravioli	square-shaped and often stuffed with cheese or sometimes meat
tagliatelle	thin and flat, these are the northern version of fettuccini
pappardelle	wider and flatter than tagliatelle
polenta	deep-fried cornmeal
risotto	creamy rice dish, comes in nearly as many flavors as pasta sauce

SECONDI (SECOND COURSES)	
agnello	lamb
bistecca	steak
coniglio	rabbit
cotoletta	breaded veal cutlet with cheese
cozze	mussels
gamberetti/gamberi	shrimps/prawns

SECONDI (SECOND COURSES)	
granchi	crab
maiale	pork
manzo	beef
osso buco	braised veal shank
ostriche	oysters
pesce spada	swordfish
pollo	chicken
polpo	octopus
prosciutto	smoked ham, available cured or cooked
salsiccia	sausage
scaloppina	cutlet
sogliola	sole
tonno	tuna
trippa	tripe (sautéed cow intestines, usually in a tomato sauce)
trota	trout
vitello	veal
vongole	clams

CONTORNI (SIDE DISHES)	
carciofe/carciofini	artichoke/artichoke hearts
carotte	carrots
cavolfiori	cauliflower
cavolo	cabbage
cetriolo	cucumber
cipolla	onion
fagioli	beans (usually white)
fagiolini	green beans
funghi	mushrooms
insalata	salad
melanzana	eggplant
patate	potatoes
piselli	peas
pomodori	tomatoes
spinaci	spinach
tartufi	truffles

FRUTTA (FRUIT)	
arancia	orange
ciliegia	cherry
fragola	strawberry
lampone	raspberry
mela	apple
pesca	peach
prugna	plum
uva	grape

DOLCI (DESSERTS)	
gelato	Italian-style ice cream
granita	ice-based fruit or coffee slushee
macedonia	fruit salad
panna cotta	flan
tiramisù	cake-like dessert drenched in *espresso*, layered with *mascarpone*

INDEX

MAP INDEX

MAP LEGEND

Hospital	Building	Thermal Bath
Hotel/Hostel	Police	Park: city, other	Cave
Camping	Post Office	Plaza/other area	Waterfall
Food	Tourist Information	Beach	Pass
Nightlife	Point of Interest	Water	Peak
Museum	Embassy/Consulate	Swamp	Mountain Range
Church	Telephone Office	Pedestrian Zone	Ranger Station
Synagogue	Airport	Steps	Archaeological Site
Theater	Bus Station	Trail	Monastery
Internet Café	Train Station	Ferry Route	Border Crossing
Bank	Ferry Landing		

ABBREVIATIONS:
Lg.   Laguna, Lago
M.N.   Monumento Nacional
Pl.   Plaza
Pq.   Parque
P.I.   Parque Internacional
P.N.   Parque Nacional
Q.   Quebrada
R.   Río
R.B.   Reserva Biológica
R.E.   Reserva Ecológica
R.F.   Reserva Forestal
R.F.S. Refugio de Fauna Silvestre
R.V.S. Refugio de Vida Silvestre
R.I.   Reserva Internacional

The Let's Go compass
always points N O R T H.

ABOUT LET'S GO

THE STUDENT TRAVEL GUIDE

Let's Go publishes the world's favorite student travel guides, written entirely by Harvard students. Armed with pens, notebooks, and a few changes of clothes stuffed into their backpacks, our student researchers go across continents, through time zones, and above expectations to seek out invaluable travel experiences for our readers. Because we are a completely student-run company, we have a unique perspective on how students travel, where they want to go, and what they're looking to do when they get there. If your dream is to grab a machete and forge through the jungles of Costa Rica, we can take you there. If you'd rather bask in the Riviera sun at a beachside cafe, we'll set you a table. In short, we write for readers who know that there's more to travel than tour buses. To keep up, visit our website, www.letsgo.com, where you can sign up to blog, post photos from your trips, and connect with the Let's Go community.

TRAVELING BEYOND TOURISM

We're on a mission to provide our readers with sharp, fresh coverage packed with socially responsible opportunities to go beyond tourism. Each guide's Beyond Tourism chapter shares ideas about responsible travel, study abroad, and how to give back to the places you visit while on the road. To help you gain a deeper connection with the places you travel, our fearless researchers scour the globe to give you the heads-up on both world-renowned and off-the-beaten-track opportunities. We've also opened our pages to respected writers and scholars to hear their takes on the countries and regions we cover, and asked travelers who have worked, studied, or volunteered abroad to contribute first-person accounts of their experiences.

FIFTY YEARS OF WISDOM

Let's Go has been on the road for 50 years and counting. We've grown a lot since publishing our first 20-page pamphlet to Europe in 1960, but five decades and 54 titles later our witty, candid guides are still researched and written entirely by students on shoestring budgets who know that train strikes, stolen luggage, food poisoning, and marriage proposals are all part of a day's work. This year, for our 50th anniversary, we're publishing 26 titles—including 6 brand new guides—brimming with editorial honesty, a commitment to students, and our irreverent style. Here's to the next 50!

THE LET'S GO COMMUNITY

More than just a travel guide company, Let's Go is a community that reaches from our headquarters in Cambridge, MA all across the globe. Our small staff of dedicated student editors, writers, and tech nerds comes together because of our shared passion for travel and our desire to help other travelers get the most out of their experience. We love it when our readers become part of the Let's Go community as well—when you travel, drop us a postcard (67 Mt. Auburn St., Cambridge, MA 02138, USA), send us an e-mail (feedback@letsgo.com), or sign up on our website (www.letsgo.com) to tell us about your adventures and discoveries.

For more information, updated travel coverage, and news from our researcher team, visit us online at www.letsgo.com.

HELPING LET'S GO. If you want to share your discoveries, suggestions, or corrections, please drop us a line. We appreciate every piece of correspondence, whether a postcard, a 10-page email, or a coconut. Visit Let's Go at **http://www.letsgo.com,** or send email to:

feedback@letsgo.com, subject: "Let's Go Italy"

Address mail to:

Let's Go Italy, 67 Mount Auburn St., Cambridge, MA 02138 , USA

In addition to the invaluable travel advice our readers share with us, many are kind enough to offer their services as researchers or editors. Unfortunately, our charter enables us to employ only currently enrolled Harvard students.

Maps by Let's Go copyright © 2010 by Let's Go, Inc.

Distributed by Publishers Group West.
Printed in Canada by Friesens Corp.

ISBN-13: 978-1-59880-312-9
ISBN-10: 1-59880-312-3
Thirtieth edition
10 9 8 7 6 5 4 3 2 1

Let's Go Italy is written by Let's Go Publications, 67 Mount Auburn St., Cambridge, MA 02138, USA.